AF600433

The Intellectual History and Rabbinic Culture of Medieval Ashkenaz

The Intellectual History and Rabbinic Culture of Medieval Ashkenaz

Ephraim Kanarfogel

Wayne State University Press Detroit

17 16 15 14 13 5 4 3 2 1

Library of Congress Cataloging-in-Publication Data

Kanarfogel, Ephraim.
The intellectual history and rabbinic culture of medieval Ashkenaz / Ephraim Kanarfogel.
p. cm.
Includes bibliographical references and index.
ISBN 978-0-8143-3024-1 (cloth : alk. paper) — ISBN 978-0-8143-3802-5 (e-book)
1. Jewish learning and scholarship—Germany—History—To 1500. 2. Jewish learning and scholarship—France, Northern—History—To 1500. 3. Jews—Germany—Intellectual life—History—To 1500. 4. Jews—France, Northern—Intellectual life—History—To 1500. 5. Jewish religious education—France, Northern—History—To 1500. 6. Jewish religious education—Germany—History—To 1500. I. Title.
BM85.G4K355 2012
296.094'0902—dc23

2012012524

∞

Designed and typeset by BookComp, Inc.
Composed in Sabon Next LT Pro and Nueva Std

Contents

	Preface	vii
	Acknowledgments	xiii
	List of Abbreviations	xvii
	Introduction: Regnant Perceptions and Empirical Evidence	1
1	Talmudic and Halakhic Studies: Internal Organization and Societal Models	37
2	Tosafist Biblical Exegesis in Northern France at the End of the Twelfth Century: Between *Peshat* and *Derash*	111
3	The Contours of Biblical Interpretation during the Early Thirteenth Century	205
4	Interpretations for a Varied Audience through the Thirteenth Century	289
5	Genres and Strategies of *Piyyut* Composition among the Tosafists	375
6	Magic and Mysticism in Tosafist Literature and Thought	445
7	Tosafist Approaches to Matters of Belief and the Implications for Popular Culture	489
	Conclusion: Ashkenazic Rabbinic Culture in Its Plenitude	531
	Index of Manuscript References	541
	Subject Index	547

Preface

While talmudic studies certainly constituted the primary area of scholarly endeavor in Ashkenaz during the twelfth and thirteenth centuries, the goal of this book is to put forward disciplinary and interdisciplinary treatments and methodologies that will lead, for the first time, to an assessment of the intellectual proclivities of Ashkenazic rabbinic culture as a whole. Sefardic (and Provençal) rabbinic culture during this period tended on the whole to be more compartmentalized. A small number of the greatest medieval Sefardic talmudists and halakhists—figures such as Maimonides, R. Meir *ha-Levi* Abulafia (Ramah), Naḥmanides, and R. Solomon ibn Adret (Rashba)—also pursued extra-talmudic disciplines such as philosophy, kabbalah, and biblical exegesis. At the same time, however, many of the leading specialists in these other disciplines were not necessarily important talmudists or halakhists. The names of Judah *ha-Levi*, Abraham bar Ḥiyya, Abraham ibn Ezra, and Abraham Abulafia, as well as the Provençal scholars Isaac the Blind (son of Rabad of Posquieres) and Yedayah *ha-Penini* of Beziers, come readily to mind in this regard.[1]

This study will demonstrate that despite the lesser degree of cultural interaction between Jews and Christians in northwestern Europe, as compared to Jews who (originally) lived in Islamic lands and their Muslim counterparts, the disciplinary interests of Ashkenazic rabbinic figures were much broader than talmudic studies alone. A significant difference between

[1] See, e.g., Nahum Arieli, "Tefisat ha-Halakhah 'eẓel R. Yehudah ha-Levi," *Da'at* 1 (1978), 43–52 (and cf. Israel Ta-Shma, *R. Zeraḥyah ha-Levi Ba'al ha-Ma'or u-Bnei Ḥugo* [Jerusalem, 1992], 142–43); Adam Shear, *The Kuzari and the Shaping of Jewish Identity* (Cambridge, 2008); Shlomo Sela, "Abraham bar Ḥiyya's Astrological Work and Thought," *Jewish Studies Quarterly* 13 (2006), 128–58; Jonathan Dauber, "'Pure Thought' in R. Abraham bar Ḥiyya and Early Kabbalah," *Journal of Jewish Studies* 60 (2009), 185–201; *R. Abraham Ibn Ezra: Studies in the Writings of a Twelfth-Century Polymath*, ed. I. Twersky and J. Harris (Cambridge, Mass., 1993); *Yesod Mora ve-Sod ha-Torah*, ed. Y. Cohen and U. Simon (Ramat Gan, 2007); Moshe Idel, *Language, Torah, and Hermeneutics in Abraham Abulafia* (Albany, N.Y., 1989); Elliot Wolfson, *Abraham Abulafia: Kabbalist and Prophet* (Los Angeles, 2000); Haviva Pedaya, *Ha-Shem veha-Miqdash be-Mishnat R. Yiẓḥaq Sagi Nahor* (Jerusalem, 2001); Daniel Abrams, *R. Asher b. David: Kol Ketavav ve-'Iyyunim be-Qabbalato* (Los Angeles, 1996); I. Twersky, "Yeda'ayah ha-Penini's Commentary on the Aggadah," [Hebrew] in *Studies in Jewish Religious and Intellectual History Presented to Alexander Altmann*, ed. S. Stein and R. Loewe (Tuscaloosa, Ala., 1979), 63–82; and Marc Saperstein, *Decoding the Rabbis* (Cambridge, Mass., 1980), 201–10.

these two orbits, however, is that those Ashkenazic scholars who pursued a range of intellectual and spiritual disciplines most often began this pursuit with very strong credentials in the study of Talmud and *halakhah*, upon which the other disciplines were then built, as a means of promulgating a larger and more variegated conception of the "multiple truths of the Torah." In tracing the scope of Ashkenazic cultural achievements, we will also get a better sense of the levels and layers of scholarship in medieval Ashkenaz. Leopold Zunz, for example, whose published volumes list and briefly describe virtually all the biblical commentaries and liturgical poetry produced in medieval Ashkenaz (that were available in his day, in both published and manuscript form), made almost no effort to separate these strands and strata, even as he strove to identify the various individual authors.[2]

A description of the contents of this book is in order. The introduction points to several factors that have contributed to the relatively narrow perceptions of Ashkenazic rabbinic culture. It sets the stage for what follows by arguing that the Tosafists and Ashkenazic rabbinic scholarship more generally advocated a wide definition of the truths that could be discovered through Torah study. In addition to subjecting the text of the Talmud to a range of questions and inquiries, different kinds of textual and conceptual methods could be deployed across a wide range of Jewish texts and disciplines, as appropriate means of arriving at truthful and meaningful interpretations. Indeed, different methods could be undertaken at the same time and even by the same rabbinic scholar without concern for how or whether the results completely comported or cohered with each other. Ultimately, all that resulted, if done faithfully and skillfully, was considered to be a part of worthwhile and truthful Torah study.

Chapter 1 begins with a discussion of the salient differences in talmudic and halakhic studies between the Tosafist centers of northern France and Germany. These differences can be observed within the methods of study and intellectual tendencies, and the institutional structures and the roles of leading rabbinic figures, as well as the degree of contact between these centers. Although differences along regional lines were sometimes manifested in the halakhic positions or *minhagim* of the Tosafists (with the Tosafists of northern France ruling in a particular way over time while those in Germany took a different view), the obvious commonalities that existed within and between these Tosafist realms meant that many specific rulings or practices did not adhere to any such pattern. Nonetheless, the significant distinctions between these centers of talmudic studies that did exist also have implications for other disciplines of study, as we shall see. In addition,

[2] See L. Zunz, *Zur Geschichte und Literatur* (Berlin, 1845); and idem, *Literaturgeschichte der synagogalen Poesie* (Berlin, 1865).

this chapter considers anew the degree of Christian scholastic influence on Tosafist dialectic, an issue that also has important implications for assessing the intellectual breadth of the Tosafists.

The next three chapters deal with aspects of biblical interpretation. Chapter 2 focuses on three late twelfth-century French Tosafists and students of Rabbenu Jacob Tam (beginning with the somewhat familiar R. Yosef *Bekhor Shor* of Orleans, as well as R. Jacob of Orleans and R. Yom Tov of Joigny) who favored (and offered) interpretations that followed a kind of *peshuto shel miqra va-ʾaggadah ha-meyashevet divrei* approach similar to that of Rashi rather than the *ʿomeq shel miqra* approach adopted by their more immediate predecessor, Rashbam. Chapter 3 discusses two leading Ashkenazic rabbinic figures with German roots, R. Judah *he-Ḥasid* and R. Isaiah di Trani, who also composed Torah commentaries with this dimension, and it compares the approaches of these five exegetes with the more talmudically inclined comments to the Torah that were typically put forward by other Tosafists at this time. The possible influences of Spanish biblical exegesis on these phases of Ashkenazic interpretation in the late twelfth and early thirteenth centuries are also noted.

Chapter 4 identifies additional Tosafists and rabbinic figures during the first half of the thirteenth century, including R. Moses of Coucy, R. Yeḥiʾel of Paris, and the brothers of Evreux, who pursued both *peshat* and *derash* in their interpretations of the text of the Torah. The Tosafist exegetes highlighted in these three chapters, who were engaged to a significant degree in the study of *peshat* (and with Rashi's commentary in particular), constitute a sizable substrate of the so-called Tosafist Torah commentaries (*perushei Baʿalei ha-Tosafot ʿal ha-Torah*, extant in a dozen or so published collections and in more than two hundred manuscripts) that began to appear around 1240 and continued into the early fourteenth century. Indeed, these Tosafist exegetes serve as a bridge between the handful of independent, classical northern French *pashtanim* of the twelfth century on the one hand and the decidedly compilatory *perushei Baʿalei ha-Tosafot ʿal ha-Torah* collections on the other.

Chapter 5 focuses on the composition of liturgical poetry (*piyyut*) by Tosafists. Some contemporary scholars have suggested that, following the First Crusade (which significantly impacted the Rhineland) as well as several persecutions in northern France (and Germany) during the mid- and late twelfth century which generated a series of commemorative liturgical compositions, the writing of *piyyut* was not maintained as a staple of Tosafist creativity, especially within northern France. Moreover, according to this view, those *piyyut* genres that commemorate catastrophe (*qinot* and *seliḥot*) far and away dominated the other forms of liturgical poetry composed during the late twelfth and thirteenth centuries, mostly by German Tosafists and Pietists. Although German Tosafists did out-produce their French counterparts overall, this chapter demonstrates that it is possible to detect clearly defined areas of interest and patterns of endeavor in both regions, as Tosafists sought to compose *piyyutim* for different occasions (both happy and sad), and for liturgical contexts that had been underrepresented in earlier *piyyut* compositions or that became newly designated as appropriate venues for *piyyutim.* Commemorative *qinot* and *seliḥot* were (unfortunately) always needed and produced, but the richness and variety of the other genres during the twelfth and thirteenth centuries, throughout Ashkenaz, are palpable. Moreover, even as pre-Crusade compositional models continued to play a role, the significant patterns of composition for a large cohort of Tosafist *piyyutim* authored in both northern France and Germany further suggest that interest in *piyyut* in this period was surely not limited to the German Pietists and their followers.

In chapter 6, I reflect on and expand some of the arguments and findings that I put forward in my *"Peering through the Lattices": Mystical, Magical, and Pietistic Dimensions in the Tosafist Period* (Wayne State University Press, 2000). As with regard to the composition of *piyyutim,* there was substantial awareness of forms of (white) magic and mysticism on the part of a number of northern French Tosafists, in addition to the strong involvement of a group of German Tosafists. As the twelfth century gave way to the thirteenth, *Ḥasidei Ashkenaz* strengthened the predisposition of certain German Tosafists in these matters, just as the interest in northern France proceeded apace. To paraphrase Yaakov Sussmann, if the thirteenth century ultimately comes to be dominated by Frenchmen in terms of talmudic studies (and German Tosafists at that time received anew the methods of their French colleagues through both direct teacher-student interactions and the increased availability of the Tosafist literature of northern France), it is a German century in the realms of prayer and mysticism, during which French Tosafists may have followed the lead of their German colleagues in these areas.[3] Indeed, the influence of Ashkenaz as a whole on esoteric studies in Spain now appears to have been far greater than Gershom Scholem and others had imagined. This influence parallels the patterns (and direction) of influence with regard to talmudic studies.

[3] See Y. Sussmann, "The Scholarly Oeuvre of Professor Ephraim Elimelech Urbach," [Hebrew] in *Ephraim Elimelech Urbach: A Bibliography* [Supplement to *Jewish Studies*, forum of the World Union of Jewish Studies, vol. 1] (Jerusalem, 1993), 61 (at n. 105); my *"Peering through the Lattices": Mystical, Magical, and Pietistic Dimensions in the Tosafist Period* (Detroit, Mich., 2000), 251–58. Cf. Abraham b. Azri'el, *'Arugat ha-Bosem*, ed. Urbach, vol. 4 (Jerusalem, 1963), 100: אין כמעט פירוש לתפילות ולפיוטים ולא חיבור על דיני תפילה ומנהגיה שנתחברו אחריו שלא תורגש בהם השפעתה של חסידות אשכנז.

With respect to matters of belief, the commonly held view is that the talmudocentricity of the Tosafists tended to mask any theological positions that they might have been inclined to offer in the course of interpreting talmudic texts. For this view, the technical methods employed by the Tosafists in the interpretation of *ʾaggadah* precluded the possibility that their interpretations could reflect anything other than the valences of the underlying talmudic texts themselves. However, given the broader, more open, and multidisciplinary approaches of the Tosafists that are demonstrated throughout this book, it should not be surprising to find (as we shall see in the seventh and final chapter) that northern French and German Tosafists (as well as the German Pietists) did in fact express a range or spectrum of views on the question anthropomorphism (as but one significant example) that runs almost from one extreme to the other. Multiple (individual) views can also be detected with respect to issues of messianism and the nature of the messianic age, although in this instance the results are generally more unified. Nonetheless, these positions most often emerge from nuanced interpretation and interdisciplinary correlation, rather than as the byproducts of technical talmudic study alone, and reflect the deeply held views of the Tosafists themselves.

Acknowledgments

Researching and writing this book has proven to be both an exhilarating and daunting task, given its wide disciplinary range and the vast amount of material found in manuscript. Over the years I have been privileged to "sit at the feet" of four leading Jerusalem scholars whose remarkable knowledge and complete mastery of both manuscript and printed texts allowed (and even encouraged) me to read and understand Ashkenazic rabbinic culture in the way that I have. They are Professors Israel Ta-Shma *z"l* and Ezra Fleischer *z"l*; and, ליבדל בין חיים לבין חיים, Professors Moshe Idel and Avraham Grossman.

A wealth of colleagues in the United States and Israel have contributed in ways large and small to this study. Citation of their monographs and articles will serve, I hope, as heartfelt (if not fully adequate) acknowledgment of their generous assistance. I must, however, single out several individuals: my friend and mentor, Professor Moshe Sokolow, of the Azrieli Graduate School of Jewish Education at Yeshiva University, who read (and proofread) the entire manuscript with remarkable dedication and offered numerous corrections and suggestions; another devoted friend, Rabbi Shmuel Klein, who read through large parts of the manuscript and saved me from a number of errors; Professor Elisabeth Hollender, of the University of Frankfurt, who provided a series of helpful comments on chapter 5; and Professor Chanita Goodblatt, of Ben-Gurion University of the Negev, whose unusual expertise at transposing and converting multilingual computer programs greatly aided in the production of this work.

The academic leadership of Yeshiva University, President Richard Joel and Provost Morton Lowengrub, and Deans David Berger and Karen Bacon of the two schools in which I am privileged to teach, the Bernard Revel Graduate School of Jewish Studies and Stern College for Women, have faithfully and generously supported my research, publications, and travel. We are all still truly bereft at the passing of E. Billi Ivry, a remarkable woman of great intelligence, commitment, warmth, and friendship.

As various ideas and conclusions of this work were taking shape, I tried out a number of them in my graduate seminars at Revel, and in my classes at the S. Daniel Abraham Honors Program of Stern. Not surprisingly, I found that the students had quite a few helpful things to say. Indeed, these discussions caused me on a number of occasions to rethink and to reformulate some of my arguments; I am very grateful to my students for their interest and input.

The rich holdings of the Mendel Gottesman Library at Yeshiva (with special thanks to Zvi Erenyi) and the unique Institute for Microfilmed Hebrew Manuscripts at the Jewish National and University Library in Jerusalem (with special thanks to Dr. Avraham David and Benjamin Richler) have always been at my disposal. I am grateful to the Hebrew University of Jerusalem, Bar-Ilan University, Ben-Gurion University of the Negev, and Haifa University, and to my colleagues at these institutions, for the steady stream of conference and research invitations and subventions that helped to defray travel expenses. I also wish to express my deep sense of *hakkarat ha-tov* to Rabbi and Mrs. Reuven Aberman of Jerusalem for their exceptional hospitality and friendship over these many years, and to Mr. Victor Geller of Jerusalem for his wise guidance and counsel.

The two years I spent as a fellow at the Katz Center for Advanced Jewish Studies at the University of Pennsylvania (in 2003–4, during an early phase of this project, and in 2010–11, as the book was being completed and sent to press), were most productive and illuminating. I salute my colleagues at CAJS and its director, Professor David Ruderman, for their sagacity and camaraderie. Kathy Wildfong, editor-in-chief at Wayne State University Press—who has shepherded all my English-language books through the publication process—and her staff have once again done an exceptional job. In the course of providing expert copyediting, Mindy Brown managed to catch and correct all kinds of substantive and subtle things, in both English and Hebrew. And Cali Orenbuch and Estee Brick of Stern College have rendered invaluable assistance throughout.

My family has been remarkably supportive and patient during the research and writing of this book. They recognize that this is what I do, and they also know that I am paying considerable attention to them, even when it appears that I have my head in the books and manuscripts. It gives me great pride to mention my family and especially the newer arrivals who were not yet on the scene for prior works. Everything begins with Devorah, because that's a very good place to start. My dear parents, Ethel and Lester Kanarfogel, are already envisioning the contents (and title) of the next book project(s), and my sister Susan has always been there to provide encouragement.

To our children, Tova and Yossi (and "the fellas," Yehudah Barak, Zechariah Alon, and Yonatan Boaz), Dovid and Hindy (and the "trips," Eliana, Yehudis Shira, and Shlomo Ezra), Moshe, Atara, Chaya, and Temima: I'm not done yet, but I'll let you know. This book is dedicated to the memories of our grandparents, Sam and Yetta Kanarfogel *a"h.* They lived their lives with the fervent hope that we would be able to study and grow, and perhaps contribute a bit of learning and "Yiddishe nachas" to the world.

E. K.
Tu B'Av, 5771

On the third day of Hanukkah 5772, not long after I received the copy-edited version of this book for review, my beloved father הכ"מ was taken suddenly from us. His brilliance, devotion, and love hover over all of my work. I know that his steadfastness, deeply held principles, clever sense of humor, and inspiration by deed will sustain all of our family in the years ahead. יהי זכרו ברוך.

Abbreviations

Journals

AJS Review	Association for Jewish Studies Review
JQR	Jewish Quarterly Review
JSQ	Jewish Studies Quarterly
MGWJ	Monatsschrift für Geschichte und Wissenschaft des Judentums
PAAJR	Proceedings of the American Academy for Jewish Research
REJ	Revue des études juives

Manuscript Collections

B.M.	British Museum
Bodl.	Bodleian Library
Cambr.	Cambridge University
JNUL	Jewish National and University Library
JTS	Jewish Theological Seminary of America

Introduction

Regnant Perceptions and Empirical Evidence

Modern appreciations of the intellectual history of medieval Ashkenazic Jewry during the twelfth and thirteenth centuries have typically focused on the protean achievements of Ashkenazic rabbinic scholars in the realms of talmudic and halakhic studies. It is fair to say that the Tosafists of northern France and Germany revolutionized the study of the Talmud through their close, critical reading and dialectical applications. In doing so, they firmly established the superiority of the Babylonian Talmud as the locus of Jewish legal traditions and derivations, even as they brought a remarkably wide range of talmudic literature and post-talmudic rabbinic works to bear on (or in line with) the teachings of the *Talmud Bavli.*

The most creative and prominent twelfth-century Tosafists, figures such as Rabbenu Jacob Tam (d. 1171), R. Isaac (Ri) of Dampierre (d. 1189), and R. Samson of Sens (Rash *mi-Shanz*, d. 1214) in northern France, and R. Eliezer b. Nathan (Raban) and his grandson R. Eliezer b. Joel *ha-Levi* (Rabiah, d. c. 1225) in Germany, have justifiably garnered the lion's share of attention from among their contemporaries and within modern historiography as well. Similarly, authors of the leading halakhic works and texts in the thirteenth century, such as R. Moses of Coucy (d. c. 1250, author of *Sefer Mizvot Gadol*), R. Isaac *Or Zaru'a* of Vienna (d. c. 1250), R. Isaac of Corbeil (d. 1270, author of *Sefer Mizvot Qatan*), and R. Meir of Rothenburg (d. 1293), who composed scores of responsa (and initiated the preservation of many others by his predecessors), have long been the focus of scholarly attention.[1]

[1] See, e.g., Julius Wellesz, "Die Decisionem R. Isaks aub Corbeil," *Jahrbuch der Judisch-Literarischen Gesellschaft* II (1911), 490–97, and Hebrew section, 1–8; idem, "Isak b. Mose Or Sarua," *MGWJ* 48 (1904), 129–44, 209–13, 361–71, 440–56, 710–12; 49 (1905), 701–6; idem, "Meir b. Baruch de Rothebourg," *REJ* 58 (1909), 236–40; 59 (1910), 42–58; 60 (1910), 53–72; Avigdor Aptowitzer, *Mavo la-Rabiah* (Jerusalem, 1938); Jacob Katz, *Exclusiveness and Tolerance* (Oxford, 1961); Haym Soloveitchik, *Halakhah, Kalkalah ve-Dimmui Azmi* (Jerusalem, 1985); and idem, *Ha-Yayin Bimei ha-Benayim: Pereq be-Toledot ha-Halakhah be-Ashkenaz* (Jerusalem, 2008).

Indeed, part of the greatness of E. E. Urbach's *Ba'alei ha-Tosafot: Toledoteihem, Ḥibbureihem, Shitatam* lies in its ability to effectively reconstruct the wider circles of figures and works that surrounded these leading authorities, which included teachers, colleagues, and students who were often important scholars in their own right. Even today, however, more than fifty years after the first edition of Urbach's *Ba'alei ha-Tosafot* was published, manuscript research and other comparative textual studies continue to uncover the existence and output of Ashkenazic rabbinic figures of significant ability whose writings were lost or are virtually unknown, and whose influence in the periods during which these works were composed (and beyond) has gone mostly uncharted and unremarked.[2]

The Longitudinal Factor: French and German Centers

The lesser-known figures and works still being discovered are most often of German or Eastern European origin. Tosafists and halakhists in northern France during the twelfth and thirteenth centuries (and their students and associates) were generally better known than their German counterparts, due in no small measure to the printing of the *Tosafot* to the standard editions of the Talmud.[3] These *Tosafot* texts were fundamentally the products of Tosafist study halls in northern France. It was through these texts that the dominance of Rabbenu Tam and Ri first emerged, and that their students, such as R. Jacob of Orleans, R. Ḥayyim *Kohen*, R. Ephraim of Regensburg, R. Isaac b. Mordekhai (Rivam) of Bohemia, R. Elḥanan b. *ha-Ri*, Rash

[2] See, e.g., *Teshuvot u-Pesaqim*, ed. Efraim Kupfer (Jerusalem, 1973), 121–22, 130, 144, 218–20, 227, 282–90, 295–97 (for R. Samuel b. Abraham *ha-Levi* of Worms, known also as R. Bonfant; cf. Simcha Emanuel, *Shivrei Luḥot: Sefarim Avudim shel Ba'alei ha-Tosafot* [Jerusalem, 2006], 181–84, and Urbach, *Ba'alei ha-Tosafot* [Jerusalem, 1980], 1:413–14); I. Ta-Shma, *Knesset Meḥqarim*, vol. 1 (Jerusalem, 2004), 224–53 (for R. Moses Fuller, among other Central and Eastern European halakhists during the thirteenth century); and Emanuel, *Shivrei Luḥot*, 166–75 (for R. Shemaryah b. R. Simḥah of Speyer), and 262–66 (for R. Menaḥem b. Natronai, known also as R. Qobil of Wurzburg).

[3] See, e.g., Haym Soloveitchik, "The Printed Page of the Talmud: The Commentaries and Their Authors," in *Printing the Talmud*, ed. S. L. Mintz and G. M. Goldstein (New York, 2005), 37–42; E. Fram, "In the Margins of the Text: Changes in the Page of the Talmud," in ibid., 91–96; and Urbach, *Ba'alei ha-Tosafot*, 1:27–31. Cf. Mordechai Breuer, *Be-Ohalei Torah* (Jerusalem, 2004), 184–206; Elchanan Reiner, "Temurot bi-Yeshivot Polin ve-Ashkenaz ba-Me'ot ha-16—ha-17 veha-Vikkuah 'al ha-Pilpul," in *Ke-Minhag Ashkenaz u-Polin* [*Sefer Yovel le-Chona Shmeruk*], ed. I. Bartal et al. (Jerusalem, 1993), 9–80; idem, "The Ashkenazic Elite at the Beginning of the Modern Era: Manuscript versus Printed Book," *Polin* 10 (1997), 85–98; Moshe Halbertal, *People of the Book: Canon, Meaning, and Authority* (Cambridge, Mass., 1997), 96–100, 116–19; and cf. Boaz Huss, "*Sefer ha-Zohar* as a Canonical, Sacred and Holy Text: Changing Perspectives of the Book of Splendor between the Thirteenth and Eighteenth Centuries," *Journal of Jewish Thought and Philosophy* 7 (1998), 257–307; and Joseph Davis, *Yom Tov Lipmann Heller* (Oxford, 2004), 76–81.

mi-Shanz and his brother R. Isaac b. Abraham (Rizba), and R. Judah Sirleon, became known to both students of the Talmud and academic scholars of Tosafist literature.[4]

Moreover, the printing of the standard *Tosafot* caused other manuscript versions of *Tosafot* to fall into disuse or to be forgotten.[5] At the same time, R. Moses of Coucy's *Sefer Mizvot Gadol* (*Semag*, first printed in Rome before 1480, and referenced in the standard editions of the Babylonian Talmud by the *Ein Mishpat* of R. Joshua Boaz),[6] allowed two earlier Tosafist halakhic works on which R. Moses of Coucy relied, *Sefer Yere'im* (by R. Eliezer of Metz) and *Sefer ha-Terumah* (by R. Barukh b. Isaac), to become better known. The same holds true for R. Moses's teacher, R. Judah Sirleon, and for other contemporaries and relatives of R. Moses, some of whom were themselves students of Rabbenu Tam or Ri. On the other hand, German and Austrian halakhic works from approximately the same period as *Semag*, such as *Sefer Rabiah* (*Sefer Avi ha-'Ezri* by R. Eliezer b. Yo'el *ha-Levi*) and *Sefer Or Zaru'a* (by Rabiah's student, R. Isaac b. Moses of Vienna, who also studied in northern France), were published only in relatively modern times, while others were not published at all.[7]

E. E. Urbach's textual forensics have shown that almost all of the key collections that formed or were incorporated into the *Tosafot* to the standard editions of the Babylonian Talmud were based in northern France. These include *Tosafot Shanz*, *Tosafot R. Yehudah Sirleon*, *Tosafot Hakhmei Evreux*, *Tosafot Rabbenu Perez*, as well as the most common collections of *Tosafot*, those edited or redacted by R. Eliezer b. Solomon *mi-Tukh* (which connotes the French locale of Touques, in Urbach's view).[8] Urbach identifies the standard

[4] For the noticeable (and in some cases almost ubiquitous) presence of these figures in the standard *Tosafot*, see Peretz Tarshish, *Ishim u-Sefarim ba-Tosafot*, ed. H. S. Neuhausen (New York, 1942), 3–9, 12–14, 27–28, 36–38, 45–50.

[5] See Benyamin Richler, "Kitvei ha-Yad shel Tosafot 'al ha-Talmud," in *Sefer Zikkaron le-Prof. Yisra'el Ta-Shma*, ed. M. Idel et al. (Alon Shvut, 2011), vol. 2, 771–73; Aharon Ahrend, "Seridim mi-Perush Ashkenazi 'al Massekhet Rosh ha-Shanah," *Qovez 'al Yad* 17 (2003), 139–43; and below, n. 24.

[6] See, e.g., Urbach, *Ba'alei ha-Tosafot*, 1:477.

[7] The first two parts of *Sefer Or Zaru'a* were published in Zhitomir in 1862, and two additional parts were published in the late 1880s. Cf. Emile Schrijver, "Some Light on the Amsterdam and London Manuscripts of Isaac ben Moses of Vienna's Or Zaru'a," *Bulletin of the John Rylands Library* 75:3 (1993), 53–82; and Simcha Emanuel, "The Manuscripts of Rabbi Isaac ben Moses of Vienna's Or Zaru'a," *Judentum* (2007), 1–8 [www.misrachi.at/judentum/geschichte_handscriften_1.php]. Sections of *Sefer Rabiah* were initially published in 1885, and Victor Aptowitzer began to publish his critical edition in Berlin in 1913. Additional sections of this work were published throughout the twentieth century (and beyond). A second major work by Rabiah, *Sefer Avi'asaf*, has been lost. See, e.g., Urbach, *Ba'alei ha-Tosafot*, 1:82–88; and S. Emanuel, *Shivrei Luhot*, 86–100.

[8] See Urbach, *Ba'alei ha-Tosafot*, 2:600–675; this chapter is titled "*Ha-Tosafot shelanu, zeman arikhatan u-meqoroteihen.*" Moreover, virtually all of the additional *Tosafot* collections that

Tosafot collections to only two tractates of the Babylonian Talmud, *Sotah* and the very brief *Tosafot* to *Horayyot*, as having originated in Germany. The only other German-based *Tosafot* found in standard editions of the Babylonian Talmud are classified as "addenda" to the main *Tosafot*, and appear on a small number of tractates. They are typically referred to as *Tosafot Yeshanim*, or as some other form of marginal compositions (*gilyonot*).[9]

---

have been published from manuscript during the twentieth century and beyond originated in northern France. These include *Tosafot Shanz* to *Pesaḥim*, *Ketubot*, *Sanhedrin*, *Makkot*, and *'Avodah Zarah* (in addition to the *Tosafot R. Elḥanan b. ha-Ri* to *'Avodah Zarah*); *Tosafot Evreux* to *Sotah*; the various collections of *Tosafot ha-Rosh*, which are fundamentally based on *Tosafot Shanz*; and *Tosafot Rabbenu Perez* (b. Elijah of Corbeil). Even the so-called *Tosafot Ḥakhmei Angliyyah* are also essentially related to those of the northern French Tosafists. (For the basic bibliographic data on all of these collections, see S. Emanuel, *Shivrei Luḥot*, 345–46.) The so-called *Tosafot Maharam ve-Rabbenu Perez 'al Massekhet Yevamot*, ed. H. Porush (Jerusalem, 1991) (= *Tosafot Maharam* in *Shitat ha-Qadmonim li-Yevamot*, ed. M. Y. Blau [New York, 1983]), contain far more French names than German ones. See Porush's introduction, 15–16; and cf. *Tosafot Yeshanim ha-Shalem 'al Massekhet Yevamot*, ed. A. Shoshana (Jerusalem, 1994), editor's introduction, 21–31, and the index, 616–17.

[9] For the *Tosafot* to *Horayyot*, see Urbach, *Ba'alei ha-Tosafot*, 2:660–61; for *Tosafot Sotah*, see below. See also 2:607, where Urbach notes that *Tosafot Yeshanim* to *'Eruvin* mention R. Meir of Rothenburg (d. 1293); his student, R. Ḥayyim b. Isaac *Or Zaru'a*; his senior colleague R. Avigdor Katz of Vienna; and other associates, including R. Yedidyah of Nuremberg, R. Judah *Kohen* of Friedberg, and the uncle of R. Eliezer *Tukh*, R. Hezekiah of Magdeburg. See also the description of *Tosafot Bava Mezi'a* (*Ba'alei ha-Tosafot*, 2:646–48), and *Tosafot Ḥullin* (2:665–66). A similar collection of names can be found in "addenda" to *Tosafot Ketubot* (2:628). Maharam's *Tosafot* to *Yoma* also mention some of his German teachers and associates (2:610–11, e.g., R. Jacob *ha-Levi* of Cologne and R. Judah *ha-Kohen* of Mainz, as well as R. Isaac *Or Zaru'a* and his teacher, R. Simḥah of Speyer; see *Tosafot Yoma* 54b, s.v. *ki*). The addenda (*Tosafot Yeshanim* to *Tosafot Shabbat* that come from the academy of Maharam [2:605]) mention Maharam himself as well as his earliest teacher, R. Isaac *Or Zaru'a*, and R. Isaac's teacher R. Simḥah of Speyer (19a, s.v. *notnin*). R. Isaac *Or Zaru'a* (who also studied in northern France) and R. Simḥah are arguably two of the most important German Tosafists in their day. And yet R. Isaac is otherwise mentioned only twice in the standard *Tosafot* to the Talmud (Urbach, 1:447, n. 79), while R. Simḥah is mentioned by name only on the two occasions just noted (in *Tosafot* edited by Maharam), and once in *Tosafot Horayyot* (cf. Urbach, 1:419, n. 46). Similarly, *Sefer Roqeaḥ*, composed by R. Simḥah's well-known contemporary, R. Eleazar of Worms, is mentioned only once in the standard *Tosafot* (see *Tosafot Shavu'ot* 46a, s.v. *'avid*, and Urbach, 2:660). Another German contemporary of R. Simḥah, R. Eliezer b. Yo'el *ha-Levi* (Rabiah), is mentioned three times (and one of these is in a *gilayon* to tractate *Niddah* 7b), although his major work, *Sefer Avi ha-'Ezri*, is cited on three additional occasions (including a reference in one instance to his grandfather Raban as well; see *Tosafot Ḥullin* 47b, s.v. *'afilu*). Raban is mentioned once more, in tractate *Shavu'ot* 26b, s.v. *'afilu*. One of Rabiah's Tosafist sons-in-law, R. Samuel b. Natronai (known as רשב"ט = Rashbat or R. Shevat), is not mentioned at all, while the other, R. Yo'el *ha-Levi* of Bonn (d. 1200, and father of Rabiah), is mentioned once (*Tosafot Yevamot* 118a, s.v. *de-kol*). See Urbach, *Ba'alei ha-Tosafot*, 2:607, 665–66, 675; P. Tarshish, *Ishim u-Sefarim ba-Tosafot*, 7, 87; and cf. *Tosafot ha-Rosh 'al Massekhet Qiddushin*, 648; *'al Massekhet Ḥullin*, 202, 222, 609; *'al Massekhet Ketubot*, 290, 323, 381; *'al Massekhet Rosh ha-Shanah*, 134, 136; and *'al Massekhet Shevu'ot*, 194. *Tosafot Sotah*, which were composed in Germany by a student of R. Meir b. Qalonymus (R. Meir was the older brother of Rivaq of Speyer, d. 1199), mention R. Yo'el *ha-Levi* once (25b, s.v. *Beit Hillel*). From his German teachers, the compiler of this collection also had access to several twelfth-century German rabbinic scholars not typically cited by *Tosafot* (including R. Samuel *he-Ḥasid*

To be sure, Israel Ta-Shma has suggested that R. Eliezer *mi-Tukh* hailed not from northern France but from Germany (Tucheim), although he agrees that the earlier *Tosafot* collections that R. Eliezer compiled and edited originated for the most part in Tosafist *battei midrash* in northern France.[10] In addition, the earliest Tosafist, R. Isaac b. Asher (Riba) *ha-Levi* of Speyer (d. 1133), was not a Frenchman.[11]

Nonetheless, leading German rabbinic scholars in the twelfth and thirteenth centuries became known mainly for the large, multifaceted, overarching, and stand-alone works they produced (e.g., *Sefer Raban*, *Sefer Rabiah*, *Sefer Or Zaruʿa*, *Sefer Mordekhai*), which contain a sometimes dizzying melange of commentary, halakhic rulings or compendia, and responsa. These medieval German halakhic works are much lengthier, bulkier, discursive, and diffuse than the glosslike *Tosafot* form of composition that was favored in northern France. Unlike their Tosafist colleagues in northern France, German rabbinic figures frequently consulted or communicated in writing with other German authorities and rabbinical courts. They also tended to include and to

b. Qalonymus); see Urbach, 1:365, 2:637–39. As noted above, several key German students of Rabbenu Tam, especially R. Ephraim of Regensburg, Ribam of Bohemia, and R. Isaac (Ri) *ha-Lavan*, are cited in collections that also include northern French students of Rabbenu Tam. See Urbach, 2:620 (*Yevamot*), 640 (*Bava Qamma*), and 661 (*Zevaḥim*).

10 See Ta-Shma, *Ha-Sifrut ha-Parshanit la-Talmud*, 2:44, 101 (n.13), 119–20; idem, *Knesset Meḥqarim*, 1:235 (n. 31), 238–39 (n. 45); and cf. A. Y. Havazelet, "Zemanam u-Meqomam shel Tosafot Tukh," *Yerushatenu* 2 (2008), 319–23. R. Eliezer Tukh's *gilyonot*, on the other hand, reflect the input and discussion of both his French and German teachers; and cf. S. Emanuel, "Unpublished Responsa of R. Meir of Rothenburg as a Source for Jewish History," in *The Jews of Europe in the Middle Ages*, ed. C. Cluse (Turnhout, 2004), 283–93.

11 See Ta-Shma, *Ha-Sifrut ha-Parshanit la-Talmud*, 1:66–70, and in *Tarbiz* 69 (2004), 501–9. Cf. Haym Soloveitchik, in *Tarbiz* 70 (2005), 529–35; Richler, "Kitvei Yad shel Tosafot," 780 (sec. 20), and 789 (sec. 55); A. Grossman, "Reshitan shel ha-Tosafot," in *Rashi: ʿIyyunim be-Yeẓirato*, ed. Z. A. Steinfeld (Ramat Gan, 1993), 57–68; and Mataniah Ghedalia, "Ḥakhmei Shpira Bimei Tatn"u ule-Aḥareihen" (Ph.D. diss., Bar Ilan University, 2007), 85–89. Riba is also the only German Tosafist who was not also a student of Rabbenu Tam to be cited frequently by the standard *Tosafot*. See Tarshish, *Ishim u-Sefarim*, 39–45. Regarding the question of Riba's creativity and his use of dialectic (and as but one of many examples that could be adduced), Riba's interpretation of the Mishnah in *Megillah* 20a as referring to the immersion of the hyssop bundle (used in the purification process, as an immersion that must be done by day) rather than to the immersion of the person who is *tamei met* (which is addressed by the Mishnah at the end of tractate *Parah*, 12:11, and can be performed in the evening as well) is as incisive and original as Rabbenu Tam's derivation, based on these two *Mishnayyot* and a passage in *Keritut* 9a, that the *tamei met* actually requires two sets of immersions (one prior to each *haza'ah* with the hyssop, and one at the end of the period of impurity). See, e.g., *Tosafot Megillah* 20a, s.v. *ve-lo tovlin*; *Tosafot Yeshanim ʿal Massekhet Yevamot*, ed. A. Shoshana (Jerusalem, 1994), 276–77 (*Yevamot* 46a), s.v. *'ein haza'ah*; and cf. *Mishneh Torah*, *hilkhot parah 'adumah*, 11:2 (with the glosses of Rabad and *Kessef Mishneh*, which also cites a responsum of R. Samson of Sens as included in his epistle to R. Meir *ha-Levi Abulafia* concerning Maimonides' *Mishneh Torah*); R. Samson's and Rosh's commentaries to *Parah* 12:11; and *Tosafot ha-Rosh ʿal Massekhet Ḥagigah*, ed. A. Shoshana (Jerusalem, 2002), 203 (*Ḥagigah* 23b, s.v. *ʿasa'uha*).

refer to their predecessors and contemporary colleagues at length, in addition to listing a wealth of personal, historical, and geographic details, as well as contemporary practices. As a result of these conventions, German halakhic works sometimes give the appearance of being slightly disorganized.[12]

In addition (and as I shall discuss further in the next chapter), German halakhic works often focused extensively on narrower areas of halakhic or judicial decision-making, and are not always as accessible or as interesting to students or nonspecialists as compared to French talmudic commentaries and halakhic compendia (such as R. Barukh b. Isaac's *Sefer ha-Terumah*, R. Moses of Coucy's *Semag*, and R. Isaac of Corbeil's *Sefer Miẓvot Qatan*).[13] At the same time, the collection process or method that produced *liqqutim*, which was vigorously pursued by thirteenth-century German works such as *Sefer Mordekhai*, had a tendency to "swallow up" earlier German halakhic materials and works, leading to the obsolescence or loss of those works, as well as obscuring the visibility of their authors.[14] To be sure, several salient

[12] These characteristics apply to works produced in Germany from the second half of the twelfth century through the mid-thirteenth century, such as the no longer extant *ʾArbaʿah Panim* by R. Ephraim of Regensburg (see Emanuel, *Shivrei Luḥot*, 289–91), *Seder ʿOlam* by R. Simḥah of Speyer (see *Teshuvot u-Pesaqim*, ed. Kupfer, *passim*, and Emanuel, 158–66), and *Sefer ha-Ḥokhmah* by R. Barukh of Mainz (see below, chapter 1, n. 6); and the extant *Sefer Rabiah*, and *Sefer Or Zaruʿa*. Indeed, the so-called *Simmanei Or Zaruʿa* (known also as *Or Zaruʿa ha-Qazar/ha-Qatan*), an abridged version of *Sefer Or Zaruʿa*, composed (c. 1300) by R. Isaac b. Moses's son R. Ḥayyim, aptly summarizes the work of the father, but follows its own order of tractates and topics, and is differently formatted. As Urbach notes (*Baʿalei ha-Tosafot*, 442–45), R. Ḥayyim undertook this project because he believed that his father's work would not be copied and circulated widely, due to its wide scope and size (and its discursive nature). On the kinds of information and details (large and small) that were typically included in German rabbinic works (and less so in French works), see also Emanuel, "Ha-Meineqet ha-Noẓriyyah Bimei ha-Benayim: Historiyyah ve-Halakhah," *Zion* 73 (2008), 29–40; and Rami Reiner, "Rabbinical Courts in France in the Twelfth Century: Centralisation and Dispersion," *Journal of Jewish Studies* 60 (2009), 316–17.

[13] *Sefer Miẓvot Qatan* (*Semaq*) was not conceived of or constructed primarily as an abridgment of *Sefer Miẓvot Gadol*. Indeed, it presents an independent selection of halakhic materials and approaches. Nonetheless, *Semaq*'s overall brevity and structural organization helped to make it a successful competitor in its day with the already popular (and relatively accessible) *Semag*. See, e.g., Urbach, *Baʿalei ha-Tosafot*, 2: 571–74; I. Ta-Shma's introduction to *Qiẓur Sefer Miẓvot Gadol le-Avraham b. Ephraim*, ed. Yehoshua Horowitz (Jerusalem, 2005), 13–21; and cf. below, chapter 4, n. 196.

[14] See Emanuel, *Shivrei Luḥot*, 6–12, who notes somewhat ironically that the style of voluminous citation which characterizes *Sefer Mordekhai* and other German *liqqutim* (and halakhic works) makes lost German works easier to re-create than lost French works, since surviving French works do not cite as much (verbatim) from their predecessors. Note that some leading *ʾaḥaronim*, e.g., *Shakh* and *Qeẓot ha-Ḥoshen*, were aware of many German Tosafists, principally through the *Sefer Mordekhai* and the fifteenth-century *Terumat ha-Deshen* (which frequently cites *Sefer Or Zaruʿa*, among other Ashkenazic compendia). See my "The Meaning and Significance of New Talmudic Insights," in *Why Study the Talmud in the 21st Century*, ed. Paul Socken (Lanham, Md., 2009), 161–76. I hope to return to this theme in a separate study.

and essential characteristics of Tosafist dialectic can be found throughout these German works, which were also partially structured along the lines of the tractates of the Talmud, even though they did not comment on or interpret the text of the Talmud in a continuous or consistent way. (And German dialectic overall was somewhat more muted than its northern French counterpart.)[15]

Unlike the halakhic codes and treatises of German origin, most of the German *Tosafot* collections of which we are currently aware have been lost, or have survived only in fragmentary fashion. These include *Tosafot R. Eliʿezer mi-Metz*,[16] *Tosafot Rivaq mi-Shpira*,[17] *Tosafot R. Shmuʾel b. Natronai*,[18] *Tosafot R. Yoʾel ha-Levi*,[19] *Tosafot R. Barukh b. Samuel mi-Magenza*,[20] *Tosafot R. Simḥah mi-Shpira*,[21] *Tosafot R. Mosheh Taku*,[22] and *Tosafot R. Eleazar mi-Vermaiza*.[23] As noted earlier, these German *Tosafot* were either pushed aside or passively discarded or ignored in favor of *Tosafot* collections from northern France.[24]

15 See, e.g., Ta-Shma, *Ha-Sifrut ha-Parshanit la-Talmud*, 2:110 (n. 29), 116–17; S. Emanuel, *Shivrei Luḥot*, 123–27; idem, *R. Eleazar mi-Vermaiza—Derashah le-Pesaḥ* (Jerusalem, 2006), 20; and cf. Y. Sussmann, "The Scholarly Oeuvre of Prof. E. E. Urbach," in *Supplement to Jewish Studies* 1 (1993), ed. D. Assaf, 39–40 (n. 63), 47–54; and H. Soloveitchik, "Catastrophe and Halakhic Creativity: Ashkenaz—1096, 1242, 1306 and 1298," *Jewish History* 12 (1998), 76–78.

16 See Emanuel, *Shivrei Luḥot*, 293–97. Although R. Eliezer was a student of Rabbenu Tam, Metz is considered to be a border locale that sometimes reflects German (Rhineland) practices, and R. Eliezer's students were, for the most part, Germans. See, e.g., Urbach, *Baʿalei ha-Tosafot*, 1:26, 152–64; Ta-Shma, *Ha-Sifrut ha-Parshanit*, 1:82; Emanuel, *Shivrei Luḥot*, 105–8, 127–29; R. Reiner, "Rabbenu Tam: Rabbotav (ha-Zarefatim) ve-Talmidav Bnei Ashkenaz" (M.A. thesis, Hebrew University, 1997), 105–13; and cf. below, chapter 1, nn. 109–11.

17 See Urbach, *Baʿalei ha-Tosafot*, 1:378; and Ta-Shma, *Ha-Sifrut ha-Parshanit la-Talmud*, 2:118.

18 Emanuel, *Shivrei Luḥot*, 60–61.

19 See A. Aptowitzer, *Mavo la-Rabiah*, 46–47; Urbach, *Baʿalei ha-Tosafot*, 1:211–12; Emanuel, *Shivrei Luḥot*, 81–86; and cf. below, chapter 1, n. 38. R. Yoʾel *ha-Levi*'s *Tosafot* contain a basic commentary (*perishah*) as well as dialectical *Tosafot*, and are based on the writings and *Tosafot* of three of his teachers, Ribam, R. Ephraim b. Isaac, and R. Moses b. Joel of Regensburg. R. Moses's son, R. Abraham, also composed *Tosafot* to *Bava Batra*. See Emanuel, *Shivrei Luḥot*, 83–84 (n. 147); and below, chapter1, n. 30. Note also the *Tosafot* composed by R. Yoʾel *ha-Levi*'s (older) relative, R. Jacob b. Isaac (Yaʿavetz), who lived in the Rhineland; see Emanuel, *Shivrei Luḥot*, 83 (n. 144), and cf. David Deblitzky, "Iggeret Rabbenu Ephraim me-Regensburg u-Teshuvat Raban," *Yerushatenu* 2 (2008), 15–16.

20 Emanuel, *Shivrei Luḥot*, 112–23.

21 See Ta-Shma, *Ha-Sifrut ha-Parshanit*, 2:116, and Emanuel, *Shivrei Luḥot*, 157.

22 Ta-Shma, *Ha-Sifrut ha-Parshanit*, and Emanuel, *Shivrei Luḥot*, 315, n. 34.

23 See Ta-Shma, *Ha-Sifrut ha-Parshanit*, and S. Emanuel, *R. Eleazar mi-Vermaiza—Derashah le-Pesaḥ*, 50–51. For the *Tosafot* of R. Meir of Rothenburg (most of which are not extant), see Urbach, *Baʿalei ha-Tosafot*, 2:563–64; Emanuel, *Shivrei Luḥot*, 41–43; and cf. B. Richler (above, n. 5), sec. 53. In sec. 54, Richler notes two folios of *Tosafot R. Hezekiah mi-Magdeburg* to tractate *Pesaḥim*, which have been found and published by Y. Lifshitz.

24 See above, n. 5. There were also thirteenth-century French *Tosafot* collections that were ostensibly "pushed out" by other northern French versions (and subsequently lost), e.g., *Tosafot R. Yeḥiʾel mi-Paris* (see Ta-Shma, *Ha-Sifrut ha-Parshanit*, 2:110–11, and Emanuel, *Shivrei Luḥot*, 187–89); and *Tosafot R. Yiẓḥaq mi-Corbeil* (Urbach, *Baʿalei ha-Tosafot*,

All these factors taken together have undoubtedly contributed to the popular perception according to which the Tosafists of northern France occupied a disproportionately dominant place as representatives of the talmudism of medieval Ashkenaz. A first step in properly sketching the intellectual history of this period must therefore be to separate and distinguish "longitudinally" between Germany and northern France in order to establish what was different between these two centers. Indeed, moving forward, it should be possible to identify important differences between eastern and western Germany, or even within different regions of northern France as well, although this largely exceeds the scope of this study.[25]

As Yaakov Sussmann has noted, Urbach was well aware of the scholarly dynamism and productivity within both the German and northern French centers (he treated developments in northern France and Germany in separate chapters within his *Ba'alei ha-Tosafot*), but he also tended to view and evaluate their intellectual characteristics, proclivities, and methods as fundamentally similar. Y. N. Epstein, on the other hand, was more inclined to try to tease out the differences between these centers, just as he did with respect to parallel centers of Torah study during both the Tannaitic and Amoraic periods.[26] Once significant distinctions have been identified with respect to form (e.g., *Tosafot* versus halakhic works) and primary goals (e.g., pursuing overarching talmudic interpretations versus providing and supporting legal decisions), it becomes clear that a number of fundamental

---

2:575, and Emanuel, *Shivrei Luḥot*, 199), which were apparently rather meager in any case. Ta-Shma notes that R. Yeḥi'el of Paris also composed *shitot* (which were more basic and less *Tosafot*-like commentaries, akin to *shitat Evreux*) to several tractates, one of which (to tractate *Mo'ed Qatan*) has survived at least in part. Cf. *Tosafot Ri ha-Zaqen ve-Talmido 'al Massekhet Shabbat*, ed. A. Shoshana (Jerusalem, 2007), editor's introduction, 53–55.

[25] See e.g., Eric Zimmer, *'Olam ke-Minhago Noheg* (Jerusalem, 1996), *passim* (for distinctions between מנהג אושטרייך and מנהג ריינוס); Y. M. Pelles, "Ẓarefat, Burgundy ve-Normandy be-Piyyutim ubi-Teqiyyot," *Yerushatenu* 2 (2008), 305–18; and Elisabeth Hollender, "Reconstructing Manuscripts: The Liturgical Fragments from Trier," in *Genizat Germania*, ed. A. Lehnardt (Leiden, 2010), 61–74.

[26] See Sussmann, "The Scholarly Oeuvre of Prof. E. E. Urbach" (above, n. 15), and see also ibid., 24–25. In Sussmann's words, Urbach considered the "world of the Tosafists" as "one big world with a unified cultural and literary character," while Epstein sought "to separate between that which is connected, to distinguish between different sources in order to determine their uniqueness," which for the Tosafist period meant highlighting the differences between northern France and Germany. Indeed, there is reason to question whether German rabbinic scholars during this period should be referred to as Tosafists, although some of this discussion is fundamentally semantic in nature. Urbach has alternating chapters for each region, which do not really come together (even as the scholars from each region do not physically meet for lengthy periods of time either), but the underlying suggestion is that they are doing the very same things. At the same time, however, Urbach includes discussion of some of the German Pietists in a chapter on the German Tosafists, which creates a rather different impression as compared to contemporary Tosafists in northern France.

similarities nonetheless exist. I shall have more to say about this issue in the next chapter.

The Latitudinal Factor: The Multiplicity of Disciplines

A second significant factor (which may be characterized as a "latitudinal" one) that has shaped the perceptions of rabbinic culture during the Tosafist period concerns the extent to which Tosafist studies were exclusively talmudocentric. Here too, as Sussmann has noted, Urbach tended to stress that Tosafist talmudic methodology and interests dominated all other areas of study as well. In Urbach's words:

> The *Tosafot* were the fruits of constant laboring in the Talmud and also in the words of *Ḥazal* and their interpreters. The [talmudic] method of the Tosafists spread out and controlled other types of literature as well. Not only are the works of legal decisions and responsa by northern French and German rabbinic scholars considered to be *Tosafot*—in terms of their method, mode of interpretation, and presentation—but even their commentaries to the Torah, to the prayers and to *piyyutim*, and even their polemical confrontations with local Christians were composed according to this approach and method.[27]

As the studies of Avraham Grossman have amply demonstrated, on the other hand, quite a few German and northern French halakhists and talmudists who flourished during the pre-Crusade period were involved in the study of Scripture (*miqra*) that went well beyond the discussions and methods found within talmudic *sugyot*, and even included nascent forms of *peshat* interpretation.[28] Many pre-Crusade rabbinic scholars in Germany composed *piyyutim*, as did a number in northern France,[29] and several

[27] Urbach, *Ba'alei ha-Tosafot*, 1:18, cited partially by Sussmann, "The Scholarly Oeuvre of Prof. E. E. Urbach," 18 (and cf. ibid., 25, concerning Urbach's keen focus on *ha-Tosafot shelanu*).

[28] See Grossman, *Ḥakhmei Ashkenaz ha-Rishonim* (Jerusalem, 1981), 226, 249–50, 288–89, 293, 323, 351–53, 412–20. As Grossman notes, Y. N. Epstein's suggestion that the study of *peshat* was limited to Worms alone is not borne out, due to the presence of R. Jacob b. Yaqar in Mainz as well. See Grossman, *Ḥakhmei Ẓarefat ha-Rishonim* (Jerusalem, 1995), 462–71, where he also notes a degree of resistance to *peshat* among certain talmudists. As is well known, twelfth-century *peshat* was limited to northern France, although we shall see (in chapter 3) involvement by German rabbinic figures in the phase of *peshat* exegesis that emerged in the late twelfth and early thirteenth centuries.

[29] See Grossman's summary statement in *Ḥakhmei Ashkenaz ha-Rishonim*, 422–23; idem, *Ḥakhmei Ẓarefat ha-Rishonim*, 76–82, 98–104, 248–49; and below, chapter 5.

rabbinic scholars in both areas did *piyyut* commentary as well.[30] Groups of rabbinic figures at the academy of Mainz in particular were familiar with aspects of *torat ha-sod* and *Hekhalot* literature,[31] as were several of their northern French counterparts.[32] Indeed, the intellectual biography of Rashi (d. 1105) includes many of these extra-talmudic disciplines, in addition to his extensive commentary on the Talmud and his halakhic responsa and decisions (*pesaqim*).[33] To put it another way, there seem to be relatively few pre-Crusade rabbinic figures who did Talmud and *halakhah* exclusively.[34]

The intellectual biographies of two of the earliest leading northern French Tosafists, Rashbam (d. c. 1160) and his brother Rabbenu Tam (d. 1171), suggest that they sought to limit or shift the range of pre-Crusade disciplines. In addition to his talmudic interpretations, which are cited frequently in *Tosafot* texts and related literature (and are occasionally referred to as *Tosafot Rabbenu Shmu'el*), Rashbam also "fills in" rather extensively for Rashi's commentary on *Bava Batra* (and elsewhere), and he perhaps composed a halakhic compendium as well.[35] In the realm of biblical interpretation, Rashbam authored an extensive commentary on the Torah and on a number of other biblical books, and a detailed grammatical work that supported his biblical exegesis.[36]

[30] See Grossman, *Ḥakhmei Ẓarefat ha-Rishonim*, 507–34. At the same time (and as Elisabeth Hollender describes in her *Piyyut Commentary in Medieval Ashkenaz* [Berlin, 2008], 40–52), most *piyyut* commentaries from the twelfth century and into the thirteenth were composed in Germany, with relatively little in this discipline emanating from northern France. Cf. below, chapter 5, nn. 283–84.

[31] See Grossman, *Ḥakhmei Ashkenaz ha-Rishonim*, 100–101, 162–64, 216, 229–30, 257, 293–95, 390–91, 423; and see below, chapter 6.

[32] See Grossman, *Ḥakhmei Ẓarefat ha-Rishonim*, 78–79, 83, 85, 104–5.

[33] See Grossman, *Ḥakhmei Ẓarefat ha-Rishonim*, ch. 4, and cf. idem, *Ḥakhmei Ashkenaz ha-Rishonim*, 420, n. 50. On Rashi and *torat ha-sod*, cf. my "Rashi's Awareness of Jewish Mystical Literature and Traditions," in *Raschi und sein Erbe*, ed. D. Krochmalnik et al. (Heidelberg, 2007), 23–34.

[34] For Rashi's immediate students, see Grossman, *Ḥakhmei Ẓarefat ha-Rishonim*, 580. All this fits quite well with the broad and varied definition of truth in Torah study and method in medieval Ashkenaz, which will be discussed in the final section of this chapter.

[35] See Urbach, *Ba'alei ha-Tosafot*, 1:45–57; Ta-Shma, *Ha-Sifrut ha-Parshanit la-Talmud*, 1:58–63; and Yehudah Felix, "Shitato ha-Metodologit veha-Meḥqarit shel Rashbam be-Perusho la-Talmud," in *'Iyyunei Miqra u-Parshanut*, vol. 8 (Ramat Gan, 2008), 503–21. Felix also describes the variegated pedagogic nature of Rashbam's *Bava Batra* commentary (and the multilayered interpretations within it), aspects that are not as readily apparent in Rashbam's biblical commentaries. See Eleazar Touitou, *Exegesis in Perpetual Motion* [Hebrew] (Ramat Gan, 2002), 51–67, and cf. below, nn. 45–46. On Rashbam's halakhic rulings, cf. Urbach, *Ba'alei ha-Tosafot*, 127 (n. 19*); S. Emanuel, *Shivrei Luḥot*, 179–80 (n. 20), and 297 (n. 350); ms. Moscow 774, fol. 125r; and ms. Moscow 333, fols. 121r–v.

[36] For the scope and nature of Rashbam's biblical commentaries, see, e.g., S. A. Poznanski, *Mavo 'al Ḥakhmei Ẓarefat Mefarshei ha-Miqra* (Warsaw, 1913), XXXIX–LI; Moshe Sokolow, "Ha-Peshatot ha-Mitḥadshim: Qeta'im Ḥadashim mi-Perush ha-Torah la-Rashbam—Ketav Yad," *'Alei*

As perceptively noted by Haim Hillel Ben-Sasson more than a half-century ago,[37] Rashbam treats scriptural interpretation as a discipline quite distinct from his talmudic interpretations (in terms of both method and form), so much so that it remains unclear whether Rashbam's preferred method of scriptural interpretation, *'omeq peshuto shel miqra*, was taught and discussed within Tosafist study halls or whether it was mainly the province of specialists or groups of *ba'alei miqra* known as "*maskilim*" (as opposed to *ba'alei talmud*), as both Rashbam and R. Yosef Qara themselves seem to indicate.[38] In a fairly lengthy passage in his Torah commentary, Rashbam writes that he interacted in a matter of scriptural interpretation with his "teachers [or colleagues] in Paris." However, this discussion completely bypasses Rashbam's own *peshat* interpretation of this verse, and deals only with midrashic texts (*midreshei halakhah*) and their interpretation. The discussion ends with Rashbam citing a similar interpretation of these Tannaitic *midrashim* by

---

Sefer 11 (1984), 73–80; *Perush Rashbam le-Sefer Iyyov*, ed. Sara Japhet, editor's introduction, 9–36; E. Toitou, *Exegesis in Perpetual Motion*, 208–25; Robert Harris, *Discerning Parallelism: A Study in Northern French Medieval Jewish Biblical Exegesis* (Providence, R.I., 2004), 55–73; Ithamar Kislev, "Perush ha-Ḥizzequni ke-'Ed Nosah le-Perush Rashbam la-Torah," in *Shai le-Sarah Japhet*, ed. H. Ben-Shammai et al. (Jerusalem, 2008), 173–93; and J. Jacobs, "Iqqaron ha-Haqdamah be-Perush Rashbam la-Torah," *'Iyyunei Miqra u-Parshanut* 8 (2008), 451–79. For Rashbam's grammatical work, see Ronela Merdler, "Sefer Dayyaqot me-Rabbenu Shmu'el: Perushei ha-Diqduq shel Rashbam la-Tanakh u-Terumato ha-Parshanit," *Shenaton le-Ḥeqer ha-Miqra veha-Mizraḥ ha-Qadum* 14 (2005), 241–55, and Yossi Leshem, "Ha-Perushim ha-Diqduqiyyim be-Perush Rashbam li-Megillat Qohelet u-Terumatam li-She'elat ha-Otentiyyut shel ha-Ḥibbur," *Shenaton le-Ḥeqer ha-Miqra veha-Mizraḥ ha-Qadum* 18 (2008), 184–207.

[37] See Ben-Sasson's review of the first edition of Urbach's *Ba'alei ha-Tosafot*, "Hanhagatah shel Torah," in *Beḥinot be-Biqqoret ha-Sifrut*, ed. S. Zemach, vol. 9 (Jerusalem, 1956), 45–46; cf. Rashbam to *Bava Batra* 47b, s. v. *havah*; 48a, s.v. *yaqriv*; and *Rashbam's Commentary to Leviticus and Numbers*, ed. M. Lockshin (Providence, R.I., 2001), 14, 231. There is a dissertation waiting to be written on Rashbam's different methods of interpretation in the three exegetical arenas in which he was active (talmudic commentary, *Tosafot* interpretation and analysis, and scriptural *peshat*). In Ben-Sasson's view, Rashbam engaged in these rather diverse methods because each one represented the approach that was most needed in his day within each area of religious literature. Aharon Mondschein, "Le-Gillui ha-Perush ha-'Avud' shel Rashbam le-Sefer Tehillim u-Pirsum Muqdam le-Mizmorim 120–136," *Tarbiz* 79 (2011), 91–141, has demonstrated that Rashbam, in his (recently identified) commentary to Psalms, presents a fair amount of Talmudic and rabbinic interpretation as well. Perhaps this was due to the fact that Rashi approached Psalms in his commentary mainly as a work of biblical poetry, and often provided a kind of literary *peshat*. In this instance, it was left to Rashbam (as was his wont) to "fill in" the rabbinic interpretations to a larger degree than he might otherwise have been inclined.

[38] See my *Jewish Education and Society in the High Middle Ages* (Detroit, Mich., 1992), 82–84. Cf. E. Touitou, *Exegesis in Perpetual Motion*, 11–15, 26–33, 72–74, 98–105, 177–81; idem, "'Al Gilgulei ha-Nosaḥ shel Perush Rashi la-Torah," *Tarbiz* 56 (1986), 216, 238–41; *Perush Rabbenu Shmu'el b. Meir le-Shir ha-Shirim*, ed. S. Japhet, editor's introduction, 78–89, 100–106; S. Japhet, *Dor Dor u-Parshanav* (Jerusalem, 2008), 35–54, 151–56, 313–27; and cf. 328–40. A pointed statement by Qara in this regard is found in his commentary to 1 Samuel, 1:20 (יליזו על פתרון זה בעלי אגדה ותלמוד שלא יניחו מה שפתרו רבותינו בראש השנה ובכמה מסכתות וילכו אחר פתרי). See also Yehoshafat Nevo, *Ha-Parshanut ha-Ẓarefatit* (Tsfat, 19994), 9–22.

R. Qalonymus of Rome (who arrived at the academy of Worms c. 1080).[39] Similarly, in a second such passage, in which Rashbam responds to a question from Anjou that was posed *lefi ha-peshat*, the issue at hand concerned the structure and style of the Torah, and could easily have been of interest to rabbinic scholars in general, without any particular affinity with Rashbam's narrower method of *peshat.* Indeed, the key prooftext cited by Rashbam in his response is a talmudic passage from tractate *Rosh ha-Shanah.*[40]

Although Rashi (who interpreted virtually the entire Bible) had students such as Yosef Qara who worked primarily or largely in the area of scriptural interpretation,[41] Rashi himself had studied Scripture (including issues of *peshuto shel miqra*) with his talmudic teacher at Mainz, R. Yaʿaqov b. Yaqar.[42] Moreover, since Rashi, in his commentary on the Bible, was also interested in presenting *ʾaggadah ha-meyashevet divrei miqra*,[43] it is often instructive to compare the parallel scriptural interpretations given by Rashi within his talmudic commentaries to those found in his biblical commentaries.[44]

Within his talmudic comments Rashbam for the most part explains the Talmud's midrashic interpretation of a verse without indicating his own very different *peshat* interpretation as it appears in his Torah commentary. On quite a few occasions, however, Rashbam will note the scriptural basis that allows for the talmudic understanding of a verse to diverge from

[39] See Rashbam to Nu. 11:35, ומדרש אגדה בספרי בסוף הפרשה . . . ומסופק לרבותי ונשאלתי עליו בפא־ריש ופירשתיו בדרשה . . . וכל דרשה זו מצאתי במכילתא . . . ושוב מצאתיה בתשובות ר' קלונימוס איש רומי כמוני ופירשתי לשואלים . . . (cited in Touitou, *Exegesis in Perpetual Motion*, 12). See also Urbach, *Baʿalei ha-Tosafot*, 1:46; and *Rashbam's Commentary on Leviticus and Numbers*, ed. M. I. Lockshin (Providence, R.I., 2001), 196–98. For R. Qalonymus b. Shabbetai of Rome's activities in Worms (in both talmudic and scriptural interpretation), see A. Grosssman, *Ḥakhmei Ashkenaz ha-Rishonim*, 348–54, and idem, *Ḥakhmei Ẓarefat ha-Rishonim*, 255, 338–40, 447–49.

[40] See Rashbam Nu. 30:2–3; Touitou, *Exegesis in Perpetual Motion*, 20 (n. 35); and Lockshin, ed., *Rashbam's Commentary on Leviticus and Numbers*, 285–88.

[41] See, e.g., Moshe Ahrend, *Le Commentaire de R. Yosef Qara sur Job*, 13–23; idem, *Perush R. Yosef Qara le-Iyyov* (Jerusalem, 1988), 26–27 (n. 25); A. Grossman, *Ḥakhmei Ẓarefat ha-Rishonim*, 171–74, 255–63.

[42] See Grossman, *Ḥakhmei Ẓarefat ha-Rishonim*, 126–28. In his commentary to *Pesaḥim* (111a), Rashbam refers to R. Yaʿaqov b. Yaqar as Rashi's "teacher of Gemara and *miqra.*"

[43] See Rashi's programmatic statement in his commentary to Genesis 3:8, and cf., e.g., Sara Kamin, *Rashi: Persuhto shel Miqra u-Midrasho shel Miqra* (Jerusalem, 1986); N. Leibowitz and M. Ahrend, *Perush Rashi la-Torah: ʿIyyunim be-Shitato*, vol. 2 (Tel Aviv, 1990), 337–43, 360–80; and below, chapter 2.

[44] See, e.g., Rashi to Genesis 21:1, and to *Bava Qamma* 92a, s.v. *paqad*, and see generally Yoel Florsheim, *Rashi on the Bible in His Commentary on the Talmud* [Hebrew], 3 vols. (Jerusalem, 1981–91); Mayer Gruber, *Rashi's Commentary on Psalms* (Philadelphia, 2007), 7–9; Lea Himmelfarb, "On Some Discrepancies between Rashi's Commentary on the Talmud and His Commentary on the Bible," *Hebrew Union College Annual* 75 (2004), 163–91; and *Perush Rashi le-Masskehet Megillah*, ed. A. Ahrend (Jerusalem, 2008), 24–25

its plain meaning.[45] He will also, on occasion, juxtapose *peshat* interpretations and rabbinic interpretations in his Torah commentary especially in halakhic contexts that are fundamentally at odds with each other, without privileging either.[46]

This broad range of sensibilities, together with the expansive, dialectical interpretations provided by Rashbam throughout his talmudic comments, represent, as Ben-Sasson had indicated, the antithesis of his scriptural comments, reflecting Rashbam's conviction that true interpretations of Torah texts and ideas can be reached through rather diverse means and methods. Indeed, this is how Rashbam's various programmatic statements or disclaimers ought to be understood: he lauds the halakhic, nonliteral approach of *Ḥazal* to the interpretation of Scripture as primary in importance even as he stresses that talmudic literature itself notes that *ʾein miqra yoẓe midei peshuto*.[47]

45 See, e.g., Rashbam's commentary to *Bava Batra* 50b; s.v. *ki kaspo*; 60b, s.v. *va-yar*; 69b, s.v. *dikhtiv va-yaqom*; 72b, s.v. *dikhtiv sadeh*; 75b, s.v. *shalosh u-sheloshim*; 78b, s.v. *ʿal ken*; 81a, s.v. *tiyuvta*; 81b, s.v. *ve-laqahta*; 84a, s.v. *ʿamoq*; 84b, s.v. *lo tisʿu*; 88b, s.v. *ve-ẓedeq*, and 89a, s.v. *tanu rabbanan*; 110a, s.v. *dikhtiv ʾish*; 110b, *ʾaḥvah ve-ʾaḥvah*; 111a, s.v. *t"l ve-yarash*; 113a, s.v. *mai mashma*; 118b, *naton titein*; 120a, s.v. *va-tehiyenah*; 121b, s.v. *ʾelai hayah*; 126b, s.v. *ve-hayah*; 127b, s.v. *yakkir*; 147a, s.v. *ve-haʿavartem*; 155b, s.v. *ve-ʿamdu*. Cf. *Rashbam's Commentary on Genesis*, ed. Lockshin, 376, n. 3; Rashbam's *Commentary on Deuteronomy*, ed. Lockshin, 144–45; and see also Lockshin, "ʿIyyun be-Gishot Shonot le-Pittaron Beʿayat ha-Yaḥas she-Bein ha-Peshat le-Vein Midrash Halakhah," *ʿIyyunei Miqra u-Parshanut*, vol. 8 (2008), ed. S. Vargon et al., 33–45. In this study, Lockshin notes and characterizes the explanations for *Ḥazal*'s method of halakhic exegesis suggested by Rashbam in his *Bava Batra* commentary (and in several places his Torah commentary) on the basis of "*yittur ha-miqra(ʾot).*" Unlike Ibn Ezra, who could not abide contradictions between contextual *peshat* and the rabbinic *midreshei halakhah*, Rashbam was more than able to justify and support *Ḥazal*'s halakhic interpretations according to the(ir) method of *yitturim*. (Lockshin also cites an example from Rashi's commentary to *Ketubot* 53a, s.v. *she-mattanah*, to show that Rashi had already embraced this approach to explain *midreshei halakhah* that did not appear to comport with the simple *peshat* of a particular verse.) See also E. Toutiou, *Exegesis in Perpetual Motion*, 51–76; and Morris Berger, "The Torah Commentary of Rabbi Samuel b. Meir" (Ph.D. diss., Harvard University, 1982), 236–59.

46 See, e.g., Rashbam's comments to Exodus 22:6–12, s.v. *ki yitten*, and to Exodus 22:13–14, s.v. *beʿalav ʾein ʿimmo*; *Rashbam's Commentary on Exodus*, ed. M. Lockshin, 253–54, 260–61; and Lockshin, "Ha-Im Hayah Yosef Bekhor Shor Pashtan?" in *Iggud*, vol. 1, ed. A. Melamed et al. (Jerusalem, 2008), 165–67.

47 See, e.g., Touitou, *Exegesis in Perpetual Motion*, 18, 68–76, 98–109; Moshe Greenberg, "Ha-Yaḥas Bein Perush Rashi le-Perush Rashbam la-Torah," in *Sefer Yiẓḥaq Aryeh Zeligmann* (Jerusalem, 1983), 559–67; Ithamar Kislev, "ʿVe-ʾAsher Sam Libbo le-Divrei Yoẓerenuʾ: Ha-Heged ha-Metodologi shel Rashbam bi-Teḥilat Perusho le-Sefer Va-yiqra u-Terumato le-Havanat Yaḥasam shel Rashi le-Perusho shel Rashbam, *Tarbiz* 73 (2004), 225–26; S. Japhet, *Dor Dor u-Parshanav*, 35–54; Martin Lockshin, *Rabbi Samuel Ben Meir's Commentary on Genesis: An Annotated Translation* (Lewiston, N.Y., 1989), 9–23 (introduction); idem, *Rashbam's Commentary on Deuteronomy* (Providence, R.I., 2004), 16–25 (introduction); and idem, "Truth or *Peshat:* Issues in Law and Exegesis," in *Law, Politics and Society in the Ancient Mediterranean World*, ed. B. Halpern and D. Hobson (Sheffield, 1993), 271–78; Yeshayahu Maori, "ʾAggadot Ḥaluqot be-Perushei

And yet, despite his conviction that truthful Torah study could be pursued over different genres using very different exegetical forms, Rashbam, in contrast to Rashi and to the rabbinic scholars of the pre-Crusade period as a whole, sought to limit the number of disciplines in which he was involved.[48] Rashbam informs his readers, in both his commentary to *Qohelet* and at the beginning of his Torah commentary, that it is best to step away from the *ḥokhmah ha-ʿamuqah* of *torat ha-sod*, especially as it is found in the areas of cosmogony and theosophy, and to concentrate instead only on more exoteric forms of study and wisdom, even as Rashbam was himself aware of an array of mystical teachings and texts and of the magical powers of Divine names.[49] Additionally, no *piyyutim* (or commentaries thereupon) from Rashbam have survived, and it appears that he was uninvolved in this important pre-Crusade discipline.[50]

This kind of disciplinary concentration is also in evidence for Rabbenu Tam to an even greater extent. According to Rabbenu Tam's well-known formulation, one fulfills the (talmudic) requirement of studying, in equal proportion, the distinct subject areas of Scripture, Mishnah, and Talmud through study of the Babylonian Talmud, since the Talmud is suffused with material from the other disciplines and its study thus entails the study of these other areas as well. Through this formulation, Rabbenu Tam is indicating here not only that study of the Talmud should predominate but also that the other bodies of sacred literature can and should be studied principally through the prism of talmudic literature and its analysis.[51]

Rashi la-Miqra," *Shenaton le-Ḥeqer ha-Miqra veha-Mizraḥ ha-Qadum* 19 (2009), 155–58, 198–206; and cf. Uriel Simon, "Le-Darko ha-Parshanit shel R. Avraham ibn Ezra ʿal pi Sheloshet Be'urav le-Pasuq Eḥad," *Sefer Bar Ilan* 6 (1968), 136–38.

[48] Note also that Rashbam's youngest brother, R. Solomon, is described as the "father of the grammarians," but appears to have played no role in the formation of *Tosafot*. See Urbach, *Baʿalei ha-Tosafot*, 1:59. On the other hand, Rashbam's father (and Rashi's son-in-law), R. Meir b. Samuel, who composed some early *Tosafot* (perhaps as the result of his training at Worms), was totally uninvolved in scriptural interpretation. See Urbach, *Baʿalei ha-Tosafot*, 1:41–45. As Urbach notes (1:40, n. 30), ms. Parma 541 makes mention of *perushim shel ḥumash she-ʿasah R. Yehudah b. Natan* [= Riban, Rashi's other son-in-law]. The comment by Riban in *Baʿalei ha-Tosafot ʿal ha-Torah*, ed. Shraga Abramson (Jerusalem, 1974), 22, 68, is a talmudic interpretation, concerning an illicit sexual relationship, that was included in this collection of Tosafist (talmudic) interpretations, which were arrayed according to order of the (halakhic) verses in the Torah portion of *Ki Teze*. See below, chapter 2, nn. 1–3.

[49] See my *"Peering through the Lattices,"* 158–61; Joseph Davis, "Philosophy, Dogma and Exegesis in Medieval Ashkenazic Judaism: The Evidence of *Sefer Hadrat ha-Qodesh*," *AJS Review* 18 (1993), 213 (n. 67); and below, chapter 6, nn. 6–10.

[50] See below, chapter 5, n. 83.

[51] See *Tosafot Qiddushin* 30a, s.v. *la zerikha*; *Tosafot Sanhedrin* 24a. s.v. *belulah*; and *Tosafot ʿAvodah Zarah* 19a, s.v. *yeshallesh*. See also R. Ḥayyim Yosef David Azulai, *Shem ha-Gedolim* (Warsaw, 1876), 116, who attributed the following statement to Rabbenu Tam: "I will engage in interpretation of the Talmud, as my revered grandfather did. I will not undertake biblical

Although Rabbenu Tam authored a commentary on the book of Job and a treatment of the philological interpretations of Menaḥem and Dunash (characterized in one manuscript as *Hakhra'ot*),[52] the comments on various Torah and other biblical verses that are properly attributed to Rabbenu Tam are almost invariably a reflection of talmudic or midrashic literature rather than an attempt at independent *peshat* interpretation of the kind typically associated with the *pashtanim* of northern France.[53] Indeed,

---

interpretation, however, since I do not have the capacity to do it." Cf. Frank Talmage, "Keep Your Sons from Scripture: The Bible in Medieval Jewish Scholarship and Spirituality," in *Understanding Scripture*, ed. C. Thoma and M. Wyschogrod (New York, 1987), 84–86.

52 See S. A. Poznanski, *Mavo 'al Ḥakhmei Ẓarefat Mefarshei ha-Miqra*, 53–54; and Urbach, *Ba'alei ha-Tosafot*, 1:107–8 (where he also perceptively notes the familial influence on Rabbenu Tam's involvement in these disciplines). This work (אתחיל הכרעות של ר"ת) was published by Z. H. Filipowski, *Teshuvot Dunash ben Labrat 'im Hakhra'ot Rabbenu Tam* (London, 1855), from a Bodleian manuscript (Bodl. 1449, fols. 165r–208v), and is extant (but untitled) in three other fairly early manuscript versions: ms. Vatican 402 (fols. 1r–23r); Parma (Palatina) 3505 (Perreau 32), 201v–220v; and ms. Florence Laurenzia Plut. 88.9, fols. 174r–221r. For the Job commentary, see Benjamin Richler, "Rabbeinu Tam's 'Lost' Commentary on the Book of Job," in *The Frank Talmage Memorial Volume*, ed. B. Walfish (Haifa, 1993), vol. 1, 191–202; I. Ta-Shma, "Perush Rabbenu Tam le-Sefer Iyyov," *Qoveẓ 'al Yad* 13 [23] (1996), 193–223; *Perush Rabbenu Shmu'el b. Meir le-Sefer Iyyov*, ed. S. Japhet (Jerusalem, 2000), editor's introduction, 52–54; Mordechai Cohen, "Maimonides versus Rashi: Philosophical and Philological-Ethical Approaches to Job," in *Between Rashi and Maimonides*, ed. E. Kanarfogel and M. Sokolow (New York, 2010), 341–42; and *Sefer Iyyov mi-Beit Midrasho shel Rabbenu Tam*, ed. Abraham Shoshana (Jerusalem, 2000 [which presents Rabbenu Tam's commentary on Job along with that of Rashi and a third commentary attributed to "the students of Rashi"]). See also Shoshana's introduction to Rabbenu Tam's commentary, 74–102. Based on comments by Ta-Shma, Shoshana (77–78) notes that there are some clear connections or points in common between Rabbenu Tam's *Sefer Hakhra'ot* and his commentary to Job. A brief and complex versified treatment of biblical vocalizations, cantillations, and accents (נגינות; the treatise begins with the phrase א-להים לי מגן בידי צר מגן, and is extant in several manuscripts) is attributed to R. Jacob b. Meir or to Rabbenu Tam (and is sometimes called חרוזי ר"ת, as in ms. Vatican 301, fols. 187r–v); see Urbach, *Ba'alei ha-Tosafot*, 1:109, and see now *Shirat Rabbenu Tam*, ed. I. Meiseles (Jerusalem, 2012), 149–66. Although these subjects are also dealt with by Rabbenu Tam in his *Hakhra'ot*, the attribution of this work in one manuscript specifies יעקב בן ר' מאיר מנורטהוזן; see ms. Bodl. 1442, fols. 91v–93r. On יעקב בן מאיר מנורטהויזן, cf. ms. St. Petersburg EVR I 192, fol. 1v; ms. Moscow 82, fols. 99v–100r; and I. Ta-Shma, *Ha-Sifrut ha-Parshanit la-Talmud*, 2:128.

53 See Poznanaski, *Mavo*, LIII (n. 2). A somewhat garbled passage in Rabbenu Tam's *Sefer ha-Yashar* (in which Rabbenu Tam makes reference to a predecessor with whom he studied who espoused a particular practice) is understood by Rami Reiner, "Rabbenu Tam: Rabbotav (ha-Zarefatim) ve-Talmidav Bnei Ashkenaz" (M.A. thesis, Hebrew University of Jerusalem, 1997), 47–49, to refer to R. Yosef Qara. Reiner suggests that Rabbenu Tam studied mostly *miqra* with Qara, since his name appears in Rabbenu Tam's halakhic writings in only one other place. The discussion in that passage, however (and in a parallel passage in ms. Paris 167; see the following note), is centered around the talmudic understanding of the biblical verses that detail the requirements of a *nazir* (as Reiner himself notes). There is no evidence that Rabbenu Tam studied distinctive forms of non-talmudic biblical interpretation (such as *peshat*) with Qara. Cf. Simcha Emanuel, "New Fragments of Unknown Biblical Commentaries from the European Genizah," in *Genizat Germania*, ed. A. Lehnardt, 211–15.

relatively few non-talmudic Torah comments from Rabbenu Tam are to be found.[54] Thus, R. Joseph Kimḥi, the father of R. David Kimḥi, writes that Rabbenu Tam "did not make an effort to penetrate [or to clarify] the depths of grammar and syntax . . . and he did not occupy himself with Scripture [*higgayon*] because 'it is a virtue and not a virtue'" (as per *Bava Meẓiʿa* 33a).[55] Unlike Rashbam, Rabbenu Tam did author a fair number of *piyyutim*,[56] although like Rashbam he also eschewed the study of *torat ha-sod*.[57] Indeed, it was perhaps in order to provide a vehicle for addressing issues of spirituality and Divine immanence without having to resort to esoteric interpretations that both Rashbam and Rabbenu Tam, like R. Yosef Qara and other students of Rashi, turned to composing interpretations on the Book of Job.[58]

The brilliant dialectical method put forward by Rabbenu Tam on the basis of the entire talmudic corpus—particularly when viewed against the overarching legalistic trend of the twelfth century, in both Jewish and general society—comes to dominate talmudic studies in northern France. Moreover, Rabbenu Tam's tendency (relative to the pre-Crusade period) to downplay other disciplines of study aside from the Talmud is also firmly entrenched among a number of his leading students, including R. Ḥayyim

[54] The Torah commentary found in ms. Paris 167 (and in variant form in ms. Moscow 362), attributed by some to Rabbenu Tam or to one of his students, was not composed by Rabbenu Tam, even as it does cite him and several of his students on a number of occasions. (Reiner's assertion, "Rabbenu Tam, Rabbotav ve-Talmidav," 49, n. 178, that Rabbenu Tam's name appears in this commentary tens of times, is inaccurate.) Moreover, most of the comments in it are based on halakhic or rabbinic (and midrashic) sources and analysis. On this commentary and its provenance, see below, chapter 2, n. 6. Similarly, the debate between Rabbenu Tam and R. Meshullam of Lunel on the use of Scripture in halakhic or *minhag* contexts does not touch on independent scriptural interpretation (*parshanut*). In any case, in his debate with R. Meshallam, Rabbenu Tam plays down the role of biblical verses taken in isolation. See R. Reiner, "Rabbenu Tam u-Bnei Doro: Qesharim, Hashpa'ot ve-Darkhei Limmudo ba-Talmud" (Ph.D. diss., Hebrew University, 2002), 283–321, and his "Pershanut ve-Halakhah: ʿIyyun Meḥudash be-Polmos Rabbenu Tam ve-R. Meshullam," *Shenaton ha-Mishpat ha-ʿIvri* 21 (1998–2000), 207–39.

[55] See Kimḥi's *Sefer Ha-Galui*, ed. H. J. Mathews (Berlin, 1887), 2–3; my *Jewish Education and Society in the High Middle Ages*, 79; and Urbach, *Baʿalei ha-Tosafot*, 1:108. Cf. Rashbam's methodological statement in his commentary to Gen. 37:2.

[56] See Urbach, 1:109–10; and below, chapter 5, nn. 74–81.

[57] See my *"Peering through the Lattices,"* 166–76, and below, chapter 6, nn. 15–27.

[58] I owe this suggestion to Shalom Buchbinder, M.D., who made it in the context of the interest expressed by a number of Rabbenu Tam's students—but not Rabbenu Tam himself—in esoteric studies, as outlined in my *"Peering through the Lattices,"* 189–208. See also Mordechai Cohen's review essay of Eleazar Touitou, *Exegesis in Perpetual Motion*, in *JQR* 98 (2008), 389–408; J. S. Penkower, "The End of Rashi's Commentary on Job: The Manuscripts and the Printed Editions," *JSQ* 10 (2003), 18–48; and the formulation by the Tosafist R. Pereẓ b. Elijah of Corbeil (d. 1298) on the subtleties of thought involved in interpreting the book of Job (cited in the *Beit Yosef* commentary to *ʾArbaʿah Turim*, *Oraḥ Ḥayyim*, at the beginning of section 554).

Kohen,[59] R. Eliezer of Metz,[60] and R. Moses of Pontoise,[61] as well as the lesser-known R. Isaac b. Barukh.[62] Among Rabbenu Tam's German and Austrian students, R. Isaac b. Mordekhai (Ribam) of Bohemia, R. Isaac *ha-Lavan*, and R. Peter b. Joseph belong in this category as well.[63]

Rabbenu Tam's greatest Tosafist associate and successor, his nephew R. Isaac b. Samuel (Ri) of Dampierre, had leanings toward *sod* and ascetic tendencies (*perishut*),[64] and he composed a number of *piyyutim* as well,[65] although his output in the realm of talmudic interpretations and formulations dominates his literary productivity by far. Moreover, as is the case for Rabbenu Tam, there are few verified *miqra* interpretations in the name of

[59] See, e.g., R. Ḥayyim's comment to Deut. 21:8 (on not seeking *ta'amei ha-mizvot* that may emerge from halakhic details), found in ms. Florence Laurenziana, Plut. II.20, fol. 251v (published and discussed in my "Torah Study and Truth in Medieval Ashkenazic Rabbinic Literature and Thought," in *Study and Knowledge in Jewish Thought*, ed. H. Kreisel [Beer Sheva, 2006], 1:111, n 18). One of R. Ḥayyim's sons (R. Aaron, who is not known as a talmudist) was the author of an extensive *piyyut* commentary. See Avraham Grossman, "Perush ha-Piyyutim le-R. Aharon b. Ḥayyim ha-Kohen," in *Be-Oraḥ Madda: Sefer Yovel le-Aharon Mirsky*, ed. Z. Malachi (Lod, 1986), 451–68. R. Ḥayyim's purported authorship of the mystical work *Sefer ha-Ḥayyim* has not been sufficiently demonstrated. See *Sefer ha-Ḥayim*, ed. Gerold Necker (Tubingen, 2001), editor's introduction, 16–29; and Necker, "Fallen Angels in the 'Book of Life,'" *JSQ* 11 (2004), 73–82. Cf. ms. Bodl. 970 (a Tosafist Torah compilation), fol. 55v (to Nu. 6:23): 'יש אומרי' שר' חיי' כהן היה אומר ברכת כהנים על מטתו בלילות על פי המדרש הנה מטתו שלשלמה ששים גיבורים סביב לה וכו' ומפרש דהיינו ששים אותיות של ברכת כהנים. Cf. *Perush Shir ha-Shirim le-Rabbenu Avigdor Kohen Ẓedek*, ed. S. A. Wertheimer (Jeursalem, 1971), 25 (3:7); and *Tosafot ha-Shalem 'al Ḥamesh Megillot*, ed. J. Gellis, vol. 1 (Jerusalem, 2000), 67–68 (secs. 5–6). Contrary to the commonly held view that places him only in northern France, R. Ḥayyim apparently spent some time in the Rhineland as well. See R. Reiner, "Rabbenu Tam u-Bnei Doro," 85–98.

[60] See Urbach, *Ba'alei ha-Tosafot*, 1:154–64. R. Eliezer does exhibit some pietistic behaviors and mystical/magic interests; see my *"Peering through the Lattices,"* 68–69, 195–97; and below, chapter 6, nn. 45–49. As Urbach notes, R. Eliezar penned some poetic stanzas to adorn sections of his *Sefer Yere'im*, but he did not compose any *piyyutim*. Cf. Menaḥem Schmelzer, *Studies in Jewish Bibliography and Medieval Hebrew Poetry* (New York, 2006) [Hebrew section], 177–87, and below, chapter 5, n. 160.

[61] See Urbach, *Ba'alei ha-Tosafot*, 1:129–32 (and esp. n. 47). For R. Moses's few comments on the Torah, which are focused on halakhic and rabbinic constructs, see below, chapter 3, n. 225.

[62] Urbach, *Ba'alei ha-Tosafot*, 1:152–53.

[63] See Ubrach, *Ba'alei ha-Tosafot*, 1:196–99, and 1:215–25; R. Reiner, "Rabbenu Tam: Rabbotav (ha-Ẓarefatim) ve-Talmidav Bnei Ashkenaz," 79–82, 96–98, 134–39 (who casts some doubt on R. Peter's non-French origins); and my "R. Judah *he-Ḥasid* and the Rabbinic Scholars in Regensburg: Interactions, Influences and Implications," *JQR* (2006), 17–37. Ribam is involved a bit with *torat ha-sod* (see below, chapter 6, n. 51), while Ri *ha-Lavan* composed fewer than a handful of *piyyutim* (below, chapter 5, n. 158), and even fewer *ḥumash* comments (below, chapter 3, nn. 244–49; and cf. my *"Peering through the Lattices,"* 52). For R. Moses *ha-Kohen* of Mainz, see below, n. 76.

[64] For Ri's *perishut* (and especially as compared to Rabbenu Tam, who did not exhibit such behaviors), see my *"Peering through the Lattices,"* 43–45, 51, 57. For Ri's mystical proclivities, see 191–95, and below, chapter 6.

[65] See below, chapter 5, nn. 129–33.

Ri that are not fundamentally talmudic or halakhic in nature.[66] Several of Ri's students followed the talmudocentric pattern of Rabbenu Tam even more closely, producing just a smattering of *piyyut*, *sod*, or biblical interpretations. These include, among others, R. Shimshon (Rash) *mi-Shanz*;[67] his brother, R. Isaac b. Abraham of Dampierre (Riẓba);[68] R. Barukh, author of *Sefer ha-Terumah*;[69] R. Solomon *ha-Qadosh* of Dreux;[70] R. Judah Sirleon;[71] and R. Joseph of Clisson.[72]

In Germany as well the earliest Tosafist, R. Isaac b. Asher *ha-Levi* (Riba, d. 1133), was involved almost exclusively in talmudic studies as far as we can

[66] See e.g., below, chapter 2, n. 6; and chapter 3, nn. 208–9, 236.

[67] See Urbach, *Ba'alei ha-Tosafot*, 1:266–318; and cf. *"Peering through the Lattices,"* 217–18. As Yaakov Sussmann and others have conclusively demonstrated, the commentary on the *Sifra* attributed to R. Samson is in fact of German origin. See Sussmann, "Rabad on *Sheqalim*? A Bibliographical and Historical Riddle," [Hebrew] in *Me'ah She'arim: Studies in Medieval Jewish Spiritual Life in Memory of Isadore Twersky*, ed. E. Fleischer et al. (Jerusalem, 2001), 147–50, 168–69, and the introduction to *Sifra de-Bei Rav*, ed. A. Shoshana, vol. 2/1 (Jerusalem, 1996), 11–13. Rash's extensive commentaries to the Mishnaic tractates of *Zera'im* and *Tahorot* speak to an unusual initiative that was nonetheless completely grounded within the realm of talmudic studies (as was his acute interest in the *Talmud Yerushalmi*). Indeed, R. Samson and his study hall also produced a fair number of *Tosafot* collections to the talmudic tractates in *Seder Qodashim* as well. See my "The *'Aliyyah* of 'Three Hundred Rabbis' in 1211: Tosafist Attitudes toward Settling in the Land of Israel," *JQR* 76 (1986), 198–200; Sussmann, "Rabad on *Sheqalim*," 131–40; my "The Scope of Talmudic Commentary in Europe during the High Middle Ages," in *Printing the Talmud*, ed. S. L. Mintz (New York, 2005), 43–52; and my "On the Study of *Seder Qodashim* in Medieval Europe," [Hebrew] in *Studies in Honor of Prof. Joseph Hacker*, ed. Y. Kaplan et al. (Jerusalem, 2012).

[68] See Urbach, *Ba'alei ha-Tosafot*, 1:261–64, 270. As Urbach notes, it is difficult to assign any *piyyutim* to Riẓba with certainty (cf. below, chapter 5). On esoteric teachings that could possibly be attributed to Riẓba, see my *"Peering through the Lattices,"* 205–7 (and below, chapter 6, n. 126). See also below, chapter 3, nn. 214–17, regarding Riẓba and *miqra*. In any case, none of these involvements is at all sustained or substantial.

[69] See Urbach, *Ba'alei ha-Tosafot*, 1:346–61. For R. Barukh's several rabbinic or midrashic interpretations of the biblical text, see below, chapter 3. As noted there, the repertoire of Ri's son and student R. Elḥanan in this regard is similar; see also Urbach, ibid., 1:253–60. Like his father, R. Elḥanan did author a number of *piyyutim* (see also below, chapter 5), although he does not seem to have been at all involved with *torat ha-sod* (as his father was).

[70] See Urbach, ibid., 1:339–40. R. Solomon's fifteen or so Torah comments (which is a relatively large number among his Tosafist fellow students of Ri) are all halakhic or talmudic in nature. See Norman Golb, *Toledot ha-Yehudim be-'Ir Rouen Bimei ha-Benayim* (Tel Aviv, 1976), appendix 7 (190–92); *Ba'alei*; and below, chapter 3, nn. 215–32.

[71] See Urbach, *Ba'alei ha-Tosafot*, 1:320–35. There is a lone reference in *Tosafot R. Yehudah Sirleon* on tractate *Berakhot* to a mystical conception of the response of *'amen*, which R. Judah in turn rejects (as *lo nehira*). See my *"Peering through the Lattices,"* 190 (n. 2).

[72] See Urbach, *Ba'alei ha-Tosafot*, 1:318–20, and cf. E. Kanarfogel and M. Sokolow, "Rashi and Maimonides Meet in a Geniza Fragment," *Tarbiz* 67 (1998), 411–16. Note also R. Jacob b. Solomon of Courson, in Urbach, *Ba'alei ha-Tosafot*, 1:316–17; *Teshuot u-Pesaqim*, ed. Kupfer, 260–61, 266, 279–81; S. Emanuel, *Shivrei Luḥot*, 264–71; and below, chapter 1, n. 106.

tell.[73] To be sure, R. Eliezer b. Nathan of Mainz (Raban) composed quite a number of *piyyutim* and an exoteric prayer commentary, in addition to his extensive talmudic interpretations and halakhic rulings. While this is perhaps at least partly due to his proximity to the pre-Crusade period, he nevertheless left no writings in *sod* or *miqra*.[74] This pattern of disciplinary concentration extends to Raban's well-known grandson Rabiah, who was also much less involved in *piyyut* composition than his grandfather.[75]

R. Moses b. Solomon *ha-Kohen* of Mainz, a leading German judge and teacher of Rabiah, also studied with Rabbenu Tam and is an important conduit for bringing Rabbenu Tam's talmudic material to Germany. He too did halakhic and talmudic studies exclusively,[76] as did Raban's relative R. Yaʿavetz (= R. Isaac b. Eliezer *ha-Levi*); his contemporary, R. Shemaryah b. Mordekhai of Speyer;[77] his son-in-law, R. Samuel b. Natronai (d. c. 1180); and R. Moses b. Yo'el of Regensburg.[78] This group of German rabbinic figures from the twelfth through early thirteenth centuries provides further support for the regnant impression that the Tosafists were exclusively talmudists, who engaged little if at all in other disciplines.

Only one or two German Tosafists during this period (aside from Raban with respect to *piyyut*) appear to have had broader scholarly interests. Rabiah's contemporary, R. Simḥah of Speyer (d. c. 1230), commented

[73] See Urbach, *Baʿalei ha-Tosafot*, 1:165–73, where a limited number of *perushei ha-miqra* are noted, and cf. above, n. 11. Riba may have been something of a Pietist; see my "*Peering through the Lattices*," 44, and cf. Shalom Spiegel, *The Last Trial* (New York, 1969), 6–7.

[74] See Urbach, *Baʿalei ha-Tosafot*, 1:173–84; chapter 5, below, for his *piyyutim*; and my "*Peering through the Lattices*," 161–65, and below, chapter 6, nn. 11–14, for his *sod*-neutral approach (which was very much in line with the approaches of Rashbam and Rabbenu Tam noted above).

[75] See Urbach, *Baʿalei ha-Tosafot*, 1:378–88. The two exegetical references to *Avi ha-ʿEzri* toward the end of the Tosafist Torah compilation *Minḥat Yehudah* (in passages attributed specifically to R. Moses of Coucy) appear to be to the commentaries of Ibn Ezra, although there are fewer than a handful of other references to biblical comments by Rabiah that are talmudic or midrashic in nature. See below, chapter 4, nn. 96–97; and Aptowitzer, *Mavo la-Rabiah*, 130–33. Rabiah exhibited aspects of *perishut* (see my "*Peering through the Lattices*," 45–51, 214–17), and was the author (as was his father, R. Yo'el) of several *qinnot*. See Aptowitzer, *Mavo la-Rabiah*, 134–39, and below, chapter 5, nn. 122–23, 127–28. The two very brief compositions reproduced by Aptowitzer, *Mavo la-Rabiah*, 140, are verses in praise of tractates *Pesaḥim* and *Sukkah* that were included in *Sefer Rabiah*. Cf. M. Schmelzer, above, n. 60.

[76] See Urbach, *Baʿalei ha-Tosafot*, 1:184–86; R. Reiner, "Rabbenu Tam: Rabbotav ha-Ẓarefatim ve-Talmidav Bnei Ashkenaz," 103–5; S. Emanuel, *Shivrei Luḥot*, 108–9; and below, chapter 1, n. 5.

[77] See Urbach, *Baʿalei ha-Tosafot*, 1:186–92, and Emanuel, *Shivrei Luḥot*, 83, 282–89. R. Shemaryah, a contemporary (and neighbor) of R. Samuel *he-Ḥasid*, provided a derivation for the Ashkenazic practice of donating charity in memory of departed souls based on a passage in *Sifrei*, which appears (and is expanded upon) in *Sefer Ḥasidim*. See I. Ta-Shma, *Minhag Ashkenaz ha-Qadmon* (Jerusalem, 1992), 301, n. 9, and my "*Peering through the Lattices*," 143 (n. 25).

[78] See Urbach, *Baʿalei ha-Tosafot*, 1:207–9; Emanuel, *Shivrei Luḥot*, 60–70, 77–81, 83–86; above, nn. 18–19; and below, chapter 1, n. 27.

on a particularly wide range of rabbinic texts, and was involved with pietistic, mystical, and magical practices and teachings, and also composed three noteworthy *seliḥot.* The careful attention paid by R. Simḥah to works of Tannaitic literature, such as the *Sifra* and other *midrashei halakhah*, and to related works associated with the talmudic order of *Qodashim*, may well reflect his association with *Ḥasidei Ashkenaz*, as do his interests in *ḥasidut* and *torat ha-sod.*[79]

Indeed, R. Simḥah's Tosafist predecessor in Speyer, R. Judah b. Qalonymus (Rivaq) b. Meir (d. c. 1198), was a member of the core Qalonymide family of the German Pietists, and interacted directly in matters of *torat ha-sod* with R. Judah *he-Ḥasid*, who left his native Speyer for Regensburg only c. 1195.[80] R. Judah *he-Ḥasid*'s varied interests are well known, and we shall have the opportunity below (in chapter 3) to carefully examine his *peshat*-like comments on the Torah in particular. His father, R. Samuel *he-Ḥasid* of Speyer (b. 1115), appears to be the earliest of the relatively few rabbinic figures in Germany during the twelfth century to engage in a wide range of disciplines beyond talmudic studies, including *miqra*, *piyyut* composition and commentary, and *midrash* (as a distinct genre), as well as *torat ha-sod* that included forms of mysticism and magic, *gematriyyot*, and *remazim.*[81] As we shall see throughout this study, several Tosafists who were associated with study halls in northern France displayed strong interests in some of these same areas toward the end of the twelfth century, well before any German Tosafists who were unassociated with either the German Pietists or the school at Speyer began to do so.

Clearly, however, the study of Talmud and the derivation of *halakhah* on the basis of this study were the main pursuits of Tosafists and other leading rabbinic figures in both northern France and Germany during the twelfth

[79] See Urbach, *Baʿalei ha-Tosafot*, 1:411–20; Emanuel, *Shivrei Luḥot*, 154–66; Y. Sussmann, "Mesoret Limmud u-Mesoret Nosaḥ shel ha-Talmud ha-Yerushalmi—Le-Birur Nusḥa'otehah shel Yerushalmi Massekhet Sheqalim," in *Meḥqarim be-Sifrut ha-Talmudit le-Regel Melot Shemonim Shanah le-Sha'ul Lieberman* (Jerusalem, 1983), 14, 34–35; idem, "Rabad on *Sheqalim*," 147–48, 166–69; my *"Peering through the Lattices,"* 82, 102–3, 107–8, 225–28; my "Returning to the Jewish Community in Medieval Ashkenaz: History and Halakhah," in *Turim: Studies in Jewish History and Literature Presented to Dr. Bernard Lander*, ed. M. Shmidman, vol. 1 (New York, 2007), 81–85; and below, chapter 6, nn. 77, 113.

[80] See Urbach, *Baʿalei ha-Tosafot*, 361–78; Sussmann, "Mesoret Limmud u-Mesoret Nosaḥ shel ha-Talmud ha-Yerushalmi," 14, 34–35; my *"Peering through the Lattices,"* 60 (n. 76), 106 (n. 26), 213–14; and cf. *Megillat Taʿanit*, ed. Vered Noam (Jerusalem, 2003), 407–14.

[81] See Urbach, *Baʿalei ha-Tosafot.* 1:192–95; Sussmann, "Rabad on *Sheqalim*," 143, 148, 150, 166–68; I. Ta-Shma, *Knesset Meḥqarim*, 1:212–17, 273–77, 290–97; my *"Peering through the Lattices,"* 48, 53, 95–96, 108–9, 143, 186, 193, 243; and my "On the Study of *Seder Qodashim* in Medieval Europe" (above, n. 67). R. Samuel's extensive interest in interpreting biblical books beyond the Torah is found only within the small circle of twelfth-century northern French *pashtanim*; see below, chapter 3.

century and beyond. The centrality of these disciplines for these leading rabbinic scholars was undoubtedly established, at least in part, on the basis of the aforementioned talmudic dictum in *Bava Meẓiʿa* 33a: העוסקין במקרא מדה ושאינה מדה במשנה מדה ונוטלין עליה שכר בגמרא אין לך מדה גדולה מזו. The Tosafists were apparently aware of others in their day who were considered to be *Baʿalei Miqra* or *Baʿalei Mishnah*, and they recognized and ratified the legitimacy of these pursuits as the study of Torah. At the same time, however, they certainly saw and considered themselves as primarily *Baʿalei Talmud*.[82]

Thus in systematically laying out and characterizing the Tosafist oeuvre for the first time, E. E. Urbach was more than justified in putting forward the talmudic and halakhic achievements of the Tosafists, and in downplaying their involvement in other areas and disciplines. At this point in time, however, manuscript evidence, along with a more sophisticated mapping and reading of both these and published texts, will demonstrate that both the level and extent of Tosafist involvement in other disciplines are such that we can no longer afford to regard them solely as an outgrowth or subfield of Tosafist talmudism as Urbach did, or as a minor portion of Tosafist endeavors more generally. In addition to presenting the manuscript data and revised analytical conclusions for the various disciplines, we must address more fully both the longitudinal and latitudinal issues and distinctions that have been raised here.

There is also a need to address more effectively the distinction between the first-level rabbinic elite in Ashkenaz, whose major concentration was in talmudic or halakhic studies but who may have also exhibited strong interests in other areas as well, and the secondary elite, who were specialists

[82] See, e.g., *Tosafot Sotah* 22a, s.v. *R. Shmuʾel bar Naḥmani*; *Tosafot Bava Meẓiʿa* 33b, s.v. *ʾakheihem*; *Sefer Or Zaruʿa* (Zhitomir, 1862), pt. 1, *ʾalfa beta*, sec. 10 (end). Cf. *Pisqei ha-Rosh* to *Berakhot* 5:1, and to *Sanhedrin* 11:3; Rashi to *Shir ha-Shirim*, 7:13, s.v. *nireh* (= Judah Rosenthal, "Perush Rashi ʿal Shir ha-Sirim," in *Sefer ha-Yovel Likhvod S. K. Mirsky*, ed. S. Bernstein and G. Churgin [New York, 1958], 182); Rashi to *Berakhot* 28b, s.v. *ha-higgayon* (and cf. Rashbam's comment to Gen. 37:2); M. Breuer, "Minʿu Beneikhem min Ha-Higayyon," in *Mikhtam le-David: Sefer Zikkaron le-R. David Ochs*, ed. Y. Gilat and E. Stern (Ramat Gan, 1982, 242–61 (= idem, *Asif* [Jerusalem, 1999], 237–59); idem, "Ha-Miqra be-Tokhnit ha-Limmudim shel ha-Yeshivah," in *Meḥqarim be-Miqra uve-Ḥinnukh Mugashim Li-Prof. Mosheh Ahrend* (Jerusalem, 1996), 223–35; Frank Talmage, "Keep Your Sons from Scripture: The Bible in Medieval Jewish Scholarship and Spirituality," in *Understanding Scripture: Explorations of Jewish and Christian Traditions of Interpretation*, ed. C. Thoma and M. Wyshogrod (New York, 1987), 81–101; E. Touitou, *Exegesis in Perpetual Motion* (above, n. 37); Eran Viezel, in *Shenaton le-Ḥeqer ha-Miqra veha-Mizraḥ ha-Qadum* 19 (2009), 329–30; and Isadore Twersky, *Studies in Jewish Law and Philosophy* (New York, 1982), 203–16. *Sefer Ḥasidim* was especially concerned about providing learning opportunities within medieval Ashkenazic society for those who were not *Baʿalei Talmud* (on the highest level). See, e.g., my "Bein Yeshivot Baʿalei ha-Tosafot le-Battei Midrashot Aḥerim be-Ashkenaz Bimei ha-Benayim," in *Yeshivot u-Battei Midrashot*, ed. I. Etkes (Jerusalem, 2006), 85–108; and above, n. 38.

in biblical or *piyyut* interpretation, or in grammatical or mystical studies, but whose involvement or productivity in talmudic and halakhic studies cannot be demonstrated.[83] As noted in the preface, one of the character-

[83] Indeed, several of these non-talmudic specialists were interdisciplinary scholars. R. Yosef Qara is an excellent example (from the period just before the Tosafists) for *miqra*, grammar, and *piyyut* interpretation; see A. Grossman, *Ḥakhmei Ẓarefat ha-Rishonim*, 254–346. Similarly, Berekhyah b. Natronai *ha-Naqdan* (who apparently hailed from Provence) spent quite a bit of time in Rouen during the late twelfth century, and was involved in scriptural interpretation (that covered much of the Bible), *piyyut* interpretation, and with several areas and texts of Jewish thought (in addition to composing a series of popular proverbs and tales). See Menachem Banitt, *Le Glossaire de Leipzig*, vol. 4 (Jerusalem, 2005), 416–17; N. Golb, *Toledot ha-Yehudim be-'Ir Rouen Bimei ha-Benayim*, 54–55, 120–44; idem, *The Jews in Medieval Normandy* (Cambridge, 1998), 324–47; and cf. J. Penkower, "The End of Rashi's Commentary to Job," *JSQ* 10 (2003), 26–31. Following Zunz (*Zur Geschichte und Literatur* [Berlin, 1845], 56), Golb holds that the (positive) reference in *Tosafot Sanhedrin* 20b, s.v. *melekh*, to an interpretation by "the *naqdan*," is to an interpretation by Berekhyah to the Book of Kings. Urbach, *Ba'alei ha-Tosafot*, 2:658, n. 61, does not raise this possibility, and is unsure to whom this refers, although he notes the presence of other *naqdanim* in medieval Ashkenaz, who were involved primarily in grammar and *piyyut* interpretation. Cf. *'Arugat ha-Bosem*, ed. Urbach, vol. 4 (Jerusalem, 1963), 62 (n. 43), 121–22, and Joseph Guttman, "Joseph b. Kalonimus: The Enigma of a Thirteenth-Century Hebrew Scribe," in *A Crown for a King*, ed. S. Sabar et al. (Jerusalem, 2000), 147–51. See also David Ben-Menachem, "Ḥibbur ha-Qonnim by R. Shimshon ha-Naqdan," *Hebrew Annual Review* 11 (1987), 9–22; Ilan Eldar, "Me-Kitvei Ashkolet ha-Diqduq ha-Ashkenazit—ha-Shimshoni," *Leshonenu* 43 (1979), 110–111, 201–10; "The Grammatical Literature of Medieval Ashkenazic Jewry," in *Hebrew in Ashkenaz*, ed. L. Glinert (New York, 1993), 26–45; Y. S. Spiegel, *'Amudim be-Toledot ha-Sefer ha'Ivri* (Ramat Gan, 2005), 105; Urbach, *Ba'alei ha-Tosafot*, 1:109, and 2:498; Rami Reiner, "'Even She-Katuv 'alehah: To'arei ha-Niftarim 'al Maẓevot Beit ha-'Almin be-Wuerzburg, 1147–1346," *Tarbiz* 78 (2009), 134–35; and see now Judith Olszowy-Schlanger, "The Science of Language among Medieval Jews," in *Science in Medieval Jewish Culture*, ed. G. Freudenthal (Cambridge, 2011), 362–63. N. Golb, *Toledot ha-Yehudim be-'Ir Rouen*, 150–55, and idem, *The Jews of Medieval Normandy*, 439–52, also recounts the career of R. Qershavyah b. Isaac *ha-Naqdan*, who was a copyist, rabbinic scribe, and author of at least one *piyyut* (but not an author of halakhic works). See also *Teshuvot u-Pesaqim*, ed. E. Kupfer (Jerusalem, 1973), 325–26; Avraham David, "Pera'ot bi-Yehudei Ẓarefat be-'Et Massa ha-Ro'im shel Shenat Yod Alef (1251)," *Tarbiz* 46 (1977), 252; below, Conclusion, n. 24; and ms. Leipzig 1099 (a biblical Hebrew/French glossary), fol. 16r. (An R. Solomon *Naqdan* is mentioned on fols. 3v and 36v; see also Banitt, *Le Glossaire de Leipzig*, 415.) Several manuscripts that contain Ashkenazic rites include *piyyutim* by R. Isaac b. Samson *ha-Naqdan*. See, e.g., ms. Munich, 422, fol. 62r; ms. Bodl. 1099, fols. 83r–84r; ms. Bodl. 1104, fols. 93r, 132r; ms. Bodl. 1147, *passim*; ms. Prague (National Library) XVII F 7, fol. 18v (in the margin); ms. Paris l'Alliance H 482 A, fols. 48v–49r; ms. Vatican 324, fol. 85v; ms. Zurich Heid. 51, fols. 99v–101v (and *piyyut* interpretation by R. Isaac *ha-Naqdan*), and see also ms. Hamburg Heb. 13, fol. 74v, in the margin, and R. Aaron b. Ḥayyim *ha-Kohen* (above, n. 59). Noteworthy Ashkenazic specialists in *torat ha-sod* and related areas of Jewish thought include R. Elḥanan b. Yaqar of London and Normandy, and R. Neḥemyah b. Solomon (R. Troestlein of Erfurt), neither of whom is cited or even mentioned, as far as I can tell, in any Ashkenazic work of talmudic or halakhic interpretation. See, e.g., my "Rabbinic Figures in Castilian Kabbalistic Pseudepigraphy: R. Yehudah he-Ḥasid and R. Elḥanan of Corbeil," *Journal of Jewish Thought and Philosophy* 3 (1993), 77–109; Y. Tzvi Langermann, "Was There No Science in Ashkenaz? The Ashkenazic Reception of Some Early-Medieval Hebrew Scientific Texts," *Yearbook of the Simon Dubnow Institute* 8 (2009), 84, 87–91; Moshe Idel, "R. Neḥemiah ben Shlomo the Prophet of Erfurt's Commentary on the Piyyut *'El Na'aleh 'Olam Tu'araz* (Remarks on the Specificity of

istics and legacies of the so-called Golden Age of Spain (and afterward in Provence as well) is that biblical exegetes, philosophers, and poets who were undistinguished as talmudists or halakhists nonetheless occupied significant places in the intellectual history of Spanish and Provençal Jewry, alongside leading talmudists. Moshe Idel has cogently suggested that first-level kabbalists should be typified by rabbinic figures such as Ramban and Rashba, who were leading talmudists as well as mystics, in contradistinction to members of the second-level elite, who only put forward important teachings or composed treatises in the realm of kabbalah.[84] Given the centrality of talmudism in medieval Ashkenaz, which rendered the Tosafists and their associates dominant, such a conception or schema may be important for Ashkenaz as well.

Nonetheless, it is not always clear who should be included within Tosafist circles, as the following examples demonstrate. Two of the most important *piyyut* commentators in Ashkenaz during the twelfth and thirteenth centuries, as identified and described by Urbach in his work on Ashkenazic *piyyut* commentary,[85] are barely discussed by him in his *Ba'alei ha-Tosafot.*

the Thought of a Forgotten Ashkenazi Author)," [Hebrew] in *Moreshet Yisra'el* 2 (2005), ed. Ortsion Bartana, 5–41; idem, "Some Forlorn Writings of a Forgotten Ashkenazi Prophet—R. Neḥemiah b. Shlomo ha-Navi," *JQR* 95 (2005), 183–96; and idem,"On Angels and Biblical Exegesis in Thirteenth-Century Ashkenaz," in *Scriptural Exegesis in Honor of Michael Fishbane*, ed. D. A. Green and L. S. Lieber (Oxford, 2009), 211–44. It should be noted that both R. Elḥanan and R. Neḥemyah, as well as Berekhyah *ha-Naqdan* and others among the non-talmudic specialists noted above, lived on the geographic periphery of the medieval Ashkenazic world. See also I. Ta-Shma, *Knesset Meḥqarim*, vol. 1, 133–56, for R. Solomon Simḥah b. Eli'ezer of Troyes, a thirteenth-century *payyetan* (b. c. 1235) and author of the lengthy and distinctive theological-mystical treatise *Sefer ha-Maskil*. Cf. Gad Freudenthal, "Ha-Avir Barukh Hu u-Barukh Shemo be-Sefer ha-Maskil le-R. Shelomoh Simḥah mi-Troyes," *Da'at* 32–33 (1994), 187–234; my "*Peering through the Lattices,*" 239–45; and Susan Einbinder, *Beautiful Death* (Princeton, 2002), 130–48, 164–66; and below, chapter 7. Although R. Solomon Simḥah indicates that his teachers were R. Meir of Rothenburg and R. Pereẓ of Corbeil, he did not produce any talmudic or halakhic literature of which we are aware, nor is he cited in any *Tosafot* (or Tosafist) sources in these areas. Finally, R. Ephraim b. Samson, an apparent associate of R. Eleazar of Worms, authored a large commentary on the Torah that is replete with *gematriyyot*, *rashei*, and *sofei tevot*, and other such *remazim*. Among these *remazim* are two for the works of Rambam, *Mishneh Torah* and *Moreh Nevukhim*, that are preceded by a *remez* for the talmudic commentaries of Rabbenu Ḥanan'el. See *Perush Rabbenu Ephraim b. Shimshon 'al ha-Torah*, ed. J. Klugmann (Jerusalem, 1992), 282–83, and cf. Idel, "On Angels and Biblical Exegetes," 213. For the little that is known about R. Ephraim, see the (unpaginated) editor's introduction, and cf. Manfred Lehmann, "Perush 'al Parashat Bo mi-Rabbenu Ephraim ben Rabbenu Shimshon ve-R. Eleazar mi-Germaiza," *Sinai* 71 (1972), 1–20.

84 See e.g., M. Idel, "Kabbalah and Elites in Thirteenth-Century Spain," *Mediterranean Historical Review* 9 (1994), 5–19; idem, "R. Mosheh b. Naḥman: Qabbalah, Halakhah u-Manhigut Ruḥanit," *Tarbiz* 64 (1995), 535–80; and cf. Boaz Huss, "Hofa'ato shel Sefer ha-Zohar," *Tarbiz* 70 (1997), 507–42.

85 See *'Arugat ha-Bosem*, ed. Urbach, vol. 4 (Jerusalem, 1963).

One of these figures is R. Abraham b. Azri'el of Bohemia, the author of *'Arugat ha-Bosem*.[86] The nontreatment of R. Abraham b. Azri'el in *Ba'alei ha-Tosafot* is perhaps justified, however, since he does not seem to have played any role in shaping the *Tosafot* or related literature, even as Urbach characterizes him as a *rosh yeshivah* who studied with Tosafists in Regensburg and Wurzburg, issued halakhic rulings together with other Tosafists, and is referred to by R. Isaac b. Moses *Or Zaru'a* as his teacher (or senior colleague).[87] It is more difficult, however, to imagine that R. Ephraim b. Jacob of Bonn (d. 1197)—who in addition to studying and interacting with Tosafists and other Ashkenazic rabbinic figures was a member (and ultimately head) of the prestigious rabbinic court in Mainz (following R. Yo'el *ha-Levi* of Bonn), and authored *pisqei halakhah*, *ḥiddushim*, responsa, and glosses to the *Talmud Yerushalmi*, in addition to his many *piyyutim* and extensive *piyyut* commentary[88]—should merit only three references in Urbach's

[86] R. Abraham b. Azri'el is mentioned seventeen separate times, without any focused discussion. Almost all these references, however, are simply to note that he was a student of certain Tosafists (and that he preserved some of their teachings), or that he had access to various *Tosafot* texts for his *piyyut* commentary. In one instance (*Ba'alei ha-Tosafot*, 1:402), a pietistic practice of R. Abraham is cited by one of his teachers, R. Eleazar of Worms,and is reflected in a passage in *Sefer Or Zaru'a*. Cf. my *"Peering through the Lattices,"* 81–82, 112–13. In another instance (1:404), R. Abraham is credited with bringing *Tosafot* that originated in the study hall of Ri to the study hall of R. Eleazar of Worms. Urbach (*Ba'alei ha-Tosafot*, 1:416) notes that *'Arugat ha-Bosem* contains significant amounts of material from R. Simḥah of Speyer's lost halakhic work *Seder 'Olam*, but does not indicate that R. Abraham b. Azri'el was a direct student of Rabbenu Simḥah. Cf. I. Ta-Shma, *Creativity and Tradition* (Cambridge, Mass., 2006), 177–78; and S. Emanuel, *Shivrei Luḥot*, 158, 160–61, 165, 171.

[87] See*'Arugat ha-Bosem*, 4:112–27. Cf. I. Ta-Shma, *Ha-Sifrut ha-Parshanit la-Talmud*, 2:118–19; S. Emanuel, *Shivrei Luḥot*, 36; and Uzi Fuchs, "'Iyyunim be-Sefer Or Zaru'a le-R. Yiẓḥaq b. Mosheh me-Vienna" (M.A. thesis, Hebrew University, 1993), 16, 19.

[88] For R. Ephraim's activities and corpus, see, e.g., A. Aptowitzer, *Mavo la-Rabiah*, 248, 319–21; *Teshuvot u-Pesaqim*, ed. E. Kupfer (Jerusalem, 1973), 70 (sec. 36); R. Reiner, "Rabbenu Tam: Rabbotav (ha-Ẓarefatim) ve-Talmidav Bnei Ashkenaz," 123–24; S. Emanuel, *Shivrei Luḥot*, 55, 65, 134, 293 (n. 329); below, n. 98; and chapter 1, nn. 40–42 (where R. Ephraim's singular status as a rabbinic judge is described: (כיון שנעשה הדבר בפני מורינו [ה"ר אפרים] והוא ב"ד חשוב). For the halakhic instructions and discussion that R. Ephraim included in his lengthy prayer and *piyyut* commentaries, see, e.g., S. E. Stern, *Sefer Me'orot ha-Rishonim* (Jerusalem, 2002), 89–91 (the blessing and procedures for *sefirat ha-'omer*); 104–8 (prayers and *halakhot* of Rosh ha-Shanah); 161–63 (laws of Ḥanukkah); and 76–77 (his commentary to the Haggadah). These pieces (and several others published by S. Y. Spitzer) are conveniently collected in S. Emanuel, "Hosafot ve-Hashlamot le-Sefer Sarei ha-Elef," *Jewish Studies Internet Journal* 1 (2002), 141(www.biu.ac.il/JS/JSIJ/1-2002/Emanuel.pdf), and see also the listings in the facsimile edition of *Ms. Hamburg 152* (= *Cod. Hebrew 17*), ed. A. N. Z. Roth (Jerusalem, 1980), editor's introduction, 20–21. See also ms. Bodl. 1104, fol. 15r, regarding the procedure for *havdalah* when the Sabbath is followed by a festival (ואף בדורנו נהגו שני בני היצהר ה"ר הילל וה"ר אפרים אחיו מבונא). Cf. S. Emanuel, *R. Eleazar mi-Vermaiza—Derashah le-Pesaḥ*, 94 (n. 177); and Naftali Wieder, *Hitgabshut Nosaḥ ha-Tefillah ba-Mizraḥ uba-Ma'arav* (Jerusalem, 1998), vol. 1, 368–86. See *Sefer ha-Qushiyyot*, ed. Y. Y. Stal (Jerusalem, 2007), 132–33 (sec. 108), for an explanation on the compositional order of the *Avinu Malkenu* prayer that was offered to students in the name of R. Hillel, and cf. below, chapter 5, n. 144.

Ba'alei ha-Tosafot, none of them in connection with talmudic studies or *halakhah*.[89]

It is possible that Urbach minimized his treatment of R. Ephraim of Bonn and R. Abraham Azri'el in the original edition of *Ba'alei ha-Tosafot* (1955) because he knew that he would be treating them more fully in the introductory volume of *'Arugat ha-Bosem* that appeared in 1963. Nonetheless, this literary separation tends to sustain the misleading impression that leading *payyetanim* or *piyyut* commentators in Ashkenaz were not necessarily significant talmudists or halakhists. Similarly, there are only two passing references in *Ba'alei ha-Tosafot* to R. Menaḥem b. Jacob of Worms (d. 1203), a venerable talmudist and rabbinic judge, and a prolific *payyetan*.[90] Indeed, the only *piyyut* author and commentator who occupies a prominent place in both *'Arugat ha-Bosem* and *Ba'alei ha-Tosafot* is R. Eliezer b. Nathan (Raban) of Mainz.[91] To be sure, Raban was a towering figure in all of these areas, but

[89] See *Ba'alei ha-Tosafot* 1:110, n. 27 (for R. Ephraim's citation of a comment on a *piyyut* made by Rabbenu Tam), 182 (where he is identified as the brother of R. Hillel b. Jacob, who is the subject of discussion), and 367 (for a description from R. Ephraim's *Sefer Zekhirah* on the death of R. Isaac b. Asher *ha-Baḥur* in Speyer in 1196). R. Ephraim's career and literary productivity are described by Urbach in *'Arugat ha-Bosem*, 4:39–72. See also E. Hollender, *Piyyut Commentary in Medieval Ashkenaz*, 46–48, and below, n. 99. Cf. Haym Soloveitchik, "Catastrophe and Halakhic Creativity: Ashkenaz—1096, 1242, 1306 and 1298," *Jewish History* 12 (1998), 82 (n. 6). After noting that R. Ephraim of Bonn "wielded Spanish [poetic] metrics more felicitously than did Rabbenu Tam," Soloveitchik asserts that R. Ephraim, however, "was not in Rabbenu Tam's league as a Tosafist." While acknowledging that "few people in the past millennium were in that league," Soloveitchik concludes that "R. Ephraim of Bonn, as a dialectician, had not the stature of his contemporaries R. Ephraim of Regensburg or R. Yo'el ha-Levi, not to speak of that of the latter's son, Ravyah." The fact is, however, that R. Ephraim of Bonn was still a part of the Tosafist enterprise, and his achievements in halakhic and talmudic interpretation should be noted and included in any comprehensive study of the Tosafists, even if he should rightfully be consigned to the "back benches" of the Tosafist study hall(s) that he attended.

[90] See *Ba'alei ha-Tosafot*, 1:370, 406, and cf., e.g., Apowitzer, *Mavo la-Rabiah*, 382–85, and below, chapter 1 n. 12; chapter 2, nn. 203–4; chapter 6, n. 66. R. Menaḥem is mentioned only once in *'Arugat ha-Bosem*, ed. Urbach 4:34, even as Urbach devotes quite a bit of space (in both of his works) to R. Menaḥem's nephew and (junior) colleague on the Worms court, R. Eleazar b. Judah, author of the halakhic compendium *Sefer Roqeaḥ* and leader of *Ḥasidei Ashkenaz*. Cf. S. Emanuel, "'Ve-Ish 'al Meqomo Mevo'ar Shemo': Le-Toledotav shel R. Barukh b. Yiẓḥaq," *Tarbiz* 69 (2000), 427; and idem, *R. Eleazar mi-Vermaiza—Derashah le-Pesaḥ*, 39–40 (n. 153), 72–73 (n. 36). To be sure, there are few written records of R. Menaḥem's halakhic rulings, and R. Eleazar of Worms did compose at least some *Tosafot*. Two other prolific Tosafist figures barely discussed by Urbach, R. Isaiah di Trani (who was connected with the study hall of R. Simḥah of Speyer and other Tosafists in Germany and northern France), and R. Avigdor b. Elijah Katz of Vienna (who was also a student of R. Simḥah), may have been sidetracked because they lived for significant periods of time in Italy. See my *"Peering through the Lattices,"* 221–28; my "Mysticism and Asceticism in Italian Rabbinic Literature of the Thirteenth Century," *Kabbalah* 6 (2001), 135–49; I. Ta-Shma, *Knesset Meḥqarim*, vol. 1, 247–48; vol. 3 (Jerusalem, 2005), 9–75; S. Emanuel, *Shivrei Luḥot*, 45–47, 155–56, 164–65, 173–81; and below, chapter 6, nn. 103–6.

[91] See *'Arugat ha-Bosem*, ed. Urbach, 4:24–39; and Urbach, *Ba'alei ha-Tosafot* (above, n. 74).

he is far from the only Ashkenazic rabbinic scholar and jurist in his day to be involved in several Torah disciplines at the highest levels, as we shall see in the chapters that follow.

Multiple Truths and Interpretations

As an ideological prolegomenon to this book, which seeks to trace the various disciplines that were pursued by Ashkenazic rabbinic scholarship in addition to Talmud and *halakhah*, and bearing in mind the example of Rashbam discussed above, we should take note of the degree to which the rabbinic elite in medieval Ashkenaz believed in and pursued the possibility of multiple truths in Torah study, whether they were engaged in a range of Torah disciplines or not. In a well-known passage in his commentary to *ʿEruvin* (13b), R. Yom Tov b. Abraham al-Ishvilli (Ritva, d. c. 1325) interprets the talmudic phrase used to characterize the halakhic debates of *Beit Hillel* and *Beit Shammai*, "these and those are the words of the Living God" (*ʾelu ve-ʾelu divrei E-lohim ḥayyim*), by citing a discussion of northern French rabbinic scholars. "The rabbis of northern France asked, how is it possible that both [views] are the words of the Living God, since one prohibits and one permits? They answered that when Moses ascended to the heavens to receive the Torah, he was shown for every [halakhic] aspect [of the Torah] forty-nine ways to prohibit and forty-nine ways to permit. Moses queried the Almighty about this, and He indicated that this [the final halakhic jurisdiction] was given to the scholars of Israel in every generation and the decision would be theirs." Ritva concludes by noting that while this is the proper exoteric rabbinic interpretation (*nakhon hu lefi ha-derash*), an esoteric understanding of this concept is to be found within mystical teachings (*uve-derekh ha-ʾemet, yesh taʿam sod ba-davar*).[92]

The discussion cited by Ritva appears in fact in *Tosafot Rabbenu Perez* to *ʿEruvin*.[93] Indeed, the Tosafist R. Pereẓ b. Elijah of Corbeil (d. 1298) notes that this interpretation is to be found within the earlier *Tosafot* of his teacher, R. Yeḥiʾel b. Joseph of Paris, who had located it in an unnamed

[92] See *Ḥiddushei ha-Ritva ʿal Massekhet ʿEruvin*, ed. M. Goldstein (Jerusalem, 1974), 107–8. Cf. R. Solomon Luria's introduction to his *Yam shel Shelomoh* (to tractates *Bava Qamma* and *Ḥullin*); Meir Raffeld, "On Some Kabbalistic Elements Underlying the Halakhic Teachings of R. Shlomo Luria," [Hebrew] *Daʿat* 36 (1996), 21–23; and Yaʿakov Elbaum, *Openness and Insularity* [Hebrew] (Jerusalem, 1990), 361.

[93] *Tosafot Rabbenu Pereẓ ʿal Massekhet ʿEruvin*, ed. S. Wilman (Bnei Brak, 1980), 16 (= ed. H. Dickman [Jerusalem, 1991], 48). On the significant usage of *Tosafot Rabbenu Pereẓ* by Ritva throughout his talmudic commentaries, see my "Between Ashkenaz and Sefarad: Tosafist Teachings in the Talmudic Commentaries of Ritva," in *Between Rashi and Maimonides: Themes in Medieval Jewish Law, Thought and Culture*, ed. E. Kanarfogel and M. Sokolow (New York, 2010), 137–73.

midrash. The most likely source for R. Yeḥi'el's interpretation is a passage in *Midrash Shoḥer Tov* to Psalms 12:7 ("the expressions of the Almighty are exceedingly pure expressions"), in which early Palestinian Amoraim describe how even youngsters in the days of David and Saul and Samuel could present forty-nine different analyses of whether a substance was ritually pure or impure, and that this ability was retained by the Tannaim R. Meir and Somkhus (Symmachus) b. Joseph.[94] The Talmud in the aforementioned passage (*'Eruvin* 13b), just prior to its characterization of the arguments of *Beit Shammai* and *Beit Hillel*, makes similar statements about R. Meir and Somkhus. R. Yeḥi'el of Paris was suggesting that the concept of more than one legitimate halakhic truth that is implicit in the conflicts between *Beit Shammai* and *Beit Hillel* may best be understood against the even larger number of halakhic truths that were established at Sinai, a backdrop to which the talmudic *sugya* itself alludes.[95]

The singular extent to which these thirteenth-century Tosafists sought to affirm the possibility and legitimacy of multiple truths through Torah study and to stress the need to pursue these truths had recognizable antecedents in medieval Ashkenaz.[96] An Ashkenazic chronicle of the late thirteenth century attributes to either R. Simeon b. Isaac *ha-Gadol*, a leading talmudist and mystical adept (and member of the pious Abun family) active in Mainz circa 1000, or perhaps to R. Abun himself, the ability to interpret each letter of the Torah in forty-nine ways. This attribution is clearly modeled after the forty-nine aspects or channels that were operant at the giving of the Torah at Mount Sinai, using mystical methodology.[97]

The forty-nine "faces" of Torah interpretation (*mem-tet panim sheha-Torah nidreshet bahem*) are representative of the way that the Jews received the truth of the Torah at Sinai, and concomitantly, of the varied ways by which they would be able to interpret the halakhic possibilities and truths of the Torah. They are also mentioned in a Tosafist Torah commentary as a

94 On this midrashic passage and its variants, see Hanan'el Mack, "Shiv'im Panim la-Torah: Li-Mehalkho shel Bittui," in *Sefer Yovel li-Khvod R. Mordekahi Breuer*, ed. M. Bar-Asher (Jerusalem, 1992), 2:452–53.

95 *Tosafot Rabbenu Perez* adds that the definition of truth or correctness is determined by whether a particular position establishes itself on the basis of scriptural (or other) proofs. Its veracity and status as a "word of the living God" remain unaffected by whether this interpretation or another had in fact been chosen for actual implementation at a particular point in time. See below, n. 102, and also the position of Rabbenu Tam in *Tosafot Sanhedrin* 17a (= *Tosafot 'Eruvin* 13b), s.v. *she-yode'a*.

96 For fuller discussion, see my "Torah Study and Truth in Medieval Ashkenazic Rabbinic Literature," in *Study and Knowledge in Jewish Thought*, ed. H. Kreisel (Beer Sheva, 2006), 109–13.

97 See *Teshuvot Maharshal*, no. 29; Avraham Grossman, *Ḥakhmei Ashkenaz ha-Rishonim* (Jerusalem, 1981), 87; and idem, *Ḥakhmei Ẓarefat ha-Rishonim* (Jerusalem, 1995), 85. On the nature and provenance of this Ashkenazic chronicle, see my *"Peering through the Lattices,"* 23–24 (n. 13). For R. Simeon's mystical proclivities, see ibid., 131–36.

means of explaining the Torah's characterization (in Lev. 23:15–16) of the festival of *Shavu'ot* as occurring at the juncture of both the counting of seven full weeks (*sheva shabbatot temimot* = 49 days) as well as at the counting of fifty days (*tisperu ḥamishim yom*). The Torah, which represents the full fifty levels of Divine wisdom (*binah*), was given to Moses on behalf of the Jewish people, who stood just below the Divine realm with only one possible level of interpretation removed, as per Psalms 8:6, "You diminished him just a bit from the Divine."[98] A passage found within collections of Ashkenazic *piyyut* commentaries, whose authors range from the late eleventh through the late twelfth century, interprets a *qerovah* by R. Eleazar Qallir for *parashat Parah* according to this notion as well.[99]

Although there are quite a number of Tosafists who were familiar with various kinds of mystical views (as we shall see in chapter 6), the notion that a legitimately received or derived Torah interpretation or rabbinic teaching represents one truth out of many possible ones is at the same time a fundamentally exoteric dimension of the precept of Torah study in Tosafist thought, and constitutes a cornerstone of Tosafist analysis and intellectual endeavor. The *Tosafot* commentary to tractate *'Eduyyot* (1:5), attributed to R. Samson of Sens, refers to the notion of an open-ended revelation in explaining the Mishnaic convention of citing the minority view in many disputes. Although the law is usually decided according to the majority, a subsequent court could decide to rule according to the minority view. Despite the fact that a majority had not concurred with this view originally,

[98] See ms. Moscow 82, fol. 32r. On this manuscript, see below, chapter 3, n. 3.

[99] See ms. Hamburg 152, fol. 24r (col. 3): אצולת אומן בצירוף זקוקה זה התורה כדכ' וכו' מזוקקה בכסף צרוף כדכ' אמרות ה' אמרות טהורות כסף צרוף בעלול . . . מזוקק שבעתים. ושבע פעמים שבע מ"ט. כך התורה נדרשת מ"ט פנים טהור ומ"ט פנים טמא כאילו היה לפרש כל מעשיה ועניינה; and on fol. 24v (col. 1), when discussing the understanding of the workings of the *parah 'adumah*: זיר שבעתיים, כלו' כתר יש לה שהיא צרופה שבעתיים דכת' בעליל לארץ מזוקק שבעתים שכל מעשיה שבעה. שיש בה ז' הזיות, ז' טבילות, ז' כיבוסין, ז' פרות, ז' כהנין, ז' טמאים, ז' טהורין שהן עולין למ"ט שהן פעמיים ז'. See also the very similar (and perhaps parallel) interpretation of Qallir's *piyyut* in ms. Parma 655, fol. 33r, col. 3: שמידת זר שבעתים מזוקקה, כתר מצו' מזוקקת ומצורפת בכתרה של תורה שבעתים. התורה נדרשת מ"ט פנים והפרה נדרשת מ"ט טהרות כיצ' שבע פעמים שבע שהם מ"ט הזאות שבעה כהנים שבעה טהורים וכו' [דף 33ב] ולא עוד אלא כיון שהיו מבקשים לשרוף הפרה . . . נמצא מ"ט פנים של טהרה היו בה לומ' שהיא שקולה כנגד כל התורה כולה. In this manuscript, the commentary to Qallir's *qerovah* begins on fol. 33r, col. 2. Additional parallels are found in two *piyyut* commentaries of northern French provenance, ms. Bodl. 1206, fols. 38r–38v (פי' מזוקק שבעתיים כלו' שבעה פעמים שבעה מ"ט שהתורה נדרשת במ"ט פנים טהור ומ"ט פנים טמא וכן מעשה של פרה שמפרש לקמן מ"ט הזא[ו]ת שבעה טבילות שבעה וכו'); and ms. Bodl. 1207, fol. 35v: כתב מצוה זיר שבעתים מזוקקה. זו מזוקקת ומצורפת שבעתים ככתרה של תורה שכת' בה כסף צרוף . . . מהו מזוקק שבעתיים התורה נדרשת בארבעים ותשע פנים ואף הפרשה הזאת יש בה מ"ט פנים טהרות . . . הרי שבעה פעמים שבעה נמצאת או' ארבעים ותשע פנים של טהרה היו בה שהיא שקולה כנגד כל התורה. Cf. *'Arugat ha-Bosem*, ed. Urbach, 4:51. On the French and German scholars whose work is represented in this commentary, see also A. Grossman, *Ḥakhmei Ẓarefat ha-Rishonim*, 332–38, 355–57, 384–87, 510–21, 525–28; and Elisabeth Hollender, *Piyyut Commentary in Medieval Ashkenaz*, 35–46. For a (later) portion of ms. Parma 655 that was composed in the thirteenth century, see below, chapter 5, n. 322.

"when another generation arrives and the majority [at that time] accepts this view, the law will be established according to them. For the entirety of the Torah was given to Moses, including [all] the reasons (*panim*) to render impure [= to prohibit], as well as all the reasons to render pure [= to permit]. And they asked him, at some point will we be able to clarify [and then decide] between the various possibilities? He responded that although the majority [in each generation] must be followed, 'these and those are the words of the Living God.'"

This passage would appear to adumbrate the Tosafist texts cited by Ritva and discussed above, although its attribution to R. Samson of Sens is far from certain.[100] Nonetheless, a similar point is made in a confirmed formulation by R. Samson, found in his somewhat polemical response to R. Meir *ha-Levi* Abulafia (Ramah) of Toledo during the early phase of the Maimonidean controversy. R. Samson writes: "The Mishnah, Talmud, Sifra, Sifrei, and Tosefta did not transmit to subsequent scholars final legal decisions (*pisqei halakhot*). Rather, they included the views of those who rendered pure and impure, those who prohibited and permitted. Since the reason for these and those were all given by the one shepherd (*me-ro'eh 'eḥad*), one who ponders them is rewarded for [the study of] all of them. Moreover, a later scholar can sometimes see what was hidden to an earlier scholar . . . for a student can see what his teacher did not see. He can sometimes sharpen (or outsmart) his teacher [*maḥkim 'et rabbo*], and focus his teaching [*u-mekhaven 'et shemu'ato*]."[101]

This formulation by R. Samson clearly accords with the possibility of multiple truths in Torah study, and the need to actively pursue those truths. Indeed, Rashi, in his talmudic commentary to tractate to *Ḥullin*, explains that the Talmud inquires about the halakhic propriety of an act that took place during the initial conquest of the land of Israel, even though

[100] Although R. Samson did author a commentary to this tractate, the one attributed to him in the standard editions of the Talmud is not his. See Urbach, *Ba'alei ha-Tosafot*, 1:297; *Sarei ha-Elef*, ed. M. M. Kasher and Y. D. Mandelbaum (Jerusalem, 1979), 1:307; *Sanhedrei Gedolah le-Massekhet Sanhedrin*, vol. 6 (*liqqutei Tosafot Shanz*), ed. Y. Lifshitz (Jerusalem, 1974), 26–29; Y. Sussmann, "Perush ha-Rabad le-Massekhet Sheqalim," in *Me'ah She'arim: Studies in Medieval Jewish Spiritual Life in Memory of Isadore Twersky*, ed. E. Fleischer et al. (Jerusalem, 2001), 169–70. Lifshitz argues that this commentary, which refers to both Rambam and Rabad, is nonetheless of Ashkenazic provenance, and was probably composed by the German-born (and trained) R. Asher b. Yeḥi'el (Rosh). He also notes the view of M. Hershler that it may have been associated with *Tosafot Rabbenu Perez*, while Sussmann suggests that the author was perhaps a student of R. Samson of Sens.

[101] See *Kitab 'al Rasa'il*, ed. J. Brill (Paris, 1871), 131–32. On the implications of this comment (and other related ones) for intellectual freedom during the Tosafist period, see my "Progress and Tradition in Medieval Ashkenaz," *Jewish History* 14 (2000), 287–92. See also Yohanan Silman, *Qol Gadol ve-lo Yasaf* (Jerusalem, 1999), 145–46; Urbach, *Ba'alei ha-Tosafot*, 2:679; and *Teshuvot Maimuniyyot le-Sefer Shoftim*, sec. 20.

no practical halakhic implications for any future event can emerge from this inquiry, simply because we are always bidden to seek the truth (or true knowledge):ואע"פ שכבר עבר, דרוש וקבל שכר הוא שצריכים אנו לעמוד על האמת.[102] An unusual talmudic interpretation by Rabbenu Tam goes so far as to suggest that even if two Torah scholars are arguing with each other (*shnei talmidei ḥakhamim ha-madgilim zeh la-zeh*) in less than constructive terms, and, as a result, may not arrive at the essential truths of the subject under study, the Almighty nonetheless loves them. Rabbenu Tam's presumption in suggesting this interpretation is that discovering the truth of Torah is the principal goal of study and is eminently within reach, at least for those who are considered *talmidei ḥakhamim*.[103]

It is suggestive that the biblical prooftext adduced by the Talmud in tractate *Shabbat* for the concept found at the core of Rabbenu Tam's interpretation—that there is Divine love even for two contentious scholars—comes from Song of Songs 2:4: "He brought me to the banquet hall and he marked me with his love (ודגלו עלי אהבה)." Several medieval Ashkenazic texts (following a passage in Talmud Yerushalmi *Sanhedrin* 4:2) point out that the *gematria* value of *ve-diglo* equals forty-nine, corresponding to the notion that the Torah may be interpreted in forty-nine different and truthful ways.[104]

[102] See Rashi to *Ḥullin* 17a, s.v. *she-hikhnisu Yisra'el*. Cf. *Tosafot ha-Rosh* and *Perush ha-Rosh*, loc. cit.; Rashi to *Ketubot* 57a, s.v. *ka-mashma lan*; and Rashi's commentary to Daniel 7:19, s.v. *'edayin*. On the use of the phrase *la'amod 'al ha-'emet* in medieval Ashkenaz, see also *Teshuvot ha-Rabiah*, #1011, s.v. *ve-'agav gerara*; *Sefer Or Zaru'a*, pt. 2, *hilkhot 'erev Shabbat*, sec. 6; *Teshuvot ha-Rosh*, 31:9, s.v. *mah she-katav*, and 107:6, s.v. *Rabbi Shelomoh*; *Teshuvot Maharaḥ Or Zaru'a*, #65, s.v. *qehillah ha-mehulalah*. See also *Tosafot R. Elḥanan* to *'Avodah Zarah* 22b, s.v. *rigla*, and cf. Yohanan Silman, *Qol Gadol ve-Lo Yasaf* (Jerusalem, 1999), 146, n. 11; Ibn Ezra's comment to Eccl. 7:3, s.v. *tov*; and the next note.

[103] See *Tosafot 'Avodah Zarah* 22b, s.v. *rigla*; *Tosafot 'al Massekhet 'Avodah Zarah le-Rabbenu Elḥanan b. Rabbenu Yiẓḥaq mi-Dampierre*, ed. D. Frankel (Husiatyn, 1901), 48–49; *Shitat ha-Qadmonim 'al Masskehet 'Avodah Zarah*, ed. M. Blau (New York, 1969), 75; Ta-Shma, *Ha-Sifrut ha-Parshanit la-Talmud*, 2:95 (n. 2); and cf. *Tosafot Bava Meẓi'a* 109b, s.v. *ve-sofer*.

[104] See, e.g., *Tosafot ha-Shalem le-Ḥamesh Megillot*, ed. Y. Gellis, vol. 2 (Jerusalem, 1991), 41–42, secs. 5, 7, 9, citing R. Eleazar of Worms and the Tosafist complilatory commentary in ms. Vatican 48 (fol. 119v, end). R. Avigdor Katz, in his commentary to the Song of Songs, ed. S. A. Wertheimer (Jerusalem, 1981), 17, interprets the first half of the verse (*hevi'ani 'el beit ha-yayin*) to mean that the Almighty brought the children of Israel to receive the Torah at Sinai, which can be interpreted in seventy facets (*she-nidreshet be-shiv'im panim*), as demonstrated by the *gematria* of the word *yayin*, which equals seventy. As I have shown in my "Torah Study and Truth," 113–16, the tradition of "seventy facets of the Torah" was usually used and favored by mystics and kabbalists who wished to explore the deeper mystical subleties of the Torah. Indeed, R. Avigdor concludes here that seventy is also the *gematria* of the word *sod* as in the verse in Psalms 25:14, סוד ה' ליראיו. Ashkenazic rabbinic scholars, however, typically referred to the notion of מ"ט פנים לתורה to underscore the multiple paths through which the truths of the Torah could be discovered and expressed. Cf. H. Mack, "Shiv'im Panim la-Torah: le-Mehalkho shel Bittui," in *Sefer ha-Yovel li-Khvod R. Mordekhai Breuer* (Jerusalem, 1992), vol. 2:452–60, and *Perush R. Avigdor b. Eliyyahu Kohen Ẓedeq [Katz] me-Vienna le-Shir ha-Shirim*, ed. S. A. Wertheimer (Jerusalem, 1971), 32 (6:9).

Israel Ta-Shma has noted that the main goal of talmudic interpretation in Western Europe during the High Middle Ages was to seek a kind of enhanced *peshat* that pursued the halakhic ramifications of the talmudic *sugya* well beyond its simple meaning. Moreover, in the medieval Jewish mindset in general, and especially within medieval Ashkenaz, *peshat, derash, remez* (and perhaps even *sod*) were equally valid ways of ascertaining and presenting the truths of the Torah, given the possibility of multiple interpretations and exegesis inherent within the Torah itself. As opposed to the methods or rules of modern interpretation, Ashkenazic rabbinic scholars believed that the truth could be revealed quite effectively by non-*peshat* approaches as well.[105]

Thus Rashbam and others could engage in "enlightened" *peshat* and other critical forms of biblical interpretation while maintaining their roles as leading Tosafists and talmudists, just as other Ashkenazic talmudists could be involved at the same time in the study of mysticism or *piyyut*.[106] Sara Japhet has identified the essence of Rashbam's interpretational strategy in his biblical commentaries as achieving "complete freedom from the [existing] exegetical traditions . . . with full allegiance to context and the interpretation of the [biblical] word based on its grammatical origins and parallel usages." Moreover, "each biblical text has only one *peshat*. The text may be considered from different perspectives and angles, but the final result must be a single and unified interpretation (*perush ʾaḥid ume-ʾuḥad*) that is the 'truth of its simple meaning' (*ʾamitat peshuto*). Therefore, multiple interpretations to one topic are not found in Rashbam's [biblical] compositions, and formulations such as *davar ʾaḥer, ʿinyan ʾaḥer*, or *perush ʾaḥer* are completely absent from his commentaries." Japhet goes on to note that although Rashi also limits the number of exegetical possibilities in his biblical commentaries, certainly as compared to the variety of different interpretations presented by midrashic texts, he, unlike Rashbam, believes in the multi-meanings of the biblical text. This approach also characterizes the commentary of R. Yosef *Bekhor Shor*, as we shall see. According to Japhet, Rashbam, in contrast, believes in the uni-meaning of the biblical text as a fundamental property of *peshat*.[107]

105 Ta-Shma, *Ha-Sifrut ha-Parshanit la-Talmud*, 1:16–21.

106 Cf. H. H. Ben-Sasson's review of Urbach's *Baʿalei ha-Tosafot* (above, n.37); I. Twersky, "Religion and Law," in *Religion in a Religious Age*, ed. S. D. Goitein (Cambridge, Mass., 1973), 69–82; Rashi's introduction to his commentary on *Shir ha-Shirim*; and the studies cited above, n. 47.

107 See S. Japhet, *Perush Rabbenu Shmuʾel b. Meir (Rashbam) le-Shir ha-Shirim* (Jerusalem, 2008), 48, 86–87. Cf. Jay Harris, *How Do We Know This?* (Albany, N.Y., 1995), 82–85; Itamar Kislev, "Ha-Ziqah bein Perusheihem shel R. Avraham Ibn Ezra ve-Rashbam: Sugyat Markivei ha-Qetoret," *Tarbiz* 78 (2009), 74–79; Eran Viezel, *The Commentary on Chronicles Attributed to Rashi* [Hebrew] (Jerusalem, 2010), 74–84; and below, chapter 2, n. 47.

Although this assessment may perhaps be correct with respect to Rashbam's biblical commentaries, it does not hold true for Rashbam's other interpretational activities, such as his talmudic commentaries and *Tosafot* formulations, even where these commentaries deal with biblical verses.[108] Thus, for example, a talmudic passage in *Bava Batra* suggests that the term *moshlim* in Numbers 21:27 refers to those who can control or rule over their own inclinations (*moshlim be-yizram*). Rashbam comments here that according to the *pashteh di-qera* (the simple, contextual meaning of the verse), this term refers to Bil'am and his prophetic colleagues who were able to control or channel their prophecies. At this point, however, the information this verse imparts in retrospect was no longer especially vital, and the verse becomes somewhat superfluous (ומיהו פרשה יתירה היא דמה צריך ליכתב זה . . . ואין צריך יותר). Nonetheless, Moses included it in the Torah so that it could serve the talmudic *derashah* (הלכך לדרשה כתבה משה רבינו).[109]

Indeed, even R. Judah *he-Ḥasid*, whose full corpus of biblical interpretations takes a variety of approaches and forms ranging from *peshat* to *sod*, was not above suggesting both a *notariqon* and an *at-bash* methodology to clarify points of interpretation within Rashi's Torah commentary.[110] The availability of this kind of interpretational freedom and variety also allowed *Ḥasidei Ashkenaz* to be comfortable with Ibn Ezra's stipulation of verses that may have been added to the Torah after the revelation at Sinai,[111] and for a number of Ashkenazic exegetes to espouse theories of biblical redaction.[112]

108 See above, nn. 45–46; and cf. Y. Jacobs, "Tosafot she-Hosif Rashbam le-Perusho la-Torah," *Tarbiz* 76 (2008), 445–64.

109 See Rashbam to *Bava Batra* 78b, s.v. *mai dikhtiv*; E. Touitou, *Exegesis in Perpetual Motion*, 59–63; and M. Berger "The Torah Commentary of Rabbi Samuel b. Meir" (above, n. 45), 241–42. In his Torah commentary, Rashbam interprets this verse (only) as a reference to those who could control or master prophecy, namely Bil'am and his colleagues (מושלי נבואות כגון בלעם וחביריו). This is essentially the interpretation of Rashi, Ibn Ezra, and *Ḥizzequni* as well, although they arrive at this interpretation by understanding the word *moshlim* (spelled here as משלים, without the *vav*) as related to *meshalim*, which was the vehicle of Bil'am's prohecy (וישא משלו ויאמר).

110 See *Perushei ha-Torah le-R. Yehudah he-Ḥasid*, ed. Y. S. Lange (Jerusalem, 1975), 70 (Ex. 1:7), 173 (Nu. 12:6), and below, chapter 3, n. 110. On the variety of biblical commentaries attributed to R. Judah *he-Ḥasid* as well as those penned by his student, R. Eleazar of Worms, see, e.g., my *Jewish Education and Society in the High Middle Ages*, ch. 6; Ivan Marcus, "Exegesis for the Few and for the Many," *Jerusalem Studies in Jewish Thought* 8 (1989), 1*–24*; *Sefer Gematriot of R. Judah the Pious* (Los Angeles, 1998), with introductions by D. Abrams and I. Ta-Shma; and Joseph Dan, *'Iyyunim be-Sifrut Ḥasidut Ashkenaz* (Ramat Gan, 1975), 44–57.

111 See, e.g., I. Ta-Shma, *Knesset Meḥqarim*, 1:273–301; and cf. Haym Soloveitchik, "Two Notes on the *Commentary of the Torah* of R. Yehudah he-Ḥasid," in *Turim: Studies in Jewish History and Literature Presented to Dr. Bernard Lander*, ed. M. Shmidman, vol. 2 (New York, 2008), 241–51.

112 See Richard Steiner, "A Jewish Theory of Biblical Redaction from Byzantium: Its Rabbinic Roots, Its Diffusion and Its Encounter with the Muslim Doctrine of Falsification," *Jewish Studies Internet Journal* 2 (2003), 123–67; R. A. Harris, "Awareness of Biblical Redaction among

A broad-based search for truth and knowledge was underway in medieval Europe during the twelfth and thirteenth centuries in precisely the same geographic area in which the Tosafists of northern France flourished. Stephen Ferruolo has argued that the various masters and faculties of the cathedral schools in Paris, and the diverse and sometimes antagonistic disciplines they represented, came together by the early thirteenth century to form the nascent university at Paris in order to "advance their mutual search for wisdom and truth" on the basis of common intellectual methods and aims. Many of these masters had come to Paris in the last quarter of the twelfth century from other leading cathedral schools, such as those at Chartres, Laon, and Rheims. These scholars came together ultimately because they believed that the pursuit of all possible forms and levels of truth was best undertaken from the vantage point of multiple disciplinary perspectives.[113] There may have been issues of professionalism and autonomy at stake for these masters that contributed to their amalgamation of several approaches which were not applicable to the Tosafists and to their study halls.[114] Nonetheless, the desire to seek truth along multiple lines, in a collaborative fashion that would help to eliminate mistakes, diminish the possibility of weak reasoning, and allow for the probing of available texts and sources, appears to have been a common goal of both the rabbinic scholars of northern France and their Christian counterparts in the cathedral schools and universities.

To be sure, Israel Ta-Shma has suggested that these developments may have been somewhat different in Germany, where the formation of the universities did not occur until the mid-fourteenth century. Indeed, the subtle

---

Rabbinic Exegetes of Northern France," [Hebrew] *Shenaton le-Ḥeqer ha-Miqra veha-Mizraḥ ha-Qadum* 13 (2000), 289–310; Ta-Shma, *Knesset Meḥqarim*, i, 1:302–13; S. Japhet, "Rashbam's Introduction to His Commentary on Lamenations," [Hebrew] *Shenaton le-Ḥeqer ha-Miqra veha-Mizraḥ ha-Qadum* 19 (2009), 242–43; and cf. E. Viezel, "The Composition of Some Books of the Bible According to Rashi," in *Rashi: The Man and His Works* [Hebrew], ed. A. Grossman and S. Japhet (Jerusalem, 2008), 139–59. At the conclusion of his study, Prof. Steiner notes that "it is striking that a theory of redaction took root in Ashkenaz but not in Sepharad. The counter-intuitive nature of this finding makes an appeal to polemical factors all the more necessary." Perhaps it was the broader Ashkenazic view (which was more open to multiple truths in Torah interpretation) that allowed some of its scholars to embrace the theory of redaction being discussed as a possibility. See also below, chapter 2, n. 102, and chapter 3, n. 10.

113 See S. C. Ferruolo, *The Origins of the University: The Schools of Paris and Their Critics, 1100–1215* (Stanford, Calif., 1985), 101–3, 125–28, 163–66, 270–71, and esp. 310–11. Cf. P. Ranft, "The Role of the Eremitic Monks in the Development of the Medieval Intellectual Tradition," in *From Cloister to Classroom: Monastic and Scholastic Approaches to Truth*, ed. E. Rozanne Elder (Kalamazoo, Mich., 1986), 80–90; and E. Kearney, "Scientia and Sapientia: Reading Sacred Scriptures at the Paraclete," in *From Cloister to Classroom*, ed. Elder, 111–20; Ora Limor, *Jews and Christians in Western Europe: Hebraica Veritas* [Hebrew] (Tel Aviv, 1993), 40–42, 61–62; and Eran Viezel, *The Commentary to Chronicles Attributed to Rashi*, 322–33.

114 Cf. my *Jewish Education and Society*, 42–54, 60–64.

differences between the nature of talmudic dialectic and its application by rabbinic scholars in northern France and those in Germany may well have been related, at least in part, to this distinction.[115] Nonetheless, a fundamental aim of dialectic, as practiced by both Tosafists and Christian scholars during the twelfth and thirteenth centuries, was to reach conclusions that were carefully tested, broad-based, and unequivocal. Dialectic was meant to minimize the possibility of error.[116]

Although there was no shortage of penetrating biblical *peshat* interpretations and talmudic dialectic to be found within medieval Ashkenaz, this book will argue that other significant methods and interpretative techniques were also employed (by the same rabbinic figures). Intellectual well-roundedness is a function of the pursuit of truth, and many Ashkenazic rabbinic scholars believed that truth could best be achieved if it was pursued along multiple interpretive and disciplinary paths. We should not be surprised to learn that some of the Tosafists were involved in quite a number of varied disciplines in addition to their talmudic and halakhic studies, much of which has received scant attention in modern scholarship. These include sustained biblical interpretation beyond the (well-known) *peshat* school of the twelfth century, the writing of *piyyut* as well as *piyyut* commentary, a range of esoteric studies, as well as focused inquiries into matters of faith and belief.

Just as the truth of the Torah is manifest in multiple halakhic interpretations, so can it also be manifest in multiple disciplines or approaches to Torah study and thought. Thus although the Tosafists and other *Ḥakhmei Ashkenaz* were axiomatically and fundamentally talmudocentric, and the leadership of the Tosafist study halls was entrusted to those rabbinic scholars whose greatest strength was in the area of talmudic studies, many of these scholars were deeply involved with other disciplines as well, as they searched for the truths of the Torah and the Jewish legal tradition. In short, Ashkenazic authors preferred not to confine themselves to a single, simple, true Torah interpretation that was based on a lone text or approach. Rather,

115 See I. Ta-Shma, "Maqbilim she-Einam Nifgashim: Yeshivot Ba'alei ha-Tosafot veha-Sevivah ha-Aqademit be-Ẓarefat ba-Me'ah ha-Shteim 'Esreh veha-Shelosh 'Esreh," in *Yeshivot u-Battei Midrashot*, ed. Etkes, 80–81; and above, n. 15.

116 See Ta-Shma, *Ha-Sifrut ha-Parshanit*, 1:90, 100, 108. Ta-Shma notes that those Christian scholars who pursued well-based strategies of textual interpretation, as well as those who were more comfortable with less textually focused allusions or intuitive interpretations (akin perhaps to *remez*), sometimes claimed a form of heavenly authority or origin for their diverse interpretations. Cf. *Sefer ha-Yashar le-Rabbanu Tam (Ḥiddushim)*, sec. 660; *Sefer Rabiah*, ed. Aptowitzer, vol. 1 (Jerusalem, 1984), sec. 391; *Teshuvot Maharam b. Barukh mi-Rothenburg*, ed. M. A. Bloch (Budapest, 1895), #947; my "Torah Truth and Study," 109 (n. 16); and below, chapter 6.

they believed in pursuing a multitude of approaches and disciplines, and in multiple "interpretational voices" within a particular text.[117]

Chapter 1 will focus more comprehensively on the differences between northern France and Germany with respect to talmudic and halakhic studies, and on the possible impact of Christian learning on talmudic studies in medieval Ashkenaz. These important "longitudinal" issues will also help set the stage for the comparison across disciplines to follow in the subsequent chapters. The ability to compare and to distinguish within the corpus of talmudic literature, and thereby to expand and correctly identify new halakhic results, formed the intellectual base of all Tosafist talmudic studies. The assumption of the Tosafists was that the Oral Law allowed for such *ḥiddushim*—that is, to identify "new" *halakhah* that was not found so overtly in the Talmud, through close readings and the application of dialectics.[118] As we shall see, this assumption also stood at the heart of the intellectual freedom that came to typify rabbinic scholarship and culture in medieval Ashkenaz.

[117] Cf. E. Hollender, *Piyyut Commentary in Medieval Ashkenaz*, 2, 7–8.

[118] See Ta-Shma, "Maqbilim she-Einam Nifgashim," 82; idem, *Knesset Meḥqarim*, 2:231–35 (where Ta-Shma notes that this is also how Spanish rabbinic scholars such as Ramban, who had contact with Tosafist *battei midrash*, came to compose their own *ḥiddushim* on the Talmud); idem, *Ha-Sifrut ha-Parshanit la-Talmud*, 1:68 (that the primary meaning of the very term *Tosafot* connotes an addendum to the halakhic process based on new insights); and my "Progress and Tradition in Medieval Ashkenaz," 302.

1

Talmudic and Halakhic Studies

Internal Organization and Societal Models

The Tosafists, best known for their brief yet incisive analytical and comparative comments (*Tosafot*) to the text of the Talmud as interpreted by Rashi, revolutionized and forever changed the study of the Talmud and the formulation of *halakhah* through their methods of close reading and wide-ranging dialectic. Although the degree to which rabbinic scholars during this period also served as the leaders of their communities with respect to temporal issues is a matter of some dispute,[1] there is no doubt that they constituted the highest level of religious authority.

As opposed to the Ashkenazic rabbinic leaders of the pre-Crusade period, who were closely linked with the Rhineland academies at Mainz and Worms in particular, the Tosafists were spread over a wider geographic area throughout northern France and Germany, and within Austria, England,

[1] See e.g., Yizhak Handelsman, "Hashqafotav shel Rabiah ʿal Darkhei Hanhagat ha-Qehillot u-Meqoman be-Hitpatḥut ha-Maḥshavah ha-Ẓibburit shel Ḥakhmei Yemei ha-Benayim," *Zion* 48 (1983), 21–45; Simcha Goldin, *Ha-Yiḥud veha-Yaḥad* (Tel Aviv, 1997), 116–20, 145–52; Moses Frank (Drori), *Qehillot Ashkenaz u-Battei Dineihen* (Tel Aviv, 1938), 35; my "Unanimity, Majority and Communal Government in Ashkenaz during the High Middle Ages: A Reassessment," *Proceedings of the American Academy for Jewish Research* 58 (1992), 79–106; and below, n. 25. In early Ashkenaz, the smaller size of the communities meant that rabbinic scholars were more likely to serve also as communal leaders. See, e.g., Avraham Grossman, *Ḥakhmei Ashkenaz ha-Rishonim* (Jerusalem, 1981), 400; Yaʿakov Blidstein, "ʿIyyunim be-Perushei Rashi: ʿInyanei Hanhagah ve-Shilton," *Eshel Beʾer Sheva* 3 (1986), 137–48; Israel Ta-Shma, "ʿAl Petur Talmidei Ḥakhamim me-Missim Bimei ha-Benayim," in *ʿIyyunim be-Sifrut Ḥazal, be-Miqra, uve-Toledot Yisraʾel*, ed. Y. D. Gilat (Ramat Gan, 1982), 318–19; and Simon Schwarzfuchs, *A Concise History of the Rabbinate* (Oxford, 1993), 8–11. Cf. *Mordekhai Gittin*, sec. 384 (= *Sefer ha-Mordekhai le-Massekhet Gittin*, ed. M. Rabinowitz [Jerusalem, 1990], 552), for the position of the Tosafist R. Isaac of Evreux (which he received from his teachers), that the *bon viri* of the community (the *shivʿah tuvei ha-ʿir*) can levy and collect biblically mandated fines (*kenasot*), even though a *beit din* could not currently do so; and see also below, n. 138.

and Italy as well. Moreover, students of the Tosafists were identified primarily by their teachers rather than with the city or town in which their academies were located. As I have demonstrated elsewhere, this change in identification parallels in many respects the shift from the primacy of the monastic schools to the primacy of the cathedral schools (and their masters) that occurred in Christian society during the mid-eleventh century, a theme to which we shall return below.[2]

Although the Tosafists in both northern France and Germany appear to be similarly regarded and equally matched as religious leaders, there is a significant distinction between them that has gone virtually unremarked in modern scholarship. In Germany noted Tosafists and other leading rabbinic scholars served as local court judges in a variety of cities and towns. These scholars sat on actual cases, communicated with other courts as needed (often compiling some kind of written record of these exchanges and interactions), and handled appeals—from individual scholars as well as from other jurisdictions—as members of a court. While there can be no doubt that leading Tosafists and rabbinic scholars in northern France also served as judges, specific references to these occurrences are quite difficult to come by from the late twelfth century—that is, from beyond the days of Rabbenu Tam until the second quarter of the thirteenth century (1180–1220). Leading northern French Tosafists in the period following Rabbenu Tam were sought out in the course of judicial appeals but, as we shall see, this function tends to support and confirm the role of the northern French Tosafists as leading scholars and teachers of Jewish law rather than as sitting jurists.

Rabbinic Courts in Germany

It is possible to identify in great detail the members of the rabbinic courts in a number of locales in Germany throughout the twelfth and thirteenth centuries. These include leading scholars in Mainz, Worms, Speyer, Cologne, Regensburg, Magdeburg, and Wurzburg, among others.[3] Moreover, a steady stream of interactions and contacts between the various sitting rabbinic courts can also be documented.

[2] See my *Jewish Education and Society in the High Middle Ages* (Detroit, Mich., 1992), 57–63, 70–72; Heinrich Fichtenau, *Heretics and Scholars in the High Middle Ages* (University Park, Pa., 1998), 268–80; and below, n. 147.

[3] A listing of this kind was compiled by M. Frank, *Qehillot Ashkenaz u-Battei Dineihen*, 142–57. The discovery of manuscript materials and the publication of numerous medieval rabbinic texts over the past seventy years afford us the opportunity to supplement (and in some cases to adjust or to correct) Frank's findings.

R. Moses b. Solomon *ha-Kohen*, who had studied in northern France with Rabbenu Tam,[4] was the senior member of the Mainz court in the second half of the twelfth century. He served together with R. Judah b. Qalonymus (Rivaq) b. Moses of Mainz, and R. Moses b. Mordekhai.[5] Following R. Moses b. Solomon's death, R. Barukh b. Samuel (d. 1221), author of the voluminous *Sefer ha-Ḥokhmah*, became a member of the court. Barukh had studied in his youth with R. Ephraim of Regensburg and with R. Judah b. Qalonymus (Rivaq) b. Meir of Speyer.[6]

Although R. Eliezer b. Joel *ha-Levi* (Rabiah, d. c. 1225) served for the most part as a judge in Cologne, he writes that at one point he presented an argument before the Mainz court for their approval. R. Barukh b. Samuel had advocated in a legal matter on behalf on some orphans who were related to him. According to Rabiah, R. Barukh was sitting with him in the study hall or *scriptorum* (*beit ha-sefer*), and Rabiah presented an halakhic argument or approach in this matter (ודנתי לפניו ולפני שאר רבותי) before R. Barukh and his other teachers, which suggested that the orphans in this case should not prevail. R. Barukh acknowledged Rabiah's point, and Rabiah spoke to him further in this matter. Rabiah subsequently ruled this way in a case that came before him in Cologne, and adduced additional support for his approach from a statement of Ri found in (*Tosafot*) *Yevamot*.[7] This formulation indicates that the Mainz court was connected in some way to an

[4] See above, Introduction, n. 76.

[5] On R. Moses b. Mordekhai's place on the Mainz court, cf. Simcha Emanuel, *Shivrei Luḥot: Sefarim Avudim shel Ba'alei ha-Tosafot* (Jerusalem, 2006), 105, 130, 138, and below, nn. 11, 15.

[6] See E. E. Urbach, *Ba'alei ha-Tosafot* (Jerusalem, 1980), 1:184–86, 389, 425–28; *Sefer Rabiah*, ed. Aptowitzer (Jerusalem, 1984), 1:171 (where R. Moses is referred to as ארי שבחבורה); and Simcha Emanuel, "R. Barukh mi-Magenẓa: Demuto shel Ḥakham 'al pi Seridei Ketavav," in *Sugyot be-Meḥqar ha-Talmud* [*Yom 'Iyyun le-Ẓiyyun Ḥamesh Shanim le-Petirato shel E. E. Urbach*] (Jerusalem, 2001), 126–31. For R. Barukh's *Tosafot*, see Emanuel, 132–33, and idem, *Shivrei Luḥot*, 112–23. As we shall see below, the son of R. Moses *ha-Kohen* (Judah of Friedberg/Wurzburg, n. 67) and the son of Rivaq of Mainz (= Eleazar of Worms, nn. 13–17), as well as R. Ephraim of Regensburg (nn. 27–28) and Rivaq of Speyer (n. 19), were also members of the rabbinic courts in their communities.

[7] See *Teshuvot Rabiah*, ed. D. Deblitzky (Bnei Brak, 1989), sec. 925 (pp. 54–56): והרב ברוך אז היה מסייע ליתומים קרוביו . . . ונתיישב אז עמי בבית הספר ודנתי לפניו ולפני שאר רבותי ר' יהודה ומורי הרב ר' משה דהא קיי"ל כרבי עקיבא דינתנו ליורשין הני מילי באותו הזמן . . . אבל בזמן הזה אפילו ינתנו ליורשים היא תוציאם מידם . . . ודע כי הודה אז הרב ר' ברוך לדבריי להסכים עמי . . . ועתה דברתי עמו . . . וגם עתה מחדש דננו כן בקולוניא . . . ובסוף יבמות מצאתי כדבריי בשם ר' יצחק מדנפירא. The expression ודנתי לפניו ולפני שאר רבותי has the connotation of an argument advanced or put forward before the other rabbinic figures for their consideration, not necessarily an indication that Rabiah participated with them in an actual court case. Cf., e.g., *Teshuvot ha-Rosh*, 4:10, on the subject of when to begin reciting *ve-ten tal u-matar* in the Diaspora: כל אלו הדברים דנתי לפני רבותי באשכנז ולא היה אדם מערער לדברי. On the other hand, the phrase וגם עתה מחדש דננו כן בקולוניא indicates that Rabiah was serving in that instance as a judge. See Aptowitzer, *Mavo la-Rabiah* (Jerusalem, 1938), 201, and cf. below, nn. 9, 43–47, 61.

academy or study hall, but that the rabbinic court was the more prominent institution of the two.[8]

R. Yaqar b. Samuel *ha-Levi* and R. She'alti'el b. Menaḥem of Cologne, as recorded in R. Barukh of Worms's *Sefer ha-Ḥokhmah*, disagreed with Rabiah with regard to a lender who had confiscated the pawn that he received from another Jew as a means of collecting monies owed to him.[9] The Mainz court, consisting of Rivaq, R. Moses b. Mordekhai, and R. Barukh b. Samuel, also argued against the view of Rabiah.[10] At some point, R. Ephraim of Bonn was in Mainz and appears to have been the fourth signatory on a written opinion of the Mainz court.[11]

The leading court in Worms in the late twelfth century consisted of the well-known *payyetan* and rabbinic scholar R. Menaḥem b. Jacob (d. 1203),[12] R. Eleazar b. Judah (d. c. 1230, author of *Sefer Roqeaḥ* and the son of Rivaq

[8] See also *Mordekhai Ḥullin*, sec. 684: מעשה בא לפני רבותינו שבמגנצא ואני ברוך דנתי לפניהם וגו'. In this instance, R. Barukh of Mainz's stringent interpretation was ratified by R. Moses *ha-Kohen* (who noted that this view was espoused in the study hall of Rabbenu Tam as well) and subsequently by R. Yo'el *ha-Levi* of Bonn (when he came to Mainz and discussed the matter with R. Barukh). Cf. S. Emanuel, *Shivrei Luḥot*, 105, n. 4.

[9] See *Mordekhai Bava Meẓi'a*, sec. 403, and Aptowitzer, *Mavo la-Rabiah*, 214–15. In this instance, R. Yaqar b. Samuel *ha-Levi* is the grandfather of the leading judge in Cologne by the same name during the second half of the thirteenth century. See I. Ta-Shma, *Knesset Meḥqarim*, vol. 1 (Jerusalem, 2004), 168 (n. 70); and below, nn. 48, 114, and chapter 5, nn. 240, 310. On R. She'alti'el and Rabiah's court, see also below, n. 45, and see *Mordekhai Ketubot*, sec. 152. For additional references to R. She'alti'el (and R. Yaqar) in *Sefer ha-Ḥokhmah* and in conjunction with Rabiah, see Aptowitzer, *Mavo la-Rabiah*, 394; S. Emanuel, *R. Eleazar mi-Vermaiza—Dereshah le-Pesaḥ* (Jerusalem, 2006), 9; idem, *Shivrei Luḥot*, 129, 132; and idem, "R. Barukh mi-Magenẓa," 141 (n. 78).

[10] See *Mordekhai Bava Meẓi'a*, sec. 338, for another written opinion from this court, with which R. Barukh personally disagreed. On secs. 403 and 338 in *Mordekhai Bava Meẓi'a*, cf. Emanuel, "R. Barukh mi-Magenẓa," 139, n. 65.

[11] See *Mordekhai Bava Batra*, secs. 467–68. Although several of the most authoritative *Mordekhai* manuscripts contain all four names (see ms. B.M. 537 [Add. 19972], fol. 65r; ms. Vercelli C235, fol. 57v, col. 2; ms. Vienna 73, fol. 53v), ms. Budapest 1 (fol. 151r) lists Ephraim instead of R. Barukh, as does ms. Vienna 72 (fol. 124r). Cf. Emanuel, *Shivrei Luḥot*, 143, n. 86. Ephraim is listed together with Rivaq and R. Moses b. Mordekhai (and without R. Barukh) in *Mordekhai Bava Batra*, sec. 576. For additional responsa from the Mainz court, see *Teshuvot Rabiah*, sec. 922 (below, n. 97); *Sefer Rabiah—Teshuvot*, vol. 2, sec. 1007 (pp. 208–10); and *Mordekhai Yevamot*, sec. 58 (= ms. Vercelli C235, fol. 226v, and ms. Brit. Mus. 537, fol. 353r), which also refers to a ruling of the Speyer court. See below, n. 19.

[12] See Aptowitzer, *Mavo la-Rabiah*, 382–84, and above, Introduction, n. 90. As Aptowitzer notes, the epitaph on R. Menaḥem's tombstone reads (in part), רבינו מנחם בן ר' יעקב אבי החכמה תנא דורש ופייטן אין חסר מאומה בתלמוד רב ובמשנה ידו הרימה. When referring to the leading rabbinic teachers of the community, the Worms *Memorbucher* mentions only R. Menaḥem and his nephew, R. Eleazar b. Judah, by name: רבינו מנחם ב"ר יעקב ורבינו אלעזר בן רבינו יהודה ושאר רבנים שהרביצו תורה בישראל. Cf. Emanuel, *R. Eleazar mi-Vermaiza—Derashah le-Pesaḥ* (Jerusalem, 2006), 39–40, 72–73 (n. 36). R. Menaḥem is also cited as a leading halakhic authority by *Sefer ha-Assufot*, whose unnamed author was apparently a student of Rabiah and R. Eleazar of Worms. See below, chapter 6, n. 67.

of Mainz), and R. Qalonymus b. Gershom.[13] Among the legal decisions circulated by this court was one concerning the identification of a corpse by a single Jewish witness who testified that he had seen and clearly recognized the corpse as a victim of war.[14] A slightly later judicial alignment in Worms included Eleazar b. Judah, Qalonymus b. Gershom, and R. Mordekhai b. Joseph. As recorded in an oft-cited responsum found in the collection of R. Ḥayyim *Or Zaruʿa*, this court sent a question on the need for unanimous agreement in matters of communal government to the Mainz court (of Rivaq, R. Moses b. Mordekhai, and R. Barukh b. Samuel) for its opinion, and to R. Eliezer b. Joel *ha-Levi* for his opinion as well.[15] In similar fashion, the Worms court sent another of its rulings in a complex case (concerning the rights of a married woman to particular assets) to the Mainz court, and to Rabiah, for their approval.[16] R. Moses *ha-Kohen* of the Mainz court, R. Eleazar *Roqeaḥ* of the Worms court, and Rabiah responded to a query concerning a *ḥaliẓah* ceremony from two otherwise unknown scholars, Samuel b. Judah and Barukh b. Binyamin.[17]

In the first half of the twelfth century, R. Isaac b. Asher *ha-Levi* (Riba, d. 1133), the earliest German Tosafist, served as a judge in Speyer.[18] Later in the twelfth century, Rivaq b. Meir of Speyer (d. 1199) sat on the court with two

[13] See Urbach, *Baʿalei ha-Tosafot*, 1:406–7. Cf. A. Aptowitzer, *Mavo la-Rabiah*, 223, 382; and M. Frank, *Qehillot Ashkenaz u-Battei Dineihen*, 144–45.

[14] See *Sefer Mordekhai ʿal Massekhet Yevamot*, secs. 89–90. This ruling was agreed to by the rabbinic court in Speyer, which was led by R. Nathan b. Simeon and R. Simḥah b. Samuel; see below, n. 19.

[15] See *Teshuvot Maharaḥ Or Zaruʿa*, #222 (found also in ms. Mont. 130, sec. 95, fols. 15r–15v); Urbach, *Baʿalei ha-Tosafot* (above, n. 13); Emanuel, *Shivrei Luḥot*, 133, n. 137; and my "The Development and Diffusion of Unanimous Agreement in Medieval Ashkenaz," in *Studies in Medieval Jewish History and Literature*, vol. 3, ed. I. Twersky and J. Harris (Cambridge, Mass., 2000), 26–28.

[16] See *Teshuvot Maharam mi-Rothenburg*, ed. Prague #576 (= *Mordekhai Ketubot*, sec. 207); *Teshuvot Rabiah*, ed. Deblitzky, sec. 923 (pp. 42–45); and Aptowitzer, *Mavo la-Rabiah*, 189–90. Although the response of the Mainz court refers to a collective judicial entity (אפי' לפי דבריכם שהבאתם שגגתם קצת בזה הדין), the question was posed by Eleazar of Worms on behalf of the court in the version found in *Teshuvot Maharam*, and by R. Isaac b. Meshullam and Qalonymus b. Gershom in the *Teshuvot Rabiah* version. It should be noted that in all these groupings, at least one member of both the Mainz and Worms courts was a lesser-known rabbinic figure.

[17] See *Sefer Rabiah—Teshuvot*, ed. Deblitzky, sec. 956, and Urbach, *Baʿalei ha-Tosafot*, 1:407. Cf. *Sefer Rabiah*, vol. 4, ed. E. Prisman and S. Y. Cohen (Brooklyn, 1963), editor's introduction, 27–28, for the suggestion that one of these two judges is Samuel b. Judah (the son of R. Judah *he-Ḥasid*), who also studied with R. Moses *ha-Kohen* of Mainz. For other appeals to Rabiah by rabbinic courts, see, e.g., *Sefer Rabiah*, vol. 4, sec. 915 (pp. 239–41); sec. 916 (where Rabiah's father, R. Joel, responds); and *Teshuvot Rabiah* (vol. 2), sec. 957 (where Rabiah's response is recorded). Cf. Isaac b. Moses, *Sefer Or Zaruʿa*, vol. 3, *pisqei Bava Meẓiʿa*, sec. 258.

[18] Urbach, *Baʿalei ha-Tosafot*, 1:190. On Riba as a Tosafist, see Urbach, 1:165–73; I. Ta-Shma, *Ha-Sifrut ha-Parshanit la-Talmud*, vol. 1 (Jerusalem, 1999), 67–70; Grossman, *Ḥakhmei Ẓarefat ha-Rishonim* (Jerusalem, 1995), 442–47; and above, Introduction, n. 11.

younger contemporaries, R. Nathan b. Simeon and R. Simḥah b. Samuel, a student of Moses b. Solomon *ha-Kohen* of Mainz.[19] R. Nathan and R. Simḥah sent several rulings to Rabiah, at his request.[20] At the same time, R. Simḥah asked Rabiah for guidance in resolving a case of disputed agency (*sheliḥut*) that was before him.[21] R. Simḥah also sent a question to R. Isaiah di Trani concerning a ruling made by other judges in Speyer which R. Simḥah considered erroneous; R. Isaiah concurred with R. Simḥah's claims.[22]

Rivaq of Mainz sent a ruling in a matter of *terefot* to a group of rabbinic scholars in Speyer for approval. These authorities included R. Shemaryah b. Mordekhai, Rivaq of Speyer, his brother Meir, and Riba *ha-Levi* (הבחור, d. 1195–96), although this ruling was probably sent to them as a loosely

[19] Urbach, *Ba'alei ha-Tosafot*, 1:369, 374, 411–12. According to a passage in *Mordekhai Bava Batra*, sec. 612–13, R. Judah b. Qalonymus arranged to have two litigants come before him in Speyer in order to hear their case. On R. Simḥah of Speyer's productivity as a Tosafist (even though he is barely mentioned in the standard *Tosafot*), including his authorship of the lost halakhic compendium, *Seder Olam*, his *tiqqunei shetarot*, and his halakhic leadership, see, e.g., Urbach, *Ba'alei ha-Tosafot*, 1:413–19; *Teshuvot u-Pesaqim*, ed. Kupfer, *passim*; I. Ta-Shma, *Knesset Meḥqarim*, 1:50, 158, 161–62, 171–73, 247–48; and 3:21–22, 40, 43, 70, 173; idem, *Halakhah, Minhag u-Meẓi'ut be-Ashkenaz, 1000–1350* (Jerusalem, 1996), 160–61, 217, 224, 236; Emanuel, *Shivrei Luḥot*, 154–84; my "The Appointment of *Ḥazzanim* in Medieval Ashkenaz: Between Communal Government and the Religious Prerogatives of the Individual," in *Spiritual Authority: Struggles over Cultural Power in Jewish Thought*, ed. H. Kreisel et al. (Beer Sheva, 2009), 5*–31*, and above, Introduction, nn. 21, 79. On R. Simḥah's blindness later in his life and its impact, see Ephraim and S. Emanuel, "Ivvaron ke-'Ilah le-Gerushin," *Massekhet* 6 (2007), 31–42. For R. Simḥah's involvement in biblical exegesis, *piyyut* composition, and mystical teachings, see below, chapter 3, nn. 234–45; chapter 5, nn. 229–32; and chapter 6, nn. 77, 113.

[20] See, e.g., Urbach, *Ba'alei ha-Tosafot*, 1:369, n. 42, and 1:412, n. 6; *Teshuvot Rabiah*, sec. 989 (pp. 200–201, with regard to the amount of drawn water that is permissible in a ritual bath), and cf. *Teshuvot u-Pesaqim me-Et Ḥakhmei Ashkenaz ve-Ẓarefat*, ed. E. Kupfer (Jerusalem, 1973), 260 (n. 1*). In another instance (*Teshuvot Rabiah*, sec. 926), Rabiah begins his question (p. 57) with the phrase אתא לידן לכן אני דן ושואל מאדוני. R. Simḥah instructed an unnamed court on the serious punishments and bans that were to be prescribed in the case of a habitual wife-beater; see *Or Zaru'a*, vol. 3, *pisqei Bava Qamma*, sec. 161, and cf. A. Grossman, *Ḥasidot u-Moredot* (Jerusalem, 2001), 390–95. See also *Or Zaru'a, pisqei Bava Qamma*, sec. 197, where another court consulted R. Simḥah with regard to the return of a watched object.

[21] See *Sefer Or Zaru'a*, vol. 3, *pisqei Bava Qamma*, sec. 300. (R. Isaac *Or Zaru'a* adds his own view in sec. 301.) R. Simḥah sent a question to R. Barukh b. Samuel of Mainz concerning a plaintiff's ability to compel the other litigant to take an oath; see *Mordekhai Shevu'ot*, sec. 772. R. Simḥah ruled in a case of theft (וכבר בא מעשה לפני רבינו שמחה ודן כר' יהושע בן לוי), and then sent his ruling to Riẓba, either for Riẓba's opinion (והודה לדבריו) or at his request (והורה לדבריו). See Urbach, *Ba'alei ha-Tosafot*, 263, n. 11*, and cf. *Mordekhai Bava Qamma*, sec. 156; and *Sefer Or Zaru'a, pisqei Bava Qamma*, sec. 449. Although R. Simḥah regularly served as a court judge, Riẓba, despite his great halakhic knowledge and expertise, apparently did not. See below, nn. 95, 104–5.

[22] See *Teshuvot ha-RiD*, ed. A. Y. Wertheimer (Jerusalem, 1975), 90. The judges in that instance wrote to R. Jacob b. Solomon of Courson. On R. Jacob, see below, nn. 50, 106.

knit group of scholars rather than as an established court.[23] This group (minus R. Shemaryah) did, however, actually function as a court on another occasion.[24] In addition, Rivaq of Speyer describes how he was selected as a judge, together with Riba *ha-Levi*, to hear the case of a widow and a business associate who had contested the disposition of the assets of her deceased husband.[25] In a later gathering of the main Speyer court, Elyaqim b. Asher *ha-Levi* replaced Rivaq.[26]

The court in Regensburg during the mid-twelfth century consisted of R. Isaac b. Mordekhai (Ribam), R. Ephraim b. Isaac, and R. Moses b. Joel,[27] who were among the German students of Rabbenu Tam, while Ribam and R. Moses also studied with R. Isaac b. Asher *ha-Levi* of Speyer.[28]

23 See *Sefer Roqeaḥ*, sec. 381; Urbach, *Ba'alei ha-Tosafot*, 1:366–67, and cf. S. Emanuel, "Hibburav ha-Hilkhatiyyim shel R. Eleazar mi-Vermaiza," *Te'udah* 16–17 (2001), 217–18 (n. 59).

24 See *Mordekhai Yevamot*, sec. 58, and cf. *Sefer Or Zaru'a*, vol. 3, *pisqei Bava Batra*, sec. 97.

25 See Urbach, *Ba'alei ha-Tosafot*, 1:367, citing Rivaq's *Sefer Yiḥusei Tanna'im va-Amora'im*: ובי־ררו בית דין אותי הסודר והרב ר' יצחק הלוי בן אשר.

26 See *Teshuvot Rabiah*, vol. 2, sec. 1007, and A. Aptowitzer, *Mavo la-Rabiah*, 216.

27 See Urbach, *Ba'alei ha-Tosafot*, 1:195–208; M. Frank, *Qehillot Ashkenaz u-Battei Dineihen*, 150. Rabbenu Tam wrote to this court; see *Sefer ha-Yashar, le-Rabbenu Tam (Heleq ha-She'elot u-Teshuvot)*, ed. S. Rosenthal (Berlin, 1898), 33. At some later point, Ribam decided a case in Prague (Bohemia) on the basis of a formulation of R. Ephraim in his halakhic work titled *'Arba'ah Panim*. See *Sefer Or Zaru'a, Bava Qamma*, sec. 413: מעשה בפרגא . . . ודן מורי הרב ר' יצחק בן מרדכי מפראגא . . . דמהימן כדברי רבינו אפרים בן יצחק (שעשה) [שכתב] בארבעה פנים; Rami Reiner, "Rabbenu Tam: Rabbotav (ha-Ẓarefatim) ve-Talmidav Bnei Ashkenaz" (M.A. thesis, Hebrew University, 1997), 81–82 (= R. Isaac *Or Zaru'a ve-Dimmui 'Azmi* [Jerusalem, 1985], 76, n. 54]). On the now lost work *'Arba'ah Panim* (devoted primarily, if not exclusively, to monetary issues), see S. Emanuel, *Shivrei Luḥot*, 289–91. See also A. Y. Goldmintz, "Ḥiddushim 'al Massekhet Bava Meẓi'a le-R. Ephraim me-Regensburg," *Moriah* 24:1–2 (2001), 3–6; and *Ohel Yeshayahu le-Bava Qamma (le-Zikhro shel H. Y. Neuman)*, ed. H. Mann (Jerusalem, 2001), 4–40.

28 Cf. Reiner, "Rabbenu Tam: Rabbotav ve-Talmidav," 72, 76, 92–94. R. Joel *ha-Levi*, father of Rabiah, based his *Tosafot* to *Bava Batra* on the teachings and *Tosafot* of these three scholars. See Emanuel, *Shivrei Luḥot*, 83–86. For additional references to the *Tosafot* of R. Moses b. Joel, see *Teshuvot Rabiah*, sec. 926, sec. 953 (p. 140), sec. 959 (beg.) The members of this *beit din* seem to have produced most of their written work in the area of *Neziqin*, which may also reflect their intensive involvement in judicial activities. See also Reiner, ibid., 82–83, n. 292, and above, Introduction, nn. 9, 19, 63. As recorded in *Sefer Or Zaru'a*, vol. 4, *pisqei Sanhedrin*, sec. 77, R. Eliezer b. Samson (of Cologne), citing a case that came before Riba *ha-Levi* as well as unnamed rabbinic decisors in Mainz, validated a *shtar* document in which the Hebrew date did not match the day of the week. Rabbenu Tam disagreed with R. Eliezer and argued that such a document must be disqualified. R. Isaac b. Moses *Or Zaru'a* then notes that Ribam and R. Moses b. Joel also disqualified this *shtar* document. In their written ruling, they maintain that a passage in the *Tosafot* of Riba to *Sanhedrin* in fact supports their position. They also relate to Rabbenu Tam's formulation in this matter. Although all the rabbinic authorities involved in this case were being consulted by an unnamed court (the written ruling of Riba and R. Moses contains the phrase וכל מה שהביאו הדיינין הראיות), only Ribam and R. Moses appear to respond as members of a court.

The subsequent court grouping in Regensburg included R. Isaac b. Jacob (Ri) *ha-Lavan* (another student of Rabbenu Tam), R. Barukh b. Isaac,[29] and R. Abraham, the son of Moses b. Joel.[30]

R. Isaac b. Moses *Or Zaruʿa* cites a responsum from Rabbenu Tam on an issue of property boundaries and concludes that "there was already a (court) case and R. Isaac *ha-Lavan* issued his ruling according to the view of Rabbenu Tam." R. Isaac *Or Zaruʿa*'s teacher R. Jonathan b. Isaac of Wurzburg also authored a responsum on this subject, in which he notes that "a case [about boundaries] came before me as well and I asked my teacher R. Isaac of Bohemia [= Ri *ha-Lavan*], and he ruled in accordance with the position of Rabbenu Tam."[31] In another instance in which R. Isaac *ha-Lavan* served as a court justice (*dayyan*), his decision to allow a particular *ketubah* to be collected was apparently questioned by Rabbenu Tam.[32]

R. Barukh b. Isaac would not allow a document of admission (*shtar hoda'ah*) to be drafted if one had admitted his debt of obligation before only two individuals, having accepted them as an informal *beit din.*[33] It should be noted that R. Ephraim b. Isaac (of the earlier judicial grouping) still sat on the Regensburg court together with R. Barukh, serving as a transitional figure between the sets of judges.[34] R. Judah *he-Ḥasid* may have subsequently taken the place of Ri *ha-Lavan* on this *beit din. Sefer Ḥasidim* records a request to

[29] On Barukh b. Isaac of Regensburg, see Reiner, "Rabbenu Tam: Rabbotav ve-Talmidav," 94–95. R. Barukh of Regensburg, who was also associated with Rabbenu Tam, should not be confused with the French Tosafist of the same name, who was a student of R. Isaac of Dampierre and the author of *Sefer ha-Terumah* (and who had been linked erroneously to the Rhineland city of Worms). On this latter R. Barukh b. Isaac, see S. Emanuel, "'Ve-Ish ʿal Meqomo Mevo'ar Shemo': Le-Toledotav shel R. Barukh b. Isaac," *Tarbiz* 69 (2000), 423–40. Note also that Ribam and Isaac b. Barukh, who also apparently sat on the Regensburg court, were signed on one of the so-called *takkanot Rabbenu Tam*; see Reiner, "Rabbenu Tam: Rabbotav ve-Talmidav," 82.

[30] Abraham was indeed a rabbinic leader, and possibly *rosh qahal* in the next generation; see, e.g., *Sefer Ḥasidim* (Parma), ed. J. Wistinetski (Frankfurt, 1924), sec. 1592 (p. 390); M. Frank, *Qehillot Ashkenaz u-Battei Dineihen*, 151–52; and below, n. 35.

[31] See *Sefer Or Zaruʿa*, vol. 3, *pisqei Bava Meẓiʿa*, sec. 359: וכבר היה מעשה ודן הרב יצחק הלבן כר"ת . . . וזו תשובת מורי רבי' יהונתן . . . גם על ידי היה מעשה ושאלני את מורי הרב ר' יצחק מבה"ם ודן כדברי ר"ת.

[32] See *Teshuvot Rabiah*, sec. 957 (p. 162): וכבר היה מעשה ברינבורג כזה, והיה ר' יצחק הלבן דיין. ונחלקו ופסק הדי(י)ן בענין זה מסברא שכתבתי. See also R. Reiner, "Rabbenu Tam," 96–97.

[33] *Sefer Or Zaruʿa*, vol. 4, *pisqei Sanhedrin*, sec. 55 (fol. 8a). See also *Sefer Or Zaruʿa*, pt. 3. *Pisqei Bava Meẓiʿa*, secs. 281, 297, and Urbach, *Baʿalei ha-Tosafot*, 1:346.

[34] See *Sefer Raban*, ed. S. Z. Ehrenreich (repr. Jerusalem, 1975), fols. 308a–c: אשר על החתום באתי על דבר המשפט אשר בא לידי על ראובן ושמעון ולוי הדרים בחצר אחד . . . ואני לפי מיעוט דעי נראה לי דאיכא לדמויי . . . החצי יטלו ראובן ושמעון והחצי האחר יחלוקו, ושכנגדי היושב עמי לדין הודה לדברי. והרציתי דברי לפני רבותינו הקצינים הרב ר' יצחק ור' משה ואומרים דגבי קרקע אין שייך לומר הדין . . . אמנם הרב אפרים מודה בדבר וכדיי הוא הרב להכריע ומבלעדי אדוני לא ירום את ידו ותורה נלמד מפי קודש ואף בזה הוצרכתי . . . היאך יחלוקו . . . לגבי זה אינם מודים . . . ולפי סברתי היה נראה לי שהדין עמהם ושאלתי לרבותי ר' יצחק ור' משה ורבותא למי שהבינהו ואמרו כמוני אך ר' אפרים ושכנגדי חלוק עלי. ואדוני לבו כלב האולם האר עיניי בה . . . והכל יבאר רבנו באר היטב, לא שאני אליעזר בן נתן כדיי להכריע ולהכניס ראשי בן ההרים וכו' ברוך בן יצחק. See also ms. JTS Rab. 673, fols. 261r–262v.

establish a proper policy with regard to the purchase of synagogue honors that was sent to "*gedolei Regensburg*," who are listed as R. Barukh (b. Isaac), R. Abraham (b. Moses), and the *Ḥasid* R. Judah.[35] During the years 1225 to 1260, the lesser-known Tosafist R. Aaron of Regensburg directed the rabbinic court, together with a R. Yeḥezqel. R. Meir of Rothenburg recognized the importance of this court, referring to it as a *beit din ha-gadol*.[36]

In Cologne, Raban's son-in-law R. Samuel b. Natronai (רשב"ט) sat on a court together with R. Eliezer b. Samson.[37] Raban's grandson, Rabiah, took the place of his father, R. Joel b. Isaac *ha-Levi*, in Cologne, ostensibly as a

[35] See *Sefer Ḥasidim* (above, n. 30); Reiner, "Rabbenu Tam," 69, 95; my "R. Judah *he-Ḥasid* and the Rabbinic Scholars of Regensburg: Interactions, Influences and Implications," *JQR* 96 (2006), 17–37. Note that R. Judah *he-Ḥasid* arrived in Regensburg no earlier than 1195. This group of rabbinic scholars is also cited as ruling on the question of when to bake the *mazot mizvah* when Passover eve falls on the Sabbath: וכן הורה ה"ר יעקב בשם ה"ר יהודה החסיד וה"ר ברוך וה"ר אברהם (ms. Bodl. 1150, fol. 18r; ms. Vatican 45, fol. 88r omits the name of R. Abraham). See also I. Ta-Shma, *Knessest Meḥqarim*, 1:251–52. For R. Abraham b. Moses of Regensburg's (no longer extant) *Tosafot* to *Bava Batra*, see S. Emanuel, *Shivrei Luḥot*, 83, n. 147. Cf. *Shiltei ha-gibborim* to the *Mordekhai li-Yevamot*, sec. 29, n. 6 (end); ms. Budapest 2*1, fol. 268r (ומצאתי כתוב בשם הר"ר אברהם מרגנשבורק על יבמה שנפלה לפני יבם משומד דלא בעינה חליצה ממנו כי במקום ערוה היא וקנאים פוגעים בה): ms. Vercelli C235, fol. 290v (col. 4); ms. Vienna 72, fol. 218v; ms. Cambridge Add. 490, fol. 74r (col. 2); ms. Bodl. 667, fol. 122v; and my "Changing Attitudes toward Apostates in Tosafist Literature of the Late Twelfth and Early Thirteenth Centuries," in *New Perspectives on Jewish-Christian Relations: Studies in Honor of David Berger*, ed. E. Carlebach and J. J. Schacter (Brill, 2012), 297–327.

[36] See M. Frank, *Qehillot Ashkenaz u-Battei Dineihen*, 151; M. Breuer, "Le-Ḥeqer ha-Tippologiyyah shel Yeshivot ha-Ma'arav Bimei ha-Benayim," in *Peraqim be-Toledot ha-Ḥevrah ha-Yehudhit*, ed. L. Etkes and Y. Salmon (Jerusalem, 1980), 46–47; Urbach, *Ba'alei ha-Tosafot*, 2:565, 608, 666: and I. Ta-Shma, *Knesset Meḥqarim*, 1:234, 239, 247–48. In a responsum addressed to R. Aaron and R. Ezekiel, R. Isaac *Or Zaru'a* (a teacher of R. Meir of Rothenburg) signs off with the phrase ועליכם מורינו ה"ר אהרן ועל ישיבתו. Within medieval rabbinic literature, there are instances in which this kind of phrasing connotes a leading scholar and his court, rather than his academy or *beit midrash*. See, e.g., Frank, ibid., 126–27; my "Rabbinic Authority and the Right to Open an Academy in Medieval Ashkenaz," *Michael* 12 (1991), 237–38; and my *Jewish Education and Society in the High Middle Ages*, 158–59 (n. 35).

[37] Raban responds to Rashbat (or R. Shevet) and R. Eliezer b. Samson about a case that had come before their court. See *Sefer Raban*, ed. Ehrenreich, responsum 48 (fol. 36), and Urbach, *Ba'alei ha-Tosafot*, 1:179. See also *Sefer Or Zaru'a*, vol. 4, *pisqei Sanhedrin*, sec. 77 (above, n. 23); *Or Zaru'a*, vol. 2, sec. 45; *Sefer Raban*, responsum 98; and ms. JTS Rab. 673, fol. 354v. R. Eliezer b. Samson maintained that the biblical requirement for litigants to stand during the presentation of their cases and testimony before the judges of the court is applicable only when the judges are considered to be truly expert (*mumḥin*). Since in R. Eliezer's view, however, there are no such experts at the present time (*veha-'idna lekka mumḥin*), neither the litigants nor the witnesses are required to stand, even when a decision is being rendered. See *Mordekhai Shevu'ot*, sec. 761. R. Eliezer's name appears immediately after Raban on the *taqqanat Rabbenu Tam*, which proscribed taking cases to non-Jewish courts: see Frank, *Qehillot Ashkenaz u-Battei Dineihen*, 148, n. 1. Raban also responds to Rashbat on a question of judicial procedure; see *Sefer Raban*, responsum 76 (fol. 58). The phrase used by Raban (responsum 17, fol. 16a), חתני ר' שמואל שהיה דן לפני, refers to a ruling in a matter of *'issur ve-heter*.

judge as well.[38] R. Joel served as the guardian (*apotropus*) for a widow, and he took her son-in-law to a *beit din ʿaraʾi* (a temporary court) in Cologne (c. 1190). R. Joel, who was normally a member of the regular or permanent court, could not serve as a judge in this case, since he was the widow's guardian. Three relatively unknown rabbinic scholars were chosen to serve on the temporary tribunal: Jacob b. Mordekhai, Gershom b. Isaac, and Moses b. Samuel. The other litigant took the case to a non-Jewish tribunal (*ʿarkaʾot*), and established courts in other locales were also involved.[39]

R. Eliezer b. Joel *ha-Levi* (Rabiah) was originally a member of the rabbinic court in Bonn when it was headed by R. Ephraim b. Jacob (following the departure of R. Joel *ha-Levi* of Bonn for Cologne).[40] R. Simḥah of Speyer appealed (in written form) to this court.[41] After Rabiah had established his own court in Cologne, he writes in a responsum that only the court of his teacher R. Ephraim of Bonn was great enough to extract payments beyond that which is implicit within Talmudic law, but his own (current) court is

[38] See Urbach, *Baʿalei ha-Tosafot*, 1:380; Aptowitzer, *Mavo La-Rabiah*, 15–16; and my *Jewish Education and Society*, 56–57. R. Joʾel also composed *Tosafot* that contain both dialectical analysis and straightforward Talmudic interpretation, which were based on materials from his three teachers in Regensburg, Ribam, R. Ephraim b. Isaac, and R. Moses b. Yoʾel. See S. Emanuel, *Shivrei Luḥot*, 81–86, and above, Introduction, n. 19. Aptowitzer, *Mavo la-Rabiah*, 44, notes two passages in *Sefer Rabiah*, which would appear to refer to R. Joel's *yeshivah* and his students, וכן דנתי לפני אבי מורי ולפני כל הישיבה, and R. Joel's comment that 'כי אני לומד לבחוריי מס' גיטין, although Aptowitzer concludes that the only student of R. Joel of whom we are aware with any certainty is his son Rabiah. See also Emanuel, *Shivrei Luḥot*, 114–16, 147–49, for R. Yoʾel's halakhic and rabbinic writings as cited by a second student, R. Barukh b. Samuel of Mainz, in his *Sefer ha-Ḥokhmah.* R. Yoʾel's extensive activity as a rabbinic judge and halakhist, and the very small number of students who can be identified as his, suggest that, similar to R. Barukh of Mainz (see below, n. 144), R. Yoʾel's judicial career far outweighed his role as the head of a study hall which, in any case, may have been adjunct to the activities of his rabbinic court.

[39] See A. Aptowitzer, *Mavo la-Rabiah*, 172–74; and below, n. 59. Note that R. Joel's father-in-law, R. Eliezer b. Nathan (Raban), sat on a court in Mainz with his father-in-law, R. Elyaqim b. Joseph. These rabbis sent rulings to France, evidence of the exchanges between scholars in Germany and northern France that did occur during the earlier period. See, e.g., *Sefer Mordekhai le-Massekhet Qiddushin*, ed. Y. Roth (Jerusalem, 1990), 215, and Alexander Shapiro, "Jewish Life in Germany in the Twelfth Century—A Study of the Even ha-Ezer of R. Eliezer b. Nathan (c. 1090–1160) as a Source for the History of the Period" (Ph.D. diss., Dropsie University, 1968), 23, 188–99.

[40] See *Mordekhai Ketubot*, sec. 152; *Sheʾelot u-Teshuvot Maharshal* (repr. Jerusalem, 1969) 65 (fol. 190: לכן רבותי יפתח דבר זה בגדולים כמותכם מורי הר"ר אפרים הישיש ומורי ה"ר אליעזר בן רבינו יואל לברר לנו); Aptowitzer, *Mavo la-Rabiah*, 8, 198, 319.

[41] See *Teshuvot Rabiah*, sec. 921. R. Simḥah's expression (p. 21), ובאתי לדון לפני רבותיי לפי עניותי, connotes the presentation of his analysis before the judges rather than indicating his participation as a judge. Indeed, Rabiah presents an argument before his teachers, not as a judge but as an advocate, in similar terms: וכן דנתי בפני רבותי והודו לדברי. See *Sefer Rabiah*, vol. 4, p. 342, and see also above, n. 7, for other examples.

not sufficiently important to do so.[42] R. Joel *ha-Levi* was the guardian for another widow and appeared before the court of his son Rabiah.[43]

R. Eliezer of Toul had been hired to work for R. Hezekiah in Boppard. R. Hezekiah then withheld Eliezer's wages for a lengthy period of time. R. Eliezer maintained that he should now receive additional monies, since he could have invested his salary had he been paid in a timely fashion. The complaint came for adjudication before Rabiah, who ruled that Hezekiah should be liable for the larger amount.[44]

R. Menaḥem b. David and R. She'alti'el b. Menaḥem were apparently members of Rabiah's court in Cologne.[45] With R. She'alti'el's concurrence, Rabiah responded to a query by R. Moses b. Mordekhai from the Mainz court about property boundaries.[46] It should also be noted that Rabiah prescribed and dispensed lashes (*malkot*) for a vow that was broken, and for eating bread baked by non-Jews on the Sabbath, unmistakable indicators of the strong authority of his court.[47] We are fortunate to have extensive records of the *shetarot* drawn up in Cologne and the proceedings undertaken to ratify them for the period from 1260 to c. 1300. These records indicate

42 See *Teshuvot Rabiah*, ed. Deblitzky, vol. 2 (Jerusalem, 2000), sec. 997; and cf. ms. JTS Rab. 673, fols. 348v–349v. Ephraim of Bonn was in Mainz, and he was the fourth signatory with Rivaq, Moses b. Mordekhai, and R. Barukh. See, e.g., *Mordekhai Bava Batra*, secs. 467–68; and above, n. 8. On R. Ephraim b. Jacob's extensive *pesaqim* and other rabbinic writings, see above, Introduction, n. 88. See also ms. Bodl. 844, fols. 32r–33r; and below, chapter 5, nn. 105–20.

43 See *Teshuvot Rabiah*, sec. 957: גם על ידי מעשה באלמנת ר' משולם בן יוסף. ואני הייתי אחד מן הדיינין, ומורי הרב אבי היה אפוטרופוס של האלמנה.

44 See *Sefer Or Zaru'a*, vol. 3, *pisqei Bava Meẓi'a*, sec. 181: והיה דן מורי רבינו אבי העזרי [=ראבי"ה] לחייב את ר' חזקיה. R. Isaac *Or Zaru'a* (and others) had different views in this matter. Cf. Urbach, *Ba'alei ha-Tosafot*, 1:335–36, n. 9, and Nahum Rakover, "Piẓẓuyim 'al 'Ikkuv Kesafim," *Torah She-be-'al Peh* 19 (1979), 136–37. Rabiah (*Teshuvot*, sec. 1005) responds to a query about a case of inheritance that was sent to him by the (unnamed) judges of Strasbourg (שאלה ששאלוני דייני שטרספורק).

45 See H. Gross in *MGWJ* 34 (1885), 370–71, and *Teshuvot Rabiah*, sec. 1007. According to Aptowitzer (*Mavo la-Rabiah*, 198, 394), Rabiah sat in judgment with others but after a certain point signed decisions by himself, as the most important or singular figure on the court. However, some of the evidence cited by Aptowitzer does not support his contention. See also above, nn. 7, 38. On R. She'alti'el, see my "Religious Leadership during the Tosafist Period: Between the Academy and the Rabbinic Court," in *Jewish Religious Leadership: Image and Reality*, ed. J. Wertheimer (New York, 2004), 268, 276; S. Emanuel, *Shivrei Luḥot*, 129, 132; and *R. Eleazar mi-Vermaiza—Derashah le-Pesaḥ*, ed. Emanuel, 9, n. 25; and below, chapter 5, n. 244.

46 See *Teshuvot Rabiah*, sec. 996, and *Sefer Or Zaru'a, pisqei Bava Meẓi'a*, sec. 197: באתי להשיב למורי הרב ר' משה כי נראה לי שכיון לדון כהלכה. ומורי הרב ר' שאלתיאל הסכימה דעתו לדעתי[נו]. Cf. *Nezer Matta'ai 'al Masskhet Bava Meẓi'a: Sefer Zikkaron le-R. N. Z. Rakow* (Jerusalem, 1991), 65–68.

47 See *Mordekhai Shevu'ot*, sec. 756 (מצאתי משם ר' אבי העזרי שצוה להלקות את ר' ישראל שנדר שלא יחזור וכו'), and *Sefer Or Zaru'a*, vol. 2, *hilkhot Yom Tov*, sec. 358 (ראיתי את מורי אבי העזרי שהיה מלקה בני אדם שאכלו פת שאפה עכו"ם בשבת); and cf. my "Rabbinic Attitudes toward Nonobservance in the Medieval Period," in *Jewish Tradition and the Nontraditional Jew*, ed. J. J. Schacter (Northvale, N.J., 1992), 14–17.

that there was a remarkably stable core group of judges, along with other figures who were available to supplement the main judges in certain cases and to provide other services such as witnessing transactions and the like. For almost all of this period, the two most active judges were R. Yaqar b. Samuel *ha-Levi* and R. Ḥayyim b. Yeḥi'el *Ḥefeẓ Zahav*, who were joined in the 1280s by R. Jacob b. Joseph.[48]

In Magdeburg during the mid-thirteenth century, R. Hezekiah b. Jacob, one of the last of the Tosafists, sat on a court together with R. Isaac *Or Zaru'a.*[49] Hezekiah and his court issued a ruling that the husband of a recalcitrant woman who refused to immerse herself in the *mikveh* (and had allowed her husband to have relations with her, claiming that she had not seen any menstrual blood) could divorce his wife without having to pay her *ketubah.* The wife tried to invalidate this ruling by appealing to other authorities, including R. Aaron of Regensburg and R. Jacob b. Solomon of

[48] See Moritz Stern and Robert Honiger, *Das Judemschreinsbuch der Laurenzpfarre zu Koln* (Berlin, 1888). Cf. S. Goldin, *Ha-Yiḥud veha-Yaḥad*, 123–24. At one point (Stern and Honiger, 554–55, entry 166, dated 1284), reference is made to the "expert judges of Cologne" (דיינים מובהקים שבקולוניא). On R. Ḥayyim b. Yeḥi'el *Ḥefeẓ Zahav*, see also below, nn. 73, 139. On R. Yaqar, see Urbach, *Ba'alei ha-Tosafot*, 578, n. 32; my *"Peering through the Lattices,"* 256; Y. M. Peles, "Teshuvah be-'Inyan Pinui mi-Qever le-Qever le-Rabbenu Yaqar b. Shmu'el ha-Levi," *Moriah* 16 [11–12] (1989), 8–9; S. Emanuel, *Shivrei Luḥot*, 255, 260–61; and I. Ta-Shma, *Knesset Meḥqarim*, 1:167–74. See also below, at nn. 66, 114. (The scholar of the same name associated with Rabiah was the grandfather of this R. Yaqar; see above, n. 9.)

[49] See I. Ta-Shma, "Le-Toledot ha-Yehudim be-Polin," 355–56, and U. Fuchs, "Shalosh Teshuvot Ḥadashot shel R. Yiẓḥaq b. Mosheh Ba'al Or Zaru'a," *Tarbiz* 70 (2001), 111, 117. Sources cited in these studies refer to another R. Isaac who served as a judge with R. Hezekiah, and also to R. Jacob ha-Kohen (of Cracow), who was a judicial expert of such magnitude that it would be inappropriate for those living in his area to seek justice elsewhere (*Sefer Or Zaru'a*, vol. 1, sec. 775: כי יש בעירך ר' יעקב הכהן שהיה מומחה לרבים). See also I. A. Agus, *Teshuvot Ba'alei ha-Tosafot* (New York, 1954), 118 (= ms. Parma 86, sec. 301), for a decision on the apportioning of taxes when one of the town members had an economic relationship with the local ruler, which is signed Isaac b. Moses b. Isaac [*Or Zaru'a*], Isaac "*talmid*" son of Moses, and Hezekiah b. Jacob. When R. Isaac *Or Zaru'a* asserts, however, דנתי לפני מורי רי יהונתן (*pisqei Sanhedrin*, sec. 68), he refers to a presentation of his Talmudic analysis and not to his serving as Judah b. Qalonymus about a case that had come before him (*Sefer Or Zaru'a, pisqei Bava Batra*, sec. 176). R. Isaac *Or Zaru'a*'s rabbinic successor in Vienna, R. Avigdor b. Elijah Katz, was also involved with rabbinic courts, especially when he lived in Italy (in locales such as Ferrara, Mantua, and Verona; cf. S. Emanuel, *Shivrei Luḥot*, 175–76). See U. Fuchs, "Shalosh Teshuvot Ḥashaot," 112–14, and see also H. J. Zimmels in *Ha-Ẓofeh le-Ḥokhmat Yisra'el* 15 (1931), 119. In a case dated *Kislev* 1239 and recorded in *Sefer Or Zaru'a*, vol. 1, sec. 745, judges from Italy turned to Isaac *Or Zaru'a* (or to R. Avigdor Katz), or perhaps R. Avigdor was one of the judges and he turned to R. Isaac. In addition, a bill of divorce was sent by R. Avigdor, and the city Sulle (Halle) was not properly included. The *get* was questioned by R. Hezekiah of Magdeburg. In his response, R. Avigdor mentions the *get* form of Ri (טופס גט והלכותיו שכתב ר"י הזקן בכתב ידו; see below, n. 118), and of "my teacher R. Eleazar of Verona." Cf. H. Gross, *Gallia Judaica* (Paris, 1897), 435; and *Germania Judaica*, ed. I. Elbogen et al. (Breslau, 1934), 125–28; and Agus, *Teshuvot Ba'alei ha-Tosafot*, 201–4.

Courson. These authorities wrote to R. Hezekiah, who in turn explained and justified his court's ruling in further detail.[50]

In Wurzburg, R. Samuel b. Menaḥem (*ha-Levi*) and Simḥah b. Gershom were members of the court.[51] Samuel (b. 1212) was a teacher of R. Meir of Rothenburg, and is cited in *Tosafot Yoma.*[52] Also serving as judges in Wurzburg were Moses Azri'el b. Eleazar *ha-Darshan*, Eleazar b. Yeḥi'el, and Ephraim b. Joel (who decided a case of marital infidelity that involved other decisors in Wurzburg and Erfurt, as well as R. Meir of Rothenburg),[53] and still others associated with R. Meir of Rothenburg, including R. Menaḥem b. Natronai (known also as R. Qovil), R. Menaḥem b. David, and R. Hillel b. Azri'el.[54]

In a number of the situations that have been discussed to this point, one rabbinic court sought the input of or otherwise interacted with another. As another example of these kinds of interactions, the judges of Speyer, R. Simḥah b. Samuel and R. Nathan b. Simeon, held that one should not presume that a war had occurred with respect to freeing an *'agunah* (deserted wife) unless the husband had been seen by his wife or by another witness in the midst or context of war (*be-qishrei milḥamah*).[55] Rabiah also

50 See E. Kupfer, *Teshuvot u-Pesaqim*, 272–81. Cf. *Mordekhai Shevu'ot*, secs. 770–71 (for two rulings, *me-pisqei R. Ḥizqiyyah*, on evidentiary and other court procedures). On R. Aaron of Regensburg, see above, n. 36.

51 See *Teshuvot Maharam*, ed. Cremona, 17 (and below, n. 129).

52 See *Tosafot Yoma* 40b, s.v. *mah*; Urbach, *Ba'alei ha-Tosafot*, 2:526; and cf. Agus, *Teshuvot Ba'alei ha-Tosafot*, 216. R. Samuel is also cited in a manuscript version of *Tosafot Bava Batra* (ms. Moscow 186, fol. 101r). He was consulted in the case of a woman whose husband had assigned all of his assets just prior to his death (as a *shekhiv me-ra*) to another person (מעשה היה בשכיב מרע . . . ונשאל אל ה"ר שמואל בן מנחם). R. Samuel responded that the woman is nonetheless entitled to collect her *ketubah*, since she would normally collect her *ketubah* from any inheritance left by the deceased to his sons (and the sons' claim to their father's inheritance is even stronger than any monies assigned through the testament of a *shekhiv me-ra*). The presence of R. Samuel in this text further supports the contention of Ya'akov Lifshitz that the *Tosafot* in question were compiled in Germany in the late thirteenth century rather than in northern France somewhat earlier (even as there is a decidedly French stratum contained in these *Tosafot*). See Lifshitz, "Tosafot Ketav-Yad le-Massekhet Bava Batra," in *Sefer Zikkaron leha-Rav Yizḥaq Nissim*, ed. Meir Benayahu, vol. 3 (Jerusalem, 1985), 28–30.

53 *Teshuvot Maimuniyyot le-Hilkhot Ishut*, 25. As Urbach notes (*Ba'alei ha-Tosafot*, 2:522), Maharam's father, Barukh b. Meir, was described (in Worms) as being "like a judge" (*ke-dayyan*), suggesting that a *dayyan* had certain prerogatives. See *Teshuvot Maharam*, ed. Cremona, #31; ed. Bloch, p. 198 (#101); and cf. Urbach, *Meḥqarim be-Madda'ei ha-Yahadut*, ed. M. D. Herr and Y. Fraenkel (Jerusalem, 1988), 2:775–76.

54 See, e.g., *Teshuvot Maharam*, ed. Prague, 92, 143 (= ed. Cremona, 23); ed. Lemberg, 108; I. Agus, *Teshuvot Ba'alei ha-Tosafot*, 145–46; S. Emanuel, *Shivrei Luḥot*, 262–66 (which identifies the lost *nimmuqim* of R. Qobil, and notes a handful of Torah comments that are attributed to R. Menachem b. Natronai, all of which are in the *remez/gematria* style). See also ms. Paris 1467 (= Warsaw 260), fol. 82v.

55 See *Sefer Rabiah*, vol. 4, 125–32, sec. 900, and *Pisqei Or Zaru'a*, ed. M. Y. Blau, vol. 1 (Brooklyn, 1997), 137–38.

espoused this view,[56] as did Menaḥem b. Jacob, Eleazar b. Judah, and Qalonymus b. Gershom, the judges of Worms in the late twelfth century.[57]

As noted above, a secondary or temporary rabbinic court (*beit din ʿaraʾi*) in Cologne issued a ruling about the allocation of a widow's assets.[58] The ruling was sent to the Mainz court (headed by R. Moses b. Solomon *ha-Kohen*), which responded positively to the ruling (*yafeh dantem ve-hiyyavtem*). R. Eleazar b. Judah, writing for Worms, raised an objection, as did the court of Regensburg. Unnamed authorities from Speyer responded, and the reaction of R. Joel *ha-Levi* and the response of Barukh b. Isaac and Abraham b. Moses of Regensburg to R. Joel are also included.[59]

Although often asked to respond to the rulings of other courts, the Mainz court occasionally asked questions of their judicial colleagues in other locales. R. Eleazar of Worms and R. David b. Qalonymus of Muenzberg responded to questions from R. Barukh b. Samuel of the Mainz court.[60] Rabiah and other members of the Cologne court responded to a query from R. Moses b. Mordekhai of Mainz on behalf of the Mainz court.[61] In another instance, R. Barukh had lent out a sum of money and later wished

[56] *Sefer Rabiah*, vol. 4, 102–3.

[57] See *Sefer Rabiah*, vol. 4, pp. 117–25, and *Pisqei Or Zaruʿa*, 138. Rabiah sent his ruling to R. Eleazar of Worms, which the Worms court accepted. Two members of the Cologne court, R. She'alti'el and Rabiah's father, R. Joel *ha-Levi*, are referred to in *Sefer Rabiah*, 117, and cf. above, n. 45. For the interaction of different *battei din*, see also above, nn. 9–10. In addition, see S. Emanuel, "Hibburav ha-Hilkhatiyyim shel R. Eleazar mi-Vermaiza," 236–37, for the seven judicial scholars involved in a complex case of *terefot* (הנפולה מקולוניא) in addition to R. Eleazar of Worms: R. Shemaryah of Speyer, Rivaq and R. Meir of Speyer, Rivaq of Mainz (Eleazar's father), Ri *ha-Lavan*, R. Joel *ha-Levi* and R. She'alti'el of Cologne. See Moshe Amar, "Polmos ha-Nefulah be-Qolonyah," *Moriah* 24, 5–6 (2002), 15–24; and S. Emanuel, *R. Eleazar mi-Vermaiza—Derashah le-Pesaḥ*, 9–10. This episode, however, is an instance of rabbinic consultation rather than a series of actions taken by organized courts. (For a responsum from R. Eleazar of Worms and his father, Rivaq of Mainz, see *Teshuvot Maharam*, ed. Prague, 872, and Urbach, *Baʿalei ha-Tosafot*, 1:365.)

[58] See A. Aptowitzer, *Mavo la-Rabiah*, 172–74; and above, n. 39.

[59] See *Teshuvot Rabiah*, vol. 2, 308–22, secs. 1031–32.

[60] See Urbach, *Baʿalei ha-Tosafot*, 1:407, and ms. JTS 678, fols. 366d–367c (מורי' רבי' יב"ק. ונש־אלתי על ראובן ושמעון שבאו לדון וטען ראובן רצועה אחת של קרקע . . . ברוך בן שמואל. כן נראה בעינינו שדבריו של ראובן אינו כלום וזוכה שמעון בשלו . . . ושלום דוד בן קלונימוס, אלעזר הקטן). R. David is mentioned only once in the standard *Tosafot* to the Talmud but was a signatory on the *Taqqanot Shu"m.* Although he seems to have been a brother of R. Judah b. Qalonymus (Rivaq) and R. Meir of Speyer, a teacher of the author of the (German) commentary on *Sifra* that was mistakenly attributed to R. Samson of Sens, and among the questioners of R. Simḥah of Speyer, R. David also appears to have had close(r) connections to the rabbinic scholars of Mainz and Worms. Cf. Urbach, *Baʿalei ha-Tosafot*, 1:274–75, 312, 315, 365–66, 413 (once again, R. David is not treated in a separate section or entry); and Emanuel, *Shivrei Luḥot*, 128 (n. 112), 133, 136 (n. 143). For R. David's scattered biblical comments (which were mainly halakhic or midrashic in nature) and for his five *piyyutim*, see below, chapter 3, nn. 247, 249, and chapter 5, nn. 241–43.

[61] See above, n. 46.

to confirm the signature of the borrower based on the attestation of his and the borrowers' relatives. An objection to the use of a relative for this purpose was raised. The question was sent to R. David b. Qalonymus and to R. Meshullam, his son. They ruled that such confirmation was acceptable, although R. Barukh himself disagreed with their reasoning.[62]

The leading German rabbinic scholar and Tosafist in the second half of the thirteenth century, R. Meir (Maharam) of Rothenburg, seems only to have answered appeals from other rabbinic courts; there is little evidence for his sitting, initially, on actual cases.[63] Occasionally, he refused to respond even to requests from other courts.[64] R. Pereẓ of Corbeil, a slightly younger contemporary of R. Meir who had also studied with him, sent material from a court case to Maharam. It was initially unclear whether R. Pereẓ was rendering a decision or simply gathering information; only once R. Pereẓ's role become clear did R. Meir respond.[65]

[62] See *Sefer Or Zaruʿa*, vol. 3, *pisqei Bava Qamma*, sec. 440. On R. Meshullam b. David, who commented on tractate *Sheqalim* (and perhaps other tractates) in the Jerusalem Talmud, see Urbach, *Baʿalei ha-Tosfot*, 1:432–33. See also *Teshuvot u-Pesaqim*, ed. Kupfer, 162–63, with regard to the return of the dowry for a young woman raised by another family, in which R. David of Muenzberg responded to R. Barukh of Mainz (שאילת הר"ר ברוך ממגנצ' לר' דוד ממינצבורג על יתומה שגידל בתוך ביתו . . . איבד בתו וממונו וכדי שלא יעמוד באותה קללה שקדו לתקנו כזה. דוד ב"ר קלונימוס); and see also Kupfer, *Teshuvot u-Pesaqim*, 319–20.

[63] For one such source, see *Teshuvot Maharam*, ed. Prague, 1009; cf. I. Agus, *Teshuvot Baʿalei ha-Tosafot*, 96–97, who attributes this passage (incorrectly) to R. Ephraim of Regensburg (as shown by S. Emanuel, "Teshuvot Maharam mi-Rothenburg Defus Prague," *Tarbiz* 57 [1988], 586, n. 132). See also Agus, *Teshuvot Baʿalei ha-Tosafot*, 147. Another passage found in *Teshuvot Maharam* (ed. Prague, 917, and with additional detail in ed. Cremona, 17), which describes the selection of a rabbinic court and the ruling that was rendered, does not include Maharam as one of its members. See below, n. 114, and cf. E. Shochetman, "Ḥovat ha-Hanmaqah," *Shenaton ha-Mishpat ha-ʿIvri* 6–7 (1979–80), 337.

[64] See E. E. Urbach, *Baʿalei ha-Tosafot*, 2:539–40. Cf. S. Goldin, *Ha-Yiḥud veha-Yaḥad*, 133–35; Kupfer, *Teshuvot u-Pesaqim*, 159–61; *Teshuvot Maharam*, ed. Cremona, 297, 311; *Mordekhai Gittin*, sec. 381 (וכן דן הר"ם); and *Mordekhai Bava Meẓiʿa*, sec. 247 (יפה דן האומר שהיתומים פטורים וכו'); and *Mordekhai Sanhedrin*, sec. 707 (and cf. E. Shochetman, "Ha-Ḥiyyuv be-Hozaʾat Mishpat bi-Pesiqat Battei ha-Din ha-Rabbaniyyim," *Shenaton ha-Mishpat ha-Ivri* 10–11 [1981–83], 266–68, and below, n. 95). One appeal begins with the phrase: כי רבו מחלוקת בישראל . . . לכן נמנינו להלך אחר ב"ד יפה אחר מהר"ם לרוטנבורג להאיר עינינו; see *Teshuvot Maharam*, ed. Prague, 92. (Note the appeal to Rabbenu Tam that begins similarly: בירותי ללכת אחר ב"ד יפה . . . אחר ר' לבית שערים . . . ומנו ר' יעקב. See *Sefer ha-Yashar*, 36, and below, n. 75.) Maharam upheld a *niddui* pronounced by a court consisting of R. Neḥemyah, R. Manoah, and R. Dan; see *Teshuvot u-Pesaqim*, ed. Kupfer, 159. On R. Dan, see (in addition to Kupfer, 159, n. 2) I. Ta-Shma, "Rabbenu Dan be-Ashkenaz uvi-Sefarad," in *Studies in Medieval Jewish Thought and Jewish Ethics Presented to Isaiah Tishby*, ed. J. Dan and J. Hacker (Jerusalem, 1986), 385–94; and my *"Peering through the Lattices": Mystical, Magical, and Pietistic Dimensions in the Tosafist Period* (Detroit, Mich., 2000), 236, 247–48. On Maharam's involvement with complex marriage and divorce cases, see, e.g., Urbach, *Baʿalei ha-Tosafot*, 2:529–34. For court procedures outlined by Maharam, see, e.g., *Teshuvot Maharam*, ed. Cremona, 297; ed. Parma, 318–19; ed. Parma, 333; and *Mordekhai Shevuʿot*, sec. 761.

[65] See Urbach, *Baʿalei ha-Tosafot*, 2:576–77. Cf. S. E. Stern, "Pesaqim me-Rabbenu Pereẓ," *Netivot Torah* 2 (1993), 37, 137 (= idem, *Meʾorot ha-Rishonim* [Jerusalem, 2002], 390).

As noted earlier, R. Meir's colleague R. Yaqar *ha-Levi* was one of the key *dayyanim* in Cologne during the mid- and late thirteenth century.[66] According to R. Meir, his teacher R. Judah b. Moses *ha-Kohen* of Friedberg/Wurzburg (son of the *dayyan* R. Moses b. *ha-Kohen* of Mainz) ruled, as the head of a *beit din*, about applying a ban of settlement (*ḥerem ha-yishuv*).[67] R. Isaac *Or Zaru'a* writes to discuss a judicial decision taken by R. Judah *ha-Kohen*, R. Meshullam b. David, and R. David b. She'alti'el concerning a betrothed woman who had been raped during the persecutions in Frankfurt (1241) and whose intended husband had married another woman.[68]

In the latter part of the thirteenth century, various judges from the communities of Speyer, Worms, and Mainz (known collectively as *qehillot Shu"m*) wrote jointly to compel the defendant (*nitba*), 'Azri'el b. Yeḥi'el, to go to a court in the locale of the claimant (*tove'a*). According to their report, the presumption in Ashkenaz from earlier times (*minhag qadmonenu*) was that a defendant may not refuse to appear before a competent court in the locale of the claimant by insisting that judges from the defendant's city or town must be present. If information needed to be obtained from the other location, the head of the court hearing the case could direct the gathering of this information. One who does not adhere to these guidelines was in contempt of court, whether he was a prominent individual or not. Even if the defendant invited the claimant to the court of one of the larger communities in the area (*mazmino la-qehillot*), the claimant could still insist on going to a competent court in or near his locale if the dispute was monetary in nature. If, however, there was a more serious offense involved, such as informing or a charge of physical harm, the defendant could choose

[66] On R. Yaqar's judicial activities in Cologne, see above, n. 48, and cf. Urbach, *Ba'alei ha-Tosafot*, 2:578. R. Meir also interacted with the judge R. Joseph b. Jacob of Cologne; see Urbach, ibid., 2:530, n. 47.

[67] *Teshuvot Maharam*, Lemberg 213: אם מורי החזיקו בישוב בתורת בית דין . . . ואם באנו להרהר אחר בית דינו צריכים אנו לדקדק אחר כל בית דין שעמד להם לישראל . . . ממורי ר' יהודה שמעתי שהיה דן כך. See Urbach, *Ba'alei ha-Tosafot*, 2:526–27, and 1:186, 433. R. Judah also apparently studied in northern France, and he cites R. Yosef of Clisson; see Urbach, 1:320. For a responsum by R. Judah preserved in a collection compiled by the students of Maharam (found in ms. Parma 86, sec. 120–21), see S. Emanuel, "Qevaẓei Teshuvot Maharam mi-Rothenburt" (M.A. thesis, Hebrew University, 1987), 75–81. See also idem, *Shivrei Luḥot*, 254, n. 143, and I. Ta-Shma, *Knesset Meḥqarim*, 1:161, for references to R. Judah *ha-Kohen* in R. Isaac b. Moses, *Sefer Or Zaru'a*. For R. Judah's presence in Wurzburg, see Rami Reiner, "'Even She-Katuv 'Alehah: To'arei ha-Niftarim 'al Maẓevot Beit ha-'Almin be-Wurzburg, 1147–1346," *Tarbiz* 78 (2009), 127–28.

[68] See *Sefer Or Zaru'a*, vol. 1, sec. 747. See also Urbach, *Ba'alei ha-Tosafot*, 1:433, and Rachel Furst, "Captivity, Conversion and Communal Identity: Sexual Angst and Religious Crisis in Frankfurt, 1241" *Jewish History* 22 (2008), 179–221. R. Isaac opens his discussion as follows: לא לחלוק על ישיבת רבותי אני בא, כי איני כדאי כי מפיכם אני חי ומימיכם אני שותה. אך באתי לדון בדבר הלכה בשעת מעשה לפני רבותי הנקובים בשם מורי ה"ר יהודה בן ה"ר משה הכהן, והישיש הנכבד מורי ה"ר משולם בן רבינו דוד, והגיבור בתורה מורי ה"ר דוד בן שאלתיאל על דבר המעשה שבא לידי רבותי'. The phrase ישיבת רבותי refers not to the study halls of these authorities but rather to their legal decisions. Cf. above, n. 36.

which larger communal court he wished to appear before, and where he thought he would be treated fairly. The Speyer judges signed on this writ are Shemaryah b. Isaac, Jacob b. Menaḥem, and Barukh b. Asher; from Worms, Samson b. Judah, Meir b. Judah, Judah b. Simeon, and Yekutiel b. Meir; and from Mainz, Isaac b. Meir and Ḥayyim b. Isaac *Or Zaruʿa*.[69]

Interestingly, the recalcitrant litigant in this instance, R. ʿAzriʾel b. Yeḥiʾel *he-Ḥasid*, was himself a rabbinic scholar and judge of some note, and he is addressed as such in the document sent to him by the judges of *qehillot Shu"m*.[70] R. ʿAzriʾel was a student of R. Meir of Rothenburg and R. Pereẓ of Corbeil, and his own court was located in Wurzburg, where he sat along with a R. Yosef b. Ḥayyim. His son-in-law, R. Jacob b. Mordekhai, was a judge in Rothenburg.[71] A grandson of R. Isaac *Or Zaruʿa*, R. Menaḥem b. Abraham of Oberlingen, allowed a woman to have the secular authorities compel her husband to appear with her before R. ʿAzriʾel's court, which was the court in their city.[72]

In the course of responding to a request for the involvement of his court, R. Ḥayyim b. Yeḥiʾel *Ḥefeẓ Zahav*, an active judge and *ʾav beit din* in Cologne, wrote to the city of Boppard and its head judge, R. Abraham, that he would have preferred that no external cases come to him. Nonetheless, the young man involved in this particular case was in the process of moving and was relatively close to Cologne. In addition, Boppard utilized the cemetery in Cologne, which entitled them also to have their cases heard there.[73]

69 See *Mordekhai Sanhedrin*, sec. 709; *Teshuvot Maharam* (Berlin, 1891), secs. 678–79 (p. 319); *Ḥamishah Quntresim*, ed. N. Coronel (Vienna, 1864), fol. 97a (in a marginal note to *Sefer Eẓ Ḥayyim le-R. Ḥayyim Or Zaruʿa*); B. Z. Dinur, *Yisraʾel ba-Golah*, vol. 2, part 3, p. 453; and the corrected text with other manuscript variants published by A. Havazelet in *Ẓefunot* 1 (1989), 13. Cf. U. Fuchs, below, n. 87.

70 מ"ו אלופנו המסובל הר"ר עזריאל בן החסיד ר' יחיאל . . . ומי שיסרב חזה הרי הוא סרבן. בין שהוא מן הקלים בין שהוא מן החשובים. On the phrase אלופנו המסובל, cf. *Berakhot* 17a.

71 See *Teshuvot Maharam*, ed. Prague, 1020, and Havazelet (in *Ẓefunot* 1), 7. See also R. Azriʾel's application of the *taqqanat Rabbenu Tam* (on returning the dowry to the wife's family where the wife passed away during the first year of marriage), recorded in *Mordekhai Qiddushin*, 551. See also Y. Cohen, "Taqqanot ha-Qahal bi-Yerushat ha-Baʿal ʾet Ishto," *Shenaton ha-Mishpat haʿIvri* 6–7 (1979–80), 148–49.

72 See M. Weinberger and A. Havazelet, "Teshuvot Ḥakhmei Ashkenaz," in *Sefer ha-Zikkaron le-R. Yaʿaqov Bezalʾel Zolty*, ed. Y. Buksboim (Jerusalem, 1987), 248–50. R. Azriʾel's commentary to tractate *Nazir* was published from a Cracow manuscript by Zvi Leitner in *Sefer Zikkaron le-R. Shmuʾel Barukh Verner*, ed. Y. Buksboim (Jerusalem, 1996), 156–62. See also S. Emanuel, *Shivrei Luḥot*, 276–78.

73 See *Teshuvot Maharam*, ed. Prague, 249: אם היה תלוי בדעתי היה רצוני שלא היה בא שום דין לפני. Cf. M. Frank, *Qehillot Ashkenaz u-Battei Dineihen*, 27; S. Goldin, *Ha-Yiḥud veha-Yaḥad*, 124; and R. Barzen et al., "The Hierarchy of Medieval Jewish Settlements Seen through Jewish and Non-Jewish Sources," *Jewish Studies* 40 (2000), 63*. This study notes that the relationship between the use of the cemetery and the court district was also discussed in rabbinic sources from northern France during the twelfth and thirteenth centuries. See also S. Schwarzfuchs, *A Concise History of the Rabbinate*, 16–17. On R. Ḥayyim b. Yeḥiʾel's judicial activities (stretching from the year

Rabbinic Courts in Northern France

As opposed to the situation in Germany, it is possible to identify leading rabbinic courts and their members in northern France by name only through the second half of the twelfth century; as we have briefly noted, this pattern changed during the last quarter of that century.[74] The Paris court in the mid-twelfth century consisted of R. Elijah b. Judah *ha-Kohen*, Rashbam, and the Provençal-born R. Meshullam b. Nathan.[75] This was the case before 1145, when Meshullam left for Melun to head his own court. R. Yom Tov b. Judah of Falaise possibly sat on R. Elijah of Paris's court at that time as well.[76] Prior to that (c. 1130), Rashbam presented arguments before "the elders of Paris," R. Mattatyahu, R. Judah b. Abraham, R. Yeḥi'el, and R. Judah b. Yom Tov.[77] Rashbam also sat on the rabbinical court in Troyes with R. Joseph b. Moses,[78] while the court of R. Elijah of Paris (c. 1160) subsequently included the lesser-known R. Moses b. Yeḥi'el.[79]

1266 through 1292), see, e.g., M. Stern and R. Honiger, *Das Judemschreinsbuch der laurenzpfarre zu Koln*, 27–29, 38–39, 43, 45, 52–57, 73–74. On R. Ḥayyim b. Yeḥi'el's rabbinic scholarship, see S. Emanuel, "Qevazei Teshvuot Maharam mi-Rothenburg," 26, 33, 35, and idem, *Shivrei Luḥot*, 265–66. See also below, n. 139.

[74] Cf. R. Reiner, "Battei ha-Din be-Ẓarefat ba-Me'ah ha-Shteim 'Esreh: Bein Rikkuz le-Pizur," in *By the Well: Studies in Jewish Philosophy and Halakhic Thought Presented to Gerald Blidstein*, ed. Uri Ehrlich et al. (Beer Sheva, 2008), 565–90 (= idem, "Rabbinical Courts in France in the Twelfth Century: Centralization and Dispersion," *Journal of Jewish Studies* 60 [2009], 298–318).

[75] See *Sefer ha-Yashar (ḥeleq ha-teshuvot)*, 24, 51; R. Reiner, "Rabbenu Tam: Rabbotav ve-Talmidav," 27–32; and Urbach, *Ba'alei ha-Tosafot*, 76, 79. Rabbenu Tam dealt with a bill of divorce that had been evaluated first by R. Yom Tov b. Judah. See Reiner, "Rabbenu Tam," 33–34.

[76] Urbach, *Ba'alei ha-Tosafot*, 1:121; and *Sefer Or Zaru'a*, vol. 2, *hilkhot yom tov*, sec. 355: ובא מעשה לפני ר' יום טוב . . . וה"ר אליהו הורה ואמר וכו'.

[77] See *Sefer Rabiah (Ḥullin)*, ed. D. Deblitzky (Bnei Brak, 1976), sec. 1143 (p. 209), and *Sefer Or Zaru'a*, vol. 1, sec. 476: נשאתי ונתתי בדבר בפני זקני פרי"ש הגאון ר' מתתיהו וכו'. Rabbenu Tam also responded to שלשה אנשי מופת בפריש, ר' יחיאל, ר' אליעזר, ר' אברהם. See *Sefer ha-Yashar*, #34.

[78] See *Sefer ha-Yashar*, ed. Rosenthal, #77. R. Joseph sent a question to Rabbenu Tam concerning a bill of divorce before the court in Troyes. See *Sefer ha-Yashar*, secs. 14–15, and cf. Urbach, *Ba'alei ha-Tosafot*, 1:114–15, 286.

[79] See *Sefer Raban*, ed. Ehrenreich, fols. 308d–9. Moses b. Yeḥ'iel was the grandson of the earlier Paris judge, R. Mattatyahu (above, n. 77). See *Maḥzor Vitry*, 247 (sec. 280), and S. S. Poznanski, *Mavo 'al Ḥakhmei Ẓarefat Mefarshei ha-Miqra* (repr. Jerusalem, 1965), 75–76. (Cf. ms. JTS Rab., 673, fol. 316r [a citation from *Tosafot R. Mosheh Paris*]; and ms. Moscow 74, fol. 49 [a grammatical comment in the name of R. Moses of Paris]; and ms. Bodl. 352 [a biblical comment from R. Moses of Paris].) Raban asked a question of this court and others about the rights and prerogatives of a homeowner concerning the use of windows (*ḥalonot*) and their airspace. Another court in northern France that was consulted by Raban was headed by R. Meshullam of Melun (and included Joseph b. Elijah, Meir b. Moses, and Meshullam's son Nathan). The Regensburg court of R. Isaac b. Mordekhai and Moses b. Jo'el was also consulted, as was Rabbenu Tam. See also *Mordekhai Bava Batra*, sec. 556; A. Aptowitzer, *Mavo la-Rabiah*, 187; and *Sefer ha-Yashar*, #94–95.

In the mid-twelfth century, R. Jacob Tam responded to a question from the Orleans court of his student R. Yosef *Bekhor Shor.* The case could not be dealt with locally in Orleans because, given the small size of the community, virtually all the males who were available to serve as judges were also related.[80] The one other qualified and available person in Orleans, a R. Solomon b. Isaac, was not interested in getting involved in this case, but did join R. Yosef of Orleans to rule in another case involving a question of inheritance.[81] The options in the first situation were either to send the case to the sitting court in Paris (which one litigant did not want) or to send it to Rabbenu Tam in Ramerupt. Rabbenu Tam agreed to handle this case, even though he did not consider his court to be a higher court (*beit ha-vaʿad*).[82]

According to a *Tosafot* passage, Rabbenu Tam sat on cases regularly as a primary judge.[83] Another passage reports that Rabbenu Tam supervised

[80] On the relatively small size of the Jewish communities in northern France during the twelfth and thirteenth centuries (and certainly as compared to the leading Jewish communities in Germany), see, e.g., S. Albeck, "Yaḥaso shel Rabbenu Tam li-Beʿayot Zemanno," *Zion* 19 (1954), 104–5; S. W. Baron, "Rashi and the Community of Troyes," in *Rashi Anniversary Volume*, ed. H. L. Ginsberg (New York, 1941), 58–62; B. Blumenkrantz, "Quartiers juifs en France (XIIe, XIIIe, XIVe siecles)," *Melanges de philosophie et de literature juives* 3–5 (1958–62), 77–86; W. C. Jordan, *The French Monarchy and the Jews* (Philadelphia, 1989), 4–8, 58–61, 183–84; A. Haverkamp, *Medieval Germany, 1056–1273* (Oxford, 1988), 170–73, 249–98; K. Stow, "The Jewish Family in the Rhineland in the High Middle Ages: Form and Function," *American Historical Review* 92 (1987), 1085–95; Michael Toch, "The Formation of the Diaspora: The Settlement of Jews in the Medieval German *Reich*," *Ashkenas* 7 (1997), 55–74; my *Jewish Education* and *Society in the High Middle Ages*, 24; and G. Nohon, "From the *Rue aux Juifs* to the *Chemin du Roy*: The Classical Age of French Jewry, 1108–1223," in *Jews and Christians in Twelfth-Century Europe*, ed. M. Signer and J. Van Engen (Notre Dame, Ind., 2001), 312–18. For Germany through the period of the First Crusade, see A. Grossman, *Ḥakhmei Ashkenaz ha-Rishonim*, 6–9.

[81] See *Teshuvot Rabiah*, sec. 925; and Aptowitzer, *Mavo la-Rabiah*, 295. Cf. ms. Vienna 73 (*Sefer Mordekhai*), fol. 36v (in a marginal gloss): טופס שטר מר"י מאורליינש התיר ללוות ברבית מתוך שטר זה; *Haggahot Mordekhai* to *Bava Meẓiʿa*, secs. 454–55; N. Rakover, "Piẓẓuyim ʿal ʿIkkuv Kesafim," 155–56; H. Soloveitchik, "Pawnbroking: A Study in Usury and of the Halakhah in Exile," *PAAJR* 38–39 (1972), 252, n. 93; and idem, *Halakhah, Kalkalah ve-Dimmui ʿAẓmi*, 68–69, n. 33.

[82] See *Sefer ha-Yashar*, #36–39. Cf. S. Goldin, *Ha-Yiḥud veha-Yaḥad*, 126–27; *Sefer Or Zaruʿa*, *pisqei Bava Meẓiʿa*, sec. 14 (שאלו בני אשתנפש לרבינו תם והשיב להם ר"ת . . . ויש לבית דין לשמוע אם פרעונו לפי דבריו וישבע על דעת ב"ד); and below, n. 87.

[83] See *Tosafot Ketubot* (69a, s.v. *ve-ʿishtiq*: מכאן רגיל היה ר"ת [בשעה] (כ)שהיה יושב בדין ואחד מבעלי דינין מגזם לחבירו ואומר כך וכך תתחייב לי בדין [וכשנגדו אינו בקי בדין], רגיל היה ר"ת [להכחיש ו]לומר שקר אתה דובר כי לא יתחייב. שאם אין לו לדיין לומר כך, מה היה מוכיח [הוכחתו] של רב מניומי מדאישתיק אמימר. Cf. *Tosafot ha-Rosh*, *Perush ha-Rosh*, *Ḥiddushei ha-Ritva*, and *Shitah Mequbbeẓet*, ad loc. (citing Rivash). See also *Sefer Or Zaruʿa, pisqei Bava Meẓiʿa*, sec. 202 (and cf. *Teshuvot Maharam*, ed. Prague, #796): נראה בעיני היתר גמור ומצוה מן המובחר לתת מחיה לבני ברית שמותר ללוה ולמלוה שיתן המשכונות ליד גוי . . . ופעמים שההפסד על מלוה ועל לוה, ששני דינין באו לפנינו בדבר זה שאבד הלוה כל אשר לו . . . ועוד ראיתי הפסד של מלוה. מעשה אירע בחתני שהלוה על המשכונות . . . וכן נגמר הדין . . . למען דעת כל אדם שהוא היתר גמור הארכתי בדבר. In this passage (which deals with a non-Jewish strawman interposed between a Jewish borrower and lender), Rabbenu Tam dispenses advice to other courts and authorities while noting actual cases that came before his court and others. At the end of the passage, Rabbenu Tam appends a *shtar* form that could be used in this type of situation. R. Isaac *Or Zaruʿa* adds that he copied

or trained judges.[84] Rabbenu Tam's student, R. Eliezer b. Samuel of Metz, describes an unusual divorce case that took place in Troyes "in the *beit din* of R. Jacob."[85] R. Isaac *Or Zaruʿa* reports that he heard of a case that came before Rabbenu Tam about whether the burial of a debtor could be held up until his heirs paid his debt. Rabbenu Tam consulted R. Shemaryah b. Mordekhai (of Speyer), who maintained that this could be done, and Rabbenu Tam accepted his view.[86] Although Rabbenu Tam asserted that his court was to be considered the leading court of the generation for purposes of executing a *prozbol*, there were other instances in which he gave equal standing to all local courts.[87]

---

the words of Rabbenu Tam from a handwritten copy made by his teacher, R. Judah Sirleon of Paris. See Soloveitchik, "Pawnbroking: A Study in Usury," 251–55, and cf. idem, *Halakhah, Kalkalah ve-Dimmui ʿAẓmi*, 136–41, and below nn. 105, 119.

[84] See *Tosafot Bava Qamma* 118a, s.v. *Rav Naḥman*: ושמע ר"י שר"ת היה מניח לדיינין לחייב היכא דליכא דררא דממונא. Cf. *Tosafot Ketubot* 105b, s.v. *mai*, and *Tosafot ha-Rosh (ad loc.)*, s.v. *ʿim domeh dayyan le-melekh she-ʾein ẓarikh kelum* (ואומר ר"ת דתרתי בעינן, שאינו צריך [דיין] ממון ולדברי תורה). On Rabbenu Tam and court procedures, see also *Sefer Or Zaruʿa, pisqei Bava Meẓiʿa*, sec. 200 (*pesaqim* of Rabiah and Rabbenu Tam, and a responsum of R. Meshullam b. Nathan of Narbonne/Melun, on paying an obligation before it is demanded in court); and *Tosafot Ketubot* 105b, s.v. *mai.* See also L. Finkelstein, *Jewish Self-Government in the Middle Ages* (New York, 1964), 194: עוד תקן ר"ת ובית דינו למכה חבירו חוץ מבית הכנסת לקונסו וכו'. This passage is, however, a part of *takkanot Rabbenu Tam* and may therefore refer to a super-communal gathering or context rather than to a local court. Cf. R. Chazan, "The Blois Incident of 1171: A Study in Jewish Intercommunal Organization," *PAAJR* 36 (1968), 13–31.

[85] See *Sefer Yere'im ha-Shalem*, vol. 1, 22 (sec. 7), and *Haggahot Maimuniyyot* to *Hilkhot Ishut*, 9:3 [1]: ושמעתי שמעשה היה בטרוייש ברבי יצחק בן הרב ר' אושעיא נכדו של ה"ר מנחם בבית דינו של רבי' יעקב ששידך בת הקטנה של ר' מוריל [מאנגליטריא] והיו לו ג' בנות קטנות ובשעת הקידושין קידש סתם ולא הזכיר אם המשודכת והיו מהם מתירין מטעם שידוכין. לא שמעו להם האוסרין ונתן גט לשלשתן. See also *Tosafot Qiddushin* 52a, s.v. *ve-hilkheta*; *Ḥiddushei ha-Rashba* to *Qiddushin* 51b; ms. JTS Rab. 673, fol. 363r; and Urbach, *Baʿalei ha-Tosafot*, 1:148. Although the court in question seems to have been a regular communal one under Rabbenu Tam's direction, it should be noted that the court was convened in Troyes (rather than Ramerupt), which was a regional judicial center (and Rabbenu Tam's residence in his later years). The issue at stake was one involving divorce, an area of Jewish law where an organized judicial presence was more common, even in northern France. See, e.g. *Sefer ha-Yashar le-Rabbenu Tam (ḥeleq ha-ḥiddushim)*, ed. Simon Schlesinger (Jerusalem, 1974), 102: והילך משפט על גט של משומד שגירש אשתו, כבר הגט והלכתו כמו שסדרתי ושלחתיו לבני פריס; ms. Montefiore 134, fol. 149v: שאלו לר"ת אם צריך לכתוב בגט שם של גוים. והשיב חלילה וכו'; fol. 150r: השיב רבינו תם לבני פריש על הגט שנכתב ויצא קול שלא נכתב; *Sefer ha-Yashar*, ed. Rosenthal, #24, 34; and below, at n. 117.

[86] See *Sefer Or Zaruʿa, pisqei Bava Batra*, sec. 199: אני יצחק המחבר בן ר' משה שמעתי שבא מעשה לפני רבינו תם בראובן וכו' . . . ונסתפק רבינו תם אם מן הדין יכול לעכב . . . ונמלך ברבינו שמריה ב"ר מרדכי והשיב לו שהדין עם שמעון, ויכול מן הדין לעכב את קבורתו . . . וקבל רבינו תם את דבריו. Isaac *Or Zaruʿa* then adds his own caveat. There is no indication of which judges or indeed whether any other judges were with Rabbenu Tam; perhaps he issued his ruling as a "singular expert" (*yaḥid mumḥeh*). Cf. above, n. 46, and below, n. 144. Note also the responsum of *rabbanei Ẓarefat* with regard to the employment terms of a *melammed*, found in *Sefer Or Zaruʿa, pisqei Bava Meẓiʿa*, sec. 242. This text reads, however, as a larger communal statement and issue, akin to a *taqqanah*, rather than the action of a local rabbinic court.

[87] See, e.g., Y. Kaplan, "Qabbalat Hakhraʿot ba-Qehillah ha-Yehudit le-Daʿat Rabbenu Tam le-Halakhah ule-Maʿaseh," *Zion* 60 (1995), 277–300; my "The Development and Diffusion

Rabbenu Tam's nephew and successor as the leader of the nascent Tosafist enterprise in northern France, R. Isaac b. Samuel of Dampierre (Ri, d. 1189), also preferred, wherever possible, that a local court hear cases that arose, rather than having them sent by messenger to other venues. Thus he writes that the court of R. Ḥayyim *Kohen* in Paris, which was the closest local court, should have heard a particular case in its jurisdiction that was sent instead to the court of R. Yosef *Bekhor Shor* in Orleans.[88] It appears from the texts assembled here that there were established courts in Paris and Orleans during the middle of the twelfth century,[89] with Rabbenu Tam and then Ri dealing with and responding to appeals, perhaps with the status of a singular expert (*yaḥid mumḥeh*). It should be noted, however, that we cannot confirm the names of any other judges (with one exception) who sat on the courts of R. Ḥayyim *Kohen* and R. Yosef *Bekhor Shor*, or the names of the judges who sat on the Troyes court after Rabbenu Tam—only that these courts were recognized as local (and regional) courts in their day.[90] And as we shall see, much of the documented activity of these courts was focused on issues of *gittin* (divorce).

Indeed, while we cannot imagine that Ri or his Tosafist heir, R. Samson (Rash) b. Abraham of Sens (d. 1214), did not sit at some point on an actual primary *beit din*, there is scant evidence to document their participation.[91] Interestingly, Ri clearly indicates that Rashbam did so, describing a *beit din*

---

of Unanimous Agreement in Medieval Ashkenaz," 21–44; and Uzi Fuchs, "Shalosh Teshuvot Ḥadashot shel R. Yiẓḥaq b. Mosheh Ba'al Or Zaru'a," *Tarbiz* 70 (2001), 127–31.

88 See Urbach, *Ba'alei ha-Tosafot*, 1:232. Urbach sees this more as a reflection of Ri's respectful nature, and his desire to insure that R. Ḥayyim's honor not be insulted.

89 Rami Reiner (above, n. 74) carefully traces the activities of these courts during this period.

90 Cf. Urbach, *Ba'alei ha-Tosafot*, 1:120, *46 (citing a passage in *Mordekhai ha-Qaẓar*): הסכימו רוב זקני', רבי אליעזר מפלג' [=חותנו של ר' שמשון מפלייזא, שהיה גיסו של ר"ת], וה"ר מנחם בן רבי' חיים הכהן, ועמהם כל גדולי צרפת, מורשה שתבע בעל דינו חייבוהו לנתבע שבועת היסת . . . לא יכול להפכה. It remains unclear, however, whether this was a court action or a larger statement of rabbinic policy that was formulated to deal with such a situation.

91 For Ri, see *Mordekhai Bava Meẓi'a*, secs. 363–64: פסק ר"י המלוה חבירו על המשכון וחזר המלוה והפקידו ללוה ונגנב או נאבד חייב המלוה . . . ומזה הטעם דן ר"י על ראובן שלוה מעות משמעון על בגדי אשתו וחזר והשאילו לו עד לאחר המועד ומת במועד . . . והחזיר לה שמעון הכל חוץ מהמלבושים ופסק ר"י שהדין עמו וכו'. Cf. Urbach, *Ba'alei ha-Tosafot*, 1:239. Ri advised others about how to transfer a pawn to a non-Jewish strawman, but does not include (as Rabbenu Tam did) that any actual cases of this kind came before a *beit din* on which he sat. See *Sefer Or Zaru'a, pisqei Bava Meẓi'a*, secs. 213–14; H. Soloveitchik, "Pawnbroking: A Study in Usury," 254–55; and above, n. 76. A responsum by R. Samson of Sens (recorded in *Sefer Or Zaru'a*, sec. 214), shows that R. Samson, like Ri, responded to appeals from others in this matter, without any indication that R. Samson sat on a case of this type himself. (R. Isaac *Or Zaru'a*'s concluding evaluation, *harei 'asah [R. Shimson] kedivrei Rabbenu Yiẓḥaq*, refers to the ruling issued by R. Samson in this responsum rather than to an actual case that came before him. Cf. Soloveitchik, "Pawnbroking," 252, n. 92.)

ruling and procedure that Rashbam initiated.[92] In establishing a comparison to the Talmudic period concerning the existence of permanent or fixed courts that were available to each community, Ri writes that since there are no longer any set court days, claims could be presented before a panel of three judges on any day of the week. Similarly, witnesses in the Talmudic period knew to appear at the court on particular days, which was no longer the case. Although this formulation suggests additional flexibility in Ri's day, it also indicates a less formal judicial structure.[93]

The rulings (*pesaqim*) that we have from Ri and Rash *mi-Shanz* in matters of monetary law and torts are formulated almost exclusively on the basis of their academic interpretations of relevant talmudic *sugyot* or in response to a query (or an appeal), and do not appear to have been derived in the course of court deliberations and decisions.[94] One of the few court cases that came before R. Samson of Sens for which we have documentation concerns the conditions under which a particular type of oath (*shevuʿat heset*) should be administered before a litigant may collect his judgment.[95]

[92] See *Mordekhai Bava Meẓiʿa*, sec. 414 (corrected according to ms. Vercelli C235): זמן ב״ד ל׳ יום . . . יש שהיו רוצים לפסוק מכאן דכל דין ופסק שחייבו ב״ד סתם לשלם ממון אינו חייב לפרוע עד שלשים יום . . . ור״י שיבש הוכחה שלהם . . . ואר״י שרשב״ם פסק דין אחד בי מיו וגבה הכל תוך ג׳ ימים. Rabbenu Tam also refers to a judicial decision of Rashbam (cited by Ri, in *Teshvuot Maharam*, ed. Prague, #358): היה פוסק ר״ת כשנפסל מטבע דינא דמלכותא דינא . . . כי כל היהודים ביניהם דנים ע״פ ר״ת. גם בשם רבי׳ שמואל היה אומר ר״ת שכך היה דן, ואם כתוב בשטר שיש לו עליו כך וכך וכו׳.

[93] See *Tosafot* (and *Tosafot Rash mi-Shanz*) *Ketubot* 3a, s.v. ועתה נוהגין לישא אף בשני :אי איכא בתי דין׳ משום דאין ב״ד קבועין ואם יש לו טענת בתולים יכול לקבול בשבת בפני שלשה כמו בשאר ימות השבוע . . . דוקא בימיהם קבעו יום הנישואין משום דעל ידי כך יתברר הדבר ויבואו עדים מתוך שמתאספים העם לב״ד ואין שייך עכשיו לומר כך. Cf. Goldin, *Ha-Yiḥud veha-Yaḥad*, 118.

[94] See, e.g., *Sefer Zaruʿa, pisqei Bava Qamma*, secs. 28, 50, 72, 134, 137, 252, 408, 411, 439; *pisqei bava Meẓiʿa*, secs. 3 (as noted by R. Judah Sirleon), 10, 38, 119, 125, 183, 189, 204, 214, 215, 218, 223 (from Ri's son R. Elḥanan, in his father's name), 252–53 (from R. Elḥanan), 276, 326; *pisqei Bava Batra*, secs. 97 (Ri responded to an appeal in the case of a *get* given by a husband who was close to death, as did Rivaq of Speyer and his brother R. Meir, and R. Eliezer of Metz), 138, 142, 162, 212. *Sefer Or Zaruʿa, pisqei Sanhedrin*, sec. 58, contains an interpretation and responsum by Ri of Speyer, Rabiah, and R. Samson of Sens. R. Isaac b. Mordekhai (Ribam), a German Tosafist and judge in Regensburg (see above, nn. 27–28), delineates a series of *beit din* rules collected in *Sefer Or Zaruʿa, pisqei Bava Batra*, secs. 222, 224, 225, 228. Although this may reflect Ribam's role as an active court judge, many of Ribam's theoretical rulings, like those of Ri, are also cited in *Sefer Or Zaruʿa*. For *pesaqim* from Rash *mi-Shanz*, see, e.g., *pisqei Bava Qamma*, secs. 123, 229; *pisqei Bava Meẓiʿa*, secs. 23, 31, 79, 203; and *pisqei Sanhedrin*, secs. 17, 53, 73. (On sec. 73, cf. *Teshuvot Maharam*, ed. Prague, 454, and E. Shochetman, "Ḥovat ha-Hanmaqah," 334, n. 50.) Cf. Chaim Sha'anan, "Pisqei Rabbenu Yeḥi'el mi-Paris be 'Inyanei Ḥoshen Mishpat," *Moriah* 18 (7–8), 3–10.

[95] See *Sefer Or Zaruʿa, pisqei Bava Meẓiʿa*, sec. 10 (R. Hai, R. Isaac Alfasi, and Rabbenu Tam all ruled the same way in theory): וכבר בא מעשה לפני רבינו שמשון בן אברהם באומר לא היו דברים מעולם ופטר אותו משבועה. R. Samson's brother Riẓba is then cited as adding a procedural instruction for the judges. Cf. below, n. 105.

Another case concerns the proper procedures for executing binding legal documents (*shetarot*).[96]

The following passages in *Sefer Or Zaru'a* allow us to easily identify and to compare the more theoretical guidance offered by French authorities with the hands-on experiences of German courts and justices. *Sefer Or Zaru'a* records a Talmudic interpretation of Ri dealing with the liability of a nonprofessional who evaluated coins for another. R. Joel *ha-Levi* suggested the same interpretation, but also asked R. Ephraim of Regensburg about this matter. R. Ephraim suggested a modified approach, and he referred to an actual case in which such a ruling was given.[97] In similar fashion, R. Samson of Sens noted that Ri *heard* a ruling of Rabbenu Tam in which he had accepted written testimony in a case that came before him. R. Joel *ha-Levi*, on the other hand, actually accepted such testimony while serving as a judge.[98]

Ri added to a responsum of Rabbenu Tam that was written in answer to an appeal sent to him about collecting an overpayment when a non-Jew is involved. At the same time, Rivaq b. Moses of Mainz asked R. Ephraim b. Isaac of Regensburg to render a decision for him in this kind of matter. It appears that Rivaq, unlike Ri, was involved with an actual case, and was turning to R. Ephraim for direct guidance.[99] In a lengthy passage, *Sefer Or Zaru'a* discusses whether any kind of oath may be taken in connection with a claim on real estate. Rabiah argued, in the name of the Geonim, that a *shevu'at heset* may be administered, and Riẓba (R. Isaac b. Abraham of Dampierre) responded similarly; Riba *ha-baḥur*, however, rejected the Geonic proofs, and R. Samuel b. Natronai (Rashbat), R. Barukh b. Samuel, and R. Simḥah of Speyer offered proofs that no oaths whatsoever can be taken in connection with land. "And my teacher Rabiah of Bonn ruled in an actual case (פסק ועבד עובדא) that no oaths are to be taken on real estate . . . it is therefore clear to us that Rabiah is correct."[100]

[96] *Sefer Or Zaru'a, pisqei Bava Batra*, sec. 55. Here too, interpretations by Rabbenu Tam, Riba *ha-Levi*, and R. Isaac b. Mordekhai are presented first. R. Isaac *Or Zaru'a* chooses to rely on the approach of Rabbenu Tam, based on the fact that an actual case came before R. Samson b. Abraham of Sens, who decided his case according to the position of Rabbenu Tam.

[97] *Sefer Or Zaru'a, pisqei Bava Qamma*, secs. 408–10.

[98] See Abraham Fuss, "Edut bi-Khtav be-Dinei Mamonot," *Shenaton ha-Mishpat ha-'Ivri* 3–4 (1975–76), 331–37.

[99] See *Sefer Or Zaru'a*, sec. 415: עתה הודיענו מורי הדין עם מי כי להוליך מנה אינו דומה. והשיב לו אמת דינו של שמעון וכו'. Cf. *Sefer Or Zaru'a, pisqei Bava Meẓi'a*, sec. 14 (above, n. 81).

[100] See *Sefer Or Zaru'a, pisqei Bava Meẓi'a*, sec. 9: ומורי רבי' אבי העזרי הוא מו' רבי' אליעזר בן יואל הלוי מבון פסק ועבד עובדא דאין נשבעין כלל על הקרקעות ואפילו שבועת היסת . . . הילכך איתברר לן כדברי מורי רבי' אבי העזרי דאין נשבעין על קרקעות כלל. See also *Teshuvot Maharam*, ed. Prague, #357–60, 369. (For #357, see the parallels in ms. Bodl. 884, fol. 150v, col. 2, and in ms. Cambridge 667.1, fol. 167v, col. 1.) In these responsa as well, Ri gives judicial advice in monetary cases but never seems to be the judge on the case itself. It should be noted generally that the largest collections of Ri's *pesaqim*

We also learn about the nature and power of local courts in northern France in the late twelfth and early thirteenth centuries, and the relative lack of participation in these courts on the part of leading rabbinic scholars, from a responsum by Ri's grandson, R. Samuel b. Elḥanan (d. 1230), who was a contemporary of R. Moses of Coucy and R. Yeḥi'el of Paris. Samuel rules that a litigant who is concerned lest he be taken advantage of in the local court by the important communal leaders (*gedolei ha-ʿir u-farnasehah*) who had invited him there, since the judges may be intimidated by the leaders and the litigant's claims may not be heard properly, can have the case heard in another city. Indeed, "it is best for the judges and the litigants to go to the next locale." Samuel supports his ruling by noting that his grandfather Ri did thusly, directing a member of the Troyes community not to appear before the court in Troyes since his legal antagonist was a communal head (*rosh ha-ʿir*) and was very influential. For similar considerations, R. Samson of Sens permitted his son-in-law who lived in Troyes not to appear at the court there, and R. Judah (Sirleon) of Paris ruled the same way on behalf of *he-ḥaver* Yom Tov *ha-nadiv.*[101]

Although R. Samuel b. Elḥanan in this responsum supports the powers of the local court for the most part, except where there may be clear indications of bias, several underlying factors must be noted. The leading Tosafists referred to are not hearing the cases themselves in Troyes or in Paris. Moreover, they are not consulting with or referring to any colleagues in these locales, as one "head of a court" to another, but are ruling from afar. Indeed, we have no record and no clue regarding who the judges on these various courts were. All of this occurs at precisely the same time that we can identify fully and precisely a large number of active courts in various German cities and towns.

Based on his close reading of a Talmudic passage, Ri discusses the issue of whether one litigant can force the second to go to another court, but the formulation is purely prescriptive.[102] In a responsum, Ri oversees the way

---

that have been preserved are in the area of ritual law and *ʾissur ve-ḥeter.* See, e.g., Simcha Emanuel, "Teshuvot shel Maharam mi-Rothenburg she-Einan shel Maharam," *Shenaton ha-Mishpat ha-ʿIvri* 21 (1998–2000), 160–64.

[101] See the responsum cited in Urbach, *Baʿalei ha-Tosafot*, 1:486 (and see also 1:254); *Tosafot Shanz le-Massekhet Sanhedrin* (*Sanhedrei Gedolah*, vol. 6), ed. Y. Lifshitz (Jerusalem, 1974), 117; and ms. JTS Rab. 673, fol. 357v. Cf. S. Goldin, *Ha-Yiḥud veha-Yaḥad*, 127–28, and ms. Cambridge Or. 71 (*Sefer Mordekhai ha-Qazar*), fol. 38r (in a marginal note) (= ms. Bodl. 672, fol. 32v): מעשה היה בטרוייש והוציא רבינו תם ורבינו שמואל נכבד עשיר מטרוייש לדון [ב]ב"ד בעיר אחרת. ואני הצעיר ראיתי ככה בטרוייש. מצא[תי] בילקוט ישן.

[102] *Mordekhai Sanhedrin*, sec. 707 (מכאן מוכיח ר"י דאם הוציא ראובן יציאותיו כדי לכוף את שמעון לדין, שמעון לא יפרע הוצאה אע"פ שראובן זכה בתביעתו דאם לא כן מאי פריך הכא וכו'); ms. JTS Rab. 673, fols. 356r–v. Cf. E. Shochetman (above, n. 64), 264–65; U. Fuchs (above, n. 87); *Teshuvot Maharam*, ed. Prague, #497; and below, nn. 155–56.

that a court distributes assets to a wife whose husband entrusted them to another person, but it is clearly not his court that originally heard the case.[103] R. Samson b. Abraham of Sens's brother, R. Isaac b. Abraham (Riẓba), refers in a responsum to what various judges (*dayyanim*) did, including R. Ḥayyim *Kohen*, strongly implying that he himself was not offering a judicial ruling in this matter.[104] Similarly, Riẓba writes to his correspondent, *he-Ḥaver* Joseph b. *he-Ḥaver* Solomon, about the procedures to be followed when monies were confiscated by the ruler from a Jew, who promptly went to a rabbinic court and accused another Jew of informing on him in a way that led to this confiscation. It is clear, however, that Riẓba himself never presided over such a case as a sitting judge.[105]

The impression fostered by all these texts is that in the period after Rashbam and Rabbenu Tam—with the exception of two of Rabbenu Tam's students, R. Yosef *Bekhor Shor* and R. Ḥayyim *Kohen*—northern French Tosafists were not especially involved with local courts, and that, indeed, these courts appear to have been mostly informal bodies, with few of their discussions preserved. Although, to be sure, the rabbinic literature of the Tosafists in northern France is often theoretical or even abstract, not even any offhand references can be found in this literature concerning the involvement of these scholars in the workings of the *battei din* that were convened during this period.

Indeed, this impression is substantially confirmed by the response of R. Samson of Sens to a question from his student, R. Jacob b. Solomon of Courson,[106] about choosing local judges and the right of a litigant to take his case to a superior court (*beit din ha-gadol*). R. Samson, who certainly responded to appeals[107] but does not appear to have sat on a fixed local court of any kind, indicated to R. Jacob that local courts are to be chosen through

103 *Teshuvot Maimuniyyot le-Hilkhot Ishut*, #21.

104 See *Sefer Or Zaru'a, pisqei Bava Meẓi'a*, secs. 262–63: השוכר סוס מחבירו ונמצא צולע זה היה מעשה והשיב רבינו יצחק בן אברהם . . . וראיתי מקצת הדיינים העולה על רוחם לפוטרו ולדמותו להכה על ידו וצמתה ידו וסופה לחזור [א]כן נראה אני בעיני כי טעות גדולה היא בידם . . . וחבל על האומרים בענין אחר דלא מצינו לא במקרא ולא במשנה ולא בתלמוד מזיק ממון חבירו והיזק ניכר שיפטר. עוד נראה בעיני דעל כרחין אפי' כעין צמתה בידו וסופה לחזור חייב וכו'. Cf. I. Agus, *Teshuvot Ba'alei ha-Tosafot*, 88–89 (#29).

105 See *Sefer Or Zaru'a, pisqei Bava Qamma*, sec. 283; and Agus, *Teshuvot Ba'alei ha-Tosafot*, 89–91 (#30). On Riẓba and Joseph b. Solomon, see my "The Development and Diffusion of Unanimous Agreement in Medieval Ashkenaz," 26. Cf. above, n. 83. Although R. Judah Sirleon preserved an important procedural ruling (and *shtar*) of Rabbenu Tam, there is again no evidence that he implemented it as a sitting judge, as Rabbenu Tam had.

106 In later years, R. Jacob lived in Germany and taught a number of students there. For his halakhic writings, see S. Emanuel, *Shivrei Luḥot*, 254–61, and cf. above, nn. 22, 50.

107 Rash *mi-Shanẓ* ruled by responsum in the distribution of the assets of a person who was near death; see, e.g., *Mordekhai Bava Batra*, secs. 668–69. So, too, he and R. Simḥah of Speyer ruled by responsum on the appropriateness of paying an exorbitant fee to a matchmaker; see *Sefer Or Zaru'a, pisqei Bava Qamma*, sec. 457.

the talmudic principle of *zabla* (זבל״א, *zeh borer lo ʾeḥad*; each litigant picks one judge and the two judges who are chosen, in turn, pick a third judge), and that if the leading scholar in a city is chosen to serve on a court, that court is akin to the *beit din ha-gadol* (a supreme court), so litigants cannot therefore petition to have their cases heard elsewhere.[108]

A case that the Tosafist R. Eliezer b. Samuel of Metz (d. 1198) participated in suggests that he served as a judge chosen through the method of *zabla.* R. Eliezer found himself hearing a case along with one of the ordinary Jewish householders in Metz who was also serving as judge (וישב עמו בדין אחד מבעלי הבתים שבעיר). The case concerned an individual who had unfairly rushed in to buy the parcel of land that a poor man had been arranging to purchase, before the poor man (who was not experienced in such matters) could complete his transaction, a situation described in the Talmud (*Qiddushin* 79a). R. Eliezer intended to rule, in accordance with the talmudic *sugya*, that while the court did not have the authority in such a situation to take the land away from the usurper, the usurper is nonetheless considered to be a *rasha.* The Metz layman sitting on this case with R. Eliezer raised an objection. "Rebbe," argued the layman, "we have not sufficiently fulfilled

[108] See *Sefer Or Zaruʿa, pisqei Bava Qamma*, sec. 436; *Teshuvot Maimuniyyot le-Sefer Shoftim*, #2; *Tosafot Shanz le-Massekhet Sanhedrin*, ed. Lifshitz, 115; ms. JTS Rab. 673, fols. 356v–357r; U. Fuchs, "Shalosh Teshuvot Ḥadashot shel R. Yiẓḥaq b. Mosheh Or Zaruʿa," 119–21; and *Mordekhai Sanhedrin*, sec. 709 (corrected according to ms. Budapest 1, fol. 197v, col. 1, and ms. Vercelli C235, fol. 94r, col. 1): האידנא . . . הגדול שבעיר חשיב בית דין הגדול כדפי׳ רבינו שמשון דמאחר שאנו רחוקים יותר מדאי, סברא הוא דגדול חשיב בית דין הגדול וכגון שהוא מומחה ויודע להוציא דין תורה לאורה [הרי זה דן בעירו] דאיכא למיחש לרמאין שלא ידחו עצמם כל שעה מן הדין באומרם לב״ד הגדול קאזילנא [ותו דלית לן מקום הועד מקום קיבוץ תלמידי חכמים שיתבייש מהם]. וכבר שאל הרב ר׳ יעקב מרבינו שמשון והשיב לו מנהג (קדם על) [חרם של] בית דין דעירנו אודיעך ע״י אחד מבני עירנו המזמין את חבירו לדין על כרחו ידון כאן ואינו יכול לדחותו לומר נלך לבית הועד או לבית דין הגדול. אך בזה יכול לדחותו שלא יטעון עד יום השלישי. אבל דיינין בוררין להם לאלתר, זה בורר לו אחד וזה בורר לו אחד. ואם אכסנאי הוא המזמין אחד מבני עירו או שני אכסנאים שמזמינים זה את זה, בוררין לאלתר וטוענין לאלתר וזה מנהג הגון וכשר מפני הרמאין עכ״ל. While acknowledging that not all locales resemble the area in which R. Samson resided (since he was unique in his generation and it is therefore difficult to derive a pattern for everyone based on what was done in his city), R. Isaac *Or Zaruʿa* suggests (see also sec. 437) that in order to prevent chicanery (*rama'in*), it is appropriate to compel both litigants to have their case heard locally and allow neither of them to petition to go to the greatest court (*beit din ha-gadol*), as R. Samson had indicated. Moreover, there is no longer a central judicial edifice or authority where leading scholars gather that could cause someone acting improperly to be embarrassed. Cf. *Sefer Or Zaruʿa, pisqei Sanhedrin*, sec. 73, citing a passage in *Sefer Raban*, ed. Ehrenreich, fol. 227c: כתב רבינו אב״ן . . . שאפי׳ אמר הלוה נדון כאן שומעין לו, דליכא האידנא מקום וועד קבוע כמו שהיה בימי חכמים שהיתה ישיבתם קבועה במקום אחד, כדתניא צדק צדק תרדוף הלוך אחר חכמים לישיבה; U. Fuchs, "Shalosh Teshuvot Ḥadashot," 127–31; and above, nn. 75, 81, 87, for other antecedent formulations in the writings of Rabbenu Tam and Ri. On the acceptance of *zabla* by R. Isaac *Or Zaruʿa* as the standard method for selecting judges and courts, see also *pisqei Bava Batra*, sec. 232 (ולא נהירא לי אלא מיד כשבירר אותו ובירכהו לישב בדין וקבל הברכה שוב אינו יכול לחזור בו, לא בעל דין ולא דיין) and *pisqei Sanhedrin*, sec. 7. It should also be noted that Isaac *Or Zaruʿa*'s son, R. Ḥayyim Eliezer, also presumes the practice of *zabla* in his treatise on judicial practices, *Sefer Eẓ (ha-) Ḥayyim.* See *Ḥamishah Quntresim*, ed. N. Coronel, fols. 97v–98v, and ms. Paris 1480, fols. 172–174r.

our obligation [to protect the poor]. We should announce in the synagogue that it is permitted to publicly castigate this person as an evil man (*rasha*), until he makes restitution [to the poor man]." R. Meir of Rothenburg, who reports this case, takes note of how this layman's proper reaction caused the usurper to return the parcel, thereby allowing the poor man to purchase it as he had intended. It is fairly apparent that two individuals had been selected as "judges" in this case, and that they had then chosen R. Eliezer of Metz, as the leading scholar in the city, to be the third judge.[109]

Although there is a reference to a judgment in monetary matters rendered by R. Eliezer of Metz and R. Joseph *Tov 'Elem* in the presence of Rabbenu Tam, this occurred during their student days at his academy.[110] While

[109] See *Teshuvuot u-Pesaqim*, ed. Kupfer, sec. 93, 151–52: שמעתי בשם ר׳ אליעזר ממץ פעם אחת ישב בדין עני המהפך בחררה . . . וישב עמו בדין אחד מבעלי הבתים שבעיר ואמר לו רבי בזה לא יצאנו ידי חובותינו. See also Kupfer's introduction, 24–25. Kupfer notes the responsum of R. Jacob Reischer (d. 1803) in his *Teshuvot Shevut Ya'akov* (pt. 2, #142), that "the practice here in the community of Metz was to never have fixed judges from time immemorial [*me-'olam umi-shanim qadmoniyyot*] but to judge according to the principle of *zabla*, with the leading scholar of the town [the *'av beit din*] being selected as the third." He also notes that R. Eliezer of Metz independently stated his *pesaq* on this issue (*Haggahot Maimuniyyot, hilkhot ḥovel u-maziq*, ch. 5, sec. 1), without any reference to the court incident. Cf. Urbach, *Ba'alei ha-Tosafot*, 1:159, and S. Goldin, *Ha-Yiḥud veha-Yaḥad*, 124. See also the passage in ms. Cambridge 3127, published by Chaim Sha'anan, "Pisqei R. Yeḥi'el mi-Paris be-'Inyanei Ḥoshen Mishpat," 4, sec. 4: ראובן הלך לבית הכנסת ותבע חבירו לדין ובררו ב״ד ונתבררו הדייני׳ וכשיצאו מבית הכנסת חזר ראובן ואמ׳ איני חפץ באותו ב״ד בשניהם ולא קבלתי כ״א דיינים כשרים. יכול ראובן לחזור בו מלקבל הדיינים עליו משום דאינם כשרים שלא קבל עליו החרם אא״כ הם כשרים.

[110] See *Teshuvot Maharam*, ed. Prague, #721, and *Sefer Or Zaru'a, pisqei Bava Meẓi'a*, sec. 71. Joseph *Tov 'Elem* here cannot be the well-known eleventh-century scholar of this name. He is possibly the biblical scholar R. Yosef Qara but more likely, from the standpoint of rabbinic courts in the twelfth century (and from the chronology as well), R. Yosef of Orleans. See A. Grossman, *Ḥakhmei Ashkenaz ha-Rishonim*, 46; Urbach, *Ba'alei ha-Tosafot*, 1:154; and R. Reiner, "Rabbenu Tam: Rabbotav ve-Talmidav," 54. The phrase in *Mordekhai Bava Qamma*, sec. 142 (= *Mordekhai ha-Shalem*, ed. A. Halpern [Jerusalem, 1992], 176, recorded from Barukh of Mainz's *Sefer ha-Ḥokhmah*), מכאן היה דן רא״ם וכן הסכימו כל הגדולים שכל ממון שלא נקנה ביד מי שהוא בייאוש, reflects an argument made by R. Eliezer that was accepted by other leading scholars, albeit not necessarily in the context of a court case. The passage (from *Sefer ha-Ḥokhmah*) that lists R. Eliezer on a court with R. Barukh (*Mordekhai Bava Batra*, sec. 507, אני ברוך ב״ר שמואל וה״ר אליעזר ישבנו יחד בדין אחד = ms. Parma 86, fols. 248–49, sec. 458) is more likely a reference to R. Eliezer b. Joel *ha-Levi* (Rabiah) than to R. Barukh's teacher, R. Eliezer of Metz. Rabiah and R. Barukh were together for other court procedures and discussions. See above, n. 7; and cf. Reiner, "Rabbenu Tam," 111 (n. 382); and S. Emanuel, "R. Barukh mi-Magenẓa," 142 (n. 83). (Note also that ms. Vercelli C235, fol. 63v, and ms. B.M. 537, fol. 76r, list ה״ר אליעזר, while ms. Vienna 72, fol. 128r [col. a] and ms. Budapest [National Library 2*] 1, fol. 156r [cols. a–c], record ה״ר אלעזר.) On R. Eliezer of Metz as a teacher (and relative, מורי קרובי) of R. Barukh, see Emanuel, *Shivrei Luḥot*, 107–8. The phrase in *Mordekhai Shabbat*, sec. 313 (where a ruling of R. Eliezer of Metz concerning a corpse that was brought to a community by boat on the Sabbath is presented), ורבינו ברוך ממגנצא דן לפניו, refers to arguments and analyses that R. Barukh offered in connection with R. Eliezer's ruling in this *hilkhot Shabbat* issue. This was clearly an (external) halakhic discussion rather than a court case. Note also *Mordekhai Ḥullin*, sec. 684. A case came before the rabbis of Mainz (*rabbotenu shebe-Magenẓa*) about a lung, ואני ברוך דנתי לפניהם. Once again, this question is one of *'issur ve-heter* rather than a case for a *beit din*. The sense of the term דנתי again seems to be

R. Eliezer does not appear to have served regularly on cases as a sitting judge, he was nonetheless consulted by other rabbinic judges, particularly those in Germany.[111]

By the second quarter of the thirteenth century, the situation in northern France began to change, returning to its own *status quo ante* and to what had been in vogue in Germany throughout the previous century. During this time R. Hezekiah of Magdeburg sent an appeal to the Tosafist R. Yeḥi'el b. Joseph of Paris, one of the first such consultations from Germany to northern France in quite a while.[112] Similarly, R. Isaac *Or Zaruʿa* sent a monetary ruling for approval to R. Yeḥi'el and to the Tosafist R. Samuel b. Solomon of Falaise, referring to them as "my teachers in Paris." R. Yeḥi'el replied that R. Isaac had ruled well, and R. Samuel began his response, "With respect to the case that came before you." Although it appears that these responses were written to R. Isaac separately, R. Yeḥi'el and R. Samuel did sit on the same Paris court, as we shall see. In any event, this renewed consultation between Germany/Austria and northern France is significant, although to be sure, R. Isaac *Or Zaruʿa* studied with leading Tosafists in both northern France and Germany, and is a bridge figure in this regard as well.[113] R. Yaqar

---

that R. Barukh advanced or argued or demonstrated a particular view before his senior rabbinic colleague. Indeed, his teacher R. Moses *ha-Kohen* later told him that this approach had been argued in northern France in the presence of Rabbenu Tam, who accepted it, and R. Joel *ha-Levi* subsequently said to R. Barukh, יפה דנת (= your analysis is correct), since this was also the approach of R. Joel's father-in-law, Raban. See also *Mordekhai Bava Batra*, sec. 578 (recorded from *Sefer ha-Ḥokhmah*, וכן דנתי). In this instance, R. Barukh refers to one of his Mainz teachers, Rivaq, by name (and perhaps includes the other senior colleagues on the Mainz court as well; see above, n. 7, and cf. Emanuel, "R. Barukh mi-Magenẓa," 126). The issue here is one of *davar she-ba le-ʿolam*, which might have been discussed in a *beit din* context, although the passage itself has the ring of a presentation and consultation rather than a formal proceeding. In his formulation R. Barukh cites a proof from מורי קרובי (= R. Eliezer of Metz).

[111] See, e.g., S. Emanuel, "R. Barukh mi-Magenẓa," 139 (n. 66), for a section from *Sefer ha-Ḥokhmah* (found in certain *Mordekhai* texts to tractate *Qiddushin*) in which a young woman was betrothed to a *kohen* and there was a problem with the *qiddushin*. R. Eliezer of Metz, who also spent some time in Mainz, was among the leading scholars consulted. See also above, n. 110.

[112] See *Mordekhai Gittin*, sec. 379, and *Teshuvot Maharam*, ed. Berlin, 210 (#145). That R. Hezekiah sent a related query to R. Avigdor Katz (sec. 380) is not surprising at all; cf. above, n. 50. R. Hezekiah may have studied with R. Samson of Coucy, although the only record that we have of this relationship concerns an issue in *hilkhot terefot*: בדק רבינו שמשון בקנה אחד ומצא בו נקבים קטנים ודנתי לפניו קיי"ל כרב באיסורי. See *Haggahot Asheri* to *Ḥullin*, 3:12, and Urbach, *Baʿalei ha-Tosafot*, 2:565 (n. 6).

[113] See *Or Zaruʿa, pisqei Bava Meẓiʿa, sec.* 180: ושלחתי דברי אלה לרבותיי שבפריש והשיבוני ועל הלואת חבירו דלוקח אדם בפחות כדתניא בתוספתא, יפה דנת וכן הוא אמת וכו'. ושלום . . . יחיאל בן יוסף אוהבך נדבה. ועל מעשה שבא לידך בראובן שחייב לשמעון מנה ליתן לו בתשרי ורוצה שמעון למכור אותה הלואה ללוי . . . נראה דליכא רבית. . . . שמואל בן שלמה (R. Isaac *Or Zaruʿa* also adds a responsum of Ri that he found on this subject.) The response by R. Yeḥi'el was sent to R. Isaac *Or Zaruʿa* as the final part of a larger responsum penned by R. Yeḥi'el which addressed several different issues raised by R. Isaac, including a case of *ḥaliẓah*. See *Sefer Or Zaruʿa*, pt. 1, sec. 773.

b. Samuel *ha-Levi* of Cologne sent a ruling about fixing the ritual bath in his city to R. Samuel of Falaise and R. Jacob b. Joseph of Verdun, and to R. Barukh b. Abraham of Mainz and several rabbinic scholars in Speyer, for their approval.[114]

Hearkening back to the days of Rabbenu Tam and his immediate students, R. Yeḥi'el of Paris was apparently involved in a court case concerning the use of a non-Jewish middleman to secure a loan between Jews with interest. Although he actually disagreed with the position taken by Rabbenu Tam in this situation, R. Yeḥi'el, like Rabbenu Tam, had the opportunity to put his view into practice as the member of a rabbinic court.[115]

R. Yeḥi'el of Paris also supervised the writing and giving of *gittin*. Qershavyahu (Cresbia) b. Isaac the scribe (*ha-naqdan*) writes that he was in Paris at the court of R. Yeḥi'el, and he was involved in the writing of many bills of divorce. Sitting with R. Yeḥi'el were R. Judah b. David of Melun and R. Samuel b. Solomon of Chateau Thierry (and Falaise). Although the two latter scholars had maintained certain practices that they received from their teachers, most of the *gittin* were written under the direction of R. Yeḥi'el, and the other scholars followed his directives.[116]

It should be noted that we have evidence that most of the leading Tosafists in northern France throughout the twelfth and thirteenth centuries supervised the writing of bills of divorce and related documents such as *gittei ḥalizah*, and even convened rabbinic courts for these purposes. Included

[114] See *Teshuvot u-Pesaqim*, ed. Kupfer, 260–69 (secs. 189–65). R. Samuel of Falaise makes reference in his response to something he had discussed with R. Yeḥi'el of Paris. This R. Yaqar b. Samuel *ha-Levi* was an older contemporary of R. Meir of Rothenburg; see above at n. 48. R. Barukh b. Abraham of Mainz was a grandson of R. Barukh b. Samuel of Mayence.

[115] See ms. Hamburg 45, fol. 183c–d (transcribed in H. Soloveitchik, *Halakhah, Kalkalah ve-Dimmui 'Azmi* [Jerusalem, 1985], 141): ר"ת היה מתיר לישראל לשלוח את הגוי אצל ישראל אחר ללוות לו מעות אפי' בידיעת המלוה והלוה. ור' [=ה"ר יחיאל מפריז] מחמיר . . . וגדולה מזאת אמ' לי ר' דאם מת הגוי והמלוה הלך וזכה במשכון ואפי' אם יביא עדים הא' ישראל השולח את המשכון שהוא שלו או' לו לאו בעל דברים דידי את. ומעשה היה בפריש במעות ה"ר יוסף ששלח המשכון ביד גוי ולוה מישראל ברבית. וכנודע הדבר למלוה לא רצה להחזיר המשכון ולא היה כח ביד ב"ד להוציא מידו. ואמרתי לו וכי לא עשו בו תקנת השוק וכו'. See also Soloveitchik, 68–71 (esp. n. 32), 83, and above, n 77. On ms. Hamburg 45, cf. S. Emanuel, *Shivrei Luḥot*, 172–75; my "*Peering through the Lattices*," 94–95, 227; and below, chapter 4, n. 193.

[116] See ms. Los Angeles/UCLA 779 (bx. 3.3), fol. 99r: אמ' קרשביהו הנקדן ב"ר יצחק הסופר אשר היה בימי הר"ם מקוצי ור' יחיאל מפריש הייתי בעיר פריש לפני מהר"ר יחיאל ב"ר יוסף מפריש והיו שפ מה"ר יהודה ב"ר דוד מעין מילון ומה"ר שמואל ב"ר שלמה מכרך טיירי ורבי' [והרבה] גיטין כתבתי לפניהם . . . אך מרוב הגיטין שהיו נעשים ברשותם לפני מהר"ר יחיאל וכו', published in *Teshuvot u-Pesaqim*, ed. Kupfer, 325–26, and in Gavriel Zinner, *Ozar Pisqei ha-Rishonim 'al Hilkhot Pesaḥ* (Brooklyn, 1985), 251 (sec. 14). See also ms. LA/UCLA 779 (bx. 3.3), fol. 92v (וכן כל הטופסי' של רבי' יחיאל מפריש וכן של רבי' פרץ תלמידו); Norman Golb, *The Jews in Medieval Normandy* (Cambridge, 1998), 444–45; and above, Introduction, n. 83.

in this list are Rabbenu Tam and R. Yosef of Orleans,[117] Ri,[118] R. Isaac b. Abraham of Dampierre (Riẓba)[119] and his brother R. Samson of Sens,[120] R. Barukh b. Isaac,[121] R. Judah Sirleon of Paris,[122] R. Yeḥi'el of Paris (as indicated here), and R. Pereẓ b. Elijah of Corbeil.[123] This one exception (of

[117] On Rabbenu Tam and R. Yosef *Bekhor Shor* of Orleans, see, e.g., Agus, *Ba'alei ha-Tosafot*, #11; *Sefer ha-Mordekhai le-Massekhet Gittin*, ed. M. Rabinowitz , 870–72; above, nn. 66, 75; *Sefer ha-Yashar le-Rabbenu Tam* (*ḥeleq ha-ḥiddushim*), ed. Schlesinger, 101–4 (*tiqqun ha-get*), 446–47 (*seder ḥaliẓah*); S. E. Stern, "Sefer Ḥaliẓah she-Sidder Rabbenu Shelomoh li-Bnei Paris," in *Zekhor le-Avraham: Qoveẓ Torani* (Jerusalem, 1994–95), 9–12; ms. L.A./UCLA 779 (bx. 3.3), fol. 103v (*'inyan ḥaliẓah mi-pi Rabbenu Tam*); and cf. E. Shochetman, "Ha-Ḥashash Le-Hoẓa'at La'az 'al ha-Rishonim ke-Shiqqul bi-Pesiqat ha-Halakhah," *Bar Ilan* 18–19 (1981), 177–79.

[118] See *Sefer ha-Mordekhai le-Massekhet Gittin*, ed. Rabinowitz, 850–56, for a letter from Ri on various *get* procedures, including the way that a rabbinic court deals with an agent appointed by the wife to receive the *get*. See also *Sefer ha-Mordekhai le-Gittin*, ed. Rabinowitz, 861; ms. LA/UCLA 779 (box 3.3), fol. 98r (והר"י היה רגיל להקריא את הגט לאחר הנתינה וקודם הנתינה); *Tosafot Alfasi le-R. Mosheh b. Yom Tov mi-London* in *Shitat ha-Qadmonim 'al Massekhet Qiddushin*, ed. M. Blau (New York, 1970), 347–49; *Teshuvot Rabiah*, sec. 929; E. Kupfer, "Hilkhot ha-Get 'asher Yasad Rabbenu Yiẓḥaq b. Shemu'el," *Qoveẓ 'al Yad*, n.s. 6, pt. 1 (1966), 123–42; *Ba'alei ha-Tosafot 'al ha-Torah*, ed. Shraga Abramson (Jerusalem, 1974), 77–81; and "Sefer ha-Get le-Rabbenu Yiẓḥaq b. Shmu'el Talmid Rabbenu Tam," in *Me-Ḥiddushei Ba'alei ha-Tosafot le-Massekhet Gittin*, ed. Y. Satz (Toronto, 1989), 113–32.

[119] *Sefer ha-Mordekhai le-Massekhet Gittin*, ed. Rabinowitz, 788–94, sec. 205. Riẓba ruled on the validity of a *get* that came from Hungary (*'ereẓ Hagar*), but asked that his ruling be shown to his brother R. Samson (of Sens) and "our Rabbis in Paris" for verification.

[120] See ms. Parma De Rossi 1334, fol. 349r: כתובה דאירכסא . . . מועתק מיד ה"ר שמשון ב"ר אברהם משאנץ (dated *Tammuz*, 1209); S. Emanuel, *Shivrei Luḥot*, 255 (n. 145); and idem, "Ha-Meineqet ha-Noẓerit Bimei ha-Benayim: Halakhah ve-Historiyyah," *Zion* 73 (2008), 36 (n. 51). See also ms. Bodl. 875 (Germany, 1299), fol. 157v, col. 2 (end): כתובה דארכתא בחתימת ה"ר שניאור וה"ר יצחק המכונה שירא פנייש; and cf. S. E. Stern, *Me'orot ha-Rishonim*, 313–17 (from R. Meir of Rothenburg). See also *Sefer Or Zaru'a*, pt. 1, sec. 778 (וכבר בא משעה לפני רבינו שמשון בן אברהם . . . באשה שהיתה רגילה להיות דעתה מטורפת . . . והשיב רבינו שמשון בתשובה וכו'); and I. Agus, *Teshuvot Ba'alei ha-Tosafot*, 78–79 (#21: עיר שהנהר חוץ לעיבורה . . . היאך כותבין בגט . . . אם העיר מסתקפת מן הנהר לכל תשמישיה . . . כותבין שם העיר . . . ושלום שמשון בן אברהם).

[121] See *Teshuvot u-Pesaqim*, ed. Kupfer, 296–97, and G. Zinner, *Oẓar Pisqei ha-Rishonim 'al Hilkhot Pesaḥ*, 250 (sec. 13). On R. Barukh b. Isaac's status as a lifelong Frenchman, see S. Emanuel, "Ve-Ish 'al Meqomo Mevo'ar Shemo" (above, n. 29).

[122] R. Judah Sirleon of Paris compensated two witnesses (who were concerned about losing a portion of their livelihood) so that they could be available to sign a *get* (מעשה בגט אחד שלא רצו העדים לחתום מחמת שהיו טרודים בצרכיהם והשכירם ר' יהדוה מפריש ונתן לכל אחד ו' פשוטים); see the sources cited in Urbach, *Ba'alei ha-Tosafot*, 1:325 (n. 47). See also above, n. 121; *Mordekhai Qiddushin*, sec. 568; *Sefer ha-Mordekhai le-Massekhet Gittin*, ed. Rabinowitz, 328–33, 859–60; *Tosafot Alfasi le-R. Mosheh b. Yom Tov mi-London*, ed. M. Blau, 322–23 (*seder ḥaliẓah me-R. Yehudah b. Yiẓḥaq*); and ms. LA/UCLA 779 (bx. 3.3), fol. 100v, regarding the form of the shoe used for *ḥaliẓah*. Other rulings with regard to the *ḥaliẓah* shoe are cited in the name of R. Samson of Sens (fol. 101r) and R. Jacob of Verdun (fol. 101v, concerning how the shoe should be tied). R. Yaqar reports how R. Samuel of Evreux tied the shoe on the basis of a case that came before him (fol. 101v: ועושים הקשר על השוק מבחוץ. בשם הר"ר יקר שראה המעשה כך לפני רבינו שמואל מאיוורה).

[123] See, above, n. 113; *Sefer ha-Mordekhai le-Gittin*, ed. Rabinowitz, 860; ms. Montefiore 140, fol. 46v: סדר חליצה ממהר"ף. יבררו שלשה דיינים בתחלה ויוסיפו עליהם עוד שנים . . . ולא יהיו קרובים . . . נשלמו דיני חליצה מלשון ממהר"ף; *Haggahot Rabbenu Pereẓ* to *Semaq*, sec. 185; and ms. L.A./UCLA 779, fol. 97v (which mentions R. Yeḥi'el, his son-in law R. Isaac b. Joseph of Corbeil [author of *Semaq*],

writing and granting *gittin*) to the pattern that we have found with respect to rabbinic courts in northern France is striking, but not surprising. The extreme consequences and unusually complicated halakhic requirements inherent in Jewish divorce law required all leading scholars, even those who were perhaps not regularly or generally involved in the local judicial process, to lend their expertise and support. Moreover, the documentation for these kinds of proceedings was equally critical, which also helps to account for the court materials and documents that have survived with regard to matters of divorce. In light of the judicial patterns that have emerged in this study, it goes without saying that these activities were also within the purview of the rabbinic courts of Germany, and there are many records of both procedures and documents from them.[124]

---

and Rabbenu Pereẓ, above, n. 116); and see also fol. 92v (= ms. Vercelli C235, fol. 355d, recorded by R. Yeḥi'el's other son-in-law, R. Joseph b. Abraham), מו' חמי רבי' יחיאל מפאריש וחתנו מורי [גי'] הר"ר יצחק היו מונעי' מלכתוב לא מעינות ולא בארות במקום שיש נהר וכו' וכן הנהיג ה"ר פרץ מקורבילי בסוף ימיו והוא הנכון . . . אם יש עיר שאין בה נהרות ולא מים שאינם שותים . . . יכתוב שם העיר הסמוכה לה ומימיו. מלשון הר"ר יחיאל; and cf. S. Emanuel, *Shivrei Luḥot*, 217, and 95v (מעשה בא לפני מהר"ף באחד שהיה חולה והחליפו שמו בחליו . . . והצריך הרב ב' גיטין אחד בשם הראשון ואחד בשם השני ונתנם שניהם ביחד; this ruling is followed by related comments from R. Menaḥem of London and Rabiah, and rulings by R. Moses b. Yom Tov of London and R. Meir of Rothenberg are found on fol. 98v). For R. Isaac of Corbeil, see also *Sefer Orḥot Ḥayyim le-R. Aharon ha-Kohen mi-Lunel*, v. 2, 171–72 (והא לך הגט מלשון הר"י מקורביל), 182–84 (*seder ḥaliẓah shel ha-Ri mi-Corbeil*); and ms. LA UCLA 779, bx. 3.3, fol. 96r (in the margin). For a possible *ma'aseh beit din* in monetary law undertaken by R. Isaac of Corbeil, see H. Soloveitchik, *Halakhah, Kalkalah ve-Dimmui 'Aẓmi*, 66 (n. 25), 145–46. See also the *pesaqim* of R. Isaac of Corbeil published by Moshe Hershler in *Sinai* 61 (1970), 246 (#21), 248 (#56); the *pesaqim* published by Chaim Sha'anan in *Ner li-Shemayah (Sefer Zikkaron le-Zikhro shel ha-Rav Shemayah Sha'anan)*, ed. Sha'anan (Bnei Brak, 1988), 11 (#4), 14–15 (#18), 19 (#36); and *Haggahot Mordekhai*, *Shevu'ot*, sec. 789 (end).

124 See, e.g., *Teshuvot u-Pesaqim*, ed. Kupfer, 213–17: סדר חליצה מן ה"ר אליעזר בן שמואל ממיץ (R. Eliezer of Metz taught in both Metz and Mainz; see R. Reiner, "Rabbenu Tam," 110–13, and above, n. 110); ms. Warsaw 258, fol. 342r: סדר חליצה של מאור הגולה ר' שמחה ב"ר שמואל משפירא, and fol. 342v: גט חליצה . . . ונראה למורי ר' שמחה; *Haggahot Mamuniyyot*, *Hilkhot Gerushin* 4 [30]: וכן כתב רבינו שמחה בטופס גט בתיקון שטרות שלו, and cf. S. Emanuel, *Shivrei Luḥot*, 161–63; *Teshuvot u-Pesaqim*, ed. Kupfer, 218–20 (סדר חליצה מנימוקי רבינו שמחה בן אברהם מוורמייזא); and I. Ta-Shma, "Qeẓat 'Inyanei R. Yiẓḥaq Or Zaru'a mi-Ketav Yad," in *Sefer ha-Zikkaron le-R. Y. Y. Frankel*, ed. Y. Buksboim (Jerusalem, 1992), 272–80. (Note that R. Samuel b. Abraham *ha-Levi* was a prime student of R. Simḥah of Speyer [see S. Emanuel, *Shivrei Luḥot*, 181–84], and that R. Simḥah studied with R. Eliezer of Metz [see Urbach, *Ba'alei ha-Tosafot*, 1:411, and Reiner, "Rabbenu Tam," 111, n. 382].) See also *Teshuvot Rabiah*, ed. Deblitzky, sec. 922. Rabiah supervised the writing of *gittin* in Cologne, and R. Barukh b. Samuel oversaw the giving of these *gittin* in Mainz. Thus, R. Barukh writes to Rabiah: דע לך אדוני הראבי"ה כי הגט אשר הובא מקולוניא גוי הביאו אלי אשר על החתום . . . ואל ידיחני אדוני על רבותיי אשר אתנו כי תאבתי דעתך לדעת הן או לאו. Further on in *Teshuvot Rabiah*, sec. 922, there is a letter from R. Joel b. Isaac *ha-Levi* to the Mainz court of Rivaq, R. Moshe b. Mordekhai, and Barukh about the writing of a *get* that was to be received (from a different court of three), and then given by R. Barukh to the woman in question. See also *Sefer Rabiah*, vol. 4, sec. 894 (and the editor's introduction, 17–18, and 46–51), for a *ḥaliẓah* form (and other related documents), as well as instructions for the judges, composed by Raban and Rabiah. See also *Sefer ha-Mordekhai le-Massekhet Gittin*, ed. Rabinowitz, 795 (sec. 206), for a question from R. Hezekiah of Magdeburg to R. Avigdor Katz concerning a *get*. Cf. ms. JTS Rab. 673,

To sum up the judicial or *beit din* situation in northern France: While there is ample evidence for appeals that were sent by local courts to leading Tosafists in northern France, there is a noticeable period during which it is virtually impossible to document any kind of established, sitting court in a particular locale, or to find any leading Tosafists playing a role on particular rabbinic courts.[125] Rashbam and Rabbenu Tam did serve as court judges, as did students of Rabbenu Tam such as R. Ḥayyim *Kohen* and R. Yosef (*Bekhor Shor*) of Orleans. From the last quarter of the twelfth century until the second quarter of the thirteenth century, however, leading Tosafists in northern France responded to appeals and issued abstract rulings, but are not identified (with truly minor exceptions) as actively sitting in judgment. It seems improbable that they never actually served as judges (*dayyanim*) on a rabbinic court. For some reason, however, these experiences were not recorded or remarked upon in the rabbinic literature of the period, as they were extensively recorded for the Tosafists and rabbinic figures in Germany. This difference in attitude, if not in actual occurrence, is nonetheless highly significant.[126]

An exception to this pattern exists with regard to bills of divorce and related matters. Here it appears that all leading Tosafists did formally

fol. 377v; *Mordekhai Gittin*, ed. Rabinowitz, 859–61; and Ta-Shma, "Qeẓat Inyanei R. Yiẓḥaq Or Zaruʿa," for procedural rulings from Raban, Rabiah, and R. Isaac *Or Zaruʿa* of Vienna. See S. E. Stern, *Me'orot ha-Rishonim*, 348–60, for *get* material in *Sefer Assufot*, and idem, "Seder Gittin le-Rabbenu Yiẓḥaq b. Rabbenu Meir he-Ḥasid," *Ẓefunot* 4:2 [14] (1992), 7–13 (= idem., *Me'orot ha-Rishonim*, 336–48). R. Isaac b. Meir appears to have been a German contemporary of R. Isaac *Or Zaruʿa*, who (like R. Isaac *Or Zaruʿa*) also studied in northern France. Cf. Urbach, *Baʿalei ha-Tosafot*, 1:487.

125 The Tosafist R. Tuvyah of Vienne, a contemporary of R. Yeḥi'el of Paris, records in the name of Riẓba (d. 1209) that young men who caused damages to each other in the course of the merriment of the Purim festival ought not be summoned to a *beit din*. See Urbach, *Baʿalei ha-Tosafot*. Although undoubtedly unintentional, this rare reference to a *beit din* during this period (in the days of Riẓba) furthers the perception that the *beit din* was not seen as a locus of path-breaking rabbinic scholarship. For the context of R. Tuvyah's ruling, cf. my "*Halakhah* and *Meẓi'ut* (Realia) in Medieval Ashkenaz: Surveying the Parameters and Defining the Limits," *Jewish Law Annual* 14 (2003), 216–24.

126 As we have noted, a number of the prominent local judges in Germany during the late twelfth century had also studied in northern France with Rabbenu Tam. Although northern French *Tosafot* literature is generally far less discursive than contemporary German halakhic compendia and commentaries (which retain a great deal of logistical as well as halakhic details), references to Tosafists as judges (if they indeed served in such a capacity, or wished to be identified as such) could easily have been included without having to recount their judicial views or decisions at length. *Tosafot* texts certainly had no difficulty communicating the fact that Rabbenu Tam was an active rabbinic judge as well; see, e.g., above, n. 86. Moreover, *Sefer Or Zaruʿa* and *Sefer Mordekhai*, which contain many details about Jewish life in northern France (as well as Germany) throughout the twelfth and thirteenth centuries, are also very limited in the way in which they record judicial activities from northern France, as has been noted throughout this study. Cf. R. Reiner, "Rabbinic Courts in France" (above, n. 74), 316–17.

participate in some way (and are identified as such), either by providing and approving documents for divorce (and perhaps *ḥaliẓah*) or even by sitting on actual cases, as we would expect leading scholars to do, and as the German Tosafists certainly did. In matters of monetary law, however, and even with respect to marital law and inheritance (apart from the dissolution of marriage), there is almost no evidence for any participation by northern French Tosafists and their students and associates from approximately 1180 until 1220.

Interestingly, these differences with respect to judicial structure and participation coincide almost precisely with a period for which it is possible to detect a strong degree of separation between the northern French and German Tosafist centers. While Urbach presumed that there was ongoing contact between the rabbinic scholars of these different areas throughout the twelfth and thirteenth centuries, and that students, texts, and rulings moved freely between them,[127] more recent scholarship has indicated that, during this period, no German students went to study in northern France as had been the case during the days of Rabbenu Tam. There were also relatively few exchanges of responsa between the German centers and their counterparts among rabbinic scholars in France; the rabbinic authors in northern France generally did not cite contemporary German rabbinic figures and vice versa. Toward the end of the first quarter of the thirteenth century, R. Isaac b. Moses *Or Zaruʿa* ends this period of disconnection by studying with Rabiah and R. Simḥah of Speyer in Germany, and by traveling to northern France to study with R. Judah Sirleon and others. In addition, R. Isaac *Or Zaruʿa* and his contemporaries in central Germany sent questions to R. Yeḥiʾel of Paris and other northern French Tosafists.[128]

[127] See, e.g., Urbach, *Baʿalei ha-Tosafot*, 1:250, 345, although cf. 372–73. As we shall see throughout this study, there is also some question as to the extent (or even the existence) of this separation in other areas of intellectual endeavor, such as biblical interpretation, liturgical composition, and mystical studies.

[128] See H. Soloveitchik, *Halakhah, Kalkalah ve-Dimmui ʿAẓmi*, 82–85, 97–100; Y. Sussmann, "Mifʿalo ha-Maddaʿi shel Professor Ephraim Elimelekh Urbach," in *Musaf Maddaʿei ha-Yaḥadut* 1, ed. D. Assaf (Jerusalem, 1993), 39 (n. 63), 48–54; S. Emanuel, "Ve-Ish ʿal Meqomo Mevʾor Shemo," 436–40; and idem, *Shivrei Luḥot*, 189, nn. 118–119. Emanuel also considers the implications of this development for the theory of Israel Ta-Shma that northern French Tosafists began to compose halakhic works at the turn of the twelfth century under the influence of the German Pietists (and Tosafists). Given the period of disconnect, it would seem that northern French and German Tosafists arrived at the decision to begin to codify their talmudic and halakhic teachings and studies independently, although German Tosafists already in the twelfth century were inclined to pursue somewhat less sharp dialectical resolutions than their northern French counterparts. Cf. Ta-Shma, *Ha-Sifrut ha-Parshanit la-Talmud*, 2:116–17; idem, *Knesset Meḥqarim*, 1:369–70 (citing Y. N. Epstein); and see also Aptowitzer, *Mavo la-Rabiah*, 261–62, 264, 288; Emanuel, *Shivrei Luḥot*, 108, 155; idem, *R. Eleazar mi-Vermaiza—Derashah le-Pesaḥ*, 22–23, 50; Rami Reiner, "From Rabbenu Tam to R. Isaac of Vienna: The Hegemony of

To be sure, northern French texts from this period of separation do refer to actions taken by rabbinic courts, but it is exceedingly difficult to identify the judges who served on them. Even if leading Tosafists did serve, few reports of their service exist, and there are no records of communication between courts, which were so common in Germany. Where we do have evidence for *beit din* activity in northern France, that evidence suggests that courts were chosen, for the most part, through *zabla*. Although there is some evidence for *zabla* practices in Germany as well,[129] we have also seen that there were many fixed, local *battei din* in Germany often headed or manned by leading rabbinic scholars. The German *beit din* policy is underscored at the end of the thirteenth century by the report of Meir of Rothenburg's student, R. Samson b. Ẓadoq, who suggests that there were German cities with two sitting or established courts.[130] The preferred German approach was to establish cohesive, long-lasting rabbinic courts as institutions that endured through the generations.[131] Reflecting this approach, *Sefer Ḥasidim* decries the poor results that *zabla* selections can often yield: judges who are not particularly knowledgeable in Jewish law, and those who are insensitive to the litigants.[132] Established courts, consisting of prominent and experienced judges, could more effectively address, if not eliminate, these shortcomings.

---

the French Talmudic School in the Twelfth Century," in *The Jews of Europe in the Middle Ages*, ed. C. Cluse (Turnhout, 2004), 273–82; Uzi Fuchs, "ʿIyyunim be-Sefer Or Zaruʿa le-R. Yiẓḥaq b. Mosheh me-Vienna" (M.A. thesis, Hebrew University, 1993), 21–28; M. M. Hoenig, "ʿAl Mahadurato ha-Ḥadashah shel Sefer ha-Maskil le-R. Mosheh b. Eleazar ha-Kohen," *Yerushatenu* 1 (2007), 214–15 (n. 43); and above, n. 21.

129 See, e.g., *Sefer Raban*, fol. 224a; *Teshuvot Maharam defus Prague*, 917 (with additional detail in *Teshuvot Maharam*, ed. Cremona, 17; Urbach, *Baʿalei ha-Tosafot*, 1:367; and cf. M. Frank, *Qehillot Ashkenaz u-Battei Dineihen*, 152, n. 1): נחנו ח"מ הובררנו להיות ב"ד בין ר' יצחק הבא בהרשאת אמו אלמנת ר' שבתי ובין ר' אברהם וכבר באו לדין (בנורנבערק) [בוורצבערק] לפני ר' שמואל ב"ר מנחם הלוי ולפני ר' שמחה ב"ר גרשם וטענו בפניהם ולא נפסק שם דין . . . וכאשר הראנו מן השמים פסקנו וחתמנו, לוי ב"ר שלמה, משה ב"ר יצחק, יוסף ב"ר יעקב; S. Goldin, *Ha-Yiḥud veha-Yaḥad*, 116–19, 130–31; and above, nn. 25, 34, 108.

130 See Samson b. Ẓadoq, *Sefer Tashbeẓ*, sec. 516; and Goldin, *Ha-Yiḥud veha-Yaḥad*, 208 (n. 15).

131 Any comparison between the judiciaries within Jewish and Christian societies must be undertaken with caution, given the very different legal systems and underlying values involved. Nonetheless, it is interesting to note the relatively organized and effective judicial system in twelfth-century Cologne (featuring the *scabini*), which played a stabilizing communal role through much of the thirteenth century. See P. Strait, *Cologne in the Twelfth Century* (Gainesville, Fla., 1974), 24, 45–46, 61–68. See also S. Schwarzfuchs, *A Concise History of the Rabbinate*, 11–12.

132 See, e.g., *Sefer Ḥasidim* (Parma), secs. 1142, 1309–10, 1312, 1315, 1374. See also below (n. 156) for *Sefer Ḥasidim*'s support for the *ḥerem ha-qehillot* with regard to *battei din*, which was a communal attempt to insure that competent judges would hear cases, and cf. *Sefer Ḥasidim* (Parma), secs. 1313 (ואין נאה להיות דיין אלא דיין סביר וחכם) and 1301 (ויש מקומות שהגוים דנים באמת ולא היהודים מפני שמעט תלמידי חכמים שם).

Accounting for the Differences

Several explanations for these differences in judicial practice and perceptions may be suggested. In a number of respects, these differences are parallel to a distinction that has already been noted in modern scholarship between northern France and Germany concerning the writing and collection of responsa. Although there is ample evidence that northern French rabbinic scholars of the twelfth and thirteenth centuries wrote legal decisions (*pesaqim*) and to a lesser extent responsa (*she'elot u-teshuvot*) in response to particular queries, collections of responsa are preserved and circulated, for the most part, only within the writings of German rabbinic scholars.[133] Put simply, the leading rabbinic scholars of northern France did not feel the need to preserve the full records or even brief descriptions of the judicial decisions they may have rendered, just as they did not preserve their responsa in a significant or systematic way. In addition, the level of actual participation by leading scholars in the judicial process in northern France during the period appears to have been much lower than in Germany. We have also seen that some of the most important sources for judicial activity in Germany are to be found within the responsa produced by leading German Tosafists and halakhists.

On the logistical or societal side, the small size of the northern French Jewish communities, in particular, must be taken into account when considering the transitory status of the rabbinic courts. Indeed, as we have seen, there were occasionally situations in which many of the members of the community were related to all potential judges.[134] In Germany, however, smaller settlements had arrangements with larger ones to provide court services for them. One guiding principle directed that a smaller settlement that buried its dead in the cemetery of a larger, more established settlement was entitled to bring its judicial needs to the larger settlement as well.[135] The small size of the communities in northern France also meant that numbers of qualified scholars were not easily found in these populations, further diminishing the possibility of maintaining established courts.[136]

133 See, e.g. H. Soloveitchik, *Halakhah, Kalkalah ve-Dimmui 'Azmi* (above, n. 128); idem, "Catastrophe and Halakhic Creativity: Ashkenaz—1096, 1242, 1306 and 1298," *Jewish History* 12 (1998), 76–78. Cf. I. Ta-Shma's introduction to *Mafteaḥ ha-She'elot veha-Teshuvot shel Ḥakhmei Ashkenaz, Ẓarefat ve-Italyah*, ed. B. Lifshitz and E. Shochetman (Jerusalem, 1977), 11–13 (= *Knesset Meḥqarim*, 1:117–25); idem, *Knesset Meḥqarim*, 2:73–74; and S. Emanuel, "Ve-Ish 'al Meqomo Mevo'ar Shemo," 426–27. The fairly recent publication of *Teshuvot ha-Rabiah* serves as a stark reminder of this distinction.

134 See above, n. 80.

135 See above, n. 73.

136 Cf. *Sefer Ḥasidim*, sec. 1301 (above, n. 132).

Another possible societal factor relates to the use of existing non-Jewish or secular courts (*ʿarkaʾot*), especially with regard to monetary matters. This practice was decried in a super-communal ordinance promulgated at a synod in Troyes around the year 1150. Although a number of prominent German rabbinic scholars and leading communal judges such as Raban of Mainz and R. Eliezer b. Samson of Cologne were included among the signatories, this ordinance, and indeed the synod itself, was initiated by Rabbenu Tam and Rashbam, and was attended primarily by northern French leaders. The ordinance forbids any Jew from bringing litigation against another Jew before non-Jewish courts, and it forbids a Jew from using any connection to these courts and the secular authorities to his advantage in his case against another Jew[137] although, to be sure, later German authorities were vehemently opposed to *ʿarkaʾot* as well.[138]

[137] See L. Finkelstein, *Jewish Self-Government in the Middle Ages*, 41–43, 150–60. The prohibition against going to *ʿarkaʾot* may have been emphasized earlier in an ordinance attributed to Rabbenu Gershom of Mainz. See M. Elon, *Ha-Mishpat ha-ʿIvri*, 2:635 (n. 24).

[138] See *Mordekhai ha-Shalem ʿal Massekhet Bava Qamma*, ed. Halpern, 244–45 (secs. 195–96): מעשה בר׳ אפרים שהלך בערכאות של גוים וקבל על ר׳ יואל להכריחו שיעשה לו דין יהודים. ומתוך כך קבל ר׳ יואל על ר׳ אפרים והפסיד ממון לר׳ אפרים במסירתו. והשיב מור״ם [=ר׳ מאיר מרוטנבורג] יפה דנתם יפה זכיתם יפה חייבתם אלופיי ומיודעי ה״ר יצחק אתה ובית דנך. ואם אנו באים לדון אחר בית דין צריכים אנו לדום אחר כל בית דין ובית דין שעמד להם לישראל מימות משה ע״ה ועד עכשיו. ונהי שאף אותו ר׳ אפרים לא טוב עשה בעמיו וראוי לימתח על העמוד כי הלך לערכאות של גוים תחלה להכריח שכנגדו אע״ג שלא הכריחו אלא לדת ישראל לא היה לו לעשות דבר זה אלא על פי קהלו או על פי הגדולים שבמלכות ויקבל עליו את הדין ללקות או ליתן ממון הכל לפי מה שהוא אדם כאשר ישיתו עליו רבותינו שבמדינה. אמנם, ר׳ יואל חייב להשיב לר׳ אפרים כל ההפסד שהפסידו כמו שפסקת וכו׳. In this case, which occurred late in the thirteenth century, a Jew went to the secular court to compel his fellow Jew to come to the Jewish court (which in turn caused the other litigant to ask the secular court to adjudicate the case according to secular law). Cf. Urbach, *Baʿalei ha-Tosafot*, 2:537, and see also ibid., 512. R. Isaac b. Pereẓ of Northampton, England (mid-thirteenth century), ruled that if an agreement had been made to hear a case in the secular court, even though this was clearly not preferred, the case could not be heard again in a *beit din* because of the principle of *dina de-malkhuta dina*. See also the *pesaq* of R. Isaac of Corbeil (d. 1280), ed. Sha'anan (above, n. 123), 26 (#26): עוד משמו, כשאדם מכה חבירו והמכה אומר אפרע לך נזק וצער ושבת ורפוי, אבל לא בושת שזהו קנס ולא מגבינן בבבל, שלא היה כופה המוכה לעשות לחבירו דין חכמים אלא מותר למוכה לשים אותו בערכאות של גוים. See also *Sefer Or Zaruʿa*, at the very beginning of pt. 3 (*hilkhot ʿarkaʾot*, based largely on earlier Sefardic authorities), and see also the responsa section at the end of pt. 1, sec. 745 (fol. 105b); and *hilkhot gittin*, sec. 705 (fol. 99b). As Urbach notes, however (*Baʿalei ha-Tosafot*, 2:513, n. 5), Maharam's student R. Asher b. Yeḥiʾel was unequivocally against any recourse to *ʿarkaʾot*. In sum, although it is difficult to demonstrate that this problem was exclusively French, the evidence from northern France is more suggestive. Cf. Zvi Avineri, "Peniyyah le-Arkaʾot," *Zion* 25 (1960), 57–60. Note also the view of R. Isaac of Evreux (*Mordekhai le-Gittin*, sec. 384; cf. above, n. 1) that the *shivʿah tuvei ha-ʿir* could assess biblically mandated fines. Cf. Isaiah di Trani, *Sefer ha-Makhriʿa*, ed. S. A. Wertheimer (Jerusalem, 1998), 473–76 (sec. 76), who insisted that no such fines could be adjudicated any longer, and R. Barukh b. Samuel of Mainz (*Mordekhai le-Gittin*, sec. 384), who would not allow biblical fines to be collected but did allow a rabbinic court to levy fines for purposes of enforcement as it saw fit. See also *Teshuvot u-Pesaqim*, ed. Kupfer, 150–51; *Sefer Or Zaruʿa, pisqei Bava Qamma*, sec. 96–97; *Teshuvot Maharam defus Prague*, #994; I. Agus, *Teshuvot Baʿalei ha-Tosafot*, 146; and *Sefer Yereʾim le-R. Eliʿezer mi-Metz*, sec. 164. On the coercive powers of the *shivʿah tuvei ha-ʿir* to extract certain types of monetary obligations, see also *Teshuvot Rabiah*, sec. 997 (above, n. 42).

In addition to these societal or logistical issues, there is a personal or ideological dimension that should be considered. In a text referred to earlier, the Cologne judge R. Ḥayyim b. Yeḥi'el *Ḥefeẓ Zahav* states that "if it were up to me, I would prefer that no case should come before me." Although R. Ḥayyim's comment in context appears to be directed to an appeal that came to him from a different city (Boppard), it points to another consideration as well. For a scholar to serve as an active communal judge raised at least the distinct possibility of his being taxed and bombarded with all kinds of cases and questions. This burdensome communal responsibility could certainly curtail the scholar's own creative scholarship.[139]

R. Ḥayyim does not, of course, directly enunciate this consideration, but the value of uninterrupted Talmudic studies or instruction, as opposed to serving the community as a rabbinic decisor or *dayyan*, was debated rather explicitly by rabbinic figures in other periods.[140] In addition, there is anecdotal evidence from the medieval period for the heavy burden placed on the scholar who served a community as both its central *rosh yeshivah* and *dayyan.*[141]

Moreover, R. Ephraim b. Samson, an Ashkenazic biblical commentator associated with R. Eleazar of Worms, interprets the advice given to Moses by his father-in-law, Yitro, to appoint lower courts and judges so that he would not have to handle all judicial cases by himself, in precisely this manner. Yitro concludes (Ex. 18:23) by asserting that only if Moses implements the proposed system would he be able to function properly as a leader. According to the literal phrasing of this verse, Moses "would be able to stand" (*ve-yakholta 'amod*). In R. Ephraim's comment, Moses would be able to stand whenever he wished and would not be required "to sit from dawn until dusk in judgment (*ba-din*), thereby forgoing his ability to engage in Torah study (*ule-vattel Talmud Torah*)."[142]

139 See above, n. 73; M. Frank, *Qehillot Ashkenaz u-Battein Dineihen*, 27–28; and B. Buchman, "Jewish Courts in Western Europe during the High Middle Ages" (M.A. thesis, Yeshiva University, 1975), 39. Cf. *Sefer Miẓvot Gadol le-R. Mosheh mi-Coucy, miẓvat 'aseh* 97: צריכין הדיינין להתרחק בכל היכולת שלא יקבלו עליהן לדון דין תורה כי מאוד נתמעטו הלבבות. In context, however, this formulation (which is based on a passage in *Talmud Yerushalmi Sanhedrin* 1:1), admonishes the *dayyan* not to attempt to judge a case according to pure Torah law (without any recourse to compromise). It does not recommend that a qualified judge attempt to "step away" from hearing cases or that he refuse to adjudicate them. Cf. *Sefer ha-Ḥinnukh, miẓvah* 116, end: ודרך החכמים הראשונים שבורחין מלהתמנות דיינים אלא במקום שאין גדול מהם.

140 See, e.g., Immanuel Etkes, "Bein Lamdanut le-Rabbanut be-Yaḥadut Lita shel ha-Me'ah ha-Yod Tet," *Zion* 53 (1988), 385–403.

141 See, e.g., *Sefer ha-Qabbalah*, ed. G. D. Cohen (Philadelphia, 1967), 47–48 (Hebrew text), referring to R. Nathan of Cordoba; and A. H. Freimann, *Ha-Rosh ve-Ze'eza'av* (Jerusalem, 1986), 32–33, focusing on R. Asher b. Yeḥi'el's career in Toledo.

142 See *Perush R. Ephraim b. Shimshon 'al ha-Torah*, ed. J. Klugmann (Jerusalem, 2000), 239, and *Tosafot ha-Shalem*, ed. Y. Gellis, vol. 8 (Jerusalem, 1990), 34. This interpretation is cited without

To my mind, however, the most compelling interpretation or explanation for the differences that we have noted between northern France and Germany relates to the intellectual lives and roles of rabbinic scholars but has a significant societal aspect as well. A crucial consideration here is the role of the rabbinic court, as opposed to the *beit midrash* or academy (*yeshivah*), as the seat of religious leadership and power within the communities of Ashkenaz. To put it simply, the notion developed in Germany that leading scholars could best serve the community, and could exert the greatest positive influence, as masters of and participants in the rabbinical courts. Many of the German scholars whom we have discussed also headed study halls or *yeshivot*, but it must be kept in mind that the largest and most prominent Tosafist study halls consisted of twenty-five or so students at one time, and the average size was more likely to be in the mid-teens.[143]

Simcha Emanuel has noted that R. Barukh b. Samuel of Mainz, a prominent judge and author of the voluminous *Sefer ha-Ḥokhmah* (which while extant only in fragments was devoted in large measure to monetary law and *Seder Neziqin*), does not seem to have had any students of whom we are aware. Emanuel concludes that R. Barukh was in fact only a judge and not an academy head at all. Indeed, R. Barukh includes a significant selection of the judicial decisions and cases of the Mainz court within *Sefer ha-Ḥokhmah*, in addition to his own talmudic interpretations and applications.[144] I suspect that the same kind of characterization may be true for R. Menaḥem b. Jacob of Worms as well (although there are almost no literary remains from him), and also in large measure for R. Joel b. Isaac *ha-Levi* of Bonn.[145] Older German contemporaries of R. Barukh, including his teacher R. Ephraim of Regensburg and R. Ephraim's colleagues on the *beit din* in Regensburg, R. Isaac b. Mordekhai and R. Moses b. Joel, did have students, just as they

---

attribution by the Tosafist Torah commentary *Moshav Zeqenim*, ed. D. Sassoon, 156. As Gellis notes, R. Ḥayyim Azulai (Ḥida) attributes this comment to R. Eleazar of Worms (who served as a communal *dayyan*; see above, nn. 13–16). See also *Nimmuqei Ḥumash le-Rabbenu Yeshayah di-Trani*, ed. C. B. Chavel (Jerusalem, 1972), 44.

143 See my *Jewish Education and Society in the High Middle Ages*, 66–67. As noted above (at n. 8), the study hall in Mainz appears to have been somewhat secondary to the rabbinic court there.

144 See S. Emanuel, "R. Barukh mi-Magenẓa," esp. 154 (= *Shivrei Luḥot*, 146).

145 See Urbach, *Ba'alei ha-Tosafot*, 1:370, 406. R. Menaḥem b. Jacob is mentioned by Urbach only twice in *Ba'alei ha-Tosafot*, once in disagreement with the suggestion by Aptowitzer that Menaḥem b. Jacob is the R. Menaḥem *he-Ḥasid* referred to by Rivaq of Speyer (in his *Sefer Yiḥusei Tanna'im va-Amora'im*), and once when listing a decision of the Worms court of which R. Menaḥem b. Jacob was a member. Aptowitzer, who was somewhat more attuned to the significance of German rabbinic communal authorities, has a fairly substantial entry on R. Menaḥem b. Jacob. See *Mavo la-Rabiah*, 382–84, and above, Introduction, n. 90. For R. Joel *ha-Levi*, see above, n. 38.

also composed and circulated *Tosafot* texts. At the same time, however, they were also active judges who were especially involved in rendering opinions and writing in the area of monetary law (*dinei mamonot*).[146]

In addition, or perhaps as a cause, leading German Tosafists and rabbinic scholars appear to have retained the notion, prevalent in the Rhineland during the pre-Crusade period, of identifying institutions (including academies) by their community or locale and its traditions rather than by the important scholars who taught in them. Thus the *rosh yeshivah* was in a less central position in Germany. In northern France, on the other hand, there was a consistent and strong belief that the *rosh yeshivah* was, in effect, the most important distinguishing aspect of an academy. The person who served as *rosh yeshivah* was more significant than the office of *rosh yeshivah* as an educational institution. Students followed leading scholars as they changed locales, and they identified with them in particular rather than with the location of the academy or its practices. Thus while it is possible to speak about the pre-Crusade Mainz commentary (*Perushei Magenza*) to various tractates, we invariably refer to *Tosafot Ri* or *Tosafot R. Yehudah Sirleon.*[147]

146 See above, nn. 27–28. Note also the curious but interesting correlation between *mishpat* and *piyyut*, found among those German rabbinic scholars who were both prolific *payyetanim* and recognized communal judges, such as R. Ephraim of Regensburg, R. Ephraim of Bonn, R. Barukh of Mainz, and R. Menaḥem b. Jacob of Worms, among others; see below, chapter 5. The state of affairs in Germany may perhaps also account for the lengthy period, between R. Barukh of Mainz (d. 1221) and Rabiah (d. c. 1225), and R. Meir of Rothenburg (d. 1293), during which there do not seem to have been any other rabbinic figures of their stature in Germany, a noticeable gap to which Simcha Emanuel called attention in his paper at the Fifteenth World Congress of Jewish Studies (Jerusalem, 2009) titled "The Sages of Germany in the Thirteenth Century: Continuity and Changes" (Hebrew). German Tosafists may not have had as many students and successors on the whole (and certainly fewer than their Tosafist counterparts in northern France) owing to their preoccupation with judicial functions and activities.

147 On *perushei Magenza*, see below, n. 216. For the pre-Crusade period, see also *Teshuvot Rabbenu Gershom Ma'or ha-Golah*, ed. S. Eidelberg (New York, 1955), 98–99 (#32): אם יש למול נער בראש השנה . . . שאירע במגנצא מילה בר"ה, ושאלו לקדושים אשר בארץ רבי' גרשום ב"ר יהודה מאור הגולה ורבינו שמעון הגדול ב"ר יצחק ורבי' יהודה הכהן שעשה ספר הדינין . . . ושאר בני הישיבה הקדושה, והורו כולם למול הנער לאחר קריאת התורה; and see also below, n. 215. For a parallel situation in the twelfth century, see *Sefer Or Zaru'a*, vol. 4, *pisqei 'avodah zarah*, sec. 262. R. Isaac *Or Zaru'a* records that when he was a young student of R. Judah Sirleon in Paris, R. Judah was approached after the prayer services, in front of his home, while a group of students and residents were in his presence. R. Judah was asked a practical question concerning *notein ta'am lifgam*, and he immediately issued a (permissive) ruling. No students offered or were called on for their opinions. For a fuller discussion of these distinctions (including parallels to educational conventions in medieval Christian society), see my *Jewish Education and Society in the High Middle Ages* (above, n. 2). As noted there as well, the so-called *Tosafot Shanz* were not the product of their locale per se but are rather the *Tosafot* composed by R. Samson of Sens, the leading student of Ri (and Rabbenu Tam), who established his *beit midrash* in Sens. See also below, nn. 222–23.

Moreover, there are a series of northern French rabbinic texts which describe how students could and should attempt to challenge the *rosh yeshivah* on the basis of their best understanding of talmudic and rabbinic texts. Scholarly reputations were to be made on the basis of intellectual and exegetical abilities and skills. According to Ri, as opposed to the talmudic period in which the teacher had access to bodies of knowledge and a depth of analysis that were not easily available to students, in his day, with the appearance and availability of talmudic commentaries and post-talmudic halakhic texts, a student could more easily achieve the ability to rule in matters of Jewish law.[148]

In the words of R. Samson of Sens, "That which was hidden to earlier scholars is sometimes revealed to later scholars . . . for a student can sometimes see what his teacher cannot from its [the Talmud's] words. He can 'outsmart' his teacher and focus his [teacher's] interpretation."[149] Indeed, the Tosafist academy heads R. Moses and R. Samuel of Evreux (d. c. 1250) wrote that demonstrations of reverence which a student must show his main teacher according to talmudic law were no longer required. "For the talmudic texts, the commentaries, the novellae, the [halakhic] composition, they are the teachers of men. And all is determined by one's perspicacity. And thus, it was usual in their locale that a student opened his own study hall without concern for the talmudic dictum that 'one who decides a matter of law in his teacher's presence is punishable by death.' Similarly, a student, on the basis of superior reasoning, can contradict his teacher."[150] According to the brothers of Evreux, the right of a student to open his own academy, in competition as it were with his teacher, is predicated solely on the ability that the student has to convincingly demonstrate his interpretations and positions with respect to talmudic literature and law. In northern France, the concept of the academy head as the central figure in the

[148] See *Sefer Semaq mi-Ẓurikh*, ed. Y. Har-Shoshanim, vol. 1 (Jerusalem, 1973), 275 (as corrected by ms. Moscow-Guenzberg 187, fols. 49v, and ms. Berlin 37 (Cat. Steinschneider), fols. 49r–v; and cf. my "Rabbinic Authority and the Right to Open an Academy in Medieval Ashkenaz," *Michael* 12 (1991), 242 (nn. 29–30).

[149] See R. Meir b. Todros *ha-Levi* Abulafia (Ramah), *Kit'ab al Ras<>il*, ed. Jehiel Brill (Paris, 1871), 131–32: ופעמים נגלים לאחרונים הצפונים לראשונים, והוי רץ למשנה ולתלמוד כי יש תלמיד רואה מה שאין רבו רואה מדבריו, מחכים את רבו ומכוין את שמועתו. See also above, Introduction, n. 101.

[150] The statement of the brothers of Evreux is found in an epistle (*'iggeret*) composed by them and preserved in *Sefer Orḥot Ḥayyim le-R. Aharon ha-Kohen mi-Lunel* (ed. Florence, repr. Jerusalem, 1986), *hilkhot Talmud Torah*, sec. 21 (fols. 29a–b): אין לנו עוד לומר מורא רבך כמורא שמים. וכל הדינים הראויין לעשות תלמיד לרבו נתבטלו כי הגמרות והפירושים והחידושין והחיבורים הם המורים אנשים והכל לפי פקחות הלבבות. ולכך היו רגילים שבעירם יחזיק התלמיד [בית] מדרש ולא אמרי' בהא כל המורה הלכה בפני רבו חייב מיתה. וכן יסתור דבריו התלמיד לרב אם יוכל לפי פלפולו. This letter is cited, with slight variation, in *Teshuvot Maharashdam, Ḥoshen Mishpat*, #1. See also Urbach, *Ba'alei ha-Tosafot*, 1:4799–80; and M. Elon, "The Law, Books and Libraries," *National Jewish Law Review* 2 (1987), 16–18.

Jewish intellectual and halakhic community reigned supreme, and was to be linked most closely to the virtuosity of the aspiring scholar.[151]

All of these phenomena relate to the issue of rabbinic leadership and power as well. Does rabbinic leadership derive primarily from one's ability to discover *ḥiddushim* (novellae), an ability that resides in the person of the academy head and his students (the model in northern France), or is leadership the province of the most authoritative source of Jewish law and tradition, a *dayyan* (judge) and his associates (the model favored in Germany)? These two aims, of course, are not mutually exclusive; the issue is really only one of emphasis.[152] Indeed, during the pre-Crusade period, the differences between northern France and Germany in these matters appear to have been much less pronounced,[153] as is the case for the second half of the thirteenth century and beyond, once the period of separation noted above had ended.

[151] For a full discussion of the formulations of Ri (including some significant variants), Rash *mi-Shanz*, and the brothers of Evreux and other related rabbinic formulations, as well as the implications for the intellectual and institutional history of medieval Ashkenazic Jewry, see my "Rabbinic Authority and the Right to Open an Academy in Medieval Ashkenaz," 233–50, and my "Progress and Tradition in Medieval Ashkenaz," *Jewish History* 14 (2000), 287–315. (Note that R. Meir of Rothenburg offers a formulation similar to that of Ri, but R. Meir focuses more on the availability of data to assist in the decision-making process than on the interpretive skills of the student. This may be a reflection, however, of Maharam's vantage point in the late thirteenth century—when Ashkenazic Jewry experienced serious reversals and decline—rather than a distinctly German view of Ri's academic conception.)

[152] Our focus on the judicial matters here has been limited to communal *battei din*, and has not taken into account *taqqanot ha-qahal* or the functioning of the *qehillah* itself as a *beit din* with respect to setting communal policy. Similarly, we have not discussed the role of rabbinic scholars in super-communal government (and the promulgating of *taqqanot*), where it may be assumed that, of necessity, leading figures would be more inclined to be involved. Nonetheless, it is interesting to note which prominent Tosafists and local communal judges are among the signatories on the various super-communal *taqqanot* promulgated during the twelfth and thirteenth centuries. See, e.g., L. Finkelstein, *Jewish Self-Government in the Middle Ages*, 42 (Raban of Mainz, Eliezer b. Samson of Cologne), 62–63 (Eleazar of Worms, Rabiah, Simḥah of Speyer, Barukh of Mainz), 155 (Rabbenu Tam, Rashbam, Raban), 165 (Rabbenu Tam), 198 (Yeḥiʾel of Paris), 223 (David b. Qalonymus of Muenzberg). Note also the roles played by a number of these rabbinic scholars in applying the תקנת רבינו תם and the תקנת קהילות שו"ם, which stipulated that the wife's family was entitled to receive back her dowry if she died within the first year of marriage. See Y. Cohen, "Taqqanot ha-Qahal bi-Yerushat ha-Baʿal ʾet Ishto" (above, n. 71), 148–50.

[153] A full analysis of pre-Crusade judicial antecedents cannot be undertaken here. There is evidence that Rashi served on a court in Troyes. He is signed on a judicial decision after a R. Zerah, an older contemporary who had been a judge in Troyes prior to Rashi's return from the academies of the Rhineland. See *Teshuvot Rashi*, ed. I. Elfenbein (New York, 1943), 74, and A. Grossman, *Ḥakhmei Ashkenaz ha-Rishonim* (Jerusalem, 1995), 131 (n. 33), for additional evidence. The Solomon b. Isaac who served as a judge with R. Yosef *Bekhor Shor* of Orleans (noted also by Grossman) is someone other than Rashi; see above, nn. 80–82. The phrases employed by Rashi, ואני איני כחולק על ישיבתו של רבי כי נוהגין איסור בהן עד שאזכה לחזור ולדון לפניו ויודה לדברי כאשר דנתי לפניו על עסקי וכו' . . . ולבסוף דנתי לפניו והודה לדברי (*Teshuvot Rashi*, #103/1, end), were offered in the context of a case of *muqzeh*, and characterize Rashi's competing interpretation of the Sabbath laws with that of his teacher, R. Isaac *ha-Levi*, rather than a court

R. Barukh b. Samuel of Mainz penned a responsum in answer to a question about a person who was doing business in England and had entrusted another person who had been with him there to take a certain amount of money back home to his wife. On the way back, the agent invested the money and made a profit through moneylending. The person who had sent the money demanded that the agent return both the principal and the interest to him, while the agent maintained that the interest was his alone, since he had undertaken sole responsibility for the loan. A *beit din* ruled that the sender was indeed entitled to the principal and to the interest. At this point, the agent summoned the judges of that court before another rabbinical court, where the original judges were asked to explain their reasoning. From this discussion it becomes clear that the original court had been chosen through *zabla.* Nonetheless, this first set of judges (presumably not the greatest of scholars) maintained that they had consulted with "many rabbis" about the case, and these rabbinic figures had agreed with the decision rendered. A complex series of negotiations ensued, which included the possibility of yet another court being chosen to decide the case. Ultimately, R. Barukh and other leading German Tosafists, including Rabiah and his father, R. Yo'el ha-*Levi*, were asked for their opinions.[154]

R. Barukh ruled in favor of the agent. Since he had taken responsibility for the money (i.e, since he made use of the money without authorization and would have been required to replace the money had it been lost), the agent is entitled to the profits earned with that money. More important for our purposes, however, is R. Barukh's response regarding whether one court can be summoned before another to question the decision of the original judges; R. Barukh states that this is completely appropriate. Moreover, according to R. Barukh, it is "a regular occurrence" (*ma'asim she-bekhol yom*) that judges' actions are questioned and that judges are brought before a second court to explain their decisions. Moreover, there is no communal enactment or rule (*ḥerem* or *takkanat ha-qehillot*) that restricts the litigant's right to appeal a court's decision. The assumption of the litigants who accepted the original court is that they would judge according to Torah law. If it was believed that they did not, their decision was subject to appeal.[155]

---

case of any kind. Cf. M. Breuer, "Le-Ḥeqer ha-Tippologiyyah shel Yeshivot ha-Ma'arav Bimei ha-Benayim," 46, and above, nn. 7, 36. *Sefer Or Zaru'a, pisqei Bava Qamma*, sec. 85, records a responsum by Rashi to three judges (*sheloshet ha-nedivim*) with respect to the *ketubah* of a woman who had developed certain blemishes. See also H. Soloveitchik, "Pawnbroking: A Study in Usury and of the Halakhah in Exile," 205–7. For the relationship between judicial practices in fifteenth-century Germany and those of the earlier (medieval) period, see Yedidyah Dinari, *Ḥakhmei Ashkenaz be-Shilhei Yemei ha-Benayim* (Jerusalem, 1984), 125–34.

154 See *Sefer Rabiah*, vol. 4, sec. 916, and *Teshuvot Rabiah*, #957 (referred to above, n. 17).

155 For the full text of this responsum, based on ms. Parma 86, see S. Emanuel, "R. Barukh mi-Magenẓa," 155–59. On appeals in the Jewish judicial system, see E. Shochetman, *Sidrei*

As noted, R. Barukh of Mainz was not the only German rabbinic decisor to respond to the case of the money-lending agent, but only his response raises this crucial larger issue. In R. Barukh's view, a local court is obligated to hear the case and to try to get it right; if they do not, however, the case can be appealed. Indeed, this is the goal of the *ḥerem ha-qehillot* mentioned by R. Barukh, which required judges to serve but did not prohibit appeals. The kind of *ḥerem ha-qehillot* to which R. Barukh refers is also described in *Sefer Ḥasidim* as a local, communal ruling.[156]

Although we cannot be certain that all or even most German communities participated in this *ḥerem ha-qehillot*, there is no evidence for such a *ḥerem ha-qehillot* anywhere within northern France. As we have seen, R. Samson of Sens held that a litigant cannot demand to take his case to a more prominent court, and must be content to present the case to a local court that was chosen via *zabla*, with the assumption that a qualified judge would be selected.[157] While German communal policy allowed the litigants

---

ha-Din (Jerusalem, 1988), 445–75, and cf. *Semag* (above, n. 139). In another formulation on this matter from his *Sefer ha-Ḥokhmah*, R. Barukh notes that since there is a standing communal ban (*ḥerem ha-qehillot*) that forces judges (who have been selected *be-zabla*, or an established court that has been requested to hear a particular case) to decide the case and prohibits them from choosing not to serve, these judges do not have to pay for their judicial errors. However, these judges do have to allow their cases to be reviewed, and they have to vacate their judgment if, upon review, it is deemed to be incorrect. See *Teshuvot Maharam*, ed. Prague, #715; *Mordekhai Sanhedrin*, sec. 666–67 (= ms. Budapest 2*1, fol. 192v). Cf. Emanuel, 158 (n. 166), and S. Goldin, *Ha-Yiḥud veha-Yaḥad*, 133.

156 See *Sefer Ḥasidim* (Parma), sec. 980 (p. 337, and cf. above, n. 132): ושמו הקהל חרם כשבעלי הדין יבררו בית דין שלא יוכלו בית דין למנוע מלישב בדין. Cf. M. Frank, *Qehillot Ashkenaz u-Battei Dineihen*, 100–103, and S. Goldin, *Ha-Yiḥud veha-Yaḥad*, 118–19.

157 See above, n. 108 (*Sefer Or Zaru'a*, vol. 3, *pisqei Bava Qamma*, sec. 436, et al.). In some versions of R. Samson's formulation, this policy is characterized as a *ḥerem beit din*. Interestingly, R. Meir of Rothenburg refers to the more limited German version of this policy as a part of *taqqanat ha-qehillot* (*Sefer Mordekhai ʿal Massekhet Sanhedrin*, sec. 707): ועוד השיב ר"מ [ר' מאיר] כך ראיתי בתקנת הקהלות שאם אחד מבעלי דינין טוען לשלוח למרחקים ויש חכם סמוך להם ורואין הדיינין שהוא מתכוין להפסיד בשכירות השליח, אין שומעין לו לפי שהדברים ניכרין שהוא מתכוין לדחייה ולהפסידו . . . אלא כופין אותו לדון בעירו. On the permissibility for a lone expert judge to rule (*yaḥid mumḥeh dan yehidi*), which is implicit in the first part of *Or Zaru'a*'s presentation of R. Samson's views, cf. above, n. 45 and at n. 79; and see S. W. Baron, *The Jewish Community* (Philadelphia, 1942), 2:215. Cf. *Teshuvot Mahari Weil*, #155, ed. Y. S. David (Jerusalem, 2001), 200. In practice, however, it seems that this was not often done, as the body of evidence in the present study suggests. According to *Sefer Or Zaru'a*, vol. 4, *pisqei Sanhedrin*, sec. 7, a *yaḥid mumḥeh* could be utilized (at least in theory) only when one of the litigants refused to come to any tribunal for judgment. See also *ʾArbaʿah Turim, Ḥoshen Mishpat*, sec. 3. To be sure, there was often a *leading* judge among the three, but he had others sitting with him on the court, at least nominally. Indeed, this possibility appears to have been part of R. Samson's assumption, according to *Sefer Or Zaru'a, pisqei Bava Qamma*, sec. 436. See also Isaiah di Trani, *Sefer ha-Makhriʿa*, ed. Wertheimer, 186–87 (sec. 32); *Perush ha-Rosh le-Sanhedrin*, 1:4; *Teshuvot Maharaḥ Or Zaru'a*, #13; M. Frank, *Qehillot Ashkenaz u-Battei Dineihen*, 20, 30–33; B. Buchman, "Jewish Courts in Western Europe during the Middle Ages," 41–42; and E. Shochetman, *Sidrei ha-Din*, 18–23. Once, however, a court had convened and

greater flexibility in selecting a court,[158] the *ḥerem ha-qehillot* stipulated that, once a court had been selected, it could not abdicate its responsibility. In this study, we have been able to note the presence of established courts during the days of R. Barukh b. Samuel and R. Judah *he-Ḥasid* only in Germany.

German Jewry was more aggressive than its northern French counterpart in forcing judges to serve, just as they were more successful in maintaining established courts throughout their communities.[159] This societal approach should be linked with the attitude of the German Tosafists and other rabbinic scholars seen throughout this discussion, who considered serving on a *beit din* to be the highest form of religious leadership.[160]

Distinctions between rabbinic scholarship in northern France and in Germany can be seen not only with respect to the larger educational,

---

issued its ruling, appeals were made either to other courts or most often to singular scholars (*gedolim*) for their guidance.

[158] See the continuation of R. Meir of Rothenburg's formulation in the above note: ע"כ אם הדיינין אומרים נשלח לחכם שבסמוך וחבירו אומר נשלח למרחוק . . . אם יש ב"ד בקי סמוך לעירם . . . אין נכון שישלח למרחוק וישכיר שליח בעשרים דינרים אע"פ שאותו חכם הרחוק חכם יותר מן החכם שבסמוך וכו'. A case cannot be sent to a more distant (superior) court or scholar if the local judges perceive that the litigant who had requested this is doing so simply to have the other litigant incur additional expenses (for messengers and so forth). For legitimate causes, however, a case could apparently be sent to a more prominent court. See also above at n. 69, where, according to long-standing German policy, an established communal court, even if distant, could be selected by the litigants in a number of situations (such as instances of a more serious offense). Cf. L. Finkelstein, *Jewish Self-Government in the Middle Ages*, 381, and above, nn. 25, 34.

[159] Compare also the nuanced difference between R. Eliezer b. Nathan of Mainz (as cited by *Teshuvot Maharam*) and R. Samson of Sens (above, n. 108) in their characterizations of the absence in their day of a *beit din ha-gadol* or *beit ha-va'ad* and the impact of that absence. For R. Samson, what is missing is a group of scholars whose collective erudition would shame any other judge or court beneath them who rules improperly. For Raban, what is missing is a central, stable place for scholars to gather so that they can arrive, through their setting, at an absolutely just decision. For R. Samson, the judge (as a person) makes the high court. For Raban, the court (as an institution) makes the judge. Cf. Rashi, *Sanhedrin* 94a, s.v. *beit ha-va'ad*, and *Tosafot Bava Qamma*, s.v. *mazi ta'in le-beit ha-din ha-gadol*. Note also the *ḥerem beit din* attributed to Rabbenu Tam (see Finkelstein, 48, 176): *maqom she-dar bah rav gadol mi-qodem, mistama yesh sham ḥerem beit din ve-danin shamah*. Any community in which a prominent rabbi is known to have lived may assume that he established a regular court (*ḥerem beit din*), so that any (current) court there may compel the residents to obey its summons and decrees. Cf. *Sefer ha-Yashar*, ed. Rosenthal, 67; and U. Fuchs (above, n. 87).

[160] Cf. Ta-Shma, *Ha-Sifrut ha-Parshanit la-Talmud*, 1:70. Ta-Shma makes a distinction between Riba, the earliest German Tosafist, who, like a judge, wished (especially as reflected in his responsa that are recorded in *Sefer Raban*) to distinguish (*le-ḥaleq ule-havdil*) between talmudic *sugyot* that appeared to be similar, in order to distill which *sugyot* were relevant to the case before him. Early northern French Tosafists, on the other hand, tended to seek similarities and connections rather than differences between the various talmudic *sugyot* and the case before them. The French Tosafists were like lawyers who wished to garner as much supporting law as possible, while Riba was like a judge who had to decide between the positions presented. His task was therefore to remove from consideration as much material as possible in order to leave only the most relevant material before him so that he could render his decision.

methodological, and literary issues that we have described to this point[161] but also with respect to more discrete positions and approaches taken in matters of Jewish law, legal interpretation, and thought.[162] Nearly twenty-five years ago, I demonstrated that Tosafist and other rabbinic attitudes toward *ʿaliyyah* during the twelfth and thirteenth centuries broke down primarily along northern French and German lines, a conclusion that subsequent scholarship has ratified and further refined.[163] Similarly, Israel Ta-Shma has shown that the halakhic sensibilities toward permitting a non-Jewish servant to raise the heat in the home on the Sabbath reflect a northern French and German divide,[164] as Simcha Emanuel has shown more recently with respect to concerns for *bittul shiddukhin.*[165]

[161] See also the studies cited above, nn. 128, 133. In my "Yeʿadei Limmud ve-Dimmui Aẓmi Eẓel Ḥakhmei ha-Talmud Be-Eiropah Bimei ha-Benayim," in the *Jubilee Volume for Prof. Yosef Hacker*, ed. Y. Kaplan et al. (Jerusalem, 2012; in press), I demonstrate that there were significant differences between northern French and German Tosafists with respect to the scope of their study of the tractates in *Seder Qodashim.*

[162] My student Pinchas Roth has suggested (in an unpublished seminar paper, "The First Crusade in Tosafist Historiography: An Unpublished Thirteenth-Century Chronicle") that the version of the chronology of the Tosafists found in ms. Bodl. 847 displays an abiding interest in the origins and development of northern French talmudic scholarship which is not seen in the parallel text found in *Teshuvot Maharshal*, #29 (in which the interest and vantage point is more German-centered). Cf. Matania Ben-Ghedalia, "Ḥakhmei Speyer Bimei Gezerot Tatnu ule-Aḥareihen" (Ph.D. diss., Bar-Ilan University, 2007), 96–100; S. Emanuel, "Shivrei Luḥot," 27; and my *"Peering through the Lattices,"* 23–24 (n. 13), 193 (n. 8), and 218 (n. 64).

[163] See my "The *ʿAliyyah* of 'Three Hundred Rabbis' in 1211: Tosafist Attitudes toward Settling in the Land of Israel," *JQR* 76 (1986), 191–215; Elḥanan Reiner, "ʿAliyyah ve-ʿAliyyah le-Regel le-Ereẓ Yisraʾel, 1099–1517" (Ph.D. diss., Hebrew University, 1988), 39–40, 59–66; I. Ta-Shma, *Knesset Meḥqarim*, 1:254–60; S. Emanuel, "Ve-Ish ʿal Meqomo Mevoʾar Shemo," 431 (n. 37), 439–40; and Rami Reiner, "Rabbenu Tam u-Bnei Doro: Qesharim, Hashpaʿot ve-Darkei Limmudo ba-Talmud" (Ph.D. diss., Hebrew University, 2002), 88–90.

[164] See Ta-Shma, *Halakhah, Minhag u-Meẓiʾut be-Ashkenaz*, 149–67. To be sure, this particular issue may also depend at least in part on both the differences in climate and in structure of the homes that were prevalent in different lands or regions. Cf. Jacob Katz, *Goi shel Shabbat*, 40, 43–57.

[165] See S. Emanuel, "Invalidating a Marriage Agreement," [Hebrew], in *Studies on the History of the Jews in Ashkenaz Presented to Eric Zimmer*, ed. G. Bacon et al. (Ramat Gan, 2008), 157–71. Cf. idem, "'Keshe-Yarad Ribbon ha-ʿOlamim le-Miẓrayim': Le-Toledotehah shel Pisqah Aḥat ba-Haggadah shel Pesaḥ," *Tarbiz* 77 (2008), 109–28. In this instance, however, the key difference between northern France and Germany (which begins to resolve itself, not so surprisingly, after the two centers become "reacquainted" in the 1220s, and disappears entirely by the end of the thirteenth century) is liturgical (i.e., within the text of the Passover *Haggadah*). Differences in liturgical rites, including some very significant ones, even between different regions within Germany itself, are fairly common in this period, especially with regard to *piyyutim.* See, e.g., *Maḥzor Sukkot, Shemini ʿAẓeret ve-Simḥat Torah*, ed. D. Goldschmidt and Y. Fraenkel (Jerusalem, 1981), editors' introduction, 9–48; E. Zimmer, *ʿOlam ke-Minhago Noheg*, 114–18; 125–28, 268–72; and Y. Sussmann (above, n. 128), 58–61. See also *Sefer Rabiah*, ed. Aptowitzer, 2:142–43, sec. 541 (tractate *Pesaḥim*): יש שנוהגין שכל [כוס] ששתו ממנו מחזיקין אותו לפגום אם לא יערה לחוץ כל מה שבכוס וימזוג יין אחר לקדש [עליו] וכן לברכת המזון וכן נוהגין בארץ צרפת וכן ראיתי נוהג מורי הרב [אליעזר] ממיץ. ומדקדקין לה מהך שמעתא . . . ויש דיחוי. ובבית אבא מרי ראיתי שלא היה מערהו לחוץ אך כשהיה שותה ממנו היה מוסיף עליו מעט יין או מים. וכן נוהגין בארץ אשכנז והניהוג שלנו נראה לי [עיקר].

Given the many similarities between the northern French and German Tosafist dialectical methods and halakhic outlook, however, there is ostensibly an even greater number of instances in which a range of German and northern French Tosafists took positions concerning both the analysis and practical applications of talmudic passages and other rabbinic sources for which such distinct geographic patterns cannot be detected, and this will hold true in more theoretical matters of rabbinic thought as well.[166] In sum it is ill-advised at this juncture to ignore the larger and smaller distinctions that separated the rabbinic scholarship of northern France and Germany, those distinctions that have been shown to exist as well as those that may yet be uncovered,[167] although one who attempts to find essential patterns

[166] See, e.g., my "Returning to the Jewish Community in Medieval Ashkenaz: History and Halakhah," in *Turim: Studies in Jewish History and Literature Presented to Dr. Bernard Lander*, ed. M. A. Shmidman (New York, 2007), 69–97 (in which the requirement or nonrequirement for immersion by a returning apostate are discussed and held by northern French and German Tosafists without much of a discernible geographic pattern); I. Ta-Shma, *Halakhah, Minhag u-Meẓi'ut be-Ashkenaz*, 201–15 (*qedushat bekhor*), 228–40 (tax exemptions for Torah scholars), 241–60 (*yemei 'eideihem*); and Eric Zimmer, *'Olam ke-Minhago Noheg*, 23–24 (headcovering for men), 48–50 (sidelocks), 100–101 (physical movements during prayer), 163–66 (sitting in the *sukkah* on *Shemini 'Aẓeret*), 243–45 (seven days of *niddah*), 253–57 (the permissibility of eating the fat that surrounds an animal's stomach), 288–89 (the way the prayer shawl is worn on the night of Yom Kippur); my "Medieval Rabbinic Conceptions of the Messianic Age: The View of the Tosafist," in *Me'ah She'arim: Studies in Medieval Jewish Spiritual Life in Memory of Isadore Twersky*, ed. E. Fleischer et al. (Jerusalem, 2001), 147–70 (in which Tosafist approaches to the messianic era consistently follow the same pattern, precisely against the approach followed by Maimonides, in both Germany and northern France); and my "Ḥishuvei ha-Qeẓ shel Ḥakhmei Ashkenaz, me-Rashi u-Bnei Doro ve-'ad li-Tequfat Ba'alei ha-Tosafot," in *Rashi, Demuto vi-Yeẓirato*, ed. A. Grossman and S. Japhet (Jerusalem, 2008), 381–400 (in which the two systems or patterns of messianic calculation practiced in Ashkenaz during this period were adopted by various Tosafists and rabbinic figures, completely irrespective of their places of origin). See also my "Unanimity, Majority and Communal Government in Ashkenaz during the High Middle Ages: A Reassessment," *PAAJR* 58 (1992), 79–106; "The Development and Diffusion of Unanimous Agreement in Medieval Ashkenaz," in *Studies in Medieval Jewish History and Literature* 3 (2001), ed. I. Twersky and J. Harris (Cambridge, Mass., 2000), 21–44; and "Halakhah and *Meẓi'ut* (Realia) in Medieval Ashkenaz," 193–224. As this last study intimates (and as do others within contemporary scholarship), while Tosafists from both northern France and Germany proposed talmudic and halakhic readings and rulings to address (and to alleviate) situations in which widespread Ashkenazic practice appeared to conflict with talmudic and rabbinic law, the Tosafists in northern France were somewhat more innovative in this endeavor. See also my "Devarim she-Bikhtav 'i Attah Rashai le-Omran 'Al Peh: Amirat ha-Pesuqim sheba-Tefillah u-Middat ha-Oryanut be-Ashkenaz ubi-Sefarad Bimei ha-Benayim," in *Rishonim ve-Aharonim: Meḥqarim be-Toledot Yisra'el Muggashim le-Avraham Grossman*, ed. Y. Hacker et al. (Jerusalem, 2009), 187–211.

[167] In addition to the various differences discussed above, see E. Zimmer, *'Olam ke-Minhago Noheg*, 193–96, 206 (regarding *minhagei 'avelut*), 228–35 (the *humrot* of *yemei dam tohar*, where firm distinctions between regions within Germany become a factor as well, and see also 296–97), 267–77 (*tefillin shel yad*); 281–86 (baking matzah). Note also the distinct German and French approaches and positions as to whether the basic Torah requirement of making *kiddush* on Friday night requires only the recitation of a text or the inclusion of wine

of difference between the Tosafists of northern France and those of Germany in every matter of legal interpretation or practice is misguided, and does so at his or her own peril. In addition, one must always be aware that fundamental differences in interpretation and practice among the different centers of rabbinic scholarship in Ashkenaz could have narrowed over time, especially as patterns of scholarly migration shifted or changed, although it is certainly possible that new regional perspectives and variations could have emerged as well.[168] The overarching studies by Israel Ta-Shma and Eric

as well. The northern French Tosafist position (that only recitation of the text is required) begins explicitly with Rabbenu Tam, and is supported by R. Elḥanan b. ha-Ri, R. Judah Sirleon, R. Moses of Coucy, and various French *Tosafot*. The German position is found in the so-called Rashi (*mefaresh*) to *Nazir* (which was composed in the Rhineland; see Urbach, *Baʿalei ha-Tosafot*, 1:41–45, and A. Grossman, *Ḥakhmei Ẓarefat ha-Rishonim*, 216, n. 275), and in R. Eliezer b. Nathan of Mainz's *Sefer Raban*, ed. Ehrenreich, fol. 288a (toward the end of tractate *Sotah*, arguing against the view of Rabbenu Tam and also citing R. Moses b. Joel of Regensburg, above, n. 27). It is also presented by R. Yosef Qara in the name of R. Qalonymus (b. Shabbetai) of Rome, whom R. Yosef met at the academy of Worms; see Grossman, *Ḥakhmei Ẓarefat ha-Rishonim*, 255. See *Sefer ha-Yashar le-Rabbenu Tam* (*ḥeleq ha-ḥiddushim*), ed. Schlesinger, 55 (sec. 62), and *Tosafot R. Yehudah Sirleon ʿal Massekhet*, ed. N. Zaks, vol. 1 (Jerusalem, 1969), 246 (to *Berakhot* 20b), and esp. n. 448. See also R. Eleazar of Worms, *Sefer ha-Roqeaḥ*, sec. 52; *Tosafot Rid* (R. Isaiah di Trani) to *Pesaḥim* 106a (*mahadura telitaʾah*); R. Isaiah's *Sefer ha-Makhriʿa*, ed. S. A. Wertheimer (Jerusalem, 1998), 441–56 (sec. 71, and cf. I. Ta-Shma, *Knesset Meḥqarim*, 3:40–43); R. Isaac b. Moses, *Sefer Or Zaruʿa*, pt. 2, *hilkhot ʿerev Shabbat*, sec. 25 (fol. 6b); and *Tosafot Shevuʿot* 20b, s.v. *nashim*. With respect to *terefot ha-reʾah*, see, e.g., R. Eleazar of Worms, *Shaʿarei Shehitah*, ed. A. Kozme (Jerusalem, 2010), 37–39 (based on ms. New York—JTS Rab. 1923 = ms. Bodl. 696, fol. 40r–41v).

168 In tracing the contacts between the two centers in the pre-Crusade period (and in the early twelfth century), Avraham Grossman, *Ḥakhmei Ẓarefat ha-Rishonim*, 542–55, 572–86, points to several significant similarities and differences in the intellectual proclivities and the methodological and disciplinary preferences of these centers at that time. The French scholars, who appear to have been influenced in this regard by Geonic writings, composed liturgical *Azharot*—which enumerate and organize the *Taryag mizvot*—and adopted forms of Spanish meter in their *piyyutim*, while their German counterparts did not. Cf. Rami Reiner, "The Acceptance of *Halakhot Gedolot* in Ashkenaz," [Hebrew] in *Study and Knowledge in Jewish Thought*, ed. H. Kreisel (Beer Sheva, 2006), vol. 2, 95–121. While a large number of customs and observances in both centers were fundamentally similar, Grossman shows that there were several recognizable differences between them, e.g., with respect to *hafrashat ḥalah*, the use of egg matzah on Passover, practical aspects of the prohibition of *yayn nesekh*, the way in which the *shofar* was blown, and whether the weekly Torah reading in the synagogue could be done from a *ḥumash*. On a larger scale, German rabbinic figures in this period placed greater emphasis on the value of good familial lineage (*yiḥus*) than did their French counterparts; cf. my *Jewish Education and Society in the High Middle Ages*, 67–69, 166–67. Although German customs came to dominate those of northern France during the second half of the eleventh century (when French students as a group tended to reach the Rhineland academies rather than the reverse), German "conservatism" at this time also meant that a narrower range of disciplines was pursued in the learned rabbinic circles there, as opposed to the broad-based study hall of Rashi in northern France. We have already seen (and will continue to see) similar kinds of developments and patterns during the Tosafist period as well.

Zimmer have consistently sought to properly discern the presence and impact of each of these factors.[169]

Christian Scholarship and the Talmudic Method of the Tosafists

The assumption that the rabbinic scholars of medieval Ashkenaz as a whole received little or no material from (and were not particularly influenced by) the Christian intellectual traditions that developed around them in northern Europe gains support when Ashkenazic rabbinic scholars are compared to their Spanish and North African counterparts, who flourished in the Islamic world. An earlier view suggests that rabbinic scholars in Ashkenaz were influenced less than their Sefardic colleagues because the surrounding culture and level of Christian education and erudition was markedly lower and much less developed or compelling than that of Muslim culture.[170] By now, however, more than eighty years after Charles Homer Haskins authored his pioneering study on the twelfth-century Renaissance that occurred within western European Christendom,[171] it is clear that Christian scholars and thinkers contributed in significant ways to a number of disciplines and produced numerous works of substance and depth, in terms of both method and content. The intellectual productivity of the Scholastics cannot be dismissed as unworthy of study or emulation.[172]

It might be suggested that the difference between Jewish learning in the Muslim and Christian worlds has to do mainly with issues of religion and society. The gap between (or perhaps the insularity of) Judaism and Christianity in both these realms made it more difficult for Jews to learn from

[169] See also David Strauss, "*Pat 'Akkum* in Medieval France and Germany" (M.A. thesis, Yeshiva University, 1979), 17–38. Note that even as the debate about immersion for the returning apostate (and his status prior to that immersion) involved German and northern French Tosafists on both sides of the issue (above, n. 166), as did the discussions of whether an ongoing apostate may borrow money from or lend money to a Jew, a group of German Tosafists alone maintained that an apostate whose brother had died childless was not required to do *ḥaliẓah* in order to allow his brother's widow to remarry. See my "Changing Attitudes toward Apostates in Tosafist Literature of the Late Twelfth and Early Thirteenth Centuries" (above, n. 35).

[170] See, e.g., Mortiz Gudemann, *Ha-Torah veha-Ḥayyim* (Warsaw, 1897), vol. 1, 22–26, 86–87.

[171] C. H. Haskins, *The Renaissance of the Twelfth Century* (Cambridge, Mass., 1927).

[172] See, e.g., *Renaissance and Renewal in the Twelfth Century*, ed. R. L Benson and G. Constable (Cambridge, Mass., 1982); S. C. Ferruolo, "The Twelfth-Century Renaissance," in *Renaissances Before the Renaissance*, ed. W. Treadgold (Stanford, Calif., 1984), 114–43; R. N. Swanson, *The Twelfth-Century Renaissance* (Manchester, 1999). Cf. Jacques Le Goff, "What Did the Twelfth-Century Renaissance Mean?" in *The Medieval World*, ed. P. Linehan and J. L. Nelson (London, 2001), 635–47, and C. S. Jaeger, "Pessimism in the Twelfth-Century 'Renaissance,'" *Speculum* 78 (2003), 1151–83. Cf. S. W. Baron, *A Social and Religious History of the Jews*, vol. 4 (New York, 1957), 149, and 311 (n. 71).

Christians, unlike the case for the Jews who lived in the Muslim world.[173] To be sure, Jews and Christians interacted regularly in the economic sphere as well as in the polemical arena,[174] and they even discussed biblical interpretations together.[175] At the same time, however, the subjects of theology and religious philosophy, which occupied a central place in Christian learning from the eleventh through the thirteenth century, presented a special problem for Jews, and were considered strictly off limits. This may account for the impression that Jews and Christians did not interact much on an intellectual plane, despite their many more mundane points of contact.

Nonetheless, the single most important factor that limited what Jews could receive from their Christian surroundings is a linguistic one. Ashkenazic Jewry as a whole (certainly during the twelfth and thirteenth centuries) did not read Latin, the lingua franca of Christian scholarship and culture.[176] To be sure, a small contingent of Jewish biblical scholars and

173 See, e.g., David Berger, "Judaism and General Culture in Medieval and Early Modern Times," in *Judaism's Encounter with Other Cultures*, ed. J. J. Schacter (Montvale, N.J., 1997), 61–123, and M. R. Cohen, *Under Crescent and Cross: The Jews in the Middle Ages* (Princeton, 1994), 129–36.

174 See, e.g., Aryeh Grabois, "The Hebraica Veritas and Jewish-Christian Intellectual Relations in the Twelfth Century," *Speculum* 50 (1975), 620–33; David Berger, "Mission to the Jews and Jewish-Christian Contacts in the Polemical Literature of the High Middle Ages," *American Historical Review* 91 (1986), 576–91; W. C. Jordan, *The French Monarchy and the Jews* (Philadelphia, 1989), 3–9; *Jews and Christians in Twelfth-Century Europe*, ed. M. Signer and J. Van Engen, 1–8; and Jonathan Elukin, *Living Together, Living Apart* (Princeton, 2007), 64–88, 152–83.

175 See Beryl Smalley, *The Study of the Bible in the Middle Ages* (Oxford, 1951), 148–72, 175–76, 197–99, 234–35; Jeremy Cohen, "Scholarship and Intolerance in the Medieval Academy: The Study and Evaluation of Judaism in European Christendom," *American Historical Review* 91 (1986), 596–600; E. Touitou, *Exegesis in Perpetual Motion* [Hebrew] (Ramat Gan, 2002),11–45, 164–76, 177–88 (and M. Cohen's review essay in *JQR* 98 [2008], 389–408); Ora Limor and Amnon Raz-Krakotzkin, *Jews and Christians in Western Europe: Encounters Between Cultures in the Middle Ages and the Renaissance* [Hebrew] (Tel Aviv, 1993), 36–60; David Malkiel, *Reconstructing Ashkenaz* (Stanford, Calif., 2009), 219–33. Cf. Curt Leviant, *King Artus* (New York, 1969), 76–79; S. J. D. Cohen, *Why Aren't Jewish Women Circumcised?* (Berkeley, Calif., 2005), 192–98 (for parallel interpretations put forward by Rupert of Deutz and Yosef *Bekhor Shor*); D. L. Goodwin, *Take Hold of the Robe of a Jew: Herbert of Bosham's Christian Hebraism* (Leiden, 2006), 1–8, 135–47, 163–67 and below, n. 244.

176 See Yizhak Baer, "Rashi veha-Meẓi'ut ha-Historit shel Zemanno," *Tarbiz* 20 (1949–50); idem, "Ha-Megammah ha-Hevratit/Datit be-Sefer Ḥasidim," *Zion* 3 (1937), 5; Ezra Shereshevsky, "Rashi and Christian Interpretation," *JQR* 61 (1970–71), 76–87; and Grabois, "The Hebraica Veritas," 632. David Berger's skepticism ("Mission to the Jews," 589, n. 86) about the degree of proof offered in these studies for Jews' knowledge of Latin is appropriate. See also Berger, "Judaism and General Culture," 119–21; Jordan, *The French Monarchy and the Jews*, 14–16; Avraham Grossman, *Ḥakhmei Ashkenaz ha-Rishonim* (Jerusalem, 1981), 424; Menaḥem Banitt, *Rashi: Interpreter of the Bible* (Tel Aviv, 1985), 6–7; and Touitou, *Exegesis in Perpetual Motion*, 37–38. Cf. Sara Kamin, "Dugma be-Perush Rashi u-Perush Origen le-Shir ha-Shirim," *Shenaton la-Miqra ule-Ḥeqer ha-Mizraḥ ha-Qadum* 7–8 (1984), 246, n. 121; *Sefer Ḥasidim* (Parma), sec. 259; Simcha Kogut, "The Language in *Sefer Ḥasidim*, Its Linguistic Background and Methods of Research," in *Studies in Medieval Jewish History and Literature*, vol. 2, ed. I. Twersky (Cambridge, Mass.,

polemicists recognized a number of verses from the Vulgate, and may have had a rudimentary knowledge of Latin. On the basis of his *lea'zim* to the book of Job, it is possible to theorize that R. Yosef Qara (c. 1050–1125, who studied in pre-Crusade Germany before moving to the Champagne region of northern France to study biblical interpretation with Rashi) may have been influenced in some of his word choices by the Vulgate.[177] As his title, intellectual orientation, and life's work suggest, however, R. Yosef Qara was much more of a biblicist than a talmudist.[178] Rashbam, who was a leading biblicist and talmudist, appears to have been aware of the Vulgate translation of a number of biblical verses, although these instances do not demonstrate that he had any real facility with Latin as a language.[179] R. Elḥanan b. Yaqar (a leader of the circle of mystics known as the *Ḥug ha-Keruv ha-Meyuḥad*, who has been traced to northwestern France and London) apparently read a number of Christian theological and philosophical treatises in Latin. However, as with R. Berekhyah *ha-Naqdan* of Normandy (whose Provençal origin and background may account for his familiarity with Latin), R. Elḥanan was a peripheral figure, both geographically and by specialty of discipline, within the intellectual world of medieval Ashkenaz.[180]

1984), 98, 101; S. Z. Leiman, "The Scroll of Fasts: The Ninth of Tebeth," *JQR* 74(1983), 191–92, n. 52; Urbach, *Ba'alei ha-Tosafot*, 1:210–11; I. Ta-Shma, "Hilkheta ke-Batra'ei—Beḥinot Historiyyot shel Kelal Mishpati," *Shenaton ha-Mishpat ha-'Ivri* 6–7 (1979–80), 417–21; and below, n. 243.

177 See Kirsten Fudeman, "The Linguistic Significance of the *Le'azim* in Joseph Kara's Job Commentary," *JQR* 93 (2003), 397–414.

178 See Moshe Ahrend, *Le Commentaries de-R. Yosef Qara sur Job*, 2–3; idem, *Perush R. Yosef Qara le-Iyyov* (Jerusalem, 1988), 26–27, n. 25; Touitou, *Exegesis in Perpetual Motion*, 27; A. Grossman, "Ha-Polmos ha-Yehudi—ha-Noẓri veha-Parshanut ha-Yehudit la-Miqra be-Ẓarefat ba-Me'ah ha-Yod Bet," 31–32; idem, *Ḥakhmei Ẓarefat ha-Rishonim*, 254–63; *'Arugat ha-Bosem*, ed. Urbach, 4:13–15; Urbach, *Ba'alei ha-Tosafot*, 1:143; and my *Jewish Education and Society in the High Middle Ages*, 184–85 (n. 126).

179 See, e.g., Rashbam to Genesis 49:10 and to Exodus 20:13; *Rabbenu Samuel ben Meir's Commentary on Genesis*, ed. M. Lockshin, 360–61, n. 1; M. Lockshin, *Rashbam's Commentary on Exodus*, 218–19, n. 24; Sara Japhet, *Dor Dor u-Parshanav* (Jerusalem, 2008), 294–309; and idem, *Perush Rashbam le-Shir ha-Shirim* (Jerusalem, 2008), 65–69. My friend and colleague Prof. Daniel Lasker has suggested, in an unpublished paper entitled "Joseph ben Nathan's *Sefer Yosef Ha-Meqanne* and the Medieval Jewish Critique of Christianity," that Joseph, a prominent north French polemicist of the mid-thirteenth century, was well-versed in Latin. The paper was delivered at a conference ("Thirteenth-Century France: Continuity and Change") held in February 2011, at the Institute for Advanced Study in Jerusalem, and will appear in a volume of the conference proceedings being edited by Judah Galinsky and Elisheva Baumgarten.

180 See Georges Vajda, "De quelques infilrations chretiennes dans l'oeuvre d'un auteur anglo-juif du XIIIe siecle," *Archives d'Histoire Doctrinale et Litterature du Moyen Age* 28 (1961), 15–34; D. Berger, "Judaism and General Culture," 121, n. 10. On Berekhyah's Latinity, see Norman Golb, *Toledot ha-Yehudim be-'Ir Rouen Bimei ha-Benayim* (Tel Aviv, 1977), 134–36, and above, Introduction, n. 83 (regarding both Berekhyah and Elḥanan).

Among the Tosafists, however, it is hard to identify even one figure other than Rashbam who had any familiarity with Latin. Indeed, German Tosafists referred to Latin using the epithet *leshon galahim*, the language of the priests. Although the degree to which Latin was felt to be out of bounds by Ashkenazic rabbinic scholars may have varied (as in the actual case of a convert to Judaism, who was still much more comfortable reading the Jewish Bible in Latin),[181] the lack of any knowledge of Latin on the part of these scholars is presumed. In Islamic lands, of course, the language of culture (Arabic) was the same as the language the Jews spoke—and to a more limited extent read—in their daily lives. As such the portal to Arabic culture was already open before them, unlike the case in the Christian world.

Against this backdrop we are now prepared to look anew at a significant issue of influence that Urbach and others have discussed but which remains unresolved. There are recognizable parallels between the methods and even the language employed by the Tosafists in their critico-dialectical interpretations of the Talmud and those used by the glossators of Church (canon) and Roman law. It is difficult, as noted, to maintain that the Tosafists were influenced directly by the literature produced by canon lawyers, but it is impossible to ignore the fact that precisely in the realm of talmudic study, which was such a central and lofty realm within medieval Ashkenazic society, we encounter both oral and written phenomena that are strikingly similar to what was found a number of years earlier in the circles of canon and Roman law.

In the first edition of his *Ba'alei ha-Tosafot*,which appeared more than fifty years ago, E. E. Urbach devoted two pages at the end of his introductory chapter to the extent to which the glossators of Roman law working with the Code of Justinian (*Corpus iuris civilis*, which generated great interest in Christian circles following the rediscovery of the *Digesta*, c. 1070)[182] might have influenced the Tosafists.[183] In his review of Urbach's work, Isadore

[181] See *Sefer Rabiah*, vol. 2, ed. V. Aptowitzer (Jerusalem, 1964), 253–56 (tractate *Megillah*), sec. 549; and Urbach, *Ba'alei ha-Tosafot*, 210–11. The discussion of the convert's question involved R. Yo'el *ha-Levi*, who encountered the convert in Wurzburg, and unnamed rabbinic colleagues of R. Yo'el in Speyer. The lenient view held that, since the convert was not yet comfortable with Hebrew, use of the Latin text constituted a kind of exigency for him, which is governed by the principle of *'et la'asot la-Shem heferu Toratekha*. Cf. my article on the levels of Hebrew literacy in medieval Ashkenaz and Sefarad ("Devarim she-Bikhtav," above, n. 166), end.

[182] See, e.g., Stephan Kuttner, *Harmony from Dissonance: An Interpretation of Medieval Canon Law* (Latrobe, Pa., 1960), 1–10; idem, "The Revival of Jurisprudence," in *Renaissance and Renewal in the Twelfth Century*, ed. Benson and Constable, 299–304; and David Knowles, *The Evolution of Medieval Thought* (New York, 1962), 156–67; James Brundage,*The Medieval Origins of the Legal Profession* (Chicago, 2008), 75–89. Cf. Beryl Smalley, *The Study of the Bible in the Middle Ages*, 52–53.

[183] See Urbach, *Ba'alei ha-Tosafot* (Jerusalem, 1955), 27–28.

Twersky points to several weaknesses in Urbach's comparison, including the notion that the Talmud is not a legal code in the way the Code of Justinian is, which impacts and changes the nature of glosses and comments on these works accordingly. Twersky briefly suggests that a better comparison might be made between the *Tosafot* and the glosses of the canon lawyers.[184]

In the expanded edition of *Ba'alei ha-Tosafot*, which appeared in 1980, Urbach included a more extensive discussion of this issue as part of a chapter on the methodology of the Tosafists which appears at the end of this edition. Based on studies by Stephan Kuttner (in the realm of canon law) and Hermann Kantorowicz (in the realm of Roman law), Urbach points to several clear parallels between the methods of the Jewish and Christians legal scholars, beginning with a close, critical reading of the text before them, followed by the resolution of contradictions that emerged from comparisons with other texts. In addition, there are some parallels among the literary concepts and terms that the various groups of scholars employed.[185] Aside from identifying the linguistic and content parallels between the methods of the glossators and the Tosafists, Urbach highlights the similar work and methods of several important canon lawyers, chief among them Gratian, who worked in Bologna during the first half of the twelfth century. In this presentation, however, Urbach maintains that there were significant but separate parallel lines of methodological development (*zeitgeist*) among the Jews and the Christians, rather than suggesting that there was any influence in either direction.[186]

Similarly, Israel Ta-Shma maintained initially that the change from the key methods of study and decision-making prevalent in Ashkenaz during the eleventh century to the more flexible dialectical method of the Tosafists in the twelfth century is quite similar to what occurred among the jurists in Pavia, Lombardy, in northern Italy, and that the Pavia school should be seen as influential.[187] It remains unclear, however, how these Italian jurists came

[184] See Twersky's review essay in *Tarbiz* 26 (1957), 219 (= Twersky, *Studies in Jewish Law and Philosophy* [Cambridge, Mass., 1982], Hebrew section, 46), and see also H. H. Ben-Sasson's review essay, "Hanhagatah shel Torah," *Beḥinot be-Biqqoret ha-Sifrut* 10 (1956), 42–43.

[185] For example, questions in the Christian texts included Latin phrases such as *queritur, dubitatur, solet queri*, with answers (*solutio*) that were introduced by Latin phrases such as *bulgarus respondit.* These words and phrases are quite similar to specific Tosafist terms, in Hebrew and Aramaic, such as *'im tomar/yesh lomar, ve-qasheh/ve-yesh lomar, maqshin ha-'olam/ve-tirez r. ploni.* Moreover, the Latin texts distinguish between *questiones decretales*, whose main goal was to lead to the resolution of contradictions (*solutio contrarium*), and *questiones disputates*, whose intention was to lead to an expansion of the legal realm through casuistic reasoning. These two aims were also part of Tosafist literature.

[186] Cf. Jose Faur, "The Legal Thinking of Tosafot: An Historical Approach, *Dinei Israel* 6 (1975), xliii–lxxii; and A. Grossman, *Ḥakhmei Ashkenaz ha-Rishonim*, 423.

[187] See I. Ta-Shma, *Ritual, Custom and Reality in Franco-Germany, 1000–1350* [Hebrew] (Jerusalem, 1996), 19–35, and idem, "Halakha and Reality—The Tosafist Experience," in *Rashi et la*

to influence developments within Jewish scholarship between the Rhineland and northern France.[188]

In one of his last articles (published posthumously), which looked at some suggestive parallels between the structures and methods of Christian educational institutions and their leaders in the High Middle Ages and their Jewish counterparts, Ta-Shma preferred to talk about "parallels that do not meet" rather than meaningful (Christian) influence. To be sure, the main focus of this article is not so much the academic methods that scholars employed but rather the institutions of higher learning themselves, and the status of scholars and scholarship within them. Clearly, there was no composite (or corporate) entity akin to the University of Paris within the Tosafist orbit. Scholarly privileges were of a very different order in Christian society, and debate within the cathedral schools was meant to be a "fight to the finish" and an argument for its own sake, none of which was the case within the Tosafist *battei midrash.* As such, Ta-Shma concludes that the similar forms of academic method and academic freedom and questioning that are found in both Jewish and Christian schools should not be seen as the result of any thread of influence between these institutions or circles. Indeed, Ta-Shma largely leaves the Tosafist *yeshivot* in Germany out of the discussion. Universities developed in Germany only in the mid-fourteenth century and beyond, although this may also help to explain the somewhat milder and less incisive dialectic that was more typical of the German Tosafists in Ta-Shma's view.[189]

Avraham Grossman has argued that the development of Tosafist dialectic should be understood primarily as an internal phenomenon. Examples

---

culture juive en France du Nord au moyen age , ed. G. Dahan et al. (Paris, 1997), 315–29. See also Ta-Shma, *Ha-Sifrut ha-Parshanit la-Talmud*, 1:81–89, and my "Halakhah and *Meẓi'ut* (Realia) in Medieval Ashkenaz," 198–201.

188 To be sure, the same question can be raised about Urbach's approach involving the glossators at Bologna. For contacts (and movement) between rabbinic scholars in Italy and in the Rhineland/Northern France in the late eleventh and early twelfth centuries, see, e.g., Avraham Grossman, *Ḥakhmei Ashkenaz ha-Rishonim*, 348–57, 382–85; idem, *Ḥakhmei Ẓarefat ha-Rishonim*, 338–39, 350–52, 539–41, 569–74; S. Emanuel, *Shivrei Luḥot*, 65–81; and cf. my "Mysticism and Asceticism in Italian Rabbinic Literature of the Thirteenth Century," *Kabbalah* 6 (2001), 135–49. Radding's theories about Pavia, especially the dating and nature of the change in its literary activities (as laid out in Radding's *The Origins of Medieval Jurisprudence: Pavia and Bolgna 850–1150* [New Haven, Conn., 1988]), on which Ta-Shma's analysis relies, have been roundly criticized. See, e.g., the reviews by B. C. Brasington in *Comitatus: A Journal of Medieval and Renaissance Studies* 20 (1989), 97–100; R. M. Fraher in *American Historical Review* 93 (1989), 732; and also Anders Winroth, *The Making of Gratian's Decretum* (Cambridge, 2000), 171–72.

189 See Ta-Shma, "Maqbilim she-Einam Nifgashim: Yeshivot Ba'alei ha-Tosafot veha-Sevivah ha-Aqademit be-Ẓarefat ba-Me'ah ha-Shteim 'Esreh veha-Shelosh 'Esreh," in *Yeshivot u-Battei Midrashot*, ed. E. Etkes (Jerusalem, 2006), 75–84. See also idem, *Ha-Sifrut ha-Parshanit la-Talmud*, 1:89–92 (and above, n. 128); and cf. H. Soloveitchik, "Catastrophe and Halakhic Creativity" (above, n. 133).

of nascent dialectic can already be found, here and there, within the writings of the academy of Worms during the late eleventh century in the name of R. Solomon b. Samson (ר' ששון), and others. From Worms, dialectic moves to northern France by way of those who studied in Worms at that time, including R. Meir b. Samuel, son-in-law of Rashi and father of Rashbam and Rabbenu Tam.[190] In addition to the proofs adduced by Grossman (found primarily in texts published by J. Mueller in *Teshuvot Ḥakhmei Ẓarefat ve-Lothaire*), we should take note of the commentary to tractate *Nazir* attributed to Rashi. This commentary reflects the Worms milieu and method (if not the specific authorship of R. Meir b. Samuel). In this commentary we find examples not only of the critical reading that became a hallmark of the method of the Tosafists but also some clear examples of the classical dialectical resolutions that were proposed by the Tosafists in which different *sugyot* in tractate *Nazir* are compared and contrasted (to *sugyot* both within and outside this tractate), using phrases such as *ʾim tomar/yesh lomar* and the like.[191] It is also possible to see Tosafist dialectic as a renewal or perhaps as a continuation of Amoraic dialectic, especially as it was practiced by Abbaye and Rava (*havayyot de-Abbaye ve-Rava*).[192] For these approaches, what was happening around the Jews within the intellectual networks of Christian society was perhaps not as influential.

Nonetheless, there are other significant parallels between the circles of talmudic scholars in Ashkenaz and the scholars of canon and Roman law in Christian society that have not received sufficient attention but can also contribute to this discussion. These comparative aspects can be found in the structure of the institutions of learning themselves and the status of teachers within them. Indeed, the nature of these institutions and the status that they conferred underwent very similar changes between the eleventh and twelfth centuries. Moreover, these changes were directly linked to the growth of the dialectical method in both Christian and Jewish circles, although we should note once again that the changes took place in Christian society a generation or so before they occurred within the institutions of Jewish learning.

190 See A. Grossman, *Ḥakhmei Ẓarefat ha-Rishonim*, 439–54, and idem, *Ḥakhmei Ashkenaz ha-Rishonim*, 343, 419.

191 See Y. N. Epstein, "Perushei ha-Rivan u-Perushei Vermaiza," *Tarbiz* 4 (1933), 153–67; Urbach, *Baʿalei ha-Tosafot*, 1:41–45; and above, n. 167. Note, e.g., this *perush* to *Nazir* 4a, s.v. *ve-harei mushba ve-ʿomed me-har Sinai*, and to *Nazir* 61b, s.v. *kol she-yesh lo taharah*.

192 See, e.g., Haym Soloveitchik, "Three Themes in the *Sefer Ḥasidim*," *AJS Review* 1 (1976), 178; idem, "Can Halakhic Texts Talk History?" *AJS Review* 3 (1979), 178; and idem, "Rabad of Posquieres: A Programmatic Essay," in *Studies in the History of Jewish Society in the Middle Ages and in the Modern Period*, ed. I. Etkes and Y. Salmon (Jerusalem, 1980), 19. Cf. Ha-Tosafai, "Ha-Pilpul," *Ha-Shiloah* 19 (1908), 138–42, and H. H. Ben-Sasson, "Hanhagatah shel Torah," 44.

Through the beginning of the eleventh century, the monastery was the center of knowledge and wisdom in the Christian world. Learned monks assimilated vast amounts of Scripture and its interpretation, as well as Church law and other bodies of knowledge, through their constant and repetitive patterns of reading and review. The monasteries encouraged the study of canon law as it existed (and even advocated its memorization), without attempting to reconcile seeming contradictions or other textual problems that appeared throughout the corpus. The goal or aim of monastic study was simply to soak up or gather as much material as was to be found, in the broadest possible way.[193]

Already at the end of the tenth century, however, cathedral schools such as the one at Chartres (under the direction of Fulbert) began to compete with the monasteries for students and attempted to establish themselves as the centers of enlightenment in Christian society. By the second half of the eleventh century, the cathedral schools won out. These educational institutions were different from the monasteries in two basic ways. First, the name and status of each school were determined not by the place in which the school was located (as was the case with the monastic schools, such as that of Bec or Cluny). Rather, the reputation of the cathedral school was dependent on the teacher(s) who taught there at a particular time.[194] Even the name of Paris as a center for higher education in the twelfth century was dependent, at its inception and at its core, on the fact that there were several great, independent teachers who taught there.[195]

Similarly, Richard Southern has argued that Chartres was a significant school only when particular masters taught there; its importance was not tied to its location or history per se. The students who wandered to France from Germany (e.g., Otto of Freising, who reached Paris c. 1125)[196] or who

[193] See D. Knowles, *The Evolution of Medieval Thought*, 79–82; R. W. Southern, *The Making of the Middle Ages* (New Haven, Conn., 1953), 185–92; Jean Leclerq, *The Love for Learning and the Desire for God* (New York, 1961), 87–93; M. D. Chenu, *Nature, Man, and Society in the Twelfth Century* (Chicago, 1968), 300–309; Lester Little, *Religious Poverty and the Profit Economy in Medieval Europe* (Ithaca, N.Y., 1978), 173–75; C. S. Jaeger, *The Envy of Angels* (Philadelphia, 1994), 21–27.

[194] See, e.g., G. Paré, A. Brunet, and P. Tremblay, *La renaissance du XIIeme siècle: Les écoles et l'enseignement* (Paris, 1933), 18–38; Chenu, *Nature, Man, and Society*, 310–20; Southern, *The Making of the Middle Ages*, 193–203; Jacques Le Goff, *Intellectuals in the Middle Ages* (Cambridge, Mass., 1993), 20–24; and Jaeger, *The Envy of Angels*, 46–48, 217–19. See Edward Grant, *God and Reason in the Middle Ages* (Cambridge, 2001), 62–65.

[195] See, e.g., R. W. Hunt, "English Learning in the Late Twelfth Century," in *Essays in Medieval History*, ed. R. W. Southern (London, 1968), 106–8; A. L. Gabriel, *Garlandia: Studies in the History of the Medieval University* (Notre Dame, Ind., 1969), 1–6; I. Ta-Shma, *Ha-Sifrut ha-Parshanit la-Talmud*, 1:105–11; and S. Ferruolo, *The Origins of the University* (above, Introduction, n. 113).

[196] See Southern, *Scholastic Humanism and the Unification of Europe* (Oxford, 1995), 208–12. Cf. Chenu, *Nature, Man, and Society*, 275; Jaeger, *The Envy of Angels*, 239.

followed certain masters (such as Peter Abelard) around northern France also confirm this phenomenon.[197] These wandering students were inclined to identify themselves more by the names of the teachers with whom they studied than by the places in which they studied. Indeed, despite the very free academic environment that was the rule in the cathedral schools, students typically thought of themselves as students of their teachers rather than of a place.[198]

The second basic difference was that even though the lessons in the cathedral schools began, as in the monastic schools, with the reading and fundamental analysis of an underlying text (*lectio*), the goal of the educational process was to pose questions in order to clarify the texts and what stood behind them, to resolve or to rectify texts or commentaries that appeared to contradict each other or other possible challenges and questions (*quasestio, disputatio*). In the study of the Bible (Jewish and Christian), Church law, or Christian theology, presenting contradictory texts and sources and the search for their resolution stood at the center of the educational process.[199]

The cultivation and use of scholastic dialectic in this way was the hallmark of the cathedral schools even before the days of Peter Abelard (who died in 1142). The canonist Ivo of Chartres (d. 1116, or perhaps 1095), who arrived at the monastery of Bec in 1060 and went to Chartres in 1090, employed this type of dialectic in his work *Panormia.* Even before, this form

[197] R. W. Southern, "The Schools of Paris and the School of Chartres," in *Renaissance and Renewal in the Twelfth Century*, ed. Benson and Constable, 113–32; idem, *Medieval Humanism* (New York, 1970), 61–85; and idem, *Scholastic Humanism*, 66–88. Others disagree, maintaining that Chartres's status was fundamentally tied to and derived from its location. See, e.g., J. Le Goff, *Intellectuals in the Middle Ages*, 48, as well as the criticisms of his position that are discussed by Southern, *Scholastic Humanism*, 88–100. All agree, however, that the university at Paris became a kind of corporate entity by the thirteenth century (in which masters of different disciplines gathered in order to unite these various forms of truth and knowledge under one roof), and from that point functioned as an educational if not societal center that was larger and more powerful than any of its individual masters. Although there were several important Tosafist teachers active around the year 1200 in the same area of Paris in which the university was located, they remained completely independent and never taught together in the same study hall as far as we can tell. See, e.g., Urbach, *Ba'alei ha-Tosafot*, 1:124–25, 274, 318–22, 348; *Teshuvot u-Pesaqim*, ed. Kupfer, 296–97; my *Jewish Education and Society*, 58; Limor and Raz-Krakotzkin, *Jews and Christians in Western Europe* (above, n. 175), 61–64; and cf. above, n. 195.

[198] See, e.g., Jaeger, *The Envy of Angels*, 239–43; Chenu, *Nature, Man, and Society*, 272–90; Southern, *Scholastic Humanism*, 163–76, 204–12; and cf. J. W. Baldwin, "Masters at Paris from 1179 to 1215: A Social Perspective," in *Renaissance and Renewal in the Twelfth Century*, ed. Benson and Constable, 138–63.

[199] See Chenu, *Nature, Man, and Society*, 291–310; Pare, Brunet, and Tremblay, *La renaissance*, 110–23; J. W. Baldwin, *Masters, Princes, and Merchants* (Princeton, 1970), 88–101; Knowles, *The Evolution of Medieval Thought*, 174–75; Ivan Illich, *In the Vineyard of the Text* (Chicago, 1993), 60–65; Le Goff, *Intellectuals in the Middle Ages*, 93–106; Ta-Shma, *Ha-Sifrut ha-Parshanit la-Talmud*, 1:97–98.

was widespread in the writings of Bernold of Constance.[200] Indeed, a number of monastic teachers during the eleventh century also employed dialectic, including Anselm of Canterbury (d. 1109) and his teacher Lafranc of Bec, who left his birthplace in Italy and reached northern France, becoming the head of the monastery at Bec in 1042, two years after Rashi's birth.[201]

In the early twelfth century, however, German monastic scholars led by Rupert (d. 1130), abbot of Deutz (located in the eastern quarter of Cologne), broadly criticized this newer method and suggested that students return to study according to the venerable monastic methods. A distinction made at a debate held at the cathedral school of Laon in 1117 caused Rupert, who was then a monk at Liege, to travel to northern France in order to publicly raise his objections. The distinction in question, made by two masters at Laon, William of Champeaux and Anselm of Laon, identified two wills of God: a permissive will (*voluntas permittens*) that tolerates evil, and an approving will (*voluntas approbans*). In Rupert's view, this was an absolute denigration of the outlook of Scripture. Such a meaningless and sterile distinction (*tam inertem divisionem*) could lead only to the blasphemous notion that God wills evil. Rupert continues by noting that he did not follow the schools of dialectic but that, even if he had mastered their knowledge, he would not make use of it, for such knowledge can only lead to the worst incongruities while adding nothing to the holiness and simplicity of the Divine truth. For Rupert, "Whatever can be thought up apart from sacred scripture or fabricated out of argumentation is unreasonable and therefore pertains in no way to the praise or acknowledgment of the omnipotence of God." Thus theology is nourished by faith, according to Rupert, and not by "reasoning" in the manner of the cathedral masters.[202]

In accordance with his mystical orientation, Rupert believed that God displayed His will to men in human history through theophany of Scripture. Rupert and likeminded monks had no desire to transform this theophany

200 See Knowles, *The Evolution of Medieval Thought*, 83–106; S. Kuttner, *Harmony from Dissonance*, 12, 24; R. Somerville and B. C. Brasington, *Prefaces to Canon Law Books in Latin Christianity* (New Haven, Conn., 1998), 111–17, 132–33; Anders Winroth, *The Making of Gratian's Decretum*, 16; and J. Brundage, *The Medieval Origins of the Legal Profession*, 194–96. On Ivo and his travels, see Southern, *Scholastic Humanism*, 252–61.

201 See Gordon Leff, *Medieval Thought* (Manchester, 1962), 93–115; Knowles, *The Evolution of Medieval Thought*, 116–48; Southern, *Scholastic Humanism*, 250–52; and Chenu, *Nature, Man, and Society*, 274–75.

202 See Chenu, *Nature, Man, and Society*, 204–10, 216–17, 270–72, 302; L. Little, *Religious Poverty*, 26–27; and cf. U. T. Holmes, "Transition in European Education," in *Twelfth-Century Europe and the Foundations of Modern Society*, ed. M. Clagett et al. (Madison, Wis., 1961), 15–38. See now Ian Wei, "From Twelfth-Century Schools to Thirteenth-Century Universities: The Disappearance of Biographical and Autobiographical Representations of Scholars," *Speculum* 86 (2011), 42–78.

into a rational theodicy that attempted to sort out the Divine attributes as the cathedral masters did.[203] At the same time, however, it must be noted that Rupert had to defend himself throughout his life against internal Christian charges that he innovated in his own reading (or *sensus*) of Scripture, against the knowledge of the Divine that had been passed down through the Church.[204] Again reflecting his involvement with mysticism, Rupert, an older contemporary of Rashbam, sometimes indicates that these "new" interpretations were revealed to him in heavenly dreams or visions.[205]

This tension concerning the use of dialectic had further repercussions within northern France. Robert of Melun, in the preface to his *Sentences* (composed c. 1160), rails against "a new type of teaching that has recently appeared which has gained inordinate popularity among certain men . . . by their strange and disgusting newness of terminology, they do not fear to divulge what they hope." Bishop Stephen of Tournai (from 1192 to 1203; he studied both canon and Roman law in Bologna in the early 1150s, and then studied in Orleans and Chartres) denounced the new method from a different perspective: "Students applaud nothing but novelties, and the masters are more intent on glory than doctrine. Everywhere they draw up new and modern summaries and supporting commentaries on theology with which they lull and deceive their listeners, as if the works of the sacred fathers did not still suffice."[206] Indeed, the schools that championed the new dialectic were characterized in reports from both the monastic and cathedral communities "as teeming with cavalier students, whose breasts swell with pride in their knowledge, who can dispute, cast doubt, redefine old usage, violate the laws of *reverentia* and *pietas* left and right, and have the nerve to contradict and show up their own teachers."[207]

More nuanced concerns about the use of dialectic were raised in northern France as part of the disputes between Bernard, abbot of Clairvaux, and Peter Abelard. Bernard characterizes Abelard's reasoning as "a war of words (*pugnae verborumi*), marred by novelties of expression (*novitates vocum*)." Despite the harshness of his words and his goal of ultimately branding Abelard a heretic (if not the head of an international conspiracy who sought to reject

203 See Chenu, *Nature, Man, and Society*, 307.

204 *Jews and Christians in Twelfth-Century Europe*, ed. Signer and Van Engen, 126–27, 154–66; Peter Classen, "*Res Gestae*, University History, Apocalypse: Visions of Past and Future," in *Renaissance and Renewal in the Twelfth Century*, ed. Benson and Constable, 404–6; Chenu, *Nature, Man, and Society*, 314–15; and my "Progress and Tradition in Medieval Ashkenaz" (above, n. 151), 287–88.

205 See Ralph Lerner, "Ecstatic Dissent," *Speculum* 67 (1992), 42–57, and Ta-Shma, *Ha-Sifrut ha-Parshanit la-Talmud*, 1:100.

206 See Chenu, *Nature, Man, and Society*, 310–11, and see also 95, 235. Cf. Jaeger, *The Envy of Angels*, 33–43, and Somerville and Brasington, *Prefaces to Canon Law Books*, 177–78.

207 See Jaeger, *The Envy of Angels*, 217, and cf. the statement by R. Samson of Sens, above, n. 149.

all authority, both religious and Divine),[208] Bernard, who was trained as a so-called new monk mainly in the Benedictine monastery of Citeaux,[209] was not against the powers of logical thinking or even the dialectical method per se, as his older German contemporary Rupert of Deutz was. Rather, Bernard was opposed to incorrect applications or mistaken manipulations of these methods, and the misguided reasoning that resulted from their overly wide use. He preached about this to students in Paris in 1140: "Flee from the midst of this Babylon and save your souls; fly to the cities of refuge [i.e., the monasteries]. You will find much more in the forests than in the books, and the rocks will teach you more than any master."[210] Moreover, as Richard Southern has observed, "St. Bernard . . . has not been given as much credit as he deserves for the trouble he took to promote masters of whom he approved."[211]

Abelard is charged by Bernard with believing that reason can accomplish more than its legitimate aims. The way of teaching the Bible should dovetail with the ordinary experiences of life. It is important to note that neither Rupert of Deutz nor Bernard participated in the newer cathedral schools. Moreover, both were inclined toward mystical teachings and study, as has already been noted for Rupert. For Bernard, mysticism was the means by which man could get above himself, through upward spiritual striving. In Bernard's words, the more profound truth that sometimes stands behind the obvious, which instructs the soul in the way it should go, militates against trying too hard to achieve explications through reasoning.[212]

In turning now to the study of Talmud in medieval Ashkenaz in the period prior to the First Crusade, we note that for rabbinic scholarship at this time (as for the monastic schools), the aim was to absorb as much as possible from biblical and talmudic literature, and to identify bona fide post-talmudic customs, without searching for or relating in a consistent way to contradictions or comparative questions. This is clearly seen in the halakhic

208 See M. T. Clanchy, *Abelard: A Medieval Life* (Oxford, 1997), 218–19, 311–13, 371.

209 See G. R. Evans, *Bernard of Clairvaux* (New York, 2000), 7–8, and Clanchy, *Abelard: A Medieval Life*, 37–38. On Bernard's non-cathedral training, see 42–43. On Citeaux, see also Chenu, *Nature, Man, and Society*, 95. On the "new monks," see *Jews and Christians in Twelfth-Century Europe*, ed. Signer and Van Engen (above, n. 204), 165.

210 See J. Le Goff, *Intellectuals in the Middle Ages*, 21–22. See also Jaeger, *The Envy of Angels*, 269–77.

211 See Southern, *Scholastic Humanism*, 170, and see also 173.

212 See Evans, *Bernard of Clairvaux*, 42–56, 71, 102–5, 141–42; Clanchy, *Abelard*, 7–9, 35–37, 40, 216, 244; Giles Constable, "Renewal and Reform in Religious Life," in *Renaissance and Renewal in the Twelfth Century*, ed. Benson and Constable, 59–60; Peter Classen, "*Res Gestae*," 404–7; Jean Leclerq, "The Renewal of Theology," in *Renaissance and Renewal in the Twelfth Century*, 71, 77–87; J. Le Goff, *Intellectuals in the Middle Ages*, 41–44, 61–62; Southern, *Scholastic Humanism*, 225–28; and Ta-Shma, *Ha-Sifrut ha-Parshanit la-Talmud*, 1:109–10.

compendia that were produced in this period, such as *Maʿaseh ha-Geonim*, and in the so-called *sifrut de-Bei Rashi*, and perhaps even within Rashi's talmudic and biblical commentaries themselves.[213] Talmudic studies in the pre-Crusade period were centered in two main *yeshivot*, Mainz and Worms. As I have demonstrated elsewhere, these academies, similar to the monasteries, were identified by their location and not on the basis of the teachers who taught there or the figures who headed them. Although the Rhineland academies of the eleventh century were few in number, they were closely tied to their communities. Academy heads (*roshei yeshivah*) came and went, but the community and its academy remained. For a lengthy period, the *yeshivot* of Mainz and Worms were the centers of learning and custom, to which both students and new teachers gravitated.[214]

A suggestive example of the significance of the academy and its locale over and above the presence of a particular rabbinic scholar or master can be seen in regard to a question that was asked in Mainz c. 1000 regarding the proper place during the prayer service for a circumcision that was to be performed on Rosh ha-Shanah: Should it occur at the end of the prayers or after the Torah reading, prior to the blowing of the *shofar*? The question was posed to the "holy scholars of the city," including Rabbenu Gershom b. Judah (d. 1028), R. Simeon b. Isaac *ha-Gadol*, and R. Judah *ha-Kohen*. According to the textual source for this episode, however, "the remainder of the holy academy" (*she'ar bnei ha-yeshivah ha-qedoshah*) was also queried. A number of the rabbinic teachers and students who were present disagreed with the view of the majority, which Rabbenu Gershom supported, and Rabbenu Gershom was compelled to explain and prove this position. Even though Rabbenu Gershom was considered to be the most outstanding scholar at Mainz in his day, the students are not referred to as the members of the *yeshivah* of Rabbenu Gershom or as the students of Rabbenu Gershom but rather as the students of the "holy academy at Mainz," who were able and entitled to voice their opinions.[215]

213 See H. Soloveitchik, "Three Themes in the *Sefer Ḥasidim*," 342–43, 348–49. The contradiction found in Rashi's commentaries to the Talmud were apparently intentional (rather than circumstantial), and usually reflect specific exegetical concerns or strategies. See, e.g., Yonah Fraenkel, *Darko shel Rashi be-Perusho la-Talmud ha-Bavli* (Jerusalem, 1980), 284–98; A. Grossman, *Ḥakhmei Ẓarefat ha-Rishonim*, 193–201, 209–10, 231–34; and see now Yeshayahu Maori, "'Aggadot Ḥaluqot' Be-Perush Rashi la-Miqra," *Shenaton le-Ḥeqer ha-Miqra veha-Mizraḥ ha-Qadum* 19 (2009), 155–207.

214 See my *Jewish Education and Society in the High Middle Ages*, 57–59.

215 See *Sefer Or Zaruʿa*, pt. 2, sec. 275. See also the annotated text and parallel sources in *Teshuvot Rabbenu Gershom*, ed. S. Eidelberg (New York, 1955), 98–100. Cf. *ʿArukh ha-Shalem*, ed. A. Kohut (Tel Aviv, 1968), vol. 1, editor's introduction, xi–xii; Grossman, *Ḥakhmei Ashkenaz ha-Rishonim*, 120; I. A. Agus, "Rabbinic Scholarship in Northern Europe," in *World History of the Jewish People: The Dark Ages*, ed. C. Roth (Ramat Gan, 1966), 193–94; *Teshuvot u-Pesaqim*,

Similarly, we now know that the surviving so-called commentaries of Rabbenu Gershom on several tractates of the Talmud are, in reality, *perushei Magenza* that were written and composed in layers over several generations in Mainz during the eleventh century, even for a period of many years after the death of Rabbenu Gershom.[216] The locale and *yeshivah* of Mainz was the central educational entity in these endeavors, over and above the presence of any individual teacher, including Rabbenu Gershom.[217]

By the second quarter of the twelfth century, with the beginning of the Tosafist enterprise, these educational entities, approaches, and values began to change. The dialectical method, which had been used in a limited way in only one academy in the Rhineland (Worms) toward the end of the eleventh century, becomes the dominant approach in the various Tosafist *battei midrash* that develop. Similarly, the reputations and presence of leading Tosafists themselves, rather than the traditions, customs, and name of a particular academy or locale, begin to draw students from Germany to northern France and back.[218] A phrase from a *piyyut* (*reshut*) for a *Shabbat ḥatan*, composed by Rashi's (and R. Meir b. Samuel's) teacher at Worms, R. Isaac b. Eliezer *ha-Levi* (d. c. 1080), may provide a literary snapshot of the incipient shift from the older, location-based institutions to the newer contexts of dialectical talmudic instruction, in which the teachers were seen as the most prominent element: "from those who study nights and days ... they are coming from city to city, to study from the mouths of rabbinic scholars" (בואם מעיר אל עיר ללמוד מפי חכמים).[219] It is also worth remembering that in Germany during the Tosafist period, where the dialectical method was a bit more restrained, the *beit din* was the preferred venue for rabbinic interaction and tutorial power, rather than the academy.[220]

In the Tosafist period, a city or town had an important, high-level academy only when a particular Tosafist or other rabbinic scholar was there. Students wandered from the study hall of one leading scholar to the study hall of another, and the rabbinic scholars themselves occasionally changed

ed. E. Kupfer, 314–15; and I. Ta-Shma, "Halakhah, Minhag u-Massoret be-Yaḥadut Ashkenaz ba-Me'ot ha-Yod Alef/Yod Bet," *Sidra* 3 (1987), 137–38.

216 See, e.g., Grossman, *Ḥakhmei Ashkenaz ha-Rishonim*, 165–74, and Ta-Shma, *Ha-Sifrut ha-Parshanit la-Talmud*, 1:35–40.

217 On the centrality and significance of *minhagim* in the *yeshivot* of the pre-Crusade period, see, e.g., Grossman, *Ḥakhmei Ashkenaz ha-Rishonim*, 412–15.

218 This was the case, for example, with the students of Rabbenu Tam who came from Regensburg and returned there following their studies. See, e.g., R. Reiner, "Rabbenu Tam: Rabbotav ve-Talmidav" (above, n. 27), 79–95.

219 For the fuller passage (on the basis of ms. Parma 586, fol. 94v), see Grossman, *Ḥakhmei Ashkenaz ha-Rishonim*, 292. See also Rashi's comment, below, n. 221.

220 See above, nn. 128, 189.

locales.[221] Thus, for example, we hear nothing about the academy or study hall in Ramerupt or Troyes once Rabbenu Tam has departed. When a situation comparable to the one in Mainz c. 1000 (described above) arose involving Riẓba of Dampierre (d. 1210) and his colleagues and students (*ha-ḥaverim veha-talmidim*), Riẓba took immediate charge of the situation. His decision was open to discussion only after the fact (at which point it emerged that Riẓba could not parry all of the questions that were raised).[222] Moreover, the talmudic comments that were produced in the academies of the Tosafists were referred to as the commentary of Rabbenu Tam or the *Tosafot* of Ri. Even though students were often responsible for copying and preserving the lectures or *ḥidduhsim* of their teachers, the written forms of *Tosafot* are always referred to as the *Tosafot* of R. so and so, the teacher. They are never referred to as the *Tosafot* of study hall or academy X, in the place or city of Y.[223]

In addition, the strong critique of *Ḥasidei Ashkenaz* against *pilpul* (dialectic) in the *Tosafot* style—especially as it appears to have developed in northern France—and the concomitant suggestion that the more monochromatic method of halakhic study prevalent in the Rhineland during the pre-Crusade period was more appropriate for most students, is similar in many respects to the critique of Rupert of Deutz and others against Christian dialectic. Especially irksome to these critics and to *Ḥasidei Ashkenaz* as well was the inflated name or reputation that could easily be acquired by

221 See, e.g., Mordechai Breuer, "Nedudei Talmidim ve-Ḥakhamim—Aqdamot le-Pereq mi-Toledot ha-Yeshivot," in *Tarbut ve-Ḥevrah be-Toledot Yisra'el Bimei ha-Benayim*, ed. R. Bonfil et al. (Jerusalem, 1989), 445–68; idem, *Be-Ohalei Torah* (Jerusalem, 2004), 431–41; and my *Jewish Education and Society*, 49–52. Rashi (d. 1105, who went from his home in northern France to the Rhineland academies) appears to refer to wandering students in his commentary to the Song of Songs (5:16, ד"א תלמידי חכמים שהקב"ה נותן להאיר עינים . . . כיונים הנודדים משובך לשובך לבקש אכלם, כך הם הולכים ממדרשו של פלוני חכם לבית המדרש של פלוני חכם לבקש לעמי תורה). See Judah Rosenthal, "Perush Rashi ʿal Shir ha-Sirim," in *Sefer ha-Yovel Likhvod S. K. Mirsky*, ed. S. Bernstein and G. Churgin (New York, 1958), 169, and cf. above, Introduction, n. 82.

222 See Urbach, *Baʿalei ha-Tosafot*, 1:264 (and above, n. 147); I. Twersky's review of Urbach (above, n. 184), in *Tarbiz* 26 (1957), 226 (= Twersky, *Studies in Jewish Law and Philosophy*, Hebrew section), 53; and my *Jewish Education and Society*, 59–60 (for additional examples).

223 The so-called *Tosafot Shanẓ* to various talmudic tractates do not weaken my argument. Rather, this is an abbreviated term for the *Tosafot* that emanated from the study hall of R. Samson b. Abraham (Rash) of Sens, the rabbinic scholar who made Sens a recognized place. See Urbach, *Baʿalei ha-Tosafot*, 1:272, and cf. ibid., 22–34. Indeed, these *Tosafot* are often called *Tosafot R. Samson of Sens* or *Tosafot Rashba* (= R. Samson b. Abraham). Cf. I. Ta-Shma, *Ha-Sifrut ha-Parshanit la-Talmud*, 2:103–7, who stresses that R. Samson often wrote his own *Tosafot* (rather than allowing his students to do so), so that he could accurately record the teachings of his teacher, Ri of Dampierre. Similarly, *Tosafot Tukh* is the abbreviated name for the groups of *Tosafot* texts that were edited by R. Eliezer of Tukh. See Urbach, *Baʿalei ha-Tosafot*, 2:584–85, and 643; Ta-Shma, *Ha-Sifrut ha-Parshanit la-Talmud*, 2:101, 119–20; and cf. above, Introduction, nn. 8, 10.

someone who was facile in presenting distinctions and intellectual manipulations. Additionally, there was great concern for the misguided conclusions (theological and dogmatic for the Christians, halakhic for the German Pietists) that might emerge from these distinctions, results that stood in opposition to the modesty that was to be expected from someone who exceled in religious and spiritual studies.[224] As was the case for Rupert, the mystical outlook of the German Pietists played a strong role in their view. They believed that their mystical forebears in Mainz, the members of the Qalonymus family and others, had a more salutary approach to Torah study and its limits. Interestingly, however, and again like Rupert, the "reactionary" exegesis of the German Pietists was often considered in its own way to be highly innovative at the same time, albeit in a different direction.

In northern France as well, and mirroring perhaps the concerns of Bernard of Clairvaux, R. Elijah b. Judah of Paris typically favored a less expansive form of logic than Rabbenu Tam did, as can be seen in several of the halakhic disputes between them. And like Bernard, R. Elijah was also associated with mystical study.[225] Moreover, R. Elijah was connected to R. Meshullam of Melun, a spirited antagonist of Rabbenu Tam in matters of halakhic proofs and the justification of popular customs, who hailed originally from Narbonne but reached northern France no later than 1130. R. Elijah and R. Meshullam sat together for a time on the rabbinic court in Paris,[226] and R. Meshullam appealed to R. Elijah and to other members of the rabbinical court in Paris for guidance and support in his confrontations with Rabbenu Tam. R. Meshullam considered R. Elijah's piety and modesty to be such that "access to the Almighty cannot be denied to the people of Israel owing to his existence."[227]

[224] See my "Progress and Tradition in Medieval Ashkenaz" (above n. 151), and see also H. Soloveitchik, "Three Themes in the *Sefer Ḥasidim*," 339–54; Ta-Shma, "Miẓvat Talmud Torah ki-Beʿayah Ḥevratit—Datit be-Sefer Ḥasidim," *Sefer Bar-Ilan* 14–15 (1977), 98–113; and Ta-Shma, *Ha-Sifrut ha-Parshanit la-Talmud*, 1:81–84. (On Rupert's intense anti-Jewish formulations throughout his corpus, see, e.g., Anna Abulafia, "The Ideology of Reform and Changing Ideas Concerning Jews in the Works of Rupert of Deutz and Hermannus Quondam Iudeus," *Jewish History* 7 [1993], 44–50, and Jeremy Cohen, *Living Letters of the Law* [Berkeley, Calif,. 1999], 271–72.)

[225] See Urbach, *Baʿalei ha-Tosafot*, 122–23; R. Reiner, "Rabbenu Tam u-Bnei Doro: Qesharim, Hashpaʿot ve-Darkei Limmudo ba-Talmud," 70–84; and cf. my *Jewish Education and Society*, 28–29. Reiner concludes that "for the most part, Rabbenu Tam's talmudic interpretations were created through the application of much broader considerations than those employed by R. Elijah." See also below, n. 231.

[226] See above, n. 75; R. Reiner, "Battei ha-Din be-Ẓarefat" (above, n. 74), 568–79; and cf. Ta-Shma, *Knesset Meḥqarim*, 1:73, for their place or role within *Maḥzor Vitry*.

[227] See *Sefer ha-Yashar*, ed. Rosenthal, 92 (הרב ר' אליהו שאין עזרה ננעלת על אדם כמותו בענווה וביראת החטא), cited in Urbach, *Baʿalei ha-Tosafot*, 1:76. R. Meshullam's own (supererogatory) piety was noted by Rabbenu Tam's student, R. Yom Tov of Joigny. See below, chapter 2, n. 219.

Rabbenu Tam also recognized the unusual spiritual qualities of R. Elijah of Paris, and on one occasion, he went along with R. Elijah (and against his own proclivities) in permitting the magical adjuration of a Divine name, which would then allow the practitioner to raise the spirit of a deceased child so that his father, who was not present at the time of the child's death, might see him one last time.[228] Nonetheless, Rabbenu Tam firmly rejected the differing ritual customs that R. Meshullam and R. Elijah proposed and apparently implemented.[229] Interestingly, although talmudic interpretations by R. Elijah are cited within northern French *Tosafot*, his halakhic rulings and responsa are cited mostly by German rabbinic authorities throughout the twelfth and thirteenth centuries.[230]

Rami Reiner has demonstrated that the series of sharp and specific debates between Rabbenu Tam and R. Meshullam (and his mentor R. Elijah) were predicated on very different approaches to several larger interpretive or analytical principles. R. Meshullam was a literalist, who required that terms be interpreted in the same way throughout all rabbinic literature. This approach impelled R. Meshullam to emend certain talmudic passages; at the same time, it allowed him to interpret midrashic passages in which these terms appeared in order to reach halakhic conclusions. Rabbenu Tam, however, tended to view the meaning of a term and its halakhic relevance in the context of the original talmudic formulations in which they appeared, with far less concern for non-talmudic variants.

R. Meshullam also considered the Bible itself (as well as Tannaitic literature) as a ready source for halakhic rulings, and as a basis for understanding and interpreting the text of the Babylonian Talmud. Rabbenu Tam vehemently objected to this structure; the Talmud alone, and its contextual interpretation, must guide the determination of the *halakhah*. At the same time, Rabbenu Tam saw custom and practice, as well as certain bodies of post-talmudic literature, as factors that could influence talmudic interpretation and halakhic decision-making, a more flexible approach than that of R. Meshullam. Finally, while Rabbenu Tam gave great weight to the external reasonability of the halakhic results derived through talmudic interpretation (an unreasonable conclusion had to be rejected, even where established custom appeared to follow this interpretation), Rabbenu Meshullam held that intuitive thinking, in and of itself, could not challenge the accepted interpretations or conclusions of the Babylonian Talmud.

[228] See Urbach, *Ba'alei ha-Tosafot*, 1:123, and my "*Peering through the Lattices*," 170–71.

[229] Urbach, ibid., 1:79, 122. Cf. my "Rabbinic Authority and the Right to Open an Academy in Medieval Ashkenaz," *Michael* 12 (1991), 239–40.

[230] See Urbach, ibid., 123–24.

In short, Rabbenu Tam rejected the approach of R. Elijah and R. Meshullam to interpret the *Bavli* only from within, and to determine normative Jewish law only in this way. For Rabbenu Tam, halakhic intuition and common sense, alongside custom and various post-talmudic collections, were all valid interpretive tools. The "extreme canonization" of the Talmud, together with the Bible and Tannaitic literature, which was presumed by Rabbenu Meshullam, was not shared by Rabbenu Tam. Although for Rabbenu Tam the Talmud was certainly the cornerstone within the world of Jewish law, there were additional factors that could properly impact and influence halakhic outcomes. *Halakhah* was much more open-ended for Rabbenu Tam, and its study and derivation, by definition, allowed for continuing innovation.[231]

Thus Rabbenu Tam writes the following (in rhyme) about R. Elijah's suggestion—strongly supported by Rabbenu Meshullam—that the seventh *ʿaliyyah* to the Torah on the Sabbath should simultaneously serve as the *ʿaliyyah* for the *maftir*: "Although he is, in my eyes, pious and modest, and he and his family are among our redeemers and the Almighty should lengthen his years, R. Elijah's suggestion, based on his interpretation of the Talmud, is not modest (*ʾeino ʿanavah*) but rather haughty (*gaʾavah*), because with it he argues against the *Tosefta*, tractate *Soferim*, and the *Geʾonim* of Sura and Pumbeditha, and it is therefore close to heresy (*qarov le-minut*)."[232] For R. Elijah, on the other hand, Rabbenu Tam's interpretation was incorrect, since he departed from the narrow, textual interpretation of the Talmud, and conflated various additional texts and sources in support of his view. As with the conflicts between Abelard and Bernard (especially in regard to the notion of negative theology),[233] the alleged "heresy" invoked by Rabbenu Tam had more to do with issues of reasoning and textual interpretation than with lapses in or abject errors of religious doctrine per se.[234]

231 See Reiner, "Parshanut ve-Halakhah: ʿIyyun me-Ḥadash be-Polmos Rabbenu Meshullam ve-Rabbenu Tam," *Shenaton ha-Mishpat ha-ʿIvri* 21 (1998–2000), 207–39, and idem, "Rabbenu Tam u-Bnei Doro," 283–321. Cf. Avi Lifshitz, "The Tosaphists' Learning Methodology/Dialectic," [Hebrew] (Ph.D. diss., Hebrew University, 2008), 223–38, 410–18. Reiner cogently theorizes that R. Isaac Alfasi's *halakhot* had a decisive impact on Rabbenu Meshullam (who hailed originally from Provence) in the matter of halakhic canonization.

232 *Sefer ha-Yashar*, 97, cited in Urbach, *Baʿalei ha-Tosafot*, 1:79. As Urbach notes (1:76), R. Meshullam also mentions R. Elijah's guidance with regard to his recommendation concerning Sabbath candle lighting (that a blessing not be made), and that the blessings for both *ʾerusin* and *nissuʾin* be recited over the same cup of wine.

233 See Evans, *Bernard of Clairvaux*, 105.

234 In light of the focus of Tosafist enterprise on resolving contradictions between divergent talmudic texts and between rabbinic texts and a number of Ashkenazic customs, it is interesting to note that Abelard wrote to Bernard on the subject of discrepancies between the Gospels, and the role and status of custom. This follows on the heels of a formulation by Anselm of

We have already noted that the timetable for the development and supersession of dialectic within Christian society, and the concomitant changes within Christian educational institutions and with regard to the status of masters and teachers, precede by at least one generation the similar changes among Ashkenazic talmudists. At this point, however, additional proof is needed to demonstrate that the Jews were familiar with or influenced by the dialectical method of the Christians per se. Before proceeding to evaluate additional evidence for this possibility, we must acknowledge that the burden of proof is lower or less acute than it was for Urbach, who wrote more than a half century ago, or even for his revised edition, which was completed nearly thirty years ago. Thanks to the research of Grossman and others, who have suggested and demonstrated that dialectic was already present in the academy of Worms in the last quarter of the eleventh century, the question is not whether the Jews learned about dialectic for the first time from Christians. Rather, the question is whether the presence of dialectic in Christian scholastic circles, especially in northern France, can explain how this methodology, which was limited to one rabbinic academy in the late eleventh century, became the dominant method of talmudic study throughout the twelfth and thirteenth centuries. Was the interest of several pre-Crusade Worms rabbinic scholars in this method developed or expanded because this method already occupied such an important place in Christian society from the mid-eleventh century and beyond?

C. S. Jaeger has focused new attention on the development of cathedral schools in Germany, and the commonalities between these schools and their better-known counterparts in northern France. Between 950 and 1015, some twelve cathedral schools arose in German urban centers, including Wurzburg, Cologne, Worms, Mayence, Speyer, Trier, Hildesheim, Regsenburg, Magdeburg, and Bamberg, and in northern France in Lieges, Rheims, and Chartres. Students of the well-known school at Chartres, in turn, were responsible for the founding or revival of other cathedral schools in northern France in the middle and later eleventh century, in locales such as Orleans, Tournai, and Troyes, and beyond that, in Paris and Laon.[235]

Speyer is the locale with which the earliest German Tosafist Riba *ha-Levi ha-Zaqen* (c. 1060–1133) is most often associated, although Avraham Grossman maintains that Riba studied at Worms as well, where he encountered

---

Canterbury (d. 1109) that custom establishes as an "ought" (i.e., "one ought to do this by custom"). See Evans, *Bernard of Clairvaux*, 141.

[235] See C. S. Jaeger, *The Envy of Angels*, 15, 46–48, 53–75. Cf. *Renaissance and Renewal in the Twelfth Century*, ed. Benson and Constable, 113–33, 144–45, 190–94.

the nascent dialectic being utilized there.[236] A recent study, however, has shown that positive evidence for Riba's activity in Speyer exists only for the period after 1110. Prior to that (from approximately 1103), Riba lived in Mainz. A manuscript passage places Riba (in 1082) in the academy at Cologne, in an open intellectual environment where older and younger students were encouraged and able to put forth new insights and interpretations.[237] For our purposes, it is important to note that, irrespective of where Riba spent his formative years (Speyer, Worms, Cologne, or Mainz), a cathedral school was proximate. To be sure the extent to which dialectic was practiced in each of these schools remains unclear. Indeed, the impact of the cathedral schools in Germany, which has not received much attention in modern scholarship, is in need of a fundamental reexamination.[238]

Nonetheless, as the case of Riba suggests, we should also look again at the connections between Jews and Christians in Western Europe in the twelfth century. In the expanded edition of his *Ba'alei ha-Tosafot*, Urbach came to the conclusion that the Tosafists did not have especially meaningful contacts with Christian legists or with scholars of dialectic. However, Urbach was focused on locating only one dimension or manifestation of such influence: Were the Jews familiar with or aware of written texts and formulations by the Christians which employed dialectic? Although Urbach was perhaps justified, at least in theory, in pursuing this narrow criterion (since influence is most easily demonstrated if an awareness of central, written texts can be shown), that degree of influence is not required in the case of the Tosafists.[239] We have seen that a form of dialectic was already being practiced within a limited circle of rabbinic scholars at Worms during the late eleventh century. Thus the issue is only whether contact with Christian dialectic was a contributing factor in the remarkable expansion and efflorescence of this approach in Jewish learning and talmudic scholarship during the twelfth century, which quickly and forcefully became the hallmark of all Tosafist *battei midrash*. There are a number of important and meaningful contacts between Jews and Christians in this regard that were not noted by Urbach.

That Jews learned dialectic in a formal way from the Christians is, as we have indicated at the outset, nearly impossible. Even if there were Torah

236 See A. Grossman, *Ḥakhmei Ashkenaz ha-Rishonim*, 399, and idem, *Ḥakhmei Ẓarefat ha-Rishonim*, 441–47.

237 See Mataniah Ben-Ghedalia, "Ḥakhmei Speyer Bimei Gezerot Tatnu ule-Aḥareihen," 85–107.

238 Cf., e.g., J. Le Goff, *Intellectuals in the Middle Ages*, 66–75, 138–42, and J. Brundage, *The Medieval Origins of the Legal Profession*, 109–10.

239 Cf. Kenneth Stow's review of my *"Peering through the Lattices,"* in *Jewish History* 16 (2002), 213–16.

scholars who could read Latin to a significant degree, there is no evidence (again, aside from the truly exceptional mystic, R. Elḥanan b. Yaqar) that they were genuinely familiar with the texts of any Christian works of theology or jurisprudence that employed dialectic. On the other hand, the literature of Jewish-Christian polemic presumes and demonstrates that small-scale disputations and dialogues were commonplace between Jewish and Christian spokesmen and scholars of varying levels.[240]

Indeed, according to one such specific account, Count Henri Rozenne of Champagne asked Rabbenu Tam three questions about scriptural interpretations. The first of these concerned the status of Ḥanokh. Henri assumed that the verse in Genesis 5:24, "And Ḥanokh walked with the Almighty, but he ceased to exist since God took him," refers to the death of Ḥanokh. He wondered why Ḥanokh died at a relatively young age for his day (at 365 years), when many in those generations lived for around nine hundred years, especially since Ḥanokh had walked in the way of the Almighty, apparently more so than others. Rabbenu Tam's response was that Hanokh did not simply die as all other men do. Rather, he was literally "taken by God" to Him, in a special and unique way, in recognition of the fact that he was the seventh (successful) generation of mankind, just as the Almighty assigned an enhanced status to the seventh day of the week and to the seventh year in the cycle of years. It is perhaps suggestive that Rabbenu Tam proposed this approach to Henri, which is based on passages in *Pesiqta Rabbati* and *Va-Yiqra Rabbah*, rather than the approach favored by Rashi in his commentary, which is based on *Bereshit Rabbah*, that Ḥanokh was taken early from his earthly existence simply because he sinned. Nonetheless, this exchange bespeaks a fairly open kind of interaction and dialogue between these figures, and should perhaps be seen as a model in this regard.[241]

240 See above, n. 174.

241 See *Tosafot ha-Shalem*, ed. Gellis, 1:178, sec. 8, citing ms. Bodl. 271/1 (IMHM #16739). The passage begins, שאל השלטון מקופניא לר"ת, and concludes, זה ענה ר"ת מנוחתו בגן עדן כבוד אל השלטון ויישרו בעיניו. See also *Perushei R. Ḥayyim Palti'el ʿal ha-Torah*, ed. Y. S. Lange (Jerusalem, 1981), 108. For an analysis of the larger cultural contexts of these consultations, see Rami Reiner, "Rabbenu Tam ve-Henri Rozen Champagne—Ha-Yelkhu Shenayim Yaḥdav Bilti ʾim Noʿadu," in *Leyl Iyyun le-Zikhrono shel Prof. Yisrael Ta-Shma*, ed. Institute for Jewish Studies, Hebrew University (Jerusalem, 2005), 29–36. Cf. Norman Golb, "Jacob Tam's Service on Behalf of the King of France at Reims and the Question of Remois Hebraic Scholarship in the Twelfth Century," http://oi.uchicago.edu.research/projects/scr/jacob_tam_2007.pdf, 1–13. On Rabbenu Tam's (similar) use of *midrashim* such as *Pesiqta* to establish the nature and role of Metatron, see Daniel Abrams, "The Boundaries of Divine Ontology: The Inclusion and Exclusion of Metatron in the Godhead," *Harvard Theological Review* 87 (1994), 298–305, and cf. below, chapter 2.

Similarly, there is specific evidence for meaningful contacts between Jewish and Christian Bible scholars, who discussed the nature of *peshat* and other styles of biblical interpretation.[242] Although there were a number of Christian Bible scholars who could read Hebrew and the Hebrew text of the Bible, Christian exegetes and Bible scholars typically report that they learned about Jewish exegetical techniques and conclusions "by heart" (and through listening); they did not learn of these techniques from the written Hebrew sources or treatises of Jewish biblical exegesis. Thus Abelard, who was among those Christian scholars who could read Hebrew to some degree, tells Heloise that he listened to a Jew who was teaching or explaining verses in the Book of Kings.[243] Eleazar Touitou and Sara Kamin have argued that, similarly, Jewish scholars absorbed techniques of Christian exegetes from their conversations with these exegetes.[244]

There is no reason to think that a similar process could not have occurred with regard to dialectic, whereby Jewish scholars *heard* from their Christian counterparts about the different forms and general methodologies of dialectic as it was applied in Christian scholarly circles. Indeed, if a circle with a radius of sixty miles is drawn around the leading cathedral schools in northern France during the twelfth century (such as Laon, Chartres, Orleans, and Paris), all of the most significant Tosafist study halls in northern France will also be found within the limits of that circle. As noted, Abelard reached Paris after having taught at Melun and at Corbeil, which was not far to the south of Paris. He also spent some time (after being condemned in 1221) in the monastery at Saint Denis, and with the Bishop of

242 See above, n. 175. See also Sara Kamin, *Jews and Christians Interpret the Bible* (Jerusalem, 1991), 13–61, and 12*–68*; and Michael Signer, "King/Messiah in Rashi's Exegesis of Psalms 2," *Prooftexts* 3 (1983), 273–78.

243 On Abelard's knowledge of Hebrew, see A. Grabois, "The Hebraica Veritas," 617 (n. 20) and 628. Cf. *A Dialogue of a Philosopher with a Jew and a Christian*, ed. P. Payer (Toronto, 1979), 9; and D. Berger, "Mission to the Jews," 584. Abelard's report to Heloise that he *listened* to a Jew teaching the Book of Kings is found in *Patrologia Latina*, vol. 178, col. 718. As described by Gilbert Dahan, things change from the Christian standpoint with the passage of time, as Latin translations of portions of Rashi's Torah commentary begin to appear after the trial of the Talmud in 1240. See *La brulement du Talmud a Paris, 1242–44*, ed. G. Dahan (Paris, 1999), 7–20, 95–120.

244 See above, nn. 175, 241. See also Gad Freudenthal's brief review of *The Cambridge Companion to Abelard* in *Aleph* 7 (2007), 353–54. Freudenthal notes that a manuscript which preserves a commentary (probably) by Abelard, "seems to record verbatim what happened in the lectures: not only comments and jokes in the vernacular, but lengthy argumentative exchanges." He concludes that "if indeed some of the instruction given by Abelard and others in that period was in the vernacular, it is possible that some Jews could have understood at least snippets of it. . . . [Moreover,] if some teaching took place in the vernacular, the assumption that developments within Scholastic philosophy [in northern France] directly influenced Jews becomes more plausible."

Troyes. The Paraclete in Champagne, where Abelard taught students prior to returning to Paris, was less than ten miles from Troyes, and Abelard was supposed to debate Bernard of Clairvaux at one point in Sens.[245] Virtually all these locales had significant Tosafist study halls within them.[246]

It is certainly possible to grasp the basic concepts, ideas, and definitions of dialectic in the course of direct conversation. Talmudists could absorb these ideas and utilize them based on their conversations with Christians or even if they simply heard about them, just as the Christians learned about and activated the principles of *peshat* methodology as they received them orally from the Jews. To be sure, Jewish and Christian biblical exegetes were working with the same basic text, which created a closer connection between them; this was not the case, of course, with regard to Christian canonists or legists and talmudic scholars. But since the dialectical method as such was not at all foreign to talmudic scholars, they could easily adjust to the extensions and developments in this realm that were being put forward by Christians.

There are other instances of important Christian educational methods or fundamental principles in Christian learning that medieval European rabbinic scholars heard about and ultimately adopted. The Italian rabbinic scholar R. Isaiah b. Mali di Trani (d. c. 1240) studied in Germany with the Tosafist R. Simḥah of Speyer at the end of the twelfth century, and also absorbed teachings of Rabbenu Tam by way of his German Tosafist students.[247] In one of his halakhic responsa, R. Isaiah presents a parable that he reports he heard from philosophers (אלא אני דן בעצמי משל הפילוסופים. שמעתי מחכמי הפילוסופים שאלו לגדול שבהם ואמרו לו וכו'), of a midget standing on the shoulders of a giant, who can see farther and understand more than the giant himself. R. Isaiah employs this parable to justify his stance that all qualified decisors of his day can question and disagree with their post-talmudic predecessors based on the precise proofs and well-based logical

[245] See J. Le Goff, *Intellectuals in the Middle Ages*, 35–36, 41–45; M. T. Clanchy, *Abelard*, 245; Southern, "The Schools of Paris and the School of Chartres," 121–23; G. R. Evans, *Bernard of Clairvaux*, 115–23. See also Jean Leclerq, "Renewal of Theology," in *Renaissance and Renewal*, ed. Benson and Constable, 78: "For Champagne in particular, it is necessary to keep in mind the personal and cultural relationships that may have existed between the cathedral school of Troyes, the abbeys of Clairvaux and the Paraclete, the court of Marie de France, and the yeshiva or rabbinical academy of Troyes." Cf. Peter Schafer, *Mirror of His Beauty* (Princeton, 2002), 157–61, 189–91, 240–41.

[246] For additional comparative perspective, Stephan Kuttner notes that canonistic treatises were produced in the last third of the twelfth century in and around Paris, Rouen, Oxford, Northampton, Cologne, and Mainz, and perhaps Troyes and Rheims. See Kuttner, "The Revival of Jurisprudence," in *Renaissance and Renewal*, ed. Benson and Constable, 316–19.

[247] See, e.g., I. Ta-Shma, *Knesset Meḥqarim*, vol. 3 (Jerusalem, 2005), 20–30, 40–48; and below, chapter 7.

arguments they put forward in interpreting the underlying talmudic texts, even though the predecessors are indeed considered to be much greater as individual scholars than their successors. Indeed, as we have seen, northern French Tosafists, including Ri of Dampierre (d. 1189), his student R. Samson of Sens (d. 1214), and the brothers of Evreux (d. c. 1250), also expressed views that fully accorded with this larger theory or approach.[248]

This parable was first put forward by Bernard of Chartres (d. 1126) and his student, William of Conches, and later by John Salisbury (d. 1180) and Peter of Blois (d. 1212), to explain how thinkers and philosophers in their day could argue with the founding fathers of philosophy and religious thought.[249] This is indeed a "big idea" that had wide support within Christian scholarship, such that Ashkenazic rabbinic scholars could easily hear about it and adopt it without any textual grounding that required the ability to read Latin. R. Isaiah's devoted follower in Italy, Zedekiah b. Abraham *ha-Rofe min ha-ʿanavim* (Anau), cites this parable in R. Isaiah's name in the introduction to his own halakhic compendium, *Shibbolei ha-Leqet* (mid-thirteenth century), making explicit that the scholars (or philosophers) from whom R. Isaiah di Trani heard this parable were non-Jews.[250]

Just prior to the appearance of the first edition of Urbach's *Baʿalei ha-Tosafot*, Shalom Albeck theorized that a basic premise of medieval scholasticism—which held that any new and, thereby, speculative legal teaching or ratification of custom had to be harmonized with existing collections and accepted sources of law—must have reached Rabbenu Tam through his personal contacts with Christian scholars.[251] In a more recent study, Talya Fishman has pointed to some suggestive parallels between the written penitential treatises and tracts of the Christians and various penitential theories and practices of the German Pietists. Fishman maintains that if, indeed, the German Pietists formulated their *tiqqunei teshuvah* under some

248 See *Teshuvot ha-Rid le-Rabbenu Yeshayah di-Trani ha-Zaqen*, ed. A. Y. Wertheimer (Jerusalem, 1972), 302–3 (responsum 62). Cf. *Teshuvot ha-Rid* 6–7 (responsum 1), and my "Progress and Tradition in Medieval Ashkenaz," *Jewish History* 114 (2000), 288–90. It should also be noted that the cathedral school at Chartres (as renovated in the thirteenth century) had a stained-glass window scene of dwarfs who were perched on the shoulders of giants; see Le Goff, *Intellectuals in the Middle Ages*,13. For the views of Ri, R. Samson, and the brother of Evreux, see above, nn. 148–50.

249 See Robert Merton, *On the Shoulders of Giants* (Chicago, 1993), 37–41, 209–23. See also Umberto Eco's forward, xiv–xv, and Abraham Melamed, *ʿAl Kitfei ʿAnaqim* (Ramat Gan, 2003), for additional bibliography.

250 See *Shibbolei ha-Leqet*, ed. S. Buber (Vilna, 1889), fol. 18r (in the introduction, = ed. S. K. Mirsky [New York, 1966], 107–8): השיב האלוף המסובל ה"ר ישעיה מטרני לחבר אחד אשר שאלהו . . . והמ־ שיל עליו במשל אשר מחכמי הגוים שהפילוסופים שאלו לגדול שבהם וכו׳. Cf. above, n. 70.

251 See S. Albeck, "Yashaso shel Rabbenu Tam le-Beʿayot Zemanno," *Zion* 19 (1954), 112–13, and cf. above, n. 241.

measure of Christian influence, this influence reached them not necessarily through the written texts of the Christians but rather through conversations in the marketplace and in other economic contexts, or when the Jews observed Christians fulfilling their penitential teachings and procedures in public and outdoor venues. Fishman suggests that the manual of penitential regimens compiled by Burchard of Worms in the early eleventh century influenced R. Eleazar of Worms, a leading figure among *Ḥasidei Ashkenaz* who wrote his penitential treatises some two hundred years after Burchard. However, Burchard's widely copied work, which was very influential within Christian society, had an impact on Jewish society not in its written form but rather because Jews learned about it by observing the practices of the Christians around them, which were in accordance with this text.[252]

Given the presence of dialectic within the Talmud itself (and the developments at the academy of Worms by the late eleventh century), Jewish awareness of and comfort with the nature and dimensions of Christian dialectic is perhaps even easier to assume than the path of acculturation that Fishman has suggested with regard to the *tiqqunei teshuvah* of *Ḥasidei Ashkenaz.*[253] Indeed, a section in *Sefer Ḥasidim* clearly shows that around 1200, Jews in Germany at least recognized the dialectic prevalent within Christian learning, and that this was a highly significant and central method of study for them.[254] As stated earlier, *Sefer Ḥasidim* strongly objects to the use of (unrestrained) *pilpul* and dialectic, especially by students who were not qualified or properly prepared to do so. In the section in question, the author of *Sefer Ḥasidim* maintains that it is inappropriate for students of Torah to be under the influence of disciplines or methods that are not in accordance with the ethos of the Torah, and especially that Jewish scholars not be unduly influenced by the "*dialeqtiqah shel goyim.*"[255]

At the end of this section, the author also decries *limmud shel nizzaḥon*, which reflects the *disputationes* that were typically conducted in the cathedral schools of the twelfth century. Although this section does not demonstrate

[252] See T. Fishman, "The Penitential System of Ḥasidei Ashkenaz and the Problem of Cultural Boundaries," *Journal of Jewish Thought and Philosophy* 8 (1999), 214–18. Cf. Eva Haverkamp, "Martyrs in Rivalry: The 1096 Martyrs and the Thebean Legend," *Jewish History* 23 (2009), 330–35.

[253] On the similarities between older Jewish ascetic (and mystical) approaches and medieval Christian practices, and the implications for influence in the medieval Jewish milieu, see, e.g., Peter Schafer, "The Ideal of Piety of the Ashkenazi Ḥasidim and Its Roots in Jewish Tradition," *Jewish History* 4 (1990), 9–23; Ivan Marcus, *Rituals of Childhood* (New Haven, Conn., 1996), 102–27; Fishman, "The Penitential System of Ḥasidei Ashkenaz," 218–23; and my "*Peering through the Lattices,*" 125–30, 253–58.

[254] See *Sefer Ḥasidim* (Parma), sec. 752; I. Ta-Shma, *Halakhah, Minhag u-Mezi'ut be-Ashkenaz*, 119–29; idem, *Ha-Sifrut ha-Parshanit la-Talmud*, 1:81–84; and my *Jewish Education and Society*, 73–75, 86–88.

[255] Cf. Haym Soloveitchik, "Three Themes in the *Sefer Ḥasidim*" (above, n. 224).

that the Jews knew about the specific details or mechanics of Christian dialectic, it does show that they recognized this as an important and effective method in the eyes of the Christians, and they were certainly familiar with it in broad terms.[256] Since the dialectical method was to be found earlier within the talmudic corpus, and among earlier rabbinic scholars in Ashkenaz as well, the Jews' familiarity with the use of this method by the Christians could well have led to additional interest on the part the Jews. It appears that Christian dialectic acted on Jewish scholarship as a kind of "enzyme," hastening, sharpening, and expanding the process of dialectical study, and it was the unfettered continuation of this process and its extension even to unqualified students that *Sefer Ḥasidim* feared.

Indeed, we can even find an example within the Christian world of the kind of process I have described. The canonist Gratian, who worked exclusively in Bologna as far as we can tell, may also have studied theological dialectic with Abelard in northern France. Gratian's *Concordia discordantium canonum* (better known by its brief name, *Decretum*) has been characterized in the following terms by David Knowles: "It was Gratian's great achievement to compile a comprehensive and fairly well arranged body of legal pronouncements, carefully grouped under leading headings of subject and topic, and to apply to them the *Sic et Non* method of dialectic [of Abelard], giving also in most cases a judgement on the issue and a brief discussion in which critical and legal principles were displayed."[257]

Richard Southern has also suggested that Gratian was influenced by Abelard's *Sic et Non.*[258] Although Gratian's presence at academic institutions in northern France is difficult to prove conclusively, Gratian's work certainly reached Paris itself by the middle of the twelfth century, as demonstrated by its citation in Peter Lombard's *Sentences*, a work that was composed in Paris no later than 1158.[259] Moreover, much of what we know about Gratian comes from Parisian sources. Indeed, there are a series of parallels between

[256] Note also, for example, the awareness by *Sefer Ḥasidim* (and R. Eleazar of Worms) of the strict discipline that was enforced in the churches during Christian prayer, a practice that *Ḥasidei Ashkenaz* sought to forcefully instill within the synagogues as well. See, e.g., Moshe Hallamish, "Siḥat Ḥullin be-Beit ha-Knesset: Meẓi'ut u-Ma'avaq," *Milet* 2 (1985), 226–27, 243–44, and my "*Peering through the Lattices*," 83–84. Cf. Ivan Marcus, "A Jewish-Christian Symbiosis: The Culture of Early Ashkenaz," in *Cultures of the Jews*, ed. D. Biale (New York, 2002), 449–501.

[257] See David Knowles, *The Evolution of Medieval Thought*, 177–78. See also S. Kuttner, *Harmony from Dissonance*, 12–26; R. W. Southern, *The Making of the Middle Ages*, 205–6; and G. Leff, *Medieval Thought*, 130–31.

[258] Southern, *Scholastic Humanism*, 284–88, 292–96.

[259] See Anders Winroth, *The Making of Gratian's Decretum*, 136–42. Winroth offers this datum in the context of his larger thesis that Gratian's *Decretum* was produced in two recensions, the first by Gratian himself, before 1140, and the second (updated) recension by his successors (such as Bernard of Pavia), which included the first recension within it. It was this second or

the books of Abelard, Ivo of Chartres, Gratian, and Peter Lombard.[260] Although Gratian was somewhat less systematic than Ivo of Chartres and others among his predecessors, he exceled at putting forth comparative analyses that led to practical conclusions (just as the literature of the *Tosafot* did).

In the same way Gratian adapted the *theological* dialectic that he perhaps learned from Abelard in northern France—and found a way to use it in his deliberations and in the writing of his major legal work—it is quite possible that the early Tosafists used the essential elements of the dialectical methods that reached them through their contact with Christians to enhance their talmudic studies. Their steady and extensive use of the method, above and beyond what had been done in Worms during the late eleventh century, as a means of inquiring from and about the texts of the Talmud, which then allowed them to suggestively interpret these texts and to issue definitive halakhic conclusions, helped the Tosafists to establish their own renaissance, leading to a sea change in the study of Talmud and Jewish law.

Having identified a series of distinctions between Germany and northern France with respect to talmudic studies, and having suggested the possible impact that Christian scholarship may have had in some of these developments, we will now turn to the other disciplines that were pursued significantly by Tosafists. Much less is known with respect to the Tosafists and these disciplines; they were clearly somewhat secondary to the centrality of the Tosafist mission, which focused on the study of Talmud and *halakhah*. Nonetheless we shall see—and perhaps be surprised initially by—the extent to which, according to both manuscript and published texts, Tosafists did participate in these other disciplines, and took the time not only to write extensively within them but also to develop and to feature particular methods and forms of interpretation and composition as well. We will begin with the Tosafist interpretations of the text of the Torah itself, an activity that we shall survey and study over three successive periods, from the end of the twelfth century (primarily in northern France), during the early thirteenth century (in Germany), and during the mid-thirteenth century in both centers.

---

fuller recension that was cited by Peter Lombard of Paris in his *Sentences*, establishing that the completion of this second recension occurred before 1158, when Peter's *Sentences* appeared. See also J. Brundage, *The Medieval Origins of the Legal Profession*, 96–105. Winroth, 144, stresses the similarity between Peter Lombard's *Sentences* in the area of theology and Gratian's *Decretum* in the area of canon law. Note that a key element of the second recension of Gratian's work was its much better grasp of Roman law. Winroth shows that the study of Roman law in Bologna was undertaken in a significant way only c. 1140, when Gratian's first recension was already nearing completion. See Winroth, *The Making of Gratian's Decretum*, 171–73.

[260] See Southern and Winroth in the two preceding notes, and see also Somerville and Brasington, *Prefaces to Canon Law Books*, 170–80.

2

Tosafist Biblical Exegesis in Northern France at the End of the Twelfth Century

Between *Peshat* and *Derash*

On a certain level we would expect the Tosafists and other leading rabbinic scholars in medieval Ashkenaz to offer interpretations of biblical verses, since this traditional intellectual endeavor was fully consonant with their central mission as interpreters of the Talmud. Indeed, scattered throughout the standard *Tosafot* on the Babylonian Talmud are numerous passages that encounter and interpret biblical verses in the context of the halakhic (and even the non-halakhic or aggadic) *sugyot* at hand. Almost forty years ago Shraga Abramson published an edition of a *Tosafot* Torah commentary (from a Bodleian manuscript) that is essentially a series of *Tosafot* comments placed according to the order of the Torah portions of *Shoftim* and *Ki Teẓe*, and which constitutes a kind of Tosafist *midrash halakhah*.[1] Much of the material found in others of the so-called Tosafist Torah commentaries (*perushei Ba'alei ha-Tosafot 'al ha-Torah*) that have been published—including compilations such as *Da'at Zeqenim*, *Hadar Zeqenim*, *Moshav Zeqenim*, *Pa'aneaḥ*

[1] See *Ba'alei Tosafot 'al ha-Torah*, ed. S. Abramson (Jerusalem, 1974), based on ms. Bodl. 2679. With respect to the development of *midreshei halakhah*, the consensus of modern scholarship holds that these texts and their scriptural derivations preceded the Mishnaic organization of Tannaitic material in a topical way. See, e.g., E. E. Urbach, "Ha-Derashah ki-Yesod ha-Halakhah u-Be'ayat ha-Soferim," in his *Me-'Olamam shel Hakhamim* (Jerusalem, 1988), 50–66, and the discussion and studies cited in David Halivni, *Midrash, Mishnah, Gemara* (Cambridge, Mass., 1986), 18–68. In the case of the Tosafists, however, there is no doubt that the talmudic *Tosafot* were the original site of their interpretive activity, while the placement of these materials into the form of Torah commentaries reflects a subsequent development.

Raza, *Tosafot/Perush ha-Rosh*, *'Imrei No'am*, and *Minḥat Yehudah*[2]—reflects *Tosafot* interpretations that are essentially of a talmudic nature as well, although as we shall see, there is a common misconception that this type of interpretation represents the sum total of these compilations.[3]

E. E. Urbach does not say much about the Torah commentaries (or comments) of individual Tosafists, asserting at least initially that he will not deal with this aspect or form of Tosafist endeavor.[4] Nonetheless, Urbach does note from time to time that, aside from the recognized *pashtanim* such as R. Samuel b. Meir (Rashbam) and R. Yosef b. Isaac *Bekhor Shor* (of Orleans),[5] a number of other northern French Tosafists were also involved with some form of *parshanut ha-miqra*.

[2] Descriptions and publication data for these and other, related, collections are conveniently located in *Tosafot ha-Shalem*, ed. Jacob Gellis, vol. 1 (Jerusalem, 1982), editor's introduction, 11–20. (For a large selection of the manuscript collections of *perushei Ba'alei ha-Tosafot 'al ha-Torah*, see ibid., 21–38, with a supplemental list in *Tosafot ha-Shalem*, ed. Gellis, vol. 11 [Jerusalem, 2002], 11.) See also S. A. Poznanski, *Mavo 'al Ḥakhmei Ẓarefat Mefarshei ha-Miqra* (Warsaw, 1913; repr. Jerusalem, 1965), XCII–CXIV (who also describes a number of important manuscript collections); J. M. Orlian, "Sefer ha-Gan" (Ph.D. diss., Yeshiva University, 1973), 117–41 (= *Sefer ha-Gan*, ed. Orlian [Jerusalem, 2009], editor's introduction, 83–97, with some addenda); and Deborah Abecassis, "Reconstructing Rashi's Commentary on Genesis from Citations in the Torah Commentaries of the Tosafists" (Ph.D. diss., Concordia University, 1999), 42–48, 247–51.

[3] In his introduction, Abramson (above, n. 1), 7–10, compares and contrasts the collection that he presents with other published collections of Tosafist Torah commentaries, an exercise that serves to foster this misconception, albeit perhaps unwittingly. Nonetheless, the fact is that many more names of Tosafists are found in these collections in and around halakhic sections (such as *parashat Mishpatim* and the like) than in narrative sections.

[4] See E. E. Urbach, *Ba'alei ha-Tosafot* (Jerusalem, 1980), 1:18. More recently, several scholars have suggested that the study of Tosafist biblical interpretation (in its fullest manifestation and forms) remains an important desideratum. See, e.g., Y. S. Lange, "Ba'alei ha-Tosafot 'al ha-Torah—Ketav Yad Paris 48," *'Alei Sefer* 5 (1978), 74; Sara Japhet, "Ḥizkuni's Commentary on the Pentateuch," [Hebrew] in *Sefer ha-Yovel li-Khvod R. Mordekhai Breuer*, ed. M. Bar-Asher et al. (Jerusalem, 1992), 1:107; idem, "The Nature and Distribution of Compilatory Commentaries," [Hebrew] in *'Iyyunei Miqra u-Parshanut*, vol. 3, ed. M. Bar-Asher et al. (Ramat Gan, 1993), 215; idem, "The Nature and Distribution of Medieval Compilatory Commentaries in Light of Rabbi Joseph Kara's Commentary on the Book of Job," in *The Midrashic Imagination*, ed. M. Fishbane (Albany, N.Y., 1993), 130, n. 76; I. Ta-Shma, *Ha-Sifrut ha-Parshanit la-Talmud*, vol. 2 (Jerusalem, 2006), 96; idem, "Maqbilim she-Einam Nifgashim: Yeshivot Ba'alei ha-Tosafot veha-Sevivah ha-Aqadema'it be-Ẓarefat ba-Me'ot ha-Sheteim 'Esreh veha-Shelosh 'Esreh," in *Yeshivot u-Battei Midrashot*, ed. I. Etkes (Jerusalem, 2007), 83, n. 10; and Hazoniel Touitou, "Minḥat Yehudah: A Commentary by R. Yehudah b. Elazar," [Hebrew] (Ph.D. diss., Bar-Ilan University, 2004), 62, n. 74.

[5] Urbach, *Ba'alei ha-Tosafot*, 1:48–49, 134–36. Urbach, 1:40, notes the simplicity of the talmudic comments composed by Rashi's son-in-law, R. Judah b. Nathan, which also included simple interpretations of the biblical verses cited by the Talmud (and indications of when the talmudic exegesis of these verses strayed from the simplest interpretation). Urbach adds (at n. 30) that the Tosafist Torah compilation found in ms. Parma 541, as reported by Solomon Schechter ("Notes on a Hebrew Commentary to the Pentateuch in a Parma Manuscript," in *Semitic Studies in Memory of Dr. Alexander Kohut*, ed. G. A. Kohut [Berlin, 1897], 486), cites an interpretation

These Tosafists include Rabbenu Tam, whose Torah comments were made almost invariably within halakhic or talmudic contexts;[6] R. Moses of Pontoise, from whom a handful of comments have been preserved;[7] R. Jacob of Orleans, who authored a relatively large number of comments;[8] R. Yom Tov of Joigny, whose biblical comments are often cited in the name of תי"ט ב= *Tosafot Yom Tov*;[9] Yom Tov's colleague from Joigny, R. Menaḥem

---

in the *Ḥumash* commentaries composed by R. Judah b. Nathan (כן מצאתי כתוב בפירושים של חומש שעשה ר' יהודה בן נתן). This interpretation, however, to Gen. 15:16 (*ve-dor revi'i yashuvu henah*), is found word for word in the Torah commentary of R. Judah *he-Ḥasid* (which he dictated to his son, R. Zalman); somehow, the name of Judah's father, Samuel, became confused in the Parma manuscript (which, as Schechter also recorded, subsequently cites other comments by R. Judah *he-Ḥasid*). See *Perushei ha-Torah le-R. Yehudah he-Ḥasid*, ed. Y. S. Lange (Jerusalem, 1975), 20; and *Tosafot ha-Shalem*, ed. Gellis, vol. 2 (Jerusalem, 1983), 70–71, sec. 2. On R. Judah *he-Ḥasid*'s Torah commentary, see below, chapter 3, and on ms. Parma 541, see below, chapter 4.

[6] Urbach, *Ba'alei ha-Tosafot*, 1:107, and see below, n. 142. Urbach's (correct) sense (following Poznanski, *Mavo*, LIII–LIV) is that Rabbenu Tam did not compose a distinct Torah commentary (as opposed to his commentary to Job; see above, Introduction, n. 52). Indeed, Urbach, ibid., 1:144, is also unwilling to attribute ms. Paris 167 (Byzantium, 1443, fols. 51v–103v—a *Tosafot*-like commentary to the Torah which presents for the most part talmudic, midrashic, and halakhic discussions according to the order of the Torah, whose colophon describes it as *Tosafot shel Rabbenu Tam*—to R. Jacob of Orleans, a student of Rabbenu Tam (who himself offered a large number of Torah interpretations; see later in this chapter). Although this commentary is characterized elsewhere in the manuscript as a *perush ha-Torah le-R. Shelomoh ha-Kohen ben R. Ya'aqov ha-Kohen* (an otherwise unknown figure), Rabbenu Tam is mentioned nearly fifteen times in the manuscript, as are a number of his students from both northern France and Germany. However, the unnamed editor or compiler does not refer to Rabbenu Tam at any point as his teacher. Cf. my *"Peering through the Lattices": Mystical, Magical, and Pietistic Dimensions in the Tosafist Period* (Detroit, Mich., 2000), 197–200; and my "Midrashic Texts and Methods in Tosafist Torah Commentaries," in *Midrash Unbounded: Transformation and Innovation*, ed. M. Fishbane and J. Weinberg (Oxford, 2012), nn. 18, 103. See also Abraham Shoshana, "Ḥiddushim 'al ha-Torah le-Rabbenu Tam z"l," *Yeshurun* 14 (2004), 15–26, for a description and publication of several passages from a parallel manuscript text, ms. Moscow 362 (Candia, 1400, fols. 125–81v); and Hazoniel Touitou, "Minḥat Yehudah," 93–94. The colophon of ms. Moscow 362 describes the work as *pesaqim shel Rabbenu Tam she-hem kemo Tosafot 'al Perush Rabbenu Shelomoh*, and the first line of this manuscript begins with the phrase *'athil ḥiddushim shel Rabbenu Tam 'al ha-Torah.* However, interpretations in the name of R. Judah *he-Ḥasid* are also included (fols. 129r, 178r), as is one from R. Yiẓḥaq *ba'al ha-ḥotam* (= R. Isaac of Corbeil, fol. 177v). For examples of the halakhic (and talmudic) considerations typically put forth by Rabbenu Tam (and Ri of Dampierre), even in narrative sections of the Torah, see *Tosafot ha-Shalem*, ed. J. Gellis, vol. 3 (Jerusalem, 1984), 142–43, secs. 1–2; 3:172, sec. 11; *Sefer ha-Gan* to Gen. 18:10 (ed. Orlian, 156), and to Gen. 38:24 (ed. Orlian, 189). See also *Pa'aneaḥ Raza* to Gen. 48:1, ed. Machon Torat ha-Rishonim (Jerusalem, 1998), 203–4, and *Tosafot ha-Shalem*, ed. Gellis, vol. 5 (Jerusalem, 1986), 11–12, sec.11; ms. Leiden 27, fols. 19v and 33r; Poznanski, LIII (n. 2); and below, chapter 3, nn. 177, 183, 193.

[7] Urbach, *Ba'alei ha-Tosafot*, 1:132.

[8] Urbach, ibid., 1:144, citing L. Zunz, *Zur Geschichte und Literatur* (Berlin, 1845) [hereafter *ZGL*], 76, 91, 93, 97.

[9] Urbach, ibid., 1:146. Urbach notes the presence of comments from R. Yom Tov in the published version of the Tosafist Torah compilation *Pa'aneaḥ Raza*, and mentions (correctly) that a larger number of comments can be found in ms. Munich 50; see below, n. 192. As we shall

b. Pereẓ;[10] R. Judah of Corbeil;[11] R. Isaac b. Abraham of Dampierre, whose comments are typically of a halakhic or midrashic nature and also focus on the cantillations (*teʿamei ha-miqra*) and *gematria*;[12] R. Solomon of Dreux, several of whose comments appear to have been taken from his talmudic *Tosafot*;[13] R. Yeḥiʾel of Paris, whose comments are cited in a number of later *Baʿalei ha-Tosafot ʿal ha-Torah* collections;[14] R. Samuel of Falaise, from whom

---

also see, the version of *Paʿaneaḥ Raza* found in ms. B.M. 9931 (Gaster 730) yields several additional comments. See, e.g., *Tosafot ha-Shalem*, ed. Y. Gellis, vol. 4 (Jerusalem, 1985), 152–53 (to Gen. 42:5), sec. 1, which records a comment found in the Tosafist Torah compilation *Moshav Zeqenim*, ed. S. Sasoon (Jerusalem, 1982), 83, in the name of ר״י, which appears in ms. B. M. 9931, fol. 21v, in the name of ה״ר יום טוב מיוני; and see also below, n. 211. Urbach also notes that R. Yom Tov was a prolific *payyetan*; see below, chapter 5.

[10] Urbach, *Baʿalei ha-Tosafot*, 1:148–49. Urbach seems to suggest that the proximity and collegiality between R. Yom Tov and R. Menaḥem in Joigny played a factor in this common activity. A much smaller number of Torah comments have survived from R. Menaḥem as compared to those of R. Yom Tov (as we shall see), and the strong *peshat* component found in R. Yom Tov's comments is completely absent from those of R. Menaḥem (although R. Menaḥem is occasionally confused with R. Yom Tov with respect to biblical interpretations; see, e.g., below, n. 127). Indeed, virtually all the comments to the Torah attributed to R. Menaḥem either explain the exegesis of the Talmud without offering any other interpretation of the verses in question or put forward and explain halakhic rulings (or are summaries of these rulings presented by others). See *Tosafot Bava Meẓiʿa* 60a, s.v. *Rava*, and *ʿArakhin* 17a, s.v. *heseg* (and cf. Urbach, *Baʿalei ha-Tosafot*, 1:149, n.53); *Moshav Zeqenim*, ed. Sasoon, 144, 350, and 391 (which is found unnamed in *Tosafot Sanhedrin* 45, s.v. *barur*); *Perushim u-Pesaqim le-Rabbenu Avigdor*, ed. Machon Harerei Qedem (Jerusalem, 1996), 42, 75, 93–94, 174, 181, 361; *Tosafot ha-Shalem*, ed. Gellis, 6:14–15, sec. 9; 8:231, sec. 12; 9:8, sec. 21; and cf. 7:43, sec. 13. Urbach also notes that Menaḥem produced a treatise on the masoretic notes to the Bible (found in ms. Leipzig 1). Cf. J. S. Penkower, "The Tosaphist R. Menaḥem of Joigny and the Masoretic Work *ʾOkhlah ve-ʾOkhlah*, the Halle Manuscript Recension," [Hebrew] in *ʿIyyunei Miqra u-Parshanut*, ed. Bar-Asher (above, n. 4), 287–315; and see *Sefer Yosef ha-Meqanne*, ed. Judah Rosenthal (Jerusalem, 1970), 114 (sec. 124), for a polemical comment attributed to R. Menaḥem.

[11] See Urbach, *Baʿalei ha-Tosafot*, 1:151, although the two corroborative references cited by Urbach in n. 50* appear to refer to *piyyutim* rather than scriptural interpretations.

[12] Urbach, ibid., 1:270 (based on Zunz, *ZGL*, 78, 89, 100). See also Riẓba's midrashic exchange with R. Solomon of Dreux, in Urbach, 1:261 (n. 4); cf. my "Midrashic Texts and Methods in Tosafist Torah Commentaries," nn. 67–69; and below, chapter 3, nn. 177, 193, 216–18. Riẓba may have composed *piyyutim*; see Zunz, *Literaturgeschichte der synagogalen Poesie* (Berlin, 1865), 335, 622; and below, chapter 5, nn. 4, 129–30. At the same time, Urbach, 1:333, notes a lone biblical comment made by Riẓba's Tosafist colleague R. Judah Sirleon, which he suggests originated with one of R. Judah's *Tosafot* or *pesaqim*. Urbach also notes (1:361) that it is unclear whether the few citations attributed to R. Barukh b. Isaac (by Zunz, *ZGL*, 88, 97) were made by R. Barukh b. Isaac, author of *Sefer ha-Terumah* (see my "Midrashic Texts and Methods," n. 20; and below, chapter 3), or by R. Barukh b. Isaac of Regensburg (see above, chapter 1, n. 28), from whom *ʿArugat ha-Bosem* cites an interpretation to a verse in Psalms.

[13] Urbach, *Baʿalei ha-Tosafot*, 1:339–40. See also Norman Golb, *Toledot ha-Yehudim be-ʿIr Rouen* (Tel Aviv, 1977), 190–92 (appendix 7). Urbach (1:260) makes the same point about the Torah comments attributed to Ri and to his son R. Elḥanan (based on Zunz, *ZGL*, 74, 91, 93, 97).

[14] Urbach, ibid., 1:460, based on Zunz, *ZGL*, 89, 100, and Poznanski, *Mavo*, CIV, who also refers to a Torah commentary compiled by one of his students (in ms. Parma 541; see below, chapter 4). Urbach notes that R. Yeḥiʾel is also linked to *pashteh di-qra*, as cited by another of his

a few comments are cited by his descendant, R. Ḥayyim (Palti'el) of Falaise, in his own extensive Torah commentary/compilation;[15] R. Moses of Coucy, who authored a nonextant commentary titled *Peshatei ha-Ram mi-Coucy*, which is cited with some frequency in R. Judah b. Eliezer's compilation, *Minḥat Yehudah*, and in other *Tosafot ʿal ha-Torah* collections;[16] and R. Moses b. Shne'ur of Evreux, and his brothers, R. Samuel and R. Isaac.[17] Urbach finds little evidence for Torah comments or interpretations among the

---

students in a *Tosafot*-like commentary to tractate *Moʿed Qatan*. For *piyyut* interpretations by R. Yeḥi'el, see below, chapter 5, nn. 283–84.

15 See Urbach, ibid., 1:465, citing studies by B. Ziemlich and H. Gross (from the late nineteenth century). Y. S. Lange, "Le-Zehuto shel R. Ḥayyim Palti'el," *ʿAlei Sefer* 8 (1981), 144–45, maintains that R. Samuel of Falaise is not the grandfather (or ancestor) of R. Ḥayyim Palti'el of Falaise but rather the grandfather of the editor of R. Ḥayyim's commentary (an otherwise unidentified student of R. Ḥayyim and R. Solomon of Chateau-Landon). In the same year (and just after the revised two-volume edition of Urbach's *Baʿalei ha-Tosafot* appeared in 1980), Lange published the extensive *Perushei ha-Torah le-R. Ḥayyim Palti'el* (Jerusalem, 1981) on the basis of several manuscripts. Three comments in the name of *mori zeqeni R. Shmu'el mi-Falaise* are included (6, 38, 298), all of which are related to (or are derivations for) halakhic practices and customs. Moreover, the handful of comments from R. Samuel of Falaise reproduced in two parallel texts—the Tosafist Torah compilation *Moshav Zeqenim*, ed. Sasoon, 180, 193, 390, 461, and *Perushim u-pesaqim ʿal ha-Torah le-Rabbenu Avigdor (Ẓarefati) [Katz]*, ed. Machon Harerei Qedem (Jerusalem, 1996), 50, 178, 252, 355, 368—are all *pisqei halakhah* (or *Tosafot*-related talmudic comments) that are attached to various verses or Torah portions rather than discrete scriptural comments. (On these parallel texts, see, e.g., Simcha Emanuel, *Shivrei Luḥot: Sefarim Avudim shel Baʿalei ha-Tosafot*, [Jerusalem, 2007], 172, n. 89; cf. Urbach, *Baʿalei ha-Tosafot*, 1:486, n. 32, and below, chapter 4.) See also *Paʿaneaḥ Raza*, ed. Machon Torat ha-Rishonim, 119 (Gen. 25:5, and cf. *Bava Batra* 133b, *Yoma* 28b), and 265–66 (Ex. 19:13, and cf. *Tosafot Pesaḥim* 6b, s.v. *'aval*). In only one instance recorded by *Paʿaneaḥ Raza* (99, to Gen. 21:14), R. Samuel of Falaise poses and resolves a seeming contradiction to Rashi's interpretation, which does not appear to have any practical halakhic relevance. Cf. below, chapter 3, n. 125.

16 Urbach, *Baʿalei ha-Tosafot*, 1:478–79 (citing Poznanski, *Mavo*, XCIII).

17 Urbach, ibid., 1:484 (citing Poznanski, ibid., XCVIII), identifies *Sefer ha-Gan* as the source of R. Moses's comments. See now *Sefer ha-Gan*, ed. Orlian, 179, 187, 234, 299. From Zunz, *ZGL*, 82, Urbach notes a reference to R. Samuel of Evreux in a *sefer leʿazim* (see also Menachem Banitt, *Le Glossaire de Leipzig*, vol. 3 [Jerusalem, 2002], 1727 [entry 22068], and vol. 4 [Jerusalem, 2005], 418), and adds another reference to R. Isaac of Evreux in *Daʿat Zeqenim*. In fact, there are quite a few additional references that can be added, and a fuller exegetical theory or approach for the brothers of Evreux can be formulated (which tends mostly toward midrashic analysis). See my "Midrashic Texts and Methods," nn. 36–38, and section 8; and below, chapter 4. In *Baʿalei ha-Tosafot*, 2:508, Urbach notes the interest in *parshanut ha-miqra* exhibited by the English Tosafist Berekhyah of Nicole (or Lincoln, England), in the few and brief talmudic *Tosafot* comments of his that have survived, as well as the citation of R. Berekhyah in *Minḥat Yehudah* to Deut. 33:24 (fol. 26a). (I could not locate the references to R. Berekhyah mentioned by Urbach, *Baʿalei ha-Tosafot*, 1:508, n. 80, in *Hadar Zeqenim* and *Daʿat Zeqenim* to Deut. 33:23.) *Minḥat Yehudah* to Deut. 32:39 (fol. 23a) cites an interpretation by R. Berekhiah b. Isaac *ha-Naqdan*, a somewhat unusual exegetical specialist (and not a Tosafist; see above, Introduction, n. 83), although another comment by R. Berekhiah *me-Nicole* is found in manuscript versions of *Minḥat Yehudah* to Lev. 1:11 (fol.3a). See Hazoniel Touitou, "Minḥat Yehudah shel R. Yehudah b. Elazar," 74.

Tosafists of Germany.[18] Moreover, as the summary and notes presented in this section have shown, Urbach, like Zunz before him, has little analysis or discussion of the interpretations and methods of the various Tosafists whose comments he does note, making it rather difficult to get any sense of historical development, not to mention exegetical style and scope, in this area of Tosafist endeavor.

Where and how did the Tosafists study *miqra*? From the scattered evidence presented by Urbach, it would seem that this study took place primarily in the context of the talmudic lectures and discussions that were presented within the study halls and academies of the Tosafists. Indeed, the connotation of the (talmudic) phrases פשטיה דקרא (the simple meaning of a verse)[19] and אין מקרא יוצא מידי פשוטו (e.g., *Shabbat* 63a), which are employed approximately fifty times by the standard *Tosafot* to the Babylonian Talmud, do not refer to the meaning of the verse according to a formal exegetical approach, such as *peshat* or *peshuto shel miqra*, but rather to the way most people would read or understand a biblical verse simply, unencumbered by the halakhic or rabbinic derivations and interpretations that were engendered through the hermeneutical rules and techniques of the Oral Law.[20]

[18] As noted above (n. 12), Urbach is unsure whether comments attributed to R. Barukh b. Isaac belong to the student of Ri (and author of *Sefer ha-Terumah*) by that name, or to R. Barukh of Regensburg. Moreover, Urbach, *Ba'alei ha-Tosafot*, 1:387, is correctly skeptical about references to Torah comments made by Rabiah (אבי העזרי), as cited in R. Moses of Coucy's commentary. In fact, these passages are from the commentary of Ibn Ezra; see below, chapter 4, nn. 18, 97. As far as the Torah comments attributed to Riva (Urbach, *Ba'alei ha-Tosafot*, 1:173), who is ostensibly Riva *ha-Levi* of Speyer (d. 1133), Urbach correctly notes that there are other Tosafists who are referred to as ריב"א; and cf. above, n. 12. Moreover, the comment to Ezekiel that R. Yosef Qara heard from Riva *ha-Levi* of Speyer (as listed by Urbach) should perhaps be viewed as a manifestation of the pre-Crusade period, during which rabbinic scholars offered comments on verses outside of the Pentateuch with some frequency (see my *Jewish Education and Society*, 80), a pursuit in which few Tosafists were involved, other than committed *pashtanim* such as Rashbam and *Bekhor Shor*. Similarly, in the absence of other parallel comments, the comments of R. Samuel b. Qalonymus *he-Ḥasid* to the Torah and to other biblical verses (Urbach, *Ba'alei ha-Tosafot*, 195) seemingly reflect the intellectual milieu of *Ḥasidei Ashkenaz* rather than that of the Tosafist academies. In *Ba'alei ha-Tosafot*, 2:585, Urbach notes that references to comments by *Tosafot Tukh* in the so-called Tosafist Torah compilations are to R. Eliezer of Tukh's talmudic *Tosafot* rather than to direct biblical comments that he composed or compiled.

[19] This phrase is found seven times within the Talmud itself. See, e.g., *'Eruvin* 23b, and cf. *Tosafot*, ad loc., s.v. *pashteh*.

[20] See, e.g., *Tosafot Berakhot* 31a, s.v. *be-maqom*; *Shabbat* 3a, s.v. *ba-'asotah*; *'Eruvin* 63a, s.v. *kol ha-notein*; *Pesaḥim* 21b, s.v. *likhtov*; *Rosh ha-Shanah* 3a, s.v. *Arad*; *Yoma* 62b, s.v. *musafin*; *Beiẓah* 20a, s.v. *lamad*; *Ketubot* 7b, s.v. *she-ne'emar*; *Ketubot* 99a, s.v. *natan*; *Yevamot* 3a, s.v. *bitto*; *Yevamot* 78a, s.v. *miẓri*; *Bava Meẓi'a* 61a, s.v. *qari*; *Sanhedrin* 42b, s.v. *melammed*; *Sanhedrin* 52o, s.v. *keshehu*; *'Avodah Zarah* 3b, s.v. *'im*; *Menaḥot* 53b, s.v. *ben yedid*; *Ḥullin* 24a, s.v. *minayin*; *Ḥullin* 98b, s.v. *de-kulei 'alma. Niddah* 42b, s.v. *mah talmud lomar. Tosafot 'Arakhin* 26a, s.v. *mai*, maintains that since the *pashteh di-qra* of the verse being discussed by the Talmud supports the halakhic interpretation of the Tanna R. Eliezer, the attempt by the Talmud to ascertain the reasoning behind R. Eliezer's position appears to be superfluous. In two instances in tractate *Ta'anit*, the use of

There is specific evidence for study of the weekly Torah portion in the French Tosafist academy of R. Meshullam of Melum, although the discussion in this instance, as well, was from a halakhic perspective.[21] The talmudic obligation to review the weekly Torah portion employing the format of *shenayim miqra ve-eḥad targum*, which was considered to be fully in effect in medieval Ashkenaz, certainly presented an opportunity to review the text of the Torah within the Tosafist academies with the commentary of Rashi alongside of or in place of the Aramaic Targum, although it remains unclear whether this was most often accomplished through organized study or on an individualized basis.[22]

At the same time, however, the standard *Tosafot* to the Babylonian Talmud cite Rashi's Torah commentary about fifty times, either to confirm or to probe the Talmud's interpretation or use of a particular verse or phrase,[23]

---

this phrase by *Tosafot* does have the connotation of more specialized *peshat* exegesis. See *Tosafot Taʿanit* 5a, s.v. *loʾavo* (in reference to Hosea 11:9, and cf. the commentaries of Rashi and R. Yosef Qara, ad loc.); *Taʿanit* 20a, s.v. *ve-neʿetarot*; and cf. *Tosafot Ḥagigah* 5b, s.v. *hen* and s.v. *va-yehi.* See also Eleazar Touitou, *Exegesis in Perpetual Motion* (Jerusalem, 2003), 163, for the coincidence of an interpretation proposed by *Tosafot Ḥullin* 95b, s.v. *ke-Eliʿezer* (on the approach of one of the Tannaim in the *sugya*) and the literary *peshat* of Rashbam to Gen. 24:22. It is suggestive that the phrase (and notion) of *pashteh di-qra* are only rarely identified in the standard *Tosafot* with the name of a particular Tosafist. Cf. *Tosafot Sanhedrin* 43b, s.v. *ʾamar* (Rabbenu Tam; see above, n. 6, and see also Urbach, "Sefer ʿArugat ha-Bosem le-R. Avraham b. Azriʾel," *Tarbiz* 10 [1939], 46, n. 130a); *Sanhedrin* 83b, s.v. *ʾein* (R. Jacob of Orleans; see above, n. 8). Regarding R. Yeḥiʾel of Paris and this phrase, see Urbach, *Baʿalei ha-Tosafot*, 1:460 (above, n. 14). On the connotation of *pashteh di-qra*, see also Sarah Kamin, *Rashi's Exegetical Categorizations* [Hebrew] (Jerusalem, 1986), 28–37; *Rashbam's Commentary on Deuteronomy*, ed. Martin Lockshin (Providence, R.I., 2004), editor's introduction, 2–3; and Moshe Ahrend, *Parshanut ha-Miqra ve-Horaʾato* (Jerusalem, 2006), 9–16.

21 See *Sefer ha-Yashar* (*ḥeleq ha-teshuvot*), ed. S. F. Rosenthal (Berlin, 1898), sec. 47:1 (כשהיינו למדין סדר זאת תהיה [תורת] המצורע). See also *Gezerot Ashkenaz ve-Ẓarefat*, ed. A. M. Habermann (Jerusalem, 1971), 164, on the study of the weekly Torah portion by R. Eleazar of Worms in his home; and Solomon Schechter, "Notes on a Hebrew Commentary to the Pentateuch in a Parma Manuscript" (above, n. 5), 485–86, regarding an apparent exchange between R. Yeḥiʾel of Paris and his students on *parashat Lekh Lekha* (and see also below, chapter 4). Cf. *R. Eleazar mi-Vermaiza, Derashah le-Pesaḥ*, ed. Simcha Emanuel (Jerusalem, 2006), editor's introduction, 45; and my "Bein Yeshivot Baʿalei ha-Tosafot le-Battei Midrash Aḥerim be-Ashkenaz Bimei ha-Benayim," in *Yeshivot u-Battei Midrashot*, ed. Etkes, 102.

22 See my *Jewish Education and Society in the High Middle Ages* (Detroit, Mich., 2007), 81–82, and 182 (n. 111); J. S. Penkower, "The Canonization of Rashi's Commentary on the Pentateuch," [Hebrew] in *Limmud ve-Daʿat be-Maḥshevet Yisraʾel*, ed. H. Kreisel (Beer Sheva, 2006), 123–46; *Sefer Or Zaruʿa le-R. Yiẓḥaq b. Mosheh* (Zhitomir, 1862), pt. 1, *hilkhot qeriʾat Shema*, sec. 11; Y. S. Lange, "Pisqei R. Yiẓḥaq mi-Corbeil," *Hamaʿayan* 16:4 (1976), 95 (sec. 8); and *Sefer Tashbeẓ le-R. Shimshon b. Ẓadoq* (Jerusalem, 1975), sec. 185.

23 See, e.g., *Tosafot Ḥagigah* 6b, s.v. *R. Aqiva*; 12a, s.v. *mi-sof*; and 16b, s.v. *ʾav*; *Tosafot Ketubot* 20b, s.v. *R. Yoḥanan*; *Tosafot Gittin* 60a, s.v. *Torah*; *Tosafot Bava Batra* 115b, s.v. *melammed*; *Tosafot Menaḥot* 94a, s.v. *ukeshe-hu.*; and Peretz Tarshish, *Ishim u-Sefarim be-Tosafot*, ed. H. S. Neuhausen (New York, 1942), 114–15.

although on occasion to critically review and even to question Rashi's Torah comments.[24] Moreover, in light of the oft-cited assertion by Rabbenu Tam that study of the Babylonian Talmud—which is suffused with biblical and Mishnaic texts—alone fulfills the dictum of R. Joshua b. Ḥananyah that one must study equal measures of the Bible, Mishnah, and Talmud, the question remains whether the study of the Bible and its interpretation, as an independent set of texts and values, constituted a significant part of the intellectual activity and mindset of the Tosafists in northern France.[25]

This question is heightened by the fact that while Rashbam and R. Yosef b. Isaac *Bekhor Shor* of Orleans were also active participants in the unfolding Tosafist discussions and analyses of talmudic texts,[26] their fellow *pashtanim*

[24] See *Tosafot Rosh ha-Shanah* 3a, s.v. *va-yishma*; *Tosafot Yoma* 4a, s.v. *nikhnesu*; *Tosafot Yoma* 5b, s.v. *bi-ketonet*; *Tosafot Ketubot* 37b, s.v. *ve-ʾaḥar*; *Tosafot Bava Batra* 117a, s.v *u-maḥzirin*; *Tosafot Menaḥot* 75a, s.v. *ke-min*. *Tosafot ʿArakhin* 15b, s.v. *hitʾavu*, presents a comment by R. Yosef Qara about the quail the Israelites received as food in the desert, which conflicts with Rashi's comment to that verse (Nu. 11:4). *Tosafot Menaḥot* 65, s.v. *ʾaḥad ʿasar*, points to a contradiction between Rashi's talmudic commentary and his Torah commentary (to Deut. 1:2). Cf. Yonah Fraenkel, *Darkhei ha-Aggadah veha-Midrash* (Tel Aviv, 1996), 1:517. For a discussion and detailed talmudic analysis of a comment by Rashi to the Torah (to Ex. 4:19), which seems to have taken place at least initially without Rashi's comment being explicitly mentioned, see *Tosafot Nedarim* 7b, s.v. *ʿaniyyut*; and *Tosafot ʿAvodah Zarah* 5a, s.v. *ʾela*. Cf. *Tosafot ha-Shalem*, ed. J. Gellis, vol. 6 (Jerusalem, 1987), 114–15; and ms. Paris 1292, fols. 49v–50r (where the discussion begins with Rashi's comment).

[25] The standard *Tosafot* to the Talmud cite *Bereshit Rabbah* tens of times; indeed, *Bereshit Rabbah* is the midrashic work most often cited by *Tosafot*. See Peretz Tarshish, *Ishim u-Sefarim ba-Tosafot*, 87–89. Most of these citations, however, are intended to explain the text of the Talmud or to provide additional rabbinic materials related to the talmudic discussion, and not as opportunities to analyze or to discuss the text of *Bereshit Rabbah* cited (or the underlying Torah verse) for its own sake. See my "Midrashic Texts and Methods in Tosafist Torah Commentaries," sec. 1. Nonetheless, there were individual Tosafists who did show particular interest in midrashic interpretation, irrespective of its connection to talmudic study. See below, chapters 3 and 4.

[26] On the Tosafist careers of Rashbam and R. Yosef b. Isaac of Orleans (who was a talmudic student of Rabbenu Tam), see Urbach, *Baʿalei ha-Tosafot*, 1:45–57, 132–40. As Urbach indicates (1:134), the identification of R. Yosef *Bekhor Shor* with the Tosafist R. Yosef of Orleans is no longer in doubt. Cf. Poznanski, *Mavo*, LVI–LVII; *Perushei R. Yosef Bekhor Shor ʿal ha-Torah* (Jerusalem, 1994), ed. Y. Nevo, editor's introduction, 1–2. In addition to the sources cited by Urbach, see the (*ʾalfa-beta*) introduction of R. Isaac b. Moses of Vienna to his *Sefer Or Zaruʿa* (Zhitomir, 1862), vol. 1, sec. 20 (fol. 4a), which cites R. Yosef *Bekhor Shor*'s grammatical and polemical interpretation to Deut. 6:4 (*Shema Yisraʾel*; see *Perushei Bekhor Shor ʿal ha-Torah*, ed. Nevo, 316–17) as ופי' ה"ר יוסף דאורליינש בפירושי החומש שלו, and cf. *Sefer Yosef ha-Meqanne*, ed. Rosenthal, 57–58. See also *Sefer Or Zaruʿa, Hilkhot ʿerev Shabbat*, pt. 2, sec. 31 (fol. 8a): וכבר היה מפרש ה"ר יוסף דאור־ליינש דכינה היינו שקורין בילחא ובלע"ז פוצ"א דכתיב והך את עפר הארץ והיה לכנים דהיינו אותם שחורים שקופצים שגדלים ע"ג קרקע, which is found in *Bekhor Shor*'s commentary to Ex. 8:12 (Nevo, 108), and is also cited in *Tosafot Shabbat* 12a, s.v. *ve-shema*, in the name of R. Yosef of Orleans. In his Torah commentary to Lev. 25:20 (ed. Nevo, 231), R. Yosef *Bekhor Shor* writes וכן פירשתי בהלכות ספיחים בפסחים. As Nevo notes, this ruling is found in *Tosafot Pesaḥim* 51b, s.v. *kol ha-sefiḥim ʾasurim*, in the name of *Bekhor Shor*'s teacher Rabbenu Tam. See also *Tosafot ha-Rosh ʿal Masskhet Pesaḥim*, ed. A. Shoshana (Jerusalem, 2006), 713, 773–80. Moreover, *Bekhor Shor*'s reference in his Torah commentary (248) to a comment of his on tractate *Ḥullin* is found in the name of R. Yosef of

in northern France during the twelfth century, R. Yosef Qara and R. Eliezer of Beaugency, apparently were not. R. Yosef Qara, as his title suggests, was akin to a professor of Bible, whose lessons were taught to so-called *maskilim* rather than to *Ba'alei Talmud.* Qara had studied at the academy of Worms in pre-Crusade Germany, but his scholarly role in the twelfth century was in the area of *peshuto shel miqra* and *piyyut* commentary.[27] There is no evidence for any involvement by R. Eliezer of Beaugency in either talmudic studies or with Tosafist academies.[28] In a study of Jewish attitudes in the twelfth century toward the election of Israel, Haim Hillel Ben-Sasson cites from R. Eliezer of Beaugency's interpretations on the books of the later prophets,

---

Orleans in *Tosafot Ḥullin* 98b–99a, s.v. *Rava* (as noted by Nevo, n. 11). A large piece of *Bekhor Shor*'s interpretation to Nu. 30:3 on the recanting of vows (ed. Nevo, 296), in which he also refers to what he saw from unnamed *gedolim* (= Rabbenu Tam, as found in *Tosafot 'Eruvin* 64b, s.v. *potḥin*; see Nevo, n. 19), is included (with attribution) in a responsum by R. Meir of Rothenburg. See *Sefer Mordekhai le-Massekhet Shavu'ot*, sec. 759 (end) (= *Maharam: Teshuvot, Pesaqim u-Minhagim*, ed. Y. Z. Kahana, vol. 2 [Jerusalem, 1960], 246–47 [*pesaqim*], sec. 177). At the end of his comment to Nu. 34:4 (Nevo, 301–2), *Bekhor Shor* çites the *Zera'im* commentary of his Tosafist colleague R. Samson of Sens (to *Mishnah Shevi'it* 6:1). See also *Bekhor Shor*'s commentary to Nu. 32:30 (Nevo, 300); to Deut. 17:17 (Nevo, 345, *ken mukheḥa ha-sugya*); and to Deut. 24:13 (Nevo, 361, *ve-khen pasqu kol ha-Ge'onim*); *Tosafot Makkot* 6a, s.v. *nirva*, and 8a, s.v. *haynu.* For two other students of R. Simḥah of Speyer (aside from R. Isaac *Or Zaru'a*) who were aware of *Bekhor Shor*'s Torah commentary, see *'Arugat ha-Bosem le-R. Avraham b. Azri'el*, ed. Urbach, vol. 4 (1963), 154, 164; and see below, chapter 3, for R. Isaiah di Trani.

27 See, e.g., Moshe Ahrend, *Perush R. Yosef Qara le-Iyyov* (Jerusalem, 1988), 17–22, 43; A. Grossman, *Ḥakhmei Ẓarefat ha-Rishonim*, 255–63; E. Touitou, *Exegesis in Perpetual Motion*, 11–13, 26–27, 51–52, 98–105 (on *maskilim* versus *Ba'alei Talmud*); Eran Viezel, *The Commentary on Chronicles Attributed to Rashi* (Jerusalem, 2010) [Hebrew], 98–99; above, Introduction, n. 38; and chapter 1, nn. 177–78. Avraham Grossman includes in his survey of northern French *pashtanim* (as S. Poznanski did before him) Rashi's student R. Shemayah, who was both a *pashtan* and a talmudist, and R. Menaḥem bar Helbo, who was not. See *Hebrew Bible: The History of its Interpretation*, ed. Magne Saebo, vol. 1, pt. 2 (Gottingen, 2000), 331–32, 356–58.

28 See, e.g., Poznanski, *Mavo*, CXXV–CXXIX; R. Harris, *Discerning Parallelism: A Study in Northern French Medieval Jewish Biblical Exegesis* (Providence, R.I., 2004), 28–30, 75–83; Yitzhak Berger, "The Contextual Exegesis of Rabbi Eliezer of Beaugency and the Climax of the Northern French *Peshat* Tradition," *JSQ* 15 (2008), 115–19; and idem, "Conceptions of Biblical Composition and Poetic Structure in the Commentary on Chronicles in Manuscript Munich 5," in *Iggud*, vol. 1, ed. A. Melammed et al. (Jerusalem, 2008), 3*–19*. To be sure, both R. Yosef Qara and R. Eliezer of Beaugency were extensively involved with the interpretation of *Nevi'im* and *Ketuvim* as well (which is more suggestive of *miqra* study and interpretation as an independent value). To a great extent, this is also the case for Rashbam (and other anonymous compilatory works that followed his methods in the thirteenth century; see Sara Japhet, *Dor Dor u-Parshanav* [Jerusalem, 2008], 313–27, 341–63), and, to a much lesser extent, for R. Yosef *Bekhor Shor* as well. Aside from R. Isaiah di Trani, no other Tosafist was significantly involved in the interpretation of biblical books other than the Pentateuch itself, although a number of *Ḥasidei Ashkenaz* most certainly were. See my "On the Role of Bible Study in Medieval Ashkenaz," in *The Frank Talmage Memorial Volume*, ed. Barry Walfish (Haifa, 1993), vol. 1, 151–66; and below, nn. 42, 199. Cf. ms. Paris BN 343 (IMHM # 2937), fols. 188v–205r; and ms. Florence Laurenziana Acq. e. Doni. 121 (IMHM #18007). Thanks to Dr. Baruch Alster for drawing my attention to these manuscripts.

pairing them with those of the Provençal biblical exegete and polemicist R. Joseph Kimḥi. In one instance, Ben-Sasson expresses surprise that when R. Eliezer, who belonged (according to Ben-Sasson) to the "circle of Tosafists in northern France," expresses himself on the greatness and splendor of Herod's Temple, he does so not by citing the relevant talmudic passage in *Bava Batra* (4a) but rather through a passage from the work of Yosippon.[29] The fact is, however, that we have no evidence whatsoever which places R. Eliezer in such a circle, nor should there be any assumption that he had the knowledge and the proclivities of a leading talmudist.

Moreover, while Rashbam and *Bekhor Shor* undoubtedly discussed their biblical interpretations with individuals and groups of students, their Torah commentaries do not reflect the ongoing give and take between teachers and students that typifies the texts of talmudic *Tosafot* and is essential to them.[30] In short, we cannot be certain that any of the business of northern French *peshat* was conducted within the framework of Tosafist institutions or circles. Indeed, it is difficult to trace or even to detect any overt relationship between the institutions of the Tosafists of northern France and the development of *peshat* or *peshuto shel miqra* there during the twelfth century.[31]

Questions concerning the development of *peshat* exegesis in northern France have been discussed anew by a number of scholars during the past three decades. Virtually all this scholarship has assumed that the phenomenon of northern French *peshat* essentially ended at the conclusion of the twelfth century, with the passing on of the handful of known *peshat* exegetes just noted.[32] Whether the search for *peshat* in northern France was

[29] See H. H. Ben-Sasson, "Yiḥud ʿAm Yisraʾel le-Daʿat Bnei ha-Meʾah ha-Yod Bet," in *Peraqim*, vol. 2, ed. E. S. Rosenthal (Jerusalem, 1969–74), 214 (n. 237), and see also, 171, 203–6, 212–18.

[30] Indeed, as noted above in the Introduction (nn. 39–40), two of the very few discussions reported by Rashbam in his Torah commentary which he had with other rabbinic figures concerned issues of midrashic or halakhic interpretation rather than matters of *peshat*.

[31] See my *Jewish Education and Society*, 82–85. Cf. S. Japhet, *Dor Dor u-Parshanav*, 328–40; Jair Haas, "Iqqaron 'Kefel ha-ʿInyan be-Milot Shonot' be-Askolah ha-Parshanit shel Ẓefon Ẓarefat," *Hebrew Union College Annual* 75 (2004), 52 (n. 4); and I. Ta-Shma, "Maqbilim she-Einam Nifgashim: Yeshivot Baʿalei ha-Tosafot veha-Sevivah ha-Aqademaʾit be-Ẓarefat ba-Meʾah ha-Shteim-ʿEsreh veha-Shlosh-ʿEsreh," in *Yeshivot u-Battei Midrashot*, ed. I. Etkes (Jerusalem, 2007), 83. Ta-Shma observes that the interpretation of *piyyut*, prayer, and *midresehi halakhah va-ʾaggadah*, as well as *parshanut ha-miqra* (mainly to the Pentateuch), took place either "in the main study hall or in the private residence of the teacher." Ta-Shma's formulation, however, does not seem to include classic *parshanut ha-peshat*, where the methods of both Yosef Qara and Rashbam, for example, spoke more (according to their own assessments) to *maskilim* than to *Baʿalei talmud*. See Rashbam's comments to Genesis 37:2; Qara's comment to 1 Samuel 1:20; above, n. 27; and in Introduction, n. 38. Given its heavy reliance on talmudic and midrashic literature, the interpretation of *piyyut* in Ashkenaz, on the other hand, did typically require the full resources of the rabbinic *beit midrash*, as Ta-Shma indicates.

[32] See, e.g., Avraham Grossman, *Ḥakhmei Ẓarefat ha-Rishonim*, 457–58, 471, 505–6, and the studies by Touitou, Yefet, and Grossman) cited in 458 (n. 4, על הדעיכה).

motivated in the main by internal intellectual considerations, including the influence of Spanish biblical exegesis, or whether the influence of Christian polemics was most crucial, modern scholarship has assumed that these motivations either had played themselves out or had been transferred to other literary forums, such as handbooks of Jewish polemics (e.g., *Sefer Yosef ha-Meqanne*), beginning with the early thirteenth century.[33] At the same time the so-called Tosafist Torah commentaries noted above, which were produced from the mid-thirteenth century and into the early fourteenth century, were seen mainly as collections of midrashic and halakhic interprerations which would appear, at first blush, to have had little in common with the earlier *pashtanim.*

In a study dealing with the compilatory commentary *Ḥizzequni* (composed by Hezekiah b. Manoaḥ),[34] Sara Japhet has argued that this work, which was composed in northern France during the last quarter of the thirteenth century, retains a strong interest in *peshat* as one of the interpretive dimensions it seeks to present. *Ḥizzequni* includes material from *Sefer ha-Gan*, a northern French exegetical work completed c. 1240 (to which we shall return); from the commentary of *Bekhor Shor* (which was a major influence on *Sefer ha-Gan*); from Rashbam; and from other Ashkenazic sources, including the Torah commentary of R. Judah *he-Ḥasid* (and obviously from Rashi as well). At the same time, *Ḥizzequni* also includes exegetical material from Abraham ibn Ezra, R. David Kimḥi (Radak), and perhaps from Naḥmanides. Although Poznanski and others had suggested that *Ḥizzequni* might have been composed in Provence, Japhet argues convincingly that the liturgical and synagogue customs included in it, the *le'azim* found in this work, and the bulk of its exegetical strategies and sources, reflect the cultural milieu of northern France or Ashkenaz.[35]

[33] For a recent summary and discussion of these trends, see Mordechai Cohen's review essay of Eleazar Touitou's *Exegesis in Perpetual Motion* in *JQR* 98 (2008), 398–408.

[34] See S. Japhet, "Perush ha-Ḥizzequni la-Torah—Li-Demuto shel ha-Ḥibbur ule-Mattarato," in *Sefer ha-Yovel li-Khevod ha-Rav Mordekhai Breuer*, ed. Moshe Bar Asher (Jerusalem, 1992), 91–111 (= idem, *Dor Dor u-Parshanav*, 364–82); idem, *Perush Rashbam le-Sefer Iyyov* (Jerusalem, 2000), 36–48; and cf. Martin Lockshin, "'Rashbam' on Job: A Reconsideration," *JSQ* 8 (2001), 80–104; Robert Harris, "The Rashbam Authorship Controversy Redux," *JQR* 95 (2005), 63–81.

[35] On the presence of the name "Manoaḥ" in Ashkenazic rabbinic texts, against the claim of Poznanski, *Mavo*, CVI (n. 3), that *Ḥizzequni* is likely to be a Provençal work since the name Manoaḥ is to be found only in that region during this period, see, e.g., *Teshuvot u-Pesaqim*, ed. Kupfer, 159 (n. 3), and cf. I. Ta-Shma, *Knesset Meḥqarim*, 2:159; Urbach, *Ba'alei ha-Tosafot*, 1:482 (n. 20), 2:666; and see also *'Arugat ha-Bosem*, 4:24 (n. 26); *Tosafot ha-Rosh 'al Massekhet Ketubot*, ed. E. Lichtenstein (Jerusalem, 1999), 169 (to *Ketubot* 23a = *Ḥiddushei ha-Ritva 'al Massekhet Ketubot*, ed. M. Goldstein, 209, *ve-hiqshu ha-Tosafot be-shem R. Manoaḥ*); Ta-Shma, *Knesset Meḥqarim*, 1:158; S. Emanuel, *Shivrei Luḥot*, 167 (regarding R. Manoaḥ *ha-Kohen*, the son-in-law of R. Simḥah of Speyer); and *Knesset Meḥqarim*, 1:244.

In assessing the nature and achievement of this exegetical work, Japhet notes that we are not much further along in understanding and evaluating Ashkenazic biblical interpretation in the thirteenth and fourteenth centuries than we were during the days of Poznanski (nearly a century ago). Poznanski felt that the so-called Tosafist commentaries of this period represent a sharp decline relative to the exegetical works of the *pashtanim* that were produced in northern France during the twelfth century. Japhet maintains, on the other hand, that although the so-called Tosafist commentaries of the thirteenth century and beyond do not typically favor strict *peshat* interpretation over other interpretational modes and forms, both *peshat* and *derash* are included in these works and are presented as two discrete and distinct exegetical methods. It seems fair to conclude that, although *midrash* is their dominant component (in addition to pieces of talmudic *Tosafot* and other halakhic interpretations), these compilations did not abandon earlier forms of *peshat* interpretation, nor did they systematically blur the differences between *peshat* and *derash*,[36] even as they restored and developed further the central and independent study of *midrash* and, to a lesser extent, *remez*, if not *sod*.[37]

Clearly, Rashi's commentary served as an important model for all of the various Tosafist Torah commentaries. Indeed, a distinguishing characteristic or aim of the so-called Tosafist commentaries, as noted already by Poznanski and as confirmed by Japhet, was to compose, in effect, *Tosafot*

[36] Japhet, "Perush ha-Ḥizzequni la-Torah," 107, n. 49, presents a fairly typical example from *Hadar Zeqenim* to Gen. 22:14 (Livorno, 1840), fol. 8a (the chapter number is misidentified in this note as Gen. 25), which begins with the phrase *ha-peshat ken hu*, after which three additional interpretations appear that are designated as *ʾaggadah*, *midrash ʾaggadah*, and *ʾaggadah ʾaḥeret.* In the two verses that are interpreted prior to this one, the phrase *yesh ba-midrash* appears several times. See also Yehoshafat Nevo, *Ha-Parshanut ha-Ẓarefatit* (Tzfat, 1994), 120–21 (regarding the *Moshav Zeqenim* collection). On the targeting of these compilations (by their second-level elite compilers) to a broader and less scholarly audience, see my "Bein Yeshivot Baʿalei ha-Tosafot le-Battei Midrash Aḥerim be-Ashkenaz," 104–6, and below, chapter 4.

[37] Thus, for example, *gematria*, which is hardly found in Rashi's Torah commentary (see C. B. Chavel, *Perushei Rashi ʿal ha-Torah* [Jerusalem, 1983], 632, s.v. *gematria*), and only somewhat more in the commentary of *Bekhor Shor* (see Poznanski, *Mavo ʿal Ḥakhmei Ẓarefat Mefarshei ha-Miqra*, LXXII, and cf. *Sefer ha-Gan*, ed. Orlian, 65, for the handful of instances in that work), is found much more frequently in the so-called Tosafist Torah collections. To be sure, *gematria* is also found in increasing amounts in the exoteric Torah commentary of R. Judah *he-Ḥasid* (and in R. Isaiah di Trani's Torah commentary as well). See below, chapter 3, and cf. I. Ta-Shma, *Knesset Meḥqarim*, 1:236–37, regarding *Paʿaneaḥ Raza.* On *gematria* and *Ḥasidei Ashkenaz* (with reference to their biblical commentaries as well), see, e.g., Daniel Abrams, "From Germany to Spain: Numerology as a Mystical Technique," *Journal of Jewish Studies* 47 (1996), 85–101; *Sefer Gematriʾot le-R. Yehudah he-Ḥasid*, introduced by D. Abrams and I. Ta-Shma (Los Angeles, 1998), 1–21; and my *"Peering through the Lattices,"* 93–97, 198–99. There is one instance of א״ת ב״ש usage in Rashbam's commentary to the Torah (to Ex. 3:15, and no instances of *gematria*). See also *Ḥizzequni* ad loc; and *Rashbam's Commentary to the Book of Exodus*, ed. M. Lockshin (Providence, R.I., 1997), 37–38.

to the Torah commentary of Rashi. Rashi's commentary itself became an object of study, and his commentary was subjected to intense, if not always consistent, scrutiny and analysis: Why did Rashi choose to make a particular comment? What were his sources and how did he use them?, and so on. The goal was to complete and to add to Rashi's commentary, similar in this regard to the *Tosafot* on the Talmud.[38] However, while the relationship between *peshat* and *derash* in Rashi's commentary is defined by such brief programmatic statements as found on Gen. 3:8, ואני לא באתי אלא לפשוטו של מקרא ולאגדה המשיבת דברי מקרא, or on Gen. 33:20, ורבותינו דרשוהו שהקב"ה קראו ליעקב אל. ודברי תורה כפטיש יפוצץ סלע מתחלקים לכמה טעמים. ואני לישב פשוטו של מקרא באתי, the Tosafist Torah commentaries do not typically define or clarify what the nature, relationship, or proportion of *peshat* and *derash* were meant to be in these works.[39]

Japhet stresses that *Ḥizzequni* and the other so-called Tosafist Torah commentaries of the thirteenth and early fourteenth centuries—whether they were the product of a single composer or editor, such as *Ḥizzequni* and *Sefer ha-Gan*, or whether, like *Da'at Zeqenim* and *Hadar Zeqenim*, they were the editorial product of one or more anonymous rabbinic figures—reflect a compilatory style. These works explicitly drew on many sources, including a variety of earlier rabbinic materials, combining and juxtaposing extracted segments from different authors and works to form a continuous commentary. The *peshat* commentaries of the twelfth century, on the other hand, beginning with that of Rashi, were self-contained commentaries composed by a single author. The retreat from *peshat* led to a concomitant change in the style of authorship, reflected in the move from individual *parshanim* to compilatory *perushim* (although there are also several thirteenth-century compilations, such as the so-called commentary of R. Yosef Qara to Job, found in ms. Lutzki 778, and perhaps others attributed to Rashbam, which primarily reflect the commentaries of twelfth-century *pashtanim*).

To be sure, *Ḥizzequni* displays a degree of uniqueness among the Tosafist Torah commentaries of its day in terms of its presentational style.[40]

[38] See Urbach, *Ba'alei ha-Tosafot*, 1:18, 2:676; Poznanski, *Mavo*, ibid.; and H. Touitou, "Minḥat Yehudah" (above, n. 4), 43–65.

[39] See also below, in the section on *Bekhor Shor.* For the ongoing discussion of whether *peshat* or midrash is more dominant within Rashi's biblical commentaries, see, e.g., Aharon Mondschein, "The Massoretes Fabricated Explanations for Full and Defective Spellings: On Abraham Ibn Ezra's Struggles Against the (Ab)use of Biblical Spelling as an Exegetical Tool," [Hebrew] *Shenaton le-Ḥeqer ha-Miqra veha-Mizraḥ ha-Qadum* 19 (2009), 282, and the literature cited in n. 173; and see also Gila Prebor, "The Use of Midrash in Rashi's Commentary to Ecclesiastes," *Shenaton le-Ḥeqer ha-Miqra*, ibid., 209–29.

[40] Japhet, "Perush ha-Ḥizzequni," 101–2, notes the reliance of this commentary on Sefardic and Provençal exegetical approaches as well, as represented by Ibn Ezra, Radak, and perhaps even Ramban. Although most other Tosafist Torah commentaries have a less sustained interest

Ḥizzequni alludes to its sources in an extremely cryptic fashion in a poetic preface to the commentary, and barely mentions any sources within the body of the work, while the Tosafist Torah commentaries generally mention a large number of rabbinic scholars and sources by name.[41] At the same time, the Tosafist Torah commentaries typically do not offer systematic commentaries to each verse and biblical phrase. Their comments are made selectively—similar again to the prevailing pattern in the *Tosafot* on the Talmud—and may contain notes or glosses, new interpretations, relevant *midrashim*, or questions and comments on Rashi. In other words, these commentaries are more akin to somewhat random "*ḥiddushim*," while *Ḥizzequni* was composed as an overarching commentary that includes a steady selection of comments—from unnamed but important predecessors—to virtually every verse, which can also serve as a companion to Rashi's commentary.

It follows from Japhet's analysis that *peshat* did not disappear in medieval Ashkenaz after the twelfth century, certainly not to the extent that contemporary scholarship has otherwise assumed. Aspects of *peshat* remained in the Tosafist Torah commentaries generally, perhaps in a more focused way in the *Ḥizzequni* commentary and certainly in more *peshat*-oriented compilations such as the so-called commentary of Qara to Job or the commentary published by Jellinek (from a Hamburg manuscript) to Esther, Ruth, and Lamentations.[42] Japhet does not engage in much discussion about those who composed the so-called Tosafist commentaries, and she does not attempt in any way to trace the roles of particular Tosafists. She suggests that Hezekiah b. Manoaḥ, about whom we know nothing from any other rabbinic contexts, was a kind of conceptual student of or successor to the twelfth-century *pashtanim* (*talmidam min ha-ketavim*), who was interested in preserving and discussing their works.[43]

In my view, however, it is possible to isolate and delineate a middle phase (from both the chronological and phenomenological standpoints) that effectively transitions from the last of the twelfth-century *pashtanim* to the so-called Tosafist Torah commentaries and compilations that were composed beginning in the middle of the thirteenth century. Although this

in *peshat* than the *Ḥizzequni* does, they will also cite these exegetes on occasion, as we shall see in the succeeding chapters. For now, see A. Lifshitz, "R. Avraham Ibn Ezra be-Perushei Ba'alei ha-Tosafot 'al ha-Torah," *Hadarom* 28 (1968), 202–21.

[41] Poznanski, *Mavo 'al Ḥakhmei Ẓarefat*, XCIII, estimates that 120 names are mentioned. The names range from the well known to those that are otherwise unknown.

[42] See Poznanski, *Mavo*, LXXXIX; and S. Japhet, *Dor Dor u-Parshanav*, 341–63.

[43] See also Japhet, "The Nature and Distribution of Medieval Compilatory Commentaries in Light of R. Joseph Kara's Commentary on the Book of Job," in *The Midrashic Imagination* (Albany, N.Y., 1993), 98–130.

middle phase may overlap with some of the earliest compilatory works, it is dominated by several individual and distinct Tosafists and Ashkenazic rabbinic figures who composed a series of comments as individual authors and not as collectors or compilers. These figures often begin with the commentary of Rashi.

Although their comments on Rashi are certainly not systematic, their interest in his commentary has two aims. The first involves the checking and correlating of Rashi's talmudic and rabbinic interpretations that are provided as part of his *'aggadah ha-meyashevet divrei miqra*. The second engages and critiques Rashi's style of *peshuto shel miqra*. At the same time, these Tosafist exegetes also offer *peshat* interpretations of their own, often in places where Rashi does not. Indeed, part of the reason this exegetical phase in Ashkenaz has not received sufficient attention to this point is that these commentaries were ultimately eclipsed by the very commentary they sought to further explain and to emulate, that of Rashi.[44]

An initial key—which will help us to isolate and bring forth this middle phase or layer of Ashkenazic biblical interpretation—is to properly understand the relationship of R. Yosef *Bekhor Shor*'s Torah commentary to Rashi's commentary. Rashbam and R. Yosef Qara were clearly aware of the Torah commentary of Rashi and reacted to it, with Qara and R. Shemayah even adding accretions or glosses to Rashi's commentaries.[45] Nonetheless, these exegetes, who were interested in a deeper and more consistent level of *peshat* than Rashi was (which is often characterized as *'omeq peshuto shel miqra*), sought to achieve this in their own commentaries using additional

[44] Cf. Eran Viezel, "Ha-Perush ha-Meyuḥas le-Rashi le-Sefer Ezra-Neḥemyah," *Jewish Studies Internet Journal* 9 (2010), 53. For a similar pattern with respect to Rashi's talmudic commentary and other contemporary Ashkenazic efforts, see, e.g., Aharon Ahrend, "Seridim mi-Perush Ashkenazi 'al Massekhet Rosh ha-Shanah," *Qovez 'al Yad* 17 [27] (2003), 139–44. In the same vein, the tens of manuscripts of Rashi's Torah commentary that have survived, versus the meager number for Rashbam's commentary (only one complete manuscript and several fragments), may be the result of Rashi's mixed approach to *peshuto shel miqra* having won many more adherents than the more radical (or pristine) form of *peshat* favored by Rashbam.

[45] See, e.g., E. Touitou, *Exegesis in Perpetual Motion*, 68–69; M. Sokolow, "'Ha-Peshatot ha-Mitḥadshim'—Qeta'im Ḥadashim mi-Perush ha-Torah la-Rasbam—Ketav Yad," *'Alei Sefer* 11 (1984), 72–80; Ithamar Kislev, "'Va-Asher Sam Libbo li-Devar Yoẓerenu': Ha-Heged ha-Methodologi shel Rashbam bi-Tehillat Perusho le-Sefer Va-Yiqra u-Terumato le-Havanat Yaḥaso shel Rashbam le-Perushav shel Rashi," *Tarbiz* 73 (2004), 225–37; Rashbam's commentary to Numbers 34:2; Avraham Grossman, *Ḥakhmei Ẓarefat ha-Rishonim*, 183–19, 210–12, 290–302, 358–76; idem, "Haggahot R. Shemayah le-Nosaḥ Perush Rashi la-Torah," *Tarbiz* 60 (1991), 67–98; *Sefer Yehoshua/Sefer Shotfim, Nosah Miqra 'al pi Keter Aram Zova*, ed. M. Cohen (Jerusalem, 1992), editor's introduction, 32*–33*; and M. Ahrend, *Perush R. Yosef Qara le-Sefer Iyyov*, 13–14. See also J. S. Penkower, "Shnei Ḥakhamim ha-Nizkarim be-Kitvei Yad shel Perushei Rashi la-Miqra—R. Yehudah ve-R. Yehudah *ha-Darshan*," in *Shai le-Sara Yefet*, ed. M. Bar-Asher et al. (Jerusalem, 2007), 233–47, and idem, "Haggahot Rashi le-Perusho la-Torah," *Jewish Studies Internet Journal* 6 (2007), 17.

methods of grammatical, literary, and contextual interpretation, and by largely eliminating references to and methods of midrashic literature.[46] As such, their commentaries and comments do not function as supercommentaries to *perush Rashi.* Indeed, these commentaries rarely engage or even mention Rashi explicitly,[47] although the extent to which Rashbam's biblical commentaries were intended as an implicit reaction to those of Rashi has recently been the subject of renewed discussion.[48]

R. Joseph *Bekhor Shor* of Orleans

R. Joseph (Yosef) *Bekhor Shor* does not present any methodological statements about the relationship between *peshat* and *derash* such as those included by Rashi, Rashbam, and R. Yosef Qara, although he does occasionally enunciate a principle of literary style or interpretation of the Torah.[49]

[46] Cf. Aharon Mondschein, "'Ve-Ein bi-Sefarav Peshat Raq Eḥad Minei Elef'—Le-Derekh ha-Hityaḥasut shelo R. Avraham Ibn Ezra le-Perush Rashi la-Torah," *'Iyyunei Miqra u-Parshanut* 5 (2000), 221–48.

[47] E. Z. Melammed, *Mefarshei ha-Miqra, Darkeihem ve-Shitoteihem* (Jerusalem, 1978), 484, lists five instances in which Rashbam mentions Rashi's commentary by name (in addition to his programmatic discussions of the goals of his and Rashi's commentaries, in Gen. 37:2 and Ex. 21:2). For the most part, however, Rashbam informs his readers in these passages that they should consult Rashi's commentary on matters of detail (regarding the *mishkan* and the priestly vestments, the sacrificial rites, and the sketching of the boundaries of the land of Israel), areas in which he (Rashbam) will comment only briefly. See also I. Kislev, above, n. 45. In similar fashion (and without mentioning Rashi's commentary by name), Rashbam, in his commentary to Lev. 13:2, notes that the various physical manifestations of leprosy do not lend themselves particularly well to *peshuto shel miqra*, and the reader should consult the essential *midrash shel ḥakhamim ve-ḥuqqoteihem ve-qabbaloteihem.* Cf., however, the commentary of R. Yosef *Bekhor Shor* on this verse (ed. Nevo, 197), which begins by citing the Tannaitic interpretations of the various leprous blemishes but ends with an insight *lefi ha-peshat.*

[48] Melammed, *Mefarshei ha-Miqra*, 484–87, adduces nearly fifteen instances in which Rashbam essentially follows or adopts a comment by Rashi (albeit without comment, and without referring to him). In another three cases, Rashbam adopts Rashi's explanation only in part (and in one such instance, Nu. 17:18, Rashbam notes that this is the comment of "my grandfather"). In ten places, Rashbam strongly disagrees with an interpretation put forward by Rashi (often in the realm of *peshat*), usually calling it a *ta'ut* or its author a *to'eh*, without ever mentioning Rashi by name, ostensibly as a matter of respect. (To this list can be added Rashbam's comment to Gen. 49:10, among others.) See also, e.g., M. Lockshin, *Rashbam's Commentary on Genesis* (Lewiston, N.Y., 1989), introduction, 13–23; idem, *Rashbam's Commentary on Exodus*, introduction, 2–4, 225; E. Touitou, *Exegesis in Perpetual Motion*, 70–72, 229–37; M. Greenberg, "Ha-Yaḥas Bein Perush Rashi le-Perush Rashbam 'al ha-Torah," in *Sefer Yiẓḥaq Aryeh Zeligmann*, ed. Y. Zakovitch and A. Rofe, vol. 2 (Jerusalem, 1983), 559–68; S. Japhet, *Perush Rashbam le-Sefer Iyyov*, 78–95; idem, *Perush Rashbam le-Shir ha-Shirim*, 54, 63–65; and Moshe Sokolow, above, n. 45.

[49] See R. Harris, *Discerning Parallelism*, 31. *Bekhor Shor* will occasionally refer to a broad principle or conception of scriptural interpretation, but there does not seem to be any pattern or consistency with regard to his use of these principles or phrases. See, e.g., Lev. 6:2 (ed. Nevo, 188; ואני לפרש לשון המקרא באתי, אלא שדבר בהווה); Ex. 25:29 (Nevo, 159; ובע' פנים התורה נדרשת ואני פירשתי אחר לשון המקרא העברי); Ex. 35:26 (Nevo, 176; קרא יתירא הוא ודרשינן ליה רבותינו וכו', and cf.

Indeed, *Bekhor Shor* appears to be a highly original exegete who was cognizant of a number of the literary forms and theories applied by Rashbam,[50] and who apparently had even greater access to Spanish works of biblical exegesis and thought than did his northern French predecessors, R. Yosef Qara and Rashbam, including those of Baḥya ibn Paquda, Judah ibn Ḥayyuj, and Avraham bar Ḥiyya, if not to the commentaries of Ibn Ezra.[51] At the same

---

above, Introduction, n. 45); Deut. 7:21 (Nevo, ed. 320, כל זה במשמעות המקרא); and cf. Deut. 9:28 (Nevo, 323: ובלשון התלמוד יש ווי'ן הרבה שהם במקום או ו'). R. Yosef *Bekhor Shor* uses the phrase of *'ein miqra yoẓe midei peshuto* once (on Gen. 48:22, ed. Nevo, 86); but this is in support of a passage in *Bereshit Rabbah* against a talmudic interpretation. Cf. Y. Nevo, "R. Yosef Bekhor Shor Parshan ha-Peshat," *Sinai* 95 (1984), 268–69.

50 See, e.g., Yonatan Jacobs, "Iqqaron ha-Haqdamah be-Perush Rashbam la-Torah," in *'Iyyunei Miqra u-Parshanut* 8, ed. S. Vargon et al. (Ramat Gan, 2008), 451–79 (and cf. Touitou, *Exegesis in Perpetual Motion*, 116, n. 13); idem, "'Lilmod Tevah me-Ḥavertah': Rashbam ki-Mefaresh ha-Miqra mi-Tokh Aẓmo," *Shenaton le-Ḥeqer ha-Miqra veha-Mizraḥ ha-Qadum* 17 (2007), 215–31; idem, "Habbatah Aḥor ki-Keli Parshani be-Perush Rashbam la-Torah," *Iggud* 1 (2008), 125–42; R. Harris, *Discerning Parallelism*, 87–98; idem, "Awareness of Biblical Redaction among Biblical Exegetes of Northern France," [Hebrew] *Shenaton le-Ḥeqer ha-Miqra veha-Mizraḥ ha-Qadum*, 13 (2000), 304–5 (and cf. Touitou, 121, n. 24), and below, n. 96. Among *Bekhor Shor*'s other rational exegetical characteristics that we shall discuss further below, Poznanski, *Mavo*, LX, notes that *Bekhor Shor* sought to neatly tie together seemingly similar events and narratives that are discussed in the Torah in disparate places. Thus *Bekhor Shor* maintains that the report of the quail in Ex. 16:13 (ed. Nevo, 125) was a mere reference to the giving of the quail in the context of the giving of the manna, since the quail were actually given (only once) as a response to the complaints about having no meat (Nu. 11:31–32). Similarly, *Bekhor Shor* maintains that the episode of Moses's staff hitting the rock and extracting water in Nu. 20 (ed. Nevo, 276) is the same as the one found in Ex. 17 (albeit from a different perspective), and *Bekhor Shor* formulates a broader principle on the Torah's propensity to refer to the same event more than once, in greater or lesser detail. Cf. also *Bekhor Shor*'s comment to Lev. 25:1 (ed. Nevo, 229), regarding those sections of the Torah that were given at *Har Sinai* versus those that were given in *Ohel Mo'ed.*

51 See, e.g., *Perushei R. Yosef Bekhor Shor 'al ha-Torah*, ed. Nevo, editor's introduction, 3; Moshe Idel, "Perush Mizmor Yod Tet bi-Tehillim le-R. Yosef Bekhor Shor," *'Alei Sefer* 9 (1981), 63–69; E. Touitou, *Exegesis in Perpetual Motion*, 46–47; and cf. M. Liber in *REJ* 58 (1909–10), 309–11; A. Grossman, "Ha-Qesharim Bein Yahadut Sefarad le-Yahadut Ashkenaz Bimei ha-Benayim," in *Moreshet Sefarad*, ed. Haim Beinart (Jerusalem, 1992), 176–77; idem, *Ḥakhmei Ẓarefat ha-Rishonim*, 472–73; Abraham Lifshitz, "R. Avraham ibn Ezra be-Perushei Ba'alei ha-Tosafot," 219–21; Meir Miyara, *Ba'alei ha-Tosafot: Rabbotenu ha-Mefarshim*, vol. 1 (Jerusalem, 1988), 242–48, 315–17; Jonathan Jacobs, "Does Rashbam's Commentary on the Torah Acknowledge the Commentaries of Rabbi Abraham Ibn Ezra," *Journal of Jewish Studies* 61 (2010), 291–307; and my "Ashkenazic Messianic Calculations from Rashi and His Generation through the Tosafist Period," [Hebrew] in *Rashi, The Man and His Work*, ed. A. Grossman and S. Japhet (Jerusalem, 2009), 2:391–93. For R. Yosef's *piyyutim* (and the aspects of Spanish *piyyut* that are present in them), see below, chapter 5. For his calculations of the *tequfot*, see, e.g., ms. Cambridge Add. 561 (fol. 225), ms. JTS 4460 (fols. 253r–254r), ms. Lund L. O. 2 (fol. 2v), ms. Zurich Heid 51/34 (fol. 104r), further described in my "Anthropomorphism and Rationalist Modes of Thought in Medieval Ashkenaz: The Case of R. Yosef Bekhor Shor," in *Yearbook of the Simon Dubnow Institute* 8 (Leipzig, 2009), 120, n. 4. In the first section of that study, I also discuss similarities between the positions of *Bekhor Shor* and Maimonides with respect to the explanation of anthropomorphic phrases in the Torah, the presentation of *ta'amei ha-mizvot*, and the tendency

time, R. Yosef *Bekhor Shor* does less grammatical analysis than his predecessors, and he presents *peshat* interpretations and those of *Ḥazal* together—even in purely narrative contexts—as Rashi does.[52]

Martin Lockshin recently authored a brief study (in Hebrew), "Was Yosef *Bekhor Shor* a *Pashtan* (*Peshat* Exegete)?" in which he sought to clarify *Bekhor Shor*'s place within northern French *peshat* exegesis of the twelfth century.[53] Citing a study by Judith Kogel in which she divides northern French exegesis into three categories—the Torah commentary of Rashi, which is replete with midrash; the more radical commentaries of Qara and Rashbam, which seek to eliminate or at least significantly minimize the use of midrash; and the return of R. Yosef *Bekhor Shor* and other Tosafists to the approach of Rashi[54]—Lockshin suggests that *Bekhor Shor* indeed appears to represent something of a "retreat" in terms of *peshat*, since midrash is clearly a much more frequent ingredient in *Bekhor Shor*'s Torah commentary than it was for Rashbam and Qara. Although Lockshin presents examples in which R. Yosef Shor implicitly criticizes an interpretation of Rashi for not being sufficiently *lefi ha-peshat*, he brings other instances in which *Bekhor Shor* retains a talmudic or midrashic interpretation, where Rashbam and Qara do not.

Highlighting several verses that are centered on halakhic issues (Ex. 21:6–8 and 22:13–14; Lev. 21:2, 6) in particular, Lockshin shows that Rashi typically puts forward interpretations that are consonant with talmudic material, while Rashbam juxtaposes the rabbinic approach with the *peshat*, thereby highlighting the tension between them.[55] For his part, *Bekhor Shor*, unlike Rashi, cites both the rabbinic interpretation and the *peshat* approach, acknowledging the tension between them while showing that the rabbinic approach is well based—and even more acceptable—thereby resolving or deflating that tension. Although this was the road not taken by Rashbam, Lockshin's study suggests that *Bekhor Shor* appreciated Rashbam's

---

to explain miracles in the Torah in accordance with natural law; see also below, n. 135. Cf. Poznanski, *Mavo*, LVI–LIX; and below, chapter 7. Idel notes (64) that despite *Bekhor Shor*'s familiarity with astronomy, he allowed for the impact of astrological phenomena as well, in ways that Maimonides certainly would not.

52 See below, n. 102. On *gematria*, see above, n. 37.

53 See M. Lockshin, "Ha-Im Hayah Yosef Bekhor Shor Pashtan?" in *Iggud: Selected Essays in Jewish Studies*, vol. 1, ed. Abraham Melammed et al. (Jerusalem, 2008), 161–72.

54 Judith Kogel, "L'utilisation du *Midrasch* dans l'exegese de la France du Nord, de Rashi au recuils des tosafistes," in *Le brulement du Talmud a Paris 1242–1244*, ed. G. Dahan (Paris, 1999), 143–59.

55 See above, Introduction, n. 46, and cf. S. Japhet, "The Tension between Rabbinic Legal Midrash and the 'Plain Meaning' (Peshat) of the Biblical Text—An Unresolved Problem in the Wake of Rashbam's Commentary on the Pentateuch," in *Sefer Moshe: The Moshe Weinfeld Jubilee Volume*, ed. C. Cohen et al. (Winona Lake, Ind., 2004), 403–25.

delineation of *peshat* even as he could not support the unchecked use of this exegetical approach, especially in halakhic contexts.[56]

This suggestive undertaking begun by Lockshin can be extended in several directions. First, there are quite a number of instances in which *Bekhor Shor* cites comments by Rashi, and explicitly reacts or responds to them, in both halakhic and narrative sections. These instances can surely help to sketch *Bekhor Shor*'s relationship with his predecessors in a more effective

[56] Lockshin notes (168–69) that there is only one example in *Bekhor Shor*'s Torah commentary of an anhalakhic interpretation (to Ex. 21:2, *uba-shanah ha-shevi'it yeẓe la-ḥofshi ḥinam*), which is understood by all rabbinic interpretations to mean that a Hebrew slave goes free in the seventh year of his servitude. *Bekhor Shor* interprets *uba-shevi 'it* to refer to the year of *shemitah* (when the master, by definition, requires less work in terms of planting and harvesting; this interpretation also appears in the so-called pseduo-Targum Yonatan). See also *Derakhim be-Parshanut ha-Miqra*, ed. Y. Nizan, Y. Nevo, and M. Gross, vol. 1 (Tel Aviv, 1999), 145, and cf. *Bekhor Shor* to Exdous 19:29, 20:30, and 24:3. Interestingly, Rashbam (who embraces several anhalakhic interpretations within his Torah commentary, including his interpretation of ועבדו לעולם, in Ex. 21:6) rejects this interpretation in his commentary to Ex. 21:2. See Poznanski, *Mavo*, XLII–XLIII, and Touitou, *Exegesis in Motion*, 187–88. See also *Bekhor Shor*'s interpretations of *parashat ha-shomrim* (Ex. 6–14), and cf. S. Japhet, *Dor Dor ve-Parshanav*, 42–44. With regard to *Bekhor Shor*'s varying contextual interpretations of the verse(s) *lo tevashel gedi ba-ḥalev 'immo* (in Ex. 23:19, 34:26, and Deut. 14:21), see R. Harris, *Discerning Parallelism*, 31–32, and cf. M. Lockshin, *Rashbam's Commentary on Exodus*, 286–87, 421. As opposed to Rashi, who interprets all three of these instances according to the halakhic guidelines prohibiting the cooking and eating of (and otherwise benefiting from) meat and milk that are cooked together, *Bekhor Shor* offers his own new contextual interpretations, but interprets the third instance (in Deuteronomy, based also on its context, as noted by Harris in n. 51) in accordance with the standard rabbinic and halakhic requirement and texts. Cf. *Perushei R. Ḥayyim Palti'el 'al ha-Torah*, 301, 340–41, 584. In an example cited by Lasker from a narrative portion (the extensive comments on the order or chronology of the flood in Gen. 8), *Bekhor Shor* explicitly notes (in Gen. 8:12) that his scenario for the flood is different than that of the Rabbis (*ve-rabbotenu pirshu*), which was also the approach presented by Rashi (*ve-hu katuv be-perush Rashi*). In similar fashion, *Bekhor Shor* presents the rabbinic interpretation (*ve-rabbotenu 'amru*) of the phrase אל מול פני המנורה יאיר שבעת הנרות (Nu. 8:2; Nevo, 251), that the three candles on each side of the middle branch of the *menorah* will shine their light toward the middle branch. This talmudic interpretation, which was also cited by Rashi (whose name is not mentioned by *Bekhor Shor* in this instance), is deemed by *Bekhor Shor* to be deficient (*yesh le-gamgem*), since the verse should have said that six candles (rather than seven) will shine toward the face of the *menorah*. *Bekhor Shor*'s proposed *peshat* interpretation, for which the reference to seven candles makes good sense, is that the candles of the *menorah* must be lit facing the show table, which was directly across from the *menorah* in the Tabernacle (*'al ha-shulḥan she-hu mul pnei ha-menorah*). This interpretation was also proposed by R. Isaiah di Trani. See *Nimmuqei Ḥumash le-Rabbenu Yeshayah*, ed. C. D. Chavel (Jerusalem, 1972), 57 (who first cites the interpretation of Rashi, *ha-Moreh*, by name), and below, chapter 3. Cf. *Ḥizzequni*, and see also *Moshav Zeqenim*, ed. Sasoon, 437, who cites the question on Rashi in the name of Ri (which probably connotes R. Isaiah rather than R. Yosef *Bekhor Shor*), and *Minḥat Yehudah* (Nu., fol. 5a), who records the solution (אל מול פני המנורה היינו השלחן) in the name of Rashbam. In the final part of his article, Lockshin points briefly to *Bekhor Shor*'s use of Spanish rationalism, and his position on anthropomorphism, and he suggests that *Bekhor Shor* was more philosophically inclined in this matter than Rashbam. Cf. my "Anthropomorphism and Rationalist Modes of Thought in Medieval Ashkenaz," and below, chapter 7.

way. Second, there are a number of other large patterns of interpretational tendencies and differences that can also help to establish the relationship between *Bekor Shor* and his predecessors more firmly and precisely.

R. Yosef *Bekhor Shor* cites Rashi by name (or simply by the title *Rabbenu*) nearly fifty times in his Torah commentary in order to adopt, explain, or even expand Rashi's view but also, in a number of instances, to reject the exegesis put forward by Rashi. He adjusts Rashi's comment to Genesis 10:9, which describes Nimrod as a warrior "before God" (*lifnei ha-Shem*). In *Bekhor Shor*'s formulation, Rashi interprets this phrase to mean that Nimrod's actions were "intended to upset the Almighty" (מכוין להכעיס). Rashi's actual formulation (following *Sifra* to *Beḥuqotai*, 2:2) is that Nimrod intended to defame God, whose existence he recognized (מתכוין להקניטו על פניו). Clearly, R. Yosef *Bekhor Shor* wished to support and perhaps to amplify Rashi's approach, which accords with the focused *Ḥazal* interpretation as well. In citing and paraphrasing Rashi in this way, R. Yosef *Bekhor Shor* is also implicitly rejecting the (*peshat*) interpretation of Rashbam that *lifnei ha-Shem* has the connotation of "throughout the world."[57] Similarly, in his comment to Genesis 42:2 (*va-yar Yosef ki yesh shever be-mizrayim*), *Bekhor Shor* cites Rashi's interpretation to Genesis 41:56 (on the phrase *va-yishbor le-mizrayim*) in his name, noting that the word (or root) *shever* connotes availability for sale or acquisition (*leshon mekhirah ve-qinyan*), and affirming that this interpretation is also appropriate for the subsequent verse as well.[58]

In Genesis 41:16, R. Yosef *Bekhor Shor* again cites Rashi's comment in his name. Joseph's claim that his seemingly extraordinary ability to interpret dreams is "without himself, for only the Almighty will respond" (בלעדי הא-להים יענה) is understood by Rashi to mean that "this wisdom is not mine, but belongs to and comes from God." *Bekhor Shor* then adds a further comment (*ve-yesh lefaresh*), that Joseph means to say that the interpretations he provides are not determined by or dependent on him but rather the Almighty. In this instance *Bekhor Shor* has amplified or enhanced Rashi's interpretation by adding a bit more description about Joseph's role in this process. The nuance of *Bekhor Shor*'s additional interpretation is essentially that of Rashbam in his commentary (אינו תלוי בי), and *Bekhor Shor* appears to be

[57] See *Derakhim be-Parshanut ha-Miqra: 'Iyyunim be-Parshanut Yemei ha-Benayim 'al ha-Torah*, ed. Y. Nevo et al. (Tel Aviv, 1999), 152–53. Rashbam bases his interpretation on Jonah 3:3. He repeats and contrasts this interpretation in his comment to Gen. 27:7, in which Isaac asserts that he will bless Yishma'el, *lifnei ha-Shem.* In that verse, Rashbam interprets this phrase to mean "in the name of God."

[58] Rashbam's interpretation to Gen. 41:56 is essentially the same as that of Rashi.

presenting it as a kind of "friendly amendment" to or extension of Rashi's comment, without mentioning Rashbam's contribution by name.[59]

R. Yosef *Bekhor Shor* suggests that the name Binyamin (as given by Jacob, in Gen. 35:18) was meant to retain at least the first part of the name that Rachel wanted her son to have (*ben 'oni*), as recorded at the beginning of that verse. *Bekhor Shor* interprets the second part of the name given by Jacob, *yamin*, to connote strength. He then notes that Rashi interpreted *yamin* as reflecting the south, and adds another biblical prooftext for this meaning (Jer. 1:14) to the one given by Rashi (Ps. 89:13), making clear that the land of Israel is the intended reference of this word (and direction). Whether *Bekhor Shor* is primarily amplifying Rashi's interpretation or using Rashi's interpretation to support his own, any exegetical differences between Rashi and *Bekhor Shor* in this instance (as in the previous one) are minimal.[60]

At the end his comment to Deuteronomy 32:6 (Nevo, 385), *Bekhor Shor* cites the three etymologies given by Rashi for the unusual word קניך, and adds a biblical verse (Nu. 24:21) and a talmudic passage (*Gittin* 6a, in accordance with Rashi's commentary *ad loc.*) in support of the second and third meanings that Rashi had provided.[61] Similarly, *Bekhor Shor* explains (on

[59] See also *Bekhor Shor*'s commentary to Gen. 1:7 (Nevo, 5); Gen. 20:11 (Nevo, 35); Gen. 27:19 (Nevo, 46); Gen. 32:9 (Nevo, 58); Gen. 32:5 (Nevo, 59); Gen. 41:45 (Nevo, 76–77, against Rashbam); Gen. 48:22 (Nevo, 86), where Rashi's unnamed comments are explained or clarified (and see also *Derakhim be-Parshanut ha-Miqra*, ed. Y. Nizan et al., 1:155); Ex. 16:1 (Nevo, 125); Ex. 17:5 (Nevo, 127); and Ex. 38:28 (Nevo, 179). See also Ex. 38:28 (Nevo, 179). My assessment of the relationship between the commentaries of *Bekhor Shor* and Rashi generally differs from that of Nevo in his introduction to *Perushei R. Yosef Bekhor Shor 'al ha-Torah*, 12, and in his "Yaḥas Perushei R. Yosef Bekhor Shor la-Torah 'el Perush Rashi," *Sinai* 93 (1983), 245–52.

[60] Cf. *Derakhim be-Parshanut ha-Miqra*, ed. Nizan, 1:154. Rashbam's interpretation to Gen. 35 (that *ben yamin* means "a son of old age," since the word ימין can be appropriately associated with the word ימים), appears to go in a completely different direction. Cf. Lockshin, *Rashbam's Commentary on Genesis*, 223. *Bekhor Shor* to Gen. 49:4 (Nevo, 87) explains Rashi's understanding of the word *paḥaz* as a noun (rather than a verb), while suggesting that in fact it is a gerundive or participial form that means the same thing. Note that Rashbam here understands the word as a participle, but (as is his wont) does not engage Rashi's interpretation (the reason Rashi thought this). See Lockshin, ibid., 351. In Ex. 10:21 (Nevo, 113), *Bekhor Shor* supports and amplifies Rashi's interpretation of the word *ve-yamesh* (לשון אמש ולילה כמו שפירש רש"י כלו' יעריב ויחשיך החושך). Note Rashbam's similar linguistic interpretation, made without any reference to Rashi (and cf. Lockshin, 97).

[61] Rashbam carefully suggests that there is only one meaning here (which coincides with the first one provided by Rashi). See Lockshin, *Rashbam's Commentary to Deuteronomy*, 174. See also *Bekhor Shor*'s comment to Nu. 13:9 (Nevo, 275), in which he cites and agrees with Rashi's interpretation concerning the preparation of the ashes of the red heifer (based on *Sifrei*), offering further support from the larger context of the verse (והכי משמע קרא). Without mentioning Rashi by name, *Bekhor Shor* to Gen. 20:11 (Nevo, 35) clarifies and adds to Rashi's interpretation (based on *Bava Qamma* 92a) as to how Abraham intuited that there was no fear of God among the people of Avimelekh in Gerar, and why he took the steps that he did.

Deut. 33:24; Nevo, 398) that the abundance of oil located in the area of the tribe of Asher to which this verse refers (וטובל בשמן רגלו) is available to both the men and the women of the tribe, who use it to beautify themselves. This explanation supports the midrashic interpretation cited by Rashi, that the beauty of the women from this tribe allowed them to be married to kings and high priests, who were anointed with olive oil when they assumed their lofty positions.

In a comment to the final chapter of the Torah (Deut. 34:2, ואת כל נפתלי ואת ארץ אפרים ומנשה ואת כל ארץ יהודה עד הים האחרון; Nevo, 399–400), *Bekhor Shor* paraphrases Rashi's interpretation (following *Sifrei*), that the Almighty showed Moses at the end of his life a series of highlights that would occur in the future, within each of the four major regions of the land of Israel. *Bekhor Shor* includes the *Sifrei*'s understanding of the final phrase in this verse (which he refers to as *darshu rabbotenu*), that עד הים האחרון should be read as עד היום האחרון ("until the final day"), meaning that Moses was shown all the things that would occur to the children of Israel, up to and including the messianic era and the end of days (עד סוף העולם). *Bekhor Shor* concludes by noting that *kol zeh katav Rashi* (who actually used the phrase עד שיחיו המתים).

In his very next comment, to Deuteronomy 34:5, *Bekhor Shor* begins by noting the two talmudic opinions about who wrote the last eight verses of the Torah (Joshua or a tearful Moses). He then notes that the next verse, which appears to gloss over the identity of the one who buried Moses (ויקבור אותו בגיא בארץ מואב) is, *lefi peshuto*, a *miqra qaẓar.* By rules of literary style, the verse simply indicates that the one who buried Moses did so at a high point in the land of Moav. *Bekhor Shor* then continues by noting that (*ve-*) *rabbotenu ʾamru ha-Qadosh Barukh hu qavro*, which is the first explanation brought by Rashi to that verse.[62] *Bekhor Shor* on Numbers 30:15 (Nevo, 298) cites a Mishnaic interpretation to the phrase "from day to day" that includes (or permits) the nullification of vows at night, followed by Rashi's *peshat* comment (אבל רבינו לפי פשוטו פירש) that a vow may be nullified only within the first twenty-four hours of its enunciation. Here *Bekhor Shor* is

[62] Rashi then presents another opinion cited by *Sifrei* (in the name of R. Yishmaʿel), that Moses buried himself. This explanation is also cited by Ibn Ezra. Note that Rashbam's comment here, as reproduced from manuscript by Moshe Sokolow ("'Ha-Peshatot ha-Mitḥadshim'—Qetaʿim Ḥadashim mi-Perush ha-Torah la-Rashbam," 78), does something quite similar to what *Bekhor Shor* does. He first presents the view (on the basis of Amos 6:12) that the one who buried Moses did so in this location, and he then suggests that either the Almighty or angels buried him. Cf. E. Touitou, *Exegesis in Perpetual Motion*, 145. At the same time, *Bekhor Shor*'s interpretation of the phrase in Deut. 34:7, לא כהתה עינו ולא נס ליחה, as referring to Moses throughout his lifetime, even at the point of old age (*lefi ha-peshat, be-ḥayyav maḥmat ziqnah*), is in clear disagreement with the approach of Rashi (following the *Sifrei*), which explains this biblical phrase to mean that even after Moses died, "the fluids within him prevented decay from occurring, and his facial appearance did not change."

ratifying Rashi's *peshat* interpretation, which is not reflected in talmudic literature.[63]

In his commentary to Numbers 23:13 (Nevo, 285), *Bekhor Shor* suggests that Balak moved Bilʿam around to three different locations in order to most effectively secure Divine approval for Bilʿam to curse as many Jews as possible, and to ensure that the merits of some of the people would not be able to protect others. Perhaps recognizing the somewhat speculative nature of his interpretation, however, *Bekhor Shor* also presents the midrashic view (found in both *Tanḥuma* and *Midrash Rabbah*) that the places to which Balak brought Bilʿam were those where tragedies would befall the Jewish people in the future. *Bekhor Shor* notes that this was the interpretation recorded by Rashi in his commentary (to Nu. 23:14, 28).

Bekhor Shor also indicates where he disagrees with Rashi in matters of interpretation, and he often specifies the nature of his critique. Rashi, following *Bereshit Rabbah*, understood the phrase in Genesis 11:2, ויהי בנסעם מקדם, to reflect that the putative builders of the Tower of Babel moved from a place called *Har ha-Qedem* (Gen. 10:30) in order to find a larger area that would accommodate their many followers. For his part *Bekhor Shor* notes (Nevo, 23; *ve-nirʾeh li*) that the various boundaries (and places) referred to throughout Genesis 10 were meant to delineate the locations the children of Noah would occupy after the dispersion (*ʾaḥar ha-palaggah*), and that *Har ha-Qedem* is identified there as belonging only to the descendants of Shem. He therefore suggests instead that *Qedem* in Genesis 11:2 refers to the area in the east, where civilization first lived following Adam's expulsion from the Garden of Eden (Gen. 3:24, וישכן מקדם לגן עדן). It was from there that the builders of the tower moved to Shinʿar (*Bavel*), since this more northern locale was wetter and less arid, making it easier for agricultural pursuits.[64]

R. Yosef *Bekhor Shor* disagrees with Rashi's interpretation of Genesis 11:7 (which he refers to as פירש רבינו; Nevo, 24). Rashi understood the final phrase in this verse as an interrogative, "and now will this project [of building the Tower of Babel] not be prevented?" *Bekhor Shor*, on the other hand, views this phrase as an assessment of the present situation. Since all the participants spoke one language and were gathered together, there was no reason to believe that this project would not move forward and would not

[63] See also Lev. 20:9 (Nevo, 217). In Nu. 31:3, *Bekhor Shor* follows a simple interpretation and contrasts it with that of a *midrash ʾaggadah* (*Tanḥuma*).

[64] Rashbam has no comment here, while Ramban raises the same objection to Rashi's interpretation as *Bekhor Shor* does (*ve-ʾein zeh nakhon*), and *Ḥizzequni* adopts *Bekhor Shor*'s approach. In Lev. 13:5 (Nevo, 198), *Bekhor Shor* cryptically suggests that the inclusion of the next phrase in this verse (לא פשה הנגע בעור) supports his interpretation of the prior phrase (והנגע עמד בעיניו) against that of Rashi. Ramban again raises the same objection, based primarily on a passage in *Sifra*.

be prevented. Therefore, the next verse indicates that, in fact, the Almighty would not allow this project to succeed. The disagreement between Rashi and *Bekhor Shor* is a relatively subtle one, but *Bekhor Shor* feels quite comfortable "correcting" Rashi's approach toward understanding this verse in context. R. Yosef *Bekhor Shor*'s numerous explicit disagreements with *peshuto shel miqra* interpretations put forward by Rashi generally take place in this same way. *Bekhor Shor* cites Rashi by name, offers some brief criticism, and then makes his own suggestion, providing a kind of sharing of "*ha-peshatot ha-mitḥadshim bekhol yom*" with or against the master Rashi.[65]

When *Bekhor Shor* openly and emphatically disagrees with Rashi's interpretation in Genesis 15:6 ("and he [Abraham] believed in the Almighty and he/He considered it as a kindness" or a good deed, *ẓedaqah*), *Bekhor Shor* refers to Rashi's interpretation not by name but as *yesh mefarshim.* Rashi understands that it was God who considered it to the credit of Abraham that he believed in Him, while *Bekhor Shor* insists that it was Abraham who considered this to be an act of great kindness, since the Almighty had bestowed a child upon him who would then inherit the land of Israel. *Bekhor Shor*'s reaction to Rashi's comment here is almost visceral: (ואין נראה לי, כי מי לא יאמין לא-ל הנאמן); and it is perhaps for this reason that *Bekhor Shor* does not mention Rashi by name in this instance.[66]

At the same time, *Bekhor Shor* (to Ex. 9:6; Nevo, 109–10) does mention Rashi by name when criticizing Rashi's approach (Ex. 9:10, citing the *Mekhilta*) to the plague of *dever.* For Rashi the statement in Exodus 9:6 that

[65] On Gen. 50:15. *Bekhor Shor* notes (Nevo, 93) that while Rashi's interpretation of the word *lu* fits the context of the verse nicely (*ve-yoshev yafeh*), this type of usage is not found within the biblical lexicon (שלא מצינו לו שהוא לשון שמא), a point that Rashi had himself conceded in his comment (ואין לו עוד דומה במקרא). In Ex. 13:16, *Bekhor Shor* (Nevo, 119) links the word *totafot* with the process of seeing, based on a talmudic passage in tractate *Megillah* 14a. He notes that Rashi linked this word with speech, based on Amos 7:16, and then adds an additional biblical verse (Isaiah 3:16) that appears to support his own view. *Ḥizzequni* again follows *Bekhor Shor*'s interpretation. See also *Bekhor Shor*'s comment Ex. 14:21 (Nevo, 121), where he cites Rashi (who follows Onkelos) and mildly disagrees in a matter of lingustic interpretation. See also Lev. 26:1 (Nevo, 233), in which *Bekhor Shor* (after mentioning Rashi's interpretation) explains the term *ʾeven maskit* differently from Rashi (who had defined it based on Ex. 33:22) according to a talmudic usage (*Megillah* 14a). Here again, Rashbam appears to suggest the very same interpretation as *Bekhor Shor* does (albeit based on Psalms 73:7).

[66] Rashbam has no comment here, while Ramban follows the approach of *Bekhor Shor*, including the substance (if not quite the tone) of his objection to Rashi's interpretation. See also *Bekhor Shor* to Ex. 33:26 (Nevo, 171), where he criticizes Rashi's interpretation of Deut. 33:9 (following *Sifrei*, referred to here only as *u-lefi ha-mefarshim*), that the Levites killed their non-Levite (maternal) relatives who participated in the sin of the golden calf. Based on his understanding of this episode (in Ex. 33), *Bekhor Shor* concludes that no relatives of the Levites whatsoever took part in this sin. *Bekhor Shor* characterizes his objection to Rashi's interpretation in the following terms: ולפי המפרשים שלא הכירם אלא הרגום צריך לדחוק . . . ואינו נראה בעיני.

"all the cattle [of the Egyptians] died" during this plague (as per Ex. 9:4) suggests that any cattle that had been taken in from the field by God-fearing Egyptians were spared. *Bekhor Shor* asserts that he considers this approach to be confused (והדבר מגומגם בעיני), since the Torah's description of the plague of hail (Ex. 9:25) explicitly states that those who did not fear God and left their cattle in the fields lost them to the hail, implying that even those Egyptians who did not fear God had some cattle remaining after the plague of *dever. Bekhor Shor* supports Rashi's approach, suggesting that perhaps even those who did not fear God might have had some cattle remaining after the plague of *dever*, because coincidentally they did not take those cattle out to the pasture at that time (על ידי מקרה שלא הוציאו אותו היום). In this instance *Bekhor Shor* tries to minimize the extent of his disagreement with Rashi, which is perhaps what allows Rashi's name to remain explicit.[67]

In Exodus 12:45 (Nevo, 117–18), *Bekhor Shor* objects to an interpretation of Rashi (ומה שפי' רש"י לא נהירא לי) on the basis of a point of talmudic law. Rashi maintains that the prohibition expressed in 12:48 (וכל ערל לא יאכל בו) refers specifically to the rule that an uncircumcised Jew—whose two brothers had previously died as a result of their circumcisions, thereby mandating as a matter of Jewish law that he, the third brother, may not be circumcised—nonetheless cannot participate in a Passover sacrifice, even though his noncircumcision is not a willful or brazen violation on his part of this precept. Rashi further notes that such a person's exclusion clearly cannot be derived from Exodus 12:43 (כל בן נכר לא יאכל בו), since this verse comes to exclude a non-Jew or an apostate (*meshummad*) who has (willfully) "made himself foreign" to the precept of circumcision if not to the very offering of the Passover sacrifice itself.

Based on a talmudic passage in tractate *Yevamot* (71a), *Bekhor Shor* maintains that an uncircumcised brother is already excluded because every *'arel* is considered to be unacceptable (literally, disgusting) in the face of the sacrificial altar, and therefore may not eat of any sacrifice (ואסור ... משום דמאים לאכול משלחנו של מקום). Indeed, this is how *Bekhor Shor* then interprets the broader prohibition in 12:48 (*ve-khol 'arel lo yokhal bo*) that all uncircumcised Jews may not partake in the Passover sacrifice, *mishum de-ma'is*, citing again this passage in tractate *Yevamot*. In this instance, *Bekhor Shor* is critical of Rashi's interpretation from his vantage points as both a talmudist and a *peshat* exegete. He is sensitive to Rashi's use of talmudic texts in halakhic contexts, as were all of the Tosafists. At the same time, however, *Bekhor Shor*'s search for *peshat* in his Torah commentary impels him to find a less narrow

[67] As noted by Nevo, several later Tosafist Torah compilations suggest other answers.

interpretation of 12:48 than Rashi's, which could nonetheless include the specific prohibition that Rashi had correctly highlighted.[68]

In a similar vein *Bekhor Shor* at first supports Rashi's interpretation to Deuteronomy 12:19 (which follows the *Sifrei*; Nevo, 331) that the Torah's requirement to support the needy Levite applies only within the land of Israel (באדמתך): "In the diaspora, however, one is not required to support him more than any other needy person." *Bekhor Shor* points out that this distinction is reasonable, since the Levite had no share or inheritance in the land of Israel itself, and others were therefore required to look out for his welfare. In the diaspora, however, no one has a particular share of the land, neither the Levites nor others, and all needy people are therefore on equal footing. However, *Bekhor Shor* then argues against Rashi, based on the talmudic interpretation found toward the end of tractate *Horayyot* (13a), which teaches that the Levite has precedence over an Israelite both in terms of his being supported and in terms of caring for and returning his lost objects. This talmudic formulation appears to be in force irrespective of whether the principals reside in the land of Israel or in the diaspora.[69]

Rashi's interpretation of the word מן (in Ex. 16:15, מן הוא) as ready and available (לשון זימון, based on parallels in Jonah 2:1 and Daniel 1:5) is disputed by *Bekhor Shor* (*ve-'ein nir'eh li*; Nevo, 126) due to the broader context of this verse, which describes how the manna initially appeared. The verse states that the people said to each other (upon seeing the manna) מן הוא, because they did not know what it was (כי לא ידעו מה הוא). Thus, *Bekhor Shor* asks, how could this term represent the definitive name that was given by the children of Israel to this substance (as Rashi's interpretation maintains)? Moreover, they could not know yet that the מן would in fact be ready and available (*mezuman*). *Bekhor Shor* therefore suggests (ולפיכך נראה לי) that the word *man* in Egyptian is equivalent to the interrogative term *mah* in Hebrew. The people asked each other "what is this?" since they indeed did not know—until Moses explained to them—that "this is the bread that God has provided for you to eat." From that point on, the מן was referred to in this way, reflecting their initial encounter with it. Although Rashi had sought to interpret this word according to a *peshat* method by identifying parallel words within the

[68] Somewhat surprisingly, Rashbam essentially follows Rashi here. See Lockshin, *Rashbam's Commentary on Exodus* (Atlanta, 1997), 124–25.

[69] This appears to be the comment of Rashbam as well (*'al admatekha* means as long as you are alive, on this earth), based on a verse later in Deuteronomy (31:13) rather than on the talmudic passage. See Lockshin, *Rashbam's Commentary on Deuteronomy* (Atlanta, 2004), 89. *Bekhor Shor* again makes no reference to Rashbam. See also *Pa'aneaḥ Raza*, 513. *Bekhor Shor*'s comments to Deut. 10:10 (Nevo, 325), Deut. 21:21 (Nevo, 354), and Deut. 27:8 (Nevo, 369) contain additional implicit analyses of Rashi's comments (with which *Bekhor Shor* does not always ultimately agree).

Bible, *Bekhor Shor* was clearly more comfortable with suggesting an Egyptian word to resolve the contextual issue. Although Rashbam, following the relatively late *Midrash Leqah Tov* and Dunash ben Labrat at least in part, also suggests this interpretation, adding two additional examples for the presence of "foreign words" in the Bible,[70] *Bekhor Shor*, following Rashbam, suggests that this phrase is based on an Egyptian cognate, although he makes no reference to any earlier exegetical works. He is content to simply propose an alternate suggestion to the interpretation of Rashi.[71]

As the examples we have presented demonstrate, it is clear that *Bekhor Shor* wished to define his work, at least in part, by inspecting Rashi's approach to *peshuto shel miqra*, and by endorsing his approach toward using material from *Ḥazal*. Although *Bekhor Shor* felt free to disagree with Rashi in matters of *peshat* and to suggest reasonable interpretations of his own, he was more hesitant to do so where strongly held rabbinic interpretations were at stake—even in narrative sections. He provides additional *peshat* support for some of Rashi's comments, and he closely questions and extends or corrects other comments by Rashi which he felt were inadequate.[72] Moreover, the model established by Rashi—of presenting both rabbinic and *peshuto shel miqra* interpretations to the same verse—greatly influenced *Bekhor Shor*, as we shall see. Although *Bekhor Shor*'s goal of seeking meaningful *peshat* interpretations often tends toward the approach of Rashbam,[73] his style of presentation remains much closer to that of Rashi.[74]

[70] Rabbenu Tam (in his *Hakhra'ot*, ed. H. Z. Filipowski [London, 1855], 20; see above, Introduction, n. 52) also appears to have accepted Dunash's basic approach in this matter. See M. Lockshin, *Rashbam's Commentary on Exodus*, 173–75.

[71] *Bekhor Shor* on Ex.11:21 (Nevo, 113) notes and accepts Rashi's linguistic interpretation of the somewhat unusual word form וימש. He also cites Rashi's linguistic interpretation of the word ולטוטפות (Ex. 13:16; Nevo, 119), but only after he had suggested an alternate. See also Ex. 32:4 (Nevo, 169), where *Bekhor Shor* cites Rashi's linguistic interpretation as *yesh mefarshim* (and then suggests another approach) and see also Lev. 4:3 (Nevo, 187); and Deut. 12:19 (Nevo, 331); Deut. 34:24 (Nevo, 398).

[72] To be sure, *Bekhor Shor* often pursues these same goals directly on the verse(s) in question, without identifying Rashi's interpretation by name. See Nevo's introduction, 12, and his notes on Genesis 1:7 (p. 5); to Nu. 16:3, 14, 15 (Nevo, 269); to Deut. 18:4 (Nevo, 345–46). Cf. M. Miyara, *Ba'alei ha-Tosafot: Rabbotenu ha-Mefarshim*, 315, n. 105; and below, n. 93.

[73] See, e.g., Ex. 12:39 (Nevo, 116, and cf. Lockshin, *Rashbam's Commentary to Exodus*, 120); Ex. 14:19 (Nevo, 121, and cf. Lockshin, 13. 135); Ex. 18:2 (Nevo, 128–29, and cf. Lockshin, 189–90); Ex. 19:13, 19:19 (Nevo, 132–33, and Lockshin, 207, 209); Ex. 25:6 (Nevo, 156); Ex. 3:27 (Nevo, 178).

[74] As Nevo points out in quite a few instances, various Tosafist compendia and collections contain comments in the name of *Bekhor Shor* that are either not found in the one surviving manuscript of his commentary, ms. Munich 52, or are found in somewhat different form. Although the authenticity of these comments is not always assured, *Bekhor Shor* responds in a number of them to a question or problem with Rashi's interpretation. See, e.g., Nevo's notes to his edition of *Perushei R. Yosef Bekhor Shor*, 169, 184, 188, 196, 204, 230, 256, 268, 278, 282. Cf. Shaul Bruchi, "Ha-Haggahot be-Perush R. Yosef Bekhor Shor la-Torah," *Megadim* 40 (2004), 75–113.

Somewhat surprisingly, *Bekhor Shor* mentions Rashbam by name only three times in his Torah commentary, each one on verses in the Book of Exodus. Moses is made aware that his smiting of the Egyptian aggressor had become known, אכן נודע הדבר (Ex. 2:14). *Bekhor Shor* interprets the unusual word *ʾakhen* to mean that what Moses had done was now clearly known (in truth, *be-ʾemet*), despite Moses's sense (and the precaution he took in looking this way and that, in 2:12) that his action would not become known. *Bekhor Shor* then cites the similar interpretation of Rashbam that he had heard in his name (*u-mishum R. Shmuʾel shamati*) that *ʾakhen* is a kind of compound word, אך כן, which again indicates that what Moses had thought would not happen had in fact occurred.

In the second instance (Ex. 3:14; Nevo, 101), concerning the meaning of the Divine name represented by *E-hyeh Asher E-hyeh*, Rashbam holds that this word and phrase are actually a Divine name. *Bekhor Shor* disagrees, however, suggesting that this phrase only represents the Tetragrammaton (*ve-Rabbenu Shmuʾel piresh . . . ve-lo nehira li*). *Bekhor Shor* justifies his interpretation against that of Rashbam by noting that accepted halakhic practice is to pronounce the word *ʾehyeh* as it is written and vocalized, but not to pronounce the Tetragrammaton in this way.[75]

In the third instance (Ex. 14:25; Nevo, 122), *Bekhor Shor* once again had "heard in the name of R. Samuel" (*u-mishum Rabbenu Shmuʾel shamati*) that the phrase ויסר את אופן מרכבותיו וינהגהו בכבדות connotes an attempt by the Egyptians to turn the wheels of their chariots around (or at least to move backward) in order to retreat and flee. Owing, however, to the many chariots lined up one in front of the other, they were unable to do so.[76] *Bekhor Shor* presents his own understanding of this phrase first, that the Egyptians removed the wheels from their chariots so that they would not sink into the depths of the sea but would remain close to the shore, which would perhaps

[75] See Lockshin, *Rashbam's Commentary to the Book of Exodus*, 38.

[76] See Lockshin, ibid., 144–45, and cf. *Ḥizzequni.* For another possible citation of Rashbam (found in glosses to *Bekhor Shor*'s commentary), see *Miqraʾot Gedolot Ha-Keter* (Jerusalem, 1992), vol. 1 (pt. 2), 89, where *Bekhor Shor*'s commentary to Gen. 36:12 contains a reference to Rashbam: ור' שמואל מצא חברים לזה הענין. However, other editions read (more accurately): ורבים שמות [ת]מצא חברים לזה הענין. See *Commentary to the Pentateuch by R. Joseph Bechor Shor*, ed. A. Jellinek (to Genesis and Exodus) (Leipzig, 1855; repr. Jerusalem, 1978), 57; and ed. Nevo, 64. The citation of a comment by R. Samuel in ed. Jellinek (to Ex. 6:13), 95–96, is correctly labeled in the text as an added gloss (הגה"ה). This comment is not found in ed. Nevo, 106, and it is shown to be a later addendum by Bruchi, "Ha-Haggahot be-Perush R. Yosef Bekhor Shor," 99–101. (In addition, the lone surviving version of Rashbam's Torah commentary does not contain this comment.) Cf. E. Viezel, "Ha-Perush ha-Meyuḥas le-Rashi le-Sefer Ezra-Neḥemyah," *Jewish Studies Internet Journal* 9 (2010), 22 (n. 88). The fact that *Bekhor Shor* refers in two (of the three) instances of his verifiable use of Rashbam's Torah commentary to comments that he "heard in the name of R. Samuel" suggests that *Bekhor Shor* may not have had a full version of Rashbam's commentary in written form.

allow them to be extricated. This effort was not successful, however, since they could not easily drive the chariots without wheels back to the banks of the sea and out of danger.

In six additional cases, *Bekhor Shor* refers to Rashbam's commentary as the view of *yesh mefarshim.* In his commentary to Genesis 37:28 (Nevo 69), *Bekhor Shor* severely criticizes Rashbam's interpretation of the chain of events that led up to the sale of Joseph. As some have suggested, *Bekhor Shor* may have omitted Rashbam's name intentionally here (similar perhaps to the instance noted above with respect to Rashi's commentary),[77] because he characterizes it as "completely contrived" (ואינו רק דברי בדאות).[78] Another less-remarked instance of this same type of critique is found earlier, in Genesis 25:34 (Nevo, 44), where Rashbam interprets (in verses 31 and 33) that Esau ate Jacob's food at the point that the *bekhorah* was sold simply as a means of ratifying this sale through the common convention of eating together and not only because of his abject hunger. *Bekhor Shor* again dismisses this interpretation as contrived (והוא בדאות בעיני).[79]

However, *Bekhor Shor* also refers to Rashbam as *yesh mefarshim*, even when his objections are less pointed. On Genesis 41:7 (Nevo, 74–75, to the phrase והנה חלום), *Bekhor Shor* provides and prefers an alternative to the *peshat* of Rashbam,[80] and similarly in Exodus 21:10 (Nevo, 138–39) he provides an alternative *peshat* to that of Rashbam, which is, again, closer to Rashi's interpretation of the meaning of ועונתה.[81] The same is true for Numbers 31:49 (Nevo, 299), where *Bekhor Shor* rejects Rashbam's *peshat* interpretation of the phrase *ve-lo nifqad mimenu 'ish* in favor of the talmudic *derashah*. Similarly, in Deuteronomy 21:23 (Nevo, 355), where Rashbam's innovative *peshat* interpretation of the phrase כי קללת אלהים תלוי (that whenever a hanged person is seen, the judges—*'elohim*—who sentenced him are cursed) is rejected by *Bekhor Shor* in favor of his own *peshat* (i.e., for not allowing one who has been hanged to remain too long in that position before burial because that will ultimately lead to a dishonoring of the Almighty), as well as the rabbinic interpretation (followed also by Rashi on this verse), both of which understand *E-lohim* in this verse as a reference to the Divine.[82]

77 See above, n. 64.

78 See E. Touitou, *Exegesis in Perpetual Motion*, 101, n. 7, who also notes that *Ḥizzequni* accepts Rashbam's interpretation and expands it. For the details of this interpretation and *Bekhor Shor*'s problems with it, see my "Midrashic Texts and Methods in Tosafist Torah Commentaries" (above, n. 6), sec. 8, and see also below, n. 111; and chapter 4, nn. 161–63.

79 See Lockshin, *Rashbam's Commentary to Genesis*, 137–38; and Touitou, *Exegesis in Perpetual Motion*, 202. Naḥmanides again does not like this interpretation.

80 See Lockshin, *Rashbam's Commentary to Genesis*, 279–80.

81 Cf. ibid., 233–34.

82 The phrase אית דמפרשי (on an etymology) in Deut. 28:20 (Nevo, 371) also perhaps refers to Rashbam. Similarly, the etymological *yesh mefarshim* in Nu. 21:30 (Nevo, 282) may refer either

In two of the three instances where Rashbam's name is explicitly mentioned by *Bekhor Shor*, and in all eight references to Rashbam as *yesh mefarshim*, *Bekhor Shor* takes issue with Rashbam's interpretation to some extent. At no point does he ratify and expand explanations by Rashbam, as he does with many of those made by Rashi. At the same time, R. Yosef *Bekhor Shor* refers to R. Yosef Qara by name on nine occasions, and almost always accepts his interpretations.[83] He also mentions the Sefardic biblical interpreter and *pashtan* R. Ovadyah (b. Samuel) eight times, which is more than Rashbam himself does.[84] In light of the findings on the explicit citations that have been presented here, the latter portion of Poznanski's assessment—that Rashi is "brought many times" (כן למשל יביא פעמים הרבה את רש"י ראש המפרשים אף יכנהו בשם רבינו סתם) by *Bekhor Shor*, and that R. Yosef and Rashbam are also mentioned "many times" (כן יזכיר פעמים הרבה את הר"י קרא ואת הרשב"ם)—appears to be imprecise. Poznanski goes on to say that *Bekhor Shor* also makes use of a goodly number of Rashbam's interpretations and methods without referring to him by name.[85] Although the second instance in which *Bekhor Shor* refers to Rashbam by name as noted above (Ex. 14:25, משום ר' שמואל שמעתי) intimates that he perhaps did not have a written copy of Rashbam's commentary in front of him, there are indeed quite a number

---

to Rashbam or to Ibn Ezra. See also *Bekhor Shor* to Gen. 46:24, where the rejected *yesh mefarshim* (*ve-'eino nir'eh*) can refer either to Targum Yonatan (or to Rashi, who cites it) or to Ibn Ezra. In addition, it is possible that Rashbam (in his comment to Ex. 13:9) may be *Bekhor Shor*'s target when he rejects an allegorical interpretation of Deut. 6:9 (Nevo, 318, attributed to *vehamefarshim*), in favor of various rabbinic *derashot* and interpretations. See Lockshin, *Rashbam's Commentary to Genesis*, 129, n.10; Touitou, *Exegesis in Perpetual Motion*, 125, n. 38, and Sara Kamin, "Ha-Polmos Neged ha-Allegoriyyah be-Divrei R. Yosef Bekhor Shor," *Jerusalem Studies in Jewish Thought* 3 (1984), 367–92.

[83] See Gen. 4:23 (ed. Nevo, 14), 14; 34:25 (62); 49:9 (88; *mishum R. Yosef Qara shamati*); Ex. 4:13 (103; *u-mishum R. Yosef Qara shamati*); 20:1 (133; *piresh R. Yosef Qara*); Deut. 14:1 (334); 28:68 (375; *piresh R. Yosef Qara*); 32:17 (387; *ve-R. Yosef Qara piresh*); 33:1 (391, *u-piresh R. Yosef Qara*). *Bekhor Shor*'s comment to Gen. 10:25 (ed. Nevo, 23) is cited in the *Da'at Zeqenim* compilation in the name of R. Yosef Qara, but this may be a transposition of names.

[84] See the listings in Nevo's introduction to his *Perushei R. Yosef Bekhor Shor*, 3, and in M. Miyara, *Ba'alei ha-Tosafot*, 246, n. 60. Cf. Touitou, *Exegesis in Perpetual Motion*, 46–47; A. Grossman, *Ḥakhmei Ẓarefat ha-Rishonim*, 473; and S. Bruchi, "Haggahot be-Perush R. Yosef Bekhor Shor," 107–12 (for both R. Ovadyah and for *Bekhor Shor*'s citation of R. Solomon Parhon's biblical dictionary).

[85] See Poznanski, *Mavo*, LIX. Poznanski refers to the data on citations found in Gotthilf Walter, *Joseph Bekhor Schor, der letzte nordfranzoesiche Bibelexeget*, vol. 1 (Breslau, 1890), 18–19, which was republished as an appendix to the third volume in the Makor edition of *Bekhor Shor*'s commentary(Jerusalem, 1978). Walter's identification (n. 6) of R. Eliezer *mi-Magenza* in *Bekhor Shor*'s commentary (to Lev. 22:25, ed. Nevo, 223) as Rashbam's German contemporary, R. Eliezer b. Nathan (Raban) of Mayence, is incorrect (even as there are some difficulties with text here). Rather, this is a reference to R. Eliezer of Beaugency, the last of the so-called *pashtanim* in northern France during the twelfth century. See N. Golb, *The Jews in Medieval Normandy* (Cambridge, 1998), 322; R. Harris, *Discerning Parallelism*, 28–33; and above, n. 28.

of instances in which *Bekhor Shor*'s interpretation is very similar to that of Rashbam.[86] Perhaps *Bekhor Shor* hardly cites Rashbam by name because he still considered the search for *peshat* undertaken by Rashbam to be a "work in progress," which did not have the quasi-canonical status of Rashi's commentary. Indeed, while *Bekhor Shor* never cites Ibn Ezra by name either (and we cannot even be certain that he had a copy of Ibn Ezra's work), he does present a number of interpretations that are very close to those of Ibn Ezra, sometimes in the name of *yesh mefarshim*.[87]

In any event, in one crucial aspect, which can be documented no fewer than three hundred times throughout his Torah commentary, *Bekhor Shor* steadfastly follows the method and style of exegesis pioneered and made famous by Rashi. Just as Rashi simultaneously pursued *peshuto shel miqra va-'aggadah ha-meyashevet divrei ha-miqra*, *Bekhor Shor* openly presents and utilizes talmudic and midrashic literature together with interpretations that he designates as (*lefi ha-*)*peshat* on almost every page of his Torah commentary, and far more frequently (to put it mildly) than either Rashbam or R. Yosef Qara do.[88] Like Rashi, *Bekhor Shor* also expresses great fealty to the rabbinic

[86] In his introduction (13), Nevo lists some twenty-five such cases. See also Walter, *Joseph Bekhor Schor*, nn.11–14; E. Touitou, *Exegesis in Perpetual Motion*, 14–15, n. 5 (to Gen. 45:24), and 44–45 (although cf. 140–41, 197, 199); and M. Miyara, *Ba'alei ha-Tosafot*, 182, 204–205. However, even if the number of these similarities can be expanded significantly, it still pales in comparison to the number of occasions on which *Bekhor Shor* implicitly follows (or supports) interpretations of Rashi, just as the number of actual citations of Rashi is much higher than the citations of Rashbam by name.

[87] See, e.g., ed. Nevo, 21 (Gen. 9:24), 173 (Ex. 33:20), 174 (Ex. 34:6, along with an approach by Rabbenu Tam found in *Tosafot Rosh ha-Shanah*), 175 (34:9), 283 (Nu. 22:7); 324 (Deut. 10:6, *ve-yesh lomar*), 369 (Deut. 26:18). See also Nevo's references to pp. 10, 11, 25, 34, 156, 218, 270. In one instance, *Sefer ha-Gan* (to Gen. 2:23, ed. Orlian, 129) records a comment in the name of *Bekhor Shor* in which he allegedly cites Ibn Ezra by name. In this instance, however, the interpretation is not found within the extant version of Ibn Ezra's commentary, and appears to have been misattributed. See *Sefer ha-Gan*, ed. Orlian, nn. 172–74; Nevo's note on p. 10 of his edition; and *Tosafot ha-Shalem*, ed. Gellis, 1:115, secs. 6, 9, 11, 13, which reveal that a similar interpretation was attributed to Rabbenu Tam as well. On the commentaries of *Bekhor Shor* and Ibn Ezra, see also Nevo, *Ha-Parshanut ha-Ẓarefatit*, 149–55 (= "Ha-Yaḥas Bein Perushei ha-Torah shel R. Yosef Bekhor Shor ve-R. Avraham Ibn Ezra," *Tarbiz* 51 [1992], 503–7); A. Meir in *Beit Miqra* 43 (1998), 264; and cf. Uriel Simon, "Transplanting the Wisdom of Spain to Christian Lands: The Failed Efforts of R. Abraham Ibn Ezra," *Simon Dubnow Institute Yearbook* 8 (2009), 181–89.

[88] At the conclusion of an illuminating paper given at the Fifteenth World Congress of Jewish Studies in Jerusalem (August 2009), Dr. Yonatan Jacobs of Bar-Ilan University suggested that, unlike Rashbam (or Rashi), *Bekhor Shor* was the first of the northern French school of *pashtanim* to offer multiple *peshatim* to a single verse. Rashbam puts forward only one *peshat* in his Torah comments (as noted by Japhet and others; see above, Introduction, n. 107), while Rashi will present a *peshat* alternative, along with a rabbinic or midrashic interpretation (as an *'aggadah ha-meyashevet divrei miqra*), rather than multiple *peshatim* (although Rashi does often present a *peshat* along with a *peshat*-like comment by Onkelos). Jacobs reported that he has identified approximately one hundred such instances in which *Bekhor Shor* offers multiple *peshatim* to a single verse, although this is still far fewer than the number of instances when

approach to biblical interpretation, as his comment to Exodus 8:15 (ed. Nevo, 109) indicates. Although there is no logical or simple reason (*lefi ha-peshat*) to explain why the Egyptian magicians could replicate the plagues of blood and frogs but could not produce the lice, *Bekhor Shor* asserts that one ought not object to or disparage (*va-ʿaleihem ʾein le-hashiv*) the talmudic and midrashic explanation (*divrei rabbotenu*, found in tractate *Sanhedrin* 67b and in *Midrash Tanḥuma* to *Va-Era*) that a magical rite of *shedim* cannot affect objects that are exceedingly small (פחות מכעדשה, as in the case of the lice), so that the magicians would be forced to exclaim to Pharaoh that this plague was from "the finger of God." It should be noted that this is also essentially how Rashi interpreted the phrase *ʾeẓba E-lohim* on the basis of *Shemot Rabbah.*[89]

Similarly, *Bekhor Shor* suggests that *lefi ha-peshat* the "three people" who came to visit Abraham (in Gen. 18:2; Nevo, 30) were actual human beings (*ʾanashim mamash*), because angels do not typically eat and rest in peoples' homes as these figures did. Indeed, the exceptional case of the angels who lodged in the home of Lot is counterbalanced by the angel who explicitly tells Manoaḥ (Judg. 13:16), "For if you will hold me back [by inviting me to your home], I will not eat your bread." Nonetheless, *Bekhor Shor* concludes by asserting that he cannot challenge the rabbinic interpretation here, that the three figures who appeared to Abraham were angels as well (אך אין להשיב על דברי רבותינו שאף הם כמלאכים), an interpretation that was again adopted by Rashi (following *Bereshit Rabbah*).[90]

In his commentary to Deuteronomy 31:28 (Nevo, 383), *Bekhor Shor* maintains that *lefi ha-peshat* the people were to be gathered by means of the trumpets to hear Moses's final words. The rabbis had asserted, however (*ʾaval rabbotenu ʾamru*), that the trumpets were hidden away already during Moses's lifetime. This tradition is also noted by Rashi to this verse, without further comment. *Bekhor Shor* then concludes that the trumpets were only an appropriate means

he juxtaposes (as Rashi constantly does) a *peshat* with a rabbinic approach. Cf. E. Viezel, "Ha-Perush ha-Meyuḥas le-Rashi le-Sefer Ezra-Neḥemyah," 56; idem, *The Commentary on Chronicles Attributed to Rashi*, 134–35; and above, n. 47. Earlier in his paper, Jacobs also noted examples in which *Bekhor Shor* pursues some of the literary approaches and forms favored by Rashbam, such as the notion of *haqdamah* (according to which the Torah narrative provides details in advance or at the beginning of the episode in which this information becomes relevant). Cf. the studies by Jacobs cited above, n. 50, and see also M. Ahrend, *Perush R. Yosef Qara le-Sefer Iyyov*, 14–15.

[89] Rashbam makes a very different (and more rationalistic) suggestion. The magicians maintained that this plague was not from Moses and Aaron but rather the result of a natural disaster. See Lockshin, *Rashbam's Commentary to Exodus*, 79.

[90] *Bekhor Shor* is not concerned here with the corporeality of angels per se. Cf. below, chapter 3, nn. 190–91, and chapter 7. As Nevo notes (based on a gloss in ms. Munich 52), there are also polemical considerations that may have impelled *Bekhor Shor* to suggest that the three figures who appeared to Abraham were human beings rather than angels. Cf. David Berger, *The Jewish-Christian Debate in the High Middle Ages* (Philadelphia, 1979), 48–51.

of convening the people in the desert, when they were all in one camp. Once they had settled in their various cities within the land of Israel, however, this method would no longer be effective (לא יועילו החצוצרות להקהיל).[91]

Here again, R. Yosef *Bekhor Shor* declines to sustain a reasonable but otherwise unsupported *peshat* interpretation in the face of a widely held rabbinic tradition that appears to contradict it, although *Bekhor Shor*'s exegetical aim may have been to simply suggest and present the *peshat* interpretation. This is similar to the methodological strategy suggested by Lockshin above, with regard to verses that were concentrated in distinctly halakhic contexts. Apparently, then, even in narrative portions, *Bekhor Shor* was hesitant to leave the tension between *peshat* and rabbinic midrash unaddressed, although he was more comfortable than Rashi in putting forward additional *peshat* options, and he sought to explain the validity and the advantage of the rabbinic interpretation in the face of an otherwise fully reasonable *peshat* interpretation.

It almost goes without saying that, where *Bekhor Shor* could present a rabbinic interpretation that coincided with the simple *peshat*, he would do so. Thus *Bekhor Shor* (Nevo, 154) interprets the phrase in Exodus 24:14, "whoever has a claim will come to them" (מי בעל דברים יגש אליהם), as that they will come to them, *lefi ha-peshat*, to be judged (*ladun*). "And the rabbis interpreted [this phrase to mean] (*ve-rabbotenu ʾamru*, in *Bava Qamma* 46b) that the litigant [who can] will submit proof to them [the judges], in support of his position (יגש ראיה אליהם)." *Bekhor Shor* then proceeds to show that this is in fact the scriptural derivation of the important juridical principle, המוציא מחבירו עליו הראיה (that a claimant must bring proof in order to extract money from his fellow litigant), and he spends a moment on related judicial procedures. The rabbinic approach clearly adds quite a bit of important additional detail, but it too ultimately stems or derives from the initial *peshat* reading, that the verse refers specifically to matters of judicial process. Similarly, *Bekhor Shor* provides a *peshat* approach toward understanding the circumstances through which the *zav* becomes purified (Lev. 14:13; Nevo, 203, ומכאן לפי הפשט), which he then notes was also derived in the *Sifra* through a rabbinic *derashah*, which is found in Rashi's comment as well. In short, similar to Rashi, *Bekhor Shor* will often cite and place a rabbinic approach alongside a *peshat* approach, in both narrative and halakhic contexts, albeit with less consistent attempts at integration.[92]

[91] The rabbinic interpretation cited here is found in passages in both *Bereshit Rabbah* and *Bamidbar Rabbah*, and in *Midrash Tanḥuma* to the portions of *Be-ha'alotkha* and *Va-Yeḥi*. See also, e.g., Gen. 19:24 (Nevo, 34); Gen. 21:33 (Nevo, 37).

[92] Note also *Bekhor Shor*'s tendency, as compared to Rashbam, to avoid anhalakhic interpretations; see above, n. 56. On rare occasions in narrative contexts, *Bekhor Shor* will strongly disagree with an established *Ḥazal* approach. See, e.g., Gen. 47:29–31 (שים נא ידך תחת ירכי; Nevo 85),

As noted above, *Bekhor Shor* frequently presents (*peshat*) interpretations that are parallel to those of Rashbam, albeit without attribution. Indeed, within narrative sections, *Bekhor Shor* will present what are essentially Rashi's and Rashbam's comments, one after the other, again without identifying them.[93] As *Bekhor Shor*'s understanding of the placement of the story of the binding of Isaac indicates, however, determining which earlier exegete's approach was preferred by *Bekhor Shor* is not always a simple matter. In his interpretation of Genesis 22:1 (Nevo, 38), *Bekhor Shor* suggests that the phrase *'aḥar ha-devarim ha-'elah* that leads into this story connects it directly with the section immediately preceding it, in which Abraham had become such an important person that kings, like Avimelekh, sought to make covenants and alliances with him. This would seem to be in accordance with Rashbam's interpretation, that the phrase *'aḥar ha-devarim ha-'eleh* "always connects events to the preceding chapter," an approach that is not consonant with the midrashic and talmudic understanding of the meaning and significance of this phrase. For Rashbam, the pact that Abraham had made with Avimelekh, which ceded to him the land of the Philistines, angered the Almighty, since the area of *'ereẓ Pelishtim* was rightfully a part of the land of Israel. Therefore He tried Abraham through the binding of Isaac.

Rashi, not wishing to make anything of a juxtaposition that *Ḥazal* did not endorse, had interpreted the "prior event" as either the remonstrations of the *satan* that Abraham was not so devout in his worship of the Almighty (in accordance with a passage in tractate *Sanhedrin*), or the fact that Isaac had committed himself to be sacrificed to the Almighty as a means of "outdoing" the circumcision that Yishma'el had undergone at the age of thirteen

---

which *Bekhor Shor* understands as a demonstration of submission or servitude, not as an oath taken while holding the *milah* (as *Ḥazal* and Rashi do). *Bekhor Shor* notes that he had already put forward this interpretation (on Gen. 24:2; Nevo, 40). There, *Bekhor Shor* mentions the rabbinic approach, and also deflects a Christian interpretation, suggesting perhaps that polemical considerations involved may have caused him to insist on his own approach. Cf. *Bekhor Shor* to Ex. 32:20 (Nevo, 170), and M. Miyara, *Ba'alei ha-Tosafot*, 1:281–82.

[93] See, e.g., Lev. 26:18 (Nevo, 236). For Rashi (following *Sifra*), the seven-fold punishments for continued sin (שבע על חטאתיכם) correspond to the seven expressions of sin delineated in prior verses (Lev. 26:14–15). For Rashbam, the number seven is a symbolic number in Scripture that represents "many," as verses in Proverbs (24:16) and Isaiah (30:26, 4:1) indicate. *Bekhor Shor* first lists the seven earlier violations at some length, citing *Sifra* by name (but not Rashi). He then briefly presents the approach taken by Rashbam (without mentioning his name either), identifying it as *lefi ha-peshat*, and citing only the verse from Proverbs in support. Once again, it appears that *Bekhor Shor* wants to make his audience aware of the *peshat* possibility, although his own preference seems to be the *Ḥazal* interpretation, which pays close attention to context. *Ḥizzequni* goes in a somewhat different direction, linking the number seven with the seventh year (and the violation of that sabbatical year), which is mentioned in a subsequent verse in this section (26:34). See also *Bekhor Shor* to Nu. 31:49 (Nevo, 299), and to Nu. 35:25 (Nevo, 303).

(in accordance with a passage in *Bereshit Rabbah*). At the same time, however, the content and substance of *Bekhor Shor*'s explanation are much closer to that of Rashi (in his first interpretation). For *Bekhor Shor*, the Almighty tested Abraham to prevent the carping of the *satan*, that Abraham and his family had been fully supported by the Almighty, so that now even kings were making pacts with him, as was explicitly said by the *satan* about Job (Job 1:9–10).[94]

In Genesis 32:2, it appears that *Bekhor Shor* comes to defend Rashi against the approach taken by Rashbam. Rashi had interpreted that the angels who came to Jacob at Maḥanayim were angels from the land of Israel, who had come to accompany him back to the land. Rashbam interprets that these angels, whom he does not identify in any way, intended to protect Jacob at this point. This is also the approach of Ibn Ezra, that the angels had come to help him along the way (לעוזרו בדרך). Naḥmanides questions Rashi's interpretation, since Jacob was still very far away from the land of Israel. Moreover, Rashi elsewhere holds (Gen. 28:12, at the beginning of *parashat Va-Yeẓe*) that angels from the land of Israel do not leave the land in order to offer protection. Naḥmanides therefore suggests that these angels appeared to Jacob only in a vision as he was about to depart the land of his enemies, to let Jacob know that he had greater heavenly support than his enemies did—an approach found in the *Moshav Zeqenim* in the name of R. Isaiah di Trani.[95]

On the other hand, R. Yosef *Bekhor Shor* comments (Nevo, 57) that these angels actually met Jacob but did not say anything to him. Their presence was merely to give him honor, as when a person returns from a faraway journey and others come out to greet him on his return. In offering this interpretation, R. Yosef *Bekhor Shor* is able to support and preserve Rashi's approach. Even though these angels may have been from the land of Israel, they appeared here not to help or even to accompany Jacob in a protective sense but merely to accord him honor.

Bekhor Shor does embrace several of Rashbam's larger *peshat* strategies, although he modifies and adjusts them, and does not follow them as consistently as Rashbam does. Among these strategies is Rashbam's frequent suggestion that the particular details of a narrative verse were given by the Torah in order to inform the reader of the significant qualities of the

94 Cf. Sara Japhet, "Perush Rashbam le-Parashat ha-ʿAqedah—Peshuto shel Miqra ʾo Midrasho," in *Ha-Miqra bi-Reʾi Mefarshav*, ed. S. Japhet (Jerusalem, 1994), 170–88. On Rashi's broad tendency to ignore juxtapositions that were not remarked upon by *Ḥazal*, see Isaac Gottlieb, *Yesh Seder la-Miqra* (Jerusalem, 2009), 12, 82, 88, and cf. Rashi to Genesis 2:15.

95 See *Moshav Zeqenim*, ed. Sassoon, 58, and see below, chapter 3, n. 118. See also M. Lockshin, *Rashbam's Commentary on Genesis*, 197.

biblical figure in question, or to provide necessary background information so that later developments that unfold in the course of the narrative can be better understood.[96] Rashbam employs terms such as להגיד חשיבותו/להודיע/ הוצרך לפרש /ללמד to introduce the reasons that the text of the Torah provides these details,[97] and he also notes the Torah's interest in highlighting broader values and personal traits, as Rashi already does.[98] In similar fashion Rashbam typically accounts for the presence of particular words and phrases in a verse through a systematic awareness of literary usages and lexicographical details throughout Scripture.[99] Rashbam often refers to these various conventions as *derekh ha-miqra/ha-pesuqim.*

Bekhor Shor delves into the motivations of biblical characters as Rashbam did.[100] However, he provides more elaborate details than Rashbam, and he also fills in the conversations (which was done already by Rashi) and the thought processes of biblical figures, providing what some have

[96] See Y. Jacobs, "Iqqaron ha-Haqdamah be-Perush Rashbam la-Torah" (above, n. 50), and see also Touitou, *Exegesis in Perpetual Motion*, 116 (n. 13).

[97] See Gen. 19:15 (the sun's position is noted to show that the angels waited a long time for Lot, because of their affection for Abraham); 20:4 (to introduce the veracity of God's later remark to Avimelekh); 23:1 (Sarah's lifespan and death introduce the episode of מערת המכפלה); 24:1 (Abraham's advanced age meant that it was time for him to marry off his son); 25:28 (the Torah introduces the early feelings of Isaac and Rivka toward their sons to prepare the reader for their actions concerning the blessing); 25:34 (Esau's foolish spurning of the *bekhorah* at this point informs the reader that his later protestations concerning the *bekhorah* were not accurate); 26:34–35 (the bitterness expressed by Isaac and Rivka over Esau's marriage prepares the reader for Rivka's strong statement that Jacob may not marry a woman from Canaan); and see also 27:30.

[98] See, e.g., Rashbam to Genesis 18:7 (the extensive details of how Abraham prepared the food for his guests were recorded by the Torah as a means of teaching about Abraham's heightened sense of caring and generosity for others). See Lockshin, *Rashbam's Commentary to Genesis*, 63.

[99] See, e.g., Rashbam to Genesis 18:6 (the word *solet* always refers to wheat), 22:1 (the words *'aḥar* and *'aḥarei* both mean that the events that follow occurred right after those in the preceding chapter); 24:22 (*beqa* always means half a *shekel*); 25:24 (the word *ve-hineh* is customarily used to introduce newly gained knowledge, and cf. Rashbam to Gen. 29:25 and 41:7); and 26:8 (*mesaḥeq* refers to sexual intercourse). In an unpublished seminar paper, my student Avi Strauss identified these sources in Rashbam's commentary as indicative, and suggested the comparisons to *Bekhor Shor* as noted below in nn. 105, 106, 108 (all of which are found in *Sefer Bereshit*). See also Yonatan Jacobs, "'Lilmod Tevah me-Ḥavertah': Rashbam ki-Mefarseh ha-Miqra be-Tokh 'Aẓmo" (above, n. 50).

[100] See Poznanski, *Mavo*, LXI–LXII, LXVII–LXVIII; M. Miyara, *Ba'alei ha-Tosafot*, 1:242–61, 284–301 (who argues for Spanish influence in these matters), and A. Grossman, *Ḥakhmei Ẓarefat*, 316–21 (who argues for the influence of R. Yosef Qara in particular). *Bekhor Shor* also puts forward quasi-rationalistic *ta'amei ha-mizvot*, and he attempts to portray the *Avot* in a consistently favorable light, perhaps for polemical purposes. Cf. my "Anthropomorphism and Rationalist Modes of Thought in Medieval Ashkenaz" (above, n. 51); and David Berger, "On the Morality of the Patriarchs in Jewish Polemic and Exegesis," in *Understanding Scripture*, ed. C. Thoma and M. Wyschogrod (New York, 1987), 49–62.

haracterized as "psychological insights."[101] *Bekhor Shor* does far less grammatical analysis than Rashbam, however, and is not especially innovative in taking note of parallelisms or double words and phrases.[102]

Bekhor Shor tends to make use of colloquial meanings rather than cross-referencing biblical words as Rashbam did.[103] Although *Bekhor Shor*

[101] See, e.g., Gen. 3:10 (on the dialogue between Adam and God following Adam's eating from the Tree of Knowledge); 7:16 (Noah was fearful to close the opening of the ark on his own—and therefore the Almighty did it—since Noah was uncertain whether all the animal species had boarded the ark, "because there is no hunter who recognizes all the species in the world," although *Bekhor Shor* also adduces a talmudic passage in this regard, which notes that the doors of the Temple courtyard "closed by themselves" when the courtyard became completely filled on the eve of Passover); 8:7 (explaining why the raven was comfortable flying "back and forth" and eating from the carcasses that were floating on the water, but was afraid to fly very far, lest it exhaust itself and plummet into the waters); 17:1–2 (Abraham should feel himself complete so that he could now be circumcised, which would function as an irrevocable sign that he is a servant to the Almighty, just as slaves have a seal on their clothing to demonstrate that they are in servitude); 22:5 (the dialogue between Abraham and Isaac on the way to the *ʿaqedah*, again adding a rabbinic interpretation as well); 24:3 (on marriage customs in the area, and why Abraham went in a different direction); 24:53 (an emotional reason for why Eliezer gave gifts to the mother and brother of Rivka but not to her father); 25:30 (the human considerations that Jacob worked through as he asked Esau to sell him the *bekhorah*); 27:24 (the reason for the precise words used by Jacob, in the guise of Esau, when speaking to Isaac); 29:13 (the things Jacob told Laban at their first meeting and his reasons for doing so); 29:17 (the minor physical weakness of Leah's eyes), 32:8 (Jacob's precise considerations in fearing Esau); and 37:20–21(the considerations of Joseph's brothers and specifically Reuven in dealing with Joseph and the pit). See also *Derakhim be-Parshanut ha-Miqra*, ed. Nizan et al., 1:156–58; Nevo's introduction, 7–8; idem, "Qavvei Parshanut Ofaniyyim le-R. Yosef Bekhor Shor," *Sinai* 52 (1989), 53–59; and cf. Mordechai Cohen, "'Gedolim Ḥiqrei Lev': Regishut Psychologit be-Perushei Ramban la-Torah ule-Iyyov," in *Teshurah le-Amos Ḥakham*, ed. M. Bar-Asher (Alon Shvut, 2007), 213–33. On Rashi's tendency to fill in biblical conversations, see Aharon Mondschein, "Le-Shitato shel Rashi be-Milui Peʿarim ba-Miqra," *Mayyim mi-Dalyo* 1 (1990), 138–43; "Le-Darko shel Rashi be-Divuvan shel Siḥot she-Nitʿalmu," in *Talpiyyot: Shenaton ha-Mikhlalah* (Tel Aviv, 1993–94), 107–16 (and the literature cited in n. 1).

[102] See Poznanski, *Mavo*, LXX–LXXII (who considers *Bekhor Shor*'s grammatical analyses to be a regression as compared to those of Rashbam), and see also M. Miyara, *Baʿalei ha-Tosafot*, 1:265–68. On parallel words and phrases, see Harris, *Discerning Parallelism*, 87–98, and cf. the studies of Amira Meir, cited in 87–88, n. 1, and Jair Haas, "Iqqaron 'Kefel ha 'Inyan be-Milot Shonot'" (above, n. 31), 51–79. *Bekhor Shor* accepts the ladder parallelism put forward by Rashbam to Gen. 49:22 (and elsewhere, all without attribution) as דרך הפסוק להתחיל דברו ואינו גומר, ואחר כך מתחיל וגומר (ed. Nevo, 91). Note also that *Bekhor Shor* assigns certain verses to Moses as the editor of the Divine word, but he does so in a much more traditional and understated way than do either Rashbam or R. Eliezer of Beaugency (or R. Judah *he-Ḥasid* for that matter). See Harris, "Mudaʿut la-Arikhat ha-Miqra Eẓel Parshanei Ẓefon Ẓarefat," *Shenaton le-Ḥeqer ha-Miqra veha-Mizraḥ ha-Qadum* 12 (2001), 301–10; M. Miyara, *Baʿalei ha-Tosafot*, 309–14; and cf. R. Steiner, "A Jewish Theory of Biblical Redaction from Byzantium: Its Rabbinic Roots, Its Diffusion and Its Encounter with the Muslim Doctrine of Falsification," *Jewish Studies, An Internet Journal* 2 (2003), 123–67; above, Introduction, n. 112; and below, chapter 3, n. 10.

[103] See, e.g., Gen. 3:11 (ed. Nevo, where *Bekhor Shor* understands the phrase מי הגיד לך כי עירום אתה not to mean "who told you that you are naked," but rather, "who told you that you are

accounts for extraneous phrases in the Torah in ways that Rashbam does,[104] he is more inclined to explain why the human figures in the Torah appear to make unexpected or seemingly extraneous remarks, or to sometimes act in unusual ways,[105] as opposed to Rashbam, who was concerned mainly with explaining the *derekh ha-miqra'ot*, or why the verses used the seemingly extraneous or unusual phrases they did. *Bekhor Shor* is more involved with providing reasons that are often quite simple, on the basis of how people might deal with the situations before them.

Thus, for example, in Genesis 3:11, *Bekhor Shor* explains that it should come as no surprise that Adam blamed Eve, and that Eve then blamed the snake, because this is also the way of thieves (כן דרך הגנבים), to inform on one another at the point at which they are caught. Similarly, in Genesis 3:14, *Bekhor Shor* suggests that God aptly punished the snake by forcing it to crawl on its belly, since this is *derekh benei 'adam*, to put a stop to scheming and collaboration by effectively separating the conspirators. Joseph was initially entrusted to the care of the sons of the maidservants (Gen. 37:2), because this was the way of important people (כן דרך הגדולים), to entrust the responsibility for a beloved younger sibling to the sons of the maidservants, so that they would take him on walks and serve him. In the very same verse, while the sons of Leah were consumed by their jealousy for Joseph, the maidservants' sons merely hated him for sharing gossip with their father about them. They did not experience deeper feelings of jealousy because "it is not typical for the sons of maidservants (כי אין דרך בני האמהות) to be jealous of the sons of the wives who were the mistresses of the maidservants."[106]

supposed to be clothed": שאין נקרא ערום אלא מי שראוי ללבוש ואין לו, אין דרך לומר על הבהמה ערומה היא כיון שאינה ראויה לגבדים . . . ואף הגדולים הלבושים בגדים גרועים קרואין עצמם ערומין לפי שאין להם בגדים הראוים להם . . . מי הגיד לך שאתה ראוי לבגדים.

[104] See, e.g., Gen. 17:24, 18:15, 29:30 (in which extra details in the verses teach laudable character traits, as well as certain liabilities if they are absent), and 27:1 (following Rashbam's principle that the earlier material is sometimes needed to explain a later verse).

[105] Both Rashbam and R. Yosef *Bekhor Shor* to Gen. 37:32 note that the verb form used (וישלחו) signifies that Joseph's brothers sent his bloodied coat back to Jacob through a messenger rather than presenting it to him themselves. Only *Bekhor Shor*, however, actually explains this behavior, as part of a calculated attempt on the part of the brothers to prevent Jacob from discovering their scheme and blaming them for the disappearance of Joseph. Rashbam does not address this issue at all.

[106] See also Gen. 4:12 (Cain was to wander, in the way of people, *derekh bnei 'adam*, who move to another place in search of success after they plant in the first locale and are not successful); 24:54 (Rivka's father did not need to speak,because he did not need to have Rivka remain any longer, since Isaac was his relative—akin to one who says to his relative, כאדם ששואל לקרובו ואומר ממני אין עיכוב, I have no objection, just check with her mother); 25:23 (fetuses give signs of their proclivities, כי כן דרך שהוולדות עושין סימן לפי המזל כמה שצריך להיות); 25:27 (Jacob was identified as a tent-dweller, since shepherds typically erect tents to protect them against the cold and the heat; and see also Gen. 37:25, it is "the way of shepherds" that some take a break

Several other sets of comments highlight *Bekhor Shor*'s tendency to seek "people" principles in broader forms to account for certain scriptural conventions, where Rashbam employs similar rules that are more narrowly text-focused. In his comment on Genesis 23:1 (which notes the passing of Sarah and specifies her age at her death), *Bekhor Shor* invokes a principle (Nevo, 39, אין דרך לכתוב מיתת הנשים אפילו צדקניות אם לא על ידי מעשה) that explains why the only deaths of women mentioned in the Torah are those of Sarah, Rachel, Devorah (the maidservant of Rivka), and Miriam. In all of these instances, there was a related issue or episode of significance that had to be transmitted (ללמד/להודיענו/על שהודיענו). Only in Sarah's case, however, was her age mentioned, since she was the most significant female figure of all. Rashbam explains the particular circumstance that required the narrative to mention Sarah's death according to the literary model of *haqdamah* (to introduce the subject of מערת המכפלה), but he does not comment any further on the special nature of Sarah or any of the other women.[107] Similarly, *Bekhor Shor* notes in Exodus 15:20 (Nevo, 124) that, when the Torah mentions the name of a woman, it also typically mentions her older brother (Nevo, 124, דרך הפסוק כשמזכיר אשה מזכיר אחיה הגדול, as found also in Gen. 36:3 and Ex. 6:23). Rashbam enunciates this principle in a different way here (and in

to eat their meals while others remain with the animals and then they swtich; at no point do they all eat together); 27:15 (as hunters typically did, Esau had two sets of clothing, one for hunting and another that he wore among people, כן דרך הציידים); 28:12 (the angels went up and down the ladder, according to the second interpretation offered by *Bekhor Shor*, because this is a convention of Hebrew linguistics, כי כן דרך העברי, to always express the act of going up before going down; and as the Talmud in tractate *Ḥullin* similarly asserts with respect to wielding the slaughterer's knife); Rashbam writes similarly here שכן דרך ארץ להזכיר עלייה קודם ירידה); 30:32 (it is not usual for a sheep to be spotted but only goats, although sheep can occasionally be brown); 30:33 (on the usual results for the conception and birth of children and sheep, כי כן דרך נשים ודרך בהמות לילד בגוון שהם רואות בשעת חימום); 32:30 (angels do not typically provide their names); 38:18 (it is the custom of important people, such as Judah, to carry a staff in their hand). See also Ex. 3:5 (Nevo, 100), where *Bekhor Shor* associates the word *na'al* with the leather gauntlets worn on the arm by knights and other officers, which was also the way that they acquired things (by removing or exchanging their gauntlets). The Torah therefore had to specify that Moses was to remove his *na'alayim* "from his feet," to distinguish these from the gauntlets/gloves that he may have been wearing on his hands. See also Y. Nevo, *Ha-Parshanut ha-Ẓarefatit*, 23–28, and Ora Limor and Amnon Raz-Krakotzkin, *Jews and Christians in Western Europe: Hebraica Veritas* [Hebrew] (Tel Aviv, 1993), 30–31. Cf. Rashi to Ex. 28:41, where he refers to the transferring of the gauntlet in the medieval context (when a knight is appointed by his feudal lord to perform a certain task or function) as a means of explaining the phrase ומלאת את ידם, used by the Torah in connection with the appointment of Aaron and his sons to their priestly roles. Indeed, Rashi already has a number of uses of *derekh ha-miqra* and related phrases that should be compared to the approaches of Rashbam and *Bekhor* as well. See Eran Viezel, "Perush ha-Meyuḥas le-Rashi le-Ezra u-Neḥemyah," 10, 37; and idem, *The Commentary on Chronicles Attributed to Rashi*, 86–93.

107 See Lockshin, *Rashbam's Commentary to Genesis*, 101.

Gen. 28:9): the firstborn or oldest son is usually mentioned together with his sister.[108]

Unlike Rashbam, for whom all explanations must emerge from the verses themselves, explanations for R. Yosef *Bekhor Shor* can be predicated on other external considerations and logic as well.[109] This is how *Bekhor Shor* understands the story of the selling of Joseph. A key aspect of *Bekhor Shor*'s interpretation is that Joseph was made to swear to his brothers that he would never reveal his identity nor attempt to contact Jacob. *Bekhor Shor* found it necessary to add this aspect to the story (based on a passage in *Midrash Tanḥuma*) because it would otherwise be impossible to explain, in terms of normal human behavior, Joseph's cruel silence during the many years that his father, Jacob, mourned his loss.[110] *Bekhor Shor* bases his contention that the brothers themselves sold Joseph, against the interpretation of Rashbam that they did not (which he characterizes as *baddui*), on Genesis 45:4, in which Joseph openly instructs his brothers not to be melancholy over the fact that they had sold him. He does not accept Rashbam's simple reading of Genesis 37:28, that the *Midyanim* sold Joseph (or Rashbam's related explanation of Gen. 45:4), because this approach cannot account for

[108] See Lockshin, *Rashbam's Commentary to Exodus*, 164, and idem, *Rashbam's Commentary to Genesis*, 162. *Bekhor Shor* notes and discusses the presence of ladder parallelism in Gen. 49:22 as part of a broad scriptural phenomenon (Nevo, 91, דרך הפסוק להתחיל דבר ואינו גומרו ואחר כך מתחיל וגומר כמו נשאו נהרות וכו' וכן בן פורת יוסף וכו'), while Rashbam, although noting that this phenomenon is found elsewhere, focuses it much more specifically here, beginning with the phrase וחוזר וכופל חצי ראש המקרא ומסיים דבורו . . . הרי פסוק זה דוגמא לחצאים בקרא. See Lockshin, *Rashbam's Commentary to Genesis*, 376, who notes that *Bekhor Shor* expresses this much more succintly, and cf. Nevo's introduction, 13, and above, n. 96. Only with regard to Nu. 24:7 (Nevo, 287), that all kings of Amalek are called Agag, just as all Egyptians kings are called Pharaoh (and all Philistine kings are called Avimelekh), do the brief statements of principle by *Bekhor Shor* and Rashbam essentially match. Indeed, on this specialized understanding of the title פרעה by Rashbam, see also Rashbam's comments to Genesis 41:10 (and Lockshin, ibid., 281–82), Gen. 41:45, Ex. 4:19; and cf. E. Viezel, "Ha-Perush ha-Meyuḥas le-Rashi le-Sefer Ezra-Neḥemyah," 9 (n. 48); and cf. *Bekhor Shor*'s comment to Gen. 21:22 (Nevo, 37). On the similar, localized connotation and use of *derekh ha-sarim* by Rashbam, see his comments to Gen. 44:15 and Ex. 7:15 (and Ex. 32:1). Cf. Morris Berger, "The Torah Commentary of R. Samuel ben Meir (Ph.D. diss., Harvard University, 1982), 83, 238–40 (and 91–94, for Rashbam's noting of the way people typically speak); Y. Jacobs, "Rashbam's Major Principles of Interpretation as Deduced from a Manuscript Fragment Discovered in 1984," *Revue des etudes juives* 170 (2011), 477–97; and S. Japhet, "Rashbam's Introduction in His Commentary to Lamentations," *Shenaton le-Ḥeqer ha-Miqra veha-Mizraḥ ha-Qadum* 19 (2009), 437–40.

[109] See Yosefa Rahaman, "Melekhet ha-Sevara be-Perush Bekhor Shor la-Torah," *Tarbiz* 53 (1984), 615–18. See also *Bekhor Shor* to Gen. 11:7 (Nevo, 24); *Sefer ha-Gan*, ed. Orlian, 144–45; and below, n. 122. Cf. S. Japhet, "Rav Leshoniyyut Halakhah u-Ma'aseh be-Perushei Rashbam la-Miqra," *Meḥqarim be-Lashon* 8 (2001), 291–93 (= idem, *Dor Dor u-Parshanav*, 159–61); and Limor and Raz-Krakotzkin, *Jews and Christians in Western Europe* (above, n. 106). For Rashbam, achieving a proper contextual interpretation requires that the meaning of a Hebrew word in the Bible cannot be derived even from terms in rabbinic Hebrew or from an Aramaic word.

[110] See *Bekhor Shor*'s comments to Gen. 37:26 and Gen. 37:28 (Nevo, 69).

Joseph's seemingly irreconcilable behavior with respect to his father. The need to allow for basic canons of human behavior and emotion (*derekh ha-ḥayyim*) takes precedence for *Bekhor Shor* over Rashbam's interpretation that follows (in his own words) *ʿomeq derekh peshuto shel miqra*, which to be sure would not countenance the emotional or "life" factor as an interpretational key here, as *Bekhor Shor* does.[111]

Similarly, *Bekhor Shor* strongly disagrees with Rashbam's interpretation (to Gen. 25:31, 33–34, which he refers to as *ve-yesh mefarshim*) that Jacob paid a sum of money for the *bekhorah* he acquired from Esau, while the bread and lentils he gave to Esau were simply a *seʿudat mekhirah* (as was the "common custom," according to Rashbam, found also in 31:46 between Jacob and Laban), to confirm that the transaction or agreement had indeed taken place.[112] *Bekhor Shor* (Nevo, 44) refers to this approach as well as בדאות בעיני, and interprets instead that Esau actually gave away his *bekhorah* for a pittance (the bread and the lentils alone), "because all the money in the world means nothing to a person, and is completely worthless to him, when his body (i.e., his very existence) is at stake (כי כל ממון שבעולם אין אדם חושב כלום ובזוי בעיניו כנגד גופו)."[113] Taken together with his less prominent reliance on grammatical analyses as a means of explaining variations in the style of the Torah, *Bekhor Shor*'s overall exegetical approach tends to read more into the text of the Torah than Rashbam does.[114]

Bekhor Shor's comments on Exodus 14:2 and 14:5, that the Jewish people were instructed by God to "return" toward Egypt (*ve-yashuvu*) in order that they not appear to have been duplicitous (איני רוצה שתהיו בדאים), since Moses had announced (in Ex. 3:18) that if the Jews were allowed to leave Egypt they would merely journey for three days, to worship God in the desert and then return. Similarly, when the Jews left Egypt at the end of the plagues, they "borrowed" the implements of the Egyptians, again suggesting

111 See Nevo's introduction, 7–8. Ramban suggests here that Joseph needed to see his prophecy play itself out and therefore could not intervene by letting his father know who and where he was. Note that *Bekhor Shor* uses the phrase *derekh ha-ʿolam* (in his commentary to Ex. 15:25) to explain the miracle of sweetening the water along more natural lines, which is parallel to Rashbam's use of the phrase *derekh ʾerez* to characterize the same kind of process (regarding the splitting of the Red Sea, in his commentary to Ex. 14:21). This difference in usage is also evident in Lev. 19:19, regarding the reason for the prohibition of *kilʾayim* according to both Rashbam and *Bekhor Shor*. Cf. Touitou, *Exegesis in Perpetual Motion*, 143–44, and above, n. 100.

112 See Lockshin, *Rashbam's Commentary to Genesis*, 137–38, who also notes the implication of this interpretation for polemics.

113 Cf. Grossman, *Ḥakhmei Ẓarefat ha-Rishonim*, 488–93; and Touitou, *Exegesis in Perpetual Motion*, 202.

114 Thus, with respect to the selling of Joseph, it is reasonable to assume that for *Bekhor Shor*, as for Rashi (s.v. וימשכו), there is a shift in the middle of Gen. 37:28, away from the *Midyanim* as the sellers, and toward the brothers themselves.

that their intent was to return at some point.[115] *Bekhor Shor* is clearly at odds here with the approach of Rashbam (to Ex. 3:11–12), who explained that God told Moses to offer Pharaoh the scenario of a three-day journey "in order to worship" simply as a means of getting Pharaoh to release the Jews. Rashbam finds another biblical example for this kind of deception in 1 Samuel 16:2, where God tells Samuel to bring a heifer with him when he went to anoint David, so that he could say that he had come to offer a sacrifice, and Saul would not immediately understand his true purpose and move to punish Samuel. Rashbam asserts that in the case of Egypt as well, God advises Moses what to say in order to get the desired result from Pharaoh without unduly exciting him.

Bekhor Shor, on the other hand, is quite concerned with the moral problem raised by this interpretational approach, and therefore interprets that the Jews actually carried out in some way what they had suggested they would do. For his part, Rashi's interpretation of Exodus 14:2 explains that the Jews "turned toward Egypt every third day," in order to trick Pharaoh into thinking that they had lost their way in the desert.[116]

Avraham Grossman has suggested that polemical considerations were at least partly behind *Bekhor Shor*'s strong efforts (following Rashbam and R. Yosef Qara) to defend the behavior of the *Avot*, serving as both a response to Christian claims and as a means of preventing members of the Jewish community from being swayed by Christian arguments. This holds true for *Bekhor Shor*'s approach to the sin of the golden calf as well, in which he proposes that the desire of the Jewish people was to create a kind of leadership figure, but not to create and serve any idolatry, which would certainly seem to be the most straightforward reading of the biblical text itself.[117] This

[115] This is again the interpretation put forward by *Ḥizzequni* as well.

[116] Cf. M. Lockshin *Rashbam's Commentary on Exodus*, ed. Lockshin, 35, and N. Leibowitz, *'Iyyunim be-Sefer Shemot* (Jerusalem, 1975), 73–75. At the same time, Rashi understands Ex. 3:12 to mean that the proof presented to Moses that God is with him (and with the people) is that they will ultimately come to serve God and to receive the Torah at this very place, Mount Sinai, which is the way that *Bekhor Shor* interprets that verse as well (Nevo, 100–101).

[117] See Grossman, *Ḥakhmei Ẓarefat ha-Rishonim*, 488–89; Poznanski, *Mavo*, LXIX–LXX (citing Gen. 1:26, 3:22, 18:2, 19:1, 24:2); and cf. D. Berger (above, n. 94), and M. Lockshin, *Rashbam's Commentary on Deuteronomy*, editor's introduction, 19–22. *Bekhor Shor*'s approach to the sin of the golden calf is adopted (without attribution) by Naḥmanides, although this approach was also taken by R. Yehudah *ha-Levi*. Cf. *Bekhor Shor*'s unattributed comment to Deut. 27:8 (Nevo, 369), which accords with one by R. Yehudah *ha-Levi* (as cited by Ibn Ezra), and similarly, see *Tosafot ha-Shalem*, ed. Gellis, 8:367, secs. 4, 6. For *Bekhor Shor*'s impact on Naḥmanides' Torah commentary, see Hillel Novetzky, "The Influence of Rabbi Joseph Bekhor Shor and Radak on Ramban's Commentary on the Torah" (M.A. thesis, Yeshiva University, 1992), 6–33. See also *Bekhor Shor* to Gen. 15:6 (Nevo, 27): the approach of Rashi (identified only as *yesh mefarshim*) is rejected (*ve-'ein nir'eh li*). Unlike Naḥmanides, however, *Bekhor Shor* does not suggest an alternate interpretation. In Gen. 48:7 (Nevo, 85), *Bekhor Shor* (like Naḥmanides to Gen. 35:16) suggests that Rachel's burial place was located in the land of the tribe of Benjamin. As Nevo

appears to be a reasonable suggestion, especially in light of *Bekhor Shor*'s overt and substantive engagement in Jewish-Christian polemics.[118]

At the same time, however, *Bekhor Shor* presumes in his commentary to Genesis 35:22 (Nevo, 63, against the approach of Rashi and Ibn Ezra, among others) that Reuven actually did cohabit with his father's maidservant and wife, Bilhah.[119] Similarly, in Genesis 37:9–10, *Bekhor Shor* depicts Joseph in very human terms, as an immature adolescent who increased his brothers' hatred for him through his senseless boasting. The brothers, in turn, are described (Gen. 37:20; Nevo, 68) as seeking to rid themselves of Joseph in a way that hardly absolves them from any wrongdoing. Perhaps *Bekhor Shor*, despite his fundamental commitment to understanding and explaining verses on the basis of common or typical human behavior, is willing to assume, as a matter of both *peshat* and anti-Christian polemics, that only Abraham, Isaac, and Jacob, whose total devotion to God is reflected in the biblical narrative, never acted sinfully. The same is not true with respect to Reuven or even Joseph, at least when he is initially introduced. Here, the logical approach requires, along with the notion of *peshat*, that normal human motivations that may lead to bad behavior (e.g., the typical frivolity of youth, the need to defend the honor of one's parents) be considered.

Indeed, in at least one instance (noted above with regard to his infrequent citation of Rashbam), *Bekhor Shor*'s overriding sense of *derekh ha-ḥayyim* (the way that people typically reacted) as a bona fide means of establishing *peshuto shel miqra* caused him to explicitly reject Rashbam's defense of Jacob's actions when Esau sold him the *bekhorah*. Rashbam sought to understand the meal that Jacob provided for Esau not as Jacob's payment

---

notes, however, this appears to be against the view of *Tosefta Sotah*, *Bereshit Rabbah*, and Rashi in his commentary (to 1 Samuel 10:2) that the gravesite was actually in the territory of the tribe of Judah.

118 See, e.g., *Sefer Yosef ha-Meqanne*, ed. Rosenthal, 79, 100, 104, 113; Shaye Cohen, "Does Rashi's Commentary Respond to Christianity? A Comparison of Rashi with Rashbam and Bekhor Shor," in *The Idea of Biblical Interpretation [Essays in Honor of James Kugel]*, ed. H. Najman and J. Newman (Leiden, 2004), 449–72; and N. Golb, *The Jews in Medieval Normandy*, 309–10.

119 Rashba (Barcelona, d. c. 1310) discusses why the Torah mentions the sin of Reuven (and the sin of Judah, among other seemingly untoward incidents) in the context of Jewish-Muslim polemic. See *She'elot u-Teshuvot ha-Rashba*, ed. Makhon Yerushalayim, vol. 8 (Jerusalem, 1997) [*teshuvot ha-ḥadashot mi-ketav yad*], 241 (#367); *Ma'amar 'al Yishma'el*, ed. Bezalel Naor (Spring Valley, N.Y., 2008), 72–74; and cf. the comments by Rashbam and Radak to Genesis 35:22. For R. Judah *he-Ḥasid*'s approach, see below, chapter 3. Note that in at least two instances, Rashbam attributes miscues to the *'avot* (which is not so explicit within the biblical text). See his comment to Gen. 22:1 (above, at n. 94, with regard to why Abraham was tested with the *'aqedah*), and to Gen. 32:29, where Rashbam understands that Jacob was lamed by the angel as punishment for his lack of faith (since he had attempted to flee). Cf. Lockshin, *Rashbam's Commentary to Genesis*, 209–10 (n. 4).

for the *bekhorah* (which would suggest that the primacy of Esau—and the institution of medieval Christendom that Esau represented—was gained by Jacob in an unfair way, by taking advantage of Esau in his moment of distress) but merely as a symbolic ratification of the agreed-upon payment that Jacob made with Esau's full agreement. In demonstrably rejecting Rashbam's approach here in favor of one that is framed by the way a person typically reacts in such a stressful situation, *Bekhor Shor* has ceded the ability to defend one of the three *Avot.* Clearly, this aspect of *Bekhor Shor*'s method was quite important to him and was even sufficient, at times, to override an overt polemical consideration, an exegetical value that was also close to *Bekhor Shor*'s heart.[120]

Rashi understands Esau's exhaustion (in Gen. 25:29, following *Bereshit Rabbah*) as a function of his involvement with killing (*ve-hu ʿayef bi-reẓiḥah*, likely including the murder of human beings as well), while *Bekhor Shor* (Nevo, 43), taking a realia-based approach, explained that Esau was tired in the way that animal hunters (*derekh ha-ẓayyadim lihyot ʿayefim*) tire in pursuit of their prey. It was not uncommon for them to wander through the forest for three or four days during these pursuits, and to be overtaken by severe hunger and thirst. Although *Bekhor Shor* bypasses the midrash cited by Rashi, his typical approach of noting the way certain types of people behave (in this instance, hunters) achieves the same kind of interpretation as the one put forward by Rashi, which could be acceptable to talmudist and *pashtan* alike.[121]

As Yosefa Rahaman has perceptively noted, the talmudic passage in *Shabbat* 63a, which mandates that students of Scripture must always keep in mind the *peshuto shel miqra* (שאין מקרא יוצא מידי פשוטו), concludes with the observation that it is also crucial to continue to study the biblical text and to explain it through *sevara* (דליגמר איניש והדר ליסביר). In Rahaman's view, *Bekhor Shor* practiced a kind of rational *sevara* approach in quite a noticeable way. She sees this especially in *Bekhor Shor*'s interpretation of the dreams of the baker and butler and Pharaoh himself (Gen. 40–41; Nevo, 72–76), and in other dream situations as well. *Bekhor Shor* interprets the biblical text like a talmudic צריכותא, which shows that the details provided by the biblical text are given in this way so that the dream interpreter (and the reader of the

[120] See above, at n. 79. Similarly, as Poznanski notes (*Mavo*, LXIII–LXIV), *Bekhor Shor* will occasionally overreach in order to deflect an anthropomorphic interpretation. Cf. below, chapter 7.

[121] Indeed, as Nevo notes, this interpretation is found in a series of Tosafist Torah compilations including *Hadar Zeqenim*, *Minḥat Yehudah*, and *Moshav Zeqenim* (as well as ms. Leiden 27). *Ḥizzequni* also follows the approach of *Bekhor Shor*, and cf. Ibn Ezra.

biblical text) will be able to properly decode and follow the key points, and to get the details right without going off the mark.

Similarly, while Rashi was unsure (in Gen. 28:5) why the Torah had to re-identify Rivka as the mother of Jacob and Esau (*'eini yodea mah melamdenu*), *Bekhor Shor* suggests that the Torah wanted to underscore that Laban was indeed the brother of the very same Rivka who was the mother of Jacob and Esau (ומגיד לך הכתוב שהוא אח לאותה רבקה שהיא אם יעקב ועשו). In Exodus 38:21 the *mishkan* is doubly identified as *mishkan ha-'edut* so that there will be no mistake about its identify. For *Bekhor Shor* the details of human life and activity that the Torah records may be decoded according to conventions of human logic and perception. This is how *Bekhor Shor* understands the kiss that Isaac requested from Jacob just before he gave his blessing (Gen. 27:26). The kiss was not simply a sign of agreement or acquiescence. For *Bekhor Shor*, Isaac used this opportunity, even at this late stage, to smell his son (since Esau smelled like the field and Jacob did not), to try to determine and to decide finally whether it was Jacob, whose voice he thought he had heard, or Esau, whose hands he thought he had felt. This type of logical approach, of course, is partly grounded in the fact that *Bekhor Shor* was also a highly trained talmudist. Indeed, in his comment to Genesis 40:12, he asserts that כל גמרא בלא סברא אינו כלום, any study without proper reasoning is worthless.[122]

Whereas Rashbam favored a minimalist approach of *derekh ha-miqra'ot* to explain variations that a *darshan* would certainly explain differently—and much more expansively—*Bekhor Shor* allows for considerations of rational and logical thinking that are often not explicitly indicated by the biblical text, and he will also assume (or read in) considerations of what we have termed *derekh ha-ḥayyim* as well. All of this, however, puts *Bekhor Shor* closer to Rashi. His logic illuminates the text in moral and human ways, and it leads to a broader and more vibrant "truth" than Rashbam's minimalist *peshat/derekh ha-miqra'ot* approach does. This was certainly the case for a decidedly talmudic or rabbinic audience that was comfortable with Rashi's commentary, as opposed to the group of exegetical *maskilim* whom Rashbam, R. Yosef Qara, and *Bekhor Shor*'s immediate and most radical colleague, R. Eliezer of Beaugency, intended to address.[123]

This is not to suggest that *Bekhor Shor* did not put forward innovative *peshatim* or interpretational strategies, which he most certainly did.[124]

122 See Y. Rahaman (above, n. 109).

123 On these *maskilim*, see above, nn. 27, 31. On the radicalism of R. Eliezer of Beaugency relative to all other twelfth-century northern French *pashtanim*, see above, nn. 28–29.

124 See, e.g., E. Touitou, *Exegesis in Perpetual Motion* [Hebrew], 14–15, n. 5, 116, n. 13, 140, 143, n. 70, 144, 154, 169, nn. 133–34, 172–73, 175, 185, 190, n. 5, 196–97, 199, 204–5. Several of

Nonetheless, the foregoing analysis and discussion help to explain what Poznanski had already noticed, that *Bekhor Shor*'s commentary is much more frequently cited in the so-called Tosafist compilations of the thirteenth and early fourteenth centuries (beginning with *Sefer ha-Gan*, c. 1240, whose affinity for *Bekhor Shor* is one of the defining characteristics of this work) than any other northern French *pashtan* of the twelfth century, including R. Yosef Qara and Rashbam.[125] The overall compatibility of *Bekhor Shor*'s commentary with Rashi's commentary (including the frequent citation of rabbinic and talmudic exegesis in ways and forms that are quite similar to Rashi's, as well as the sizable number of direct references to Rashi), along-side *Bekhor Shor*'s distinctively "human" (perhaps anthropological) method of *peshat*, were undoubtedly among the key factors that contributed to these conclusions.

Indeed, as Poznanski goes on to note, a number of later *Tosafist* Torah compilations such as *Hadar Zeqenim*, the commentary of *R. Ḥayyim Palti'el*, *Minḥat Yehudah*, and especially *Moshav Zeqenim*, contain comments attributed to *Bekhor Shor* that are not found in ms. Munich 52, the only full and authentic manuscript of *Bekhor Shor*'s commentary to the Torah that is extant. In several of these passages, *Bekhor Shor*'s comment is purported to be a question on Rashi's commentary, or a response to it.[126]

Although it is often difficult to verify whether these comments are authentic,[127] this is, in part, how the Tosafist compilations viewed the com-

---

these novel interpretations are within the realm of Jewish-Christian polemics; cf. above, nn. 109–110. Yonatan Jacobs (above, n. 88) has also indicated that *Bekhor Shor* may have moved past the achievements of Qara and Rashbam regarding the use and application of certain literary principles. See also Y. Nevo, *Ha-Parshanut ha-Ẓarefatit*, 30–43, although cf. R. Harris, above, n. 102. Note also *Bekhor Shor* to Ex. 32:20 (Nevo, 170), where both Rashi and Rashbam mention only the rabbinic view that the children of Israel were purposely given to drink from the waters into which the ashes of the golden calf were strewn (שנתכוין לבודקן כסוטות), while *Bekhor Shor* first argues, *lefi ha-peshat*, that the drinking of the ashes of the golden calf was unintended happenstance. *Ḥizzequni* presents this *peshat* view only, without referring to the talmudic interpretation. See also Ibn Ezra's short commentary; *Ḥizzequni* to Deut. 9:21p; and *Derakhim be-Parshanut ha-Miqra*, ed. Y. Nizan et al., 1:148–49.

[125] See Poznanski, *Mavo*, LXXIII: הנה כי כן יתראה לפנינו ר' יוסף בכור שור עומד על הגבול בין פשטני צפון צרפת וביו בעלי התוספות לתורה שבאו אחריהם . . . ולכן לא נתפלא אם בעלי התוספות התשמשו הרבה בפירושיו ומבי־אים אותו ואת פירושיו פעמים אין מספר (והרבה פעמים מאוד גם בלי הזכרת שמו); and see also M. Miyara, *Ba'alei ha-Tosafot*, 1:318–23. For *Sefer ha-Gan*'s heavy citation of (and reliance on) *Bekhor Shor*'s Torah commentary (and the relationship between these works), see *Sefer ha-Gan*, ed. Orlian, 42–48.

[126] See Poznanski, *Mavo*, LXXIII–IV (beginning with the phrase וביניהם גם באורים כאלו שאינם נמצאים בפירושו); Nevo's notes to *Perushei R. Yosef Bekhor Shor*, ed. Nevo, 124–25, 184, 196, 230, 256–57, 282. See also 7, 110; and cf. above, nn. 74, 90, 244.

[127] See, e.g., the comment (and question on Rashi) to Nu. 15:38, attributed to *Bekhor Shor* by *Moshav Zeqenim* (as noted by Nevo, 267–68). According to this passage, the eight strings of the *ẓiẓit* represent the eight days that the Jewish people waited from the time of their exodus until they sang the Song of the Sea. *Bekhor Shor* questions this linkage, since the sea was split on the

mentary of *Bekhor Shor*: as an analysis of Rashi's commentary—if not as some kind of supercommentary—and perhaps even as an extension or a continuation of it. Indeed, as we shall see further below, there are several Tosafist collections still in manuscript that were characterized as or considered to be versions of *Bekhor Shor*'s Torah commentary. Although each manuscript is somewhat different, the common denominator among all of them seems to be that a core of comments taken from *Bekhor Shor*'s authentic commentary served as the base, to which additional comments by Tosafists and other *Ḥakhmei Ashkenaz*, were then added.[128]

---

seventh day after the exodus (and for this reason, the common practice is to read the Torah portion of the Song of the Sea on the seventh day of Passover). *Bekhor Shor* responds that the exodus technically began with the slaughtering of the Passover sacrifice on the fourteenth day of Nisan, so that the seventh day of Passover was actually the eighth day of the Jews' redemption. The problem of verification in this instance is complicated by a number of factors and details. Rashi to Ex. 14:5 explains that they went into the sea on the eve of the seventh day, and on the morning of the seventh day, they sang the *shirah*. In Nu. 15:41, however, Rashi, at the end of a lengthy citation from R. Moses *ha-Darshan*, writes that the eight strings of the *ẓiẓit* represent the eight days that it took from the exodus from Egypt (משיצאו ממצרים עד שירדו לים) until the day that they got to sing the *shirah*, and so *Bekhor Shor*'s comment is, in effect, also mediating between the two different approaches found within Rashi. Note also that *Pa'aneaḥ Raza*, ed. Machon Torat ha-Rishonim, 253 (to Ex. 14:5, and see also *Tosafot ha-Shalem*, ed. Gellis, 7:183, sec. 9), presents the resolution attributed to R. Yosef *Bekhor Shor* by *Moshav Zeqenim* to R. Jacob of Orleans (who was also a student of Rabbenu Tam) instead. On the blurring of these names (especially in *Pa'aneaḥ Raza*, where sometimes only the word *Orleans* appears), see below in this chapter. See also ms. B.M. 9931, fol. 37v (a version of *Pa'aneaḥ Raza* in manuscript), where following this solution in Rashi (which is unattributed there), R. Yom Tov of Joigny (yet another student of Rabbenu Tam) proposes a completely different solution, on the basis of what he saw in the "*ḥiddushim ha-qadmonim*" (אבל ה"ר יום טוב מיואני תיר' שראה בחידושים הקדמונים), referring perhaps to the text of R. Moses *ha-Darshan* or to a venerable version of Rashi's commentary: דהוה כתי' ביה הכי ח' חוטים יש בציצית כנגד ח' ימים משאמרו שירה על הים דלאחר שאמרו שירה על הים שהו ח' ימים ליקח בזה שבים. According to the solution of R. Yom Tov, the *ẓiẓit* represent the eight days following the singing of the *shirah*, not the number of days leading up to it. On R. Yom Tov of Joigny's commentary to the Torah, see below in this chapter. *Moshav Zeqenim* (to Ex. 14:5) records this answer in the name of R. Menaḥem of Joigny (ובשם ר' מנחם מיואני שמעתי שראה בפי' הקדמונים), while *Moshav Zeqenim* (to Nu. 15:41) refers to R. Yosef *Bekhor*'s answer there simply as a *yesh 'omrim*; see Gellis, 182, sec. 7, and below. Apparently, this question or issue must have been "making the rounds." See also *Ḥizzequni* to Nu.15:41, who raises the contradiction within Rashi (ואם תאמר הרי בפרשת בשלח פרש"י וכו') but proposes a different starting point for the count than in the resolution attributed to R. Yosef *Bekhor Shor*. See also ms. B.M. 9931, fols. 103r–v (to Lev. 25:13), which has a question by *Bekhor Shor* on Rashi's commentary that is not noted by Nevo (231): בשנת היובל הזאת. פרש"י והלא כבר נאמר ושבתם איש אל אחוזתו אלא לרבות המוכר שדהו ובא בנו וגואלו שחוזרת לאביו ביובל. שאל ר' יוסף מאורליינש אמאי איצטריך קרא שחוזרת והלא מק"ו שמעינן. ומה מקדיש שדה אחוזה אינה יוצאה ביובל וכו'. See also ms. B.M. 9931, fols. 20v and 66r.

128 Among these manuscripts are ms. Vatican 45, ms. Hamburg 45 (*peshatim*), and ms. Leiden 27. See the brief descriptions in *Tosafot ha-Shalem*, ed. Gellis, vol. 1, editor's introduction, 25, 26, 29. Vatican 45 is certainly a later compilatory text, with pieces from the *Minḥat Yehudah* compilation and the commentary of R. Ḥayyim Palti'el, as well as from *Sefer ha-Gan* and *Ḥizzequni*; see the *Catalogue of Manuscripts in the Vatican Library*, ed. B. Richler (Jerusalem, 2009), 31–32. Likewise, the *peshatim* in Hamburg 45 are replete with comments from R. Judah *he-Ḥasid*

All that remains is to highlight an additional dimension of *Bekhor Shor*'s Torah commentary, which further reflects its compatibility with and interest for rabbinic scholars who had strong backgrounds in talmudic and halakhic studies. It is not surprising that R. Yosef *Bekhor Shor* cited a wealth of talmudic and rabbinic sources in his comments to legal portions of the Torah,[129] since even Rashbam did something similar in halakhic contexts.[130] More significant is that a large percentage of the more than three hundred instances in which *Bekhor Shor* juxtaposes rabbinic teachings and *peshat* interpretations within his Torah commentary is found within narrative contexts, a number of which have been noted above.[131] A most interesting

(d. 1217 in Regensburg) and others who lived later than *Bekhor Shor* and were completely unrelated; on this manuscript, see below, chapter 3, n. 249, and chapter 4, n. 193. Similarly, see Y. Nevo, "Ketav-Yad Leiden 27 ha-Meyuḥas le-R. Yosef Bekhor Shor." Although this manuscript (= Or. 4765, Byzantium, 1400, IMHM #17371) contains a number of interpretations that correlate with those of *Bekhor Shor* (and see fol. 2v, יוליכני א-להי במישור בהחילי בכור שור), as well as a number of additional *peshat* interpretations from R. Yosef *Porat* (a name that may or may not connote R. Yosef *Bekhor Shor* as well), there is also quite a bit of *gematria*. Moreover, this manuscript also mentions all kinds of other rabbinic figures and works as well (from the late twelfth through the mid-thirteenth century) such as Ibn Ezra (fol. 79v); Rambam (fol. 73v); R. Judah *he-Ḥasid* (fols. 20r, 32r, 76r); several students of Ri, including R. Barukh *Ba'al ha-Terumah* (fol. 82v); R. Samson b. Abraham of Sens (רשב"א, fol. 46r); R. Solomon of Dreux (fols. 7r, 25v); R. Samson of Coucy (fol. 104v); *Sefer ha-Gan* (fols. 15r, 39r); and R. David of Muenzberg and R. Jacob of Chinon (fol. 67); and below, chapter 4, n. 2. Cf. ms. Paris 167 (above, n. 6), and see also ms. Moscow 303 (below, chapter 3), for its extensive inclusion of unnamed pieces by *Bekhor Shor.*

129 See, e.g., *Bekhor Shor*'s commentary to Ex. 12:18, 19, 42 (Nevo, 116–17). In Ex. 21:10 (Nevo, 138–39), *Bekhor Shor* implicitly disagrees with Rashi about the woman from whom marital rights cannot be withheld according to the verse. As Nevo notes, their positions are actually two competing views of Tannaim within the *Mekhilta.* See also, e.g., Lev. 11:16, 29 (Nevo, 195); Lev. 15:13 (Nevo, 203); Lev. 19:26 (Nevo, 216); Lev. 20:21 (Nevo, 218); Lev. 21:2 (Nevo, 219); Lev. 21:5 (Nevo, 220); Lev. 21:18 (221); Lev. 22:23 (223); Lev. 23:13 (Nevo, 224); and Lev. 25:21, 22, 25 (Nevo, 231). In Lev. 25:20, *Bekhor Shor* refers to one of his talmudic comments, וכן פירשתי בהלכות ספיחין בפסחים, an interpretation that can be found in *Tosafot Pesaḥim* 51b, s.v. *kol ha-sefihin 'asurim* in the name of *Bekhor Shor*'s talmudic teacher, Rabbenu Tam. Similarly, in Nu. 30:3 (Nevo, 296), *Bekhor Shor* follows a linguistic interpretation of Rashi (against that of Rashbam) regarding the nullification of vows, and he cites a procedure "that I saw in the name of *gedolim*," which corresponds to a halakhic interpretation of his teacher Rabbenu Tam; see above, n. 26. See also Nu. 6:3 (Nevo, 248); Nu. 30:7 (Nevo, 298); Num. 35:4 (Nevo, 302–3); Deut. 4:1 (Nevo, 313); Deut. 16:3, 4, 8, 10 (Nevo, 340–41); 23:16, 18, 20, 24; 24:8, 13, citing a geonic ruling (Nevo, 358–61)

130 See Eleazar Touitou, *Exegesis in Perpetual Motion*, 177–88. Like Rashbam, *Bekhor Shor* will include some of his unique motivational interpretations in these contexts as well. In Ex. 12:12 (Nevo, 117), he adds to the talmudic interpretation of *leil shimurim* (that it will safeguard the Jewish people from *maziqin*) that the children of Israel will keep and preserve this night each year, in order to perform the appropriate *mizvot* on it (= the seder), as a means of commemorating their redemption at the hands of the Almighty.

131 See above, nn. 89–92, and see also *Bekhor Shor*'s comments to a series of verses in the portions of *Bamidbar* and *Naso* (Nu. 3:39, 4:3, 4:12, 5:3, 6:25, 6:27, 7:18–19; Nevo, 243–45, 249–50), and to *parashat Balak* (Nu. 22:18; 23:10, 23:13, 21; 24:6, 17–18; Nevo, 284–88); and see also Deut. 31:12 (Nevo, 381), regarding the age of the children to be brought to the *hakhel*

aspect of *Bekhor Shor*'s exegetical method concerns how he presents talmudic and rabbinic sources not just to accompany *peshat* interpretations as possible and sometimes preferred options, but as vehicles for putting forward a basic (*peshat*) interpretation that resolves exegetical questions and dilemmas within narrative sections of the Torah, constituting a kind of *halakhah ha-meyashevet divrei miqra* (to paraphrase Rashi's well-known phrase). We have encountered a bit of this already, but it is appropriate to conclude our treatment of *Bekhor Shor* with a clear and highly indicative example of this approach.

Following *Bereshit Rabbah* (85:6, יהודה התחיל במצות יבום תחלה), which is based on the phrase in Genesis 38:8, *ve-yabbem ʾotah*, *Bekhor Shor* (to Gen. 38:13; Nevo, 70) suggests that there was a fully developed structure of pre-Sinaitic *yibbum* operant with respect to Tamar, according to which any male member of the immediate family of a husband who had died leaving his wife childless—including the husband's father—might undertake *yibbum*. Thus when Judah did not allow his third son, Shelah, to marry Tamar (Gen. 38:11), he himself should have performed *yibbum*. Indeed, *Bekhor Shor* notes that even after the Torah was given, and *yibbum* was thereby limited or permitted only to one of the dead husband's brothers, more distant male relatives (who were not otherwise prohibited from marrying her) were encouraged to step forward to marry her as a form of *yibbum*, where no brother was able to do so. This is precisely what Boaz did in the case of Ruth. Implied at this point by *Bekhor Shor* is that the assignation between Tamar and Judah was not a promiscuous, unfortunate, or inappropriate episode, as many other commentators, including Rashi, understood it to be.[132]

In his comment to Genesis 38:26 (Nevo, 71), *Bekhor Shor* makes this last point explicit. He interprets the phrase *ẓadqah mimeni* (following the approach of Rashbam rather than that of Rashi) to mean that Tamar was judged by Judah to be more righteous or correct than he was, since he had not given her to his son Shelah, and she was therefore completely justified in attempting to insure that he would have relations with her as part of the requirement of *yibbum*. For *Bekhor Shor*, Judah could have continued to live with Tamar, since their relationship was ultimately a permitted one through

ceremony. On the implications of providing these exegetical options, cf. S. Kamin, *Rashi's Exegetical Categorizations* (above, n. 22), 158–208, and J. Haas (above, n. 31), 62, 68, 72–77.

[132] In his Arabic translation of the Torah, Saʿadyah Gaon (as recorded in the *Ḥumash Torat Ḥayyim* to Gen. 38:8) interprets the phrase ויבם אותה as completely unrelated to the notion of *yibbum*. He interprets this phrase to mean ובנה ממנה, apparently suggesting that the *mem* in *ve-yabbem* could be switched with the letter *nun* (as does occur in other biblical phrases and contexts). For Rashi's understanding of the degree of *yibbum* present, see Naḥmanides' critique in his commentary to Gen. 38:8–9, and cf. *Perushei R. Ḥayyim Paltiʾel*, 120 (= *Tosafot ha-Shalem*, ed. Gellis, 4:63, sec. 3).

the agency of *yibbum*. *Bekhor Shor* therefore explains the concluding phrase in this verse, that Judah did not continue to live with Tamar (*ve-lo yasaf ʿod le-daʿatah*), as a reflection of Judah's sense that Tamar had the status of an *ʾishah qatalanit* since two of his sons had died while married to her. He did not want to place himself in this position, even though the relationship itself was considered to be a fundamentally permitted one as indicated.[133]

It should be noted that *Bekhor Shor* here clearly adumbrates the exegetical approach of Ramban. For Ramban, however, aspects of *torat ha-sod* (especially with regard to the relationship between the precept of *yibbum* and the mystical phenomenon of *gilgul neshamot*, the transmigration of souls) are fully intertwined with his exegesis of these verses, rendering this as an outstanding example of where *peshat* and *sod* coincide for Naḥmanides.[134] For *Bekhor Shor*, the *sod* element is completely absent, and his exegetical approach is ultimately an excellent example of *ʾaggadah ha-meshavet divrei miqra*. As we shall see, *Bekhor Shor*'s approach here was also adopted (and expanded upon, based on a passage in the *Pesiqta*) by another Tosafist and contemporary of Naḥmanides, R. Yeḥiʾel of Paris.[135]

Bekhor Shor's preserving of the reputation of Judah and Tamar by suggesting that their relationship was fundamentally permitted through the

[133] Cf. Avraham Grossman, *Ḥasidot u-Moredot* (Jerusalem, 2001), 476. See also 487–94, regarding the halakhic status of the *ʾishah qatlanit* in medieval Ashkenaz.

[134] On the influence of R. Yosef *Bekhor Shor* on Ramban, see Novetzky, "The Influence of Rabbi Joseph Bekhor Shor and Radak," above, n. 117. Radak, another mostly unnamed source for Ramban's Torah commentary, comments very briefly on Gen. 38:8. See *Perushei R. David Qimhi ʿal ha-Torah*, ed. M. Kamelhar (Jerusalem, 1970), 182: נראה כי הדבר של יבום היה משפט הקדמונים קודם שניתנה התורה (clearly with *Bereshit Rabbah* 85 in mind). The expansive nature of Ramban's comment to Gen. 38:8–9, however, seems to owe quite a bit of its specifics to the comment by *Bekhor Shor.* Moreover, Ramban, in his comment to Gen. 38:26 (*ẓadqah mimeni*), rejects Rashi's interpretation that "she is correct, since the child is from me," and suggests instead, exactly as *Bekhor Shor* does, that it reflects the fact that Tamar was more righteous here than Judah, since Judah should have allowed his son Shelah to marry her through *yibbum.* And if Shelah did not wish to undertake this, Judah himself should have done so. Ramban also notes (again like *Bekhor Shor*) that Judah chose not to remain with Tamar (even though their relationship was completely appropriate and permitted). See also E. Touitou, *Exegesis in Perpetual Motion*, 204. Rashbam interprets *ẓadqah mimeni* as *Bekhor Shor* does (and unlike Rashi; see M. Lockshin, *Rashbam's Commentary to Genesis*, 268), but does not suggest at any point that this was an instance of *yibbum* (except in an errant variant recorded in *Perushei R. Ḥayyim Paltiʾel*, 124, n. 75). On the intersection of *peshat* and *sod* in Ramban's Torah commentary (and specifically in this instance), cf. my "On the Assessment of R. Moses b. Naḥman (Naḥmanides) and His Literary Oeuvre," *Jewish Book Annual* 54 (1996–97), 71 (and the literature cited in n. 18).

[135] See *Tosafot ha-Shalem*, ed. Gellis, 4:84, 86–87, secs. 5, 18, 20, and cf. *Sefer ha-Gan*, ed. Orlian, 188; and below, chapter 4, nn. 118–19. In at least two instances (sacrifices and *ʿeglah ʿarufah*), the *taʿamei ha-miẓvot* provided by *Bekhor Shor* in his Torah commentary were precisely in accord with those rationalistic ones of Maimonides rather than with those mystical ones of Naḥmanides. See my "Anthropomorphism and Rationalist Modes of Thought" (above, n. 51), 122–23 (nn. 9–10), and below, chapter 7.

concept of *yibbum* and by presenting his supportive exegesis was not accidental; it reflects a fairly consistent goal of his commentary, as we have noted. Indeed, using another exegetical strategy that is consistently employed throughout his Torah commentary as well, *Bekhor Shor* puts forward a psychological, "nature of people" (*derekh ha-ḥayyim*) consideration to explain why the Torah bothers to note (in Gen. 38:13) that Judah sought out female companionship specifically at the point that he was overseeing the shearing of his flocks, a period that was characterized by great joy and large feasts as described, for example, in two different verses and incidents in the Book of Samuel. These experiences, in turn, often caused the men to become aroused.[136] All the various exegetical considerations of *Bekhor Shor* merge here into a highly original, yet simple and contextual interpretation for this unusual incident.

To end this section where we began, it must be remembered that R. Yosef *Bekhor Shor* of Orleans was a direct Tosafist student of Rabbenu Tam who was cited in *Tosafot* with some frequency, and who died somewhere around the year 1200.[137] Well before the compilatory Tosafist Torah collections (which frequently cite *Bekhor Shor*) were edited, however, other individual Tosafists were interested in subjecting Rashi's Torah commentary to analysis, and in creating *peshat* commentaries that were also sensitive to the interpretations of *Ḥazal* and to the notion of *'aggadah ha-meyashevet divrei miqra* in ways similar to those of Rashi. To be sure, few of these Tosafists had the precise background—including exposure to certain Spanish teachings—and exegetical sensibilities that *Bekhor Shor* had, and, as we shall see, their efforts have gone largely unnoticed. After all, in the face of the commentaries of Rashi, Rashbam, and *Bekhor Shor*, and when measured against them, getting noticed is not a simple matter. Nonetheless, the existence of a group of such works and comments (largely still in manuscript) suggests that these Tosafists wanted to produce additional and competing voices in the area of Torah commentary, which would nonetheless be closer to the methods and style of *Bekhor Shor* and Rashi than to the commentary of Rashbam. Irrespective of whether history has been kind to these works or whether the verdict of history is correct, these works constitute an important latitudinal step or link in terms of the intellectual history of Ashkenazic Jewry during the late twelfth and early to mid-thirteenth centuries, at precisely the time when the bulk of the talmudic *Tosafot* and related

136 This interpretation is also found in *Ḥizzequni* to Gen. 38:13. Cf. E. Touitou, *Exegesis in Perpetual Motion*, 154.

137 Cf. Rami Reiner, "Rabbenu Tam u-Bnei Doro: Qesharim, Hashpa'ot ve-Darkhei Limmud ba-Talmud" (Ph.D. diss., Hebrew University of Jerusalem, 2002), 151–52, who suggests, based on his activities, that R. Yosef *Bekhor Shor* was born in the early 1120s.

works were being created by some of these same rabbinic figures and their colleagues.

R. Jacob of Orleans

One such Tosafist was R. Jacob of Orleans,[138] an exact contemporary of R. Joseph *Bekhor Shor* who hailed from the same locale as R. Joseph[139] and was also a student in Rabbenu Tam's *beit midrash*. R. Jacob relocated at some point to England and died as a martyr in London during the coronation of Richard the Lionheart in 1189. Cited even more frequently in *Tosafot* texts than R. Yosef of Orleans, R. Jacob had particular interest and expertise in the interpretation of talmudic passages within *Seder Qodashim* and related *sugyot*. Among his halakhic innovations, R. Jacob created a loan document that was designed to legally circumvent the problem of usury, and he was counted among those northern French Tosafists (along with R. Yom Tov of Joigny, as we shall see below) who allowed Jewish adults to benefit from the hearth when the heat was raised on the Sabbath by a non-Jewish servant for his or her own benefit.[140]

R. Jacob's numerous comments to the Torah have not survived in a separate commentary or treatise, but they were included piecemeal in a

[138] The name of R. Jacob's father is not mentioned in the literature of the *Tosafot*. See, however, the French liturgies found in ms. Parma 403 (#13059), fol. 12r–v (in the margin), and in ms. Vatican 324, fol. 5r (in the bottom margin), which record a liturgical custom for *pesuqei de-zimra* on the Sabbath and festivals that was initiated by R. Solomon, father of Jacob of Orleans: ה"ר שלמה אביו של ה"ר יעקב מאורליינש היה נוהג לומר כאן בין ויהי נועם [תהלים צ:יז, עד סוף תהלים צא, ארך ימים אשביעהו] להללוי-ה שם ה' [תהלים קלא:ה] יברכך ה' מציון עושה שמים וארץ [תהלים קלד:ג, והוא סוף הפרק]. R. Solomon bases his practice on the fact that the Talmud (*Pesaḥim* 117a) does not consider the word הללויה to be the opening word of Ps. 135:1 but rather the final word of the prior verse, Ps. 134:3. This passage about R. Solomon's practice does not appear, however, in a related manuscript, ms. Lund L. O. 2 (IMHM #34100). On these manuscripts, cf. S. Emanuel, *Shivrei Luḥot*, 31 (n. 93) and 199 (n. 56). See also ms. Paris 752 (#12057), fol. 37 (*ʿinyanei tefillah*), regarding R. Jacob of Orleans's doubling the verse (recited in *pesqei de-zimrah*) of *ʾorekh yamim ʾasbiʿehu* (Ps. 91:16). Note also that the father of the later Tosafist R. Jacob of Courson (who studied in northern France with R. Samson of Sens and subsequently taught in Germany) was also named Solomon. See Emanuel, *Shivrei Luḥot*, 254–61, and above, chapter 1, nn. 80, 106.

[139] On the role of Orleans during the Maimonidean controversy, see below, chapter 7, n. 105.

[140] See Urbach, *Baʿalei ha-Tosafot*, 1:142–44; I. Ta-Shma in *Encyclopedia Judaica* (Jerusalem, 1972), 9:1234; idem, *Halakhah, Minhag u-Meziʾut be-Ashkenaz, 1000–1350* (Jerusalem, 1996), 163; Pinchas Roth, "Perush ʿal Massekhet Qinim le-Eḥad mi-Baʿalei ha-Tosafot," *Netuʿim* 6 (2000), 9–16; and H. Soloveitchik, *Pawnbroking: A Study in the Interrelationship between Halakhah, Economic Activity, and Communal Self-Image* [Hebrew] (Jerusalem, 1985), 68–69 (n. 33). Cf. *Tosafot Pesaḥim* 22a, s.v. *R. Shimʿon*; *Tosafot ha-Rosh*, ed. A. Shoshana (Jerusalem, 2006), ad loc.; and *Ḥiddushei Rabbenu Yonah ʿal Massekhet Sanhedrin* (59a), for a rather unique approach by R. Jacob concerning the prohibition of eating the sciatic nerve and its applicability to Noachides.

number of published Tosafist Torah compilations and in quite a few collections still in manuscript.[141] Like R. Yosef *Bekhor Shor*, R. Jacob of Orleans was more committed to this area of endeavor than their most influential talmudic teacher, Rabbenu Tam. Indeed, within the collections of Tosafist Torah commentaries, R. Jacob is often referred to as Rabbenu (Jacob) Tam of Orleans.[142]

R. Isaac b. Judah *ha-Levi*, compiler of the Tosafist Torah commentary known as *Pa'aneaḥ Raza* (which was apparently composed in northern France during the last decades of the thirteenth century), states in the introduction to his work that he called it by this name because he would

141 Through citations by Zunz (*ZGL*, 76, 91, 93, 97), Urbach, *Ba'alei ha-Tosafot*, 1:144, was aware that R. Jacob's comments appear in a variety of Tosafist compilations, especially *Pa'aneaḥ Raza* and *Minḥat Yehudah* (and that he was one of the unidentified commentators relied upon by *Ḥizzequni*), but Urbach does not attempt to characterize R. Jacob's comments in any way. See also Henri Gross, *Gallia Judaica* (Paris, 1897), 36. Urbach notes correctly that R. Jacob was not the editor or compiler of ms. Paris 167; cf. above, n. 6; I. Ta-Shma, *Knesset Meḥqarim*, 1, 235–37; and Poznanski, *Mavo*, LIII–LIV, and LVII–LVIII (n. 4), who also does not deal at all with the substance of R. Jacob's comments. Quite a number of citations appear in manuscripts that were used in the preparation of *Perushei R. Ḥayyim Palti'el 'al ha-Torah*, ed. Y. S. Lange (actually compiled by a student of R. Ḥayyim Palti'el), which was published in 1981, not long after the revised, two-volume edition of Urbach's *Ba'alei ha-Tosafot* appeared. See the editor's introduction, 10–11. Although a number of comments by R. Jacob of Orleans are found in this work without his name (and R. Jacob's name is associated with a particular comment only in other collections), there are places in *Perushei R. Ḥayyim Palti'el*, ed. Lange, where ר"י connotes ר' יעקב מאורליינש. See the index, 650 (n. 3), and 653 (n. 10). Hazoniel Touitou, "Minḥat Yehudah shel R. Yehudah b. Elazar," 92–95, has a brief treatment of R. Jacob's exegetical method and its impact on the *Minḥat Yehudah* compilation (which was composed in northern France in 1313; see Touitou, 9–11). Touitou suggests, based on several passages in *Minḥat Yehudah*, that R. Jacob's comments were available in written form, if not in a distinct treatise.

142 As noted above (n. 6; and see also chapter 1, n. 54), it appears that Rabbenu Tam (and Ri) did not attempt to systematically interpret the Torah outside the realm or context of talmudic studies. Indeed, references to Rabbenu Tam in the so-called Tosafist Torah compilations are often to R. Jacob "Tam" of Orleans. (Another student of Rabbenu Tam, R. Jacob of Corbeil, was also referred to occasionally as R. Jacob Tam of Corbeil; and cf. above, Introduction, n. 52.) See, e.g., Poznanski, *Mavo*, 53; Touitou, *Minḥat Yehudah*, 80–81 (n. 74); *Perushei R. Ḥayyim Palti'el*, 34, 44, 69–70, 107, 111, 312, 411, 426, 499, 502, 507, 532, 583, 598, 611; *Tosafot ha-Shalem*, ed. Gellis, 1:2, sec. 5; 1:42, sec. 7. See also *Tosafot ha-Shalem*, ed. Gellis, 2:1, sec. 7; 2:97, sec. 1; 2:124, sec. 11; 2:133–34, sec. 8; 2:138–39, sec. 6; 2:166–67, sec. 1; 2:257, sec. 2; 2:283, sec. 11; 3:6–7, sec. 6 (in which the initials ר"י refer either to R. Yehudah *he-Ḥasid* or to R. Yeshayah di-Trani); 3:124, sec. 9; 3:82, sec. 8; 5:14, sec. 1; 5:20, sec. 7, 5:87, sec. 1; 7:100, sec. 10. The reference to Rabbenu Tam in *Tosafot ha-Shalem*, 1:177–78, sec. 7, is from a passage in *Tosafot Yevamot* (where Rabbenu Tam comments on the nature of Metatron in talmudic and *piyyut* literature, and the relationship between Metatron and Hanokh; cf. *Perushei R. Ḥayyim Palti'el*, ed. Lange, 20–21), and see also the reference in 1:178, sec. 8, to a piece of Rabbenu Tam's polemical response to Count Henri of Champagne (above, chapter 1, n. 241). Polemical comments made by others were also attributed to Rabbenu Tam. See, e.g., ms. Munich 50, fol. 95r (and the parallel passage in ms. B.M. 9931), for a polemical comment by R. Yosef Qara (based on Gen. 47:31 and 48:2), and see *Tosafot ha-Shalem*, ed. Gellis, 5:9, sec. 5, for the attribution to Rabbenu Tam. Cf. *Nizzaḥon Yashan*, ed. David Berger (Philadelphia, 1979), 248.

"reveal hidden things," and because the *gematria* value of his name, Isaac, (208) is equal to both the word פענח and the word רזא. He also lists the exegetes whose interpretations he will present: וכללתי בו מה ששמעתי מרבותי ומ־ דברי ר[י]"ץ בחידושיו ומדברי ר' יעקב מאורליינש ופי' רבי' בכור שור וקצת מה שמצא' בג"ן שחיבר הרב מצרפת כל דבר במקומו כאשר סייעני מן השמים. וקצת פשטי' וגמטריות מדברי רבי' יהודה החסיד ומדברי ה"ר אלעזר נזכרים בו כדי שיהא כערוגה מלאה בשמים. ומעט מזעיר הוספתי אני הלוי הנזכר וכו'. The first identifiable figure among these principal authors is R. Jacob of Orleans. While R. Isaac b. Judah *ha-Levi* does not seem to attribute a full commentary to R. Jacob (as he does to R. Yosef *Bekhor Shor*), he assigns R. Jacob a fairly important role in his work, which he suggests is larger than that of R. Judah *he-Ḥasid* and his student, R. Eleazar of Worms, if not quite as varied. R. Isaac's roster of earlier commentators and their places in his work are fairly complete, although as we shall see, there is one additional northern French Tosafist who figures fairly prominently in *Pa'aneaḥ Raza*, R. Yom Tov of Joigny, who is not mentioned on this list. A slight complication in identifying R. Isaac *ha-Levi*'s sources arises, since a number of comments in both the published and manuscript editions of *Pa'aneaḥ Raza* are attributed simply to Orleans. It is sometimes difficult to determine with certainty if these comments belong to the more prolific R. Yosef *Bekhor Shor* or to R. Jacob b. Solomon, who is the only rabbinic figure specifically identified in the introduction as hailing from Orleans.[143]

[143] I have corrected the introduction as it appears in most printed editions of *Pa'aneaḥ Raza* (including the Machon Yerushalayim edition, published in Jerusalem in 1998 [p. 1], which is the published version of *Pa'aneaḥ Raza* that is cited throughout this study unless otherwise indicated) on the basis of the slightly enhanced introductory paragraph, which is actually found at the end of an enhanced manuscript version of this work, ms. Bodl. 2344, fol. 144r. (On this manuscript, cf. I. Ta-Shma, *Knesset Meḥqarim*, 1:240.) We know next to nothing about R. Isaac *ha-Levi* (other than that he seems to have lived in northern France in the last decades of the thirteenth century) or about his teachers. Ta-Shma (above. n. 141) struggles with the identification of רי"ץ, and offers an inventive but ultimately unconvincing suggestion. It is quite possible, however, that this name represents a little-known contemporary of R. Isaac *ha-Levi*, and is connected to R. Isaac's teachers. There are indeed quite a few commonly named individuals within this collection whose identities we cannot ascertain but who seem to be teachers or colleagues of the compiler (who refers to himself in the text not as Isaac but as Levi, as he indicates in his opening statement). As such, R. Jacob of Orleans may be the most senior of the exegetical predecessors and sources listed by R. Isaac *ha-Levi.* See also below at R. Judah *he-Ḥasid* (chapter 3, n. 7) and at R. Eleazar of Worms (chapter 4, nn. 205, 247); in the version of the introduction found in the Machon Yerushalayim edition (among others), R. Eleazar's work is characterized as *peratim.* The title *Pa'aneaḥ Raza* (revealer of secrets) also reflects the amalgam of *peshatim* and other exoteric interpretations together with the more esoteric concepts and *gematri'ot* that are found throughout this work (as well as issues and uses of the occult; see, e.g, R. Samuel of Falaise's interpretation to Ex. 20:13, in *Tosafot ha-Shalem*, ed. Gellis, 8:115–16, secs. 10, 13). See my *"Peering through the Lattices,"* 181, 248–49; and Joy Rochwarger, "Sefer Pa'aneaḥ Raza and Biblical Exegesis in Medieval Ashkenaz" (M.A. thesis, Touro College/Jerusalem, 2000), 43–51, 109–17. On the problem of the otherwise unidentified Orleans comments, see also Poznanski, above, n. 141.

Many of the extant comments of R. Jacob of Orleans were directed toward Rashi's commentary on the Torah (even more frequently than R. Yosef *Bekhor Shor*'s were), although they are neither as numerous nor as consistent to characterize them as a full-fledged supercommentary.[144] Moreover, many of R. Jacob's observations with respect to Rashi's commentary are essentially talmudic or rabbinic in nature. Although they seek to verify or to amplify this aspect or dimension of Rashi's exegesis, a number of them could easily have been made at least initially within the course of talmudic study.[145] Others, however, can be classified as structural or *peshat*-like comments or queries that were focused on Rashi's commentary, and made as free-standing observations to the text of the Torah itself. What follows is a description and analysis of a representative sample of the more than fifty of these kinds of comments by R. Jacob, taken almost exclusively from narrative or non-halakhic contexts.

In his opening comment to Genesis 1:1, Rashi accounts for the Torah's beginning with the Creation story, rather than with the first *mizvah* precept given to Moses on behalf of the people (in Ex. 12), to designate the new month and thereby to fix the order of the calendar, as might have been expected in what is fundamentally a repository of law. A key element in Rashi's framing of this issue may be questioned, however, since the precept of circumcision (and the prohibition of eating the sciatic nerve, based on Jacob's fight with the angel), as well as the so-called *sheva mizvot bnei Noaḥ*, were commanded already in the book of Genesis, and well before the precept of designating the start of a month upon seeing the new moon. Although this question is found anonymously in a number of the so-called Tosafist Torah commentaries, an enriched manuscript version of *Paʿaneaḥ Raza* (ms. Bodl. 2344) records this question in the name of R. Jacob of Orleans. Various Tosafist Torah compilations suggest the response that Rashi's formulation is quite apt, since the precept of circumcision was given in the Book of Genesis only to Abraham and his sons, just as the prohibition

144 On the nature of medieval supercommentaries to Rashi's Torah commentary, see H. Touitou, "Minḥat Yehudah," 3–8, 60–65; Eric Lawee, "The Reception of Rashi's Commentary on the Torah in Spain," *JQR* 97 (2007), 33–66; and idem, "From Sepharad to Ashkenaz: A Case Study in the Rashi Supercommentary Tradition," *AJS Review* 30 (2000), 393–425.

145 See, e.g., *Tosafot ha-Shalem*, ed. Gellis, vol. 1, 273, sec. 1, for clarification of a rabbinic reference in Rashi to Gen. 9:23, in light of what appears to be conflicting talmudic sources. Similarly, R. Jacob provides talmudic or rabbinic background information (and deflects possible contradictions) for Rashi's comments in *Tosafot ha-Shalem*, ed. Gellis, 2:191, sec. 3; 2:198, sec. 4; and 2:201, sec. 1. In *Tosafot ha-Shalem*, ed. Gellis, vol. 7, a series of talmudic and midrashic questions and interpretations on Rashi and on the verses themselves are found in the name R. Jacob of Orleans. See 7:74, sec. 7 (based on a passage in the standard *Tosafot* and *Tosafot Rash mi-Shanz* to *Pesaḥim* 41b); 7:86, sec. 2; 7:95, sec. 5; 7:109–10, sec. 3; and 7:256, sec. 4. See also *Tosafot ha-Shalem*, ed. Gellis, 8:215.

concerning the consumption of the *gid ha-nasheh* was enunciated at that point to Jacob alone.[146]

In Genesis 1:11 the Almighty instructs that the land should give forth trees that bear fruit. The Tosafist Torah compilation *Minḥat Yehudah* notes that the precise intention of this verse is somewhat unclear since there were any number of trees created at this time that were not fruit-bearing, and then proceeds to cite a simple observation about the wording of this verse in the name of Rabbenu Tam of Orleans. This verse conveys the sense that, for the most part, the trees being created would forth give fruit (עץ עושה פרי). At no point, however, does the verse say that *all* trees (*kol ʿeẓ*) created at this time would give forth fruit.[147]

The Torah records that the flood began in the second month of the six hundredth year in the life of Noah (Gen. 7:11). Some twenty-five verses later, however, the Torah notes that the waters receded in the first month of the six-hundred-and-first year (Gen. 8:13), without mentioning that this numerical reckoning was being done according to the lifetime or the years of Noah. The Tosafist Torah compilation *Minḥat Yehudah* cites Rabbenu (Jacob) Tam of Orleans, who explains that the Torah intentionally omitted the reference to Noah in the later verse, because during the period of the flood, Noah's life was not a normal one.[148]

Citing *Bereshit Rabbah*, Rashi writes that Noah had brought grape vines and fig shoots with him into the ark, and it was from these roots that Noah

[146] See *Tosafot ha-Shalem*, ed. Gellis, 1:1, sec. 1, and *Perushei R. Ḥayyim Palti'el*, ed. Lange, 1. *Perushei R. Ḥayyim Palti'el*, 3, records an additional question from R. Jacob of Orleans on Rashi's characterization (in this same comment) of the charge that the nations of the world might level, that the Jewish people had stolen the land of Israel from them (*listim attem*). Since Noah's son and grandson Ḥam and Kenaʿan were to be subjugated to Shem, their assets became the property of their master, and the land of Israel rightfully belonged to the descendants of Shem. See also ms. Vatican (Urban) 21, fol. 1r (והקשה ר"ת מאורליינש) = R. Judah b. Eleazar, *Minḥat Yehudah* (repr. Jerusalem, 1967), Genesis, fol. 1a. *Paʿaneaḥ Raza*, 47, records another question raised by R. Jacob of Orleans, on Rashi's comment to Gen. 6:13 (with an answer suggested by the compiler, [R. Isaac ha-] Levi). See also *Tosafot ha-Shalem*, ed. Gellis, 1:206, sec. 12. The first question on Rashi 1:1 (with a brief version of the answer noted here) is found in the Cambridge manuscript (669.2), which contains R. Judah *he-Ḥasid*'s Torah commentary that he transmitted to his son R. Zalman. See *Perushei ha-Torah le-R. Yehudah he-Ḥasid*, ed. Y. S. Lange (Jerusalem, 1975), 2; and below, chapter 3.

[147] See *Tosafot ha-Shalem*, ed. Gellis, 1:42, sec. 7; *Minḥat Yehudah*, Gen., fols. 1b–2a; and ms. Vatican (Urban) 21, fol. 1v. The version of *Minḥat Yehudah* preserved in ms. Budapest Kaufmann A 31 cites this piece simply (and incorrectly) in the name of Rabbenu Tam. *Perushei R. Ḥayyim Palti'el*, ed. Lange, 16, questions Rashi's comment to Genesis 6:13, that when promiscuity prevails (as in the generation of Noah), an evil spirit prevails that eliminates both sinners and innocents. As R. Jacob of Orleans notes, however, only those members of Noah's family who entered the ark were considered to be innocent, and they were all saved. The answer suggested is that there were any number of young children alive at the time of the flood who were blameless, but who perished nonetheless (and they were the object of Rashi's comment). See also *Tosafot ha-Shalem*, ed. Gellis, 1:206, sec. 12.

[148] See *Tosafot ha-Shalem*, ed. Gellis, 1:253, sec. 2 (לפי שכל ימות המבול לא היו ימי נח חיים).

planted his vineyard after the flood (Gen. 9:20). R. Jacob of Orleans explains that Noah took these two species in particular with him into the ark in order to preserve them, because these species, more than other plantings, are ruined by excessive water. *Ḥizzequni*, writing a century later, presents the explanation of R. Jacob without attribution, and provides another similar explanation, that these species generally have a more difficult time taking root as compared to other plants.[149]

When Abraham arrives in the land of Canaan, the Torah notes that he passed through the land until he reached Shekhem (Gen. 12:6). Based on a midrashic source, Rashi explains that Abraham went there to pray for the sons of Jacob, who would wage a battle there in the future (in connection with the episode involving Dina). R. Jacob of Orleans wonders how Abraham can then say to God later on in this portion (Gen. 15:3) that he is concerned that he will have no children. He answers that when he first arrived in the land, Abraham was confident in the promise made to him by God, that He would make Abraham a great nation in the land of Israel. Later on, however, after not having any children for a lengthy period of time, Abraham despaired that perhaps he would indeed remain childless due to his misdeeds, similar to the sentiment expressed by Jacob (in Gen. 32:11, as interpreted by Rashi) that he had become "diminished" (*qatonti*) by virtue of his actions, and that he therefore might ultimately fall prey to Esau.[150]

[149] See *Tosafot ha-Shalem*, ed. Gellis, 1:271, sec. 5 (= *Minḥat Yehudah*, Gen., fol. 4b, and ms. Vatican [Urban] 21, fol. 10r). *Minḥat Yehudah* records the first explanation in the name of Rabbenu Tam of Orleans, and the second in the name of *Ḥizzequni*. In his systematic supercommentary to Rashi, R. Elijah Mizraḥi also suggests the explanation given by R. Jacob of Orleans, without attribution. See also *Perushei R. Ḥayyim Palti'el*, ed. Lange, 25. Rashi interprets Gen. 9:23 (following *Midrash Tanḥuma*), that Shem's descendants in particular merited the precept of *ẓiẓit* because of the key role that Shem played in covering his father's nakedness with a garment. Here, R. Jacob questions Rashi's choice of this midrashic interpretation, since the Talmud (in tractate *Sotah* 17a) links the precept of *ẓiẓit* to a proper action taken by Abraham. The answer suggested by R. Jacob (see Lange, 25, n. 23) links and harmonizes these two rabbinic sources (thus removing the question on Rashi).

[150] See *Tosafot ha-Shalem*, ed. Gellis, vol. 2, 11, sec. 58; *Perushei R. Ḥayyim Palti'el*, 30; and cf. *Tosafot ha-Shalem*, ed. Gellis, vol. 4, 241, sec. 1, for another striking example of this type of questioning in the name of Rabbenu Tam of Orleans (on Rashi to Gen. 46:9). Once again, *Ḥizzequni* to Gen. 15:3 suggests the same explanation as R. Jacob of Orleans does. *Pa'aneaḥ Raza*, 114, contains an instance (on Gen. 24:22) in which R. Jacob of Orleans questions the consistency of Targum Onkelos regarding the word *nezem* in *parashat Ḥayyei Sarah* and in *parashat Va-Yaqhel*; see *Tosafot ha-Shalem*, ed. Gellis, 2:264, sec. 10. In *Perushei R. Ḥayyim Palti'el*, ed. Lange, 34 (and see also *Tosafot ha-Shalem*, ed. Gellis, 2:97, sec. 4), R. Jacob wonders why Abraham waited to circumcise himself until God commanded him to do so if, according to the Talmud (*Yoma* 28b), "Abraham kept the entire Torah including *'eruv tavshilin*." R. Jacob makes the interesting suggestion that once he was circumcised, Abraham certainly did endeavor to fulfill all other precepts. Prior to his circumcision, however, Abraham was unable to do so.

In this instance, R. Jacob of Orleans is evaluating Rashi's commentary for its consistency across other Torah verses and contexts. R. Jacob, however, is not beyond disagreeing outright with an exegetical approach taken by Rashi. *Minḥat Yehudah* (to Gen. 31:52) records R. Jacob's disagreement with a grammatical comment made by Rashi, on the usage and meaning of the word *ʾim* in this verse (אם אני לא אעבור עליך את הגל הזה ואם אתה לא תעבור אלי את הגל הזה).[151] In another instance, without mentioning Rashi's comment, R. Jacob of Orleans suggests that Abraham's statement to Efron (in Gen. 23:13) that "I have given you the money for the field" ought to be read as a question: Have I yet given you the money, which causes you to act as if I have? Rashi interpreted this verse to mean that Abraham wanted to make sure that he paid for the field and that he did not receive it from Efron for free. He therefore tells Efron that the money is "ready to go," and he would like to pay it already. R. Jacob achieves a similar interpretation by deftly reading the conversation between Abraham and Efron into the verse itself: "Have I yet given you the money? No, but take it from me now."[152]

In a halakhic context, R. Jacob of Orleans (as recorded in *Paʿaneaḥ Raza*) probes the implications of Isaac asking Esau to take his hunting implements and slaughter animals for a meal (Gen. 27:3). The Talmud in tractate *Ḥullin* 4b seeks to establish that one is permitted to eat from the *sheḥitah* of a Jewish idolater based on an episode recorded in the biblical book of 1 Chronicles (involving Aḥav and Yehoshafat). R. Jacob wonders why the Talmud cannot prove from the request of Isaac to Esau (which is found within the Torah itself) that such a *sheḥitah* is indeed permitted. He answers that, in fact, Isaac never got the chance to eat from Esau's *sheḥitah*, since Jacob stepped in first. Isaac's special righteousness was rewarded here by God's intervention (and the appearance of Jacob), which prevented his partaking from the animal slaughtered by Esau. The Torah's earlier description (Gen. 25:28), that Isaac loved Esau "because his [Esau's] hunted food was in his mouth," refers to a period before Esau practiced idolatry.[153] To be sure, this kind of comment, given its halakhic dimensions, might have been made by R. Jacob in the course of analyzing the talmudic discussion on the status of the *sheḥitah* of an idolater or some related issue, rather than in the course of reviewing the Torah portion or otherwise studying the biblical text for its own sake.

[151] See *Tosafot ha-Shalem*, ed. Gellis, 3:200–201, sec. 7 (= *Minḥat Yehudah*, Gen. fol. 32a), and cf. *Tosafot ha-Shalem*, 3:120–21, sec. 7 (הפשט כך הוא, as found in ms. Bodl. 2343), and sec. 12 (ר' אהרן בשם ר' יעקב, from ms. Bodl. 2344). For another grammatical comment by R. Jacob (dealing with a matter of gender), see *Tosafot ha-Shalem*, ed. Gellis, 6:30, sec. 5 (to Ex. 1:21), ויעש להם בתים (= *Minḥat Yehudah*, Exodus, fol. 2b). Cf. *Tosafot ha-Shalem*, ed. Gellis, sec. 3; and *Ḥizzequni*; and below, n. 158.

[152] See *Paʿaneaḥ Raza*, 109; *Tosafot ha-Shalem*, ed. Gellis, 2:240, sec. 3, and see also *Ḥizzequni*. See also R. Jacob's *peshat* interpretation of Gen. 23:17–18, in *Tosafot ha-Shalem*, 2:243, sec. 4.

[153] See *Paʿaneaḥ Raza*, 130; *Perushei R. Ḥayyim Paltiʾel*, 76 (n. 8); and cf. 81 (n. 14), and 83 (n. 45).

In a purely scriptural or *peshat* context, however, R. Jacob Tam of Orleans compares the recapitulation of Joseph's statements offered by Judah at the beginning of *parashat Va-Yigash* with the original statements that Joseph had made to his brothers. According to Judah, Joseph asked that Jacob's youngest son, Benjamin, be brought to Egypt, "so that I may place my eyes upon him" (ואשימה עיני עליו; Gen. 44:21). Rashi (to Gen. 44:18) understands this phrase to mean that Joseph would thereby protect him. In fact, however, Joseph himself never actually uttered this phrase. R. Jacob of Orleans therefore puts forward a different interpretation from that of Rashi (without explicitly noting Rashi's commentary). Judah's charge against his brother at the beginning of *Va-Yigash* was that Joseph's intention had been that he merely wanted to see the lad, after which he would allow him to move on without any delay. It was *as if* Joseph had said, "Let me just place my eyes upon him."[154]

The question asked by Joseph after he revealed himself to his brothers, "Is my father alive?" (העוד אבי חי; Gen. 45:3), is understood by R. Jacob of Orleans to be different from the question he had asked of them earlier, "Is your elderly father well?" (השלום אביכם הזקן, Gen. 43:27). Joseph's earlier question was whether Jacob was still alive. His question to his brothers at the point that he revealed himself was whether his father was well and still vigorous. R. Jacob cites a verse in Leviticus (13:10) and a talmudic *sugya* in tractate *Ḥullin* (7a) to demonstrate that the word חי connotes wellness in particular, and not simply a basic state of existence.[155]

R. Jacob of Orleans accounts for the fact that a singular form of the verb "to be" is used at the very beginning of *parashat Va-Yeḥi* (Gen. 47:28), in the phrase "and the years of Jacob numbered one hundred and forty-seven"

[154] See *Tosafot ha-Shalem*, ed. Gellis, vol. 4, 204, sec. 7, from ms. JTS Lutzki 791: אלא כך פתרונו כאילו אמרת לשים עיניך עליו כלומר לראותו בלבד ולא לעכבו, ואתה מעכבו. Cf. Ibn Ezra's comment to this verse, ואראה אותו. (As Gellis notes, the published version of *Minḥat Yehudah*, as well as two other manuscripts, record this in the name of Rabbenu Tam.) Cf. *Tosafot ha-Shalem*, ed. Gellis, 4:141, and *Perushei R. Ḥayyim Palti'el*, 71–72, 80, 90, 94, for additional aspects of R. Jacob's interaction with Rashi's commentary.

[155] See *Tosafot ha-Shalem*, ed. Gellis, 4:212, secs. 5–6, and *Perushei R. Ḥayyim Palti'el*, ed. Lange, 144. This passage is again found inaccurately in *Minḥat Yehudah*, Gen., fol. 44b, in the name of Rabbanu Tam. R. Jacob of Orleans questions the midrashic assertion that Joseph did not buy (and thereby take control of) the lands of the Egyptian priests (Gen. 47:22) since they had vindicated him with regard to the accusations of Potiphar's wife, because the verse itself states that these lands were a right or entitlement of the *kohanim* that had been given to them by Pharaoh (כי חק לכהנים מאת פרעה) which could not be rescinded. See *Moshav Zeqenim*, ed. Sassoon, 95, and *Tosafot ha-Shalem*, ed. Gellis, 4:259–60, secs. 1, 4. R. Jacob also questions Rashi's interpretation of Jacob's blessing to Reuben (Gen. 49:3, to the phrase *ve-reshit 'oni*)—that Reuben was conceived from the very first drop of Jacob's semen—on the basis of a series of talmudic texts having to do with a woman's virginity and the possibility of impregnation from the first act of intercourse. R. Jacob ultimately succeeds in confirming Rashi's interpretation. See *Tosafot ha-Shalem*, ed. Gellis, 5:38–39, and *Perushei R. Ḥayyim Palti'el*, 158.

(ויהי ימי יעקב שני חייו), while the lifespans of Abraham and Isaac are presented using the plural form of this verb (ויהיו ימי חייו). R. Jacob explains this difference as a reflection of the fact that, by his own admission to Pharaoh, Jacob had not lived a good and lengthy life (Gen. 47:9), as compared to the lifespans of his father and grandfather. Moreover, the only fully peaceful or positive periods of Jacob's life correspond to the numerical value of the word ויהי (= 31), which represent the fourteen years in which he studied in the "academy of Shem and ʿEver" and the seventeen years during which he was reunited with Joseph in Egypt.[156] Like R. Yosef *Bekhor Shor*, R. Jacob considered the use of *gematria* to be an appropriate method of supporting his goal of close biblical interpretation.[157]

Returning to the realm of *peshat*, R. Jacob of Orleans offers a somewhat unusual interpretation to explain the "houses" that were built in connection with the efforts the Jewish midwives undertook to avoid the killing of male children at birth (Ex. 1:20). Rashi and Ibn Ezra (and similarly, the Talmud in tractate *Sotah*, as well as *Sifre*) explain that the phrase "and he made for them houses" in the second part of this verse (ויעש להם בתים) refers to houses provided by the Almighty for the midwives as a reward for their actions. Rashbam interprets that Pharaoh was the one who built these houses for the midwives, to place them under a kind of house arrest. Like Rashbam, R. Jacob understands the verse to mean that Pharaoh built these homes as a result of the actions taken by the midwives; but he did so, according to R. Jacob, in order to place an Egyptian home—whose residents could serve as informants—between every two Jewish homes, as an effective means of ascertaining when Jewish babies were being born, since their cries could also be heard by their immediate neighbors.

Although two late midrashic collections (*Leqaḥ Tov* and *Sekhel Tov*) propose this type of interpretation, R. Jacob does not cite them by name, basing his interpretation instead on the grammatical anomaly in this verse, in which the possessive form (להם, for them) is masculine. Had the homes been for the midwives, the text should have used the feminine form (להן). Rather, the actions of the midwives caused houses to be built on their account, which would be occupied by others who could serve as spies.[158] This

156 *Tosafot ha-Shalem*, ed. Gellis, 5:3, sec. 15.

157 See above, n. 37.

158 See *Tosafot ha-Shalem*, ed. Gellis, vol. 6, 30, sec. 5 (= *Minḥat Yehudah*, Ex., fol. 2b), and see also *Tosafot ha-Shalem*, ed. Gellis, sec. 3 (citing the similar exegetical approach found in ms. Cambr. 669.2). As was his wont, R. Jacob also refers to a talmudic passage that notes how the cries of Moses caused the Egyptian babies to cry as well, so that they could no longer be hidden by their mothers. Cf. M. Lockshin, *Rashbam's Commentary to the Book of Exodus*, ed. Lockshin, 16–17; *Tosafot ha-Shalem* ed. Gellis, sec. 7 (citing ms. Bodl. 2344); and *Ḥizzequni*, ad loc., both of which follow the approach of Rashbam).

is another example (similar to the different questions asked by Joseph about Jacob's status) of how R. Jacob of Orleans comes to offer a kind of realia-based interpretation, in view of a particular word or form that the Torah chose to use.

R. Jacob analyzes Rashi's contention that the plague of boils affected both humans and livestock (Ex. 9:10), despite the Torah's earlier assertion (9:6) that the Egyptian livestock perished during the previous plague of pestilence (*dever*). Rashi, following the *Mekhilta*, is of the opinion that God-fearing Egyptians brought their livestock indoors and were thus spared from the pestilence, as the Torah later states explicitly about the hail (9:20). R. Jacob upholds Rashi's interpretation by means of a realia-based explanation: Pestilence is a likelier cause of injury among animals than hail. Therefore, anyone who was God-fearing enough to take his livestock indoors in the face of the hail would certainly have done so in the face of pestilence. Thus there was no need for the Torah to make explicit reference to this since the inference is obvious.[159] Interestingly, Rashi's interpretation had been questioned by R. Yosef *Bekhor Shor* (as noted earlier), who considered it to be forced or confused (והוא מגומגם בעיני). The first to argue in defense of Rashi here, on the basis of a kind of *derekh ʾereẓ* approach, was *Bekhor Shor*'s contemporary Tosafist colleague, R. Jacob of Orleans.[160]

R. Jacob questions the rabbinic interpretation cited by Rashi (from *Sotah* 11a, as an *ʾaggadah ha-meyashevet divrei ha-miqra*) to the phrase, "let us outsmart him" (Ex. 1:10, *havah nitḥakmah lo*): "Let us outsmart the Savior of Israel, who swore that He would never again bring a flood [for the purpose of destructive Divine punishment]." According to this approach, the Egyptians reasoned that if they were to kill the Jewish children through the agency of water, God would not be able to retaliate against them by way of water because of His prior oath. Without suggesting a solution, R. Jacob notes that those who built the Tower of Babel, which occurred after the period of the flood, were punished, according to a passage in the Jerusalem Talmud and other midrashic texts, by the "waters of the ocean." Therefore, the Egyptians should not have been so confident in their understanding of the parameters of God's vengeance.[161] Although the discussion here proceeds fundamentally along the lines of midrashic interpretation, R. Jacob is concerned mostly with understanding or verifying Rashi's interpretation of the verse.[162]

159 See *Tosafot ha-Shalem*, ed. Gellis, 6:240–41, sec. 3 (= *Minḥat Yehudah*, Ex., fol. 9b).

160 See *Perushei R. Yosef Bekhor Shor*, ed. Nevo, 109–10 (and above, n. 67).

161 *Perushei R. Ḥayyim Palti'el*, ed. Lange, 170. See also ibid., 188 (n. 12); 195 (n. 20); and cf. 189 (n. 2, Ex. 6:1), where R. Jacob questions a *peshtuo shel miqra* approach in Rashi.

162 Similarly, R. Jacob supports Rashi's rabbinic interpretation of Ex. 2:1, that Amram had originally separated from Yokheved as a result of Pharaoh's decree (even though the Talmud

In a naturalistic vein, R. Jacob explains why the Torah notes that all the frogs died following their plague (Ex. 8:9), while the murrain was simply "removed" (ויסר הערוב, Ex.8:27) after that plague had ended. Many additional frogs had to be created in Egypt for the plague in which they were involved (as per Ex. 7:28, "the Nile gave forth frogs," ושרץ היאור צפרדעים). Thus, once the plague had concluded, there remained far more frogs in Egypt than was typical, and most of them had to perish. The animals that constituted the murrain, on the other hand, were not created especially for this plague but were able to migrate to Egypt from other places. When the plague concluded, they could simply return to their places of origin. Another possible way to explain the different fates of these creatures is that had the animals that comprised the murrain died in Egypt, the Egyptians would then have been able to benefit from their skins.[163]

Rabbenu Tam of Orleans proposed a correction or emendation to the text of Rashi's commentary to Exodus 9:14. Following the plague of boils, God instructs Moses to tell Pharaoh that he would now bring "all my plagues to your heart" (את כל מגפותי אל לבך). According to the standard texts, Rashi interprets this to mean that we learn from here that the plague of the firstborn (מכת בכורות) was equivalent to all the other plagues. An apparent problem with Rashi's comment is that there were several plagues yet to come before the plague of the firstborn, beginning with the plague of hail. R. Jacob of Orleans suggests that, in fact, the word בכורות in Rashi's comment should be vocalized and read as *bekhurot*, those that had ripened, which refers to the effects that the hail had on destroying crops that had already ripened. According to the Torah (Ex. 9:31–32), the hail destroyed only the flax and barley crops, since these crops were already ripe, with their stalks firm and exposed. The wheat and the spelt crops, however, which were to ripen later, were still closed and were therefore not struck.[164]

---

strongly decries divorce), because loss of life was at stake. See *Perushei R. Ḥayyim Palti'el*, 173, n. 2. He also questions (but ultimately supports) both the content and consistency of Rashi's interpretation and timing of the appearance of the manna. See *Perushei R. Ḥayyim Palti'el*, 243 (n. 6); 244 (n. 15); 246 (n. 53); and cf. 256 (n. 3). R. Jacob's question on Rashi to Ex. 12:6 is a purely talmudic one, concerning how the principle of *sheluḥo shel 'adam ke-moto* is derived. See below, chapter 3, n. 205.

163 See *Perushei R. Ḥayyim Palti'el*, 200, n. 43. The second interpretation is found in some editions of Rashi; see *Perushei Rashi*, ed. Chavel, 197. R. Jacob also wondered why Pharaoh did not call his magicians to perform this plague as he did with the earlier plagues; see *Perushei R. Ḥayyim Palti'el*, 200, n. 47, and cf. *Tosafot ha-Shalem*, ed. Gellis, 6:232. In *parashat Bo*, R. Jacob raised several questions about Rashi's interpretation (or the Torah's formulation) of the Passover sacrifice and its observance. These issues are all based within talmudic and halakhic literature. Indeed, in at least one instance, R. Jacob's discussion is recorded in a *Tosafot* text. See *Perushei R. Ḥayyim Palti'el*, 217 (n. 58); 218 (n. 81); 221 (n. 124).

164 See *Minḥat Yehudah*, Ex., fol. 9b.

Other Tosafist exegetes, colleagues, and successors of R. Jacob offered similar solutions.[165] Indeed, R. Yosef *Bekhor Shor*, without referring to Rashi by name, explains that the hail was a multipronged plague that had multiple effects. It fell on and could kill both people and animals. It could smash houses and trees, and it could destroy vegetation within the fields.[166] This is similar to the approach taken by Rashbam, who focuses on the multiple types of damage that could be delivered by the diverse physical elements that comprised the hail.[167]

The Tosafist Torah compilation *Da'at Zeqenim* records a literary interpretation (to Ex. 15:11) "that I found written in the name of Rabbenu Tam of Orleans." The phrase "Who is like You among the gods" (*mi khamokha ba-'elim ha-Shem*) appears in close proximity to the phrases "You blew with your wind and covered them with the sea" and "by the wind of Your nostrils the waters piled up" (Ex. 15:10), in order to highlight the full extent of this miracle. Air blown from the nostrils is typically warm. Nonetheless, in this instance, the water was congealed (or frozen) by this air. The breath that is blown from the mouth usally emerges as cold air, and yet in this instance, the blown wind caused the congealed water to return to its liquid state. All of this is completely against the laws of the natural world, in which cold air freezes water, and warm air causes it to melt. Thus the Torah's phrase (at the end of 15:11), "great praises for the One who performs miracles," is readily understood.[168]

165 See *Nimmuqei Ḥumash le-Rabbenu Yeshayah*, ed. Chavel, 37, which emends the Rashi text to read מכת בצורת. This also refers to the plague of hail, which can significantly destroy crops and thereby cause a famine. Cf. the editor's notes, and below, chapter 3, n. 153. The printed edition of *Pa'aneaḥ Raza*, 233, contains R. Jacob's emendation, without attributing it to him. A certain R. Abraham, however, wrote that he saw a copy of Rashi's commentary *in his handwriting* (בכתב ידו), in which the phrase was indeed written מכת מיתת הבכורות. *Moshav Zeqenim*, ed. Sassoon, 119–20, records an emendation of the phrase to read מכת בכירות (which is similar to the approach of R. Jacob of Orleans), although it also brings support for reading the phrase in Rashi as is, since the plague of hail had not yet been announced, and this reading is consistent with another interpretation of Rashi (to tractate *Makkot*). The so-called *Tosafot/Perush ha-Rosh 'al ha-Torah* at the end of *parashat va-Era* (fol. 27a) notes both types of emendations but suggests that the one put forward by Rid is less forced than the reading favored by R. Jacob of Orleans. See also *Perushei R. Ḥayyim Palti'el*, 202. R. Jacob of Orleans's vocalization is cited in his name in R. Eliyyahu Mizraḥi's supercommentary to Rashi.

166 *Perushei R. Yosef Bekhor Shor 'al ha-Torah*, ed. Nevo, 111.

167 Rashbam's comment reads: מגפותי. מיני חבלות והכאות אש וברד ואבני אלגביש וגופרית ושלג וקיטור. Cf. M. Lockshin, *Rashbam's Commentary to Exodus*, 86. While Rashbam and R. Yosef *Bekhor Shor* offered a different approach without mentioning Rashi by name or relating directly to his comment, R. Jacob of Orleans (and Rid) attempted to correct the text of Rashi itself in order to put forward a more precise interpretation. Cf. *Tosafot ha-Shalem*, ed. Gellis, 6:243–44; Meir Raffeld, "Le-Parshanut Perush Rashi, Bein Rishonim u-Me'uḥarim," *'Iyyunei Miqra u-Parshanut* 8 (2008), ed. Vargon, 393–407 (I am grateful to Prof. Eric Lawee for this reference); and below, chapter 3, n. 154.

168 See *Tosafot ha-Shalem*, ed. Gellis, 7:229, sec. 1. This interpretation is also found, without attribution, in *Ḥizzequni*. Cf. Ibn Ezra's short commentary to Ex. 15:10. On the seemingly anthropomorphic nature of this comment and its connotations, see below, chapter 7.

R. Jacob amplifies Rashi's example at the beginning of *parashat Yitro* (Ex. 18:31), on the incorruptible judge who "hates bribes."[169] He also indirectly justifies Rashi's interpretation of the order of the phrases in Exodus 19:13, in which the act of stoning appears to precede the victim's being pushed down to the place where the stoning occurs, through his interpretation and application of the rabbinic principle *'ein muqdam u-me'uḥar ba-Torah.*[170] In this instance, variant *Tosafot* texts cite R. Jacob's approach in his name.[171] Not surprisingly, virtually all of the comments attributed to R. Jacob of Orleans on *parashat Mishpatim* are talmudic or halakhic in nature.[172]

Most of R. Jacob's comments to the verses at the end of the Book of Exodus (which describe and detail the construction of the Tabernacle and the fabrication of the priestly vestments) deal with the technical specifications and properties of the various implements and garments as recorded in rabbinic literature, including those comments that relate primarily to Rashi's Torah commentary. Given the particular interest that R. Jacob of Orleans had in the *sugyot* of *Seder Qodashim* (as noted above), this is to be expected, as is the presence of a number of these biblical comments by R. Jacob in talmudic *Tosafot.*[173] R. Jacob also wonders at the end of the Book of Exodus why the disposition and placement of most of the materials and

[169] *Tosafot ha-Shalem*, ed. Gellis, 8:31, sec. 7 (cited from the edition of *Pa'aneaḥ Raza* found in ms. B.M. 9931/Gaster 730; cf. below).

[170] See *Tosafot ha-Shalem*, ed. Gellis, 8:52, sec. 6 (citing *Minḥat Yehudah*, which also refers to the commentary of *Ḥizzequni*). See also *Minḥat Yehudah* to Genesis 6:3, 18:3; and *Tosafot ha-Shalem*, ed. Gellis, 1:187; 2:112, sec. 4 (= ms. Moscow 362, fol. 128r).

[171] See *Tosafot ha-Rashba (me-Rabbenu Shimshon mi-Shanz) 'al Massekhet Pesaḥim*, ed. E. D. Rabinowitz Te'omim (Jerusalem, 1956), 14 (to *Pesaḥim* 6b, s.v. *'aval*); *Tosafot ha-Rosh 'al Massekhet Pesaḥim*, ed. Avraham Shoshana (Jerusalem, 1996), 87; and cf. the standard *Tosafot* to *Pesaḥim* 6b, s.v. *'aval* (which does not mention R. Jacob's name).

[172] See *Perushei R. Ḥayyim Palti'el*, ed. Lange, 271 (n. 38); 272 (n. 45); 278 (n. 138 = *Tosafot ha-Shalem*, ed. Gellis, 8:180); 282 (n. 213, on the insertion of the injunction against kidnapping between the prohibitions of hitting one's parents and cursing them; this comment is also attributed to R. Yosef *Bekhor Shor* and R. Isaiah di Trani, and is attributed by the *Ba'al ha-Turim* to R. Sa'adyah); 291 (an interpretation by *Midrash Tanḥuma* that includes a *gematria* and applies the verse that describes the obligations of an unpaid watchmen [Ex. 22:8] to the misdeeds of Aaron and the Jewish people at the sin of the golden calf, cited also in the Torah commentary of R. Judah *he-Ḥasid*). In a comment to Ex. 24:6, R. Jacob suggests that the Jews underwent both circumcision and immersion prior to their receiving the Torah.

[173] See *Tosafot ha-Shalem*, ed. Gellis, 9:42–43, sec. 6 (from *Tosafot Yoma* 72a, s.v. *ha ketiv*); 9:48, sec. 1; 9:161, sec. 5 (from *Tosafot 'Avodah Zarah* 34a, s.v. *ba-meh*); 9:196, sec. 7 (a linguistic query on Rashi's interpretation; see also *Perushei R. Ḥayyim Palti'el*, 321, n. 48, and 322, n. 64); 9:205, sec. 1 (in connection with an interpretation by R. Eliyyahu as well); 9:208–9, sec. 6 (and cf. 9:132–33, sec. 6); 10:16 (R. Jacob questions Rashi's chronology from a talmudic passage in tractate *'Arakhin*; see also *Perushei R. Ḥayyim Palti'el*, 328, n. 41, and 334, n. 1); 10:151; and 10:250. In *Minḥat Yehudah* to Exodus, fol. 39 (and cf. *Perushei R. Ḥayyim Palti'el*, 310, and esp. n. 56, which also attaches a *teshuvah le-minim* to this interpretation), R. Jacob compares the cherubs described in the Torah (Ex. 25:18) to those of Solomon's Temple, as described in 1 Kings 6.

implements for the *Mishkan* are mentioned by the Torah, while others are not included.[174]

Similarly, the many sacrificial and other technical requirements found in the opening portions of the Book of Leviticus, and the way Rashi interprets them, elicited a number of queries, resolutions, and verifications from R. Jacob of Orleans.[175] Nonetheless, R. Jacob also raises a number of narrower exegetical issues as well. Rashi's comment to Leviticus 14:4, that the Torah's requirement for the healed leper to bring kosher birds (*ẓipporim tehorot*) as a sacrifice is intended to exclude his bringing nonkosher birds, evinces R. Jacob's criticism that this comment is superfluous. R. Jacob suggests that *tehorot* (literally, pure) might have been taken in this context to mean a bird that is physically unblemished, and Rashi therefore needed to point out that a nonkosher bird of any type, even an unblemished one, is in fact proscribed. R. Jacob sharpens his question by noting that, according to the Talmud in tractate *Ḥullin*, the term *ẓipporim* always connotes kosher birds as a matter of convention. He then provides a solution for Rashi, which takes this factor into account as well.[176] R. Jacob questions the purpose and meaning of the verse "and he atoned for the holy sanctuary" (Lev. 16:33), as well as Rashi's interpretation and that of the Talmud in tractate *Shavu'ot*, invoking a talmudic interpretation of his teacher Rabbenu Tam (of Ramerupt) in the process.[177]

R. Jacob of Orleans interprets the precept of "love your neighbor as yourself" in *parashat Qedoshim* (Lev. 19:18) according to the *Sifra* on that verse: "A great principle of the Torah is to love your neighbor as yourself, but a greater principle is 'for in the image of God did He make man' (Gen. 9:6)." R. Jacob explains this *Sifra* passage by noting that the principle of loving one's neighbor as oneself is to be understood as formulated by Hillel (*Shabbat* 31a), "that which is hateful to you do not do to another." If, however, a person is cruel-hearted or crass and does not care about himself, he will not have mercy on others either. Just as he may harm or embarrass himself, he may do the same to others. The phrase in Genesis 9:6, "for in the image of God did He make man," is meant to counteract that kind of negative reasoning.[178]

174 See *Perushei R. Ḥayyim Palti'el*, ed. Lange, 346.

175 See *Perushei R. Ḥayyim Palti'el*, ed. Lange, 350, 353 (n. 99, cited also in the name of Rid); 363 (n. 71); 378 (n. 73); 409. See ibid., 433, regarding Rashi' s explanation of the prohibition against the *kohanim* defiling themselves through contact with a corpse (*parashat Emor*, Leviticus 21:4), and see also 436, and 449–50 (regarding Rashi's explanation of *yovel*).

176 See *Perushei R. Ḥayyim Palti'el*, 402. See also ibid., 415–16 (and n. 38); and *Tosafot ha-Shalem*, ed. Gellis, vol. 12 (Jerusalem, 2009), 251–52, sec. 12.

177 See *Perushei R. Ḥayyim Palti'el*, 416–17.

178 See *Perushei R. Ḥayyim Palti'el*, 426–27. *Moshav Zeqenim*, ad loc., records a similar kind of interpretation in the name of Rashbam (which is not found, however, in any extant version

A number of exegetical comments and questions are put forward by R. Jacob in *parashat Be-Ḥuqqotai.* Rashi's comment on the verse that contains the blessing, "And your threshing shall reach to the vintage and the vintage shall reach to the sowing time" (והשיג לכם דיש את בציר ובציר ישיג את זרע; Lev. 26:5), is that the threshing will be so bountiful that it will take until the time of the vintage to complete, just as the vintage will last until it is time to plant again. R. Jacob notes, however, that according to the Talmud in *Bava Meẓiʿa*, the vintage and planting seasons typically overlap.[179]

In the realm of *peshat* interpretation, R. Jacob of Orleans understands the phrase in the *tokhehah* (admonition), "I will break your powerful pride" (ושברתי את גאון עזכם; Lev. 26:19), as connoting the good land and abundant produce that God had given to the Jewish people, which will be diminished if they sin. This interpretation is supported by a verse in Ezekiel (16:49), which links the pride of the Jewish people to the goodness of their land. R. Jacob notes that this interpretation has contextual support in addition, since at the end of the verse in Leviticus, the Torah notes that the sins will cause "your land to become like brass" (ואת ארצכם כנחשה). Although R. Jacob makes no mention of this, Rashbam interprets Leviticus 26:19 in the very same way (*lefi ha-peshat*), citing the verse in Ezekiel 16 (and Lev. 26:26 as well) against the midrashic interpretation of Rashi, which associates the source of pride (that can become diminished through sin) with the Temple.[180]

At the beginning of the Book of Numbers, R. Jacob of Orleans notes that the princes of each tribe were enumerated according to the chronological order of the sons of Jacob, even as the various censuses in this book of the Pentateuch were listed according to the organization of the encampment and the order of the flags.[181] He supports Rashi's interpretation of Numbers 7:2 ("they stood over the countings"), that it was the princes who stood with Moses and Aaron to supervise the counting of the tribes, based on the role that Moses played in writing down the Torah at the end of his life. Even though this section in *parashat Naso* describes the appointment of the princes when the Tabernacle was dedicated (which occurred in the

---

of Rashbam's Torah commentary), and related interpretations in the name of Rabbenu Tam's student, R. Menaḥem of Joigny (see above, n. 10).

[179] See *Perushei R. Ḥayyim Palti'el*, ed. Lange, 453. Lange speculates (in n. 10) that R. Jacob is reflecting the realia in northern France and Babylonia, which may have been different from the situation in the land of Israel. R. Jacob questions Rashi's exegetical consistency in Lev. 26:8; see *Perushei R. Ḥayyim Palti'el*, 454–55, n. 26; and the Talmudic underpinnings of Rashi's interpretations to Lev. 27:17 (in terms of the order of the verses), and 27: 20–21. See also *Perushei R. Ḥayyim Palti'el*, 461 (nn. 41, 44, 52).

[180] See *Perushei R. Ḥayyim Palti'el*, 456; *Perush ha-Torah asher Katav ha-Rashbam*, ed. David Rosin (Breslau, 1882), 166–67; and cf. M. Lockshin, *Rashbam's Commentary to the Books of Leviticus and Numbers*, 140–41.

[181] *Perushei R. Ḥayyim Palti'el*, 466 (n. 35).

first month of the second year in the desert) and the counting of the tribes, and although the designation of the princes for this purpose did not actually occur until the second month, by the time Moses wrote the Torah, the princes had been appointed and the counting had come to pass, and so he included them already in this verse.[182]

On the other hand, R. Jacob questions Rashi's interpretation of Numbers 8:25 (that at the age of fifty, a Levite should no longer work, ולא יעבוד עוד) to mean that even though the Levite at that age could no longer be involved in carrying the implements of the Tabernacle, he could still participate in activities such as singing and closing the gates. R. Jacob reasons that, if so, the Levitical families of Gershon and Merari, which were never involved in the task of carrying (which was the exclusive role of the family of Kehat), should have been able to continue with their Levitical activities even past the age of fifty, a suggestion that would seem to contradict the plain meaning of the verse in question. Several answers are suggested in this exegetical passage, although it is unclear if any of these come from R. Jacob himself.[183]

R. Jacob makes a sharp observation about God's statement in Numbers 17:20—similar again to an interpretation of Rashbam—that the test involving the presentation of staves to determine the leadership of the Jewish people would serve to remove the complaints made by the children of Israel. This statement would seem to refer, however, only to the complaints made about the 250 supporters of Koraḥ, who perished after offering the *qetoret*, despite the fact that they were instructed to present these *qetoret* offerings by Moses and Aaron. There was, however, an additional complaint, recorded several verses later (17:27), that was not answered by this test.[184]

A somewhat different (*peshat*) interpretation from those put forward by Rashi and R. Yosef *Bekhor Shor* is suggested by R. Jacob for the two double phrases found in Numbers 27:17. Moses asks the Almighty to appoint a successor who would lead the Jewish people into battle, who would literally "go out and return before them," as well as one "who would take them out and bring them in." Rashi suggests (following *Sifrei*) that this repetitive phrasing

[182] See *Minḥat Yehudah*, Numbers, fol. 4a (מ"מ כשתב משה את התורה [לסוף מ' שנה] כבר נתבררו וכתב מקרא זה . . . כפר"ת מאורליינש); and cf. *Perushei R. Ḥayyim Palti'el*, 481 (nn. 9–10).

[183] *Perushei R. Ḥayyim Palti'el*, 487, and cf. Maharal of Prague, *Gur Aryeh*, in *Sefer Ozar Perushim 'al ha-Torah Mizraḥi* (New York, 1965), vol. 2 (Nu.), fols. 14a–b. See also *Perushei R. Ḥayyim Palti'el*, 564 (n. 7).

[184] See *Perushei R. Ḥayyim Palti'el*, 523–24, n. 18 (with reference to *Minḥat Yehudah*). See also Rashbam to 17:6, 17:17, and 17:27–28. R. Jacob questions (and explains) Rashi's interpretation of the number of non-red hairs that disqualify a red heifer from being perfect (*temimah*, Nu. 19:1) on the basis of several Mishnaic and talmudic texts. See *Perushei R. Ḥayyim Palti'el*, 528–29 (n. 26), and see also 551 (n. 2).

conveys the notion that the people would go physically out to war and return with this person in the lead, and they would also spiritually leave and return due to the merits of this leader. Alternatively (following *Bamidbar Rabbah*), Rashi maintains that Moses wished to stress that this leader would also be able "to bring them in" to the land of Israel, which Moses could not do. *Bekhor Shor* (similar to Ibn Ezra) interprets that the second doubling connotes the idea that this leader would be completely in charge, such that the leader of the military effort would also take full direction in every aspect from this overall leader. R. Jacob of Orleans suggests a different distinction, however, on the basis of two other biblical verses. While the successor to Moses—who would serve as the king—would indeed lead the way in war (based on 1 Sam. 18:16, which is cited by Rashi among other verses), the *ʾurim ve-turim* would guide or determine the leaving and returning of the people themselves (as Nu. 27:21 indicates, ושאל לו במשפט האורים . . . על פיו יצאו ועל פיו יבאו, a phrase that corresponds to the second one in the verse at hand).[185]

R. Jacob wonders why the Jewish people were apparently allowed to use the food utensils seized in the wars against Siḥon and ʿOg, but were not allowed to use the utensils they captured from Midian until these were properly immersed and made kosher (Nu. 31:22–23). He suggests, based on a *sugya* in tractate *Ḥullin* (17a), that during the war with Siḥon and ʿOg, the Jewish people were permitted to eat even certain forms of swine to sustain themselves (and thus did not need to make kosher the utensils seized at that time).[186]

The Tosafist Torah collection compiled by a student of R. Ḥayyim Palti'el (c. 1300) presents two interpretations on the blessings given by Moses to the tribes at the end of the Torah in the name of Ibn Ezra, although neither of these is found in the extant commentary of Ibn Ezra to Deuteronomy. The first, to Deuteronomy 33:9, explains the phrase in the blessing to Levi, "you will say to your father and mother that you have not seen them." Rashi had explained that this refers to the sin of the golden calf, where the Levites

[185] See *Minḥat Yehuda* (Numbers) fol. 24a: כ"פ ר"ת מאורלי' ורש"פ [=ורש"י פירש] בע"א. See also *Perushei ha-Torah le-R. Ḥayyim Palti'el*, ed. Lange, 560 (n. 15), where a similar interpretation (without the other scriptural references) is associated with R. Berekhyah *ha-Naqdan*; see above, Introduction, n. 83, and below, chapter 4. Cf. Rashi, *Bekhor Shor* and Ibn Ezra to Nu. 27:21.

[186] See *Perushei R. Ḥayyim Palti'el*, 564–65. R. Jacob's solution is questioned, since this allowance was made only during the ongoing war to conquer the land of Israel in the days of Joshua. The suggestion is made that during the war with Siḥon and ʿOg, only animals (and not utensils) were captured, as opposed to the war with Midyan, where both kinds of property were taken. In his Torah commentary, loc. cit., Naḥmanides (who was aware of certain Tosafist Torah commentaries and texts; see e.g., above, n. 135; and below, chapter 4, n. 3) raises this question, and suggests a somewhat different approach, based on the same *sugya* in tractate *Ḥullin*. See also Maimonides, *Mishneh Torah, Hilkhot Melakhim*, 8:1; *Sefer ha-Ḥinnukh*, sec. 527 (end); and *Teshuvot ha-Radvaz*, vol. 5, sec. 2205.

killed those who participated even if they were their elders or relatives (who were not from the tribe of Levi). The interpretation attributed to Ibn Ezra suggests that this refers to the *kohen gadol*, who could not defile himself even to his parents, and to his closest relatives when they died; he had to make himself like a stranger to them.[187]

The second interpretation attributed to Ibn Ezra explains why the territory of Joseph was singled out for blessing by Moses more than that of any other tribe (as per Deut. 33:13, "his land is blessed by God"). Adam, who heeded the improper advice of his wife, was informed that the land would become cursed because of him (Gen. 3:17). Joseph, on the other hand, who did not heed the entreaties of the wife of Potiphar, merited that his land should be blessed. In *Minḥat Yehudah*, this interpretation is attributed to Rabbenu Tam of Orleans.[188]

Often using Rashi as a foil, and always interested in rabbinic and halakhic *derash*, R. Jacob of Orleans nonetheless puts forward a number of *peshat* interpretations, several of which are similar to those of Rashbam, Ibn Ezra, and, of course, Rashi himself. Although R. Jacob's comments are far less expansive than those of R. Yosef *Bekhor Shor*, his interest in *miqra* as a distinct discipline, separate from matters of talmudic study and law, is recognizable and substantive. As we shall now see, another student of Rabbenu Tam, R. Yom Tov of Joigny, was even more interested in forms of *peshat* interpretation. At the same time, R. Yom Tov appears to have been somewhat less involved in verifying and troubleshooting Rashi's Torah commentary, as compared both to R. Jacob of Orleans and to R. Yosef *Bekhor Shor.*

R. Yom Tov of Joigny

R. Yom Tov b. Isaac of Joigny, who met his death during the pogroms at York in March 1190, was a Tosafist colleague of R. Jacob of Orleans who em-

[187] See *Perushei R. Ḥayyim Palti'el*, 623. Another interpretation of this blessing to the tribe of Levi, also attributed in some variants to Ibn Ezra, stresses that the Levites must steadfastly serve in the Temple from ages 20 to 50, which diminishes their ability to serve and honor their parents. See ibid., 623, n. 44, and ms. B.M. 9931, fol. 182r. Cf. my *Jewish Education and Society in the High Middle Ages*, 104–5 (comparing the interpretation to this verse offered by *Sefer Ḥasidim* and *Sefer Ḥuqqei ha-Torah*), and below, chapter 3, n. 184.

[188] See *Minḥat Yehudah* (Deut.), fol. 24b, and *Perushei R. Ḥayyim Palti'el*, 623, n. 49. Interestingly, *Moshav Zeqenim*, ed. Sassoon, 516, points to a *sugya* in *Zevaḥim* (118b) which stresses Joseph's virtuosity in this regard, and attributes the overall interpretation of R. Jacob of Orleans to R. Judah *he-Ḥasid.* Cf. *Perushei ha-Torah le-R. Yehudah he-Ḥasid*, ed. Lange (Jerusalem, 1975), 210–11. As Lange notes (211, n. 6), both ms. JTS Lutzki 791 and ms. JTS 794 attribute this interpretation to Rabbenu Tam (which points to R. Jacob Tam of Orleans rather than to R. Judah *ha-Ḥasid*). On the use of Ibn Ezra by later Tosafists, see below, chapter 4, n. 122.

igrated from northern France to England.[189] R. Yom Tov is cited in the standard *Tosafot* to several talmudic tractates, in the *Tosafot* of R. Judah Sirleon to tractate *Berakhot*, and in the writings of German Tosafists and halakhists of the late thirteenth century, including *Sefer Rabiah*, the *hilkhot semaḥot* of R. Meir of Rothenburg, and *Sefer Mordekhai*. His interpretation to a verse in Leviticus (which has halakhic implications) is cited in *Sefer Rabiah* under the acronym תיט"ב (= *Tosafot Yom Tov*).[190] R. Yom Tov testifies that even as his father, R. Isaac, and R. Meshullam of Melun were extremely pious (*she-hayu perushim*), they allowed themselves to benefit from a fire that a non-Jewish servant had stoked on the Sabbath solely for the purpose of benefiting another Jew, a leniency that went even further than that of Rabbenu Tam in this matter.[191] As we shall see in chapter 5, R. Yom Tov also composed a series of *piyyutim*.

Unlike R. Yosef *Bekhor Shor* and R. Jacob of Orleans, R. Yom Tov of Joigny is not mentioned by the compiler of *Paʿaneaḥ Raza* (R. Isaac b. Judah *ha-Levi*) as one of the exegetes whose work would be featured in his compilation.[192] Nonetheless, the published version of *Paʿaneaḥ Raza* does include a number of comments from R. Yom Tov, often using the acronym (ר') תיט"ב (R. Teitav). As we shall soon see, however, a much larger number of interpretations are found in a series of manuscript texts that appear to be expanded or enhanced versions of *Paʿaneaḥ Raza*, ms. B.M. 9931 (Gaster 730), ms. Bodl. 2344, ms. Munich 50, and ms. St. Petersburg EVR I 22. To this point, the bulk of R. Yom Tov's more than seventy-five comments to the Torah remain unidentified and unremarked by modern scholarship.[193]

[189] See Urbach, *Baʿalei ha-Tosafot*, 1:133. Cf. Susan Einbinder, *Beautiful Death* (Princeton, 2002), 29–30, 51–52, 57–59. The *payyetan* R. Joseph of Chartres composed an elegy on the death of R. Yom Tov.

[190] See Urbach, *Baʿalei ha-Tosafot*, 1:145–46, and A. Aptowitzer, *Mavo la-Rabiah*, 270, 350–51. Aptowitzer suggests that the acronym תיט"ב was perhaps meant to hint at R. Yom Tov's name while referring to his father as well. תולדות יצחק יום טוב.

[191] See Urbach, ibid.; J. Katz, *Goy shel Shabbat* (Jerusalem, 1984), 49–50, I. Ta-Shma, *Halakhah, Minhag u-Meziʾut be-Ashkenaz, 1000–1350* (Jerusalem, 1996), 163–65; my *"Peering through the Lattices,"* 46–47; and above, chapter 1, n. 164. As these studies indicate, R. Jacob of Orleans supported this leniency as well.

[192] On this introduction, see above, n. 143.

[193] For a description of ms. B.M. 9931 (IMHM #6987, written in fourteenth-century Ashkenazic hand), see Moses Gaster, *Handlist of Gaster Manuscripts* (Hebrew section; London, 1995), fol. 55b. In addition to those of R. Yom Tov, many comments by R. Judah *he-Ḥasid*, and R. Jacob and R. Joseph are included, as well as comments from other leading French and German Tosafists and rabbinic figures such as R. Yeḥiʾel of Paris and R. Nathan Official (fol. 166v); R. Tuvyah of Vienne (fols. 55r, 129v, 158v); R. Eleazar of Worms (fol. 176r); R. Samuel Bamberg (fols. 16r, 18r, 21r, 61v); R. Simḥah of Speyer (fol. 104r), and his student, R. Isaiah b. Mail di Trani (fol. 54v); R. Yaqar *ha-Levi* (fol. 27r); R. Isaac Fuller (fol. 123v); R. Solomon of Cologne (fol. 102v); as well as several other lesser known or unknown names. There are references to a teaching of R. Meir of Rothenburg (fol. 96v, ותירץ מהר"ם מרוטנבורג) and to the practice of

Most of the comments by R. Teitav found in ms. B.M. 9931 are clustered in the book of Deuteronomy (as is the case for the published editions of *Pa'aneah Raza*),[194] and several are decidedly *peshat*-like. The special anathemas pronounced against a person who beats his friend in private (מכה רעהו בסתר, Deut. 27:24, which Rashi, following the so-called Targum Yonatan, understands as a reference to the "secret" attack engendered by *leshon ha-ra*), and against one who forms an idol but hides it away (האיש אשר יעשה פסל ומסכה ושם בסתר; Deut. 27:15), are interpreted together by R. Teitav (in what appears to be a variation on the approach of Rashbam) to take into account the typical behavior of an aggressor who will not attempt to harm his victim in public because of the potential punishment that a *beit din* might mete out, just as the idolater knows that public worship will cause him to be put to death by the court. These violators will therefore conspire to harm another person only in private or to serve the idol privately, where it is possible that they may be able to escape human judgment and punishment. These secret behaviors (which are no less destructive) are thus covered by the special anathemas, which allow for their punishment by Divine decree even when the rabbinic courts are not able to try the perpetrators and adjudicate such acts.[195]

After explaining (as Ibn Ezra does) that the phrase "at the end of seven years you will observe a *shemitah*" (Deut. 15:1) actually refers to the end of

---

Regensburg (fol. 152r), and the compiler of this commentary notes at one point (fol. 16r) that his teacher was R. Yedidyah (of Nuremberg, a student of Maharam). On fol. 97r, a halakhic ruling of Maimonides (regarding the nature of the *met mizvah*, for which a *kohen* is permitted to defile himself) is mentioned, which is found already in *Sefer ha-Gan*; see *Sefer ha-Gan*, ed. Orlian, 253 (to Lev. 21:4), and below, chapter 7, n. 16. Note that several of the pieces in the name of R. Teitav (which in this manuscript are grouped at the end of the Torah) are interspersed with or juxtaposed to comments from R. Judah *he-Hasid*; see, e.g., fols. 156v, 171v, 179v. for Munich 50 (= 01692, dated 1552); Y. S. Lange, "Le-Zehuto shel R. Hayyim Palti'el," *'Alei Sefer* 8 (1981), 142–43. Ms. St. Petersburg, National Library, EVR I 22 (= IMHM #50864, Ashkenaz, 13th–14th century), is a Torah commentary through *Ki Teze*. Many rabbinic scholars and exegetes from northern France are mentioned (as well as several from Germany), including Rashi, R. Yosef Qara, R. Yosef *Bekhor Shor*, R. Jacob of Orleans, R. Yosef of Clisson, R. Simon of Joinville, R. Aaron *ha-Zarefat* (compiler of *Sefer ha-Gan*), R. Samuel of Falaise, R. Aaron *ha-Zarefati*, R. Yehudah *he-Hasid* (sometimes referred to as יפר"ח), Isaac *mi-Morat* (ממורט, who is associated with the circle of R. Judah *he-Hasid*; see I. Ta-Shma, *Knesset Mehqarim*, 245–48, and below, chapter 3), n. 1. Yehudah *mi-Vermaiza*, Troestlein *ha-Navi*, R. Solomon of Chateau Landon (קצטלנדון, a student of R. Yehi'el of Paris and R. Hayyim Palti'el; see S. Emanuel, *Shivrei Luhot*, 31, 198, and below, chapter 4, n. 146.), and R. Asher *ha-Levi* of Osnabruck (fols. 58r, and 61v, identified by the compiler as his uncle), as well as a series of lesser or otherwise unknown rabbinic figures (cf. my "Bein Yeshivot Ba'alei ha-Tosafot le-Battei Midrash Aherim be-Ashkenaz Bimei ha-Benayim," 104–6).

194 Cf. Zunz, *ZGL*, 94–95, and below, nn. 217–18.

195 See ms. B.M. 9931, fol. 171v: 'ארור מכה רעהו בסתר. שיש למנוע לעשות בגלוי. שדיינים יענשוהו כדאמ' התוקע לחבירו נותן לו מנה . . . ושם בסתר. שאם היה עושה בגלוי ימיתוהו ב"ד ודבר הכתוב בהוה. Cf. the commentaries of Ibn Ezra, Yosef *Bekhor Shor*, and *Hizzequni*, and *Rashbam's Commentary on Deuteronomy*, ed. Lockshin, 153–54.

the sixth and the beginning of the seventh year—and that similarly *Hakhel*, which is held on *Sukkot* after the end of the sabbatical year, is still identified (in Deut. 31:10) as "at the time of *shemitah*"—R. Teitav explains why the Torah (in Deut. 31:12) mandates the presence of women and children in Jerusalem only for *Hakhel*. In the other years of the agricultural cycle, these groups of people were needed at home, to take in the wheat and vegetables and other produce of the fields that had been harvested, making sure that these items were properly stored so that they would not rot or be stolen. Thus only the men were obligated to go to Jerusalem for the *Sukkot* festival each year. At the end of the year of *shemitah*, however, when all the produce was still ownerless (*hefker*), and could not be harvested and stored (and the women and children had, in any case, not been to Jerusalem for six years), the women and children were required to come to Jerusalem to listen and learn. No one had to worry then about the fields at all, and everyone was able to go together. This is a kind of *ta'amei ha-mizvot* or *derekh 'erez* approach, offered on the basis of the agricultural realia.[196]

In Deuteronomy 32:14, R. Teitav explains the phrase "with the fat of the kidneys of wheat" (עם חלב כליות חטה) along linguistic lines. The *kelayot* (kidneys) connote desire, as in Psalms 84:3, "my soul desires" (כלתה נפשי); 2 Samuel 13:39, "and David desired to go out to Avshalom" (ותכל דוד, in addition to other verses); the Targum Yerushalmi to the verse in Daniel 9:23, "for you are desirous" (כי חמודות אתה); and perhaps to Genesis 2:2, *va-yekhal E-lohim*, "and God completed his work." This grammatical or literal approach to Deuteronomy 32:14, that this wheat produce is much desired, is again an expanded version of Rashbam's comment to this verse ("the coveted, choice wheat"). Rashbam also cites the same prooftexts from Samuel and Psalm 84 (and another from Ps. 73:26, "my body yearns," כלה), although he does not include the Targum Yonatan passage.[197] R. Yom Tov has similarly nuanced

[196] See ms. B.M. 9931, fol. 176v. This approach is found in the commentaries of *Bekhor Shor* and *Ḥizzequni* (unattributed), in briefer form. *Bekhor Shor* also interprets *lefi ha-peshat* that the children (*taf*) are youngsters aged 14 or 15 (rather than babies and toddlers, as per the rabbinic interpretation). See *Perushei R. Yosef Bekhor Shor 'al ha-Torah*, ed. Y. Nevo (Jerusalem, 1994), 381 (Deut. 31, 10–12), and cf. Naḥmanides' commentary to Deut. 31:14. For a similar kind of interpretation based on agricultural realia (and *ta'amei ha-miḥvot*), see below, chapter 3, nn. 75–76.

[197] See ms. B.M. 9931, fol. 178v. *Ḥizzequni* presents the approach of Rashbam, as well as the differing approach of R. Yosef *Bekhor Shor*, that these crops are similar to kidneys because of the narrowings and creases in them. (R. Yosef *Bekhor Shor*'s prooftext comes from Ezekiel 27:17.) Cf. *Rashbam's Commentary to Deuteronomy*, ed. Lockshin, 180. See also ms. B.M. 9931, fol. 180v, (to Deut. 32:37), ואמר האומות אי אלהימו של האומות. וחבירו סלו סלו. This appears to be similar to the interpretation reproduced in *Ḥizzequni*, but against that of Rashbam and *Bekhor Shor* (and Ramban).

linguistic and ideational interpretations for the blessings of Zevulun (Deut. 33:19) and Gad (33:20).[198]

R. Teitav connects the two phrases in the blessing of Joseph found in the first half of Deuteronomy 33:16 (*umi-meged ʾereẓ u-meloʾah u-reẓon shokhni seneh*), that the land's produce and vegetation would be plentiful as a manifestation or sign of the One who appeared in the burning bush, in a somewhat more nuanced way than Rashi did. Rashi explains that the blessings or fullness of the land occur only with the acquiescence of the Almighty, who first appeared to Moses in the burning bush. R. Teitav accepts the first aspect (without mentioning Rashi by name), that the fullness of the crops in the fields is not possible without the will of God, and he finds additional biblical support for this from Judges 6:3–4. R. Teitav then adds, however, that God's presence in the treetops helped David in his battle with the Philistines (2 Samuel 5:24), as had been the case with the burning bush and Egypt, and he again supports his approach with a citation from the Targum.[199] Here too,

[198] See ms. B.M. 9931, fol. 183v: קוריהו . . . כאשה מניקתה את בנה בחלב יושבים מניק יהיה ה"פ יינקו. וינקתם גוים בזכור וכן ושבעתם תינקו למען יניקה. This interpretation is found in abbreviated form in the printed edition of *Paʿaneaḥ Raza*, 561, in the name of *Teitav*. The next comment in ms. B.M. 9931, to the verse *barukh marḥiv Gad* (פי' ברוך כל מי שמרחיב דרך לגד כדי שלא יפגע בו, שהרי כל הפוגע בו לרעה אינו נמלט כמו שנ' וטרף זרוע אף קדקד ודומה ללביא שאין אדם רשאי לעמוד כנגדו. תיטב), appears in similarly abbreviated from in the printed edition but without the identifier *Teitav*. On the powers of the lion according to this formulation, cf. *Quntres zekher ʿasah le-nifleʾotav le-R. Yehudah he-Ḥasid*, in I. Ta-Shma, *Knesset Meḥqarim*, 1:197–98. The printed edition of *Paʿaneaḥ Raza* does not cite comments of *Teitav* to two other places in this chapter (verses 1 and 4), which are found in ms. B.M. 9931. In verse 1 (fol. 182r), R. Yom Tov notes that Moses is referred to specifically here as *ʾish ha-Elohim* to indicate that these blessings were not delivered by Moses on his own account but were transmitted to him by the Almighty, or to suggest that Moses's blessings were worthy of being fulfilled since he was a true man of God; cf. the commentary of Ibn Ezra. In verse 4, R. Teitav puts forward Moses's status as a king of Israel (as reflected in 33:5, ויהי בישורון מלך as well, and in other verses). R. Teitav's approach is against Rashi's (and *Bekhor Shor*'s) interpretation of 33:5, that God is the King of Israel in context here, but this is the approach taken by Ibn Ezra, and cf. *Ḥizzequni*.

[199] See ms. B.M. 9931, fol. 183r: ארץ ומלואה. תבואה הגדילה בבקעה כגון שדה הלבן ואם אין רצונו של מקום מה מועיל כל אלה הענין שנ' אם זרע ישראל ועלה מדין ועמלק ובני קדם וישחיתו את יבול הארץ [שופטים ו: ג-ד]. לכך נאמ' ורצון שוכני סנה רצון הקב"ה שנגלה אליו בסנה. והזכיר שכינתו על אילנות מפני אותה חרבה שנגלה על הסנה. לכך כתוב ויהי כשמעך את קול צעדה בראשי הבכאים (שמואל ב', ה:כד) תר'[גום] האילנות שתשמש שם השכינה בימי פלשתים. תיט"ב. Cf. Rashi's commentary to 2 Samuel 5:24. Throughout his comments to the Torah, R. Yom Tov's extensive use of both *Nakh* and Targum is striking. As Rashi did, the twelfth-century *pashtanim* (including Rashbam and Qara) wrote commentaries to many biblical books outside the Pentateuch (and all the extant comments of R. Eliezer of Beaugency are to prophetic works, as are several other compilatory *peshat* commentaries from the early thirteenth century). While R. Yosef *Bekhor Shor* authored a commentary to Psalms (which is only partially extant) and to perhaps other biblical books as well, only R. Isaiah di Trani commented on a significant number of works beyond the Pentateuch among the group of late twelfth- and thirteenth-century Tosafist exegetes under discussion in these chapters. See below, chapter 3, nn. 97, 110, 120.

R. Teitav's approach is similar (although not identical) to that of R. Yosef *Bekhor Shor.*[200]

R. Yom Tov occasionally confirms interpretations of Rashi (and expands upon them) in both narrative and halakhic contexts,[201] although not nearly to the extent that R. Jacob of Orleans does. Rather, closer to the more creative style of R. Yosef *Bekhor Shor* (who also works with Rashi's commentary as we have seen), R. Yom Tov mainly puts forward his own interpretations. Like *Bekhor Shor*, R. Yom Tov's *peshat* interpretations sometimes parallel those of Rashbam. And like Rashbam, R. Yom Tov relies heavily on other verses throughout the Bible as the arbiters of biblical linguistics and style (in addition to various citations from the Aramaic *targumim*). Although R. Yom Tov also puts forward ideas about *ta'amei ha-mizvot* in his comments to the Torah (as we shall see in what follows), he is certainly not as committed to a systematic search for *'omeq peshuto shel miqra* as Rashbam was.[202]

[200] See *Perushei R. Yosef Bekhor Shor*, ed. Nevo, 396. *Bekhor Shor* also presents Rashi's approach in brief form but goes on to suggest (*lefi peshuto*) that the Almighty wishes to dwell among the bushes in the land of Joseph rather than within the towering cedars of other lands. *Bekhor Shor* also links these two ideas. The Will of God (who dwelled in the burning bush) will now in effect reside in the area of Joseph, as represented by Joshua and Shiloh. In addition, *Bekhor Shor* notes that most of the kings of Israel came from the tribe of Ephraim (son of Joseph).

[201] See, e.g., ms. B.M. 9931, fol. 157v: כי בגלל הדבר הזה יברכך ה' א-להיך בשמינית בכל מעשה ידיך. בתוספתא דפאה [ד:יז] גרסי' אמ' ליתן ונתן נותנין לו שכר אמירה ושכר מעשה. אמ' ליתן ולא הספיק בידו ליתן נותנים לו שכר אמירה כשכר מעשה. לא אמ' ליתן אבל אומ' לאחרים תנו נותנים לו שכר על כך שנ' בגלל הדבר הזה. תיט"ב. R. Yom Tov extends Rashi's point (based on the *Sifrei*), according to a fuller citation of a passage in the *Tosefta.* See also ms. Leiden 27, fol. 55v (found similarly in *Tosafot ha-Shalem*, ed. Gellis, 7:90–91, sec. 6, based on the published edition of the Tosafist Torah compilation *Hadar Zeqenim*). Some question Rashi's interpretation of *shiv'at yamim mazot tokhelu* (Ex. 12:15), in which he compares this phrase to *sheshet yamim tokhal mazot* (in Ex. 16:8), and concludes that there is no obligation to eat *mazah* on the seventh day of Passover, although *hamez* may still not be eaten. Indeed, Rashi proceeds to derive that the obligation to eat *mazah* is limited to the first day of Passover alone. Although R. Isaac of Evreux emends Rashi's derivation, "R. Yom Tov confirms *perush Rashi*." For R. Isaac of Evreux's more midrash-oriented exegetical style, see below, chapter 4.

[202] On *ta'amei ha-mizvot* in Rashbam's commentary, see E. Touitou, *Exegesis in Perpetual Motion*, 180–88. For a very different exegetical approach by R. Yom Tov, see ms. Parma 541, fol. 86r–v (to Nu. 3:39, *'asher paqad Mosheh ve-Aharon*). The word *ve-Aharon* has masoretic dots above it, which Rashi understands (on the basis of a *Baraita* cited in *Bekhorot* 4a) to reflect the fact that Aaron was not included in the census of the Levites: שמעתי מר' יום טוב לפיכך נקוד על אהרן שלפי שלא מנה את הלויים בצווי של הקב"ה כי פקודת הלויים לא נצטוית אלא למשה בלבד כמו שנ' ויאמר ה' אל משה פקוד את בני לוי. וכאן כתו' אשר פקד משה ואהרן על פי ה' ואהרן לא היה על פי ה', לכך נקוד עליו. אבל לגבי פקודת בני ישראל נאמרה למשה ולאהרן שנ' תפקדו אותם אתה ואהרן על כן אינו נקוד בפקודת בני ישראל; see also below for additional examples. (For similar attention to masoretic conventions in the exegesis of R. Yeḥi'el of Paris, see below, chapter 4, n. 144). See also ms. Vatican 138, fol. 19v (end, to Nu. 3:15, *peqod 'et benei Levi*): משה חילק לאהרן כבוד ולקחו למנותם. אבל למנות כל ישראל הוא נצטוה שנ' תפקדו אותם לצבאותם אתה ואהרן. This is found much more briefly in the name of R. Teitav, in the published edition of *Pa'aneaḥ Raza*, ed. Machon Torat ha-Rishonim, 409.

The material from R. Teitav included in ms. St. Petersburg EVR I 22 begins in the Book of Leviticus, and an analysis of several passages from that manuscript follows.[203] Rashi notes at the beginning of Leviticus (1:2), following *Sifra*, that the Torah lists specific types of domestic animals that can be brought as sacrifices (צאן, בקר, בהמה) in order to exclude kosher animals of the wild (חיות) from being brought as sacrifices. Without citing Rashi by name, R. Teitav offers an explanation for this exclusion on the basis of rabbinic thought. According to a passage in *Midrash Tadshe* (which is cited by Rashi in his commentary to Gen. 1:22), nondomesticated animals (*ḥayyot*) as a group did not receive a blessing, during the account of the Creation, that they should be fruitful and multiply, since God knew that the snake would behave improperly. Thus with respect to sacrifices as well, the *ḥayyah* is not acceptable. In addition, there are two practical corollaries: the *ḥelev* (fat) of kosher *ḥayyot* is permissible for consumption, even as the *ḥelev* of domesticated animals (*behemot*, which are acceptable for sacrifices) is not. And similarly, since a *ḥayyah* cannot be brought on the sacrifical altar, its blood (as opposed to that of a *behemah*) must be covered at the time of ritual slaughter. At the same time kosher fish cannot be brought as any type of sacrifice, since it has neither blood nor fat.[204]

Imitating the *peshuto shel miqra* approach taken by Rashi (although without mentioning his name, and employing a different set of details), R. Teitav presents several ways to explain the Torah's unusual phrase prohibiting slanderous speech (לא תלך רכיל בעמך; Lev. 19:16). His preferred interpretation, presented on the basis of the Targum (once again) as "do not eat cakes," reflects the notion that bearers of evil speech accomplish their mission by eating in the homes of those who wish to hear their damaging words. R. Teitav supports the Targumic interpretation with linguistic proofs from both biblical and rabbinic texts.[205]

203 There is at least one reference in this manuscript to רי"ט (fol. 47v, following a comment by Ibn Ezra to Ex. 20:3) that does not connote R. Yom Tov of Joigny. See *Tosafot ha-Shalem*, ed. Gellis, 8:84, sec. 2.

204 See ms. St. Petersburg EVR I 22, fol. 63r. This explanation is then followed by a passage from *Sifra*, which suggests simply that God did not wish to trouble His children by making them bring sacrifices from the hard-to-catch *ḥayyot* but rather from the much more easily catchable *behemot*. This *Sifra* is cited R. Yosef *Bekhor Shor* in his commentary (ed. Nevo, 184), and see also *Ḥizzequni*. On *ta'amei ha-mizvot* in the Torah commentary of *Bekhor Shor*, cf. above, nn. 51, 100, 135.

205 See ms. St. Petersburg, fol. 80v. Cf. Rashi (that the gossip is like a spy, and רכיל is a variant of the root רג"ל) and Rashbam (that the gossip is like a peddler, who goes from city to city hawking his merchandise); cf. *Rashbam's Commentary to Leviticus and Numbers*, ed. Lockshin, 103. R. Yom Tov of Joigny does something quite similar here, both linguistically and conceptually. Note the fuller version of this passage, found in yet another version of *Pa'aneaḥ Raza*, ms.

R. Teitav's understanding of the woman whom Moses married (כי אשה כושית לקח), which raised the ire of Miriam (Nu. 12:1), follows that of Rashbam, who argues that this woman was not Ẓipporah, as Rashi and others maintained. Rather, according to R. Teitav, Ẓipporah had died, and Moses married another woman to serve him. He was careful to marry her, however, only for this purpose, and not for the purpose of having relations with her (which also accords with Rashbam's analysis), and thus did not even know about her physical appearance or her origins. Miriam and Aaron, however, were not aware of this arrangement, and they therefore criticized Moses.[206]

A polemical comment attributed to R. Yom Tov (on a verse toward the beginning of the Book of Genesis) also bears mentioning. On the complex verse of Genesis 6:6, "and the Almighty regretted [or comforted Himself, following Rashi], that He created man" (וינחם ה' כי עשה את האדם), "and the Almighty was saddened [or the Almighty caused man to be saddened, following Rashi]" (ויתעצב אל לבו),[207] a northern French Tosafist Torah compilation notes that Christian polemicists cited this verse (among other verses) as a proof that God regrets or rethinks His covenant and changes His utterances. "But R. Yom Tov explains that this expression means to convey that the Almighty was comforted that He had created man in the earthly realm, so that man's heart absorbed all the sadness that had been generated by his own actions. Had man been created in the heavenly realm, the angels would have been saddened, as would their Creator." R. Yom Tov follows the interpretation of Rashi in its first part (which also effectively responds to the Christian claim), but he suggests an even more tightly contextual explanation for the Almighty's comfort than Rashi does. The Almighty decided to

---

Parma 1051 (fol. 81v): לא תלך רכיל. למה נקט לשון הילוך לפי שהנחש היה רכיל ונקצצו רגליו. לכך רכיל שלא יארע לו כדרך שאירע לנחש. ורבותי' פי' לילך לביתו ולשמוע ולומר. ד"א לא תלך רכיל ומתרגמי' לא תיכול קורצין פי' לא תאכל עוגות כי דרך המלשינים לאכול בבית מקבל לשון הרע כדכתי' מחנפי לעגי מעג יד חרק עלי שנימו [תהלים לה:טז]. וקורצין עוגות כמו מקרצות זו בזו וכן השרץ בתנור והקרץ ביניהין וקורצין כמו קריצין פני פטורין כי מתחלף. תיט"ב.

[206] Ms. St. Petersburg, fol. 97v. Once again, a fuller version is found in ms. Parma 1051, fol. 100v: מתה צפורה ולקח אשה אחרת לשרתו ולא לתשמיש . . . ועל שם שזאת היתה מזרע חם ובני חם כוש ומצרים לכן גינוהו מרים ואהרן. ומשה לא ידע שכושית היא שלא שימש עמה. תיט"ב. Cf. the comment by Rashbam: הכושית שהיא ממשפחת חם . . . כדכתיב ב[ספר מדרש] דברי הימים דמשה רבנו, שמלך בארץ כוש ארבעים שנה ולקח מלכה אחת ולא שכב עמה כמו שכתוב שם, והם לא ידעו כשדיברו בו שלא נזקק לה. זהו עיקר פשוטו. שאם בשביל צפורה דיברו, מה צורך לפרש כי אשה כושית לקח וכי [עד] עתה לא ידענו כי צפורה מדינית היא. Ramban essentially agrees with Rashbam's objections, while Ibn Ezra entertains both possibilities (but prefers the possibility that it does refer to Ẓipporah). *Bekhor Shor* (Nevo, 258) suggests an entirely different kind of *peshat* here.

[207] This simple interpretation of the verse (reflected in the initial translation here), as an example of *dibrah Torah ki-leshon bnei ʾadam*, is suggested by both Ibn Ezra and Ramban. Rashi, in his first explanation (following the Targum) reverses the meaning: The Almighty was comforted that He had created man in the earthly realm and had not placed him in the heavenly realm, where he would have caused a rebellion, and He decided to make man sad.

sadden man because he had engendered such sadness himself. Fortunately for the world, this sadness did not extend into the heavenly realm, but remained only in the heart of man.[208]

We now turn to the collection of interpretations by R. Yom Tov found in ms. Munich 50. At the beginning of *parashat Miqez*, Rashi interprets (following *Midrash Rabbah*) that the shaving of Joseph as he was taken to meet to Pharaoh (Gen, 41:14) was done to give proper honor to royalty (*kevod ha-malkhut*). R. Teitav wonders, according to the talmudic datum that Joseph was released from jail on Rosh ha-Shanah (found in tractate *Rosh ha-Shanah* 11a), how could Joseph be shaved on *yom tov*? He suggests that Joseph's release did occur on Rosh ha-Shanah itself, but that he did not appear before Pharaoh until the next day, and thus had the opportunity to be shaved after the holiday was over. However, R. Teitav also allows that the "fear of the kingship" might have been sufficient to allow Joseph to be shaved by others on the day of Rosh ha-Shanah itself.[209] The interpretation attributed here to R. Teitav, which seeks to reconcile a talmudic source with the biblical text (and perhaps to explain Rashi's interpretation in addition), is found in another manuscript in the name of R. Yosef Qara.[210]

R. Yom Tov poses a *peshat*-oriented question (and response) on Genesis 42:6, where the Torah notes that Joseph was both the ruler (*shalit*) and the provider (*mashbir*) for all of Egypt. Since these two titles were now in the hands of the same person, it would seem to be unecessary to list both of them. R. Teitav provides an intrigue-filled answer, which focuses on the realia of the day. The brothers considered buying their wheat from agents or middlemen, who would typically buy supplies of wheat directly from Joseph and then sell it to others outside of Egypt for a profit. In doing this,

208 See ms. Bodl. 270 (IMHM #1673), *Ḥiddushei Ẓarefat* (Ashkenaz, late thirteenth century; on the similarity of this collection to the published edition of *Hadar Zeqenim*, see Poznanski, *Mavo ʿal Ḥakhmei Ẓarefat Mefarshei ha-Miqra*, CVIII1), fol. 3r: וינחם ה' כי עשה את האדם. כאן המינים פוקרים . . . ואו' הרי"ט דהכי קאמר וינחם כי עשה כלו' נמחה היא לפניו מן מה שעשאו בארץ דעל ידי כך כל העצבון יהיה אל לבו של אדם, דאי עשאו בשמים היה העצבון אל לבו של המלאכים ואל מי שבראו. ולפיכך קאי ויתעצב אל לבו אל לבו של אדם. See also *Sefer Yosef ha-Meqanne*, ed. Rosenthal, 37–38. Cf. *Tosafot ha-shalem*, ed. Gellis, 1:189–90, sec. 4, for two related manuscript versions (without attribution), and 1:189, sec. 1 (where both printed and manuscript texts attribute this interpretation to ר"ש, which is perhaps a miscopied version of ר' יו"ט); and see also *Perushei R. Ḥayyim Paltiʾel*, ed Lange, 14, 457–48. On R. Yom Tov's polemical comments, see also *Sefer Yosef ha-Meqanne*, 31 (to Gen. 1:26), where R. Yom Tov suggests (in an exegetical strategy similar to that of R. Yosef *Bekhor Shor*), that the plural verb *naʿaseh* is found only with regard to the creation of man. For R. Yom Tov, Moses is speaking here, saying that God commanded us to create man (i.e., human beings will give birth to man). See *Tosafot ha-Shalem*, ed. Gellis, 1:2–63, sec. 16; E. Touitou, *Exegesis in Perpetual Motion*, 121 (n. 24); and cf. R. Harris, "Awareness of Biblical Redaction" (above, n. 50), 289–310.

209 Ms. Munich 50, fol. 84v.

210 See ms. JTS Lutzki 791 (fol. 42r), cited in *Tosafot ha-Shalem*, ed. Gellis, 4:127.

the brothers would have been able to avoid any direct contact with Joseph, whom they feared might try to accuse them of nefarious actions (as he ultimately did). Joseph, for his part, anticipated his brothers' thinking, and therefore ordered that all those coming to Egypt to buy wheat were permitted to buy only directly from his supply, and only according to their own needs. In this way, no agents could become involved with any resales. Thus Joseph was literally (and this was noteworthy) both the ruler and the provider, since he personally provided the wheat to all those who were in need and collected their monies, without the possibility of any middlemen.[211]

When Jacob heard from his sons that Joseph was still alive, and he saw the royal wagons laden with provisions that Joseph had sent him, his reaction is phrased as רב עוד יוסף בני חי (Gen. 45:28). The word *rav* is somewhat difficult to interpret in context. Rashi understands it to mean that "I will have much additional joy," since it was now clear that Joseph was still alive, and both Ibn Ezra and R. Yosef *Bekhor Shor* (following Targum Onkelos) interpreted this word in similar fashion. Rashbam suggests that this word connotes that "it is enough" time that my heart has been depressed, for it is now certain that Joseph is alive. Rashbam adds that "other interpretations [*peshatot*] have been suggested here, but they are contrived and foolish [*hevel*]."[212] Another *peshat* approach, attributed to R. Teitav by ms. Munich 50, is appended to Rashbam's commentary in the name of *'ani ha-za'ir*: "You [my sons] say that Joseph is alive and that he is a ruler in Egypt; it is enough (*rav*) that he is still alive, even if he is not a ruler."[213] The question remains whether R. Yom Tov is himself the "צעיר" who added this comment directly to the commentary of Rashbam.[214]

211 Ms. Munich 50, fols. 86v–87r: ויבאו בני ישראל לשבור בתוך הבאים וכתיב בתריה ויוסף הוא השליט והוא המשביר. והק' הר''ר י''ט ומה בא זה להשמיענו הכא שיוסף הוא השליט וכי איני יודע שהוא המשביר? אלא הכי פי' ר' יו''ט מיוני וי''ל דבא להשמיענו משום דכתי' בתוך הבאים [78א] פי' הבא לשבור תבואה מיוסף כדי להרויח בה ולמכרו לאחרים בדמים יקרים. ואחי יוסף אמרו נקנה מן הבאים לקנות תבואה ובמצרים לא נבוא, שמא יפגע בנו יוסף שנמכר למצרים ויקבול עלינו שגנבנו אותו ומסרנו אותו. ויותר טוב שניתן לאלו הבאים לקנות תבואה תדיר במעט רווח ולא נצטרך לבוא למצרים. והרגיש יוסף בדבר ואמ' שמא יקנו אחיו מן הבאים הנה וצוה לבאים אחר התבואה שלא יקנה יותר מכדי צורכם ולא ימכרו לאחרים וצוה לכל עובר ושב שלא יקנה אלא ממנו ומאז בעל כרחם יבואו לשם אחי יוסף וצריכים לקנות ממנו ובזה משמע כאן שיוסף הוא השליט והוא המשביר כי בעצמו היה מוסר לכולם. ה''ר יום טוב. See also *Tosafot ha-Shalem*, ed. Gellis, vol. 4, 152–53, sec. 1; *Ḥizzequni*, who presents a briefer form of this interpretation without attribution; and above, n. 9. This interpretation is found in *Moshav Zeqenim* to Gen. 42:3 in the name of Ri (שאל הר''י . . . ופי'), although it is also properly attributed in ms. B.M. 9931, fol. 21v, to R. Yom Tov of Joigny: שאל ה''ר יום טוב מיוני מה בא להשמיענו כאן שיוסף הוא השליט והוא המשביר לכולם. וכי איני יודע שהוא שליט והוא המשביר משום דכתי' לשבר בתוך הבאים ופי' הבאים לקנות תבואה מיוסף וכו'.

212 Cf. *Rabbi Samuel b. Meir's Commentary on Genesis*, ed. M. Lockshin, 322.

213 See ms. Munich 50, fol. 91v. R. Teitav's comment appears without attribution in several Tosafist Torah compilations still in manuscript, and in *Minḥat Yehudah* (see *Tosafot ha-Shalem*, ed. Gellis, 4:233, sec. 4), and in the *Ḥizzequni* commentary as well.

214 Cf. *Perush ha-Torah 'asher katav ha-Rashbam*, ed. Rosin, 65 (note ב, and n. 15).

R. Teitav explains Pharaoh's comment to Joseph (which combines several seemingly diverse elements) similarly: "And if you know that there are men of distinction [*ʾanshei ḥayyil*] among them, you may place them as officers over my flocks" (Gen. 47:6). Rashi understands the term *ʾanshei ḥayyil* to mean that they are very capable in their profession as shepherds.[215] Rashbam understands the phrase to mean that they are worthy (*reʾuyim*) in terms of both bravery and leadership, as in the verse describing Ruth (Ruth 3:11), "for you are an *ʾeshet ḥayyil*." Extending these two approaches (and displaying a clear sense of realia that is typical of Rashbam's exegetical use of *derekh ʾereẓ*, if not *Bekhor Shor*'s use of *derekh ha-ḥayyim*), R. Teitav notes that shepherds must typically traverse deserts and areas that are frequented by wild animals and dangerous robbers. Also, the sheep sometimes fall into faults and crevices, and bravery is required to extract them.[216]

The comments by R. Yom Tov of Joigny to the Book of Genesis found in ms. Munich 50 relate only to the concluding *parashiyyot* of the book, those that deal with Joseph, his rise to power in Egypt, and his reunion with Jacob. Nonetheless, as we have seen, this manuscript presents a noticeable cluster of comments on these portions, although it remains unclear whether R. Teitav's comments were gathered in some kind of treatise or simply reported here in his name. A similar pattern emerges in this manuscript with respect to the Book of Exodus. Before *parashat Ki Tissa*, less than a handful of comments are included,[217] although there are additional scattered

[215] *Ḥizzequni* adopts this interpretation of Rashi, noting that *ḥayyil* connotes broad competence that does not have a military dimension (similar to the connotation of the phrase *ʾeshet ḥayyil mi yimẓa*, in Proverbs 31:10). See also Radak and *Gur Aryeh*, ad loc.

[216] See ms. Munich 50, fol. 93r, and cf. *Tosafot ha-Shalem*, ed. Gellis, vol. 4, 253. Rashbam's comment is followed by a note, ואני הצעיר מצאתי תרגום, שרי מקנה רבני חילא ואין צורך לפירוש רבינו; see *Perush ha-Rashbam*, ed. Rosin, 66 (note ג, and n. 13), and cf. above, n. 214. *Minhat Yehudah* cites R. Moses of Coucy who, like *Ḥizzequni*, considers and rejects the confluence of military bravery and shepherding. Later in the same folio in Munich 50, a contextual interpretation by R. Teitav (on Gen. 47:14) is found: ויבא יוסף את הכסף ביתה פרעה. שלא יחשדוהו שיעשיר את אחיו ובית אביו מן הממון שאסף במוכרו התבואה לארץ. תיט"ב. Cf. *Tosafot ha-Shalem*, ed. Gellis, 4:257, sec. 2 (citing *Moshav Zeqenim*, which presents this interpretation without attribution). A similar kind of contextual interpretation by R. Teitav is found in ms. Munich 50 on fol. 95r (to Gen. 48:8, "and [Jacob] asked who are they"), which is again quite similar to those of Rashbam and Ibn Ezra (and different from that of Rashi): [וירא ישראל את בני יוסף] ויאמר מי אלה. רואה ואינו רואה, מכיר ואינו מכיר, לפיכך לא רצה לברך בטעות, לכך שאל. תיט"ב; and cf. *Tosafot ha-Shalem*, ed. Gellis, 5:17–18. See also fol. 100r (Genesis 50:5), בקברי אשר כריתי. לשון סעודה, כלו' כסעודה אשר נתתי לעשו קניתי קברי, כמו ויכרה להם כרה גדולה [מלכים ב', ו:כג] (and cf. *Tosafot ha-Shalem*, 5:84); and (also on) fol. 100r (to Genesis 50:10): ויעש לאביו אבל שבעת ימים. כל זמן שהיה מתו מוטל לפניו הוי אונן ולא אבל לפי שספדו שם מספד גדול וכתב כאן הצדיק גרם לו ושלוחי מצוה היו. לכך הזכיר אבל גדול.

[217] See ms. Munich 50, fol. 117r (Ex. 12:31), ויקרא למשה ולאהרן לילה. יכול שדחקו לצאת בלילה ת"ל ואתם לא תצאו איש מפתח ביתו עד בקר. תיט"ב, and fol. 120v (Ex. 14:19): ויסע מלאך הא-להים. ולמעלה הוא אומר וה' הולך לפניהם וכו' הרי שנתן למלאך רשות להשחית בשמו של הקב"ה כאילו הוא בעצמו וכן מצינו בכמה מקומות. וילך מאחריהם. ותימ' הלא במקום אחד קורא למלאך עמוד הענן וכתוב בו ויעמד. אך עמוד אש בא בתחלת

references to interpretations of R. Teitav on prior portions of the Book of Exodus in other manuscripts.[218] One of these, an interpretation of the Torah's legal procedure for piercing the ear of an *ʿeved ʿivri*, again follows the (*peshat*) strategy of *derekh ʾereẓ*. The ear was pierced in the doorway of the owner so that neither the slave nor another owner could make fraudulent claims about the ownership of the slave. The ear was not commonly subject to injury, thereby short-circuiting a false claim that he was not a slave and that his blemish had been caused by an injury rather than by his owner's act of piercing. At the same time, another owner could not make a claim on this slave, since the piercing of the slave's ear matched only the doorpost of his true owner.[219]

Beginning with *parashat Ki Tissa*, however, we find another cluster of comments from R. Teitav in this manuscript. On Exodus 30:12, concerning whether the Levites (who were not included in the regular census of the people) still had to contribute the half *shekel*, R. Teitav suggests that, according to the view that the Levites were required to contribute, they had to give the half *shekel* for every child who reached the age of one month (the age from which the Levites were counted in their special census), even as Israelites had to give the half *shekel* only from the age of twenty, which is the age at which they were counted.[220]

Next come a series of comments on Moses's request to apprehend the Almighty (Ex. 33:18; הראני נא את כבודך). R. Teitav notes that Moses's request

---

הלילה ולכך קראהו מלאך שיורד עתה משמים כדי להאיר. ובלכתו אחריהם להאיר למצרים כי עמוד הענן מפסיק ביניהם כי הוא נוסע לפניהם פי' לפני מצרים ועומד אחריהם פי' מאחרי ישראל כדי להפסיק. ובזה הפי' יתיישב הכל. בשם החסיד ה"ר יום טוב. Cf. *Tosafot ha-Shalem*, ed. Gellis, 7:196–97, secs. 3, 4, 7, for similar questions and interpretations by Rashbam, R. Isaiah di Trani, and ms. Hamburg 45 (below, chapter 4, n. 193). See also fol. 124v (Ex. 17:9), וצא הלחם בעמלק. פי' צא חוץ למחנה שלא יבואו עלינו תחת הגבעה. ואותה הגבעה הוא הצור שהכה משה. תיט"ב.

[218] See, e.g., ms. Leiden 27, fol 55v (above, n. 204), and ms. B.M. 9931, fol. 37v (above, n. 127).

[219] See ms. Florence-Laurenziana, Plut II 20 (IMHM #20365), fol. 195v (in a section of the commentary that is associated with R. Yeḥi'el of Paris; see S. Emanuel, *Shivrei Luḥot*, 187, and below, chapter 4): ורצע אדוניו את אזנו במרצע. וה"ר יום טוב מפרש לפי הפשט אוזן דנקט לפי שאם היה רוצעו במקום אחר יכול לומר העבד חתרתי עצמי. אבל באוזן, אין זה מקום שיוכל העבד לומר דבר זה אז הוא ניכר לעבדו. וכזה מפרש לפי הפשט את הדלת, שאם היה רוצעו בדבר אחר יוכל אדם לערער עליו לומר שלי הוא. אבל עכשיו מדת אזנו ניכרת בדלת אדוניו. Just prior in this manuscript, a similar interpretation to that of Rashi is suggested, that the ear was chosen because it had heard at Sinai not to steal (and theft was often the cause of an individual's being sold initially into slavery). R. Teitav's *derekh ʾereẓ* approach here is even more practical and detailed than those of Rashbam and *Bekhor Shor*. See *Rashbam's Commentary on Exodus*, ed. M. Lockshin, 229–30.

[220] Ms. Munich 50, fol. 162v–163r: זה יתנו כל העובר. י"מ כל העובר על מנינא ולא נמנו שבט לוי. וי"מ כל דעבר בימא ואפי' שבט לוי נתנו. ורבותינו דרשו ז"ה י"ב מלמד שי"ב [שבטים] יתנו. מה"ר משה [וכן הוא בפענח רזא הנדפס, עמ' רצז.] ולפי ש"ס אתי שפיר דנתינה לא היה אלא לצורך קרבנות. ועי"ל דלמ"ד היו [הלוים] שוקלים יש לפרש הפקודים לכל חד וחד, כדיני ישראל מבן עשרים ולוי מבן חדש. תיט"ב. This is a fairly simple approach to the verse, which takes the talmudic discussion into account as well.

was itself somewhat inappropriate (*she-lo ka-halakhah*), as expressed by the Tanna R. Yehoshua b. Qorhah (in *Berakhot* 7a), who notes that the Almighty in effect said to Moses at this point, "When I wanted to reveal myself to you [at the burning bush], you did not want to see me" (Ex. 3:6; ויסתר משה פניו כי ירא מהביט אל א-להים). And yet Moses was apparently never punished or even censured for this request.[221] Indeed, R. Teitav maintains that the goodness that the Almighty passed over the face of Moses (Ex. 33:19) consisted of the rays of His splendor, which in turn radiated from the face of Moses when he descended with the second set of tablets (Ex. 34:29).[222]

In a highly original and suggestive comment, R. Teitav interprets the phrase *ki lo yir'ani ha-'adam va-ḥai*, "that no man can see Me and live" (Ex. 33:20), to mean that if a man were to see the Almighty, he would not wish

221 See ms. Munich 50, fol. 168r. Rashbam wonders how Moses had the temerity (היאך מלאו לבו) to ask to apprehend God now, since the Torah had essentially praised Moses when he hid his face away (in Ex. 3:6). Rashbam suggests that Moses undertook this initiative only to insure that the Divine covenant would remain intact on several levels (and see also Rashi). Rashbam is ostensibly following the conflicting view in *Berakhot* 7a of R. Samuel bar Nachmeni, in the name of R. Yonatan, that Moses was rewarded with a holy appearance (קלסתר פנים) that caused the Jewish people to be afraid to look at him, because he restrained himself from looking at the Almighty (and was afraid to do so) when He appeared to him in the burning bush. Cf. *Tosafot ha-Shalem*, ed. Gellis, 6:74, sec. 10 (and the passage cited there from *Midrash Tanḥuma*); *Perushei R. Ḥayyim Palti'el*, ed. Lange, 179, n. 19; M. Lockshin, *Rashbam's Commentary on Exodus* (Atlanta, 1997), 412, n. 26. *Pa'aneaḥ Raza*, 221 (to Ex. 3:6), in the name of R. Jacob (of Orleans?), highlights the completely contradictory conclusions and biblical interpretations that emerge from these two different talmudic interpretations (as does *Moshav Zeqenim*, 108 [to Ex. 3:6], without attribution). R. Isaiah di Trani (to Ex. 33:18, ed. Chavel, 49, cited also by *Moshav Zeqenim*, 215, in R. Isaiah's name) proposes a developmental or psychological solution to the exegetical problem raised here. Moses's shyness at the beginning of his career, when he covered his face because he was afraid to look (Ex. 3:6), was directly opposed to his more confrontational demeanor following the sin of the golden calf. R. Isaiah explains that, early on at the burning bush, Moses was insecure and not at all self-reliant. By the time the sin of the golden calf occurred, however, Moses had already dealt directly with the Divine presence and was confident that his righteousness would sustain him. See below, chapter 3. This interpretation is subsequently found (taking the two different Talmudic opinions into account and thereby resolving them) in ms. Hamburg 45; see *Tosafot ha-Shalem*, ed. Gellis, vol. 6:74–75, sec. 14. Without connecting the two biblical episodes, *Bekhor Shor* appears to follow this type of approach as well. In Ex. 3:6 (Nevo, 100), *Bekhor Shor* interprets Moses's fear as stemming from the custom that "the student should not raise his eyes and face in the presence of his teacher." In *Ki Tissa* (Nevo, 173) *Bekhor Shor* comments that Moses requested to see the Divine presence "since I wish to see and to hear." Clearly, Moses had evolved over time as a confidant of the Almighty. Cf. *Tosafot ha-Shalem*, ed. Gellis, 10:110–13.

222 See ms. Munich 50, fol. 168r. Just prior to the comment of R. Teitav, R. Judah *he-Ḥasid* is cited, applying a combined *sofei tevot*/א"ת ב"ש technique to the phrase אעביר כל טובי על פניך that yields the word נפשם. Cf. *Perushei R. Yehudah he-Ḥasid 'al ha-Torah*, ed. Y. S. Lange, 125 (the word טובי in א"ת ב"ש yields the word נפשם). These exegetical techniques, in turn, support the interpretation of this verse by the Talmud (*Menaḥot* 29b) that the Almighty would pass the souls of all the righteous before Moses (and forgive them). On these techniques in R. Judah's Torah commentary, see below, chapter 3.

to remain in this human world. Immediately upon seeing the Almighty and His Presence, the person would wish to die so that he could proceed to the world where the Divine Presence resides.[223] R. Yosef *Bekhor Shor* offered two interpretations of this phrase. The first (following *Sifrei*) is that no one can see God, neither man nor angels, who are also considered to be living beings, even though some of them may live forever. This is also the interpretation presented by Ibn Ezra in his long commentary to the Book of Exodus (in the name of *ʾaḥerim ʾomrim*). *Bekhor Shor* then presents a second approach in the name of *yesh mefarshim* (also found in the comment of Ibn Ezra, in the name of *yesh ʾomrim*), that if one does apprehend God, he will live forever. *Bekhor Shor* rebuts this interpretation by citing Judges 13:22, in which Manoaḥ tells his wife that "we will perish for we have seen God," which suggests that if man sees God, he will not live beyond that event but will die. Ibn Ezra likewise disparages this interpretation as being against the meaning of the text in Exodus 33:20 as well. Indeed, Ibn Ezra in this same passage had initially interpreted the verse in accordance with Manoaḥ's statement, that there can be no future life after one has seen God.[224] In any case, R. Yom Tov's interpretation surely stands out as a unique and sensitive interpretation of this verse.

Although the St. Petersburg manuscript records several substantive comments from R. Yom Tov to the first half of the Book of Leviticus (including some interactions with Rashi's commentary, as we have seen), there is only one very brief comment to this part of the Torah from R. Yom Tov found in ms. Munich 50.[225] The comments from R. Teitav in ms. Munich

[223] Ms. Munich 50, fol. 168r. The manuscript first cites a comment of the *Sifra*, noting that even angels cannot see Him: פי' ואפי' מלאכים בדאי' ת"כ. ועי"ל כי לא יראני האדם וחי כלומר לא יבקש להיות בעולם הזה כי מיד כשיראה אותו ושכינתו, יתאוה למות כדי לבוא אליו לאותו עולם. תיט"ב. In a comment to Ex. 33:21 (fol. 168v), R. Teitav explains the intent of the defective spelling of the term *kevodi* (כבדי) in Ex. 33:22: ועי"ל והיה בעבור כבודי כאדם הדומה ויעבור בזכוכית ואמ' חכמי' משה ראה באספקלריא המאירה ולכך כתי' כבודי חסר ו' שלא היה כבודו ממש אלא כמודרך באספקלריא. תיט"ב. Note also the similar interpretation presented in the name of R. Jacob of Orleans, ופני לא יראו. שלא תראה באספקלריא המאירה שרואה את חבירו בפניו ומתבונן בו יפה יפה. מה"ר יעקב מאורליינש; and cf. Ramban to Ex. 33:18. R. Teitav also has two comments on the construction of the *mishkan* (fols. 171v–172r), one concerning the donations (35:22) and one concerning the building itself (36:23): ויבואו האנשים על הנשים. רבו כל המביאים אנשים ונשים שהיו הולכים כאילו הם נשואים. תיט"ב; עשרים קרשים. ובצו[ו]אה כתי' עשרים כרש [כו:יח] פי' מכוון הכל קרש אחד ולא יכלו לעשותם כך. לכך אומ' בעשייה עשרים קרשים פי' שעשרים קרשים כל אחד ואחד נראה בפני עצמו. תיט"ב.

[224] See also *Bekhor Shor*'s commentary to Genesis 1:26, and cf. Lockshin, "Ha-Im Hayah Yosef Bekhor Shor Pashtan?" (above, n. 53), 170–71, and below, chapter 7. On *Bekhor Shor*'s (un)awareness of Ibn Ezra's commentary, cf. above, n. 87.

[225] See ms. Munich 50, fol. 180r (Lev. 2:6), ויצק[ת] עליה שמן [מנחה היא] לפי שהשמן יבלל בכולה. תיט"ב, and note also two comments found in ms. B.M. 9931. The first is on fol. 73v (Lev. 12:2): אשה כי תזריע . . . אשה מזרעת תחלה יולדת בן זכר. זכר מזרעת תחלה וכו'. י"מ כשהאשה מתאוה לאיש קודם תלד זכר וכן איפכא וראיה מהאי דאמרי' בהשוכר את הפועלים דרבי יוחנן וכו' כלו' שיתנו לב ומדה ומחשבה . . . ור' יום טוב פי' שלעולם הזכר בא מן האיש והנקבה מן האשה ומי שמזריע תחלה המזריע אחריו מבטלו. על כן כשהיא מזרעת תחלה בא

resume in earnest, however, with a series that appears in *parashat Emor* (Lev., chapter 23). First, the spelling anomaly found in Leviticus 23:13 (which appears to have gone unremarked by others)—in which the word *ve-nisko* (ונסכה, "and its libation") is spelled with a *heh* at the end but is vocalized as if there were a *vav*—is understood by R. Teitav as part of a larger pattern of biblical style. The masculine form ending in *vav* that is more typically found has as its antecedent the masculine word for wine (*yayin*). In this instance, however, the word is spelled in the feminine form (ending in *heh*), since it modifies the feminine noun *minḥah* (offering) that it accompanies.[226]

In a comment to Leviticus 23:34, R. Teitav derives that while there must be joy (*Simḥah*) on every festival, the festival of *Sukkot* requires even more intense joy (*Simḥah shel Simḥah*). He learns this from several scriptural cues that mandate staying in Jerusalem for all seven days of the festival, which is not the case for either Passover or *Shavu'ot* (when a stay of one day is sufficient). This difference is supported by the fact that the sacrifices for each day of *Sukkot* are considered to be distinct, and also because *Shemini 'Aẓeret* is considered to be a festival in its own right. Although R. Teitav includes and discusses halakhic positions here as well, his explanation is essentially based on a series of close readings of the biblical text, over several verses.[227] R. Teitav also presents three distinct interpretations concerning the identity, crime, and punishment of the blasphemer described at the end of *parashat Emor* (chapter 24).[228] At the beginning of *parashat Bahar* (and on the basis of Rashi's comment to Lev. 25:1), R. Teitav appears to distinguish between those *mizvot* that were given at Sinai and discussed there, and others in the Book of Leviticus that were centered on and presented in the *Ohel Mo'ed*. The bulk of this comment is virtually identical to *Bekhor Shor*'s comment to Leviticus 25:1 (Nevo, 231), and it is possible that R. Teitav's

אז זרע האיש ומבטלו וכן איפכא. וראייה מההיא דהרוצה שיהיו בניו זכרים יבעול וישנה בשלהי עירובין ופר"ש וכו' מזרעת תחלה בביאה שניה. והג"ן פי' בשם אברהם אבן עזרא שיש באשה ז' חדרים, ג' מימין וג' משמאל ואחד באמצע וכו'. (The printed edition of *Pa'aneaḥ Raza*, 398–99, does not include R. Yom Tov's rabbinic analysis in this matter, but begins with the comment of Ibn Ezra, as cited by *Sefer ha-Gan.*) See also fol. 76r (= ms. Parma 1051, fol. 75r) (Lev. 14:44): ובא הכהן וראה. פר"ש דבא ללמד על שעמד בעיניו בשבוע הראשון ופשה בשני. והק' ה"ר יום טוב א"כ מאי איריא פשה בשני' אפי' עמד בעיניו נמי תולין וקוצה כדמוכח בתו"כ. According to these parallel passages, R. Yom Tov's question on Rashi (from the *Sifra*) is answered by R. Avraham of Toul (which is near Metz). For a reference to this little-known rabbinic figure by R. Isaac *Or Zaru'a*, see S. Emanuel, *Shivrei Luḥot*, 254, and cf. Urbach, *Ba'alei ha-Tosafot*, 353.

226 Ms. Munich 50, fol. 212r.

227 Ms. Munich 50, fol. 213r.

228 Ms. Munich 50, fols. 214r–215v. R. Teitav's exegetical suggestions for the different punishments prescribed for blasphemy (under different conditions) is close to that of Ibn Ezra, cited also by R. Yeḥi'el of Paris; see below, chapter 4, n. 122.

comment comprises only the last interpretational option that appears just before his name, which was appended to the comment by *Bekhor Shor.*[229]

Like Rashi, R. Teitav questions why the Torah (in Lev. 25:9) needed to characterize the day that the *shofar* is sounded during the Jubilee year as both the tenth day of the seventh month and as Yom Kippur. Rashi explains that this was done to underscore that, unlike the blowing of the *shofar* outside the precincts of the Sanhedrin, which is prohibited on the Sabbath, the *shofar* of *yovel* is blown in all areas, even if Yom Kippur occurs that year on the Sabbath. R. Teitav suggests more simply that this double identification was done to ensure that the *shofar* would be sounded by day (*be-yom ha-kippurim*) and not at night. He also explains the seeming inconsistency between the singular form of the verb signifying the blowing of the *shofar* at the beginning of the verse (והעברת) and the plural form at the end of this verse (תעבירו). The *shofar* is blown first in Jerusalem alone, and is then sounded in all other locales. Here again, R. Teitav's exegetical method makes much of a grammatical nuance.[230]

R. Teitav makes a halakhic inference from Leviticus 25:55 that while a Jew cannot sell himself as a slave in perpetuity, he can sell himself as a servant (לשמשות) in this way, since this form of servitude does not require a bill of manumission (גט שחרור) at the point of release, as does an *ʿeved kenaʿani.*[231] Following Rashi's interpretation of Leviticus 26:14 (with the interpretive addendum of the *Sifra*), "and if you do not listen to me, to work at the study of Torah" (*ve-ʾim lo tishmeʿu li, lihyot ʿamelim ba-Torah*), R. Teitav questions the implication of the word *li* (= the phrase "to me," which is ostensibly unecessary) in this verse. He suggests that this refers to one who knows his Creator and intentionally rebels against Him.[232] Returning to Leviticus 25:3, R. Teitav explains the use of the feminine possessive form תבואתה (her wheat) rather than תבואתו (his wheat) or תבואתם (their wheat), because this refers to the produce of each year in the six-year agricultural cycle, and the feminine form is thus appropriate.[233]

229 Ms. Munich 50, fols. 215r–v: פרש"י לפי שהשמטת קרקע לא נשנית בערבות מואב . . . אבל אלו הפר־ שיות בהר ובחקותי לא שייכים כ"כ לאהל מועד ולא לכהנים לכך נא' בהר סיני. ואותו הדבר בשמיטות ויובלות וערכין ששייכי בכהנים שהכהנים מקדשים אותם ליובל כתי' והעברת שופר תרועה וכתי' בני אהרן הכהנים יתקעו בחצוצרות וגם הכהנים מעריכין אחרי ימים לכך נצטרפו כאן ולא תיפוק אדעתיה דבאהל מועד נאמר אלא בסיני נאמרו. ועי"ל בהר סיני לפי שמדבר במצוות ושם נתנו אבל לקמן במדבר במנין של ישראל כתי' במדבר סיני. תיט"ב. The extent to which this passage is actually playing off Rashi, whose comment is cited at the beginning of this passage but not in the commentary of *Bekhor Shor*, is unclear. Cf. *Paʿaneaḥ Raza*, 390, for a briefer treatment in which no names are mentioned.

230 Ms. Munich 50, fol. 216r. Note also Naḥmanides' criticism of Rashi's solution.

231 Ms. Munich 50, fol. 217v.

232 Ms. Munich 50, fol. 219r. Cf. Rashi to Gen. 10:10.

233 Ms. Munich 50, fol. 221r. Ibn Ezra notes that the feminine form here goes back to the feminine word "the land" in the previous verse.

Eighteen comments by R. Teitav are recorded in ms. Munich 50 on *Sefer Bamidbar*, the largest number for any one book of the Pentateuch. Although there is some clustering here as well, these references are spread throughout the book and are not grouped mostly toward the end. In the verse that names the first prince to bring his sacrifice at the dedication of the *mishkan*, Naḥshon b. ʿAminadav from the tribe of Judah (Nu. 7:12), the title *nasi* does not appear. R. Teitav suggests that this title was omitted for reasons of modesty, to diminish boastfulness.[234]

Referring to the service of the Levites, the Torah writes (in Nu. 8:26), "and he will serve (ושרת) his brethren in the tent of assembly." Here, R. Teitav offers a masoretic interpretation. The word *ve-sheret* is found only in this verse and in Deuteronomy 18:7, "the Levite will serve [*ve-sheret*] in the name of his God," in the context of his helping the *Kohanim*. These passages, taken together, are intended to equate the roles of the *Kohanim* and the Levites in the Temple.[235] We have seen that another type of masoretic interpretation, also suggested in connection with the service of the Levites, is found elsewhere in the name of R. Yom Tov.[236]

R. Teitav supplements Rashi's comment on Numbers 10:35. Following the Talmud in tractate *Shabbat* (116a), Rashi explains that the brief two-verse section beginning with the phrase ויהי בנסוע הארון (visibly bracketed in the text of the Torah scroll by upside down, reversed forms of the letter *nun*) was inserted into its place in *parashat Be-Haʿalotekha*, even though this section does not really belong here from the chronological standpoint. This was intended to separate between the negative sections that came both before and after. R. Teitav adds that the form of the reversed *nun* itself conveys this message. The Jews were originally scheduled and positioned to enter Israel a mere three days after they reached the desert. Instead, however, they moved backward (both figuratively and literally), due to their misdeeds.[237]

[234] Ms. Munich 50, fol. 231r. *Moshav Zeqenim*, 432, cites a similar interpretation in the name of the later halakhist R. Asher b. Yeḥi'el (Rosh). R. Teitav's comment to Nu. 3:1 (*ve-'eleh toledot Moshe ve-Aharon*) is found on fol. 225r.

[235] Ms. Munich 50, fol. 233v: ושרת את אחיו. ושרת ב׳ במסורה הא׳ דהכא ואידך ושרת בשם ה׳ א-להיו. כלו׳ כהן בשירותו ולוי בשרותו דהא הוזכרו לוים כאן כנגד ד׳ מקומות ששורתים בבית המקדש. תיט״ב. (To this point, I have not been able to locate this interpretation in the commentaries of contemporary Ashkenazic *baʿalei masorah.*)

[236] See ms. Parma 541, above, n. 202.

[237] Ms. Munich 50, fol. 236v: ויהי בנסוע הארון. פי׳ רש״י למה נכתב כאן כדי להפסיק בין פורענות לפורענות. ופורענות ראשון כתיב ויסעו מהר ה׳ מלמד שסרו מאחרי השם ית׳ כדפי׳ רש״י. ועי״ל ויהי בנסוע הארון נ׳ הפוכה. היה להם ליכנס לארץ מיד תוך ג׳ ימים והלכו לאחור ולא לפניהם. תיט״ב. This section in the manuscript subsequently mentions Rabbenu Tam, who cites a passage from the *Midrash Yelamdenu* that characterizes the first negative action of the Jewish people (recorded in Nu. 10:33, "and they traveled [away] from the mountain of the Lord," and discussed in *Shabbat* 116a by R. Ḥama b. Ḥanina), כתינוק שברח מלפני רבו. Cf. *Tosafot Shabbat* 116a, s.v. *porʿanut*, which cites a variant of

R. Teitav also presents Rashi's interpretation to Numbers 11:1, "and the fire of the Lord burned in them, and it consumed the edge of the camp" (ותבער בם אש ה' ותאכל בקצה המחנה), although in this instance he agrees with Rashi only in part. Rashi suggests two approaches (as found initially in *Sifrei*) to the punishment this verse describes. The first approach understands the word *qeẓeh* to be related to the word *muqẓin*, outcasts. The fringe of the camp that was destroyed consisted only of estranged, lowly members of the people, the *ʿerev rav.* R. Teitav suggests instead, in accordance with the second approach found in Rashi, that the word *qeẓeh* is linked to the word *qeẓinim*, officers, indicating that this punishment affected the leaders of the people. R. Teitav further supports this interpretation with a verse in Psalms, which refers to those who disputed Moses at that time and the punishment they received, in terms very similar to those found in Numbers 11:1, "and a fire burned in their midst" (ותבער בה בעדתם; Ps. 106:18). Moreover, the rabbinic interpretation of this verse in Psalms is that *ʿedah* (as the root of *ʿadatam*) connotes members of the Sanhedrin. Indeed, as R. Teitav notes, Rashi himself interpreted that when Moses was instructed to invest the group of seventy elders with his spirit (Nu. 11:16), he was in fact investing a second such group. This was because the first group of elders had perished in the fires of Tavʿerah (Nu. 11:3).[238]

R. Teitav employs a *gematria* interpretation of Numbers 14:27 to derive the number of men required for a quorum,[239] and he has another masoretic interpretation based on Numbers 17:2, "and he [Eleazar] should raise up

---

the *Yelamdenu* passage (כתינוק היוצא מבית הספר שבורח והולך לו, כך בורחקים מהר סיני . . . שלמדו הרבה תורה בסיני) in the name of Rabbenu Tam's leading student, Ri of Dampierre. R. Jacob of Orleans is also mentioned at the end of the passage in ms. Munich 50, perhaps as the presenter of all those different elements.

[238] See ms. Munich 50, fol. 238r: מי יתן כל עם ה' נביאים כאלו כי יתן את רוחו עליהם כמו על אותם שנים. כי לע' זקנים לא נתן את רוחו עליהם כמו על אותם שנים ולא היה נוטל מן הרוחי אשר בקרבו. ועי"ל אספה לי שבעים איש והאחרונים מתו. ופי' בקצה המחנה במוקצה שבמחנה כנגד ערב רב אבל לשאר בני אדם לא. והכא משמע קצינים שבמחנה. וכן בדוד הוא אומר ותבער אש בעדתו, ועדה אלו סנהדרין. תיט"ב. In this instance as well, only the interpretation that begins with the phrase *ʿal yesh lomar* can be attributed to R. Teitav with certainty.

[239] Ms. Munich 50, fol. 247v: עד מתי לעדה. מכאן שאין עדה פחות מי' וכן עדה במילוי עין דלת הא בגימט' עשר . . . וכן א'ב'ו'א אליך וברכתיך עולה יו"ד. לפיכך דבר שבקדושה לא יהא פחות מעשרה. תיט"ב. These elements of *gematria* and *milui*, which are staples of the German Pietists (see, e.g., Ivan Marcus, "Exegesis for the Few and for the Many: Judah he-Ḥasid's Biblical Commentaries," *Jerusalem Studies in Jewish Thought* 8 [1989], 1*–24*, and below, chapter 3), are relatively rare for R. Yom Tov, although he does present a number of masoretic comments (that involve both words and markings), as we have seen. On this *gematria*, see also *Sefer Ḥuqqei ha-Torah* (in my *Jewish Education and Society in the High Middle Ages*, 108, lines 56–57, and the discussion of the origin of *Sefer Ḥuqqei ha-Torah* in Appendix A, 101–5). See also ms. Munich 50, fol. 251v (Nu. 16:11): כי תלינו עליו [הכתיב בוי"ו, תלונו]. כלומר וי וי למהרהר על רבו ועליו אתם מהרהרים. ועוד שעל ו' אתם חולקים, משה ואהרן, אלעזר ואיתמר, נחשון ואליצפן. תיט"ב. This is yet another "masoretic *vav*" interpretation, found also in *Paʿaneaḥ Raza*, 445 (without attribution).

the pans" (of the 250 followers of Koraḥ; וירם את המחתות). The word *ve-yarem* appears only twice in the Bible, here and in 1 Samuel, 2:10, "and He shall raise up the horn of his anointed" (וירם קרן משיחו), which rabbinic literature applies to the reversal of the destruction of the Temple in the messianic age. The implication of the usage here is that the messiah will also raise up members of Koraḥ's entourage at the time the Temple is rebuilt.[240]

In a halakhic vein, R. Teitav derives from Numbers 18:21 and 23 that the Levite must perform his services during *shemitah* and *yovel*, even though there are no tithes separated for the Levites in those years,[241] and he suggests what appears to be an unusual midrashic approach to Moses hitting the rock (Nu. 20:11): Moses wanted the rock to give forth blood and not water.[242] R. Teitav provides support for Rashi's interpretation to Numbers 21:1 concerning what the king of ʿArad heard that caused him to attack the Jews (i.e., the passing of Aaron and the departure of the *ʿananei ha-kavod*),[243] as well as Rashi's understanding of what Balak meant when he

240 Ms. Munich 50, fol. 253v: וזה הגיד לנו המסורת.וירם את המחתות וירם קרן משיחו. ואת האש זו שלהבת שעל הקטרות כדדרשי' פרק כיצד צולין אי אש יכול שלהבת ת"ל גחלי אש. תיט"ב. A more extensive interpretation of these usages is found in the masoretic commentary by R. Meir of Rothenberg to this verse. *R. Meir b. Barukh mi-Rothenburg*, ed. I. Z. Kahana, vol. 1 (Jerusalem, 1957), 27–28.

241 Ms. Munich 50, fol. 256v: ועבד הלוי. להשמעינו שצריך לעבוד אף בשמיטין וביובלות אע"פ שאין [דיני] מעשר נהוגים. תיט"ב. *Paʿaneaḥ Raza*, 552, includes this comment, without attribution. An addendum there asserts, ומכאן שגם בזמן הזה שאין בהמ"ק קיים ישרת הלוי לכהנים. Cf. I. Ta-Shma, *Ha-Nigleh shebe-Nistar* (Tel Aviv, 2001), 25, regarding the early Ashkenazic origins for the custom of the Levites washing the hands of the *kohanim* in preparation for the *birkat kohanim.*

242 Ms. Munich 50, fol. 259r: ד"א ויך את הסלע. ולא רצה מים לצאת כי אם דם שנא' הן הכה צור ויזובו מים [תהלים עח:כ], ואין זבה אלא דם שנא' אשה כי תזוב דמה וכו'. ולא הואיל זכות משה ואהרן לפי שעברו את פי ה'. באתה מרים להתפלל לפני ה' ואמרה לפני' רבש"ע זכור שהחייתי בניך במצרים והיו מלים את התינוקות והמילה גורמת חיים שנא' ואומר לך בדמייך חיי. תיט"ב

243 Ms. Munich 50, fol. 259v: וישמע הכנעני מלך ערד וכו'. פי' רש"י התייר הגדול, ופי' ר"י זה היה אהרן. ומיד כשמת אהרן התייר, מיד וישמע הכנעני ועשה מלחמה עמהם ובשבילו היה הענן הולך לפניהם. וכשמת, מסולק הענן מישראל. תיט"ב. The identity of Ri in this passage is uncertain. The standard texts of Rashi read simply, שמע שמת אהרן ונסתלקו ענני הכבוד (as per *Rosh ha-Shanah* 3a). *Paʿaneaḥ Raza*, 456 (which does not include the name of R. Teitav), reads, פרש"י התייר הגדול וכו' פי' ר"י חסיד שזהו אהרן שבזכותו היה הענן המתייר אותם וכשמת אהרן נסתלק מיד וכו', and see also *Perushei ha-Torah le-R. Yehudah he-Ḥasid*, ed. Lange, 183. As Lange notes, Aaron as *ha-tayyar ha-gadol* is found in *Yerushalmi Sotah* 1:10. This passage perhaps implies a connection between R. Teitav and R. Judah *he-Ḥasid* (although R. Teitav was somewhat older than R. Judah). *Moshav Zeqenim*, 471, cites R. Yosef *Bekhor Shor*, who wonders what forced Rashi to accept this interpretation (אמאי דוחקו לפרש מיתת אהרן); he should have interpreted instead (*ki-peshuto*) that what the Canaanite king heard was that the Jews had reached the point of *derekh ha-ʾatarim.* Two solutions for Rashi are then suggested. First, Rashi had in mind here the parallel verse in Nu. 33:40, which reads וישמע הכנעני מלך ערד והוא יושב בנגב בארץ כנען [בבא בני ישראל]. The sense of this verse is that the king had heard about something other than the arrival of Israel. (Rashi there repeats the Talmudic interpretation that he heard about the death of Aaron and the concomitant loss of the protective clouds; this verse appears immediately after the Torah records the death of Aaron, and Rashi further suggests that this explains why the impact of Aaron's death on מלך ערד is repeated here.) The second suggestion is that Rashi was following the interpretation of the *Sifrei*, that *derekh ha-ʾatarim* refers

said to Bil'am, "for I know that whatever you bless is blessed, and whatever you curse is cursed" (Nu. 22:6), in a manner that is identical to the comment of R. Yosef *Bekhor Shor*.[244]

R. Teitav has an interesting rabbinic interpretation of Bil'am's response to the angel as he became aware of his presence: "I have sinned because I did not know that you were standing before me on the road" (Nu. 22:34). Rashi, based on *Midrash Tanḥuma*, interprets this to be yet another unflattering assessment of Bil'am's ability (or inability) to know the intentions of the Divine, an assessment that he was forced to grudgingly acknowledge by the appearance of the angel. R. Teitav interprets Bil'am's response from a different perspective. He notes that if Bil'am did not know of the angel's presence until the angel alerted him, it follows that he did not really sin, contrary to his own statement. R. Teitav explains, however, that according to talmudic law, a Noachide is culpable for behavior that he should have learned but did not.[245] Bil'am was admitting to the angel that he should have been able to understand from all of the unusual occurrences around him that something was amiss even before the angel appeared to him, and he is therefore culpable.[246] R. Teitav also draws a suggestive comparison between Bil'am's limited ability to offer blessings (Nu. 23:13) and the fuller blessings extended by King David (Ps. 113:2), and notes some subtle differ-

---

also to the path of the *tayyar ha-gadol* (meaning the *'anan*), which directed the Jews on their way. Cf. *Perushei R. Ḥayyim Palti'el*, ed. Lange, 535–36. Both R. Teitav and *Bekhor Shor* defend Rashi's interpretation in this instance, although this comment of *Bekhor Shor* does not appear in the main manuscript of his commentary (Munich 52); see *Perushei R. Yosef Bekhor Shor*, ed. Nevo, 278. On Rashi as *tayyar ha-gadol*, see, e.g., *Perushei R. Ḥayyim Palti'el*, 205 (to Ex. 9:30), and R. Menaḥem ibn Zeraḥ's introduction to his *Zedah la-Derekh* (repr. Jerusalem, 1977), fol. 3b (וקודם זמן רבינו שלמה התייר הגדול מעיר טרוי"ש היו לומדים בפירושי רבינו גרשום מאור הגולה . . . ושרתה רוחי הקודש על רבינו שלמה).

[244] Ms. Munich 50, fol. 263v: כי ידעתי את אשר תברך מברך ואשר תאור יואר. לפי שנתנבא על מואב שיפול ביד סיחון. תיט"ב. This interpretation is also found in *Pa'aneaḥ Raza*, 459, without attribution (and in *Da'at Zeqenim* to Nu., fol. 18b). Rashi, following *Midrash Tanḥuma*, notes that Bil'am had helped Siḥon defeat Moav (*'azarto le-hakkot 'et Moav*) which gave Balak an indication of the extent of his powers. R. Teitav understands Bil'am's privileging Siḥon as a function of his favorable prophecy; and see also *Perushei R. Yosef Bekhor Shor*, ed. Nevo, 283. Cf. *Moshav Zeqenim*, 476, and Rashi and Rashbam to Nu. 21:27.

[245] See *Bava Qamma* 92a (based on the verbal exchange between Abraham and Avimelekh), and cf. *Avot de-R. Natan*, chapter 31 (end).

[246] Ms. Munich 50, fol. 265r: חטאתי כי לא ידעתי אי אתה נצב לקראתי. תימ' אם כן שלא ידע לא חטא. וי"ל דבן נח נהרג על דבר שיש לו ללמוד ולא למד. הכא נמי היה לו להבין על מה כל השנווים האלו. תיט"ב. This interpretation is presented briefly in *Pa'aneaḥ Raza*, 462 (without attribution), and in *Moshav Zeqenim*, 478 (again without attribution), which cites this interpretation as proof (אלא מכאן אזהרה לבן נח) for the rabbinic notion (as per *Bava Qamma* 92a) that a Noachide must learn from past experiences and act accordingly. See also *Perushei R. Ḥayyim Palti'el*, 544–45, and cf. *Ḥizzequni*, who explains similarly that Bil'am should have understood from his troubles to this point why he was not succeeding.

ences between the different places that Balak took Bilʿam to carry out his mission (Nu. 23:14).[247]

R. Teitav has three rather different types of comments concerning the war against Midyan and its spoils, as described in Numbers 31. The first (on Nu. 31:18) is a kind of halakhic analysis regarding whether the female Midianites who had never had relations (and did not have to be put to death) were then permitted even to *kohanim*, based also on the parameters of the *ʾeshet yefat toʾar.*[248] The second comment suggests (based on the defective spelling of the word וממחצ[י]ת in Nu. 31:30) that the portion of the spoils that went to those who actively participated in the war was marked in such a way as to designate it more valuable or praiseworthy than that of the rest of the people, since those who fought had risked their lives to fulfill the religious requirement and precept of going to war. Similarly, the thirty-six thousand heads of cattle (half of the total) that were awarded to those who fought in the war were singled out by the definite article, והבקר (Nu. 31:38), while the half that was distributed among the rest of the people was simply designated as ובקר (Nu. 31:44). The extra *heh* underscores the notion that the spoils of those who actually fought in the war were considered to be more exalted. This is once again a sharp and unusual kind of exegetical argumentation that is based both on the precise characteristics of the masoretic texts as well as considerations of realia (*derekh ʾereẓ*).[249] R. Teitav's third comment, on the phrase כל כלי מעשה (Nu. 31:51), notes that the word *keli* appears eighteen times in the Torah, signifying the eighteen blessings of the *ʿAmidah*, which are desirous and effective vessels (כלי חפץ). The word *keli* is also an acrostic for *kohanim, leviyyim, yisraʾelim.*[250] We can see that R. Teitav

247 See ms. Munich 50, fol. 266r: וקבנו לי משם. אכולו קאי על כן את אשר תברך מברך כלפי מעלה. אבל דוד המלך בירך בלב שלם שנא' יחי שם ה' מבורך מעתה ועד עולם. והודה להקב"ה שלם. תיט"ב, and ויקחו שדה הצופים. לפי שבראשונה ובשנייה נאמר מקום ע"ז במות מעל ראש פעור. לכך נאמ' ויקח כלו' עתה אראך מקום מפלתם כלו' שם יכעיסו בוראם ולכך מאריך הלשון כ"כ. תיט"ב

248 Ms. Munich 50, fols. 279v–280r: החיו לכם. לכל צרכיהם ופנחס היה עמהם כדדרשינן לעיל. ומה בכך והלא כדין אותו ביפת תואר לרב בפ"ק דקידושין ואפילו ביאה שנייה דהואיל ואשתרייה אשתרייה אע"ג דשאר גיורת לא חזינו לכהונה דבעי קידושין לכהן. מיהו ביפת תואר תפשוט מהכא מדכתיב החיו לכם ופנחס היה עמהם. ויש לומר דבירושלמי יש בהלכה שלא הותר ביפת תואר אלא לאחר שחלקו. תיט"ב. This discussion might easily have taken place within the context of talmudic study; cf. *Tosafot Qiddushin* 21b, s.v. *be-biʾah sheniyyah*; *Tosafot Tukh Qiddushin*, ed. A. Z. Sheinfeld (Jerusalem, 1982), 58 (ad loc.); and *Tosafot ha-Rosh*, s.v. *ve-giyyoret.* Somewhat uncharacteristically, *Ḥizzequni* here, as well as *Moshav Zeqenim*, 490, cite a passage from *Sifrei* that R. Shimʿon bar Yoḥai derived from this verse, that a female convert who converted before the age of three was permitted to marry a *kohen.*

249 Ms. Munich 50, fol. 281v: וממחצת. צ' מצוינת ומסומנת בעין כדי לעשות היכירא על אותם אנשי מלחמה שהוא יותר משובח משל העדה האלו, נסתכנו וקיימו המצוה להלחם. לכך במחצית העדה כתוב והבקר שלשים ושש אלף לכך כתוב והבקר ה' יתירה כי היא היתה יותר מעולה. תיט"ב. Cf. A. Mondschein, "The Massoretes Fabricated Explanations" (above, n. 39), 284–86.

250 Ms. Munich 50, fol. 282r: כלי י"ח פעמים בקרי' כנגד י"ח ברכות והם כלי חפץ. כל"י ראשי תיבות כהנים ישראלים לוים. תיט"ב.

(at least based on his extant comments) has gone from offering Rashbam-like comments on the Book of Exodus to more masoretic-like comments on the Book of Numbers which are much closer to those typically associated with the German Pietists. However, both systems are highlighted by quite a number of sharp observations overall. It would seem that R. Teitav was fully comfortable with pursuing a variety of valid interpretations of the Torah, while traveling along different interpretational paths at the same time.

There are only seven comments from R. Teitav on Deuteronomy in Munich 50, and all of them are centered in the last part of the book, and especially in the last portion, *Ve-Zot ha-Berakhah*. Many of these comments are also linguistic or letter-based. The first, at the beginning of *parashat Ki Teẓe*, notes that the letters that spell "the hated" (wife, who gives birth to the firstborn son), לשניאה (in Deut. 21:15), also form the words or phrase לי שנאה ("she has become hateful to me"), which suggests that the hatefulness was engendered by inappropriate actions on her part.[251] In Deuteronomy 22:19 the word הוציא in the phrase *ki hoẓi shem ra* ("for he has brought out an evil name") is spelled *plene*, with the *yod*. In Deuteronomy 22:14, when the charge is initially made, *ve-hoẓi* (*'alehah shem ra*; "and he brought out an evil name against her") is spelled without the *yod*. R. Teitav notes that the first spelling reflects that initially it is unclear whose claim is true. In the later verse, however, the husband's charge has been shown to be false, and it is thus a fully libelous charge on his part, hence the *plene* spelling.[252]

In Deuteronomy 28:2, the Torah asserts that one who observes the law will be overtaken by blessing (ובאו עליך כל הברכות האלה והשיגך), with the word *ve-hisigukha* spelled defectively (without a *vav*). In Deuteronomy28:15, however, referring to the curses that will befall the Jewish people if they do not observe the law, the word *ve-hisigukha* is spelled *plene* (with a *vav*). R. Teitav explains this distinction in line with the rabbinic aphorism (*Qiddushin* 39b) that there is no meaningful reward in this world for the performance of *mizvot* (*sekhar mizvah be-hai 'alma lekka*). Thus the punishments that may

[251] Ms. Munich 50, fol. 302r: לשניאה. איותיות לי שנאה כלו' שנאה היא בעיניו אם מעשיה היו מכוערין. תיט"ב. This simple comment is found in *Pa'aneaḥ Raza* (without attribution), 530. Cf. Rashi to *Qiddushin* 68a, s.v. *senu'ah* (שנשואיה שנואים לפני המקום); *Perush ha-Roqeaḥ 'al ha-Torah*, ed. Klugman, 231: שנואה אותיות נשואה, שנואה בנישואיה; and *Perush Rabbenu Ephraim 'al ha-Torah*, ed. Klugman, 200 (*me-Ḥakhmei Ashkenaz*).

[252] Ms. Munich 50, fol. 305r: כי הוציא שם רע. כאן הוציא מלא י' ולמעלה חסר י', שעדיין לא נודע הוצאת שם רע עם מי הדין. תיט"ב. Note the different approach of *Perush Roqeaḥ 'al ha-Torah*, 234 (found also in the *Ba'al ha-Turim*) to explain the defective spelling (in Deut. 22:14). The *yod* is missing when the charge is first made, to signify that the Ten (*yod*) Commandments have, in effect, been violated when such a false charge is made. Indeed, our forefather's fate was not sealed following the sin of the golden calf until they gave and accepted a bad report about the land of Israel (*dibbat ha-'areẓ ra'ah*, as per *'Arakhin* 15a).

occur will be full ones, but the rewards that are given (in this world) will be only partial ones.[253]

R. Teitav interprets "when the most High divided their inheritance to the nation, when He separated the sons of Adam" (Deut. 32:8) as referring to the generation of the Tower of Babel that came after the flood. The *dor ha-palagah* had been given their inheritance following the flood, but then had to be scattered. This interpretation seems to follow the one suggested by Rashi (on the basis of *Sifrei*), and is different from the one put forward by Rashbam, who sees the second phrase as describing the days of Abraham, after Noah had died, at which time the boundaries of the nations were established.[254]

R. Teitav opens his comments to *parashat Ve-Zot ha-Berakhah* with a homiletical or midrashic notion. In the phrase, "This is the blessing [*berakhah*] that Moses blessed" (Deut. 33:1), the word *berakhah* may also be vocalized as *berekhah*, a pool that purifies those who are impure. Thus the atmosphere of Torah purifies those who are impure.[255] As noted above in connection with ms. B.M. 9931, R. Teitav has several nuanced linguistic comments about the blessings of Moses to the tribes of Israel which do not appear, however, in ms. Munich 50.[256] The final comment by R. Yom Tov found in ms. Munich 50 is on the verse toward the very end of the Torah (Deut. 34:7) indicating that Moses was 120 years old when he died. R. Teitav asserts that Moses's lifespan was measured against the 120 days (all told) he spent on Mount Sinai with the Almighty. He lived for this lengthy period of years based on the notion of one year for each day, *yom la-shanah, yom la-shanah*. In repeating this phrase, R. Teitav shows that he was undoubtedly aware that he was applying this to Moses in a rather different way than the Torah intended it in Numbers 14:34. According to that verse, for each of the

253 Ms. Munich 50, fol. 312v: כל הברכות האלה והשיגוך. כתי' חסר ו'. אבל אצל הקללות כתי' מלא ו', ששכר מצוה בהאי עלמא ליכא. לכך בברכות חסר, אבל הקללות באות בהאי עלמא לכך מלא. תיט"ב. Cf. *Perush ha-Roqeaḥ ʿal ha-Torah*, ed. Klugmann, 250–51.

254 Ms. Munich 50, fol. 319v: בהנחל עליון גוים. את נחלתן. בהפרידו בני אדם אחר המבול זה היה דור ההפלגה. תיט"ב. R. Yosef *Bekhor Shor*, ed. Nevo, 385, interprets the second phrase as referring to the *dor ha-haflagah*, as R. Teitav does, and perhaps applies the first phrase to the *dor ha-haflagah* as well, as Ibn Ezra does. Cf. *Rashbam's Commentary on Deuteronomy*, ed. M. Lockshin, 174, n. 18. See ms. Munich 50, fol. 320v, for R. Teitav's interpretation of Deut. 32:21.

255 Ms. Munich 50, fol. 320v: הברכה אשר בירך משה. אל תקרי הברכה אלא הבריכה, כמו בריכת המים המטהרת טמאים. אויר התורה מטהרת את הטמאים. תיט"ב. This is the first and only *ʾal tiqrei* by R. Yom Tov that I have encountered.

256 See above, nn. 198–99. *Paʿaneaḥ Raza*, 556, cites (by name) an interpretation of R. Teitav of Deut. 33:1 where Moses is referred to as *ʾish ha-E-lohim* in this verse to show that these were not his personal blessings but were delivered at the request of the Almighty. At the same time, these blessings were so worthwhile (and destined to take effect) particularly because of Moses's genuinely exalted status. See also *Paʿaneaḥ Raza*, 557, for R. Teitav's comment to Deut. 33:4 (תורה צוה לנו משה).

forty days that the spies surveyed the land, the Jewish people would spend one year in the desert (*yom la-shanah, yom la-shanah*).[257] To the end, Moses remained far superior to his charges.

R. Yom Tov of Joigny—whose exegesis on the Torah was not discussed at all by S. A. Poznanski in his classic *Mavo ʿal Ḥakhmei Ẓarefat Mefrashei ha-Miqra*, or by any other modern scholars of medieval *parshanut ha-miqra*, as far as I can tell—displays several different types of exegetical techniques. Most significantly, R. Yom Tov appears to imitate and meaningfully engage the *peshat* methods pursued by his predecessors Rashi and Rashbam, and by his contemporary, R. Yosef *Bekhor Shor*. He has some interesting *peshat* interpretations that attempt to take into account the thoughts or motivations of biblical figures and characters, and others that are realia-based, although he does not use the term *derekh ʾereẓ*, or related phrases, to characterize them.

R. Teitav often comes close to the *ʿomeq peshuto shel miqra* approach favored by Rashbam (which was not the case for his contemporary, R. Jacob of Orleans), but he is not a consistent adherent of this approach. He "follows up" or explains Rashi's comment on a number of occasions, although far less frequently than R. Jacob of Orleans does (and less even than *Bekhor Shor* does). Although R. Teitav presents a number of talmudic and halakhic interpretations, there is little *derash* found in his comments (similar to R. Yosef *Bekhor Shor* in this dimension, and different from R. Jacob of Orleans); and one does not have the sense that any of his interpretations were necessarily offered in the course of talmudic studies. In addition, R. Teitav presents a collection of masoretic and *gematria* interpretations reminiscent of those by *Ḥasidei Ashkenaz*, whose founders, R. Samuel b. Qalonyumus *he-Ḥasid* (b. c. 1115) and his son, R. Yehudah (d. 1217), were active mainly in Rhineland Germany and especially in Speyer, but had some contact with northern France.[258] These are not fanciful calculations, however; they were often intended to resolve exegetical problems in the verses to which they were applied. Most of the multiple exegetical approaches and methods pursued by R. Teitav can perhaps be seen in Rashi's Torah commentary, but R. Teitav offers no programmatic insights into his methods and work.

The movement for the study of intensive *peshat* in the twelfth century, which included Rashi, R. Yosef *Qara*, and Rashbam, was concentrated almost exclusively in northern France. The late-twelfth century (Tosafist) variation that we have identified and discussed in this chapter was also centered

[257] Ms. Munich 50, fol. 327r: ומשה בן מאה ועשרים שנה וגו'. כנגד ק"כ הימים שהיה בסיני לכך חי כל השנים יום לשנה יום לשנה. תיט"ב.

[258] Cf. *Taʿamei Mesoret ha-Miqra le-R. Yehudah he-Ḥasid*, ed. Y. S. Lange (Jerusalem, 1981), editor's introduction, 9–11. For R. Samuel and R. Judah's contacts with northern France, see, e.g., Urbach, *Baʿalei ha-Tosafot*, 192–93, 237.

in northern France. It includes three (talmudic) students of Rabbenu Tam who had other associations, similarities, and connections among them as well. To be sure, R. Yosef *Bekhor Shor* of Orleans composed a fairly complete commentary to the Torah, while we cannot be certain of what the fullest versions of the comments by R. Jacob of Orleans and R. Yom Tov of Joigny looked like. In the next chapter, however, we shall see that the same interest in *peshat*, in Rashi's commentary, and in *'aggadah ha-meyashevet divrei miqra* (in addition to some relatively new approaches to halakhic and *gematria* interpretations) was also present among rabbinic figures and Tosafists in Germany during the early thirteenth century, in two somewhat unlikely places: a Torah commentary of R. Judah *he-Ḥasid* and the *Nimmuqei Ḥumash* by R. Isaiah di Trani, who studied in Speyer with the leading German Tosafist, R. Simḥah b. Samuel. These interests were not typical of many Tosafists in northern France and Germany, as we shall also see, but the combination of these two figures, along with the three in northern France whose exegetical interests have been studied in this chapter, constitute a formidable unit among Ashkenazic rabbinic scholars who saw value in undertaking literary exegesis of the text of the Torah as a distinct and nuanced discipline, following the activities of the twelfth-century *pashtanim* in northern France.

3

The Contours of Biblical Interpretation during the Early Thirteenth Century

The Torah commentary that R. Judah b. Samuel *he-Ḥasid* (d. 1217) developed and shared with other members of his circle in Regensburg (including R. Isaac [b. Ezekiel *mi-Morat*] of Russia and R. Mordekhai of Poland),[1] and which he transmitted to his son R. Moses Zal(t)man (who transcribed it in a form of *reportatio*), contains quite a number of interpretations that are fundamentally exoteric, and that are characterized by a form of the Hebrew term *peshat.*[2] Indeed, one of the two principal manuscripts of this commentary, ms. Moscow 82, is introduced by the phrase *zehu peshatim meha-R. Yehudah he-Ḥasid.*[3] This is so despite the prominence of R. Judah as

[1] On these figures and their association with R. Judah, see, e.g., I. Ta-Shma, *Knesset Meḥqarim*, vol. 1 (Jerusalem, 2004), 245–48; *Perushei ha-Torah le-R. Yehudah he-Ḥasid*, ed. Y. S. Lange (Jerusalem, 1975), 86, 94, 124–25 (where R. Isaac of Russia authenticates one comment by R. Judah and rejects another), 165, 214 (s.v. *R. Yiẓḥaq me-Russia*), and the editor's introduction, 8; my "Bein Yeshivot Ba'alei ha-Tosafot le-Battei Midrashot Aḥerim be-Ashkenaz Bimei ha-Benayim," in *Yeshivot u-Battei Midrashot*, ed. I. Etkes (Jerusalem, 2006), 106, n. 8; *Pa'aneaḥ Raza*, ed. Machon Torat ha-Rishonim (Jerusalem, 1998), 260 (and see also 219); *Perushim u-Pesaqim le-Rabbenu Avigdor 'al ha-Torah*, ed. Machon Harerei Qedem (Jerusalem, 1996), 82, 84; and below, nn. 60, 85.

[2] See Ivan Marcus, "Exegesis for the Few and for the Many: Judah he-Ḥasid's Biblical Commentaries," *Jerusalem Studies in Jewish Thought* 8 (1989), 1*–24*. Cf. Aharon Mondschein, "The Massoretes Fabricated Explanations for Full and Defective Spellings: On Abraham Ibn Ezra's Struggles Against the (Ab)use of Biblical Spelling as an Exegetical Tool," [Hebrew] *Shenaton le-Ḥeqer ha-Miqra veha-Mizraḥ ha-Qadum* 19 (2009), 306.

[3] See ms. Moscow 82, fol. 62r, and *Perushei ha-Torah le-R. Yehudah he-Ḥasid*, ed. Y. S. Lange (Jerusalem, 1975), editor's introduction, 7.

a leading figure in the esoteric chain of the German Pietist tradition[4] and the presence of several highly unusual or even eccentric interpretations in this commentary.[5] Moreover, the brief masoretic commentary compiled by R. Judah *he-Ḥasid* titled *Taʿamei Mesoret ha-Miqra*, which contains *remazim* and other word and letter manipulations similar in some respects to those put forward by R. Yom Tov Joigny (R. Teitav), as noted at the end of the previous chapter, hardly presents any esoteric interpretations or issues.[6] Similarly, as noted in the previous chapter, R. Isaac b. Judah *ha-Levi*, the compiler of *Paʿaneaḥ Raza*, characterizes the material that he included from R. Judah as *peshatim u-gematriʾot me-divrei R. Yehudah he-Ḥasid.*[7]

Other leading figures among the German Pietists formulated more esoteric dimensions in the realm of biblical commentary, in particular Judah's leading Pietist student, Eleazar of Worms (in his exegetical works such as *Sefer ha-Ḥokhmah*), and another student of Judah (or Eleazar), who composed the commentary to the Torah that has been attributed to Eleazar.[8] To

[4] See, e.g., *Perushei Siddur ha-Tefillah la-Roqeaḥ*, ed. M. Hershler (Jerusalem, 1992), vol. 2, 228–29; *Teshuvot Maharshal*, #29; Jacob Freimann's introduction to *Sefer Ḥasidim*, ed. J. Wistenetzki (Frankfurt, 1924), 5–9; Joseph Dan, *Torat ha-Sod shel Ḥasidut Ashkenaz* (Jerusalem, 1968), 14–20, 40–43; my "Rabbinic Figures in Castilian Kabbalistic Pseudepigraphy: R. Yehudah *he-Ḥasid* and R. Elḥanan of Corbeil," *Journal of Jewish Thought and Philosophy* 3 (1993), 84–86; E. Wolfson, *Through a Speculum That Shines* (Princeton, 1994) 188–97, 231–32, 268, n. 341.

[5] See, e.g., Haym Soloveitchik, "Two Notes on the *Commentary on the Torah* of R. Yehudah he-Ḥasid," in *Turim: Studies in Jewish History and Literature Presented to Dr. Bernard A. Lander*, ed. M. A. Shmidman, vol. 2 (New York, 2008), 241–51.

[6] See *Taʿamei Massoret ha-Miqra le-R. Yehudah he-Ḥasid*, ed. Y. S. Lange (Jerusalem, 1981). Rashi's commentary is mentioned twice (16, 36), as is a comment of R. Yosef Qara (69, found in the Torah commentary of *Bekhor Shor*), and cf. below, n. 10. Interestingly, two of the references in this commentary to quasi-mystical or magical techniques are interpolations attributed specifically to rabbinic figures other than R. Judah *he-Ḥasid*, such as R. Abraham *ha-Navi* of Cologne (15–16) and R. Yeḥiʾel b. Moses (28; see also *Perushei ha-Torah*, ed. Lange, 206, and *Tosafot ha-Shalem*, ed. Gellis, 3:227). See also *Taʿamei Massoret*, 65–66, and cf. my "*Peering through the Lattices: Mystical, Magical, and Pietistic Dimensions in the Tosafist Period* (Detroit, Mich., 2000), 179–81, n. 10. Poznanski obviously did not treat R. Judah's commentaries in his study of the *pashtanim* of northern France.

[7] See above, chapter 2, n. 143. On R. Judah's *gematria* interpretations, see J. Freimann (above, n. 4), and *Sefer Gematriʾot le-R. Yehudah he-Ḥasid*, introduced by D. Abrams and I. Ta-Shma (Los Angeles, 1998). Cf. Simcha Emanuel, "Ha-Polmos shel Ḥasidei Ashkenaz ʿal Nosaḥ ha-Tefillah," *Meḥqerei Talmud* 3 (2005), vol. 2, 591–92, 604–6; and Aharon Mondschein, "The Massoretes Fabricated Explanations," 306.

[8] On this commentary, see J. Dan, "Perush ha-Torah le-R. Eleazar mi-Germaiza," *Qiryat Sefer* 59 (1984), 644; idem, "The Ashkenazi Hasidic 'Gates of Wisdom,'" in *Hommages a Georges Vajda*, ed. Gerard Nahon and Charles Touati (Louvain, 1980), 183–89; idem, "Sefer ha-Ḥokhmah le-R. Eleazar mi-Worms u-Mashmaʿuto le-Toledot Toratah shel Ḥasidut Ashkenaz," *Zion* 29 (1964), 168–81; David Segal, *Sefer Sodei Razei Semukhim* (Jerusalem, 2001), 31–69 (who maintains, against the view of Dan, that the author of the Torah commentary attributed to R. Eleazar of Worms was one of his students rather than another student of R. Judah *he-Ḥasid*); A. Mondschein, "The Massoretes Fabricated Explanations," 308 (n. 292); Moshe Idel, *Ben: Sonship and*

be sure, Eleazar's commentaries also contain quite a bit of fundamentally exoteric interpretations (*she'ar ha-peshat* is included as one of the many exegetical methodologies associated with Eleazar in his *Sefer ha-Ḥokmah*),[9] and we shall see in the next chapter that Eleazar also had distinct interests in the realm of midrashic interpretation. Nonetheless, the essential difference in the exegetical foci of R. Judah and R. Eleazar is clear, and has been explained by Ivan Marcus as a function of the different goals the German Pietists had in transmitting their esoteric lore, and the difficulties they encountered in doing so.[10]

R. Judah *he-Ḥasid*'s Exoteric Comments to the Torah

In the comments R. Judah *he-Ḥasid* transmitted to his son Zal(t)man, he intended to appeal primarily to the "many" rather than to the few, to use Marcus's terms. To do so, Judah resorted to the full range of exegetical strategies: *derash/midrash* (based on classical rabbinic sources and concepts, as well as his own midrashic expansions); *peshat* (based primarily on the immediate context, or on word usages elsewhere in the Bible); and methods of *remez* or *sod* that included, for the most part, derivations by way of *gematria*,[11] *rashei*

Jewish Mysticism (London, 2007), 218–35; and idem, "On Angels and Biblical Exegesis in Thirteenth-Century Ashkenaz," in *Scriptural Exegesis: The Shapes of Culture and the Religious Imagination* , ed. D. Green and L. S. Lieber (Oxford, 2009), 233–34 (n. 9). Cf. Y. Y. Stal, *Sodei Ḥumash le-Talmidei R. Yehudah he-Ḥasid* (Jerusalem, 2009), 3–52. On the esoteric aspects found in R. Eleazar of Worms's Torah commentaries, see also Elliot Wolfson, *Through a Speculum That Shines*, 214–69.

9 See also at the end of chapter 4 (n. 205), regarding R. Eleazar of Worms and ms. Vatican 123; and cf. Ivan Marcus, "The Song of Songs in German Hasidism and the School of Rashi: A Preliminary Comparison," in *The Frank Talmage Memorial Volume*, ed. B. Walfish (Haifa, 1993), vol. 1, 181–89.

10 See Marcus, "Exegesis for the Few and for the Many," n. 2. On *peshat* in the commentary of R. Judah *he-Ḥasid*, see also G. Brin, "Qavvim le-Perush ha-Torah shel R. Yehudah he-Ḥasid," *Te'udah* 3 (1989), 215–18; and idem, "'Iyyun be-Perushei R. Yehudah he-Ḥasid la-Torah," *Sinai* 88 (1981), 1. On R. Judah's "enlightened" theories of biblical redaction and authorship (following Ibn Ezra, and perhaps Rashbam), see Brin, "Qavvim," 221–26; idem, "'Iyyun," 5–7; H. Soloveitchik, "Two Notes on the *Commentary on the Torah* of R. Yehudah he-Ḥasid," n. 5; I. Ta-Shma, *Knesset Meḥqarim*, 273–313; Uriel Simon, "Shenayim Oḥazim be-Sod Sheneim 'Asar shel R. Avraham Ibn Ezra," *Megadim* 51 (2010), 77–85; I. J. Yuval, "The Orality of Jewish Oral Law: From Pedagogy to Ideology," in *Judaism, Christianity and Islam in the Course of History*, ed. L. Gall and D. Willoweit (Munich, 2011), 256–57; and cf. above, chapter 2, n. 102. See now Simcha Emanuel, "New Fragments of Unknown Biblical Commentaries from the European Genizah," in *Genizat Germania—Hebrew and Aramaic Binding Fragments from Germany in Context*, ed. A. Lehnardt (Leiden, 2010), 209, with respect to R. Eleazar of Worms's view on the authorship of the Book of Psalms.

11 See, e.g., *Perushei ha-Torah le-R. Yehudah he-Ḥasid*, ed. Lange, 11 (Gen. 5:4); 34 (Gen. 24:61); 206 (Deut. 21:22); 210 (Deut. 32:7).

and *sofei tevot*,[12] and other forms of letter manipulation and combination.[13] Of these elements, however, interpretations characterized as *peshat* are the most prevalent in the material Judah *he-Ḥasid* taught to his son. Indeed, the term *peshat* appears more than thirty times in this material, while forms of the term *midrash*, *remez*, and *sod* appear only three times each.[14]

Marcus further notes that forms of *peshat* methodology appear to be operant even when R. Judah *he-Ḥasid* does not explicitly employ this term. Thus R. Judah rejects the interpretation of the phrase והנחש היה ערום (Gen. 3:1, favored by Rashi, Ibn Ezra, R. Yosef *Bekhor Shor*, and Radak, among others), that the snake was actually sly or clever (possessed of a kind of *ḥokhmah* or *ʿormah*), because this interpretation interrupts the flow of the narrative. Although Rashi does not specify whence the snake's cleverness derived, Ibn Ezra maintains that God had given the snake this capacity during Creation, just as He had assigned the capacity for intelligence to man. *Ḥizzequni* suggests that the snake had somehow managed to eat from the Tree of Knowledge, while a number of other authorities (including Maimonides) linked the snake with the *satan* or some other negative but clever angelic figure.[15]

R. Judah *he-Ḥasid* insists, however, that the snake could not have been more clever or shrewd than any other animal, since shrewdness is not a characteristic or ability found within the animal kingdom.[16] Moreover, the

[12] See, e.g., *Perushei ha-Torah*, ed. Lange, 83 (Ex. 12:37); 121 (Ex. 31:17); 155–56 (Lev. 25:17; in this instance, the halakhic ramifications that emerged from R. Judah's *sofei tevot* interpretation were disputed by Judah's younger contemporary, R. Simḥah of Speyer); 208 (Deut. 30:12).

[13] See, e.g., *Perushei ha-Torah*, ed. Lange, 11 (Gen. 6:17); 106 (Ex. 22:16); 166 (Nu. 6:24); 204 (Deut. 16:19 and Deut. 17:15); 205 (Deut. 21:14); and cf. above, chapter 2, n. 222. For an excellent example of R. Judah's extension of midrashic literature (for pietistic purposes, with regard to the punishment of ʿEr and Onan in Gen. 38), see *Perushei ha-Torah*, ed. Lange, 52–53; below, n. 115; and below, chapter 6, nn. 82–83.

[14] In *Perushei ha-Torah*, ed. Lange, 18 (Gen. 12:6), 80 (Ex. 10:12), *sodot* of Ibn Ezra are presented and discussed by R. Judah *he-Ḥasid.* Judah's comment to Gen. 1:9 is characterized in ms. Paris 260 (a manuscript version of *Moshav Zeqenim*) as *sod* (ed. Lange, 5, n. 53).

[15] See Maimonides, *Moreh Nevukhim*, 2:30; R. Saʿadyah Gaon and R. Solomon ibn Gabirol, as cited by Ibn Ezra; ms. Vatican 506 (cited in *Tosafot ha-Shalem*, ed. Gellis, vol. 1, p. 121, sec. 7); and the two Ashkenazic commentaries cited in *Tosafot ha-Shalem*, ed. Gellis, 1:121, secs. 2–3, which note that *naḥash* is equivalent in *gematria* to *satan*. Another such commentary notes that the *gematria* equivalent of the word *ʿarum* is *yeshu*, since both the snake and Jesus wished this world to be lost, the one physically and the other spiritually. Cf. Naphtali Wieder, *Hitgabshut Nosaḥ ha-Tefillah ba-Mizraḥ uba-Maʿarav* (Jerusalem, 1998), vol. 2, 494–95. Note that according to R. Zal(t)man, however, R. Judah *he-Ḥasid* (to Gen. 3:20; ed. Lange, 7) also held that the snake, like Eve, knew all the languages of the animals because they had both actually seen the Tree of Knowledge, as opposed to Adam, who did not know the animals' languages, since he had tasted the fruit but had not actually seen the tree.

[16] On Judah *he-Ḥasid*'s unusual familiarity with and interest in the properties and characteristics of various animals (as part of his larger interest in natural or quasi-scientific phenomena), see I. Ta-Shma, *Knesset Meḥqarim*, 1:181–207, and cf. Y. Y. Stal, *Amarot Tehorot Ḥizoniyyot u-Penimiyyot* (Jerusalem, 2006), 1–236. Radak argues that there were different levels of cleverness

presence of the conjunctive *vav* at the beginning of this verse (*veha-naḥash*) typically suggests that this section is connected to the previous one, a connection made also by Rashi (following *Bereshit Rabbah*). In addressing these issues, R. Judah interprets this phrase according to its simple or literal meaning, "and the snake was naked" (*ʿarum*), in the sense that its body was hairless and without any fur, more so than virtually any other animal or beast of the field. In this respect, the snake's skin was most similar to that of Adam and Eve, which explains the snake's jealousy toward them. This section is indeed closely connected to the previous one, in which Adam and Eve recognized their nakedness owing to the revealing nature of their relatively hairless skin.[17]

In light of the expanded interest in various types of *peshat* or *peshuto shel miqra* (and in Rashi's commentary) that we have found among Tosafists in northern France during the late twelfth century, and aside from the writings of the small circle of previously known northern French *pashtanim*, it is useful and important to characterize the *peshat* aspects of R. Judah's Torah commentary in order to more accurately assess its relevance to this series of Tosafist exegetical commentaries. Like the comments of *Bekhor Shor* and R. Jacob of Orleans, comments by R. Judah *he-Ḥasid* are cited with great frequency by the so-called Tosafist Torah compilations of the thirteenth and early fourteenth centuries, a point not lost on Y. S. Lange, who compiled his edition of R. Judah's commentary taking into account a number of these compilations, both in print and in manuscript.[18] Like R. Yosef *Bekhor Shor*, R. Judah *he-Ḥasid* displays familiarity with Spanish sources in the areas of Jewish thought and biblical exegesis as well.[19]

---

among the beasts of the wild (חיות), who were (as a group) much more intelligent than domestic animals.

[17] See *Perushei ha-Torah le-R. Yehudah he-Ḥasid ʿal ha-Torah*, ed. Lange, 6. See also Gellis, vol. 1, 121, sec. 4, and 1:122, sec. 12; *Perushei ha-Torah*, ed. Lange, 32; and below, n. 169.

[18] Ms. B.M. 9931 (an expanded *Paʿaneaḥ Raza* text; see above, chapter 2, n. 193), which Lange did not use, contains a number of comments directly attributed to R. Judah which are not found in the other texts Lange used. I will include a number of these comments, as well as others from additional *Paʿaneaḥ Raza* manuscripts not included by Lange. Cf. Joy Rochwarger, "Sefer Paʿaneaḥ Raza and Biblical Exegesis in Medieval Ashkenaz" (M.A. thesis, Touro College in Jerusalem, 2000), 54–60.

[19] See Dan, *Torat ha-Sod shel Ḥasidut Ashkenaz* (Tel Aviv, 1968), 18–19, 29–31, 114–16, 138–45; Wolfson, *Through a Speculum That Shines*, 93, 97; above, nn. 10, 14; and below, n. 88. For Abraham ibn Ezra's influence on R. Judah's leading student, R. Eleazar of Worms, in the realm of biblical studies, see my *Jewish Education and Society in the High Middle Ages* (Detroit, Mich., 2007), 88–89. R. Saʿadyah Gaon, who was also cited by *Ḥasidei Ashkenaz* with some frequency (see, e.g., Dan, *Torat ha-Sod shel Ḥasidut Ashkenaz*, 11–12, 22–24, 166–68, I. Ta-Shma, *Knesset Meḥqarim*, 1:182–84, 214; and my *"Peering through the Lattices,"* 219, n. 68), is mentioned once in R. Judah's exoteric Torah commentary (ed. Lange, 97). See below, n. 63.

R. Judah *he-Ḥasid*'s involvement with "northern French" *peshat* would seem, *prima facie*, to be a bit anomalous or unexpected. Indeed, we shall see that leading Rhineland scholars during the twelfth century were not involved with *peshat* for the most part, even as a number of rabbinic scholars in Mainz and Worms during the pre-Crusade period had been.[20] The fact is, however, that R. Judah *he-Ḥasid*'s attitude toward intellectual developments in northern France is somewhat more nuanced than has been assumed. Although R. Judah was clearly concerned about the unchecked spread of Tosafist dialectic especially as it was practiced by unqualified or lesser students, he nonetheless adopted a number of older French customs and approaches in place of those that were more typical in the Rhineland. Similarly, his concern with establishing proper prayer and his criticism of errant rites did not necessarily single out French custom; on occasion he actually prefers the French rite. Hence his interest in *peshat*—especially in light of the disinterest among his contemporary rabbinic colleagues in Germany—is perhaps another such preference.[21] Similarly, although there is not a single reference to Rashi in *Sefer Ḥasidim* (a somewhat surprising omission to be sure),[22] R. Judah refers to Rashi with a degree of frequency in his own Torah commentary, as we shall see.

Identifying the components of this Torah commentary of R. Judah *he-Ḥasid* is not a simple task. In the main, Lange published R. Judah's comments as they are found in two manuscripts, ms. Cambridge 669.2 and ms. Moscow 82. Quite a number of comments in these manuscripts are explicitly labeled as having been transmitted by R. Judah to his son R. Zal(t)man (through phrases such as "my father explained to me" or "my father asked," and so on), while others are labeled as having been uttered by R. Judah himself or otherwise transmitted by his students. Lange supplements the material in these two manuscripts with comments that are also specifically attributed to R. Judah *he-Ḥasid* in various Tosafist Torah compilations.[23]

[20] See above, Introduction, nn. 28, 73; and below, at the end of chapter 3.

[21] See Eric Zimmer, *'Olam ke-Minhago Noheg* (Jerusalem, 1996), 276–77, 282–83, 286, 296–97 (and cf. my review in *Jewish Quarterly Review* 89 [1998], 205–6, and my "R. Judah *he-Ḥasid* and the Rabbinic Scholars of Regensburg," *JQR* 96 [2006], 34); *'Arugat ha-Bosem*, ed. Urbach, vol. 4 (Jerusalem, 1963), 88–93; I. Ta-Shma, *Knesset Meḥqarim*, 1:208–23; S. Emanuel, "Ha-Polmos shel Ḥasidei Ashkenaz," 609–19; and cf. Ta-Shma, *Halakhah, Minhag u-Meẓi'ut be-Ashkenaz, 1000–1350* (Jerusalem, 1996), 119–24; Haym Soloveitchik, "Three Themes in the *Sefer Ḥasidim*," *AJS Review* 1 (1976), 330–35, 350–52; and my "On the Study of *Seder Qodashim* in Medieval Europe," [Hebrew] in *Jubilee Volume for Prof. Yosef Hacker*, ed. Y. Kaplan et al. (Jerusalem, 2012; in press), part two (end).

[22] See Ta-Shma, *Halakhah, Minhag u-Meẓi'ut be-Ashkenaz, 1000–1350*, 128–29.

[23] See above, n. 18. Lange also presents *gematria*-like comments from R. Judah *he-Ḥasid* that are found in R. Abraham b. Azri'el's *piyyut* commentary, *'Arugat ha-Bosem*, in the name of רי"ח בש"ם ניחוח (= ר' יהודה חסיד בן שמואל). See ed. Lange, 4, 5, 82, 88, 148–49.

At the same time Lange also includes interpretations from the Moscow and Cambridge manuscripts in which R. Judah *he-Ḥasid* is not explicitly mentioned. As with many of the Torah commentaries that were produced in both northern France and Germany during the thirteenth century, names of contemporary Tosafists or other rabbinic scholars were added or linked by editors and copyists. These addenda are found not only within commentaries that were intended as compilatory works but also in cases where the basic commentary being copied belonged to a single author. This is the case with ms. Moscow 82 and especially with ms. Cambridge 669.2.[24]

My methodological assumption with regard to these two manuscripts is that only those comments in which R. Judah's name is explicitly mentioned (or referred to by R. Zal[t]man), either in the main manuscript collections or in passages by him that are recorded in the various Tosafist compilations, will be treated as such. Indeed, there are a number of passages in the Cambridge manuscript that are similar to other comments made by R. Judah or to his exegetical approaches—leading Lange to include them in his edition[25]—which actually belong to contemporaries of R. Judah or even

[24] Cf. above, chapter 2, n. 34.

[25] See Lange's introduction, 10–11. The Cambridge manuscript begins by reproducing the first comment of Rashi, in which R. Isaac questions why the Torah began here and not with the first *mizvah* in Exodus 12. Just as R. Jacob of Orleans did (see above, chapter 2, n. 126), the Cambridge manuscript questions R. Isaac's assumption that the first *mizvah* was not recorded until Exodus 12, since circumcision and various Noachide precepts are mentioned and presumed already in the book of Genesis, and a similar answer is suggested (ed. Lange, 2). The Cambridge commentary then notes that *ba'alei midrashim* looked for the midrashic source of R. Isaac's statement but did not find it. There is a tradition, however, that R. Solomon (Rashi) in fact was citing all of this in the name of his father. Indeed, by citing his father in this way (*'amar R. Yizḥaq*), Rashi was able to begin his commentary to the Torah with an *'alef* (and to then finish it with the letter *tav*). As Lange notes (2, n. 19), the source of R. Isaac's comment appears to be found in *Midrash Tanḥuma* (ed. Buber, ch. 11), and see also *Tosafot ha-Shalem*, ed. Gellis, 1:1 (and Lange, 2, n. 21). In the next comment in the Cambridge manuscript, a simple but profound interpretation (introduced by the phrase אלא כך הפשט) is found on the beginning phrase of the second verse in Genesis, *va-ha'arez haytah tohu va-vohu.* This *peshat* discussion is cited anonymously in *Hadar Zeqenim* (as noted by Lange, 2, n. 25), and ms. Bodl. 2343 (see below, chapter 4 n. 124) records this explanation in the name of Ibn Ezra (although it is not found in his extant commentaries to this verse). See *Tosafot ha-Shalem*, ed. Gellis, 1:18, sec. 6. On R. Judah *he-Ḥasid*'s use of Ibn Ezra, see below. Finally, like Rashi and R. Jacob of Orleans, the Cambridge manuscript also solves basic *peshat* questions with appropriate *midrashim.* See, e.g., Gen. 1:8 (ed. Lange, 4–5) and Gen. 2:3 (ed. Lange, 6). The Cambridge manuscript also deals with Rashi's commentary to Gen. 13:10 (ed. Lange, 19); 15:17 (Lange, 20); 18:22 (Lange, 21); 19:26 (Lange, 25); Gen. 21:7 (Lange, 26); 25:22 (Lange, 37); 25:27–28 (Lange, 37–38); 36:24 (Lange, 48); 37:12 (Lange, 49); 37:18 (Lange, 50); 48:9 (Lange, 64); 49:10 (Lange, 66); 49:22 and 50:10 (Lange, 68); Ex. 1:21 (Lange, 72–73); 2:14 and 2:20 (Lange, 74); 4:9 (Lange, 76); 6:3 and 7:27 (Lange, 77); 8:15 (Lange, 78); 9:22 and 9:24 (Lange, 79); 10:22 (Lange, 80); 12:29 (Lange, 82–83); 14:5 (Lange, 86); 20:1 (Lange, 98); 21:1 (Lange, 103); 21:19, 21:22, 21:30, 23:8, 23:11, 23:21 (Lange, 107–8); 34:21 (Lange, 128); Lev. 1:1–2, 1:4, 1:8, 1:10, 1:14–15, and 2:6 (Lange,

later Ashkenazic figures, as occasionally noted by Lange himself.[26] It is therefore difficult at best to consider any anonymous or unattributed comments as belonging to R. Judah, points of similarity in content notwithstanding. This methodological caveat aside, the scope and specific interpretational strategies R. Judah employed in the comments he transmitted to his son and to others (and those that are attributed directly to him in other collections) form a fairly unified methodological commentary, as we shall see.

The *peshat* comment to Genesis 3:1 discussed above (on the nature of the snake) is found in two versions of the compilatory Tosafist Torah commentary *Moshav Zeqenim*, both of which cite R. Judah *he-Ḥasid* by name.[27] These two works also contain a passage in which R. Judah *he-Ḥasid*, without mentioning Rashi, questions and explains the midrashic text in *Bereshit Rabbah* (ch. 22), which suggests that one female twin was born together with Cain, and two females twins were born with Abel, which forms the basis of Rashi's comment at the end of Genesis 4:1.[28]

Without mentioning Rashi by name again, R. Judah *he-Ḥasid* (as found in ms. Warsaw 204) explains and amplifies the comment made by Rashi to Genesis 4:15, that God added a letter of His name to the name of Cain.[29] Similarly, R. Judah includes an additional dimension to the midrashic passage cited by Rashi on Genesis 5:29, as an explanation for the Torah's derivation of Noah's name.[30]

135–37); 22:3 (Lange, 151); 26:16, and 27:13, 18 (Lange, 158–59); Nu. 15:32 (Lange, 176); 18:32 (Lange, 179); 32:12 (Lange, 194).

[26] See, e.g., ed. Lange, 8 (Ri *ha-Lavan* and R. Elḥanan b. ha-Ri, from his *Tosafot* to *'Avodah Zarah*, and see also 56); 13 (Rabbenu Tam; and see also 204, n. 7, which involves R. Yosef *Bekhor Shor* as well); 18 (question on Rashi, and response from the author of *Sefer ha-Gan*); 23, n. 29 (R. Jacob *ha-Gizbar* of Montrevaille); 25, n. 57 (R. Yosef Qara); 46 (n. 24), 55 (n. 94); 90 (n. 75), 146 (n. 4), 172, nn. 44–45 (R. Yosef *Bekhor Shor*; as we shall see, there are occasions in which R. Judah *he-Ḥasid* almost appears to play off R. Yosef *Bekhor Shor*); 146, n. 1 (R. Yeḥi'el of Paris), 156 (to Lev. 25:17, R. Simḥah of Speyer); 206 (to Deut. 22:12, 24, R. Simḥah of Speyer and R. Yeḥi'el of Paris); and 191 (an addendum from R. Solomon b. Samuel to Nu. 25:12 in the name of R. Eleazar of Worms). Cf. I. Marcus, "Exegesis for the Few and for the Many," 7* (n. 16), and 10*.

[27] See *Moshav Zeqenim* ed. S. Sasoon (Jerusalem, 1982), 3; and ms. Paris 260, as noted by Lange (above, n. 17).

[28] See *Perushei ha-Torah le-R. Yehudah he-Ḥasid*, ed. Lange, 7–8. As Lange notes (8, n. 88), only the initials ר"י are found in *Pa'aneaḥ Raza* (rather than רי"ח). See also, ed. Lange, 35 (Gen. 25:6), and *Ta'amei Mesoret ha-Miqra le-R. Yehudah he-Ḥasid*, 16 (Gen. 4:10).

[29] *Perushei ha-Torah le-R. Yehudah he-Ḥasid*, ed. Lange, 9. See also ed. Lange, 11 (Gen. 6:9), and 16 (Gen. 11:1). In Gen. 4:15, we encounter for the second time R. Judah *he-Ḥasid*, as cited by his son R. Zal(t)man, recorded in both the Cambridge and Moscow manuscripts (*piresh 'avi*; the first such occurrence is in Gen. 3:20, see above, n. 15). As noted by Lange, this comment is also found in ms. Vatican 45 (which has quite a number of comments in the name of R. Yehudah *he-Ḥasid*), and in ms. Bodl. 2344, an enhanced version of *Pa'aneaḥ Raza*. On the nature of this manuscript, see above, chapter 2, n. 143.

[30] See *Perushei ha-Torah*, ed. Lange, 9. At the same time, the Cambridge manuscript (without referring to R. Judah *he-Ḥasid*; see ed. Lange, 11) compares and contrasts Rashi's assertion (in

R. Judah *he-Ḥasid*'s father, R. Samuel *he-Ḥasid*, expresses precisely the same concerns as Rashi in determining the timing of the flood (Gen. 8:4–5).[31] In Genesis 9:18, R. Judah focuses on the "question according to the *peshat*" (*ha-qushya lefi ha-peshat*) as to why Kenaʿan alone was identified as the son of Ḥam, and, even more pointedly, why Kenaʿan was cursed, since he did not actively participate in the episode involving Noah's drunkeness.[32] In Genesis 10:13, R. Judah *he-Ḥasid* deals with the grammatical problem of plural names that appear to be attached to the sons of Miẓraʾim named in this verse and the next (ומצרים ילד את לודים ואת ענמים ואת להבים וכו'), and in Gen. 46:23 regarding the sons of Dan (ובני דן חושים), but in a different way than R. Yosef *Bekhor Shor* does. *Bekhor Shor* maintains that there are more than a few instances within the biblical corpus where the grammatical rules concerning the agreement of nouns, adjectives, and verbs with respect to gender and number are disregarded, including the plural names found in these verses.[33] R. Judah, on the other hand, suggests that each of the figures who was given a plural-sounding name had a twin. The various sets of twins then married each other so that whole families named after the initial child or children were created in this way.[34]

---

his first comment on Gen. 6:13) that the fate of the generation of the flood was sealed by its licentiousness, with the following assertion (in his second comment to that verse) that ascribed their sealed fate to their pernicious acts of theft. It is suggested that both factors together contributed to the result, or that perhaps each person stole his friend's spouse so that both acts contributed to their downfall. On the other hand, this manuscript (ed. Lange, 11) also records without attribution that the one who interprets the *ẓohar* on the ark (Gen. 6:16) as a precious stone that provided light (the second view presented by Rashi there) is mistaken, since the verb found in this verse, *taʿaseh*, does not fit this meaning. Similarly, the one who holds that the צוהר was a window (the first view presented by Rashi) is also mistaken, since the sun and the moon did not function during the flood. Rather, *ẓohar* means oil: that oil should be collected and prepared for use in the ark. This oil would serve as the fuel source for maintaining life. Cf. *Tosafot ha-Shalem*, ed. Gellis, 1:210.

31 *Perushei ha-Torah*, ed. Lange, 12. See also G. Brin, "ʿIyyun be-Perusho shel R. Yehudah he-Ḥasid la-Torah," 10. The text (in ms. Paris 260) reads הקשה אבין של הרי"ח rather than אבי הקשה (as R. Zalman usually indicates).

32 *Perushei ha-Torah*, ed. Lange, 14 (Gen. 9:18). Both the Moscow and Cambridge manuscripts here record אבי הקשה as usual. In Gen. 9:23 (Lange, ibid.), a question (found in the Moscow manuscript) is raised on Rashi's suggestion that the Jewish people merited the precept of wearing the *tallit* because of Shem's role in covering Noah. As we have seen, however, this question is found in several texts in the name of R. Jacob of Orleans; cf. above, chapter 2, n. 149. This may well be an extraneous interpolation into R. Judah's commentary.

33 See *Perushei R. Yosef Bekhor Shor* to Gen. 1:26, ed. Nevo, 6–7. *Bekhor Shor* uses these patterns of biblical grammar to respond to a polemical challenge regarding the possible multiplicity of the Divine. See also *Perushei Bekhor Shor* (to Gen. 46:15), ed. Nevo, 83.

34 *Perushei ha-Torah*, ed. Lange, 15–16. R. Judah adds that in the case of the sons of Dan (ובני דן חושים), the second son, Shuham, is mentioned in Nu. 26:42. Cf. ed. Lange, 24 (to Gen. 19:13); ed. Lange, 61–62 (to Gen. 46:15); *Tosafot ha-Shalem*, ed. Gellis, 4:244, sec. 6; 4:245, sec. 4; and

Like R. Yosef *Bekhor Shor*, R. Judah *he-Ḥasid* asks why the Almighty was more upset with Sarah for laughing at the news of her impending pregnancy (Gen. 18:13) than He was with Abraham, who also laughed earlier upon hearing the news (Gen. 17:7). *Bekhor Shor* suggests that since Abraham's laughter was accompanied by falling on his face (*va-yippol ʿal panav*) and bowing, he was showing that he believed this would indeed occur, and his laughter was a sign of joy that the Almighty would change the natural process in his favor. R. Judah *he-Ḥasid*, on the other hand, assumes that Sarah's laughter was similarly a sign of happiness. The difference in the Almighty's response is due to the fact that at the point when Sarah laughed, she had already resumed having menstrual blood (as per Rashi's commentary to Gen. 18:8, based on *Bereshit Rabbah* and *Bava Meẓiʿa* 87a), and it was at that point that she started to spread the news to other women about the change in her status. The Almighty was concerned with why she had shared the news at this point. His preferred method was to have miracles occur quietly and without fanfare, and He chided Sarah for revealing and reveling in a miracle that was a rather unusual happening. Sarah initially denied expressing her joy to others, because she was afraid the event might now not occur. Although the Almighty repeated that she had done this, His promise to her would nonetheless remain in place, and she would have a child.[35]

R. Judah *he-Ḥasid* raises the same kind of *peshat* issue here as *Bekhor Shor* does. Unlike *Bekhor Shor*, however, R. Judah resolves the problem in accordance with Rashi's commentary (Gen. 18:8) and as a kind of extension to it, including Rashi's reliance here on an *ʾaggadah ha-meyashevet divrei miqra*. R. Judah *he-Ḥasid* also suggests this interpretation (as Rashi himself does on occasion) as part of a larger point or program of piety. As noted by Lange, a section in *Sefer Ḥasidim* advises that one ought not share with his wife impending good news that he receives in a dream or in some form of angelic revelation (*gillui Eliyahu*) lest she reveal this to others, since Divine miracles are not typically done in a public fashion.[36] Although R. Judah's own sense of *peshat* is clearly developed, we have already seen that he sometimes follows Rashi's commentary even more closely than R. Yosef *Bekhor Shor* does. Nonetheless, R. Yosef *Bekhor Shor*'s polemical concern about not portraying the *Avot* in a negative light may also have been a factor in the specific direction his interpretation took.[37]

Perushei ha-Torah, ed. Lange, 24 (to Gen. 19:13). See also below, n. 145, for a similar *peshat* approach to Gen. 46:23 by R. Isaiah di Trani (= *Tosafot ha-Shalem*, ed. Gellis 4:244, sec. 1).

[35] *Perushei ha-Torah*, ed. Lange, 21–22.

[36] See *Sefer Ḥasidim* (Parma), ed. Wistinetski, sec. 386 (= *Sefer Ḥasidim* [Bologna], ed. Margoliot, sec. 447).

[37] See above, chapter 2, n. 100.

Interestingly, R. Abraham b. Azri'el of Bohemia adduces a *gematria* from his teacher R. Judah b. Samuel *he-Ḥasid* (רי״ח בש״ם ניחוח)[38] that supports the rabbinic interpretation in tractate *Ḥullin* which Rashi cites in his Torah commentary to Genesis 28:11 (*va-yiqaḥ me-'avnei ha-maqom*) to explain the use of the singular form of the word for stone (*va-yiqaḥ 'et ha-'even*) used in 28:18. The stones that Jacob had gathered to place under his head fought with each other for primacy of position in this role until the Almighty combined them into a single stone, which upon arising Jacob took to make into an altar. R. Judah's *gematria* equates the phrase ויקח את האבן with the phrase כל אבנים היו אחת.[39]

R. Judah's use of a *gematria* here to confirm Rashi's interpretation is surely a function of the many different levels or modes of truth that characterized Ashkenazic Torah study, and we shall have occasion to see additional examples of this phenomenon within R. Judah's Torah commentary. It should be noted that in at least one instance (Gen.14:14), Rashi himself presents a *gematria* (put forward in *Bereshit Rabbah* and elsewhere) as an *'aggadah ha-meyashevet divrei miqra*. The "318" men who came to Abraham's aid according to the verse were represented by the powerful Eliezer alone, since 318 is the *gematria* of Eliezer's name.

The Paris manuscript version of the Tosafist Torah collection *Moshav Zeqenim* records the following interpretation of Reuven's actions with respect to Bilhah (Gen. 35:22), in the name of R. Yehudah *he-Ḥasid* (בשם הרי״ח): "According to the *peshat* [*lefi ha-peshat*], Reuven did not sin even with respect to moving the beds,"[40] as Rashi interpreted (and he certainly did not actually live with her, as both *Bekhor Shor* and Radak suggested).[41] A simple reading of the verse(s) yields (והכי מידריש פשטיה דקרא) that at the point when Jacob dwelled in the land (as recorded at the beginning of Gen. 35:22 and leading up to the actions of Reuven), Rachel died; Reuven left his father's home and went his own way because he saw Rachel's maid Bilhah becoming his father's consort, and he did not want to witness the denigration of his mother, Leah. Thus Reuven left (*va-yelekh Re'uven*), but it was Jacob who had relations with Bilhah (*va-yishkav 'et Bilhah*). When Jacob heard that Reuven was upset due to the perceived denigration of his mother (*tava 'elbon 'immo*)—which is the intent of the next phrase, in Genesis 35:22, "and Jacob heard" (*va-yishma Yisra'el*)—he sent for Reuven. Upon his return, Reuven found that Jacob now had twelve sons altogether (as recorded in the final part of Gen. 35:22, *va-yihyu bnei Ya'aqov shneim 'asar*), whereas he

38 Cf. above, n. 23.

39 See *Perushei ha-Torah*, ed. Lange, 42; and cf. *Tosafot ha-Shalem*, ed. Gellis, 3:97–98.

40 See ms. Paris 260, fol. 74v.

41 See above, chapter 2, n. 119.

had only eleven when Reuven left. The reunion of Jacob and Reuven was successful, because Jacob spoke well of (or to) Reuven.

R. Judah's *peshat* interpretation here is quite nuanced and creative, even as it serves to "protect" Reuven by suggesting that his only miscue or misdeed was in leaving his father.[42] We shall see numerous other example of this unique and carefully calibrated, syncopated style of interpretation on the part of R. Judah *he-Ḥasid*, which accounts for every nuance of the verse in question by assigning different phrases or pieces to different figures on the scene.[43]

In explaining or justifying Judah's proposed punishment to burn Tamar for her actions (Gen. 38:24, הוציאוה ותשרף), Rashi presents the view of R. Meir (cited in *Midrash Rabbah*) that since Tamar was the daughter of Shem, who had the status of a *kohen*, this form of capital punishment was mandated for the sin of adultery. In ms. Vatican 45 (which contains a number of comments by R. Judah *he-Ḥasid*),[44] this interpretation of Rashi is cited by name, and is subjected to a series of pointed questions. Since Tamar was neither married nor affianced (*'arusah*), why was she guilty of halakhic adultery and deserving of death? On the other hand, when Judah learned that the woman in question was his daughter-in-law Tamar, why did he then release her from punishment, since this relationship was forbidden for Noachides as well? In any case, the uniform mode of capital punishment for all such violations committed by a Noachide was death by the sword (*sayyif*), according to one rabbinic view, and death by asphyxiation (*ḥeneq*) according to a second view. Death by burning (*serefah*), however, is not indicated by any rabbinic view.[45]

A *yesh mefarshim* is then presented which suggests that the court of Shem had decreed that all Noachides who had relations with non-Jews were to be burned, but this was not the case for a (promiscuous) relationship with

[42] See *Perushei ha-Torah*, ed. Lange, 48, and cf. the commentary of Ramban. R. Jacob b. Asher, who had access to the teachings and writings of R. Judah *he-Ḥasid* (see, e.g., my *"Peering through the Lattices,"* 245–47) cites this interpretation (with an insignificant variation) in *Perush ha-Tur he-'Arukh*, ed. Y. K. Reinitz (Jerusalem, 1961), 76, in the name of R. Yehudah *he-Ḥasid*. After presenting two alternate interpretations of this verse, *Pa'aneaḥ Raza*, 160, records the name of ר"י of Orleans after the final interpretation, which is quite similar to that of R. Judah *he-Ḥasid*. Cf. ed. Lange, 48 (n. 50), and 60 (n. 11). As it often does, *Moshav Zeqenim*, ed. Sasson, 63, attributes this comment of R. Judah *he-Ḥasid* simply (and imprecisely) to ר"י.

[43] On the one hand, R. Judah *he-Ḥasid*'s interpretation of the details of the sale of Joseph (Gen. 37:28, ed. Lange, 51) comports with the approach of *Bekhor Shor*, incorporating the notion found in the *Tanḥuma*, that the brothers swore Joseph to secrecy under penalty of *herem* (and cf. *Sefer Ḥasidim*, ed. Wistinetski, sec. 1961). See above, chapter 2, n. 110. On the other hand, however, R. Judah appears to agree with the basic premise of Rashbam, that the brothers did not sell Joseph directly to the Egyptians (with which *Bekhor Shor* strongly disagrees), although R. Judah does not account for the actions of the various groups of merchants in the same precise way that Rashbam does.

[44] See, e.g., above, n. 29, and below, n. 49.

[45] See *Perushei ha-Torah*, ed. Lange, 53.

a Jew. Hence Judah removed his demand for *serefah* when he found out that he was the male participant. Although R. Judah's initials (ר״ח) appear at this point in the manuscript, which suggests that the preceding was his interpretation, Y. S. Lange cogently suggests that in this instance R. Judah's name actually precedes his view.[46] The exegetical solution that follows is once again a linguistically simple one and is consistent, perhaps, with medieval realia as well: the burning prescribed by Judah for Tamar was not a form of capital punishment at all. Rather, Judah suggested that a sign be singed into her cheeks (as a kind of ad hoc penalty), a suggestion that he abandoned when he found out that it was his daughter-in-law who was involved.[47]

The correctness of Lange's textual observation is borne out by looking at the fuller version of R. Judah *he-Ḥasid*'s comment to this episode as it appears in both the Cambridge and Moscow manuscript versions of R. Judah's Torah commentary. At the end of a lengthy comment from his father on the intent of Judah's statement that "[Tamar] is more righteous than me" (צדקה ממני, Gen. 38:26), R. Zal(t)man presents his father's view on Tamar's punishment:

> And my father also said, why did [Judah] not say here, "she should be taken out and burned *by fire*" (הוציאוה ותשרף באש) as the Torah writes regarding the [punishment for the] daughter of a *kohen* [in Lev. 21:9, where the Torah states, "and the daughter of a *kohen* who has profaned herself by becoming a harlot . . . she shall be burned in fire], באש תשרף"? Rather, according to the *peshat*, [Judah] did not command that Tamar be [put to death by being] burnt, but only that she be singed about her cheeks and teeth in the way that thieves are punished, although the context does not imply this (אבל אינו משמע כן).

R. Judah *he-Ḥasid* suggests a simple yet innovative *peshat*-like solution to the problem (which relies also on common societal practice, *derekh 'erez*) that he nonetheless acknowledges does not fit so well within the larger context of this section, since it appears from the context that a death penalty was at issue.[48]

46 *Perushei R. Yosef Bekhor Shor*, ed. Nevo, 71, for example, maintains that death by burning was the prescribed punishment for promiscuity in the period prior to the giving of the Torah (כך היה דינם קודם מתן תורה).

47 See also G. Brin, "'Iyyun be-Perushei R. Yehudah he-Ḥasid la-Torah," 3.

48 See *Perushei ha-Torah*, ed. Lange, 54. As Lange notes (54, n. 88), both versions of this striking interpretation are cited in *Moshav Zeqenim*, one in the name of R. Judah *he-Ḥasid* and the other from החסיד, and by R. Jacob *ba'al ha-Turim* in both the long and short versions of his Torah commentary, in the name of R(abbenu) Yehudah *he-Ḥasid*. Cf. *Tosafot ha-Shalem*, ed. Gellis, 4:80, sec. 15; 4:85, sec. 9, and *Ḥizzequni* to Gen. 38:24. For R. Judah's unique understanding of the

In response to or as an amplification of Rashi's comment to Genesis 41:50 ("And two sons were born to Joseph prior to the coming of the years of famine"), "since it is forbidden [according to the Talmud in tractate *Taʿanit* 11a] to engage in marital relations during a time of famine," R. Judah *he-Ḥasid* limits this prohibition to someone like Joseph, who knew for certain that there would be a famine because of the dream of Pharaoh. Levi, on the other hand, who did not have nearly as clear an awareness of the situation in advance, was not prohibited from having relations, and therefore Yokheved was born as the children of Israel entered Egypt (as per the *sugyot* in *Sotah* 12a and *Bava Batra* 120a and 123b). In a second version of this comment, R. Judah's formulation is that Joseph knew when the famine would end and was therefore enjoined until that time, while Levi did not, and he could not calculate or even estimate how long he would have to abstain. Thus marital relations were not prohibited for him.[49]

Like Rashbam and R. Yosef *Bekhor Shor*, R. Judah *he-Ḥasid* seeks the etymology of the word *nashani* in Genesis 41:51, used in connection with the troubles that Joseph had experienced in Egypt. R. Judah rejects the explanation put forth by *Bekhor Shor* (without mentioning his name)[50] that *nashani* means to forget (his suffering). It would not have been especially flattering for Joseph to praise God simply for allowing him to forget his travails. Instead, R. Judah suggests that this word has the meaning or sense of jumping. The Almighty quickly and totally removed Joseph's troubles; and they thus appeared to "jump" away. R. Judah cites the verse in Jeremiah

---

culpability of ʿEr and Onan according to the midrashic view that they were under the age of 13 (ed. Lange, 52–53, and *Tosafot ha-Shalem*, ed. Gellis, 4:63–64), see Haym Soloveitchik, "Three Themes in the *Sefer Ḥasidim*," 324–25, and cf. my *"Peering through the Lattices,"* 104–5.

49 See *Perushei ha-Torah*, ed. Lange, 56. The first version is found in ms. Strasbourg 44 (a Pietist Torah commentary attributed to R. Eleazar of Worms), in ms. Bodl. 270 (a manuscript form of the Tosafist Torah compilation *Hadar Zeqenim*, as well as in the published version of this work, fol. 19v), in ms. Vatican 45, and in *Daʿat Zeqenim* (to Genesis, fol. 41b; see *Tosafot ha-Shalem*, ed. Gellis, 4:144, sec. 6). The second version is found in ms. Cambridge 669.2 and ms. Moscow 82. *Paʿaneaḥ Raza*, 183–84; *Perushei R. Ḥayyim Paltiʾel*, ed. Lange, 133–34; and *Minḥat Yehudah*, Gen. fol. 41b, also record a different answer to this question from Ri's martyred Tosafist son, R. Elḥanan (d. 1184), which had apparently been given in connection with the talmudic discussion of this principle in *Taʿanit* 11a. R. Elḥanan's answer (which focuses on the remorse that Joseph should have felt and displayed, since he did not know the status of his family during the famine, while Levi was aware that the family was in fact managing to survive) is found (anonymously) in *Ḥizzequni*. This answer is also cited by R. Samuel Bamberg in connection with the *sugya* in *Taʿanit* in ms. B.M. 9931. See *Tosafot ha-Shalem*, ed. Gellis, 4:145, sec. 10. Another answer (based on the requirements and parameters of the precept of procreation) is found in ms. Vatican 45 (and see also *Moshav Zeqenim*, 82), while *Tosafot* to *Taʿanit* (11a, s.v. *ʾasur*) regards this as a high but non-required form of pious behavior (*ḥasidut*) on the part of Joseph (דלכ"ע לא הוי אסור אלא למי שרוצה לנהוג עצמו בחסידות ויוסף לא שימש אבל שאר אנשים שימשו). Cf. below, n. 206.

50 See *Perushei Bekhor Shor ʿal ha-Torah*, ed. Nevo, 77.

51:30, נשתה גבורתם, "the bravery of the Babylonians quickly left them," as an example of this usage.[51]

On Genesis 46:26–27—"All of the souls who came with Jacob into Egypt, who came out of his loins besides Jacob's sons' wives, all the souls were sixty-six. And the sons of Joseph who were born to him in Egypt were two souls; all of the souls of the house of Jacob who came into Egypt were seventy"—R. Zal(t)man reports the following questions from his father: If the verse mentions "those who came out of his loins," why does it include the wives of Jacob's sons; what is their purpose here? Also, the next verse refers to the sons of Joseph who were born to him *in* Egypt, before announcing that the total number of members of the house of Jacob who came to Egypt was seventy.

R. Judah suggests, according to the *peshat* (*lefi ha-peshat*), that the number sixty-six (in verse 26) does not include Joseph, nor does it include the spouses of the married sons of Jacob. This is the meaning of "besides Jacob's son's wives" (מלבד נשי בני יעקב); they were excluded from this count since, in rabbinic thought, husband and wife are counted as one. On the other hand, Dinah and Serah bat Asher (who were single at this point) were included in this count. Verse 27, however, which presents the total of seventy, means to include the four wives of Jacob's married sons (who were also their nieces), in addition to Jacob's daughters. R. Judah justifies this interpretation by noting the parallel verse in Deuteronomy 10:22, "with seventy souls your forefathers went down to Egypt." Clearly, Joseph and his progeny are not to be included, since they did not go down to Egypt at this time. R. Judah also finds support for this approach from the verse in Exodus 1:5, "for the souls who came from the loins of Jacob are seventy, and Joseph was [already] in Egypt." Not including Joseph, there were seventy souls.[52] As he did regarding the exchange between Jacob and Reuben about Bilhah, R. Judah *he-Ḥasid* shifts the perspective of the verses (or even individual phrases) to accommodate the differences in detail that are detected in a close reading of the Torah's presentation.

R. Zal(t)man cites his father as asking why Genesis 47:8 (the verse in which Pharaoh asked Jacob, "How many are the years of your life?") was included in the Torah. R. Judah's response is to recreate an implicit dialogue between the two that is reflected only sparingly within the Torah itself. When Jacob came to Pharaoh, he proposed the following: If you will allow me to return to the burial land of my forefathers after the famine has

[51] *Perushei ha-Torah*, ed. Lange, 57. As Lange points out (57, n. 14*), this is precisely how Rashi interprets the verse in Jeremiah. Rashbam and Ibn Ezra understand this word in Genesis 41 as the granting of grace (חנני), while Radak interprets similarly to *Bekhor Shor*.

[52] See *Perushei ha-Torah*, ed. Lange, 62, and *Tosafot ha-Shalem*, ed. Gellis, 4:245, sec. 3.

ended, that will be very good. But if you will not allow this to happen, now that I have seen Joseph, I will simply purchase wheat from you here as in the past, and I will return to my home. Pharaoh responds by saying that he was surprised that a person as elderly as Jacob would be proposing as his first choice a plan that presumes that he would live for another five years until the famine was over. Jacob responds in turn that Pharaoh should not be surprised, since he had not yet reached the age of his forefathers. His appearance as a very elderly person was due to the tribulations of his life, which caused the appearance of old age to come upon him early. Hearing this, Pharaoh acceded to Jacob's request, and for this reason, Jacob blessed Pharaoh (Gen. 47:10) as a sign of his gratitude. Jacob's initial blessing of Pharaoh when they first met (Gen. 47:7), however, was simply a statement of greeting. R. Judah concludes his innovative conflation of the discussion here by enunciating an exegetical principle: "Do not be surprised that this [entire dialogue] is not written explicitly, because that is a characteristic of Torah. From the response, you can know [and reconstruct] the question." The reconstruction of the dialogue undertaken here by R. Judah is once again suggested by the "syncopation" or seeming disjointedness of the verses in question.[53]

R. Judah *he-Ḥasid* understood Genesis 48:22, "And *I have given you* one portion more than any of your brothers (ואני נתתי לך שכם אחד על אחיך) which I took out of the hand of the Emorites with my sword and with my bow," to have been written by Moses in the fortieth year of the sojourn in the desert, just prior to his own death. Moses knew that Jacob had also said (Gen. 48:5) that "Ephraim and Menasheh will be to me like Reuven and Shim'on," signifying that Joseph's sons would inherit his double portion as a firstborn. Therefore, Moses decided to give the kingdom of 'Og in the Bashan, which he had recently conquered, to "half the tribe of Menasheh," as a sign that he had already begun to fulfill Jacob's instructions, since any land given to the tribe of Menasheh beyond that of Ephraim was considered part of the double portion of the *bekhorah*. Moses then instructed Joshua and the twelve dividers of the main body of the land of Israel to give land to the tribe of

[53] See *Perushei ha-Torah*, ed. Lange, 62–63 (concluding with his methodological insight, ואל תתמה שלא נכתב בפירוש כי כך היא המדה בתורה שמתוך התשובה יש לדעת את השאלה), and see also *Tosafot ha-Shalem*, ed. Gellis, 4:254, sec. 3. This passage, including the methodological statement, is found in both main manuscripts (Cambridge 669.2 and Moscow 82) of R. Judah's commentary (and it is also found in his name in an abridged form in *Pa'aneaḥ Raza*, 199, and in *Moshav Zeqenim*, ed. Sassoon, 94). On dialogue reconstruction in the commentaries of Rashi and *Bekhor Shor* and the use of such reconstruction to better understand the "motivations" of biblical characters, see above, chapter 2, n. 101. R. Judah *he-Ḥasid*'s point here, about the difference in Jacob's blessings of Pharaoh, is made in a different way by Rashi to Gen. 47:7 and 47:10; and cf. *Perushei Bekhor Shor*, ed. Nevo, 84.

Ephraim, and to give half the tribe of Menasheh the remaining portion in the land itself that was coming to them.[54]

A comment found at the beginning of Exodus in ms. Vatican 45, in the name of R. Judah *he-Ḥasid* (ר״יח), employs *remez* techniques to provide two sources or verifications for Rashi's comment (to Ex. 1:7, based on various *midrashim*) that the prolific Jewish women in Egypt gave birth to six children at once. First, the verse in 1 Chronicles 4:17 lists the birth of Miriam and two other children (ostensibly Aaron and Moses), and the word *ʾet* is found three times in naming these children, yielding a (*remez*) total of six. Second, the reverse *notariqon* of the word ותמלא in Exodus 1:7 ("and the land became full of them"), yields the phase אשה לעולם מתעברת תאומים ו׳. R. Judah further explains, in a more contextual vein, the phrase that "the land became full of them" (ותמלא הארץ אותם) at the end of the verse in an impressionistic sense, seeking to fill in an informational gap. At first they worked and studied (separately) inside their homes, but after a while, they appeared and went to the market in unison, walking ten abreast and then twenty abreast, so that it indeed seemed to the Egyptians that the land was full of them.[55]

R. Zal(t)man presents another excellent example of his father's "syncopated" *peshat* method which also seeks to fill in the narrative on Exodus 2:6, "And she opened [the basket] and she saw the child [*yeled*], and behold the youth [*naʿar*] was crying." According to R. Judah *he-Ḥasid*, the child/*yeled* was baby Moses, but the youth/*naʿar* who was crying was the three-year-old Aaron, who was sitting on the bank of the river (or on a camel, according to a variant reading) to see what would happen to Moses. Aaron could sit fairly close, since the Egyptians would not automatically recognize him as a Jew. Miriam (who was older), however, had to stand and observe from afar

[54] See *Perushei ha-Torah*, ed. Lange, 64–65; above, n. 10; above, chapter 2, nn. 102, 208; and below, n. 61. Rashi interprets the somewhat unusual word for *portion* that is used here (*shekhem*) as the *bekhorah*, whereby Joseph's son would receive two shares. See also *Perushei R. Yosef Bekhor Shor*, ed. Nevo, 86: בחרבי ובקשתי אין מקרא יוצא מידי פשוטו כי בודאי במלחמה לקחו אבל לא נודע היכן. Once again, it would seem that R. Judah *he-Ḥasid* is trying to address the exegetical question raised by *Bekhor Shor*, although he does so in a very different way.

[55] See *Perushei ha-Torah*, ed. Lange, 70, and cf. *Tosafot ha-Shalem*, ed. Gellis, 6:9–10. For another instance in which R. Judah uses a form of letter manipulation like *notariqon* to confirm a simple midrashic interpretation suggested by Rashi, see above, n. 39, and below, n. 84. Also in ms. Vatican 45, R. Judah *he-Ḥasid*'s interpretation of Exodus 1:12, that the Egyptians believed that the onerous work forced upon the Jews would itself lead to their numerical diminution, is characterized as *lefi ha-peshat.* R. Judah also assumes as obvious that the Jewish midwives Shifra and Pu'ah (Ex. 1:15) must have become converts to Judaism. Otherwise, how could they have acceded to Pharaoh's request to kill the Jewish children? This assumption is supported by Exodus 1:17, "and the midwives became fearers of God," suggesting that they were initially not of this mind. See *Perushei ha-Torah*, ed. Lange, 72. For an example in the methodology of R. Yosef *Bekhor Shor* of injecting this kind of logical/behavioral assumption (*sevara*) in order to properly understand a verse, see above, chapter 2, n. 110.

(ותתצב אחותו מרחוק, Ex. 2:4), so that she would not be recognized. When the basket was opened by the daughter of Pharaoh, and she saw the baby in it, the youth/*na'ar* (Aaron) who was near the baby could no longer restrain himself and began to cry. The daughter of Pharaoh had feelings of mercy, since she understood that Aaron was crying because he was afraid lest she drown the *yeled* (the baby Moses). Because of the concern shown by Aaron, the daughter of Pharaoh realized that the baby must be a Jewish child rather than a child of unclear origins.[56]

R. Judah *he-Ḥasid* also supports, explains, and qualifies a series of Rashi's comments in the portions of *Shemot*, *Va-Era*, *Bo*, and *Beshalaḥ*. His pietistic conclusion (found also in *Sefer Ḥasidim*), that one may not punish another through magical means unless it is clear that no righteous progeny will be descended from him, follows precisely Rashi's interpretation of Exodus 2:12 (based on *Shemot Rabbah*).[57] Rashi interprets Exodus 2:16, which refers to Yitro as a priest of *Midyan*, to mean that Yitro had left his idolatrous practices and had been excommunicated by his former correligionists. R. Judah *he-Ḥasid*, after citing Rashi, presents a passage from the *Mekhilta* which suggests that this break or change in status was perhaps not a total one. Rather, Yitro and Moses initially agreed that one of Moses's children would be a full-fledged Jew, while the other would remain uncircumcised and akin to a *ger toshav*. Thus the names of Moses's sons mentioned in Exodus 18:3–4 are characterized separately as the "name of one was Gershom," "and the name of one was Eliezer," rather than simply referring to Eliezer as Moses's second son.[58]

[56] See *Perushei ha-Torah*, ed. Lange, 73, and *Tosafot ha-Shalem*, ed. Gellis, 6:43, secs. 4, 8; ms. Hamburg 45 (*peshatim*), fol. 35r; *Nimmueqi ha-Rid*, ed. Chavel, 35; and cf. Rashbam (and *Tosafot ha-Shalem*, ed. Gellis, 6:42, sec. 1), and below, n. 148. The notion that the crying youth was specifically Aaron and not Moses (which is followed also by *Ḥizzequni*) is found in *Midrash Avkir*, a source that struck strong roots in Germany and with *Ḥasidei Ashkenaz* in particular. See my *"Peering through the Lattices,"* 138–39 (n. 13); Amos Geulah, "Lost Aggadic Works Known Only from Ashkenaz: *Midrash Abkir, Midrash Esfa* and *Devarim Zuta*," [Hebrew] (Ph.D. diss., Hebrew University, 2006), pt. 2, 44–45; *Perush ha-Roqeaḥ 'al ha-Torah*, 2:14; and cf. *Perush Rabbenu Ephraim 'al ha-Torah*, ed. J. Klugmann (Jerusalem, 2000), 181; G. Brin, "'Iyyun be-Perushei R. Yehudah he-Ḥasid la-Torah," 10–13; and below, nn. 149–50. R. Yosef *Bekhor Shor* suggests (on Ex. 2:4) that Miriam did not herself stand watch but sent a maidservant in her stead. *Pa'aneaḥ Raza*, 220, and *Perush Ba'al ha-Turim 'al ha-Torah* (in *Perush ha-Tur he-*'Arukh), ed. Reinitz, 1:141, include a *gematria* that supports R. Judah *he-Ḥasid*'s interpretation: נער בוכה בגימטריא זה אהרן הכהן. Ms. Hamburg 45, cited in *Tosafot ha-Shalem*, ed. Gellis, 6:43, sec. 8, suggests (*lefi ha-peshat*) that a second baby, the son of a neighbor, was also in the basket with Moses (since Yokheved agreed to try to save his life as well). Thus the *yeled* was the (smaller) Egyptian baby, and the *na'ar* was Moses, who looked robust compared to the smaller Egyptian boy. This interpretation beautifully accounts for the exclamation by the daughter of Pharaoh that Moses was *mi-yaldei ha-'ivrim zeh* (since the other child was not). See below, chapter 4.

[57] See *Perushei ha-Torah*, ed. Lange, 73, and cf. my *"Peering through the Lattices,"* 208–14.

[58] See *Perushei ha-Torah*, ed. Lange, 74; *Tosafot ha-Shalem*, ed. Gellis, 6:54–55, secs. 2, 4; and 8:10–11, sec. 54. See also R. Judah *he-Ḥasid*'s questioning of Rashi in Ex. 14:5, ed. Lange, 86.

R. Zal(t)man also brings interpretations from his father, characterized as *peshat*, that he heard from members of his father's *Ḥumash* circle, which included a number of rabbinic scholars who hailed from Eastern Europe, as noted above:[59]

> R. Isaac of Russia recounted for me the *peshat* [to Exodus 15:26, "all of the diseases that I brought upon Egypt I will not bring upon you, for I am the Lord who heals you"]. The phrase "I will not bring upon you" refers to one who serves Him in order to be rewarded, while "I am the Lord who heals you" refers to one who serves Him without any expectation of reward. For the one who serves without expectation of reward, I will do better such that if illness weighs heavily upon him, I will completely heal him. Similarly, the verse [in Deut. 7:12] begins with the plural form, "if you will listen to these judgments and keep and do them." Later in this verse, however, the singular form is used: "the Lord your God will keep for [or with] you the covenant and the kindness that He swore to your forefathers." Whoever serves Me and keeps My statutes without expectation of reward, out of love and not out of fear, I will sustain him by keeping the covenant and the kindness.[60]

R. Zal(t)man cites his father's unusual interpretation on Exodus, chapter 16, which is reminiscent of R. Judah's interpretation to Genesis 48 (on the inheritance of the tribe of Menasheh, noted above). After discussing the people's complaints about food and presenting the detailed description of the manna for much of the chapter, the Torah records three verses (Ex. 16:32–34) that contain Moses's instruction to preserve a jar of the manna in the holy ark as a remembrance of the manna, followed by another verse (Ex. 16:35), which records that the people ate the manna for forty years until they came to the land of Israel. R. Judah suggests that these verses about

[59] See above, n. 1, and see *Perushei ha-Torah*, ed. Lange, 91, 165.

[60] See *Perushei ha-Torah*, ed. Lange, 88. In some manuscripts, this interpretation is "signed" by מהר"ם ברי"ח (= R. Moses, son of R. Judah *he-Ḥasid*). See *Tosafot ha-Shalem*, ed. Gellis, 7:252, sec. 10. Cf. the passages from ms. Vatican 506 and ms. Hamburg 45 in *Tosafot ha-Shalem*, 7:253, secs. 12–13. In the prior passage in ed. Lange, 88, on the verse "and your sanctuary Lord that you have made to dwell in" (Ex.15:17), R. Zal(t)man writes, "from here my father interpreted" (*mi-kan pashat mori 'avi*; in *Pa'aneaḥ Raza*, 255, "from here ר"י said") "that they saw a finished Temple at the Red Sea, similar to the (third) one that would be built in the future. This is what R. Isaac of Russia told me." See also *Tosafot ha-Shalem*, ed. Gellis, 7:238–39, sec. 8. R. Judah's interpretation (*lefi ha-peshat*) of Ex. 16:18 ("he that gathered much had nothing left over, and he that gathered little had nothing lacking"), that the one who gathered too much always discarded the extra, and the one who gathered too little always made sure to fill his utensils (which appears to be against Rashi's interpretation to Ex. 16:17–18), is cited in some texts in the name of R. Isaiah di Trani. See Lange, 89 (n. 60); Gellis, 6:272, sec. 1; and below, n. 159.

preserving the manna were actually composed in the fortieth year of the Jews' sojourn in the desert.[61] They were placed here somewhat tangentially (*ʾagav gerara*), following the main discussion of the giving of the manna at the beginning of the Jews' sojourn in the desert, which is chronologically correct. R. Zal(t)man then adds that he found this same approach in the *yesod* of R. Samuel b. Meir (*kakh perush mori ʾavi, ve-shuv mazati bi-yesodo shel R. Shmuʾel b. Meir ken*).[62]

R. Judah *he-Ḥasid* inquires, citing R. Saʿadyah Gaon (*mi-shem R. Saʿadyah*), why Moses had to tell God that the Jewish people could not go up onto Mount Sinai (Ex. 19:23), since they had already been warned (twice) about this by God (in Ex. 19:12 and 19:21). "Did Moses think that God Himself did not know that He had commanded this limitation, or did Moses think that God had forgotten?" R. Isaac of Russia informed R. Zal(t)man that R. Judah *heḤasid* had explained that Moses did this in order to learn why God had in fact issued this warning, as well as why it was necessary to warn the people twice. According to the *pashteh di-qra* as presented by R. Judah, God told Moses, "go down and warn the people" (Ex. 19:21) not to ascend Mount Sinai. Moses thought that, since God was instructing him again at this point to go down and warn the people, he himself was now to be included in this restriction as well. Therefore, he states (in verse 23) that the people already knew not to go up, which was his way of asking if this meant that absolutely no one (including him) could ascend. God then responds by saying (in verse 24), "go down and ascend together with Aaron." The Jewish people as a whole may not ascend, but you and Aaron should do so.

[61] See *Perushei ha-Torah*, ed. Lange, 89–90 (beginning with the phrase אילו ג' פסוקים נכתבו בשנת ארבעים). Both the Cambridge and Moscow manuscripts specify that these three verses, which are identified (according to their content) as verses 32–33 and 35, were written in the fortieth year. Since verse 34 simply confirms that the jar was put into the ark by Aaron as God had commanded Moses, it is clear that this verse is a part of the later section as well. The final verse about the manna in this chapter, verse 36, consists of a statement about the manna's measurements, and thus belongs with the initial instructions and discussion.

[62] As Lange notes (*Perushei ha-Torah*, 90, n. 72), this comment is not found in the extant version of Rashbam's Torah commentary, although Rashbam, like Rashi and Ibn Ezra (in both his commentaries) does appear to suggest that the event in verses 33 and 34 (the placing of the jar in the ark) took place quite a bit later than the other events in this chapter, and that these verses were placed in this chapter for literary reasons rather than as a function of chronology. See M. Lockshin, *Rashbam's Commentary on Exodus*, 182. (On the literary connotation of the term *yesod*, see Y. S. Spiegel, *ʿAmudim be-Toldot ha-Sefer ha-ʿIvri* [Ramat Gan, 2005], 452–55.) R. Judah's comment is found verbatim (albeit without attribution) in ms. Hamburg 45. See *Tosafot ha-Shalem*, ed. Gellis, 7:287, sec. 2. In the Moscow manuscript to Ex. 17:3 ("why have you taken us out of Egypt, to kill us and our children and our cattle by thirst," ed. Lange, 90, and *Tosafot ha-Shalem*, ed. Gellis, 7:295, sec. 3), Abraham ibn Ezra is cited as ratifying the view of the Tanna R. Judah (found in the *Mekhilta*), that the Jewish people here considered their animals as dear to them as their own lives. This comment is not found, however, in the extant commentaries of Ibn Ezra, nor is it presented in the name of R. Judah *he-Ḥasid.*

A related explanation attributed to R. Judah *he-Ḥasid* is that Moses's point (in verse 23) was that, since Aaron was to remain with the people, he would be able to make certain that they not ascend, and additional warnings would not be needed. God answered that indeed, had Aaron remained with the people, He would not have been so concerned. But since Aaron would be joining Moses at God's request (as per the first half of verse 24), leaving the people like "a flock without a shepherd," with no one to restrain them, it became necessary to issue multiple warnings to the people and to the *kohanim* as well. As he completes filling in all the details of the implicit dialogue that stood behind these verses, R. Judah explicitly notes the literary structure of the Torah here, that the second verse is meant to explain the reasoning behind the earlier one (ופסוק השני נתינת טעם לדבר הוא).[63]

In view of Rashi's comment at the beginning of *parashat Mishpatim* (Ex. 21:3, based on the *Mekhilta*), that a master may not give a *shifḥah kena'anit* to a slave who comes into his servitude unmarried, R. Judah lends a psychological dimension to this halakhic requirement. Had this ruling not been in place, young men who chanced upon a beautiful maidservant might have sold themselves into slavery, a situation to which the Almighty is averse, in order to be given this woman as a *shifḥah*.[64]

Toward the end of *parashat Mishpatim*, the giving of the Torah is discussed once again. Exodus 24:1 reads, "And to Moses he said [*ve-'el Mosheh*

[63] See *Perushei ha-Torah*, ed. Lange, 97–98 (which reconstructs this comment based on both the Cambridge and Moscow manuscripts, as well as the version of *Moshav Zeqenim* found in ms. Paris 260). See also *Tosafot ha-Shalem*, ed. Gellis, 8:71–72, sec. 1 (where this interpretation is associated in ms. Munich 62 with *Sefer ha-Gan*), and *Perushei R. Ḥayyim Palti'el*, ed. Lange, 259. Ibn Ezra cites this question in the name of R. Sa'adyah Gaon, but suggests a different answer, as does Rashbam (without mentioning R. Sa'adyah's name); cf. Lockshin, *Rashbam's Commentary on Exodus*, 210–12. Ramban, in his comment to verse 23, implicitly tries to deflect this question by interpreting these verses differently than Rashi does; and see also *Ḥizzequni* to Ex. 19: 24. R. Yosef *Bekhor Shor* (Ex. 19:24, ed. Nevo, 133) notes simply that "God repeatedly warned the people so that there would be no misstep during the giving of the Torah." For R. Judah's awareness of R. Sa'adyah Gaon's teachings, see above, n. 19. Cf. R. Judah *he-Ḥasid*'s more talmudic analysis of Rashi's comment to Ex. 18:13, in *Ta'amei Mesoret ha-Miqra le-R. Yehudah he-Ḥasid*, ed. Lange, 36.

[64] See *Perushei ha-Torah*, ed. Lange, 103–4; *Tosafot ha-Shalem*, ed. Gellis, 8:154–55, sec. 1; and cf. *Ḥizzequni.* In *Pa'aneaḥ Raza*, 274, this interpretation is presented in the names of R. Judah *he-Ḥasid* and R. Moses, leading Lange to suggest (104, n.11) that it was put forward by R. Moses of Coucy in R. Judah's name. Although this is possible from the chronological standpoint, and R. Moses of Coucy had a number of connections and affinities with *Ḥasidei Ashkenaz* (see, e.g., my *"Peering through the Lattices,"* 68–82), it is much more likely that R. Moses here refers either to R. Moses Zal(t)man or to the otherwise unidentified R. Moses, who appears to have been a contemporary of *Pa'aneaḥ Raza*'s compiler, R. Isaac *ha-Lev*; and is frequently cited in this work. See my "Midrashic Texts and Methods in Tosafist Torah Commentaries," in *Midrash Unbound: Transformation and Innovation*, ed. M. Fishbane and J. Weinberg (Oxford, 2012; in press), section five.

ʾamar], ascend to God, you and Aaron and the seventy elders." R. Judah *he-Ḥasid* (as recorded in *Moshav Zeqenim*) notes that the Torah does not indicate who gave Moses this instruction to ascend to God. Following the so-called Targum Yonatan, R. Judah suggests that it was the angelic figure Mikhaʾel who told Moses to ascend, because Mikhaʾel was the angel whom God had sent to lead the Jewish people on their journey: "My angel will go before you and bring you to the land" (כי ילך מלאכי לפניך, Ex. 23:20). R. Judah points out the letters of the word מלאכי are precisely those of מיכאל. He adds that God had originally wanted to send Metatron *sar ha-panim*, but since Metatron judges all the heavenly realms, and there is no mercy in this judgment, Moses had requested that the Almighty send an angel of mercy, and so Mikhaʾel was sent instead. "It was thus Mikhaʾel who told Moses to ascend." In this instance, R. Judah uses his interest and expertise in angelology, and his penchant for correlating the letters in various words, to resolve a basic interpretational (*peshat*) problem.[65]

R. Zal(t)man reports (as recorded in ms. Cambridge 669.2 and in ms. B.M. 9931) that R. Judah *he-Ḥasid* interpreted, according to the *peshat*, that the text read by Moses in Exodus 24:7 ("And he [Moses] took the book of the covenant, and he read it in earshot of the people") consisted of the Ten Commandments (פירש מ"א לפי הפשט אילו עשרת הדברות). The response by the people in this verse, "we will do and we will hear," connotes that they would certainly keep these commandments and laws, but that they still needed to hear more details about them because these principles and requirements were stated very broadly (רק צריכים אנו לשמוע יותר טוב כי בסתם דיבר). Thus, for example, "does 'do not murder' include only Jews or non-Jews as well, and does it include even a newborn who cannot survive [*nefel*]?" Many such distinctions and details need to be imparted with respect to the prohibitions of adultery and theft as well. "This is what we still need to hear (וזהו ונשמע עדיין)." Like Rashbam and other *pashtanim*, R. Judah departs here from the well-known rabbinic interpretation of *naʿaseh ve-nishma* (in *Shabbat* 88a), that the Jews were committed to observing the commandments even though they had not yet heard them.[66]

[65] See *Perushei ha-Torah*, ed. Lange, 109, and *Tosafot ha-Shalem*, ed. Gellis, 8:356–57, sec. 3. See also Ibn Ezra (in his short commentary) and *Perushei R. Yosef Bekhor Shor*, ed. Nevo, 153, who resolve this problem differently, on the basis of other biblical verses. *Ḥizzequni* refers to this verse as a *miqra qaẓar*, adding (in consonance with the approach of R. Judah *he-Ḥasid*) that "it was an angel" (*malʾakh ʾeḥad*) who spoke to Moses.

[66] *Perushei ha-Torah*, ed. Lange, 109, and *Tosafot ha-Shalem*, ed. Gellis, 8:361, sec. 1 (based on ms. B.M. 9931, fol. 65v). In Rashbam's words, "we will perform what was spoken and we will also hear what will be commanded to us moving forward (*mi-kan ule-haba*) and fulfill it." See Lockshin, *Rashbam's Commentary to Exodus*, 299; and see also Ibn Ezra to this verse. In the following comment in *Perushei ha-Torah*, ed. Lange (found in ms. Moscow 82 to *parashat Yitro*,

A passage in *Moshav Zeqenim* presents an interpretation of R. Yosef *Bekhor Shor* that is not found in ms. Munich 52 (from which the extant commentary of *Bekhor Shor* was published).[67] According to this passage, R. Yosef inquired why the Torah uses a singular form of the verb "to make" (*ve-ʿasita*) for each of the implements of the Tabernacle except the ark, where the plural form is used (*ve-ʿasu*, Ex. 25:10). The answer attributed to *Bekhor Shor* is that the ark contains the Torah, which all are required to honor and fulfill. Hence a plural verb is used. *Moshav Zeqenim* presents another answer, that King Solomon was able to reproduce all the implements of the Tabernacle in similar form, except for the ark. The passage in *Moshav Zeqenim* then continues, "And R. Judah *he-Ḥasid* (הרי"ח) explained that there is a hint [*remez*] here to the three crowns [of Torah, *kehunah*, and *malkhut*, as per *Avot* 4:17]. As *Ḥazal* derived (in *Yoma* 72b and elsewhere), the ark, the table, and the altar each had a border or rim (*zer*) around it. The table represents the kingship of David, the altar is the precinct of Aaron, while the ark, symbolizing Torah, is ready and available to all. Thus the plural form of *ve-ʿasu* is used to suggest that all who want to participate in the study of Torah may do so." At the same time, the singular form *ve-ʿasita* is also found in connection with the ark in the following verse, Exodus 25:11, "and you shall make upon it [the ark] a golden rim," *ve-ʿasita zer zahav saviv*. This indicates that the Torah is the highest of the three crowns. Once again, R. Judah addresses the same linguistic problem raised by *pashtanim* (including Rashbam), albeit with a different resolution.[68]

In the realm of masoretic interpretation, R. Judah *he-Ḥasid* notes that the phrase ויקחו אליך ("and you shall take unto you," Ex. 27:20) is found in this verse with respect to the pure olive oil to be used for the menorah in the Tabernacle, and in Numbers 19:2 with respect to the precept of the red heifer (ויקחו אליך פרה אדומה), suggesting some connection between the two. The connection is identified by R. Judah as a point of comparison and contrast. The olive oil in the Tabernacle was not needed by God for light but was needed by those people who served in it, while the *parah ʾadumah* was needed by the children of Israel to purify themselves from the sin of the golden calf. Thus in both these instances, the phrase "and you shall take unto you" is appropriate. The donation of the Tabernacle itself, however,

and without any attribution to R. Judah *he-Ḥasid*), the *peshat* of *naʿaseh ve-nishma* is given as "that which is dependent on hearing we will listen to, that which is dependent on action we will do."

[67] See above, chapter 2, n. 129.

[68] *Perushei ha-Torah*, ed. Lange, 112. Cf. *Daʿat Zeqenim* and *Tosafot ha-Shalem*, ed. Gellis, 9:28–29, secs. 1, 6, and ed. Lange, 55, n. 94. Rashbam explains the unique use of *ve-ʿasu* as a function of the fact that the ark was the essence of the Tabernacle, whose formation was mandated in Exodus 25:8 by the phrase *ve-ʿasu li miqdash*. See also the comment of Ramban.

was a *zorekh ha-Shekhinah* (i.e., a place for the *Shekinah* to reside), and therefore the phrase employed there by God is ויקחו לי (Ex. 25:2), "and you shall take the donation for Me."[69]

R. Judah *he-Ḥasid* raises the same question as Rashi (and *Bekhor Shor*) concerning the placement of the head-plate, *ẓiẓ* (ציץ), on the *Kohen Gadol.* The verse in Exodus 28:37 suggests that this plate is placed on the cord of turquoise wool (ושמת אותו על פתיל תכלת), while the verse in Exodus 39:31 suggests that the turquoise wool (*petil*) is placed on the head-plate (ויתנו עליו פתיל תכלת). Both R. Judah and Rashi resolve this contradiction by detailing the compositions of the *ẓiẓ* and the *petil* in a way that allows for both perspectives to be accurate.[70]

On the verse in Exodus 32:32, "and if not, blot me out please from the book that You have written," R. Zal(t)man notes that בכאן אינו אומר מ"א לפי הפשט אלא רק לפי המדרש, "here my father does not present the *peshat* but interprets only according to the *midrash*" (= *Bereshit Rabbah* 26:6, on the verse [Gen. 6:3], that "[man's] days [following the flood] would be 120 years"). According to this *midrash*, that verse refers specifically to the lifespan of Moses. Moses's argument is that, before he was born, God had limited man's lifespan during the generation of the flood (*dor ha-mabul*) to 120 years. As such, Moses's generation should therefore also retain the possibility of living for 120 years (as he would), since they were surely no worse than that generation. If, however, God now does not wish to retain the period of 120 years even for Moses's generation, He should blot out Moses's name, "for what will the succeeding generations be able to say?" God accepted Moses's argument from fairness, along with his prayer. R. Zal(t)man's introductory remark implies that this is a somewhat rare deviation by R. Judah, from the realm of *peshat* to that of midrash.[71]

[69] See *Perushei ha-Torah*, ed. Lange, 113–14, and *Tosafot ha-Shalem*, ed. Gellis, 9:151, sec. 17. This approach (minus the reference to the red heifer) is found in *Ḥizzequni* as well. The initial part of this approach, that the light of the Tabernacle was not needed by God, is found in *Midrash Tanḥuma*, and is discussed by R. Jacob of Orleans in ms. Bodl. 2344. See *Tosafot ha-Shalem*, ed. Gellis, 9:149–50, sec. 13.

[70] See *Perushei ha-Torah*, ed. Lange, 115–16; and see also Rashbam to Ex. 28:37. *Perushei Bekhor Shor 'al ha-Torah*, ed. Nevo, 165, leaves the question unresolved.

[71] See *Perushei ha-Torah*, ed. Lange, 123; and *Tosafot ha-Shalem*, ed. Gellis, 10:87, sec. 2. On Moses throwing down the tablets (Ex. 32:19), *Moshav Zeqenim*, 211, cites a fairly typical moralistic lesson for which R. Judah *he-Ḥasid* is well known (found also, in this instance, in *Sefer Ḥasidim*, ed. Wistinetski, sec. 125)—that if a person is carrying a Torah scroll and sees people sinning, but he cannot rush to prevent them from sinning because he is carrying the Torah, it is better for him to cast the Torah from his hands to prevent them from sinning, As we have seen, however, this type of moralistic interpretation, which is so common in *Sefer Ḥasidim*, is far from the dominant mode of scriptural interpretation in R. Judah's Torah commentary that is the focus of our discussion here.

Building on the definitions given by Rashi (following *Yoma* 36b) to the thirteen Divine attributes (Ex. 34:7), in which *'avon* is defined as a purposeful sin, *pesha* is defined as a sin born from rebellion, and *ḥata'ah* refers to inadvertent sins (*shegagot*), R. Judah *he-Ḥasid* (as recorded in ms. Vatican 45) notes, however, that the word *ḥata'ah* is also found in the Torah as connoting an intentional sin, as in Exodus 32:31 (אנא חטא העם הזה חטאה גדולה) concerning the sin of the golden calf, where it would be inaccurate to say that the Jewish people were all inadvertent idolaters. R. Judah neatly suggests that when *ḥata'ah* appears together with *'avon* and *pesha* (both of which are clearly intentional), *ḥata'ah* has the meaning of an unintentional sin. When *ḥata'ah* appears by itself, however, it may also connote an intentional sin.[72]

R. Judah *he-Ḥasid* interprets the phrase *va-yidom Aharon* (Lev. 10:3) to mean that Aaron waited (and not simply that he was silent), as in Joshua 10:13, *va-yidom ha-shemesh* (the sun waited to set). Since no one knew why the deaths occurred, Moses said that he would inquire of God. The Divine response was that once they had died, there was no point in asking. They simply came near to God and expired (Ex. 16:1). In any event, Aaron waited until this inquiry to God was made.[73] Here again R. Judah fleshes out the considerations that are behind the biblical text and the actions of the biblical figures.

In *parashat Emor* (Lev. 21:14), R. Judah suggests a psychological explanation—similar to the way that he understood the inability of an unmarried Hebrew slave to be given a *shifḥah kena'anit* by his master—for the prohibition against a *kohen gadol* marrying a widow, even as a regular *kohen* was permitted to do so. Since the *kohen gadol* knew the ineffable Name of God and recited it on Yom Kippur, he might be moved to utilize it (at that time) in order to kill the husband of a married woman so that he might marry her.[74]

[72] See *Perushei ha-Torah*, ed. Lange, 126–27, and cf. Ibn Ezra's long commentary, ad loc. R. Judah interpretation of Ex. 34:26, *lo tevashel gedi ba-ḥalev 'immo* (*Perushei ha-Torah*, ed. Lange, 128, and see also 129, n. 124), is quite close to the contextual, non-halakhic interpretation of R. Yosef *Bekhor Shor* (ed. Nevo, 176), that the first fruits should be brought quickly, and should not be given additional time to ripen and mature. Cf. G. Brinn, "'Iyyun be-Perushei R. Yehudah he-Ḥasid," 13–14; R. A. Harris, *Discerning Parallelism: A Study in Northern French Medieval Jewish Biblical Exegesis* (Providence, R.I., 2004), 31–32; and above, chapter 2, n. 56.

[73] See *Perushei ha-Torah*, ed. Lange, 140–41 (from ms. Vatican 45). Interestingly, the word *va-yidom* appears only in these two biblical verses, so this constitutes another example of how masoretic patterns can be used to support a *peshat* interpretation. Cf. *Ta'amei Mesoret ha-Miqra le-R. Yehudah he-Ḥasid*, ed. Lange, 41. R. Meir (Maharam) of Rothenburg offers a more midrashic interpretation in his masoretic commentary. Rashbam (followed by *Ḥizzequni*) interprets that Aaron did not cry, based on the phrase in Ezekiel 24:17, *he-'aneq dom*. Naḥmanides derives that Aaron stifled his crying, based on a verse in Lamentations 2:18.

[74] This explanation is reproduced in *Perushei ha-Torah*, ed. Lange, 150–51 (with slight variations), from several different manuscripts and texts. Cf. ed. Lange, 207 (Deut. 24:1), for R. Judah's interpretation of the Torah's prohibition against a man remarrying his ex-wife only when she had married another man in between. In ms. B.M. 9931, fol. 101v, another realia-based

Later in that same portion, R. Judah asks why there is nothing equivalent to *Shemini ʿAzeret* in connection with Passover, and why only the festival of *Shavuʿot* is dependent on a prior counting of the days. He answers the first question by arguing, in effect, that *Shavuʿot* enables the bringing of wheat offerings that could not have been brought as effectively on Passover, since the growing season had only begun. Thus one of the two loaves brought on *Shavuʿot* is for that festival, and the other serves as a make-up for Passover. *Shavuʿot* then becomes the occasion when we fufill God's will in this regard (*ki-reẓono*), and functions also as a kind of *ʿaẓeret*, in the sense of adjunct to the previous festival.[75]

Counting precedes only *Shavuʿot*, according to R. Judah *he-Ḥasid*, since people were typically in their homes for Passover, Rosh ha-Shanah, and *Sukkot*, and they were aware of any changes in the system of intercalation. Prior to *Shavuʿot*, however, when people remained far away in the fields, involved with the threshing, harvesting, and plowing, no one would be able to let these temporary villagers (*kefariyyim*) know whether the month of *Iyyar* was full or defective. Therefore the Torah required that they remember the day of Passover when they came up to Jerusalem for the festival, and when all the villages gathered together for the cutting of the *ʿomer*, and word of this was widespread. If the people of Israel then simply counted fifty days from that evening of the cutting of the *ʿomer*, they would know clearly when it was time to return to their homes for *Shavuʿot.* This interpretation, which was later abbreviated by both R. Yaʿakov *Baʿal ha-Turim* and R. David Abudarham, is based on a *derekh ʾereẓ* approach to the biblical period, yet another instance in which R. Judah *he-Ḥasid* presents this kind of realia-based interpretation.[76]

---

reason (not included by Lange in his edition) why a widow was prohibited to the *kohen gadol* is attributed to (R. Judah *he-*) *Ḥasid*, and is characterized as *lefi ha-peshat.* During the period of the Temple, when the precepts of *terumot* and *maʿasrot*, and the special status of *qodashim* meats, were all in effect, no *kohen* married a widow (whose deceased husband had been a *Yisraʾel*), since she was "like a [newly initiated] convert" (*ke-gerei de-Yisraʾel*) with respect to these precepts, and would not or did not observe them carefully [ולא היתה נזהר(ו)ת יפה בענין תרומות ומעשרות]. A virgin who had never been married, however, even if she was not from a family of *kohanim*, could be properly initiated and guided by the *kohen gadol* in these matters, according to his standards (אבל בתולת ישר' הוא יכול להדריכה כמו שרוצה). Cf. E. Touitou, *Exegesis in Perpetual Motion* (Jerusalem, 2003), 180–88; and above, chapter 2, nn. 51, 100, 135, 202.

75 *Perushei ha-Torah*, ed. Lange, 151. See also *Perushei ha-Torah le-R. Yosef Bekhor Shor*, 225: וצוה הק' שיספרו בכל שנה לחבב עליהם התורה שנתן להם כלי חמדה שבו נברא העולם. כך שמעתי מאבא מורי.

76 See *Perushei ha-Torah*, ed. Lange, 152 (to Lev. 23:16); *Perush ha-Tur ha-ʿArukh ʿal ha-Torah* (Jerusalem, 1961), 243; and *Sefer Abudarham ha-Shalem* (Jerusalem, 1995), 241. Cf. above, n. 47, and below, n. 92. In a passage preserved by *peshatei R. Mosheh mi-Coucy* (cf. above, n. 64, and below, chapter 4), R. Judah *he-Ḥasid* explains the sum of 10,000 bars of silver that Haman wished to collect (Esther 3:9) on the basis of the *shekalim* that were collected in Lev. 27:3; see ed. Lange, 159.

The Tosafist Torah compilation *Moshav Zeqenim* presents a cluster of interpretations, at the beginning of the Book of Numbers, attributed to R. Judah *he-Ḥasid*. R. Judah explains why, in the census at the beginning of the Book of Numbers (Nu. 1:10), the princes of both Ephraim and Menasheh are linked to Joseph, while in the naming of the spies (Nu. 13:8, 11), the spy of Ephraim (Yehoshua bin Nun) is mentioned several verses prior to the spy of Menasheh (Gadi ben Susi), who is also listed as representing the tribe of Joseph. R. Judah notes that the spy from Menasheh was among those who issued a negative report, described by the Torah (Nu. 13:32) as *dibbat ha-ʾarez*. Similarly, Joseph issued a negative report (characterized also as *dibbah*) to his father about his brothers (Gen. 37:2): *va-yave Yosef ʾet dibbatam raʿah ʾel ʾavihem.*[77]

R. Judah also asks why the prince from the tribe of Gad is initially called Elyasaf ben Deʿuʾel (during the census in Nu. 1:14) but is later called Elyasaf ben Reʿuʾel (in Nu. 2:14) when the encampment is described. His answer, in this instance based on a rabbinic tradition, is that since Elyasaf, owing to his good deeds, merited burial in the vicinity of Moses and Aaron (Deut. 33:21, as per *Sifrei*, sec. 355, and *Sotah* 13b), who were known as "friends of the Lord" (Ps. 139:17), Elyasaf's father's name was shifted to Reʿuʾel, which indicates that he too was a friend (*reʿa*) of God.[78]

R. Judah questions the difference between the counting of the tribe of Simeon and all the other tribes. In every other instance, the summary word used by the Torah to express the final count is *pequdeihem* alone. Only in the case of Simeon, however, is the word preceded by the word *pekudav* (Nu. 1:22–23). R. Judah suggests that this obvious difference hints that their tribal family would be diminished by the promiscuous actions of Zimri in the days of Pinḥas (Nu. 25:14).[79]

77 *Perushei ha-Torah*, ed. Lange, 160 (= *Moshav Zeqenim*, ed. Sasson, 423). R. Judah's solution can also be found (without attribution) in ms. Cambridge 82 and ms. Moscow 669.2, on Nu. 13:11; see ed. Lange, 174, and see also *Ḥizzequni* there. In the *Moshav Zeqenim* passage, R. Judah *he-Ḥasid* appears to be answering the question of an otherwise unidentified ר"י. Cf. ed. Lange, 172 (n. 37), and below, n. 79. In addition, R. Judah's solution is further questioned on the basis of a verse in *parashat Masʿei* (Nu. 34:23).

78 See *Moshav Zeqenim*, 423. Another answer is also suggested without attribution (*ve-li nirʾeh*) that the way of Scripture is to make these kinds of changes between *daled* and *raish* (so that *Dodanim* in Gen. 10:4 becomes *Rodanim* in 1 Chronicles 1:7), although a reason for that change is also suggested from a passage in *Torat Kohanim.*

79 *Perushei ha-Torah*, ed. Lange, 160. *Moshav Zeqenim* cites several additional linguistic distinctions and differences, including two regarding the encampment of Ephraim and Menasheh in Nu. 2; see also ed. Lange, 161 (there is a question here from ר"י as well, as above in n. 77). In ed. Lange, 162, a passage in the Cambridge and Moscow manuscripts records an interpretation of R. Judah (on Nu. 4:6) concerning the poles on the ark (as opposed to the poles on the show table and the altar), which his son R. Zal(t)man remembered only after R. Judah had passed away. Another passage in *Moshav Zeqenim*, on this same verse, questions other differences in

The final interpretation in this section recorded by *Moshav Zeqenim* concerns the reference in Numbers 4:18 to the Levitical family of Kehat as a tribe (אל תכריתו את שבט משפחות הקהתי מתוך הלוים). R. Judah wonders about this seemingly inaccurate appellation. His answer is that this description teaches that just as a tribe whose place of encampment is in the south cannot camp in the north, it may be derived from here that the various Levitical families could not deviate from their places of encampment either. Although a *pashtan* such as Rashbam might not resonate to the fine linguistic and grammatical distinctions put forward by R. Judah *he-Ḥasid* in these instances, Rashi and others might well do so.[80]

According to a *peshat* attributed in ms. B.M. 9931 to (R. Yehudah *he-*) *Ḥasid*, the verse at the end of *Naso* (Nu. 7:89)—which reports that when Moses came into the *ʾohel moʿed*, he would hear the voice of the Lord speaking to him from between the two cherubs—must be understood in light of the first verse in the Book of Leviticus, which states that the Lord spoke to Moses "from the *ʾohel moʿed*." When Moses stood outside the tent, he perceived (*nirʾah lo*) that the voice was coming to him from the *ʾohel moʿed*. When Moses was in the *ʾohel moʿed*, however, he perceived that the voice was coming to him from between the two cherubs. According to R. Judah *he-Ḥasid*, this reflects the "typical state of [human] affairs" (וכן אורח מילתא). When a person is outside a home, he cannot ascertain with any precision (אינו יודע לכוון בצמצום) the source of a voice that he hears from within the house. Once again, R. Judah *he-Ḥasid* has put forward a realia-based or psychological explanation that reflects the typical state of human affairs.[81]

At the end of *parashat Be-haʿalotekha* (Nu. 12:6), God says to Aaron and Miriam, שמעו נא דברי (hear my words). Rashi comments (following the *Sifrei*) that the word *na* signifies a request (*baqqashah*). God was requesting that Aaron and Miriam listen to Him. According to the version of *Moshav Zeqenim* found in ms. Paris 260, R. Judah *he-Ḥasid* asked, "From whence does Rashi know here that *na* connotes a *baqqashah*?" (since this does not seem to

scriptural details between these implements, including when the article *ʾet* is used. Cf. below, n. 92.

[80] See also *Perushei ha-Torah*, ed. Lange 166, n. 17 (to Nu. 6:23), where R. Judah's letter distinction and its implication (found in *Moshav Zeqenim*, ed. Sasson, 431) is recorded in *Paʿaneaḥ Raza*, 423, in the name of R. Aaron *ha-Ẓarefati* (author of *Sefer ha-Gan*); cf. above, nn. 26, 63.

[81] See ms. B.M. 9931, fol. 112v (which, as noted above, was not used by Lange in his edition). Cf. Rashi to Exodus 25:22, who raises a similar question, and see also *Moshav Zeqenim*, 230 (to Lev. 1:1), and especially *Ḥizzequni*, who essentially adopts this explanation (without attribution). Although R. Judah is most often referred to in ms. B.M. 9931 (Gaster 730) simply as *Ḥasid*, there are instances in which a fuller version of his name is included. See, e.g., ms. B.M. Gaster 9931, fol. 121v (to Nu. 14:9, which is not found in ed. Lange; but see also *Perushei R. Ḥayyim Paltiʾel*, ed. Lange, 510). Another interpretation from the *Ḥasid* (that is also not found in ed. Lange) appears on the same manuscript folio.

be obvious from the context of the verse itself).[82] R. Judah explains that the *gematria* of the *at-bash* result of the word *na* yields the *gematria* equivalent of the word *baqqashah.*[83] As we have seen above, R. Judah *he-Ḥasid* will occasionally mobilize techniques like *gematria*, *at-bash*, or *notariqon* to explain Rashi's findings, and even to suggest or to confirm a *peshat* interpretation.[84] He was clearly unafraid to merge these very different modes of scriptural interpretation in order to achieve a satisfactory interpretation.

In Numbers 14:20, R. Zal(t)man cites another interpretation from his father, as transmitted by R. Isaac of Russia. "And God said, I have forgiven you according to your word" (סלחתי כדבריך). R. Judah asserts that the *peshat* here is this (כך הפשט): *seliḥah* is not the same as *meḥilah. Seliḥah* means that additional time is given for repentance that will lead to complete forgiveness, while *meḥilah* means that the forgiveness is total. This is the meaning of the liturgical formulation of סלח לנו, מחל לנו, as well as אבינו מלכינו סלח ומחל לכל עוונותינו. Indeed, this is the proper way to seek forgiveness, to request it bit by bit at the beginning, in order to extend the time, so that if penitence is ultimately accomplished, there can be complete forgiveness. In this instance, God had initially wanted to eliminate the Jewish people completely until Moses had argued that His failure to preserve the people who had left Egypt would be seen as a *ḥillul ha-Shem.* Therefore, God acceded by saying *סלחתי כדבריך*. I will give them time, during which I will collect the debt that is due Me by having them die in the desert, but I will not destroy them immediately and totally as I had intended. R. Judah points to some additional examples of Moses's successful interventions (including the one from Ex. 32:32 noted above), and he speaks a bit more about the nature of *meḥilah.*[85]

R. Judah *he-Ḥasid* also compares and contrasts the sin of the spies with the sin of the golden calf. In both cases, the Jewish people expressed remorse and regretted their misdeeds. Yet in the instance of the spies, they were punished by the sword when they tried to move forward to Israel, while after the sin of the golden calf, they were able to continue to move forward merely with the warning that "on the day that I punish, I will punish" (Ex. 32:34). R. Judah attributes this difference to the fact that, following the

82 Perhaps Rashi derives this meaning from the context when this word is used twice, several verses later (Nu. 12:13), where Moses beseeches God to heal Miriam (and see Rashi, *Bekhor Shor*, and *Ḥizzequni*, ad loc.).

83 See *Perushei ha-Torah*, ed. Lange, 173, and cf. Ibn Ezra.

84 See, e.g., above, nn. 39, 55.

85 See *Perushei ha-Torah*, ed. Lange, 174–75. Cf. Rashbam, Ibn Ezra, and *Bekhor Shor*, whose overall interpretations (that time has been gained, either to prolong their punishment or to secure further repentance) are the same as R. Judah's, even as their linguistic analyses are a bit different.

sin of the golden calf, the people intuitively regretted what they had done and spontaneously repented. In the case of the spies, however, they grieved and repented only when they saw that the spies had died, which had caused them to become fearful and therefore to repent.[86]

According to R. Judah, Koraḥ and his immediate followers were punished by being swallowed up by the earth—rather than being consumed by fire, as were the 250 followers who offered the incense—since they wished to elevate themselves over all others and therefore literally needed to be brought down. In a similar measure, the sinful king Uzziah, who wished to enter the Holy of Holies, was afflicted with leprosy (2 Chronicles 26:16–21), which caused him to be sent out from all the various camps.[87]

In *parashat Ḥuqqat*, R. Zal(t)man presents a lengthy discussion from his father dealing with the dominant interpretation (*lefi peshat ha-ʿolam*) that Moses and Aaron died only because they hit the rock. In the course of his discussion, R. Judah cites an interpretation by Abraham ibn Ezra in his name.[88] R. Judah demonstrates that Balak saw firsthand (*lefi ha-peshat ra'ah mamash*) what the Jewish people had done to the Emorites (Nu. 22:2), and was not simply relying on the reports of others, as several other commentators imply, among them Rashi.[89] R. Judah does this by comparing two seemingly contradictory verses. The first, in the Book of Joshua 24:9, states that "Balak arose and fought with Israel." The second, in the Book of Judges (11:24), reads, "Are you better than Balak ben Ẓippor, king of Moab? Did he ever fight with the Jewish people or do battle with them?" R. Judah explains that from the time he became the king of Moab, Balak did not fight against

[86] See *Perushei ha-Torah*, ed. Lange, 175. In an addendum to the Cambridge manuscript (see Lange, n. 21), the Tosafist R. Tuvya of Vienne questioned R. Judah's interpretation, because in the case of the golden calf as well, God afflicted and killed those who had made the calf. If so, the regret expressed there was also only because the Jews had seen that some of their brethren had died. The answer given (perhaps on behalf of the approach of R. Judah *he-Ḥasid*) is that, nonetheless, the repentance there was more complete, as evidenced by the fact that the people did nothing else wrong at that time. In the case of the spies, however, immediately after they grieved and repented, they did wrong when they "presumed to go up to the hilltop" (Nu. 14:44), against the explicit directive of Moses not to do so. This is one of several examples of direct French interaction with R. Judah *he-Ḥasid*'s Torah commentary.

[87] See ms. B.M. 9931, fol. 125r. *Moshav Zeqenim*, ed. Sasson, 464, records the question in the name of ר"י, while the answer is given in the name of R. Samuel (although it is difficult to imagine that this refers to R. Judah's father, R. Samuel b. Qalonymus; see below, n. 91). Cf. ed. Lange, 178 (to Nu. 17:5), and *Moshav Zeqenim*, ad loc.

[88] See *Perushei ha-Torah*, ed. Lange, 180–82. See also R. Judah's *peshat* distinction in Nu. 21:8–9 (ed. Lange, 184) between the use of *naḥash* and *saraf*, and cf. Ibn Ezra. On R. Judah's use of Ibn Ezra, see above, n. 19. R. Judah's comment is found in ms. Moscow 121, fol. 26v; in *Perushei R. Ḥayyim Palti'el*, 536; and in *Moshav Zeqenim*, ed. Sasson, 471–72 (and elsewhere), in the name of ר"י.

[89] *Ḥizzequni* explicitly interprets that "he saw" means that "he heard," as in Ex. 20:14, "and all the people saw the voices."

the Jewish people. However, prior to his ascension to the throne of Moab, Balak was Siḥon's military general. Siḥon (and Balak as well) did do battle with Israel. When Balak saw that Siḥon had been killed, he escaped and hid himself away. Here again, R. Judah clarifies the precise meaning of a verse in the Torah by taking other biblical verses into account in order to provide appropriate background.[90]

In *parashat Re'eh*, R. Zal(t)man cites an interpretation from R. Judah *he-Ḥasid* in the name of his father (= R. Zal(t)man's grandfather), R. Samuel *he-Ḥasid*,[91] that accounts for a subtle textual difference in the way the Torah presents the nonkosher species of birds in *Re'eh* and in *parashat Shemini*. In Deuteronomy 14:12, the Torah lists three of the nonkosher birds of prey (different species of vultures) as הנשר והפרס והעזניה. In Leviticus 11:13, however, the wording of the verse includes the definite article, את הנשר ואת הפרס ואת העזניה. R. Samuel explains that the section in Leviticus (located in the portion that begins with *va-yehi ba-yom ha-shmini* = the eighth day of the consecration of the Tabernacle, on the first day of Nisan) reflects the end of the first year of the Jews' sojourn in the desert. At that time Moses actually pointed out to them the various species of the wild as he noted their kosher status; hence the use of the definite article. The Book of Deuteronomy, however, reflects the fortieth year after the exodus, when the Jews were already close to the inhabited land of Canaan, where birds of prey were no longer common. Therefore Moses was not able to point them out, and the article *'et* was not used in the Torah's formulation in *parashat Re'eh*.[92] In his masoretic commentary, R. Judah makes note of the definite articles that are found in *parashat Re'eh* in the next two verses (14:13–14) with regard to the *'ayah* and the raven (ואת כל עורב למינו) to suggest that these birds too were found closer to settled areas, and were thus pointed out by Moses at this later time.[93]

We have seen quite a few instances in which R. Judah explains particular phrasings and potential linguistic anomalies as a function of when the

[90] See also *Perushei ha-Torah*, ed. Lange, 198, where R. Judah interprets the events of Deut. 2:8 in accordance with a verse in 2 Chronicles 8:17.

[91] For R. Judah's citation of explanations from his father, see also *Pa'aneaḥ Raza*, 52 (to Gen. 7:10, against the view of Rashi), that the flood was preceded by thunder and lightning, which was followed by the clouds opening up and the water descending to earth, but cf. *Perushei ha-Torah*, ed. Lange, 12. See also above, n. 51.

[92] See *Perushei ha-Torah*, ed. Lange, 203, and cf. G. Brin, "'Iyyun be-Perushei R. Yehudah *he-Ḥasid* 'al ha-Torah," 7–8. Brin, 8–9, lists three other instances in which R. Judah describes (in practical terms) the Jews' state of existence in the desert, including Ex. 29:46–47 (ed. Lange, 116), on which R. Judah suggests that already in Egypt, where they acquired some of the assets of the Egyptians during the plagues, God instructed the Israelites to donate materials that would be needed for building the Tabernacle, which were otherwise unavailable in the desert (שלא תתמה לפי הפשט אנה לקחו במדבר עצי שיטים).

[93] See *Ta'amei Mesoret ha-Miqra le-R. Yehudah he-Ḥasid*, ed. Lange, 73.

verse was dictated. We have also seen R. Judah's efforts to correlate similar portions within the Torah that appear to have slight variations, and we have further seen that R. Judah was not afraid to suggest an interpretation based on the realia or circumstances experienced by the children of Israel while the Torah was being given and at other times. This section in *parashat Re'eh* is an excellent example of all of these exegetical characteristics or strategies coming together.

R. Judah *he-Ḥasid* (as recorded in ms. Vatican 45 and *Moshav Zeqenim*) has an interesting observation on the concept of *ben sorer u-moreh* (Deut. 21:18–21). In light of the talmudic view that there was never actually a *ben soreh u-moreh* nor would there ever be one (*Sanhedrin* 71a), why was this portion included in the Torah? R. Judah suggests that this portion comes to support the talmudic doctrine that a rabbinic court may inflict both corporal and noncorporal punishments that are not strictly in accordance with Jewish law in order to prevent abuses from occurring at a particular time (*makkin ve-ʿonshin shelo min ha-din*, as per the *sugya* in *Yevamot* 90b). The stated punishment for the *ben sorer u-moreh* was stoning, which is not really in accordance with Jewish law (*shelo min ha-din*) but was prescribed as a theoretical necessity by the Torah in that case, since such a young man could well end up as a highway robber. For R. Judah *he-Ḥasid* this unusual and theoretical case strengthens the power of the Jewish court to prescribe unusual punishments as mandated by the times and circumstances in which it functioned.[94]

In a passage found in ms. B.M. 9931, R. Judah *he-Ḥasid* questions Rashi's interpretation (following *Sifrei*) of the phrase "an Aramean tried to destroy my father" (Deut. 26:5) as a reference to Laban, who tried to harm Jacob. The verse links this activity with the sojourn of the Jewish people in Egypt, which did not occur in the days of Laban; Ibn Ezra raises the very same question. In response R. Judah *he-Ḥasid* suggests that the reference here is to Joseph, who was born in Aram and sold into slavery in Egypt, thus precipitating the descent into Egypt of his father, Jacob.[95]

[94] See *Perushei ha-Torah*, ed. Lange, 205. Cf. the passage by R. Ḥayyim *Kohen* in ms. Florence (above, Introduction, n. 59), who holds more broadly (with regard to *ben sorer u-moreh* and other unusual cases) that no logical reasoning to explain these kinds of punishments and details is possible. Later in *parashat Ki Teze* (Deut. 23:2), ed. Lange, 207, R. Judah presents a masoretic interpretation in which he notes that the phrase that defines the time for the *baʿal qeri* to immerse himself according to this verse, *lifnot ʿerev* (as evening comes in), is found in only one other place in the Torah (Gen. 24:63, "and Isaac went out to pray in the field toward evening" [*lifnot erev*]). These two passages inform each other, indicating that it is best to immerse oneself prior to prayer as well. Cf. Maharam's comment to Gen. 24:63, and *Baʿal ha-Turim*, ed. Reinitz, 1:61. For R. Judah's emphasis on the need for purification before prayer, see, e.g., E. Zimmer, *ʿOlam ke-Minhago Noheg*, 132–40.

[95] See ms. B.M. 9931, fol. 169v. Once again, R. Judah works here directly with Rashi's commentary.

R. Judah *he-Ḥasid* explains that the territory of the tribe of Joseph will be blessed more than that of any other tribe (Deut. 33:13) because Joseph resisted the advances of the wife of Potiphar. In doing so Joseph also threw off the broader curse of the earth that Adam had received when he was convinced by Eve to sin. Joseph, who did not succumb, merited having this curse eliminated. As we have noted above, a similar interpretation is attributed to both R. Jacob of Orleans and to Ibn Ezra. As our extensive interpretational analysis has shown, these correlations are far from coincidental.[96]

The Torah commentary that R. Judah *he-Ḥasid* transmitted to his son R. Zal(t)man is noteworthy for the multiple approaches it takes in interpreting the biblical text. Like R. Yom Tov of Joigny's comments, it stands as a suggestive blend of *peshat* and *gematria* or masoretic comments, although R. Judah employs these diverse methods even more than R. Yom Tov does. The large number of *peshat* comments we have encountered (and their quality) are certainly sufficient to link R. Judah *he-Ḥasid*'s efforts in this area of *parshanut ha-miqra* to the second wave of Tosafist *pashtanim* that began with R. Yosef *Bekhor Shor*, although R. Judah is the first German figure, and the first not to be a student of Rabbenu Tam, who can be included in this group.[97]

Indeed, as has been noted, R. Judah's Torah commentary is cited throughout the wide range of Tosafist Torah compilations, including those whose editors or compilers hailed from northern France (such as *Pa'aneaḥ Raza*, *Hadar Zeqenim*, and *Da'at Zeqenim*).[98] As another indicative example of this kind of

[96] *Perushei ha-Torah*, ed. Lange, 210–11, and cf. above, chapter 2, n.188.

[97] The author of the commentary to Chronicles in ms. Munich 5 appears to have been a student of R. Yosef Qara (from the first or classical wave of northern French *pashtanim*), as well as of members of *Ḥasidei Ashkenaz*. See I. Ta-Shma, *Knesset Meḥqarim*, 1:290–301; my "*Peering through the Lattices*," 95–96 (n. 7); and cf. E. Viezel, *The Commentary on Chronicles Attributed to Rashi* (Jerusalem, 2010), 305–33; and above, chapter 2, n. 28. As the comments to the *Haftarot* that also appear in R. Judah's commentary suggest (in addition to other, even more substantial evidence), *Ḥasidei Ashkenaz*, like the classical group of northern French *pashtanim*, were interested in interpreting books of the Bible beyond the Pentateuch, which was not quite the same for some of the French *pashtanim* in the second wave. Note, however, R. Yosef *Bekhor Shor*'s commentary on Psalms (above, chapter 2, n. 51), and see below regarding R. Isaiah di Trani's commentary on *Nakh*.

[98] See, e.g., *Da'at Zeqenim (me-Rabbotenu Ba'alei ha-Tosafot)*, Genesis, fols. 4a, 18a, 24a, 25b, 41b; Exodus, fol. 37a; *Hadar Zeqenim*, fols. 11a, 17b, 19b; and cf. Y. Nevo, "Darkhei Parshanuto shel Hadar Zeqenim la-Torah," *Sinai* 101 (1998), 23; and above, n. 7, for *Pa'aneaḥ Raza* (ms. B.M. 9931 is an enhanced version of this compilation), and cf. *Perushei R. Ḥayyim Palti'el*, ed. Lange, editor's introduction, 11. On the chronology of these compositions, see *Sefer ha-Gan*, ed. M. Orlian (Jerusalem, 2009), 85–87; 93–97; and my "Midrashic Texts and Methods in Tosafist Torah Commentaries" (above, n. 64), n. 47. A large selection of comments by R. Judah can be found in ms. Hamburg 45 (which is attributed, incorrectly, to R. Yosef *Bekhor Shor*; see below, chapter 4), and see also ms. Moscow 121 (which is associated with the *Moshav Zeqenim* collection). In many of these manuscript collections, R. Zal(t)man is not mentioned at all, and the interpretations are attributed simply to *(He-)Ḥasid*. For two earlier Tosafist Torah compilations that cite R. Judah *he-Ḥasid* (ms. Moscow 362 and ms. Leiden 27), see above, chapter 2, nn. 6, 128.

integration and inclusion, a passage in ms. Bodl. 270 (known as *Ḥiddushei Ẓarefat*, the contents of which are generally similar to those of *Hadar Zeqenim*) juxtaposes the commentary of Rashi (*perush ha-quntres*) with the *perush* of R. Judah *he-Ḥasid*. Shortly thereafter, the *Ḥiddushei Ẓarefat* cite "the book of R. Judah *he-Ḥasid*" (= *Sefer Ḥasidim*). After the second such citation of *Sefer Ḥasidim*, Rashbam's commentary to Genesis 26:5 is presented.[99] R. Judah *he-Ḥasid*'s Torah commentary has also been shown by Zunz and others to be one of the unnamed sources that the *Ḥizzequni* commentary utilized.[100]

To be sure the Torah interpretations R. Judah *he-Ḥasid* transmitted to his son R. Zal(t)man were not systematically focused on *peshuto shel miqra*. Indeed, from time to time it is possible to detect interpretations that principally reflect and transmit the ideological underpinnings of the Pietist movement.[101] Moreover, R. Judah's designated *peshat* interpretations are certainly less broadly contextual than those of Rashi, although we have encountered some rather interesting techniques that R. Judah employed to account for specific terms found in the Torah and for the ostensible dialogue or other information that stood "behind" various verses. Most significantly, R. Judah was not the only rabbinic figure associated with the Rhineland at the turn of the twelfth century who had a strong interest in developing and offering *peshat* interpretations. It is to a second such figure, R. Isaiah b. Mali di Trani, whom we now turn.

R. Isaiah di Trani

Over the past three decades, we have learned quite a bit of new information about R. Isaiah b. Mali (Emanuel) di Trani (Rid), the Italian Tosafist and halakhist, thanks in large measure to the efforts of the late Israel Ta-Shma. Indeed, chapters 2 through 5 of the third volume of Ta-Shma's collected studies are focused on the life and works of R. Isaiah.[102] R. Isaiah composed

[99] See ms. Bodl. 270, fols. 9r (and cf. *Perushei ha-Torah le-R. Yehudah he-Ḥasid*, ed. Lange, 34–35), 9b, 11a (Jacob's tricking of Esau to receive his blessing is akin to the passage in *Sefer Ḥasidim* which allows a *ẓaddiq* to trick a *rasha* in order to take away a Torah scroll or other *miẓvah* object that is in the hands of the *rasha*).

[100] See S. Japhet, "Ḥizkuni's Commentary on the Pentateuch," [Hebrew] in *Rabbi Mordechai Breuer Festschrift*, ed. Moshe Bar-Asher et al. (Jerusalem, 1992), 92, n. 6.

[101] See, e.g., ms. B.M. 9931, fol. 152v, to Deut. 7:7 (citing R. Judah by name). Since God (in the book of Genesis) had compared the Jewish people to the stars—which are inherently multitudinous—why does He state here that He did not desire the Jews because of their large numbers? The answer given is that the Jewish people in fact have fewer *ḥasidim* among them than other nations do, but God nonetheless desires them greatly (וי"ל לא מרוב חסידים שבכם חשק ה' בכם כי אתם המעט מכל העמים). Cf. *Perushei ha-Torah*, ed. Lange, for a rather different interpretation of this (not specifically attributed to R. Judah *he-Ḥasid*), as found in ms. Moscow 82.

[102] See Ta-Shma, *Knesset Meḥqarim*, vol. 3 (Jerusalem, 2005), 9–62.

a Torah commentary that displays marked similarities in approach and method to that of R. Judah *he-Ḥasid*—and to those of the late twelfth-century northern French Tosafists surveyed in the previous chapter—at virtually the same time.[103] Before proceeding to analyze this commentary, it is helpful to briefly review several aspects of R. Isaiah's biography, to situate this work in its proper historical and literary contexts.

Although R. Isaiah's lifespan cannot be established with precision, it appears that he was born in Italy between the years 1165 and 1170, and passed away no earlier than the 1230s (but certainly before 1250). He was in Israel between 1185 and 1190, returning there toward the end of his life.[104] Although R. Isaiah spent most of his life in Italy and Byzantium,[105] he also spent some time early in his career—following his return from Israel in 1190—studying in Rhineland Germany, principally with R. Simḥah of Speyer (who was a slightly older contemporary). It was there that R. Isaiah encountered R. Isaac b. Moses of Vienna, another student of R. Simḥah, with whom he maintained subsequent literary contacts,[106] and it was there, in all likelihood, that he became familiar with the teachings of several leading German students of Rabbenu Tam, including R. Isaac b. Mordekhai (Ribam) of Bohemia and R. Isaac *ha-Lavan*, among others. Through them, he also acquired an acquaintance with the work of their teacher, Rabbenu Tam.[107]

Ta-Shma has much to say in his studies about *Tosafot Rid* and the various versions (*mahadurot*) in which they were produced by R. Isaiah, and he characterizes the Ashkenazic, Sefardic, and Italian materials and methods used in the compilation of those *Tosafot.* He suggests that Rid composed his

103 See Ta-Shma, "Sefer Nimmuqei Ḥumash le-Rabbenu Yeshayah di Trani," *Qiryat Sefer* 64 (1992–93), 751–53 (= *Knesset Meḥqarim*, 3:20–23).

104 See Ta-Shma, *Knesset Meḥqarim*, 3:9–15. Ta-Shma also notes that his father's name (Mali) is a kind of nickname for Emanuel (or for the Italian name, Manueli).

105 On R. Isaiah's activities there, see Ta-Shma, *Knesset Meḥqarim*, ibid., and see also Steven Bowman, *The Jews of Byzantium, 1204–1453* (Tuscaloosa, Ala., 1985), 121–27.

106 See also S. Emanuel, *Shivrei Luḥot: Sefarim Avudim shel Ba'alei ha-Tosafot* (Jerusalem, 2007), 155–56, 163–65.

107 See Ta-Shma, *Knesset Meḥqarim*, 3:40–43. At the same time, Rid's teachings were unknown within the *Tosafot* of northern France, and his name is not mentioned at all in the standard *Tosafot* on the Babylonian Talmud. Aside from citations by several of his rabbinic successors in Italy and Byzantium (including his grandson R. Isaiah b. Elijah [Riaz] and R. Zedekiah b. Abraham *ha-Rofe*), R. Isaiah is not cited much by his contemporaries, with the exception of two other students of R. Simḥah of Speyer, R. Abraham b. Azri'el of Bohemia (in his *Sefer 'Arugat ha-Bosem*) and R. Isaac b. Moses of Vienna in his *Sefer Or Zaru'a*. Other German Tosafists cited R. Isaiah from these figure or works; see *Knesset Meḥqarim*, 3:48. Interestingly, as Ta-Shma notes, the Spanish talmudist Ritva (d. c. 1325) occasionally cites material from *Tosafot Rid* in the name of ר' ישעיה/ישעיא/אושיעא אשכנזי. Cf. Urbach, *Ba'alei ha-Tosafot*, 1:148, n. 25, and my "Between Ashkenaz and Sefarad: Tosafist Teachings in the Talmudic Commentaries of Ritva," in *Between Rashi and Maimonides: Themes in Medieval Jewish Thought, Literature and Exegesis*, ed. E. Kanarfogel and M. Sokolow (New York, 2010), 260–62.

Tosafot during the first quarter of the thirteenth century, prior to the collections of his legal rulings (*pesqaim*, including also *Sefer ha-Makhria*), which reflect a more distinctly Italian or Byzantine milieu.[108] Ta-Shma dates this commentary to a relatively early phase of Rid's career, prior to the writing of his talmudic *ḥiddushim* and halakhic works, and perhaps while he was still studying in Ashkenaz or just after his return to Italy, in the early years of the thirteenth century. He bases his assessment on ms. Paris 660 and three parallel manuscripts, as well as ms. Moscow 303, which he regarded as a much fuller version of the commentary—a subject to which we shall return. Rid's talmudic works mention his Torah commentary on a number of occasions, while his Torah commentary does not refer to his talmudic writings. Almost all the rabbinic figures cited by name in Rid's Torah commentary are Ashkenazic, with most of them coming from the circle of R. Simḥah of Speyer (who is cited twice) and his students. In addition, R. Judah *he-Ḥasid* and Rabbenu Tam are cited a handful of times each, and R. Yosef *Bekhor Shor* is mentioned by name twice.[109]

Thus the common exegetical characteristics between Rid's Torah commentary and the contemporary Ashkenazic exegetical material we have studied to this point are far from coincidental.[110] For example, Rid questions the concern expressed in Genesis 3:22 that, since man had eaten from the Tree of Knowledge, he must now be sent out of the Garden of Eden so that he would not eat from the Tree of Life. Since, however, man had been proscribed earlier only from eating from the Tree of Knowledge (Gen. 2:16–17), perhaps Adam and Eve had already eaten from the Tree of Life and had already acquired immortality? Rid's response is that the Tree of Life would not grant eternal life if one ate from it alone. Rather, it served as a kind of antidote, similar to medicinal antidotes that could be effective only if eaten by man after he ate from the Tree of Knowledge. It could not,

[108] See *Knesset Meḥqarim*, 3:24–26.

[109] See Ta-Shma, "Sefer Nimmuqei Ḥumash le-Rabbenu Yeshayah di Trani." Rabbenu Tam and other members of his circle are mentioned, as are R. Yosef Qara and Ibn Ezra. As Ta-Shma also notes, the manuscript copyist apparently included comments from several later Tosafists, such as R. Meir of Rothenburg and R. Isaac *ba'al ha-ḥotam* (= R. Isaac of Corbeil), who are each mentioned once. There are also marginal notes (integrated into the body of the text in some manuscripts) from two subsequent rabbinic scholars of Italian origin, R. Zedekiah b. Abraham and R. Avigdor Katz of Vienna, who was also a student of R. Simḥah of Speyer. Cf. my "Mysticism and Asceticism in Italian Rabbinic Literature of the Thirteenth Century," *Kabbalah* 6 (2001), 135–49.

[110] Urbach, who refers to R. Isaiah in his *Ba'alei ha-Tosafot* only in passing, makes no reference to R. Isaiah's Torah commentary. Meir Miyara, *Ba'alei ha-Tosafot: Mif'alam ha-Torani u-Perusheihem la-Torah vela-Nevi'im* (Jerusalem, 1998), 191–222, deals mostly with Rid's commentaries to the rest of the Bible. Cf. E. Z. Melammed, "Le-Perush Nakh shel R. Yeshayah mi-Trani," in his *Meḥqarim ba-Miqra be-Targumim ubi-Mefarshav* (Jerusalem, 1984), 420–42, and see also below, chapter 7.

however, serve to immortalize man if he ate from it before eating from the Tree of Knowledge. This interpretation is also found in the commentary of R. Yosef *Bekhor Shor.*[111]

The same holds true for Rid's interpretation of why Abraham was so quick to have his guests wash their feet, even before he invited them to rest (Gen. 18:4). Rid questions the interpretation of Rashi (*piresh ha-moreh*), following *Bereshit Rabbah*, who held that they were Ishmaelite idolaters who worshiped the dust on their feet. Yishma'el at this point did not yet have any children or descendants. Thus Rid explains instead (ונראה לי לפי הפשט) that since these figures appeared in the heat of the day, and it was not yet time to turn in for the evening, Abraham first invited them to wash and freshen up from their arduous trek, which would help mitigate the tiredness caused by their travels (בעבור עייפות הדרך). Rid's *peshat* comment here is again the same as the one offered by *Bekhor Shor* (who does not refer to Rashi).[112]

Rid interprets the verse in Genesis 32:32, which repeats the fact that Jacob was limping after his encounter with the angel, *lefi peshuto*, that is, that Jacob could have left the locale of Penu'el, where the confrontation with the angel occurred, even before dawn. However, this verse notes that Jacob was delayed until dawn because of his limp, which slowed his pace. This same

[111] See *Nimmuqei Ḥumash le-Rabbenu Yeshayah*, ed. C. B. Chavel (Jerusalem, 1972), 10; ms. Moscow 303, fol. 60r; and ms. Breslau 102, fol. 4v. See also Rid's comments to Gen. 2:2 (found in ms. Paris 260 without attribution; see Lange, "Sefer Moshav Zeqenim," *Ha-Ma'ayan* 12 [1972], 84), and 2:7 (found also in ms. Moscow 303, fol. 59v, ms. Breslau 102, fol. 3v, and ms. Paris 260 as cited in Lange, ibid.). A gloss by R. Zedekiah b. Abraham, author of *Shibbolei ha-Leqet*, suggests, based on 3:17, that Adam and Eve, for whatever reason, had in fact not yet eaten from the Tree of Life. Cf. *Perushei R. Yosef Bekhor Shor*, ed. Nevo, 12–13. As Chavel had noted, this also appears in *Moshav Zeqenim*, 1 (to Gen. 2:16), in the name of R. Yosef *Bekhor Shor.* See also *Moshav Zeqenim*, 6 (to Gen. 3:22), where a truncated version of part of Rid's comment appears, without attribution (which, as Nevo notes, also appears in *Hadar Zeqenim* and *Minḥat Yehudah*). See also R. Barukh b. Isaac's solution to this problem on the basis of the Targum, below, n. 194. Ms. Moscow 303, fol. 60r (to Gen. 7:2 and 7:9) includes the unattributed interpretation of *Bekhor Shor* as to why seven of each kosher species were taken into Noah's ark as opposed to only two of each nonkosher (ed. Nevo, 17). This interpretation is also found in ms. Warsaw 204 (see *Tosafot ha-Shalem*, ed. Gellis, 1:219, sec. 7), and in *Ḥizzequni*, but it is not found in Chavel's edition of *Nimmuqei Ḥumash le-R. Yeshayah* (= ms. Paris 660 and its variants). Ms. Moscow 303, fol. 60v (to Gen. 7:16) also includes the unattributed interpretation of R. Yosef *Bekhor Shor* (ed. Nevo, 17–18, cited also in *Bekhor Shor*'s name in *Moshav Zeqenim*, 11). See also ms. Moscow 303, fol. 60v, for *Bekhor Shor*'s comment to Gen. 8:9 (ed. Nevo, 19), that Noah grabbed the returning dove with his hand to see whether there was any dirt or dust on its feet or wings, which would indicate that the land had begun to dry and that the flood waters had receded.

[112] See *Nimmuqei Ḥumash*, ed. Chavel, 17, and cf. *Perushei R. Yosef Bekhor Shor*, ed. Nevo, 31: יקח נא מעט מים לנקות רגליכם וגם טוב לעייפות רחיצת הרגלים See also Ramban (שיוקח מעט מים לרחוץ רגליהם מעט מפני החום); *Ḥizzequni* (עת השרב היה . . . וזיעה מצויה ברגליהם של עוברי דרכים); and *Tosafot ha-Shalem*, ed. Gellis, 2:113, sec. 7. In ms. Moscow 303, fol. 66r (to Gen. 24:14), a close grammatical interpretation is put forward that is found in *Perushei R. Yosef Bekhor Shor 'al ha-Torah*, ed. Nevo, 41. This interpretation is also found without attribution in *Moshav Zeqenim*, 32.

interpretation is cited in *Minḥat Yehudah* in the name of R. (Jacob) Tam of Orleans, namely that the limp is repeated by the Torah to explain that Jacob was delayed in leaving Penu'el because walking was difficult for him.[113]

In *parashat Va-Yeshev* (Gen. 38:7),[114] Rid addresses the same concern raised by R. Judah *he-Ḥasid* (on the basis of *Seder 'Olam*), that 'Er and Onan were too young to be punished in such a severe way. *Seder 'Olam* indicates that 'Er and Onan were eight or nine years old at the time of their marriages to Tamar, leading R. Judah *he-Ḥasid* to explain, uniquely, that even such young people can be held fully accountable for their actions if their wisdom exceeded their years.[115] Rid's chronology yields a slightly different result, that they were no older than fourteen. Nonetheless, Rid notes that this kind of final and irrevocable punishment is not appropriate unless the person in question is twenty years old—a concern raised later by *Ḥizzequni* as well. Rid's solution is that 'Er and Onan were punished at this precocious age to prevent the commission of future sins, a fate that befell the younger people during the generation of the flood as well.

C. B. Chavel published an edition of *Nimmuqei Ḥumash le-Rabbenu Yeshayah* (Jerusalem, 1972), from ms. Paris 660. This manuscript was the basis for the transcription of this commentary by R. Ḥayyim Yosef David Azulai (Ḥida) in his *Pnei David* as well,[116] and it also contains a number of glosses from R. Zedekiah b. Abraham *ha-Rofe*, author of *Shibbolei ha-Leqet*, and from his associate R. Avidgor Katz as well.[117] In his introduction, Chavel notes that two later Tosafist Torah compilations, *'Imrei No'am* and *Moshav Zeqenim*, contain quite a number of R. Isaiah's comments, even though the

[113] See *Nimmuqei Ḥumash*, ed. Chavel, 26; ms. Breslau 102, fol. 28v; and ms. Moscow 303, fols. 68r–68v. As Chavel notes, *Minḥat Yehudah* presents this interpretation in the name of R. Jacob of Orleans (Gen.), fols. 32b–33a, and see also *Perushei R. Yosef Bekhor Shor*, ed. Nevo, 60. Rashbam interprets that Jacob's limp became apparent or visible only at dawn. For additional affinities between Rid and R. Jacob of Orleans, see below, nn. 153, 181.

[114] *Nimmuqei Ḥumash*, ed. Chavel, 28.

[115] *Perushei ha-Torah le-R. Yehudah he-Ḥasid*, ed. Lange, 52–53, and cf. above, n. 49. This interpretation is found in *Minḥat Yehudah* (and in ms. Leiden 27), among other Tosafist Torah compilations.

[116] See *Pnei David* (Livrno, 1792). Ḥida notes that there are additional Torah comments from Rid within his talmudic commentaries, suggesting (without any additional proof) that Rid composed different *mahadurot* of his Torah commentary, as was certainly the case for his talmudic *Tosafot*; see also *Nimmuqei Ḥumash*, ed. Chavel, editor's introduction, 6, n. 21. Chavel further suggests (in his introduction, 8) that this development perhaps accounts for the comments in *Moshav Zeqenim*, in the name of R. Isaiah, that are not found in ms. Paris 660. Cf. I. Ta-Shma, *Knesset Meḥqarim*, 1:171–72, who maintains that these comments are from R. Isaiah (*mi-*) Weil (a lesser-known contemporary of R. Meir of Rothenburg and R. Pereẓ of Corbeil). We shall provide some additional possibilities below, on the basis of other manuscripts.

[117] See Chavel's introduction, 5, and 61–62, in the body of the text. See also Ta-Shma, *Knesset Meḥqarim*, 3:21, 23, 70.

ʾImrei Noʿam collection never quotes R. Isaiah by name. Indeed, even *Moshav Zeqenim*, which contains some sixty-five comments from R. Isaiah (as found in ms. Paris 660), mentions his name only thirteen times.[118]

As for Rid's methodology, Chavel notes that the majority of his pithy comments are notes to or criticisms of Rashi's Torah commentary. Rashi is usually referred to—as was often the case in the talmudic *Tosafot ha-Rid* as well—as *ha-Moreh*, the teacher par excellence. Rid will sometimes establish the correct text of Rashi. On occasion he will reject Rashi's interpretation and suggest another instead. In other instances, Rashi is not mentioned at all, and Rid offers a *peshat* interpretation of his own design. Rid also offers a number of *gematria* interpretations.[119]

Chavel sees Rid's responses and reactions to Rashi's commentary as quite similar to those of Naḥmanides, although to be sure Naḥmanides' treatment of Rashi's commentary is much more extensive. Naḥmanides raises issues and problems in terms of *halakhah*, *ʾaggadah*, and even linguistics in great depth, which hardly occurs in the much briefer and narrower comments authored by R. Isaiah. Nonetheless, Chavel concludes that "in essence, they together (and in the same ways) try to clarify and locate Rashi's commentary." Noting that the efforts to provide "supercommentary" to Rashi by both Naḥmanides and Rid were continued in subsequent centuries by a number of rabbinic figures, Chavel lists a large number of references to R. Isaiah's comments (all from the Book of Leviticus) in the supercommentary on Rashi by R. Eliyyahu Mizraḥi. Based on A. Wertheimer's dating of Rid's commentary to *Nakh* (which locates Rid in the second half of the thirteenth century, and his date of death as no later than 1272),[120] Chavel incorrectly sees Naḥmanides as a precise contemporary of Rid.

In fact, however, we now know from the research of Ta-Shma (noted above) and others that Rid flourished in the first half of the thirteenth century, and that his Torah commentary was composed at the very beginning of the century. Chavel was perhaps influenced in his chronology by a halakhic

118 As we have seen, however, with regard to other Tosafists and rabbinic scholars whose names begin with the letter *yod* (see above, chapter 2, nn. 6, 56, 141, 142), there are also sections in *Moshav Zeqenim* attributed simply to ר"י that in fact belong to R. Isaiah di Trani, and we have noted a number of these in this chapter. See, e.g., above, nn. 77, 79, 118; and see also below, n. 142.

119 See *Nimmuqei Ḥumash*, ed. Chavel, editor's introduction, 3–8.

120 Published in Jerusalem in 1959, editor's introduction, 23; see also E. Z. Melammed (above, n. 110), and S. Z. Leiman in *Encyclopedia Miqraʾit*, vol. 8 (Jerusalem, 1982), 708. I. Ta-Shma, *Encyclopedia Judaica* (Jerusalem, 1972), 9:74, writes that the *Nakh* commentaries were apparently composed by R. Isaiah b. Elijah (Riaz), the grandson of R. Isaiah d. Trani (which would mean that the commentaries themselves should be dated to the late thirteenth century). Cf. below, n. 131, 161.

comment of R. Isaac of Corbeil (*ba'al ha-ḥotam*) to Leviticus 21:9, which was apparently a gloss that was copied into the body of the text. In any case, Rid wrote his commentary well before Ramban did. Indeed, as we have already begun to see, Rid's methodology puts him in the class of northern French (and German) Tosafists and rabbinic figures who were working with Rashi and with *peshuto shel miqra* at this time; however, as Chavel intuits, Rid may have been the closest in this group to producing a genuine supercommentary on Rashi, although his efforts are not nearly as systematic as the later *Mizraḥi* and *Gur Aryeh* commentaries.

Before proceeding to analyze Rid's commentary further, I should mention several telling statistics. There are nearly 150 comments made by Rid all told, as recorded in ms. Paris 660 and its closest parallel, ms. Breslau 102: sixty on Genesis, forty on Exodus, twenty each for Leviticus and Numbers, and ten on the Book of Deuteronomy. Rid's comments can be broken into five categories (and the number of comments in each category follows): (1) review and clarification of Rashi's talmudic and other rabbinic references and usages (thirty-five comments); (2) clarification of Rashi's *peshat* method (including the problem of contradictions in his commentary; thirty comments); (3) R. Isaiah's own *peshat* interpretations, which also include chronologies of biblical events(forty comments); (4) comments on various laws and customs related to the text of the Torah (thirty comments); and (5) *gematria* interpretations (five comments), as well as those related mainly to matters of *sod* or Jewish thought (nearly five comments).

As noted above, I. Ta-Shma considers ms. Moscow 303, which is nearly twice as large as ms. Paris 660 (and makes use of the word *peshat* frequently), to be the fuller version of R. Isaiah di Trani's Torah commentary. In fact, however, many of the additional comments in this manuscript are similar to those of R. Yosef *Bekhor Shor*, and I suspect that it is ultimately a kind of composite or compilation of R. Isaiah's commentary along with that of *Bekhor Shor*, which were apparently considered by the compiler(s) to be quite similar in style and otherwise compatible.[121] Our analysis will proceed according to ms. Paris 660, with pieces from Moscow 303 also included as warranted.

[121] For Tosafist Torah compilations that are built on or around the commentary of *Bekhor Shor*, see, e.g., ms. Leiden 27, Vatican 45; and above, chapter 2, n. 131. The so-called *peshatim* section in ms. Hamburg 45 is also attributed erroneously to *Bekhor Shor* (and perhaps to R. Avigdor Katz of Vienna as well, who is definitely the author or compiler of the *pesaqim* section that is found in this manuscript; see below, n. 250). The comments of *Bekhor Shor* are reproduced in the *peshatim* section of ms. Hamburg 45 (for the most part) without attribution. Two concentrated sections are found at the beginning of the books of Exodus and Numbers. See, e.g., fol. 34r (to Ex. 1:11, ed. Nevo, 97–98), and cf. *Tosafot ha-Shalem*, ed. Gellis, 6:17, sec. 2. (Fol. 34v cites Ibn Ezra by name to Ex. 1:15 [cf. *Tosafot ha-Shalem*, 6:25, sec. 11], and also records

Four of the five comments made by R. Isaiah to *parashat Bereshit* (in ms. Paris 660) are of a *peshat* nature or deal directly with Rashi's commentary. We have already seen Rid's interpretation to Genesis 3:22, which is quite similar to the comment made by R. Yosef *Bekhor Shor* to this verse. Rid interprets the phrase (Gen. 4:15), "and God gave to Cain a sign" (literally, a letter, *ʾot*), to mean that he was given a letter from the name of God. His mother had called him קין, based on her statement that "I have acquired (קניתי) a man-child from God." Technically, she and Adam should have therefore called him קן (from the root קנה). The *yod* that formed קין was given to him from the name of God prospectively, to protect him in all circumstances.[122] Rashi had interpreted that God inscribed a letter of His name on Cain's forehead, but Rid does not cite this.[123] At the same time, R. Judah *he-Ḥasid*

---

an interpretation to Ex. 1:16 [without attribution] which is found in ms. 2344 in the name of [R. Jacob of] Orleans; see *Tosafot ha-Shalem*, ed. Gellis, 6:26–27, sec. 8.) See also fol. 36r (to Ex. 3:13–14), which cites *peshat* comments by *Bekhor Shor* to both of these verses verbatim (ed. Nevo, 101, and see also *Tosafot ha-Shalem*, 6:82, sec. 3, and 6:86, sec. 3), including a comment of Rashbam as well (found also partially in ms. Leiden 27), and fol. 36v (to Ex. 4:21, with the parallel phrase in Ex. 7:3), and see ed. Nevo, 106; *Tosafot ha-Shalem*, 6:118, sec. 8 and 182, sec. 3. On fol. 44r, the *peshatim* present the unusual approach of *Bekhor Shor* to the mentioning of the quail in Ex. 16:13 (ed. Nevo, 125, and see above, chapter 2, n. 50). Cf. *Tosafot ha-Shalem*, 7:267, sec. 1, and *Paʿaneaḥ Raza* to Nu. 11:31. The *peshatim* here also present *Bekhor Shor*'s objection and response to Rashi's definition of the word *man* (in Ex. 6:15), which argues that it is related to its Egyptian cognate (Nevo, 126). On Nu. 4:37, the *peshatim* (fol. 81r–v) cite *Bekhor Shor* by name (which is unusual), concerning the differing descriptions of the counting of the various families of Levites in this chapter, and the roles of Moses and Aaron (ed. Nevo, 244, to Nu. 4:49). Nevo notes that this comment appears only in a gloss to ms. Munich 52, but he includes it within the body of the commentary because it comports with *Bekhor Shor*'s tendency to pay close attention to the literary structure of the Torah. The attribution to *Bekhor Shor* by name in ms. Hamburg 45 would strongly support Nevo's contention. Cf. *Perushei R. Ḥayyim Paltiʾel*, ed. Lange, 471–72. The *peshatim* to Nu. 8:11 (ms. Hamburg 45, fol. 83v) explain this verse in similar fashion to *Bekhor Shor* (ed. Nevo, 252, and cf. *Perushei R. Ḥayyim Paltiʾel*, 487). (Interestingly, one of the two explicit references to *Bekhor Shor* in the verified *pesaqim* of R. Avigdor [ed. Machon Harerei Qedem, 225], to Nu. 12:4 [ed. Nevo, 258], is also found unnamed in the *peshatim* [fol. 85v].) The *peshatim* also cite *Bekhor Shor* by name at the beginning of *parashat Shelaḥ* (Nu. 16:2), where *Bekhor Shor* clarifies Rashi's interpretation that Moses wished to send the spies initially, while the Almighty did not (ed. Nevo, 261, and cf. Naḥmanides), and in connection with Nu. 34:4 (ms. Hamburg 45, fol. 99r), concerning the boundaries of the land of Israel (ed. Nevo, 301–2; *Bekhor Shor*'s second interpretation here is the one cited in ms. Hamburg 45). In addition to these kinds of references to *Bekhor Shor*, the *peshatim* also refer extensively (by name and without attribution) to interpretations of R. Judah *he-Ḥasid*, and to a smaller number of interpretations by R. Isaiah di Trani. I intend to treat the contents of this manuscript in a separate study.

[122] See *Nimmuqei Ḥumash*, ed. Chavel, 11; ms. Moscow 303, fol. 60r; ms. Breslau 102, fol. 5r. Chavel notes here as well that this comment is found without attribution in *Moshav Zeqenim*, 7.

[123] Cf. Ibn Ezra and *Ḥizzequni*; God gave Cain a sign that he accepted, which the Torah does not divulge. See also *Perushei R. Yosef Bekhor Shor*, ed. Nevo, 14: God gave Cain some kind of sign in heaven or on earth which caused him to be confident that he would not be killed. Rid, like Rashi, understands *ʾot* more literally and provides a contextual source for his interpretation.

cites Rashi's comment without attribution, and then presents the same interpretation as Rid, almost verbatim.[124]

In Genesis 9:3 ("Every living thing that moves will be for you [Noah and his family] to eat, like green vegetation I have given you everything"), Rid notes Rashi's comment (המורה פירש)[125] that Adam, on the other hand, had been permitted to eat only forms of green vegetation, but was not permitted to slaughter or to eat any meat. Rid questions this assessment of Rashi, because the Talmud in tractate *Sanhedrin* (56b) derives from Genesis 2:16 that Adam was prohibited from eating *'ever min ha-ḥai* (a limb from a living animal), implying that he must have been permitted to eat meat from an animal that was slaughtered. Rid suggests, therefore—to perhaps preserve at least the spirit of Rashi's comment if not the specifics—that Adam was not allowed to slaughter meat for consumption, but when he came upon an animal that had already been slaughtered (= killed), he was allowed to partake of it. This is typical of Rid, verifying and even adjusting Rashi's talmudic assumptions or interpretations within his Torah commentary where they appear to be unclear or problematic.[126]

Five of eight of Rid's comments to *parashat Lekh Lekha*, beginning with the phrase המורה פירש, either confirm or challenge Rashi on the level of *peshat.* For example, contrary to Rashi's suggestion that Lot (in Gen. 13:11, ויסע לוט מקדם) was traveling from east to west, Rid assumes that since Lot was going to the Jordan Valley, which was to the east of where Abraham was at the time, in *Beit El*, Lot actually traveled from west to east. The meaning of the Torah's phrase is that Lot was going *toward qedem* and not from it. Indeed, this is also the meaning of the phrase מקדם לבית אל in Genesis 12:8.[127] In a passage in ms. Moscow 303 (to Gen. 12:15), an interpretation of R. Yosef

[124] See above, n. 29, and cf. *Tosafot ha-Shalem*, ed. Gellis, 1:165, sec. 8. Ms. Moscow 303, fol. 63v, cites (as an addendum) a letter-based interpretation in the name of R. Judah (וה"ר יהודה החסיד פי' דסופי תיבות והתחלת תיבות אורח כנשים [בראשית יח:יא] עולה נידה) before noting a different interpretation in the name of R. Isaiah (אבל אני מצאתי זאת הקושי' מתורצת בתוספות רבי' ישעיה בענין אחר). Two other comments from R. Isaiah found only in ms. Moscow 303, fols. 61r–v, are also found in ms. Cambridge 669 (to Gen. 12:5 and 12:3; see *Perushei ha-Torah le-R. Yehudah he-Ḥasid*, ed. Lange 17–19), although these are not presented specifically in the name of R. Judah *he-Ḥasid.* Cf. above, at n. 24. Ms. Paris 660 (ed. Chavel, 55) and ms. Moscow 303, fol. 85r (end) cite R. Judah *he-Ḥasid*'s comment to Lev. 21:14 (see above, 74) in a marginal gloss.

[125] As noted above, *ha-moreh* is the way Rid most commonly refers to Rashi (in his talmudic writings as well), although he will also refer to Rashi's commentaries as פרש"י. This perhaps reflects Rid's "outsider" status within Ashkenaz, and also that his awareness of Rashi is essentially through German rather than French Tosafist sources.

[126] *Nimmuqei Ḥumash*, ed. Chavel, 12–13. Cf. the *Gur Aryeh* and *Levush ha-Orah* supercommentaries, which discuss this resolution, without mentioning Rid by name.

[127] *Nimmuqei Ḥumash*, ed. Chavel, 13; ms. Breslau 102, fol. 11r; ms. Moscow 303, fol. 61v. This question is again found in *Mizraḥi.* Ibn Ezra assumes that Sedom was Lot's immediate destination, which is to the west of Beit El.

Bekhor Shor is cited by name. This interpretation accounts for the nuanced difference between the reaction of Pharaoh upon discovering that Sarah was Abraham's wife and not his sister, as compared to Avimelekh's reaction (in Gen. 20:4) to the same situation.[128]

In Genesis 13:14, "God said to Abraham after Lot separated from him, lift your eyes and view the place where you are," indicating that the entire land would be given to his descendants. Rashi, based on the *Midrash Tanḥuma*, notes "that as long as the wicked one [Lot] was together with Abraham, God did not speak with him," and that He later resumed speaking with Abraham. Rid notes, however, that God had spoken with Abraham toward the beginning of *Lekh Lekha* (Gen. 12:7), "And God appeared to Abraham and told him that this land would be given to his progeny." Rid suggests the following *peshat* interpretation (ולי נראה שזה פירושו לפי הפשט): God spoke with Abraham immediately upon Lot's departure, because Abraham was troubled by his separation from Lot. The import of God's appearance at this point was to tell Abraham not to be troubled, to "cheer up" so to speak, since the entire land would be given to his progeny. Rid also suggests an alternate approach, that Lot was initially righteous (and hence God was able to speak with Abraham earlier on in Lot's association with him, as in Gen. 12:7). Only later did Lot's status deteriorate, preventing God from speaking with Abraham until Lot had departed.[129] It should be noted that the first approach of Rid is not compatible with Rashi's comment (based on *Tanḥuma*), while the second one is.[130]

128 See ms. Moscow 303, fol. 61v: ותקח האשה בית פרעה. תימה למה לא פירשו ופרעה לא קרב אליה כמו שהגיד גבי אבימלך, ואבימלך לא קרב אליה. פי' הרב יוסף בכור שור בית פרעה כלו' לבית הובאה ולא למטתו כי קפצו עליו יסורין ופירש [ממנה] כאילו שנא' ופרעה לא הקריב אליה. See *Perushei R. Yosef Bekhor Shor*, ed. Nevo, 25, where this interpretation appears verbatim, and cf. *Tosafot ha-Shalem*, 2:21–22, secs. 6, 9, and 2:174–75 (citing ms. Vatican 45); *Ḥizzequni* to Gen. 20:4; and ms. Moscow 303 (to Gen. 20:4), fol. 63v.

129 *Nimmuqei Ḥumash*, ed. Chavel (hereafter Chavel), 14; ms. Breslau 102, fol. 11v; ms. Moscow 303, fol. 61v (end). As Chavel notes, this precise comment, without attribution, is found in *Moshav Zeqenim*, 17, one of many such examples.

130 See Chavel, 14. In this portion, Rid also notes (and leaves unresolved; see Chavel, 15) a conflict between Rashi's comment to Gen. 14:14 (where he defines the word וירק based on similar word forms in Lev. 26:33 and Ex. 15:9) and Rashi's own comment to Ex. 15:9 (where he defines the word אריק in a different way), as well as a postulate by Rashi in Gen. 15:10 (that other nations are compared to animals such as cows, rams, and goats, while the Jewish people are compared to birds), which seems to contradict Ezekiel 34:31, where the Jewish people are compared to livestock. Chavel, ibid., could not find anyone who resolves this contradiction, although it is perhaps possible to suggest that Rashi means that the Jewish nation is compared to birds only in the context of other nations who are being compared to animals. When the Jewish people alone are being described, however, they may be compared to other kosher animals as well. Rid offers an interpretation to Gen. 16:2 that he characterizes as ונראה לי לפי הפשט. See Chavel, 16; ms. Breslau 102, fol. 12v; and ms. Moscow 303, fol. 62v. See also the use of this phrase by Rid (in Gen. 18:4), above, n. 113. At the beginning of *parashat va-Yera* (Gen. 18:1),

When Abraham bargains with God about saving Sodom, Rashi explains (Gen. 18:29) that the initial number of fifty people put forward by Abraham meant that at least ten righteous men were needed in each of the five cities or districts that comprised Sodom. As Abraham reduced the numbers, however, he was essentially asking for the same easement from God each time. Why then did he have to repeat each request? Rid's answer, that Abraham made one large request in which he simply lowered the number of districts to be saved, adumbrates what Ramban later suggests in his commentary.[131]

Rid's opening comments to the portions of *Ḥayyei Sarah*, *Toledot,* and *Va-Yishlaḥ* are *gematria*-based.[132] The defective spelling of Efron (without a *vav*, in the phrase in Gen. 23:16, "and Avraham paid Efron") yields a *gematria* total of 400, which is equal to the 400 *shekalim* that Abraham gave to Efron to acquire the *me'arat ha-makhpelah*: In Rid's words, "And therefore, Efron was written in this fashion, so that his name testified to his actions."[133] Similarly, Rid (or perhaps a gloss to his commentary) notes that the word *holid* in Genesis 25:19 (Abraham gave birth to, *holid 'et*, Isaac) is equivalent in *gematria* to the word *domeh.* As Rashi notes (based on Tanḥuma), Isaac's physical appearance was quite similar to that of Abraham (*domeh le-Avraham*), to thwart the denigrating claim made by some that Abraham was not really

---

Rid suggests that the phrase (כחום היום) is very difficult to interpret according to the *peshat* (מאוד קשה לפי הפשט); the verse should have said בחום היום, meaning at the time of the day's greatest heat. Rid notes that he heard a fitting *derash* on this word (*derash na'eh*), that *ke-ḥom ha-yom* refers to that great day described by the prophet Malachi (3:19) as "a day for God is coming that will burn like a furnace." This would also account for the interpretation put forward by Rashi (*ha-moreh*) to Gen. 16:2, that God took the sun out of its case (*hozi ḥamah mi-nartiqah*). See Chavel, 17; ms. Breslau 102, fol. 13r; ms. Moscow 303, fol. 62v; and cf. *Tosafot ha-Shalem*, ed. Gellis, 2:107.

131 See Chavel, 19. Here again, as Chavel notes, there is similar discussion in the classic early modern supercommentaries. In several places in this portion, R. Zedekiah b. Abraham glosses several talmudic issues and refers to *Ḥakhmei Zarefat*; see Chavel, 18–21, and ms. Moscow 303, fol. 63v. See *Moshav Zeqenim*, 26 (to Gen. 19:14), for a question and interpretation in the name of R. Isaiah that are close to those of Rashbam and *Bekhor Shor*; cf. above, nn. 121, 128. This interpretation is also found in the name of R. Isaiah b. Mali in the Torah commentary of his grandson, R. Isaiah b. Elijah. See ms. Cambridge 377, fol. 20r, and *Tosafot ha-Shalem*, ed. Gellis, 2:157, sec. 4.

132 This pattern was followed even more consistently and expansively by R. Jacob b. Asher as well. His *gematria* comments (referred to as the *perush ha-Tur ha-qaẓar*) were listed at the beginning of each portion, while his broader exegetical commentary (*perush ha-Tur ha-'Arukh*) came afterward. See Aharon Ahrend, "Ha-Perush ha-Qaẓar shel Ba'al ha-Turim la-Torah," *Mahanayim* 3 (1993), 180–87, and Yehudah Shaviv, "Perush ha-Arokh shel Ba'al ha-Turim la-Torah," *Mahanayim* 3 (1993), 170–79.

133 Chavel, 21. This simple and exegetically direct *gematria* is found later in *Ba'al ha-Turim*, ed. Y. K. Reinitz, 1:55; in *Hadar Zeqenim*, s.v. *'asher biqẓeh sadehu* (without attribution); and in *Ḥizzequni* as well. As noted by Reinitz, n. 15, this *gematria* is also found in the commentary attributed to Rashi to Chronicles 1:16:11.

his father. These are nonfanciful and fairly obvious *gematria* forms, which are therefore quite effective in an exegetical context as well.[134]

Similarly, at the beginning of *parashat Va-Yishlaḥ* (Gen. 32:11), Jacob tells Esau that he had originally "crossed this Jordan with (only) my staff" (*be-maqli*, connoting that he was completely bereft), but that presently his considerable assets had been divided into two camps. Rid notes that *be-maqli* is equal to the *gematria* of Jacob, suggesting that it was in Jacob's own merit that he returned to the land of Israel with such great assets. Indeed, it is for this reason that *be-maqli* was used here by the Torah, rather than a form of the more common word for a staff, *mateh*.[135]

In *parashat Toledot*, Rid questions the validity of Rashi's well-known interpretation of Genesis 25:22 (following *Bereshit Rabbah*), that when Jacob was in Rivka's womb, he kicked whenever she passed a *beit midrash*, while Esau kicked when she passed a house of idolatry. Rashi's approach was based on a talmudic discussion (*Sanhedrin* 91a) in which R. Judah the Prince came to regard the view of the Emperor Antoninus as correct, that the evil inclination enters a person only after he is born. If so, how could Rashi have adopted the notion that Esau, *in utero*, wished to emerge at a place of idolatry, which does not accord with the final disposition of this talmudic passage?[136] Rid also suggests a response to Rashi's assertion that he did not know what the final phrase "the mother of Jacob and Esau" (in the verse "And Isaac sent Jacob, and he went to Padan Aram to Laban son of Betu'el the Aramean, the brother of Rivka, the mother of Jacob and Esau," Gen. 28:5) was meant to convey. Rid suggests that it was a reflection of Jacob's propriety (*'al shem kashruto shel Ya'aqov*) that Rivka was identified here as the mother of Jacob, just as Rivka's identification as the sister of Lavan reflected the wickedness of Esau. Jacob was among the minority while Esau was from the majority with respect to the talmudic teaching (*Bava Batra* 110a) that most sons are similar to their mother's brother. It is also possible that since Rivka had mercy for both of her sons, she is referred to here as the mother of Jacob

134 Chavel, 23. Rid presents several scriptural chronologies, most often playing off those of Rashi, although occasionally without reference to him. In Gen. 25:20, for example (Chavel, ibid.), Rid begins with Rashi's comment on Isaac's age at the *'aqedah*, then moves into the *Tosafot* discussion concerning Rivka's age when she married Isaac. See my "Midrashic Texts and Methods in Tosafist Torah Commentaries," sec. 6. This is, of course, as much a talmudic discussion as a biblical one.

135 Chavel, 26. This follows Rashi's *peshat* approach to this verse (against the midrash that he also cites), that "I had no gold or silver or livestock when I crossed the Jordan." On the *gematria* itself, cf. *Perush ha-Roqeaḥ*, ed. J. Klugmann, 1:240; *Ba'al ha-Turim*, ed. Reinitz, 1:87, and the published edition of *Pa'aneaḥ Raza*, 154; and *Perushei R. Ḥayyim Palti'el*, ed. Lange, 99. At the beginning of *parashat Va-Yeshev*, ed. Chavel, 27 (to Gen. 37:17), there is also a *gematria* on the brothers of Joseph, but this is in a gloss by R. Zedekiah b. Abraham, the author of *Shibbolei ha-Leqet*.

136 Chavel, 24, and cf. *Gur Aryeh* and *Levush ha-Orah*, ad loc.

and Esau, as the verse states (Gen. 27:45), "why should I lose you both in the same day?"[137]

Several dynamic *peshatim* are put forward by Rid in *parashat Va-Yishlaḥ.*[138] In Genesis 33:19, Jacob buys the area in which he had pitched his tent from the sons of Ḥamor, who was the father of Shekhem. Rid raises a thoughtful question. Since Jacob intended to be in this area only for a short while, why was it necessary for him to purchase the land that he used for lodging? There is certainly no indication that Jacob felt the need to acquire every place where he pitched his tent. Rid answers that since Jacob built an altar there, he therefore did not want this holy place to be destroyed or defaced. By acquiring this area formally, he was able to insure that it would be protected. On the other hand, the locations where Abraham and Isaac built their altars (Gen. 12:8, 26:25) did not have to be acquired, since they were built in outlying, ownerless places (מקום הפקר דהיינו בהר שאין שם אדון).[139] Based on a similar kind of concern, Rid explains that Jacob buried Rachel on the way to Bethlehem (Gen. 35:19, *be-derekh Efratah hi Beit Laḥem*) and did not bring her into the city itself—even though it was fairly near—because he did not wish to reside in that place even if he could purchase a burial plot there. It was inevitable that, after a while, the land in this area would be stolen and then turned into a field or vineyard, which would constitute a desecration of her grave. Jacob therefore buried Rachel near the road, at a site that would not be made into a field or vineyard.[140]

[137] Chavel, ibid. The second comment here may be a gloss to the body of the text.

[138] We have already noted R. Isaiah's comment to Gen. 32:32 (which is characterized as *lefi peshuto*), above, n. 113.

[139] See Chavel, 26. This interpretation is also found, without attribution, in *Moshav Zeqenim*, 61, and cf. *Tosafot ha-Shalem*, ed. Gellis, 3:242, sec. 3. As Chavel notes, no other commentary seems to make this scriptural distinction, although Ibn Ezra understands this action as a broad indication of scriptural approbation for acquiring a piece of land in Israel (להודיע כי מעלה גדולה יש לארץ ישראל ומי שיש לו חלק בה חשוב הוא כחלק עולם הבא).

[140] Chavel, 26–27, and see also *Moshav Zeqenim*, 63, and *Tosafot ha-Shalem*, ed. Gellis, 3:266, sec. 2. (Immediately prior in *Moshav Zeqenim*, R. Isaiah's name is mentioned in connection with the naming of Benjamin [Gen. 35:18], although this comment is not found in any of the manuscripts of Rid's Torah commentary; cf. below.) *Ḥizzequni* explains that Jacob did not want to move the body of Rachel at all because the blood from childbirth would leak out, causing disrespect to the deceased. See also ms. Bodl. 268 in *Torat ha-Shalem*, ed. Gellis, 3:266, sec. 1. Rashbam and R. Yosef *Bekhor Shor* (ed. Nevo, 63), on the other hand, suggest that the phrase *kivrat 'erez* (in Gen. 35:16, where Rachel gave birth) means that there was actually quite a distance between the place where Rachel expired and Bethlehem. Rashi, Ibn Ezra, Radak, and Ramban seem to reject this interpretation; see *Rashbam's Commentary on Genesis*, ed. Lockshin, 222. Ms. Moscow 303, fol. 69r, to Gen. 35:29, distinguishes between this verse, where the first-born Esau is mentioned before the more righteous Jacob with regard to the burial of Isaac, and Gen. 25:9, where the more righteous Isaac is mentioned before Yishma'el with regard to the burial of Abraham, even though Yishma'el was certainly older. The first explanation given for these differences based on the order of birth is that both Esau and Jacob were born from the same mother, while Yishma'el was the son of Abraham's concubine Hagar. Although two

At the end of Pharaoh's dream about the stalks of wheat (Gen. 41:7), the Torah writes, "and Pharaoh awoke and behold it was a dream" (*ve-hineh ḥalom*). This phrase, however, is not found when Pharaoh awoke from his dream about the cows (in Gen. 41:4). Rid explains that cows, as animate objects, could at least theoretically eat other cows. Therefore, that scenario was not immediately characterized as a dream. Stalks of wheat, however, which are inanimate objects, could not possibly eat other stalks of wheat. Thus Pharaoh immediately realized that this vision must have been a dream.[141] Rid's approach seeks to resolve problems raised by Rashi, Rashbam, and R. Yosef *Bekhor Shor*.[142]

Rid writes that Rashi interprets (*piresh ha-moreh*) the anomalous phrase in Genesis 46:23, ובני דן חושים, to mean that Dan actually had two sons. Although this comment is not found in the extant versions of Rashi, Ibn Ezra raises the possibility that Dan had two sons, one of whom died.[143] The Torah therefore notes that Dan had two sons, but lists only the one

---

other answers are suggested, this explanation is found also in *Perushei ha-Torah le-R. Yosef Bekhor Shor*, ed. Nevo, 63. Another similar affinity (in terms of *peshat*) is found between Rid's verified comment to Gen. 36:24 (Chavel, 27; ms. Breslau 102, fol. 37r; and ms. Moscow 303, fol. 69v) and the commentary of *Bekhor Shor*, ed. Nevo, 65.

141 Chavel, 29. As Chavel notes, this interpretation is found (without attribution) in both *Ḥizzequni* and in the Tosafist compilation *Da'at Zeqenim*. For other examples of Rid's *peshatim* that are found without attribution in *Da'at Zeqenim*, see, Chavel, e.g., 13, 30, 36.

142 *Bekhor Shor* asserts that, in fact, the thinner stalks did not swallow the bulkier ones but rather appeared to completely envelop or cover them, since stalks cannot in reality swallow other stalks, and dreams do not reveal circumstances that cannot actually occur (דבשבלים לא שייך בליעה ממש אלא כסוי ואין דרך להראות דבר שאינו נוהג בעולם לאדם). Similar to Rashi, *Bekhor Shor* explains that the phrase *ve-hineh ḥalom* signifies that Pharaoh's dreaming had concluded. He also cites the view of *ve-yesh mefarshim* (referring to Rashbam), that Pharaoh did not realize that he was dreaming until he awoke after the second part of his dream (since the word *ve-hineh* usually refers in the Torah to a newly gained realization). See *Rashbam's Commentary on Genesis*, ed. Lockshin, 279–80, and see also *Tosafot ha-Shalem*, ed. Gellis, 4:120–21, secs. 4, 6. Unlike Rashi, who understood the phrase אל תרגזו בדרך (in Gen. 45:24) to mean that Joseph was expressing concern that the brothers should not be in conflict on their way home (in accordance with the rabbinic interpretation that they should not become embroiled in any halakhic debates or disputes), ms. Moscow 303, fols. 71r–v, interprets this more simply as "do not be afraid on the way lest someone take from you the grain that you are bringing back home, for I [Joseph] am the ruler of Egypt and I will command that it should be returned to you or I will give you other wheat to replace it." Another example of this meaning for the root רגז is adduced from Deut. 28:65 (לב רגז, and its targumic interpretation). This is precisely the first (and much preferred) interpretation found in *Perushei R. Yosef Bekhor Shor* (to Gen. 45:24), ed. Nevo, 83, which is also mentioned briefly by Rashbam (based on Ps. 99:1, and see also *Sefer ha-Gan*, ed. Orlian, 195). Rid's talmudic analysis of Rashi's comment to Gen. 45:27 (based on a passage in the *Yerushalmi*; see Chavel, 31; ms. Breslau 102, fol. 37v; ms. Moscow 303, fol. 71v; and *Moshav Zeqenim*, 92) is cited in ms. JTS 794 in the name of ר"י (and is also found in ms. Cambridge 377). See *Tosafot ha-Shalem*, ed. Gellis, 4:230, sec. 8.

143 Cf. *Perushei ha-Torah le-R. Yehudah he-Ḥasid 'al ha-Torah*, ed. Lange, 15–16 (Gen. 9:13); *Tosafot ha-Shalem*, ed. Gellis, 4:244, sec. 6 (to Gen. 46:23); and above, n. 34.

(named Ḥushim) who survived. Rid rejects this possibility, since the verse in Numbers 26:8 reads, "and the sons of Falu, Eliav." In this instance, there was certainly only one son, since the very next verse (Nu. 26:9) immediately lists the sons of Eliav, making it impossible that Eliav had any brothers. Rid notes a similar phenomenon in Chronicles 1:2:8, which is also discussed in *Bava Batra* (143b).[144] In his commentary to Genesis 1:26, R. Yosef *Bekhor Shor* had noted both of the Torah verses mentioned by Rid as examples of the use of a plural noun when referring to a single subject, the same point made by Rid here, and *Bekhor Shor* does the same in his commentary to Genesis 46:15, noting that Jacob's female child is characterized by the plural term *benotav* as well, even though he had only one daugher.[145]

Early in the book of Exodus (2:6), a problematic reference is encountered: "And she opened [the basket] and saw the child (*'et ha-yeled*), and behold the young man (*na'ar*) was crying." Rashi understood that both references (*yeled* and *na'ar*) were to Moses; although he was a young baby, his voice was like that of a *na'ar* (as reported in an aggadic discussion in tractate *Sotah* 12b).[146] Similarly, Ibn Ezra suggests (in his long commentary) that Moses's limbs were larger than those of an infant, making it appear that a *na'ar* (and not a *yeled*) was crying. Rashbam criticizes the view of one who interprets (*ha-mefaresh*, an implicit reference to Rashi's view) that Pharaoh's daughter saw a *yeled* who acted in some way like a *na'ar.* Rather, she checked to see whether the child (*yeled*, a generic term for a child) was a boy or a girl. She noticed that he was a boy (a *na'ar*) who already appeared to be circumcised. Rashbam cites a verse in Judges 13:8 that links the terms *yeled* and *na'ar* in this way (i.e., a newborn boy can also be referred to as a *na'ar*). He does not, however, fundamentally disagree with Rashi that both of these terms refer to Moses.[147]

144 Chavel, 31–32; ms. Breslau 102, fol. 38r; and ms. Moscow 303, fol. 72r. *Ḥizzequni* to Gen. 46:23 follows Ibn Ezra's approach. In Gen. 46:7, however, where Jacob's only daughter, Dina, is characterized as *benotav* (his daughters), *Ḥizzequni* insists that Gen. 46:23 and Nu. 26:8, as well as this verse, refer to only one child. Indeed, this rule is cited in the published version of *Pa'aneaḥ Raza*, 198, in the name of *Sefer ha-Gan*, and see also *Tosafot ha-Shalem*, ed. Gellis, 4:244, secs. 1–2 (and the above note).

145 *Perushei R. Yosef Bekhor Shor 'al ha-Torah*, ed. Nevo, 83.

146 Naḥmanides notes that the talmudic *sugya* in *Sotah* ultimately rejects this assertion, because a particularly loud or thick voice would have disqualified Moses from his duty as a Levite to sing. He therefore suggests that Moses was crying not like an infant but with the intensity and urgency of an older child (which caused the daughter of Pharaoh to have even greater mercy on him). Cf. *Hadar Zeqenim*, and the next note.

147 See Chavel, 35. Although this appears in ms. Paris 660 only as a gloss, it is found in Rid's name in ms. Breslau 102 (fol. 44v). Cf. Lockshin, *Rashbam's Commentary on Exodus*, 22–24. This also appears to be the approach of *Bekhor Shor* (ed. Nevo, 99). On the implications of the terms *yeled* and *na'ar* in medieval Jewish literature, cf. my *Jewish Education and Society in the High Middle Ages*, ch. 1.

Rid, on the other hand, pursues a different direction here. He suggests that the *yeled* was indeed Moses, but that the crying *na'ar* was his older brother, Aaron. Aaron, who was not an infant, was standing on the banks of the Nile, openly crying about what he saw happening to his baby brother (as opposed to his older sister, Miriam, who was hiding and watching out of sight).[148] As we have seen, this was also the suggestive *peshat* approach taken by R. Judah *he-Ḥasid*.[149]

Rid also deals with the question raised by Exodus 7:22, as to where the magicians of Egypt found water to turn into blood, since all the water in Egypt had ostensibly been turned into blood during the plague (as per Ex. 7:19, that water was in all the basins and receptacles as well). Rid suggests that the magicians got their water by digging around the blood-filled Nile, as described in Exodus 7:24.[150] Although others simply assumed that the magicians were able to acquire water from a different place, R. Yosef *Bekhor Shor* presents this problem and suggests that the water turned into blood throughout the land of Egypt only for a short period of time, after which it all turned back to water. The magicians then took some of this water and turned it back into blood. Once this blood turned back to water again, Pharaoh did not pay any attention to what had been done during the plague.[151] The Tosafist Torah compilation *Moshav Zeqenim* mentions the views of both R. Yosef *Bekhor Shor* and R. Isaiah by name, as well as several other approaches without attribution.[152]

148 See Chavel, 35. Chavel notes that in addition to the midrashic source for this interpretation (*Midrash Avkir*, adduced by M. M. Kasher in his *Torah Shelemah*) and the view of Rid, *Ḥizzequni* also interprets the verse in this way. On the passage in *Midrash Avkir* (a work that greatly impacted *Ḥasidei Ashkenaz*; cf. the next note), see above, n. 56.

149 See *Perushei ha-Torah le-R. Yehudah he-Ḥasid* ed. Lange, 73 (beginning with the phrase 'פי' אבי לפי הפשט), and above, n. 56.

150 See Chavel, 36, and see also *Hadar Zeqenim* and *Da'at Zeqenim* (which include this approach without attribution).

151 See *Perushei R. Yosef Bekhor Shor*, ed. Nevo, 107. R. Elyaqim, the teacher of R. Judah b. Eleazar (who was the compiler of *Minḥat Yehudah*), cites a *Tanḥuma* passage that the magicians got their water from the Israelites, whose water had not turned into blood. This approach is also found in ms. Hamburg 45, along with the unattributed comment of *Bekhor Shor*, that the Nile turned to blood only for a short period of time and then returned to its normal state. See also *Tosafot ha-Shalem*, ed. Gellis, 6:200, secs. 1–4.

152 See *Moshav Zeqenim*, 116, which also raises questions on these views. R. Yosef *Bekhor Shor*'s view is also cited in *Perushei R. Ḥayyim Palti'el*, ed. Lange, 196. Note Rid's understanding of the form of the name of God in Exodus 6:3, *lefi peshuto* (Chavel 35; ms. Breslau 102, fol. 47r; ms. Moscow 303, fol. 73v; and cf. *Tosafot ha-Shalem*, ed. Gellis, 6:154, sec. 22). Ms. Moscow 303 (fol. 73r) alone interprets the houses that were made in connection with the God-fearing midwives (*va-ya'as lahem batim*, Ex. 1:21), *lefi peshuto*, to mean that Pharaoh constructed these houses for the Egyptians, so that they could hear the sounds of the Jewish children being born and eliminate them. A similar interpretation is found in *Minḥat Yehudah*, Ex., fol. 2b, in the name of R. Jacob of Orleans (see above, chapter 2, n. 158), and see also the commentary of R. Judah *he-Ḥasid* (*Perushei ha-Torah le-R. Yehudah he-Ḥasid*, ed. Lange, 72–73).

R. Isaiah makes a textual emendation within Rashi's commentary to Exodus 9:14. The standard text of Rashi seems to suggest that the Torah's use of "all the plagues" that would be visited upon the Egyptians refers specifically to the plague of the firstborn (מכת בכורות), "which was equal to all of the other plagues." R. Jacob of Orleans had suggested that these words should be vocalized differently (*makkat bekhurot*), so that they would apply to the plague of hail that was actually the next to come, while Rashbam and *Bekhor Shor* found other ways to understand hail as a multifaceted plague, either in terms of the multiple impacts that it could have or its multiple physical elements.[153]

R. Isaiah di Trani does something quite similar to what R. Jacob of Orleans has done. He maintains that *makkat bekhorot* is a mistaken reading (ואינו כן אלא טעות סופר . . . אלא טעות הוא), since hail, not the plague of the firstborn, was the next plague to come. R. Isaiah suggests that the correct reading in Rashi should be מכת בצורת (changing the *kaf* to a *zaddiq*), since the main impact of the plague of hail, as the Torah indicates, was in the creation of a famine (*bazoret*). In this respect, hail was as severe a plague as all the prior ones combined.[154]

Rid's comments to *parashat Bo* are focused mainly on the Passover sacrifice (Ex., ch. 12), and, by definition, most of his comments here are *halakhah*-based. He also has a comment in this section (Ex. 12:26) that deals with the interpretation of the text of the *Haggadah.*[155] Nonetheless, Rid also deals with a contradiction between two exegetical passages in Rashi. Here again he resolves the problem by suggesting a different reading in one of the Rashi passages.[156]

Rashi to Exodus10:14 interprets the phrase, ואחריו לא יהיה כן (that there would never be an affliction of locusts like the one in Egypt) to mean that even though the verse in Joel 2:2 describes a locust plague that would be

[153] See above, chapter 2, nn. 164–67.

[154] See Chavel 37; ms. Breslau 102, fol. 49v; ms. Moscow 303, fol. 73v; and cf. above, n. 114. *Perush [ha-Meyuḥas le] ha-Rosh ʿal ha-Torah*, in *Hadar Zeqenim* (Livorno, 1840), fol. 27a, notes both emendations without attribution but seems to favor the approach of Rid over the one suggested by R. Jacob of Orleans, while *Perushei R. Ḥayyim Paltiʾel*, ed. Lange, 202, favors the approach of R. Jacob of Orleans. See also *Tosafot ha-Shalem*, ed. Gellis, 6:243–44, and R. Solomon Luria, *Yeriʿot Shelomoh* (Bnei Brak, 1984), fol.52.

[155] Chavel, 41.

[156] Chavel, 38–39. Rashi asserts (Ex. 11:4) that God spoke to Moses at midnight (בעמדו לפני פרעה נאמר לו), when he was with Pharaoh. And yet, Rashi later insists (Ex. 12:1) that there was no contact between God and Moses while Moses was within the idolatrous precincts of Egypt proper (ומה תפלה קלה לא התפלל בתוך הכרך, דיבור חמור לא כל שכן). Rid corrects the text of Rashi in 11:4 to read that Moses received the words of God earlier, and then reported them to Pharaoh only at midnight (דה"ג בפירושים, בעמדו לפני פרעה, בעומדו לפני פרעה אמרה לו, דמשמע אמרה לו משה לפרעה ולא נאמרה לו באותה שעה).

unlike anything that had ever occurred before (כמוהו לא נהיה לעולם), that plague was unprecedented in that it consisted of several different species of locusts, while the plague in Egypt contained only one species and was still remarkably and uniquely destructive. Rid questions Rashi's interpretation, because according to Psalms 78:46–47, the Egyptian plague of locusts also consisted of more than one species. He therefore suggests that Moses's claim that there would never be another plague of locusts like it connotes that there would never be such a plague in that same place, in Egypt. Elsewhere in the world, however, a more severe plague might be possible. Similarly, the claim in the Book of Joel that the plague of locusts was unprecedented was limited to the land of Israel in which that plague occurred.[157] R. Yosef *Bekhor Shor* includes Rashi's interpretation (with attribution) as a second approach (*yesh lefaresh*), but his first answer to this question (*ve-yesh lomar*) is the same as the approach of Rid: במצרים לא היה כמו של משה ובארץ ישראל לא היה כמו של יואל.[158]

An interesting exegetical observation is made by Rid concerning Rashi's comment on Exodus 15:25, "there [in Marah] He gave him statutes and laws." On the basis of different rabbinic *midrashim*, Rashi notes that in Marah, God gave the Jews several laws and statutes, including the precepts of *parah 'adumah* and the Sabbath, and the rules of civil law (as Rashi notes on the basis of different rabbinic *midrashim*). Rid observes that Rashi's interpretation here is contradicted by his subsequent interpretation of Exodus 16:22. There, the *nesi'im* came to Moses to inform him (*va-yagidu le-Mosheh*) that two portions of manna were available on Friday. In explaining their confusion, Rashi cites the words of the *Mekhilta*, *mah yom mi-yomayim*, why is this day, Friday, different from the day before, on which only one portion of *man* appeared per person? Rashi explains the confusion of the *nesi'im* by suggesting that this episode shows that Moses had not yet taught the

[157] See Chavel, 38; ms. Breslau 102, fol. 50r; ms. Moscow 303, fol. 74r. *Moshav Zeqenim*, 122, cites this answer without attribution (as does *Minḥat Yehudah*, Ex. fol. 10b), among several other approaches. These include the fact that Joel's plague had certain types of locusts that Moses's plague did not; or that the species called *'arbeh* was unusually numerous and powerful in Moses's plague but not in the later one; or that the locusts in Moses's plague were more numerous, but those in the later plague were physically larger. A solution attributed in *Moshav Zeqenim* to R. Yeḥi'el of Paris suggests that the locusts during Moses's plague appeared one species at a time, while those in Joel's plague came in mixed together. This passage is also included in ms. Moscow, fol. 74r (and is certainly a later interpolation). *Pa'aneaḥ Raza*, 239, also records the view of R. Yeḥi'el, albeit in the name of R. Ḥayyim (= R. Ḥayyim Palti'el). See *Perushei R. Ḥayyim Palti'el*, ed. Lange, 208–9, and below, chapter 4. See also *Ḥizzequni*, and *Tosafot ha-Shalem*, ed. Gellis, 7:17–18. In *Tosafot ha-Shalem*, 7:17, sec. 4, a *gematria* is cited from R. Eleazar of Worms, that the word ואחריו is equivalent to אפילו בימי יואל, while the *gematria* of לא יהיה כן is equivalent to זהו מין אחד (and the last two letters of אחריו, together with the following word, לא, spell יואל). See also Maharshal, *Yeri'ot Shelomoh*, fol. 53.

[158] See *Perushei Bekhor Shor* to Exodus 10:19, ed. Nevo, 113. This is also found in *Sefer ha-Gan*, ed. Orlian, 226 (to Ex. 10:14).

Sabbath law, that harvesting crops is prohibited, because he had indeed instructed them (in Ex. 16:5) that they would have to collect two portions on Friday. Rid's explanation for this apparent contradiction in Rashi's words is that this second interpretation is *derash* (*ve-yesh lomar ki derash hu*); that is, Rashi offered two different interpretations for these two verses, the first based on *peshat* and the second on *derash*. Thus one need not pose a contradiction between two different comments that were based, in essence, on two different exegetical methodologies.[159]

Despite the many affinities we have seen already between R. Isaiah di Trani and R. Yosef *Bekhor Shor*, there are a number of times when R. Isaiah in his commentary will abandon his commitment to forms of *peshat*, or to his focused questioning and validation of Rashi's comments, in order to present additional aspects of halakhic or midrashic exegesis. A representative example of this approach can be seen within Rid's commentary to the beginning of *parashat Yitro*. The Torah refers to the fact that Yitro took his daughter back to Moses, "after he sent her away" (אחר שלוחיה, Ex. 18:2). Rashi, following the *Mekhilta*, comments that Moses "sent her away" when God commanded him to return to Egypt. At that point, Aaron advised Moses that it was inadvisable to bring his family to Egypt now, and so Ẓipporah was sent back to her father's home. In this sense, the *Mekhilta* is being used by Rashi as an *ʾaggadah ha-meyashevet divrei miqra*, by supplying the information that Ẓipporah was being sent away at some earlier point. Indeed, Rashbam suggests this without reference to either the *Mekhilta* or to Rashi.

[159] See Chavel, 42–43; ms. Breslau 102, fol. 57v; and ms. Moscow 303, fol. 75v. *Moshav Zeqenim*, 144, reproduces this passage without attribution and, as noted by Chavel, concludes that *ʾein meshivin ʿal ha-derash*. *Moshav Zeqenim* then cites a question from (R. Jacob of) Orleans (as does *Paʿaneaḥ Raza*, 255, and ms. Bodl. 2344, cited in *Tosafot ha-Shalem*, ed. Gellis 7:250, sec. 13, and see also secs. 15, 18, and 7:249, sec. 10), that the Talmud asserts (as does *Tanḥuma*) that the ashes of the red heifer will come and atone for the sin of the golden calf, suggesting that the laws of the red heifer were not given until after the sin of the golden calf. At the same time, *Moshav Zeqenim* also cites a question in the name of R. Yosef *Bekhor Shor* concerning how we know that the Jews were commanded about the red heifer at Marah. The answer given is that, earlier in this same verse, a bitter tree was used to sweeten the water in Marah. Moses inquired from God (as this same verse begins, *va-yiẓʿaq ʾel ha-Shem*) as to how a bitter tree would be able to achieve this. The Almighty answered that He is about to give the Jewish people another precept that involves the same concept or idea, i.e., it purifies the impure and renders the pure impure. Cf. *Tosafot ha-Shalem*, ed. Gellis, 7:248, secs. 1–2, and 249–50, sec. 11. As is often the case, this responding passage in *Moshav Zeqenim* is not found in the complete commentary of R. Yosef *Bekhor Shor* (in ms. Munich 52). Indeed, *Bekhor Shor* assumes there (ed. Nevo, 124) that the tree was inherently sweet. In this way, the Almighty, as He prefers to do, performed the more "natural" miracle of placing something sweet into something bitter to sweeten it, rather than simply doing this miracle without the cover of any kind of natural process. Cf. above, chapter 2. (See *Perushei ha-Torah le-R. Yehudah he-Ḥasid*, ed. Lange, 89: לפי הפשט. ולא העדיף המרבה שהיה משליך המותר והממעיט לא החסיר שהיה חוזר ומלקט עד שהיה מתמלא מדותיו [Ex. 16:18]. As Lange notes [n. 60], this is similar to the comment of Rid, as preserved by Ḥida in his *Pnei David*.)

Adopting a narrower *peshat* approach, R. Yosef *Bekhor Shor* defines the word שלוחיה as the assets (and property) with which a father sends his daughter from his home (at the time of marriage). Indeed, the word שלוחים is used this way in 1 Kings (9:16) in connection with one of Solomon's wives. Thus the verse conveys the idea that, despite the efforts expended by Yitro to provide for his daughter when he sent her into marriage, her husband, Moses, was apparently delayed in coming for her and in protecting these assets, and so Yitro brought Ẓipporah to Moses at this time.[160]

Rid, on the other hand, pursues the *Mekhilta* well beyond its use by Rashi. According to at least one Tannaitic opinion found in this *Mekhilta*, Moses gave Ẓipporah a bill of divorce when he sent her back. At the same time, according to the Talmud in tractate *Zevaḥim* (102a) and tractate *ʿAvodah Zarah* (34a), Moses functioned as a *kohen* during the period of the consecration of the Tabernacle. Thus, Rid wonders, how could Moses re-marry Ẓipporah on her return since, as a *kohen*, Moses was prohibited from marrying a woman who was divorced? (Rid is clearly following the interpretation that Yitro arrived to meet Moses only after the Torah was given, despite the appearance of this episode within the text of the Torah prior to the events at Mount Sinai.) Rid's brief answer is that Moses divorced Ẓipporah only conditionally. There is additional discussion in Tosafist Torah compilations about why this type of divorce would not have disqualified Ẓipporah to Moses—as a *kohen*—as it typically does, but these addenda may not be from R. Isaiah.[161]

160 See *Perushei R. Yosef Bekhor ʿal ha-Torah*, ed. Nevo, 128–29. This interpretation is also found in *Sefer ha-Gan*, ed. Orlian, 238. See also ms. Bodl. 271/1 (cited in *Tosafot ha-Shalem*, ed. Gellis, 6:6, secs. 3–5).

161 See Chavel, 43; ms. Breslau 102, fol. 59v; ms. Moscow 303, fol. 76v. Cf. *Moshav Zeqenim*, 151; *ʾImrei Noʿam*, 51 (neither of which cites Rid by name); and *Tosafot ha-Shalem*, ed. Gellis, 8:5–6, sec. 1. *ʾImrei Noʿam* also notes that there would be no such problem if the episode of Zipporah's return occurred before the Torah was given. Until he served in the Tabernacle (which was built after the Torah was given), Moses did not have the status of a *kohen* in any case. See also *Paʿaneaḥ Raza*, 260. *Moshav Zeqenim* contains a critical question attributed to R. Isaiah on part of Rashi's comment to this verse (which does not appear in extant versions of Rashi). This is an example of what led I. Ta-Shma to suggest (see above, n. 116) that this reference (and others like it in *Moshav Zeqenim*) to R. Isaiah refers not to Rid but to R. Isaiah (*me-*) Weil. Cf., however, ms. Cambridge 377 (a Torah commentary associated with Rid's grandson, R. Isaiah b. Elijah), fols. 33v–34r = *Moshav Zeqenim*, 150–51 (Ex. 18:2, in the name of R. Isaiah); and fol. 43r = *Moshav Zeqenim*, 218 (Ex. 34:30, in the name of R. Isaiah, *lefi ha-peshat*). Passages such as these suggest that the otherwise unidentified references to R. Isaiah in *Moshav Zeqenim* refer to Rid's grandson, R. Isaiah the younger, or perhaps even to R. Isaiah the elder himself, in comments that were preserved only by his grandson's commentary. See also above, nn. 131, 142; and below, nn. 169, 172. (Ms. Cambridge 377 refers once to R. Isaiah the elder by name [ר' ישעיה ב"מ= בן מלי], on fol. 31r.) Ms. Moscow 303, fol. 76v, explains that Moses called his second son Eliezer (since "the Almighty saved me from the sword of Pharaoh," Ex. 18:4), even though the circumstances behind this name occurred before the sentiments that led him to call his

When Yitro tells Moses that he and the people will become worn out with the existing judicial system, the Torah's phrasing, נבול תבול גם אתה גם העם הזה אשר עמך (Ex. 18:18), was constructed, according to the *Mekhilta*, to include Aaron, Ḥur, and the seventy elders in the anticipated breakdown. This rabbinic interpretation is cited by Rashi in his commentary. As is his wont, Rid questions this interpretation, however, because Ḥur had already died on 17 Tammuz, at the point of the sin of the golden calf (Ex. 32:15), while Yitro's advice was not given until just after the second *luḥot* were given, on the following Yom Kippur. Rid indicates that he heard (*ve-shamati*) that there was a variant of the *Mekhilta* passage which did not have any reference to Ḥur, and included only Moses, Aaron, and the seventy elders.

Rid then raises an additional question that emerges from his analysis. How could Aaron and the seventy elders have judged the people at any time prior to Moses descending with the second set of *luḥot*? Only after Yom Kippur, when Moses descended with the *luḥot*, could he begin to teach the Torah to Aaron and to the elders. Rid suggests that this rabbinic interpretation of this verse is totally in the realm of *derash* (*ha-kol derash*). In actuality, Moses alone taught and judged the people at this point, as Yitro says to Moses, "and you [alone] shall make known the statutes of the law and His ruling" (והודעת להם את חוקי הא-להים ואת תורותיו).[162]

---

first son Gershom (because he felt like a stranger in Midyan, Ex. 18:3, where he had escaped after killing the Egyptian), based on the notion that until Pharaoh was dead (which occurred after both his sons were born), Moses could not be absolutely certain that he had indeed been spared by the Almighty from "the sword of Pharaoh." Once again, this is the interpretation offered by R. Yosef *Bekhor Shor* (ed. Nevo, 129), although it does not appear anywhere in Rid's name or in other related collections of Rid's interpretations to the Torah. Similarly, ms. Moscow 303, fol. 176v, explains that the Torah does not specifically mention Moses as a participant in the meal Yitro shared with Aaron and the elders (Ex. 18:12) in the same way that Rashbam and R. Yosef *Bekhor Shor* (and Ibn Ezra in his long commentary) do. See *Tosafot ha-Shalem*, ed. Gellis, 6: 20, secs. 2, 4, and cf. M. Lockshin, *Rashbam's Commentary on Exodus*, 194.

[162] Chavel, 44; ms. Breslau 102, fol. 60r; ms. Moscow 303, fol. 76v. As Chavel notes, R. Elijah *Mizraḥi* raises the same first question as Rid, and notes that our *Mekhilta* text (which mentions Hur) contains an error. *Moshav Zeqenim*, 154–55, cites the entire discussion (and both questions) in the name of R. Yeshayah (and there can be no doubt that the reference is to R. Isaiah di Trani), although the suggestion is also made that the prevalent text of the *Mekhilta* (which includes the name of Ḥur) can be understood in a hypothetical way. Had Ḥur, an important, capable judge (*dayyan ḥashuv*), still been alive, he would nonetheless have also been overwhelmed. Rid's material is essentially found in *Ḥizzequni* (see above, nn. 23, 29, and below, n. 50), without attribution. See also *Sefer ha-Gan*, ed. Orlian, 238; *Hadar Zeqenim*, in the name of *Sefer ha-Gan*; and *Perushei R. Ḥayyim Palti'el*, 254, in the name of R. Yosef *ha-Kohen*, father of R. Aaron, author of the Gan (who holds the hypothetical interpretation noted above); and *Pa'aneaḥ Raza*, 263–64 (which holds Rid's view), in the name of the compiler, Levi (= R. Isaac b. Judah *ha-Levi*); and see *Tosafot ha-Shalem*, ed. Gellis, 6: 26–27. Unlike Rid, who will get involved in this kind of interpretation because of his dedication to Rashi, R. Yosef *Bekhor Shor* (ed. Nevo, 130) explains simply that *navol tibbol* means that you and the people will not be able to suffer this system, or perhaps, as derived from Gen. 11:7 (and the Tower of Babel), ונבלה שם שפתם,

R. Isaiah raises the same basic textual question put forward by R. Jacob of Orleans to Exodus 19:13 where, according to Rashi, stoning the one who comes in contact with the mountain is mentioned before pushing him down to the place of stoning (כי סקול יסקל או ירה יירה). R. Jacob deals with this issue in terms of the precision of the order of things within biblical verses (*yesh/'ein muqdam u-me'uḥar ba-Torah*).[163] Rid explains, *lefi peshuto*, that these actions refer not to the punishment of such a person but to his initial apprehension after the crime. Since no one can get near the mountain to remove him, he must be killed from a distance by throwing stones (סקול יסקל) or by shooting an arrow (ירה יירה). Thus the order of the verse is correct.[164] Rid's interpretation here is the same as that of Rashbam and R. Yosef *Bekhor Shor.*[165]

Rashi interpreted Exodus 20:21 to mean that the altar of earth referred to by this verse was actually a copper-covered wooden altar that was to be anchored in the ground (as per R. Yishma'el's view in the *Mekhilta*), or, alternatively, that this altar was meant to be filled with earth when the Jews camped (to give it greater stability), but that this earth was to be removed when traveling. Rid questions this second view of the *moreh* (Rashi), because when the Jews traveled, they were specifically instructed to clean the altar (Nu. 4:13, *ve-dishnu 'et ha-mizbeaḥ*). If the dirt had to be removed (as per the second view), why was the instruction to clean it even necessary? Therefore, Rid suggests, the first interpretation presented by Rashi, that the altar was to be anchored in the ground, is to be preferred. Here Rid is adumbrating the tactic of later supercommentaries to assess the strengths and weaknesses of multiple approaches that are included by Rashi.[166]

---

you and the people will become greatly confused, *mevulbalim.* They will call out to Moses, he will not know whom to answer, they will not know with whom they should be checking, and so on. This interpretation is cited in the very next passage in Moscow 303, fols. 76v–77r. This passage also cites Rabbenu Tam (and is perhaps related to his grammatical *hakhra'ot*; cf. S. Japhet, *Dor Dor u-Parshanav* (Jerusalem, 2008), 328–40), who associates *navol tibbol* with Gen. 18:12 (אחרי בלותי), meaning that this process will make everyone grow old. This interpretation is found (unattributed) in *Pa'aneaḥ Raza*, 263, and in *'Imrei No'am*, 51, in the name of Rabbenu Tam.

163 See above, chapter 2, n. 170.

164 See Chavel, 44; ms. Breslau 102, fol. 60v; ms. Moscow 303, fol. 77r.

165 See Lockshin, *Rashbam's Commentary on Exodus*, ed. Lockshin, 207, and *Perushei ha-Torah le-R. Yosef Bekhor Shor*, ed. Nevo, 132. This interpretation is found also in Ibn Ezra and in *Ḥizzequni.* Moscow 303, fol. 77r, cites R. Yosef Qara's distinction between the first two commandments that were heard by the people directly from the Almighty and, as such, are expressed in second person, and the remaining commandments that are expressed in the third person. This is found in the commentary of *Bekhor Shor* (in R. Yosef Qara's name), ed. Nevo, 133.

166 See Chavel, 46; ms. Moscow 303, fol. 78r; and *Moshav Zeqenim*, 169 (without attribution). Interpretations by R. Jacob of Orleans, to this verse at the end of Yitro and to the end of Terumah (Ex. 27:10), are included in ms. Moscow 303, fols. 78r, 80r.

Most of Rid's nearly forty extant comments to the Book of Exodus are located in the first half of the book, through *parashat Yitro.* There are five comments in *Mishpatim*, one each to *Terumah* and *Tezaveh*, two to *Ki Tissa*, and none on *Va-Yaqhel* and *Pequdei*, which essentially recapitulate the building of the *mishkan.* Although the comments to *Mishpatim* are all halakhic in nature, there are some noteworthy *peshat* comments as well. Rid compares Exodus 33:18, where Moses asks in a forthright manner to see the Divine glory (הראני נא את כבודיך), to Exodus 3:6, where Moses is reported to have covered his face in fear when God appeared to him in the burning bush (ויסתר משה פניו כי ירא מהביט אל הא-להים). Rid explains that Moses was afraid early in his career, because he had had no such experience. By the end of the Book of Exodus, however, Moses had already dealt with the *Shekhinah* on many occasions, and he was confident that his righteousness would allow him to do so without any ill effects.[167]

Most of R. Isaiah's twenty or so comments to the Book of Leviticus understandably involve talmudic interpretations and halakhic conclusions, especially as they relate to Rashi's commentary on the sacrificial order. Rashi explains that Moses and Aaron reentered the tent of assembly on the eighth day of the *milu'im* for the *mishkan* in order for Moses to instruct Aaron on the proper procedures for the incense (*qetoret*). Rid questions why this service could not have been taught to Aaron during the prior seven days of the *milu'im*, when all the other services in the *mishkan* were taught to him by Moses. Indeed, the *qetoret* was meant to be offered between the throwing of the blood and the burning of the limbs, both of which had been practiced during the seven days.

Moreover, it is difficult to imagine that the *mishkan* was functioning during the seven days while the *qetoret*, a vital part of the *'avodah*, was not being offered. Rid suggests that, during the seven days of the *milu'im*, only sacrifices for individuals were brought (*qorbanot yaḥid*), while the incense was offered only in conjunction with an *'olat zibbur.* Also, the fire from the outer altar had to be brought to the inner altar, where the incense was then

[167] Chavel, 49, and cf. above, chapter 2, n. 160. See also *Moshav Zeqenim*, 214–15. Moses's assertion (in Ex. 33:12) that the Almighty had not told him who would accompany the children of Israel to the land of Israel would appear to be contradicted by God's statements (in Ex. 23:20, prior to the sin of the golden calf, and in Ex. 33:2, following this sin) that He would send an angel to guide them. R. Judah *he-Ḥasid* answers that Ex. 33:12 is out of order (אין מוקדם ומאוחר בתורה) and was actually said prior to both of the other verses noted. See *Perushei ha-Torah le-R. Yehudah he-Ḥasid*, ed. Lange, 124–25. The passage in *Moshav Zeqenim* also presents an answer from R. Isaiah (שכך פשט הפסוקים האלו) that in Ex. 33:12, Moses was asking about more than just the identity of the angelic figure who would lead them; he wanted to be certain that the Almighty would get over the sin of the people, and that Moses would indeed find favor in His eyes as had been promised.

prepared; during the seven days of the *milu'im*, there was no fire yet on the outside altar. The outside altar stood ready, and the wood and the meat of the sacrifices were placed on it in anticipation of the miracle of the fire, which would come down from heaven to ignite the fire on this altar; this would occur on the eighth day of the *milu'im*, as recorded in the very next verse, Leviticus 9:24. For these reasons the *qetoret* was not brought during the seven days but only on the eighth. The precision of the preparations for the *'avodah* detailed here by Rid is striking.[168]

Rid had occasion to offer his sharp lingustic observations on Leviticus as well. Like Rashi, Rid suggests that the terms קרחתו and גבחתו, typically translated as baldness and eyebrows, are used here with respect to clothing that was infected with leprosy (in Lev. 13:55), since they refer to the age of the clothes involved. *Qaraḥto* is used to signify older clothing, since these clothes are "bald" of the hair or fur that originally covered them. New clothes are referred to as "eyebrows," because the level of the hair or fur on them is still high (גבוה or raised, גבו). Indeed, Rid notes that the letters *ḥet* and *heh* are sometimes interchanged (so that the Hebrew words גבח and גבה are linguistically related as well).[169]

In Leviticus 19:16 Rid explains the Targum's rendering of the phrase לא תלך רכיל, as לא תיכול קורצין. On the basis of Jeremiah 46:20 and *Yoma* 31b, R. Isaiah suggests that verb form of קרץ used here means to kill or to slaughter. This imagery makes good sense, because one who slanders another is, in effect, slaughtering him and eating his flesh. As noted above, Rashi and other Tosafist *pashtanim* also highlight this phrase, but they link it to eating

168 See Chavel, 51; ms. Breslau 102, fol. 92v; ms. Moscow 303, fol. 82r; and *Moshav Zeqenim*, 272, which cites this passage in the name of R. Yeshayah. See also *Gur Aryeh*, who cites this in the name of R. Isaiah's commentary to Leviticus, and cf. *Mizraḥi* and *Levush ha-Orah*. The comment is also found without attribution in the published edition of *Pa'aneaḥ Raza*, 351 (מצאתי). On the very first verse in Leviticus, ms. Moscow 303, fols. 81v–82r, cites a comment of R. Yosef *Bekhor Shor* by name (פי' ר' יוסף בכור שור הפשט; see ed. Nevo, 183–84) which links the usages in this verse to the final verse in the Book of Exodus. As was his wont, *Bekhor Shor* also includes the rabbinic interpretation of this verse. See also ms. Moscow 303, fol. 83r (to Lev. 14:7), which reproduces the comment of *Bekhor Shor* (ed. Nevo, 200), albeit without attribution. At the same time, *Moshav Zeqenim*, 275 (to Lev. 10:5) cites a comment in the name of R. Isaiah that the tunics used to remove the bodies of Nadav and Avihu were those of the deceased and not those of Misha'el and Elzafan (who did the removal), since Levites did not have special tunics that they wore during their service. This accords with Rashi's comment, which notes that the clothing of the deceased was not physically burned by the fire that erupted (only their souls were burned), and is found in *Ḥizzequni*, without attribution.

169 See Chavel, 53. In Lev. 13:4 (see Chavel, 52; ms. Breslau 102, fol. 95v; ms. Moscow 303, fol. 83r; and ms. Cambridge 377, fol. 45r), Rid again responds to Rashi's statement (and his quandary) on the phrase ועמוק אין מראיה מן העור לא ידעתי פירושו. White typically appears as a deep color. In this instance, however, since the color was not coming from below the skin (because the hair had not turned white according to the verse), the Torah asserts that its appearance was not deep.

cakes (אכילת קורצין), since the bearer of tales typically moves from place to place, eating and conversing with others. Rid's approach is highly original, even within this group.[170]

Rid begins his commentary to the Book of Numbers by noting, as several Tosafists do, that the census numbers are rounded to the nearest five or ten. Rid posits that the Torah does indeed round off numbers, as seen, for example, with regard to "you shall count fifty days" (Lev. 23:16, which actually connotes forty-nine days), or "he shall be lashed [a maximum of] forty," when in fact the maximum number of lashes is thirty-nine (Deut. 25:3).[171]

R. Isaiah understands the phrase in Numbers 8:2, that the seven candles of the menorah will cast light "opposite the menorah's face" (אל מול פני המנורה יאירו שבעת הנרות), differently from Rashi. Rashi explains (*piresh ha-moreh*) that this refers to the fact that the six candles or branches (three on each side) faced the middle branch (*qaneh*) that had the seventh candle on it. Rid questions Rashi's interpretation on the grounds that the verse should have said, according to this view, that the six candles should cast light on the *pnei ha-menorah*. Rid maintains instead that (*u-lefi peshuto*) the spot that is opposite the menorah's face, *'el mul pnei ha-menorah*, is actually where the show table stood (opposite from the *menorah* in the *qodesh*). The Torah was thus instructing that the front of the *menorah* should be turned toward the table so that it would be illuminated, "as a candelabra illuminates the table

[170] Chavel, 53. Cf. Rashi, Rashbam, *Ḥizzequni*, and Ramban; and above, chapter 2, n. 208, for R. Yom Tov of Joigny. In Lev. 19:20, Rid defines the phrase *biqqoret tihyeh* based on an interpretation that he heard (*shamati*), which Chavel identifies as a comment by Ibn Ezra. Note also Rid's positive approach (in Lev. 19:26) to uses of *kokhavim u-mazzalot* (as opposed to *shedim*), and cf. my *"Peering through the Lattices,"* 238, and below, chapter 7. Ms. Moscow 303, fol. 86r, reproduces the unattributed comment of R. Yosef *Bekhor Shor* (ed. Nevo, 231–32) to Lev. 25:29, the first part of which is found in *Ḥizzequni.* This is the first of a series of anonymous, near-verbatim citations from *Bekhor Shor* (running through fol. 87r) to verses in the portions of *Behar and Beḥuqotai.* These citations are found to Lev. 25:55 (ed. Nevo, 233); Lev. 26:3–9 (ed. Nevo, 234–35). The comment from *Bekhor Shor* to Lev. 26:8, on the ratio of Jewish pursuers to their enemies (which is in a positive context), is similar to a comment of Rid to Ex. 20:6 (Chavel, 45, citing Rabbenu Tam, a direct teacher of *Bekhor Shor*) on this kind of ratio, which also discussed the verse here. Nonetheless, the rest of the citations from *Bekhor Shor* here are not confirmed as the work of R. Isaiah but may well be the interpolations of a compiler, editor, or copyist, as we have noted above.

[171] Chavel, 57: תימה וכי אפשר שלא היה חסר אחד או שנים מן הכללים שאומר כאן או יותר. ויש לומר שאין הכתו' מקפיד בזה כדכתי' תספרו חמישים יום ואינן אלא מ"ט. וכן ארבעים יכנו והם ל"ט. *Pisqei ha-Rosh*, *Pesaḥim* 10:40, puts forward the same larger theory with respect to *sefirat ha-ʿomer*, lashes, and other rounded biblical numbers (ולי נראה). See the narrower solution for *sefirat ha-ʿomer* proposed by Ri, in *Moshav Zeqenim*, 384–85; and see *Pa'aneaḥ Raza*, 385 (in the name of Ri's father, R. Samuel).

of kings."[172] Rashbam presents the same interpretation both here and in his commentary to Exodus 25:37.[173]

Moreover, the *peshuto shel miqra* interpretation cited by Rid is found, again, in precisely the same terms in the commentary of R. Yosef *Bekhor Shor*, and designated *lefi ha-peshat.* For *Bekhor Shor* as well, the *shulḥan* is the locus of *'el mul pnei ha-menorah.* He questions the view of Rashi (אבל יש לגמגם), albeit without mentioning Rashi by name, referring to his interpretation simply as *ve-rabbotenu 'amru* in the same way that Rid does, and concludes, as Rid does, that according to this interpretation involving the *shulḥan*, the word "seven" in the verse makes perfect sense.[174]

Rid continues to verify details in Rashi's commentary on the basis of talmudic and rabbinic literature. Rashi on Numbers 9:1 explains (*piresh ha-moreh*) that the Torah did not open the Book of Numbers with the observance of the second Passover described here, since this would have reflected badly on the children Israel for whom this was the only Passover observed in the desert until they entered the land of Israel in the fortieth year of their sojourn. Rid notes that Rashi stresses (in Ex. 12:25) that the Torah itself associates the observance of the Passover sacrifice with entering the land of Israel (והיה כי תבואו אל הארץ). If so, why was the fact that the Jewish people did not observe Passover in the desert after the second year, until they reached the land of Israel, a derogatory insinuation? Rid explains, on the basis of a *sugya* in tractate *Yevamot* (72a), that the healing north wind did not blow during the years when the Jews were in the desert, as part of their punishment for participating in the sin of the golden calf. Without this wind, circumcision could not be performed during all the years the Jews were in the desert (after the first year), and that prevented them from bringing

[172] Chavel, 57, and cf. the passage in ms. Cambridge 377 cited in *Tosafot ha-Shalem*, ed. Gellis, 9:77, sec. 8. Rid also cites an alternate interpretation (*ve-yesh 'omrim*), which focuses on a different structural aspect of the menorah. Various supercommentaries on Rashi deal with the problem raised by Rid. *Moshav Zeqenim*, 437–38, has the question and answer in the name of Ri (= R. Yeshayah), and *Ḥizzequni* is noted there as being close to "Ri" as well, while a different answer is reported in the name of Rosh. See also *Perushei R. Ḥayyim Palti'el*, ed. Lange, 484.

[173] See M. Lockshin, *Rashbam's Commentary on Exodus*, 322–23; idem, *Rashbam's Commentary on Leviticus and Numbers*, 181; and cf. *Minḥat Yehudah*, Nu., fol. 5a. *Tosafot Menaḥot* 28b, s.v. *govhah*, attributes this interpretation, based on talmudic considerations, to Rabbenu Tam, although this attribution is contested.

[174] *Perushei ha-Torah le-R. Yosef Bekhor Shor*, ed. Nevo, 251. See also *Ḥizzequni*, and *Bekhor Shor*'s comment to Ex. 25:36, ed. Nevo, 160 (והאיר על עבר פניה. כנגד השולחן שהוא כנגד פניה . . . כי להאיר על השולחן היתה המנורה ונראה לפי הפשט . . . וכל הפתילות נתונות לצד השולחן). *Pa'aneaḥ Raza*, 420, cites this interpretation in the name of R. Meir. Cf. above, chapter 2, n. 56.

the Passover sacrifice. Thus the absence of a Passover sacrifice in the desert implies bad behavior on the part of the Jewish people.[175]

In Numbers 11:4, where the people ask, "Who will feed us meat?" Rid notes, on the basis of Exodus 16:13, that the people were already given quail to eat in their first year in the desert. Rid therefore suggests that this initial supply of quail had been depleted by this time. As noted by Ḥida, this answer is also suggested by *Tosafot 'Arakhin* (15b), s.v. התאוו, in the name R. Yosef Qara.[176]

In Numbers 11:23, Rid offers an unusual insight to solve a problem within Rashi's commentary. He establishes the dialogue between God and Moses, begun by Rashi, as follows: God needed to provide both meat and fish; otherwise the people would have felt that something was missing, since they fondly recalled the fish and meat they had eaten in Egypt (Nu. 11:4–5). God, however, said (in 11:21) that He would stop their complaints by giving them meat alone, and Moses wondered how this would be effective. In verse 23, God indicates that He will give them a type of meat that also had a taste of fish within it. Rid notes (as per *Ḥullin* 27b) that these quail (and other birds) were created from alluvial mud (רקק), which gave them the taste of both meat and fish. Thus the people were satisfied with quail meat alone, as God had promised. Indeed, these were birds that had the characteristics of both meat that had to be slaughtered and fish that could be gathered from the sea, precisely as Moses had indicated was necessary to satisfy the people.[177] Rid's completion of the dialogue here from a number of different directions is reminiscent of R. Judah *he-Ḥasid.*

[175] See Chavel, 59, and see Rashi's commentary to *Yevamot*, ad loc., and to Joshua 5:4. *Moshav Zeqenim*, 439–40, again has this question and answer in the name of ר"י = R. Yeshayah. *Moshav Zeqenim* also records a different answer to this question from *Bekhor Shor* (who seems to be responding to Rashi as well). Had the Jewish people not sinned regarding the spies and not made the complaints against Moses, among other sins, they would still have been able to enter the land of Israel immediately, and would have offered the Passover sacrifice there. This comment is not found, however, in Munich 52 (ed. Nevo, 253). The answer attributed to *Bekhor Shor* by *Moshav Zeqeni* is attributed to *Sefer ha-Gan* in *Pa'aneaḥ Raza*, 421, and see also *Sefer ha-Gan*, ed. Orlian, 296; *Perushei R. Ḥayyim Palti'el*, ed. Lange, 489, and *Ḥizzequni.*

[176] Chavel, 59; ms. Breslau 102, fol. 120r; ms. Moscow 303, fols. 90r–v. As Chavel also notes, Naḥmanides (in Ex. 16:12) writes similarly that this first wave of quail was not satisfying (לא היה לשובע). This question is raised in R. Yeshaya's name in *Moshav Zeqenim*, 145 (to Ex. 16:8), but a different answer is suggested. *Ḥizzequni* again has Rid's answer, albeit without attribution. As noted in chapter 2 with regard to R. Yom Tov of Joigny (nn. 197, 211–13, 246), it is quite possible that R. Isaiah di Trani was another of *Ḥizzequni*'s unidentified sources, as the many references in this chapter (and in Chavel's edition of R. Isaiah's commentary) suggest. Cf. above, n. 141.

[177] Chavel, 59. Rid's comment to Nu. 12:14 (Chavel, 60, and ms. Moscow 303, fol. 90r, on the period of leprosy for Miriam) begins with a rabbinic interpretation from Rabbenu Tam (on the basis of *Niddah* 31a), and a brief embellishment. *'Imrei No'am* begins with Rabbenu Tam, followed by a question from R. Yosef *Bekhor Shor* (that comports with his own comment, ed. Nevo, 260–61, but is focused differently). In *Moshav Zeqenim*, 448–49, Rashi's comment to this

R. Isaiah's brief linguistic interpretation of Numbers 17:25 (ותכל תלו־ נתם), that the form used here by the Torah is an imperative, follows the comment of Rashbam, which appears to be a critique of Rashi.[178] Similarly, in the one comment found in ms. Paris 660 to *parashat Ḥuqqat* (Nu. 21:30), Rid puts forward a grammatical critique of Rashi's interpretation, and suggests another approach that is found also in Rashbam.[179] In the sole comment found in ms. Paris 660 to the portion of *Balak*, Rid suggests a sensible *derash* through which he reconciles the verse in Numbers 24:2, "and Bilʿam lifted up his eyes," with the verses that describe Bilʿam as *shetum ha-ʿayin* (i.e., as having one eye that was either closed or put out). Until Bilʿam thought about cursing the Jewish people, his eyesight was normal, and both his eyes were functioning. From the point that he decided to curse the Jewish people, however, one eye became closed.[180] Thus Rid continues to work both sides of the aisle so to speak, *peshat* and *derash*, and particularly *derash* that is *meyashev divrei miqra.*

In *parashat Matot*, Rid questions why the Jewish people were commanded to purify the utensils they captured from Midian but were not required to do so in their battle against Siḥon and ʿOg. He suggests that since all of the Jewish people were involved in conquering Siḥon and ʿOg, they were allowed to partake even of nonkosher foods to sustain themselves, according to the talmudic dictate in tractate *Hullin* 17a, and impurity of the utensils was likewise allowed in such a public context (*tumʾah hutrah be-ẓibbur*). The war against Midian, however, involved a fighting force of only 12,000 men; therefore, no such allowances were made.[181]

In *parashat Masʿei*, R. Isaiah implicitly disagrees with Rashi's interpretation of Numbers 35:32, "You shall not accept ransom to flee to a city of

---

verse is cited first, followed by a question from ר"י and responses from R. Isaac b. Abraham (Riẓba), among others. *Hadar Zeqenim* cites R. Aaron (author of *Sefer ha-Gan*) and R. Barukh b. Isaac; see below, n. 193. Note also the parallels between Rid and R. Yosef *Bekhor Shor* in their interpretations of Nu. 15:34 (at the end of *parashat Shelaḥ*), concerning the correct form of capital punishment for the individual who had gathered wood on the Sabbath. See Chavel, 62; ms. Moscow 303, fol. 91r; and cf. *Perushei ha-Torah le-R. Yosef Bekhor Shor*, ed. Nevo, 267; *Moshav Zeqenim*, 460; *ʾImrei Noʿam*, 152–53.

178 Chavel, 63; ms. Moscow 303, fol. 91v; and cf. Lockshin, *Rashbam's Commentary on Leviticus and Numbers*, 238–39.

179 See Chavel, 63. *Bekhor Shor* (ed. Nevo, 282), and *Ḥizzequni* present both approaches.

180 Chavel, ibid., provides some vague midrashic sources for this interpretation, as does Ḥida. See also *Perushei R. Ḥayyim Paltiʾel*, 548, which suggests *Midrash ha-Gadol* as a source. Ms. Moscow 303, fol. 92r, and *Moshav Zeqenim*, 478 (without attribution), record a grammatical comment on the word *va-yitnaḥem* in this portion (Nu. 23:19), which is quite close to an interpretation found in the commentary of *Bekhor Shor* (ed. Nevo, 285).

181 Chavel, 64–65. He notes that Ramban makes the same distinction. This answer is found almost word for word in *Minḥat Yehudah* without attribution (Nu., fol. 27a), and in *Perushei R. Ḥayyim Paltiʾel*, 564, in the name of R. Jacob of Orleans. Cf. above, nn. 114, 153. See also *Sefer ha-Gan*, ed. Orlian, 325, and *Hadar Zeqenim*.

refuge." Rid understands this to mean that one who had been convicted of an intentional killing should not be permitted to buy his way into a city of refuge and thereby forestall his execution. Rashi's interpretation, whose correctness was openly questioned in subsequent Tosafist Torah compilations, is that this refers to one who killed by accident and had indeed legitimately run to a city of refuge, and who now wishes to "buy his way out" of the city.[182]

Virtually all of Rid's ten comments on the Book of Deuteronomy are talmudic in nature, whether as observations or questions on Rashi's commentary, or as direct comparisons between the Oral and Written Law. On Deuteronomy 18:2, which asserts that *kohanim* and *leviyyim* will not have a landed inheritance among their brethren, because God is their inheritance, Rid cites an interpretation of Rabbenu Tam (found in his *Sefer ha-Yashar*) to a passage in *Sifrei* (cited by Rashi on this verse), whose connotation is unclear. Here, Rid is simply acting as the good Tosafist and literary student of Rabbenu Tam that he was.[183]

At the same time Rid's final discussion in his Torah commentary (נראה לי) to Moses's blessing to the tribe of Levi—"The one who said of his father and mother I have not seen you, and to his brothers he did not give recognition" (Deut. 33:9)—is close to a formulation of R. Judah *he-Ḥasid* found in *Sefer Ḥasidim*. The Levites, who were devoted students and teachers of Torah, started to study in their youth, away from home, and they remained in the study halls for many years. Upon their return home, they do not recognize their parents or their brothers. These extensive periods of uninter-

[182] See Chavel, 65; ms. Breslau 102, fol. 141r; and ms. Moscow 303, fol. 94v. Ramban, in one interpretation, appears to support Rashi's approach, while Rashbam and *Ḥizzequni* subscribe to Rid's approach. R. Yosef *Bekhor Shor* (ed. Nevo, 304) suggests that the person in this case had run (away from the family of his victim) to the city of refuge as he was supposed to do, allowing the rabbinic court to now proceed to judge his case and determine whether he should remain in the city of refuge or be executed. It is at this point that the Torah instructs that payment should not be taken so that he will be allowed to remain in the city of refuge in any case. See also *Moshav Zeqenim*, 492–93.

[183] See Chavel, 66, and his notes. See also Rid's citation of Rabbenu Tam in explaining the punishment of Miriam in Chavel, 60 (and above, n. 77), and see also his implicit reference to Rabbenu Tam in the next passage on the spies carrying the fruit of the land (based on *Tosafot Shanz*). In this regard, see also Chavel, 43 (Ex. 18:7), and 45 (Ex. 20:6). On Rid's use of *Sefer ha-Yashar*, cf. Emanuel, *Shivrei Luḥot*, 29. A passage in ms. Moscow 303, fol. 97v (to Deut. 21:9, found partially in *Moshav Zeqenim*, 405), cites a talmudic analysis of Rashi's Torah comment by Rid's contemporary, R. Moses of Bohemia (or R. Moses Taku, in the *Moshav Zeqenim* passage). See also Rid's comment to Deut. 21:23 (Chavel, 67), in which he suggests (*lefi ha-peshat*) that the cursing associated with people seeing someone who was hanged means that the judges (*elohim*) who pronounced this sentence would be cursed. In a prior comment he explains Rashi's interpretation (that since man was created in the image of God, the Almighty would be blasphemed) in a way that eliminates any possibility of anthropomorphism. See below, chapter 7, n. 99.

rupted study are confirmed by the end of this verse, "for they have guarded your sayings, meaning the Torah, and they have protected your covenant. The covenant also refers to the Torah, as the verse (Jeremiah 33:25) states, 'If not for My covenant [of the Torah], I would not have established the parameters of heaven and earth.'"[184]

Contemporary Tosafist Developments in the Realms of *Derash* and Talmudic Interpretation of the Torah

Several comments by R. Barukh b. Isaac, a Tosafist student of Ri of Dampierre and author of *Sefer ha-Terumah* (who died en route to Israel c. 1211),[185] are found in *Sefer ha-Gan*, a northern French Torah compilation edited c. 1240 by R. Aaron b. Yose *ha-Kohen.*[186] The first, to Genesis 18:8, relates to the angels who were served a meal by Abraham. The Talmud (*Bava Meẓiʿa* 86b) asserts that the angels only appeared to be eating this food, in order not to deviate from the common earthly practice. The standard *Tosafot* to *Bava Meẓiʿa* (which were compiled and edited by R. Eliezer *Tukh*, based in part on *Tosafot Shanẓ*)[187] contrast this *sugya* with a passage in the midrashic collection *Seder Eliyyahu Rabbah* which rejects this approach, and insists that the angels uncharacteristically ate in this instance out of respect for Abraham (*mipnei kevodo shel Avraham*).[188] Extant versions of *Bereshit Rabbah* follow the talmudic approach, that the angels merely appeared to be eating.[189]

184 Chavel, 69; ms. Moscow 303, fol. 99r; and *Moshav Zeqenim*, 516, where the unattributed comment is introduced as *lefi ha-peshat.* For the presence of this unique interpretation in *Sefer Ḥasidim* (and in *Sefer Ḥuqqei ha-Torah*), see my *Jewish Education and Society in the High Middle Ages*, 104–5. Ms. Moscow 303, fols. 97v–98r, cites R. Judah *he-Ḥasid*'s interpretation on the punishment of a *ben sorer u-moreh* (Deut. 21:18). Cf. *Perushei ha-Torah le-R. Yehudah he-Ḥasid*, ed. Lange, 205.

185 See E. E. Urbach, *Baʿalei ha-Tosafot*, 1:347–54, for R. Barukh's *Sefer ha-Terumah* and for a listing of his many *Tosafot* (including the standard *Tosafot* to tractate *Zevaḥim*), and see Simcha Emanuel, "'Ve-Ish ʿal Meqomo Mevoʾar Shem': Le-Toledotav shel R. Barukh b. Yiẓḥaq," *Tarbiz* 69 (2000), 423–40, on R. Barukh's entirely northern French provenance. For the year and circumstances of R. Barukh's death, see I. Ta-Shma, "Keroniqah Ḥadashah li-Tequfat Baʿalei ha-Tosafot," *Shalem* 3 (1981), 319–22, and cf. my "The *ʿAliyyah* of 'Three Hundred Rabbis' in 1210–11 and Tosafist Attitudes toward Settlement in the Land of Israel," *Jewish Quarterly Review* 76 (1986), 195–215. On R. Barukh's comments to the Torah, cf. Leopold Zunz, *Zur Geschichte und Literatur* (Berlin, 1845), 88, 97.

186 On this work, see *Sefer ha-Gan*, ed. Orlian, editor's introduction, 19–29. This work is also a source for comments by northern French Tosafists in the first half of the thirteenth century, such as the brothers of Evreux. See below, chapter 4, and my "Midrashic Texts in Tosafist Torah Commentaries," sec. 8.

187 See Urbach, *Baʿalei ha-Tosafot*, 2: 646–48.

188 See *Tosafot Bava Meẓiʿa* 86b, s.v. *nirʾin ke-ʾokhlin*; *Pesiqta Rabbati*, ch. 25, end; and *Ḥizzequni* to Genesis, ad loc.

189 See *Bereshit Rabbah*, ed. J. Theodor and Ch. Albeck (Jerusalem, 1996), 411.

A *Tosafot*-like Torah commentary associated with the school of Rabbenu Tam presents the talmudic position, as well as the approach of the *Sefer Eliyyahu Rabbah*, and suggests that demonstrating proper respect for Abraham was at the core of both views.[190] *Sefer ha-Gan* cites R. Barukh b. Isaac, whose version of *Bereshit Rabbah* maintained that the angels actually did eat, in full accordance with the earthly practice.[191] All of the Tosafists mentioned here, including R. Barukh, were working with midrashic texts in an effort to clarify the various talmudic and rabbinic positions in this matter.

The same holds true for other interpretations by R. Barukh included in *Sefer ha-Gan*. Immediately after recording an interpretation to Exodus 21:28 (*lefi ha-peshat*; see Rashi and Rashbam) to explain the limited liability of the owner of a *shor tam* that has killed someone, *Sefer ha-Gan* (to Ex. 21:29) presents a question in the name of Rabbenu Barukh. According to the talmudic position that most oxen are not easily watched and restrained (*Bava Qamma* 15a, 45b), why did the Torah not exempt the owner from full payment for damages caused while this animal was walking or eating (*shen ve-regel*), as is the case in a situation of goring (*qeren*), for which the owner pays only half the damages? R. Barukh responds to his own question by noting that the Torah did ease the owner's burden in this realm by declaring him exempt from damages caused by *shen* and *regel* that are committed in the public domain.[192] This, too, is a form of rabbinic/halakhic interpretation that could easily have been addressed or discussed in the course of talmudic study rather than in a forum focused on biblical interpretation. This is also the case for R. Barukh b. Isaac's comment to Numbers 12:14, which is also recorded by *Sefer ha-Gan*.[193]

190 See ms. Paris 167, fol. 49r: נראין כאוכלין מטעם כבודו של אברהם. תנא דבי אליהו רבה קמאי שהיו אוכלין ממש משום כבודו של אברהם (= ms. Moscow/Ginzburg 362, fol. 128r); and *Tosafot ha-Shalem*, ed. Gellis, vol. 2 (Jerusalem, 1983), 123, sec. 19.

191 See *Sefer ha-Gan*, ed. Orlian, 155: וממורי רבינו ברוך בה״ר יצחק שמעתי בב״ר דודאי אכלו כדי שלא לשנות מן המנהג. *Tosafot ha-Shalem*, ed. Gellis, 2:122, sec. 16, erroneously includes this passage in the name of R. Barukh b. Isaac at the beginning of a citation from ms. Bodl. 268 (a Torah commentary attributed to R. Eleazar of Worms). Cf. *Perush ha-Roqeaḥ 'al ha-Torah*, ed. J. Klugmann, vol. 1 (Jerusalem, 1979), 152–53. Note the completely different considerations here, of both *peshat* and polemics, in *Perushei R. Yosef Bekhor Shor 'al ha-Torah*, ed. Nevo, 30.

192 See *Sefer ha-Gan*, ed. Orlian, 245–46; *Tosafot ha-Shalem*, ed. Gellis, vol. 8 (Jerusalem, 1990), 232, sec. 13 (and cf. *Tosafot ha-Shalem*, 8:222, sec. 2); ms. B.M. Or. 9931 (Gaster 730), fol. 59r; and ms. Florence Laurenziana, Plut. II.20, fol. 204r.

193 *Sefer ha-Gan*, ed. Orlian, 301: ואמ׳ לי רבינו ברוך ב״ר יצחק דבשני הסגרות די בי״ג יום והכי אמרינן אין בהסגרות יותר מי״ג יום דיום שביעי עולה לכאן ולכאן. See also ms. Leiden 27, fol. 82v: ואומ׳ הרב ר׳ אהרן [בן יוסי הכהן, בעל ספר הגן] די״ד יום וכו׳. ועוד או׳ בשם הרב ר׳ ברוך בן יצחק דבשתי הסגרות די בי״ג יום והכי אמ׳ . . . דיום ז׳ עולה לכאן ולכאן; ms. Bodl. 2344 (an enhanced version of the Tosafist Torah commentary, *Pa'aneaḥ Raza*), fol. 111v: ואמ׳ לו רבינו ברוך דבשני הסגרות די בי״ג ימים והכי אמרי׳ אין יותר מי״ד יום דיום ז׳ עולה לכאן ולכאן. ג״ן; ms. Vatican (Neofiti) 8, fol. 219v; and *Perushei ha-Torah le-R. Ḥayyim Palti'el*,

A fourth comment attributed by *Sefer ha-Gan* to R. Barukh b. Isaac concerns the Aramaic translation of the phrase, "and the Tree of Life was in the midst of the garden" (*be-tokh ha-gan*, Gen. 2:9). R. Barukh, among others, notes a deviation in the style of Targum Onkelos, which usually translates the Hebrew word *be-tokh* into Aramaic as בגו, which means "inside" or "within," but in this instance employs the Aramaic word במציעות, which means, literally, in the middle. A related question is raised in connection with Genesis 3:22, which expresses God's concern that once man had eaten from the Tree of Knowledge, he might also eat from the Tree of Life. Why wasn't God concerned about this possibility even if man had not eaten from the Tree of Knowledge? Like the Tree of Knowledge, the Tree of Life was ostensibly available to man as he wandered through the garden. R. Barukh's answer to both questions is that, in fact, the Tree of Knowledge surrounded the Tree of Life, which was located precisely in the middle of the garden (as Onkelos's translation indicates). Therefore, only "when the boundary of the Tree of Knowledge was pierced" was there concern that man might eat from the Tree of Life, which had heretofore been completely surrounded and inviolate.[194]

---

ed. Lange, 502. As the fuller passage preserved in *Sefer ha-Gan* and in ms. Leiden shows, this discussion began with a passage in *Sifrei* (that formed the core of Rashi's comment to this verse) about why it might have been appropriate for Miriam to remain "outside the camp" (after she had questioned Moses and, by implication, the Almighty Himself) for two weeks rather than just for one. Prior to citing R. Barukh b. Isaac's view, the fuller passage then cites a talmudic comment by Rabbenu Tam in this matter (found in *Tosafot Bava Qamma* 25a, s.v. *qal va-homer*, and cited also in *Nimmuqei Ḥumash le-Rid*, ed. Chavel, 60), a question (again, borne of talmudic reasoning) by R. Yosef *Bekhor Shor* (who was also a Tosafist student of Rabbenu Tam), and a response by R. Aaron *ha-Kohen.* As Lange points out (n. 67), the Tosafist compilation *Moshav Zeqenim* presents a formulation quite similar to that of R. Barukh in the name of his contemporary (and fellow Tosafist student of Ri), R. Isaac b. Abraham (Riẓba). The ms. Leiden version, however, reads *ve-kasheh li* while the *Sefer ha-Gan/R. Ḥayyim Palti'el* version reads *ve-hiqsheh/ve-qasheh le-R. Yosef Bekhor Shor.* R. Aaron *ha-Kohen* (*ba'al Sefer ha-Gan*) and R. Barukh then appear to respond to *Bekhor Shor*'s question(s). In his own Torah commentary, *Bekhor Shor* (ed. Nevo, 260–61) does raise the fourteen-day possibility, but answers it with an application of the talmudic principle of דיו לבא מן הדין להיות כנדון (and similarly in *Perushei R. Ḥayyim Palti'el*). For *Bekhor Shor*, however, the talmudic analysis leads to his *peshat* interpretation, while for the other Tosafists involved, this discussion remains squarely within the realm of talmudic studies. Note that in this instance, as in the first one, R. Aaron b. Yose *ha-Kohen* appears to have heard this interpretation directly from R. Barukh b. Isaac.

194 Neither R. Barukh's name nor his interpretation of this verse is found in the Vienna manuscript (28/Heb. 19) of *Sefer ha-Gan* (and hence none of this appears in the edition of *Sefer ha-Gan* published by Orlian; see his introduction, 107). The interpretation itself is found in the Nuremberg manuscript of *Sefer ha-Gan* (ms. Nuremberg 5), and in *Perushei ha-Torah le-R. Ḥayyim Palti'el*, ed. Lange 7 (which names R. Sa'adyah as the proponent of this interpretation). The name of R. Barukh *ba'al ha-Terumah* is associated with this interpretation in *Moshav Zeqenim*, 6 (to Gen. 3:22); in ms. Warsaw 260; and in *'Imrei No'am.* (On this Tosafist compilation, see *Sefer ha-Gan*, ed. Orlian, editor's introduction, 89.) See *Tosafot ha-Shalem*, ed. Gellis, 1:100–101, sec. 7, and 1:146, sec. 8.

In this instance, R. Barukh's interpretation was not linked to or motivated by a talmudic *sugya*, although it was occasioned by an unusual passage in Targum Onkelos. Review of Targum Onkelos to the weekly Torah portion was itself a talmudic requirement (*Berakhot* 8a–8b) that was firmly in vogue among the Tosafists of medieval Ashkenaz.[195] Moreover, it is instructive to compare R. Barukh's answer here to the approach of two of the Tosafists whose biblical exegesis has been studied to this point, R. Yosef *Bekhor Shor* and R. Isaiah di Trani. These two exegetes, who were inclined to present *peshat* interpretations alongside talmudic and midrashic analyses in connection with Rashi's comments, raise the very same question that R. Barukh does here. Both *Bekhor Shor* and Rid respond, however, with a kind of *derekh ʾereẓ* interpretation, namely that the eternal life vouchsafed by eating from the Tree of Life was effective only for one who had previously eaten from the Tree of Knowledge. For one who had not done so, however, eating from the Tree of Life would be ineffective, just as a particular medication or antidote helps only the one who has been exposed to or ingested a particular substance but does nothing for a person who has not had that experience. Indeed, it may in fact cause harm to that person.[196] For R. Barukh b. Isaac, the main issue or focus here is the unusual finding in Targum Onkelos in Genesis 2:9, which can also explain the later verse in Genesis 3:22.[197] For *Bekhor Shor* and Rid, however, the question raised by Genesis 3:22 is addressed by a point of logical interpretation.[198]

Two late thirteenth-century and early fourteenth-century Tosafist Torah compilations, *Hadar Zeqenim* and *Minḥat Yehudah*, also cite R. Barukh b. Isaac as asking why the song of *Haʾazinu* is different from all other biblical songs (*mi-kol ha-shirot sheba-Torah*). In every other song, the one(s) who said it are mentioned within it: "And Israel sang" (Nu 21:18); the song of the sea in *Beshalaḥ* (Ex. 15:1, "Then Moses and the children of Israel sang");

[195] See, e.g., J. S. Penkower, "The Canonization of Rashi's Commentary on the Pentateuch," [Hebrew] in *Study and Knowledge in Jewish Thought*, ed. H. Kreisel (Beer Sheva, 2006), vol. 2, 123–46; my *Jewish Education and Society*, 81–82, and 182, n. 111; R. Isaac b. Moses, *Sefer Or Zaruʿa* (Zhitomir, 1862), pt. 1, *hilkhot qeriʾat shema*, sec. 11; and R. Samson b. Ẓadoq, *Sefer Tashbeẓ*, sec. 185.

[196] See *Perushei R. Yosef Bekhor Shor ʿal ha-Torah*, ed. Nevo, 12–13; *Nimmuqei Ḥumash le-Rid*, ed. Chavel, 10; and above, n. 111.

[197] For another (albeit unnamed) interpretation associated with the Targum, see *Moshav Zeqenim*, 1, and *Tosafot ha-Shalem*, ed. Gellis, 1:101, sec. 8.

[198] There are several interpretations found in *Perush/Tosafot ha-Rosh* and *Hadar Zeqenim* (both of which were compiled in the late thirteenth century; see, e.g., *Sefer ha-Gan*, ed. Orlian, 85, 95) in the name of (*mori*) R. Barukh *Ẓarefati* (especially in the portions of *Yitro* and *Mishpatim*), some of which are described as *peshat.* See, e.g., *Tosafot ha-Shalem*, ed. Gellis, 2:198, and 8:40, 75, 161, 163. As far as I can tell, however, this name does not refer to R. Barukh b. Isaac, author of *Sefer ha-Terumah*, or to any other Tosafist named R. Barukh. It is likely that the reference is to a lesser rabbinic figure from the second half of the thirteenth century.

the song of Devorah (Judges 5:1, "And Devorah sang"); the song of David (2 Samuel, 22:1, "David spoke to God the words of this song"). In the song of *Ha'azinu*, however, no "singer" is mentioned. R. Barukh answers that the name of Moses is hinted at by the letter headings to the first six verses of *Ha'azinu* (Deut. 32:1–6). The *heh* of *Ha'azinu*, the *yod* of *ya'arof ka-matar*, the *kaf* of *ki shem*, the *heh* of *ha-zur*—these four "first letters" add up to forty in *gematria*, equaling and representing the letter *mem*. Adding the *shin* that begins the fifth verse (*shiḥet lo*), and the *heh* of the sixth verse (*hala-Shem tigmelu zot*), spells out, along with the *mem* derived from the first four verses, משה. Since this song contains some harsh elements of rebuke (*u-lefi she-yesh be-shirah zo qashot*), his name is not written out explicitly but is only hinted at (*be-remez*).[199] This indeed constitutes a most intricate kind of traditional letter or *remez* interpretation, although several other Tosafist collections, including one version of the earlier *Sefer ha-Gan*, attribute this passage to the Tosafist R. Isaac b. Barukh, a student of Rabbenu Tam, rather than to R. Barukh b. Isaac.[200]

Two other Tosafist students of Ri, his son Elḥanan and R. Solomon b. Judah (*ha-Qadosh*) of Dreux, from whom we also have a number of Torah comments, appear to follow the same exegetical model as R. Barukh b. Isaac. Although they interact a bit more with Rashi's Torah commentary, their comments emerge from and reflect talmudic (*Tosafot*) contexts of study. For instance, Rashi interprets the plural verb form in God's statement, "the blood of your brother (קול דמי אחיך) is shouting to me (צועקים אלי)" (Gen. 4:10), to include Abel's blood, as well as the blood of his unborn offspring. Several manuscripts record that R. Elḥanan questioned this interpretation on the basis of the talmudic statement (*Yevamot* 62a) that the Messiah will not arrive until all souls have emerged in bodily form. If so, Abel's unborn offspring would eventually live, and the only unavenged blood remaining would be that of Abel himself. Among the answers given is that, had these offspring been born earlier than the premessianic era (as scheduled), they would perhaps have contributed to their generation and merited reward

199 See *Hadar Zeqenim* (Livorno, 1840), fol. 75a (and cf. the comments in the so-called *Tosafot ha-Rosh 'al ha-Torah*, on the very same folio), and *Minḥat Yehudah* (Deut.), fols. 21b–22a. Cf. R. Yosef Qara to Judges 5:4, in *Miqra'ot Gedolot ha-Keter*, ed. M. Cohen (Ramat Gan, 1992), 107: חיזרתי על כל השירות שנאמרו על הנסים שנעשו לישראל ולא מצאתי שידבר דברי שירה אלא מן המאורע.

200 See *Sefer ha-Gan*, ed. Orlian, 362; *Pa'aneaḥ Raza*, 551; *Perushei ha-Torah le-R. Ḥayyim Palti'el*, ed. Lange, 615. The seemingly brief version of *Sefer ha-Gan* found in ms. Moscow 268, fol. 90v, retains the name R. Barukh b. Isaac. On R. Isaac b. Barukh, see Urbach, *Ba'alei ha-Tosafot*, 1:96, 152–53. Urbach, 1:361, implausibly suggests that the comments attributed to R. Barukh by Zunz (see above, n. 186) may have been by R. Barukh b. Isaac of Regensburg, from whom a comment to a verse in Psalms is recorded in *'Arugat ha-Bosem*, ed. Urbach, 1:167, n. 1; see above, chapter 2, nn. 12, 18.

that was lost with the death of Abel. Similarly, had they lived in an earlier period, any punishments for their sins would have been deferred to a later age, in accordance with the rabbinic teaching (in tractate *Shabbat* 89b and *Bereshit Rabbah* 26:2) that punishments in this period of the existence of mankind were not earned until a person reached the age of 100.[201] It would appear that R. Elḥanan raised these questions in connection with the *Tosafot* he composed and the talmudic *sugyot* he interpreted.[202]

Rashi interprets the phrase "three men" in Genesis 18:2 to mean that each of the three angels who came to visit Abraham had a different task or mission. In *Tosafot Bava Meẓiʿa*,[203] R. Elḥanan questions this avenue of interpretation in light of subsequent verses in chapter 19, in which at least two angels helped Lot and his family leave Sodom, even as only one seems to have been in charge of destroying the city (Gen. 19:22). They suggest that two angels were indeed assigned to take Lot out of the city, Mikhaʾel to accompany him to Ẓoʿar, and Gabriel to encourage him to hurry.[204]

Two sons were born to Joseph before the famine in Egypt worsened (Gen. 41:50). Rashi derives from here, in accordance with the talmudic formulation (*Taʿanit* 11a), that it is forbidden to have sexual relations during a time of famine. R. Elḥanan questions this interpretation on the basis that Yokheved was born to Levi as the family of Jacob went down to Egypt, and yet at the time of her conception, the famine in Egypt had already begun. The answer he gives is that Joseph would certainly not have had relations, since he assumed that others were already being affected by the famine. Levi, however, knew that there was sufficient food (and no shortage) within his father's house (*hayah yodeʿa she-hayah lo ule-beit ʾaviv dai/shelo hayah*

[201] See *Tosafot ha-Shalem*, ed. Gellis 1:161, secs. 1, 3; and *Perushei R. Ḥayyim Paltiʾel*, ed. Lange, 11. At least one manuscript (Bodl. 271/2) attributes this question to R. Elḥanan's father, Ri. This question (raised against the Talmud in *Sanhedrin* 37a rather than Rashi) is also found in ms. Moscow 82 and ms. Strasbourg 44, manuscripts that contain many pieces of the Torah commentary of R. Judah *he-Ḥasid*. See *Perushei ha-Torah le-R. Yehudah he-Ḥasid*, ed. Lange, 8.

[202] See *Tosafot ʿAvodah Zarah* 5a, s.v. *ʾein*; *Moshav Zeqenim*, 7; and *Tosafot ha-Shalem*, 1:161, sec. 5. The standard *Tosafot* to *ʿAvodah Zarah* are based on R. Elḥanan's *Tosafot* (see Urbach, *Baʿalei ha-Tosafot*, 2:654–57), although the extant edition of *Tosafot R. Elḥanan* to *ʿAvodah Zarah* does not contain this passage. See, however, *Tosafot Niddah* 13b, s.v. *ʿad she-yikhlu*, and *Tosafot Yeshanim ʿal Massekhet Yevamot*, ed. A. Shoshana (Jerusalem, 1994), 372 (to *Yevamot* 62a). See also S. Emanuel, *Shivrei Luḥot*, 253, n. 139, for a possible reference in *Minḥat Yehudah* (Gen., fol. 19a, to Gen. 21:4, s.v. *la-moʿed*, and the variant reading in ms. B.M. 190, fol. 44v: פי' רבי' אלחנן בן מורי רבינו יצחק בסוד העיבור שיסד) to a work on *sod ha-ʿibbur* that was composed by R. Elḥanan. Cf. above, chapter 2, n. 51, for calendric calculations by R. Yosef *Bekhor Shor*, and see ms. Moscow 365 (IMHM #43035) for *ʿevronot* by Rashbam.

[203] *Tosafot*, *Bava Meẓiʿa* 86b, s.v. *ha-hu*.

[204] See *Tosafot ha-Shalem*, ed. Gellis, 2:110; sec. 9, 2:159, sec.4; and Urbach, *Baʿalei ha-Tosafot*, 2:646.

maḥsor lo le-beit ʾaviv), and he was therefore not prohibited from having relations.[205]

Rashi interprets that Moses was almost killed by God (Ex. 4:24) because he had neglected to circumcise his son Eliezer. The Talmud (*Nedarim* 31b), however, rejects this possibility, since Moses would not have been able to travel to Egypt had he performed the circumcision. *Moshav Zeqenim* contains responses based on the talmudic *sugya* from both R. Elḥanan and R. Eliezer of Metz, Rabbenu Tam's student. For R. Elḥanan, this occurred when Aaron met Moses on the way to Egpyt and tried to convince him that he should leave his wife and child behind in that locale. Thus the circumcision could have been performed at that point, since the child was to remain there with his mother. Similarly for R. Eliezer of Metz, the place of lodging was close enough to Egypt that Moses could have performed the circumcision and then brought his son to Egypt, without any risk to the child.[206]

R. Elḥanan, as cited by *Tosafot*, also participated in a talmudic analysis of Rashi's comment to Exodus 12:6—"and they slaughtered it [the pascal sacrifice], all of the community of Israel"—about the derivation of the important principle *sheluḥo shel ʾadam ke-moto.*[207] According to yet another passage in *Moshav Zeqenim*, Rashi's interpretation to Exodus 19:17 ("and they stood at the bottom of the mountain"), that God placed the mountain over their heads like a barrel to force them to accept the Torah, was questioned by a variety of rabbinic figures, since the Jewish people had already said "we will do all that the Lord spoke" (Ex. 19:8). R. Isaiah di Trani, following a passage in *Midrash Tanḥuma*, suggests the Jewish people had committed themselves previously only to the Written Law but not to the Oral Law. R. Yosef

205 See *Sefer ha Gan*, ed. Orlian, 192 (הקשה אבא מארי בשם הרב ר' אלחנן וכו' ואמר בשמו וכו'); *Tosafot ha-Shalem*, ed. Gellis, 4:144–45, secs. 7, 10; ms. Parma 1051, fol. 21v; *Moshav Zeqenim*, 82; and *Perushei R. Ḥayyim Paltiʾel*, 133–34. (This appears to be the lone citation of R. Elḥanan within *Sefer ha-Gan.*) As Gellis notes in sec. 10, Ms. B.M. 9931, fol. 21r, which cites R. Elḥanan's question in a decidedly talmudic context (אמ' במסכת תענית מכאן דאסור לשמש מטתו בשני רעבון והקשה ה"ר אלחנן א"כ היאך לוי שימש מטתו), also cites the answer in the name of R. Samuel Bamberg. The same question was also answered by R. Judah *he-Ḥasid*, in a similar way. Indeed, R. Elḥanan's question and response appear in the ms. Cambridge 669.2, which also contains sections of R. Judah *he-Ḥasid*'s commentary. See *Perushei ha-Torah le-R. Yehudah he-Ḥasid*, ed. Lange, 56; *Tosafot Shalem*, ed. Gellis 4:144, sec. 6; *Hadar Zeqenim*, 82; and cf. ms. Moscow 303, fol. 71r, and above, n. 49. Ms. Cambridge 404, fol. 38v, citing *Sefer ha-Gan* and R. Elḥanan, exempts Levi from this prohibition since it is still before the Torah was given (although Joseph observed it nonetheless).

206 See *Moshav Zeqenim*, 110, and *Tosafot ha-Shalem*, ed. Gellis, 6:120, sec. 5. Note the completely different approach taken by R. Isaac of Evreux to explain Rashi's interpretation, below, chapter 4, n. 178.

207 See *Tosafot Yevamot* 101b, s.v. *ve-qarʾu*; *Tosafot ʿArakhin* 2a, s.v. *qorbano*; Urbach, *Baʿalei ha-Tosafot*, 2:620, 670; and *Tosafot ha-Shalem*, ed. Gellis, 7:64–65, sec. 8. As Gellis notes, Rabbenu Tam of Orleans (and possibly Rabbenu Tam himself) were also involved in this discussion, which is also reflected in *Tosafot Shanz/Tosafot ha-Rosh* to *Qiddushin* 41b, s.v. *mi-kan.*

Bekhor Shor maintains that the prior statement of acceptance applies only to what was included in the Ten Commandments, while others argued that only those laws that were given at Marah had been previously accepted. R. Elḥanan, citing a talmudic passage in tractate *Shabbat*, maintains that the Jews had recanted the earlier statement of acceptance.[208]

At the beginning of *parashat Balaq*, *Moshav Zeqenim* cites Rashi's comment to Deuteronomy 2:9 ("do not afflict Moab and do not drag them into war"), that only war itself could not be initiated by the children of Israel, whereas threatening Moab or otherwise causing them to fear Israel was permitted. Rabbenu Tam and R. Elḥanan are cited as raising a series of questions regarding this explanation from a number of talmudic and midrashic texts, and R. Elḥanan's father (Ri of Dampierre) is cited as answering some of them.[209] In this instance, as in many of the others just cited, since the biblical interpretations and formulations come from pieces of talmudic *Tosafot*, it is likely that R. Elḥanan's comments on Rashi, and for that matter, on the Torah itself, were made initially in the context of talmudic interpretations or discussions. The various Tosafist Torah compilations, led in this last instance by *Moshav Zeqenim*,[210] then gathered and assigned R. Elḥanan's comments to the appropriate verses, just as the Tannaitic *midreshei halakhah* broke down various halakhic units and organized the information according to the sequence of the Torah's verses.[211] This was the case for a number

[208] See *Tosafot ha-Shalem*, ed. Gellis, 8:63–64; *Moshav Zeqenim*, 162 (which contains all of these names); and *Pa'aneaḥ Raza*, 266–67 (which mentions only R. Elḥanan by name). *Bekhor Shor*'s approach is not found in ms. Munich 52, and R. Isaiah's is not found in ms. Paris 660, ed. Chavel, although it is found in ms. Moscow 303, fol. 77r. Cf. ms. St. Petersburg EVR I 22, fol. 46v; ms. Parma 1051, fol. 49r; ms. Hamburg 45, fol. 46v (which mentions both Rid and *Bekhor Shor*); Urbach, *Ba'alei ha-Tosafot*, 2:603; and *Tosafot Shabbat* 88a, s.v. *kafah*. The *Tosafot* passage presents a version of R. Elḥanan's solution without attribution, linking it to a *sugya* at the beginning of tractate *'Avodah Zarah* 2b, which raises the possibility that R. Elḥanan formulated his approach as part of his *Tosafot* to that tractate (although there is no reference to R. Elḥanan in any of the extant versions of *Tosafot 'Avodah Zarah* on this point). Several *pesaqim* of R. Elḥanan in the laws of blessings (often in response to questions or positions of his father, R. Isaac of Dampierre [ר"י]) are found in the *perushim* and *pesaqim* of R. Avigdor of Vienna (where R. Isaac is often referred to as ר"ץ). See ms. B.M. 243, fol. 222r, and *Perushim u-Pesaqim 'al ha-Torah le-Rabbenu Avigdor*, 368–69 (*pesaq* #378). See also *Perushim u-Pesaqim*, 439 (*pesaq* 485–86), and 464 (*pesaq* #545, שאלה לר"ץ כהן היאך כהן מצי לברך ברכת המזון הא לא נטלו חלק בארץ. והשיב ה"ר אלחנן בנו נטלו חלקם בערי המגרש), and cf. 173 (*pesaq* #215–17).

[209] See *Moshav Zeqenim*, 475–76. The formulations of Rabbenu Tam, R. Elḥanan, and Ri (as intimated in the *Moshav Zeqenim* passage) come directly from *Tosafot Bava Qamma* 38r, s.v. *nasa*. The *Moshav Zeqenim* passage is also found in ms. Munich 50, fol. 263r, and in ms. B.M. 9931, fols. 133r–v. Cf. Ta-Shma, *Knesset Meḥqarim*, 1:235–37.

[210] See also the parallel manuscript, ms. Mantua 36, fol. 162: פ' כי תבוא פ' ביכורים. ר' יוסף אמור להיות כאן פי' רב הלל . . . וכן פי' ר"ץ. פי' י"א על גר אחר שנתנו כוס לברך דיכול לומר כר' יהודה . . . וזו שאלה שאלו לר"ץ . . . היאך כהן מצי לברך ברכת הארץ הא לא נטלו חלק בארץ. והשיב ה"ר אלחנן וכו'.

[211] For this phenomenon (and the comparison to *midreshei ha-Tanna'im*), see above, at the opening of chapter 2.

of other Tosafists as well; R. Elḥanan is perhaps more noticeable in this regard, since he issued a series of these comments.

R. Solomon b. Judah (*ha-Qadosh*) of Dreux, another student of Ri *ha-Zaqen*, was one of the recipients of R. Meir Abulafia's letter about Maimonides' *Sefer ha-Madda*ʿ, which reached Rash *mi-Shanẓ* (c. 1203) as well.[212] R. Solomon is also mentioned with some frequency in the standard *Tosafot* to the Talmud, and in other *Tosafot* collections as well, and about fifteen of his comments to the Torah have survived.[213] Several of these comments relate to the chronology of Noah's life and the flood. R. Solomon questioned his colleague R. Isaac b. Abraham of Dampierre (Riẓba) about the connotation of the word *tamim* as it was applied to Noah (Gen. 6:9) and as it was defined by a passage in *Bereshit Rabbah* at the beginning of *parashat Noaḥ* (30:8).[214] This midrashic passage puts forward the principle that anyone who was characterized as *tamim* in the Bible lived to a lifetime that was perfectly divisible by seven. As R. Solomon notes, this principle works for Abraham (Gen. 17:1, 175 years), Jacob (Gen. 25:27, 147 years), and Job (Job 1:1, 140 years), but it does not seem to work for Noah, who lived for 950 years (Gen. 9:29), a number that is not divisble by seven. Riẓba justified the midrashic passage to R. Solomon by arguing that Noah's status as a *tamim* is to be counted only from the point in the Torah where he was given this appellation, when he was instructed to construct the ark. The construction took 120 years, and Noah lived for an additional 350 years after the flood, for a total of 470 years. The year of the flood itself must be deducted from this total, however, because the order of creation (and normal human existence) was effectively suspended during this year. The remaining number, 469, is indeed perfectly divisible by seven.[215]

212 See Urbach, *Baʿalei ha-Tosafot*, 1:337–38; Bernard Septimus, *Hispano-Jewish Culture in Transition* (Cambridge, Mass., 1982), 49; Norman Golb, *Toledot ha-Yehudim be-ʿIr Rouen Bimei ha-Benayim* (Tel Aviv, 1976), 105–19; and cf. my *"Peering through the Lattices,"* 97–98.

213 See Urbach, *Baʿalei ha-Tosafot*, 1:339–40, and Golb, *Toledot ha-Yehudim*, appendix 7, 190–92.

214 See *Midrash Rabbah* 30:8 = ed. Theodor-Albeck, 1:273: תמים. בר חוטה אמר כל מי שנ' בו תמים השלים שנותיו למידת שבוע.

215 See ms. Moscow 268, fol. 79r: תמים. אמ' בב"ר כל מי שנאמר בו תמים בידוע שנשלמו שנותיו למדת השבוע. וישאל ה"ר שלמה מדרויש לה"ר ריצב"א הפירוש. והשיב לו ששנותיו הולכים לו בשביעיות באברהם שחי קע"ה שנה. והקשה לו מנח שחי תשע מאות וחמישים שנה והם ה' שנים יתירים על השביעיות. י"ל שיש לחשוב משעה שנאמר לו תמים דהיינו כשאמר ה' יתברך לעשות התיבה והוא מתעסק בה מאה ועשרים שנה וש"נ שנה אחר המבול הרי לך ת"ע. סלק שנת המבול שאינה נחשבת לפי שנתשנו בה סדרי בראשית והנשארים הולכים לשביעיות. A similar version of this passage is found in the so-called *Perush ha-Rosh ʿal ha-Torah* (*shaʾal R. Shelomo la-Riva*). Urbach's reference to *Hadar Zeqenim* (in *Baʿalei ha-Tosafot*, 261 n. 4) is inaccurate. See also *Perushei R. Ḥayyim Paltiʾel ʿal ha-Torah*, ed. Lange, 15), *Daʿat Zeqenim* (= *Rabbotenu Baʿalei ha-Tosafot*), Genesis, fol. 5b (with R. Isaac b. Abraham's name, but without the name of R. Solomon of Dreux), and other Tosafist Torah compilations (including ms. Bodl. 268, fol. 21r, which links this interpretation to a R. Mordekhai *ha-Ẓarefati* and to *Midrash Leqaḥ Tov*, and refers to

Without mentioning either R. Solomon of Dreux or Riẓba,[216] a version of *Sefer ha-Gan* cites and explains the same passage in *Bereshit Rabbah*, and proposes a different answer than Riẓba's to the question that had been raised by R. Solomon: Noah's lifespan with regard to *tamim* comprises only the period that he lived after the flood, which is explicitly mentioned in the Torah as 350 years (Gen. 9:28).[217] The concern of *Sefer ha-Gan* (as of Riẓba

---

the dividing of the lives of Abraham and Noah into *shemitot*). See *Tosafot ha-Shalem*, ed. Gellis, 1:198, sec. 30, and cf. ms. Bodl. 283, sec. 3r, and *Ḥizzequni.*

[216] Cf., however, ms. Bodl. 2344, fols. 31r–v (to Gen. 25:27, *ve-Ya'aqov 'ish tam*), which cites the explanations of R. Isaac b. Abraham in the name of *Sefer ha-Gan*: ויעקב איש תם. כתיב במדרש כל מקום שנא' בו תמים הוכלים שנותיו לאחר שבוע. ופי' ר' יצחק בן אברהם כתי' והיה תמים וחי קע"ה שהן שבוע. ויעקב איש תם וחי קמ"ז דהיינו שבועיות. ואיוב איש תמים וישר חי ק"מ שנה שהם שבועיות. ואמ' ר' יצחק בן אברהם דאין למנות עיקר מנין של נח כי אם מן המבול ואילך, דכל מה שנברא קודם נתבטל. ומשם ואילך חי ש"נ שנים והיינו שבועיות. ג"ן.

[217] See *Sefer ha-Gan*, ed. Orlian, 137, and *Tosafot ha-Shalem*, ed. Gellis, 1:198, sec. 29. (On *Sefer ha-Gan*'s use of *Bereshit Rabbah*, cf. *Sefer ha-Gan*, ed. Orlian, 32–35, and more broadly in my "Midrashic Texts and Methods in Tosafist Torah Commentaries," sec. 1.) Gellis notes that this passage is also found in ms. Bodl. 2343 (above, n. 25), in the name of R. Aḥai. R. Isaac b. Abraham of Dampierre (Riẓba) is mentioned by name (or by the acronym Riba) three times in *Sefer ha-Gan:* (1) to Gen. 25:23 (*ve-rav ya'avod ẓa'ir*; ed. Orlian, 170), where he indicates that this blessing will last forever, which is why to this very day, men and woman from Esau function as servants for the Jews while the reverse does not occur, a point that should not be mentioned openly (see also Gellis, *Tosafot ha-Shalem*, 3:14, and *Pa'aneaḥ Raza*, 123); (2) in a detailed comment to Gen. 31:33 (ed. Orlian, 178), on the positioning of the tents of Rachel and Leah according to *Bereshit Rabbah* and as cited by Rashi, which follows Rashbam's *peshat* interpretation that the verse changes the order of things in order to avoid the interruption within the narrative (cf. *Rashbam's Commentary to Genesis*, ed. M. Lockshin, 193); and (3) in a halakhic discussion between Riẓba and Ri (on Lev. 19:27; ed. Orlian, 281) regarding the use of scissors and a razor to cut the *pe'ot* of the head and face (which includes the citation of *Tosafot* to *Shavu'ot* 2b and to *Nazir* 40b). R. Solomon of Dreux is also mentioned three times in *Sefer ha-Gan*: to Gen. 31:52 (ed. Orlian, 179), and a related comment to Ex. 24:8 (ed. Orlian, 249, and see below, chapter 4, nn. 106, 109), and to Lev. 27:29 (ed. Orlian, 289), on the separation of *ḥallah.* Generally speaking, however, the Torah comments and interpretations made by Riẓba were even fewer (and less exegetically focused) than those of R. Solomon, and most were overtly halakhic in nature and form. See, e.g., *Tosafot ha-Shalem*, ed. Gellis, 4:240, sec. 1 (Riẓba and R. Ḥayyim [*Kohen*] established *simanim* about the worms that are found in certain fruits, based on the names given to the sons of Issachar); 9:141, secs. 8–9 (on the height of certain implements in the *mishkan*; *Moshav Zeqenim*, 382, 389, 460; *Perushim u-Pesaqim le-Rabbenu Avigdor*, 169 (*pesaq* #205); 176 (#220); 243 (#264); 248(#268), 305 (#313); 370 (#380); 389 (#420); 406 (#448); 455 (#508); 477 (#594). See also ms. Florence Laurenziana, Plut. II.20, fol. 205v (in the section of *parashat Mishpatim*, associated with R. Yeḥi'el of Paris; see below, chapter 4), and fol. 236v (to Nu. 24:17); in this instance, Riẓba suggests that the *bnei Shet* in this verse received their name on the basis of Isaiah 20:5, perhaps the only instance in which Riẓba offers this kind of close interpretation, similar to that of Ibn Ezra. Indeed, Riẓba's brother, R. Samson of Sens, is hardly identified with any distinct *parshanut ha-miqra* either. Although R. Samson's statements from his *Tosafot* are cited on occasion by Tosafist Torah compilations such as *Minḥat Yehudah* (Gen., fol. 16a), most references to R. Samson in these compilations are to Ri's student, R. Samson of Coucy. See S. A. Poznanski, *Mavo 'al Ḥakhmei Ẓarefat Mefarshei ha-Miqra*, 97, n. 1, and cf. the comment by R. Samson *ha-Naqdan* (above, Introduction, n. 83) to Gen. 47:29 (recorded in *Moshav Zeqenim*, 96), based on *Sefer Yeẓirah*.

and R. Solomon) seems to lie mostly with explicating the brief passage in *Bereshit Rabbah*, and providing clear examples of what the midrashic passage means, before tackling the more difficult calculation for Noah. Biblical commentators, including Rashi, R. Yosef *Bekhor Shor*, R. Isaiah di Trani, and Naḥmanides, attempted to construct an overarching chronology and sequence of the milestones and duration of the flood on the basis of the fairly cryptic verses found in the first half of chapter 8 in Genesis, and as described in *Bereshit Rabbah* and *Seder ʿOlam*. So did several other northern French Tosafists, most notably Rabbenu Tam and R. Solomon of Dreux.[218]

Rashi explains (Gen. 28:17) that Mount Moriah was uprooted and transferred to Bet El when Jacob was there (אני אומר שהר סיני נעקר ובא לכאן), based on a passage in *Ḥullin* 91b, that the land miraculously "jumped" toward Jacob. R. Solomon of Dreux subjects this view to strong questioning from talmudic literature. After presenting at length a series of talmudic passages that would appear to contradict Rashi's claim, R. Solomon concludes that Rashi's interpretation is nevertheless correct, and that it indeed reflects a measure of holy inspiration (האמת פירש ורוח הקודש נזרקה בו).[219] The only problem that remains for R. Solomon is that the supporting passage in tracate *Ḥullin* does not confirm, in his view, Rashi's otherwise correct solution.[220] Clearly, the context of this discussion, too, is completely talmudic.

Sefer ha-Gan reports (in two places) in the name of R. Moses of Evreux that a R. Solomon b. Abraham (rather than R. Solomon b. Judah) coined a scriptural "principle" or rule (היה כייל כלל, on the verse *ʿed ha-gal ha-zeh*, Gen. 31:52), that whenever a covenant is made and confirmed by some kind of physical witness, any violation of that covenant is exacted by or through that witness. However, the later *Hadar Zeqenim* compilation and at least one manuscript variant assign this comment simply to R. Solomon of Dreux (or perhaps Troyes). The larger view or pattern established here, which involves a series of verses and is based on talmudic and midrashic texts, is similar in some respects to R. Solomon of Dreux's analysis of the use of *tamim* and

[218] See *Perushei R. Yosef Bekhor Shor ʿal ha-Torah*, ed. Nevo, 18–20; *Nimmuqei Ḥumash le-Rabbenu Yeshayah*, ed. Chavel, 11–12; *Tosafot ha-Shalem*, 1:237–49. For Rabbenu Tam, see esp. 1:240, sec. 8; 243, sec. 3 (ms. Paris 167); 244, sec. 1; 248–49, secs. 1–2; and see also *Perushei R. Ḥayyim Paltiʾel*, ed. Lange, 20–21. For R. Solomon of Dreux's chronology, see ms. Bodl. 271, fol. 126r, and ms. Bodl. 2344 (= *Tosafot ha-Shalem*, 1:241–42, sec. 12), following a formulation (*yesod*) by R. Yose, the father of the compiler of *Sefer ha-Gan*, R. Aaron; *Tosafot ha-Shalem*, 1:244, sec. 6; 1:245, sec. 1 (end, and cf. 1:240–41, sec. 6, and *Sefer ha-Gan*, ed. Orlian, 139–40); and see also ms. Leiden 27, fol. 104v.

[219] Cf. my *"Peering through the Lattices,"* 152–53.

[220] See *Tosafot ha-Shalem*, ed. Gellis, 3:116–17, sec. 17; *Minḥat Yehudah* (Gen.) 28b (in which Riba's teacher R. Elyaqim then reviews the analysis of *ha-Qadosh mi-Dreux* at length); and Urbach, *Baʿalei ha-Tosafot*, 1:339–40, n. 34 (on the basis of ms. Paris 168). Cf. Ramban and Mizraḥi to Gen. 28:17.

the duration of the flood. Nonetheless, it is more likely that the architect of this principle was actually R. Solomon b. Abraham of Troyes, the brother of Riẓba and R. Samson (b. Abraham) of Sens.[221]

Five comments by R. Solomon of Dreux to the Book of Exodus are extant, all of which are fundamentally halakhic and could easily have been made in the course and context of talmudic study. R. Solomon is referred to at the end of the lengthy comment on the status of eating maẓẓah after the first day of Passover (Ex. 12:15).[222] He has a halakhic discussion on the conditions of a Hebrew slave (Ex. 21:2, based on a passage in the *Mekhilta*) which differs from Rashi's comment on this verse,[223] and three other comments to *parashat Mishpatim.* The first, made in the context of Exodus 21:12 (מכה איש ומת מות יומת), discusses the status of a minor who commits murder. The minor is not punished, even though a *ben sorer u-moreh* who is also a minor is.[224] The next is a discussion about eating the meat of an ox that is to be stoned (Ex. 21:28), in conjunction with the laws of *ben pequʿah*, which is essentially found in *Tosafot* texts as well.[225] Finally, an explanation is pro-

[221] See *Sefer ha-Gan*, ed. Orlian, 179, 249 (to Ex. 24:8); *Tosafot ha-Shalem*, ed. Gellis, 3:200, sec. 2 (based on ms. Bodl. 270); *Hadar Zeqenim*, fol. 13b. Urbach, *Baʿalei ha-Tosafot*, 340, n. 34, maintains (correctly) that the author of this rule is R. Solomon b. Abraham of Troyes, brother of Rash *mi-Shanz* (cf. *Baʿalei ha-Tosafot*, 1:344). Note, however, the confusion in Poznanski, *Mavo*, CII–CIII (n. 2). The very slight difference in the Hebrew spellings of Troyes and Dreux created part of the confusion in this regard. See also below, chapter 4, n. 185.

[222] See *Minḥat Yehudah*, Ex., fol. 14b, and *Tosafot ha-Shalem*, ed. Gellis, 7:89–90, sec. 5. This lengthy halakhic comment and discussion also mentions Rabbenu Tam, R. Isaac (Ri), R. Eleazar of Worms, and R. Moses of Evreux. See also below, chapter 4.

[223] See *Hadar Zeqenim*, fol. 36b (= ms. Florence Laurenziana, fols. 193v–194r). On this manuscript and section, cf. above, chapter 2, n. 219.

[224] R. Solomon's comment is found in R. Judah b. Eleazer's *Minḥat Yehudah*, Ex., fol. 31a, and is presented by Judah's main teacher, R. Elyaqim, in conjunction with the *sugya* in tractate *Sanhedrin* about *ben sorer u-moreh.* See also *Tosafot ha-Shalem*, ed. Gellis, 8:193, sec. 6 (end). Ri and R. Moses of Coucy's *Sefer Miẓvot Gadol* are also referred to in this passage.

[225] See *Minḥat Yehudah*, Ex., 34a. See also *Tosafot ha-Shalem*, 8:228–29, secs. 5–7. Rabbenu Tam and Rashbam are also mentioned in this discussion, as are the *Tosafot* of הר"ם בן אברהם (also referred to as תוספות הר"ם נשיאה). The author of these *Tosafot* is Rabbenu Tam's student, R. Moses b. Abraham of Pontoise (Pointe Mir). See Urbach, *Baʿalei ha-Tosafot*, 1:131–32, and 2:640, 645, and see also *Tosafot Bava Qamma* 41a, s.v. *ʾeini.* Fewer than ten comments to the Torah by R. Moses are extant (several of which appear in *Minḥat Yehudah*), mainly in halakhic contexts: (1) See *Tosafot ha-Shalem*, ed. Gellis, 8:243–248, secs. 6, 10, 15–16 (to Ex. 21:33–34), as well as ms. Moscow 898, fol. 60b, and ms. Parma 541, fol. 60b (some of which refer to R. Jacob of Pontoise rather than to R. Moses), which also cite another student of Rabbenu Tam, R. Judah of Corbeil; and cf. *Tosafot Bava Qamma* 10, s.v. *sheha-shor* and *Tosafot Zevaḥim* 71a, s.v. *ubi-terefah.* (2) See also *Tosafot ha-Shalem*, 8:306 (to Ex. 22:28), sec. 11 (= ms. Cambr. 669, in the name of R. Moses), on the halakhic definition of דמעך (and see also Rashi and Ramban; although the standard text of Rashi does not commit to any definition, some manuscript passages attribute a definition to him). See also the enriched *Minḥat Yehudah* manuscript, ms. JTS 791, fol. 61r, and the published version of *Minḥat Yehudah*, Ex. fol. 37b; ms. Parma 1051, fol. 57r. *Tosafot ha-Shalem*, ed. Gellis, 8:304–5, secs. 7–9, and *Tosafot Temurah* 4a, s.v. *meleʾatkha*, which cites R. Moses of Pontoise in

vided in the name of *ha-Qadosh mi-Dreux* which has clear similarities to material found in a talmudic *Tosafot* passage for the oath that is required in a case of partial admission (Ex. 22:8).[226]

Rashi (Ex. 30:14–16) distinguishes between two censuses, one taken after Yom Kippur—at the point when the donations to the *mishkan* commenced—and another during the following Iyyar, after the *mishkan* had begun operation. He also addresses the difficulties involved in reconciling the ages of those being counted in each census, asking whether their ages were established by their date of birth or by a point on the calendar. Here, *Ha-Qadosh mi-Dreux* introduces a talmudic passage in tractate *ʿArakhin* which suggests that the date of birth was to be used.[227]

---

disagreement with Rashi (in his talmudic commentary). (3) See also ms. Moscow 303, fol. 76v, to Ex. 16:25–26, where a R. Moses argues with Rabbenu Tam about the requirements and parameters of *seʿudah shelishit.* This also refers ostensibly to R. Moses of Pontoise; see *Teshuvot Maharam mi-Rothenburg defus Prague*, #473, and S. Emanuel, "Teshuvot shel Maharam she-Einam shel Maharam," *Shenaton ha-Mishpat ha-ʿIvri*, 21 (1998–2000), 161–63, and cf. *Tosafot ha-Shalem*, ed. Gellis, 7:279–82, and *Moshav Zeqenim*, 146–47. (4) See also *Minḥat Yehudah*, Lev., fol. 15b (and *ʾImrei Noʿam*, 108), citing R. Moses of Pontoise on technical procedures of the *seder ha-ʿavodah* (in Lev. 16:12). (5) See ms. JTS 791 to Gen. 44:18 (כי כמוך כפרעה), cited in *Tosafot ha-Shalem*, ed. Gellis, 4:200, sec. 23, where R. Moses of Pontoise supports Rashi's comment, based on a verse in Proverbs (the published edition of *Minḥat Yehudah*, Gen., fol., cites ר"י מפונטויש"א). (6) R. Moses of Pontoise is one of several figures cited in *Moshav Zeqenim*, 151–52, on the naming of Moses's sons based on the event that had occurred to Moses (Ex. 18:3–4); *Bekhor Shor*, R. Jacob of Orleans, and R. Judah *he-Ḥasid* are also mentioned. See *Perushei ha-Torah le-R. Yehudah he-Ḥasid*, ed. Lange, 91 (and n. 4), and *Tosafot ha-Shalem*, ed. Gellis, 8:9, sec. 2, and 8:10–11. Similar to R. Yehudah *he-Ḥasid*, R. Moses enunciates the principle that a more immediate salvation is commemorated first, before a greater deliverance that had occurred earlier. (7) The only close linguistic comment attributed to R. Moses was occasioned by a passage in the Targum to Deut. 32:5 (cf. above at R. Barukh b. Isaac), and is preserved in ms. Moscow 268, fol. 90v: תרגו' חבילו להון ולא ליה. וק' לה"ר משה מפונטייזא דלפי שחת לו לא בניו מומם. וכן זה היה לכתוב הראשון בא' והשני בוי"ו. לכן פי' כן. שחת לו כשמשחית האדם לו עצמו הוא משחית לא בניו מומם כי בני מום שלהם הוי שהקב"ה אומר עליהם כי לא בניו הם כשחוטאים. וכן אמר הושע כי היא לא אשתי והם לא בני. This comment is also found in R. Moses's name (in briefer form) in *Daʿat Zeqenim/Rabbotenu Baʿalei ha-Tosafot*, Deut. fol. 21b. (See also ms. Bodl. 1083 [#17690], fol. 123r.) Following the *mizvot ʿaseh* section of the *ʾazharot* (for *Shavuʿot*) by R. Elijah the elder of Le Mans (אמת יהגה חכי), which concludes with a prayer by R. Elijah to fear the Almighty and to come near to Him and to His precepts, a final rhymed addendum by R. Moses of Pontoise appears: זאת החריזה שייסד ה"ר משה מפונטייזא להשלים מצוות עשה: ב(מ)ציון ינופף אחד לכל החוברים, רבו מדת סמיכה וב(ב)מות סרים. שוו באשה לבד מסוטה ונזירים. לא כן לכו נא הגברים. This brief poetic piece, which is found in an unusual venue for Tosafist *payyetanim*, is published in Isaac Meiseles, *Shirat ha-Mizvot: ʾAzharot R. Eliyyahu ha-Zaqen* (Jerusalem, 2001), 63–64 (from ms. Montefiore 220). On the (halakhic) intention of R. Moses's addendum, see *Maḥzor Shavuʿot*, ed. Y. Fraenkel (Jerusalem, 2000), 664 (note to line 96), and cf. below, chapter 5, n. 42.

226 See *Tosafot ha-Shalem*, ed. Gellis, 8:273, sec. 8 (from ms. Hamburg 45 and its parallel, ms. B.M. 243). See also *Tosafot Bava Meziʿa* 3b, s.v. *be-kuleih.*

227 See *Hadar Zeqenim*, fols. 43a–b, and *Tosafot ha-Shalem*, ed. Gellis, 10:15–16, sec. 7. See also *Tosafot Pesaḥim* 23b, s.v. *de-ha*, citing the views of both R. Solomon of Dreux and Ri, on the basis of Lev. 10:16.

R. Solomon is cited both in the *Moshav Zeqenim* compilation to Leviticus 23:14 and in the earlier *Perushim u-Pesaqim le-R. Avigdor Katz* as allowing the consumption of beer without concern for the *ḥadash* deadline, since most people in the world, even if not in the immediate region, plant the crops used in the production of beer well before the month of *Nisan*.[228] As Urbach notes,[229] there is ample reason to assume that this was taken from his talmudic *Tosafot*. Similarly, R. Solomon of Dreux's discussion of the punishment for blaspheming (Lev. 24:12–15) is essentially talmudic,[230] as is his discussion of the precept of the giving of *ḥalah* (Lev. 27:30).[231] So too is R. Solomon's discussion of the appropriate punishment to give the מקושש עצים (Nu. 15:32–34), although here he is perhaps playing off Rashi's comment as well.[232]

A number of leading northern French Tosafists, such as Riẓba of Dampierre and his brother R. Samson of Sens, appear to have commented on Torah verses only sporadically, and exclusively within the context and through the prism of talmudic studies and analysis. Although R. Barukh b. Isaac, R. Elḥanan b. *ha-Ri*, and R. Solomon b. Judah of Dreux commented for the most part in such halakhic contexts, it is possible to identify a small body of exegetical comments from them, and to get a sense of some of their methods and preferences, as well as their use of midrash. Nonetheless, even these Tosafists did not make their comments outside the framework of talmudic studies or the review of the Torah portion that they undertook each week, often along with Rashi's commentary. Thus this model of Tosafist interpretation of the Pentateuch remains fundamentally different from what we have identified for R. Joseph and R. Jacob of Orleans and R. Yom Tov of Joigny, who produced a far greater volume of exegtical comments and, more important, pursued forms of *peshuto shel miqra* and the study of the text of the Torah—and perhaps Rashi's commentary—independently, to some extent, from the *shiurim* in talmudic studies that constituted "the

228 See *Moshav Zeqenim*, 382; and *Perushim u-Pesaqim le-R. Avigdor*, 169 (*pesaq* #205). In both texts, R. Solomon's ruling follows a lenient ruling in this matter (for a different consideration) by Riẓba; cf. above, n. 218. On the parallels in halakhic materials and ruling between these texts (and two other related works found in ms. B.M. 243 and ms. Mantua 36), see Simcha Emanuel, *Shivrei Luḥot*; 172, n. 89; my *"Peering through the Lattices,"* 94, n. 2; and below.

229 See Urbach, *Baʿalei ha-Tosafot*, 1:340, at n. 35, and cf. Golb, *Toledot ha-Yehudim be-ʿIr Rouen*, 117, for the assessment that, as opposed to Rashbam, who endeavored always to remain within the *peshuto shel miqra* in his Torah commentary, R. Solomon was most interested in elucidating aspects of the Oral Law as they emerged from the *Torah she-bikhtav*, and in supporting Rashi's commentary in a traditional yet learned way.

230 See *Hadar Zeqenim*, fol. 52a.

231 See *Sefer ha-Gan*, ed. Orlian, 289–90 (in the name of *he-Ḥasid ha-R. Shelomoh mi-Dreux*); *Hadar Zeqenim*, fol. 52b; and *Perushei R. Ḥayyim Paltiʾel*, ed. Lange, 462.

232 See ms. Moscow 82, fol. 36v.

main event" within Tosafist *battei midrash*. We will continue to identify these kinds of different models among Tosafists in northern France during the thirteenth century as well, as we shall see in the next chapter.

We have identified two significant rabbinic scholars from the Rhineland who pursued forms of *peshat* at the turn of the twelfth century, R. Judah *he-Ḥasid* and R. Isaiah di Trani, and we can easily add Judah's closest student, R. Eleazar of Worms, who advocated a variety of different forms of biblical exegesis including *peshat*, as we will note further at the end of the next chapter.[233] On the other hand, there were few German Tosafists, if any, whose interpretation of *miqra* was particularly focused or noteworthy outside the realm of talmudic studies. As an example, we shall look at the small number of Torah interpretations that have been preserved from R. Simḥah b. Samuel of Speyer.

R. Simḥah, as noted, was the teacher of R. Isaiah di Trani, and he interacted with the circle of R. Judah *he-Ḥasid*, who had lived for a time in Speyer. Moreover, R. Simḥah's involvement with the study and interpretation of the Talmud Yerushalmi and the *Sifra*, among other curricular broadenings within the realms of rabbinic and talmudic studies, may well reflect the impact of *Ḥasidei Ashkenaz*, in addition to his pietistic practices and mystical leanings.[234] Nonetheless, R. Simḥah does not appear to have produced a particularly noteworthy number of comments on the Torah, let alone a whole corpus.

In Genesis 3:14, Rashi himself engages with the talmudic interpretation of the verse. God moves directly to indict and to punish the snake (*ki ʿasita zot*), without any questioning or discussion of why the snake acted

233 See, e.g., Marcus, "Exegesis for the Few and for the Many" (above, n. 2); the literature cited above, nn. 8–9; and my "On the Role of Bible Study in Medieval Ashkenaz," in *The Frank Talmage Memorial Volume*, ed. B. Walfish, vol. 1, 157–58, 164–66.

234 See, e.g., Yaʿakov Sussman, "Rabad on *Shekalim*? A Bibliographical and Historical Riddle," in *Meʾah Sheʿarim: Studies in Medieval Jewish Spirituality in Memory of Isadore Twersky*, ed. E. Fleischer (Jerusalem, 2001), 140–52, 166–70; my "The Appointment of *Ḥazzanim* in Medieval Ashkenaz: Communal Policy and Individual Religious Prerogatives," in *Spiritual Authority: Struggles over Cultural Power in Jewish Thought*, ed. H. Kreisel (Beer Sheva, 2009), 5–31; my "*Peering through the Lattices*," 102–11, 225–28; and my "On the Study of *Seder Qodashim* in Medieval Europe (above, n. 21)." In this study, I argue that the so-called Speyer school was more Tannaitic in terms of its rabbinic self-image, while the northern French Tosafists considered themselves to be more like Amoraim, designations that have both methodological and disciplinary ramifications. Thus, while the Germans extensively studied and commented on *midrashei halakhah*, *Talmud Yerushalmi*, and some Palestinian *midrashim* (together with a fair measure of involvement in *torat ha-sod*), northern French Tosafists interpreted all of the Babylonian Talmud (and even the orders of *Zeraʿim* and *Taharot*). Similarly, the Frenchmen appear to have been more committed overall to works of basic scriptural interpretation than their German counterparts were, although the extent to which this effort takes place away from talmudic texts and discussions (and the degree to which midrash may be used *le-yashev ʾet divrei ha-miqra*) varies, even within northern France itself, as we have seen.

as he did, as there had been in the case of both Adam and Eve (3:11 and 3:13). As Rashi notes, the Talmud *Sanhedrin* (29a), derived from here that we are not obligated to seek any merits on behalf of a "beguiler and seducer" (*mesit*). In theory, the snake could have tried to deflect the blame by arguing that Adam and Eve should have listened to the Almighty's instructions about the Tree of Knowledge rather than to the inferior snake (*divrei ha-rav ve-divrei ha-talmid divrei mi shom'in*), but he was not given an opportunity to do so. As we shall see, R. Moses of Coucy raises a problem with this explanation, namely that the snake was not like a human "beguiler and seducer," since he probably had a heightened sense of what Eve would do.[235]

A related question attributed to R. Simḥah represents a broader point of *halakhah*. According to the passage in tractate *Sanhedrin*, every human *mesit* should indeed be able to offer the same defense, namely that the people should ultimately have listened to God's Torah with regard to the prohibition of idolatry rather than to his attempt at suasion. An answer is suggested in the name of a R. Isaac (whose identity is unclear) that only the snake could have made this claim, since he himself was not commanded to observe the prohibition at hand. A human *mesit*, however, is just as constrained from committing idolatry as his potential victims.[236]

In Genesis 25:26, the Torah writes, "and he called him [*va-yiqra shemo*] Jacob." Since the prior verse stated that Isaac and Rivka called their first son Esau, Rashi, based on a passage in *Midrash Tanḥuma* at the beginning of the Book of Exodus, comments that the Almighty is the One who gave Jacob his name. This would appear, however, to be in conflict with a passage in the Talmud Yerushalmi, according to which God did not change Isaac's name, as He did for Abraham and Jacob, because the latter two were given their names by their parents, while only Isaac's name was revealed to his parents by God (Gen. 17:19). *Moshav Zeqenim* presents several answers to this question, including an anonymous one that suggests that God prescribed Isaac's

[235] See below, chapter 4, n. 9.

[236] See ms. Moscow 303, which contains many comments from R. Isaiah di Trani (as noted above), fol. 59v. See also *'Imrei No'am*, 2 (which records the answer in the name of ר"י), and *Perushei R. Ḥayyim Palti'el*, ed. Lange, 8–9. It is certainly possible that R. Isaac is R. Simḥah's student R. Isaac *Or Zaru'a*, who is cited three other times in this manuscript; see I. Ta-Shma, *Knesset Meḥqarim*, 3:22. See also ms. Moscow 303, fol. 82v and *'Imrei No'am*, 98 (to Lev. 12:2), and Moscow 303, fol. 85v (to Lev. 22:28). In Moscow 303 (fol. 61r), a comment of R. Isaiah to Gen. 11:32 (ed. Chavel, 13, and ms. Breslau 102, fol. 9v) is cited in the name of ר"י. This occurs in other instances as well, and especially in the *Moshav Zeqenim* collection. See e.g., *Nimmuqei Ḥumash le-Rabbenu Yeshayah* (to Nu. 9:1), ed. Chavel, 59; ms. Breslau 102; ms. Moscow 303, fol. 90r; and *Moshav Zeqenim*, 439. At the same time, however, these positions also appear in northern French *Tosafot* (*Sanhedrin* 29a, s.v. *divrei*) and Torah compilations; see *Tosafot ha-Shalem*, ed. Gellis, 1:132–33, secs. 2–3. And so it is at least possible (although still unlikely) that Ri is Ri of Dampierre, and R. Simḥah may refer to a northern French rabbinic figure by that name.

name even before he was conceived, while Jacob's name was given only after his birth. Rabbenu Simḥah, in consonance with Rashi, suggests that God did not give the name Jacob, but the name Israel.[237]

Moshav Zeqenim records a halakhic discussion by R. Simḥah of Speyer (*Rabbenu Simḥah me-Ashpira*) with regard to circumcision on the Sabbath, based on Leviticus 12:3,[238] and a similar point of law with respect to the defilement of a *kohen*, based on Leviticus 21:2.[239] On Leviticus 23:28 (that one may not slaughter an animal and its offspring on the same day), R. Simḥah raises a sharp halakhic question. How can we slaughter any pregnant animal, since the Talmud (in tractate *Niddah*) asserts that the fetus dies prior to the mother and therefore, de facto, the parent and child would be killed on the same day? The answer given is that the phrase *mi-kol ha-behemah tokhelu* (Lev. 11:2–3) allows for this contingency as well.[240] R. Simḥah is also mentioned in two of the manuscripts that contain R. Judah *he-Ḥasid*'s Torah commentary, as following up with a halakhic point about *'ona'ah* being a sixth of an item's value. This follows R. Judah *he-Ḥasid*'s *sofei tevot* derivation in Leviticus 25:17, that a sixth is the measure of *'ona'ah*. R. Simḥah challenged R. Judah's *remez* from this verse, but ultimately left it intact.[241]

In connection with the verse, "they [the *kohanim*] will place my Name on the children of Israel and I will bless them" (Nu. 6:27), the Talmud Yerushalmi notes (*Gittin* 5:9) that one should not worry if a *kohen* who has sinned, even grievously, is giving the priestly blessing alone, since God says, in effect, that He is the one giving the blessing (*va-'ani 'avarkhem*). R. Simḥah maintains that although the Babylonian Talmud (*Berakhot* 32b), based on Isaiah 1:15, "your hands [of the priestly blessing] are filled with blood," pointedly prohibits a *kohen* who has killed someone from giving the priestly blessing, this applies only to the *kohen* who has willfully killed and is unrepentant (*'omed be-merdo*), while the Jerusalem Talmud passage, which seems to allow sinners to participate, refers to a murderer who has repented. This was a matter of debate among halakhists in medieval Ashkenaz; indeed, the passage in *Moshav Zeqenim* that presents R. Simḥah's view

[237] See *Moshav Zeqenim*, 38, and cf. *Tosafot ha-Shalem*, ed. Gellis, 3:22–23, secs. 11–12.

[238] *Moshav Zeqenim*, 292. See also the comment on the prior verse attributed to R. Simḥah in ms. Bodl. 274 cited in *Tosafot ha-Shalem*, ed. Gellis 12:164, sec. 16 (and in *Tosafot ha-Shalem*, 12:171, sec. 27*, citing the *'Imrei No'am* compilation), which is again purely talmudic and halakhic.

[239] *Moshav Zeqenim*, 368. This is also found in R. Simḥah's name in the parallel *Perushim u-Pesaqim le-R. Avigdor Katz*, 164–65 (*pesaq* #200). R. Avigdor Katz was a student of R. Simḥah; see above, n. 109. See also *Perushim u-Pesaqim*, 397 (#431).

[240] *Moshav Zeqenim*, 379.

[241] See *Perushei ha-Torah le-R. Yehudah he-Ḥasid*, ed. Lange, 155–56 (אל תונו איש את עמיתו ויראת ס"ת שתות. מכאן לאונאה שאינה אלא פחותה משתות. מפי הרי"ח. והקשה מה"ר שמחה על טעם זה מפרק איזהו נשך וכו'), and see also 206 (Deut. 22:12)

also notes the restrictive view within Ashkenazic rabbinic sources in this matter.[242]

Rashi, following *Midrash Tanhuma*, interprets Moses's seeming uncertainty—"will we extract water for you from this rock?" (Nu. 20:10)—to reflect the fact that the rock in question concealed itself among other rocks when the well of Miriam ended its service, and Moses and Aaron did not recognize it. In light of the widespread talmudic axiom[243] that the Almighty does not place these kinds of glitches (*taqqalah*) in the paths of the righteous (or even in front of their animals), how did this entire boondoggle occur, ultimately costing Moses his life? Ms. Moscow 303 notes that an interpretation by Rabbenu Simḥah of this talmudic axiom serves to answer the question. God does not bring a *taqqalah* without provocation. In this instance, however, Moses brought the *taqqalah* upon himself.[244] Finally, a discussion between R. Jonathan (b. Isaac of Wurzburg) and R. Simḥah is recorded with regard to the halakhic interpretation or import of the word *yaḥdav* in Deuteronomy 22:10 ("do not plow with an ox and a donkey *yaḥdav* [together]"), but this too is purely halakhic exegesis.[245]

Less than a handful of comments have survived in the name R. Isaac b. Jacob *ha-Lavan* of Regensburg, one of a group of Rabbenu Tam's students who hailed from Germany and Bohemia,[246] but they are nonetheless more suggestive. Speaking to Cain, the Almighty says (Gen. 4:7), "If you improve you will surely be forgiven; but if you do not improve yourself, sin rests at the door [*le-petaḥ ḥatat rovez*]. Its desire is toward you, yet you can conquer it." R. Isaac explains that the *pashteh di-qra* of this verse connects it directly to the one preceding it, where God asked Cain, "Why are you annoyed and why has your countenance fallen?" R. Isaac then proceeds to explain the word *ḥatat* as a sacrifice and to entirely reconstruct the flow of the verse. The message to Cain is that if his offering is made in a better way, God will surely accept it. And even if he does not have the wherewithal to improve

[242] See *Moshav Zeqenim*, 432 (= ms.Moscow, 121, fols. 16v–17a; along with ms. Paris 260, this manuscript appears to be a partial variant of *Moshav Zeqenim*).

[243] *Yevamot* 99b, *Ketubot* 28b, *Ḥullin* 8b.

[244] See ms. Moscow 303, fol. 92v: פר"ש לפי שלא היו מכירין אותו לפי שהלך לו הסלע וישב לו בין הסלעים. וקש' אמאי נעשית זאת התקלה למשה רבינו והלא אין הקב"ה מביא תקלה אף לבהמתן של צדיקים וכ"ש לצדיקים עצמן וזו תקלה גדולה למשה שהרי מת עליה. אמנם רבי' שמחה פי' האי דאמ' אין הקב"ה מביא תקלה וכו' ה"פ אין הקב"ה מביא תקלה. ועל ידי משה באה תקלה לעצמו. Cf. *Perushei R. Ḥayyim Palti'el*, ed. Lange 534. R. Simḥah is cited only three times in this fuller version of Rid's commentary; see Ta-Shma, *Knesset Meḥqarim*, 3:22, and above, n. 237.

[245] See *Moshav Zeqenim*, 507 (= ms. Moscow 121, fols. 40b–41). R. Jonathan, who appears twice in ms. Moscow 303, is another of R. Isaac *Or Zaru'a*'s teachers; see Ta-Shma, *Knesset Meḥqarim*, 1:161–63, and S. Emanuel, *Shivrei Luḥot*, 112 (n. 44), 164 (n. 39), 269.

[246] See Rami Reiner, "Rabbenu Tam: Rabbotav (ha-Ẓarefatim) ve-Talmidav Bnei Ashkenaz" (M.A. thesis, Hebrew University, 1997), 96–98; and see above, chapter 1, nn. 30–32, 59.

(*ʾein lekha bameh le-hetiv ve-lashuv*), this is the "opening" at which the *ḥatat* rests. You can still bring the sacrifice, and that will begin your repentance process. Lest Cain believe that his brother, Abel, who controls the flocks, would not give him an animal for this purpose, "*his* desire is toward you," which means that Abel wants to give it to Cain to help him. In any case, Cain will be able to prevail on Abel to let him have an animal, since he controls the grazing grounds and the produce (= you can conquer him). Although there is a talmudic dimension here as well, the approach R. Isaac *ha-Lavan* proposes interprets the possessive forms in this verse in different and subtle ways, reminiscent of the method of R. Judah *he-Ḥasid.*[247]

R. Isaac *ha-Lavan* also presents a sensitive interpretation of Exodus 6:7, the opening of *parashat va-Era.* R. Isaac interprets that while God appeared to the *Avot* and made commitments to them using both the name *E-l Shadai* and the Tetragrammaton, He only fulfilled the promises for which the former name had been used, such as the promise that they would be fruitful and multiply, in Genesis 35:11 and Exodus 1:7. Although R. Isaac does not refer to Rashi here, his approach also responds to a question raised against the comment of Rashi, that the Tetragrammaton had never been used with the *Avot.* In fact, the Tetragrammaton was used when God told Abraham to leave the land of Canaan with the promise that he would be a great nation (Gen. 11:1–2), and that he would be given the land of Canaan (Gen. 35:11). According to R. Isaac's approach, these promises were still unfulfilled.[248] Perhaps additional comments from R. Isaac *ha-Lavan* will be found in the future, but the very small sample of albeit creative comments that we have from him suggests that non-halakhic or non-talmudic interpretation

247 See *Tosafot ha-Shalem*, 1:156, sec. 3. This passage is found in ms. Paris 48; see Y. S. Lange, "Perushei Baʿalei ha-Tosafot ʿal ha-Torah—Ketav Yad Paris 48," *ʿAlei Sefer* 5 (1978), 80. Aside from Rashbam and *Bekhor* (and a single reference to Rambam), virtually all of the Tosafists and rabbinic figures mentioned by name in this brief collection are German (e.g., R. David of Muenzberg, R. Eliezer of Bohemia, R. Avraham b. Yequtiʾel, and R. Zal(t)man, son of R. Judah *he-Ḥasid*), a rare occurrence in and of itself with regard to Tosafist Torah compilations; see *Perushei ha-Torah le-R. Yehudah he-Ḥasid*, ed. Lange, 73–88. (R. David of Muenzberg is also mentioned in the somewhat parallel collection, ms. Bodl. 271/8, fol. 123v, although this version cites a number of northern French Tosafists as well, including R. Solomon of Dreux. See also below, n. 250.) Ri *ha-Lavan*'s passage is also found in ms. Cambridge 669.2, which contains the Torah commentary of R. Judah *he-Ḥasid*; see *Perushei ha-Torah le-R. Yehudah he-Ḥasid*, ed. Lange, 8.

248 See ms. Hamburg 45 (הר"ר יצחק הלבן פירש הפשט כך) in *Tosafot ha-Shalem*, ed. Gellis, 6:151, sec. 16, and ms. Munich 50 (מפי ה"ר יצחק הלבן), in *Tosafot ha-Shalem*, 6:150, sec. 11. In both instances, R. Isaac's interpretation is followed by one from Rabbenu Yonah (*veha-R. Yonah piresh ha-peshat*). Hamburg 45 then presents a comment from R. Yosef *Bekhor Shor*, followed by a midrash (see *Tosafot ha-Shalem*, 6:152). On the *peshatim* found within ms. Hamburg 45, see the next note.

of Scripture was not a heavy priority for most figures within the German Tosafist milieu.[249]

Indeed, although Aptowitzer lists seven Torah interpretations in the name of *Avi ha-ʿEzri* (Rabiah),[250] the final three, which are cited by R. Moses of Coucy in his comments to *parashat Ve-Zot ha-Berakhah*, are actually offered by R. Abraham ibn Ezra,[251] as is the fourth (to Ex. 20:22), which appears in the name of *Avi ha-ʿEzri* in ms. Munich 50 (fol. 134r). The third is essentially a question on a midrashic interpretation to Genesis43:17, based on Rashi's commentary to *Avot*,[252] and the first two are *gematria/remez* traditions on Genesis 3:18 and 3:22, noted by the Tosafist Torah compilation that

[249] In addition to the extensive comments by R. Yom Tov of Joigny (above, chapter 2) and comments by other French Tosafists (including, e.g., R. Tuvyah of Vienne, fol. 96v), as well as a large number of comments by R. Judah *he-Ḥasid* (as befits a version of *Paʿaneaḥ Raza*; see, e.g., fols. 4r, 21r, 43v, 47v, 48r, 60r, 65v, 67r, 78r, 85r), two by his father, R. Samuel *he-Ḥasid* (fols. 14r, 35r), and one by the Pietist associate, R. Ephraim of Samson (fol. 49r, in support of Rashi), ms. Munich 50 also has a comment by R. David of Muenzberg to Gen. 43:23 (fol. 88v, and see also *Tosafot ha-Shalem*, ed. Gellis, 4:177, sec. 1, citing ms. Bodl. 2344 and *Moshav Zeqenim*). See also *Moshav Zeqenim*, 38, 76. Another version of *Paʿaneaḥ Raza* that cites R. Judah *he-Ḥasid* quite heavily, ms. B.M. 9931, was apparently edited by a student of the German Tosafist R. Yedidyah of Nuremberg (who also studied in northern France with R. Yeḥi'el of Paris and the brothers of Evreux; see Urbach, *Baʿalei ha-Tosafot*, 2:566–70). See especially fol. 16r, where the editor cites his teacher R. Yedidyah, in the name of R. Samuel Bamberg (who in turn cites a teaching of R. Judah *he-Ḥasid*). See above, chapter 2, n. 196; and my *"Peering through the Lattices,"* 105 (n. 24). Among the leading figures in the later Tosafist Torah compilations, R. Ḥayyim Palti'el was from Germany, although his student (who compiled the so-called *Perushei R. Ḥayyim Palti'el*) was also a student of R. Solomon of Chateau-Landon (and R. Ḥayyim Palti'el himself spent time in and had affinities for the communities in northern France), which might explain the large number of French scholars whose comments appear in this work. See, e.g., Y. S. Lange, "Le-Zehuto shel R. Ḥayyim Palti'el," *'Alei Sefer* 8 (1980), 140–46; E. Zimmer, *'Olam ke-Minhago Noheg*, 271, 276–77, 282–83, 296–97; S. Emanuel, *Shivrei Luḥot*, 219; and below, chapter 4. The *peshatim* in Hamburg 45 (which contain quite a bit of northern French material) are attributed erroneously to R. Yosef *Bekhor* and perhaps to R. Avigdor Katz of Vienna (who actually hailed from northern France) as well. See, e.g., H. J. Zimmels, "Ketav Yad Hamburg Cod. Hebr. 45 ve-Yaḥaso le-R. Avigdor Katz," in *Ma'amarim le-Zikhron R. Ẓvi Perez Chajes* (Vienna, 1931), 248–61; my "Mysticism and Asceticism in Italian Rabbinic Literature of the Thirteenth Century" (above, n. 109); Emanuel, *Shivrei Luḥot*, 173–81; and below, chapter 4, nn. 148, 193. It would appear that the anonymous *Moshav Zeqenim* collection (along with its two manuscript variants, ms. Paris 260 and ms. Moscow 121), which was not compiled until at least the mid-fourteenth century (see, e.g., *Sefer ha-Gan*, ed. Orlian, 93–94, and I. Ta-Shema, *Knesset Meḥqarim*, 1:171–72, 235–36), has the most German material of all, including a very large number of comments by R. Judah *he-Ḥasid* and R. Isaiah di Trani, as we have noted throughout this chapter (in addition, however, to a similarly large number of comments from R. Yosef *Bekhor Shor* and from R. Jacob of Orleans).

[250] See Avigdor Aptowitzer, *Mavo la-Rabiah* (Jerusalem, 1938), 130–33.

[251] See below, chapter 4, nn. 96–97.

[252] See *Daʿat Zeqenim*, fol. 43a, and *Tosafot ha-Shalem*, ed. Gellis, 175–76, sec. 1. A similar point is made in two versions of *Minḥat Yehudah*, based on a teaching of R. Judah *he-Ḥasid*. See *Tosafot ha-Shalem*, 176, sec. 2–3.

is attributed to R. Asher b. Yeḥi'el (Rosh).[253] There is not one basic, focused scriptural interpretation among the lot.

The lack of such exegetical interpretation in Germany during this period does not, of course, minimize or undermine the work of R. Judah *he-Ḥasid* and R. Isaiah di Trani. Indeed, even among northern French Tosafists, there was a range of approaches taken to scriptural interpretation, as we have seen, and as is to be expected in the dynamic and variegated world of interpretation throughout medieval Ashkenaz. Nonetheless, we have encountered a group of important Ashkenazic rabbinic figures in both northern France and Germany who sought to continue and to expand the kind of *peshuto shel miqra* approach that had been made popular by Rashi, consisting of explicit *peshat* comments and the use of talmudic-midrashic sources.

As we shall see in the next chapter, these developments continue as the thirteenth century unfolds, albeit mainly in northern France, although several northern French Tosafists begin to rely more heavily on midrash as well. Indeed, the mid-thirteenth century also marks the appearance of the so-called Tosafist Torah compilations. The earliest of these, such as the one that featured the "students of Rabbenu Tam" (ms. Paris 167= ms. Moscow 362) and R. Aaron *ha-Kohen*'s *Sefer ha-Gan* (which was composed c. 1240), tend to provide instances of discrete scriptural interpretation (including examples of *peshuto shel miqra* and *'aggadah ha-meyashevet divrei miqra*), together with high-level Tosafist talmudic studies or midrashic analyses, as we have seen.

By the late thirteenth century, however, while the growing number of these compilations retained elements of *peshat*, midrashic and talmudic interpretations, often as presented by lesser-known or anonymous later figures, become noticeably more prevalent. As we shall discuss, it is quite possible that this shift, in terms of both genre and method, was an attempt by members of the secondary rabbinic elite to bring Tosafist interpretation (of both the Torah and the Talmud) to more of a popular audience, by shortening and varying the interpretational strategies and results found in these works, and by playing up midrashic and talmudic stories and accounts. These are less methodologically demanding of the reader, while they provide him

[253] The scholarly consensus is that the R. Asher who composed this work is probably not the famous halakhist R. Asher b. Yeḥi'el, and it is possible that this work emanated from northern France rather than from Germany, although, like *Moshav Zeqenim*, it refers to a number of Spanish works, including Naḥmanides' Torah commentary. See, e.g., A. H. Freimann, *R. Asher b. Yeḥi'el ve-Ze'eza'av* (Jerusalem, 1986), 129; *Tosafot ha-Shalem*, ed. Gellis, vol. 1, editor's introduction, 20; *Sefer ha-Gan*, ed. M. Orlian, 95–96; *Sarei ha-Elef*, ed. M. M. Kasher and Y. D. Mandelbaum (Jerusalem, 1979), 1:67; and I. Ta-Shma, *Knesset Meḥqarim*, 2:163.

with a wealth of interesting (and practical halakhic) information, and also with a better sense of the revolutionary methods of talmudic and scriptural interpretation that the Tosafists had put forward.

Thus while these compilations are, on the one hand, less concise, they are, on the other hand, collections of great variety that could conceivably appeal to a wider audience. The best examples of such collections are *Daʿat Zeqenim*, *Hadar Zeqenim*, *Perush ha-Rosh*, and perhaps *Minḥat Yehudah*. To be sure, however, some of these later collections retained a more controlled, traditional presentation of exegetical comments, reflecting both *peshat* and *derash*. *Ḥizzequni* is certainly in this category, as are *Paʿaneaḥ Raza*, *Perushei R. Ḥayyim Palti'el*, and *Moshav Zeqenim*. However, as opposed to *Ḥizzequni*, the three latter works also contain a great deal of halakhic discussion and Tosafist talmudic methodology (albeit in digest form), in addition to elements of *gematria*, *remez*, and even *sod*.[254]

[254] For a closer look at the midrashic elements and methods in these collections, see my "Midrashic Texts and Methods in Tosafist Torah Commentaries," (above, n. 64).

4

Interpretations for a Varied Audience through the Thirteenth Century

As the thirteenth century unfolds, the first of the so-called Tosafist Torah compilations begin to appear. Included among these are the collection attributed to the study hall (or to the students) of Rabbenu Tam (found in ms. Paris 167 and ms. Moscow 322, which contains some later names as well);[1] *Sefer ha-Gan*, composed or edited by R. Aaron b. Yose *ha-Kohen* c. 1240 (which reflects the clear influence of R. Yosef *Bekhor Shor*);[2] and the contemporary ms. Leiden 27 and ms. Vatican 45 (which were incorrectly attributed to R. Yosef *Bekhor Shor*, even as the presence of his comments in them is also noticeable).[3] As we have seen, these collections and many of the Tosafists cited in them present a good deal of rabbinic interpretation and *remez* together with instances and examples of *peshat* interpretation, and serve in this regard as partial models for the fairly steady flow of Tosafist Torah compilations that would follow during the late thirteenth and early fourteenth centuries.[4]

[1] See above, chapter 2, n. 6.

[2] See *Sefer ha-Gan*, ed. M. Orlian (Jerusalem, 2009), editor's introduction, 24, 42–48.

[3] Ms. Vatican 45 is described in its colophon as הילך ליקוטים מלקח טוב מבכור שור ומג"ן. Cf. *Tosafot ha-Shalem*, ed. Gellis, vol. 1 (Jerusalem, 1982), editor's introduction, 26; above, chapter 2, n. 128; and below, n. 193, regarding ms. Hamburg 45. In *Naḥmanides on Genesis: The Art of Biblical Portraiture* (Providence, R.I., 2010), 6, my colleague Michelle Levine has noted the apparent use by Naḥmanides of the Tosafist collections found in ms. Leiden 27 and ms. Vatican 45 (in particular). The dating of these compilations to c. 1240 certainly comports with their use by Naḥmanides in his Torah commentary.

[4] On the published versions of these compilations, which include *Daʿat Zeqenim*, *Hadar Zeqenim*, *Paʿaneaḥ Raza*, *Perushei R. Ḥayyim Paltiʾel*, *Perush ha-Rosh*, *ʾImrei Noʿam*, *Perushim u-Peshatim le-R. Yaʿaqov me-Vienna*, *Minḥat Yehudah*, and *Moshav Zeqenim*, among others, see, e.g., *Sefer ha-Gan*, ed. Orlian, editor's introduction, 83–97; and above, chapter 2, n. 2.

At the same time there were Tosafists during the mid-thirteenth century who continued to pursue the more focused study of *peshuto shel miqra va-ʾaggadah ha-meyashevet divrei miqra*, of the type that we have seen from R. Yosef *Bekhor Shor*, R. Jacob of Orleans, and R. Yom Tov of Joigny in northern France, and from R. Judah *he-Ḥasid* and R. Isaiah di Trani as well. Embedded in the Tosafist Torah compilation *Minḥat Yehudah*, which was completed by an otherwise unknown R. Judah b. Eliezer (or Eleazar) in 1313,[5] are nearly eighty comments from R. Moses of Coucy (d. c. 1250), most often cited as פשטי ר׳ משה מקוצי.[6]

R. Moses of Coucy

In his brief discussion of R. Moses's comments to the Torah, Poznanski notes that there are also comments from R. Moses found in ms. JTS Adler 501 (= ms. Lutzki 791), often in the name of R. Moses *ha-Darshan*, and in the published compilation titled *ʾImrei Noʿam*, especially to the last part of *Sefer Shemot*. He also correctly cautions, however, that comments found in other Tosafist Torah compilations in the name of R. Moses (or R. Moses *ha-Darshan*) are most often not by R. Moses of Coucy. Presenting fewer than a handful of examples, Poznanski maintains that most of the *peshatei R. Mosheh mi-Coucy* are *ʿal pi derash*,[7] an assessment that has

[5] On this work, see Hazoniel Touitou, "*Minḥat Yehudah*: A Commentary by Rabbi Yehudah ben El[e]azar" [Hebrew] (Ph.D. diss., Bar-Ilan University, 2004); and see also idem, "Qavvim le-Darko shel ha-Riva be-Perusho la-Torah," in *ʿIyyunei Miqra u-Parshanut* vol. 8, ed. S. Vargon et al. (Ramat Gan, 2008), 589–605.

[6] The Book of Numbers contains the largest number of comments (nearly twenty-five), while Genesis has the fewest (ten), and each of the remaining books of the Pentateuch has approximately fifteen comments by R. Moses. This is a somewhat uncommon pattern among the group of Ashkenazic rabbinic *pashtanim* whom we have been studying (and is certainly anomalous for Rashbam), although we cannot be certain that all of R. Moses's original comments to the Torah are to be found within *Minḥat Yehudah*.

[7] See S. A. Poznanski, *Mavo ʿal Ḥakhmei Ẓarefat Mefarshei ha-Miqra* (Warsaw, 1913), XCIII–XCIV, CX–CXI. On ms. Adler 501, see also Heinrich Gross, "Ein handschriftlicher, tossafistischer Commentar zum Pentateuach," *MGWJ* 45 (1901), 364–73. Y. S. Lange, in the introduction to his edition of *Perushei R. Ḥayyim Paltiʾel* (Jerusalem, 1981), 10–11, notes that both R. Moses of Coucy and R. Jacob of Orleans are mentioned by name far less than their actual impact on this collection, and that the name R. Moses in this collection refers occasionally to the Tosafist R. Moses of Evreux. R. Moses of Coucy was legitimately referred to as *ha-Darshan* on any number of occasions (a title more consistently and typically applied to the eleventh-century R. Moses *ha-Darshan* of Provence), owing to the missions that he undertook in Spain (and in northern Europe) to preach fuller observance of the commandments; see, e.g., I. Ta-Shma, *Knesset Meḥqarim*, vol. 2 (Jerusalem, 2004), 114–18, 149–56. For additional biographical and compositional details about R. Moses of Coucy, see Urbach, *Baʿalei ha-Tosafot* (Jerusalem, 1980), 1:465–79, and cf. my *"Peering through the Lattices": Mystical, Magical, and Pietistic Dimensions in the Tosafist Period* (Detroit, Mich., 2000), 68–82.

been questioned, also on the basis of only a few specific samples, by Judah Galinsky.[8]

Many of the comments that are found under the name of *peshatei R. Mosheh mi-Coucy* in R. Judah b. Eliezer's *Minḥat Yehudah*, and in other collections of the *Perushei Ba'alei ha-Tosafot 'al ha-Torah*, are investigations or explanations of Rashi's interpretations, some on the basis of talmudic or rabbinic texts,[9] and others along the lines of *peshat* exegesis.[10] We have seen in the previous chapters that R. Jacob of Orleans and R. Isaiah di Trani were especially interested in challenging and verifying aspects of Rashi's commentary, although all the exegetes we have discussed to this point interacted with Rashi's commentary in some significant ways. Indeed, we shall have occasion throughout this chapter to note the many similar and parallel approaches and points made by R. Moses and this group of earlier colleagues, although it is not always clear which of these commentaries R. Moses had before him. R. Moses's deep appreciation for Rashi's Torah commentary led

[8] See Y. D. Galinsky, "Rabbenu Mosheh mi-Coucy ke-Ḥasid, Darshan u-Polmosan: Hebbetim me-'Olamo ha-Maḥshavti u-Pe'iluto ha-Ẓibburit" (M.A. thesis, Yeshiva University, 1991), 4–5. Cf. H. Touitou, "*Minḥat Yehudah*," 96–103.

[9] See, e.g., *Minḥat Yehudah* (Jerusalem, 1967) to Genesis 3:14 (fols. 3b–4a): כי עשית זאת. פרש"י [עיין סנהדרין דף כט ע"א] מכאן שאין טוענין למסית [ש]אם שאלו למה עשית זאת היה לו להשיב דברי הרב ודברי התלמיד מי שומעין. וא"ת היאך למדנו מכאן שאין טוענין למסית והא (לא היה) [אין] מסית אלא לע"ז. וי"ל שהנחש היה מסית לע"ז דכתי' והייתם כא-להים יודעי טוב ורע. וא"ת מה היה בלבו של הנחש אם היה יודע שחוה תעשה ציוויו . . . וי"ל שהיה יודע שתעשה חוה ציוויו ואפ"ה נלמד ממנו למסית אחר . . . לפי שהיתה כוונתו להרע היה לכתוב כי יען ברוע לבבך עשית זאת ומדלא כתב הכי ש"מ דנלמוד ממנו למסית אחר ואין הדבר תלוי ברוע הלב. מצאתי קושיא זו ותירוצין הללו בפשטי הר"ם מקוצי. The final comment of *Minḥat Yehudah* strongly suggests that *peshatei ha-Ram mi-Coucy* was a written record or work. Cf. *Moshav Zeqenim*, 4 (to Gen. 3:4), where the comment is found in the name of ה"ר משה. It appears without a name in *Perushei R. Ḥayyim Palti'el*, ed. Lange, 8–9. As Lange notes, there are parallel formulations in *Tosafot Hakhmei Angliyyah* to *Sanhedrin* 29a, and in *Tosafot Shanz*, ad loc. There is also discussion in the standard *Tosafot* to *Sanhedrin*. A manuscript version of *Minḥat Yehudah* (ms. JTS 787) assigns the names of Ri and R. Simḥah of Speyer to the discussion found in *Tosafot Sanhedrin*. See *Tosafot ha-Shalem*, ed. Gellis, 1:132–33, sec. 2, and above, chapter 3, nn. 235–36. All of this has implications for whether the discussion by R. Moses of Coucy was undertaken initially within the context of biblical or talmudic studies; see n. 10, below. Cf. *Ḥizzequni*, who concludes his unattributed interpretation by establishing that the snake was indeed interested in causing Eve to do idolatry.

[10] See, e.g., the late-thirteenth century Tosafist Torah compilation of R. Isaac b. Judah *ha-Levi*, *Pa'aneaḥ Raza*, ed. Machon Torat ha-Rishonim (Jerusalem, 1998) 54 (to Genesis 8:4), in the name of R. Moses b. הר"י [=Moses b. R. Ya'akov of Coucy], and cf. *Perushei R. Ḥayyim Palti'el*, ed. Lange, 19: בשבעה עשר יום לחודש. פרש"י שהיתה אמה נחסרה בד' ימים. וא"ת אם כן כפי' זה לא היה שום הר בעולם גבוה יותר מט"ו אמה דהא ב[חודש ה]עשירי היינו באב באחד לחדש נראו ראשי ההרים ובאחד בתשרי חרבו המים הרי בס' ימים כלו כל המים שהיו נגד ההרים. [ויש לומר שהיו הרים גבוהים יותר.] ואולי כשבא לחלל ההרים [מפני עובי ההרים המפסיקים בהם וממעטים אותם] היו המים [שבין ההרים] יותר כלים מהרה. See also *Ḥizzequni*, who asks the same question and then proceeds to offer this same explanation at greater length, and *Tosafot ha-Shalem*, ed. Gellis, 1:240–41, sec. 10, which presents a briefer version of this passage without R. Moses's name, from another manuscript version of *Minḥat Yehudah* (ms. Munich 62).

to his suggestion to his teachers—who concurred—that it would be very useful to substitute the recitation and review of Rashi's commentary to the weekly Torah portion in place of the recitation of the Aramaic Targum, in fulfillment of the talmudic requirement to review the weekly Torah portion through *shenayim miqra ve-ʾeḥad targum.*[11]

In addition to his ongoing engagement with Rashi's commentary, R. Moses of Coucy offers a goodly number of simple exegetical interpretations of his own, which are similar in method and style to those of his Tosafist colleagues who shared this interest. Thus, for example, R. Moses writes that the rainbow was chosen by God to be the sign to man that He would never again bring about a flood to destroy the world, because the rainbow is produced by the union of fire and water. Just as the rainbow mediates and makes peace between these normally hostile elements, so too the rainbow will serve as a sign that there is peace in the world. This passage appears in *Minḥat Yehudah* with the note that it is found "in the commentary of R. Moses of Coucy" (*be-perush ha-Ram mi-Coucy*), suggesting that R. Judah b. Eliezer had before him a written composition of some sort.[12] When Abraham tells the king of Sodom that he will not take any gifts or assets from him, "save only [*bilʿadai*] what the young men have eaten and the share of the men who went with me" (Gen. 14:24), *Minḥat Yehudah*, citing R. Moses of Coucy, explains that the unusual word *bilʿadai* conveys the notion that Abraham is able to vouch only for himself; he had taken nothing from the king. He did not know, however, if the young men with him had taken anything.[13]

A number of R. Moses of Coucy's halakhic comments on the Torah are associated with his major halakhic work, *Sefer Mizvot Gadol* (*Semag*). For example, the question is raised, in connection with Genesis 18:9, as to how the angels could have asked Abraham, "Where is your wife Sarah?" in light of the *sugya* (*Qiddushin* 70b) that prohibits inquiring about a married

[11] See, e.g., my *Jewish Education and Society in the High Middle Ages* (Detroit, Mich., 1992), 82, and 182 (n. 12); and J. S. Penkower, "The Canonization of Rashi's Commentary on the Pentateuch," [Hebrew] in *Study and Knowledge in Jewish Thought*, ed. H. Kreisel (Beer Sheva, 2006), vol. 2, 140–44. For the (mistaken) possibility that R. Moses's father, R. Jacob, was a member of the family of Rashi, see A. Grossman, *Ḥakhmei Ẓarefat ha-Rishonim* (Jerusalem, 1995), 124 (n. 9).

[12] See *Minḥat Yehudah* (to Gen. 9:13), fol.9a (= Gellis, 1:267, sec. 2): את קשתי נתתי בענן. לכך ניתן סימן בקשת לפי שהוא עשוי מאש וממים ועושים שלום ביניהם כך הוא סימן שיש שלום בעולם. בפי' הר"ם. In *Perushei R. Ḥayyim Paltiʾel*, 24, a similar kind of interpretation is presented in the name of R. Jacob of Orleans, in response to an observation that "the rainbow is actually a sign of conflict and not of peace, as per the verse in Lamentations 2:4, 'He bent his bow [*keshet*] like an enemy.'" Cf. *Tosafot ha-Shalem*, ed. Gellis, 1:268, sec. 6.

[13] See *Minḥat Yehudah* (Genesis) fol. 12b. *Minḥat Yehudah* notes that this explanation is found explicitly in the commentary (or the *peshatim*) of R. Moses of Coucy (כך מפורש בפר"ם מקוצי), once again pointing to a written (commentary) text (of a *peshat* nature).

woman's well-being even in the presence of her husband. *Minḥat Yehudah* suggests that perhaps the situation with angels is different, since they do not have an evil inclination. The solution found in *Semag* is also presented: while the prohibition entails sending greetings to the woman, even through her husband, asking her husband about her welfare is permitted.[14]

On occasion, *Minḥat Yehudah* will present an interpretation given by R. Moses of Coucy in his Torah commentary which can be supplemented by an interpretive passage found in *Sefer Mizvot Gadol.* In Deuteronomy 2:28–30, Moses recounts that he had requested Siḥon, the king of the Amorites, to allow the Jewish people direct passage through his land, and to provide food and water for which he would be compensated, just as the children of Esau in *Seʿir* and the Moabites in *ʿAr* had done—a request Siḥon refused. As Rashi notes, the children of Esau did not allow the Jewish people to pass through their land, but they did sell them food and water for their journey. *Minḥat Yehudah* questions these assertions further, since the Torah indicates (Deut. 23:4–5) that Jewish women may not marry Amonite or Moabite men for three generations after their conversion to Judaism, because Amon and Moab did not provide food and water for the Jewish people. *Minḥat Yehudah* suggests that while this was the problem with respect to Amon, the restriction on Moabites stemmed only from the final clause in that verse in Deuteronomy 23:5, "and because they hired Bilʿam son of Beʿor from Aram Naharayim to curse you."

A question from R. Moses of Coucy is then presented, based on a talmudic passage (*Yevamot* 76b–77a) that preserves the purity of King David's

[14] See *Minḥat Yehudah* (Genesis), fol. 16a; *Semag, Mizvot lo taʿaseh* 126, fol. 43c; and cf. *Perushei R. Ḥayyim Paltiʾel*, 44. This resolution is also found in *Tosafot Qiddushin* (70b), s.v. *ʾein* (without attribution). R. Isaiah di Trani (Rid), in his *Nimmuqei Ḥumash*, ed. D. B. Chavel (Jerusalem, 1972), 18, proposes the same resolution as that found in *Tosafot Bava Meziʿa* 87a, s.v. *ʿal yedei baʿalah*: whereas asking a husband about his wife's welfare is also prohibited, asking him (only) about her whereabouts (as the angels did) is permitted (although Rid notes that this resolution does not comport with the *sugya* in *Qiddushin*). See also *Tosafot ha-Shalem*, ed. Gellis, vol. 2, 123, secs. 1–2. Rashi interprets Gen. 16:6, "and when Sarah dealt harshly with her [Hagar], she fled from before her," to mean that "Sarah made harsh demands on her." R. Elyaqim, the teacher of R. Judah b. Eliezer, raises the question as to how the righteous Sarah could engage in this type of behavior. Based on Rashi's comment two verses earlier ("and [Hagar] viewed her mistress with disdain"), the suggestion is made that Sarah's treatment of Hagar was justified and permitted. The prooftext for this is given (either by R. Elyaqim or by the author of *Minḥat Yehudah*) as *Sefer Semag*, in the matter of the prohibition of *lo tonu ʾet ʿamitekha*—that one may not speak antagonistically to his fellow). *Semag, lo taʿaseh* 171, fol. 61c, cites a midrash that if one speaks to another with disdain, the speaker is not considered to be a fellow of the second person, and he may in turn act antagonistically as well (דאיתא במדרש שאם הונה אותך אדם אתה רשאי להונותו שאינו קרוי עמיתך). An additional citation from *Sefer Mizvot Gadol* is found in *Minḥat Yehudah* (Exodus), fol. 31: ואמנם כבר הרגיש ר"מ מקוצי בקושי' זו שפי' בספרו וז"ל תניא איש פרט לקטן פחות מבן ט' שנים שהנבעלת פטורה שלפטור קטן אינו צריך שהרי אינו בר עונשין עכ"ל = *Semag, Mizvot lo taʿaseh* 103, fol. 35a; and see below, n. 17.

lineage even though he was descended from Ruth the Moabite. Although male Moabite converts were restricted from immediately marrying Jewish women, female converts such as Ruth could immediately marry Jewish men, since the issue of withholding food and water applied only to men, who made and implemented this decision, and not to women. However, this talmudic passage clearly assumes that the nation of Moab was also guilty of withholding food and water from the Jewish people, against the reading of Deuteronomy 23:5, which restricted their male converts only because they had hired Bilʿam.

The author of *Minḥat Yehudah* embarks on a fairly lengthy attempt to resolve this problem. Included in this resolution is what he "found in *Semag* in the name of R. Joseph of Chartres." In this passage, *Semag* presents the approach suggested earlier by *Minḥat Yehudah*, that Amon's malfeasance was in not providing food and water, while Moab was guilty of hiring Bilʿam. Moreover, since women were not involved in either of these endeavors, they are immediately permitted to marry Jewish men in accordance with a passage in the Yerushalmi. *Minḥat Yehudah* then suggests that the talmudic passage in *Yevamot* should be understood and interpreted in the same way. Moab was guilty only of hiring Bilʿam, while Amon's crime was in not providing food and water, and women were uninvolved in either of these decisions.[15]

On the basis of this passage in *Minḥat Yehudah*, R. Ḥayyim Yosef David Azulai (Ḥida, d. 1806) questions whether the R. Moses of Coucy found in *Minḥat Yehudah* is the same figure as the author of *Semag*, since the *Semag* passage ostensibly answers the question posed initially by R. Moses.[16] In fact, however, *Minḥat Yehudah* is simply bringing together a biblical comment by R. Moses (in connection with a talmudic interpretation) and a passage in *Semag*, in order to resolve his larger dilemma with regard to the verse in question, although this particular instance suggests that R. Moses offered his comments to the Torah prior to his completion of the *Sefer Miẓvot Gadol* (c. 1240), which was composed toward the end of his life.[17]

[15] See *Minḥat Yehudah* (Deut.), fol. 3b (מצאתי בסמ"ג בשם הר"ר יוסף מקרפנטרא"ס); in ms. Vatican [Urban 21], fol. 144r, the passage reads: ואמנם מצאתי בספר מצוות גדול בשם ה"ר יוסף מקשטרש, and see also ms. B.M. 190); and *Semag, Miẓvot lo taʿaseh*, 113–14 (Venice, 1547), fols. 39b–40a. See also *Sefer Miẓvot Gadol ha-Shalem*, ed. Machon Yerushalayim, vol. 2 (Jerusalem, 2003), 186–87: והטעם מפרש המקרא על דבר אשר לא קדמו אתכם בלכם ובמים וה"ר יוסף מקארטרש [מ"ק: והרב ר' יוסף מקרטש] היה אומר כי בעמון הוא טעם זה כי מתוך המקרא משמע כי מואבים קדמו וכו'.

[16] See *Shem ha-Gedolim* (Warsaw, 1876), *maʿarekhet ha-gedolim* (ר"מ מקוצי) fol. 51a (sec. 179).

[17] See also *Minḥat Yehudah* (Deut.), fol. 12a (= ms. JTS Lutzki 794, fol. 111v), on the prohibition of returning to Egypt (as reflected in Deut. 17:16). This passage includes a citation of *Semag, Miẓvot lo taʿaseh* 227 (fol. 68b), that concludes with the lenient position of R. Eliezer of Metz: אם לא נפרש כפי' ר' אליעזר ממיץ לא תוסיפון וגו' לא אסרה תורה אלא בדרך [זו] כלו' מארץ ישראל לארץ מצרים אבל משאר ארצות מותר. כך מצאתי בסמ"ג שיסד ר"מ מקוצי. Although ms. JTS Lutzki 794, fol. 111v,

Overall, R. Moses of Coucy's *peshatim* rarely cite his Tosafist predecessors or contemporary Ashkenazic rabbinic figures by name.[18] R. Moses's desire, however, to work with Rashi's comments is clear. When the third son of Leah is born, the Torah states, "Now this time my husband will be joined to me (ילוה אישי אלי) because I have borne him three sons; therefore [*'al ken*] his name was called Levi" (Gen. 29:34) Rashi understood Leah's remark to mean that, since Jacob's four wives, who were prophetesses according to *Midrash Tanḥuma*, knew that he would have twelve children all told, Jacob would now have no complaint with Leah, since she had fulfilled her childbearing responsibilities. R. Moses of Coucy questions this explanation, however, since if each of the wives would ultimately have three children, and Leah was just doing her share, why then would this birth have particularly drawn Jacob to Leah? R. Moses therefore suggests that with the birth of Levi, Jacob would literally be joined to Leah, since it would be difficult for her to take care of three children without Jacob's help. Two children could still be physically cared for with relative ease by Leah and by her maid. Using Rashi's comment as a starting point, R. Moses suggests a different interpretation, based not on the approach of the *Tanḥuma* but on the common reality of child-rearing and family dynamics.[19]

---

cites this only in the name of י"מ, on fol. 116r, it cites the position of *Semag* by name (*mizvat 'aseh* 140, fol. 202b), which disagrees with the comment of Rashi (Deut. 26:11), that a convert to Judaism brings the first fruits (*bikkurim*) but does not recite the accompanying formula.

[18] See the list compiled by H. Touitou, "*Minḥat Yehudah*," 99, in which barely a handful of Ashkenazic figures are listed, none of whom are cited more than twice. The lone reference to a comment by R. Yehudah *he-Ḥasid* appears on the phrase מבן עשרים שנה found in Lev. 27:3 (fol. 24b) and not in Numbers 32:11 (as recorded in Touitou, "*Minḥat Yehudah*," n. 131). As we shall see below (n. 97), *'Avi ha-'Ezri* as cited by R. Moses of Coucy refers to Ibn Ezra rather than to Rabiah. (Ibn Ezra is cited overall by *Minḥat Yehudah* with some frequency; see, e.g., below, nn. 29, 48.) The two references in *parashat Qoraḥ* to R. Moses's unnamed teacher (*rabbo*) may indeed be to R. Moses's main talmudic teacher, R. Judah Sirleon, as Touitou suggests, although R. Judah's own roster of Torah comments is hardly extensive (see above, chapter 2, n. 12), and his impact on R. Moses's commentary on the basis of these two comments is minimal in any case; cf. below, n. 65. The reference to ר' יוסף מקרפנטראס (Touitou, ibid., n. 135) is to a passage from R. Moses's *Sefer Mizvot Gadol* (see above, n. 15), where the more accurate reference is to to ר' יוסף מקרטרש. On R. Yosef of Chartres, cf. Urbach, *Ba'alei ha-Tosafot*, 1:145. In addition to the two references by R. Moses to comments by R. Berekhyah *ha-Naqdan* noted by Touitou ("*Minḥat Yehudah*," n. 133), ms. JTS Lutzki 791 includes another; see below, n. 88.

[19] See ms. JTS Lutzki 791, fol. 27v: הק' ר' משה מקוצי על פ"ה שפי' דד' נשים היו ומגיע לחלקה ג', שהרי נראה לו' תלוה אישי שאיני יכול לשאת רק ב' וצריך הוא לטפל עמי. עי"מ אני ושפחתי נטפל בב' וצריך בעלי לטפל בג'. In *Minḥat Yehudah* (Gen.), fol. 30a, R. Moses's basic exegesis is reproduced, without the connection to Rashi's commentary: הפעם ילוה אישי אלי כי ילדתי וגו'. כלומר איני יכולה לשאת עול רק משני בנים וא"כ עכשיו שילדתי שלשה בנים צריך שיטפל עמי בעלי. כך פי' ר"מ מקוצי. This is also the case in ms. Vatican (Urban) 21, fols. 35r–v: עשכיו בעלי יצטרך לטפל עמי כי איני יכולה להחזיק יותר מב' בנים. כפר"מ מקוצי. . . . ורשב"ם פי' בענין אחר וכו'. See also *Tosafot ha-Shalem*, ed. Gellis, 3:150, sec. 2; *Perushei R. Ḥayyim Palti'el*, ed. Lange, 90, which adds (anonymously from ms. Hamburg 40, and see *Tosafot ha-Shalem*, 3:150, sec. 5) that when the third son is born, the first son would surely be

Rashi's comment on the words *ʿal ken qara shemo Levi* (Gen. 29:34), following *Bereshit Rabbah*, is that "anyone about whom it is said *ʿal ken* was numerous in population, except for Levi, for the ark would annihilate them [*sheha-ʾaron hayah mekhaleh ʾotam*]." Rashi's observation is that the work of the Levites in carrying and caring for the ark, in which the slightest lack of respect or procedural misstep could result in the loss of life, is what kept the population of the Levites small. This interpretation can be questioned, however, because even prior to their assignment to carry the ark, the tribe of the Levi was the smallest of all. R. Moses of Coucy justifies Rashi's interpretation here on the basis of an interpretation put forward by Rashi at the beginning of the Book of Exodus. There Rashi notes that the Levites were not included in the suffering brought about by the back-breaking work decreed by the Egyptians. As such, they were not part of the Divine plan to increase the populations of those tribes that were being afflicted (Ex. 1:12). Thus the tribe of Levi was indeed small, even prior to their work with the ark. In this instance, R. Moses of Coucy supports Rashi's interpretation in Genesis by showing that it is fully consistent with another of Rashi's comments on the Book Exodus.[20]

Pharaoh tells Joseph (Gen. 47:6), "and if you know any able men (אנשי חיל) among them [your brothers], appoint them as managers of the livestock that belongs to me (ושמתם שרי מקנה על אשר לי)." Rashi interprets the phrase *ʾanshei ḥayyil* as "capable men, who are expert at their occupation of herding sheep (בקיאין באומנותן לרעות צאן)." R. Moses of Coucy notes that others interpret the phrase *ʾanshei ḥayyil* more literally, as an indicator of their abilities as brave fighting men. R. Moses initially objects to this interpretation, because it is unreasonable to suggest that livestock managers also need to be brave soldiers. At the same time, R. Moses also implicitly criticizes

old enough for his father to have to begin to teach him Torah and other religious observances and values, while Leah would deal with the two younger ones.

[20] See *Minḥat Yehudah* (Gen.), fol. 30a, and see also *Tosafot ha-Shalem*, ed. Gellis, 3:150, sec. 6. At the beginning of *parashat Va-Yigash* (*Minḥat Yehudah*, fol. 44a = *Tosafot ha-Shalem*, ed. Gellis, 4:201, sec. 1), a question from *Ḥizzequni* is raised in connection with Gen. 44:19 in which Judah asserts, "my master [Joseph] had asked his servants [the brothers], do you have a father or a brother?" In fact, however, the Torah does not record that Joseph had actually asked these questions. An answer is cited from *peshatei ha-Ra"m mi-Coucy*, that since Joseph had now accused the brothers of being spies, they had to account, in any case, for whether they had a father or brother. *Minḥat Yehudah* then presents an additional solution in the name of his teacher R. Elyaqim. (Although R. Moses lived well before Hezekiah b. Manoaḥ, it is not uncommon for *Minḥat Yehudah*, as a compilatory work, to present earlier authorities who provide answers to later questions; cf. H. Touitou, "*Minḥat Yehudah*," 5–9, 129–32.) Interestingly, *Minḥat Yehudah*, fols. 44a–b (and ms. JTS Lutzki 791), records a similar explanation in the name of Rabbenu (Jacob) Tam (of Orleans) to explain Joseph's claim in Gen. 44:21 that he had told the brothers something originally, which is not included in the text of the Torah. See *Tosafot ha-Shalem*, ed. Gellis, 4:204, sec. 7; and above, chapter 2, n. 154.

Rashi's comment, because of the Torah's assertion that "all shepherds are an abomination in Egypt" (Gen. 46:34)

These concerns lead R. Moses to suggest that the term שרי מקנה is derived from the root word קנאה, jealousy, since "the nature of brave fighting men is to be jealous of those who are as brave as they are." R. Moses's nuanced interpretation, which supports an approach not taken by Rashi, is that Pharaoh was asking Joseph to let him know if any of his brothers was as brave a fighter as Pharaoh, so that he could assign them as officers in his army, even though he was inherently jealous of their abilities as warriors. R. Moses also notes, however, that Rashi's interpretation was motivated by a desire to achieve the full contextual meaning of the verse, since he also interprets the phrase at the end of the verse, "over that which belongs to me" to mean "over my flocks." Although R. Moses prefers his own interpretation of the somewhat problematic phrase *ʾanshei ḥayyil*, an interpretation that parallels those of Rashbam, R. Yosef *Bekhor Shor*, and R. Yom Tov of Joigny, he acknowledges that Rashi's interpretation of this last phrase, *ʿal ʾasher li*, works well in terms of the larger context of the verse (*piresh Rashi ke-mashmaʿo*).[21]

As noted, however, R. Moses of Coucy will also put forward his own interpretations, without reference to Rashi's commentary. Jacob's blessing to the tribe of Naftali reads, "Naftali is a hind set off, who delivers beautiful sayings" (Gen. 49:21). Rashi, based on *Bereshit Rabbah*, identifies the content of this blessing with the valley of Ginossar in the portion of the tribe of Naftali, "which is as quick to ripen its fruits as the hind, which is quick at running." Without referring to Rashi at all, R. Moses of Coucy pursues a very different direction and dimension in his interpretation. "This verse hints that the prophetess Devorah, who would rule over Israel, will come from this tribe. It is for this reason that the hind [*ʾayalah*] in this verse is written in the feminine form. Similarly, the word *ʾishah* is formed by the first letters [*rashei tevot*] of the [second, third, and fourth] words [in this verse], *ʾayalah sheluḥah ha-noten*." In this instance, R. Moses considers *remez* and *rashei tevot*

21 See *Minḥat Yehudah* (Gen.), fol. 47a. *Minḥat Yehudah* then cites his mentor R. Elyaqim, who attempts to interpret the last part of the verse in context, while following the approach of R. Moses of Coucy. See also *Perushei R. Ḥayyim Paltiʾel ʿal ha-Torah*, ed. Lange, 150. The version of R. Moses's comment found in ms. JTS Lutzki 794, fol. 13r (in which the questions on Rashi are asked by R. Moses but the author of the answer is not specifically identified), adds a rather remarkable scriptural prooftext that links the words *miqneh* and *kinʾah*: סמל הקנאה המקנה (Ezek. 8:3). Cf. *Tosafot ha-Shalem*, ed. Gellis, 4:253; *Rashbam's Commentary on Genesis*, ed. M. Lockshin (Lewiston, N.Y., 1989), 328–29; *Perushei R. Yosef Bekhor Shor ʿal ha-Torah*, ed. Nevo, 84; and above, chapter 2, nn. 214–16, for R. Yom Tov of Joigny. Ms. JTS Lutzki 794 contains material from R. Moses of Coucy, R. Yosef *Bekhor Shor*, and R. Judah *he-Ḥasid*. See, e.g., *Tosafot ha-Shalem*, ed. Gellis, vol. 1 (introduction), 32, and below.

to be the keys to the interpretation of the verse.[22] The same *rashei tevot* interpretation is found in the so-called *Perush ha-Roqeaḥ ʿal ha-Torah*, composed by a student of either R. Judah *he-Ḥasid* or R. Eleazar of Worms, which adds additional *gematriʾot* in support.[23]

R. Moses notes a linguistic inconsistency in the verse "who made man's mouth, or who makes a man dumb or deaf or seeing or blind" (Ex. 4:11). The verse presents two of man's major faculties and their absence, one who speaks versus one who is dumb, and one who sees (*piqeaḥ*) versus one who is blind. This verse, however, omits one who hears, including only one who is deaf. In his *peshatim*, R. Moses explains that the term *piqeaḥ* represents the opposite states of both blindness and deafness. Support for his contention is drawn from two verses in Isaiah 42: verse 20, in which a form of *piqeaḥ* is used in connection with the ears, and verse 7, in which a form of this word is used in connection with the eyes.[24] This approach, including the prooftexts from Isaiah 42, is reproduced, without attribution, by *Ḥizzequni*.[25]

[22] See *Minḥat Yehudah* (Gen.), fols. 50b–51a, ending with the phrase כך מפורש בפשטי הר"מ מקוצי. This phrase strongly suggests once again that R. Moses's interpretations were produced or collected in written form. See also *Tosafot ha-Shalem*, ed. Gellis, 5:69–70. Other texts, including the Cambridge and Moscow manuscripts that contain R. Judah *he-Ḥasid*'s Torah commentary (see *Perushei ha-Torah le-R. Yehudah he-Ḥasid*, ed. Lange, 67), suggest that Devorah made special use of the soldiers of Naftali (and Zevulun) because they were fleet of foot (as per Judges 4:6). Indeed, this is essentially how Rashbam interprets the blessing given to Naftali, that this tribe will have warriors who are fleet-footed like hinds (based on 1 Chronicles 12:9, and without any reference to Devorah); and see also R. Yosef *Bekhor Shor* in his second interpretation (ed. Nevo, 90–91). *Bekhor Shor*'s first interpretation (and that of *Sefer ha-Gan*, ed. Orlian, 207) is the same as that of Rashi.

[23] See *Perush ha-Roqeaḥ ʿal ha-Torah*, ed. J. Klugmann, vol. 1 (Bnei Brak, 1978), 319. On the author of this commentary, see above, chapter 2, n. 2. This multifaceted commentary also records (1:313) the more conventional "fleet-footed" interpretation (קל ברגליו במלחמה כאילה; see the above note). *Paʿaneaḥ Raza*, 209, sees the *rashei tevot* of *ʾishah* as an indication that Naftali had many daughters. The word *ʾayalah* is seen as an inference for the messianic era, which will arrive speedily.

[24] See *Minḥat Yehudah* (Exodus), fol 5a. This is the lone example of *peshat* from R. Moses of Coucy noted by Poznanski (above, n. 7). Although this same comment is found in ms. Hamburg 40 in the name of Maharam (see *Perushei R. Ḥayyim Paltiʾel*, 184–85), there is no reason to doubt its association with R. Moses of Coucy, since it is cited by *Minḥat Yehudah* from his written treatise (מפרש בפשטי ר"מ מקוצי). The acronym *Maharam* may simply refer here to מורנו הרב משה [מקוצי]. Moreover, there is no evidence for its association with R. Meir of Rothenburg, although it is of course possible that he or someone else adopted this interpretation and shared it with others without attribution. Cf. *Perushei R. Ḥayyim Paltiʾel*, ed. Lange, 275. To be sure, *Minḥat Yehudah* was roughly contemporaneous with the commentary of R. Ḥayyim Palti'el (which was recorded by one of his students), and there is a measure of difficulty in identifying the figures behind the *rashei tevot* ר"ם/מהר"ם, which appear (with some frequency) in *Perushei R. Ḥayyim Paltiʾel*. See Lange's introduction, 10–11, and idem, "Le-Zehuto shel R. Ḥayyim Palti'el," *ʿAlei Sefer* 8 (1980), 140–46.

[25] Cf. Sara Japhet, "Ḥizkuni's Commentary on the Pentateuch—Its Genre and Purpose," [Hebrew], in *Rabbi Mordekhai Breuer Festschrift*, ed. M. Bar Asher et al. (Jerusalem, 1992), vol. 1, 92.

In Exodus 10:4, Moses and Aaron come before Pharaoh and announce in the name of God that if Pharaoh does not release the Jews, the plague of locusts would begin on the morrow. Both *Hadar Zeqenim* and *Minḥat Yehudah* note that there was never any discussion recorded in the Torah between God and Moses about bringing on this plague at this point. The answer given by these compilations, in the name of R. Yosef *Bekhor Shor*, is that God did actually command Moses to initiate this plague, as He did with all the others. For the sake of brevity, however (*le-qaẓer ha-devarim*), this instruction is not mentioned in the Torah, in order to include instead what Pharaoh's aides told him, "Do you not know yet that Egypt is destroyed?" (Ex. 10:7). This also explains Pharaoh's response to Moses and Aaron, "Let the Lord be so with you" (Ex. 10:10), "because the way of Scripture is to limit its words."[26]

Minḥat Yehudah, however, first presents R. Moses of Coucy's explanation for this seeming omission, as cited from פשטי הר"ם מקוצי, that the plague of hail did not destroy all of the crops (Ex. 9:31–32), since Pharaoh had expressed a degree of resignation at that time before returning to his intransigence. Therefore, Moses now tells Pharaoh that "if you will not release my people because you saw that the plague of hail left some of your crops intact, God will bring a plague tomorrow [i.e., the locusts] that will spare nothing." This is the meaning of the verse, "and [the locusts] ate every plant

[26] See *Hadar Zeqenim*, fol. 2b, and *Minḥat Yehudah* (Ex.), fol. 10a. According to *Minḥat Yehudah* (fol. 10b), this principle also explains Moses's later statement, "This is what God had spoken, I sanctify Myself through those nearest to Me" (Lev. 10:3), even though we do not have a record of God actually saying this to Moses. In the version of *Bekhor Shor*'s complete Torah commentary published from ms. Munich 52 (ed. Nevo, 112, to Ex. 10:2), R. Yosef simply presents an axiom that he heard from the Spanish exegete R. Ovadyah to explain the absence of God's description of the plague here. There are many prophecies that the prophets revealed, without indicating where (or when) God transmitted these prophecies to them. The same is true, for example, with respect to Moses and the manna (see Ex. 16:16, 23, 32). See also *Tosafot ha-Shalem*, ed. Gellis, 7:7, secs. 3–4. Two manuscripts attribute an interpretation to Rashbam (which is not found in Rashbam's extant Torah commentary), that the command to bring the three final plagues is included in the phrase "and the signs that I placed upon them" in Ex. 10:2. *Moshav Zeqenim*, 124, attributes to הר"מ the question that Rashbam raised in connection with the differences between Ex. 11:5 and Ex. 12:29. In warning about the plague of the firstborn, the firstborn of the maidservants (who would be killed) are described as being located "behind the grindstones," while the firstborn of the "captives" who were killed had been located among the pits (*be-beit ha-bor*). Rashbam's resolution is that these two groups are precisely the same; the children of the maidservants, who worked at the grindstone, were kept in these pits (and they were killed there). The very similar resolution found in *Moshav Zeqenim* is that by day, when the warning about the plague was enunciated, these children were located at the grindstone. At night, when the decree was carried out, they were in the pits (where they were lodged in order to prevent their escape). In ms. B.M. 190, this interpretation is presented (= כ"נ כן נמצא) from the *peshatim* of R"M *ha-darshan* (בפשטי הר"מ הדרשן). I thank Dr. Itamar Kislev for this reference. Cf. *Minḥat Yehudah* (Ex.), fol. 11b.

of the land and all the fruits of the tree that the hail had left" (Ex. 10:15). This verse clearly suggests that the plague of locusts was a more severe continuation of the plague of hail. While *Bekhor Shor* explains the lacuna here through a larger axiom of biblical style, R. Moses offers a narrower interpretation that fits especially well within the biblical context.

This comment and the prior one by R. Moses are fundamentally *peshat*-oriented interpretations. At the same time, given his talmudic background and his fealty to Rashi's commentary, it is not surprising that R. Moses of Coucy is also quite interested in presenting what might be characterized as *'aggadah ha-meyashevet divrei miqra.* During the plague of the firstborn, the Jewish people were completely protected by God. The Torah emphasizes this by indicating that at that time, "not even a dog shall move its tongue, against neither man nor beast" (Ex. 11:7). Rashbam, Ibn Ezra, and *Bekhor Shor* interpret this imagery to mean that even as the angel of death was actively killing the Egyptian firstborn, the Jews experienced no harm whatsoever, not even from the barking of a dangerous dog.[27] R. Moses of Coucy also notes that the angel of death was operating actively at this time since "there was no [Egyptian] house where there was not a death" (Ex. 12:30). Nonetheless, R. Moses turns to a talmudic interpretation to explain the scriptural imagery. The Talmud maintains (*Bava Qamma* 60b) that when the angel of death comes to a city, the dogs instinctively bark, מלאך המות בא לעיר כלבים צועקים. In the case of the plague of the firstborn, however, even this most common reaction did not occur, so as not to disturb the Jews. "This is what is written (כך כתיב) in the *peshatei ha-Ra"m mi-Coucy.*"[28]

[27] See *Rashbam's Commentary on Exodus: An Annotated Translation*, ed. M. Lockshin (Atlanta, 1997), 101, and *Perushei Bekhor Shor*, ed. Nevo, 114. See also *Ḥizzequni*, who asserts that dogs tend to bark particularly after midnight.

[28] See *Minḥat Yehudah* (Ex.), fols. 11b–12a. Note yet again the indication of R. Moses's written corpus. *Minḥat Yehudah* then presents an approach taken by Rabbenu Menaḥem מגוע, and a third attributed simply to *morenu.* A more precise version of this entire passage is found in ms. JTS Lutzki 791, fol. 64r–v: לא יחרץ כלב לשונו. כלו' אע"פ שמלאך המות בא לעיר כדכתי' כי אין בית אשר אין שם מת ואמ' בפ' הכונס מלאך המות בעיר כלבים צועקים אפי' הכי לא חרץ. כ"פ הר"מ הדרשן. רבי' מנחם מגוייני פי' אע"פ דדרכן של כלבים לצעוק בלילה לא חרצו. ואנשי מצרים אע"פ שדרכן לישון בלילה צעקו כדכתי' ותהי צעקה גדולה במצרים. ורבי' בנימין מקנוורביל פי' אע"פ שדרכן לנבוח בלילה כשרואין בני אדם ומקל בידם ובישראל כתי' ומקלכם בידכם [לא נבחו בהם]. As noted by Poznanski (above, n. 7), R. Moses of Coucy is typically referred to in this manuscript as R. Mosheh *ha-Darshan*. The second view is that of R. Menaḥem of Joigny (the spelling of *Joigny* in *Minḥat Yehudah* is defective; in the manuscript, it is an unusual, exaggerated transliteration of the French). The third view is that of R. Benjamin of Canterbury. See *Tosafot ha-Shalem*, ed. Gellis, 7:34, sec. 13, which cites this passage from ms. B.M. 190. Here, the locations of R. Menaḥem of Joigny (יואני) and R. Benjamin of Canterbury (קנטבורייא) are spelled in the more usual way (even as the details of the interpretations are thinner, and R. Moses's comment is attributed to פשטי הר"ם דרשן). As noted above (chapter 2, nn. 10, 181), R. Menaḥem of Joigny's biblical exegesis is occasionally cited (see also *Tosafot ha-Shalem*, ed. Gellis 7:182, sec. 7, and 263–64, sec. 9, which is fundamentally a *pesaq* by R. Menaḥem), although his name is sometimes interchanged with that of R. Yom

Minḥat Yehudah notes that the specifics in the final commandments of *lo taḥmod* are organized differently in the earlier and later versions of the Ten Commandments. In the first set of commandments (Ex. 20:13), coveting a neighbor's house is listed first, followed by his wife, his servants, his animals, and all that he has. This order reflects the typical course of life. A home is purchased first, followed by marriage, the acquisition of servants, and then livestock. In the commandments in *parashat Va-Etḥanan* (Deut. 5:17), however, the wife is mentioned first, followed by the house, and then the servants. This follows the order of their importance, or the extent to which they are typically desired. The passage in *Minḥat Yehudah* notes that this distinction comes from the commentary of Ibn Ezra.[29]

Minḥat Yehudah then cites R. Moses of Coucy, who notes another difference between the two versions. The second set includes fields, while the first version does not.[30] R. Moses explains this omission because at the point where the first version appeared in the Book of Exodus, the Jewish people did not yet have any fields in their possession, since they were not close to entering the land of Israel. When the second set of commandments was recorded in the Book of Deuteronomy, however, the Jewish people were very close to entering the land of Israel where they would have fields, and so the fields were included in the commandments at that point. This explanation is quite reminiscent of the "realia" explanation offered by R. Judah *he-Ḥasid*, who lived in the generation prior to R. Moses of Coucy, with respect to the different listings of nonkosher birds in Leviticus and Deuteronomy.[31]

To this point, we have reviewed pieces of R. Moses of Coucy's exegesis to narrative portions of the Torah. In *parashat Mishpatim*, R. Moses continues

---

Tov, the more prolific biblical commentator from Joigny. R. Benjamin of Canterbury, whom Urbach identifies also as R. Benjamin of Cambridge, studied in Rabbenu Tam's *beit midrash*, and was also involved in the study of grammar and vocalization; see Urbach, *Baʿalei ha-Tosafot*, 1:109–10; 2:494, 498, 500, and cf. *The Jewish Communities of Medieval England: Collected Essays of R. B. Dobson*, ed. H. Birkett (York, 2011), 108. (My thanks to Pinchas Roth for this reference.) R. Benjamin's interpretation also appears (in his name) in ms. Vatican 21; see *Tosafot ha-Shalem*, ed. Gellis, 7:43, sec. 11. *Ḥizzequni* to Ex. 11:7 presents an amalgam of the interpretations attributed to R. Menaḥem and R. Benjamin (without any names, as was his wont). Of the three, which all employ a kind of *derekh ʾerez* approach (on the nature of how dogs react), only that of R. Moses of Coucy relies fundamentally on a talmudic axiom. *Paʿaneaḥ Raza*, 242, has a less elaborate version of this approach, presented in the name of R. Ḥayyim (Paltiʾel) in the name of R. Samuel. Cf. *Tosafot ha-Shalem*, ed. Gellis, 7:41, sec. 2, and *Moshav Zeqenim*, 125.

29 See *Minḥat Yehudah* (Ex.), fol. 26a. Ibn Ezra's interpretation is found at the end of his long commentary to Ex. 20:1. See also Ramban to Ex. 20:13; Rambam, *Mishneh Torah, Hilkhot Deʿot*, 5:11; and *Tosafot ha-Shalem*, ed. Gellis, 8:117, sec. 1, and 8:120, sec. 10.

30 This accords with Ibn Ezra's approach to the second set of commandments, since the fields are included after one's wife and home, but before the acquisition of servants.

31 See *Perushei R. Yehudah he-Ḥasid ʿal ha-Torah*, ed. Lange, 203 (to Deut. 14:12); *Tosafot ha-Shalem*, ed. Gellis, 8:120, sec. 10; and above, chapter 3, nn. 92–93.

to work both with Rashi's commentary and with the text of the Torah itself. In the first verse (Ex. 21:1), "And these are the laws that you shall place before them," Rashi, following the Talmud in tractate *Gittin*, interprets that "before them" means that it is forbidden to bring cases before non-Jewish courts and judges even if they are familiar with the tenets of Jewish monetary law. The question is raised as to why Rashi needed to derive this from a verse of the Torah, since even a convert to Judaism is unfit to serve as a judge according to the Talmud in tractate *Qiddushin.* R. Moses of Coucy answers that a convert is unfit to serve as a judge only in situations where Jews from birth who are competent to serve as judges are present. Where no such competent Jews are present, however, a competent convert may serve. Indeed, Shemaʿayah and Avtalyon were converts who served as the leading judges of Israel in their day, since no other Jew was as important (*ḥashuv kemotam*, i.e., as knowledgeable) as they were.[32]

In the next verse, Rashi wishes to establish whether the term *ʿeved ʿivri* connotes a slave who is fully Jewish, an *ʿeved ʿivri* who goes free after six years of work, or the slave of a Jewish person, meaning an *ʿeved kenaʿani*, who typically does not go free but who may also go free after six years if he were sold to another Jewish owner. Based on a parallel section in Deuteronomy 15, where the slave is characterized as "your brother the Hebrew," Rashi concludes, following the *Mekhilta*, that the Torah speaks here of a Jew who became a slave. Indeed, how could Rashi have considered the possibility that the portion here speaks of an *ʿeved kenaʿani*? According to the end of this section (Ex. 21:6), this same slave may become manumitted and work until the jubilee year. Given the well-known aphorism of Rabban Yoḥanan b. Zakkai cited by Rashi to this verse, that the ear of such a slave is pierced to show the shortcomings of "the ear that heard at Mount Sinai the verse for the children of Israel are slaves only to Me," it is clear that only a full Jew, an *ʿeved ʿivri*, can be included in the process of manumission. R. Moses of Coucy suggests that, nonetheless, one might have thought than an *ʿeved kenaʿani* can be manumitted as well, since the *ʿeved kenaʿani* is less important than an *ʿeved ʿivri.*[33]

In describing the obligations of a watchman, the Torah states that if a wild animal mauls the animal that a watchman is watching, יביאהו עד, literally, the watchman should bring the carcass of the dead animal as evidence

[32] See *Minḥat Yehudah* (Ex.), fol. 27a, and *Tosafot ha-Shalem*, ed. Gellis, 8:143, sec. 31. The passage ends with [כך פירש ר' משה מקוצי=] כפר"ם.

[33] See *Minḥat Yehudah* (Ex.), fols. 27a–b (= Gellis, 8:145, sec. 2): פרש"י . . . וקשיא היכי ס"ד דעבד כנעני יהא נרצע . . . וי"ל דס"ד שהיה נרצע אפילו שלא שמע משום דזיל טפי מעבד עברי. כפר"ם. In ms. JTS Lutzki 791, fol. 82v, the passage is attributed to הר"ם הדרשן. See above, nn. 7, 28.

(Ex. 22:12). Rashi, however, explains this phrase to mean that the watchman should bring witnesses that the animal was mauled by accident (*be-'ones*), that is, that there was no reasonable way for the watchman to have prevented this from happening, and the watchman is then exempt from paying for the dead animal. This interpretation would seem to be superfluous, however, since a few verses earlier (Ex. 22:9), the Torah had said that if the animal in the watchman's charge dies or is hurt or is driven away by thieves (נשבר או נשבה), meaning that if an accident occurs which the watchman could not normally have prevented, the watchman is exempt from having to pay, provided that he takes an oath that he did not put his own hand to his neighbor's goods. R. Moses of Coucy explains that the later verse, which speaks of the need to bring witnesses, teaches that where there are witnesses, the watchman *must* bring them. The Torah accepts and believes a watchman's oath and frees him from payment only on the basis where there are no witnesses. R. Moses notes that this is also the implication of the Talmud in *Bava Mezi'a* (83a).[34]

The Torah speaks in *parashat Mishpatim* about not taking advantage of orphans and widows: "If they cry out to God against such abuse, He will surely hear their cry" (= כי אם צעוק יצעק אלי שמוע אשמע צעקתו; Ex. 22:22). Similarly, the Torah cautions that a lender must return at nightfall the covering that was received as a pledge from a poor borrower who has no other such covering. Here too, the Torah states, using the same terms as before, that if the poor man's night garment is not returned, and he cries out to God, "I will surely hear his cry" (Ex. 22:26). In this instance, however, the Torah adds a phrase: "I will surely hear his cry, because I am gracious" (כי חנון אני). R. Moses of Coucy explains the difference between these two situations. In the case of the poor borrower, God should not intervene according to the letter of the law, because a lender is entitled to take a pledge that by law remains with him, until the loan is repaid. Nonetheless, God states that He will hear the poor borrower's cry, "because I am gracious," and He will therefore supralegally act to protect him (*lifnim mi-shurat ha-din*). In the case of the widow and the orphan, however, God does not have to summon his graciousness in order to intervene. Here, the Almighty must hear their cries about the abuse against them and intervene according to the letter of the law, since taking advantage of them is inherently prohibited. This

[34] See *Minhat Yehudah* (Ex.), fols. 36b–37 (= *Tosafot ha-Shalem*, ed. Gellis, 8:276, sec. 3); and ms. JTS Lutzki 794, fol. 29v. In this instance as well, the comment is attributed at the end, as in the prior two pieces from *parashat Mishpatim* (and the piece in *parashat Yitro* on the Ten Commandments), to כפר"ם מקוצי rather than to פשטי הר"ם מקוצי, suggesting perhaps that these were originally halakhic or talmudic interpretations by R. Moses, which may not have been developed or presented separately from his more exegetical *peshatim*.

precise distinction, in almost identical terms, is made by both Rashbam and R. Yosef *Bekhor Shor* to Exodus 22:26.[35]

In the last section of the Book of Exodus, R. Moses amplifies a comment of Rashi on the features of the poles that ran along the ark,[36] as well as a halakhic comment related to the sabbatical year.[37] He also offers an interesting interpretation of Exodus 33:5, which followed the sin of the golden calf: "now take off your ornaments (עדיך) from upon you." Rashi, following the Talmud in tractate *Shabbat*, suggests that these ornaments were the crowns that had been given to the Jewish people at Mount Sinai when they uttered "*naʿaseh ve-nishma.*" Rashbam and Ibn Ezra, followed by *Bekhor Shor* and Ramban, understood these ornaments to be the personal jewelry that they had worn for the special occasion of receiving the Torah.[38] This jewelry now had to be removed, however, as a sign of mourning and regret.

R. Moses of Coucy, perhaps mediating between the interpretation of Rashi, that these were the crowns that had been bestowed from heaven, and the understanding of the group of commentators, that these were personal items, suggests that the ornaments being referred to were in fact the blood of the covenant that had been sprinkled on their clothing by Moses at the time of the giving of the Torah, the *sefer ha-berit* (Ex. 24:6–8). This blood had originally indicated that the Jews were prepared to keep the entire Torah, and so the clothing on which it was found now needed to be removed. Indeed, some wise people had already removed these articles on their own

[35] See *Minḥat Yehudah* (Ex.), fols. 37a–b, כך פי' ר"מ מקוצי, and cf. *Rashbam's Commentary on Exodus*, ed. Lockshin, 269–70, and *Perushei R. Yosef Bekhor Shor*, ed. Nevo, 150. This again suggests (cf. above, n. 21) that R. Moses was unaware of Rashbam's commentary (and perhaps *Bekhor Shor*'s commentary as well), although *Semag* prominently cites the comment of Rashbam to Deut. 20:19 in identifying the types of trees that may not be cut down during a military siege. See *Semag, Mizvot lo-taʿaseh*, #229, and cf. Eleazar Touitou, *Ha-Peshatot ha-Mithadshim be-khol Yom: ʿIyyunim be-Perusho shel Rashbam la-Torah* (Jerusalem, 2003), 75 (n. 9), 174. See also the gloss to *Tosafot Rosh ha-Shanah* 7b, s.v. *shalosh*. *Bekhor Shor*, ed. Nevo, 150, adds a reference to Eccl. 10:2 (which states, in positive terms, that if the lender does return the garment in the evening, the borrower will bless him and he will be considered righteous), which is not mentioned by either Rashbam or R. Moses of Coucy. Cf. *Perushei R. Ḥayyim Palti'el*, ed. Lange, 295; *Nimmuqei Ḥumash le-Rabbenu Yeshayah*, ed. Chavel, 47–48; ms. Moscow 303, fol. 79v (= ms. Breslau 102, fol. 67r); and *Tosafot ha-Shalem*, ed. Gellis, 8:301–2, sec. 4.

[36] See *Minḥat Yehudah* (Ex.), fol. 39b, and *'Imrei Noʿam* (Jerusalem, 1970), 64 (= *Tosafot ha-Shalem*, Gellis, vol. 9, p. 41), ור"מ מקוצי פי'. Cf. *Tosafot Yoma* 72b, s.v. *di-khtiv*, and *Nimmuqei Ḥumash le-Rabbenu Yeshayah*, ed. Chavel, 48.

[37] *Minḥat Yehudah* (Ex.), fol. 48a, כ"פ ר"מ מקוצי.

[38] See *Rashbam's Commentary on Exodus*, ed. Lockshin, 405, and *Perushei R. Yosef Bekhor Shor*, ed. Nevo, 172.

once the sin of the golden calf occurred (Ex. 33:4). Now, God commanded that all the people should do so.[39]

In Exodus 39:32, the Torah states that "the work of the tabernacle of the tent of meeting was completed." The word for completion used by the Torah is ותכל. R. Moses of Coucy noticed, however, that with respect to the completion of Solomon's Temple, the verse uses the word *va-tishlam* (ותשלם כל המלאכה, 1 Kings 7:51). R. Moses explains, according to the *Midrash Yelamdenu*, that when the *mishkan* was completed in the month of Nissan, the month of Tishrei was upset that no such completion had occurred in it. The Almighty promised that Tishrei would experience a similar completion. When Solomon's Temple was indeed completed in Tishrei, the word *va-tishlam*, which also connotes a form of compensation, was specifically used to signify that the Almighty had thereby fulfilled His vow.[40] In this instance, R. Moses's sharp observation leads to a *peshat* question, even though his solution is distinctly midrashic.

R. Moses continues his close exegetical comments on the Book of Leviticus. He notes that the Torah does not specify that a burnt offering brought from goats or sheep must be flayed (Lev. 1, 10–11), since this requirement had already been mentioned with regard to a burnt offering brought from herds of cattle (Lev. 1:6). At the same time, however, the Torah specifies that the goats or sheep being offered must be cut into pieces (Lev. 1:12), even though this requirement had also been mentioned for cattle, in the very same verse that required flaying. R. Moses explains that had the Torah not specified that a burnt offering from these animals must also be cut into

39 *Minḥat Yehudah* (Ex.), fol. 46a (= ms. Vatican [Urban] 21, fol. 99v): הורד עדיך מעליך. ר"מ מקוצי פירש שהעדי הוא דם הברית שהיה על בגדיהם, דומה כי קיימו כל המצוות והתורה. והחכמים בהם הורידו מעצמם כשחטאו בעגל כמו שנא' ולא שתו איש עדיו עליו. ועכשיו צוה המקום לכולם שיורידוהו לפי שעברו על אנכי ולא יהיה לך. Cf. *Tosafot ha-Shalem*, ed. Gellis, 10:94–95, sec. 5. This interpretation is also found in *ʾImrei Noʿam*, 71–72 (*ve-Rabbenu Mosheh mi-Coucy piresh*), and in *Paʿaneaḥ Raza*, 305, without attribution.

40 See ms. JTS Lutski 791, fols. 100v–101r: בפי' הר"ם איתא בתכלית המשכן כתי' ותכל ובתכלית המקדש כתי' ותשלם מפ' בילמדינו שמלאכת המשכן נסתיימה באחד בניסן והיה חדש תשרי מתרעם שלא נעשה בו שום דבר והבטיחו הב"ה שישלימו בו בו מלאכת המקדש וזהו ותשלם ששילם הב"ה נדרו. See also *ʾImrei Noʿam*, 76, cited in *Tosafot ha-Shalem*, ed. Gellis, 10:247, sec. 7. In *Minḥat Yehudah* (Ex.), fol. 50a, this interpretation is found in briefer form (and without the reference to *Midrash Yelamdenu*) and concludes (as in the *ʾImrei Noʿam* version), והיינו ותשלם ששלם בנדרו. כך מצאתי בפשטי ר' משה מקוצי. Cf. the prior passage in ms. Lutski 791, fol. 100v (Ex. 40:31): ורחצו ממנו משה ואהרן ובניו. פ"ה יום שמיני למילואים הושוו כולם לכהונה. ובפ"ב דזבחים פי' רש"י . . . שלא שהיה משה כהן ביום שמיני למילואים. ופלגותא דתנאי בזב־חים פרק טבול יום אם כהן היה. בפי' הר"ם. This comment appears in *Minḥat Yehudah* (Ex.), fol. 50b, without the attribution to ר"ם (and see also *Moshav Zeqenim*, 226–27), although it is likely that this comment, which seeks to rectify a seeming contradiction between Rashi in his Torah commentary and in his talmudic commentary, was by R. Moses of Coucy as well. Cf. Poznanski, *Mavo*, XCIII, and Lange, *Perushei R. Ḥayyim Paltiʾel* (above, n. 24).

pieces, one might have thought that this requirement did not apply here, since sheep and goats have smaller bodies and fewer limbs than cattle.[41]

R. Moses engages Rashi's comment, following *Sifra* to Leviticus 11:11 ("and they shall be abominable to you"), that a prohibited species or food remains so even in a mixture, if it imparts flavor (*noten ta'am*). This rule, however, appears to be derived from a verse in Numbers (6:3), dealing with the laws pertaining to a *nazir* who consumes an admixture of grape products. R. Moses suggests that it is perhaps necessary for the derivation from Leviticus 11:11 as well, since there is also an issue of how much actual volume of the prohibited species must still be present.[42] Always the halakhist, R. Moses is deeply interested in this aspect of biblical interpretation, as was Rashi.

Similarly, R. Moses discusses the midrashic passage in *Va-Yiqra Rabbah* in the name of R. Simlai that forms the basis of Rashi's comment to the beginning of *parashat Tazri'a* (Lev. 12:2, *'ishah ki tazri'a*). Since the creation of man occurred after all the animals and fowl were created, the regulations that apply to man (*torato*) concerning the purity of his body are presented in the Book of Leviticus after the teachings concerning the purity and *kashrut* of the animal kingdom, which are found earlier in *parashat Shemini.* The question may be raised, however, that if this axiom is so, the presentation of the laws of purity in *parashat Tazri'a* itself should have begun with those that are applicable to men rather than those that pertain to women, since man was created first. R. Moses responds that once the pure and impure species within the animal kingdom have been identified, and the discussion of the purity of man now begins, it is appropriate to start with the status of childbirth (*'ishah ki tazri'a*), since this marks the beginning of man's existence.[43]

Rashi comments, following *Sifra*, that when the leper is sent to sit "outside the camp" (Lev. 13:46), this means that his place is outside all three camps: the

[41] *Minḥat Yehudah* (Leviticus), fol. 3a: לפי שעולת הצאן אין איברים כל כך כמו עולת הבקר. הילכך אם לא נאמר בו נתוח היית אומר שאינה צריכה נתוח. כך פי' ר"מ מקוצי.

[42] *Minḥat Yehudah* (Lev.), fol. 9a, and *Tosafot ha-Shalem*, ed. Gellis, vol. 12 (Jerusalem, 2009), 112, sec. 1 (from ms. B.M. 243). The passage concludes כך פירש הר"ר משה מקוצי, although just prior to this, the name מהר"ר אהרן is mentioned. This perhaps suggests that R. Moses might have had access to *Sefer ha-Gan*, although no such comment appears there on this verse; see *Sefer ha-Gan*, ed. Orlian, 274. See also *Tosafot ha-Shalem*, 12:288–89, sec. 6–7, for another comment from *peshatei ha-Ram* (to Lev. 14:46), found in ms. B.M. 243.

[43] *Minḥat Yehudah* (Lev.), fol. 10b: ור"מ מקוצי פי' וז"ל [= וזה לשונו] וכו', and see *'Imrei No'am*, 98, and *Tosafot ha-Shalem*, ed. Gellis, 12:162, sec. 12 (on the basis of ms. Vatican 21). The prior, unattributed answer in *Minḥat Yehudah* suggests that since most women give birth but relatively few men become lepers (the next topic in the portion), it is appropriate to begin with the phenomenon that is more common. R. Moses of Coucy is cited as offering another interpretation ([עוד פי' רמ"מ [= עוד פירש ר' משה מקוצי), following a passage in *Vayiqra Rabbah* to *Meẓora*, sec. 15) related to the content and structure of the portion of *Meẓora*. The juxtaposition of the laws of leprosy to the laws of *niddah* teaches that one who has relations with his wife when she is a *niddah* will have children who contract leprosy.

camp of the *Shekhinah*, the camp of the Levites, and the general camp of the people. R. Moses wonders how it is possible to consider a person "sent out" of the camp of the *Shekhinah*, since a person cannot enter this camp in any case. He therefore suggests that *maḥaneh Shekhinah* connotes the courtyard of the *mishkan*, the עזרה, where any properly purified person could go to offer his Passover sacrifice. R. Moses adds that the talmudic injunction that no one may occupy the עזרה except Davidic kings (*Yoma* 71a) means that only they are permitted to remain in that area for a lengthy period of time.[44]

The Torah introduces the type of leprosy that can appear in houses with the phrase, "When you will enter the land of Canaan ... I will put the plague of leprosy in the house of the land of your possession" (Lev. 14:34). The condition of being in the land of Israel, however, is not stated with respect to the leprosies that affected a person's body or clothing. R. Moses of Coucy explains this distinction based on the physical situation of the Jewish people. In the desert, the Jews had no homes. On the other hand, leprosy of the body or of one's clothing could be experienced in the desert as well. Once again, and as other *pashtanim* did, R. Moses notes that the verse expresses its requirements according to the particular location or realistic situation in which the Jewish people found themselves at that time.[45]

R. Moses uses his commentary to provide scriptural justification for performing the Yom Kippur *ʿavodah* during the period of the Second Temple, when there was no ark or covering for the ark (*kapporet*). As others had noted, these implements would seem to be critical to the performance of the *ʿavodah*, which is characterized, in any case, as a required statute (*ḥuqqah*, Lev. 16:29) that cannot be changed or modified. R. Moses derives his allowance from Leviticus16:3, "thus shall Aaron come into the holy place," based on an interpretation of *Sifra*, which appears to conflict with Rashi's relatively rare *gematria* hint on this verse.[46]

[44] *Minḥat Yehudah* (Lev.), fol. 12b: כך פי' ר"מ מקוצי. (The attributed source for this passage [*Daʿat Zeqenim*] in *Tosafot ha-Shalem*, ed. Gellis, 12:233, sec. 7, is incorrect.)

[45] *Minḥat Yehudah* (Lev.), fol. 13b. כפר"מ מקוצי; and cf. above, n. 25. Rashi here presents a well-known *ʾaggadah ha-meyashevet divrei miqra* (found in *Sifra*) on the treasures that would be uncovered in the walls of the homes of the Jews (which had been left there by the Emori while the Jews were wandering in the desert) when the walls were torn down due to the procedures for dealing with leprosy. The Almighty would put the blemishes of leprosy in the homes of the Jews so that they would be ultimately enriched. See Ibn Ezra for another *peshat* solution, and cf. *Bekhor Shor* (ed. Nevo, 201), as well as Ramban.

[46] See *Minḥat Yehudah* (Lev.), fol. 15b (to Lev. 16:15, "and he will sprinkle it [the blood] on the *kapporet*"): כך פי' רבינו משה מקוצי. See also ms. JTS Lutzki 791, fol. 111r: מה שהעולם מקשים היאך היו עובדים בבית שני וכו'. אלא הכי איתא בת"כ בזאת יבוא. מה"ר יצחק פשטי הר"ם. (This is perhaps a citation from R. Moses's *peshatim* by R. Isaac of Evreux; cf. below, n. 172.) *Minḥat Yehudah* (fol. 15r, to Lev. 16:3) also cites Rashi's (contradictory) *gematria* approach, along with the view of R. Jacob of Orleans. Cf. *Paʿaneaḥ Raza*, 370.

Rashi, like many other medieval commentators, understands the phrase "so that the land will not vomit you out also when you defile it, as it had vomited out the nations before you" (Lev. 18:28) as a warning to the Jewish people to make sure that they do not defile the land as others did, lest they share the same fate as those nations. According to a simple (mis-)reading, however, the verse appears to be saying that if the Jewish people sin there, they would not be vomited out as others were. To undermine this reading, R. Moses links the verse to the one after it ("for whoever shall commit any of these abominations, those that commit them will be cut off from among their people") and interprets it in the following way. If the Jews commit these abominations, being vomited from the land in the way that others were is an insufficient punishment; rather, those Jews who do so will be completely cut off.[47]

A cluster of interpretations by R. Moses of Coucy is found to the end of *parashat Qedoshim* and the beginning of *parashat Emor.* The forbidden relations mentioned at the end of *Qedoshim* are typically listed together with their punishments. An exception to this pattern is the verse "you shall not uncover the nakedness of your mother's sister or your father's sister, for he uncovers his near kin, they shall bear their iniquity" (עונם ישאו, Lev. 20:19). *Minḥat Yehudah* cites an interpretation in the name of Abraham ibn Ezra that when Moses wrote the Torah, he did not want to include the punishment for relations with a father's sister in deference to his father, Amram, who had married his aunt (Ex. 6:20). Since Moses omitted the punishment for a father's sister, he omitted it with regard to a mother's sister as well. According to *Minḥat Yehudah*, Ibn Ezra adds that Moses also did not include here the punishment for having relations with two sisters, since the children of Israel were descended from Jacob, who had married two sisters. This passage ends with the phrase כך פי' ר"מ מקוצי. Since the extant commentary of Ibn Ezra notes these omissions but does not provide these explanations, noting only that והמשכיל יבין גם דברי הקבלה אמת, it is possible that R. Moses of Coucy originated these specific explanations for Ibn Ezra's observations.[48]

[47] *Minḥat Yehudah* (Lev.), fol. 16a, כלו' דלא סגי בהקאה אלא כל אשר יעשה מכל התועבות האלו ונכרתו. Additional clarification of R. Moses's approach is provided by ms. JTS Lutzki 791, fol. 112r. See also *Perushei R. Ḥayyim Palti'el*, ed. Lange, 422 (based on ms. Hamburg 40): כלומר אל תהיו סבורים שתקיא אתכם כך ולא יותר כאשר קאה אותם שלפניכם, אלא ברעה גדולה ובעונש גדול תקיא אתכם כמו שמפרש ונכרתו וכו'. As the editor notes (n. 35), a version of this passage is attributed to R. Yosef *Bekhor Shor* by *Moshav Zeqenim*, 340, although this is not found in the main manuscript (ms. Munich 52) of *Bekhor Shor*'s commentary. See *Perushei R. Yosef Bekhor Shor*, ed. Nevo, 211.

[48] See *Minḥat Yehudah* (Lev.), fol. 18b. The rabbinic tradition (*qabbalah*) to which Ibn Ezra refers is found in *Sifra*, that when the Torah characterizes a punishment as עונו ישא (as is the case here), *karet* is indicated. On R. Moses's citation of Ibn Ezra, cf. above, n. 18, and below, n. 96. On the citation of Ibn Ezra by other northern French Tosafists at this time, see below, n. 122.

Rashi interprets the phrase "who was never with a man" in Leviticus 21:3 to mean a woman who never had relations. A *kohen* must defile himself to his sister upon her death, if this was her status. R. Moses of Coucy questions the need for Rashi's interpretation, since the Torah in this verse had already characterized the sister as a virgin, ולאחותו הבתולה. R. Moses explains that Rashi's comment allows for the *kohen* to defile himself to his sister if she had lost the signs of her virginity as she matured (upon becoming a *bogeret*) or through injury (*mukkat ʿeẓ*), as long as she had not had relations.[49] Here, as in several instances noted above, R. Moses's aim was to serve as a kind of supercommentary on Rashi.[50]

Kohanim may eat *terumah* only when they are ritually pure. According to Rashi, this is the intent of Leviticus 22:9: "They shall keep my charge, lest they bear sin for it and die, if they profane it." Rashi also points to the tradition of the Oral Law (*Sanhedrin* 83a), that the punishment of death for eating impure *terumah* is administered divinely (*mitah bidei shamayim*). R. Moses of Coucy again questions Rashi's interpretation in light of the Oral Law principle that any time the Torah records a punishment of death without any further clarification or discussion, it is assumed to be death by strangulation (חנק), which is carried out by the Sanhedrin court. R. Moses goes on to demonstrate that the particular form of the word for death here (*u-metu*) is not included in the talmudic rule, which applies only when the word *yumat* is used. Although death for a false prophet is formulated similarly as *u-met* (Deut. 18:18), and a false prophet dies through the *mitat beit din* of strangulation, R. Moses explains that the death penalty for the false prophet receives additional clarification from the verse immediately preceding it (אנכי אדרוש מעמו, Deut. 18:19).[51] Once again, R. Moses, like R. Isaiah di Trani and R. Jacob of Orleans before him, is involved here with verifying the details of Rashi's commentary in order to make sure that it is fully understood, and that its technical nuances are accurate and properly appreciated.

49 *Minḥat Yehudah* (Lev.), fol. 19a, כ"פ ר"מ מקוצי. *Minḥat Yehudah*'s mentor, R. Elyaqim, suggests that Rashi's interpretation would include the more unusual situation of a woman who never had vaginal intercourse (נבעלה שלא כדרכה).

50 Maharal of Prague (d. 1609), in his classic supercommentary to Rashi, *Gur Aryeh*, links this comment of Rashi to his earlier one in the verse on the word *ha-qerovah*, which means that even if she is an *ʾarusah*, her brother the *kohen* may defile himself (as long as she has not yet undergone *nissuʾin* and had marital relations). See also *Sefer ha-Zikkaron ʿal Perush Rashi la-Ḥumash* (by the Spanish exile, R. Avraham Bakarat), ed. M. Phillip (Bnei Brak, 1985), pt. 2 (Leviticus), 72–73.

51 *Minḥat Yehudah* (Lev.), fol. 20a, כפר"מ מקוצי. In two succeeding comments, to Lev. 22:14 and Lev. 22:23 (*Minḥat Yehudah*, ibid.), R. Moses responds to talmudic questions relative to the contents of these verses. This is also the case in *Minḥat Yehudah*, fol. 23b (Lev. 25:46).

As Rid and other Ashkenazic rabbinic figures interested in *peshat* exegesis did, R. Moses considers the interpretation of Rabbenu Tam, offered in a talmudic context, which mediates between the two different proportions found in Leviticus 26:8, in which the Torah details the successes the Jewish people can have in defeating their enemies if they do the will of God: "Five of you shall chase a hundred, and a hundred of you shall cause ten thousand to run, and your enemies shall fall before you by the sword," and the verse in *parashat Ha'azinu* (Deut. 32:30), "How can one man chase a thousand and two put ten thousand to flight, unless their Rock has sold them and the Lord has shut them out?" According to Rabbenu Tam, the verse in Leviticus indicates that when the Jews are pursuers, their enemies will fall before them by the sword. Thus one pursuer can deal effectively only with a maximum of one hundred. In *Ha'azinu*, however, where the Jews are the ones being pursued, the verse does not say that the pursuers will kill the Jews, only that they will force them to flee (*yirdof*). That is an easier goal to accomplish, and it is therefore possible for one person to cause even a thousand others to flee. Similarly, the even smaller ratio found there, that two can affect ten thousand, is possible because the two are causing the enemy to disperse and thereby to escape—*yanisu* in the language of the verse. Allowing the enemy to escape is not as difficult or as arduous as forcing them to flee, and therefore the ratio can be even smaller. The notion of escaping as opposed to fleeing is established by Leviticus 26:17, ונסתם ואין רודף אתכם.[52]

On the basis of careful contextual analysis, R. Moses of Coucy maintains instead that the verse in *Ha'azinu* reflects the highly impressive powers of the Jewish people during the messianic era rather than the prowess of their enemies, which the other nations should have been able to anticipate. The passage in *Minḥat Yehudah* concludes by noting that Rashi in *Ha'azinu* interprets the verse as reflecting the weakness of Israel, as Rabbenu Tam did. Thus the solution attributed to Rabbenu Tam, in this instance, is more

[52] In several places (*Yoma* 76a, *Sotah* 11a, *Sanhedrin* 100b), the Talmud discusses the notion that *middah tovah* is typically greater than *middat ha-por'anut*. The discussion here in the name of Rabbenu Tam is found in *Tosafot Sotah* 11a, s.v. *ule-'olam* (which identifies this as a passage from Rabbenu Tam's *Sefer ha-Yashar*; cf. Urbach, *Ba'alei ha-Tosafot*, 1:101, 2:637–39; and S. Emanuel, *Shivrei Luḥot*, 29). The contradiction between these two verses, and the resolution of Rabbenu Tam (without attribution), is also found in the Torah commentary of Rabbenu Tam's talmudic student, R. Yosef *Bekhor Shor* (Nevo, 234–35). *Perushei ha-Torah le-R. Ḥayyim Palti'el*, ed. Y. S. Lange (Jerusalem, 1981), 454, attributes both the question and the answer of Rabbenu Tam to his brother Rashbam, although these are not found in Rashbam's extant Torah commentary; see ed. Lange, 454, n. 21. Lange also notes that Rid (in his *Nimmuqei Ḥumash*, 45, to Ex.20:5, *ve-'oseh ḥesed la-'alafim* = ms. Moscow 303, fols. 77r–v) cites this in the name of Rabbenu Tam, and see above, chapter 3, n. 109. *Moshav Zeqenim*, 415–16, cites this in the name of Ri (= R. Isaiah di Trani, or perhaps Rabbenu Tam's leading talmudic student, Ri of Dampierre). See also *Tosafot ha-Shalem*, ed. Gellis, 8:90–92.

effective for reconciling the interpretations of Rashi on the two seemingly contradictory verses, even as the solution proposed by R. Moses of Coucy reflects a greater degree of originality.[53]

At the same time, R. Moses also includes by name, and in full, the suggestion and detailed proofs by R. Judah *he-Ḥasid* to explain the sum (of 10,000 silver pieces, עשרת אלפים ככר כסף) that Haman offered for exterminating the Jews (Esther 3:9). As R. Judah discovered, this sum, calculated according to the specifications found in Leviticus 27:3, accords precisely with the monetary evaluation (*ʿerekh*) of the 600,000 males between the ages of twenty and sixty, the conventional figure used to represent the male population of the Jewish people when they left Egypt (ששים רבוא), which Haman reasoned was also an appropriate representation of the population of the Jewish people in his day.[54]

As opposed to Rashi, who presents two midrashic explanations for the separate counting of the Levites mandated at the beginning of the Book of Numbers (1:49), R. Moses of Coucy presents a more directly contextual approach. Because service in the Tabernacle was incumbent upon the Levites, they did not serve in the army. Since the main census was defined as one that was to include "all that are able to go forth to war in Israel" (Nu. 1:3), the Levites were excluded by definition. Moreover, the Levites were the "keepers of the vessels" (*shomrei ha-kelim*), as the following verse notes, "you shall appoint the Levites over the tabernacle of testimony and over all its

[53] *Minḥat Yehudah* (Lev.), fols. 24a–24b, ור"מ מקוצי פי' דהתם נמי היא מדה טובה. See also ms. JTS Lutzki 794, fol. 66r: פר"ת הכא במדה טובה . . . והתם במדת פורענות לא נאמר בה הריגה אלא רדיפה והוא קלה יותר מן ההריגה ולכך אומר איכה ירדוף . . . וי"מ דהכא רודפים והורגים והתם גבי פורענות אינם הורגים. ור"מ מקוצי פירש כי אף שם מדה טובה כי מדבר על פורענות אומות העולם. איכה ירדוף איש אחד ישראל אלף מן האומות. See also ms. JTS Lutzki 794, fol. 73v, where R. Moses of Coucy cites a rabbinic explanation in the name of Rabbenu Tam which links the defective spelling of בהעלתך in Nu. 8:2 with the *plene* spelling of העלוך in Ex. 32:4, 8.

[54] *Minḥat Yehudah* (Lev.), fol. 24b: כך מצאתי בפשטי ר"מ מקוצי, וכבר פרשתי בפרשת משפטים כמה עולה שקל, found also in ms. Vatican 45. See *Perushei ha-Torah le-R. Yehudah he-Ḥasid*, ed. Lange, 159. This comment appears in expanded form in R. Abraham b. Azriel's *ʿArugat ha-Bosem* (ed. Urbach, 2:290), with R. Zal(t)man citing R. his father's suggestion that Haman calculated his monetary demand on the basis of his nuanced estimation of the total population of the Jewish people: אמר אבי, המן היה בקי בתורת משה. אמר סתם חשבון של ישראל ששים רבוא ואע"פ שנהרגו מהם בשעת חורבן אינן יכולין להיות פחות; see also ed. Lange, 133–34. The passage in *ʿArugat ha-Bosem* adduces additional support from R. Eleazar Qailir's *qerovah* to *parashat Sheqalim*, while the passage found in *Minḥat Yehudah* refers to a *yoẓer* for *parashat Zakhor*. It is likely that these *piyyut* references were not provided by R. Judah *he-Ḥasid* in his original formulation; the passage in *ʿArugat ha-Bosem* also provides additional proof from Rashi's commentary to the end of Exodus. H. Touitou, "*Minḥat Yehudah*," 75 (n. 37), records four other passages by R. Judah *he-Ḥasid* (three in Genesis and one in Exodus) that are found in *Minḥat Yehudah* (although he does not mention this one from the end of Leviticus). It would appear that *Minḥat Yehudah* became aware of this interpretation by R. Judah from the *peshatei R. Mosheh mi-Coucy*. See also below, n. 79.

vessels and over all that belongs to it" (Nu. 1:50). Thus the Levites did not go out to war and therefore had to be separately counted.[55]

A series of comments by R. Moses of Coucy, which all conclude with the notation כפר"ם מקוצי, is preserved in *Minḥat Yehudah* at the beginning of *parashat Shelaḥ* concerning the selection of the spies from each tribe. As the choices are presented beginning with the tribe of Reuven in Numbers 13:4, R. Moses wonders why these men, who are identified in the previous verse as the *nesi'im* from each tribe (*kol nasi bahem*), are completely different from the *nesi'im* who are listed in *parashat Naso* as having presented the gifts from each tribe for the dedication of the *mishkan*, beginning with Naḥshon b. ʿAminadav in Numbers 7:12. R. Moses rejects the notion that all those princes had passed away and were replaced by those listed here, since there is no indication of this whatsoever. He therefore suggests that the designation כל נשיא בהם is akin to כל אשר נשאו לבו (in Ex. 36:2), which describes those who volunteered to work on fabricating the implements of the Tabernacle. Here too, the men in question were highly regarded or well-positioned volunteers, who were then approved and ratified for this spy mission.[56] A similar *peshat* solution is offered by R. Yosef *Bekhor Shor* to Numbers 13:3, where the spies are characterized as "the heads of the children of Israel," ראשי בני ישראל המה. *Bekhor Shor* suggests that they were possibly *sarei 'alafim*, since they were clearly not the formal heads of the tribes who were chosen at the beginning of the book of Numbers and who also donated the gifts to the *mishkan* in *parashat Naso.*[57]

R. Moses also points to a seeming lack of organization in the order of the spies. The naming of the representative from the tribe of Ephraim (Nu. 13:9) comes right after the representative of Yissachar, a son of Leah. Next

[55] *Minḥat Yehudah* (Numbers), fols. 1b–2a:פרש"י כדאי הוא לגיון מלך וכו'. ד"א צפה הקב"ה שעתידה לעמוד גזירה וכו' [= הפירוש השני ברש"י]. ד"א את מטה לוי לא תפקוד לפי שפקודת המשכן עליהם לפיכך לא יצאו לצבא. ואני אומר לפי שהיו שומרי כלים כמו שמפרש ואתה הפקד את הלוים על משכן העדות ועל כל כליו ועל כל אשר לו כדרך יושבי' על הכלים. כך פר"מ מקוצי. Although it is possible that R. Moses's reason begins only with the phrase *va-'ani 'omer* (and is distinct from their nonservice in the army), *Ḥizzequni*, whose frequent use of R. Moses's comments has been noted, combines elements from both pieces into one formulation (as his second explanation): לפי שאין מהם יוצא צבא אלא שומרים וחונים סביב למשכן כדרך היושב על הכלים. Cf. Rashbam's comment to Nu. 1:47: ומפרש טעם כי לא ילכו בצבא המלחמה אלא הפקד את הלוים על משכן העדות, and *Rashbam's Commentary to Leviticus and Numbers*, ed. M. Lockshin (Providence, R.I., 2001), 157. *Ḥizzequni*'s first explanation follows that of R. Yosef *Bekhor Shor* (Nevo, 242), that the Levites had to be counted separately since the ages for their inclusion in a census (at one month or at the age of thirty) were different from those of the rest of the people (for whom the census began at the age of twenty). A similar distinction was also made by R. Yom Tov of Joigny; see above, chapter 2, n. 220.

[56] *Minḥat Yehudah* (Nu.), fol. 9b (= ms. Vatican [Urban] 21, fol. 126v; and see also ms. Frankfurt Hebr. Oct. 100, fol. 119r).

[57] See *Perushei R. Yosef Bekhor Shor*, ed. Nevo, 261. This interpretation is found in *Ḥizzequni* as well.

Benjamin follows, and only afterward Zevulun, another son of Leah, who should have been listed with Yissachar. After Zevulun we find Menasheh, who should have been listed together with Ephraim. R. Moses maintains that this indiscriminate mixing (*ʿirbuvyah*) was a clever psychological ploy on Moses's part. This new order would serve to bind and keep the representatives of each tribe together for this mission, which in turn would instill fear in the nations, by showing the equality and common purpose of all the tribes, through mixing their order and breaking down existing familial divisions.[58] R. Moses also asks why the Torah repeats after the list was completed, "these are the names of the men" (Nu. 13:16), since the list had started with the phrase "And these are their names" (Nu. 13:4). R. Moses suggests, as does Ibn Ezra, that this was done to emphasize that Moses changed only Joshua's name from Hosea, as recorded in the second half of Numbers 13:16. No other names were changed.[59]

Indeed, R. Moses of Coucy notes further that Joshua was already called by this name in the Torah prior to this episode. That is because by the time Moses wrote the Torah, Joshua's name had been changed, and he adjusted the earlier portions accordingly. Moses mentioned the name Hosea only in the listing of the spies, to let us know that this was Joshua's original name and that it was changed at this point.[60]

[58] *Minḥat Yehudah* (Nu.), fol. 9b: This kind of psychological exegesis or insight is also suggested by *Bekhor Shor* and by R. Judah *he-Ḥasid*. See, e.g., *Perushei R. Yosef Bekhor Shor ʿal ha-Torah*, ed. Nevo, introduction, 7–8, and above, chapter 3, nn. 74, 81.

[59] *Minḥat Yehudah* (Nu.), fol. 9b, and ms. JTS Lutzki 794, fol. 76r: אלא [כך] פי' אלה שמות האנשים ולא שינה משמותם אך ויקרא משה להושע בן נון יהושע.

[60] *Minḥat Yehudah*, ibid., and ms. JTS Lutzki 794, ibid.: כשכתב משה את התורה כבר נשתנה שמו ולכך כתב יהושע בכל מקום חוץ מענין המרגלים . . . להודיעך שכך היה שמו מתחלה. Cf. *Perushei R. Ḥayyim Palti'el*, ed. Lange, 504–5, in which the comment of Rashi (that Moses changed Hosea's name to Joshua as a kind of prayer that he should not join with the negative report of the other spies) and the comment of R. Moses of Coucy are included together. Cf. Robert Harris, "Awareness of Biblical Redaction among Biblical Exegetes of Northern France," [Hebrew] in *Shenaton le-Ḥeqer ha-Miqra veha-Mizraḥ ha-Qadum*, 13 (2000), 289–310, and above, n. 48; above, chapter 2, n. 102; and chapter 3, n. 54. Both Rashbam and R. Yosef *Bekhor Shor* suggest a different resolution (*lefi ha-peshat*, as *Bekhor Shor* notes). Moses changed Joshua's name after he was appointed to be Moses's aide and was successful, just as the kings of Egypt and Babylonia changed the name of Joseph and Daniel (and his friends), when they found favor in the eyes of these rulers and entered into their respective services. (*Bekhor Shor* adds the fact that God changed the names of Abraham, Sarah, and Jacob after they found favor in his eyes, as well as in the cases of Nehemiah and Zedekiah.) R. Moses of Coucy compares and resolves Rashi's understanding of the halakhic valence of the word *reshit*, as it is found concerning the separation of *ḥalah* (in Rashi's commentary to Nu. 15:21), with Rashi's understanding of this word, as it appears with regard to the taking of *terumah*. See *Minḥat Yehudah* (Nu.), fol. 11a. R. Moses also reconciles Rashi's enumeration (based on *ʿArakhin* 15a–b) of the ten times the people tested Moses (Nu. 14:22) with the Mishnah in *Pirqei Avot*, which discusses the ten times "our forefathers tested the Almighty in the desert"; see ms. JTS, fol. 791, fol. 130v. This passage is also found in ms. Moscow 303, fol. 91r, and in *Moshav Zeqenim*, 457, in the name of ר"י (= R. Isaiah).

There is also a series of comments from R. Moses of Coucy on *parashat Koraḥ*. Unlike Rashi, who held that most of the 250 followers of Koraḥ (Nu. 16:2) were important figures from the tribe of Reuven, which was a neighbor of the tribe of Levi in the encampment of the Jewish people, and Rashbam, who held that the 250 were all Levites from the family branch of Koraḥ, R. Moses of Coucy suggests that Korah formed the cohort of his followers by choosing 23 people (who formed a "small Sanhedrin" of 23) from each of the other eleven tribes, for a total of 253; the tribe of Levi, which was the focus of his argument and ire, was obviously excluded. The three people above the number of 250 were Datan, Aviram, and On ben Pelet, all of whom are mentioned in Numbers 16:1.[61]

Both *Minḥat Yehudah* and ms. JTS Lutzki 791 attribute to *peshatei Rabbenu Mosheh mi-Coucy* the intricate and interesting explanation found in Rashi's commentary about why and how Moses proposed that the members of Koraḥ's group take up fire-pans of incense (Nu. 16:6),[62] an explanation that is rooted in *Midrash Tanḥuma*. It is difficult to prove that this explanation was not put forward by Rashi, but several points should be made. First, it is not found in the earliest printed edition of Rashi.[63] Second, the number of Koraḥ's men referred to in this passage in *Minḥat Yehudah* and ms. JTS Lutzki 791 is 253, in accordance with the unique number that R. Moses had suggested (as noted in the preceding paragraph). Moreover, there are quite a few comments produced by R. Moses on this entire episode, as we shall see.[64]

From the unusual doubled construction of Numbers 16:16, in which Moses says to Koraḥ, "You and all your company shall be before the Lord, you and they and Aaron tomorrow," R. Moses suggests that we can learn Koraḥ's response to Moses's question in Numbers 16:11, Why are you and your company against the Lord, and what is your complaint against Aaron?

[61] *Minḥat Yehudah* (Nu.), fol. 13a: בירר קרח מכל שבט ושבט כ"ג אנשי' שהם סנהדרי קטנה לבד משבט לוי לפי שעליהם תערמתו . . . והג' היתירים על החמישים ומאתים איש הם דתן ואבירם ואון בן פלט שהשלימו לקשר רשעים. כך פ"ר משה מקוצי. R. Moses's interpretation is adopted by *Ḥizzequni*. See also *Perushei R. Ḥayyim Palti'el*, 519. R. Yosef *Bekhor Shor* held that (*lefi ha-peshat*) On ben Pelet was part of the group of 250 (ed. Nevo, 268). *Moshav Zeqenim*, 462 (which overall contains only two comments in the name of R. Moses *ha-Darshan* and none in the name of R. Moses of Coucy), cites the comment of R. Moses of Coucy (inaccurately) in the name of *Bekhor Shor*.

[62] See *Minḥat Yehudah* (Nu.), fol. 13a, and ms. JTS Lutzki 791, fol. 132r, in the name of 'פש הר"ם.

[63] See *Perushei Rashi 'al ha-Torah*, ed. C. D. Chavel (Jerusalem, 1983), 456.

[64] In the standard editions of Rashi, the number of Koraḥ's group is recorded here as 250, reflecting the total number of the group according to Rashi at the beginning of Nu. 16. As such, it remains unclear which commentary text was adjusted, but the mere fact that the commentaries of Rashi and R. Moses of Coucy are intertwined in this way is an indication of the perceived relationship between these commentaries.

Koraḥ initially tells Moses here, "Why should my group and I go there? I have no complaint against God but only to Aaron. If Aaron comes to the *beit ha-va'ad*, I will go as well, and whoever God chooses will be holy." Moses then informs Koraḥ that Aaron will also be there. This is the meaning of the second phrase in this verse, "you and they and Aaron tomorrow." This reconstruction of the "behind the scenes" or implicit dialogue between Moses and Koraḥ, which we have also encountered in the commentaries of *Bekhor Shor*, R. Judah *he-Ḥasid*, and R. Isaiah di Trani, is cited in this instance from the commentary of R. Moses of Coucy, "in the name of his teacher."[65]

R. Moses notes that while Numbers 16:32 includes "all the men that belonged to Koraḥ" among those who were swallowed up by the earth, Numbers 26:10 links Koraḥ with the group that died by fire. R. Moses explains that, indeed, Koraḥ was both burned and swallowed up, as the Talmud describes in *Sanhedrin* 110a. Had he not been burned, those who perished in this way would have had a complaint, since he brought this disaster upon them; had he not been buried, that group would have complained similarly. In this instance, R. Moses provides additional scriptural evidence to support the talmudic approach.[66]

In the same context, R. Moses of Coucy provides a parable that responds to the question raised by R. Yosef Qara as to why the 250 men who offered the incense were killed by fire, while Datan and Aviram experienced the harsher death of being swallowed up by the depths of the earth. The point of R. Moses's parable is that the 250 men agreed at least to follow Moses's instructions concerning the test of the incense, while Datan and

[65] See *Minḥat Yehudah* (Nu.), fol. 13b (= ms. Vatican [Urban] 21, fol. 129v): תימ' למה אמר והם אלא מכפל הלשון למדנו תשובתו של קרח. כשא"ל משה אתה וכל עדתך היו וגו' השיב לו קרח מדוע אלך לשם אני וכל עדתי הלא אינני מעורר אלא על אהרן. אך אם יבוא אהרן לבית הועד אלך לשם ואשר יבחר השם הוא הקדוש עד שא"ל משה שגם אהרן יהיה שם. כפר"מ בשם רבו. This passage is found in ms. JTS Lutzki 791, fol. 132v, in the name of פשטי הר"ם. Cf. *Perushei R. Ḥayyim Palti'el*, ed. Lange, 521–22; above, chapter 2, n. 101 (for *Bekhor Shor*), and chapter 3, nn. 53, 63, 127 (for R. Judah *he-Ḥasid* and R. Isaiah di Trani). In *Minḥat Yehudah* (Nu.), fol. 13b, (again in the name of his teacher) and in ms. JTS Lutzki 791, fol. 132v, R. Moses distinguishes chronologically between the term *hibadlu* (Nu. 16:21), through which God tells Moses and Aaron to separate themselves from Koraḥ and his men, and the term *heromu* (Nu. 17:10), which is used later as the Torah's term for separation from the evil congregation. At first, before the swallowing up of Koraḥ and his men, the groups were intermingled in the camps, and physical separation was required. However, once Koraḥ himself had been defeated, the instruction was *heromu*. This signifies not merely the separation, which had already been accomplished, but rather an intensification (*haramah*) of the removal process, which had begun following the separation from Koraḥ. Cf. *Perushei R. Ḥayyim Palti'el*, 522–23. These are the only two passages in *pesahtei R. Mosheh mi-Coucy* that refer to his teacher (*rabbo*). The identity of this teacher, however, remains unclear, especially in light of the fact that R. Moses's primary teacher of Talmud, R. Judah Sirleon, did not offer many Torah interpretations altogether, and those we have are almost exclusively based on talmudic or rabbinic exegesis. Cf. above, n. 18.

[66] *Minḥat Yehudah* (Nu.), fol. 14a (כפר"מ מקוצי = ms. Vatican [Urban 21], fol. 130r).

Aviram adamantly refused to do anything that Moses instructed (Nu. 16:12, *lo na'aleh*).[67]

R. Moses reconciles an apparent contradiction between a verse in *parashat Ḥuqqat* (Nu. 20:21) and another in *parashat Devarim* (Deut. 2:29). The verse in *Ḥuqqat* suggests that the Jews did not pass through the land of Esau on their way to Israel (ויט ישראל מעליו). And yet the verse in *Devarim* has the Jewish people asking Siḥon to sell food and water to them, just as the descendants of Esau (who live in Se'ir) did, implying that the Jews did pass through the land of Esau. R. Moses's explanation, similar to that of R. Yosef *Bekhor Shor*, is that the Jews did not pass through the land of Esau (as per Nu. 21:4, *lisbov 'et 'erez Edom*), only that they traveled along the border of their land, stopping in the border town of Arnon (Nu. 21:14). The reference to what Esau did for the Jewish people in *Devarim* is to the food that the Edomites supplied the Israelites there on the border, and not to any pathway taken through the Edomites' land, which they did not provide. R. Moses concludes by noting that this is how Rashi interpreted the verse in *parashat Devarim*. He considers his comment to be an extension or confirmation of Rashi's interpretation.[68]

Ms. JTS Lutzki 791 contains six additional comments to *parashat Ḥuqqat* in the name of פשטי הר"ם, which in this manuscript connotes פשטי ר' משה מקוצי as we have seen, that are not found in the published edition of *Minḥat Yehudah*. The first is a way of approaching the paradoxical nature of the *parah 'adumah*, which causes the impure person to become pure while rendering the pure preparer impure, by comparison to other natural phenomena that cause contradictory reactions or results.[69] The second is a brief

[67] See *Minḥat Yehudah* (Nu.), fol. 14a (הקשה הרב יוסף קרא); ms. JTS Lutzki 791, fol. 132v; and ms. JTS Lutzki 794, fol. 81v. R. Judah *he-Ḥasid* (above, chapter 3, n. 87), presents a different resolution for this same question. R. Moses of Coucy discusses a comment of Rashi in *parashat Ḥuqqat* which appears to be otherwise self-evident. See *Minḥat Yehudah* (Nu.) fol. 15a (לשון פשטי הר"ם); JTS Lutzki 791, fol. 133r (פשטי הר"ם); and ms. JTS Lutzki 794, fol. 82v (פר"מ מקוצי).

[68] See *Minḥat Yehudah* (Nu.), 16a (כפר"מ מקוצי); ms. JTS Lutzki 791, fol. 135v (פש' הר"ם); and ms. JTS Lutzki 794, 83v. There is a subtle variation between the printed and manuscript texts. The printed version concludes: ומה שנא' כאשר עשו לי בני עשו וגו' קאי אארנון ולא קאי אדרך כמו שפרש"י בפרשת דברים, while the manuscript version reads: דכתי' כאשר עשו לי קאי אמזון ולא אדרך. וכן פרש"י בפרשת דברים. See *Perushei R. Yosef Bekhor Shor*, ed. Nevo, 311; Rashi to Nu. 21:13, and Ibn Ezra to Deut. 2:29 (who suggests a different approach).

[69] Ms. JTS Lutzki 791, fol. 134r: אם ישאלך שואל כיצד מעשה פרה שמטהרת טמאים ומטמאה טהורים. תשובה: כי . . . מעשים כאלו בכל יום כי האש מקרשת החלב המתכת והבדיל. והמים מלחלח עצי ארזים ומרטב ומצמק עצי תאנים ומיבשם. ויש אוכל המשביע הרעב והמרעיב השבע ופעמים מרפאים החולה מחליאים הבריא. Cf. *Perushei R. Ḥayyim Palti'el*, ed. Lange, 527, where this comment appears (in ms. Hamburg 40) without attribution. On *ta'amei ha-mizvot* and R. Moses of Coucy, cf. Yehuda Galinsky, "'Ve-Lihyot Lefanekha 'Eved Ne'eman kol ha-Yamim': Pereq be-Haguto ha-Datit shel R. Mosheh mi-Coucy," *Da'at* 42 (1999), 13–22, and Jeffrey Woolf, "Maimonides Revised: The Case of the *Sefer Miswot Gadol*," *Harvard Theological Review* 90 (1997), 175–203.

but arcane talmudic analysis of the phrase ושחט אותו לפניו (Nu. 19:3), pointing to what can be derived from this verse about those who are eligible to slaughter the red heifer, and the conditions of eligibility.[70] The next comment similarly assesses the ramifications of the *gezerah shavah* that links the death of Miriam (Nu. 20:1) to *ʿeglah ʿarufah*.[71]

R. Moses cites Rashi's comment to Numbers 20:11, i.e., that Moses and Aaron spoke to the rock before hitting it. Because this was not the rock that God had designated, very little water came forth, and they therefore decided to hit the rock. If so, however, what sinful act did Moses commit? R. Moses of Coucy suggests that Moses should have sought permission from God before hitting the rock. Moses mistakenly thought that God wanted him to do this. Indeed, this is what he had been instructed earlier in Refidim (Ex. 17:6), והכית בצור ויצאו ממנו מים. In this instance, however, God wanted Moses to point the rock out with his staff, but not to strike it.[72]

R. Moses reconstructs the dialogue between Israel and Edom in Numbers 20:14, "You know all the travail that has befallen us." Thus, the Jews argued, you need not be jealous of us, since the blessings of Isaac to Jacob have not been fulfilled in us. Edom nonetheless responded, "Lest I come out against you with the sword." For it is clear that the blessing that Isaac gave to Esau, "that you will live by your sword," has indeed been fulfilled within us.[73]

In his final comment in this unit, R. Moses of Coucy proposes two insightful interpretations of Moses's request to Edom to traverse their land without eating from the fields or vineyards that they would pass through, and without drinking any well water (Nu. 20:17). First, potable well water was an expensive commodity in this region, a point also made by Rashbam. Moses did expect, however, that the Jews would be able to drink from natural bodies of water that they found along the way. Alternatively, there are

70 Ms. JTS Lutzki 791, fol. 134r. Cf. *Perushei R. Ḥayyim Paltiʾel*, p. 529. As we have noted, the term פשטי הר"ם was associated on occasion even with interpretations by R. Moses that mainly involved talmudic analysis. See, e.g., above, nn. 9, 51.

71 Ms. JTS Lutzki 791, fol. 134r. Cf. *Moshav Zeqenim* to Nu. 20:1.

72 Ms. JTS Lutzki 791, fol. 135r: פ"ה שדברו אל הסלע להוציא מים ולא הוציא. וק' א"כ למה פשע משה? צ"ל שלא היה לו לחכות עד שיעשה ברשות הב"ה. ומשה טעה וסבר שצוה הב"ה להכות הסלע כמו שאמ' לו ברפידים והכית בצור. וזה לא היה, שהב"ה לא צוה [כאן] מטה אלא להראות להם. *Moshav Zeqenim*, 470 (to Nu. 20:12), cites the same question, and a similar interpretation, in the name of *Bekhor Shor*. See *Perushei R. Yosef Bekhor Shor ʿal ha-Torah*, ed. Nevo, 276. On the association of comments by R. Moses of Coucy with R. Yosef *Bekhor Shor* in the *Moshav Zeqenim* compilation, cf. above, nn. 47, 61. Note also the difference of opinion between R. Yosef *Bekhor Shor* and Naḥmanides about whether there was one episode involving hitting a rock or two separate ones (with the other account found in Ex. 17). R. Moses, like Ramban, clearly holds that there were two such incidents.

73 Ms. JTS Lutzki 791, fol. 135r: את כל התלאה. כלו' אין לך לקנא בשביל הברכות כי לא נתקיימו בנו. והוא ענה פן החרב אצא לקראתך כי הברכה על דעת חרבך נתקיימה.

those, including Rashi, who interpret that Moses meant the Jews would not drink from their own well, the well of Miriam, which accompanied them. Moses promised that the Jews would instead purchase their water, which would be more profitable for Edom.[74] Medieval Ashkenazic commentaries occasionally slacken when they reach *Sefer Bamidbar*, as is the case, for example, with Rashbam, R. Isaiah di Trani, and others. The number of comments by R. Moses of Coucy in the portions of *Koraḥ* and *Ḥuqqat*, and indeed, in *Sefer Bamidbar* as a whole, relative to the total number of comments that we have from him, is therefore noteworthy.

Basic parallelism suggests that *Bnei Yisra'el*, who are mentioned explicitly in the second half of Numbers 22:3 as irksome to Moab, are also the unidentified nation of whom Moab was deeply afraid according to the first half of the verse (ויגר מואב מפני העם), because they were so numerous (*ki rav hu*). R. Moses of Coucy notes, however, that according to Rashi in *parashat Beshalaḥ* (Ex. 15:15, "the leaders of Moab were seized by fear"), Israel was not interested in attacking or pursuing Moab (*she-harei lo ʿaleihem holkhim*). R. Moses of Coucy therefore suggests that Moab (in Nu. 22:3) was in fact afraid of Balak, who was from the nation of Midyan, which was Moab's traditional enemy (as Rashi indicates in Nu. 22:4). Or perhaps Moab was afraid of those people who were settled around them. As the following verse suggests, "their congregation will lick up all that are around us." Moreover, Israel received Divine instruction (Deut. 2:9) not to afflict Moab or to fight with them. Although Rashi interprets that verse to mean that Israel was permitted to do things to cause Moab to fear them but were not permitted to actually attack or engage them in warfare, R. Moses of Coucy suggests a sequence of events that allow the various interpretations of Rashi (in Exodus, Numbers, and Deuteronomy) to remain unified and consistent.[75]

God tells Bilʿam, "If the men [of Midyan] come to call you [*liqro lekha*], go with them" (*qum lekh 'ittam*; Nu. 22:20). And yet earlier (Nu. 22:12), God had said to Bilʿam, "Do not go with them" for the purpose of cursing the Jewish people. R. Moses of Coucy explains that verse 20 means that if they come to ask for your advice—which is the connotation of the word *qeri'ah*, as in Genesis 31:4, "and Jacob called [*va-yiqra*] for Leah and Rachel to come to the field," i.e., that he sought their counsel—you may go with them, but you may not go to curse the Jewish people.[76] Different solutions to this

[74] Ms. JTS Lutzki 791, fol. 135v: לא נשתה מי באר שהם יקרים אך מימיך המצויים בדרך נשתה. וי"א מי באר פי' בארה של מרים ההולכת עמנו אך נקנה ממך מים כדי שתרויח. R. Moses here follows the approaches of both Rashi and Rashbam. Cf. *Ḥizzequni*, and above, n. 35.

[75] See *Minḥat Yehudah* (Nu.), fol. 18a; ms. JTS Lutzki 794, fol. 85r (ותירץ ר"מ מקוצי . . . כפר"מ מקוצי); ms. Vatican (Urban 21), fol. 132v; and cf. *Ḥizzequni*.

[76] *Minḥat Yehudah* (Nu.), fol. 19a (כפר"מ מקוצי).

seeming contradiction, on the basis of other scriptural analogues, were proposed by Ibn Ezra in the name of R. Saʿadyah Gaon and in his own name.

In the first verse in *parashat Pinḥas* (Nu. 25:11), the Torah specifies that Pinḥas was descended directly from Aaron. Rashi explains, following the Talmud in tractate *Sanhedrin*, that this was done because members of other tribes were ridiculing Pinhas, saying that he was descended on his mother's side from Jethro (Puti'el), who had been an idolater. Hence the Torah stresses Pinhas's priestly lineage through Aaron. R. Moses of Coucy questions this interpretation of Rashi, since it is well known that Jewish lineage and tribal ancestry follow the paternal side. He notes, however, that Rashi's approach contains an important nuance. The claim of the other tribes could have been that Pinhas's mother was a convert, since she was descended from Jethro. A convert may not marry a *kohen*, and any male child from that union has the status of a non-*kohen* (*ḥalal*). Therefore, it was necessary for the Torah to indicate Pinhas's descent from Aaron, to show that his *kehunah* was completely intact.[77] Similarly, R. Moses himself interprets God's statement about Pinhas, "behold I am giving him My covenant of peace" (Nu. 25:12), as a move to allay Pinhas's concern that, since his hands had blood on them, and a *kohen* who killed someone could not pronounce the priestly blessing according to R. Yoḥanan's uncontested ruling in *Berakhot* 32b, he might lose his *kehunah*.[78]

In the census of the tribe of Levi found in *parashat Pinḥas*, the Torah writes that the wife of Amram was Yokheved, the daughter of Levi, who was born to him in Egypt (Nu. 26:59). The Hebrew construction of the last phrase in this verse is rather unusual. The verse should have said אשר יולדה ללוי במצרים, who was born to Levi in Egypt, but the verse actually reads, אשר ילדה אותה ללוי במצרים, who gave birth to her to Levi in Egypt. In ms. JTS Lutzki 791, the explanation presented from *peshatei R. Mosheh mi-Coucy*, which is also suggested by R. Judah *he-Ḥasid* in his Torah commentary, is that Otah must have been the name of Levi's wife: "Otah gave birth to her [Yokheved] for Levi in Egypt," which precisely, if somewhat boldly, fits the grammatical structure of the sentence.[79]

[77] See *Minḥat Yehudah* (Nu.), fol. 21b; ms. JTS Lutzki 791, fol. 139v (and see also ms. JTS Lutzki 794, fol. 90v): פינחס בן אלעזר בן אהרן הכהן. פרש"י לפי שהיו שבטים מבזין אותו אומרים הראיתם בן פוטי וכו'. לפיכך בא הכתוב ויחסו אחר אהרן עכ"ל. ודבר תימא הוא דפשיטא דמייחסין אותו אחר האב. ונראה לי שלכך יחסו אחר האב שלא תאמר אמו גיורת היתה שהיתה מבנות פוטיאל וגיורת אסורה לכהן וא"כ היה חלל. לפיכך הוצרך ליחסו. פש' הר"ם/ כפר"מ מקוצי.

[78] See *Minḥat Yehudah* (Nu.), fols. 21b–22a (and see also ms. JTS Lutzki 794, fol. 91r): הנני נותן לו את בריתי שלום. לפי שכפיו נגואלו בדם וכהן שהרג את הנפש לא ישא כפיו והיה ירא שמא יפסיד כהונתו לכך נתן לו הקב"ה את בריתו שלום. *Ḥizzequni* adopts this approach without attribution. See also *Perushei R. Ḥayyim Palti'el*, 554.

[79] See ms. JTS Lutzki 791, fol. 140r: אשר ילדה אותה ללוי במצרים. ק' דהל"ל אשר ילדה ללוי במצרים. ונראה דאותה היה שמה של אשת לוי. This explanation (which is not recorded in *Minḥat Yehudah*)

R. Moses of Coucy questions the Torah's assertion in Numbers 26:64 that, in the census taken in *ʿArvot Moʾav* after the episode involving Pinhas, "no one was included who had been counted by Moses and Aaron in the Sinai desert," since all those who had been included in the counting then were above the age of twenty, and had by now passed away. Rashi notes that this verse is accurate only with respect to men, because according to *Midrash Tanḥuma* the women were not included in the decree made at the time of the spies—that all those who were above the age of twenty would perish in the desert—since the women loved the land of Israel. R. Moses of Coucy raises a more fundamental question, however, that he leaves unanswered. There were several men who were born in the days of Jacob and who were much more than sixty years old at the time of the spies, such as Makhir and Ya'ir, who were also not included in the Divine decree due to their more advanced age and who were therefore still alive, even though they had been counted by Moses and Aaron in the Sinai desert. A possible solution, that men above the age of sixty were not counted and included in the later census in *ʿArvot Moʾav*, is also not tenable, because Joshua himself was more than sixty at this time, and he was included in this census.[80]

R. Moses of Coucy addresses the highly unusual opening of *parashat Matot* (Nu. 30:2). Instead of the Torah writing as is typical that "God spoke to Moses saying" and that He initiated the discussion, this portion begins with Moses speaking: "And Moses spoke to the heads of the tribes of the children of Israel saying," with Moses proceeding directly to speak about the laws of vows. R. Moses of Coucy explains that this verse must be connected to the final verses in the preceding *parashah* of *Pinḥas* (Nu. 29:39 and 30:1). There, Moses had mentioned the voluntary offerings that had to be brought on the festivals, in addition to the sacrifices for the festivals themselves, so

---

is found as one possible explanation (*yesh ʾomrim*) in the Cambridge manuscript of R. Judah *he-Ḥasid*'s commentary to the Torah, ed. Y. S. Lange, 61–62. Cf. G. Brin, "ʿIyyun be-Perushei R. Yehudah he-Ḥasid la-Torah," *Sinai* 88 (1981), 10; and see above, chapter 3, n. 34. This passage maintains that there is a verse in Chronicles (which Lange could not locate) which lists Otah as the name of a man. It is also found in *Sefer ha-Gan*, ed. Orlian, 321, citing an unidentified *midrash* (*ve-yesh ba-midrash de-Otah shem ʾishto shel Levi*). Several later Tosafist Torah collections (as well as ms. JTS Lutzki 794) cite this explanation from the unidentified *midrash*, while the printed edition of *Paʿaneaḥ Raza*, 471, cites it in the name of a *midrash* "that the author of *Sefer ha-Gan* heard from his teacher." See also *Perushei R. Yosef Bekhor Shor*, ed. Nevo, 291, which suggests that this verse is a *miqra qaẓar* (a shortened verse), which should be understood as if it were written, "that Levi's wife bore to him in Egypt" (*ʾasher yaldah lo ʾishto le-Levi be-Miẓrayyim*). *Perushei R. Ḥayyim Paltiʾel*, ed. Lange, 559, cites the explanation of *Bekhor Shor* (anonymously), but prefers the explanation that Otah was the name of Levi's wife, because otherwise the word *ʾotah* would appear to be completely superfluous. Cf. Rashbam's comment to Gen. 49:10 (עד כי יבא שילה).

80 See *Minḥat Yehudah* (Nu.), fol. 23b (כך מצאתי בפשטי ר"מ מקוצי), and ms. JTS Lutzki 794, fol. 92r.

that they should not become overdue (משום בל תאחר). He then spoke to the heads of the tribes, who were also the judges, in order to instruct the people in the laws of vows. He conveyed to them that God had commanded him to make sure that the people bring forward their voluntary commitments on the festivals, lest they become overdue, and therefore the people had to become familiar immediately with the laws of vows.[81] This is yet another excellent example of the kind of contextual *peshat* that is found in R. Moses of Coucy's Torah commentary; in this instance, as in some others, it is quite similar to the interpretation put forward by Rashbam.

R. Moses makes a double comment related to Numbers 31:2, in which Moses is told by God to "execute the vengeance of the children of Israel on the Midianites." The first part, which reads something into the biblical text, addresses the juxtaposition of this command to the portion dealing with the nullification of vows at the beginning of *parashat Matot*. R. Moses indicates that Moses was led to believe that perhaps God was considering the nullification of His vow, made in the presence of His Heavenly entourage, that Moses would not go into the land of Israel, since at this point Moses had already reached the lands of Siḥon and ʿOg, which would become part of the land of Israel on the eastern shore of the Jordan River. God's response, however, is that Moses's presence here was only to accomplish the Jews' revenge on Midyan. His oath, which instructed that Moses not cross the Jordan River, would remain intact. R. Moses of Coucy's second remark is a more *peshat*-like analysis of the text. Although Moses himself was commanded to seek the vengeance of Israel (*neqom niqmat Yisra'el*), the next verse states that Moses went to the people and told them to prepare armed men (חלוצים) who would go and exact this vengeance. Moses had grown up partially in Midian, and it would therefore have been inappropriate for him to "bite the hand that fed him" and that had personally sustained him, in this way.[82]

81 See *Minḥat Yehudah* (Nu.), fol. 26a, and ms. JTS Lutzki 791, fol. 143r: לפי הפשט היכן מצינו שצוה הקב"ה למשה כן שלא מצי' שום פרש' שמתחלה כן שלא כתוב למעלה וידבר ה' אל משה לאמר. וי"ל וכו'. Cf. Ramban's commentary, ad loc.

82 See ms. JTS Lutzki 791, fol. 143r (הקב"ה אמר לו נקום אתה בעצמך והוא שלח אחרים דכתי' וישלח אותם משה וגו' וע"י שנתגדל במדין חדל לו דאמרי' אינשי בירא דשתית מטה לא תשדי ביה קלא. פש' הר"ם); *Minḥat Yehudah* (Numbers), fol. 26b; and ms. JTS Lutzki 794, fol. 94v. In a comment to Nu. 31:50, R. Moses distinguishes between the girdles (perhaps chastity belts) that were captured from Midyan, which Moses accepted as holy donations, and the mirrors that had been used in sexual contexts that he did not wish to accept (see Ex. 38:8, and Rashi's comment ad loc.) until he was explicitly instructed to do so. R. Moses's explanation is that these items were not worn against the reproductive organs but were a kind of external mold. See *Minḥat Yehudah*, fol.27b (ואומר הר"מ מקוצי היכן קיבל משה כומז שהיה לאותו מקום לקרבן והלא לא קבל המראות הצובאות שעשה מהם הכיור כי אם על פי הדיבור. נרא' כי כומז ועגיל אינו ממש אצל הרחם אלא מנגד הדד על כנגדה וכנגד בית הרחם); *ʾImrei Noʿam*, 172; and ms. JTS Lutzki 791, fol. 145r. Cf. *Perushei R. Ḥayyim Paltiʾel*, ed. Lange, 345–46; *Moshav Zeqenim*, 222–23; and *Tosafot ha-Shalem*, ed. Gellis, 10:214, secs. 5–6.

R. Moses of Coucy's extant comments to Deuteronomy, which are fewer than his comments to Numbers but more numerous than his comments to Genesis, are concentrated in four portions. ʿOg, king of Bashan, lived in a place called *ʿAshtarot* (Deut. 1:4). Rashi interprets this word to mean crisis and difficulty, and he therefore identifies this place as *ʿAshterot Qarnaʾim*, which is mentioned in Genesis (14:5), and has the connotation of horns. Indeed, the giants who defeated Amrafel were from there. R. Moses of Coucy explains, on the other hand, that *lefi ha-peshat*, *ʿAshtarot* has the connotation of grazing land (*mirʿeh*) as we find in the phrase צאנך עשתרות, located several chapters away, in Deuteronomy 7:13, as translated by Onkelos. In addition, *Ḥazal* held (*Ḥullin* 84b) that the name for *ʿAshtarot* reflects the fact that this place made its owners wealthy.[83] Since this was a place for grazing, it was requested by the tribes of Reuven and Gad for their flocks. R. Moses here proposes a meaning that is etymologically more nuanced than the one suggested by Rashi, supporting his choice with prooftexts from both biblical and rabbinic literature.[84]

The attacking Amorites are compared in Deuteronomy 1:44 to bees: "They chased after you as bees do, and they beat you down in Seʿir as far as Ḥormah." Rashi understands this comparison to mean that just as a bee dies immediately upon stinging someone, so too the warriors of the Emori will die as soon as they touch you. *Ḥizzequni* explains that, in context, Rashi's interpretation means that even though the Amorites had inherent weaknesses, as the comparison to bees indicates, they were still able to defeat Israel at this point. R. Moses of Coucy, on the other hand, explains that just as bees swarm—that is, one leads the way and the others follow—so too with the Emori. As the verse in *parashat Shelaḥ* states (Nu. 14:45), "The Amalekites and the Canaanites who dwell in the mountain descended and they smote them and discomfited them as far as Ḥormah."[85] *Ḥizzequni* cites this view as well (as always, without referring to R. Moses by name), adding, as *Bekhor Shor* interprets, that the Emori, like bees, were able to wound the Jews but were unable to kill them.[86] Once again, R. Moses is in the company of several of the *pashtanim* of his day, and his approach is adopted by *Ḥizzequni*.

[83] The interpretations of Onkelos and *Ḥazal* are the second and third options presented by Rashi to Deut. 7:13. The first, from Menaḥem ben Saruq, interprets this term in the sense of the choicest (of the flock), citing Gen.14:5 (*ʿasterot qarnayim*). Cf. Ibn Ezra, who cites Onkelos, as well as an astrological interpretation from an unnamed Spanish exegete.

[84] See *Minḥat Yehudah* (Deut.), fol. 2a (ור"מ מקוצי פי' לפי הפשט), and ms. JTS Lutzki 791, fol. 147r.

[85] *Minḥat Yehudah* (Deut.), fol. 2b (פי' ר"מ מקוצי), and *ʾImrei Noʿam*, 176.

[86] See *Perushei R. Yosef Bekhor Shor*, ed. Nevo, 309–10.

Rashbam explained that ʿOg's cradle (*ʿarso*) was located in *Rabbat Benei Amon* (Deut. 3:11), because it had remained there from when ʿOg was a child, as a kind of memento. R. Moses of Coucy understood *ʿarso* to refer to ʿOg's present bed. ʿOg had heard that God had commanded Israel not to fight or come into conflict with *Benei Amon* (Deut. 2:19), and so he put his bed there out of fear, because he knew the Jews would not be able to come after him there.[87]

We have two comments from R. Moses toward the end of *parashat Re'eh.* Rashi interprets the phrase that characterizes the added value or worth of an *ʿeved ʿivri* that makes it hard for his master to part with him, *ki mishneh sekhar sakhir ʿavadkha shesh shanim* (Deut. 15:18), in accordance with the *Sifrei.* An *ʿeved ʿivri* works for his master by day and by night, by day in terms of service and by night through having children with a *shifḥah kenaʿanit.* For this approach, the phrase *mishneh sekhar sakhir* means that an *ʿeved ʿivri* does double service for his master during his six-year stint, and this is the source of his value. R. Moses of Coucy suggests an interpretation that appears to be even simpler. The *ʿeved ʿivri* works for twice or double the time of a regular hired hand, a *sakhir*, whose term of employment is limited to three years, as defined by a verse in Isaiah (16:14: "in three years, which are the years of a hired hand," *sakhir*). This interpretation, including the prooftext from Isaiah, is proposed by both Ibn Ezra and *Bekhor Shor*, although it was rejected by Rashbam.[88]

As Rashi and Ibn Ezra do, R. Moses of Coucy explains the inclusion of a reference to the exodus from Egypt within the Torah's description of

[87] *Minḥat Yehudah* (Deut.), fol. 3b (כתב ר"מ מקוצי); ms. Vatican (Urban 21), fol. 146r; and ms. JTS Lutzki 794, fol. 98v. The verb *katav* again suggests that we are dealing with a written commentary. See *Rashbam's Commentary on Deuteronomy*, ed. M. Lockshin (Providence, R.I., 2004), 46–47, and cf. *Perushei R. Yosef Bekhor Shor*, ed. Nevo, 311 (followed by *Ḥizzequni*), that ʿOg's bed was placed in *Rabbat Benei ʿAmon*, since this city had a wall made of iron around it.

[88] See *Minḥat Yehudah* (Deut.), fol. 11a (ור' משה מקוצי פירש . . . שהרי ג' שנים שנ' שכר שכיר כדכתוב בישעיה . . . וזה עבדך שש שנים). Cf. ms. JTS Lutzki 791, fol. 154v: כי משנה שכר שכיר. שהרי ג' שנים שני שכיר כדכתי' בישעיה (טז:יד) שלש שנים כשני שכיר וזה עבדך שש שנים. ורש"י פי' בע"א כי דרך משכירים לשכור ג' שנים ואין ג' שנים בלא עיבור . . . כי אין לוקח מעשר עד שנה ג'. ה"ר ברכיה, and *Perushei R. Yosef Bekhor Shor*, ed. Nevo, 339. *Perushei R. Ḥayyim Palti'el*, ed. Lange, 586, characterizes the approach of R. Moses (and his predecessors) as *pashteh di-qera*. Rashbam's rejection of this interpretation is due in part to another verse in Isaiah (2:16), which suggests the term of a hired hand is only one year. Cf. *Rashbam's Commentary on Deuteronomy*, ed. M. Lockshin, 99–100. On R. Moses of Coucy's use of R. Berekhyah's interpretations to Deuteronomy, see also *Minḥat Yehudah* to Deut. 27:13 (fol. 18a; the passage concludes, כפר"מ מקוצי), and to Deut. 32:39 (fols. 23a–b; and see below, n. 95), and cf. N. Golb, *The Jews in Medieval Normandy* (Cambridge, 1998), 333–34; and above, Introduction, n. 83. (In ms. B.M. 190, the second comment found in *Minḥat Yehudah* to Deut. 27:13, on the various ארורים, is also included as part of פשטי הר"ם.) See *Perushei R. Ḥayyim Palti'el*, ed. Lange, 560, n. 15, for a comment of R. Berekhyah to Nu. 27:17, although this is found already in similar form in the name of R. Jacob of Orleans; see above, chapter 2, n. 185.

the festival of *Shavu'ot* in Deuteronomy 16:12. Rashi explains the connection in a general way. God is stressing that he redeemed the Jewish people from Egypt in order for them to observe these precepts that were contained in the Torah. Ibn Ezra maintains that the reference to the Exodus here is not because of *Shavu'ot* per se, but rather because, in the prior verse, which describes the joy to be experienced in Jerusalem on *Shavu'ot*, the Torah instructs that the entire household, including one's servants, be included. R. Moses of Coucy, on the other hand, suggests a particular connection between *Shavu'ot* and the Exodus. Lest one say, how can I go up to Jerusalem at this crucial time at the beginning of the harvest season, and leave my harvesting in order to make the journey, remember that you were slaves in Egypt. You had nothing there, until God showed you His kindness. The specific connection suggested by R. Moses is presented and amplified by *Ḥizzequni*.[89]

R. Moses of Coucy explains the focus in *parashat Shoftim* on excluding from war only those who had built a new home, planted a vineyard, or betrothed a woman (Deut. 20:5–7), as opposed to others who were in the midst of fulfilling other new *mizvot* (e.g., one who had a firstborn son but had not yet redeemed him, or one who had acquired a *tallit* but had not yet put *ẓiẓit* on the garment). Moses saw that these three particular elements would be part of his address of rebuke to the Jewish people (the *tokheḥah* in *parashat Ki Tavo*): those who had betrothed women would see them given to others, those who built homes would not dwell in them, and those who had planted vineyards would see them harvested by others (Deut. 28:30). Therefore, Moses instructed the Jews that only people in these specific three situations should not go to war, because if they were killed in battle, it would be said that the *tokhehah* given by Moses is already affecting the Jewish people, and they can no longer succeed in battle.[90]

A trenchant question is posed by R. Moses on the portion of the *'eglah 'arufah* which deals with an unsolved murder. If the elders who come to

[89] See *Minḥat Yehudah* (Deut.), fol. 11a; and ms. JTS Lutzki 791, fol. 155r: מה ענין יציאת מצרים אצל שבועות? וי"ל שלא תאמר איך אעלה ואבטל מן הקציר. לכך נאמ' וזכרת..ולא היה לך כלום עד שחנך המקום יתברך. פש' הר"ם. Cf. *Bekhor Shor* Nevo, 341: "when you find yourself in a state of *simḥah*, remember your servitude in Egypt when you had no time to rest and to rejoice, until God redeemed you from there." *Ḥizzequni*, who follows precisely the approach of R. Moses here (without attribution), adds that all the other festivals of the Jewish year have key precepts (*maẓah*, *sukkah*, *shofar*, fasting on Yom Kippur) reminding us that only through God's favor did we leave Egypt. *Shavu'ot*, however, does not have any such cue (*'ein bo shum remez*). Thus the verse on the Exodus is included here, with the connotation suggested by R. Moses. For *Ḥizzequni*'s use of R. Moses of Coucy's comments, see above, nn. 10, 25, 55, 57, 61, 78; and the next note.

[90] See *Minḥat Yehudah* (Deut.), fol. 13a (כ"פ ר"מ מקוצי), found also (unnamed) in *Ḥizzequni*. *Perushei R. Ḥayyim Palti'el*, ed. Lange, 593, contains a more extensive answer in the name of מהר"ח, which briefly mentions this approach as well.

the scene state that "our hands have spilled no blood" (*yadenu lo shafkhu*, Deut. 21:7), why is any further expiation required, as is requested in the following verse (*kapper le-ʿamkha Yisraʾel*)? *Minḥat Yehudah* suggests that since every Jew is responsible for the welfare of other Jews, there is still some level of culpability that attaches to the populace at large. R. Moses of Coucy suggests, however, *lefi peshuto*, that the word *kapper* here has the meaning of *galeh*, to reveal. The elders are asking God to reveal to His people who the killer is, for as long as there is no accurate knowledge, the *goʾel ha-dam* may kill someone who is not deserving of death. R. Moses finds proof for the use of *kapper* in this way from a verse in Isaiah 28:18, וכפר בריתכם את מות, which is translated in this way by Targum Yonatan b. Uziʾel.[91] In addition to providing these insightful *peshat* comments, R. Moses also deals in *parashat Shoftim* with the proper meaning of a passage in *Sifrei* and with a seeming contradiction in Rashi's commentary,[92] and he cites without embellishment a comment made by Ibn Ezra.[93]

The sinfulness of the Jewish people is characterized in *parashat Haʾazinu* (Deut. 32:18) as "you are unmindful of the Rock that begot you, and you have forgotten the God that formed you" (צור ילדך תשי ותשכח א-ל מחוללך). R. Moses of Coucy provides a suggestive interpretation of this verse, based on a word play. The letter *yod* in the word תשי, unmindful, is a small one according to the masoretic tradition (יו"ד זעירא). The letters *tav*, *shin*, and the smaller or defective *yod*, can be understood to represent the midrashic phrase and concept of תש ידי הצייר, the artist's hands have become weakened. The form of a fetus develops in the first forty days of gestation. An adulterer who has relations with a woman in this period of gestation forces the

[91] *Minḥat Yehudah* (Deut.) fols. 13b–14a. R. Yosef Qara translates *ve-khuppar* in Isaiah 28:18 as "cleaning and removal" (לשון קינוח וסילוק), and see also Ibn Ezra there. See also R. Yosef *Bekhor Shor*, whose approach to finding the murderer follows that of Rambam (in *Guide for the Perplexed*, as cited by Naḥmanides), and see below, chapter 7.

[92] R. Moses's identification of the lands that *shevet Levi* could not inherit (Deut. 18:1–2, and see Rashi's interpretation based on the *Sifrei*) is linked to that of Rabbenu Tam in his *Sefer ha-Yashar*. See *Perushei R. Ḥayyim Paltiʾel*, ed. Lange 591, n. 4, and cf. *Nimmuqei Ḥumash le-Rabbenu Yeshayah*, ed. Chavel, 66; *Perushei R. Yosef Bekhor Shor*, ed. Nevo, 345; and above, n. 46. In ms. JTS Lutzki 794, fol. 111v, and *Minḥat Yehudah* (Deut.), fol. 11b, R. Moses resolves a seeming contradiction between Rashi's view on the timing of the punishment of a *zaqen mamre* (Deut. 17:13) and his view with regard to the punishment of a *ben sorer u-moreh* at the beginning of *parashat Ki Teze*.

[93] See ms. JTS Lutzki 791, fol. 157v: לא תשיג. פי' א"ע שע"י הסגת גבול בא לידי ריב ומכות ורציחה על כן נסמכה פרשה זו אחריו עין בעין נפש בנפש. פש' הר"ם. This is Ibn Ezra's comment to Deut. 19:14, that encroachment on the boundaries of others (*hasagat gevul*) can lead to further conflicts (both physical and legalistic) and even to death, as indicated also by the fact that these kinds of damages are mentioned at the end of the ensuing section in *parashat Shoftim* (19:21, *nefesh be-nefesh*, *ʿayin be-ʿayin*, and so on).

Divine artist, who has initially formed the face of the child in the image of the father, to now recast the face in the image of the adulterer.[94]

R. Moses carefully traces the parallelism in Deuteronomy32:39, "See now that I, even I, am He (ראו עתה כי אני אני הוא), and there is no god with me, I kill and make alive (אני אמית ואחיה), I wound and I heal (מחצתי ואני ארפא), and there is no one who can deliver out of My hand (ואין מידי מציל)," and notes that the first *'ani* at the beginning of the verse goes with "I kill and make alive" (*'ani 'amit va-aḥayeh*), while the second *'ani* goes with the *'ani* of *maḥazti va-'ani 'erpah* ("I wound and I heal"). A second related comment here by R. Moses, citing R. Berekhyah *ha-Naqdan*, explains that since the enemies of Israel in this portion are always referred to in the plural (e.g., in the prior verse, let them rise up and help you, יקומו ויעזרוכם), God states unequivocally in this verse "there is no other god with me." Since the enemies say in the prior verse that their gods should drink the libations of their drink offerings, God says (in Deut. 32:42) "My arrows will be drunk with the blood of the enemies, but I will not drink their offerings." Similarly, the enemies say, in the prior verse, that their gods eat the fat of their sacrifices, and so God says (in Deut. 32:42), "I do not eat, but my swords eats flesh" (וחרבי תאכל בשר). In this instance, R. Moses traces the parallelism that is demonstrated over several phrases and verses.[95]

R. Moses of Coucy makes several comments at the beginning of *parashat Ve-Zot ha-Berakhah* that are linked to comments cited in the name of *'Avi ha-'Ezri.* Rashi interprets the brief blessing to Reuven (33:6) to mean that he should live in this world (*yeḥi Reuven*) and should not die in the next world (*ve'al yamot*), and that his number should be included among the other tribes (ויהי מתיו מספר)—that is, he shouldn't be excluded because of the episode with Bilhah. *Rabbenu 'Avi ha-'Ezri* (Ibn Ezra), as cited by R. Moses of Coucy, explains that the term for the negative in *ve'al yamot* carries over to the phrase *vihi metav mispar* (= *ve'al yehi metav mispar*), a construction that can be found in other verses such as Psalms 6:2. Thus the latter phrase means that Reuven's number should not be small but should rather be exceedingly large. R. Moses of Coucy's interpretation of the blessing is that Reuven should live, and not die in war; rather the number of his people

[94] See *Minḥat Yehudah* (Deut.), fol. 22b (כפר"מ מקוצי), and ms. JTS Lutzki 791, fol. 160v ('פש הר"ם). The midrashic discussion is found in *Bamidbar Rabbah* to *Naso*, sec. 9, and in *Tanḥuma* to *Naso*, ed. S. Buber, sec. 6.

[95] See *Minḥat Yehudah*, fols. 23a–b; ms. JTS Lutzki 791, fol. 160v; and above, n. 88. Cf. R. Harris, *Discerning Parallelism: A Study in Northern French Medieval Jewish Biblical Exegesis* (Providence, R.I., 2004), 40–42, 60–65, 89–98; Jair Haas, "Iqqaron 'Kefel 'Inyan be-Milim Shonot' be-Asqolah ha-Parshanit shel Ẓefon Ẓarefat," *Hebrew Union College Annual* 75 (2004), 51–79; and above, n. 75. An anonymous interpretation to Deut. 32:43 found in *Minḥat Yehudah*, fol. 23b, appears in ms. Vatican 21 in the name of R. Moses of Coucy

who go to war is always the same number that returns. Furthermore, the unusual phrase in the next verse, *ve-zot li-Yehudah*, "and this is for Judah" (Deut. 33:37, followed by the phrase, "O God, hear Judah's voice and bring him to his people"), connects Judah's blessing to that of Reuven in the following way. Moses is saying that this same blessing of losing no one in war which was given to Reuven should also be given to Judah. Thus God should hear Judah's voice when he goes to war, and he should be brought home to his people, signifying that none of his warriors will be lost either. This comment is again presented by R. Moses of Coucy in the name of *ʾAvi ha-ʿEzri* (Ibn Ezra).[96]

In addition, R. Moses of Coucy discusses the fact that Moses does not mention Simeon in his blessings. Even though Jacob in his blessings had grouped Simeon together with his close brother, Levi, their linkage in that context was a fundamentally negative one; they were "brothers in anger" (Gen. 49:6). R. Moses explains that both Simeon and Levi had essentially lost the possibility of a positive blessing from Jacob because of their actions regarding Joseph (*ʾarur ʾappam ki ʿaz*, Gen. 49:7). In the eyes of Moses, however, Levi now merited a blessing, since the tribe of Levi had stood up so clearly during the sin of the golden calf when they gathered together to follow Moses. This is the meaning of the phrase, "to give to you a blessing today" (*ve-latet ʿaleikhem ha-yom berakhah*, Ex. 32:29), that is, to restore to you the blessing that you had lost over the selling of Joseph. Thus Moses blesses Levi, but Simeon's blessing is still not merited. Moreover, Zimri was descended from Simeon, which further underscores that this tribe did not now deserve a blessing. R. Moses of Coucy again cites this interpretation in the name of *ʾAvi ha-ʿEzri.*[97]

[96] See *Minḥat Yehudah*, fol. 24a: ורבי' אבי העזרי פי' . . . ור' משה מקוצי פי' . . . כפר"מ מקוצי בשם אבי העזרי. Ms. JTS Lutzki 791, fol. 162r, cites R. Moses's interpretations in the name of *peshatei R. Mosheh*, without mentioning *ʾAvi ha-ʿEzri*, although ms. Frankfurt Hebr. Oct. 100, fol. 157v, does (כפר"ם בשם אבי העזרי); see the next note. See also *Perushei* R. Yosef *Bekhor Shor*, ed. Nevo, 393. *Bekhor Shor* presents the same interpretation to the blessing of Reuven as R. Moses of Coucy does. He notes explicitly that the war being referred to here by Moses is the war that he would fight crossing the Jordan as a *ḥaluẓ* on behalf of the other tribes. *Bekhor Shor* presents the interpretation attributed to *ʾAvi ha-ʿEzri* as an (unnamed) *yesh ʾomrim* (cf. above, chapter 2, n. 87), and he also presents the interpretation attributed by R. Moses of Coucy to *ʾAvi ha-ʿEzri* on the blessing of Judah. Judah will suffer no losses in any wars for the land of Israel (just as Reuven would not), and God will surely hear Judah when he calls during the war. In this instance, *Ḥizzequni* follows more closely the formulation of *Bekhor Shor* rather than that of R. Moses as he usually does.

[97] See *Minḥat Yehudah*, fol. 24b: כפר"מ מקוצי בשם אבי העזרי. In ms. JTS Lutzki 791, fol. 162v, *ʾAvi ha-ʿEzri* is again not mentioned, although it is included again in ms. Frankfurt Hebr. Oct. 100in the above note; כפר"ם בשם אבי העזרי). See above, chapter 3, nn. 250–51, for the incorrect attribution of these comments to R. Eliezer b. Joʾel *ha-Levi* (Rabiah), an older, German Tosafist contemporary of R. Moses of Coucy. Cf. *Bekhor Shor*'s commentary, ed. Nevo, 394; Ibn Ezra refers to this as well in 33:8. Ibn Ezra was also cited by name on a handful of occasions in *Sefer*

There are no other recognized Tosafists or other leading rabbinic figures in Ashkenaz during this period who produced the volume and array of *peshat*-like comments, centered to a large extent around Rashi's commentary and its methods, that we have seen from R. Yosef *Bekhor Shor*, R. Jacob of Orleans, R. Yom of Joigny, R. Judah *he-Ḥasid*, R. Isaiah di Trani, and R. Moses of Coucy. We should note that this group is a bit larger than the classical northern French *pashtanim* of the twelfth century who are known to us, even though its members are not as consistently dedicated to the pursuit of *peshat*.

In addition, and as we shall now see, several northern French Tosafist contemporaries and colleagues of R. Moses of Coucy, including R. Yeḥi'el of Paris and R. Moses and R. Isaac b. Shne'ur of Evreux,[98] evinced a noticeable interest in biblical interpretation, much of it seemingly independent of talmudic or halakhic studies. To be sure, the incidence of *peshat* interpretations in comments by R. Yeḥi'el and the brothers of Evreux to the Torah is much less frequent than what we have seen among their Tosafist predecessors and contemporaries. Indeed, together with the compilatory commentary *Sefer ha-Gan*, which contains a mixture of *peshat* and *derash* with quite a bit of the latter, R. Yeḥi'el and the brothers of Evreux herald the transition to the more diffuse Tosafist Torah compilatory commentaries of the mid-thirteenth century and beyond, which were produced in both Germany and northern France.

R. Yeḥi'el of Paris

R. Yeḥi'el b. Joseph of Paris has recently begun to emerge as a more multifaceted Tosafist and rabbinic figure than heretofore thought. Known for his *pesaqim* and legal rulings, in addition to his participation in the so-called Trial of the Talmud in 1240, R. Yeḥi'el also composed *Tosafot* that are extant, and others that are no longer extant.[99] He provided commentaries to a

---

ha-Gan, which was compiled in northern France at the same time as R. Moses of Coucy's Torah commentary; see *Sefer ha-Gan*, ed. Orlian, 129, 192, 200, 276, 279. For the commentaries and works of Ibn Ezra that were composed during his stay in Rouen and London (from 1154–60), see Shlomo Sela and Gad Freudenthal, "Abraham Ibn Ezra's Scholarly Writings: A Chronological Listing," *Aleph* 6 (2006), 13–55. On the citation of Ibn Ezra by R. Yeḥi'el of Paris, another French contemporary of R. Moses, see below, n. 122.

[98] On their connections, see Urbach, *Ba'alei ha-Tosafot*, 1:461, 465, 485; S. Emanuel, *Shivrei Luḥot*, 193–97; and see above, chapter 1, n. 116.

[99] On R. Yeḥiel's *Tosafot* and *pesaqim*, see Simcha Emanuel, *Shivrei Luḥot*, 187–98; idem, "R. Yeḥi'el mi-Paris: Toledotav ve-Ziqato le-Ereẓ Yisra'el," *Shalem* 8 (2009), 86–89; I. Ta-Shma, *Ha-Sifrut ha-Parshanit la-Talmud*, vol. 2 (Jerusalem, 2001), 110–12, and cf. Urbach, *Ba'alei ha-Tosafot*, 458–60, and *Tosafot ha-Rosh 'al Massekhet Pesaḥim*, ed. A. Shoshana (Jerusalem, 1997), 834, 843, 922, 976, and the editor's introduction, 25–28. Ms. Bodl. Qu. 635, fols. 17r–v (*'inyanei gittin*), includes *get* forms by R. Jacob of Corbeil (a student of R. Jacob of Courson), R. Pereẓ

number of *piyyutim*, some of which reflect familiarity with mystical teachings.[100] There are also records of additional polemical encounters and exchanges in which R. Yeḥi'el participated.[101] R. Yeḥi'el died sometime before 1265. He set out for the land of Israel but did not reach it, and, indeed, appears to have been forced to return to France due to his failing health.[102]

In addition, R. Yeḥi'el's extant comments to the Torah are more extensive and varied than those of many other Tosafists. To be sure, more than a few are related to halakhic verses and issues, although there are also a number of comments on narrative sections of the Torah, including several that are dedicated to the search for *peshat*, as we shall see. One version of comments to *parashat Mishpatim*, found in a Tosafist Torah commentary in a Florence manuscript, concludes with the phrase, זה סדור משפטים שסדר הר"ר יחיאל אשר הלך לארץ הצבי ברוך השם אשר עזרני לסיימו.[103]

Several observations are in order about this section of commentary. The bulk of the material presented here is explicitly halakhic and is entitled *siddur mishpatim*—a compendium of law—that could have been discussed either in the context of talmudic study or during a review of the weekly Torah portion. It is also unclear whether R. Yeḥi'el was responsible for compiling all of this section or only certain parts. One of the first comments in this section, for example, comes from Rabbenu Pereẓ b. Elijah of Corbeil, who died in 1298, more than thirty years after R. Yeḥi'el, and discusses Rashi's opening remark to this portion, that *ve-'eleh ha-mishpatim* "adds to what

---

of Corbeil, and R. Yeḥ'iel of Paris. Cf. Urbach, *Ba'alei ha-Tosafot*, 1:461; Emanuel, *Shivrei Luḥot*, 217–18; and above, chapter 1, nn. 116–23.

100 See below, chapter 5, nn. 283–84, and chapter 6, nn. 128–30. See also ms. Hamburg 144 (#882; Ashkenaz, 13th century), which begins with *qinnot* for the ninth of Av by R. Eleazar *ha-Qalir*, followed by *qinnot* from several German Tosafists and rabbinic figures including R. Eliezer b. Nathan (fol. 20v), R. Barukh b. Samuel of Mainz (fol. 26v), and R. Abraham b. Samuel *he-Ḥasid* of Speyer (fols. 33r and 50r). A *qinah*, זכור איפה ארמון נוף by R. Yeḥi'el b. Yosef, appears on fol. 50v, although cf. below, chapter 5, n. 281. See also ms. Paris 312, fols. 235v–236v (סימני כתבי הקברות אשר הביאם ה"ר יעקב שליח נאמן מר' יחיאל מפריז). A legendary tale about R. Yeḥi'el is found in ms. Montefiore 479, fol. 189r, from Gedalyah ibn Yaḥya's *Shalshelet ha-Qabbalah*.

101 See ms. Bodl. 271/1, fol. 27v, for a תשובת ר' יחיאל אל מין ומשומד, and cf. Poznanski, *Mavo*, 111. See also *Sefer Yosef ha-Meqanne*, ed. Judah Rosenthal (Jerusalem, 1970), 53, 67 (גלח אחד אמר לרבינו יחיאל מפריס); and ms. Vatican 324 (Ashkenaz, 1398), fol. 278r (תשובות הר"ר יחיאל מפריס לפול המין), which begins a somewhat different, truncated version of the trial of the Talmud than the one that has been published as *Vikkuaḥ R. Yeḥi'el mi-Paris*. Cf. Yehuda Galinsky, "Mishpat ha-Talmud bi-Shenat 1240 be-Paris," *Shenaton ha-Mishpat ha-'Ivri* 22 (2001–3), 45–69.

102 See S. Emanuel, "R. Yeḥi'el mi-Paris," 89–99, and idem, *Shivrei Luḥot*, 185–86. The "ten questions asked by R. Eliezer with regard to resurrection" that appear in ms. Vatican 324 just before the version of R. Yeḥi'el's disputation (see the above note) have nothing to do with R. Yeḥi'el.

103 See ms. Florence/Laurenziana Plut. II.20 (#20365, Sefarad, 13th–14th centuries), fol. 208r. Cf. S. Emanuel, *Shivrei Luḥot*, 187 (n. 9), and Urbach, *Ba'alei ha-Tosafot*, 1:458–60.

came before it."[104] A number of other recognized northern French Tosafists from the late twelfth and early thirteenth centuries are cited within this unit. One of them is Rashba, an acronym that connotes either R. Samson b. Abraham of Sens or his brother, R. Solomon b. Abraham of Troyes. Rashba discusses the exclusion of women from serving as *dayyanim*, as implied by the phrase *ʾasher tasim lifneihem*, which serves to exclude both non-Jews and women, and the distinction between a Jewish slave who is sold by the court (and must be freed after six years) and a Jewish slave who sold himself, whose enslavement is not limited by any term. R. Solomon of Dreux, whose comments in these halakhic contexts have been noted,[105] is also mentioned several times, as are Riẓba and Ri, as well as a R. Barukh (which most likely refers to the author of *Sefer ha-Terumah*, R. Barukh b. Isaac), and R. Moses and R. Samuel, who were R. Yeḥiʾel's Tosafist colleagues, the brothers of Evreux.[106]

R. Yeḥiʾel is cited in the body of this treatise or section in connection with the comment of Rashi to Exodus 21:6. Rashi writes that the slave's right ear is pierced if he wishes to stay with his master beyond his initial term of servitude, based on a linkage with the leper. Just as the leper's right ear receives the blood used in his purification process, so too the right ear is the one that is pierced in the case of slavery. R. Yeḥiʾel, verifying the details in Rashi's comment, asks why this is not learned from the dedication ceremony of the *mishkan*, in which the right ear of the *kohen* received the blood of consecration (Lev. 8:24)? He responds that it would be inappropriate to learn non-Temple procedures from the procedures that were in effect in the Temple or the *mishkan*. A certain R. Nathan questioned whether there is any association between slavery and leprosy that would justify the linkage of these procedures. His son (who was also named R. Yeḥiʾel) answered that since leprosy appears because of slanderous speech, and the slave's perpetual state of slavery is also occasioned by his speech—since he had declared "I love my master, my wife and my children, and I do not wish to go free" (Ex. 21:25)—this is a most appropriate linkage. Others explain (*ve-yesh mefarshim*) the connection on the basis of the similarity of letters and the implied relationship between the Hebrew word for awl, מרצע, and the word for leper, מצ[ו]רע.[107]

[104] See ms. Florence, fols. 192r–v. The versions or variations closest to this comment, found in *Tosafot ha-Shalem*, ed. Gellis, 8:139, do not mention the name of Rabbenu Pereẓ.

[105] On these comments by R. Solomon, see above, chapter 3, nn. 223–26.

[106] For the comment by R. Barukh to *parashat Mishpatim*, see above, chapter 3, n. 192. For the brothers of Evreux, see below.

[107] Ms. Florence, fol. 195v. The identities of R. Nathan and his son Yeḥiʾel, who followed up on R. Yeḥiʾel's comment, are unclear, and there is no mention of these names in *Tosafot ha-Shalem*, ed. Gellis, 8:168–69. *Tosafot ha-Shalem*, 169, sec. 16, presents the comment about

This section of Torah commentary also reproduces a *peshat* interpretation by R. Yom Tov of Joigny, noted above in our treatment of R. Yom Tov's commentary, as to why the slave's ear is pierced, and why this is done at the doorpost. Simply put, this procedure makes it impossible for the *'eved* to later claim that the piercing was self-inflicted. At the same time, no other owner can claim that he did the piercing on this slave, since the door frame of the genuine owner precisely fits and reflects the specific piercing of this slave's ear.[108] Similarly, an unattributed *peshat* is presented as to why a female servant may not serve her master past her initial term, in addition to an analysis by R. Solomon *ha-Qadosh* of Dreux of the talmudic dictum (*Qiddushin* 21b) that other utensils besides an awl may be used.[109]

Another interpretation labeled as *lefi ha-peshat* accounts for the internal order of Exodus 21:14–17 and its significance. This sequence of verses begins with the crime of intentional murder, and then moves to kidnapping and selling the victim, which is less heinous than outright murder, and finally to cursing one's parents, which is (merely) an act of speech. Nonetheless, the punishment of death in all three cases is the same.[110] Also *lefi ha-peshat*, there is no punishment for one who kills a criminal who tunnels into his house (Ex. 22:1), and there is no obligation incumbent upon him to try to stop the thief in less harmful ways, because this break-in occurred at night. If the thief came to steal by day, however, when other means to dispatch him

the similar Hebrew letters in the words *awl* and *leper* from the commentary of R. Ephraim b. Samson, an associate of R. Eleazar of Worms and *Ḥasidut Ashkenaz*, whose Torah commentary contains quite a bit of letter manipulation and other forms of *remazim*. See above, Introduction, n. 84 (end). In *Moshav Zeqenim*, 191 (to Ex. 21:29 = *Tosafot ha-Shalem*, ed. Gellis, 8:236, sec. 12), R. Yeḥi'el is cited as questioning Rashi's halakhic analysis of the text of this verse, based on a talmudic passage in tractate *Bava Qamma*, although no answer is provided. Immediately following this comment, *Bekhor Shor* is cited in an explanation of another halakhic detail found in Rashi.

108 See fol. 195v: [פרש"י] אוזן ששמעה לא תגנוב. וי"מ דמ"מ בן נח מוזהר על לא תגנוב וכו'. וי"ל כי אוזן ששמעה לא תגנוב מפי משה רבי' שא"ל הקב"ה בסיני. וה"ר יום טוב מפרש לפי הפשט אוזן דנקט לפי שאם היה רוצעו במקום אחר יוכל לומר העבד צפתי עצמי או חתרתי עצמי. אבל באוזן אין זה מקום שיוכל לו' העבד דבר אז הוא עבד לעבד. ובזה מפרש לפי הפשט אל הדלת לפי שאם היה רוצעו ממקום אחר יכול אדם לערער עליו לו' שלי הוא ואני רצע־תיו. אבל עתה ייאמר האדון שלי הוא והנה מדת אזנו בדלת שלי. See also above, chapter 2, n. 219. *Ḥizzequni*, without attribution, notes that piercing the ear will prevent the possibility of self-infliction, while Ibn Ezra, in his short commentary, suggests that this procedure marks the door of the actual owner, preventing any confusion with regard to ownership (as does *Hadar Zeqenim*, also without attribution; see *Tosafot ha-Shalem*, ed. Gellis, 8:166, sec. 5). *Bekhor Shor* suggests (ed. Nevo, 138) that use of the doorway serves to publicize the matter.

109 See fol. 196r–v. The talmudic analysis found in *Minḥat Yehudah* in the name of *ha-Qadosh mi-Dreux* to Exodus 21:12 (מכה איש ומת), cited in *Tosafot ha-Shalem*, ed. Gellis, 8:193, sec. 6 (and see also above, chapter 3, n. 224), is not found in this manuscript.

110 See fol. 198v: ולפי הפשט בתחלה כתי' וכי יזיד איש איירי ברוצח ואח"כ בגונב שהוא קל ממנה ואח"כ במקלל אביו שאינו אלא דיבור בעלמיא.

are available, the one who kills him is responsible.[111] A polemical comment by one of the members of the Official family (who were well known in mid-thirteenth century France for their political and polemical activities) is also included.[112] In sum, while the bulk of the comments in *parashat Mishpatim* within the section associated with R. Yeḥi'el of Paris are focused, as we might expect, on the laws and specifications found in the portion, there is an attempt at *peshat* as well, although only R. Yom Tov of Joigny is mentioned by name in this regard. Following these comments on *Mishpatim* in the Florence manuscript, a second very brief commentary of similar nature appears. This is then followed by a third set of comments to *Mishpatim*, which consist mainly of *gematria* interpretations, including some that are associated explicitly with the German Pietists.[113]

In terms of R. Yeḥi'el's own exegetical methods, however, it is instructive to turn to a comment found earlier in this manuscript, to Genesis 38:26.[114] In this verse, in which Judah acknowledges that Tamar was more correct than he was (צדקה ממני), Rashi interprets the phrase to mean that, according to Judah, Tamar was vindicated because she was pregnant with his child. The comment in ms. Florence, which is quite similar to a comment on this verse found in a manuscript version of the Tosafist Torah compilation *Hadar Zeqenim*, explains instead that Judah maintained that Tamar should not be punished (she was righteous, *ẓadqah*) because their tryst was consummated through *qiddushin.*[115] Their relations were thereby permitted according to Jewish law (*be-heter 'astah*), and she did not act promiscuously (*derekh zenut*). At the same time, however, a R. Moses[116] notes that *qiddushin* cannot be given to one's daughter-in-law in any case. Therefore, Judah's

[111] See fol. 204r: אם במחתרת. לפי הפשט ר"ל לילה לכך נכנס בכותלו [ביום] ולא הצילו באחד מאיבריו או לתפסו חי אז יש לו דמים אם בא. This comment is made by Rashbam and *Bekhor Shor* (and Ibn Ezra as well), against the *Mekhilta*, that it does not have to be night. See *Tosafot ha-Shalem*, ed. Gellis, 8:255, sec. 4, and *Rashbam's Commentary on Exodus*, ed. Lockshin, 249–50.

[112] See fol. 201v, and cf. *Sefer Yosef ha-Meqanne*, ed. Y. Rosenthal (Jerusalem, 1970), 49–50, and David Berger, *The Jewish-Christian Debate in the High Middle Ages* (Philadelphia, 1979), 66, 255.

[113] This third set begins on fol. 210r. As an example, the *gematria* of the word *mohar* (in the phrase in Ex. 22:16, כמהר הבתולות, according to the marriage contract of virgins), as noted by a R. Moses, is equal to ר' זוזים (which is the amount of the standard *ketubah*). R. Judah *he-Ḥasid* adds that the word *mohar* is spelled without a *vav* to demonstrate that כמה ר' הבתולות, the *ketubah* of virgins is in the amount of two hundred (*reish*) *zuz* (*kamah ketubbat ha-betulot reish*). Another *gematria* associated with *Ḥasidei Ashkenaz* is found on Exodus 23:20, where several angels are linked to the phrase, הנה אנכי שולח מלאך לפניך. Cf. *Tosafot ha-Shalem*, ed. Gellis, 8:343–44, sec. 11, from ms. Bodl. 268 (the so-called *Perush ha-Roqeaḥ 'al ha-Torah*).

[114] See ms. Florence, fol. 168v.

[115] For this passage and its variants, see *Tosafot ha-Shalem*, ed. Gellis, 4:87, sec. 22. (In *REJ* 49 [1904], 33–50, I. Levi lists a number of manuscript versions of *Hadar Zeqenim*, as well as the rabbinic figures cited.)

[116] This is perhaps R. Moses of Paris, although it is sometimes difficult to definitively identify exegetes named R. Moses within Tosafist Torah compilations. Cf. above, chapter 3.

statement should be understood to mean that since her child is from him and not from a non-Jew, she does not deserve the punishment of burning (*serefah*) that had been first proposed.[117]

According to a passage in a Bodleian manuscript, R. Yeḥi'el of Paris raises a similar issue. What was Judah's argument according to Rashi's interpretation that "since the child is from me, she is now free from punishment"? Their relationship was still illicit, if not promiscuous. R. Yeḥi'el explains, however, that since Judah believed that his sons had consummated their marriages with Tamar, she had been legally married to them. Accordingly, even in the pre-Sinaitic period, Tamar was now eligible for *yibbum* and, as such, she was prohibited to marry or to have relations with any other man, until a *yavam* (or *go'el*) released her. Indeed, this was precisely the situation of Ruth and Boaz. What Judah did not know, however, until Tamar proved that she had relations with him, was that his sons had not had marital relations with her, and were therefore not formally married to her. This proposed chain of events also explains a number of other statements made by Judah. The passage concludes by noting that although *yibbum* does not appear to have been formally commanded, and therefore Tamar should not have been punished in any event, a passage found in the *Pesiqta* suggests that this precept was given to Judah even before the Torah was given, just as Abraham and Isaac were instructed to be circumcised, and Jacob did not eat from the sciatic nerve, and so on.[118]

As noted above in chapter 2, R. Yosef *Bekhor Shor* had also interpreted the correctness of Tamar's actions vis-à-vis Judah on the basis of the notion of pre-Sinaitic *yibbum*, which meant that Judah himself should have performed *yibbum* if he did not want to give Tamar to his third son, Shelah. Both *Bekhor Shor* and R. Yeḥi'el of Paris employ this rabbinic approach and analysis as a kind of *'aggadah/halakhah ha-meyashevet divrei miqra*, to address

[117] Another possibility is also suggested. Since 'Er and Onan never had marital relations with Tamar, she retained her status as a single (nonmarried) woman.

[118] See ms. Bodl. 274, cited in *Tosafot ha-Shalem*, ed. Gellis, 4:87, sec. 20. A brief version of the first part of this passage, without R. Yeḥi'el's name, is found in *Pa'aneaḥ Raza*, 174; other Tosafist Torah commentaries in manuscript take up aspects of this issue and offer similar solutions. See *Tosafot ha-Shalem*, 4:84–86, and see also ms. Gaster 9931, fol. 18r, in the name of R. Samuel Bamberg. Ms. Bodl. 271/2 (cited in *Tosafot ha-Shalem*, 4:87, sec. 18) writes that "in those days, another family member could perform *yibbum*," although there is no reference to Boaz and Ruth as there is in the passage associated with R. Yeḥi'el. The question raised by R. Yeḥi'el had been raised by R. Judah *he-Ḥasid*, although his answer was rather different. See Lange, 53–54 (and above, chapter 3, nn. 45–47), and see also ms. Parma 541, fol. 31r: הק' ר' יהודה החסיד מהו צדקה ממני, וכי בשביל שזינתה ממנו לא תשרף. Since this Parma compilation appears to have been composed by a student of R. Yeḥi'el of Paris (as we shall soon see), he was perhaps sensitized to this issue from two different directions.

the various contextual and linguistic challenges that this portion of the Torah presents.[119]

There is also evidence, however, of R. Yeḥi'el's interest in forms of more pointed *peshat* interpretation. A Paris manuscript contains a treatise titled *Teʿamim shel Ḥumash*,[120] which was composed by a student or follower of R. Samuel *he-Ḥasid* and his sons, R. Abraham (R. Eshel) and R. Judah *he-Ḥasid.* Although there had been some scholarly debate regarding the authorship and dating of this treatise, Israel Ta-Shma has established definitively that the author of this treatise—and several sections that follow, dealing mostly with Divine names as well as a few difficult passages in Ibn Ezra's Torah commentary—is R. Solomon b. Samuel *ha-Ẓarefati*, father of the Tosafist R. Samuel of Falaise. A Frenchman by birth, R. Solomon made his way to Germany to study with members of the German Pietists, especially R. Eleazar of Worms. The commentary contains quite a bit of *gematria*, in addition to *sod* and exoteric materials, similar to other Torah commentaries associated with *Ḥasidei Ashkenaz*, and both R. Samuel *he-Ḥasid* and R. Judah *he-Ḥasid* are cited by name.[121]

R. Solomon reports the contact that he had with R. Yeḥi'el of Paris concerning a *peshat* interpretation suggested by Ibn Ezra: "R. Yeḥi'el b. Joseph

[119] See above, chapter 2, n. 135. It is likely that the interpretation of *Bekhor Shor*, or perhaps R. Yeḥi'el's interpretation, influenced Naḥmanides' exegetical approach to this section, in which *yibbum* plays a significant role in both its esoteric and exoteric dimensions; cf. my "On the Assessment of R. Moses b. Naḥman and His Literary Oeuvre," *Jewish Book Annual* 54 (1996–97), 71. Ramban works with the expanded precept of *yibbum* at this time; he mentions Ruth and Boaz; and he explains Tamar's "correctness" in the way that these Tosafist exegetes do. We have noted (above, chapter 2, n. 117) that Naḥmanides certainly appears to have received exegetical material from *Bekhor Shor*. Although Ramban does not cite R. Yeḥi'el in his talmudic commentaries, which were completed at a relatively early point in his career (see I. Ta-Shma, *Ha-Sifrut ha-Parshanit la-Talmud*, 2:29–45, and cf. *Ḥiddushei ha-Ramban le-Massekhet Ketubot*, ed. E. Chwat [Jerusalem, 1993], editor's introduction, 32–37), it is quite possible that he was influenced in his Torah commentary (which was completed toward the end of his life and perhaps in Israel, as passages in this commentary suggest) by R. Yeḥi'el as well. For Ramban's awareness of and contact with R. Yeḥi'el of Paris (and his northern French Tosafist contemporaries, R. Moses and R. Samuel of Evreux) via his relative, R. Yonah of Gerona, see, e.g., Ramban's sermon for Rosh ha-Shanah in *Kitvei ha-Ramban*, ed. C. Chavel (Jerusalem, 1968), 1:228 (ודבר זה חדשתי אותו בילדותי והרציתי הדבר לפני רבני צרפת של ה"ר הרב ר' משה ב"ר שניאור ואל אחיו ר' שמואל ואל הרב ר' יחיאל בפירש על ידי קרובי הרב ר' יונה שלמד שם); and cf. Shalem Yahalom, "Ha-Ramban u-Baʿalei ha-Tosafot be-Akko: Ha-Narativ ha-Histori bi-Drashat ha-Ramban le-Rosh ha-Shanah," *Shalem* 8 (2008), 100–125.

[120] See ms. Paris BN 353, fols. 68v–81v. Sections from this manuscript treatise were published by I. Levi in *REJ* 49 (1904), 231–43.

[121] See Ta-Shma, *Knesset Meḥqarim*, vol. 1, 273–81, which is a lightly revised version of idem, "Mashehu ʿal Biqqoret ha-Miqra be-Ashkenaz Bimei ha-Benayim," in *The Bible in Light of Its Interpreters* [Hebrew], ed. S. Japhet (Jerusalem, 1994), 453–59. The earlier scholarly debate is documented and discussed briefly by A. Grossman, *Ḥakhmei Ashkenaz ha-Rishonim* (Jerusalem, 1981), 86–87 (n. 36).

told me in the name of Avraham ibn Ezra about an interpretative solution (*pittaron*) for these two verses [Lev. 24:15–16], *lefi ha-peshat.*" The first verse appears to suggest that one who blasphemes the name of God known as *E-lohim* (*'ish 'ish ki yekallel E-lohav*) is not subjected to punishment by an earthly court (*ve-nasa ḥet'o*). The following verse, on the other hand, which also refers to one who specifies and blasphemes the Divine name (*ve-noqev shem ha-Shem*), mandates the punishment of public stoning. The interpretation of Ibn Ezra reported by R. Yeḥi'el to R. Solomon, which is found, in essence, in the commentary of Ibn Ezra to Leviticus 24:15, is that in the first verse, the blasphemer is left to be punished by Heaven, where his intent can be known with certitude. An earthly court cannot be absolutely certain if his intent was to blaspheme God Himself or only to revile a judge, since judges are also referred to in the Torah by the term *'elohim.* In the second verse, however, where the blasphemer invokes an unequivocal Divine name, the punishment of stoning can be prescribed and carried out by the earthly *beit din.*[122]

R. Solomon (or the copyist) notes, however, that the Talmud (*Sanhedrin* 56a) does not seem to understand these verses in this manner. Rather, while the second verse refers to one who blasphemes the Tetragrammaton (the *Shem ha-Meyuḥad*) after having been properly warned not to do so, the first verse, as Rashi also interprets, refers to a case where there was no warning, and the punishment of *karet* (*ve-nasa 'avono*) must therefore be imposed by Heaven. R. Yeḥi'el's willingness in this instance to embrace a *peshat* interpretation (following Ibn Ezra), in light of the other available rabbinic interpretations, is striking.[123]

[122] Ms. Paris 353, fol. 77r: ר' יחיאל ב"ר יוסף אמר לי משמו של ר' אברהם אבן עזרא פתרון לאלו שני מקראות [ויקרא כד:טו-טז] לפי הפשט כנגד איש איש כי יקלל א-להיו ונשא חטאו אדם המוציא מפיו א-להים ומברך אין לנו להרגו על זה, כי אין לברר מחשבתו וכוונתו זולתי הבורא. כי אין אנו יודעים אם כוונתו היתה כלפי יוצרו או על דיינין לכן ישא חטאו וגביית חובותיה ביד שמים הוא. אבל ונוקב שם ה', המבטא בשפתיו שם הקודש ומברך, על זה אין לגמגם לפיכך מות יומת כי מחשבתו גלויה לכל. לפיכ' רגום ירגמוהו כל העדה. On R. Solomon b. Samuel (and his son, R. Samuel of Falaise), cf. my "*Peering through the Lattices,*" 94–102. On the influence of Ibn Ezra in Ashkenaz during the thirteenth century, see Ta-Shma, *Knesset Meḥqarim*, 1:277–29; Shraga Abramson, "Iggeret ha-Qodesh ha-Meyuḥeset la-Ramban," *Sinai* 90 (1982), 244–49; Abraham Lifshitz, "R. Avraham Ibn Ezra be-Perushei Ba'alei ha-Tosafot 'al ha-Torah," *Hadarom* 28 (1968), 202–21; and cf. N. Golb, *The Jews in Medieval Normandy*, 252–308; Uriel Simon, "Transplanting the Wisdom of Spain to Christian Lands: The Failed Efforts of Ibn Ezra," *Simon Dubnow Institute Yearbook* 8 (2009), 181–89; and A. Mondschein, "The Massoretes Fabricated Explanations for Full and Defective Spellings: On Abraham Ibn Ezra's Struggles Against the (Ab)use of Biblical Spelling as an Exegetical Tool," [Hebrew] *Shenaton le-Heqer ha-Miqra veha-Mizraḥ ha-Qadum* 19 (2009), (above, chapter 2, n. 39), 309–11.

[123] Ms. Paris 353, fol. 77r. Rashbam similarly distinguishes (*lefi peshuto*) between the blaspheming of a lesser form of the Divine name, as opposed to an explicit Name (סתם בכנוי בלא פירוש שם מובהק), while *Ḥizzequni* adopts the approach of Ibn Ezra. Indeed, the approach of Ibn Ezra was adumbrated by R. Yom Tov of Joigny; see above, chapter 2, n. 228. *Bekhor Shor* suggests

There are two other manuscripts that contain Torah commentaries compiled by rabbinic scholars who are identified as students or colleagues of R. Yeḥi'el of Paris. These may also shed light on R. Yeḥi'el's exegetical activities, and the model that he set for his students. The first of these is a brief treatise called *Peshatim la-Torah*, found at the beginning of a Bodleian manuscript,[124] whose compiler, R. Isaac b. Ḥayyim, is described as a student of both (his uncle) R. Moses of Coucy and R. Yeḥi'el of Paris.[125] These *peshatim* contain selected comments from the beginning of the Torah through *parashat Beshalah*, although not surprisingly, and as we have seen, these *peshatim* also owe a bit to rabbinic literature.

Rashi interprets God's statement to the snake (Gen. 3:14), "You are more cursed than any domestic animal [*mi-kol ha-behemah*] and from any beast of the wild [*umi-kol ḥayyat ha-sadeh*]," to mean that if the snake was to be more cursed than any domestic animal, he would certainly be more lowly than the beasts of the wild (*lo kol she-ken*). Rashi cites the talmudic discussion in tractate *Bekhorot* that the gestation period for a snake lasts for seven years (the first edition of Rashi adds here, "seven times longer than that of a horse, and many more times longer than a *ḥayyah*, many of which give birth in a period of fifty days") as emblematic of this curse, which makes the snake significantly worse off than all other animals. The compiler of *Peshatim le-Torah* seeks to pinpoint the precise meaning and implication of the phrase *lo kol she-ken* in Rashi's comment. He cites what he heard from R. Moses of Evreux, a contemporary of R. Yeḥi'el of Paris,[126] that if the snake was to be more cursed than a domestic animal, which is completely under man's dominion and control, and can be used by man for hard labor, the snake was certainly worse off by definition than the nondomesticated *ḥayyah*, which is typically free from man's domination.[127]

---

another approach (ed. Nevo, 228), that *ve-nasa ḥet'o* in the first verse refers to the lesser punishment of lashes, which is fitting for one who curses a judge, *elohim*, although he also notes, without attribution, the interpretation followed by both Rashi and the Talmud, that this verse refers to one who was not properly warned (*be-lo ʿedim ve-hatraʾah*). On R. Yeḥi'el's use of the term *pashteh di-qera* in a talmudic formulation, see above, chapter 2, n. 14.

124 Ms. Bodl. 2343 (IMHM #21407), fols. 1–16v.

125 See ms. Bodl. 2343, fols. 16r–v, and below, n. 133. Cf. S. Poznanski, *Mavo ʿal Ḥakhmei Ẓarefat Mefarshei ha-Miqra*, XCIV, and *Tosafot ha-Shalem*, ed. Gellis, vol. 1, editor's introduction, 24. This commentary also mentions Ibn Ezra, R. Eleazar of Worms, and R. Samuel of Falaise (fol. 6r, and Rashbam and R. Moses of Evreux, as we shall see), along with several lesser-known Ashkenazic figures. See also below, n. 133.

126 See, e.g., Urbach, *Baʿalei ha-Tosafot*, 1:479–80; S. Emanuel, *Shivrei Luḥot*, 191–98; and below.

127 Ms. Bodl. 2343, fol. 3r: ארור אתה מכל הבהמה ומכל חית השדה. [פרש"י] אם מבהמה נתקלל מחיה לא כל שכן. יש לשאול מהו לא כל שכן. ושמעתי בשם הרב ר' משה דאיברא אם מבהמה שאיננה חפשית מן האדם שהיא ברשות ידו לכל עבודת פרך. ואם ממנה נתקלל, מחיה שהיא חפשית מן אדם לא כל שכן (= *Tosafot ha-Shalem*, ed. Gellis, 1:134, sec. 9). The passage in *Tosafot ha-Shalem*, ed. Gellis, 12:268, sec. 3, which is misattributed

Peshatim la-Torah cites three interpretations that reflect Rashbam's method of *ʿomeq peshuto shel miqra* in his name (Rabbenu Shmu'el). The first (to Gen. 12:3, "all of the families of the earth will be blessed through you," *ve-nivrekhu vekha kol mishpeḥot ha-ʾadamah*) is that the meaning of the word *ve-nivrekhu* here does not reflect a form of blessing but rather connotes intermingling, as in the phrase in rabbinic Hebrew, *mavrikh u-markiv.* Rashbam bases his understanding on the grammatical structure of this word, and therefore interprets the verse, unlike the approach of Rashi, to mean that Abraham's family will mix with the families of the earth.[128] Rashbam understands Genesis 23:20, "And the field and the cave in it were established for Abraham [*va-yaqam ha-sadeh veha-meʿarah*] as a burial plot from the sons of Ḥet [*la-ʾaḥuzat qever meʾet bnei Ḥet*]," to mean that while the land belonged to Abraham immediately after he paid the purchase price, it was not deeded to him by the sons of Het as a burial plot until he actually buried Sarah there.[129]

R. Isaac b. Ḥayyim cites an interpretation from Rashbam that *lefi ha-peshat*, Eliezer, the servant of Abraham, recounted the events of his encounter with Rivka exactly as they happened; a seeming discrepancy between the unfolding of their meeting and the way Eliezer reported it presents no problem. The Torah records in Genesis 24:22 that once Rivka had completed watering the camels, Eliezer took the nose ring and bracelets in hand (*va-yiqaḥ ha-ʾish*) in order to have them ready, since he knew his mission was succeeding. He only placed them on Rivka, however, once he had asked Rivka (Gen. 24:24) who her parents were, but it was unnecessary for the Torah to confirm this transaction. Thus Eliezer's report (Gen. 24:47) that he placed the nose ring and the bracelets on Rivka (*va-ʾasim*) after he ascertained who her parents were is not an indication (as Rashi suggests in Gen. 24:47) that Eliezer changed the order of events in his report to avoid being questioned by Rivka's family as to why he gave her the jewelry before he

to ms. Bodl. 2343 (and is identified as *mi-pi ha-R. Mosheh*), should correctly be assigned to ms. Bodl. 2344 (and is found in *Paʿaneaḥ Raza*, 366, *mi-pi Maharam*).

[128] Ms. Bodl. 2343, fol. 5r, and cf. Itamar Kislev, "Perush ha-Ḥizzequni ke-ʿEd Nosah le-Perush Rashbam la-Torah," in *Shai le-Sarah Yefet*, ed. M. Bar-Asher et al. (Jerusalem, 2008), 191–92. Rashbam also interprets this phrase in this way in Gen. 28:14. Rashbam's comment here comes from a lost section of his full Torah commentary. See *Rashbam's Commentary on Genesis*, ed. M. Lockshin, 165–66, and *Tosafot ha-Shalem*, ed. Gellis, 2:8, sec. 15. As Gellis notes, this comment also appears in ms. Parma 541, which was compiled by another student of R. Yeḥi'el, as we shall see shortly below. R. Yosef *Bekhor Shor*, ed. Nevo, 25, follows Rashi's interpretational approach.

[129] Ms. Bodl. 2343, fol. 7r. Cf. the comments of R. Judah *he-Ḥasid* and ms. Bodl. 271/2 in *Tosafot ha-Shalem*, ed. Gellis, 2:244, and see also *Perushei R. Yosef Bekhor Shor*, ed. Nevo, 40.

knew who she and her family were. Rather, this was how the events actually unfolded.[130]

In addition to presenting two other unnamed interpretations to Genesis 37 that are termed *lefi ha-peshat*,[131] the *Peshatim la-Torah* treatise also cites comments from R. Moses *ha-Kohen* ibn Chiqatilia and from R. Joseph Kimḥi, who is cited occasionally in other Tosafist Torah commentaries on the books of Genesis and Exodus. Since the comment by R. Moses *ha-Kohen* comes from the commentary of Ibn Ezra, its presence here, in a commentary from the circle of R. Yeḥi'el of Paris, is not surprising.[132]

R. Isaac b. Ḥayyim identifies his teachers by name in three comments found toward the end of his treatise. "According to my teacher and uncle R. Moses of Coucy, the Torah wrote 'and [the *tefillin shel rosh*] shall be for a remembrance between your eyes' [Ex. 13:9] to teach that the less devoted [*ha-qalim*], who typically need to be reminded more, should be especially careful in keeping this precept. Similarly, the *tefillin* are also referred to as *totafot* [in Ex. 13:16], which in rabbinic Hebrew connotes seeing."[133]

[130] Ms. Bodl. 2343, fol. 7v. See the text also in *Tosafot ha-Shalem*, ed. Gellis, 2:274, sec. 3. In the standard edition of Rashbam, this comment appears at the earlier verse (Gen. 24:22), on the word *va-yiqaḥ*. In this version, Rashbam notes that the correct order of the story is the one told by Eliezer (in Gen. 24:47). Not wanting to interrupt his words and Rivka's answers, the Torah changes the chronological order a bit at that point. See *Rashbam's Commentary on Genesis*, ed. Lockshin, 116. As Lockshin notes, Rashbam's approach (against that of Rashi) is favored exegetically by R. Yosef *Bekhor Shor* (who defines *va-yiqaḥ* as *hizmin latet*, precisely as Rashbam does according to ms. Bodl. 2343; see ed. Nevo, 41); by *Tosafot* (and *Tosafot ha-Rosh* to) *Ḥullin* 95b, s.v. *ke-Eli'ezer* (which explain the problem away as a case of *'ein muqdam u-me'uḥar ba-Torah*); and by Naḥmanides. In ms. Munich 62, this interpretation, as against that of Rashi, is attributed simply to *mori* (= R. Ḥayyim Palti'el). See *Tosafot ha-Shalem*, ed. Gellis, 2:274, sec. 5, and *Perushei R. Ḥayyim Palti'el 'al ha-Torah*, ed. Lange, 63.

[131] Ms. Bodl. 2343, fol. 11v. The first, to Gen. 37:14 (cited also in *Tosafot ha-Shalem*, ed. Gellis, 4:28, sec. 12), leads to a rabbinic aphorism and word play: וישלחהו מעמק חברון. לפי הפשט הלך עמו עד העמק ומשם שלחו ואמר לו לך לשלום. מכאן אמרו רבותינו אלמלא לא ליוה יעקב ליוסף היה ניזוק. וכך דרשו כי יעקב בחר לו י-ה אותיות לויה. The second, to Genesis 37:26 (cf. *Tosafot ha-Shalem*, 4:42, sec. 7), is rather original: וכסינו את דמו. הפשט וכסינו לשון כיס, שנשים בכיסו את דמי המכר.

[132] For R. Joseph Kimḥi, see fol. 15r. Cf., e.g., *Tosafot ha-Shalem*, ed. Gellis, 1:96, sec. 4; 1:101, sec. 8; 1:110, sec. 7; 1:147, sec. 1; 1:154, sec. 2; 1:187, sec. 1; 5:41, sec. 11; 1:46, sec. 8; 8:64, sec. 9; and S. Japhet, "Ḥizkuni's Commentary on the Pentateuch" (above, n. 25), 101–2. R. Moses *ha-Kohen* is mentioned on fol. 16r, with respect to the *ḥataf qomaẓ* in the phrase עזי וזמרת (Ex. 15:2); Ibn Ezra brings the approach of R. Moses in his short commentary to that verse. Ms. Bodl. 2343 presents the reasonable rabbinic interpretation put forward by R. Elḥanan (son of Ri) to address the different approaches taken by Joseph and Levi with respect to having children during the time of famine in Egypt, albeit without attribution; see above, chapter 3, n. 205.

[133] Ms. Bodl. 2343, fol. 16r, and see also Gellis, 7:150, sec. 6: ולזכרון בין עיניך. כתב מורי דודי הרב ר' משה מקוצי כי לכך כתי' ולכרון לו' כי במצות תפילין יזהרו הקלים, אותם הצריכים יותר זכרון. ולטוטפות לשון ראיה בלשון חכמים וכו' וראו כל עמי הארץ כי שם ה' נקרא עליך ויראו ממך וכו'. This comment is undoubtedly a reflection of R. Moses of Coucy's avowed commitment to ensure that the precept of *tefillin* (among others) should be observed regularly and punctiliously, especially by those Jews who were typically less observant. See, e.g., my "Rabbinic Attitudes toward Nonobservance in the

The first comment cited by R. Isaac in the name of his teacher, R. Yeḥi'el of Paris, is a polemical one, made in connection with Exodus14:7, "and [Pharaoh] took six hundred of his chosen chariots." Rashi, following the *Mekhilta*, explains that these horses were still available for this purpose because those Egyptians who feared God (during the plagues of *dever* and *barad*) brought their animals inside, where they survived. As Rashi (following the *Mekhilta*) further notes, the Tanna R. Simeon derives from here that even the good among the nations should be eliminated, because those Egyptians who were God-fearing had no difficulty in using their horses to chase after the Jews at the Red Sea. A question is raised, however, that according to a talmudic *sugya* in tractate *'Avodah Zarah*, non-Jews may not be killed by Jews without reason. And if the allowance was being made here since it was considered to be a time of war, the fact is that anyone fighting against a Jew may be killed during wartime (including another Jew), because of the principle "if one comes to kill you, rise up and kill him first."[134] R. Isaac notes that "this question was put to my teacher R. Yeḥi'el by a heretic." R. Yeḥi'el responded that this episode is the source for the aphorism that *tov shebagoyim harog*; it reflects what the other nations would like to do to the Jewish people (הרוג את ישראל). The proper halakhic procedure for Jews to follow, which does not include the wanton killing of Gentiles, is formulated according to the *sugya* in tractate *'Avodah Zarah*.[135]

The second comment that R. Isaac received from R. Yeḥi'el addresses a more typical exegetical problem, in Exodus 15:26, "for I am the God that heals you." Since God had said earlier in this verse, "I will not place upon you the sicknesses that you suffered in Egypt," there should be no need then for God to heal them from illness in addition. Rashi, in the second of his approaches to this verse, which is labeled *lefi peshuto*, understands this to mean that the Almighty, by providing the Torah and the *Mizvot* through which man can be saved from punishment, is akin to a doctor who cautions his patient against eating certain foods, lest he fall ill. R. Yeḥi'el, without

Medieval Period," in *Jewish Tradition and the Nontraditional Jew*, ed. J. J. Schacter (Northvale, N.J., 1992), 9–10, 24–25 (n. 62). Indeed, the interpretation presented here in R. Moses's name appears to be a paraphrase of one of his *derashot*, which he recorded in his *Sefer Mizvot Gadol* (Venice, 1547), *mizvat 'aseh* 3 (fol. 96d): עוד זאת דרשתי להם כי יותר חפץ הקדוש ברוך הוא באדם רשע שיניח תפילין מאדם צדיק. ועיקר תפילין נצטוו להיו' זכרון לרשעים ולישרם דרך טובה ויותר הם צריכים זכר וחיזוק מאותם שגדלו כל ימיהם ביראת שמים . . . וכתוב בה ולזכרון ללמד שעיקר חיוב תפילין לאותם שצריכים יותר זכר.

[134] This question is recorded in the *Nimmuqei Ḥumash* by R. Isaiah di Trani, ed. Chavel, 42, and in ms. Hamburg 45 (in the so-called *peshatim le-R. Avigdor Katz*), fol. 42v. See below, n. 147.

[135] Ms. Bodl. 2343, fol. 16r: ויקח שש מאות רכב בחור. פר"ש מאין היה להם מהירא את דבר ה'. מכאן אמרו טוב [שבגוים] הרוג. שאל [מין] למורי ה"ר יחיאל מתוך פי' רש"י דמכם מותר לגוי כבר כת' הבא להרגך השכם להרגו וכאן כת' טוב שבגוים הרוג. השיב אין הפי' כך אלא מכאן יש ללמוד טוב [שבגוים] הרוג את ישראל, כשר שבנחשים רצוץ את מוחו של אדם. Cf. *Tosafot ha-Shalem*, ed. Gellis, 7:184–85, sec. 1.

mentioning Rashi, extends this approach in a more naturalistic vein: "My teacher R. Yeḥi'el told me that the Divine healing here refers to maintaining a salutary diet, through which healthy people conduct themselves in such a way that they do not become sick."[136]

Ms. Parma (De Rossi) 541 contains another collection of biblical interpretations that appears to have been compiled by a student of R. Yeḥi'el of Paris. The collection consists of individual comments, both *peshat* and *derash*, as well as lengthy midrashic citations. Virtually all the rabbinic scholars cited by name in this compilation are from northern France. The few exceptions are several comments that are cited from the Torah commentary of R. Judah *he-Ḥasid*, a lone halakhic comment found in the name of R. Judah (b. Qalonymus; Rivaq) of Speyer, and two references to rabbinic scholars from Rome. On the basis of two passages in the manuscript, Solomon Schechter suggested that the compiler was a R. Netan'el, who refers to R. Yeḥi'el of Paris as his teacher.[137] R. Yeḥi'el of Paris sent responsa to R. Netan'el of Chinon, who is mentioned a number of times in *Tosafot*; they were consulted jointly in the case of an individual who refused to perform *ḥaliẓah*; and they were both consulted by R. Moses of Evreux.[138]

We can perhaps get a better sense of R. Yeḥi'el's place in this commentary by examining more closely some of the rabbinic figures who are cited. Early on, this text cites a non-halakhic comment from R. Yeḥi'el's predecessor as the head of the Tosafist academy in Paris—who served just prior to R. Yeḥi'el's main teacher, R. Judah Sirleon—R. Isaac b. Abraham (Riẓba) of Dampierre, whose presence in Tosafist Torah commentaries is fairly rare, especially in non-halakhic contexts.[139] Noah was characterized as *tamim* (in Gen. 6:9). *Bereshit Rabbah* posits that all those referred to by the epithet *tamim* lived to ages divisible by seven. This is true for Abraham, for Jacob, and ostensibly for Job. But as Riẓba noted, Noah's life was not divisible by seven. The answer suggested is that the years that Noah lived before the flood did not figure into this characterization, since the world was to be destroyed.[140]

136 See ms. Bodl. 2343, fols. 16r–v (*Tosfot ha-Shalem*, ed. Gellis, 7:253, sec. 11): ואמר לי מורי הר"ר יחיאל רופאיך אדיאטירי, שמור הבריאים להתנהג בדרך שלא יחלו. Couched in these terms, R. Yeḥi'el's interpretation perhaps anticipates Ramban's question against Rashi's *peshuto shel miqra* approach.

137 See S. Schechter, "Notes on a Hebrew Commentary to the Pentateuch in a Parma Manuscript," in *Semitic Studies in Memory of Alexander Kohut*, ed. G. A. Kohut (Berlin, 1897), 485–94. The pagination of this manuscript, as it is presently represented in the Institute for Microfilms of Hebrew Manuscripts at the Jewish National Library in Jerusalem, differs from that followed by Schechter (usually by about two pages).

138 See Urbach, *Ba'alei ha-Tosafot*, 1:458–59, 480–81, and cf. S. Emanuel, *Shivrei Luḥot*, 191 (and the literature cited in n. 20); and below, chapter 5, nn. 274–80.

139 See above, chapter 3, nn. 178, 192, 217, 228, and at n. 232.

140 See ms. Parma 541, fol. 6v. Cf. *Tosafot ha-Shalem*, ed. Gellis, 1:198, sec. 30; and above, chapter 3, n. 214, for a full discussion of the Tosafist interpretations of this midrashic passage and

A comment by R. Joseph of Paris, ostensibly the son of R. Yeḥi'el,[141] is presented on Genesis 13:7, which juxtaposes two seemingly unrelated developments: "And there was a conflict between the shepherds of Abraham and the shepherds of Lot, and the Canaanites and the Perizites were then in the land." R. Joseph writes that, *lefi ha-peshat*, the Torah means to indicate that the conflict at this time was pointless and ill-advised, since they were then living in the land among the Canaanites and the Perizites, who were well-fortified. On the other hand, according to Rashi's interpretation that the argument broke out because the shepherds of Lot were accustomed to shepherding by means of thievery, the Torah means to indicate here that Abraham had not yet merited the full land, and that is why the Canaanites and Perizites still lived there. Although the land had already been given to Shem, and it is not possible to steal land in the absolute sense, it is possible to conquer and hold land by means of warfare. R. Joseph is thus comparing and contrasting the approach of Rashi with a deeper *peshat* approach.[142] Another comment attributed to R. Joseph of Paris, in a different manuscript collection, also has a *peshat* dimension.[143]

A lengthy passage in ms. Parma 541 on Abraham's age at the time of the "covenant between the parts" (the ברית בין הבתרים, Gen. 17:1) appears in the name of R. Yeḥi'el. The suggestion that Abraham was seventy years old (as per Rashi to Ex. 12:40) does not jibe with a number of other verses and rabbinic sources. Especially problematic is the time interval between this event and Abraham's war with the five kings, and the verse which notes that Abraham left Ḥaran at age seventy-five. The compiler then indicates what he saw *bi-yesod(ei) de-Rabbenu Shmu'el* (Rashbam) to confirm that Abraham was indeed seventy years old at the time of the covenant. In fact, the covenant preceded the war with the kings by four years. Proof for this approach may

verse. Schechter does not make note of this comment but does record (on p. 487) a subsequent passage in *parashat Bo*, in which ריב"א (an acronym that can refer to R. Isaac b. Abraham of Dampierre, and is understood as such by Schechter) interprets the significance of the (mnemonic) *simanim* given for the ten plagues by the Tanna R. Judah. However, fuller versions of this passage contain not only the name of Raban of Mainz but also those of R. Judah *he-Ḥasid* and Raban's grandson Rabiah, strongly suggesting that Riba in this instance refers to the early German Tosafist R. Isaac b. Asher *ha-Levi* rather than to the French Tosafist Riẓba. See *Tosafot ha-Shalem—Haggadah shel Pesaḥ*, ed. Y. Gellis (Jerusalem, 1989), 99, sec. 5.

141 On R. Joseph b. Yeḥi'el of Paris, R. Yeḥi'el's eldest son, who was named for R. Yeḥi'el's father, see Urbach, *Ba'alei ha-Tosafot*, 1:456–57; S. Emanuel, *Shivrei Luḥot*, 186; and below, chapter 6, nn. 282, 284.

142 See ms. Parma 541, fol. 20v, and *Tosafot ha-Shalem*, ed. Gellis, 2:28, sec. 6. Cf. *Bekhor Shor*, Ibn Ezra, and *Ḥizzequni*, ad loc.

143 See ms. Vatican 45, fol. 22v: ולקחו מן הדם ונתנו על שתי המזוזות ועל המשקוף. כאן הקדים מזוזה למשקוף ולמטה כשאמר מצות פסח לישראל שינה משה לשונו מלשון הקב"ה שאמר אם אקדים להם . . . יבאו לטעות . . . לפיכך הקדים להם משקוף למזוזות וכו' (= *Minḥat Yehudah*, Ex., fols. 13a–b, כך שמעתי בשם הר"ר יוסף מפריש); and *Tosafot ha-Shalem*, Gellis, 7:67, sec. 7.

be found in the *Seder ʿOlam* and other rabbinic texts. Once again, however, the ages and times are questioned with respect to Abraham leaving Haran. Therefore, the compiler concludes, my teacher R. Yeḥiʾel of Paris explained (*tirez mori ve-rabbi ha-Rav R. Yeḥiʾel mi-Paris*) that Abraham left Ḥaran a total of three times, once when he was seventy (although he later returned); once when he was seventy-four (he conquered the kings that year and then immediately returned to Ḥaran); and, finally, when he left for good at the age of seventy-five, as indicated in the verse. R. Yeḥiʾel's approach resolves a variety of scriptural questions as well as the *Seder ʿOlam* text. At the end of the day, however, R. Yeḥiʾel has addressed a *peshat* problem that began with Rashi's interpretation.[144]

There is also a passage in ms. Parma 541, in the name of מורי הרב ר״י, which may refer to R. Yeḥiʾel. This comment concerns R"Y's response to a masoretic tradition based on a midrashic passage, which nonetheless has a basis in a *peshat* distinction between the prophecies of Moses and Bilʿam.[145] Another student of R. Yeḥiʾel of Paris, R. Solomon of Chateau-Landon (which is located to the west of Sens, about fifty miles south of Paris), was also involved with *parshanut ha-miqra*, although he does not cite any interpretations from R. Yeḥiʾel by name as far as I can tell.[146] Indeed, most of the comments associated with R. Solomon are talmudic or midrashic in nature, although he works with comments by Rashi, and those of R. Jacob of Orleans as well, especially as reflected in R. Isaac *ha-Levi*'s *Paʿaneaḥ Raza*. R. Solomon of Chateau-Landon and R. Ḥayyim Paltiʾel were also the teachers of the anonymous figure who assembled the voluminous Tosafist Torah compilation published by Y. S. Lange under the name *Perushei ha-Torah le-R. Ḥayyim Paltiʾel*, although R. Solomon is mentioned only three times by

[144] Ms. Parma 541, fols. 11v–12v; *Tosafot ha-Shalem*, ed. Gellis, 2:55, sec. 8; and cf. *Tosafot Berakhot* 7b, s.v. *lo*.

[145] Ms. Parma 541, fol. 70v: במסורת א׳ דויקרא קטנה. והוה או׳ מורי ה״ר ר״י לולי שהיו אומרים שאני חולק על המסורה, הייתי כותבה גדולה שבגדולות לפי שבמדרש מחלק בין נביאי ישראל לבין נביאי אומות העולם. וממקרא זה ילפי׳ דנביאי אומות העולם קורא בהם בלשון גנאי כמו ויקר א-להים אל בלעם כמו מקרה לילה. ובנביאי ישראל בלשון טהרה בלשון שמלאכי השרת משתמשין בו וקרא זה אל זה אף כאן ויקרא. Cf. *Moshav Zeqenim*, 228, for an interpretation by R. Eleazar of Worms which suggests (based on a passage in *Midrash Tanḥuma*) that ויקר is also an indication of full (Jewish) prophecy. At the same time, however, *Moshav Zeqenim*, 229, also presents an interpretation by R. Yosef *Bekhor Shor* that is quite similar to what is found here in ms. Parma, in its comparison between the prophecies of Moses and Bilʿam (and in the linguistic forms that characterized them), although this passage is not found in the key manuscript of *Bekhor Shor*'s commentary (ms. Munich 52). See also the interpretation of R. Nathan b. Yosef (Official) preserved in *Sefer ha-Gan*, ed. Orlian, 268. On R. Yeḥiʾel's use of midrash, see also below.

[146] On R. Solomon, who also authored *pesaqim*, see Emanuel, *Shivrei Luḥot*, 31, 198; and cf. Urbach, *Baʿalei ha-Tosafot*, 1:456 (n. 32).

name in that collection while R. Ḥayyim Palti'el is mentioned more than a hundred times.[147]

Interpretations in the name of R. Yeḥi'el of Paris are scattered within several published collections of Tosafist Torah compilations as well. In Exodus 10:14, the locusts in Egypt are described as "after them there will never be anything like it." A number of *parshanim* compare the locusts in Egypt to those described in the Book of Joel, which the verse (Joel 2:2) describes as unprecedented (*kamohu lo nihyah me-ʿolam*). The Tosafist Torah compilation *Moshav Zeqenim* notes that R. Yeḥi'el identified a unique aspect in each case, by suggesting that those in the days of Moses arrived in smaller, separate groups, species by species, while those in Joel's day came in one very large, mixed swarm. However, the total number from each separate species in Moses's day was larger than the number from each species in Joel's day.[148]

Several compilations contain a *peshat* comment from R. Yeḥi'el about the naming of Moses's sons, Gershom and Eliezer (Ex. 18:3–4), in conjunction with Moses's writing of the Torah. Yitro brings Zipporah to Moses, together with their two sons. The first is named Gershom, "because he [Moses] said [*ki 'amar*] I was a stranger [*ger hayiti*] in a foreign land." And the name given to the other one was Eliezer, "because the God of my father helped me, and saved me from the sword of Pharaoh." R. Yeḥi'el notes that when Moses's second son, Eliezer, was named, the phrase *ki 'amar* (because he said) is not included, as it was at the naming of Gershom. R. Yeḥi'el

[147] See *Perushei R. Ḥayyim Palti'el*, ed. Lange, editor's introduction, 9–10; and Lange, "Le-Zehuto shel R. Ḥayyim Palti'el," *ʿAlei Sefer* 8 (1980), 144–46. See also *Perusehi R. Ḥayyim Palti'el*, ed. Lange, 180 (Ex. 3:12); 222 (Ex. 12:29 = *Tosafot ha-Shalem*, ed. Gellis 7:119, sec. 8); 496 (Nu. 11:22); 498 (Nu. 11:31); and *Tosafot ha-Shalem*, ed Gellis, 2:97, sec. 1; 4:121–22; 8:173, sec. 11; 8:189, sec. 11.

[148] See *Moshav Zeqenim*, 122 (וה״ר יחיאל תי׳ של משה רבינו לא באו יחד בערבוביא אלא כל מין אחד לבדו. ואותו מין אחד שבא במצרים היה מרובה יותר ממין אחד של יואל = *Tosafot ha-Shalem*, ed. Gellis, 7:17, sec. 6). Similar answers and approaches are found in the *peshatim* contained in the Ashkenazic compilation ms. Hamburg 45, fol. 39v (although none of them are attributed to a particular Tosafist): the locusts in Egypt were all from one species (and was the largest such group ever), while those in the Book of Joel came together from several different species (which is essentially the interpretation followed by Rashi); the ones in Egypt all came together, while those in Joel's day came species by species (which was the interpretation suggested by R. Isaiah di Trani, as a response to or as an explanation of Rashi, above, chapter 3, n. 157); the ones in Moses's day were more numerous overall, but those in Joel's time acted in a more crazed way (*be-shigaʿon yoter*). See also *Tosafot ha-Shalem*, ed. Gellis, 7:18–19. Two *pesaqim* of R. Yeḥi'el are found in the ms. B.M. 243 on fol. 108r (this manuscript is parallel to the *perushim u-pesaqim* that are found in ms. Hamburg 45; see below, n. 193), regarding the taking of *ḥalah* from nonleavened batters, and on fol. 200r, regarding the power of a single witness to testify in matters of *issur ve-heter.* In addition, B.M. 243, fol. 137r, contains a response that R. Yeḥi'el gave to a heretic (cf. above, n. 134), concerning the expiation associated with the new moon. For these and other citations from R. Yeḥi'el, see *Perushim u-Pesaqim le-Rabbenu Avigdor*, ed. Machon Harerei Qedem, 68, 243 292, 390, 423.

explains that "since Moses wrote his own book and said all the time that 'the God of my father helps me,' had he written *ki 'amar*, this would imply that he expressed this only at the time [that this son was born]." Although the phrase *Moshe katav sifro* is found in the Talmud (in *Bava Batra* 14b), R. Yeḥi'el is apparently comfortable with the notion of Moses as the *kotev ha-Torah*, a concept espoused by several earlier northern French Tosafist *pashtanim*, including Rashbam, R. Yosef *Bekhor Shor*, R. Yom Tov of Joigny, and R. Moses of Coucy.[149] A passage in the *Da'at Zeqenim* collection to Exodus 27:4, on the nettings and rings used for carrying the altar, records a question raised by R. Yeḥi'el in an effort to get the text of the verse to jibe with its talmudic analysis.[150]

The fourteenth-century Tosafist Torah compilation known as *'Imrei No'am* attributes to R. Yeḥi'el an exegetical resolution of Genesis 11:11—as to why the deaths of those who lived before the flood were explicitly mentioned by the Torah, while those who lived after the flood were noted in terms of the children they had, but their deaths were not mentioned at all. The same resolution is also attributed by R. Judah *he-Ḥasid*'s son, R. Zal(t)man, and by other Tosafist compilations to R. Judah *he-Ḥasid*. Although it is possible that the initials for R. Judah *he-Ḥasid* (רי"ח) came to be mistakenly identified with R. Yeḥi'el ('ר' יח), it is also possible that these two rabbinic figures actually offered a similar solution.[151] Ms. Munich 50 has a question of halakhic detail from R. Yeḥi'el that also appears in one of the main manuscripts that contains R. Judah *he-Ḥasid*'s Torah commentary, ms. Moscow 82, as to why the Torah ties the fate of the betrothed woman

[149] See *Ḥazi Menasheh*, ed. Menashe Grossberg (London, 1901), 42 (Ex. 10:14) = *Minḥat Yehudah* (Ex.), fol. 22a: כי א-להי אבי בעזרי. לא [נ]אמר כי אמר וכו' כמו כי אמר גר הייתי בארץ נכריה לפי שמשה כתב את ספרו והיה אומר כל שעה א-להי אבי בעזרי [ואלו] (ולא) כתב אמר משה [משמע ש]אמר לפי שעה. בשם ה"ר יחיאל. See also ms. Parma 541, fol. 55v, and *Tosafot ha-Shalem*, ed. Gellis, 8:11, sec. 9. In ibid., sec. 10, a different answer to this question is recorded in the name of R. Judah *he-Ḥasid* (which is also found in ms. Hamburg 45); see *Perushei ha-Torah le-R. Yehudah he-Ḥasid*, ed. Lange, 91. See also *Moshav Zeqenim*, 152, for an interpretation in the name of R. Jacob of Orleans. On the issue of Mosaic authorship in northern France, see above, n. 60; and above, chapter 2, n. 102, 208.

[150] See *Da'at Zeqenim* to Exodus, fol. 41a; *Tosafot ha-Shalem*, ed. Gellis, vol. 9 (Jerusalem, 1993), 125, sec. 5. An additional manuscript version of R. Yeḥi'el's comment is found in *Tosafot ha-Shalem*, 9:38, sec. 12.

[151] See *'Imre No'am*, ed. M. Harris (Jerusalem, 1970), 6; *Tosafot ha-Shalem*, ed. Gellis, 1:293–94, sec. 1; and cf. *Perushei R. Yehudah he-Ḥasid 'al ha-Torah*, ed. Lange, 16 (which cites both the Moscow and Cambridge manuscripts that contain R. Judah's commentary, as well as *Pa'aneaḥ Raza* and *Moshav Zeqenim*); and ms. St. Petersburg, EVR I 22, fol. 7r. See also *Sefer ha-Gan*, ed. Orlian, 145, who presents a solution to this problem (צריך ליתן טעם לפי הפשט) in the name of *ha-Rav Rabbenu Yosef Bekhor Shor* (which does not appear, however, in the commentary of *Bekhor Shor* as found in ms. Munich 52; see ed. Nevo, 24, and the editor's notes there). The muddling of R. Judah's and R. Yeḥi'el's initials may also have occurred with regard to certain esoteric teachings, although as additional texts indicate, R. Yeḥi'el was himself involved in this area of endeavor as well. See below, chapter 6, n. 129.

who has been raped in an inhabited area to whether or not she calls out (Deut. 32:24), as opposed to making her status dependent on whether she had been properly warned about the punishment for her willful participation. In this instance, however, the comment is never actually attributed to R. Judah but immediately precedes a comment by R. Judah *he-Ḥasid* to Deuteronomy 23:2.[152]

Indeed, *'Imrei No'am* records a rabbinic interpretation by R. Yeḥi'el (attached to Rashi's comment) concerning the juxtaposition of the Sabbath and the *mishkan* in *parashat Va-Yaqhel* which is not attributed to any other Ashkenazic rabbinic figure.[153] So does ms. Moscow 82, regarding the two offerings brought by a woman who had given birth (Lev. 12:8, *'eḥad le-'olah ve-'eḥad le-ḥatat*). Rashi, based on a talmudic passage in the name of Rava (*Zevaḥim* 90a), explains that the order indicated here (the *'olah* is mentioned first and the *ḥatat* second) is only for purposes of designating sanctification (לקריאת=למקראה שם). However, the *ḥatat* must certainly be offered before the *'olah*.

R. Yeḥi'el of Paris understands the talmudic passage to mean that the order of the offerings found in the Torah reflects the fact that they proceed to some extent according to the circumstances of those bringing them (למקראה= *leshon miqreh*). In this section of the Torah (Lev. 12:6–8), a woman of means brings a year-old lamb for an *'olah* and either a dove or a pigeon for the *ḥatat*, while a poor woman brings either two doves or two pigeons, for both the *'olah* and the *ḥatat*, depending on what she can afford, just as the wealthier women brings either one pigeon or one dove for her *ḥatat*. Since these details vary according to circumstance, they are listed only after the *'olah* lamb for a woman of means, which is a fixed offering that is not affected in any way by availability. R. Yeḥi'el's appreciation of the larger scriptural context plays a significant role in his interpretation of the talmudic passage.[154]

152 See ms. Munich 50, fol. 305v, and ms. B.M. 9931, fol. 166r–v: צעקה הנערה המאורשה. הקשה הרב רבינו יחיאל מפריזא אם קבלה עליה התראה אפילו בשדה תהרג. ואם לא התרו בה, אפילו בעיר תפטר. ותירץ שבאו עדים בסוף ביאה והתרו בה וקבלה התראה וכו'. ומיירי בעדים חלשים או בקיימי בתרי עברי דנהרא דאל"כ, היה להם להצילה בנפשו של בועל. [לא יבוא פצוע דכא וגו'] וקשה למה אסרתו תורה הואיל ואין מולידין ואשה אינה מצווה על פו"ר חסיד מדרבנן. *Perushei R. Yehudah he-Ḥasid*, ed. Lange, 206–7, based on ms. Moscow 82, records the first passage as a question put forward by an unknown R. Yeḥi'el b. Moses to R. Yeḥi'el (of Paris), and the second question without any specific attribution to R. Judah.

153 See *'Imre No'am*, 74. See also *Tosafot ha-Shalem*, ed. Gellis, 10:168, sec. 4: ויקהל. פרש"י למה נסמכה פרשת שבת למשכן לומר לך שאינו דוחה שבת. והקשה ר' יחיאל דאמאי צריך סמיכה והלא בנין המשכן הוי עשה ושבת הוי עשה ולא תעשה ואין עשה דוחה לא תעשה ועשה. ותי' דאצטריך סמיכה דאי לאו הכי הוי יליף מק"ו וכו'.

154 Ms. Moscow 82, fol. 30v: אחד לעולה ואחד לחטאת. פרש"י למקראה הקדימה הכתוב פי' לקריאה קודם לחטאת היינו קריאת שם. אבל להקרבה חטאת קודם. לכן גבי ע"ז כתוב שם שבכל מקום שתמצא העולה אותו החטאת בלא אלף לפי שהוא חלוק וכן אחרים. וה"ר יחיאל מפריש פי' לשון מקרה לפי שעשירה מבאיה כבש בן שנתו לעולה ושלה מקרה היא אם יש לה ב' תורים או ב' בני יונה. See also Rashi to *Zevaḥim* 90a, s.v. *le-miqra'ah*; *Hadar*

Several manuscripts contain a quasi-halakhic question from R. Yeḥi'el on a verse in *Sefer Bamidbar.* How could Aaron wear his priestly garments when he ascended Hor ha-Har prior to his death (Nu. 20:27), since wearing them out of the precincts of the *mishkan* was prohibited? R. Yeḥi'el responds that this is prohibited only when the *kohen* is still involved in doing the actual service. When the service is not ongoing, however, there is no such prohibition. R. Yeḥi'el's second suggestion is that this was a kind of *sui generis* situation (*hora'at sha'ah*), which was not subject to the fixed regulations concerning these garments.[155]

In the realm of midrashic interpretation, the Tosafist compilation *Da'at Zeqenim me-Rabbotenu Ba'alei ha-Tosafot* notes Rashi's comment to Numbers 21:34, that Moses should not fear doing battle with 'Og, even though 'Og had the merit of letting Abraham know that his nephew Lot had been captured (Gen. 14:13, according to the interpretation found in *Midrash Tanḥuma* that 'Og was the survivor, *ha-palit* of the giants [*refa'im*], who later informed Abraham about Lot). 'Og's brother Siḥon, on the other hand, had no such merit, and therefore Israel fought against him without any trepidation (Nu. 21:23). *Midrash Rabbah*, however, suggests that 'Og was referred to as the survivor because had had managed to survive the flood. While Rashi (Gen. 7:23) provides a substantive *remez* that suggests that 'Og survived the flood, there is no such indication concerning his brother Siḥon. At this point, *Da'at Zeqenim* cites the view of R. Yeḥi'el that while 'Og was born prior to the flood, his mother was pregnant with Siḥon during the period

Zeqenim, fol. 48b; and *Tosafot ha-Shalem*, ed. Gellis, vol. 12 (Jerusalem, 2009), 192, sec. 3. *Minḥat Yehudah*, Lev. 11a, cites ריב"א, who also understands מקראה as מקרה, but with a different application. If it happened that the *'olah* was offered before the *ḥatat* (בדיעבד), these sacrifices are nonetheless accepted. Cf. *Tosafot ha-Shalem*, 12:192, sec. 4; and H. Touitou, "*Minḥat Yehudah*," 77 (n. 54).

155 See, e.g., ms. Bodl. 270, fol. 75v: פ' חקת. הקשה מורנו ה"ר יחיאל מפריש היאך היה אהרן לובש בגדים בהר ההר, הא אין יוצאים בהם חוץ לעזרה כלל. וי"ל דהא שהם מקדשים דוקא בשעת עבודה אבל שלא בשעת עבודה אין חומרא בבגדים מצאתם חוץ. This passage appears in ms. Vatican 45, fol. 55r, with the additional answer: וכן אמרי' בבני אהרן שכת' בבגדיהם כלו' בגדיהם עליהם כהונתם עליהם אין בגדיהם עליהם אין כהונתם עליהם וכו'. א"נ י"ל הוראת שעה היתה. כל זה מפ' ר' יחיאל מפריש. See also ms. Jerusalem Karlin 688 (IMHM #73995, to *parashat Ḥuqqat*), and cf. *Yoma* 69a, on the meeting of the *Kohen Gadol* (while wearing his garments) with Alexander the Great (outside of Jerusalem). A similar kind of question, regarding the reward given to *Pinḥas* (in Nu. 25:11), is also resolved by R. Yeḥi'el (as recorded in *Moshav Zeqenim*, 480): והיתה לו ולזרעו אחריו. וא"ת והלא כבר נתנה כהונה לזרעו שנ' [שמות כט:כט] ובגדי הקדש אשר לאהרן יהיו לבניו אחריו וכו'. וי"ל לפי שהרג זמרי סבור היה שלא יקריב עוד קרבן כדתנן [סנהדרין דף לה ע"ב] כהן שהרג את הנפש לא ישא את כפיו. ולכן הוצרך לשנותו לומר לו הנני נותן לו את בריתי שלום שלא יערער אדם על כהונתו. ור' יחיאל מפריש אומ' דגברא קטילא קטל ולא היתה רציחה דהבא על ארמית קנאין פוגעין בו וזש"ה תחת אשר קנא לא-להיו.

of the flood. She then married one of the sons of Noah, and gave birth to Siḥon in the ark.[156]

R. Yeḥi'el's comment here was intended as much to correlate the various midrashic traditions and formulations regarding ʿOg and Siḥon as it was to support Rashi's interpretation. Indeed, R. Yeḥi'el was apparently quite involved with the study of midrash as well. An unidentified German rabbinic student records his efforts at verifying a passage in *Bereshit Rabbah* that had been cited by Rashi in his Torah commentary but which did not appear in full in the student's copy of *Bereshit Rabbah.* The student thought that his copy was perhaps defective. When he reached France, however, he checked the *Bereshit Rabbah* texts that belonged to his Tosafist teachers, R. Yeḥi'el of Paris and R. Tuvyah of Vienne, and found them both to be the same as his. The student then offered his own suggestion to fill in the lacuna.[157]

156 See *Daʿat Zeqenim—Rabbotenu Baʿalei ha-Tosafot* to Numbers, fol. 18a: ויאמר ה' אל תירא אותו. פרש"י לכך הוצרך לו' אל תירא אותו מה שאין הוצרך לו' מסיחון לפי שהיה ירא פן יעמוד לו זכות שהגיד [עוג] לאברהם אבינו שנשבה לוט [כדכתי' ויבא הפליט וכו'] . . . ומיהו תימ' למ"ד דעוג נקרא פליט על שנפלט מן המבול דבמס' נדה מסיק דעוג וסיחון אחי הוו. וא"כ סיחון פלט מן המבול [גם כן] דבשלמא עוג מצינו סמך ורמז כדאיתא בפר' נח דפי' רש"י [בר' ז:כג] וישאר אך נח שעולה בגימ' עוג. אבל לסיחון לא מצינו סמך ורמז. ואו' ה"ר יחיאל בן יוסף שעוג נולד קודם המבול ואמו היתה מעוברת מסיחון בשעת המבול והלכה ונשאת לאחד מבני נח וכבר היתה מעוברת מאותן בני הא־להים אשר לקחו מבנות האדם ונולד סיחון בתיבה. Cf. *Sefer ha-Gan*, ed. Orlian, 312–13. Interestingly, *Daʿat Zeqenim* to Gen. 7:23, fol. 7a, cites the *gematria* that links ʿOg to Noah in the name of R. Judah *he-Ḥasid* (rather than in Rashi's name). The attribution to R. Judah *he-Ḥasid* appears to be correct (and this *gematria* does not appear at all in extant texts of Rashi); see *Perushei ha-Torah le-R. Yehudah he-Ḥasid*, ed. Lange, 12, and cf. *Perushei R. Ḥayyim Palti'el ʿal ha-Torah*, ed. Lange, 19. In one of his interpretations to Gen. 14:13 (*va-yavo ha-palit*), Rashi mentions the rabbinic view (which he cites from *Midrash Rabbah*), that ʿOg came to be known as the *palit* since he had "escaped from the generation of the flood" and survived, but he does not provide any additional support for it. The resolution attributed here to R. Yeḥi'el is found without attribution in the Torah commentary of Rosh, fol. 4b.

157 See ms. Paris 260 (a variant of *Moshav Zeqenim*), fols. 92r, to Gen. 44:8 ("the money that we found in our sacks we brought to you from the land of Canaan in order to return it, and so why would we then steal silver and gold from the master's home?"). Rashi comments that this is one of ten *kal va-ḥomer* formulations found in the Torah, which are all included in *Bereshit Rabbah* (*ve-hem mefurashim bi-Bereshit Rabbah*). On fol. 92v, the student reports that only nine are to be found in his copy: והנה לפי המנין שמונה בב"ר אין בהם כי אם ט' ק"ו. ואמרתי שמא חסר בב"ר שלי. וכשבאתי לצרפת ראיתי בב"ר של מורי ה"ר יחיאל וגם בב"ר של מורי ה"ר טוביה והיה כתוב כמו בשלי. ונ"ל דזה ק"ו חסר בספרי' והנה שני מלאכים לא עמדו לפנינו וכו'. In the published edition of *Moshav Zeqenim*, 87 (= *Tosafot ha-Shalem*, ed. Gellis, 4:186–87), this passage is found without the names of R. Yeḥi'el and R. Tuvyah (וכשבאתי לצרפת ראיתי באחרים והיה כתוב כשלי), although it does contain the name of the student narrator's uncle (והגדתי לדודי ה"ר יצחק והיה לו קשה כמו כן). On the relationship between R. Yeḥi'el and R. Tuvyah (and perhaps the identity of their student as well), see Urbach, *Baʿalei ha-Tosafot*, 1:486–87, and see also S. Emanuel, "R. Yeḥi'el mi-Paris" (above, n. 100), 94–98. (The first line of Urbach, 1:487, is missing in some editions: בקשרים אמיצים עם ר' יחיאל עמד ר' טוביה בן אליהו מויאנה.) Statements such as those found in *Sefer Ḥasidim* (ed. Parma), sec. 1667 (הרי יש דברים שאינם בפירוש בתלמוד וישנם במדרשים), and in *Sefer Rabiah*, vol. 2, 333, sec. 595 (וכל שאינו בקי במדרשים ובספרים חיצונים אין לו לסתור ולהרוס בין הקדמונים ומנהגם ואם ריק הוא ממנו ריק), refer to the significance of *midrashim* in a halakhic (or talmudic) context.

In sum, R. Yeḥi'el of Paris put forward a number of *peshat* interpretations, including several that followed the commentaries of Rashbam, Ibn Ezra, and R. Judah *he-Ḥasid.* He does quite a bit of Rashi analysis, in both *peshat* and rabbinic interpretations, and he had an abiding interest in midrashic interpretation as well. R. Yeḥi'el's individual comments appear to be somewhat parallel to the slightly earlier Tosafist Torah compilation, *Sefer ha-Gan*, although his comments are certainly not as frequent or as systematic as those found in *Sefer ha-Gan.*[158]

The Tosafist Academy at Evreux

The brothers R. Moses (d. c. 1250), R. Samuel, and R. Isaac b. Shne'ur headed an active Tosafist study hall in Evreux (Normandy). They developed two different types of *Tosafot*, promoted ethical and ascetic doctrines that have much in common with the teachings of the German Pietists, and compiled and edited their own *pesaqim* as well as those of their colleague, R. Yeḥi'el of Paris.[159] There is also an unremarked group of exegetical comments from R. Moses and R. Isaac, which display a clear and consistent interest in *midrash 'aggadah* as a tool of biblical interpretation, clearly distinguished from the *peshat* elementsdetected in the comments of R. Yeḥi'el of Paris, and certainly distinct from the methods of the six Tosafists and rabbinic figures of the late twelfth through the thirteenth centuries whose methods were surveyed above. The latter, however, are also dissimilar from those of other northern French Tosafists who, perhaps following the lead of Rabbenu Tam and his circle, took a decidedly talmudocentric approach in their interpretation of biblical verses, as we have seen. Indeed, the biblical method at Evreux may represent the point of interface between or the transition from the approach of the Tosafist exegetes of the mid-twelfth and early thirteenth centuries and the midrashic expansion that comes to dominate the compilatory *perushei*

[158] The treatise found in Paris 1408, fols. 159r–168r, which concludes with the phrase, עד כאן מפרישות ה"ר יחיאל, is a collection of *Tosafot* from R. Yeḥi'el to tractate *Mo'ed Qatan*, rather than biblical interpretations. See S. Emanuel, *Shivrei Luḥot*, 188–89. Indeed, immediately following these *Tosafot* in this manuscript is a halakhic correspondence between R. Avigdor Katz of Vienna and R. Ḥayyim Palti'el b. Barukh; see Emanuel, *Shivrei Luḥot*, 219 (n. 2). The comment attributed in *Ta'amei Mesoret ha-Miqra*, ed. Y. S. Lange (Jerusalem, 1981), 28, to R. Yeḥi'el in the name of R. Meir (concerning the angel who asked Jacob his name, in Gen. 32:28), שאל את שמו ללחוש על מכתו שכך דרך המתלחשים לרפואה, does not appear to refer to R. Yeḥi'el of Paris.

[159] On the academy and methodology at Evreux, see Urbach, *Ba'alei ha-Tosafot*, 1:479–85; I. Ta-Shma, *Knesset Meḥqarim*, vol. 2 (Jerusalem, 2004), 110–118; my *Jewish Education and Society in the Middle Ages*, 74–79, 172–80; my *"Peering through the Lattices,"* 59–68; and S. Emanuel, *Shivrei Luḥot*, 193–97.

Ba'alei ha-Tosafot 'al ha-Torah, which were produced during the second half of the thirteenth century and beyond.[160]

A good example of these changes and developments can be seen with regard to the interpretation of the sale of Joseph toward the end of Genesis 37. At issue here, for many exegetes, were the nationalities and the number of groups that appeared to be involved in the selling of Joseph by his brothers, and the actual transfer of Joseph to Egypt. Reference is made at various points in the Torah to מדנים, מדינים, and ישמעאלים. In addition, the sequence or the stages of the transaction are confusing. In Genesis 37:27, for example, the brothers speak of selling Joseph to the *Yishma'elim*, but in the following verse, the Torah writes that merchants from among the *Midyanim* took Joseph out of the pit and sold him to the *Yishma'elim*, who brought him down to Egypt. At the same time, Genesis 37:36 states that the *Medanim* were the ones who sold Joseph to Egypt.

Rashbam (to Gen. 37:28), following his stated exegetical goal of presenting *'omeq peshuto shel miqra*, suggests that while the brothers were eating a meal while waiting for the *Yishma'elim* to arrive, a group of *Midyanim* happened upon Joseph in the pit and removed him, unbeknown to his brothers, and then sold him themselves to the *Yishma'elim*, who in turn sold him into slavery in Egypt. Although the brothers then did not actually sell Joseph into slavery in Egypt, their course of action certainly led to this result. Alternatively, and according to Genesis 45:4, where Joseph specifically attributes his being sold into slavery in Egypt to his brothers, Rashbam suggests that the brothers first instructed those *Midyanim* who came along only to remove Joseph from the pit, and they themselves sold him to the *Yishma'elim.* Rashbam (to Gen. 37:36) further notes that according to the *peshat* the *Medanim* and *Midyanim* were kin, while the *Medanim*, who sold him to Egypt, and the *Yishma'elim*, who transported him to Egypt, were identical (*ki sheneihem 'eḥad hem lefi ha-peshat*). Thus, the removal of Joseph from the pit, and his sale and transfer to Egypt, were essentially accomplished by two groups of related merchants.[161]

160 For a scriptural analysis by R. Isaac of Evreux of the talmudic interpretation of a series of verses, see, e.g., *Tosafot Qiddushin* 61b, s.v. בשלמא.

161 See M. Lockshin, *Rashbam's Commentary on Genesis: An Annotated Translation* (Lewiston, N.Y., 1989), 257–58, 260. As Lockshin notes (260, n. 3), Rashi also appears to think that there were only two groups, but he labels them differently. Rashbam is also directing his comment against Rashi's view, that it was the brothers themselves who removed Joseph from the pit, a point made (without attribution) by the later *Ḥizzequni* as well (Lockshin, 258, n. 2). Rashbam is also cited in *Da'at Zeqenim—Rabbotenu Ba'alei ha-Tosafot*, Gen., fol. 36b; *Minḥat Yehudah* (on the same page); *Hadar Zeqenim*, fol. 17a; and *Perush (Tosafot) ha-Rosh* (on the same page).

R. Yosef *Bekhor Shor* (to Gen. 37:28) summarizes Rashbam's approach (in the name of *yesh mefarshim*), but rejects it as a "self-invention" (בדאות) that is "not worthwhile" (וכל זה איננו שוה לי; see Esther 5:13).[162] Rather, as he had already explained (in Gen. 37:25), *Bekhor Shor* holds that the three groups of merchants represented three brothers, all of whom had been born from the concubines of Abraham, Hagar, and Qeturah, and these groups were therefore all considered to be one nation (אומה אחת היו). Thus there was really only one consortium of merchants involved here (חבורה באותה), which contained representatives from each of these larger families. The Torah is referring only to this one larger nation or group, alternately using the three individual and different names of its constitituents.[163]

In his Torah commentary (to Gen. 37:28), R. Judah *he-Ḥasid* suggests a similar approach, albeit from a different direction.[164] R. Judah was troubled by Joseph's seemingly untrue statement to Pharaoh's butler (Gen. 40:15) that he reached Egypt "because I had been kidnapped [*ki gunov gunavti*] from the land of the Hebrews." Therefore R. Judah presents an interpretation that is "according to the *peshat*, to explain what had occurred" (*'ela lefi ha-peshat kakh hayah ma'aseh*). While eating their meal, the brothers saw a caravan of *Yishma'elim* and they decided to sell Joseph to them. They made Joseph swear that he would neither tell nor write their father without their permission about this arrangement, and they enacted a *herem* among themselves that they would not tell. While they were involved with the *Yishma'elim* in writing up the sale, a group of *Medanim* passed by and looked into the pit where Joseph was, in search of water. They saw Joseph in the pit and removed him. Fearful that they would be pursued by whoever put Joseph into the pit in the first place, the *Medanim* quickly sold Joseph to the *Yishama'elim* for twenty pieces of silver, a relatively small sum.

Leaving aside the embellishments with regard to Joseph being made to swear an oath that he would not tell his father about what had transpired, and the *herem* enacted among the brothers (which are midrashic and

162 See *Perushei R. Yosef Bekhor Shor 'al ha-Torah*, ed. Nevo, 68–69. Cf. Lockshin, 257 (n. 3); E. Touitou, *Exegesis in Perpetual Motion*, 100, 246; and above, chapter 2, nn. 110–11.

163 *Bekhor Shor*'s comments to Gen. 37:25 are found in his name in *Moshav Zeqenim*, 72 (along with some other unnamed alternatives), and unnamed in *Tosafot ha-Rosh*. This is also the interpretation of Ibn Ezra (and Radak) to Gen. 37:28, although it is unclear whether *Bekhor Shor* had Ibn Ezra's commentary before him. See, e.g., *Perushei R. Yosef Bekhor Shor 'al ha-Torah*, ed. Nevo, editor's introduction, 10; *Bekhor Shor*'s commentary, 10 (to Gen. 2:24, and Nevo's note); *Tosafot ha-Shalem*, ed. Gellis, 1:115, secs. 9, 11; 1:277–78, sec. 3; and cf. above, n. 123, and above, chapter 2, n. 87.

164 See *Perushei ha-Torah le-R. Yehudah he-Ḥasid*, ed. Lange, 51. This piece is cited by *Moshav Zeqenim*, 72, in the name of R. Yehudah *he-Ḥasid* in two passages, found just before and just after *Bekhor Shor*'s interpretation. See also *Tosafot ha-Shalem*, ed. Gellis, 4:45–46, sec. 9; and above, chapter 3, n. 43.

pietistic approaches that represent an aspect of this story which is discussed further in *Sefer Ḥasidim*),[165] R. Judah *he-Ḥasid*'s *peshat* here essentially comports with the first approach taken by Rashbam. Indeed, R. Moses Zal(t)man asked his father how he then understands Genesis 45:4, where Joseph identifies himself to the brothers "as the one whom you sold here [to Egypt]." As Rashbam does, R. Judah answers that the brothers' throwing Joseph into the pit initially is what caused him to be sold into Egypt, making them responsible, in effect, for his sale. Indeed, R. Judah *he-Ḥasid* adduces support for this type of causality as an indication of larger responsibility from the case of Moses being unable to cross the Jordan along with the children of Israel.

Sefer ha-Gan, which was edited by the northern French rabbinic figure R. Aaron b. Yose *ha-Kohen* circa 1240, making it perhaps the earliest of the so-called thirteenth-century Tosafist Torah compilations,[166] seeks to reconcile Genesis 37:36, which states that the *Medanim* sold Joseph to Egypt, with a later verse (39:1), according to which Potiphar acquired Joseph from the *Yishma'elim* who had brought him down to Egypt. The first answer recorded by *Sefer ha-Gan*, which is characterized as *lefi ha-peshat*, is that the *Yishma'elim* had sold him to the *Medanim*, who brought him down to Egypt for sale. *Sefer ha-Gan* then presents an unidentified midrash that appears to be a passage from *Bereshit Rabbah* found (in extant versions) at the later verse about Potiphar.[167] This midrash portrays a kind of racial problem that the

[165] See *Sefer Ḥasidim* (Parma), ed. J. Wistinetski (Frankfurt, 1924), sec. 1961, and the references to *Midrash Tanḥuma* and *Pirqei de-R. Eli'ezer* in *Perushei ha-Torah*, ed. Lange, 51 (nn. 39–40).

[166] On the dating of *Sefer ha-Gan* (and the identity and family background of its compiler), see *Sefer ha-Gan*, ed. Orlian, 24–29. On the role of R. Aaron's father and brother in this work, see also, e.g., *Tosafot ha-Shalem*, ed. Gellis, 1:241 (sec. 12 = ms. Bodl. 271, fols. 125v–126r, כל זה מיסוד ה"ר יוסי אבי ה"ר הכהן אשר יסד הגן); 3:32 (sec. 2); 3:155–56 (sec. 7); ms. Leiden 27, fol. 19v; and below, n. 169. The Tosafists whom R. Aaron appears to cite directly (which include R. Barukh b. Isaac, R. Yosef of Clisson, R. Samson of Coucy, R. Jacob of Dreux, R. Isaac *ha-Kohen* of Provins, R. Judah b. Isaac Sirleon, R. Jacob of Provins, R. Moses of Evreux, R. Nathan b. Joseph, and R. Netan'el of Chinon) all fall within the period of 1180–1240. Note that on p. 244, the citation reads, "I heard that R. Jacob of Orleans asked," and on p. 156, "I heard from my father in the name of R. Isaac b. Samuel." The references to R. Samson b. Abraham of Sens on that page are indirect citations. Although the precise identity of "R. Natronai, the son of my uncle R. Jacob *ha-Qadosh*" (p. 227) is unclear, a son of the Tosafist R. Jacob *ha-Qadosh* of Corbeil (see Urbach, *Ba'alei ha-Tosafot*, 149–50) would fit this time frame as well. On the methodology of *Sefer ha-Gan*, and its focused use of both *peshat* and *derash*, see Orlian, 51–72.

[167] The later *Perush* (or *Tosafot*) *R. Asher* (*ha-Rosh*) compilation to Gen. 37:28 (fol. 16b, "and they sold Joseph to the *Yishma'elim* for twenty pieces of silver") cites and identifies this *midrash* as *Bereshit Rabbah*. Cf. M. M. Kasher, *Torah Shelemah*, vol. 6 (Jerusalem, 1938), 144. On the nature of *Perush R. Asher* and its attribution to R. Asher b. Yeḥi'el, see, e.g., A. H. Freimann, *R. Asher b. Yeḥi'el ve-Ze'eza'av* (Jerusalem, 1986), 129; *Tosafot ha-Shalem*, vol. 1, editor's introduction, 20; *Sefer ha-Gan*, ed. Orlian, 95–96; *Sarei ha-Elef*, ed. M. M. Kasher and Y. D. Mandelbaum (Jerusalem, 1979), 1:67; and I. Ta-Shma, *Knesset Meḥqarim*, 2:163. The scholarly consensus is that

Egyptians had with the dark-skinned *Yishma'elim* selling them fair-skinned Joseph as a slave. Although Joseph was technically in the possession of the *Yishama'elim*, the Egyptians required the *Medanim* to act as guarantors on behalf of the *Yishma'elim* for this sale, in order to overcome this difficulty.[168] Thus the Torah can credibly assign this sale to both groups.

R. Aaron *ha-Kohen*, the compiler of *Sefer ha-Gan*, offers this interpretation as one that he heard from his brother R. Jacob, who had himself heard it in the name of R. Moses b. Shne'ur of Evreux.[169] As we shall see, R. Moses and his brother R. Isaac were inclined to put forward midrashic interpretations of the Torah, and to expand or otherwise manipulate passages in *Bereshit Rabbah*, even as this particular selection from *Bereshit Rabbah* might be fairly characterized as an *'aggadah ha-meyashevet divrei miqra.* Although subsequent Tosafist Torah compilations on this episode include many of the earlier *peshatim* that have been noted, few cite the focused midrashic approach of *Sefer ha-Gan*/R. Moses of Evreux.[170] Rather, these later compilations tend to link this passage in *Bereshit Rabbah* to another and to present additional *midrashim*, creating a much more diffuse midrashic picture and discussion. This was done, in part, to explain or to amplify Rashi's approach

---

the R. Asher who may have composed this work was probably not the halakhist R. Asher b. Yeḥi'el, and it is possible that the work emanated from northern France rather than from Germany (although, like *Moshav Zeqenim*, it also refers to a number of Spanish writings, including Naḥmanides' Torah commentary).

168 *Bereshit Rabbah* 86:3, ed. Theodor-Albeck, 1055 (to Gen. 39:1), has the Egyptian official Potiphar, who acquired Joseph from the *Yishma'elim*, make a very similar point from the other direction. Upon seeing the fair-skinned Joseph being offered for sale by the dark-skinned *Yishma'elim*, Potiphar sensed that Joseph was not really a slave, and he cleverly requested a guarantor for the sale in the event that Joseph had been stolen or kidnapped, and was not rightfully in the possession of the *Yishma'elim*.

169 See *Sefer ha-Gan*, ed. Orlian, "Sefer ha-Gan," 187: ומה שכתוב והמדנים מכרו אותו [אל מצרים] לפוטיפר ובמקום אחר כתוב מיד הישמעאלים אשר הורידוהו שמה [בראשית לט:א] לפי הפשט הא דכתב והמדנים מכרו אותו למצרים היינו לימשעאלים להוריד למצרים. ויש במדרש כי הישמעלאים היו מוחזקים ממנו והורידו למצרים למכרו. אמרו המצריים גורמני מוכר כותי ואין כותי מוכר גורמני. כלו' דרך הלבן למכור שחור כי הלבן הוא הבן חורין והשחור הוא העבד אתמה אין כאן עבד תנו ערב. המדנים ערבו הדבר לכן הוא אומר והמדנים מכרו אותו. כך שמעתי מאחי ה"ר יעקב ששמע משם ה"ר משה ב"ר שניאור ז"ל. See also Orlian, ibid., 122 (n. 18).

170 *Perushei ha-Torah le-R. Ḥayyim Palti'el*, ed. Lange, 124 (to Gen. 39:1), cites R. Moses b. Shne'ur by name (based on ms. Munich 62; cf. *Tosafot ha-Shalem*, ed. Gellis, 4:57, sec. 2). *Pa'aneaḥ Raza*, 168, cites this interpretation in the name of ה"ר יעקב ג"ן. See also ms. Florence/Laurenziana Plut. II,20, fol. 171r: וא"ת למה כתוב המדנים מכרו אותו אל מצרים, היה לו לו' המדינים. ופי' רשב"א כי מדן ומדין וישמעאל אוחת היא. In this manuscript, "Rashba" (who is also cited, e.g., on fol. 193r, at the beginning of *Mishpatim* in a purely halakhic context; cf. *Tosafot ha-Shalem*, ed. Gellis, 8:145) may refer either to the exegete R. Solomon b. Abraham of Troyes or to his better-known brother, R. Samson b. Abraham of Sens; cf. above, chapter 3, n. 221. It is highly unlikely that "Rashba" is a misspelling of "Rashbam" in this instance, since the interpretation attributed to him is that of *Bekhor Shor* (which was against that of Rashbam), although see also ms. Leiden 27, fol. 46r.

to this series of events, but new midrashic directions and solutions were also put forward that had little to do with Rashi's commentary.[171]

The focused use of *Midrash Rabbah* by the brothers of Evreux can also be seen in connection with the advance made by Potiphar's wife to Joseph, when he returned to the house of Potiphar and no one of the household staff was there (*ve-'ein 'ish me-'anshei ha-bayit sham ba-bayit*, Gen. 39:11). The *Hadar Zeqenim* compilation notes a *peshat* approach, which understands the phrase "no one of the household staff was there" to mean simply that Joseph was alone in the house with the wife of Potiphar. Ri (= R. Isaac) of Evreux interprets, however, that Joseph's "manhood was removed" (*nutal zikhruto*). The phrase *'ein 'ish*, according to this approach, connotes that Joseph was "not a man." As R. Isaac explains, Joseph's reproductive organ became suddenly and miraculously covered with a membrane and was rendered ineffective, thus preventing him from sinning with the wife of Potiphar.[172] Neither the published version of *Hadar Zeqenim* nor any identifiable manuscript source of this Tosafist Torah compilation notes the fact that R. Isaac of Evreux's interpretation is an extension of a passage in *Bereshit Rabbah*.[173]

[171] See, e.g., *Moshav Zeqenim*, 71–72 (to Gen. 37:25); *Tosafot ha-Shalem*, ed. Gellis, 4:44–46, secs. 6–7, 10; and see also *Perushei R. Ḥayyim Palti'el*, 117–18 (to Gen. 37:27). See also ms. Bodl. 2343 (to Gen.37:36), reproduced in *Tosafot ha-Shalem*, 4:57, sec. 3. Although this collection, compiled by a student of R. Moses of Coucy and R. Yeḥi'el, does not cite R. Moses of Evreux's approach here, it does cite (fol. 3r) R. Moses's explanation of Rashi's comment concerning the punishment of the snake (Gen. 3:14). See above, n. 128. On the more diffuse midrashic approaches of the later so-called Tosafist Torah commentaries, see my "Midrashic Texts and Methods in Tosafist Torah Commentaries," in *Midrash Unbound: Transformations and Innovations*, ed. Michael Fishbane and Joanna Weinberg (Oxford, 2012; in press).

[172] *Hadar Zeqenim*, fol. 18b: ואין איש מאנשי הבית שם בבית. הפשט שלא היה בבית רק יוסף. והר"י מאיוורא מפרש מלמד שבדק עצמו ומצא שאינו איש שבאותה שעה נוטל זכרותו למונעו מן החטא. The beginning of the passage in *Bereshit Rabbah* (87:7, ed. Theodor-Albeck, 1072–73) reads: ואין איש. בדק את עצמו ולא מצא את עצמו איש. The midrash then offers three rabbinic interpretations of this somewhat enigmatic passage, each supported by verses that testify to Joseph's own resolve, specifically in the terms being suggested: אמר ר' שמואל [בר נחמני] נמתחה הקשת וחזרה. ר' יצחק אומר נתפזר זרעו ויצא דרך צפורניו. ר' הונא אמר איקונין של אביו ראה ונצטנן דמו. R. Isaac of Evreux's interpretation matches none of these views exactly. It is either his own understanding of the initial phrase in *Bereshit Rabbah*, or it is perhaps his adaptation, in more graphic and miraculous terms, of Joseph's sudden inability to function sexually, according to the first interpretation in the midrash (by R. Samuel). On the presentation of both *peshat* and *derash* in this passage in *Hadar Zeqenim*, cf. Sara Japhet, above, chapter 2, n. 36. *Sotah* 36b records these three opinions in the names of other Amoraim, but combines them in a different way. *Tosafot Sotah* 36b, s.v. *be-'otah*, presents R. Moses *ha-Darshan*'s interpretation of Joseph's response, which follows the psychological approach that Joseph saw the image of his father's face before him and was unable to sin.

[173] See *Tosafot ha-Shalem*, ed. Gellis, vol. 4 (Jerusalem, 1985), 97, sec. 9, and cf. Kasher, *Torah Shelemah*, 6:1501. The name of R. Isaac of Evreux is cited in full in ms. Vatican 48, fol. 35v; Ms. Moscow 268, fol. 81v. Ms. B.M. 190, fol. 40r; ms. JTS Lutzki 791, fol. 40r; and ms. Moscow 898, fol. 29v, cite this in the name of ר"י Evreux, and ms. Munich 50, fol. 82v, reads הר"י מאייברא.

This same interpretation, that Joseph checked himself and found that his manhood had become covered and rendered ineffective, headed by an attribution to an unnamed midrash (*yesh ba-midrash*), is found in a variant *Tosafot* commentary to the Talmud, the so-called *Tosafot Evreux* to tractate *Sotah.* These *Tosafot* were composed in the study hall of the brothers of Evreux in the mid-thirteenth century, and this comment comes at a point where an aggadic passage in the Talmud is discussing Joseph's actions in the house of Potiphar.[174] What we have here then is a talmudic interpretation from Evreux that was incorporated into a Tosafist Torah commentary, as well as another significant use of *Bereshit Rabbah* by a Tosafist, irrespective of the precise text of this midrash that R. Isaac had before him. The commitment of this Tosafist *beit midrash* to the study and interpretation of *Bereshit Rabbah*, and its incorporation into both biblical and talmudic interpretations, is once again evident.[175] In this instance, it is the Tosafist R. Isaac of Evreux himself who favors a more miraculous and dramatic perspective on the biblical episode, and not merely the compiler of the Tosafist Torah commentary who cites this interpretation alongside the *peshat.* In this instance, Rashi is also among those exegetes who favored a nonmiraculous, psychological approach.[176]

Like his brother R. Moses,[177] R. Isaac of Evreux also interacted with comments to the Torah made by Rashi in both narrative and halakhic sections,

[174] See *Tosafot Evreux ʿal Massekhet Sotah*, ed. Yaʿakov Lifshitz (Jerusalem, 1969), 100 (36b, s.v. *ve-ʾein ʾish me-ʾanshei ha-bayit*): יש במדרש שבדק יוסף את עצמו מעשה של איש, שלא היה לו מילה שמצא את עצמו טומטום.

[175] In his comments to the *Tosafot Evreux* passage cited in the preceding note, Y. Lifshitz suggests (100, n. 88) that since R. Isaac of Evreux's interpretation is not found so clearly in the midrash, this passage should perhaps begin with the phrase *yesh le-faresh* rather than *yesh ba-midrash*. Such an emendation, however, aside from not being indicated on any other level, fails to take into account the strong affinity that the Tosafist academy at Evreux had for *Bereshit Rabbah* and its interpretation. Although the piece about Joseph and the wife of Potiphar derives from *Tosafot Evreux*, and R. Moses of Evreux is cited by name four times in *Sefer ha-Gan* and had some contact with its compiler (see above, n. 166; *Sefer ha-Gan*, ed. Orlian, 99; and below, n. 183), this interpretation is not found there.

[176] See Rashi to Gen. 39:11 ("he beheld the image of his father"); and cf. M. Lockshin, *Rashbam's Commentary on Genesis*, 128; *Tosafot ha-Shalem*, ed. Gellis, 4:97, sec. 10; N. Leibowitz, *ʿIyyunim be-Sefer Shemot* (Jerusalem, 1983), 512–13; and Morris Berger, "The Torah Commentary of R. Samuel b. Meir," (Ph.D. diss., Harvard University, 1982), 200–201. Rashbam (to Gen. 39:10, followed by *Bekhor Shor* to Gen. 39:11, ed. Nevo, 72) suggests that Joseph ended up alone in the house with the wife of Potiphar through happenstance, although Rashbam also cites a *midrash ʾaggadah* (= *Bereshit Rabbah*) that everyone else had gone out that day to witness the Nile overflowing its banks. Cf. Lockshin, *Rashbam's Commentary on Genesis*, 272 (n. 3)

[177] See above, n. 128; *Tosafot ha-Shalem*, ed. Gellis, 7:89, sec. 5; *Tosafot Beiẓah* 21b, s.v. *lakhem* (citing both R. Moses and R. Samuel of Evreux = *Tosafot ha-Shalem*, 7:94, sec. 1); ms. Moscow 268, fol. 92r (citing R. Ḥayyim, the son of R. Moses of Evreux, in the name of his father, on *parashat Shelaḥ*); *Tosafot ha-Shalem ʿal Massekhet Sotah*, ed. Y. Lifshitz, editor's introduction, 27–28; *Perushei ha-Torah le-R. Ḥayyim Paltiʾel*, ed. Lange, editor's introduction, 11; and Urbach, *Baʿalei*

sometimes explaining or amplifying his explanations and at other times disagreeing with them. Following the approach of the Talmud in tractate *Nedarim*, Rashi to Exodus 4:24 explains why God threatened Moses with death as he returned from Midyan to Egypt and made his way to a place of lodging (*va-yehi ba-derekh ba-malon*). Rashi attributes this to the fact that Moses was lax, tending first to the lodging issues (*lefi she-nitʿaseq ma-malon teḥilah*), and only then to the requirement to circumcise his son. R. Isaac of Evreux understands Rashi to mean that since Moses had already heeded the Almighty's instruction to leave Midyan (4:18), he now had the time to undertake the circumcision of his son, even though this would have delayed his vital journey.[178]

Rashi to Exodus 12:15 makes note of an apparent contradiction within the Torah about whether *maẓah* should be eaten on Passover for seven days, as this verse seems to indicate, or for six days, as per Deuteronomy16:8. Based on the *Mekhilta*, Rashi derives from this that eating *maẓah* on the seventh day, and indeed on all the days of Passover except for the first, is optional, so long as leaven is not consumed. Based on a series of textual questions, R. Isaac of Evreux derives the optional aspect of *maẓah* from a different verse (Ex. 12:18), and notes that his approach does not comport with that of Rashi.[179]

In the Song of the Sea (Ex. 15:8), the Torah characterizes the water as being piled up or heaped (*neʿermu mayim*). Rashi, following Onkelos, interprets the word *neʿermu* as a form of *ʿarmimut* or cleverness. The cleverness of the water is understood by some to mean that it arranged itself in a way that would fool the Egyptians into entering the sea, or that it covered only

---

ha-Tosafot, 1:484. See also See Menachem Banitt, *Le Glossaire de Leipzig*, vol. 4 (Jerusalem, 2005), 418, for a French gloss interpretation by R. Moses to the Book of Esther. This glossary, which was composed in Rouen toward the end of the thirteenth century, contains many *leʿazim* that are found initially in Rashi's commentaries. See also vol. 3 (Jerusalem, 2001), 1727, for the fuller context of R. Moses's gloss; and see also above, Introduction, n. 83.

178 See ms. Moscow 268, fol. 82r: [פרש"י] ולמה נענש לפי שנתעסק במלון תחלה. [פי'] מה"ר מאייברא שנענש לפי שמיד שנסע ביום ראשון כבר קיים מצות המקום שאמ' לו לך וא"כ היה יכול למולו ביום הראשון שנסע. Cf. *Tosafot ha-Shalem*, ed. Gellis, 6:119, sec. 1–3; and ms. Vatican 45 in the next note.

179 See Moscow 82, fol. 15v (found also in *Hadar Zeqenim*, fol. 29b): פ"ה כתוב אחד אומר שבעת ימים תאכל מצות וכתוב אחד אומר ששת ימים תאכל למדתנו על שביעי שהוא רשות . . . לכן פי' הר"י מאיוורא דששת ימים רשות מדכתי' בערב תאכלו מצות משמע מכאן ואילך אינו מחויב לאכול. ואין זה כפי' הקונטרוס. The passage concludes, ומה"ר יום טוב מקיים פי' רש"י. It is unclear, however, whether this refers to R. Yom Tov of Joigny or to R. Yom Tov, the son of Rashi's son-in-law R. Judah b. Nathan, or to some other rabbinic figure of this name. Cf. above, chapter 2, n. 217, and ms. Leiden 27, fols. 55v–56r: לכן נראה לי דששת ימים רשות . . . ומורי הרב שי' מקיים פרש"י. See also *Tosafot ha-Shalem*, ed. Gellis, vol. 7 (Jerusalem, 1988), 90–91, sec. 6; ms. Vatican 45, fol. 22v (ואומר הרב יצחק מאיוורא פסח מצרים מקחו בעשור . . . כדי שישהו ג' ימים לאחר המילה קודם שיצאו לדרך) [= *Tosafot ha-Shalem*, 7:55, sec. 8]; *Daʿat Zeqenim*, Ex., fol. 13a; *Tosafot ha-Shalem*, 7:64, sec. 7 (citing *Daʿat Zeqenim*); and *Tosafot ha-Shalem ʿal Massekhet Sotah*, ed. Y. Lifshitz, editor's introduction, 34–35, n. 21.

the Egyptians and not the Jews.[180] In any case, Rashi also puts forward a more *peshat*-like approach. According to the "sense of clarity of the verse" (לצחות המקרא), *ne'ermu* is akin to the phrase in the Song of Songs (7:3), "a pile of wheat" (*'aremat ḥittim*), as evidenced also by the phrase *niẓvu kemo ned nozlim*, that the flowing water stood straight as a wall. *Hadar Zeqenim*, without mentioning Rashi by name, as is often its wont, comments first that *ne'ermu* is like a pile of wheat (*kemo 'aremat hittim*).[181] *Hadar Zeqenim* then proceeds to deal with the translation of Onkelos, which it finds somewhat difficult to explain, since cleverness is not a trait that can be easily applied to water. Citing from *Sefer ha-Gan*, *Hadar Zeqenim* presents the view of R. Meir b. Shne'ur, that there is a midrash which maintains that the water itself became intelligent, and offered its own song.[182] The original text of *Sefer ha-Gan* contains the correct name of the source of the attribution, R. Moses b. Shne'ur of Evreux. Once again, a leader of the Tosafist academy at Evreux has provided an even more miraculous midrashic interpretation than the one proposed by Rashi, not to mention Rashbam and other *pashtanim*.[183]

Another passage in *Sefer ha-Gan* further testifies to the sensitivity of R. Moses of Evreux with regard to rabbinic traditions and scriptural interpretation. *Sefer ha-Gan*, to Genesis 31:52,[184] records a principle put forward

180 See *Torah Shelemah*, vol. 14 (New York, 1951), 125, and *Perushei ha-Torah le-R. Ḥayyim Palti'el*, ed. Lange, 239–40.

181 This is the interpretation given by Rashbam and Ibn Ezra using the same prooftext, and it is also found in Menaḥem b. Saruq's *Maḥberet*. See M. Lockshin, *Rashbam's Commentary on Exodus*, 156, who suggests that these commentators are thereby avoiding Onkelos's approach. This interpretation is also found in the name of R. Yosef Qara. See *Tosafot ha-Shalem*, ed. Gellis, 7:226, sec. 9, and cf. the interpretation from ms. Hamburg 45 found in sec. 5 (*lefi ha-peshat*).

182 *Hadar Zeqenim*, fol. 32a: נערמו מי כמו ערימת מים. ועל מה שתרגם אונקלוס חכימו מיא קשה מה חכמה שייכא במים. ואו' ה"ר מאיר ב"ר שניאור דיש במדרש שנכנסה בהם ערמימות של חכמה ואמרו שירה. ג"ן. וי"מ שהחכמה היתה כאשר נצבו כמו נד נוזלים. Note that the core of both interpretations given by Rashi and *Hadar Zeqenim* are also found in the *Mekhilta*. A later Tosafist Torah compilation, *Peshatim u-Perushim 'al Ḥamishah Ḥumshei Torah le-R. Ya'aqov me-Vienna*, ed. M. Grossman (Mainz, 1888), 68, cites anonymously the view attributed by *Hadar Zeqenim* to R. Meir b. Shne'ur ('נערמו מים תרג חכימא מיא ומה היא חכמתם שאמרו שירה וכן במדרש), as does *Da'at Zeqenim* (Ex., fol. 18b). See also ms. Bodl. 271/1, fol. 14v; *Tosafot ha-Shalem*, ed. Gellis, 7:227, sec. 11; and Poznanski, *Mavo*, XCVIII.

183 See *Sefer ha-Gan*, ed. Orlian, 234: 'על מה שתרגם אונקלוס חכימו מיא, נערמו לש' ערימת חטים, וקש מה שחכמה שייכא במים. וא"ל ה"ר משה ב"ר שניאור דיש במדרש נע'[רמו שנכנסה בהם] ערמימות של חכמה ואמרו שירה. The passage in ms. Vienna 19/Heb. 28 to Ex. 15:8 may read = ואו' הר"ר משה rather than וא"ל (= ואמר לי) as Orlian has it. Of the three other comments from R. Moses of Evreux that *Sefer ha-Gan* records, two were told by R. Moses directly to the compiler R. Aaron (see the next note and below, nn. 188–89), while the other one was told to R. Aaron's brother R. Jacob by R. Moses (above, n. 170). The other major manuscript of *Sefer ha-Gan*, ms. Nuremberg 5, does not contain comments to the Book of Exodus. Cf. *Sefer ha-Gan*, ed. Orlian, 107, and *Tosafot ha-Shalem*, ed. Gellis, vol. 1, editor's introduction, 33.

184 See *Sefer ha-Gan*, ed. Orlian, 179; Poznanski, *Mavo*, CII; *Tosafot ha-Shalem*, ed. Gellis, 3:200, sec. 2. See also the variants in *Perushei R. Ḥayyim Palti'el*, ed. Lange, 543; *Pa'aneaḥ Raza*, 150; and *Moshav Zeqenim*, 57.

either by the Tosafist R. Solomon (b. Judah) of Dreux or by R. Solomon (b. Abraham) of Troyes, the brother of R. Samson of Sens.[185] Any time Scripture indicates that an *ʿed*—a sign or a witness—has been established to mark the forming of a covenant, the one who violates that covenant will be punished by the very same sign or substance that was used to establish the covenant or testimony in the first place. Thus, for example, the covenant established with stone by Joshua (Joshua 24:27), to confirm that the Jewish people in the land of Israel would not desert the Almighty, meant that anyone who committed idolatry would be punished by stoning (as per Deut. 17:7). Upon hearing this prinicple, R. Moses of Evreux was greatly perplexed and troubled (*meʾod huqshah be-ʿeinav ve-niẓtaʿer bah*) on account of the covenant of stone (*ʿed ha-gal ha-zeh*) that was established between Jacob and Laban as described by the verse in Genesis 31:52. According to the talmudic view (*Sanhedrin* 105a) that Bilʿam and Laban were one and the same, Laban violated his earlier covenant with Jacob when, as Bilʿam, he sought to curse Jacob's descendants. At no time, however, do we find that Laban/Bilʿam was punished for his violation by the stones of the original covenant.

This passage then reports that R. Moses of Evreux was told in a dream to go and look in (*Midrash*) *Bereshit Zuta* (*ʿad she-herʾu lo ba-ḥalomo puq ve-doq bi-Bereshit Zuta*).[186] R. Moses was able to locate this slim volume (*maẓa sefer qatan*), in which it was written that a sword had been stuck into the stone, to seal the covenant between Laban and Jacob (*she-naʿaẓu ḥerev be-tokh ha-gal le-ʿiqqar keritat berit*). The stone fence or border into which Bilʿam's leg was rammed by his donkey (Nu. 22:25) was the very stone of that covenant, and the sword that killed Bilʿam (Nu. 31:8, *ve-ʾet Bilʿam ben Beʾor hargu be-harev*, which intimates that the particular sword in question was a known one that had a history) was the very sword that had been stuck into the rock. In light of this, Rashi interprets Numbers 22:24, "a fence on this and a fence on that [side]" (*gader mi-zeh ve-gader mi-zeh*), with the words "that a standard fence is made of stone" (*setam geder shel ʾavanim hu*), to hint (*ve-ramaz*) that Bilʿam/Laban was being punished at this point via the stone fence, for violating his covenant with Jacob.[187]

185 For R. Solomon b. Judah, see above, chapter 3, n. 213–20. For R. Solomon b. Abraham, see chapter 3, n. 221. See also Urbach, *Baʿalei ha-Tosafot*, 1:344, and 1:340, n. 4, and cf. Poznanski, *Mavo*, CII–CIII (n. 2).

186 For a fuller discussion of this and numerous related passages, and the contexts in which Ashkenazic rabbinic authorities relied on dreams and shared their contents, see my "Dreams as a Determinant of Jewish Law and Practice in Northern Europe during the High Middle Ages," in *Studies in Medieval Jewish Intellectual and Social History: A Festschrift in Honor of Professor Robert Chazan*, ed. D. Engel and E. Wolfson (Leiden, 2012), 111–43.

187 The passage concludes, כך שמע[תי] ממה"ר משה ב"ר שניאור. On Bilʿam and Laban, see also *Tosafot ha-Shalem*, ed. Gellis, 6:14–15, sec. 9. *Sefer ha-Gan*, ed. Orlian, 249, reprises this

In a fourth citation from R. Moses of Evreux (כך שמעתי מפי הר"ר משה בן שניאור), *Sefer ha-Gan* presents a straightforward interpretation of Numbers 11:23, in which God asks Moses, in a seemingly harsh way, "Are you trying to shorten the hand of God?" Moses appears to be wondering (in Nu. 11:21–22) how it would be possible to provide sufficient food in a readily available manner, now that God in His anger had indicated that He would give them a month's supply of food in one day, which they would then have to gather and prepare. R. Moses of Evreux explains the phrase *ha-yad ha-Shem tiqzar* to mean that just as God can provide, He can withhold until His words are heeded, as the following verses demonstrate, in which the quail were provided in very large yet easily accessible amounts. R. Moses of Evreux adds the comment of R. Nissim Gaon. This section shows that God and Moses were in fact "on the same page." Moses's inquiry was only about how the logistics would work out (*be-ʾeizeh ẓad yigmeru bnei ʾadam ʾet ha-davar*), and was not a statement of distrust or disbelief. R. Moses's comment here is intended principally to explain and to defend the words of Moses, following the approach of R. Nissim Gaon, and to integrate them within the larger episode.[188] In his brief comment on Numbers11:23, on the other hand, R. Yosef *Bekhor Shor*, who often tries to defend the statements and actions of our forefathers, views the Almighty's response to Moses as a kind of rebuke: "For I have on the earth many creatures of which you are unaware."[189]

Extending from the earliest of the Tosafist Torah commentaries, which had its roots in the circle or study hall of Rabbenu Tam (ms. Paris 167 = ms. Moscow 362), through the various (talmudic) *Tosafot* and the later Tosafist Torah compilations, scores of *midrashim* were cited by Tosafists with great frequency.[190] What is suggestive, however, about the use of *midrashim*

---

interpretation on Exodus 24:8 without reference to R. Moses of Evreux. The Jewish people were sprinkled with blood at Mount Sinai to signify that one who does not keep the Torah will pay with his blood, as confirmed by both scriptural and aggadic texts. This passage concludes: "And this constitutes a large proof (וראיה גדולה היא to what we explained in the name of R. Solomon b. Abraham regarding *ʿed ha-gal ha-zeh* [Gen. 31:52]) that one who violates a covenant will be punished by the substance used to seal the covenant." See also *Tosafot ha-Shalem*, ed. Gellis, 8:363, sec. 1, and cf. *Hadar Zeqenim* to Ex. 24:8 (fol. 48a, citing *Sefer ha-Gan*), and to Nu. 24:8 (fol. 59b, citing an unidentified midrash).

188 See *Sefer ha-Gan*, ed. Orlian, 299, and see also *Paʿaneaḥ Raza*, 426.

189 *Perushei R. Yosef Bekhor Shor*, ed. Nevo, 257. On *Bekhor Shor*'s general tendency to defend the actions of the *ʾavot* (and some notable exceptions), see above, chapter 2, nn. 117–20.

190 Two indicative examples from ms. Paris 167 (and the parallel ms. Moscow 362; see above, chapter 2, n. 6) concern the eating done by the angels who came to visit Abraham (cf. above, chapter 3, n. 190), and the age of Rivka when she married Isaac. See ms. Paris 167, fol. 54r (= ms. Moscow 362, fol. 182r, and cf. *Tosafot ha-Shalem*, ed. Gellis, 2:123, sec. 19); and fols. 55r–v (= ms. Moscow 362, fols. 128r–v); cf. *Tosafot ha-Shalem*, ed. Gellis, 3:6, sec. 4. See also my "Midrashic Texts and Methods in Tosafist Torah Commentaries" (above, n. 171), sec. I (end) and sec. VI.

in the academy at Evreux, unlike the commentary produced by the circle of Rabbenu Tam, is that the *midrashim* appear to have been selected and interpreted not simply as an extension of talmudic study and interpretation, but with the goal of consistent scriptural interpretation as well. The same can be said for the early Tosafist Torah compilation *Sefer ha-Gan*, which features the exegetical work of *Ḥakhmei Evreux*. In this respect, the brothers of Evreux can perhaps be seen as an outgrowth of the six late twelfth- and early thirteenth-century Tosafists and rabbinic figures that were featured earlier.

Tosafist Torah Commentaries of the Mid-Thirteenth Century

As we have seen throughout our discussions to this point, there were always Tosafists who engaged in the interpretation of biblical verses as part of talmudic study and interpretation. Beginning with the northern French *pashtanim*, however, Tosafists began to look at the interpretation of the biblical text in its own right. Ultimately, however, the methods favored by Rashi and *Bekhor Shor*, rather than those of R. Yosef Qara and Rashbam, became predominant in this endeavor. Both R. Yeḥi'el of Paris and the brothers of Evreux, who were not so involved in *peshat* interpretation, also considered the interpretation of the Torah on its own terms to be a worthy goal.

The later compilatory Tosafist Torah works, which were produced in both Germany and northern France from the middle of the thirteenth century onward, focus much more on *derash* than they do on *peshat*, with the exception of Hezekiah b. Manoaḥ's *Ḥizzequni*. Indeed, it is not uncommon for these compilations to begin a passage with what the midrash says (or what the Talmud says), pushing the biblical text into the background, and citing both exegetical and homiletical *midrashim*.[191] Overall, however, these commentaries contain, as we have seen, a range of materials in different proportions, as well as several sometimes muddled strata, which can be identified as follows: the work of the twelfth-century *pashtanim*; the comments produced by the group of Tosafist *pashtanim*, and other leading rabbinic scholars in both northern France and Germany, who have been the focus of the present study as well as those of their more Midrash-minded Tosafist colleagues and successors; and the interpretations of other, later, and lesser rabbinic scholars, who perhaps themselves served as, or assisted, the compilers of the collections. Although we have succeeded in the present study in further identifying and highlighting the stratum of Tosafist *pashtanim* and

[191] On this distinction, see, e.g., Hanoch Albeck, *Mavo li-Bereshit Rabbah* (Jerusalem, 1965), 1, and Amos Geulah, "Midreshei Aggadah Avudim ha-Yedu'im me-Ashkenaz Bilvad: Avkir, Esfah u-Devarim Zuta" (Ph.D. diss., Hebrew University, 2007), vol. 1, 36–41.

related colleagues which effectively begins with R.Yosef *Bekhor Shor* and extends through R. Moses of Coucy and the brothers of Evreux, a full literary and stylistic analysis of the so-called Tosafist Torah compilations, along with a complete correlation of the many manuscript texts in which they are to be found, are beyond the scope of this study.

Nonetheless, as I have argued elsewhere, the many midrashic interpretations and expansions found in these later Tosafist Torah compilations, along with talmudic and *Tosafot* interpretations of biblical verses and the measure of *peshat* exegesis that is contained in them as well, were meant to yield works that were more popular or broad-based than the commentaries produced by the *pashtanim* of northern France and their immediate Tosafist successors. The Tosafist Torah compilations were apparently intended to attract readers who were below the level of the highest rabbinic elites. Indeed, these compilations may well reflect the efforts of the second-level elite in Ashkenaz at providing to a wider audience various kinds of Tosafist-like materials—halakhic, talmudic, midrashic, and exegetical—associated with and arrayed around the text of the Torah.[192]

Indeed, there is evidence from the mid- to late thirteenth century for several large collections from Germany and Austria, with individual authors who were designed to present Tosafist material primarily in the realm of *halakhah* but also in the realms of midrash and *'aggadah*, arranged according to the verses and order of the Torah. It would appear that these works as well were intended to reach an audience wider than that of the rabbinic elite who populated the most prestigious or advanced (talmudic) study halls. These works include the *Perushim u-Pesaqim* by R. Avigdor Katz of Vienna,[193] the

[192] See my "Midrashic Texts and Methods in Tosafist Torah Commentaries," sec. X; my "Between the Tosafist Academies and Other *Battei Midrash* in Ashkenaz in the Middle Ages," [Hebrew] in *Yeshivot and Battei Midrash*, ed. I. Etkes (Jerusalem, 2006), 99–106; my *Jewish Education and Society in the High Middle Ages*, 80–85; and cf. H. Touitou, "*Minḥat Yehudah*," 3–7, 60–66.

[193] See S. Emanuel, *Shivrei Luḥot*, 175–81, and my *"Peering through the Lattices,"* 95–98, 225–27. This work was published under the title *Perushim u-Pesaqim le-R. Avigdor [Ẓarefati]*, ed. I. Herskovitz (Jerusalem, 1996), on the basis of ms. Hamburg 45, and ms. B.M. 243. The attribution of the as yet unpublished *peshatim* in ms. Hamburg to R. Avidgor (and indeed, the very nature of these comments) is less certain. A number of passages from this work (which mention earlier Tosafist interpretations and exegetes) have been cited in the present study, and I intend to publish a fuller evaluation of this text separately. R. Avidgor cites quite a number of northern French and German Tosafists by name in his *Perushim u-Pesaqim*, most often in halakhic contexts. As listed in Herskovitz's index (536–37), *Bekhor Shor*'s Torah commentary is cited only once, while Rashbam is cited more than ten times, although many of these citations refer to his commentary to *Bava Batra* (or to comments made by Rashbam in *Tosafot*) rather than to his Torah commentary. Interestingly, there is a core of halakhic material on various verses throughout the fourteenth-century *Moshav Zeqenim* collection which parallels material found in both ms. Hamburg 45 and ms. B.M. 243 (as well as ms. Mantua 36). See, e.g., Emanuel, 172 (n. 89).

no longer extant *Kol Bo* by R. Shemaryah, the son of R. Simḥah of Speyer,[194] and the *Derashot u-Pisqei Halakhot* by R. Ḥayyim b. Isaac *Or Zaruʿa*.[195] This group of works also parallels the halakhic abridgements in northern France during the second half of the thirteenth century, which exist in both published and manuscript forms. The best-known work among these is the *Sefer Miẓvot Qatan* by R. Isaac of Corbeil, whose intended appeal to a larger and generally less knowledgeable audience was explicitly noted, and promoted, within the period of its composition.[196]

R. Eleazar b. Judah of Worms

Although most of what we have seen in this chapter regarding developments in biblical interpretation has been centered in northern France, cultivation of midrashic exegesis in Germany during the first half of the thirteenth century also proceeded apace. Indeed, we can point to an excellent yet unknown specimen of German exegesis that contains neither the pronounced *peshat* component found in the Torah commentary by R. Judah *he-Ḥasid*, which was discussed at length in chapter 3, nor the unbridled *derash* found in the later Tosafist Torah collections that were compiled in both Germany and northern France, although some words of introduction are in order.

The lengthy Torah commentary that has been published under the title *Perush ha-Roqeaḥ ʿal ha-Torah* was composed not by R. Eleazar of Worms (d. c. 1235) but rather by another student of R. Judah *he-Ḥasid* or by a student of R. Eleazar himself,[197] even as this work opens with the methodological *Sefer ha-Ḥokhmah* that includes the "seventy-three gates" of Torah interpretation, a text that was composed by R. Eleazar of Worms.[198] This commentary contains quite a bit of *gematria*, *rashei/sofei tevot*, *notariqon*, and so on, as well as a fair amount of *torat ha-sod*, although it also contains

194 On this work, see Emanuel, *Shivrei Luḥot*, 166–74.

195 This work was published in a critical edition by Y. S. Lange (Jerusalem, 1973), and by M. Abitan (Jerusalem, 2002). Of the three works noted here, this one appears to have the smallest amount of non-halakhic exegesis and discussion. Cf. Noah Goldstein, "R. Ḥayyim Eliezer b. Isaac Or Zarua, His Life and Work" (D.H.L. diss., Yeshiva University, 1959), 36–37.

196 See, e.g., I. Ta-Shma, "Devarim ʿal ha-Semag, ʿal Qiẓur ha-Semag ve-ʿal Sifrut ha-Qiẓurim," in *Qiẓur Sefer Miẓvot Gadol le-R. Avraham b. Ephraim*, ed. Y. Horowitz (Jerusalem, 2005), 13–21; idem, *Knesset Meḥqarim*, 2:114, n. 9; and Urbach, *Baʿalei ha-Tosafot*, 2:571–74. Other examples of works (of *pesaqim*) in this category are the unattributed *Sefer ha-Niyyar* (which has been published, although additional manuscripts are extant), and ms. Warsaw 258 (Ashkenaz, 1303), fols. 210r–223v (= ms. Moscow 983, fols. 42r–58r; Vatican 183, fols. 99r–126r; ms. Cambridge Or. 791, fols. 26v–31r). On this larger literary phenomenon, cf. Kirsten Fudeman, *Vernacular Voices: Language and Identity in Medieval French Jewish Communities* (Philadelphia, 2010), 132–35.

197 On this commentary and its authorship, see above, chapter 3, n. 8.

198 See Joseph Dan, *ʿIyyunim be-Sifrut Ḥasidut Ashkenaz* (Ramat Gan, 1975), 44–57.

some examples of *peshat* as per the methodological introduction in *Sefer ha-Ḥokhmah*, which includes designations such as *she'ar ha-peshat* and *she'ar ha-leqet*. The commentary also cites R. Isaac *ha-Navi* of *Ẓarefat*, among other figures from northern France.[199] We do have quite a few esoteric biblical comments from R. Eleazar of Worms that are found mostly in his various works of *torat ha-sod*. An exceptionally prolific author of halakhic, esoteric, and biblical studies, R. Eleazar also composed commentaries to the Book of Psalms,[200] to the Book of Ezekiel,[201] and perhaps to the five *megillot*, as well as a commentary to *Midrash Eikhah Rabbah*.[202]

As we have had occasion to note, *Moshav Zeqenim*, a multilayered, fourteenth-century compilatory collection, preserves quite a bit of exegetical material from R. Yosef *Bekhor Shor*, R. Judah *he-Ḥasid*, and R. Isaiah di Trani.[203] As supplemented by a Paris manuscript that contains an alternate version of *Moshav Zeqenim*,[204] another exegetical layer, not nearly as large as these but discernible nonetheless, consists of a series of exoteric comments by R. Eleazar of Worms. Indeed, only from the following pieces in *Moshav Zeqenim* are we aware of this "basic" Torah commentary produced by R. Eleazar, which consists mostly of moralistic *derash*, in passages that are not typically found in the lengthy Torah commentary associated with his school, as described above.[205]

199 See, e.g., *Perush Roqeaḥ 'al ha-Torah*, ed. J. Klugmann (New York, 1981), 2:229 (to Lev. 11:8, שאלתי את ר' יצחק [הנביא] מצרפת), and see also 2:221 (בתורת כהנים בי"ג מקומות באילו דיבר הקב"ה עם אהרן וכנגדן בתורה י"ג מיעוטין. והקשה לי הנביא מצרפת והא י"ו הן והם רמוזים במסורת הגדולה ואילו הן). A R. Mordekhai *Ẓarefati* is also cited, and R. Joseph Kimḥi is mentioned once.

200 See S. Emanuel, "New Fragments of the Unknown Biblical Commentaries from the European Genizah," in *Genizat Germania—Hebrew and Aramaic Binding Fragments from Germany in Context*, ed. A. Lehnardt (Leiden, 2010), 207–11.

201 See Emanuel, *R. Eleazar mi-Vermaiza—Derashah le-Pesaḥ* (Jerusalem, 2006), 1 (n. 2.)

202 See Emanuel, ibid., 22 (n. 27); and cf. Dan, *'Iyyunim be-Sifrut Ḥasidut Ashkenaz*, 56, n. 53; and *Sifrei R. Eleazar Ba'al ha-Roqeaḥ*, ed. S. Eizenbach, vol. 2 (Jerusalem, 2004). In his elegy for his martyred wife, Dulce, R. Eleazar refers to his weekly review of the Torah portion; see A. M. Habermann, *Sefer Gezerot Ashkenaz ve-Ẓarefat* (Jerusalem, 1945), 64.

203 See, e.g., above, chapter 2, n. 126; and chapter 3, nn. 27, 40, 65, 118, 152.

204 Ms. Paris BN 260 (IMHM #26739, Byzantium, fifteenth century, from *Bereshit* to *Bamidbar*). Sections of this manuscript were published by Y. S. Lange, "Sefer Moshav Zeqenim," *Ha-Ma'ayan* 12 (1972), 75–95. The names found in this version are essentially the same as those in the printed version of *Moshav Zeqenim*, with R. Jacob (b. Asher) *Ba'al ha-Turim* (d. c. 1350) as the latest name cited. Cf. I. Ta-Shma, *Knessest Meḥqarim*, 1:235–36.

205 Ms. Vatican 123, fols. 31v–76v, contains a brief, multifaceted commentary to the Torah by R. Eleazar of Worms that is divided into "gates of interpretation," and contains mostly *gematriot* and *remazim*, as well as *peshat* interpretations, which are designated as such. Dr. Amos Geulah has indicated to me his intention to publish and to discuss this commentary, especially its *peshat* facet. For now, see his "Midreshei Aggadah Avudim," vol. 2, 15–16, and the examples of *gematria* and *remez* that he presents throughout this volume of texts.

Only one comment by R. Eleazar is preserved in *Moshav Zeqenim* to *Sefer Bereshit.* Abraham tells Sarah (Gen. 12:13), "Please say that you are my sister." In fact, however, Abraham should have instructed her to say to the Egyptians that "he is my brother." R. Eleazar of Worms explains that Abraham initially wanted Sarah to say that she was his sister rather than his wife, but she would not agree to prevaricate. Therefore, he asked her to remain silent and not to contradict him if he were to say "she is my sister."[206]

The next comment from R. Eleazar in *Moshav Zeqenim* is found at the very end of the Book of Exodus, and is a type of *remez.*[207] The Torah indicates (Ex. 40:35) that Moses could not enter the tent of assembly (*'ohel mo'ed*), because the cloud rested upon it (*ki shakhan 'alav he-'anan*). This suggests that if even Moses could not enter, Aaron and his sons certainly (*kol she-ken*) could not enter. R. Isaiah (di Trani) questions this assumption and interpretation because, if so, how could the candles be lit and the showbread be arrayed on its table, which was being done in an ongoing way at this point? R. Eleazar of Worms interprets that the cloud did not rest there—which indeed would have prevented anyone from entering—for more than a short period of time (*ki 'im sha'ah*). This interpretation is suggested by the *rashei tevot* of the words *shakhan 'alav he-'anan*, which spell out the word *sha'ah.* Interestingly, R. Eleazar appears to be responding to a question or issue that also concerned Rashbam,[208] and that is also raised in

[206] See *Moshav Zeqenim*, 17 (in the name of R. Eliezer of Worms, a typical spelling/printing error in this and related texts), and *Tosafot ha-Shalem*, ed. Gellis, 2:19, sec. 2. *Pa'aneaḥ Raza*, 71–72, cites this interpretation in the name of מוהר״ר יודא [מ]ווירמיישא, as do ms. Bodl. 2344, and *Perushei R. Ḥayyim Palti'el*, ed. Lange, 31. Lange, 31, n. 54, suggests that R. Eleazar heard this comment from his teacher R. Judah *he-Ḥasid*, but there is no source that attributes this to R Judah. Cf. *Perushei R. Yehudah he-Ḥasid 'al ha-Torah*, ed. Lange, 18–19. Ms. Paris 260, fol. 30, preserves this comment without attribution, but there is also a lacuna at this point in the manuscript. Ms. Moscow 898 (sixteenth century, in a Sefardic hand), titled *Ḥiddushei Ẓarefat* (and generally similar to *Hadar Zeqenim*, fol. 11b), cites a לשון מפי ר' אלעזר מגרמייזא on the first verse in *Va-Yera* (Gen. 18:1), ישב פתח האוהל. The word *yoshev* is written without a *vav* to signify that Abraham wanted to stand up (as in the form *yashav*, he was sitting and now he wanted to stand). The Almighty responded that Abraham should remain seated (and He would stand, which would be a sign for the efficacy of the judicial system of Abraham's children, as Rashi explains). This grammatical explanation is brought anonymously in *Hadar Zeqenim* (fol. 6b), and in other Tosafist Torah compilations. See *Tosafot ha-Shalem*, ed. Gellis, 2:106, secs. 13, 15.

[207] See *Moshav Zeqenim*, 227, and ms. Paris 260, fol. 191v.

[208] The somewhat similar second answer found in the *Moshav Zeqenim* texts (*ve-'od yesh lomar*), which does not seem to have been put forward by R. Eleazar (that after the cloud rested on the tent, it alighted and moved to the holy ark between the cherubs), is the interpretation suggested by Rashbam. When the *'ohel mo'ed* was assembled, the cloud immediately set upon it to demonstrate God's love for Israel. Afterward, the cloud departed the *'ohel mo'ed* and settled upon the ark between the cherubs (as per Ex. 25:22). Following that, Moses and the *kohanim* were able to enter. Rashbam notes that this precise pattern of events is repeated when the First Temple was completed, as described in 1 Kings 8:11. See M. Lockshin, *Rashbam's Commentary on Exodus*, 436–37, and cf. *Tosafot ha-Shalem*, ed. Gellis, 10:262, secs. 1, 3 (citing ms. B.M. 9931

the Moscow manuscript that contains the expanded version of R. Isaiah di Trani's Torah commentary, whose Ashkenazic orientation has been amply demonstrated.[209]

The published edition of *Moshav Zeqenim* contains only one comment to the book of Deuteronomy in the name of R. Eleazar of Worms (to Deut. 32:6), a midrashic exposition on the role of the angel Mikha'el in bringing the souls of martyrs before the heavenly throne,[210] while a manuscript variant suggests a psychological approach in R. Eleazar's name for the fact that *ʿedim zomemim* are put to death only if the individual whom they sought to convict has not yet himself been put to death on the basis of their false testimony (כאשר זמם ולא כאשר עשה; Deut. 19:19).[211] There are, however, more than forty comments to the Book of Leviticus and more than twenty comments to the Book of Numbers, raising the question whether this emphasis on *Torat Kohanim* and beyond was based on the singular thought of *Ḥasidei Ashkenaz* or simply a function of extant literary remnants.[212] In any case, a digest of these more than sixty comments follows.

There are thirteen comments in *parashat Va-Yiqra* itself. Most of these are brief midrashic formulations or *gematria*, which are closely tied to the words of the biblical text. The unusual spelling of the word *va-yiqra* in the first verse of the book, ויקר followed by a small *ʾaleph* is explained by R. Eleazar according to a passage in *Tanḥuma* that four things are referred to as

---

and ms. Hamburg 45). This *gematria* is also found briefly in the so-called *Perush R. Eleazar Roqeaḥ ʿal ha-Torah*, ed. Klugmann, 2:198 (and is included in the *shaʿar rosh-sof*), but it has a different connotation there: כי שכן עליו הענן, לקדש המקום. שכן עליו הענן התחלתן שעה כי שעה גדולה עמד כן.

[209] See ms. Moscow 303, fol. 81v. (This passage is not found in ms. Paris 660, from which C. D. Chavel published his edition of *Nimmuqei R. Yeshayah*; cf. above, chapter 3, nn. 109, 117.) The Moscow manuscript also includes the response by R. Eleazar of Worms (involving the *rashei tevot*). See also *ʾImrei Noʿam*, 76: פירש ה"ר אלעזר שלא שכן עליו אלא שעה אחת ואח"כ היה מסתלק והיו נכנסים ומתקנים הצריך, כי ש'כן ע'ליו ה'ענן ראשי תיבות שעה.

[210] See *Moshav Zeqenim*, 515: הלא הוא אביך קניך. יש לשאול ממי קנאם. וכתב ה"ר אל(י)עזר מוורמשא כשהב"ה נתן לכל מלאך אומה, אז נפלו ישראל למיכאל. אמר הב"ה למיכאל מכור לי אומה שלך ואעשה אותך שר וכהן ברקיע וכן עשה. וזהו הלא הוא אביך קניך. ומכאן שמיכאל שר ברקיע שנ' בדניאל (י:כה) כי אם מיכאל שרכם וכהן שמקריב הנפשות הנהרגים על קידוש השם ית' והנשמה עולה לרקיע אל הא-ל והנפש אל תחת כסא הכבוד. Cf. Reuven Margoliot, *Malʾakhei ʿElyon* (Jerusalem, 1988), 108–9, 113–14, 119–20.

[211] See ms. Moscow 121, fols. 39v–40r. The passage itself is found, without attribution, in *Moshav Zeqenim*, 504–5. Ms. Moscow 121 (IMHM #6801, Byzantium, 1403), fols. 1r–45b, is a Tosafist Torah compilation that begins (only) in *parashat Tazariʿa*, but continues through the end of the Torah. It appears, at least in part, to be another variant of the *Moshav Zeqenim* commentary. Cf. below, nn. 233, 242, 245, 247.

[212] On the significance of the study of *Torat Kohanim* and *Sifrei* (and Tannaitic *midreshei halakhah* generally) in the thought of *Ḥasidei Ashkenaz* and their associates, see *Sefer Or Zaruʿa*, pt. 1, *Hilkhot Qeriʾat Shema*, sec. 6 (fol. 11a); Y. Sussmann, "Rabad on *Sheqalim*? A Bibliographical and Historical Riddle," [Hebrew] in *Meʾah Sheʿarim: Studies in Medieval Jewish Spiritual Life in Memory of Isadore Twersky*, ed. E. Fleischer et al. (Jerusalem, 2001), 149–52, 168–69; and my "On the Study of *Seder Qodashim* in Medieval Europe," [Hebrew] in *Studies in Honor of Prof. Joseph Hacker*, ed. Y. Kaplan et al. (Jerusalem, 2012; in press).

yaqar, one of them being prophecy.[213] In the second verse, the phrase "When a person offers a sacrifice" (*'adam ki yaqriv mi-kem*), is interpreted, based on a passage in tractate *Shabbat*, to mean that such a person is identified with Adam, who was the first to offer a sacrifice for his sin. This remark is similar to Rashi's on this phrase, which follows *Midrash Rabbah*.[214] "And the innards and appendages should be washed" (*yirḥaz*, Lev. 1:9) suggests to R. Eleazar that no sacrifices have efficacy if the person who is bringing them does not also cleanse himself from sin, since the *gematria* of the word *yirḥaz* is equal to *be-yiẓro*, namely that the person must turn his *yeẓer* away from all nefarious thoughts.[215]

R. Eleazar also explains the symbolism behind various details of the sacrifices, and he makes spiritual observations as well. Thus he explains that the Torah's requirement for an offering brought by a prince (*nasi*) who has sinned must be brought in the very same place as the burnt offering (Lev. 4:24), in order not to embarrass the prince publicly (*shelo le-halbin panav be-rabbim*). Had he brought this offering in another locale, all would have known that he had sinned.[216]

Moshav Zeqenim records four comments in the name of R. Eleazar of Worms to *parashat Ẓav*, three of which appear also in ms. Paris 260, and most of which deal with the special status of Aaron in receiving certain precepts directly. On Leviticus 8:2–3, R. Eleazar asks why it was necessary to gather together all of the Jewish people in order to have Aaron dressed in the priestly vestments before them. His response was that this raised the status of Aaron in their eyes and demonstrated to the Jewish people that

213 *Moshav Zeqenim*, 228. *Tanḥuma* bases its association on 1 Samuel 3:1, *u-dvar ha-Shem hayah yaqar*. See also *Moshav Zeqenim*, 235 (to Lev. 1:5 and 1:7), and 237 (to Lev. 1:10).

214 *Moshav Zeqenim*, 231. See also *Moshav Zeqenim*, 248 (to Lev. 4:23).

215 *Moshav Zeqenim*, 237.

216 *Moshav Zeqenim*, 248. See also 247 (to Lev. 4:4). The essential point of *shelo le-halbin panav* is made, without the supporting *gematria*, in *Sotah* 32b. (It is also found, without the *gematria*, in the so-called *Perush R. Eleazar Roqeaḥ ʿal ha-Torah*, ed. Klugmann, 2:211, in the context of *shaʿar semukhim*.) See also *Moshav Zeqenim*, 238 (Lev. 1:14). Naḥmanides is noted as suggesting that sacrifices brought from birds are to come from only two (of the kosher) species, doves and pigeons, because these birds are most available and common. Eleazar of Worms suggests that these species were designated because the Jewish people are compared by the Bible to birds (generally) when they sin, but they are compared specifically to doves when they do God's will. Similarly, biblical verses suggest that the two pigeons represent the oral Torah and the written Torah. The doves will therefore serve to atone for the sins of the Jews (who are favorably compared to doves) as will the pigeons, which remind the Almighty of His two *Torot* and will thereby achieve forgiveness for errors of omission as well as commission. R. Eleazar explains in a similar way why the slaughter of the sin offering that consisted of a bird was done using the fingernail (*meliqah*); see *Moshav Zeqenim*, 239 (to Lev. 1:15), and see also *Moshav Zeqenim*, 244 (Lev. 3:3). About half of R. Eleazar's comments to *parashat Va-Yiqra* are also found in ms. Paris 260, without significant variation.

he had been chosen to do the Divine service and that God had completely forgiven Aaron for his role in the sin of the golden calf.[217] At the same time, R. Eleazar explains that Moses, Aaron, Aaron's sons, and the elders were called together at the beginning of *parashat Shemini* (Lev. 9:1) on the final day of the consecration of the *mishkan*, but that the entirety of the children of Israel was not assembled at that time, so that He could review with Aaron his performance at the time of the sin of the golden calf. The Almighty did want to publicize this, but He did so only in front of this circumspect group of elders and others. But if this was so, why didn't God speak to Aaron alone about this? Following an important theme of *Ḥasidei Ashkenaz*, R. Eleazar states that this was done "in order that [Aaron] be embarrassed [at least] in front of them, so that he could receive expiation." Not surprisingly, R. Eleazar of Worms points to details of the Torah text as evidence to support a fundamental penitential doctrine of the German Pietists, that a sinner must be embarrassed or humiliated by his sin in order to achieve full expiation.[218]

R. Eleazar interprets the signs of kosher and nonkosher animals found in *parashat Shemini* in broader terms, to represent differences between the Jewish people and the other nations of the world.[219] Similarly, various constructs of leprosy, found in *Tazri'a/Meẓora*, are interpreted by R. Eleazar in broader ways, as methods of insuring proper comportment: "the clothing of a Jew should not be as pretentious as those of a knight." A Jew's clothing should identify him as a Jew, which will help him to control his impulses.[220]

[217] See *Moshav Zeqenim*, 265, and ms. Paris 260, fol. 201r, and cf. Ramban and *Ḥizzequni*.

[218] See *Moshav Zeqenim* 268 (and ms. Paris 260, fol. 201r), and see now *Tosafot 'al ha-Torah*, ed. Gellis, vol. 12 (Jerusalem, 2009), 4 (sec. 5). Cf. Haym Soloveitchik, "Three Themes in the *Sefer Ḥasidim*," *AJS Review* 1 (1976), 325–30, and my "R. Judah *he-Ḥasid* and the Rabbinic Scholars of Regensburg: Interactions, Influences and Implications," *JQR* 96 (2006), 27–78. See also, similarly, *Moshav Zeqenim*, 263 (to Lev. 7:20), 273 (Lev. 10:3), and 345 (Lev. 19:5).

[219] See *Moshav Zeqenim* 281 (Lev. 11:3), 282 (Lev. 11:9), 284 (Lev. 11:19). This last passage associates the *Ḥasidah* with the practice of sending one out of ten of her offspring down to earth (and giving *ma'aser* in this sense). This dimension is also found in the so-called *Perush R. Eleazar Roqeaḥ 'al ha-Torah*, 2:230–31 (*sha'ar ha-marbeh veha-mam'it*) and in the *Hilkhot Ḥasidut* of *Sefer Roqeaḥ* as well. However, the passage by R. Eleazar in *Moshav Zeqenim* also links the *Ḥasidah* to the so-called *ḥayyot ha-qodesh* on the basis of an elaborate *gematria*. See also *Tosafot ha-Shalem*, ed. Gellis, 12:122, sec. 1.

[220] See *Moshav Zeqenim*, 298 (Lev. 13:2), and *Tosafot ha-Shalem*, ed. Gellis, 12:161–62, sec. 11. See also *Moshav Zeqenim*, 305 (Lev. 13:47), and *Tosafot ha-Shalem*, ed. Gellis, 12:233, sec. 1. In this instance, R. Eleazar cites a talmudic passage with Rashi's commentary to support his analysis and offers his suggestive approach, even as he notes that *'ein miqra yoẓe midei peshuto*. For references to knights or noblemen (*parashim*) in *Sefer Ḥasidim*, see, e.g., *Sefer Ḥasidim* (Parma), secs. 359, 611, 985. In this passage, R. Eleazar also notes (positively) the priestly vestments (בגדי כומרי יש"ו), which have crosses on them that clearly identify the wearers as members of the Christian faith. See David Berger, *The Jewish-Christian Debate in the High Middle Ages*, 27, and cf. below, n. 226.

R. Eleazar briefly interprets the entire section on leprous blemishes that can be found in a home (Lev. 14:34–53), on the basis of various verses in the Books of the Prophets, as referring to the fate of the first two Temples as well as the forthcoming messianic deliverance.[221] At the same time, R. Eleazar interprets the phrase "two live birds" (*shtei ẓipporim ḥayot*, in Lev. 14:4, which Rashi explains was meant to eliminate the possibility of bringing a *terefah*) to reflect instead the mindset of the one bringing these animals as a sacrifice, that they should be brought quickly (*zerizut*), since it is obvious that the animals must be brought initially as fully live offerings.[222]

Fifteen comments are recorded for the portions of *Qedoshim*, *Emor*, and *Behar.* Several of these are either pietistic or refer back to creation and its implications for the lives of the Jewish people, as has been noted for several of the comments above.[223] There are, however, several that are unique, and occasionally even *peshat*-like. *Moshav Zeqenim* to Leviticus 19:19 cites both Naḥmanides and Maimonides on the possible reason or rationale for the precept of *shatnez*, which prohibits the specific mixture of linen and wool within a garment. An interpretation is then brought in the name of R. Eleazar of Worms, that wool and linen were highlighted when Cain killed his brother, Abel. Cain brought his offering from the fruit of the land (flax seeds), while Abel brought his from his best sheep, which are covered by wool.[224] Once again, this same interpretation is found in the Moscow manuscript version of R. Isaiah di Trani's Torah commentary.[225]

Similarly, *Moshav Zeqenim* cites R. Abraham [Ibn Ezra]'s contention that the prohibition against shaving off one's sidelocks and beard completely (Lev. 19:27) was intended to keep the Jewish nation separate from others; facial hair was meant to enhance the visage of human beings, and it is therefore inappropriate to remove this hair completely. *Moshav Zeqenim* then cites the view of R. Eleazar of Worms, that the Almighty knew that the Christian monks or clergymen (כומרי יש"ו) would completely cut off the *pe'ot* on their heads, and therefore the Torah prohibited this. In effect, the Torah prohibited

221 See *Moshav Zeqenim*, 309–10, and *Tosafot ha-Shalem*, ed. Gellis, 12:268, sec. 3.

222 See *Moshav Zeqenim*, 307, and *Tosafot ha-Shalem*, ed. Gellis, 12:250, sec. 5, and cf. Ibn Ezra and Ramban.

223 See *Moshav Zeqenim*, 346 (Lev. 19:12), 358 (Lev. 19:29), 359 (Lev. 19:32), 378 (Lev. 23:27), 380 (Lev. 22:27: 387 (Lev. 23:27). 399 (Lev. 25:1). There is also one *sofei tevot* application (409, Lev. 25:34, not found in the so-called *Perush R. Eleazar Roqeaḥ 'al ha-Torah*), and one halakhic derivation (411, Lev. 25:46).

224 *Moshav Zeqenim*, 351–52.

225 See ms. Moscow 303, fol. 98v, in the name of *yesh mefarshin*. See also ms. Breslau 102, fol. 159r (in a marginal note). It is possible that R. Eleazar is the *yesh mefarshin* here, since he is roughly a contemporary of Rid, and was present in Worms when Rid studied with R. Simḥah of Speyer c. 1200. See also above, n. 209.

this removal as a means of separating the pure from the impure.[226] A similar interpretation was offered by R. Yosef *Bekhor Shor.*[227]

R. Eleazar of Worms wonders why the Torah (at the beginning of *Emor*) first discusses the occasions when a *kohen hedyot* may become impure, such as on the death of a close family member, and only then discusses the status of the more important *kohen gadol.* R. Eleazar explains that since the *kohen gadol* may never willfully make himself impure, as opposed to the *kohen hedyot* who is required to do so under certain limited circumstances of personal mourning, the Torah juxtaposed the possible impurity of the *kohen hedyot* with impurities described at the very end of the prior portion, *parashat Qedoshim*, a kind of *semikhut ha-parashiyyot.*[228] Once again, R. Yosef *Bekhor Shor* (Nevo, 219) makes a similar point about the impurities that separate Israel from the other the nations at the end of *Qedoshim*, and the status of the *kohen hedyot* as compared to the rest of the Jewish people when it comes to the impurities discussed at the beginning of *Emor*. Prior to this, *Moshav Zeqenim* presents a completely different reason, in the name of R. Judah *he-Ḥasid*, as to why the discussion of *ʾov ve-yidʿoni* (in the final verse of *Qedoshim*) is juxtaposed with the first verse of *parashat Emor* that follows.[229]

Moshav Zeqenim records two comments from R. Eleazar of Worms on the episode of the blasphemer at the end of *Emor.* R. Eleazar explains the word used by the Torah for the act of blaspheming (in Lev. 24:11), *va-yiqqov*, to mean literally that he punched a hole (*neqev*), since the blasphemer wrote down the Divine name and blasphemed it by stabbing it (*she-katav ha-Shem ve-daqar bo*).[230] In the next verse, R. Eleazar understands Moses's

226 See *Moshav Zeqenim*, 357, and cf. above, n. 219. *Ḥasidei Ashkenaz* were especially sensitive to shaving off one's beard. See, e.g., Eric Zimmer, *ʿOlam ke-Minhago Noheg* (Ramat Gan, 1996), 44–50.

227 See *Perushei R. Yosef Bekhor Shor ʿal ha-Torah*, ed. Nevo, 216: כמו שעושין הכומרים לחוק ע"ז הוא. והקפיד עליו הכתוב שלא נלך בחקותם. On R. Yosef *Bekhor Shor* as a polemicist, see, e.g., *Sefer Yosef ha-Meqanne*, ed. J. Rosenthal (Jerusalem, 1970), 79, 104, 113, and above. chapter 2.

228 *Moshav Zeqenim*, 365.

229 *Ḥizzequni* essentially follows R. Judah *he-Ḥasid*'s reason, while Seforno sounds similar to R. Eleazar of Worms. Interestingly, the so-called *Perush R. Eleazar Roqeaḥ ʿal ha-Torah*, ed. Klugmann, 2:274, explains the juxtaposition the way that R. Judah *he-Ḥasid* does (and not as R. Eleazar of Worms does).

230 See *Moshav Zeqenim*, 397, and ms. Paris 260, fol. 227v. In both the published and manuscript versions, this comment of R. Eleazar is found between two comments of R. Yosef *Bekhor Shor* on this section. The imagery here is perhaps taken from Titus's blaspheming the Divine in the Holy of Holies (according to *Gittin* 56b) by stabbing the *parokhet* (ונטל סייף וגידר את הפרוכת). See also *Sefer Assufot* (composed by an anonymous student of Rabiah and R. Eleazar of Worms), in ms. Montefiore 134, fol. 113, col. 4 (in explaining why the *mezuzah* is completely covered when placed on the doorpost): ועוד נראה מפני שבזמן הזה שאנו דרים בין אומות העולם והם עושים לרעתינו ולהכעיסנו ונועצים בתוך הנקב סכינים ומקרקרים אחריהם וחותכין הקלף [של המזוזה], מוטב לכסותו לגמרי. I owe this latter suggestion to my student Pinchas Roth. Cf. Rashi and Ibn Ezra to Lev. 24:11, who both offer a more conventional *peshat*-like approach.

hesitation to rule until he consulted with the Almighty, since Moses was indeed unsure if the blasphemer deserved to be killed for his sin. The witnesses who had warned him about this act warned him that it is prohibited to curse one's father, and it is therefore certainly prohibited to blaspheme the Divine. Moses was unsure whether he should be judged as a purposeful offender or as a *shogeg*, since he had no intention of honoring his human father either, and may not have realized that both he and his father must honor God (and not blaspheme) as well.[231]

The more than twenty comments from R. Eleazar of Worms to the Book of Numbers recorded by *Moshav Zeqenim* also begin with a *peshat* dimension. On the very first verse of the book, R. Eleazar wonders why it took until the beginning of the second month of the second year for God to count the Jews. His explanation, very similar to that of Rashi, is that until this point, the Jews were busy with preparing for the service of the *mishkan* and with erecting it, and with the offerings brought by the princes of each tribe to dedicate the altar.[232] At the same time, R. Eleazar notes that the three different forms of the verb שלח in Numbers 5:2–3 (וישלחו, תשלחו, תשלחום) indicate that the various impure figures listed need to be sent out of all three of the camps (מחנה כהונה, מחנה לויה, מחנה ישראל).[233]

R. Eleazar of Worms asks with regard to Numbers 7:89 ("and when Moses came to the tent of assembly to speak with Him," *le-dabber ʾitto*) why the Torah did not specify with whom Moses was speaking, namely God. He answers that this was a reflection of the modesty of Moses, who did not want to write that he was able to speak with the Almighty whenever he wished. Thus the Torah also writes in this verse that "Moses heard the voice" and does not specify that Moses heard the voice of God.[234] R. Eleazar asks with regard to Numbers 8:12, which describes the offerings that were brought at the election of the Levites to atone for them (*le-khapper ʿal ha-leviyyim*), what was their sin? He suggests that their only sin occurred during the attack on Shekhem in the days of Jacob. In Egypt, they observed all the laws, including the precept of circumcision (as per Deut. 33:9, *u-britkha yinẓoru*).[235]

231 *Moshav Zeqenim*, 397, and ms. Paris 260, fol. 228r. Cf. Rashi and *Ḥizzequni*.

232 See *Moshav Zeqenim*, 422, and ms. Paris 260, fol. 237r (for R. Eleazar's comment on Nu. 1:2 as well).

233 *Moshav Zeqenim*, 428; ms. Paris 260, fol. 246r; and cf. ms. Moscow 121, fol. 15v. In *Moshav Zeqenim*, 430 (Nu. 5:18), and ms. Paris 260, fol. 249r, R. Eleazar explains the reasoning for the uncovering of the *sotah*'s hair (as a kind of *middah ke-neged middah*) on the basis of a talmudic passage.

234 See *Moshav Zeqenim*, 435, and ms. Paris 260, fol. 257r.

235 *Moshav Zeqenim*, 439, and ms. Paris 260, fol. 260r.

In Numbers 10:2, R. Eleazar explains the use of the seemingly superfluous word "make for *you* trumpets" (*ʿaseh lekha hazozrot*), so that "these trumpets will be for your benefit and for your good." As long as you don't have trumpets, individual messengers have to be sent out. Now, people can be gathered together at one time.[236] Here again, R. Yosef *Bekhor Shor* (Nevo, 255) offers exactly the same (*peshat*) interpretation.[237] In Numbers 10:35, R. Eleazar asks why the verse reads, "and when the ark moved" (*va-yehi binsoʿa ha-ʾaron*). The verse should have read, "and when those who were carrying the ark moved." Rather, the ark essentially transported itself. Those who were appointed to carry the ark merely seemed to be doing so. This is a kind of *ʾaggadah ha-meyashevet divrei miqra*, which makes use of a talmudic teaching (*Sotah* 35a, "the ark carries those who carry it") to solve the apparent structural problem in the verse.[238]

R. Eleazar defines the word מתאוננים (in Nu. 11:1) as related to the word אנינות. They were mourning, as if their deceased was arrayed before them prior to burial. Once again, this is exactly like the comment by *Bekhor Shor.*[239] Similarly, R. Eleazar asks why Moses instructed the spies (Nu. 13:19) to determine whether the land was good or bad (*ha-tovah hi ʾim raʿah*). Surely Moses knew that the Jewish people had been promised a good land of milk and honey. He answers that Moses wanted them to ascertain if the land was good for its inhabitants. There are some very good and rich lands (*she-tovah meʾod u-shemenah*) that nonetheless raise weak or ill people. The spies responded that, indeed, this land consumes its inhabitants. Any foreigner who attempts to live there and was not raised there from his youth will not survive.[240] Rashi understood Moses to be asking here not about the land's produce, which was certainly good, but about whether there were springs and other healthy water sources. Once again, however, R. Yosef *BekhorShor* (Nevo, 261) goes in the same direction as R. Eleazar: is its air good (*ʾim ʾavirah tovah*), and are the people who live there healthy or infirmed?[241]

[236] *Moshav Zeqenim*, 442, and ms. Paris 260, fol. 263v.

[237] See also *Ḥizzequni*, and cf. Rashi to Gen. 12:1 (לך לך. לטובתך ולהנאתך.)

[238] See *Moshav Zeqenim*, 444, and ms. Paris 260, fol. 266r. In *Moshav Zeqenim*, 444 and 447, R. Eleazar carefully explains what food the people were really asking for (in Lev. 11:5), and why they were given quail (Lev. 11:31). The second passage (only) is also found in ms. Paris 260, fol. 271v.

[239] R. Eleazar's comment is found in ms. Paris 260, fol. 226v (but not in the published edition of *Moshav Zeqenim*). See *Perushei R. Yosef Bekhor Shor*, ed. Nevo, 256: כאוננים על מת, היו קצרי רוח ומתאבלים על שהיה רוצה הקב״ה להכניסם לארץ ויבאו למלחמה כי היו יריאים ומקטני אמונה. Cf. Rashi, Rashbam, Ibn Ezra, and Ramban.

[240] See *Moshav Zeqenim*, 451, and ms. Paris 260, fols. 277v–278r.

[241] In a comment to Nu. 16:19 (*Moshav Zeqenim*, 463), R. Eleazar explains the need for the glory of God to appear to the entire assemblage as a means of deflecting the claim that might

In Numbers 17:23, the staff of Aaron gave forth a flower, *va-yoze peraḥ*. R. Eleazar of Worms asks why it was necessary to state this. The same verse had said earlier that the staff had flowered, *ve-hineh paraḥ*. R. Eleazar explains that people might have thought that perhaps Moses had switched the staffs, taking one that had flowered earlier and now writing on it the name of Aaron and presenting it. The Almighty knew what these people were thinking, and He therefore miraculously performed a miracle within a miracle, which caused the staff of Aaron to flower now, right before their eyes.[242] This is also the sense of the next phrase in the verse, *va-yazez ziz*, that the staff flowered in front of their eyes, a suggestion which is also made by Rashbam.[243]

At the end of *parashat Korah* (Nu. 18:31), R. Eleazar defines the Torah's assertion that the tithes and other gifts given to the Levites are "in place of your work" (*ḥelef ʿavodatkhem*) in the tent of assembly, to mean that if they had a share in the land, they would have worked that land. Now, however, since they do the work of the Almighty, the tithes are the Levites' share from the working of the land, which is actually done only by others.[244]

When the people did not have water, the Torah notes that Moses and Aaron "fell on their faces and the glory of God appeared to them" (Nu. 20:6). R. Eleazar raises a comparative question. In this verse, the falling occurs prior to their apprehending the glory, while in the later case of Bilʿam (Nu. 24:4), the verses states that he saw God and then fell (*maḥazeh Sha-dai yeḥezeh, nofel u-glui ʿenayim*). R. Eleazar explains that, in fact, Bilʿam did not deserve to see the splendor of the glory of God. He did not have the strength to stand, but rather he fell immediately, at the very beginning of this vision. In the case of Moses and Aaron, however, as they sensed that the Divine splendor wished to appear, they fell on their faces because of the glory of the *Shekhinah*, as servants first fall in front of their masters and only then

be put forth,that Moses killed Koraḥ and his group through the use of the ineffable Divine name. In fact, however, Moses was later accused of killing these people (in Nu. 17:6). Similarly, in Nu. 17:3 (*Moshav Zeqenim*, 464), R. Eleazar explains the Torah's description of those who presented the pans of incense as sinners (*ḥatta'im*). If a *nazir* who withheld himself from eating certain foods is referred to by the Torah as a sinner, these people, who brought about their own deaths, are certainly to be characterized as such.

242 *Moshav Zeqenim*, 464, and ms. Paris 260, fol. 291v, and see also ms. Moscow 121, fols. 23v–24r. *Moshav Zeqenim* also presents a question on this verse from *mori ha-R. Aharon* (and see also ms. Paris, loc. cit.)

243 See *Rashbam's Commentary to Leviticus and Numbers*, ed. Lockshin, 237. *Moshav Zeqenim* (in the above note) cites a similar interpretation in the name of *Bekhor Shor*, although it is not found explicitly in the published edition of *Bekhor Shor*'s commentary (ed. Nevo, 271).

244 *Moshav Zeqenim*, 466, and ms. Paris 260, fol. 293r. On Nu. 19:21 (*Moshav Zeqenim*, 468), R. Eleazar explains the verse at hand on the basis of the talmudic *sugyot* in tractates *Niddah* and *Yoma*.

come to greet them. Indeed, after Moses and Aaron fell, the Divine glory appeared to them. But Bilʿam did not see anything once he fell.[245]

In the manuscript version of *Moshav Zeqenim*, the next piece deals with the Almighty's instructions to Moses to provide water for the people (Nu. 20:8). From the fact that the Almighty told Moses to extract water for the people (*ve-hoẓeta lahem*), Moses derived incorrectly that he should tell the people (Nu. 20:10), "Can we extract water from this rock? (*noẓi lakhem mayim?*)," meaning that "the Almighty and I will." Had Moses merely said, "Will I be able to extract water for you?" he might not have been punished. Moses sinned, and was punished, by linking himself to the Almighty in this endeavor. R. Eleazar also inquires (as found in the published edition of *Moshav Zeqenim* as well) as to why Aaron was also punished as a result of this episode. Moses alone spoke to the rock, and he was the one who hit it. Rather, Aaron heard Moses say, "Will we extract water from this rock?" thereby linking himself to the Almighty, and yet Aaron remained silent and did not protest this linkage.[246]

Finally, R. Eleazar comments on the phrasing in Nu. 21:8, where God tells Moses "to make for you [*lekha*] a snake," which would serve as an antidote for the venomous snakes (*ha-neḥashim ha-serafim*) that had attacked the people. Typically, *lekha* signifies that something will be to your enjoyment, as at the beginning of *parashat Lekh Lekha* (Gen. 12:1), and as R. Eleazar had interpreted above, in Numbers 10:2. What good is accomplished for Moses by his making this snake? Rather, Moses was also afraid of or worried about these snakes because of the concept that "once they were permitted to destroy, there is no distinction made between a righteous person and a sinner." God understood the concern that was in Moses's heart, and therefore He said *lekha*, to signify that no harm would come to any innocent people from these snakes, thereby allaying Moses's fears.

R. Eleazar also suggests a kind of aggadic interpretation. Moses understood that he was to make the "antidote" snake from copper, from the fact that God had told him to make a *saraf* and not a *naḥash*. In fact, however, God did not use the word *snake* in His instruction to Moses, as a means of honoring or exculpating Moses. When Moses tried to delay accepting his mission to confront Pharaoh in order to lead the Jews out of Egypt, his staff was turned into a snake (Ex. 4:3). Similarly, when Moses put off circumcising his son, a snake was sent to swallow him, according to rabbinic teachings cited, for example, by Rashi to Exodus 4:24. Here too, snakes were sent

[245] See *Moshav Zeqenim*, 470, and ms. Paris 260, fol. 295r. See also ms. Moscow 121, fol. 25v, and cf. *Ḥizzequni* and *Bekhor Shor*.

[246] A similar question about the fate of Moses is raised by *Moshav Zeqenim* in the name of *Bekhor Shor*, and Rashi'scommentary is also mentioned in this context.

because of the malfeasance of the people. However, in His instructions to Moses, the Almighty used the word *saraf* rather than *naḥash*, in order not to remind us of those two earlier shortcomings of Moses, and Moses also understood that this was done for his benefit.[247]

Considerable work remains to be done in identifying and extracting the comments of various Tosafists and other Ashkenazic rabbinic figures from the many manuscripts and published editions of the so-called *Perushei Ba'alei ha-Tosafot 'al ha-Torah*. In light of our findings in the realm of biblical studies and interpretation in medieval Ashkenaz, however, we would not be surprised to learn of additional material that reflects an active interest in understanding the text of the Torah in its own right on the part of additional rabbinic scholars. At the same time, such research will also undoubtedly shed further light on the role that the Tosafist Torah compilations played, beginning in the mid-thirteenth century, in bringing the biblical, Talmudic, and midrashic interpretations by the rabbinic elites to other layers and levels of Ashkenazic society.

For now, however, we will move to another area of intellectual endeavor and rabbinic creativity in medieval Ashkenaz, the writing of liturgical poetry (*piyyutim*) by leading talmudists and halakhists. Here again, the regnant perception has tended to limit the extent of this activity, both geographically and conceptually, in ways that are not borne out when a fuller measure of texts, both published and still in manuscript, is brought to bear.

247 See *Moshav Zeqenim*, 471–72; ms. Paris 260, fol. 298v; and ms. Moscow 121, fol. 26r. Just before this comment by R. Eleazar of Worms, these texts present (with slight variation) a question from *Bekhor Shor* (not found in the body of his commentary, which is contained in ms. Munich 52) as to why snakes were sent more than any other creature to exact punishment. *Bekhor Shor* answers that since even the greatest delicacies turn into dirt in the mouth of the snake (as per the verse in Isaiah 65:25, ונחש עפר לחמו), this creature was most appropriate to exact payment from the אוכלי המן, since the מן tasted like all kinds of delicacies in their mouths. (Prior to this comment, a comment from R. Judah *he-Ḥasid* appears, as it is found in *Perushei R. Yehudah he-Ḥasid*, ed. Lange, 183, and as is typical for the varied and changing strata in *Moshav Zeqenim*.) In the programmatic introduction to his work, R. Isaac *ha-Levi*, the compiler of *Pa'aneaḥ Raza*, notes (at the end of his brief list of sources) that he would also include some material from R. Eleazar of Worms (which are characterized as *peratim* in the published version of this introduction), to accompany the *gemtari'ot* and *peshatim* by R. Judah *he-Ḥasid*. Cf. above, chapter 2, n. 143, and chapter 3, n. 7. These are hard to come by, although there are four comments attributed to R. Eliezer (sic) in *Sefer Bamidbar* (see *Pa'aneaḥ Raza*, ed. Machon Torat ha-Rishonim, 429, 430, 460, 470, and cf. above, n. 205). None of these correspond, however, to the citations found in *Moshav Zeqenim*, and the entire matter requires further investigation. Additional interpretations by R. Eleazar can be found in ms. Manchester/Gaster 1831 (IMHM #16057, which is parallel to ms. Strasbourg 44).

5

Genres and Strategies of *Piyyut* Composition among the Tosafists

In his seminal study on the Tosafists, E. E. Urbach refers to some fourteen Tosafists who composed *piyyutim*, evenly divided between those who hailed from northern France and those who were from Germany. This is not a very large number when measured against the total number of Tosafists known to us, although several figures mentioned by Urbach are particularly well known or important. The Frenchmen mentioned by Urbach are connected, for the most part, to Rabbenu Tam and his school, while the Germans are members of Rabiah's family or others among his circle of contemporaries. In most instances, Urbach simply notes, based on the studies of Zunz, that the Tosafist in question composed a number of *piyyutim*.[1] That number

[1] Among twelfth-century Tosafist *payyetanim* in northern France, Urbach notes Rabbenu Tam (*Ba'alei ha-Tosafot* [Jerusalem, 1980], 1:110), whose relatively large number of *piyyutim*, as well as the possible Spanish influences in terms of both rhyme and meter, are also mentioned; R. Elijah b. Judah of Paris (ibid., 1:124), who is not to be confused with the much more prolific eleventh-century *payyetan* R. Elijah b. Menaḥem of Le Mans (and see also A. Grossman, *Ḥakhmei Ẓarefat ha-Rishonim* [Jerusalem, 1995], 98–105); R. Joseph of Orleans (*Ba'alei ha-Tosafot*, 1:140), whose polemical perspectives are also mentioned; and R. Yom Tov of Joigny (ibid., 1:146), characterized as a productive *payyetan* whose *piyyutim* included two that were written in Aramaic and one commemorating the incident at Blois in 1171. For Rabbenu Tam's student Ri (and Ri's son Elḥanan, and his student Riẓba, d. 1210), see below, at nn. 3–4. Among northern French Tosafists during the thirteenth century, Urbach, *Ba'alei ha-Tosafot*, 1:492, mentions only R. Tuvyah of Vienne, "whose six seliḥot, which Zunz lists and characterizes as excellent in language and style, also reflect the persecutions of his day." See also *Ba'alei ha-Tosafot*, 1:212, where Urbach notes that Rabiah's father, R. Yo'el *ha-Levi*, "was also a *payyetan*, who composed six *seliḥot* and one *qinah* that have reached us," and 1:387, concerning Rabiah himself, about whom Urbach writes that "like most *ḥakhmei ha-dor* in Ashkenaz Rabiah also composed *piyyutim*, six of which are known." Urbach's references to other, more central *payyetanim* among the German Tosafists will be reviewed shortly, in the body of the text.

is most often not a large one, even as the nature of this genre and the way that its literary remnants are identified require that the possibility of finding additional compositions by a particular author be kept open. Thus, for example, Urbach writes about Raban's son-in-law R. Samuel b. Natronai (known as Rashbat or R. Shevat) that "only one of his *piyyutim* is known, a *seliḥah* for *Yom Kippur.*"[2]

These brief comments usually appear after Urbach has described in great detail the various achievements of these Tosafists in the realms of talmudic interpretation and *halakhah.* At the very end of a 33-page chapter on Rabbenu Tam's leading student (and nephew), Ri (R. Isaac of Dampierre), his son Elḥanan, and their talmudic writings, Urbach writes that "father and son made an effort [*nisu 'et koḥam*] at writing *piyyutim* in the style of the generation." In a note, the reader is referred to the works of Zunz, Landshuth, and Davidson, which reveal that, although several *piyyutim* attributed to Isaac b. Samuel may not be those of Ri, father and son nonetheless did manage to author more than fifteen *piyyutim* between them.[3] Similarly, Urbach writes that Ri's student R. Isaac b. Abraham (Riẓba) "should perhaps be counted among the *payyetanim*," indicating in his note that Zunz lists seventeen figures named Isaac b. Abraham who composed *piyyutim*, while implying at the same time that none of them may be the Tosafist known as Riẓba.[4]

Intended or not, Urbach's presentation fosters the impression that the involvement of northern French Tosafists in the writing of *piyyut* was peripheral, certainly as compared to their contributions in the realm of talmudic interpretation, and was largely confined to the twelfth century. The German Tosafists fare a bit better. Urbach refers to Raban as a prolific author of liturgical poems (*payyetan poreh*) for whom Zunz counts twenty-four *piyyutim* and *seliḥot*, including several that reflect the persecution and the martyrdom during the First Crusade.[5] Urbach devotes half a paragraph to the *piyyutim* of R. Ephraim of Regensburg, whose use of meter perhaps reflects the influence of his main talmudic teacher, Rabbenu Tam, *piyyutim*

[2] Urbach, *Ba'alei ha-Tosafot*, 1:209. On Rashbat's origins in southern Italy, and for additional fragments of his *Tosafot* and other halakhic writings, see Simcha Emanuel, *Shivrei Luḥot: Sefarim Avudim shel Ba'alei ha-Tosafot* (Jerusalem, 2007), 60–81. Despite his contact with Italian halakhists who were also *payyetanim*, the dearth of Rashbat's own *piyyut* compositions suggests that he remained uninfluenced by them in this area of endeavor. See Emanuel, *Shivrei Luḥot*, 67, n. 80, and cf. *Piyyutei R. Yeḥi'el b. Avraham me-Roma*, ed. Avraham Fraenkel (Jerusalem, 2007), editor's introduction, 1–7, 65–73.

[3] Urbach *Ba'alei ha-Tosafot*, 1:260. In his next and last sentence of the chapter, Urbach writes that the biblical comments attributed to Ri and Elḥanan in the so-called Tosafist Torah commentaries are taken from their talmudic *Tosafot*, and should not be construed as evidence that they authored any distinct biblical commentaries either. See also above, chapter 3.

[4] Ibid., 1:270.

[5] Ibid., 1:181–82.

that Zunz had characterized as "superior to the compositions of all of his German contemporaries and most of those in northern France."[6]

Urbach also notes the contributions of R. Barukh b. Samuel of Mainz (d. 1221), "who excelled as a *payyetan*, and whose *seliḥot* reflected the decrees and troubles that occurred prior to his time and in his day." R. Barukh based his *piyyutim* not only on scriptural linguistics and themes but also on halakhic and midrashic sources; indeed, he composed an entire *piyyut* that was based on a talmudic *sugya*.[7] Urbach records Zunz's positive evaluation of the writing style ("a light and flowing form") of R. Simḥah of Speyer (d. c. 1230) in his *seliḥot*.[8] Finally, in a single paragraph of four sentences, Urbach takes note of the nearly twenty *piyyutim*, *qinot*, and *seliḥot* composed by R. Meir of Rothenburg (d. 1293), as well as Maharam's commentaries to the *piyyutim* of others, which appear to reflect the influence of *Ḥasidei Ashkenaz*.[9]

To be sure, Urbach has much more to say about *piyyut* composition in the introductory volume to his edition of *'Arugat ha-Bosem*, the lengthy *piyyut*-commentary compiled by R. Abraham b. Azri'el, a student of the German Pietists and R. Simḥah of Speyer who composed his work circa 1230. In that volume, Urbach discusses other figures who were associated with Tosafist study halls, such as R. Ephraim of Bonn,[10] a prolific *payyetan*, rabbinic scholar, and judge to whom he barely refers in his *Ba'alei ha-Tosafot*,[11] and he also describes the affinity that the German Pietists had for *piyyut* as authors, and as interpreters or commentators.[12] If we place Urbach's *'Arugat ha-Bosem* alongside his *Ba'alei ha-Tosafot*, an implied dichotomy emerges. The German Pietists, and other specialists, did *piyyut* in Ashkenaz during the twelfth and thirteenth centuries, while the Tosafists, especially in northern France during the generations after Rabbenu Tam, essentially did not.[13]

[6] Ibid., 1:206–7.

[7] Ibid., 1:428–29.

[8] Ibid., 1:419. Urbach writes that Leopold Zunz (*Literaturegeschichte de synagogalen poesie* [Berlin 1865; hereafter cited as *LG*], 311) listed ten *seliḥot* for R. Simḥah, when in fact only three are mentioned; see below, nn. 230–31. Urbach apparently confused R. Simḥah's compositions with the ten *piyyutim* by R. Solomon *ha-na'ar* b. Abun; see Zunz, *LG*, 311–12. Urbach mentions a *seliḥah* by R. David of Muenzberg in passing (*Ba'alei ha-Tosafot*, 1:366).

[9] Urbach, *Ba'alei ha-Tosafot*, 2:564. (The reference to Zunz, *LG*, should be to pp. 359–61.)

[10] *'Arugat ha-Bosem le-R. Avraham b. Azri'el*, ed. Urbach, vol. 4 (Jerusalem, 1963), 39–58.

[11] See Urbach, *Ba'alei ha-Tosafot*, 1:110, 182, 367. R. Ephraim was a student of Rashbat, and perhaps of R. Yo'el *ha-Levi* and R. Samuel b. Qalonymus *he-Ḥasid* as well. See Avigdor Aptowitzer, *Mavo la-Rabiah* (Jerusalem, 1938), 45, and *'Arugat ha-Bosem*, ed. Urbach, 4:39–40. For R. Ephraim's activities as a Tosafist, halakhist, and rabbinic judge (and for his non-*piyyut* corpus), see above, Introduction, nn. 88–89; and chapter 1, nn. 11, 40, 42.

[12] *'Arugat ha-Bosem*, 4:73–111.

[13] Cf. Yaacov Sussmann, "The Scholarly Oeuvre of Professor Ephraim Elimelech Urbach," [Hebrew] *E. E. Urbach: A Bio-Bibliography, Supplement to Jewish Studies* [Forum of the World

From the standpoint of intellectual history, however, the most crucial consideration is not simply how Tosafist *piyyut* composition and output compare with their talmudic and halakhic writings. The question is whether the Tosafists had a genuine interest in the writing of *piyyut* alongside their obvious interest in the realms of Talmud and *halakhah*. Only by identifying fully those Tosafists who wrote *piyyutim* as well as their compositions, by studying the nature and patterns of the *piyyutim* that were written, and by comparing Tosafist *piyyut* composition to the writing of *piyyut* in pre-Crusade Ashkenaz can this question be properly addressed.

Even as the primacy of talmudic study and halakhic analysis within the Tosafist oeuvre is undeniable, manuscript evidence, coupled with a careful review of published materials, reveals that more than forty Tosafists and rabbinic scholars in both northern France and Germany, of varying reputations and importance, composed a large and suggestive corpus of *piyyutim*. Among the figures in this cohort who are not so well known are R. Isaac b. Isaac of Chinon; R. Menaḥem b. Jacob of Worms; R. Samuel b. Abraham *ha-Levi* Bonfant; his son, R. Yaqar b. Samuel *ha-Levi*; and R. Avigdor b. Elijah Katz of Vienna.[14]

Menaḥem Schmelzer has recently surveyed the Ashkenazic *piyyutim* that were written for personal, celebratory occasions—especially the

---

Union of Jewish Studies] 1 (1993), 55–62. Susan Einbinder, *Beautiful Death: Jewish Poetry and Martyrdom in Medieval France* (Princeton, 2002), 28–30, 34–37, 49–52, 57–64, 70–74, has demonstrated that Tosafist commemorations of various persecutions and acts of martyrdom during the twelfth and thirteenth centuries in *seliḥot* and *qinot* were part of a dynamic process that involved both German and northern French rabbinic scholars and Tosafists. However, not all of these figures were leading talmudists or halakhists (e.g., Gershom b. Isaac of Cologne; R. Ephraim of Bonn's brother, Hillel b. Jacob of Bonn; and Solomon Simḥah of Troyes), and several others were in fact specialists, whose literary contributions were made only in the realm of *piyyut* or biblical interpretation (e.g., Joseph of Chartres and Isaac bar Shalom). For Hillel of Bonn, see *'Arugat ha-Bosem*, ed. Urbach, 4:31–35; Urbach, *Ba'alei ha-Tosafot*, 1:182; *Sefer ha-Qushyot*, ed. Y. Y. Stal (Jerusalem, 2007), 133 (sec. 168); and *R. Eleazar mi-Vermaiza—Derashah le-Pesaḥ*, ed. S. Emanuel (Jerusalem, 2006), 94 (n. 177). For Joseph of Chartres, see, e.g., Zunz, *LG*, 470 (and see also ibid., 311–12, 467–69, for other nothern French specialists in *piyyut*); Urbach, *Ba'alei ha-Tosafot*, 1:145 (and see also 1:226, for R. Yehosefyah *ha-Ger*); *Tosafot ha-Shalem*, ed. J. Gellis, vol. 1 (Jerusalem, 1982),198, sec. 3; 6:65, sec. 3; and Samuel Poznanski, *Mavo 'al Ḥakhmei Ẓarefat Mefrashei ha-Miqra* (Warsaw, 1913), CXI. Cf. Tova Beeri, "Remarks on Ezra Fleischer's Research on Medieval Hebrew Liturgical Poetry," [Hebrew] *Jewish Studies* 45 (2008), 145–46, n. 41; and above, Introduction, n. 83.

[14] For Isaac of Chinon, see, e.g., my *"Peering through the Lattices": Mystical, Magical, and Pietistic Dimensions in the Tosafist Period* (Detroit, Mich., 2000), 174–77. For Menaḥem of Worms, see above, Introduction, n. 90; chapter 1, n. 145; and below. For R. Bonfant (a leading student of R. Simḥah of Speyer), see my "Returning to the Jewish Community in Medieval Ashkenaz: History and Halakhah," in *Turim: Studies in Jewish History and Literature Presented to Dr. Bernard A. Lander*, ed. M. Shmidman (New York, 2007), 83–85; S. Emanuel, *Shivrei Luḥot* 181–84; and above, Introduction, n. 2. (For R. Bonfant's son Yaqar, see Emanuel, *Shivrei Luḥot*, 258–61, and above, chapter 1, n. 114.) For R. Avigdor Katz, see my *"Peering through the Lattices,"* 107–9, 221–27; Emanuel, *Shivrei Luḥot*, 173–81; and above, chapter 4, n. 193. Several of these rabbinic scholars were also involved in mystical studies and practices, as we shall see below in chapter 6.

Shabbat ḥatan and Sabbaths on which a circumcision was performed—in the pre-Crusade period and beyond. As Schmelzer notes, the existence of these liturgical poems corrects the perception that Ashkenazic *payyetanim* composed *seliḥot* and *qinot* almost exclusively. A number of these poems have been discovered only recently in manuscript, and were unknown to Zunz and others. Moreover, while later Ashkenazic liturgies and *Maḥzorim* often retained and included newly composed penitential *piyyutim* or *seliḥot*, they tended to discard those *piyyutim* that had been written to celebrate these more "personal" or individual life events. This series of rejections over the long term may have also been predicated in part on the fact that the *piyyutim* for these life events were typically composed as part of the *yoẓerot* within the *Shema* or in the *kedushah* of *Musaf*, which meant that they had to be included as part of the fixed liturgy on the Sabbath after a wedding, or on a Sabbath on which a circumcision took place. The liturgical venue for *seliḥot*, on the other hand, was most often a separate or additional section of the prayers. These addenda were therefore more easily retained, as opposed to compositions that were meant to "interrupt" the fixed *tefillot*. Indeed, venerable, long-standing *yoẓerot* and *kedushtot* that clearly predated the period of the High Middle Ages were often allowed to remain in these sensitive positions—becoming, in effect, themselves part of the fixed liturgy—and were not easily displaced by newer compositions.

Perhaps in part to address this concern, authors of celebratory *piyyutim* from the late eleventh century onward developed new forms and venues through which to attach their compositions within the fixed liturgy of the Sabbath and festivals. In order not to compete too directly with the existing, older *piyyutim* that had already been included within the body of the liturgy, they situated their *piyyutim* around the *Nishmat* prayer just prior to the *Shema*, or within the *Shema* at places where predecessors had not written *piyyutim*, or at the point of [*Ani ha-Shem*] *E-loheikhem* at the end of the *kedushah* for the *Musaf* prayer. Several other newer venues were associated with the Torah service. *Reshuyyot* were composed for when the groom was called to the Torah and similarly for the so-called *ḥatanei Torah* on *Simḥat Torah*. *Reshuyyot*, and other *piyyutim*, were also developed for *Shavu'ot* and for the seventh day of Passover, known as the *Yom va-Yosha*, when Ashkenazic liturgies routinely retained the reading of an Aramaic translation of the Torah readings, which included the Decalogue on *Shavu'ot* and the Song of the Sea on Passover, among other notable passages, as well as Aramaic translations of the *Haftarot* for those occasions.[15]

[15] See M. Schmelzer, "Mashehu 'al Piyyutim le-Nisu'in be-Ashkenaz," in *Meḥqarim be-Sifrut Yisra'el Muggashim le-Avraham Holtz*, ed. Z. Ginor (New York, 2003), 31–52 (= Schmelzer, *Studies in Jewish Bibliography and Medieval Hebrew Poetry* [New York, 2006], Hebrew section, 190–208). In this study, Schmelzer highlights the liturgical poems found in ms. JTS 8972, many of which

Schmelzer characterizes the overall scope of medieval Ashkenazic *piyyut* as follows: *piyyutim* for festivals (especially for occasions that were not covered by the classical *payyetanim*, such as *piyyutim* for *yom tov sheni*); *ma'arivim* for the festivals (since the somewhat lesser status of the evening service meant that it was still available to support additional liturgical compositions); *yozerot* and *zulatot* for special Sabbaths such as those between Passover and *Shavu'ot* (when many persecutions occurred in Ashkenaz, beginning with those related to the First Crusade); and, of course, *seliḥot.* In addition, it turns out there were also quite a number of *piyyutim* produced (that have survived mostly in manuscript) for the wedding Sabbath. These were mainly *yozerot*, which consisted of the body of the *yozer*, the *'ofan*, and the *zulat.* Additional places within the *Shabbat ḥatan* liturgy, close to or within the *Shema*, were also enhanced by *piyyutim* as noted, including *Ha-Melekh*, *E-l 'adon*, and *La-E-l 'asher shavat*, as well as the *E-loheikhem* in the *kedushah* of *Musaf.* And there were also new compositions in connection with the *'aliyyah* of the groom to the Torah on that Sabbath (*reshuyyot*).[16]

The Ashkenazic wedding and circumcision *piyyutim* remained mostly in manuscript, since they were often not incorporated into formal, ongoing liturgies. Schmelzer estimates that the total number of these "happy" *piyyutim* approaches one hundred.[17] He has identified a significant selection of them (including several heretofore unknown) chronologically, by author and then by genre, especially as they are found in ms. Bodl. 1099, a western Ashkenazic liturgy composed during the lifetime of Meir of Rothenburg (d. 1293).[18] Among the Tosafist *payyetanim* represented in this manuscript—all of whom are German—are Raban, R. Judah b. Qalonymus (Rivaq of Magenza), R. Ephraim of Regensburg, R. Ephraim of Bonn, R. Menaḥem

are unknown from other sources; cf. below, n. 294. On the practice and extent of providing Aramaic translations for the Torah readings (and *Haftarot*) on Passover and *Shavu'ot* within medieval Ashkenaz, see, e.g., *Maḥzor Vitry*, ed. S. Hurwitz (Nuremberg, 1923), 158ff., 304ff; *Sefer ha-Oreh*, ed. S. Buber (Lemberg, 1905), 43 (1:56); *Tosafot Megillah* 24a, s.v. *ve-'im*; and below, n. 45. Cf. Ezra Fleischer, *Shirat ha-Qodesh ha-'Ivrit Bimei ha-Benayim* (Jerusalem, 2008), 179–80.

16 For the genres prevalent in Ashkenazic *piyyut* (including the newer ones), cf. Fleisher, *Shirat ha-Qodesh*, 442–73. Fleisher, *Ha-Yozerot be-Hithavvutan ve-Hipatḥutan*, 618, also notes that many *yozerot* from the early *payyetanei Erez Yisra'el* did not seem to reach Italy or Ashkenaz by the medieval period, leaving room for new compositions in this area. See also A. Fraenkel's assessment of the genres prevalent in Italy during the tenth through twelfth centuries, in his introduction to *Piyyutei R. Yeḥi'el b. Avraham me-Roma* (Jerusalem, 2007), 8–13. On Ashkenazic *piyyutim* for the Sabbaths between Passover and *Shavu'ot*, see Yonah and Abraham Fraenkel, *Ha-Tefillah veha-Piyyut be-Maḥzor Nuernberg* (Jerusalem, 2008), 73–75.

17 The "founder" of these genres in medieval Ashkenaz was R. Simeon *ha-Gadol* of Mainz; see below. Cf. Fraenkel, *Ha-Tefillah veha-Piyyut*, 54–56.

18 Schmelzer also notes similar collections in Bodl. 1149, Moscow 611, and JTS 9303 (and see also ms. Verona [Seminario Maggiore] 34 [#32864], which Schmelzer does not treat). Ms. Bodl 1099 is the most varied and best organized within this group of manuscripts.

b. Jacob, R. Barukh b. Samuel of Mainz, R. Yaqar b. Samuel *ha-Levi*, as well as R. Eleazar of Worms. Late eleventh-century predecessors found in this manuscript include R. Meshullam b. Moses of Mainz, R. Meir b. Isaac *Shaẓ*, and R. Qalonymus b. Judah of Worms, and there are two earlier German *payyetanim* represented as well.[19]

Before I proceed to present the full complement of *piyyutim* that were in fact composed by the Tosafists in both northern France and Germany during the twelfth and thirteenth centuries (for all occasions, happy and sad), and to consider the implications of these findings, it is helpful, as Schmelzer's research suggests, to begin with an overview of the compositions of pre-Crusade *payyetanim.* The nature and venues of their compositions will allow us to identify and analyze the patterns of composition by the Tosafists, and to assess their involvement with *piyyut* most accurately.

Pre-Crusade Antecedents

It has been well established that the ranks of Ashkenazic rabbinic scholarship during the pre-Crusade period boasted a number of highly accomplished *payyetanim.* As we have noted throughout this study, a crucial factor in understanding the intellectual history of the Tosafist period is the extent to which the Tosafists continued or changed the methods and disciplines that were prevalent during the earlier period. A focused overview of the types of poems that were composed during the pre-Crusade period will enable us to better evaluate the *piyyut* compositions from the Tosafist period itself.

Franco-German *payyetanim* in the tenth and eleventh centuries were very conscious of the works and styles of their predecessors, especially those of R. Eleazar *ha-Qallir.*[20] As earlier liturgical poems became accepted as unimpeachable parts of the fixed liturgy on Sabbaths and festivals, and were included in such major prayers as the *Shema* and the repetition of the *'Amidah*, some leading Ashkenazic rabbinic authors who wished to express

[19] See M. Schmelzer, "Piyyutim le-Nisu'in le-Rishonei Ḥakhmei Ashkenaz," in *Sefer Zikkaron le-Aharon Mirsky*, ed. E. Hazan and Y. Yahalom (Jerusalem, 2007), 173–85.

[20] On the status and stature of *Qallir* in medieval Ashkenaz, see, e.g., Ruth Langer, "Kalir Was a Tanna: Rabbenu Tam's Invocation of Antiquity in Defense of the Ashkenazi Payyetanic Tradition," *Hebrew Union College Annual* 67 (1996), 95–106; Avraham Grossman, *Ḥakhmei Ẓarefat ha-Rishonim*, 331–40, 519–22, 534–36; Ezra Fleischer, "Tefillah u-Piyyut be-Maḥzor Vermaiza," in *Introductory Volume to the Worms Maḥzor*, [Hebrew] ed. Malachi Beit Arie (Jerusalem, 1985), 37–38; idem, *Shirat ha-Qodesh ha-'Ivrit Bimei ha-Benayim*, 442–54; Yosef Yahalom, *Poetry and Society in Jewish Galilee of Late Antiquity* [Hebrew] (Jerusalem, 1999), 115–16; and cf. R. Joseph Soloveitchik, *The Lord Is Righteous in All His Ways: Reflections on the Tish'ah be-Av Kinot*, ed. J. J. Schacter (New York, 2007), 137–42.

themselves in *piyyut* form focused almost exclusively on writing penitential prayers (*seliḥot* and *teḥinnot*) or elegies (*qinot*) that often commemorated particular persecutions or communal tragedies. These compositions were intended to be recited as part of the supplementary liturgy on occasions that marked those tragedies, including fast days (from *ʿAsarah be-Tevet* to *Tishʿah be-Av*), during the penitential periods surrounding Rosh ha-Shanah and Yom Kippur (when special groups of *seliḥot* were recited each day), and throughout the day on Yom Kippur itself.[21] In addition, in the pre-Crusade period, a number of *zulatot* (placed toward the end of *Shema*, usually in conjunction with the phrase *ʾein E-lohim zulatekha*) were added to the fixed liturgy for Sabbaths that occurred during periods of communal mourning observances, such as *Shabbat Ḥazon* or the Sabbaths between Passover and *Shavuʿot* (the period of *sefirat ha-ʿomer*).[22]

All of Rabbenu Gershom b. Judah's ten extant liturgical compositions are *seliḥot*, as are Rashi's seven *seliḥot* and *qinot*, several of which perhaps reflect events associated with the First Crusade in 1096. However, the notion expressed within modern scholarship, that the limited scope of these compositions is an indication that they were relatively simple or artistically unimaginative, requires modification.[23] Four of Rabbenu Gershom's *seliḥot* appear as part of the Yom Kippur service in various Ashkenazic liturgies.[24] In one of these, a *seliḥah* for the afternoon service (גדול עוני ולחטוא הוספתי/ הוספתי אשמה ותרב רעתי/ רעתי רבה וללקות חויבתי/ חיובתי גלות ורבצי שכחתי/ שכחתי מפעלות ה' עושי וכו'), each line begins with the word that concludes the previous line. This stylistic convention, known as שרשור (*shirshur*), originated in the classical period of *piyyut* and was further employed by Spanish *payyetanim* and by R. Gershom's contemporary in Mainz, R. Simeon *ha-Gadol*.[25] Three of Rashi's *seliḥot*, including a *petiḥah* for *erev* Rosh ha-Shanah and another

[21] See Ezra Fleischer, *Shirat ha-Qodesh*, 468–71.

[22] See Fleischer, *Shirat ha-Qodesh*, 458–59, and below, nn. 169–70.

[23] See A. Grossman, *Ḥakhmei Ẓarefat ha-Rishonim*, 248–49, and Avraham David, "Historical Records of the Persecutions during the First Crusade in Hebrew Printed Works and Manuscripts," [Hebrew] in *Yehudim mul ha-Ẓelav*, ed. Y. T. Assis et al. (Jerusalem, 2000), 197–98 (secs. 7, 17, 19). A small number of other *piyyutim*, under the name *Shelomoh*, may also have been authored by Rashi. See A. M. Habermann, *Piyyutei Rashi* (Jerusalem, 1941), 202, and cf. Sara Kamin, *Peshuto shel Miqra u-Midrasho shel Miqra* (Jerusalem, 1986), 262 (n. 123). On the quality of Rashi's *piyyutim*, cf. Grossman, *Ḥakhmei Ashkenaz ha-Rishonim* (Jerusalem, 1981), 161–62; and cf. H. Soloveitchik, "Three Themes in the *Sefer Ḥasidim*," *AJS Review* 1 (1976), 345 (n. 112).

[24] See *Maḥzor le-Yamim Noraʾim*, ed. D. Goldschmidt (Jerusalem, 1970), vol. 2 (Yom Kippur), 214–17, 514–15, 566–68, 766–68.

[25] See e.g., Fleischer, *Shirat ha-Qodesh*, 128–32, 221–28, 302–8, 373–82. On R. Simeon's use of this form, see also below, n. 28.

for the Fast of Gedalyah,[26] have a single, unified rhyme throughout, referred to as a *ḥaruz mavriaḥ* or a *ḥaruz 'aḥid*. Although this technique is found already in the classical period, its use in Ashkenaz (which actually increases through the twelfth and thirteenth centuries as we shall see) owes much to the prominence of this convention within Spanish *piyyut* (and Arabic poetry), hearkening back to the *piyyutim* of R. Sa'adyah Gaon. This form is considered to be more artistically creative than some others, precisely because of the way that it limits and thereby challenges the author's ability to express his thoughts in poetic style.[27]

Several rabbinic authors during the pre-Crusade period composed *piyyutim* that reflected their abiding interest in mystical teachings. Liturgical poems provided a vehicle for these authors to convey mystical themes and aspects in veiled linguistic forms. A prominent exemplar of this approach is R. Simeon b. Isaac (*ha-Gadol*) of Mainz, who composed his *piyyutim* circa 1000.[28] Recent research suggests that a number of pre-Crusade Ashkenazic *payyetanim* and their contemporaries in Italy were aware of the developments in this field that were occurring in Spain, akin to their awareness of aspects of Spanish biblical exegesis.[29] In addition, pre-Crusade rabbinic figures occasionally used *piyyutim* as a vehicle to summarize or to highlight the halakhic dicta and observances associated with festivals and more somber occasions as well.[30]

26 See *Seder ha-Seliḥot ke-Minhag Lita*, ed. D. Goldschmidt (Jerusalem, 1965), sec. 23 (65–66, 'ה אמרת שובו בני שובבים/ א-להי הצב-אות נורא בעליונים), and sec. 46 (139–40, אז טרם בארץ נמתחו נבלי שכבים/ בארץ עוד לא דובקו רגבים).

27 See, e.g., Fleischer, *Shirat ha-Qodesh*, 343–44, 436–37; Aharon Mirsky, *Ha-Piyyut* (Jerusalem, 1990), 316–40; and Ephraim Hazan, *Leshon ha-Shirah ha-'Ivrit bi-Sefarad* [History of the Hebrew Language: The Medieval Division] (Tel Aviv, 2003), 37–44. Cf. *Piyyutei R. Avraham b. Yehi'el mi-Roma*, ed. Y. Fraenkel, editor's introduction, 25–26 (nn. 151–52); and below. On the importance of *piyyut* and *piyyut* interpretation in Rashi's intellectual life, see Elisabeth Hollender, "Commentary on a 'Lost' Piyyut: Considering the Transmission of Teachings and Texts in Rashi's Bet Midrash," in *Raschi und seine Erbe*, ed. D. Krochmalnik et al.(Heidelberg, 2007), 47–63, and Y. Fraenkel, "Ha-Piyyut veha-Perush: Li-Meqorot ha-Aggadah be-Perusho shel Rashi 'al ha-Torah," in *'Iyyunei Miqra u-Parshanut*, vol. 8, ed. S. Vargon et al. (Ramat Gan, 2005), 475–90.

28 For Rashi's predecessors (especially in Mainz) who pursued mystical studies, see A. Grossman, *Ḥakhmei Ashkenaz ha-Rishonim*, 76–80, 86–88, 94, 100–101, 162–64, 229–30, 293–95, 390–91, and my "Rashi's Awareness of Jewish Mystical Literature and Traditions," in *Raschi und seine Erbe*, 26–29.

29 See, e.g., Grossman, "Ha-Qesharim Bein Yahadut Sefarad le-Yahadut Ashkenaz Bimei ha-Benayim," in *Moreshet Sefarad*, ed. H. Beinart (Jerusalem, 1992), 176–77; idem, *Ḥakhmei Ẓarefat ha-Rishonim*, 98–102; *Piyyutei R. Yeḥi'el b. Avraham me-Roma*, ed. Fraenkel, 25–29, 66–68; and Fleischer, *Shira ha-Qodesh*, above, n. 25.

30 See e.g., the next note (for R. Yosef *Tov 'Elem*'s *qerovah* for *Shabbat ha-Gadol*, which details the laws of preparing for Passover and the observances of the *Seder*), and below, n. 51 (for R. Meir *Shaẓ*'s *seliḥah* on the technical requirements of the *tamid* offerings).

R. Yosef (b. Samuel) *Tov 'Elem* (Bonfils), who flourished in central and northern France during the first half of the eleventh century, is an excellent example of a more variegated *payyetan* in this period, as opposed to Rabbenu Gershom and Rashi, who pursued the *seliḥot*-only pattern. R. Yosef *Tov 'Elem* composed more than forty *piyyutim*. These include insertions into the morning *Shema* on special Sabbaths and festivals (*yoẓerot* and *zulatot*), and even *qerovot* and *kedushtot* that were inserted into the repetition of the *'Amidah*, in addition to *seliḥot*.[31] Ezra Fleischer has noted the influence of both Italian and Spanish *payyetanim* on Yosef *Tov 'Elem*.[32] Yosef also includes several mystical allusions in his *piyyutim*, although these are not central to his liturgical corpus.[33]

Nonetheless, even as accomplished a *payyetan* as R. Yosef *Tov 'Elem* had to contend with the large number of *piyyutim* from the earlier periods that had already become incorporated into the main body of Ashkenazic prayer liturgies, and which could not be dislodged by newer compositions.

[31] See, e.g., A. Grossman, *Ḥakhmei Ẓarefat ha-Rishonim*, 76–81; M. Schmelzer, *Studies in Jewish Bibliography* [Hebrew section], 138, 141, 146–52; and Fraenkel, *Ha-Tefillah veha-Piyyut be-Maḥzor Nuernberg*, 61–63. The best known of R. Yosef *Tov 'Elem*'s *qerovot* (and perhaps of all his *piyyutim*) is actually a *qedushta* (recited prior to the *silluq*) for *Shabbat ha-Gadol*, א-להי הרוחות לכל בשר, which concludes with the stanza חסל סידור פסח כהלכתו (and was introduced by the *reshut* אבוא בחיל). The extensive commentary to this *piyyut* by the thirteenth-century Tosafist R. Samuel of Falaise, extant in two slightly different versions (see *Sefer Or Zaru'a* [Zhitomir, 1862], pt. 2, sec. 256, and Gavriel Zinner, *Oẓar Pisqei ha-Rishonim 'al Hilkhot Pesaḥ* [Brooklyn, 1985], 43–147, based primarily on ms. Vatican 266; see Zinner, 31–33), contributed to its notoriety. Cf. *Tosafot 'Avodah Zarah* 74b, s.v. *ve-darshu* (וכן פירשתי בסדר ביעור חמץ בקרובץ שבת הגדול שיסד רבינו טוב עלם). Some of R. Yosef's *yoẓerot* (e.g., for *Shabbat ha-Gadol* and for *Shavu'ot*) were moved to other venues (see Fraenkel, *Ha-Tefillah veha-Piyyut be-Maḥzor Nuernberg*, 61–63). For *qerovot* by R. Yosef for the first two days of Passover, see *Maḥzor Pesaḥ*, ed. Yonah Fraenkel (Jerusalem, 1993), 153–63, 170–77. For R. Yosef's eschatological *qedushta* for the seventh day of Passover (with a single rhyme throughout, referred to as a *ḥaruz 'aḥid* or *ḥaruz mavriaḥ*), see *Maḥzor Pesaḥ*, ed. Fraenkel, 553–55, and cf. Schmelzer, *Studies*, 145. On R. Yosef's *piyyutim* for the festivals and High Holy Days, see *Maḥzor Shavu'ot*, ed. Fraenkel, 716, and see *Seder ha-Seliḥot ke-Minhag Lita*, ed. D. Goldschmidt (Jerusalem, 1965), sec. 56 (162–63), a *seliḥah* by R. Yosef for the Fast of Gedalyah with a *siyyomet miqra'it*, also referred to as a *soger min ha-miqra*. This literary technique, in which each stanza concludes with a biblical verse (or phrase) is frequently found in classical as well as Spanish liturgical poetry. See e.g., Fleischer, *Shirat ha-Qodesh ha-'Ivrit Bimei ha-Benayim*, 131, 221–23, 357, 362–63, 440–41; and cf. A. M. Habermann, *'Iyyunim ba-Shirah uba-Piyyut* (Jerusalem, 1972), 235–36.

[32] See Fleischer, *Ha-Yoẓerot*, 614–16, 623–25. Fleischer notes (ibid., 614, n. 21, and idem, *Shirat ha-Qodesh*, 411, 437–38), that the Spanish conventions that Yosef adopted in his *Hoshanah* (see below, n. 37) and in his ryhmed *ma'arivim* (below, n. 35) faithfully imitate the *piyyutim* of R. Yosef ibn Avitur. See also Fleischer, *Ha-Yoẓerot*, 645 (n. 21); and the end of the above note.

[33] See Grossman, *Ḥakhmei Ẓarefat ha-Rishonim*, 79–80. R. Yosef's level of interest and involvement in *torat ha-sod* is markedly lower than that of R. Simeon b. Isaac *ha-Gadol* of Mainz (who lived one generation before R. Yosef) or R. Meir b. Isaac *Shaẓ* of Worms (who flourished one generation after R. Yosef); see above, n. 28.

In response, Yosef experimented with newer constructions of the *yozer.*[34] In addition he composed a number of relatively brief but intricately rhymed *maʿarivim* for the evening services on *Pesaḥ*, *Sukkot*, and *Shavuʿot*, as well as Rosh ha-Shanah. This genre of *piyyut* had received little attention prior to Yosef, and was not cultivated by either Italian or Spanish *payyetanim*; indeed, only two such compositions from the east reached early Ashkenazic *Maḥzorim.*[35] As we shall see, R. Yosef *Tov ʿElem* served in turn as a model in this regard for a series of northern French Tosafists.[36] R. Yosef also composed a *Hoshanah* for *Shabbat Ḥol ha-Moʿed Sukkot.*[37]

Like Yosef *Tov ʿElem*, R. Meir b. Isaac *Shaliaḥ Ẓibbur* (*Shaẓ*), the prayer leader of the Worms community and a notable rabbinic scholar there during the second half of the eleventh century, composed *yoẓerot* (and *ʾofanim*) and *qerovot* (and *shivʿatot*) to be inserted into the *Shema* and *the ʿAmidah* during morning services on special Sabbaths (e.g., *Shabbat Rosh Ḥodesh* and *Shabbat Naḥamu*) and festivals—in one instance, an *ʾofan* for *Shavuʿot*, אדיר ונאה, was moved to the Sabbath following this festival, at least in eastern German prayer rites[38]—as well as *seliḥot.*[39] Indeed, R. Meir's poetic inser-

[34] See Fleischer, *Ha-Yoẓerot*, 643–44.

[35] See Fleischer, *Shirat ha-Qodesh*, 463; Leon Weinberger, *Jewish Hymnography* (London, 2000), 182–83; and cf. *Piyyutei R. Yeḥiʾel b. Avraham mi-Roma*, ed. A. Fraenkel, 13. For R. Yosef's *maʿarivim*, see Daniel Goldschmidt, *Meḥqerei Tefillah u-Piyyut* (Jerusalem, 1978), 381–83 (= *Maḥzor Pesaḥ*, ed. Y. Fraenkel, 394–95); *Maḥzor Rosh ha-Shanah*, ed. D. Goldschmidt (Jerusalem, 1970), editor's introduction, 14–16; *Maḥzor Sukkot*, ed. D. Goldschmidt (Jerusalem, 1981), 5–9; *Maḥzor Shavuʿot*, ed. Y. Fraenkel (Jerusalem, 2000), 10–15; Grossman, *Ḥakhmei Ẓarefat ha-Rishonim*, 79; Weinberger, *Jewish Hymnology*, 158–59; Fraenkel, *Ha-Tefillah veha-Piyyut be-Maḥzor Nuernberg*, 60–61; and below, n. 42.

[36] Cf. Y. Fraenkel, *Ha-Tefillah veha-Piyyut be-Maḥzor Nuernberg*, n. 334.

[37] See *Maḥzor Sukkot, Shemini ʿAzeret ve-Simḥat Torah*, ed. D. Goldschmidt and Y. Fraenkel (Jerusalem, 1981), 214–15 (כהושעת טמון גמא לשדים צמא).

[38] Grossman, *Ḥakhmei Ashkenaz ha-Rishonim*, 294–95; Fleischer, *Ha-Yoẓerot*, 616, 625, 644–46; Weinberger, *Jewish Hymnography*, 13–14, 160–61, 165–66, 177–79; Schmelzer, *Studies* [Hebrew section], 143–44; idem, "Piyyutim le-Nisu'in le-Rishonei Ḥakhmei Ashkenaz," 176. In n. 10 of the latter study, Schmelzer notes that not every *ʾofan* for a wedding refers specifically to that occasion, and thus could be (and actually were) moved to commemorate other occasions. Once such *ʾofan* by R. Meir was moved to *Shabbat Ḥol ha-Moʿed Sukkot*. See *Maḥzor Sukkot*, ed. Goldschmidt, 261–62. See similarly Schmelzer, "Piyyutim le-Nisu'in le-Rishonei Ḥakhmei Ashkenaz," 177–78, nn. 17, 20, on the shift of an *ʾofan* for a groom by R. Ephraim of Bonn to *Shavuʿot*, and for the similar shift of an *ʾofan* by R. Eleazar of Worms. On R. Meir Shaẓ's *shivaʿtot* for *Shabbat Zakhor* and *Shabbat Parah*, see also Fraenkel, *Ha-Tefillah veha-Piyyut be-Maḥzor Nuernberg*, 64. For his *yoẓerot* (and related compositions) for special Sabbaths, see ibid., 65–67, 70. On R. Meir's *yoẓer* for *Shabbat Naḥamu*, ארוממך א-ל חי, אספרה שמך לאחי, אחידך בהוד שבחי (which has a *siyyomet miqraʾit*), see also M. Y. Rosenwasser, "Perush u-Meqorot le-Yoẓer Shabbat Naḥamu she-Ḥibbero R. Meir b. Yiẓḥaq Baʿal ha-Aqdamot," *Yerushatenu* 2 (2008), 259–67, and below, n. 56.

[39] Eight of R. Meir's *seliḥot* found their way into the liturgy for Yom Kippur, mostly during the afternoon service. See *Maḥzor le-Yamim Noraʾim*, ed. Goldschmidt, 259–60, 558, 636–37, 640–42, 657–59, 668–70, 672–74, 679; and cf. below, n. 55.

tions into the *ʿAmidah* appear to have been the last ones to be composed in medieval Ashkenaz, signifying that this weighty genre had now been exhausted by earlier *payyetanim* and was, in any case, now considered closed to further addenda. His *yoẓer* for *Shabbat Ḥol ha-Moʿed Sukkot* represents his interest in composing *piyyutim* for occasions that were still "open and available" despite the presence of earlier *piyyutim* for the festivals.[40] R. Meir incorporated mystical teachings within his corpus of nearly fifty *piyyutim* to a greater extent than Yosef *Tov ʿElem* did.[41] Like R. Yosef, however, R. Meir also employed Spanish stylistic conventions especially in terms of meter, although the artistic success of some of these attempts has been debated by modern scholarship.[42] This important new characteristic of Spanish *piyyut*

[40] See *Maḥzor Sukkot*, ed. Goldschmidt, 241–46 (את השם הנכבד [והנורא] נאה לתהלותיו), with a *siyyomet miqraʾit*, and cf. Fraenkel, *Ha-Tefillah veha-Piyyut be-Maḥzor Nuernberg*, 66. The eastern Ashkenazic rite moved this composition to the Sabbath between Yom Kippur and *Sukkot*, for which there does not seem to have been much competition at all.

[41] See Grossman, *Ḥakhmei Ashkenaz ha-Rishonim*, 293–95; and above, n. 35.

[42] A. M. Habermann, *ʿIyyunim ba-Shirah uba-Piyyut*, 226–28; Fleischer, *Shirat ha-Qodesh ha-ʿIvrit Bimei ha-Benayim*, 435–366; idem, *Ha-Yoẓerot*, 615, n. 23, 645. R. Meir was the first Ashkenazic *payyetan* to employ the complex, repeating Spanish rhyme pattern that is described as *meʿen ʾezori*, together with a *siyyum miqraʾit* (while R. Yosef *Tov ʿElem* was the first in Ashkenaz to use the *meʿen ʾezori* pattern alone). Cf. Fleischer, *Ha-Yoẓerot*, 670, n. 33; idem, *Shirat ha-Qodesh*, 350–51; and idem, "ʿIyyunim bi-Shlabei ʿAliyyatah ve-Hitqabbalutah shel Shir ha-Ezor ba-Shirah ha-ʿIvrit shel Yemei ha-Benayim," *Milet* 1 (1983), 191–95. According to Fleischer (*Ha-Yozerot*, 645, n. 21), R. Meir *Shaẓ* was also the first to employ a Spanish form of *mishqal ha-kamuti* (= משקל היתדות והתנועות, and see also Fleischer, *Shirat ha-Qodesh*, 341). Fleischer (*Ha-Yozerot*, 649–50), also notes within the *piyyutim* of R. Meir a unique (and difficult) rhyme form that changes with every two words. There was also a late eleventh-century *payyetan* in northern France named R. Meir b. Isaac (of Orleans), and there is discussion about which *piyyutim* should be attributed to him. See, e.g., L. Zunz, *LG*, 251; idem, *Die synagogale Poesie des Mitelalters* (Frankfurt, 1920), 184; A. L. Landshuth, *ʿAmmudei ʿAvodah* (Berlin, 1857), 167; and cf. N. Golb, *The Jews in Medieval Normandy* (Oxford, 1998), 480, 485. Use of Spanish *piyyut* conventions by this (French) R. Meir would be readily understood, given their use already by R. Yosef *Tov ʿElem*. Several *seliḥot* and *teḥinot* by R. Meir b. Isaac were published in *Leqet Piyyutei Seliḥot*, ed. D. Goldschmidt and A. Fraenkel (Jerusalem, 1993), vol. 1, 379–94; see below, n. 50. Fraenkel maintains (vol. 2, 793–813) that this R. Meir was in fact R. Meir *Shaẓ*. He reasons that R. Meir was one of the first Germans to be influenced by Spanish methods, since this had already occurred earlier in France (with R. Yosef *Tov ʿElem* and R. Elijah *ha-Zaqen* of Le Mans). To be sure, it is possible that this influence reached Germany via northern France, and R. Meir *Shaẓ* may have played a role in this (if he reached northern France himself). Indeed, this is what seems to have occurred with R. Ephraim of Regensburg, a leading student of Rabbenu Tam in northern France in talmudic studies who may also have learned about Spanish *piyyut* stylistics from Rabbenu Tam. R. Ephraim returned to Regensburg, where he apparently influenced the liturgical styles of his talmudic students, R. Joel *ha-Levi* and R. Barukh of Mainz. See Urbach, *Baʿalei ha-Tosafot*, 1:207, and below. Cf., however, A. Grossman, *Ḥakhmei Ẓarefat ha-Rishonim*, 111–12, and idem, "R. Netanʾel me-Qinon: Mi-Gedolei Baʿalei ha-Tosafot be-Ẓarefat ba-Meʾah ha-Yod Gimmel," *Meḥqerei Talmud* 3 (2005), 186 (n. 46). Grossman doubts that both *payyetanim* named Meir b. Isaac were the same figure. (R. Meir b. Isaac of Orleans was the son of R. Isaac b. Menaḥem of Le Mans, and the Isaac b. Meir who wrote *piyyutim* about the First Crusade was perhaps the son of this R. Meir. See Zunz, *LG*, 310; Landshuth, *ʿAmmudei ʿAvodah*, 123–24; and below, n. 84.)

also becomes even more evident in Ashkenazic circles as the Tosafist period unfolds, indicating the increase of Spanish influence in this regard.

R. Meir composed *piyyutim* in other less developed forms or areas as well, as R. Yosef *Tov 'Elem* did. These include several compositions that were recited on the Sabbath following a wedding (the so-called *Shabbat ḥatan*), when the new groom was called to the Torah in accordance with Ashkenazic custom,[43] or that served as introductions to various sections of the prayers or synagogue services, including *reshuyyot* recited on *Simḥat Torah* for those who received *ʿaliyyot* to mark either the end or the new beginning of the yearly cycle of the reading of the Torah.[44]

As noted above, the custom in both northern France and Germany was to recite an Aramaic translation of the Torah reading (the so-called Targum) on the seventh day of *Pesaḥ* and on the first day of *Shavuʿot* (which was highlighted by the Decalogue), as well as an Aramaic translation of the *Haftarah* on the seventh day of *Pesaḥ* and the second day of *Shavuʿot*.[45] Aramaic *piyyutim*, also known as *reshuyyot*, were recited to introduce these translations, and R. Meir composed several such Aramaic *reshuyyot*.[46] The best known of

Grossman, *Ḥakhmei Ẓarefat*, 41–42 (n. 79), questions the evidence that R. Meir *Shaẓ* left Worms for France (as Fraenkel had suggested), although it is possible that his origins were in northern France. See also below, regarding R. Menaḥem b. Makhir (whose *piyyutim* also reflect Spanish influence); and below, at n. 50.

43 On the *Shabbat ḥatan* and its *piyyutim*, see Schmelzer, "Piyyutim le-Nisu'in," 173–75. For R. Meir's three compositions for the *ḥatan* (which were meant to be recited during the *Shema* prayer), see ibid., 176.

44 See, e.g., *Maḥzor Sukkot*, 446–48, for the *ḥatan Torah* (מושך חסד ליודעיו וצדקה לחושבי שמו); 459–60, for the *ḥatan Bereshit* (מקדים וראש לקוראים זוכה ועומד וקורא); and the editor's introduction, 27. The earliest such *reshuyyot* in Ashkenaz were composed by R. Simeon *ha-Gadol* of Mainz; see, e.g., Fraenkel, *Ha-Tefillah veha-Piyyut be-Maḥzor Nuernberg*, 55–56, and cf. 79–80. On the social tensions and issues that could accompany the designation of these honors, see, e.g., *Maḥzor Vitry*, 457–58; and *Sefer Ḥasidim* (Parma), ed. J. Wistinetski (Frankfurt, 1924), secs. 470–71.

45 On the *minhag Ashkenaz* to recite an Aramaic translation of the Torah reading on the seventh day of Passover and the first day of *Shavuʿot* (and of the *Haftorah* on the second day of *Shavuʿot*), see *Maḥzor Pesaḥ*, ed. Fraenkel, editor's introduction, 20–21; *Maḥzor Shavuʿot*, ed. Fraenkel, editor's introduction, 28–35; and E. Fleischer, "Tefillah u-Piyyut be-Maḥzor Vermaiza," 32; and above, n. 15.

46 For R. Meir's Aramaic introduction to the Torah reading for the seventh day of Passover (אילו פומי נימי בני נשא רשמי, with a *ḥaruz mavriaḥ*), see *Maḥzor Pesaḥ*, ed. Fraenkel, 608–10. (See also ms. Giessen Cod. 892 [#38878], fols. 128r–130v. Fols. 131r–132v contain a *reshut* for the Aramaic translation of the *Haftarah* for *Shavuʿot*, אתא דוגמא וריבותא, by the French *payyetan* R. Reuven of Chartres.) As my doctoral student Gabriel Wasserman has pointed out, the opening lines of this *piyyut* focus on the inability of language (whether written or spoken) to fully express the inner experience of God's miraculous actions, the same theme found at the beginning of R. Meir's *Aqdamut millin* for *Shavuʿot* (in the next note). For R. Meir's Aramaic introduction to the Targum at end of the first *ʿaliyyah* on the seventh day of Passover (אבונן דבשמיא ובריין ברי בוכרי קריין, with a *ḥaruz mavriaḥ*), see *Maḥzor Pesaḥ*, 616–18. For R. Meir's lengthier Aramaic introduction to the Targum of the *Shirat ha-Yam* itself, אלהא עלם דמלקדמין במימריה עלמא ברא (which also has a *ḥaruz mavriaḥ*), see *Maḥzor Pesaḥ*, 624–29.

these is *Aqdamut millin*, which introduces the Torah reading on the first day of *Shavu'ot*.[47]

Unlike R. Yosef *Tov 'Elem*, however, R. Meir *Shaliaḥ Ẓibbur* appears to have composed very few complete *ma'arivim*.[48] He did, however, innovate the "*bikkur*" form that was added at the end of certain *ma'arivim*, at the blessing of *ha-pores sukkat shalom*, a form that was unknown in Spanish *piyyut*,[49] as well as the *'aqedah* form for penitential *seliḥot* during the period of the High Holidays.[50]

Moreover, R. Meir captures, in a mere fifty-four lines, the essence of the two daily *tamid* offerings (based on the teachings of tractate *Tamid*), in a *seliḥah* titled תפלה תקח תחנה תבחר תמור ניחוח תמיד השחר. This *seliḥah*, which was composed according to a form of quantitative meter, is found toward the end of the standard *seliḥot* grouping for *erev* Rosh ha-Shanah.[51] These various innovations were undoubtedly undertaken in response to the perceived need to develop *piyyut* forms that had not been exhausted during the earlier centuries and to invigorate older venues as well. Indeed, as we shall see moving forward, R. Meir *Shaz* of Worms was perhaps an inspiration for northern French *payyetanim* in the twelfth century, who wrote *bikkurim* and

47 See *Maḥzor Shavu'ot*, ed. Fraenkel, 385–95; Grossman, *Ḥakhmei Ẓarefat ha-Rishonim*, 425; and Weinberger, *Jewish Hymnology*, 179–81. R. Meir's Aramaic *piyyutim* may also have served, at least partially, to couch some of his mystical ideas in less explicit or obvious terms. See Fleischer, "Tefillah u-Piyyut be-Maḥzor Vermaiza," 39; and above, n. 15. For R. Meir's *piyyut* to the Aramaic translation of the second commandment, see *Maḥzor Shavu'ot*, ed. Fraenkel, 428–34 (מישך שדרך ועבד נגו / מדאורייתא דמשה אסתכלו והגו). As Fraenkel notes in his introduction, 30, this *piyyut* appears in a number of northern French rites as well, while *Aqdamut* does not (and is also mostly absent from eastern German rites; cf. Fraenkel, *Ha-Tefillah veha-Piyyut be-Maḥzor Nuernberg*, 69). For R. Meir's *yoẓer* for the second day of *Shavu'ot*, see *Maḥzor Shavu'ot*, 114–25; for his *'ofan*, see 169–72.

48 See, e.g., *Maḥzor Pesaḥ*, ed. Fraenkel, 15–17 (אזכרה שנות עולמים ימים מקדם, with five words in every half-line), and 24–31 (ליל שמורים אור ישראל קדוש אימה נדגלות, with a *siyyomet miqra'it*).

49 See E. Fleischer, *Shirat ha-Qodesh*, 463–66, and Fraenkel, *Ha-Tefillah veha-Piyyut be-Maḥzor Nuernberg*, 68–69. Ashkenazic *bikkurim* often dealt with halakhic themes. Thus, for example, R. Meir's *bikkur* for the second night of *Pesaḥ* (which contains a *siyyum miqra'it*), deals with the *'omer* offering. See *Maḥzor Pesaḥ*, ed. Fraenkel, 32–36 (אור יום הנף ספירה הכשרה בנוגהים).

50 See Fleischer, *Shirat ha-Qodesh ha-'Ivrit Bimei ha-Benayim*, 469–70; L. Weinberger, *Jewish Hymnography*, 160–61, 184–85. For R. Meir's *seliḥot*, see *Leqet Piyyutei Seliḥot*, 379–94 (אין תשורה; להביא; אליך יהב משעני; הנה כעיני עבדים; לך מלא עולם; תמו פסו; תמרת סנסנה). See also *Seder Seliḥot*, ed. Goldschmidt (fifth day of *'aseret yemei teshuvah*) for אמץ יוסיף טהר ידים וכחו יגדל ויישר (which was attributed to R. Meir by R. Eleazar of Worms).

51 See *Seder ha-Seliḥot*, ed. Goldschmidt, sec. 44, 132–36; L. Weinberger, *Jewish Hymnography*, 166; Grossman, "R. Netan'el me-Qinon" (above, n. 42); and below, n. 276. Although R. Meir is not characterized as a leading halakhist of his day, a halakhic tradition of his has survived, and the *piyyut* תפלה תקח speaks further to his talmudic knowledge and expertise. R. Isaac was described within the writings of *Ḥasidei Ashkenaz* as בקי היה בסודות במדרשים ובטעמים, and he offered corrections and addenda to various liturgical texts. See A. Grossman, *Ḥakhmei Ashkenaz ha-Rishonim*, 292–96.

Aramaic *piyyutim* that were associated with *Pesaḥ* and *Shavuʿot*. The link between the development of Tosafist dialectic in northern France during the twelfth century and the academy of Worms in particular during the late eleventh century has been described above in the first chapter.

A similar compositional pattern to that of R. Meir *Shaẓ* can be found in the *piyyutim* of R. Menaḥem b. Makhir, a younger contemporary of Rashi who studied in Mainz but was active primarily in Bohemia and Regensburg, which were included in the geographic area of the so-called eastern German liturgical rite. Menaḥem authored more than twenty *piyyutim* overall[52] including *yoẓerot*, *ʾofanim*, and *zulatot* for special Sabbaths, such as *Shabbat Shuvah*,[53] *Shabbat ha-Gadol* (as well as a *yoẓer* for the period before Passover),[54] *Shabbat Naḥamu*,[55] and the second *Shabbat* of Ḥanukkah. None of these occasions were especially popular venues for *piyyutim* heretofore, and were thus considered particularly felicitous for new compositions; indeed, new compositions for other venues were occasionally redirected to one of these occasions if found to be relevant.[56] In his *yoẓer* for Ḥanukkah, R. Menaḥem portrays in dramatic fashion the decrees of Antiochus and the revolt of the Hasmoneans, based on *Megillat Antiochus* and other lesser-known *midrashim* that were available to Ashkenazic rabbinic scholarship during this period.[57]

52 See L. Zunz, *LG*, 158–59, and A. Grossman, *Ḥakhmei Ashkenaz ha-Rishonim*, 373, n. 63, for listings of R. Menaḥem's *piyyutim*.

53 See *Maḥzor le-Yamim Noraʾim*, 308, 313, 315. The *zulat* by R. Menaḥem has a word from the root שוב at the end of each stanza, as do those by the subsequent German *payyetanim* R. Eliezer b. Nathan (*Maḥzor*, 305, and below, n. 88) and R. Eleazar of Worms (*Maḥzor le-Yamim Noraʾim*, 323, and below, n. 180).

54 R. Menaḥem's *yoẓer* for the Sabbath(s) before Passover, אורי וישעי אגילה בישועתו, was recently published (along with a thorough discussion of its midrashic sources and its historical and eschatological themes) by M. Schmelzer, *Studies in Jewish Bibliography*, [Hebrew section] 138–53. Each stanza consists of a triplet, along with a *siyyomet miqraʾit*. (Cf. below, n. 289, for R. Meir of Rothenburg's *yoẓer* for *Shabbat Sheqalim*.) Schmelzer, ibid., 154–61, discusses (and publishes) an otherwise unknown *zulat* for *Shabbat ha-Gadol* from R. Menaḥem, אמון נוא הובא נזיר אחים אדניי / אנוס על פי הדיבור ראש איתניי / בא בעמק חברון לקיים עצה ותנאי / כי היתה סיבה מאת ה' [מלכים א, יב:טו]. In this *piyyut*, each stanza has four lines, along with a *siyyomet miqraʾit*. See also the יוצר להפסקה מר' מנחם בן מכיר, אור זרוע זרוח כבודו, in ms. JTS 9303, fol. 110v; ms. Bodl. 1025, fol. 15v; and ms. Verona 34, fol. 63r.

55 R. Menaḥem's *yoẓer* begins with the phrase, אל א-ל ש-די אתחנן, which alludes to the name of the Torah portion for *Shabbat Naḥamu* (*Va-Etḥanan*), and his *ʾofan* is titled שאו מנחה. Cf. E. Fleischer, *Ha-Yoẓerot*, 611 (n.13), and above, n. 38, for R. Meir *Shaẓ*'s *yoẓer* for this Sabbath.

56 Cf. Fraenkel, *Ha-Tefillah veha-Piyyut be-Maḥzor Nuernberg*, 70. Fraenkel notes that R. Meir *Shaẓ* also composed a *yoẓer* (and a *zulat*) for this Sabbath (see above, n. 38), but R. Menaḥem's *yoẓer* was selected for *Shabbat Naḥamu* in the eastern rite.

57 אודך כי עניתני חייתני. See Fleischer, *Ha-Yoẓerot*, 658, and L. Weinberger, *Jewish Hymnology*, 172. Menaḥem's *zulat* for Ḥanukkah is titled אין מושיע וגואל.

R. Menaḥem also composed a *Hoshanah* for the Sabbath of *Ḥol ha-Mo'ed Sukkot*;[58] a *bikkur* for *Shemini 'Aẓeret* (with six words in each line and a biblical phrase, a *siyyomet miqra'it*, at the end of each stanza);[59] the earliest (Ashkenazic) poetic insertion for the *Nishmat* prayer on the morning of *Simḥat Torah*, in which each stanza ends with a phrase from Psalms 19:8–10 (תורת ה' תמימה וגו') and with a single rhyme throughout (*ḥaruz 'aḥid/mavriaḥ*);[60] a *reshut* for *Simḥat Torah* (again with a *ḥaruz 'aḥid*);[61] and another *reshut* for the Sabbath of the *ḥatan* or a circumcision; as well as *seliḥot* for Yom Kippur[62] and for the seventeenth of *Tammuz*;[63] and *qinot*, including one authored by Menaḥem toward the end of his life (with rhymed couplets and then triplets, and alternating refrains) that describes and commemorates the events of 1096.[64] R. Menaḥem's *seliḥah* for the fast of Esther, אדם בקום עלינו חיל אחז־תנו לרעוד (which has a *siyyomet miqra'it*), is referred to without attribution in a *Tosafot* passage.[65] Overall, his *piyyutim* often employ Spanish style and meter, and he appears to follow specific conventions favored by R. Yosef ibn Avitur (as R. Yosef *Tov 'Elem* did) in terms of both genre and style.[66]

Rashi's northern French student, R. Jacob b. Samson, who was also a teacher of Rashi's grandson, Rabbenu Tam, authored several Aramaic *piyyutim* and *reshuyyot* on the Ten Commandments and their Aramaic translation that were recited on *Shavu'ot*, as well as his own commentaries to

[58] See *Maḥzor Sukkot*, ed. Fraenkel, 186–89; and see below, n. 174, for a similar composition by R. Samuel *he-Ḥasid*.

[59] *Maḥzor Sukkot*, ed. Fraenkel, 322–24.

[60] *Maḥzor Sukkot*, ed. Fraenkel, 331–32, מה אהבתי מעון ביתך חי גואלי (on the theme of ניסוך המים). On this (uncommon) genre or venue and its Sefardic provenance, see E. Fleischer, *Shirat ha-Qodesh*, 461–63, and Weinberger, *Jewish Hymnology*, 160.

[61] *Maḥzor Sukkot*, ed. Fraenkel, 453–55, מרשות מרומם על כל ברכה ושירה נורא על כל תהלה וזמרה.

[62] See *Maḥzor le-Yamim Nora'im*, ed. Fraenkel, 674.

[63] אמרר בבכי מפני יד שלוחה בעי בנאצי בתוך ביתו בבגדי וקבעי. See *Sefer ha-Dema'ot*, ed. S. Bernfeld, vol. 1 (Berlin, 1924), 250.

[64] אבל אעורר אנינות אמרר אויה לי. See A. David, "Historical Records of the Persecutions," (above, n. 23), 197 (entry 2); A. M. Habermann, *Gezerot Ashkenaz ve-Ẓarefat* (Jerusalem, 1945), 63; and Weinberger, *Jewish Hymnology*, 159.

[65] See *Tosafot Ḥagigah* 11a, s.v. *be-rum*; and cf. Israel Davidson, *Oẓar ha-Shirah veha-Piyyut mi-Zeman Kitvei ha-Qodesh 'ad Reshit ha-Haskalah*, vol. 1 (New York, 1924), 55 (1158א).

[66] See E. Fleischer, *Shirat ha-Qodesh*, 438; idem, *Ha-Yoẓerot*, 616, 635, 658–59 (n. 8), 667–68 (alternating rhymes in each line, with a *siyyomet miqra'it*, using verses that begin with the word *va-'ani*), 670 (use of an intricate rhyme pattern formulated by R. Solomon ibn Gabirol), 685, n. 7; L. Weinberger, *Jewish Hymnology*, 160, 178–79; M. Schmelzer, *Meḥqarim*, 154; Fraenkel, *Ha-Tefillah veha-Piyyut be-Maḥzor Nuernberg*, 71; and cf. above, n. 31. Grossman, *Ḥakhmei Ashkenaz ha-Rishonim*, 373–74, characterizes R. Menaḥem b. Makhir as a *payyetan poreh*. At the same time, he notes that R. Menaḥem's brother, R. Nathan, apparently authored only one *piyyut*, an Aramaic *reshut* to the *Haftarah* for the seventh day of Passover. See *Maḥzor Vitry*, 159, sec. 168 (נצחן קרביא ומרי מלכיא שולטניה בדר ודר ובמדור עילאה =*Maḥzor Pesaḥ*, ed. Fraenkel, 652–54); ms. Verona 34, fol. 250r; and Davidson, *Oẓar ha-Shirah veha-Piyyut*, 3:453 (579נ). As Grossman notes, however, R. Nathan was also involved in *piyyut* interpretation.

some of these compositions.[67] Nonetheless, R. Jacob's prolific Rhineland contemporary, R. Qalonymus b. Judah (*ha-baḥur*) of Worms (d. 1126), who authored approximately thirty *piyyutim*, followed more closely the compositional model of Rabbenu Gershom and Rashi. He produced mostly penitential and commemorative compositions: *zulatot* for the period of *sefirat ha-ʿomer*, a *seliḥah* for the seventeenth of Tammuz, and several *qinot* for the ninth of Av, including three that commemorated the events of 1096. The best known of these, מי יתן ראשי מים, stresses the unified defiance of the many martyrs at that time; the loss of both young girls and women in this way, and of "tender young boys" who studied "Torah and Scripture [= *Nakh*], and Mishnah and *ʾaggadah*" as well as the Talmud; and the general degradation of the Torah that resulted.[68] In addition, R. Qalonymus composed a *seliḥah* for Yom Kippur.[69] His unpublished *seliḥah* for the eve of Rosh ha-Shanah (ממעמקי איום קראתיך) is a direct imitation of R. Gershom's *Zekhor Berit* composition for that day (with the double refrain, ושוב ברח־/והשב שבות אהלי יעקב מים על שארית ישראל).[70] To be sure, R. Qalonymus also produced a *yoẓer*, *ʾofan*, and *zulat* for a Sabbath *brit milah* or for a *Shabbat ḥatan*, another *yoẓer* and three *ʾofanim* for a *ḥatan*, and a *reshut le-ḥatan*, as well as an *E-loheikhem* for the *kedushah* during *Musaf*, but these represent only a quarter of his total *piyyut* output. As such, since virtually all of R. Qalonymus's liturgical

67 See Grossman, *Ḥakhmei Ẓarefat ha-Rishonim*, 413, 424–25 (based on texts in *Maḥzor Vitry*, and in ms. Parma 159). Cf. M. Schmelzer, *Meḥqarim*, 3–4; *Maḥzor le-Shavuʿot*, ed. Fraenkel, 554–60, and the editor's introduction, 33. On R. Jacob and Rabbenu Tam, see also below, chapter 7, n. 38.

68 For R. Qalonymus's *qinot* on 1096, see A. David (above, n. 23), 198, secs. 13, 14, 18; Habermann, *Gezerot Ashkenaz ve-Ẓarefat*, 63–69; and S. Einbinder, *Beautiful Death*, 20, 83–84, 163. R. Qalonymus's corpus of *piyyutim* is listed (and briefly described) by Zunz, *LG*, 165–66, 255–56. The *seliḥah* for 17 Tammuz begins אפפוני מצוקות זו מזו. The *zulatot* for the period of *sefirat ha-ʿomer* (אז כעברתה בארץ פתרוסים; אבודים בקש בארץ שבים; איומה כנגדגלות במוסת גדולות; זולתך בעלונו באף ובחרי בך לבד נזכיר בואם להצהיר; and cf. above, n. 22) also include one that mentions the destruction of Jerusalem in 1099 during the Crusader battles, אין זולתך לגאול גואל חזק. R. Qalonymus b. Judah does not seem to have been a leading talmudic master, although he may also have been associated with mystical or pietistic teachings. See A. Grossman, *Ḥakhmei Ashkenaz ha-Rishonim*, 37–38 (n. 44), 379–80 (n. 83); and Zunz, *LG*, 164, n. 11. On the use of the term *miqra* to represent specifically *Nakh*, cf. the prayer commentary of R. Eleazar of Worms, cited in *ʿArugat ha-Bosem*, ed. Urbach, 4:111.

69 For R. Qalonymus's *seliḥah* for the morning of Yom Kippur, אדברה תחנונים כרש ואבכה, see *Maḥzor le-Yamim Noraʾim*, ed. Goldschmidt, 2:277. See ibid., 2:646–47, for a *seliḥah* for *minḥah*, את הקול קול יעקב נוהם / בידי עשו בהם מתלהם (which is actually one of R. Qalonymus's compositions about the events of 1096 in the Rhineland; see the above note).

70 Cf. D. Goldschmidt, *Meḥqerei Tefillah u-Piyyut* (Jerusalem, 1980), 341 (n. 1). As Goldschmidt notes, R. Gershom's *Zekhor Brit* spawned several additional imitators in Ashkenaz (and elsewhere), including R. Eleazar of Worms, אות ברית (a *pizmon li-berit milah*, when a circumcision occurs on a fast day; see below, n. 180), and R. Samuel b. Abraham *ha-Levi* Bonfant, in his שש אנכי (a *seliḥah* for *minḥah* on Yom Kippur; see below, n. 237). See also Zunz, *Der Ritus des synagogalen Gottesdienstes* (Berlin, 1859), 143.

compositions were composed in the years after 1096, he is a transitional figure who begins to produce *piyyutim* for "personal *semaḥot*," although not yet for festivals.[71]

In concluding our discussion of pre-Crusade *piyyut* composition, it is instructive to again focus on the issue of novelty. Ezra Fleischer has noted that *seliḥot* and *qinot* were always "in demand," both because they commemorated current and ongoing events and because the *Tish'ah be-Av* and penitential *seliḥot* liturgies (which also included the recitation of *seliḥot* throughout Yom Kippur) were typically expanded or changed with much greater frequency than the *piyyutim* that were associated with the prayers of the so-called fixed liturgy. Thus those pre-Crusade scholars who concentrated on *seliḥot* and *qinot* were attempting to make contributions in liturgical areas and forms that were still relatively available, as were those who favored newer genres, such as *ma'arivim*, *reshuyyot*, and, to a certain extent, even *yozerot*, which had been bypassed by some of the earliest *payyetanim* in favor of *piyyutim* for the *'Amidah* itself.[72]

It should also be noted that there were periods of time prior to the First Crusade in which very few *piyyutim* were written in Ashkenaz. Even at the academy of Mainz, which produced the largest number of *piyyutim* during the pre-Crusade period, there were virtually no *piyyutim* composed during the middle third of the eleventh century, despite the presence of a number of leading scholars there, including R. Eliezer *ha-Gadol*, R. Ya'akov b. Yakar, and R. Isaac b. Judah. Indeed, R. Eliezer and R. Ya'akov were both involved in mystical studies, an interest that is often associated with the writing of *piyyut* in this period.[73]

To be sure, not everyone could be—or wanted to be—a liturgical poet. In addition, these gaps may have been a function of the need to prevent or to avoid "*piyyut* overload," since periods of active and innovative literary

[71] See Elisabeth Hollender, "Piyyut Commentary in the Nuremberg Maḥzor," to appear in a volume on the Nuremberg Maḥzor edited by Evelyn Cohen. Cf. M. Schmelzer, "Piyyutim le-Nisu'in," 176, sec. 5. Fleischer, *Ha-Yozerot*, 640 (n. 10), notes that the stylistic technique used by R. Qalonymus in his *yozer le-Shabbat ḥatunah*, לך ה' הגדולה אורות מאופל במען אירשתה (= ms. Paris 644, fol. 134r), is reminiscent of an artistic tactic employed by the venerable Italian *payyetan* Amittai. See also Fleischer, 654 (n. 45), for another strophic imitation of the Italian school in another of R. Qalonymus's *yozerot*, אור תורה הבהיקה במאור (= ms. Paris 644, fol. 100r, and ms. Paris 648, fol. 70r). And see M. Schmelzer, "Piyyut Yoẓer la-Nisu'in le-Rabbana Qalonymus ha-Baḥur ben Rabbana Yehudah," in *Tifferet Yisra'el: Sefer Yovel Likhvod Yisra'el Francus*, ed. J. Roth et al. (New York, 2010), 275–88, for a detailed literary and manuscript analysis of לך ה' הגדולה (which also includes a listing of the nine additional manuscripts in which it appears).

[72] See esp. Fleischer, *Ha-Yozerot*, 607–17, and idem, "Tefillah u-Piyyut be-Maḥzor Vermaiza," 37–40.

[73] See A. Grossman, *Ḥakhmei Ashkenaz ha-Rishonim*, 422–23, and cf. above, n. 28. It was precisely during this period, however, that R. Meir *Shaẓ* produced his many *piyyutim* in Worms, as described above.

composition are often followed, quite naturally, by quieter periods. Nonetheless, it is significant that there were recognizable gaps in both time and place with respect to the writing of *piyyut* in the pre-Crusade period, just as we have been able to discern clearly identifiable patterns for the *piyyutim* that were composed.

The Twelfth Century

Indeed, as we move to the period of the Tosafists, we encounter many of the very same kinds of compositional patterns and issues that have been identified for the pre-Crusade period. Rashi's grandson R. Jacob b. Meir of Ramerupt (Rabbenu Tam, 1100–1171) composed far more *piyyutim* than Rashi did (nearly twenty-five, as compared to Rashi's seven or so).[74] Even more significant to my mind, however, is the fact that Rabbenu Tam's *piyyutim* were written in forms other than just the *seliḥot* genre that was favored by Rashi. Rabbenu Tam composed *yoẓerot* and *ʾofanim* for the festivals,[75] including a relatively unusual form for this period known as a *meʾorah* (which was meant to be recited just prior to the phrase and blessing of *ʾor ḥadash*

[74] L. Zunz, *LG*, 265–67, assigns only eleven *piyyutim* to Rabbenu Tam. However, additional *piyyutim* in the name of Jacob have been attributed to him, based primarily on similarities in style to others that Rabbenu Tam composed, and others have been identified from manuscript texts which Zunz did not have. As a result, I. Davidson, *Oẓar ha-Shirah veha-Piyyut*, 4:415–16, assigns thirty-one *piyyutim* to Rabbenu Tam, although he is unsure about four of these attributions. On the poetics found in *Sefer ha-Yashar*, Rabbenu Tam's grammatical work, and his exchange with Ibn Ezra regarding quantitative metrics, see, e.g., Urbach, *Baʿalei ha-Tosafot*, 1:107–11; L. Weinberger, *Jewish Hymnography*, 166–67; and R. Langer, "Kalir Was a Tanna" (above, n. 20). E. Fleischer, *Shirat ha-Qodesh ha-ʿIvrit Bimei ha-Benayim*, 436–37, notes Rabbenu Tam's use of the Sefardic *shirei ʾezor* and related rhyme schemes (similar to the usage by R. Meir *Shaz*). Cf. Fleischer, 344–55; idem, *Ha-Yoẓerot*, 670 (n. 33); below, nn.79, 82; and below at R. Eliezer b. Nathan of Mainz (Raban), n. 87. An edited collection of Rabbenu Tam's *piyyutim* and other samples of his versification, *Shirat Rabbenu Tam*, ed. Isaac Meiseles (Jerusalem, 2012), appeared after the present study was in copyedited form. Thus I have only been able to make occasional references to it. Meiseles addresses virtually all of these issues of attribution, meter, and poetic style in his prologue (pp. 7–11), and in his brief introductory remarks (and notes) to each composition.

[75] An *ʾofan* for *Shemini ʿAẓeret*, יחיד ערץ יסוד ארץ ברוב חכמה ותושיה, is found in ms. Parma 1198 (a thirteenth-century French *Maḥzor* that has *piyyutim* from R. Yosef *Tov ʿElem*, R. Elijah *ha-zaqen* of Le Mans, and several early Italian *payyetanim*), fols. 133r–v; and see also *Maḥzor Sukkot*, ed. Goldschmidt, 259–60, and the editor's introduction, 33; and *Shirat Rabbenu Tam*, ed. Meiseles, 24–27. A French manuscript includes this *piyyut* for *Shabbat Ḥol ha-Moʿed Sukkot* (as does a later Austrian rite), while another French manuscript records it for *Shavuʿot* (and some German *siddurim* list it for the second Sabbath after Passover). See *ʿArugat ha-Bosem*, ed. Urbach, 2:196–99, for an Ashkenazic commentary to this *piyyut*. In ms. Bodl. 1147 (a German liturgy; see below, nn. 168, 184, 195), fol. 78v, this *yoẓer* is assigned to the period of special Torah readings prior to Passover (-יוצר להפסקה שניה, יחיד ערץ יסוד ארץ וכו'). See also *Maḥzor Pesaḥ*, ed. Fraenkel, 447–49, for a metered *ʾofan* (with a refrain) for the seventh day of Passover, ידועי שם / בבור נשם / ובנקיון רעיונים, that has been attributed to Rabbenu Tam.

'al ẓion ta'ir in the morning *Shema*) for the second Sabbath of Ḥanukkah,[76] and another such metered composition for *Shavu'ot*.[77] He also wrote a post-*havdalah* poem that was to be recited at the end of the Sabbath,[78] *ma'arivim* for *Sukkot*,[79] and a number of Aramaic *piyyutim*—to introduce the Targum of the *Haftarah* on the seventh day of Passover and on the second day of *Shavu'ot*—which feature internal rhyme systems or a coordinated refrain, as well as a single rhyme throughout, at the end of each line (*ḥaruz mavriaḥ*).[80] The best known of Rabbenu Tam's compositions in this genre is יציב פתגם.[81]

[76] On the *me'orah* for the second Sabbath of Ḥanukkah (which may have been composed as an 'ofan and assigned to that occasion only later), יום הודו וכבודו ונחת ידיו יראה, see ms. Parma 1198, fols. 161r–v; ms. Bodl. 1151, fol. 45v; ms. Parma 605, fol. 106v; ms. Moscow 611 (a Worms rite), fol. 9v; ms. Verona 34, fol. 115v; ms. Moscow 201, fol. 42v; ms. Vatican 308; and *Shirat Rabbenu Tam*, ed. Meiseles, 66–70. For other *piyyutim* for Ḥanukkah, see above, n. 57, and below, nn. 129, 165.

[77] This *me'orah*, יום נגלה / צור מעלה / להנחיל דת לכמיהם, has a form of Spanish meter; see *Maḥzor Shavu'ot*, ed. Fraenkel, 160–62, and the editor's introduction, 21; and *Shirat Rabbenu Tam*, ed. Meiseles, 45–50. On the *me'orah* form (and related *'ahavah* form, which was inserted immediately prior to the *Shema*), see Fleischer, *Ha-Yoẓerot*, 673–83. The earliest European *payyetanim* may not have known about this form at all, and even later ones, such as R. Simeon b. Isaac *ha-Gadol* (c. 1000), made use of this form only sparingly. Fleischer, *Ha-Yoẓerot*, 677–80, also discusses the compositions of this type that were produced by R. Ephraim of Bonn (d. 1197), a younger German contemporary of Rabbenu Tam; see below.

[78] See ms. Parma 352, fols. 61v–63r, יד ושם חיש חדשם. This *havdalah* appears (unnamed) in *Maḥzor Vitry*, 189 (following one attributed to Ibn Ezra), but yields the acrostic יעקב חזק. See *Shirat Rabbenu Tam*, ed. Meiseles, 97–101. For similar compositions by Ri, see below, n. 128, and cf. E. Fleischer, *Shirat ha-Qodesh*, 412, 472, and L. Weinberger, *Jewish Hymnography*, 134–35, 173–74, for the possible Sefardic origins of this genre. (There are also two other *piyyutim* for a circumcision in the name of Jacob that are found in ms. Parma 352, fol. 72r, יצו הקב"ה את ברכתו לבן נולד, and fol. 65r, יחד ישאו צופים; see also below, n. 158.)

[79] See *Maḥzor Sukkot*, ed. Goldschmidt, 46–48, 315–17. The first of these, א-להים ה' לו עיני מחכות, has a verse at the end of each stanza (*siyyomet miqra'it*). The second, אדיר ונאור עוטה אור כאדרת, is a *ma'ariv* for *Shemini 'Aẓeret/Simḥat Torah*. Both are preserved in *Maḥzor Vitry*, ms. Reggio; see *Maḥzor Sukkot*, editor's introduction, 29–30, secs. 9, 17; and *Shirat Rabbenu Tam*, ed. Meiseles, 15–23, 28–36. The second *ma'ariv*, אדיר ונאור, is also found in ms. Parma 1265, fol. 77r, and is cited by *Tosafot Sukkah* 48a, s.v. *regel* (ור"ת יסד במעריב של שמיני עצרת); and similarly by *Tosafot Rosh ha-Shanah* 4b, s.v. פז"ר; and *Tosafot Yoma* 3a, s.v. פז"ר. See also the parallel *Tosafot* passage in *Ḥagigah* 17a, and ms. Moscow 109, fol. 496r, and cf. Y. S. Spiegel, "Birur be-Divrei ha-Payyetan 'u-teshuvah, u-tefillah u-ẓedaqah ma'avirin 'et ro'a ha-gezerah' ve-'al Kefifut ha-Payyetanim la-Halakhah," *Netu'im* 8 (2002), 23–42, and Landshuth, *'Ammudei 'Avodah*, 108. See also *Maḥzor Sukkot*, ed. Goldschmidt, 477–79, for a poem attributed to Rabbenu Tam (by Zunz), ה' בו מעיני יעטה תהלה כמדו (to be recited on *Simḥat Torah* when the Torah scrolls are finally returned to the ark just prior to *Musaf*), which contains a Spanish rhyme-form, the so-called חרוז מעין אזורי. Cf. above, n. 74.

[80] See *Maḥzor Pesaḥ*, 651–52 (אי יממיא ומיא כי מילנין), and cf. the editor's introduction, 45; and see also *Shirat Rabbenu Tam*, ed. Meisles, 42–44; *Maḥzor Shavu'ot*, 587–89 (ייתון בני עממין למשאל בשלומיו), and ibid., 589–91 (יהודון כל נשמי למריה כולא שמיה, with an established meter as well). See also the editor's introduction, 34–35; *Shirat Rabbenu Tam*, ed. Meiseles, 55–62; and ms. Parma 924 (Ashkenaz, 13th century), fols. 371v–372v.

[81] See *Maḥzor Pesaḥ*, ed. Fraenkel, 632–34 (= *Maḥzor Shavu'ot*, ed. Fraenkel, 570–72); and *Shirat Rabbenu Tam*, ed. Meiseles, 51–54. Although Rabbenu Tam's authorship of *Yeẓiv pitgam* had

Rabbenu Tam clearly wished to take advantage of the available opportunities and venues for *piyyutim* within the prayer service, bypassing those areas that had been covered in large measure by earlier authors, although he did compose several *seliḥot* as well.[82] Rabbenu Tam's older brother, Rashbam, on the other hand, composed no *piyyutim* at all, as far as we can tell.[83] Their middle brother, Isaac, who passed away at a relatively young age, wrote a total of three *piyyutim* (two of which are *seliḥot*), while their father, R. Meir b. Samuel, who had studied in Worms during the late eleventh century, produced but a single *qinah*. R. Meir, Rashbam, and R. Isaac (and R. Isaac's son as well) were involved, albeit to a limited extent, in offering comments on *piyyutim*.[84] Thus Rabbenu Tam's concerted involvement in

---

been questioned (with some attributing it to a R. Ya'aqov *ha-Levi*, based on an extra, corrupt line; cf. E. Katz in *Sinai* 53 [1963], 276–78), E. Fleischer, "Tefillah u-Piyyut be-Maḥzor Vermaiza," 39, notes that the attribution to Rabbenu Tam is by now certain. Cf. *Shirat Rabbenu Tam*, ed. Meiseles, 37–41.

[82] For Rabbenu Tam's *seliḥot*, see, e.g., ms. Parma 588, sec. 30, and ms. Hamburg 137 (Heb. 409; Ashkenaz 13th century), fol. 8v (אשמרה אליך עזי אלם לפני גוזזי). See also ms. Parma 855 (a thirteenth-century northern French *Maḥzor*), fols. 228v–229v; ms. Parma 1318, fol. 104v, שמך [נורא] ביום אירא; and *Shirat Rabbenu Tam*, ed. Meiseles, 77–86. On the proper wording of this composition, cf. Landshuth, *'Ammudei' Avodah*, 108. Note also the *seliḥah*, יגוני ומר חכי נדודי וגרושי ואזכיר שמך מלכי, which according to E. Fleischer, "'Iyyunim bi-Shlabei 'Aliyyatah ve-Hitqablutah shel Ẓurat Shir ha-Ezor be-Shirat ha-'Ivrit shel Yemei ha-Benayim," above n. 42, 179, also shows Spanish influence (in terms of חרוז מעין אזורי). See also *Shirat Rabbenu Tam*, ed. Meiseles, 63–65, where this is identified as a פיוט לחג הסוכות; and cf. ibid., 87–93.

[83] Rashbam did, however, compose some verses to conclude books within his Torah commentary and in his grammatical work, ספר הדייקות, which were similar to the verses composed by R. Yosef *Bekhor Shor* to the end of various portions in his Torah commentary (see below, n. 150). See, e.g., Jonathan Jacobs, "Tosafot she-Hosif Rashbam le-Perusho la-Torah," *Tarbiz* 66 (2007), 465–69. Cf. *Shirat Rabbenu Tam*, ed. Meiseles, 107–31, 138–39.

[84] R. Meir b. Samuel's *qinah* begins אבוא לפניך שומע תפלה; see Davidson, *Oẓar ha-Shirah veha-Piyyut*, 1:8 (24:א). One of Isaac b. Meir's *seliḥot*, אל-הי עושי נוצרי לפניך מה אמר מיוצרי (*Maḥzor le-Yamim Nora'im*, ed. Goldschmidt, 2:535), was recited on *Musaf* of Yom Kippur, and the other, ישראל עמך תחנה עורכים (commemorating the persecutions of 1096), was recited on the first fast of בה"ב (*sheni qamma*), and on the fifth day of *seliḥot* prior to Rosh ha-Shanah. See, e.g., A. M. Habermann, *Be-Ran—Yahad* (Jerusalem, 1945), 152; *Sefer ha-Seliḥot ke-Minhag Lita*, ed. D. Goldschmidt (Jerusalem, 1965), 44–46 (sec. 14); and ms. St. Petersburg (#69720, Institute of Oriental Studies of the Russian Academy), D 101, fol. 167v. This *seliḥah* is not included in A. David's listing ("Historical Records of the Persecutions," above, n. 23), 197–98; cf. Zunz, *LG*, 303. R. Isaac b. Meir's third composition was an *'ofan* titled י-ה שוכן שחקים; see Davidson, *Oẓar ha-Shirah veha-Piyyut*, 2:308 (1124:י). Ms. Moscow 611, a western German rite that contains *piyyutim* from a number of German authors (above, nn. 18, 74), includes (in section 134) an *E-loheikhem* piece to the end of the *kedushah le-musaf*, א-להיכם ישרי לב באות ברית חתם (cf., e.g., Fleisher *Shirat ha-Qodesh*, 448–49); a *piyyut* for the end of the reader's repetition of the *'Amidah*, יושב מרומי צמצם מתקוממי (sec. 141); and a *zulat* for a *Shabbat* (sec. 218), all attributed to an Isaac b. Meir. Note, however, that R. Meir b. Isaac *Shaẓ* also had a son named Isaac, who was killed in 1096; see Grossman, *Ḥakhmei Ashkenaz ha-Rishonim*, 292, and cf. above, n. 42. On Meir b. Samuel's (relatively few) *piyyut* commentaries, see Grossman, *Ḥakhmei Ẓarefat ha-Rishonim*, 170. For commentaries by the son of R. Isaac b. Meir (which also utilized material by Rabbenu Tam),

piyyut composition was not simply a matter of familial tradition or pre dilection but rather a considered and concentrated effort on his part to participate in this discipline, an approach that stands in clear contrast to his more restrictive approaches to mystical and biblical studies.[85]

The same variety in *piyyut* composition seen in the range of *piyyutim* by Rabbenu Tam can also found at this time in the Rhineland, in the literary corpus of the leading German Tosafist R. Eliezer b. Nathan (Raban) of Mainz. Raban was a prolific *payyetan* who authored close to thirty *piyyutim*, including *ma'arivim* for *Pesaḥ* and *Shavu'ot*;[86] a *yoẓer*, *'ofan*, and *zulat* (and a *reshut*) for a *Shabbat ḥatan*; another set of *yoẓerot* to mark a *brit milah* that took place on the Sabbath;[87] and a third set for *Shabbat Shuvah*.[88] Indeed, Ezra Fleischer concludes that "in the first half of the twelfth century, the compositions of R. Menaḥem b. Makhir of Regensburg and Raban ... made a noticeable contribution toward solidifying the contours of the *yoẓer* in Ashkenaz."[89] Raban also authored several *qinot* to commemorate the events of 1096,[90] and *seliḥot* for the *Musaf* service on Yom Kippur; fully a third of

---

see Grossman, *Ḥakhmei Ashkenaz ha-Rishonim*, 135, n. 47. For one such commentary by R. Isaac b. Meir himself, see *'Arugat ha-Bosem*, ed. Urbach, 4:12–13 (which also includes remnants of comments made by Rabbenu Tam). See Elisabeth Hollender, *Piyyut Commentary in Medieval Ashkenaz* (Berlin, 2008), 53, for a possible comment by Rashbam. Rashbam was involved to some extent in interpreting *piyyutim* (as cited by R. Shemayah), although he does not appear to have left any written compilation or record of these; see also A. Grossman, *Ḥakhmei Ashkenaz*, 533. See *'Arugat ha-Bosem*, ed. Urbach, 4:8–11, for comments by R. Meir b. Samuel, R. Isaac b. Meir, and Rabbenu Tam.

85 See above, chapter 2, n. 6; below, chapter 6, nn. 3, 15–18; and cf. H. Soloveitchik, "Three Themes in the *Sefer Ḥasidim*," 352; and below, n. 155.

86 See *Maḥzor Pesaḥ*, 368–71 (and the editor's introduction, 24), and *Maḥzor Shavu'ot*, 19–33, for a *ma'ariv* and a lengthy *bikkur* (on the theme of bringing the *bikkurim*). For the body of the *ma'ariv*, which begins א-ל א-להים ה' דבר ויקרא ארץ, see also ms. Paris (Cluny Museum) 12290 (#14772), fols. 169r–v; and ms. Verona 34, fols. 205v–206r. The *bikkur*, אשריך ישראל מי כמוך עם סגו־לתו, has a *siyyomet miqra'it*. See also Fraenkel, *Ha-Tefillah veha-Piyyut be-Maḥzor Nuernberg*, 68.

87 See M. Schmelzer, "Piyyutim le-Nisu'in le-Rishonei Ḥakhmei Ashkenaz," 177 (based on ms. Bodl. 1099 and 1149, and ms. Moscow 611); ms. Paris (Cluny Museum) 12290 (#14772), fols. 202v–205v; ms. Verona 34, fols. 15v–19v; and E. Fleischer, *Ha-Yoẓerot*, 624 (n. 32), 646 (including a שרשור), 668–70, 682 (a שיר איזור; Fleischer makes use of the Bodl. mss., as well as ms. Paris 647, among others, and cf. above, n. 74). See also Fraenkel, *Ha-Tefillah veha-Piyyut be-Maḥzor Nuernberg*, 80.

88 See *Maḥzor le-Yamim Nora'im*, ed. Goldschmidt, 1:301–7 (see also above, n. 53, and Fleischer, *Ha-Yoẓerot*, 667, n. 28, and 685, n. 7), and cf. Matania Ben-Ghedaliah, "Ha-Reqa ha-Histori li-Ketivat Sefer Even ha-'Ezer," (M.A. thesis, Touro College, 2002), 69–72.

89 See Fleischer, *Ha-Yoẓerot*, 616. Raban also composed a *yoẓer* for *Shabbat Naḥamu*; cf. above, n. 55.

90 See A. David, "Historical Records of the Persecutions," (above, n. 23), 197–98 secs. 6 (אך טוב לישראל) and 11 (א-להים באזנינו שמענו אבותינו ספרו לנו, which was recited as a *zulat* for the Sabbath before the seventeenth of Tammuz or for *Shabbat Ḥazon*; cf. below, n. 128). See also *Leqet Piyyutei Seliḥot*, ed. D. Goldschmidt and A. Fraenkel (Jerusalem, 1992), 1:64–74: אודה עלי פשעי (a *shlishiyyah* triplet, with a *soger* that has a form of the root שמע); אודך ואמתך הניחנו (a triplet

his liturgical compositions were *seliḥot* and *qinot*.[91] In addition, Raban was the author of an extant (more prose-like) Crusade chronicle, and he was a thorough interpreter of *piyyutim* as well.[92]

A younger contemporary of Raban, R. Eliezer b. Samson of Cologne, who served on the Cologne rabbinic court with Raban's son-in-law R. Samuel b. Natronai, and was also a signatory of the ordinances promulgated by Rabbenu Tam and Rashbam in Troyes in 1150,[93] composed a *ma'ariv* and a *bikkur* for *Sukkot*,[94] a *bikkur* for Passover, and an Aramaic *reshut* to the *Haftarah* on *Shavu'ot*, but apparently no *seliḥot*.[95] R. Eliezer is the only German Tosafist known to have authored such an Aramaic *reshut*.[96] Indeed,

---

with a *siyyomet miqra'it* that begins with the word או or ואו); אך טוב א-להים לישראל (in which the third line of each stanza contains a verse that begins with the word למה, and the fourth line has a verse beginning with a form of the word אבי); א-ל א-להי הרוחות (a triplet with a *siyyomet miqra'it* that has a form of the word סליחה); תבוא אנקת אסיריך (a triplet, with a *soger min ha-miqra* that begins with אל or ואל); and תודיעני אורח חיים ומוסר (another triplet with similar endings). For references by Raban to the persecutions of 1096 even in a *zulat* that he composed for a circumcision that took place on the Sabbath, see Matania Ben-Ghedaliah, "Ha-Reqa ha-Histori li-Ketivat Sefer Even ha-'Ezer," 51–52.

91 *Maḥzor le-Yamim Nora'im*, 2:507–10, 520–22. L. Zunz, *LG*, 259, counts twenty-four compositions for Raban all told, while I. Davidson, *Oẓar ha-Shirah veha-Piyyut*, 4:364, counts a total of twenty-eight. See also Habermann, *Gezerot Ashkenaz ve-Ẓarefat*, 107–8 (את הברית ואת השבועה).

92 See e.g., A. David, "Historical Records of the Persecutions," (above, n. 23), 193–97; *'Arugat ha-Bosem*, ed. Urbach, 4:24–39; and E. Hollender, *Piyyut Commentary in Medieval Ashkenaz*, 45–46.

93 See Urbach, *Ba'alei ha-Tosafot*, 1:179, and above, chapter 1, nn. 37, 137.

94 For R. Eliezer b. Samson's *ma'ariv* for the second night of *Sukkot*, חג האסיף תקופת השנה בשמחה להרבות שושנה . . . סוכה אזכירה מעללי נורא (the body of which has a *ḥaruz mavriaḥ*), see *Maḥzor Sukkot*, ed. Goldschmidt, 14–18, and ms. Moscow 611, fols. 197r–v. This *ma'ariv* also has a *bikkur* addendum by R. Eliezer (אדברה ואעירה בירחי קדם אזכיר, *Maḥzor Sukkot*, 18–20, and see also the editor's introduction, 28), which describes the laws of *ma'aser* in Jerusalem (and has a *siyyomet miqra'it*). See ms. Parma 1274, fol. 136r, where the *ma'ariv* חג האסיף תקופת השנה is headed by the phrase, יסד ר' שמשון ב"ר אליעזר מקולוניא נהרריינוס. See also ms. Bodl. 1099, fols. 42r–44v, and ms. Parma 605, fol. 187r, in which חג האסיף לר' אליעזר בן שמשון is designated for "a ma'ariv for the second [night] of Sukkot or first [night], if it occurs on the Sabbath." Cf. ms. Modena, State Archive 769 (four folios).

95 For R. Eliezer's *bikkur* for *Pesaḥ*, אשירה נא לידידי, see *Maḥzor Pesaḥ*, ed. Fraenkel, 405–10 (with a *siyyomet miqra'it*), and the editor's introduction, 27. For R. Eliezer's Aramaic *reshut* to the Aramaic Targum of the *Haftarah* (on the second day of *Shavu'ot*) אזגד מתורגמנא / בעי הרמנא (which has both a *ḥaruz mavriaḥ* and an internal rhyme in the style of Rabbenu Tam's *reshuyyot*, as well as kind of Spanish meter), see *Maḥzor Shavu'ot*, ed. Fraenkel, 580–86, and the editor's introduction, 34.

96 The only other German *payyetan* to compose this type of *reshut* (for Passover) is R. Nathan b. R. Makhir, the brother of R. Menaḥem b. Makhir of Regensburg; see above, n. 66. Moreover, as Y. Fraenkel notes (in his introduction to *Maḥzor Pesaḥ*, 27, n. 52), there is another R. Eliezer b. Samson at this time who hailed from Falaise. He was the son-in-law of Rabbenu Tam's brother-in-law, R. Samson of Falaise, and is mentioned in the standard *Tosafot* to *Bava Batra*; see Urbach, *Ba'alei ha-Tosafot*, 1:118–20. Fraenkel further notes that the *bikkhur* described in the above note is found (only) in a French *Maḥzor* (ms. B.M. Or. 2735), and is attributed there

the pattern of his *piyyut* compositions appears to be most similar to that of the northern French Tosafist R. Elḥanan (d. 1184), son of Ri of Dampierre, a point to which we shall return below.

Another contemporary of Raban who corresponded with him in halakhic matters and possibly with R. Tam as well,[97] R. Joseph b. Nathan *Ḥazzan* of Wurzburg, was the author of nearly fifteen carefully metered *piyyutim.*[98] These include a *ma'ariv* and a *bikkur* for *Shemini 'Aẓeret* (with a *siyyomet miqra'it* throughout; the *bikkur* focuses on the *simḥat beit ha-sho'evah* that was celebrated in the Temple); two *reshuyyot* for *Simḥat Torah* (one to fete the *ḥatan Torah* and the other for the *ḥatan Bereshit*, and each with a *ḥaruz mavriaḥ*);[99] a *yoẓer*, *'ofan*, *zulat*, *reshut*, and *E-loheikhem* for a *Shabbat ḥatan* (which have been only partially published);[100] and five *seliḥot*: a *petiḥah* that

---

to R. Eliezer b. Samson מפלאג״י (= Falaise), even though Zunz, *LG*, 137, holds that this *piyyut* is among those composed by R. Eliezer b. Samson of Cologne.

[97] For R. Joseph b. Nathan's correspondence with Raban in two matters of monetary law, see *Sefer Raban*, ed. Ehrenreich (repr. Jerusalem, 1975), fols. 298b–299b; and S. Emanuel, *Shivrei Luḥot*, 73–74 (n. 106). There is some question as to whether this Joseph is the Joseph (or Yose) of טרנטו/טרינטו in Italy, who corresponded with Rabbenu Tam and whose ruling in matters of nonkosher brine is cited by Rabiah (and indeed, whether Joseph b. Natan *Ḥazzan* of Wurzburg was originally from Italy or from Tirnau in central Europe). See Aptowitzer, *Mavo la-Rabiah*, 257, 352; L. Zunz, *LG*, 271; I. Elbogen et al., *Germania Judaica*, vol. 1 (Tubingen, 1963), 481–82; Emanuel, *Shivrei Luḥot*, 73–74; and Rami Reiner, "Even she-Katuv 'Alehah: Te'arei ha-Niftarim 'al Maẓevot Beit ha-'Almin be-Wurzburg, 1147–1346," *Tarbiz* 78 (2009), 141 (sec. 2.5).

[98] The modern treatments of Joseph's *piyyutim* are conveniently found in Emanuel, *Shivrei Luḥot*, 74 (n. 7). The editors of *Leqet Piyyutei Seliḥot* (2:782–83) dispute the attribution of one of the *seliḥot* by Zunz (*LG*, 273) and Davidson, *Oẓar ha-Shirah veha-Piyyut*, 1:86 (1854:א), to this author (אומן בעמדו להתחנן לפניך, below, n. 101), since this composition is found only in a manuscript of a French *seliḥot* rite (ms. Parma 654, fol. 67), while all of R. Joseph's other *piyyutim* are found in manuscripts of German rites and (*seliḥot*) collections. In addition, virtually all of Joseph's compositions are tightly metered (as has been noted), while the one is question is not.

[99] See *Maḥzor le-Sukkot*, ed. Goldschmidt, 289–97 (שמיני אותותיו ומעשיו בספר כתובים, and the *bikkur* that begins, אודות באר המים אות היא לאזרחיים, and cf. ms. Vatican 320, fols. 530v–531r); 444–46 (מרשות יסד ארץ בחכמה ונצב בעדת א-ל); 455–58 (מרשות אומר עצתו תקום מגיד אחרית מראשית). A commentary to שמיני אותותיו/אודות באר מים, which deals with a range of *Sukkot* themes (from the sacrifical rites to *simḥat beit ha-sho'evah*), can be found in ms. Parma 541 (#13218, Ashkenaz, 13th–14th centuries), fols. 256r–262r; ms. Bodl. 1208 (Ashkenaz, 15th century), fols. 8r–14r; ms. Lund 2 (Ashkenaz, 1407), fols. 69r–73r; and cf. *'Arugat ha-Bosem*, ed. Urbach, 4:59–60; E. Hollender, *Clavis Commentatorium of Hebrew Liturgical Poetry in Manuscript* (Leiden, 2005), 127, 901; and idem, *Piyyut Commentary in Medieval Ashkenaz*, 52. Although the author of this commentary is otherwise unidentified, references are found in it to a comment by Rashi to Psalms and to his talmudic comments, as well as those of R. Isaac b. Asher *ha-Levi* (Riva *ha-Zaqen*) of Speyer. See, e.g., ms. Lund 2, fols. 72r, 73r, and ms. Bodl. 1208, fol. 13r. This *piyyut* commentary is followed closely by one from R. Meir of Rothenburg to the *piyyut* אודך כי אנפת (see ms. Bodl. 1208, fols. 16r–18r), in which R. Meir cites his father, R. Barukh.

[100] See Schmelzer, "Piyyutim le-Nisu'in," 177, sec. 8 (based on ms. Bodl. 1099); ms. Verona 34, fols. 76r–78r (for his *yoẓer*, אביעה חידות מקדם); and cf. Zunz, *LG*, 271–73. For R. Yosef's *E-loheikhem* (א-להיכם יוסף ידו שנית), see ms. Prague (National Library), VI EA 2, sec. 117. The first half of the *yoẓer* and *'ofan* were published by Abraham Katsch, "Unpublished Poems of Ashkenazic Poets of the Thirteenth and Fourteenth Centuries from a Manuscript in

commemorates the events of 1096, a triplet for the ten days of penitence with a *siyyomet miqra'it* in which each verse contains the word *boker*, another in which nearly every phrase is of biblical or talmudic origin, another in which each stanza ends with a biblical phrase from Exodus, chapters 32–34 (relating to Moses's entreaty of the Almighty and the thirteen Divine attributes that were invoked), and a *seliḥah* for the tenth of Tevet.[101]

In sum, one third of R. Joseph *Ḥazzan*'s liturgical poetry was composed for festivals, a second third for joyous personal occasions, and the remaining third was devoted to *seliḥot.* Thus the distribution or balance of R. Joseph's *piyyut* corpus follows precisely the compositional pattern or makeup of Raban's nearly thirty *piyyutim.* This suggests that *piyyut* composition at this point during the Tosafist period in Germany was governed, at least in part, by certain larger conventions or approaches.

R. Ephraim b. Jacob (b. Qalonymus) of Bonn (1133–97), a prominent German rabbinic judge who studied with Raban's sons-in-law, the Tosafists R. Samuel b. Natronai and R. Joel b. Isaac *ha-Levi*, served in both Mainz and Bonn. He also lived for a time in Speyer, where he issued halakhic rulings as well.[102] In addition to his extensive *piyyut* commentaries,[103] which occasionally reflect the give-and-take typical within a rabbinic academy,[104] R. Ephraim composed more than twenty-five *piyyutim.*

the Ginzburg Collection," *JQR* 58 (1967), 89–94. On this manuscript, ms. Ginburg 1041, see also Simon Bernstein, "Piyyutim 'Atiqim me-Osef Kitvei ha-Yad ha-Baron Ginzburg," *Sinai* 50 (1962), 405–21. I thank Prof. Elisabeth Hollender for these last two references.

[101] See ms. Parma 588, sec. 10 (מרבינו יוסף חזן ב"ר נתן), for the *petiḥah*, א-ל ארך אפים נוצר חסד לאלפים, published by A. M. Habermann in *Gezerot Ashkenaz ve-Ẓarefat*, 89–90, and cf. A. David, "Historical Records of the Persecutions" (above, n. 23), 198, sec. 8. Three *seliḥot* are published in *Leqet Piyyutei Seliḥot*, ed. Fraenkel, 1:275–80: the שלישיה (for the ten days of penitence), תבוא לפניך שועת אנקת אסיר, אגורה עולמים באהליך (with the rich assortment of biblical and talmudic phrases); and אומן בעמדו להתחנן לפניך (which relates to Ex. 32–34). On the *seliḥah* for the tenth of Tevet, אפפו עלי רעות בקושי באין מספר כפפו, see Zunz, *LG*, 273, and I. Davidson, *Oẓar ha-Shirah veha-Piyyut*, 1:326 (1854:א). Note the *seliḥah* for the tenth of Tevet by R. Eleazar of Worms, with a very similar opening (אפפו עלינו רעות). See Davidson, ibid. (7160:א); I. Meiseles, *Shirat ha-Roqeah* (Jerusalem, 1993), 142–45; and below, nn. 180, 183.

[102] See A. Aptowitzer, *Mavo la-Rabiah*, 319; above, Introduction, nn. 89–90; and chapter 1, nn. 40–42. For R. Ephraim's interest in *torat ha-sod*, see below, chapter 6. For R. Ephraim's use of *gematria* in a manner similar to that of *Ḥasidei Ashkenaz*, see *Maḥzor Vitry*, 519; *'Arugat ha-Bosem*, ed. Urbach, 4:110, n. 30; and below, chapter 6, n. 61. See also ms. Bodl. 2797/15 (#16716), fol. 54r: דרוש על דגלי השבטים מנימוקי רבינו אפירם יליכ"ה. ד' דגלים כנגד ד' יסודות עולם. והם י"ב שבטים כנגד י"ב מזלות וכנגד י"ב [אבני] אפוד שנא' והאבנים תהיינה על שמות בני ישראל. R. Isaac b. Moses of Vienna cites the tale of the composition and transmission of *U-netaneh Toqef*, as he found it in "the handwritten account of R. Ephraim b. Jacob of Bonn"; see *Sefer Or Zaru'a*, pt. 2, *hilkhot Rosh ha-Shanah*, sec. 276 (fol. 63a), and cf. M. Schmelzer, *Studies in Jewish Bibliography*, 188–89, 230*–32*, for the link between R. Ephraim's *piyyut*, *Ta-shma marei 'alma*, and *U-netaneh Toqef.*

[103] See, e.g., E. Hollender, *Piyyut Commentary in Medieval Ashkenaz*, 46–48; *'Arugat ha-Bosem*, ed. Urbach, 4:39–58; and above in the Introduction, n. 99.

[104] See, e.g., ms. Hamburg 152, fol. 6v: ע"א [ענין אחר] שמעתי מ"ר [מפי רבי] לכך נקט הפייט אודך כי אנפת בי כי אמשול לך דבר למה הוא דומה וכו'. Cf. *'Arugat ha-Bosem*, ed. Urbach, 4:69–70; above, Introduction

In his broad assessment of R. Ephraim of Bonn's *piyyutim*, A. M. Habermann noted that they exhibit the salient Ashkenazic characteristic of including both talmudic conceptions and language in their composition. Indeed, talmudic and Aramaic phrases became an organic, essential aspect of these compositions, even as R. Ephraim has a tendency to employ Sefardic meter as well. Similar to his older contemporary, R. Ephraim b. Isaac of Regensburg, R. Ephraim of Bonn composed quite a number of metered *piyyutim*, occasionally providing earlier liturgical tunes or structures that were meant to guide their recitation.[105]

R. Ephraim's compositions include a series of *seliḥot*, *ʿaqedot*, and commemorative *qinot* (fourteen in all) for tragedies that occurred in both Germany and northern France;[106] for the ninth of Av[107] (including one, with a

(n. 99), and below, Conclusion (n. 7). Although R. Ephraim's rabbinic training and career took place completely within Germany, his awareness of Rabbenu Tam and his teachings (in terms of *piyyut* and *halakhah*), as reflected in both Ephraim's *piyyut* commentaries and in his *Sefer Zekhirah*, is noteworthy. See, e.g., Rami Reiner, "Rabbenu Tam: Rabbotav (ha-Ẓarefatim) ve-Talmidav Bnei Ashkenaz" (M.A. thesis, Hebrew University of Jerusalem, 1997), 123–24, and ms. Bodl. 1606, fol. 273, for a commentary to the thirteen Divine *middot*, similar to the one by Rabbenu Tam. As noted by Susan Einbinder (below, n. 106), R. Ephraim identifies two of the martyrs at Blois as students of Rashbam and Rabbenu Tam. Cf. below, n. 144.

[105] See A. M. Habermann, "Piyyutei R. Ephraim b. Yaʿaqov mi-Bona," *Yediʿot ha-Makhon le-Ḥeqer ha-Shirah ha-ʿIvrit bi-Yerushalayim* 7 (1958), 217–18.

[106] For the corpus of R. Ephraim's *piyyutim*, see Habermann, "Piyyutei R. Ephraim b. Yaʿakov mi-Bona," 219–96, and Zunz, *LG*, 288–93. Habermann also published eleven of Ephraim's *seliḥot* and *qinot* (for various fast days and days of supplication, including two for the martyrs at Blois in 1171, אשיחה במר נפשי/עולותיכם וזבחיכם לרצון על מזבחי, and נפשי למי אוי למי אבוי), together with an edition of R. Ephraim's *Sefer Zekhirah*, a narrative account of a series of persecutions in Western Europe between the years 1171 and 1196. See Habermann, *Sefer Zekhirah, Seliḥot ve-qinot* (Jerusalem, 1970). In this collection, Habermann also points out Ephraim's use of שרשור and Spanish meter; see pp. 58, 60, 70, 96, and below, n. 108. Susan Einbinder, *Beautiful Death*, 52–54, 63–64, discusses Ephraim's *qinot* for Blois, as well as his related treatments in *Sefer Zekirah* (ibid., 31, 45, 48, 50). Cf. Robert Chazan, *Medieval Stereotypes and Modern Antisemitism* (Berkeley, Calif., 1997), 23–30, 54–57, 68–69). See also the *qinah* about the Blois incident by Ephraim's brother Hillel, אמוני שלומי ישראל (noted in Einbinder, *Beautiful Death*, 20–21, 28, 51, 55–57, 62–64), which was recited during *Musaf* of Yom Kippur (*Maḥzor le-Yamim Nora'im*, ed. Goldschmidt, 2:551–54); and *Leqet Piyyutei Seliḥot*, ed. Goldschmidt and Fraenkel, 1:180–81, for a possible *seliḥah* by Hillel for *Taʿanit Esther*, אתה הוא א-להי הראשונים/ מפליא פלאות בכל זמנים/ בעמוד צורר להשמיד זרע אמונים/ נשים ישישים ונערים וזקנים; on Hillel's authorship of this *seliḥah*, cf. ibid., 2:778. For Hillel's *maʿariv* for Rosh ha-Shanah, מלך א-להים הופיע מציון (*Maḥzor le-Yamim Nora'im*, ed. Goldschmidt, 1:21), see also ms. Jerusalem/Schocken 19522, fol. 84v; ms. Bodl. 1038, fol. 29v; and ms. Vatican 326, fol. 87v. Ephraim and Hillel are referred to as שני בני יצהר in ms. Bodl. 1104, fols. 15r–v (in a marginal note: וכן הנהיג רבינו גרשום ב"ר יהודה מאור הגולה וכן נהגו הרבה חכמים אחריו לברך עצי בשמים. ואף בדורנו נהגו שני בני יצהר ה"ר הילל וה"ר אפרים מבונא ושאר חכמי' שבדורם לברך עצי בשמים). Cf. above, Introduction, n. 88, for this passage, as well as an instruction given by Hillel regarding the composition of *Avinu Malkenu*.

[107] See אמרתי הנה באתי בשירתי בצאתי ממצרים / איכה ישבה בדד בכיתי בצאתי מירושלים . . . איכה קינה לשיר תהפך ותהי עוד לנחמתי בשובי לירושלים (Habermann, "Piyyutei R. Ephraim b. Yaʿakov mi-Bona," 225–26); and אשיחה במר נפשי יגוני / אני הגבר ראה עני / א-לי א-לי למה עזבתני, which petitions the Almighty

siyyomet miqra'it, about the *'asarah harugei malkhut*, which links their deaths to the martyrs during the period of the First Crusade, as well as to the tragedies suffered during the destruction of the Second Temple at the hands of Titus and during the days of Trajan and Hadrian);[108] for *'asarah be-Tevet* and the penitential season as well;[109] and a *ma'ariv* for Rosh ha-Shanah.[110]

As noted, R. Ephraim of Bonn had a predilection for incorporating talmudic phrases and fairly complex halakhic dicta into the poetics within his *seliḥot*, reflecting quite openly the nexus between the many possibilities for expressing truthful Torah study and interpretation and the writing of *piyyut*.[111] In addition, R. Ephraim composed an unusually ornate,

---

to retain and remember the blood of those who died in the sanctification of His name, קבל בפורפרך דמי המטהרים לשמך (Habermann, ibid., 260–64; and cf. *Midrash Tehillim*, 9:13, and Yisrael Yuval, "Ha-Naqam veha-Qelalah, ha-Dam veha-'Alilah," *Zion* 58 [1992–93], 55–60).

108 איכה ישבה בדד עגונה / רבתי עם מקוננת קינה/ הוי אריאל קרית חנה; see Habermann, ibid., 227–31, and Alter Velner, *'Asarah Harugei Malkhut* (Jerusalem, 2005), 327–33. This *qinah* refers to the עשרה צדיקים שתותי אדמה, but mentions only R. Aqiva by name. The section relating to 1096 begins, בשנת תתנ"ו לטבח נתננו / עדת קדושיו לשמך קדשנו / יגענו ולא הונח לנו, and continues, פשטו צוארם שמע ישראל כהשמיעו / יחד האב והבן בהתחברם נפגעו / דמים בדמים נגעו. The *qinah* is based on a passage in the *petiḥta* of *Eikhah Rabbah*, sec. 24, and was meant to be chanted according to the tune of a *qinah* commemorating the events of 1096 by Raban's teacher, R. Jacob b. Isaac *ha-Levi*, אוי לי על שברי (below, n. 121). Note also an elegy by R. Ephraim for those who were killed in another locale (קינה על קדושי סולי), לבי חללי לי. See Habermann, ibid., 218, and *Sefer ha-Dema'ot*, ed. Bernfeld, 1:221. E. Fleischer, *Shirat ha-Qodesh*, 483–84, uses a passage from a *qinah* by R. Ephraim to highlight the rhetorical techniques and emotional sensitivities employed (together) by Ashkenazic *payyetanim*.

109 A *seliḥah* for the tenth of Tevet in Spanish meter, איומה נדגלה לך היתה סגולה (Habermann, ibid., 231–32), has a *siyyomet miqra'it*, as does an *'aqedah*, את אבותי אני מזכיר לפניך היום (Habermann, ibid., 264–68). A *seliḥah* (*ḥatanu*) about the *'asarah harugei malkhut*, אמנה אני חטאתי לה' אך לקחתי כפלים בכל עוני (Habermann, ibid., 243–49, and Velner, *'Asarah Harugei Malkhut*, 315–25) has a *shirshur*, as well as a *siyyomet miqra'it*. This composition mentions and describes the deaths of R. Shim'on b. Gamli'el and R. Yishma'el, who were killed at the time of the destruction of the Second Temple, as well as R. Ḥananyah b. Tradyon, Ḥuẓpit *ha-meturgeman*, and R. Eliezer b. Shamu'a, who were victims of the Hadrianic persecutions. Using talmudic terminologies (such as אלו הן הנסקלים והנחנקים), the *seliḥah* links these martyrs with those who perished in persecutions that took place in Ashkenaz during the years 1190, 1192, and 1196, and expresses a basic tenet of Ashkenazic martyrdom: קדוש השיב מוטב שאמות ביסורים, ולא אעבור על דת חברים. See also Habermann, ibid., 249–52, for a *seliḥah* connected to *Zekhor Brit*; 254–56, for another *seliḥah* with a *shirshur*, אני בחסדך אבוא ביתך לשקוד על דלתותיך; and 263–64, for a *seliḥah* with a *ḥaruz 'aḥid*, סלח נא אשמתינו רבה הטה אזנך בקשתנו הקשיבה. In the *seliḥah* אהבתי כי ישמע, the *payyetan* seeks complete repentance, unlike the repentance of Ninveh (as interpreted in a negative light by passages in *Yerushalmi* [*Ta'anit* 2:1] and *Avot de-Rabbi Nathan* [ch. 41]), or the repentance of Cain: השיבנו אליך בתשובה שלמה שלא כתשובת נינוה ועובד אדמה. See also below, n. 111.

110 See *Maḥzor le-Yamim Nora'im*, ed. Goldschmidt, 1:18–20 (כס[א] ה' אורי וישעי ממי אירא ואוחילא = Habermann, ibid., 221–24; and see also ms. Verona 34, fol. 212v–213r). The main core of this *ma'ariv* is a triplet, which ends with a biblical phrase that contains a form of the word *melekh*.

111 אשיחה במר נפש יגוני (above, n. 109) contains talmudic-based phrases such as ואפילו חובל ומע־ביר תשלומי ארבעה וחמשה. The same is true for a *seliḥah* by R. Ephraim for *'erev* Rosh ha-Shanah, אני עבדך בן אמתך / ברוב חסדך אבוא ביתך (Habermann, ibid., 256–60), which refers to complex talmudic constructs and phrases such as איסור חל על איסור כולל ומוסיף אלי (*Ḥullin* 113b, *Yevamot* 32b);

metered *ʾahavah* for *Shavuʿot* with a single rhyme throughout (in which each of its seventy-three stiches ends with a form of the word *ʾahavah*)[112] and two *ʾofanim* for a *Shabbat ḥatan*. One of these *ʾofanim* was also recited on *Shavuʿot*, and contains several clear references to *Hekhalot* literature.[113] The second *ʾofan* has at least one formulation that is based on a passage in *Hekhalot* literature as well.[114] R. Ephraim also composed a *piyyut* for *E-l ʾadon* on a *Shabbat ḥatan*,[115] a lengthy, four-part *reshut* for the *ʿaliyyah* of a *ḥatan* to the Torah,[116] two poetic introductions to the grace after meals (*birkat ha-*

אפטרופוס שמנהו אבי יתומים (*Mishnah Gittin* 5:4); פקדונו ביד אחר [ה]והלא אין אדם רוצה שיהי (*Bava Meẓiʿa* 37a); וכבר בא חכם לדרוש במערב (*ʿEruvin* 36b, from a *sugya* dealing with *ʿeruvei teḥumin*); as well as numerous biblical phrases. In context, these usages are meant to highlight the significant presence of Torah study in Western Europe, as a means of achieving expiation from sin (as the *seliḥah* indicates, for example, רחום הכינו לך בימה וסניגורים להתקרב). See also Ephraim's Aramaic *teḥinnah* (for the ten days of penitence), תא שמע מרי עלמא (Habermann, ibid., 283–85), for talmudic phrases such as לכמה אבות נזיקין ונזק צררא (*Bava Qamma* 2a, 3b), and מתפגלת בפגול ונותר ונשפך הדם בעזרה (*Zevaḥim* 45a–46b; and cf. above, n. 102). For an additional such *teḥinnah*, תחלי תורה תתנני ברה בעד עם נברא לא-ל הנורא . . . שלומים תתמים ברעים תמים לך בדמים להכניס ברחמים (with Spanish meter), see Habermann, ibid., 292–94, and cf. Fraenkel, *Ha-Tefillah veha-Piyyut be-Maḥzor Nuernberg*, 115 (n. 516), for the spread of Ephraim's *teḥinot* into eastern German rites. On *piyyut* interpretation and truthful Torah study in the writings of R. Ephraim, cf. above, Introduction, n. 99.

112 Habermann, ibid., 234–36, and see also ms. Bodl. 1149, fols. 200v–202v (אחרת להבוחר מר' אפרים): איומתי אהבתיך יונתי אהנה נשגבה/ האמרתני והאמרתיך באחת חטיבה. The preceding composition in ms. Bodl. 1149 is a *ha-boher* (= an *ʾahavah*) by R.Yehudah *ha-Levi*. As Fleischer also notes (*Ha-Yozerot*, 677–80), each stanza in this *piyyut* has its starting letter doubled, so that Ephraim's name is spelled out by the first two words in each stanza. In addition, each stanza ends with a biblical verse that concludes with the word *ʾahavah*, and the final word in each stanza is the same as the first word in that stanza (which, in turn, rhymes with the beginning word of the next stanza). Fleischer characterizes R. Ephraim's poetics in this instance as "a virtuoso performance . . . and a fine example of the high artistic level that was achieved by Ashkenazic *piyyut* composition at its best." See also Fleischer, *Ha-Yoẓerot*, 674–75, for R. Ephraim's preservation or recapitulation of R. Simeon ha-Gadol's *meʾorah* and *ʾahavah* forms, as part of R. Ephraim's interest in the earlier history of Ashkenazic *piyyutim*.

113 See Habermann, ibid., 232–33, and ms. Bodl. 1149, fols. 165v–166v: אימתו קדושתי תהלתו יספרו, פאר גוחם בכל כוחם שמו גדול יפארו (in Spanish meter). Lines 12 and 13 in this *piyyut* read: ינשק צור / דמות היצור / בכס עצור והוא נכבד. As Habermann notes, this formulation is parallel to a passage in an *ʾofan* for *Shavuʿot* by R. Simeon b. Isaac of Mainz, and draws on a passage in *Hekhalot Rabbati* (8:3= *Synopse Zur Hekhalot Literatur*, ed. P. Schafer [Tubingen, 1982]), 164; and see also A. Y. Wertheimer, *Battei Midrashot* (Jerusalem, 1968), 122–23 (= *Pirqei Hekhalot Rabbati*, 35:1): מה עדות אתם רואים אתי, מה אני עושה לקלסתר פניו של יעקב אביהם שהיא חקוקה לי על כסא כבודי. כי בשעה שאתם אומרים לפני קדוש כורע אני עליה ומנשקה ומחבבה.

114 See ms. Bodl. 1149, fol. 170r (בניגון אחד קדוש), and Habermann, ibid., 241–42: א-ל אחד יחיד ומיוחד שמו / פעמים בכל יום בפי עמו / רם ונשא בשרפי מרומו / יברכו חיות לעמתם ממקומו. See lines 5–7 (and Habermann's notes) for the *Hekahlot* reference, and cf. lines 9–10.

115 א-ל אדון בורא עליונים ותחתונים/ פתח דברו האיר מתוך ראשונים (Habermann, 238, ibid., and see also idem, *Be-Ran—Yaḥad*, 166). This poem has a *ḥaruz ʾaḥid*; cf. Fleischer on this genre.

116 See Habermann, "Piyyutei R. Ephraim b. Yaʿakov mi-Bona," 274–82 (sec. 25), and ms. Bodl. 1149, fol. 229r–233r: רשות לחתן מר' אפרים ב"ר יעקב, מרשות א-להי עולם שמים וארץ קנה בהבראם לא יעף ולא יגע לכוננה. Cf. Fleischer, *Ha-Yoẓerot*, 616–17, L. Weinberger, *Jewish Hymnography*, 13, 163–64, 184–85; and M. Schmelzer, "Piyyutim li-Nesu'in," 177.

mazon) following a circumcision (and for the *ha-raḥaman* addenda toward the end of the *birkat ha-mazon*),[117] an *E-loheikhem* (for the *kedushah* to *Musaf* on the Sabbath),[118] a metered ברכו addendum for *Sukkot*,[119] and an Aramaic *piyyut* with a single rhyme for the Targumic translation of the first of the Ten Commandments.[120] Clearly, R. Ephraim of Bonn's compositions were quite varied, and similar in many respects to those of another of his older German contemporaries, Raban.

In contrast Raban's Tosafist relative and teacher, R. Jacob b. Isaac *ha-Levi* (Ya'avetz, who was perhaps the youngest son of Rashi's teacher, R. Isaac *ha-Levi* of Worms), composed only *qinot*.[121] Moreover, Raban's son-in-law R. Joel b. Isaac *ha-Levi* (d. 1200),[122] his grandson Rabiah (d. c. 1225),[123]

117 See Habermann, ibid., 236–37 (אך טוב א-להים לישראל בשבתם על כסאותם סביב לשלחן א-ל, with a *ḥaruz 'aḥid*); 239–41 (א-להים צוית לידידך בחירך את בריתי תשמר חק בשאריך, and cf. ms. Parma 908, fol. 61v); and Habermann, ibid., 268–70, secs. 22–23, for the *ha-raḥaman* addenda.

118 Zunz, *LG*, 290, sec. 9b, has one titled א-להיכם אל כל מקום גדולתו, and cf. above, n. 16.

119 See Habermann, ibid., 243, and ms. Bodl. 1149, fol. 191v (אמונים באורו לכן עליו תסמכו שבחו תערכו בית ישראל ברכו את ה'). In his note to line 3, Habermann suggests an esoteric passage from *Sefer Yeẓirah* as the basis for R. Ephraim's formulation. On this genre (which perhaps reflects Spanish influence), cf. Fleischer, *Shirat ha-Qodesh*, 142, 144, 369, 472, and below, n. 138.

120 See *Maḥzor Shavu'ot*, ed. Fraenkel, 416 (אנא אליפית אוריתי לעמא), which has a *ḥaruz mavriaḥ*. See also the editor's introduction, 29–30, and Habermann, ibid., 252–54.

121 On the identity of R. Jacob b. Isaac *ha-Levi*, see Aptowitzer, *Mavo la-Rabiah*, 354–56; Urbach, *Ba'alei ha-Tosafot*, 1:186–89 (who also describes his *Tosafot*); Grossman, *Ḥakhmei Ashkenaz ha-Rishonim*, 272, 354–57; and Matania Ben-Ghedalia, "Ha-Reqa ha-Histori li-Ketivat Sefer Even ha-'Ezer," 41–44. See also the chain of tradition recorded in *Teshuvot Maharshal* #29, and cf. S. Emanuel, *Shivrei Luḥot*, 53, n. 7. See also Emanuel, 83, for R. Jacob's *Tosafot*; 233, n. 56, for one of R. Jacob's *pesaqim*; as well as ms. Montefiore 101, fols. 57v–58r. R. Jacob composed a *qinah* for the ninth of Av, on the persecutions at Worms in 1096, אוי לי על שברי / נחלה וגברה מכתי / ממני אמרר בבכי. See A. David, "Historical Records of the Persecutions" (above, n. 23), 197, sec. 4; Urbach, *Ba'alei ha-Tosafot*, 1:188; the Worms rite found in ms. Prague (National Library) VII EA2 right after *Megillat Eikhah*, and also in ms. Parma 586, fols. 163r–165r; ms. Vatican 319, sec. 31; and ms. Vatican 312, fols. 55r–56r. A second *qinah* for the ninth of Av by Jacob b. Isaac *ha-Levi*, אדרת תפארתי כותרת התורה (which is not listed by I. Davidson), is found in ms. Parma 635, sec. 22.

122 Aptowitzer, *Mavo la-Rabiah*, 47, lists seven *piyyutim* by R. Yo'el (which is one more than Zunz had recorded). Four of them are included in the standard *seliḥot* rites for *erev* Rosh ha-Shanah and *Ẓom Gedalyah*. See *Seder ha-Seliḥot*, ed. Goldschmidt, secs. 28 (74–78), 30 (80–83), 31 (83–88), 55 (158–61). R. Yo'el also composed an *'aqedah*, אכן ה' צדיק יבחן; another *seliḥah*, שמעה קול תחנוני; and a *qinah* (שלישיה) for the martyrs at Cologne in 1147 (קינה על גזירת קולוניא יבכיון מר מלאכי שלום ואבות, בניגון מי ימלל). See, e.g., ms. Parma 585, fol. 156r; ms. Bodl. 1025, fol. 154v; Habermann, *Be-Ran—Yaḥad*, 154; and idem., *Gezerot Ashkenaz ve-Ẓarefat*, 109–12. For commentaries to R. Yo'el's *seliḥot*, see E. Hollender, *Clavis Commentatorium of Hebrew Liturgical Poetry in Manuscript*, 266, 306, 369.

123 See Aptowitzer, *Mavo la-Rabiah*, 134–39, who publishes (and analyzes) four of Rabiah's *piyyutim*: a *pizmon* for a circumcision during the ten days of penitence or perhaps on a fast day, אל תפר בריתך אתנו (see ms. Parma 588, sec. 13); another *pizmon* for a circumcision that occurs on a fast day, א-להינו א-ל ש-די ברוך הוא (found in ms. Leiden Scal. 413, fols. 159v–160r, and ms. Bodl. 1098, fols. 49r–49v); an *'aqedah*, אמרתי כבר יכבדך שוע והילך . . . קראתי בשמך לי אתה (see *Leqet Piyyutei Seliḥot*, ed. Goldschmidt and Fraenkel, 56–59); and a *qinah* that commemorates the events of 1096, הרג רב ויום טבוח בתתנ"ו נגזרה גזירה; see also below, n. 128. Another *seliḥah* by

and one of their judicial colleagues, Gershom b. Isaac, also wrote only *seliḥot* and *qinot.*[124] Owing perhaps to R. Joel's close tutorial relationship with R. Ephraim of Regensburg,[125] whose extensive use of Spanish poetic techniques will be noted and discussed below,[126] two of R. Joel's *seliḥot* contain a *siyyomet miqra'it*, while a third—which mourns the loss of the *ʿasarah harugei malkhut*, and is typically recited on the Fast of Gedalyah—has stanzas that end with either a biblical or mishnaic phrase, in addition to employing the literary technique of *shirshur.*[127] Only three stanzas from Rabiah's *qinah* that commemorates the events of 1096 (which begins יום הרג וטבוח רב, covering the letters *heh* through *ʿayin*) have survived. We know of their existence

Rabiah, אפפוני חבלי מות מדני (a *shelishiyyah* with a *soger miqra'it*), includes a word with a form of the verb ברך at the conlusion of each stanza; see *Leqet Piyyutei Seliḥhot*, 59–63, and ms. Parma 588, sec. 135. See ms. Vatican 319, sec. 47: איכה יועם ומשחת מראה מהרב ר' אל[י]עזר בן הרב ר' יואל מעיר בונא. Aptowitzer, *Mavo la-Rabiah*, 134, 140, also notes that Rabiah composed two brief poetic preambles to introduce the tractates *Pesaḥim* and *Sukkah* in his *Sefer Rabiah*, in addition to the rhetorical flourishes with which he sometimes began his responsa. None of these, of course, is a full-fledged *piyyut.* Cf. M. Schmelzer, *Meqarim*, 177–87, for the seven such introductory poems (almost like *reshuyyot*) that Rivaq of Speyer included in his *Sefer Yiḥusei Tanna'im ve-Amora'im*. Similarly, Rabiah's teacher, R. Eliezer of Metz, included eleven poetic introductions in his *Sefer Yere'im*. See also *Perushei R. Yosef Bekhor Shor ʿal ha-Torah*, ed. Y. Nevo (Jerusalem, 1994), where each of the Torah portions in the books of Genesis and Exodus concludes with a brief poem, as does the portion of *Devarim*. See also Jonathan Jacob, "Tosafot she-Hosif Rashbam le-Perusho la-Torah," *Tarbiz* 66 (2007), 468–69, and below, n. 160.

124 Gershom b. Isaac was a member of the *beit din ʿara'i* that was established in Cologne to hear a case in which R. Yo'el, a member of the permanent court, was the guardian of a widow who needed to have her case adjudicated (thus necessitating the second, temporary court; see above, chapter 1, n. 39). Gershom composed two elegies for Blois, איש לבוש הבדים (see *Leqet Piyyutei Seliḥot*, ed. Goldschmidt and Fraenkel, 1:137–43; each stanza concludes with a verse that contains a form of the word אש), and a sequel, גאל לך אתה את גאולתי (*Leqet Piyyutei Seliḥot*, 143–48; here too there is a *soger min ha-miqra* that contains the word *'esh*); and a *teḥinnah* with a *ḥaruz 'aḥid*, אבואה ואכרעה ברגל ישרה (*Leqet Piyyutei Seliḥot*, 1:149–52). Although Zunz (*LG*, 294) definitively attributes this *teḥinnah* to Gershom, cf. *Leqet Piyyutei Seliḥot*, 2:777. On Gershom's Blois elegies, cf. Einbinder, *Beautiful Death*, 28–29, 42, n. 46, 51–52, 59–64, 166. Although Gershom's elegies clearly allude to a variety of talmudic sources (and also refer explicitly to *tofsei ha-Torah*), Gershom is among the least established of the rabbinic scholars who were the authors of the various Blois laments, a group that includes R. Barukh of Mainz, R. Ephraim of Bonn (and his brother Hillel), R. Yosef *Bekhor Shor* of Orleans, and R. Yom Tov of Joigny.

125 See Urbach, *Baʿalei ha-Tosafot*, 1:201–3, 210–12.

126 See below, n. 162.

127 See *Seder ha-Seliḥot*, ed. Goldschmidt, sec. 28 (א-ל אלו-ה דלפה עיני אשוה ויאמר הנני); sec. 30 (א-להים יראה לו שה פזורה ויושע); and sec. 55 (a *ḥatanu*, יקרו רעיך רב מחולל / אדום לה' ולא אתחלל / באויב אשר בעמי מסתולל / על זאת יתפלל). The Mishnaic phrases in the *ḥatanu* come from tractates *Makkot*, *Zevaḥim*, *Sanhedrin*, and *Nedarim*, and several of the verses that mark the ends of stanzas come from the Book of Job. R. Yo'el alludes to R. Aqiva and his fellow martyrs in a number of phrases, but he mentions only R. Yishma'el and R. Shimʿon b. Gamli'el by name, at the very end of his composition. See A. Veller, *ʿAsarah Harugei Malkhut*, 303–10. On the Spanish influences reflected in R. Yo'el's liturgical compositions, see also Fraenkel, *Ha-Tefillah veha-Piyyut be-Maḥzor Nuernberg*, 116, 118–19. R. Yo'el's second son, Uri, was martyred in Cologne in 1216. See, e.g., my "*Peering through the Lattices,*" 165.

because these stanzas were appended to Raban's *zulat* for the Sabbath before the fast of the seventeenth of Tammuz or for *Shabbat Ḥazon.*[128]

Nonetheless, this last group of German authors at the turn of the twelfth century, as compared to Raban and R. Ephraim of Bonn, serves to establish that the two broad patterns of *piyyut* composition which were evident in the pre-Crusade period and in northern France through the mid-twelfth century—of *seliḥot* only on the one hand, and of a more varied output that relates to both festive and somber occasions on the other—were both represented in Germany as well. Moreover, within both Germany and northern France, these patterns could vary even within leading Tosafist families and between teachers and their students. The decision to compose *piyyutim* was a most personal one on some level, and was surely not the same as a commitment to halakhic or biblical study and formulation. At the same time, the consistent presence of these compositional patterns throughout the twelfth century, which takes quite a few Tosafists into account as we have seen, suggests that this discipline had not lost its attractiveness for Ashkenazic talmudic scholars with the transition from the pre-Crusade period. Our survey of German Tosafist *payyetanim* has already extended to the first quarter of the thirteenth century. A significant group of Rabbenu Tam's students, as well as some of their students, also composed *piyyutim*, from the last quarter of the twelfth century through the first quarter of the thirteenth century, and it is to their literary productivity that we now turn.

The Students of Rabbenu Tam

Among Rabbenu Tam's northern French talmudic students who were also *payyetanim*, his nephew R. Isaac b. Samuel of Dampierre (Ri, d. 1189) composed a series of *piyyutim.* Several of the unique forms that had been favored by Rabbenu Tam were produced by Ri as well, including *piyyutim* that were assigned to the second Sabbath of Ḥanukkah, and post-*havdalot.*[129] Ri also

[128] See, e.g., ms. Paris (Cluny Museum) 12290, fols. 244r–245v. For Raban's *zulat*, א-להים באזנינו שמענו אבותינו ספרו לנו, see above, n. 90. See also A. David, "Historical Records of the Persecutions" (above, n. 23), secs. 11, 16 (where הרג רב ויום טבוח is listed without attribution). See also the marginal note to ms. Bodl. 1099, fol. 81r: זולת זה יסד רבי' אב"ן ושלשה פרקים הללו יסד ר' אבי העזרי בן בתו; Habermann, *Gezerot Ashkenaz ve-Ẓarefat*, 82–84; and Aptowitzer, *Mavo la-Rabiah*, 134.

[129] For Ri's *yoẓer* for the second Sabbath of Ḥanukkah, see Davidson, *Oẓar ha-Shirah veha-Piyyut*, 1:115 (2443:א), אחורה שמעוני חכמי ונבוני. See also ms. Modena (Archivio di Stato), 416–21 (a western Ashkenazic rite, from *Shemini ʿAẓeret* to *Ḥanukkah*), at the beginning of 419. Another *piyyut* for the second Shabbat of Ḥanukkah that has been attributed to Ri, יתנו צדקות י-ה בה' חוסים, is a so-called *shalom* insertion at the end of the *ʿAmidah*, which is typically found only within Sefardic liturgies. See Landshuth, *ʿAmmudei ʿAvodah*, 127; Davidson, *Oẓar ha-Shirah veha-Piyyut*, 2:459 (4348:י); and cf. E. Fleischer, *Shirat ha-Qodesh*, 385. For Ri's *havdalah* poem for *Moẓaʾei Shabbat*, אבי סגני כהונה ולויה (with the refrain איש הנביא אליה), see ms. Parma 352, fols.

composed an Aramaic *reshut* for the Targum of the *Haftarah* on *Shavu'ot*, as Rabbenu Tam did.[130] Moreover, he composed several addenda to the reader's repetition of the *'Amidah*, a rather rare venue for *piyyutim* by this time. These include an introductory *silluq* and three inserts to the *kedushah* of the morning service for the first days of Passover (which contain single and internal rhymes as well as a *siyyomet miqra'it* and *shirshur*),[131] and a *qerovah* for the reader's repetition during *Musaf* on the first day of Passover, just after the prayer for dew (also with a *haruz mavriah*).[132] Ri also composed a *pizmon*

36r–37r; *Mahzor Vitry*, ed. S. Hurwitz (Warsaw, 1923), vol. 1 (*liqutei batar liqutei*), 181; cf. Davidson, ibid., 1:4 (56:א). Another *havdalah le-Motza'ei Shabbat* (with the same refrain), titled 'יד ה' היתה עלי צפויה, is recorded in Davidson, ibid., 2:271 (275:י), and in ms. Parma 352, fol. 37v–39a. Indeed, ms. Parma 352 contains *piyyut* material from other students of Rabbenu Tam (including R. Ephraim of Regensburg, and Ri ha-Lavan; see below, nn. 158, 168), as well as a *havdalah* from Rabbenu Tam himself (above, n. 78). See also Davidson, ibid., 2:351 (2003:י), for יונה בחגוי סלע נחבאה, written either by Ri or by his student R. Isaac b. Abraham (Rizba) of Dampierre (for Purim), found in *Mahzor Vitry*, 220 (and attributed there to רבינו יצחק מדנפירא), and see the next note. As noted already above, identification of Ri's *piyyutim* is not always a simple matter, in part because Rizba was also from Dampierre, and in part because the father of R. Meir *Shaz* was also named Isaac b. Samuel; see e.g., Zunz, *LG*, 168–69, 262, 283; Urbach, *Ba'alei ha-Tosafot*, 1:260; and below, n. 133. Note also the Provençal *payyetan* named R. Isaac b. Samuel *ha-Levi*; see Binyamin Bar-Tikva, *Genres and Topics in Provençal and Catalonian Piyyut* [Hebrew] (Beer Sheva, 2009), 44.

130 E. Fleischer, "Tefillah u-Piyyut be-Mahzor Vermaiza," 33, 39, identifies the Aramaic *reshut* for the *Haftarah* on the seventh day of Passover (found on fol. 102 of the Worms Mahzor), אלימו כעין דמנכון כזיז (which has a *haruz mavriah* and an internal rhyme scheme, and is also found, unattributed, in *Mahzor Vitry*, 164–65), as a *piyyut* of Ri, as does Y. Fraenkel in the introduction to his *Mahzor Pesah*, 45, sec. 5. In the body of this *Mahzor*, however (*Mahzor Pesah*, 638), it is noted that while ms. Bodl. 2373 (Laud. Or. 321) identifies this composition as רשות למפטיר דרבינו יצחק מדנפור, ms. Verona 34 attributes this to Ri's student, Rizba (רבינו יצחק ברבי אברהם הבחור מדנפירא, although it is difficult to identify any other *piyyutim* written by Rizba). Cf. Urbach, *Ba'alei ha-Tosafot*, 1:270 (n. 46); Zunz, *LG*, 335, 622; and Landshuth, *'Ammudei 'Avodah*, 69. For a comment attributed to Rizba on a *piyyut*, see Zunz, *Der Ritus des synagogalen Gottesdienstes*, 197, and Fraenkel, *Ha-Tefillah veha-Piyyut be-Mahzor Nuerenberg*, 174. Rizba also cites (and explains) *piyyutim* in his *Tosafot* comments (as other Tosafists do), but it does not appear that he authored more sustained *piyyut* commentaries.

131 Ri's poetic inserts to the *kedushah* include: א-ל נא אסירים הוצאת בכושרות ביד רמה בקול שרים ושרות (which has a *haruz mavriah*); יצקדו ויתהללו במלך רם ונשא חסין קחת גוי מקרב גוי ניסה (which has a *haruz mavriah* and an internal rhyme); יצאת לישע עמך באין מעצור (which has a *siyyomet miqra'it*); and his *silluq*, תוסיף ידך לקנות שאר / שאר יעקב בשבטך רעה (with a שרשור); see *Mahzor Pesah*, ed. Fraenkel, 126–34. As Fraenkel notes in his introduction, 36, not all of the poetic sections intended by Ri to be added to a particular *qedushta* by Qallir have survived. See above, n. 31, for the *qedushtot* produced by R. Yosef *Tov 'Elem*.

132 For Ri's insert for the *'Amidah* (following the prayer for dew), יצלצלו חובבים קול שמחים וגילים / זבול כוננו רועים להמוני דגלים / טבח יובל שי אילים ועגלים / ויעלו בשנה מדי שלש רגלים (with a *haruz mavriah*), see *Mahzor Pesah*, 243–44; Davidson, *Ozar ha-Shirah veha-Piyyut*, 2:421, 3538:י; and *Mahzor Vitry*, 298–99 (where it is unattributed). See also Davidson, 2:430 (3743:י), for a *zulat* by Ri for the seventh day of Passover, יראה טהורה יראו הנורא.

for Yom Kippur, among other *seliḥot.*[133] Similarly, Ri's son Elḥanan (who died a martyr's death in 1184) composed a *ma'ariv* for the last days of *Pesaḥ* which has a biblical phrase embedded in each line,[134] an Aramaic *reshut* for the *Haftarah* on the second day of *Shavu'ot* with Spanish meter (and a *ḥaruz 'aḥid*),[135] an opening *seliḥah* for the ten days of penitence,[136] and a *reshut* for the recitation of ברכו on the eve of a festival,[137] a genre that reflects Sefardic infuence.[138]

The eight extant *piyyutim* produced by another of Rabbenu Tam's students in northern France, R. Yom Tov b. Isaac of Joigny—who settled in England circa 1180 and died a martyr's death in York in 1190, and whose

133 See *Maḥzor le-Yamim Nora'im*, ed. Goldschmidt, 2:562, יחביאנו צל ידו תחת כנפי השכינה. This *pizmon* was apparently designated for the *Musaf* service, but it is included in a number of rites for *Ne'ilah*. Ri's other *seliḥot* include אליך ה׳ אזעק וצרתי אזכיר (see *Leqet Piyyutei Seliḥot*, 1:357–59); שמע הא-להים קול רנינו (Davidson, *Ozar ha-Shirah veha-Piyyut*, 3:58, 1260:ל); לעמו ישראל יצו ה׳ סליחה (Davidson, ibid., 3:489, 1758:ש); שקר החן והבל היופי (Davidson, ibid., 3:510, 5016:ש, and cf. *Maḥzor Vitry*, ed. Hurwitz, vol. 1, *liqqutei batar liqqutei*, 182). The attribution of two additional (unrhymed) *seliḥot* to Ri remains unconfirmed: א-לי א-לי אזון אנקתי (Davidson, ibid., 1:226, 4900:א), and אליך ה׳ אקרא בעטוף לבי (Davidson, ibid., 1:231, 5016:א). See also *Leqet Piyyutei Seliḥot*, 1:359–61, and 2:809. Davidson, ibid., 1:183 (3954:א) attributes the *pizmon*, א-ל עוררה נא ולבוש ישע, to Ri's student, R. Judah Sirleon of Paris; see also *Leqet Piyyutei Seliḥot*, 1:217–19. This *seliḥah* appears (as does the above-noted אליך ה׳ אעזק) in ms. Parma 654, vol. 2 (fol. 215), which contains compositions from a number of other northern French Tosafists including R. Yom Tov of Joigny, R. Tuvyah of Vienne, and R. Isaac b. Isaac of Chinon, among others. See above, nn. 98–99; and below, nn. 144, 148, 152, 264–66, 272. A young Jerusalem scholar, Avraham Levin, has tentatively suggested on the basis of additional manuscript evidence that some of these *seliḥot* attributed to Ri were composed by an eleventh-century northern French *payyetan* of the same name. I thank my student Gabriel Wasserman for bringing Levin's efforts to my attention.

134 See *Maḥzor Pesaḥ*, ed. Goldschmidt, 387–90, אזכיר צדקתך ה׳ לבדיך / ברוגז רחם תזכור עבדיך / גבור שבענו בבוקר חסדך / ולערב אל תנח ידיך.

135 See *Maḥzor Shavu'ot*, ed. Fraenkel, 576–79, beginning with the phrase אבובא לחרי דמרא and concluding with the phrase הן לא מתידע סברא אלמלא תרגומאי. This *piyyut* has two fixed rhymes in each line that alternate throughout.

136 For this *petiḥah* (typically assigned to the fourth day), אשת נעורים האהובה / אשר ארשתה ברב מוהר ורב טובה / ואיך אתה יושבת עלובה / געולה מאוסה ועזובה, see *Seder ha-Seliḥot*, ed. Goldschmidt, 211 (sec. 78), and ms. Prague 246, fol. 4r. Cf. Habermann, *Be-Ran—Yaḥad*, 161; Zunz, *Literaturgeschichte*, 287–88; and Hollender, *Clavis Commentatorium of Hebrew Liturgical Poetry in Manuscript*, 504 (entries 8964–69).

137 See ms. Bodl. 1149, fol. 189v (אחי שאו משאת [קומו] רננו וברכו את ה׳ לשמך א-ל תן כבוד); Davidson, *Ozar ha-Shirah veha-Piyyut*, 1:118 (493:א); and *Maḥzor Vitry*, 568. Two *piyyutim* are attributed to an Elḥanan, and are possibly by R. Elḥanan b. Isaac: א-ל לעמך רצה (Davidson, ibid., 1:174, 3257:א), and א-ל נורא ואיום יצו עזו (Davidson, ibid., 1:181, 3908:א), an unusual *reshut* for the *Haftarah* of *parashat Shemini*. Note also a *me'orah* by R. Samuel b. Isaac for a *Shabbat ḥatan*, שובי נא מכל פינה. See Fraenkel, *Ha-Tefillah veha-Piyyut be-Maḥzor Nuerenberg*, 55; Zunz, *LG*, 313; and cf. Urbach, *Ba'alei ha-Tosafot*, 1:248.

138 See above, n. 119, and E. Fleischer, *Shirat ha-Qodesh ha-'Ivrit Bimei ha-Benayim*, 400, 466. *Piyyutim* for *kaddish* and *barkhu* (among other genres) by R. Judah *ha-Levi* (ר׳ יהודה קשטילין) are also present in ms. Bodl. 1149, and in the parallel ms. Bodl. 1099 (fols. 85v, 87v, 90v, 93v, 147r) as well. See also below, n. 295.

comments to the Torah were discussed above in chapter 2—adhere to the compositional pattern of Ri and R. Elḥanan. R. Yom Tov's *piyyutim* include an Aramaic *reshut* (to the Sixth Commandment). This is a complex composition that begins with a passage in the *Mekhilta* which compares the commandments that appear side by side on the *luḥot ha-berit*, in this instance, *ʾanokhi* and *lo tirẓaḥ*. R. Yom Tov paraphrases quite a bit of halakhic and talmudic material here, in addition to putting forward a number of wordplays.[139] He also composed a metered *reshut* to the *Haftarah* on the second day of *Shavuʿot*,[140] a *seliḥah* for the night of Yom Kippur with Spanish meter that displays specific similarities to the liturgical poetry of R. Yehudah *ha-Levi*,[141] three additional *seliḥot*,[142] a *reshut* for *kaddish* on the festivals,[143] as well as a *qinah* that commemorated the burning of the Jews at Blois in 1171, which also displays familiarity with aspects of Spanish poetics in both the strophic form of this lament and its quantitative meter. As both R. Ephraim of Bonn and his brother Hillel did, R. Yom Tov identifies two of the heroic Blois martyrs by name, Yeḥiʾel and Yequtiʾel (who are described by R. Ephraim as students of "R. Jacob and R. Meir").[144]

[139] See *Maḥzor Shavuʿot*, ed. Fraenkel, 476, ארישא דמגילתא [=עשרת הדברות] איתחזי חתימות ידא דב־ריינא. See also ms. B.M. Or. 2735, fol. 43v, and ms. B.M. Add. 11639, fol. 218. This *piyyut* was transposed into Hebrew and analyzed by Avraham Tal, "Piyyut Arami le-Shavuʿot," *Leshonenu* 38 (1974), 257–68. Cf. M. Schmelzer, *Meḥqarim*, 2–3. R. Yom Tov embedded his name in several *piyyutim* as R. Yom Tov b. Isaac *ha-Qadosh*. On the connotation of *ha-Qadosh* with respect to R. Yom Tov's father, R. Isaac, see my *"Peering through the Lattices,"* 46–47.

[140] See *Maḥzor Shavuʿot*, 573–75, יציב אבעה קדם קודשא דבריך הוא יבני מקדשא, and cf. above, n. 81.

[141] See *Maḥzor le-Yamim Noraʾim*, ed. Goldschmidt, 2:28–30 (אמנם כן יצר שוכן בנו; in some versions, this *seliḥah* begins with יום יום ידרושון לך טוב ומעוז). This composition is described and analyzed by Y. Fraenkel in his *Maʿayanot le-Yamim Noraʾim* (Jerusalem, 1968), 497ff., and see also D. Goldschmidt, *Meḥqerei Tefillah u-Piyyut*, 372–74 (= *Leshonenu* 32 [1971], 312–15), who notes the stylistic affinities with techniques of R. Yehudah *ha-Levi*. This composition may originally been a *maʿariv*, which then transitioned into a *seliḥah* that was recited after the *ʿAmidah*. See also L. Weinberger, *Jewish Hymnology*, 189, and L. Zunz, *LG*, 286–87.

[142] תפארתך לבל תבחן (Davidson, *Ozar ha-Shirah veha-Piyyut*, 3:537, 454:ת); אביוני אדם (Davidson, ibid., 1:3, 203:א); and י-ה רעיון לבך מעשות מי יחדיל (Davidson, ibid., 2:308, 1114:י).

[143] יגדל כחך ניב דל בורא לעם לך נבדל; see Davidson, ibid., 2:267 (199:י), and cf. above, n. 138, on the origins of this genre.

[144] On this *qinah*, י-ה תשפוך חמתך, and its similarities to Spanish poetics, see Haim Schirmann, *Qinot ʿal ha-Gezerot be-Ereẓ Yisraʾel, Afriqah, Sefarad, Ashkenaz, Ẓarefat* (Jerusalem, 1939), 13–15. See also ms. Parma 654, sec. 251; S. Einbinder, *Beautiful Death*, 51, 55–59, 66 (n. 21); and above, n. 104. Einbinder notes that the familiarity with Spanish poetics reflected in this composition is found also in some of the *piyyutim* of R. Yom Tov's teacher, Rabbenu Tam, and in those of other students of Rabbenu Tam, as we have seen. Einbinder also notes that Yom Tov was himself eulogized as a martyr in a *piyyut* by Joseph of Chartres on the persecutions of York in 1190. See also L. Weinberger, *Jewish Hymnology*, 14, 190. Urbach, *Baʿalei ha-Tosafot*, 1:146, assigns a guideline concerning the text of the Friday night *ʿAmidah* that appears in *Maḥzor Vitry*, 143 (sec. 155), to R. Yom Tov of Joigny. This attribution, however, is uncertain. The comment in *Maḥzor Vitry* is attributed to "my teacher R. Yom Tov" (כך קבלתי ממורי ר׳ יו״ט), which may refer to R. Yom Tov b. Judah, the son of (Rashi's son-in-law) Rivan (cf. *Baʿalei ha-Tosafot* 1:120–22).

At the same time, R. Eliezer b. Solomon, a possible student of Rabbenu Tam who sent him halakhic questions, composed a *reshut* for *Ma'ariv* (to ברכו) on the *yamim nora'im*, with a *haruz 'ahid*,[145] and a *pizmon* for the ten days of penitence that employs Sefardic meter and a *siyyomet miqra'it*, as it weaves together biblical and talmudic conceptions and phrases about sin and repentance.[146] Similarly, R. Joseph b. Isaac (*Bekhor Shor*) of Orleans, another of Rabbenu Tam's direct students, composed a *Hoshanah*, א-ל נערץ בסוד קדושים רבה ברך אום מיוחדת ברוח נדיבה, which has a single repeating rhyme (a *haruz mavriah*) throughout,[147] along with six *selihot* and one *qinah*.

The best known of R. Joseph's *selihot*, אדון מועד כתקח מישרים לשפוט בתעצומיך (for *erev* Rosh ha-Shanah), has a *siyyomet miqra'it* throughout.[148] The second half of this composition, which begins with the letter *mem* (מרבים צרכי עמך ודעתם קצרה / מחסורם ומשאלותם בל יוכלו לספרה / נא בינה הגיגנו טרם נקרא / הא-ל הגדול

We have discussed Yom Tov of Joigny's extensive comments to the Torah above, at the end of chapter 2. Ms. Parma (de Rossi) 403, fols. 137v–143r, contains a commentary to several of the Aramaic *piyyutim* on the Ten Commandments by R. Moses b. Moses, the son-in-law of Yom Tov of Joigny (which appears along with a comment by R. Shemayah, a prolific *piyyut* commentator and student of Rashi), שלש הדברות פי' רבינו משה בן משה והינו חתנו של ר' יום טוב מי(ג)וני. Cf. Urbach, *Ba'alei ha-Tosafot*, 1:255, who notes that an "otherwise unknown" R. Moses b. Moses is cited by R. Elhanan, son of Ri, in his *Tosafot*.

145 See *Mahzor Vitry*, 566 (אמרו לא-להים עם אחריו נוחים). See also Zunz, *LG*, 293–94, and Davidson, *Ozar ha-Shirah veha-Piyyut*, 1:268 (5868:א).

146 See *Seder Selihot*, ed. Goldschmidt, 226–28 (sec. 84), for the fourth day of the ten days of penitence (בין כסה לעשור השלכנו רוע שאור, צדקנו במשפט באור החיים לאור), and see also Fraenkel, *Ha-Tefillah veha-Piyyut be-Mahzor Nuernberg*, 122. R. Eli'ezer's question to Rabbenu Tam (which begins with a poetic opening) is recorded in *Sefer ha-Yashar*, ed. Rosenthal, 131–33 (sec. 58); cf. Urbach, *Ba'alei ha-Tosafot*, 1:61.

147 See *Mahzor Sukkot*, ed. Goldschmidt, 207–8. This genre, as we have seen, was also pursued by two venerable Ashkenazic *payyetanim*, R. Yosef *Tov 'Elem* and R. Menahem b. Makhir, and is essentially one of supplication (which also reflects Spanish *piyyut*). See above, nn. 37, 58. On R. Yosef *Bekhor Shor*'s exposure to Spanish methodologies of biblical interpretation and thought, see above, chapter 2. The only other well-known twelfth-century Ashkenazic rabbinic figure to compose a *Hoshana* was R. Samuel *he-Hasid*; see below, n. 174.

148 In *Tarbiz* 9 (1937–38), 323–42, Abraham Habermann published five of *Bekhor Shor*'s *selihot* that are found in ms. Paris 654. The *selihah* for *erev* Rosh ha-Shanah (which according to some versions begins with the phrase אדון כתקח מועד לשפוט משירים בתעצומיך) is found there on p. 325. See also *Sefer ha-Selihot*, ed. Goldschmidt, 69–71 (secs. 25–26); ms. Vatican 316, fol. 3v; ms. JNUL Heb. 4*1125, fol. 77 (sec. 27); ms. Prague (Museum) 250 (#46940; in this eastern Ashkenazic rite, this *selihah* is listed during the morning service on Yom Kippur, with the second half repeated during *Ne'ilah* as well); and ms. Bologna (Archive) 165 (which contains a number of Ashkenazic *piyyut* fragments from the twelfth and thirteenth centuries). Habermann also published the *selihot* א-ל אדון רב העלילה . . . והוציאנו ה' מיגון לשמחה ה' שמעה . . . אל-הי הרחמים והסליחות; א-להי הא-להים ואדוני האדונים (found also in Habermann, *Be-Ran—Yahad*, 147, and in *Leqet Piyyutei Selihot*, ed. Goldschmidt and Fraenkel, 1:265–68); אין לבנון די בער; and . . . א-להים ממכון שבתך וישוב ממרומים לירושלים ברחמים (and see also ms. Parma 855, fol. 304v, and *Leqet Piyyutei Selihot*, 1:268–71). *Leqet Piyyut Selihot*, 1:271–74, also contains an *'aqedah*, ה' אורי וישעי וגאוות חרבי, that was not published by Habermann. On *Bekhor Shor*'s authorship of the *'aqedah*, cf. *Leqet Piyyutei Selihot*, 2:780–82, and Zunz, *LG*, 282–83.

הגבור והנורא), was also recited during *Ne'ilah.*[149] As Urbach has noted, R. Joseph *Bekhor Shor*'s *seliḥot*, like his Torah commentary, reflect the vicissitudes of his time, although his *qinah* for the martyrs of Blois, ה' אליך עיני ישברו, is particularly suggestive in this regard, as Susan Einbinder has demonstrated. Just as *Bekhor Shor*, in his Torah commentary, often sought to minimize the miracles that occurred to various biblical figures,[150] *Bekhor Shor*'s *qinah* for Blois plays down the miraculous aspects of the martyrs' deaths, such as the imperviousness of the bodies of the scholars to the fire at the stake (which were highlighted in other *piyyutim* about this event), stressing instead the physical ordeals of fire and water that the martyrs endured and the great faith they displayed.[151]

The pattern of writing only *seliḥot* continues with *Bekhor Shor*'s son R. Abraham, who also studied with Rabbenu Tam and was the father-in-law of R. Judah Sirleon of Paris (d. 1224), a leading student of Ri. R. Abraham composed two *seliḥot*, including one for the tenth of *Tevet.*[152] R. Eliezer b. Aaron of Burgundy was one of the recipients of the letter sent in 1203 by R. Meir b. Todros *ha-Levi* Abulafiah (Ramah) of Toledo to R. Samson of Sens and other northern French rabbinic figures in the context of the nascent Maimonidean controversy, and he authored the no longer extant halakhic work *Sha'arei ha-Panim*, which focuses on *hilkhot 'issur ve-heter.*[153] R. Eliezer also appears to have composed only *seliḥot.*[154] Nonetheless, it is quite clear

149 See *Maḥzor le-Yamim Nora'im*, ed. Goldschmidt, 2:761–63, and the above note; and cf. *Berakhot* 30b.

150 See, e.g., S. A. Poznanski, *Mavo 'al Ḥakhmei Ẓarefat Mefarshei ha-Miqra*, LXVII; *Perushei R. Yosef Bekhor Shor 'al ha-Torah*, ed. Nevo, editor's introduction, 15; and above, chapter 2, n. 51.

151 See Urbach, *Ba'alei ha-Tosafot*, 1:140, and Einbinder, *Beautfiul Death*, 30, 52, 63 69 (nn. 58–59). *Bekhor Shor*'s elegy for the martyrs of Blois, ה' אליך עיני ישברו, was not included by Habermann in his collection, but is found in *Leqet Piyyutei Seliḥot*, 1:263–65. For *Bekhor Shor*'s brief poetic summations in his Torah commentary, see above, n. 123. For his reckonings of the *tequfot*, see my "Anthropomorphism and Rationalist Modes of Thought in Medieval Ashkenaz: The Case of R. Yosef *Bekhor Shor*," *Simon Dubnow Institute Yearbook* 8 (2009), 120 (n. 4).

152 On the talmudic teachings of R. Abraham b. Yosef *Bekhor Shor* (and his connection to R. Judah Sirleon), see Urbach, *Ba'alei ha-Tosafot*, 1:40–42, 322. See also ms. Parma 1237, fols. 46r–46v, חלוקות בגירושין, חתום אני הצעיר מתלמידי הדור, אברהם בן יוסף. Abraham's *seliḥot* are אדון עולם ומלואו עם בשמך (Davidson, *Ozar ha-Shirah veha-Piyyut*, 1:30, 588:א), and נקראו הרם למעלה, איך נמכרו ביד אויביהם, גוי עז פנים שולט עליהם (Davidson, ibid., 1:133, 2831:א), for the tenth of *Tevet*. A *payyetan* of the same name from southern Germany (d. 1298) composed a so-called Zionide *qinah* for the ninth of Av (following the model of R. Judah *ha-Levi*), ציון הלא תשאלי לשלום אמוניך (Davidson, ibid., 3:321, 2913:צ, and cf. below, n. 183), as well as a *reshut le-ḥatan*, מרשות אב ורם א-ל עליון (Davidson, ibid., 3:182, 2441:מ). Cf. Zunz, *LG*, 494; M. Schmelzer, "Piyyutei Nisu'in," 178, sec. 16; and ms. Hamburg 130 (#1044). Ms. Hamburg 130 also contains *yoẓerot* by R. Samuel *Ḥazzan* of Erfurt (below, n. 333), R. Meir of Rothenburg, and Isaac *ha-Naqdan* (see above, Introduction, n. 83). Note also Abraham b. Joseph of Burgos, who wrote on *'iqqrei ha-'emunah* (as reflected in ms. Vatican 214 [Byzantium, 1394], fols. 216v–220v), and hailed from a Sefardic milieu.

153 See S. Emanuel, *Shivrei Luḥot*, 240–41. As Emanuel notes, *Sha'arei ha-Panim* may be the earliest example of this type of limited or discrete halakhic treatise to be produced by a Tosafist.

154 R. Eli'ezer's *piyyutim* include two *petiḥot* (ה' א-להי צב-אות צור עולמים, and ה' א-להי ישראל שוכן שמי מעלה), and a *seliḥah* for Yom Kippur (אתה שופט ברום עולם מעונך). See *Leqet Piyyutei Seliḥot*, ed.

from the compositions of R. Yom Tov of Joigny, Ri, and R. Elḥanan that interest in a range and variety of *piyyut* forms among Tosafists in northern France did not end with Rabbenu Tam.[155]

Interestingly, the group of important students who studied with Rabbenu Tam (and with R. Isaac b. Asher *ha-Levi* of Speyer) and subsequently (re-)settled in Germany, in either Regensburg or in the Rhineland,[156] produced very few *piyyutim*, with one notable exception, as we shall see. R. Isaac b. Mordekhai (Ribam) of Bohemia composed only a single *maʿariv* (with a *shirshur* from one stanza to the next) for *Shabbat Ḥol ha-Moʿed* (dealing with the laws of *Shabbat* and *Yom Tov*), without focusing specifically on either *Sukkot* or *Pesaḥ*.[157] R. Isaac b. Jacob of Prague (known as Ri *ha-Lavan*) composed a *seliḥah*, and a *zemer* for the Sabbath.[158] R. Eliezer b. Samuel of Metz

---

Fraenkel and Goldschmidt, 1:49–54, and cf. 2:772 for the possibility of an additional *petiḥah*. These compositions are found only in ms. Parma 654, which typically reflects a northern French rite, as we have seen (e.g., above, nn. 133, 144; and see also below, n. 266). Cf. Zunz, *LG*, 304, and Norman Golb, *The Jews of Normandy*, 485 (n. 170).

155 Cf. Haym Soloveitchik, "Three Themes in the *Sefer Ḥasidim*," *AJS Review* 1 (1976), 352 (in characterizing the perceived declining state of *piyyut* composition and recitation, among other imbalances that *Sefer Ḥasidim* sought to address and correct): "Piyyut never struck deep roots in France. Rashi's generation and the generation of his early pupils and younger contemporaries—R. Meir of Rameru, Rashbam and R. Joseph Kara—were raised in an Ashkenazic world and, faithful to their upbringing, they either composed or interpreted religious poetry. Their successors—R. Isaac of Dampierre, R. Samson of Sens, the French Tosafists—had little contact with the Rhineland, knew next to nothing of its traditions, and evinced no interest in *piyyut*. [In a note: Rabbenu Tam is a transitional figure in this regard.] From the days of R. Isaac to those of the exile in 1306, poetry is noticeably absent from the center of the French stage. With the French conquest of Germany [dated, on p. 349, to the second quarter of the thirteenth century], piyyut becomes peripheral even in the Rhineland." Needless to say, the details of *piyyut* composition put forward in the present chapter suggest that this assessment needs to be revised. See below (beginning at n. 251) on the writing of *piyyut* in northern France during the thirteenth century, and *passim* on the precise patterns and circles of ongoing *piyyut* composition in Germany as well. See also M. Schmelzer, "Piyyutei Nisu'in," 179–82.

156 On this cohort of students, see Rami Reiner, "Rabbenu Tam: Rabbotav (ha-Ẓarefatim) ve-Talmidav Benei Ashkenaz," esp. 68–70, 99–103, 125–30; and my "Rabbi Judah he-Ḥasid and the Rabbinic Scholars of Regensburg: Interactions, Influences and Implications," *JQR* 96 (2006), 17–37.

157 Ribam's *maʿariv*, יושבי קצוות יראו מאותותיך המצויינין, appears in *Maḥzor Vitry*, 579–80. See also *Maḥzor Pesaḥ*, ed. Fraenkel, 281–86, and the editor's introduction, 23, sec. 5. This *maʿariv* was mistakenly attributed by Israel Davidson (*Oẓar ha-Shirah veha-Piyyut*, 2377:י) to the thirteenth-century northern French Tosafist Isaac b. Isaac of Chinon, who composed a *bikkur* addendum for the evening service on *Ḥol ha-Moʿed* (see below, n. 264), ימים מקדם אזכרה, that is found in *Maḥzor Vitry*, 580–81, immediately after the Ribam's *maʿariv*. Cf. *Maḥzor Pesaḥ*, 287–89, and the editor's introduction, 26, sec. 3. On Ribam's involvement in *torat ha-sod*, see Urbach, *Baʿalei ha-Tosafot*, 1:199; and below, chapter 6, n. 51.

158 See *Leqet Piyyutei Seliḥot*, ed. Goldschmidt and Fraenkel, 1:339–43 (for the *pizmon*, אמונת מלכים נתת למשיסת שוטניך), and see also *Maḥzor Nuernberg*, 311–42 (and Y. and A. Fraenkel's study, *Ha-Tefillah veha-Piyyut be-Maḥzor Nuernberg*, 115–16). A second *seliḥah* that has been attributed to R. Isaac b. Jacob, אתאונן ביום זה שנהרגו עדתי בחרבם הגירוני בעון פקודתי, commemorates the persecution in Wiener-Neustadt in 1230. See *Sefer ha-Demaʿot*, ed. S. Bernfeld, 1:270–73, and

(d. 1198), whose base of operations in the Lorraine region—and some of his rabbinic experiences and teachings in addition—hovered between northern France and Germany,[159] wrote no *piyyutim*, although he did include some poetic codas in his *Sefer Yere'im*.[160]

The lone exception among Rabbenu Tam's German students is the highly prolific *payyetan* R. Ephraim b. Isaac of Regensburg (d. 1175), who was not much younger than Rabbenu Tam himself.[161] R. Ephraim, whose *piyyutim* owe a great deal to Spanish stylistics and are considered by modern scholarship to be among the most graceful ever produced by an Ashkenazic *payyetan*, authored more than thirty *piyyutim*.[162] These include an innovative *bikkur* (that weaved together several halakhic themes) for the seventh (or eighth) day of Passover;[163] another for *Shavu'ot*;[164] an *'ahavah* for *Shabbat*

I. Davidson, *Ozar ha-Shirah veha-Piyyut*, 1:392 (8623:א). This *seliḥah*, however, could not have been composed by Ri *ha-Lavan*, since he certainly died before 1200. Ri *ha-Lavan*'s *zemer*, ירוחם יתום, found in ms. Parma 352, fols. 69v–70r, is perhaps for *moẓa'ei Shabbat*, similar to the one composed by Rabbenu Tam that is also found in ms. Parma 352. See above, n. 78, and see also Zunz, *LG*, 313, 489.

159 See Urbach, *Ba'alei ha-Tosafot*, 1:154–61; R. Reiner, "Rabbenu Tam," 105–13; and cf. above, chapter 1.

160 There are a total of eleven such sections in *Sefer Yere'im* which are similar in structure to the *reshuyyot* for a *ḥatan*. See M. Schmelzer, *Studies in Jewish Bibliography and Medieval Hebrew Poetry* [Hebrew section], 177–87. Schmelzer discusses and analyzes the seven such poems found in Rivaq of Speyer's *Sefer Yiḥusei Tanna'im va-Amora'im*. Schmelzer (178–79, n. 11) also refers to similar compositions found in works such as *Sefer ha-Terumah*, *Sefer Rabiah*, *Sefer Shibbolei ha-Leqet*, and *Sefer Keritot*. See also above, n. 123.

161 On R. Ephraim's relationship with Rabbenu Tam, his rabbinic writings, and his travels throughout Germany and northern France, see Reiner, "Rabbenu Tam," 82–92, and Urbach, *Ba'alei ha-Tosafot*, 1:199–207. See also S. Emanuel, *Shivrei Luḥot*, 58–60, 289–91. Ephraim is cited in *Ḥiddushei ha-Ritva* to *'Eruvin* 31b, s.v. *nitnan* (and elsewhere) as R. Ephraim *Ẓarefati*. See also my "Between Ashkenaz and Sefarad: Tosafist Teachings in the Talmudic Commentaries of Ritva," in *Between Rashi and Maimonides: Themes in Medieval Jewish Thought, Literature and Exegesis*, ed. E. Kanarfogel and M. Sokolow (New York, 2010), 246 (n. 30), and 248 (n. 34).

162 See A. M. Habermann, "Piyyutei R. Ephraim b. Isaac mi-Regensburg," *Yedi'ot ha-Makhon le-Ḥeqer ha-Shirah ha-'Ivrit* 4 (1938), 127–95; E. Fleischer, *Ha-Yoẓerot*, 616–17, 650, 688–89; idem, *Shirat ha-Qodesh*, 436–37, 452, 458; L. Weinberger, *Jewish Hymnography*, 13–14, 161–63, 176–78. In his introductory remarks (p. 124), Habermann cogently suggests that Ephraim learned about aspects of meter from his (talmudic) teacher Rabbenu Tam as well.

163 See *Maḥzor Pesaḥ*, ed. Fraenkel, 402–4 (אסיר אלקנה אביאסף / חרפת עם לו נכסף/מזמור לאסף, with biblical phrases in the last piece of each stanza). See also Weinberger, *Jewish Hymnography*, 161, and Habermann, "Piyyutei R. Ephraim b. Isaac mi-Regensburg," 127–28. As Fraenkel notes in his introduction (26–27), R. Ephraim added his *bikkur* addendum to an existing *ma'ariv* not at the blessing of *ha-pores sukkat shalom* (where the *bikkur* form was typically situated) but rather (in a more innovative way) at the prior blessing of *ga'al Yisra'el*.

164 See *Maḥzor Shavu'ot*, ed. Fraenkel, 55–58 (= Habermann, ibid., 138–40) את קולך שמעתי, תמונתך עיני לא ראתה (with a biblical verse at the end of each stanza that contains the word *har* or *Sinai*), which was again meant to be placed in the *ge'ulah* blessing rather than at the end of *Shema*. See Fraenkel's introduction, 16, sec. 1; idem, *Ha-Tefillah veha-Piyyut be-Maḥzor Nuernberg*, 68; and ms. Vatican 323, fols. 153v–154r.

Ḥanukkah (or for the *Shabbat* on which the portion of *Be-Haʿalotekha* was read, an underutilized *piyyut* venue that is found also among Rabbenu Tam's corpus of *piyyutim*);[165] a *yoẓer* and a *zulat* for *Shabbat Rosh Ḥodesh* (which, like *Shabbat Ḥanukkah*, had not been covered so thoroughly in classical *piyyut* literature);[166] a metered *yoẓer* and two *zulatot* for a *Shabbat ḥatan* (one of which was metered);[167] and a metered *zemer* for the Sabbath.[168]

R. Ephraim of Regensburg also composed an *ʾahavah* for the Sabbath prior to *Shavuʿot*, which was the final Sabbath of the *sefirat ha-ʿomer* mourning period as it was observed in Ashkenaz;[169] several *ʾofanim* and *zulatot* for the Sabbaths between *Pesaḥ* and *Shavuʿot* (on the suffering and future redemption of the Jewish people, a *seliḥot*-like theme for the period of *sefirat ha-ʿomer*);[170] and some twenty *seliḥot*, *ʿaqedot*, *baqqashot*, and *pizmonim*

165 אמור ישועתך לנפשי (Habermann, ibid., 173–75). See also ms. St. Petersburg (Russian National Library) EVR IV 1 (IMHM #69479), fol. 167r; and cf. above, n. 76.

166 אמיתת חסדיך היקרים ידועים לכל and אשר במאמרות אימץ גבורות/ אשר יצר אור ויצר נר עורכים לחלפני וניכרים (Habermann, ibid., 184–87). The second composition is also found in Habermann, *Be-Ran—Yaḥad*, 158. See also Fraenkel, *Ha-Tefillah veha-Piyyut be-Maḥzor Nuernberg*, 70 (n. 387); and ms. St. Petersburg RNL EVR IV 1, fols. 155r–158v. On *piyyutim* for *Shabbat Rosh Ḥodesh*, cf. above, n. 38 (at R. Meir *Shaẓ*). E. Fleischer, *Ha-Yoẓerot*, 650 (n. 32) highlights the couplet form found in אשר במאמרות, which is also found in R. Ephraim's *yoẓer* for a *ḥatan*, אשר ברא / אורה יקרה (see the next note).

167 For the *yoẓer*, see M. Schmelzer, "Piyyutim le-Nisu'in," 177, sec. 9, and Habermann, "Piyyutei R. Ephraim b. Isaac mi-Regensburg,," 187–88. See Habermann, 190–91, for the metered *zulat*, אשיחה עם לבבי ויחפש רוחי עת מתי אויבי משכל את כוחי, which argues for the larger salavation of the Jewish people, just as the Almighty preserves the bride and groom. For the second *zulat*, אחותי כלה קראני נחי, see Habermann, 188–90, and cf. Fraenkel, *Ha-Tefillah veha-Piyyut be-Maḥzor Nuernberg*, 55.

168 אשר לו ים ויבשת / וכל מעשה ימי ששת / וצפנת לו מפולשת / וכל נעשה במרחשת (Habermann, ibid., 191–92, and see also ms. Parma 352, fols. 19r–v). The final stanza reads,חזות קרית באולמו / ויום כולו ולכבוד שמ ו/ מנחה היא בעולמ ו/ האלף לך שלמה. All told, the number of *piyyutim* composed by R. Ephraim for festivals and joyous occasions comes to fewer than ten.

169 See Habermann, ibid., 137–38, and ms. Bodl. 1147, fol. 37v,אותך כל היום קוינו / לשמך ולזכרך אוינו / אתה ה' אתה אבינו. E. Fleischer, *Ha-Yoẓerot*, 683 (n. 26, and see also 695), notes that this *ʾahavah* of R. Ephraim for the *Shabbat* prior to *Shavuʿot* (in which the end of each stanza is the plaintive phrase, 'עד מתי ה) is labeled in ms. Paris 646 as זולת לרבינו אפרים, ויש אומרים אותו להודות לך וליחדך באהבה. Note that in other manuscripts, this *piyyut* is designated for the *Shabbat* prior to the seventeenth of Tammuz, or for *Shabbat Ḥazon*. See, e.g., ms. Paris (Cluny Museum) 12290, fols. 242v–244r; ms. Verona 34, fols. 202v–204r (for the שבת על פני הגזירה); and cf. above, n. 90 (Raban).

170 See Fleischer, *Ha-Yoẓerot*, 689, and Weinberger, *Jewish Hymnography*, 162–63; See also, e.g., אזור נקמות חגור חימות (Habermann, ibid., 128–30, and ms. Parma 605, fol. 171r; a *pizmon* for 23 Nisan, the first Monday of the fast days of בה"ב following Passover, with Spanish meter and a refrain); א-להים לא אדע זולתיך / מושיע אין בלתך / גאל לך את גאוליך (Habermann, 132–34; a *zulat*, for the fifth Sabbath after Passover); and three other *zulatot*:א-ל א-לי למה אנחתי, for the fifth Sabbath after Passover (Habermann, 135–36); א-להי בך, for the fourth Sabbath after Passover (Habermann, 130–32); and (the metered) אשיחה עם לבבי / ויחפש ברוחי / עד מתי אויבי / מכשיל את כוחי (Habermann, 190–91, and idem, *Be-Ran—Yaḥad*, 157). Habermann notes a number of references in these *piyyutim* to the events of 1096.

for the *Yamim Nora'im* period, including several *seliḥot* for *Musaf* on Yom Kippur[171] and for other fast days.[172] These somber genres—which include R. Ephraim's *yoẓerot* for the Sabbaths during the *sefirah* period—comprise nearly three-quarters of the *piyyutim* produced by R. Ephraim.

Piyyut Writing in Germany during the First Half of the Thirteenth Century

As we leave the twelfth century and move further into the thirteenth century, we need to carefully consider the *piyyut* output of the German Pietists.

[171] See *Maḥzor le-Yamim Nora'im*, 2:530–31 (= Habermann, "Piyyutei R. Ephraim b. Isaac mi-Regensburg," 151, אין פה להשיב ולא פנים / בבושת עלומי פני לבנים, with a *ḥaruz mavriaḥ*, and cf. above, n. 26, at Rashi); *Maḥzor le-Yamim Nora'im*, 2:548–50 (= Habermann, ibid., 152–53, א-להי העברים / נקרא בכל עברים / בלבות נשברים / לכו נא הגברים, with Spanish meter and a similar *ḥaruz 'aḥid*); *Maḥzor le-Yamim Nora'im*, 2:555–57 (אני אני המדבר וקרבי משתבר, with Spanish meter), and 2:560–61 (= Habermann, 155–56, אני הוא המדבר / וקרבי משתבר / ואת מלין אחבר / ולב עם פה שוה, again with Spanish meter and a different *ḥaruz 'aḥid*). See also Habermann, 156–58, for a *pizmon* for Yom Kippur (אתה הוא א-ל ראי), in which each stanza ends with the phrase אליך ה' שועתי ובבקר, and see the next note.

[172] R. Ephraim composed two *seliḥot* for the tenth of Tevet, אבותי כי בטחו בשם ה' צורי / גדלו והצליחו וגם עשו פרי (which has a Sefardic חרוז מעין אזורי; Habermann, "Piyyutei R. Ephraim b. Isaac mi-Regensburg," 175–82), and the metered שמע עליון לקול אביון (Habermann, 183–84), and another *seliḥah*, אומללה יושבת בגולה (with a *siyyomet miqra'it*); see *Leqet Piyyutei Seliḥot*, ed. Goldschmidt and Fraenkel, 113–17. Several additional *seliḥot* were associated with the eve of Rosh ha-Shanah and the ten days of penitence: ה' שומרי לביתך נאוה / שמירת קודש כמו נר מצוה (Habermann, 148ff); א-ל אמונה עזרה הבה / לעמך כלם הטיבה / יחדיו למשפט נקרבה (Habermann, 140–41 = *Seder ha-Seliḥot*, ed. Goldschmidt, 78–80, sec. 29, with a biblical phrase at the end of each triplet, which contains a form of the word *mishpat*). An *'aqedah* (for the Fast of Gedalyah), אם אפס רובע הקן / אהל שכן אם רקן / אל נא נאבדה על כן / יש לנו אב זקן (Habermann, 141–47), was revised twice by R. Ephraim, showing his dedication to his craft. See also *Seder ha-Seliḥot*, 151–53 (sec. 52), and ms. Prague 246, fols. 72r and 92v. See also the *pizmon*, אם בניך חטאו אתה הוא א-ל לי (Habermann, 158–58); and a שלישיה, א-להים ה' חילי / יוצרי ומחוללי / לך אני וכל אשר לי (Habermann, 146–47 = *Seder ha-Seliḥot*, 238–240. sec. 90, with a *siyyomet miqra'it* at the conclusion of each line, for the fourth day of penitence); and another for the fifth day, א-דני שומרי (Habermann, 148–50). Other *seliḥot* include אומנות אבותי תפסתי במצוק (Habermann, 162–65, with a *ḥaruz 'aḥid*); איומתך כבולה בגולה (Habermann, 167–70, and cf. Yosef Yahalom, *Poetry and Society in Jewish Galilee in Late Antiquity* [Hebrew], 362, n. 7); אסוף עברה ואב עברה (Habermann, 170–71); אשר אין לו תמורה והוא יהיה והיה (Habermann, 159–62, with Spanish meter and a *ḥaruz mavriaḥ*, described in E. Fleischer, *Shirat ha-Qodesh*, 436); and אם יוספים אנחנו לעמוד לשרת בשמו (Habermann, 153–54, for *Musaf* on Yom Kippur). R. Ephraim's son, R. Moses (see Urbach, *Ba'alei ha-Tosafot*, 1:207, and my *"Peering through the Lattices,"* 112), composed a *seliḥah*, גואל דמי דומי לדמי (with a *siyyomet miqra'it*), to commemorate a decree that occurred in his day. See *Leqet Piyyutei Seliḥot* ed. Goldschmidt and Fraenkel, 2:463–64. Habermann, 193, also attributes the *seliḥah*, מגיני וקרן ישעי, to R. Moses b. Ephraim; cf. *Leqet Piyyutei Seliḥot*, ed. Goldschmidt and Fraenkel, 2:814. Whatever the similarities between father and son in terms of pietism, these did not extend to *piyyut* composition. Cf. ms. St. Petersburg RNL EVR IV 1, fol. 166r, for an אופן for the last day of Passover, מחוללת מהוללת נאדרי מוקדם, that is attributed to ר' משה בן הרב אפרים. However, in *Maḥzor Pesaḥ*, ed. 453–54, this composition is attributed to a R. Moses b. Isaac.

R. Judah *he-Ḥasid* authored several esoteric or magical supplications and prayers, including the *Shir ha-Kavod*,[173] which has also been attributed to his father, R. Samuel *he-Ḥasid*, who was the author of a series of *Shirei Yiḥud*.[174] In terms of traditional *piyyutim*, however, R. Judah may have composed an *E-loheikhem* for *Shabbat Bereshit* (= the first Sabbath after *Sukkot*), which was an underutilized venue, although elsewhere this *piyyut* is ascribed to R. Judah (b. Samuel) *ha-Levi* (= R. Yehudah *ha-Levi*).[175] R. Judah *he-Ḥasid* did compose an *E-loheikhem* for *Shabbat Naḥamu*, and perhaps another such addendum to the *kedushah* on *Shabbat Ḥol ha-Mo'ed Sukkot*,[176] and fewer than a handful of *seliḥot*.[177] On the other hand, R. Judah *he-Ḥasid*'s brother,

[173] See Zunz, *LG*, 300. Included among the supplications are a *viddui* found in ms. Paris l'Alliance 482, fol. 33, and ms. Vatican Rossiana 356, fol. 2v; and a *tefillah u-teḥinnah* (which begins יוצרי ברוב רחמיך כבוש אפך מזעמך . . . תעביר את חטאתי סלח נא על כל פשעי כפר לעונותי חלצני מיסורין ומרוחות וממזיקין), found, e.g., in ms. Parma 1138, fol. 139v, and in ms. B.M. Add. 26883 (= Margoliouth 640, *Catalogue*, 2:255). Cf. my *"Peering through the Lattices,"* 73, n. 112. See also ms. Prague 45, fol. 145v (in a section titled *tefillot me-R. Yehudah he-Ḥasid*), for a *baqqashah*, אזכרה יום מותי. Several magical *tefillat ha-derekh* forms are also attributed to R. Judah *he-Ḥasid*; see, e.g., ms. Bodl. 1098, fol. 77r (beginning בשם ה' א-להי ישראל). A *shir ha-yiḥud* is attributed to R. Judah; see, e.g., ms. Bodl. 1105, fols. 419v–420v.

[174] See *Kitvei Avraham Epstein*, ed. A. M. Habermann, vol. 1 (Jerusalem, 1950), 263; J. Dan, *Shir ha-Yiḥud* (Jerusalem, 1981), 7–26; Y. Y. Stal, *Sefer Gematriot le-R. Yehudah he-Ḥasid* (Jerusalem, 2005), vol. 1, 22–28 (introduction); and I. Davidson, *Ozar ha-Shirah veha-Piyyut*, 1:362 (8004:א). Aside from the *Shirei Yiḥud*, R. Samuel *he-Ḥasid* was himself the author of fewer than a handful of *piyyutim*. For his *Hoshanah* (כהושעת אב המון השליך עליה יהב), see, e.g., *Maḥzor Sukkot*, ed. Goldschmidt, 184–5 (and see also the editor's introduction, 39); ms. Parma 908, fol. 124r; ms. Moscow 201, fol. 230r. On this *piyyut* form, cf. above, nn. 37, 58, 147, and see also *Piyyutei R. Yeḥi'el b. Avraham me-Roma*, A. Fraenkel, editor's introduction, 13. Some have attributed to R. Samuel *he-Ḥasid* a *magen* (שפרם רם ברוחו וברך יום מנוחו, in which each stanza contains a verse that ends with the word כמוהו) that was to be recited before the *Magen Avot* prayer on a Friday evening that coincided with the second day of *Shavu'ot*, all in all a fairly rare *piyyut* form and venue; cf. E. Fleischer, "'Itturei Piyyut le-Magen Avot," *Tarbiz* 45 (1976), 89–105; and idem, *Shirat ha-Qodesh ha-'Ivrit Bimei ha-Benayim*, 466–67. This *piyyut*, however, is correctly attributed to the martyr R. Samuel *Ḥazzan* Devlin of Erfurt (d. c. 1280); see ms. Parma (de Rossi) 586, fols. 171r–v; ms. Bodl. 1099, fol. 93r; Zunz, *LG*, 465, and Davidson, *Ozar ha-Shirah veha-Piyyut*, 3:50 (2114:ש).

[175] See I. Davidson, *Ozar ha-Shirah veha-Piyyut*, 1:230 (4590:א), א-להיכם ישכיל עבדו. The attribution to R. Yehudah of Castile (קשטילין, = R. Yehudah *ha-Levi*) is found in ms. Parma 1274, fol. 206v.

[176] See Davidson, *Ozar ha-Shirah veha-Piyyut*, 1:209 (4577: א),א-להים יוסיף ידו לקבץ נפוצותיכם, and *Maḥzor Sukkot*, ed. Goldschmidt, 286 (א-להיכם ישיב שלם סוכו ומעונתו). On this genre, cf. above, nn. 71, 100, 118.

[177] A *seliḥah* for Yom Kippur, א-להים בישראל גדול יחודך תשגבנו צדקתיך (with a *ḥaruz 'aḥid*), is most often attributed to R. Judah *he-Ḥasid* (although it is occasionally attributed to R. Eleazar of Worms); see Zunz (above, n. 173); *Maḥzor le-Yamim Nora'im*, ed. Goldschmidt, 2:237–38; S. Baer, *Seder 'Avodat Yisra'el*, 243; and my *"Peering through the Lattices"* (above, n. 173), for additional manuscript evidence. Another of R. Judah's *seliḥot*, דמעתי יכבה חרון אפך ממך (sometimes formulated as יכבה דמעתי), originates in *Sefer Ḥasidim* (Parma), sec. 41 (= *Sefer Ḥasidim* [Bologna], sec. 171). Despite the small number of verified *piyyutim* by R. Judah, E. Fleischer, *Ha-Yozerot*, 608, n. 4, and idem, *Shirat ha-Qodesh*, 431, includes him in a group of significant

R. Abraham b. Samuel *he-Ḥasid* (referred to on occasion in halakhic sources as ר' אשל), was a much more active *payyetan* than either his brother or his father, composing more than ten (albeit relatively brief) *seliḥot* and *qinot.*[178]

Moreover, R. Judah's *he-Ḥasid*'s leading Pietist student, R. Eleazar b. Judah of Worms (d. c. 1230), who composed *Tosafot* and halakhic works (including *Sefer Roqeaḥ*), and served as a key member of the rabbinic court in Worms and as the *ḥazzan* of the community,[179] composed more the fifty *piyyutim.* The vast majority of R. Eleazar's *piyyut* compositions revolve around penitential or commemorative themes, quite similar to the pattern we have just seen for R. Ephraim of Regensburg, in which nearly three-quarters of the *piyyutim* were *seliḥot*-related. Thus Eleazar of Worms authored some thirty-five *seliḥot* and *qinot*, including five *seliḥot* for the day of Yom Kippur—and a series of *seliḥot* for the ten days of penitence and for other fast days, including the Fast of Gedalyah, the tenth of Tevet, the Fast of Esther, and the seventeenth of Tammuz—as well as an *'ofan* and a *zulat* for *Shabbat Shuvah.*[180] He also composed an *'ofan* (אף אורח משפטיך ה' קוינוך) and a *zulat*

Ashkenazic *payyetanim*, albeit without providing any specific data about his compositions. Cf. L. Weinberger, *Jewish Hymnography*, 169, 175–76, and A. Freimann's bibliographic introduction to *Sefer Ḥasidim* (Parma), ed. J. Wistinetski (Frankfurt, 1924), 8–9. On the significance of the proper recitation of *piyyut* in *Sefer Ḥasidim* (and indeed, that only the *piyyutim* penned by proper authors should be recited), see H. Soloveitchik, "Three Themes in the *Sefer Ḥasidim*," 330–35, 345–46, and I. Marcus, *Piety and Society* (Leiden, 1980), 98–101.

178 The *seliḥot* can be found in *Leqet Piyyutei Seliḥot*, ed. Goldschmidt and Fraenkel: אבל אשמים אנחנו לפניך עליון (10–11, with a *siyyomet miqra'it*); א-להים מארץ שבינו (11–13, a *shlishiyah* with a *siyyomet miqra'it*, and cf. S. Abramson's extensive analysis of a phrase in this *seliḥah* [כי פס ערך הקצובות] in *Leshonenu le-'Am* 18 [1966], 67–71); אם עונינו כבדו מנשוא (13–15, a *ḥatanu*, with a *siyyomet miqra'it* and a *shirshur*);את שיחי אשפוך לפניך (15–17, with a *siyyomet miqra'it*); תחל כל מפעליך (17–19, with a *siyyomet miqra'it*); and תפוצת ישראל פוטרת שפה(20–23). The *qinot* include: איש ישראל בגרון (Davidson, *Oẓar ha-Shirah veha-Piyyut*, 1:146, 1473:א); אלכה וירדתי אל ההרים ואבכה (Davidson, 1:236, 5141:א), and see also ms. Parma 1104, fol. 38v;-אמרות ה' נחמות הבאות תמהר ותחיש ה' צב אות (Davidson, 1:269, 5905:א); and את התמוז מבכות (for 1096; see Davidson, 1:395, 8524:א). Cf. Zunz, *LG*, 284. In addition, Rivaq composed an *'ahavah* for the Sabbath after *Shavu'ot* to mark another persecution, אשר יחדיו עם ידידיו עובדים לו אחד שכם (Davidson, 1:373, 8250:א). On R. Abraham b. Samuel's halakhic writings, see Urbach, *Ba'alei ha-Tosafot*, 362–64; S. Emanuel, *R. Eleazar mi-Vermaiza—Derashah le-Pesaḥ*, 24–24, 72, 101; idem, *Shivrei Luḥot*, 55, 60, 285, 287; *Teshuvot u-Pesaqim*, ed. E. Kupfer (Jerusalem, 1973), 33, 49, 85, 201.

179 See above, chapter 1, nn. 13, 57, 252. See also S. Emanuel, *R. Eleazar mi-Vermaiza—Derashah le-Pesaḥ*, 1–41. On R. Eleazar as *ḥazzan*, see esp. ibid., 3 (n. 9), and 5–6 (n. 19); on his *Tosafot*, and use (or non-use) of northern French material, see esp. 22–23, 50–51, 117.

180 For the *'ofan* (אור ישראל וקדושו), see *Shirat ha-Roqeaḥ*, ed. I. Meiseles (Jerusalem, 1993), 31–33. For the *zulat*, see *Maḥzor le-Yamim Nora'im*, ed. Goldschmidt, 1:322–25 (ה' מעון אתה), and Meiseles, 51–56. The *'ofan* has the word *qadosh* at the end of every stanza, while the *zulat* has a form of the word *shuv* at the end of (virtually) every stanza; cf. above, n. 53. For the *seliḥot* for Yom Kippur, see Meiseles, 108–16 (ה' ה' א-להי בך חסיתי, in several versions); 117–120 (ה' א-להי אברהם, with a verse that concludes with the word *minḥah* at the end of each stanza); 121–25 (אין כמוך בשמים ממעל); 126–28 (אך בך לדל עזרה); 129–33 (אנא ה' הא-ל הגדול והנורא). The full corpus

(אודה שמך עליון נפלאות הפלאת, with a *siyyomet miqra'it*) for *Shabbat Ḥazon* and to commemorate the deliverance of the Worms community from persecution in 1201, and a *zulat* for the Sabbath at the end of Sivan on which the persecution in Erfurt of 1221 was commemorated.[181]

Only ten *piyyutim* in Eleazar's very large corpus are not associated with persecutions and recovery, or with penitential themes. These include *ma'arivim* for *Sukkot*, *Shemini 'Azeret*, and *Pesaḥ*; one set of *piyyutim* for the *Shema* that are not linked to any particular event or Sabbath; two *E-loheikhem* addenda to the *kedushah* for *Musaf* on the Sabbath (one for when a circumcision occurs); a *yozer* and a *zulat* for a *Shabbat ḥatan*; and a *zulat* for *parashat Shoftim* (אילת אהבים ויעלת חן בחבה), on which the *Haftarah* of

of R. Eleazar's *seliḥot* and *qinot* has been conveniently collected by Meiseles in his *Shirat ha-Roqeaḥ* (see also below, n. 183; there are several additional *piyyutim* by R. Eleazar found in ms. Moscow 611, as we shall see below, which was not used by Meiseles). A helpful breakdown of R. Eleazar's *piyyutim* according to genre (and occasion) is found in Meiseles, 313–15. In addition, nearly twenty of Eleazar's *seliḥot* were published in *Leqet Piyyutei Seliḥot*, ed. Goldschmidt and Fraenkel, 74–112. Among Eleazar's *qinot* is אשת חיל עטרת בעלה בת נדיבים (Meiseles, 226–32), an elegy for his wife, Dolce, and daughter, who were killed in 1197. See Habermann, *Gezerot Ashkenaz ve-Ẓarefat*, 165–67; and cf. I. Marcus, "Mothers, Martyrs and Moneylenders: Some Jewish Women in Medieval Europe," *Conservative Judaism* 38:3 (1986), 34–45; Judith Baskin, "Some Parallels in the Education of Medieval Jewish and Christian Women," *Jewish History* 5 (1991), 41–51; and Y. Y. Stal, "Amirat 'Nishmat kol Ḥai' bi-Yemot ha-Ḥol uve-Khol Yom," *Yerushatenu* 5 (2011), 202–14. Eleazar's *seliḥot* cover the cycle of fast days of the year (cf. above, n. 101) and the penitential periods before Rosh ha-Shanah and Yom Kippur (including an *'aqedah* and two *pizmonim*), and also include (as noted) *piyyutim* for both *Shabbat Shuvah* and *Shabbat Ḥazon*. See also ms. Moscow 611, fols. 31r, 51v. For R. Eleazar's *piyyutim* for Rosh ha-Shanah and Yom Kippur, see also *Maḥzor le-Yamim Nora'im*, ed. Goldschmidt, 1:16–17 (a *ma'ariv*, אשרי העם ידועי תרועה לפתוחו, and see ms. Moscow 611, fol. 190r); 1:258–59 (a *pizmon* for a circumcision on Rosh ha-Shanah or on a fast day), אות ברית ביני ובינך אבינו, connected to the *piyyut* of *Zekhor Brit* by Rabbenu Gershom and its refrain); 2:283–84 (את מדותיך זכור ושמע רנון, a *pizmon* for a circumcision on Yom Kippur again with the *Zekhor Brit* component and refrain); 559–60 (for *Musaf*, which is an addendum to a *piyyut* by R. Meir b. Isaac *Shaz*); 2:643 (for *Minḥah*, imitating a composition by R. Shelomoh *ha-Bavli*). R. Eleazar also composed a *reshut* for *Ha-melekh*, and two *piyyutim* for *shevah notnim lo*; see Meiseles, *Shirat ha-Roqeah*, 19–26 (the second of these two, 'אהללה ה, has a *ḥaruz 'aḥid*), and cf. E. Fleischer, *Shirat ha-Qodesh*, 460–62. For Eleazar's *yozer* and *zulat* for a *ḥatan*, see Meiseles, 38–44 (את מי נועץ), and 60–64 (אילת אהבים), and cf. M. Schmelzer, "Piyyutim le-Nisu'in," 178, n. 20, who notes that Eleazar's *Shema Yisra'el* (an unspecified *'ofan* published in Meiseles, 27–30) is found in ms. Moscow 611, among various Ashkenazic wedding *piyyutim*. Like his teacher R. Judah *he-Ḥasid*, R. Eleazar composed several penitential and mystical prayers as well.

[181] R. Eleazar's *zulat* for this occasion begins זולתך אין א-ל צדיק ומושיע / ברגז רחם זכור ואל תשפיע גאלנו משחת ואל תרשיע/ דרכיך הוראת טוב ורב להושיע /; see Meiseles, *Shirat ha-Roqeaḥ*, 45–50. R. Solomon b. Abraham (a rabbinic correspondent of R. Barukh b. Samuel of Mainz; see Urbach, *Ba'alei ha-Tosafot*, 1:427, and *Teshuvot u-Pesaqim*, ed. Kupfer, 226) also authored a *qinah* to commemorate this event, א-להים חיים אצים בי נוגשים. These two pieces were published together by A. M. Habermann, *Gezerot Ashkenaz ve-Ẓarefat*, 168–71. For R. Eleazar's *'ofan* and *zulat* for *Shabbat Ḥazon*, see Meiseles, 34–37, 56–59; and see also ms. Verona 34, fols. 112r–v.

consolation from Isaiah 51:12–52:11 is read.[182] R. Eleazar's compositional style was also apparently influenced significantly by Spanish style and metrics, although to a lesser extent than R. Ephraim of Regensburg.[183]

R. Eleazar's father, R. Judah b. Qalonymus of Mainz (Rivaq b. Moses, d. c. 1200), was a student of the early German Tosafist and halakhist

[182] On the somewhat unusual *zulat* for *Shoftim* (אני ראשון ואני אחרון, in which each stanza ends with a form of the word נחם), see Meiseles, *Shirat ha-Roqeah*, 65–70 (and see also ms. Verona 34, fol. 113v). See Meiseles, 38–44, and 60–64, for the *Shabbat ḥatan*; ibid., 27–30, for the *'ofan* (about the songs of the angels) whose temporal connection is unclear; and in the next note for R. Eleazar's two *E-loheikhem* compositions. The core of R. Eleazar's *ma'ariv* for *Shemini 'Aẓeret* (which begins ארחמך ה' חזקי אתה משגבי; see *Maḥzor Sukkot*, ed. Goldschmidt, 305–7) is analyzed in E. Hazan and B. Bar-Tikva, *Shirat ha-Halakhah* (Ramat Gan, 1991), 45–52. Each stanza ends with the biblical phrase ביום השמיני עצרת (Nu. 29:35), and the second rhyme in each stich is a biblical phrase. This *piyyut* is replete with midrashic and halakhic references, as R. Eleazar seeks to explain the character of *'aẓeret* according to rabbinic thought. E. Hazan and B. Bar-Tikva, *Shirat ha-Halakhah* (Ramat Gan, 1991), 53–54, present and discuss R. Eleazar's *bikkur* addendum that follows. For R. Eleazar's festival *piyyutim* (all *ma'arivim*, each of which has a kind of refrain), see Meiseles, 80–107, and see also *Maḥzor Sukkot*, ed. Goldschmidt, 27–30 (אתה לבדך עטית אור לכללה), and 305–10 (for *Shemini 'Aẓeret*, ארחמך ה' חזקי אתה משגבי, as noted above, and a *bikkur*, אדברה נא שלום בך ירושלים החביבה); and *Maḥzor Pesach*, ed. Fraenkel 363–67 (אמונת אומן לעם זו רם זכרת, with a *soger min ha-miqra*, and see also ms. Moscow 611, fol. 176v, sec. 219, and ms. Bodl. 1025, fol. 79r), followed by two pieces by R. Yehudah *ha-Levi*. There are relatively few references to R. Eleazar's *piyyutim* in Fleischer, *Ha-Yoẓerot*, 608, 625, 685 (n. 7). For R. Eleazar's extensive prayer commentaries (which also include numerous *piyyut* commentaries), see, e.g., *Perushei Siddurei ha-Tefillah la-Roqeah*, ed. M. Hershler (Jerusalem, 1992); *'Arugat ha-Bosem*, ed. Urbach, 4: 100–111, 115–16; and E. Hollender, *Piyyut Commentary in Medieval Ashkenaz*, 49–50.

[183] The *ḥaruz 'aḥid* convention found in the *yoẓer* אהללה ה' (see the above note) is also found in a *qinah* for the ninth of Av that occurs after the Sabbath, בליל זה סר נגהי (Meiseles, *Shirat ha-Roqeaḥ*, 159–60); R. Eleazar's addendum to the *qinah* of R. Qalonymus b. Judah (*mi yitein roshi mayim*) on the persecutions of 1096, קהלות הקודש הרגיתם היום בזכרה (Meiseles, 268–70); R. Eleazar's two *E-loheikhem* poems, for the *kedushah le-musaf Shabbat* when a circumcision takes place, א-להיכם יוסיף כס י-ה (Meiseles, 70–71, and cf. ms. Bodl. 1099, fol. 146v), whose theme is the return of the exile and the rebuilding of Jerusalem; and א-להיכם תפארתו ממעל ואין בלעדו (Meiseles, 72–73). R. Eleazar's *zulat* for *Shabbat Ḥazon* (אודה שמך עליון; Meiseles, 56–59, and see above, n. 181) concludes each stanza with biblical phrases, as does a *seliḥah* for the ten days of penitence, אליך נקרא חונן ומרחם (Meiseles, 175–78). See the above note for the *zulat* for *Shabbat Naḥamu*, אני ראשון ואני אחרון, in which each stanza ends with a verse that contains a form of the root נחם, and see above, n. 181, for a *seliḥah* for Yom Kippur, ה' א-להי אברהם, in which each stanza ends with the word מנחה. In another *seliḥah*, possibly written in connection with a siege that occurred in Mainz in 1188, תאות ענוים שמעת במכלל יופי (Meiseles, 237–40), and in yet another *seliḥah*, אנא הא-ל הגדול (212–16), each stanza concludes with a verse that ends with the word *tamid*. See also the *ma'ariv* for Rosh ha-Shanah, אשרי העם יודעי תרועה לפתותו/ בקול שופר בכסא לכמור חמלתו (Meiseles, 74–79), and in the above note. A *seliḥah*, א-להים אקרא וה' נסיכי (Meiseles, 197–202), concludes each stanza with a biblical phrase that ends with the word *E-lohim*, and this word then begins the next stanza as well (שרשור). A *seliḥah* for the Fast of Gedalyah, אשריך ישראל מי מטהרך מעונותיך (Meiseles, 137–41), has each stanza end with a verse that begins with the word *le-ma'an*. Finally, Eleazar's *qinah*, ציון הלא תשאלי לשלום עלוביך (Meiseles, 259–67), is an imitation of R. Judah *ha-Levi*'s well-known Zionide poem, ציון הלא תשאלי לשלום אסיריך, in terms of both rhyme and meter (in addition to similarity in the opening line). Moreover, it has a *ḥaruz 'aḥid* throughout. See also the *seliḥah*, א-להים אל תרחק ממני (Meiseles, 192–96).

R. Shemaryah b. Mordekhai of Speyer; indeed, Rivaq copied his teacher's lost *sefer pesaqim.* Rivaq became a member of the rabbinic court headed by R. Moses *ha-Kohen* of Mainz and later headed the court himself, where he was joined by R. Ephraim of Bonn and R. Barukh of Mainz.[184] Rivaq of Mainz authored close to twenty *piyyutim.* Like his son R. Eleazar of Worms after him, he wrote mainly *seliḥot* and *qinot*, along with a set of *yoẓerot* for a *Shabbat ḥatan*, and two additional *'ofanim* for a circumcision that occurred on the Sabbath.[185] As such, the numerous *piyyut* compositions of R. Eleazar of Worms and his father are to be found mostly in the realm of additional penitentials and elegies, and to mark special occasions that occurred on a

[184] See S. Emanuel, *Shivrei Luḥot*, 133–34 (nn. 137, 139), 285–88; idem, *R. Eleazar mi-Vermaiza—Derashah le-Pesaḥ*, 20, 44, n. 175, 48–49, 60, 122, n. 383; Urbach, *Ba'alei ha-Tosafot*, 1:365–69, 379, 388–89; *Teshuvot R. Ḥayyim Or Zaru'a*, #222; and above, chapter 1, nn. 5, 7, 10, 15, 59. R. Judah b. Qalonymus of Mainz is also included in the esoteric chain of tradition of *Ḥasidei Ashkenaz*, although R. Eleazar of Worms barely refers to his father in his prayer commentary; see *'Arugat ha-Bosem*, ed. Urbach, 4:107–9. Urbach notes that an *'ofan* by Rivaq of Mainz (יקר גדלו, which Urbach characterizes as *kulo sod*; see the next note) was copied by R. Eleazar of Worms's student R. Abraham b. Azri'el into his *'Arugat ha-Bosem* (ed. Urbach, 1:136), together with a full commentary by R. Eleazar, and additional comments from Abraham b. Azri'el.

[185] See *Leqet Piyyutei Seliḥot*, ed. Goldschmidt and Fraenkel, for an *'aqedah*, איתן האזרחי השכיל (1:219–21), followed by a series of nine *seliḥot*: אמ״י עכ״ר תכנס לפניך מדת רחמים (221–23); אם עוני נאדם (223–25); אנחתי מאוד רבה הגדלתי פשעי חובה (225–27); אנקת זעקת בני בחוניך (227–28); יאחז צדיק דרכו (228–30); ידידות נפשך תתה ביד אוי־בים (230–32, which is listed as a *baqqashah*); ישראל עמך נתונים בגולה (232–34); תופסים עמך אומנות אבותיהם (234–35) (235–37). There is an additional *seliḥah*, אנוש כחציר ימיו אחרי תוהו טועה (Davidson, *Oẓar ha-Shirah veha-Piyyut*, 1:295, 6471:א); and a *qinah* for the ninth of Av (commemorating the attacks against Jews that occurred in Speyer in 1196), אל אבל אקרא וקינה (Davidson, 1:155, 3307:א). Cf. Haim Schirmann, *Qinot 'al ha-Gezerot*, 16–19; A. M. Habermann, *Gezerot Ashkenaz ve-Ẓarefat* (Jerusalem, 1945), 155–58; S. Einbinder, *Beautiful Death*, 36–37; and Urbach, *Ba'alei ha-Tosafot*, 1:368. For Rivaq's *yoẓer*, *'ofan*, *zulat*, and *reshut* for a *Shabbat ḥatan*, see M. Schmelzer, "Piyyutim le-Nisu'in," 177, sec. 6. The *'ofan le-ḥatan me-Rivaq b. Mosheh* (see, e.g., ms. Bodl. 1099, fol. 118v), ידודון ותרשישים טובלים באישים וזה מזה מרשים קדושתם משלשלים, contains *Hekhalot* motifs and phrases on the immersion of the angels in fire prior to their offering praises (and an overall listing of angelic figures), which are similar to those found in compositions by R. Ephraim of Bonn (above, nn. 113–14) and R. Barukh of Mainz and R. Meir of Rothenburg (below, nn. 200, 298–99): וניגון אלים בשיר מסל־לים ומנצחים ארלאים ומתחדדים חשמלאים ואומר׳ קדוש קדוש קדוש . . . מיכאל וגבריאל שתקיאל וברדיאל וברקיאל ושדריאל שרי א-ל. See also ms. Bodl. 1099, fols. 76r–78r (= ms. Bodl. 1147, fols. 25v–26r), לברית מילה מריב״ק בן משה. ישראל חביבים כמלאים אהובים בכל עונה מרבים שירה ערבים (with a *ḥaruz 'aḥid*). Rivaq's second *'ofan* for a circumcision is titled למי יאתה (Davidson, *Oẓar ha-Shirah veha-Piyyut*, 3:50, 1103:ל), and cf. ms. Moscow 611, secs. 215–18. Rivaq's *zulat le-ḥatan*, אמה העבריה נכבשה בקטנותה (see, e.g., ms. Bodl. 1099, fols. 124r–v), compares the *ketubah* that the groom gives his bride in love to the redemption of the Jewish people by the Almighty, during which He released the nation from servitude (formulated according to the release of a female bondwoman), as well as the prayerful expression that the terms of the "ketubah" between the Almighty and the Jewish people will be renewed in perpetuity, so that the Jewish people will be able to dwell in happiness together with the Almighty. Cf. Habermann, *'Ateret Renanim* (Jerusalem, 1967), 30–31, and idem, "Shtei Tefillot la-Yehidim veha-Piyyutim ha-Qeshurim Lahem," *Qoveẓ 'al Yad* 8 (1975), 237–50. For an esoteric *'ofan* by Rivaq, יקר גודלו ורוב חילו, see the above note.

particular Sabbath, with far fewer meant to be linked to the permanent liturgy for festivals or to other celebratory contexts, as was also the case for R. Ephraim of Regensburg.[186]

Two students of R. Ephraim who were older contemporaries of R. Eleazar of Worms, R. Barukh b. Samuel of Mainz (d. 1221) and R. Menaḥem b. Jacob of Worms (d. 1203), were almost as prolific as R. Eleazar in their composition of *piyyutim*. R. Barukh, a leading judge and halakhist who authored the voluminous but no longer extant *Sefer ha-Ḥokhmah*, composed some thirty *piyyutim*.[187] The distribution of R. Barukh's *piyyutim* differs only

[186] Note the very modest *piyyut* output of R. Eleazar of Worms's contemporary, R. Moses b. Ḥisdai Taku. R. Moses served as the rabbinic leader in Regensburg and authored *Tosafot* to *Nedarim*, as well as *pesaqim* and responsa, much of which is no longer extant. See Urbach, *Ba'alei ha-Tosafot*, 420–25; my "Appointment of *Ḥazzanim* in Medieval Ashkenaz: Communal Policy and Individual Religious Prerogatives," in *Spiritual Authority: Struggles over Cultural Power in Jewish Thought*, ed. H. Kreisel et al. (Beer Sheva, 2009), 5–31; and above, Introduction, n. 2. In matters of thought, R. Moses was an antagonist of R. Judah *he-Ḥasid*, as evidenced by his *Ketav Tamim*; see below, chapter 7. He composed only two *seliḥot*—an *avinu malkenu* sequence for *minḥah* of Yom Kippur (beginning אבינו מלכנו אנקת עמך) in which each stanza concludes with a scriptural phrase (see *Maḥzor le-Yamim Nora'im*, 2:680–82; Fraenkel, *Ha-Tefillah veha-Piyyut be-Maḥzor Nuernberg*, 117; and cf. E. Hollender, *Clavis Commentatorium of Hebrew Liturgical Poetry in Manuscript*, 65, secs. 322–26), and a *seliḥah* for the Fast of Esther, אזון אנקת נאנחים, that is recorded in Zunz, *Literaturgeschichte*, 317—as well as a recently discovered *ma'ariv* for *Shemini 'Aẓeret/Simḥat Torah* (א-להי צורי אקוה). See M. Schmelzer, *Meḥqarim*, 170–76 (and esp. 170, n. 3). R. Moses's apparent comment to a *piyyut*, recorded in ms. Parma de Rossi 1131, fol. 60v, is instead a technical instruction for the prayer service of the High Holidays. See also R. Moses's practice for the recitation of *piyyutim* on *erev Pesaḥ* that occurs on the Sabbath (in ms. Warsaw [Jewish Historical Institute] 240, fol. 62r), cited by S. Emanuel, *R. Eleazar mi-Vermaiza—Derashah le-Pesaḥ*, 77 (n. 57); idem, *Shivrei Luḥot*, 218–19 (n. 18); ms. Cambridge Dd. 13.7, fol. 8v; and ms. JTS Rab. 1489, fol. 222r.

[187] See A. M. Habermann, "Piyyutei Rabbenu Barukh b. Samuel mi-Magenẓa," *Yedi'ot ha-Makhon le-Ḥeqer ha-Shirah ha-'Ivrit* 6 (1945), 58–159; L. Weinberger, *Jewish Hymnography*, 13, 164–67, 186; and Urbach, *Ba'alei ha-Tosafot*, 428–29. Urbach notes that although R. Barukh is never mentioned in the standard *Tosafot* (cf. above, Introduction, nn. 12, 20), his *piyyutim* contain not only biblical themes and stylistics but also halakhic and midrashic ones. See also Habermann, 56 (who notes, in addition, the impact of various earlier *payyetanim* on R. Barukh). Indeed, R. Barukh based an entire *piyyut*, בראש אילן משוררת אני בינה מאושרת, on a talmudic *sugya* (*Bava Batra* 25b; cf. Maharsha, *ḥiddushei 'aggadot, ad loc.*, fol. 7b, and above, n. 51). R. Barukh's talmudic and halakhic methods and writings are discussed extensively in S. Emanuel, *Shivrei Luḥot*, 104–46. R. Barukh studied with R. Eliezer of Metz and asked questions of him. He also studied with R. Isaac b. Mordekhai of Bohemia, R. Ephraim of Regesnburg, and Rivaq of Speyer. R. Barukh received teachings of Rabbenu Tam through R. Moses *ha-Kohen mi-Magenẓa*, with whom he sat on the Mainz court; see also above, chapter 1. On R. Barukh's *piyyutim*, see E. Fleischer, *Ha-Yoẓerot*, 616–17, and 624 (regarding a *yoẓer le-ḥatan* that had been misidentfied as a *zulat*; cf. Zunz, *LG*, 260 [sec. 7], and 306 [sec. 2]; Habermann, "Piyyutei Rabbenu Barukh b. Samuel mi-Magenẓa," 64–69; and below, n. 196). As Fleischer further notes (630–31, n. 18), this *yoẓer* maintains a single rhyme (a *ḥaruz 'aḥid*, שים and סים) throughout all of its eighty-nine lines. See also Schmelzer, *Meḥqarim*, 180, n. 13, who notes that R. Barukh included acrostics of his name in a number of places in the middle of his *piyyutim* (and not only toward the end as a kind of signature, which is more typical).

slightly from those of Eleazar of Worms. R. Barukh composed a similarly large percentage of *seliḥot* and *qinot*, including a lament for the martyrs in Blois (1171)[188] and those of Boppard and Speyer (1196),[189] as well as a composition marking a persecution that occurred in Wurzburg prior to 1221;[190] two lengthy metered *seliḥot* for the ten days of penitence in Spanish meter, each with the same rhyme throughout;[191] and a metered *seliḥah* for *Musaf* on Yom Kippur with a single rhyme.[192] R. Barukh also composed a *zulat* for the Sabbath of *parashat Bahar* (which always falls toward the end of the *sefirat ha-ʿomer* period, within two or three weeks of *Shavuʿot*), comparing the redemption of fields in the Torah portion to the need for the Almighty to redeem His "firstborn" (*ha-ben ha-bekhor bo yavo ve-yigʾalo*, signifying the Children of Israel), in light of the suffering and persecutions that they have endured;[193] a *seliḥah* for the period after Passover; and a penitential *seder tamid*.[194]

188 אש אוכלה אש (Habermann, "Piyyutei Rabbenu Barukh b. Samuel mi-Magenẓa," 137–40, sec. 25). Cf. ibid., 52–54; S. Einbinder, *Beautiful Death*, 52, 62–64, 164; and below, n. 192. This again suggests that the German Tosafists who wrote elegies did so for events in northern France as well. Cf. above, n. 106.

189 איככה אוכל וראיתי בידים (Habermann, ibid., 96–99, sec. 14, and cf. ibid., 54–55; each stanza ends with א-דוני. Cf. R. Chazan, *Medieval Stereotypes and Medieval Antisemitism*, 56–57.

190 בינות אריות (Habermann, ibid., 146–48, sec. 28, and cf. ibid., 55–56). This *seliḥah* was composed as an elegy to R. Isaac b. Asher (*ha-Levi*) *ha-baḥur*, who perished at this time in Wurzburg *ʿal qiddush ha-Shem*. Cf. Urbach, *Baʿalei ha-Tosafot*, 1:366–68.

191 בטרם הר וגבעה/ ברואה התשובה / רפואה נבחנת בדוקה וחשובה (Habermann, ibid., 122–25, sec. 22); and נולדו הרים ונבראו ברואה הרפואה החשובה / רפואה נבחנת ובדוקה והיא נקראת תשובה (Habermann, 125–29, sec. 23).

192 אני הוא השואל בעד בית ישראל, אני אדרוש אל א-ל ואשים דברתי (Habermann, ibid., 129–33, sec. 24 = *Maḥzor le-Yamim Noraʾim*, ed. Goldschmidt, 2:516–19). Among R. Barukh's other *seliḥot* and *qinot* are אצבעותי שפלו ואשיותי נפלו . . . אוי מה היה לנו (Habermann, 86–90, for the ninth of Av); לך ה' הצדקה (Habermann, 152–56, a *taḥanun* with Spanish meter), אליך ה' נפשי אשא בדמע ומשמע ודומה ומשא (Habermann, 101–2), אם החלנו בלא רחוקה (Habermann, 103–9), and אשכ[ו]ל מבושל שריג וענב (Habermann, 140–43), all with a *siyyomet miqraʾit*; אתה הרואה בעלבון נעלבים אתה האומר שובו בנים משובבים (Habermann, 116–19, for the fifth day of the ten days of penitence), and an *ʿaqedah* for that day, בנין המזבח אם נהרס ובנין החטא אם נדרש (Habermann, 119–21); אבקש אקשקש אנקש דלתות (Habermann, 90–93); אמרתי אל לבי לנפשי שובי שובי כי איך אעלה אל אבי (Habermann, 113–16); a *petiḥah*, ה' א-להי הצב-אות נערץ בסוד קדושים א-ל אדון על כל המעשים . . . חסדיך נזכיר מחילתך מבקשים תמוכים על רחמיך ופניך אנו דורשים (Habermann, 93–96, with a *ḥaruz ʾaḥid*, similar to the *petiḥah* of Rashi and the later example by R. Bonfant, below, n. 238); a *pizmon*, אין כא-ל ישורון אשר שם עבים רכובו (to be chanted according to the tune of *shofet kol ha-ʾareẓ*), in which each stich ends with the phrase שיח הגיוני עד הא-להים יבא (Habermann, 99–100); and a *seliḥot* that begins with a talmudic phrase, בכל מערבין ומשתתפין לצער מחילות (Habermann, 149–52). Fraenkel, *Ha-Tefillah veha-Piyyut be-Maḥzor Nuernberg*, 115–16, seeks to account for the fact that the many *seliḥot* composed by leading Rhineland *payyetanim* such as R. Eleazar and R. Menaḥem of Worms, R. Barukh of Mainz, and R. Simḥah of Speyer did not appear in any significant way in eastern German rites.

193 אחרי נמכר גאלה תהיה לו (Habermann, ibid., 83–85, sec. 10). See also idem, *Be-Ran—Yaḥad*, 167; ms. Bodl. 1099, fols. 78v–80v; and ms. Bodl. 1149, fols. 36r–v.

194 For the *seliḥah* אליך ה' נפשי אשא / במרר ומשמע ודומה ומשא, see ms. Parma 585, fol. 167v, and Habermann, "Piyyutei R. Barukh b. Samuel mi-Magenẓa," 101–2 (sec. 16). For the *tamid*,

Unlike R. Eleazar of Worms, R. Barukh did not compose any *maʿarivim.*[195] He did, however, author a *yoẓer*, *ʾofan*, and *zulat* for a *Shabbat ḥatan*,[196] as well as two *reshuyyot* (both with a *ḥaruz ʾaḥid*), to mark both the *ḥatan*'s ascent to the Torah and his descent, which chart the ultimate success that Joseph experienced due to Divine guidance,[197] and an *E-loheikhem* for the *kedushah* on that Sabbath with a single rhyme,[198] in addition to a metered *ʾofan* for a circumcision that took place on the Sabbath.[199] The two *ʾofanim* R. Barukh composed, for a *ḥatan* and for a circumcision on the Sabbath, contain a series of clear references to *Hekhalot* literature.[200] R. Barukh

---

בחר לך עליון בהגיון אביון / כעולת התמיד עשויה בציון (with Spanish meter), see Habermann, 143–46; and cf. above, n. 51.

[195] Habermann, ibid., 157–58, tentatively assigns a *barkhu* composition (cf. above, n. 138) to R. Barukh of Mainz, ברוך שמו והכל רוממו והכל נותן עוז לעמו ויברך אותם מפומו, which has a *ḥaruz ʾaḥid* (as many of these brief compositions do). Each of the six brief stanzas concludes with the biblical phrase ברוך כבוד ה' ממקומו.

[196] See Habermann, ibid., 60–61 (sec. 2, an *ʾofan*, בנים לאביהם ישראל קדושים הם, and see below, n. 200); 62–64 (sec. 3), and ms. Bodl. 1147, fols. 39r–v (a *zulat*, בת נדיב הוכלאה בארץ פתרוסים, with a *siyyomet miqraʾit* on the theme of redemption of the Jewish people and their release, which is comparable to the release of a female bondwoman, וישימו עליה שרי מסים . . . מכרוה כשפחה ויש לשחררה, and cf. above, n. 185, at Rivaq of Mainz); 64–69 (sec. 4, an *ʿezrat le-Shabbat ḥatunah*, with a single rhyme throughout, אומן באמון ימן מעשים אליכם אישים אביעה מיוששים). In ms. Bodl. 1149, fols. 154v–156r, however, this last composition (which has a single rhyme over its eighty-nine lines) is introduced as a יוצר לחתן מרבינו ברוך בניגון איחד (and see also ms. Verona 34, fols. 81r, 92v). Cf. E. Fleischer, *Ha-Yoẓerot*, 624 (n. 32), and above, n. 187; and M. Schmelzer, "Piyyutim le-Nisuʾin," 178, sec. 12.

[197] R. Barukh's lengthy *reshut* for the *ḥatan*'s *ʿaliyyah la-Torah* begins מרשות א-ל אל-הי ישראל אין קץ ואין חקר לתבונתו, בנה בשמים מעלותיו יסד על ארץ אגודתו (Habermann, ibid., 69–76, sec. 5 = ms. Bodl. 1149, fols. 225v–228v), while the poem to accompany the *ḥatan*'s descent from the *bimah* (Habermann, 77–78, sec. 7 = ms. Bodl. 1149, fols. 237v–238r) begins ביום טובה ונחמה אלומתך קמה, ידעתיך מלא חכמה, ראיתיך כמלאך צור. R. Barukh also composed a brief single-rhyme *mi she-berakh* to be recited for the groom. See Habermann, 76 (sec. 6, במקהלות ברכו בני ברית בגיל מורא ברעד, noted by Schmelzer, *Meḥqarim*, 199, n. 39, from ms. JTS 8972), and Fraenkel, *Ha-Tefillah veha-Piyyut be-Maḥzor Nuernberg*, 79. The Nuremberg *Maḥzor* also includes a similar composition by R. Yehudah *ha-Levi*.

[198] א-להיכם ברוך סודו וברוך כבודו וטעמו (Habermann, ibid., 78, sec. 8, and see also ms. Bodl. 1099, fol. 144r).

[199] ברית כרות בתיו חרות עלי שרות בני אלים (Habermann, ibid., 79–82, sec. 9, and the next note), and ms. Bodl. 1099, fols. 73v–74v. The two halves of this *piyyut* each have their own *ḥaruz ʾaḥid*. The *ʾofan* for a groom, בנים לאביהם ישראל קדושים הם / קימו וקבלו עליהם / להקדישו בסודיהם (Habermann, sec. 2), apparently also doubled for a circumcision on the Sabbath. Note also the Sabbath *zemer*, *Barukh E-l elyon ʾasher natan menuḥah* (Habermann, 55–59).

[200] See my *"Peering through the Lattices,"* 106, n. 25; my "Esotericism and Magic in Ashkenazic Prayer during the Tosafist Period," [Hebrew] in *Meḥqarim be-Toledot Yehudei Ashkenaz*, ed. G. Bacon et al. (Ramat Gan, 2008), 203–6, and Habermann, ibid., 60–61(sec. 2), and 79–82 (sec. 9). In addition to a poetic paraphrase of the *Hekahlot* passage referred to by R. Ephraim of Bonn (above, n. 113), R. Barukh includes *Hekhalot* references to the heavenly figures שמעיאל, גליצור, אדירון, and the numerous immersions in fire of various angelic figures prior to their recitation of praise to the Divine. Cf. *Synopse*, ed. Schafer, secs. 790–96; the *ʾofan* by R. Simeon b. Isaac of Mainz, שביבי שלהבת / חצובי להבות, and his *zulat*, אמהות עת נכבשה הבת הנאה / על ידי גלגול לסונה הובאה in

made use of Spanish meter in nearly a third of his *piyyutim*;[201] the conduit for these techniques was likely R. Ephraim of Regensburg.[202]

R. Menaḥem b. Jacob of Worms—either an uncle of R. Eleazar b. Judah *Roqeaḥ* of Worms or the uncle of Eleazar's father—was the senior member of the Worms rabbinical court on which R. Eleazar b. Judah also sat, and a leading rabbinic authority and halakhic decisor of his day. Indeed, the epitaph on his tombstone reads in part, רבינו מנחם בן ר' יעקב אבי החכמה, תנא דורש ופייטן אין חסר מאומה, בתלמוד רב ובמשנה ידו הרימה; and the Worms *Memorbucher* prominently singles out the names of R. Menaḥem b. Jacob and R. Eleazar b. Judah (in that order) for memorial recognition, together with the otherwise unidentified שאר הרבנים שהרביצו תורה בישראל.[203]

R. Menaḥem composed more than thirty *piyyutim*. In a number of Ashkenazic *piyyut* collections or rites found in manuscript, R. Menaḥem's name is one of the few names (and sometimes the only name) noted explicitly at the beginning of his *piyyutim*, ostensibly a sign of the esteem in which they were held.[204] R. Menaḥem composed a *ma'ariv* and a *bikkur* for the last day(s) of Passover, both with a *siyyomet miqra'it*.[205] M. Schmelzer points

Habermann, *Piyyutei R. Shim'on b. Yiẓḥaq* (Jerusalem, 1938), 58–61 (secs. 2–3); and above, n. 186 (Rivaq b. Moses of Mainz). R. Barukh's son, R. Samuel Bamberg, was a halakhist and prolific commentator on the prayers (and on *piyyutim*, although he does not seem to have composed any *piyyutim*). See Urbach, *Ba'alei ha-Tosafot*, 1:429–32, *'Arugat ha-Bosem*, ed. Urbach, 35, n. 74, 59, 69 n.98, 71; S. Emanuel, "Polmos shel Ḥasidei Ashkenaz 'al Nosaḥ ha-Tefillah," in *Meḥqerei Talmud*, vol. 3., ed. Y. Sussmann and D. Rosenthal (Jerusalem, 2005), 2:622–24; idem, *Shivrei Luḥot*, 106–7, 262–66; and my *"Peering through the Lattices,"* 103–5.

201 Cf. Habermann, "Piyyutei Rabbenu Barukh mi-Magenẓa," 57, 159.

202 Habermann, ibid., 49, 56–57.

203 See Aptowitzer, *Mavo la-Rabiah*, 382–84, 407 (and cf. Grossman, *Ḥakhmei Ashkenaz ha-Rishonim*, 329); *Mordekhai li Yevamot*, sec. 89; above, Introduction, n. 90, and in chapter 1, nn. 12, 57, 145; and *R. Eleazar mi-Vermaiza—Derashah le-Pesaḥ*, ed. S. Emanuel, 39–40, 72–73. R. Eleazar cites a comment on a *piyyut* by R. Menaḥem (which he indicates was part of R. Menaḥem's commentary to the *piyyutim* of R. Meir *shaliaḥ ẓibbur* of Worms). Cf. *'Arugat ha-Bosem*, ed. Urbach, 4:33–34 (n. 69). R. Menaḥem's practices on eating dairy and meat foods on *Shavu'ot* is recorded both by R. Eleazar (in his *Ma'aseh Roqeaḥ*) and by his student, the author of *Sefer Asufot*. See also below, chapter 6 (nn. 62–67), and *Sefer ha-Qushyot*, ed. Stal (above, n. 13), 167–68 (sec. 215).

204 See, e.g., ms. Prague 246, fol. 157v, and below, nn. 207, 209.

205 See *Maḥzor Pesaḥ*, ed. Fraenkel, 347–55; ms. Paris (Cluny Museum) 12290 (#14772), fols. 160r–v; ms. Moscow 611, fols. 182v–184r; and ms. Verona 34, fols. 193r–v. The *ma'ariv* begins אורי וישעי על הים נגלה, while the *bikkur* (with a *ḥaruz 'aḥid*, on the pilgrimage to Jerusalem and the Temple) begins מתי אבוא ואראה פני א-להים להקבילה. E. Fleischer, *Ha-Yoẓerot*, 55, suggests that the *ma'ariv* was originally written for the seventh night of Passover, but as often occurs, it was listed in some liturgies for the eighth night as well. See also Fleischer, "Prayer and Piyyut in the Worms Maḥzor," [Hebrew] in the Introductory Volume to *Worms Maḥzor* (ms. JNUL $4^0$781), ed. M. Beit Arie (Jerusalem, 1985), 31. See also ms. Giessen (#38878), fols. 87r–v, in which R. Menaḥem's *ma'ariv* is followed by one from R. Eleazar of Worms (אמונת אומן, fols. 88v–89v), for the eighth day of Passover; see also I. Meiseles, *Shirat ha-Roqeaḥ*, 99–107.

to a passage in the *ma'ariv* which suggests that R. Menaḥem subscribed to the doctrine of the German Pietists concerning the revelation of hidden miracles (*zekher 'asah le-nifle'otav*) that would occur at the end of days.[206]

R. Menaḥem b. Jacob also composed a series of *yoẓerot*, *'ofanim*, and *reshuyyot* for a *ḥatan*, as well as a *zulat*,[207] two commemorative *'ahavot* for the *Shabbat* prior to *Shavu'ot*,[208] a *yoẓer* for *Shabbat Shuvah* with a *siyyomet miqra'it*, an *'ofan* and a *zulat*,[209] as well as a number of *seliḥot*. These include three metered *teḥinot* for the end of the *seliḥot* service (one of which is also designated as a *tamid*),[210] a *seliḥah* for the ten days of penitence with a *siy-*

[206] See Schmelzer, *Meḥqarim*, 144–45. On R. Menaḥem and *sod*, see my *"Peering through the Lattices,"* 132, n. 3, and below, chapter 6.

[207] See Schmelzer, "Piyyutim le-Nisu'in," 177–78 (sec. 11), and cf. ms. Bodl. 1149, fols. 143v–144v (יוצר אחר לחתן מר' מנחם בן יעקב. מי ימלל גבורות א-להי עולם מלכותו בכל משלה); and Schmelzer, 183–85); fols. 161v–165v (יוצר לחתן מרבינו מנחם בניגוד אחיד. א-להי לעולם אודך בהגיוניי אזמרך כבוד בלהקת אמוני); fols. 214r–218r (רשות לחתן מר' מנחם ב"ר יעקב. מרשות מעונה א-להי קדם עד דכא); and fols. 233v–237v (רשות לחתן מר' מנחם ב"ר יעקב. איום ונורא קצת נוראותיו אספרה אשר דוק וחלק לכבודו ברא). See also ms. Verona 34, fols. 95r, 97v, 100r. As further evidence for his stature in Ashkenaz as a *payyetan*, R. Menaḥem is the only *payyetan* for whom two sets of wedding *yoẓerot* are included as part of the collection preserved in ms. Bodl. 1099 (just as two sets of his wedding *piyyutim* are preserved in ms. Bodl. 1149). Note also R. Menaḥem's *E-loheikhem* for a *ḥatan* (א-להיכם משרתיו שואלים איה מקומו) in Zunz, *LG*, 296 (sec. 16); and see also ms. Jerusalem Schocken 19522 (SH 73), fol. 146r. A third *yoẓer* noted by Schmelzer, אלה תולדות בהרבאם פעולתו, was also designated for a Sabbath on which a circumcision took place. L. Weinberger's claim (in his *Jewish Hymnography*, 174), that R. Menaḥem b. Jacob composed a *ma'ariv* for Purim (ליל שיכורים הוא זה הלילה לשמוח ביין הטוב ובגילה), found in *Maḥzor Vitry*, ed. Hurwitz, 583–84, is belied by the fact that the *koteret* to this *piyyut* in *Maḥzor Vitry* reads, ממעמד ר' מנחם בן אהרן ז"ל.

[208] See E. Fleischer, *Ha-Yoẓerot*, 683 (אליך עין נשאתי . . . את אשר יאהב ה'). This *'ahavah*, found in ms. Bodl. 1149, fol. 50r (and cf. Zunz, *LG*, 295, sec. 9), has the same fine stylistic construction as the commemorative *'ahavah* by R. Ephraim of Regensburg (above, n. 169), אותך כל היום קוינו. See also Fleischer, *Ha-Yoẓerot*, 625, where conventions employed by R. Menaḥem b. Jacob are linked to those of Raban, R. Eleazar of Worms, and R. Meir of Rothenburg. The second *'ahavah* by R. Menaḥem, for the Sabbath before *Shavu'ot*, is titled אהבתיך על כן . . . סגולתי משכתיך חסד. See Fraenkel, *Ha-Tefillah veha-Piyyut be-Maḥzor Nuernberg*, 74, and Zunz, *LG*, 296, sec. 10.

[209] For the *yoẓer*, אלהי ישענו נוראות מאויים אות ברבבה דגול ומסוים (with a biblical phrase at the end of each stanza), see *Maḥzor le-Yamim Nora'im*, ed. Goldschmidt, 1:318–20. In ms. Bodl. 1149, fol. 72r–75v, this is introduced as a יוצר לשבת שובה מר' מנחם ב"ר יעקב ב"ר שלמה. See also ms. Parma 605, fols. 123r–125v; ms. Paris BN 648, fols. 57r–59v; ms. Bodl. 1025, fol. 215r; and ms. Verona 34, fols. 107v–108r. For the *'ofan*, מכון כסא בהוד נושא, see ms. Paris BN 648, fol. 60r–61r, and see fol. 61v for the *zulat* (to be recited in the ניגון of אהובה אני לפניך). See also the private Jerusalem manuscript collection C (film #41225 at the Institute for Microfilmed Hebrew Manuscripts in the National Library of Israel), fols. 86v–87r.

[210] א-להים הבט בשעבוד גלות / ירודי עפר ודלי דלות (*Leqet Piyyutei Seliḥot*, ed. Goldschmidt and Fraenkel, 1:406–8). The identifying acrostic found within this piece reads "Ẓemaḥ b. Jacob" (rather than Menaḥem). Ẓemaḥ and Menaḥem, however, have the same *gematria* value, and R. Menaḥem included this equivalent "nickname" in several of his other *seliḥot*; see *Leqet Piyyutei Seliḥot*, ed. Goldschmidt and Fraenkel, 2:813. For the (lengthy) *teḥinnah/tamid*, אשיחה עם לבבי ורוחי חפש, see *Leqet Piyyutei Seliḥot*, ed. Goldschmidt and Fraenkel, 1:413–17. The final *teḥinnah*, אשרי העם בחרם הא-ל / וגדול קרבם קדוש ישראל (*Leqet Piyyutei Seliḥot*, ed. Goldschmidt and Fraenkel, 1:418–21), is not noted by either Zunz or Davidson.

yomet miqra'it (= *hava'ah min ha-miqra ba-soger*),[211] another in which each stanza concludes with a biblical verse that ends with the word (*le-*)*ʿolam*,[212] an *ʿaqedah* with a *siyyomet miqra'it*,[213] a *seliḥah* for *erev* Rosh ha-Shanah, another for the Fast of Gedalyah, and a *ḥatanu* (חטאנו) that commemorates the deaths of ten martyrs.[214] In addition, R. Menaḥem composed three *pizmonim*: one for a circumcision that occurs on a fast day, in which each stanza concludes with a verse ending with the word (*ha-*)*brit*,[215] and a second for the seventeenth of Tammuz with a *siyyomet miqra'it*.[216]

The third *pizmon* by R. Menaḥem, also with a *siyyomet miqra'it*, was modeled after the *Zekhor Brit pizmon* by Rabbenu Gershom for *erev* Rosh ha-Shanah (with the double refrain, והשב שבות אהלי יעקב / ושוב ברחמים אל שארית ישראל). R. Menaḥem's version refers similarly to several themes: the destruction of the Temple by the Romans, contemporary persecutions at the hands of the Christians, and calls for Divine vengeance. It begins with the phrase מיד איש שעיר [= עשו] דרוש נפש אדם. The next four brief stanzas begin with the following phrases: חמול זנוחים קדומים, בית היכל יקטרג מהרסיו, מתי תקום תנקש ותרומם, מושיע וגואל, and כמהפכת סדום תן אדום ואת גבולו. Similarly, the various stanzas conclude with the phrases כאשר עשו לי בני עשו, קום מה לך נרדם ונמסו הרים מדמם, ונתתי נקמתי באדום ביד ישראל, and finally, נקמת ה' היא נקמת היכלו.[217]

R. Menaḥem also composed an elegy for the martyrs of Boppard (1179) and York (1190), in which these martyrs are linked and compared to the sons

211 אמת ראש דברך נורא ואיום/ באחרית הימים מצאנו דברך עליון/ גם צר לנו באנו משבר וכליון/ יום צרה ותוכחה ונאצה היום (*Leqet Piyyutei Seliḥot*, ed. Goldschmidt and Fraenkel, 1:408–9).

212 אנחנו הדבקים בה' כגדול ועבות / מים רבים לא יוכלו האהבה לכבות (*Leqet Piyyutei Seliḥot*, ed. Goldschmidt and Fraenkel, 1:410–12).

213 את דבר קדשך זכור והבטחת / שבועת איתן אשר מקדם נוכחת (*Leqet Piyyutei Seliḥot*, ed. Goldschmidt and Fraenkel, 1:422–25).

214 אם יתקע שופר בעיר וחרדו עם ומחנות (Zunz, *LG*, 296, sec. 10, and Davidson, *Oẓar ha-Shirah veha-Piyyut*, 1:246 [5363א]); את צום השביעי (Zunz, ibid., 297, sec. 28, and Davidson, 1:389 [8594:א]). For the *ḥatanu*, אל א-להים אצעקה במלולי (which has a *siyyomet miqra'it*, as well as a *shirshur* between the stanzas), see Zunz, ibid., 296, sec. 22, and A. Velner, *ʿAsarah Harugei Malkhut*, 335–42. The order of the deaths of the martyrs in this *ḥatanu* differs from the standard *Eleh Ezkerah*, and there is discussion about burying R. Aqiva on Yom Kippur eve. Perhaps for this reason, there were rites that listed this *piyyut* for recitation on that day. See, e.g., *Minhagot Vermaiza le-R. Yuda Loew Kircheim*, ed. I. M. Peles (Jerusalem, 1987), 134, 349 (חטאנו אל א-להים אצעקה). For another *seliḥah* by R. Menaḥem, איככה רחמיך התאפקו, see A. M. Habermann, *Gezerot Ashkenaz ve-Ẓarefat*, 239–40.

215 מבור תשלח אסירי / עבור פשע לשארית / נקה טהור עוני / תרבה עלי בורית (*Leqet Piyyutei Seliḥot*, ed. Goldschmidt and Fraenkel, 1:426–27, to be recited according to the tune of *ha-Shofet kol ha-'areẓ*).

216 משנה שברון הושברתי ונתתי לבוז (*Leqet Piyyutei Seliḥot*, ed. Goldschmidt and Fraenkel, 1:429–30). See also ms. Modena 30 (PH#6854), אבכה יומם ולילה חללי בת עמי.

217 See *Leqet Piyyutei Seliḥot*, ed. Goldschmidt and Fraenkel, 1:428. D. Goldschmidt, *Meḥqerei Tefillah u-Piyyut* (Jerusalem, 1980), 341–44, demonstrates that this *pizmon* form actually originated with Rabbenu Gershom's Italian predecessor, R. Solomon *ha-Bavli*. Goldschmidt's list of those who imitated Rabbenu Gershom's work (341, n. 1) does not include this composition by R. Menaḥem b. Jacob.

of Aaron (Nadav and Avihu) on the one hand, and to Ḥananyah, Misha'el, and Azaryah on the other;[218] and a liturgical poem that marked the end of the siege of Worms in March 1201.[219] In one of R. Menaḥem's three *qinot* for the ninth of Av, marking the destruction of the Temple, the final stich of each stanza consists of a biblical phrase that ends with the word *bayit.*[220]

The percentage of R. Menaḥem of Worms's *piyyutim* that are not *seliḥot* or *qinot* (or commemorative *'ahavot* and elegies) is not nearly as high as that of Raban. This signifies that R. Menaḥem's output was not as well balanced as Raban's, and he remains more similar in this regard to R. Eleazar of Worms, R. Baruch of Mainz, and R. Ephraim of Regensburg. Nonetheless, Ezra Fleischer has linked the *piyyutim* of R. Menaḥem to those of Raban in terms of their structure and significance, and he has suggested that they are very deserving of a critical edition and close literary treatment. Indeed, the importance of R. Menaḥem's *piyyutim* within medieval Ashkenaz is further underscored by the comments and interpretations that were offered to several of them.[221]

R. Nathan b. Isaac was a lesser-known *dayyan* from Mainz, who was nonetheless a signatory (along with Rabiah, R. Simḥah of Speyer, and other leading Tosafists and rabbinic authorities) to the so-called *takkanot Shu"m* that were promulgated in the Rhineland in the 1220s. In addition, R. Nathan and his judicial colleague in Mainz, R. Eleazar b. Simeon, presented a matter that had come before them (concerning the wife of an impotent husband who wanted a divorce) to Rabiah for his imput.[222] R. Nathan composed at least five *piyyutim*, and perhaps as many as eight.[223] Three of these

[218] אללי לי כי באו רגע אלמון ושכול. See ms. Vatican 312, fols. 72r–73v; ms. Vatican 319, sec. 46; ms. Parma 586, fol. 171v; S. Einbinder, *Beautiful Death*, 29–30; and R. Chazan (above, n. 180), 54–55.

[219] מצור באתה העיר (Zunz, *LG*, 296, sec. 21).

[220] מעוני שמים שחקים יזבלוך מלאים מהודך והם לא יכלכלוך ואף כי הבית (Zunz, *LG*, 296, sec. 20). R. Menaḥem's two other *qinot* for the ninth of Av are אשים לבי לספר ומאספכם א-להי ישראל כתוב על יד נביאך קול צופיך נשאו (Zunz, *LG*, sec. 19, and cf. ms. Vatican 319, sec. 53), and אוי לבנים סוכלו/ משלחן אב גלו (Zunz, *LG*, sec. 17).

[221] See Fleischer, "Prayer and Piyyut in the Worms Maḥzor," 40, n. 176, and cf. Tova Beeri, "Remarks on Ezra Fleischer's Research on Medieval Hebrew Liturgical Poetry," [Hebrew] *Jewish Studies* 45 (2008), 145–46 (n. 41). For comments on R. Menaḥem's *piyyutim*, see E. Hollender, *Clavis Commentatorium of Hebrew Liturgical Poetry in Manuscript*, 126 (to the *ma'ariv* for the seventh day of Passover, אודה חסדו); 168 (to the *ma'ariv* for the seventh day of Passover, אורי וישעי על הים נגלה); 333 (to the *zulat* for *Shabbat ha-Gadol*, אמון נוא הובא); 514–15 (to the *seliḥah* for the Fast of Gedalyah, את צום השביעי); 816 (to the *ma'ariv* for the seventh day of Passover, מתי ואבוא).

[222] See Urbach, *Ba'alei ha-Tosafot*, 1:382; A. Aptowitzer, *Mavo la-Rabiah*, 315; Louis Finkelstein, *Jewish Self-Government in the Middle Ages* (New York, 1964), 250; and cf. A. Grossman, *Ḥasidot u-Mordot* (Jerusalem, 2001), 418–21.

[223] See I. Davidson, *Oẓar ha-Shirah veha-Piyyut*, 4:453; Zunz, *LG*, 332–33; and cf. A. M. Habermann, *Piyyutim Nivḥarim le-Ḥagim ule-Mo'adim* (Lod, 1992), 26–27.

are *seliḥot* (with a *siyyomet miqra'it*) for the penitential period of the *Yamim Nora'im.*[224] An additional *seliḥah*, a *teḥinnah* for the Fast of Esther,[225] and a *qerovah* for the *'Amidah* of *Ta'anit Esther* are found in the name of R. Nathan b. Isaac only in Provençal prayer rites, and were likely the products of a Provençal *payyetan* of the same name.[226]

The remaining *piyyutim* composed by R. Nathan b. Isaac of Mainz were for "happy" occasions. These consist of a *yoẓer* and a *zulat* for a *Shabbat ḥatan*,[227] and perhaps an addendum to the *Nishmat* prayer on *Shavu'ot.*[228] The fact that virtually half of R. Nathan's *piyyut* output was intended for these occasional venues takes on added significance when we consider that several other German Tosafists and rabbinic judges during this period composed only *seliḥot* and *qinot.*

R. Simḥah of Speyer (d. c. 1230), a leading halakhist and talmudist with an array of important students, composed three *seliḥot* that were written,

224 See *Leqet Piyyutei Seliḥot*, ed. Goldschmidt and Fraenkel, 2:505–9, for איככה אוכל וראיתי ערך מענית . . . ובקדוש ישראל תתהלל, and see also ms. Cremona (Archives) 56 (IMHM #34136, from book bindings). As noted by the editors, this composition has phrases such as וישימו אותות בקרב (see Psalms 74:4), which serve as allusions to the Crusaders and their symbols, as well as a series of expressions about the misdeeds of Edom, and references to the *'Aqedah*. For the א-להים ,שלישיה שלח עזרה . . . וברכת ה' היא תעשיר, see *Leqet Piyyutei Seliḥot*, ed. Goldschmidt and Fraenkel, 2:509–11, and see also ms. Hamburg Cod. Heb. 39 (#26291), and ms. Modena 20, (PH#6854). For the שלישיה ,אנכי עפר ואפר חטאי עצמו מלספר, see *Leqet Piyyutei Seliḥot*, ed. Goldschmidt and Fraenkel, 2:511–13, and ms. Parma 588, sec. 217. On this manuscript, cf. above, nn. 82, 101, 123.

225 See Zunz, *LG*, 587 (ה' נין בוזה זמם), and ms. Parma 1117 (a fifteenth-century Provençal *Maḥzor*), fol. 152r.

226 See Davidson, *Oẓar ha-Shirah veha-Piyyut*, 2:470 (182:כ), כי א-לי אבלי המיר לגילה, and ms. Vatican 553 (Provence, 1389), fol. 8v. Cf. Binyamin Bar-Tikva, *Genres and Topics in Provençal and Catalonian Piyyut*, [Hebrew] (Beer Sheva, 2009), 64, 297. Note also that *qerovot* were produced by hardly any Ashkenazic *payyetantim* after R. Meir *Shaẓ* of Worms (who was active in the second half of the eleventh century). Cf. *Piyyutei R. Yeḥi'el b. Avraham me-Roma*, ed. A. Fraenkel, editor's introduction, 11.

227 See Schmelzer, "Piyyutim le-Nisu'in," 178 (sec. 14); ms. Moscow 611, secs. 203–4 (fols. 73r–75r), and Zunz, *LG*, 332 (א-להינו מלך העולם אספרה תהלותיו . . . יודוך ה' כל מעשיך, and אודה ה' על עזוז נוראותיו . . . ומשירי אהודנו). These are found in the manuscript after an *'ofan* and a *reshut* by R. Ephraim of Bonn (sec. 199), and before four *'ofanim* and a *yoẓer* from R. Judah *ha-Levi* (whose *piyyutim* were widely appreciated in medieval Ashkenaz, along with those of Ibn Gabirol and Ibn Ezra; see, e.g., Schmelzer, *Meḥqarim*, 194–98, and E. Fleischer, *Ha-Yoẓerot*, 670–71, 680–83, 704–6), a *yoẓer* and an *'ofan* for a circumcision on the Sabbath by R. Menaḥem b. Jacob (secs. 209–10), and an *'ofan* by Rivaq. Although there are quite a number of German authors in these manuscripts, there are also *piyyutim* from *Ha-Levi* and from R. Joseph Kimḥi (in a different hand). See also ms. Bodl. 1149, fols. 246r–248v (beginning יוצר מר' נתן בן יצחק זקיני); and ms. Verona 34, fols. 73r–75r (beginning יוצר לשבת חתן מר' נתן ב"ר יצחק מגרמיישא).

228 נשמת נעימה פנימה תמימה קהילה קדושה; see Davidson, *Oẓar ha-Shirah veha-Piyyut*, 3:233 (788:ג), but cf. Zunz, *LG*, 727 (in the Hebrew index, 107). On this genre and venue in Ashkenaz, see E. Fleischer, *Shirat ha-Qodesh ha-'Ivrit Bimei ha-Benayim*, 461–63; idem, *Ha-Yoẓerot*, 626, n.40; and cf. Bar-Tikva, *Genres and Topics*, 93–99; and *Maḥzor Shavu'ot*, ed. Fraenkel, 90–92. Similarities have been noted by these modern scholars between Ashkenazic *piyyutim* for *Nishmat* and those of the Sefardic *payyetan* R. Joseph ibn Avitur. See also Schmelzer, *Meḥqarim*, 193–96.

according to Zunz, in "light and flowing language."[229] One of these makes explicit reference to those who perpetrated the growing number of persecutions in his day, including a ritual murder charge,[230] and another is a *petiḥah* that was intended either for *erev* Yom Kippur or for *Kol Nidrei.*[231] R. Simḥah also composed a brief elegy for his teacher, R. Abraham b. Samuel *he-Ḥasid*, which he included in one of his responsa.[232]

R. Simḥah's student R. Samuel b. Abraham *ha-Levi* of Worms (c. 1200–1275, known also as R. Bonfant) is mentioned only once in passing in Urbach's *Ba'alei ha-Tosafot.*[233] Nonetheless, recent manuscript research, as it has elucidated the fuller range of R. Simḥah's own rabbinic writings, has revealed that R. Bonfant composed *ḥiddushim* and *nimmuqim* to several talmudic tractates which remain largely lost, as well as a *seder ḥalizah*, and that he also issued a number of *pesaqim.*[234] Four of R. Samuel's *piyyutim* have been identified with certainty. He authored one of the commemorative elegies for the martyrs in Frankfurt who died *'al kiddush ha-Shem* in the spring of 1241, and a *zulat* for the Sabbath nearest 13 Sivan, the date on which this

229 See Zunz, *LG*, 311.

230 שמך הגדול יעמוד לנו בעת צרה, in *Leqet Piyyutei Seliḥot*, ed. Goldschmidt and Fraenkel, 2:640–42, as a response to an *'alilat dam*. The second stanza begins with the phrase חנית חריקה ולפי חרב עדתך חילשה / מיתות מאמורות אחרות פילשה. A subsequent stanza begins with the phrase מתגוללים עלינו מתנפלים ומעלילים, and the following stanza raises the need for Divine revenge (ואם בגוי אשר כזה לא תתנקם / קיים דברך ומילתך הקם / ידין בגוים מלא גלויות). On the decrees in R. Simḥah's day that may be reflected here, see R. Chazan, *Medieval Stereotypes*, 55–57 (and note especially the incident in Speyer itself in 1196).

231 כי על רחמיך הרבים אנו סמוכים ובצדקותיך אנו תמוכים (Davidson, *Oẓar ha-Shirah veha-Piyyut*, 2:473, 220:כ, and cf. *Maḥzor le-Yamim Nora'im*, 2:18). R. Simḥah's third *seliḥah* is titled את חטאי אני מזכיר, and ends with the phrase אל נא תשיבנו ריקם מלפניך. See also *'Arugat ha-Bosem*, ed. Urbach, 4:165, for the frequent references made by a student of R. Simḥah, R. Abraham b. Azri'el (in his *piyyut* commentary), to R. Simḥah's no longer extant halakhic work, *Seder 'Olam*. On *Seder 'Olam*, see S. Emanuel, *Shivrei Luḥot*, 158–66, and cf. above, chapter 1, n. 19.

232 See Urbach, *Ba'alei ha-Tosafot*, 1:411–12. The responsum is preserved in *Sefer Or Zaru'a* (pt. 1, sec. 760), composed by another of R. Simḥah's students, R. Isaac b. Moshe *Or Zaru'a*. On R. Simḥah's connections and affinities with R. Yehudah *he-Ḥasid* (and *ḥasidut Ashkenaz*), cf. Urbach, *Ba'alei ha-Tosafot*, 1:412–13, 419, and my "Appointment of *Ḥazzanim* in Medieval Ashkenaz," 25 (n. 44).

233 Urbach, *Ba'alei ha-Tosafot*, 1:413–14, notes the report of R. Isaac *Or Zaru'a* of Vienna that while he was living (and studying) in R. Simḥah's home in Speyer, R. Samuel came along on a Friday to ask R. Simḥah about a *she'elah* that had occurred in his own home (in Speyer) at that time. Cf. I. Ta-Shma, *Knesset Meḥqarim*, vol. 1, 161–62, 170–71; *Teshuvot u-Pesaqim*, ed. E. Kupfer, 62, n. 1; and my *Jewish Education and Society*, 66–67.

234 See *Teshuvot u-Pesaqim*, ed. Kupfer, 121–22, 129–32, 144, 174, n.6, 218–20, 227, 282–89, 290, 295–96; S. Emanuel, *Shivrei Luḥot*, 181–84; and idem, "Teshuvot Maharam she-Einan shel ha-Maharam," *Shenaton ha-Mishpat ha-'Ivri* 21 (1998–2000), 173–76. See also my "Returning to the Jewish Community in Medieval Ashkenaz: History and Halakhah" (above, n. 14), 81–87, and Rachel Furst, "Captivity, Conversion and Communal Identity: Sexual Angst and Religious Crisis in Frankfurt, 1241," *Jewish History* 22 (2008), 206–10.

tragedy occurred.[235] Some of those who converted to Christianity at this time later returned to Judaism, and both R. Simḥah of Speyer and R. Judah b. Moses *ha-Kohen* (of Friedberg and Wurzburg, who also authored one of the commemorative *piyyutim*, as we shall see shortly) issued responsa rulings related to this episode.[236]

R. Bonfant also composed a *qinah* for the ninth of Av,[237] and he authored a *petiḥah* for the *seliḥot* of the ten days of penitence with a *ḥaruz ʾaḥid/mavriaḥ*, similar to those authored by Rashi.[238] An unusual *ʾahavah* for *parashat Va-Yera*, which is centered on the account of the binding of Isaac—a highly significant martyrological symbol in medieval Ashkenaz—has also been attributed to R. Bonfant.[239] R. Bonfant's son was R. Yaqar b. Samuel *ha-Levi* of Cologne, an important rabbinic judge and *payyetan* in the second half of the thirteenth century, as we shall see.[240]

235 אין לנו א-להים עוד זולתיך / מושיע וגואל אפס אין בלתך/ בעמים הורעתה עוד נפלאותיך. See ms. Bodl. 1149, fols. 41r–43r (ומורי הרב ר׳ בשמואל ב״ר אברהם הלוי הוא יסדו); Habermann, *Gezerot Ashkenaz ve-Ẓarefat*, 176–78; and S. Bernfeld, *Sefer ha-Demaʿot*, 1:301–5; and cf. 1:295–99.

236 S. Einbinder, *Beautiful Death*, 21, and 40 (n. 6), notes that Bernfeld published all (three) of the commemorative poems about this episode, and that the case of the converts who returned subsequently is discussed in G. Blidstein, "The Personal Status of Captive and Apostate Women in Medieval Jewish Law," [Hebrew] *Shenaton ha-Mishpat ha-ʿIvri*, 3–4 (1976–77), 85–104. See also Urbach, *Baʿalei ha-Tosafot*, 1:433; R. Furst (above, n. 234), 214 (n. 14); and cf. my "Returning to the Jewish Community," (above, n. 14), 81–87. The third elegy for the martyrs of Frankfurt, אשא בכי ונהי ואומר אויה, is attributed in ms. Parma 1104, fol. 52v (and in ms. Jerusalem, private collection C [#41225], fol. 52v, and ms. Cremona [State Archives], 32–66 [#34136]) to אורשרגו; cf. below, n. 321. A fourth commemorative poem that apparently deals with this episode as well, א-ל נקמות לפנים הופעת / ואותי בגולה הנחת / עד מאוד עלי קצפת / בכל לב נועצים/ גזירות עלי להעצים / בקרדומות באו כחוטבי עצים / גם בברזל יחד תופסים (and unremarked by Einbinder), is found (unattributed) in ms. Prague 246, fols. 20r–20v. See also Davidson, *Oẓar ha-Shirah veha-Piyyut*, 3943:א.

237 אשיחה ואה[י]מה במר נפש אתבונן/אתאונן. See I. Davidson, *Oẓar ha-Shirah veha-Piyyut*, 7905:א (and cf. Zunz, *LG*, 341); ms. Vatican 312, fol. 68r; ms. Vatican 319, sec. 52; and ms. Parma 1104, fol. 37v, where R. Samuel's *seliḥah* immediately precedes the *seliḥah* אלכה וירדתי על ההרים ואבכה by R. Abraham b. Samuel *he-Ḥasid* (fol. 38v); cf. above, n. 178.

238 שחרנוך בקשנוך יוצר הרים / מגיד לאדם שיח ודברים . . . קחנו דברים בשילום פרים / תמוכים בטוחים ולרחמיך מסברים. See *Seder ha-Seliḥot*, ed. Goldschmidt, 191–92 (sec. 69, as the *petiḥah* for the third of the ten days), and ms. Prague 246, fol. 4v. This relatively short *petiḥah* is replete with biblical and talmudic phrases as well, as are Rashi's penitential *petiḥot* (which also had a *ḥaruz ʾaḥid*); cf. above, nn. 26, 192. For comments to this *petiḥah*, see E. Hollender, *Clavis Commentatorium of Hebrew Liturgical Poetry in Manuscript*, secs. 16752–59.

239 See ms. Prague 250, שננו לשונם בני אונם ואת אונם לא השבת (to be found following various *yoẓerot* for *Shemini ʿAẓeret* and the Sabbath of *parashat Bereshit*, and prior to the *piyyutim* for Ḥanukkah), and Davidson, *Oẓar ha-Shirah veha-Piyyut*, 3:500 (1986:ש). The refrain is a paraphrase of the biblical verse ובכן קח נא את בנך את יחידך אשר אהבת. The manuscript initially attributes this poem to R. Shmu'el *ha-Nagid* (as does שי״ר), but then specifies R. Samuel b. Abraham *ha-Levi* as its author. Cf. E. Fleischer, *Ha-Yoẓerot*, 538 (n. 18). See also ms. Parma 1264, fol. 165v, where this poem is attributed simply to Samuel, and *Siddur Kol Bo le-Ḥag ha-Sukkot*, vol. 3 (New York, 1953), following a *yoẓer le-Shabbat Bereshit* (where Samuel is again identified as R. Samuel b. Abraham *ha-Levi*).

240 See below, nn. 309–21.

Like R. Joel *ha-Levi* of Bonn and his son Rabiah, and R. Simḥah of Speyer and his student R. Bonfant *ha-Levi*, three other contemporary German *dayyanim*, whose judicial and other rabbinic activities have been noted above, also composed only *seliḥot.* Among R. David b. Qalonymus of Muenzburg's five such compositions are an *ʿaqedah* with a *siyyomet miqraʾit*,[241] a metered *teḥinnah/tamid* found in two different versions,[242] and a metered *pizmon* for the tenth of Tevet with a *siyyomet miqraʾit* and an intricate internal (Sefardic) rhyme scheme (a חרוז מעין אזורי).[243] R. Sheʾaltiʾel b. Menaḥem of Cologne, a colleague of Rabiah, composed a total of eight *seliḥot*, four of which were intended for the end of the *seliḥot* service, two of the so-called *ḥatanu* genre, and two *teḥinot*, one of which is a *tamid.*[244]

The *dayyan*, communal leader, and Tosafist R. Judah b. Moses *ha-Kohen* of Wurzburg was a teacher of R. Meir of Rothenburg. R. Judah was the son of a student of Rabbenu Tam, R. Moses b. Solomon *ha-Kohen* of Mainz, himself a leading judge.[245] R. Judah *ha-Kohen* composed two *qinot*, one in memory of the martyrs in Frankfurt in 1241[246] and another on the destruction of Jerusalem (for *Tishʿah be-Av*),[247] as well as a *seliḥah.*[248]

241 אחד היה אברהם וירש את הארץ. See *Leqet Piyyutei Seliḥot*, ed. Goldschmidt and Fraenkel, 1:166–69; Davidson, *Oẓar ha-Shirah veha-Piyyut*, 1:114, 2406א (and cf. Davidson, 2407:א, for a similarly titled *seliḥah* by Rivaq of Mainz). See also א-להים אל דמי לך (Davidson, *Oẓar ha-Shirah veha-Piyyut*, vol. 4, 79, 1228:א*), and ארוכה תצמיח צרי וסם יפה (Davidson, 1:340, 7497:א).

242 דברך האמן למקדש שמם מכונך קומם מעונך רומם (*Leqet Piyyutei Seliḥot*, ed. Goldschmidt and Fraenkel, 1:169–76, and cf. Zunz, *LG*, 326). See also ms. Parma 588, fol. 63v, and ms. Berlin 9, fol. 15. Cf. Urbach, *Baʿalei ha-Tosafot*, 1:366, who notes R. David's pedigree—as it emerges from this *seliḥah*—as the son of R. Qalonymus b. Meir (of Speyer). R. David apparently left Speyer fairly early in his training, heading first to Mainz and then to Muenzberg. See also above, chapter 1, nn. 60–62; and chapter 3, nn. 247, 249.

243 ישראל כניתו רענן יפה פרי; see *Leqet Piyyutei Seliḥot*, ed. Goldschmidt and Fraenkel, 1:176–79. On R. David, see also ibid., 2:777–78.

244 R. Sheʾaltiʾel b. Menaḥem's *seliḥot* are listed in Zunz, *LG*, 270–71. They are published in *Leqet Piyyutei Seliḥot*, ed. Goldschmidt and Fraenkel, 2:551–74 (and the note on 2:744), from ms. Bodl. 1154. These include: חטאנו-אהמה לפניך שברי כי הגדיל צרי ;ה' א-להים עד ביתך אעלה ואדדם; אשיחה ;חטאנו-אנחנו נמקים מפני פשעינו ;א-להים חיים ומלך עולם (תחנה/תמיד) ;אודך בעמים בערץ (שלישיה) תערב ישועה תקרב (תחנה) ;שביבי אש באימה וגלגלים בקולם ;ואביטה אורחותיך הטובים. Cf. Fraenkel, *Ha-Tefillah veha-Piyyut be-Maḥzor Nuernberg*, 115; and above, chapter 1, nn. 9, 45. This R. Sheʾaltiʾel (who is not mentioned at all in Urbach's *Baʿalei ha-Tosafot*) should not be confused with the thirteenth-century northern French or German *payyetan* R. Sheʾaltiʾel b. Levi (see Zunz, *LG*, 495), who authored a *geʾulah* for a Sabbath during *sefirah* (שאגת אריה וקול שחל ולביא), recorded in the Nuremberg *Maḥzor*, 76, and in Habermann, *Piyyutim Nivḥarim*, 132–33.

245 See Urbach, *Baʿalei ha-Tosafot*, 1:186, 320, 2:526–27, 565, 607, 611, 646, 666, and cf. S. Emanuel, *Shivrei Luḥot*, 108–9. On the judicial activities (and locale) of R. Judah *ha-Kohen*, see above, chapter 1, nn. 67–68.

246 ואתאונן ואקונן מרה ואלילה ואזעק הילל נהי ונהיה חמס ושוד, על שבר שהיה בכרך וורנקפורט מאפילה לראש אלף ששית לבריאת עולם בשלשה יום לירח דם (cf. above, n. 236), published in *Sefer ha-Demaʿot*, ed. Bernfeld, vol. 3 (Berlin, 1926), 332–35. See also ms. Parma 585, fol. 154r (and cf. above, nn. 122, 194); and ms. Bodl. 1025, fol. 154r.

247 איכה בדד ישבה עיר ירושלים חרבה (Zunz, *LG*, 479).

248 נפלה נפלה עטרת ראשנו (Zunz, ibid., and see also ms. Bodl. 1025 [#22611], fol. 159v).

In sum, the same established patterns of *piyyut* composition and authorship prevalent in the Rhineland during the pre-Crusade period and in the twelfth century were continued by German Tosafists and rabbinic scholars through the first half of the thirteenth century.[249] As we have seen in a number of instances, however, awareness of the Tosafists and rabbinic figures who were involved in this activity emerges mainly from materials found in manuscript, just as the halakhic writings of some of these figures cannot be detected or fully appreciated without recourse to manuscript references and citations.[250]

Northern France in the Thirteenth Century

Piyyut composition was hardly absent among the Tosafists in northern France during the thirteenth century.[251] Once again, however, the availability and incumbent status of earlier *piyyutim* on the one hand and the need to commemorate new tragedies on the other played a significant role in the nature of the *piyyutim* that were produced. The compositional model that had been favored by R. Yom Tov of Joigny, Ri, and his son R. Elḥanan, which stressed *maʿarivim* and *reshuyyot*, with fewer *seliḥot* and *qinot*, had a number of adherents among northern French Tosafists in the thirteenth century as well. Included in this group are R. Solomon *ha-Qadosh* b. Judah of Dreux (a student of Ri), who wrote an *ʾahavah* for *Shabbat Naḥamu*,[252] and an Aramaic *piyyut* for the Targum of the Tenth Commandment (on *Shavuʿot*), with a single rhyme.[253] R. Solomon b. Samuel, father of the Tosafist R. Samuel

[249] Two *seliḥot*, א-היה אשר א-היה and א-להי תחלתי אל תחרוש (and perhaps a third, אזנך הטה והקשב), as well as a *yoẓer* for the Sabbath (*hafsaqah*) between *parashat Zakhor* and *parashat Parah* (אביעה נפלות), and one for the Sabbath prior to Rosh ha-Shanah, are found in *Maḥzor Nuernberg* in the name of Isaac b. Moses. These (and an additional *seliḥah*, אם תוציא יקר; see *Leqet Piyyutei Seliḥot*, ed. Fraenkel and Goldschmidt, 1:362–69, and cf. 2:790–91) are attributed by Fraenkel, *Ha-Tefillah veha-Piyyut be-Maḥzor Nuernberg*, 116–17, to the Tosafist R. Isaac b. Moses *Or Zaruʿa* of Vienna (who was student of R. Simḥah of Speyer as well; cf. above, nn. 232–33). In addition, a *maʿariv* for *Shemini ʿAẓeret* with a *siyyomet miqraʾit* (א-להים דבר בקול ערב; see *Maḥzor Sukkot*, ed. Goldschmidt, 318–20), and another for *Shavuʿot* (with an internal rhyme scheme and a partial *ḥaruz mavriaḥ*; see *Maḥzor Shavuʿot*, ed. Fraenkel, 34–37), are also attributed to an author by this name. Nonetheless, the attribution of these *piyyutim* to R. Isaac b. Moses of Vienna remains uncertain. Cf. above, nn. 31, 102, for R. Isaac's involvement in the preservation and transmission of *piyyutim*.

[250] Note also the *piyyut* commentary (to the halakhic *piyyut* for *Shabbat ha-Gadol*, אדיר דר מתו-חים) by R. Simḥah of Speyer's student, R. Yequtiʾel. See Simcha Emanuel, "Keshe-Yarad Ribbon ha-ʿOlamim le-Miẓrayim: Le-Toledotehah shel Pisqah ʾAḥat be-Haggadah shel Pesaḥ," *Tarbiz* 77 (2008), 122–23, and cf. *Tosafot Zevaḥim* 95b, s.v. *ʿirah*; *Tosafot ʿAvodah Zarah* 74b, s.v. *darash*; and above, n. 31.

[251] Cf. above, n. 155.

[252] שתי פעמים מקוימים בכל יום על המונינו (ms. Bodl. 1150, fol. 81v, and cf. above, n. 55, 176).

[253] אלהא דאבהתי לך מהודא ומשבח אנא. See *Maḥzor Shavuʿot*, ed. Fraenkel, 541–48, and see also the editor's introduction, 33. Cf. ms. Cambridge Add. 561 (a thirteenth-century *siddur*), fol. 66r, for

of Falaise,[254] composed a *bikkur* for *Pesaḥ*;[255] an Aramaic *reshut* for the Targum of the *Haftarah* on the seventh day of *Pesaḥ* with a single rhyme (in the style of R. Meir *Shaẓ*'s *Aqdamut millin*) that concludes with the phrase, וכד (מ)פרש בר עוזיאל וגלי מסתרתא / מפומיה דקודשא בריך הוא דדיליה מלכותא;[256] and a Spanish-metered *pizmon* for *ʿaseret yemei teshuvah* patterned after a *piyyut* by R. Judah *ha-Levi* (י-ה שמך ארוממך) that was also recited at least partially during *Neʿilah*.[257]

The mid-thirteenth-century Tosafist R. Isaac b. Isaac of Chinon, who is linked to the study hall at Evreux,[258] and whose *piyyutim* have been preserved for the most part in the published edition of *Maḥzor Vitry* (a relatively late version of this ritual compendium), composed a series of *maʿarivim* and related *piyyutim*. These include a complete *maʿariv* for *Sukkot*,[259] a separate *bikkur*-like addendum (*tosefet*) on the theme of *simḥat beit ha-shoʾevah*,[260] a

---

a ritual comment by *Ha-Qadosh mi-Dreux* together with R. Netanʾel of Chinon on the proper procedure for making the blessing over the *maẓah* at the Passover *Seder*. For R. Solomon of Dreux's approach to biblical exegesis, see above, in the final section of chapter 3.

254 On R. Solomon b. Samuel, see my *"Peering through the Lattices,"* 94–103.

255 See *Maḥzor Pesaḥ*, ed. Fraenkel, 399–401, אזכרך גואל באורך זמן גאולתי. See also the editor's introduction, 26; ms. Vatican 323, fols. 151v–152r; and Fraenkel, *Ha-Tefillah veha-Piyyut be-Maḥzor Nuernberg*, 68 (n. 379). R. Samuel of Falaise perhaps composed a *reshut* to the *qerovah*, *Eimat Norʾotekha* (by R. Meshullam b. Qalonymus; see Zunz, *LG*, 496, and Davidson, 3:158, 1924:צ), in addition to his lengthy halakhic commentary to R. Yosef *Tov ʿElem*'s *yoẓer* for *Shabbat ha-Gadol*, א-להי הרוחות לכל בשר; see above, n. 31.

256 See *Maḥzor Pesaḥ*, ed. Fraenkel, 649–50, אלהא מקמא בעינא רשותא בתריה ממרן דהכא בי כנישתא (with a *ḥaruz mavriaḥ*, in the style of R. Meir *Shaẓ*'s *Aqadamut millin*). See also *Maḥzor Vitry*, 163–64 (secs. 177–78), for the text of this *piyyut* together with a commentary. Cf. *ʿArugat ha-Bosem*, ed. Urbach, 4:12, 82 (n. 62).

257 ישמיענו סלחתי יושב בסתר עליון; see *Seder ha-Seliḥot*, ed. Goldschmidt, 48–50 (sec. 16); *Maḥzor le-Yamim Noraʾim*, ed. Goldschmidt, 2:775 (where it is placed in *Neʿilah*, just after Ri of Dampierre's יחביאנו צל ידו תחת כנפי השכינה, above, n. 133); and Fraenkel, *Ha-Tefillah veha-Piyyut be-Maḥzor Nuernberg*, 122. R. Solomon b. Samuel's *piyyut* compositions reflect the style of northern France (from whence he hailed, and to which he returned later in life, maintaining a connection with R. Yeḥiʾel of Paris), despite his affinities (and the time that he spent studying) with R. Samuel and R. Judah *he-Ḥasid* and others associated with *Ḥasidei Ashkenaz*; see below, chapter 6. R. Solomon did author a prayer commentary, as well as a *gematria/remazim* style Torah commentary, *Teʿamim shel Torah*. See I. Ta-Shma, *Knesset Meḥqarim*, 1:274–78; Zunz, *LG*, 287; and above, chapter 4, nn. 120–23.

258 See Henri Gross, *Gallia Judaica* (Paris, 1897), 580–81; *Tosafot Rabbenu Pereẓ le-Massekhet Bava Meẓiʿa*, ed. H. Hershler (Jerusalem, 1970), editor's introduction, 12; ms. Vatican Urban 27, fol. 25v; *Sefer Or Zaruʿa, pisqei Bava Qamma*, sec. 315; Urbach, *Baʿalei ha-Tosafot*, 2:615, 636, 673; N. Golb, *The Jews in Medieval Normandy*, 515–16; Colette Sirat, "Un Rituel Juif de France: Le Manuscrit Hébreu 633 de la Bibliothèque Nationale de Paris," *REJ* 119 (1961), 30–33; and below, chapter 6, n. 129.

259 See *Maḥzor Sukkot*, ed. Goldschmidt, 33–35, א-ל א-להים [ה'] במקראו / בנה הדומו וקרה כסאו; *Maḥzor Vitry*, ed. S. Hurwitz, 578; and Zunz, *LG*, 553.

260 See *Maḥzor Sukkot*, ed. Goldschmidt, 35–38, אזכרה נגינותי לילות וימים בנין מפאר מחמד עולמים. See also the editor's introduction, 29, sec. 6; *Maḥzor Vitry*, ed. Hurwitz, 578–79; and cf. Zunz, *LG*, 331, 352.

full *ma'ariv* for *Simḥat Torah*,[261] and perhaps a *tosefet* for *Shemini 'Aẓeret* as well, on the cycle of festivals.[262]

R. Isaac also wrote a *bikkur* for the first night of Passover, on the laws of offering the Passover sacrifice, which he attached to a *bikkur* by R. Meir b. Isaac *Shaẓ* of Worms, אזכרה שנות ימים מקדם. It is referred to as a *tosefet le-tosefet*, and the acrostic to this poem reads, אני יצחק בן רבי יצחק משואבי מימיו.[263] R. Isaac authored another such *tosefet* on the changing of the show bread (the *leḥem ha-panim*) in the Temple on the Sabbath, which was apparently meant for *Shabbat Ḥol ha-Mo'ed Pesaḥ*.[264] A *bikkur* for *Shavu'ot* should also perhaps be attributed to R. Isaac.[265] He wrote several mystical prayers and supplications,[266] as well a single *pizmon* with a *siyyomet miqra'it*.[267]

Nonetheless, the *seliḥot*-only model, present in northern France during the twelfth century in the *piyyutim* of R. Joseph *Bekhor Shor* of Orleans, and continued in the writings of his son Abraham and others,[268] is found in the mid-thirteenth century as well, in the compositions of two of R. Isaac of Chinon's Tosafist contemporaries. R. Tuvyah of Vienne[269] composed six penitential *pizmonim* and *seliḥot*, which Zunz characterized as "excellent in style and language, written in commemoration of the persecutions and

261 אצנו לסלדך ולעבור בחילה (Zunz, ibid., 331). The text of the *ma'ariv*, which appears in ms. Paris 634, was not available to the editor when *Maḥzor Sukkot*, ed. Goldschmidt, was published. See *Maḥzor Shavu'ot*, ed. Fraenkel, editor's introduction, 17 (n. 78).

262 See *Maḥzor Sukkot*, ed. Goldschmidt, 320–22, יספת ה' לגוי נכבדת (which was meant to be appended to the *ma'ariv* by the eleventh-century *payyetan* R. Isaac b. Moses, א-להים דבר בקול ערב). Cf. the editor's introduction, 30, sec. 19a; *Maḥzor Vitry*, ed. Hurwitz, 581–82; and Zunz, *LG*, 331.

263 See *Maḥzor Pesaḥ*, ed. Fraenkel, 17–18, אומר אף אני כשומע ולא כמורה / נגד זקיננו בכתב קורא; the editor's introduction, 25, sec. 1a; *Maḥzor Vitry*, ed. Hurwitz, 570; and Zunz, ibid.

264 See *Maḥzor Pesaḥ*, ed. Fraenkel, 287–89, ימים מקדם אזכרה ואספרה צבי קדש עטרת תפארה; the editor's introduction, 26; *Maḥzor Vitry*, ed. Hurwitz, 580–81; and cf. above, n. 157. On the dating and composition of *Maḥzor Vitry*, see, e.g., I. Ta-Shma, *Knesset Meḥqarim*, 1:62–86.

265 See *Maḥzor Shavu'ot*, ed. Fraenkel, 62–64, ימות עולמים שנים קדמוניות (for which the acrostic reads, יצחק בן יצחק בן מרדכי בן ישי בן מרדכי בן שלמה). Cf. Sirat (above, n. 258), and Zunz, *LG*, 331–32.

266 See my *"Peering through the Lattices,"* 174–77, and Sirat, "Un Rituel Juif de France," 35–36.

267 See *Leqet Piyyutei Seliḥot*, ed. Goldschmidt and Fraenkel, 1:343–47 (= ms. Parma 654, fol. 258), יחיד רם ומתנשא / לובש צדקה ומתכסה. Cf. ms. Parma 885, fol. 125; ms. Parma 855, fol. 161r; and ms. St. Petersburg Evr. I 134, fols. 34r–34v.

268 See above, nn. 152–54.

269 On R. Tuvyah's activities as Tosafist and halakhist, see Urbach, *Ba'alei ha-Tosafot*, 1:486–92; my "Halakhah and Meẓi'ut (Realia) in Medieval Ashkenaz: Surveying the Parameters and Defining the Limits," *Jewish Law Annual* 14 (2003), 216–24; *Qiẓur Sefer Miẓvot Gadol*, ed. Y. Horowitz (Jerusalem, 2005), editor's introduction, 2–7; S. Emanuel, "R. Yeḥi'el mi-Paris: Toledotav ve-Ziqato le-Ereẓ Yisra'el," *Shalem* 8 (2008), 95–98; and my "R. Tobia de Vienne et R. Yeḥi'el de Paris: La créativité des Tossafistes dans une période d'incertitude," *Les cahiers du judaïsme* 31 (2011), 4–17.

decrees that took place during his lifetime."[270] Two of these have alternating rhymes within each stanza,[271] and a third has an additional repeating rhyme pattern at the end of each stanza.[272] One of R. Tuvyah's three remaining compositions is metered.[273]

Similarly, R. Netan'el b. Joseph of Chinon (c. 1180–1260, and, like R. Isaac of Chinon, linked to the academy of Evreux) composed five *piyyutim* for the penitential season.[274] These include a *shir ha-yiḥud* with a single rhyme throughout[275] and a *seder ha-tamid* for the end of the *seliḥot* on *erev* Rosh ha-Shanah, which replaced that of R. Meir *Shaẓ* in some French rites.[276] As Avraham Grossman has carefully noted, both of these compositions emphasize *inter alia* that the Divine throne is incomplete until Israel's enemies are destroyed—with a clear indication that contemporary Christendom is to be included in this fate and that prayer following the destruction of the Temple takes the place of the sacrificial rites. In addition, it describes the suffering of the Jewish people at this point and requests their redemption.[277]

[270] See Zunz, *LG*, 303–4, cited by Urbach, *Ba'alei ha-Tosafot*, 1:492.

[271] א-ל הכיל נלאיתי / זעם מלאתני (*Leqet Piyyutei Seliḥot*, ed. Goldschmidt and Fraenkel, 1:191–93); טבעתי ביוון מצולות ים זעמיך (ibid., 1:195–97).

[272] טמנו פח לי / בו נלכדתי (*Leqet Piyyutei Seliḥot*, ed. Goldschmidt and Fraenkel, 1:198–99), with a (Sefardic) חרוז מעין אזורי.

[273] שעה שועי אביר ישעי (*Leqet Piyyutei Seliḥot*, ed. Goldschmidt and Fraenkel, 1:199–201). R. Tuvyah's two other *seliḥot* are אריד לפני ה' אהמה בשיחי (*Leqet Piyyutei Seliḥot*, ed. Goldschmidt and Fraenkel, 1:193–95), and תסתיר טלאיך מרגשת מרעים / שדדום שללום וקרעום קרעים (ibid., 1:201–2). All six of R. Tuvyah's *seliḥot* are found in ms. Parma 654.

[274] See A. Grossman, "R. Netan'el me-Chinon: Mi-Gedolei Ba'alei ha-Tosafot be-Ẓarefat ba-Me'ah ha-Yod Gimmel" (above, n. 42), 174–89; and my *"Peering through the Lattices,"* 177–78 (n. 104). See also *Tosafot Yeshanim ha-Shalem 'al Massekhet Yevamot*, ed. A. Shoshana (Jerusalem, 1994), editor's introduction, 22–24. R. Netan'el is mentioned some fifteen times in this Tosafist collection, and several times in a related one, *Tosafot Maharam ve-Rabbenu Pereẓ 'al Massekhet Yevamot*, ed. H. Porush (Jerusalem, 1991). The sensitive discussion among R. Netan'el, R. Yeḥi'el of Paris, and R. Isaac b. Todros (regarding a *ḥaliẓah* that was being withheld in lieu of an appropriate payment), noted by Grossman (175, n. 6, and 184, n. 41) on the basis of passages in *Teshuvot Mahariq* and *Teshuvot Binyamin Zev*, is also attested in earlier manuscripts texts. See ms. Bodl. 672 (*Qiẓur Mordekhai le-R. Shmu'el Schlettstadt*; Ashkenaz, 1393), fol. 89r (in the margin), and cf. S. Emanuel, *Shivrei Luḥot*, 189 (n. 20).

[275] See A. M. Habermann, *Sefer ha-Yiḥud veha-Kavod* (Jerusalem, 1948), 75–85. This composition is often referred to as יה מן הקר"ן [= הקדוש ר' נתנאל], since the rhyme throughout is formed by the letters *yod* and *heh*. See also ms. Parma 740, fol. 198v; ms. Bodl. 2502 (after the fixed liturgy and various *piyyutim*); ms. Parma 3515 (following the *seliḥot* section); and ms. Toronto 3-013, fols. 37–49.

[276] See, e.g., ms. Parma 963, fols. 429v–431r; ms. Cambridge Add. 394, fols. 88r–96r; ms. Bodl. 2502, fols. 12v–13v; ms. Parma 254, fols. 185v–186r; and cf. Grossman "R. Netan'el me-Qinon," above, n. 42), 185–89. R. Netan'el's *Tamid* begins with the phrase תמיד קרוב לעמך נדרש (and is referred to as תמיד מן הקר"ן). For R. Meir *Shaẓ*'s *Tamid* (which was sometimes replaced by R. Netan'el's *Tamid*), see above, n. 51 (and cf. ms. Parma 254, fols. 186v–188r).

[277] See Grossman, ibid. For the mystical dimensions of these two *piyyutim* (which may have contributed to R. Netan'el's being referred to as *ha-Qadosh*), see my *"Peering through the Lattices,"* 177 (n. 104).

R. Netan'el also composed a *reshut* for the *Musaf* service to be recited following the morning service on Rosh ha-Shanah or Yom Kippur,[278] as well as a *teḥinnah* and another *seliḥah.*[279] The relatively unified or limited focus and venues for all of these *piyyutim* further supports Grossman's sense that none of these should be attributed to R. Netan'el b. Joseph's grandson of the same name (in the late thirteenth and early fourteenth centuries), as had been suggested in some earlier scholarship.[280]

Despite his close association with R. Tuvyah of Vienne and with the brothers of Evreux, R. Yeḥi'el of Paris apparently did not compose any *piyyutim*,[281] although his son Yosef composed an eschatological *ma'ariv* for the last day of *Pesaḥ*, in which each stanza ends with a biblical verse.[282] R. Yeḥi'el was somewhat involved, however, together with at least one of his students,[283] in commenting on *piyyutim.*[284]

278 נחנו תמיד ניחל א-ל תשועות הושיע. See ms. Melun 14 (after the morning service for Yom Kippur); ms. Bodl. 1250, fol. 63v; ms. Parma 1250, fol. 63v (as a *reshut* for the *kedushah* of *musaf*); ms. Parma 1259, fol. 60r (after *Avinu Malkenu*, at the end of the morning service for Rosh ha-Shanah); ms. Parma 1654, fol. 61v (in the margin, designated as נוסח מיוחד לתפלת ר"ה החל במוצ"ש מיסוד הקדוש ר' נתנאל מקינון; and Zunz, *LG*, 363.

279 ה' א-להי צ-באות מי כמכה (Zunz, ibid.), and אנוש יצרו רע היעמוד אם עוונות תשמר (Davidson, *Oẓar ha-Shirah veha-Piyyut*, 1:293, 6414:א).

280 For a *seder tequfot* attributed to R. Netan'el b. Yosef of Chinon, see ms. Cambridge Add. 667.1, fol. 191v.

281 See זכור איפה ארמון יפה נוף, found in ms. Hamburg 144 (Cod. Heb. 23), fol. 50r, attributed to Yeḥi'el b. Joseph. This manuscript contains *qinot* from a number of prominent German *payyetanim*, including Raban, R. Abraham b. Samuel (*he-Ḥasid*) of Speyer, and R. Barukh of Mainz; see also Zunz, *LG*, 508. Although the author of this *qinah* had the same name as R. Yeḥi'el (b. Joseph) of Paris, he was in fact a grandson of R. Mordekhai b. Hillel (d. 1298), and a descendant of Rabiah. Similarly, the *reshut* for a *ḥatan* attributed to Yeḥi'el in ms. Bodl. 1099 (as noted by Schmelzer, "Piyyutim le-Nisu'in," 179, and see also Zunz, *LG*, 468) does not appear to have been composed by R. Yeḥi'el of Paris since (among other reasons) virtually all the *payyentanim* reflected in this manuscript were from Germany. For R. Yeḥi'el's *Tosafot* and other halakhic writings, see Urbach, *Ba'alei ha-Tosafot*, 1:448–87 (the last line on p. 486 is missing in some editions and should read, בקשרים אמיצים עם ר' יחיאל מפאריס עמד ר' טוביה ב"ר אליהו מויאנה); S. Emanuel, *Shivrei Luḥot*, 185–98; and above, chapter 1.

282 See *Maḥzor Pesaḥ*, ed. Fraenkel, 408–10, יוסיף ה' שנית ישע ימינו בגבורות / בזרוע יקבץ טלאיו החונים בגדרות, and the editor's introduction, 27; Urbach, *Ba'alei ha-Tosafot*, 1:456–57; and cf. M. Schmelzer, *Meḥqarim*, 145.

283 See below, n. 321.

284 See ms. Paris l'Alliance 133, cited in Colette Sirat, "Un nouveau manuscrit du Maḥzor Vitry," *REJ* 125 (1966), 262; I. Ta-Shma, "Li-Meqorotav ha-Sifrutiyyim shel Sefer ha-Zohar," *Tarbiz* 60 (1991), 663–65 (and below, chapter 6, n. 126); *'Arugat ha-Bosem*, ed. Urbach, 4:38–39 (n. 82); ms. Bodl. 1211, fol. 9r; ms. Vatican 285, fol. 183v; ms. Pessaro (State Archive) 31 (copied by a student of R. Yeḥi'el's son, Yosef), fol. 20; M. M. Hoenig, "'Al Mahadurato ha-Ḥadashah shel Sefer ha-Maskil (Sefer Ḥasidim) le-R. Mosheh b. Eleazar ha-Kohen," *Yerushatenu* 1 (2007), 221–23; and cf. S. Emanuel, "Ḥeshbon ha-Luaḥ ve-Ḥeshbon ha-Qeẓ—Polmos Yehudi-Noẓri bi-Shenat 1100," *Zion* 63 (1998), 152 (n. 41).

The Late Thirteenth Century

To conclude our discussion on the writing of *piyyut* in Tosafist circles, it should be noted that even during the latter part of the thirteenth century, a number of leading rabbinic figures, in both Germany and northern France,[285] continued to emerge as prolific and versatile *payyetanim.* The German Tosafist and *dayyan* R. Samuel b. Menaḥem of Wurzburg, who was one of R. Meir of Rothenburg's German teachers along with R. Judah b. Moses *ha-Kohen*,[286] authored several *piyyutim*, including a *seliḥah*,[287] an *E-loheikhem* for *Musaf* on the Sabbath,[288] and a *mi khamokha* for *Pesaḥ.*[289]

R. Meir of Rothenburg composed some nineteen *piyyutim.* He wrote no *maʿarivim*, but he composed *yoẓerot* for a number of less-heralded special occasions. One lengthy *yoẓer*, which was assigned to a so-called off Sabbath (*Shabbat hafsaqah*) during the period in the month of Adar in which the four special Torah portions were read, has a *siyyomet miqra'it* throughout, and highlights the centrality of the Temple and its service and the celebration of the festivals in Jerusalem.[290] Abraham Fraenkel has cogently suggested that this *piyyut* was originally written by R. Meir for *Parashat Sheqalim* but was not placed there in Ashkenazic rites, since there was an earlier *piyyut* that was customarily recited on this occasion. Fraenkel notes that R. Meir's *piyyut* focuses quite a bit on material found in tractate *Sheqalim*, and he further suggests that the extensive discussion and praise of Jerusalem and the land of Israel—as the home of the Temple, the Divine presence, and the Jewish people—reflect Maharam's own attempt to settle in the land of Israel. The influences of both R. Meir *Shaẓ* and R. Yehudah

[285] The spate of persecutions in northern Europe in the last decades of the thirteenth century led to the composition of a range of commemorative *piyyutim* by several rabbinic authors, some of whom had peripheral connections to the Tosafist enterprise. See, e.g., S. Einbinder, *Beautiful Death*, 126–48; idem, "Meir b. Elijah of Norwich: Persecution and Poetry among Medieval English Jews," *Journal of Medieval History* 26.2 (2000), 145–62 (and cf. Urbach, *Baʿalei ha-Tosafot*, 2:513, n. 12*, and I. Ta-Shma, *Knesset Meḥqarim*, 1:272, 274); and Einbinder, "On the Borders of Exile: The Poetry of Solomon of Simḥah of Troyes," in *Medieval Constructions in Gender and Identity: Essays in Honor of Joan Ferrante*, ed. T. Barolini (Tempe, Ariz., 2005), 69–85. On Solomon Simḥah of Troyes, see above, Introduction (n. 83); and below, chapter 7.

[286] See Urbach, *Baʿalei ha-Tosafot*, 2:526, 610; *Teshuvot u-Pesaqim*, ed. E. Kupfer, 164–67; S. Emanuel, *Shivrei Luḥot*, 236 (n. 68); above, chapter 1, nn. 51–52; and ms. Paris 405, fol. 47v, שמעתי מפי זקני ר׳ שמואל בן מנחם.

[287] א-להים אל דמי לך במאריכי (Zunz, *LG*, 330, and Davidson, *Oẓar ha-Shirah veha-Piyyut*, 1:212 [4630:א]).

[288] א-להיכם שליט בעולמו (Zunz, ibid., and Davidson, *Oẓar ha-Shirah veha-Piyyut*, 1:210, 4602:א).

[289] ש-די שוכן עליונים מביט כל תחתונים ויודע כל צפונים (Davidson, *Oẓar ha-Shirah veha-Piyyut*, 3:422, 426:ש).

[290] אורות מאופל הזריח מהודו. See *Qoveẓ Shirei ha-Maharam mi-Rothenburg she-Nidpesu, veshebe-Kitvei Yad* (Jerusalem, 1993), 7–11; and cf. ms. Bodl. 1025, fol. 39v.

ha-Levi on R. Meir with regard to this type of literary expression are similarly on display.[291]

R. Meir also composed a *yozer* for the Sabbath between Yom Kippur and *Sukkot*, a Sabbath that was hardly represented within prior *piyyutim*. This *yozer* blends themes from both of these festivals.[292] He also wrote an *ʾofan* for *Shabbat Shirah*,[293] a *meʾorah* for a *Shabbat ḥatan* that imitates a similar composition by R. Yehudah *ha-Levi*,[294] two *ʾahavot* (each with a *siyyomet miqraʾit*),[295] a *geuʾlah* for a *Shabbat ḥatan* in the style of a *geʾulah* by R. Yehudah *ha-Levi* (יונה נושאתה),[296] a *yozer* composed by R. Meir during the period of his imprisonment toward the end of his life,[297] and a *zulat* for *parashat Reʾeh*.[298]

In addition, R. Meir wrote an *ʾofan* (with a *siyyomet miqraʾit*) that contains a variety of themes from *Hekhalot* literature,[299] an *E-loheikhem* for a

291 See A. Fraenkel's *piyyut* blog, shittuf.piyyut.org.il/story/1306; I thank my student Gabriel Wasserman for bringing this information to my attention. On the study of tractate *Sheqalim* in medieval Ashkenaz, see, e.g., Y. Sussmann, "Rabad on Shekalim? A Bibliographical and Historical Riddle," [Hebrew] in *Meʾah Sheʿarim: Studies in Medieval Jewish Spiritual Life in Memory of Isadore Twersky*, ed. E. Fleischer et al. (Jerusalem, 2001), 131–70; and my "The Scope of Talmudic Commentary in Europe during the High Middle Ages," in *Printing the Talmud*, ed. S. Mintz and G. Goldstein (New York, 2005), 43–53. On R. Meir and the land of Israel, see, e.g., my "The *ʿAliyyah* of 'Three Hundred Rabbis' in 1211: Tosafist Attitudes toward the Land of Israel," *JQR* 76 (1986), 206–15; A. Grossman, "Ziqato shel Maharam mi-Rothenburg ʾel Ereẓ Yisraʾel," *Cathedra* 84 (1997), 63–84; and below, nn. 294, 296, 306.

292 אליך תשוקתי לשמך ולזכרך תאוותי. See *Qoveẓ Shirei ha-Maharam*, 12–14; and ms. Bodl. 1025, fol. 300r.

293 אין מספר לגדודיו ואין קצה למרכבת היכלו. See *Qoveẓ Shirei ha-Maharam*, 26–28, and ms. Bodl. 1099, fols. 115r–v.

294 התנערי מעפרים לבשי ציון שביה. See *Qoveẓ Shirei Maharam*, 17–18; ms. Bodl. 1099, fol. 88v; Ezra Fleischer, *Ha-Yoẓerot be-Hithavvutam ve-Hitpatḥutam* (Jerusalem, 1984), 681–82; and M. Schmelzer, *Meḥqarim*, 197 (based on JTS 8972, where the end of the opening phrase reads, לבשי עוזך שבייה). This *meʾorah* is preceded immediately in ms. Bodl. 1099 by אור חדש מר׳ יהודה קשטלין, and is followed by two *ʾahavot* by R. Meir (see the next note), and then by an *ʾahavah* by R. Judah *ha-Levi* (fols. 90v–91v). It is preceded in ms. JTS 8972 by the *meʾorah* of R. Judah *ha-Levi* (אמרות הא-ל טהרות . . . והיה לו לאור עולם ראיה/ ולעין כל חי שנייה / שוב לעיר ציון בנויה), which it imitates. See Schmelzer, *Meḥqarim*, 198 (n. 27).

295 ממך תוחלתי לא נכזבה and מעט שיר מה יכילך ולא יכלכלוך גבורים כי טל אורות טליך. See *Qoveẓ Shirei Maharam*, 19–20; and ms. Bodl. 1099, fols. 89r–90v.

296 מעלה מים אי חסדיך. See *Qoveẓ Shirei ha-Maharam*, 21–22; ms. Bodl. 1099, fol. 92r; and Fleischer, *Ha-Yoẓerot*, 704–6.

297 ארחמך ה׳ חזקי / צור לבבי וחלקי / תדבק לשוני לחכי / לצמאי אליך וחשקי (which was composed כשהיה [ר׳ מאיר] תפוס בוושבורק). See *Qoveẓ Shirei Maharam*, 30–32; and cf. I. A. Agus, *R. Meir of Rothenburg*, 1:125–27, 150–53. The occurrence of *parashat Reʾeh* during the period of the "seven *Haftarot* of consolation" (*shivʿah di-neḥemta*), between the ninth of Av and the High Holy Days, combines to make this *piyyut* especially appropriate and timely.

298 This *zulat*, אמת ונכון ויציב וקיים, ends with the phrase חזק ואמץ. See *Qoveẓ Shirei Maharam*, 33–35, and ms. Paris 391, fols. 76v–77r.

299 אופני הוד כרובי הדר וגלגלי מרכבה ברעש גדול תתנשאו לומת שרפי להבה. See *Qoveẓ Shirei Maharam*, 23, and ms. Bodl. 1099, fols. 114r–v. Among the *Hekhalot* motifs are: זכי טוהר טבילין הגיון כקול מים רבים חזות בנועם ה׳ לבקר בהיכל מלך ואולם . . . טהורי מעלה בדוקי שס״ה בסולם אש לעלות יורדי מרכבה בלבבם מסילותם.

Shabbat ḥatan that also reflects a *Hekhalot* passage,[300] and a *reshut* for the end of the *Nishmat* prayer on the Sabbath of a circumcision.[301] R. Meir's *seliḥot* for Yom Kippur include a lengthy *seliḥah* for the afternoon service with a *ḥaruz mavriaḥ*,[302] another lengthy *seliḥah* with a *ḥaruz ʾaḥid* for *Neʿilah* (which is associated with Rabbenu Gershom's *Zekhor brit*),[303] a second *seliḥah* for *Neʿilah* associated with *Zekhor brit*,[304] and an addendum for the final blessing of the *ʿAmidah* during *Neʿilah*, in which each stanza ends with the word *shalom*.[305] R. Meir's three *qinot* for the ninth of Av include the well-known *Shaʾali serufah ba-ʾesh* that commemorated the burning of the Talmud in Paris in 1242 (and was modeled after *R. Yehudah ha-Levi*'s Zionide poem, ציון הלא תשאלי),[306] an elegy to mark the plundering of a Jewish settlement circa 1235 that apparently occurred as the result of a charge of host desecration,[307] and one that depicts the destruction of Jerusalem.[308]

R. Meir's slightly older contemporary, R. Yaqar *ha-Levi* of Cologne, the son of R. Samuel b. Abraham *ha-Levi* (Bonfant) of Worms,[309] was a

---

This *piyyut* also mentions צבאי היכלות and שומרי היכלות, and it concludes, ברוכים אתם יורדי מרכבה אם תגידו סוד זה לבני במאמר קדישין שאו עיניכם למעוני ואני באתי בדרביך נשאתי עיני. Cf. above, n. 200.

300 א-להיכם משרתיו אש לוהט והוא אש אוכלה. See *Qovez Shirei ha-Maharam*, 29, and ms. Bodl. 1099, fols. 145r–v. The *Hekhalot* motif is found toward the end, קלסתר פני יעקב נושק בחשק. Cf. above, nn. 113–14, 185, 200. On R. Meir's affinity for mysticism and *Hekhalot* literature, see my "*Peering through the Lattices*," 235–40, and below, chapter 6, nn. 138–43.

301 מי מצרף כאש. See *Qovez Shirei Maharam*, 15, and ms. Bodl. 1099, fol. 83v.

302 וותיק וחסיד אתה תתעטף חסידותיך. See *Qovez Shirei Maharam*, 42–46; ms. Vatican 315, fols. 252r–255r; and see also *Maḥzor le-Yamim Noraʾim*, ed. Goldschmidt, 2:653.

303 ותערב פגיעת תפלת זהר אמונים ישרך. See *Qovez Shirei Maharam*, 47–48; *Maḥzor le-Yamim Noraʾim*, ed. Goldschmidt, 2:768–70; and cf. above, n. 70.

304 ואור פניך תאיר. See *Qovez Shirei Maharam*, 49–50, and see *Maḥzor le-Yamim Noraʾim*, ed. Goldschmidt, 2:770–71.

305 ה' ממרומו יפרוס שלמה. See *Qovez Shirei Maharam*, 50–52; *Maḥzor le-Yamim Noraʾim*, ed. Goldschmidt, 2:786–88; and ms. Bodl. 1099, fol. 147v (following a similar composition by R. Judah *ha-Levi*).

306 For שאלי שרופה באש, see *Qovez Shirei Maharam*, 40–41, and see Fleischer, *Ha-Yozerot*, 681 (n. 19), on the similarities between this *qinah* and ציון הלא תשאלי by *Ha-Levi*. Cf. Fleischer, 616, 653 (n. 43), 704–7.

307 אחבירה מילין ואספר מעשה י-ה. See *Qovez Shirei Maharam*, 37–39, and cf. A. M. Habermann, *Gezerot Ashkenaz ve-Zarefat*, 180–83.

308 הורידו מאין הפוגות דמעות כנחל עיני. See *Qovez Shirei ha-Maharam*, 36; ms. Parma (de Rossi) 1104, fol. 46r; Vatican 312, fol. 63v; and Prague (Museum) 120, fol. 133v.

309 See I. Ta-Shma, *Knesset Meḥqarim*, 1:161–62, 167–74. R. Yaqar was addressed by R. Meir of Rothenburg in his responsa, and material by R. Yaqar is included within the responsa collections associated with R. Meir; see, e.g., *Teshuvot Maharam*, ed. Cremona, nos. 80, 164, 160. See also ms. Hamburg 189 (Cod. Heb. 184), fol. 49r, for a document from R. Yaqar *ha-Levi*, followed by a *get* form from Maharam.

communal judge[310] and a *baʿal sod.*[311] R. Yaqar produced a variegated corpus of *piyyutim*, much of which is still in manuscript. Among these *piyyutim* are an *E-loheikhem* for the end of the *kedushah le-musaf* on a *Shabbat ḥatan* (with a *ḥaruz ʾaḥid*), and another *E-loheikehm* for the Sabbath of a circumcision.[312] Indeed, a manuscript passage asserts that the custom in Mainz was not to recite any *E-loheikhem* addendum to the *kedushah* with three exceptions: when *Rosh Hodesh* occurred on the Sabbath, when there was a *Shabbat nissuʾin* that celebrated a new marriage, and when there was a circumcision on the Sabbath. For these occasions, the *E-loheikhem* formulated by (*she-yasad*) R. Yaqar of Cologne was instituted and recited by R. Yaqar's son, R. Bonfant *ha-Levi he-Ḥazzan.*[313]

R. Yaqar *ha-Levi* also composed a *yoẓer*,[314] an *ʾofan*,[315] and a *zulat*[316] for a *Shabbat ḥatan.* R. Yaqar's poem to fete the *ḥatan bereshit* on *Simḥat Torah* (with Spanish meter, a *ḥaruz ʾaḥid*, and an internal rhyme scheme) has a set of stanzas (beginning with the phrase והכלה צבי חן לה סגלת עזרתך, and including the phrase שבע ימים ובנעימים תבלה את שנותיו) that could be added, so that it could also serve as a *reshut* for a bridegroom.[317] Like R. Meir of Rothenburg, R. Yaqar also composed a *geʾulah*—a relatively rare *piyyut* form in medieval Ashkenaz—for a *Shabbat ḥatan.*[318]

In terms of commemorative *piyyutim*, R. Yaqar authored a *zulat* for the Sabbath after the twentieth of Tammuz, the day on which the persecution referred to as *gezerat Pforzheim* (*Purzin*; in Baden, western Germany) occurred in 1267,[319] and two *qinot*, which are interspersed in a Cluny manuscript

310 On R. Yaqar's halakhic writings and judicial activities, see S. Emanuel, *Shivrei Luḥot*, 255–56, 258, 260–61, 268, and above, chapter 1, nn. 48, 114. As Urbach notes (*Baʿalei ha-Tosafot*, 2:578), this R. Yaqar should not be confused with R. Yaqar of Chinon, who was a colleague of R. Samuel of Evreux and R. Yeḥiʾel of Paris (and a teacher of R. Pereẓ of Corbeil).

311 See my *"Peering through the Lattices,"* 248, and below, chapter 6, n. 162.

312 See ms. Bodl. 1149, fol. 146v, א-להיכם יחיד ונישא מכל נעלם, and ms. Bodl. 1107–8, fol. 244r [= ms. Bodl. 1106, fols. 154v–155r], א-להיכם יוצרי בבטן (with the note, *zeh ha-piyyut ʿasah mori ha-R. Yaqar ha-Levi*).

313 See ms. Hamburg 86 (Cod. Hebr. 37), fol. 72v, cited in S. Emanuel, *Shivrei Luḥot*, 181 (n. 128). This description ostensibly refers to א-להיכם יוצרי בבטן (in the above note).

314 See ms. Bodl. 1099, fol. 98 (= ms. Bodl. 1149, fol. 110r), אקדם ואיכף בשירה עריבה (found among a series of similar compositions that begin at fol. 95). See also Zunz, *LG*, 487; and ms. Bodl. 1106, fol. 154r, זה הפיוט עשה מורי ה"ר יקר הלוי (=Bodl. 1107, fol. 244v).

315 א-ל נערץ במרומי זבולים. See ms. Bodl. 1149, fol. 110v (which also notes that this *ʾofan* was set to the *niggun* of *ʾeḥad qadosh*), and Zunz, *LG*, 488.

316 See ms. Bodl. 1149, fols. 125v–126r, אהובה כלולה משובת חסדים, שמחת יחיד שמחת רבים. Cf. Zunz, ibid.; and M. Schmelzer, "Piyyutim le-Nisuʾin," 178, sec. 15, who notes these three marriage *piyyutim* as well.

317 יפה נוף תאות עין יליד חתן דמותך. See *Maḥzor Sukkot*, ed. Goldschmidt, 464–66.

318 ימינך א-לי גואלי רוממה תסיר מדוה [מסוה] כלימה (Zunz, *LG*, 488), and cf. above, n. 296.

319 See *Sefer ha-Demaʿot*, ed. S. Bernfeld, 1:322–25; A. M. Habermann, *Gezerot Ashkenaz ve-Ẓarefat*, 191–93; and ms. Bodl. 1149, fols. 55v–57r, beginning with זולת לגזירת פורצהיים יפרצנה פרץ

together with *qinot* by Ibn Gabirol, R. Yehudah *ha-Levi*, and R. Menaḥem b. Jacob of Worms.[320] In addition, one of the authors of the *piyyut* commentary found in ms. Parma 655 identifies himself as a student of both R. Yeḥi'el of Paris and R. Yaqar.[321] It should be noted that seven of R. Yaqar's ten *piyyut* compositions were focused on happy occasions.

R. Meir of Rothenburg's student R. Ḥayyim Palti'el b. Jacob was of French origin and ultimately settled in central Europe. This R. Ḥayyim Palti'el, who also had an affinity for *Ḥasidei Ashkenaz*, produced a treatise on customs (which retains many French practices, as opposed to those of the Rhineland, and includes numerous liturgical and synagogue customs). In addition, one of his students produced a lengthy Tosafist Torah compilation.[322] Another contemporary rabbinic scholar named R. Ḥayyim Palti'el, whose father's name was Barukh, was a halakhist who issued responsa (including one addressed to R. Meir of Rothenburg's colleague, R. Avigdor

---

על פני פרץ לכ' בתמוז נטבחו נגררו ונ(א)פנו. אזכרה א-להים נגינתי וכו'. This *zulat* concludes: נחם תנחם בחיריך נעורימו לחדשה, אויביך תמחץ ושברי החבישה, כמאז הפכת ים ליבשה, אילתי א-להי לעזרתי חושה, followed by the "signature" (found also on other *piyyutim* by R. Yaqar), יקר הלוי העלוב בן שמואל (along with the instruction that this was to be chanted using the tune [בניגון] of the *piyyut* titled נחם ינוחם). As Habermann notes, a *qinah* by R. Abraham b. Barukh, the brother of R. Meir of Rothenburg (אזעק במר לב), about a pogrom in Pforzheim, which mentions the deaths of R. Samuel *ha-Levi* and his son R. Yaqar, apparently refers to another pogrom that occurred there in 1271. See also Zunz, *LG*, 488; and Ta-Shma, *Knesset Meḥqarim*, above, n. 309.

320 See ms. Paris (Cluny Museum) 12290, fols. 346v–348v, קינה שיסד הרב ר' יקר הלוי בן הרב ר' שמואל ציון ה' לכם בחר מעוניך, and cf. above, n. 306. This *qinah*, which also concludes with the "signature," וחתם בה יקר בן שמואל העלוב נחם ינוחם, is followed immediately in the manuscript (which is a *siddur minhag Vermaiza*) by a *qinah* for the ninth of Av by Ibn Gabirol, שכורת ולא מיין. Ibn Gabirol's *qinah* is then followed (on fol. 349r) by another from R. Yaqar *ha-Levi*, הקינה הזאת יסד הרב יקר הלוי על חורבן בית המקדש והריגת בני ישראל ויהודה, אבל אעורר / אנינות אגרר / בבכי אמרר/ בחמת צורר, that is also signed יקר בן הרב שמואל נחם ינוחם. This is then followed by a *qinah* from R. Menaḥem of Worms, מעוני שמים שחקים יזבלוך מלאים מהודך (above, n. 220), and another by R. Judah *ha-Levi*, יום אכפי הכבדת, whose *piyyutim* and *qinot* are found throughout this manuscript. Cf. M. Schmelzer, *Meḥqarim*, 197–98; and above, n. 64.

321 On fol. 161v of ms. Parma 655, the composer writes אני הכותב שמעתי, while a parallel passage found in both ms. Bodl. 1128 (fol. 32v) and ms. Bodl. 1148 (fol. 160v) reads: שמעתי אני הכותב אורשרגו ב"ר אשר. In ms. Parma 655, Orsherago cites [ממורי] ה"ר יקר הלוי in ms. Parma 655, fols. 145r, 151v, and 158v. He also notes a comment that he heard from his teacher, R. Yeḥi'el of Paris (fol. 158r, ואני הכותב שמעתי מפי מורי הר"ר יחיאל מפריס), and another that he heard from R. Eleazar of Worms (fol. 152r, שמעתי מפי ר' אלעזר בן רבינו יב"ק). See *Hebrew Manuscripts in the Biblioteca Palatina in Parma*, ed. B. Richler (Jerusalem, 2001), 299 (#1134, with slightly different manuscript pagination); and see also S. Emanuel as cited above, in n. 284, "Ḥeshbon ha-Luaḥ ve-Ḥeshbon ha-Qeẓ—Polmos Yehudi-Noẓri bi-Shenat 1100." This same Orsherago is ostensibly the author of a *qinah* commemorating the persecution that occurred in Frankfurt in 1241 (see above, n. 236). Cf. *Teshuvot u-Pesaqim*, ed. Kupfer, 271.

322 See E. Zimmer, *'Olam ke-Minhago Noheg*, 271, 277, 282–83, 296–97; S. Emanuel, *Shivrei Luḥot*, 219–27; D. Goldschmidt, *Meḥqerei Tefillah u-Piyyut*, 38–60; Y. S. Lange, "Li-Zehuto shel R. Ḥayyim Palti'el," *'Alei Sefer* 8 (1980), 140–46; and above, chapter 4, n. 147. Urbach refers to him in only one instance; see *Ba'alei ha-Tosafot*, 2:582.

Katz of Vienna) as well as a *payyetan*.[323] Indeed, R. Ḥayyim Palti'el b. Barukh was apparently a teacher or mentor of the scribe who compiled and copied the so-called *Maḥzor Nuernberg* in 1331.[324]

R. Ḥayyim Palti'el b. Barukh composed a series of *piyyutim*, including *'ahavot* and *ge'ulot* for the *Shema* on *Shabbat Shirah* and for the following *Shabbat* (*parashat Yitro*), on which the *'aseret ha-dibrot* are read.[325] The use of these venues and forms marks a degree of innovation within Ashkenazic *piyyut*.[326] R. Ḥayyim Palti'el b. Barukh also composed a *reshut* for the *ḥatan Bereshit* on *Simḥat Torah*, but no *seliḥot*.[327]

R. Avigdor b. Elijah Katz of Vienna, a thirteenth-century halakhist who hailed from France and lived and taught for a period in Italy before becoming the rabbi of Vienna, had extensive contact with R. Meir of Rothenburg and other Tosafists in both Germany and northern France.[328] He composed a *ma'ariv* for *Simḥat Torah*,[329] a *reshut* for *barkhu*,[330] a *havdalah*,[331] and two *seliḥot*.[332] Here again, R. Avigdor clearly sought to compose *piyyutim* for venues that were still available and viable.

Our discussion in this chapter has omitted—except on rare occasion, in order to provide a point of comparison or contrast—those twelfth- and thirteenth-century Tosafists who composed fewer than three *piyyutim*. Nor have we included *piyyutim* that were composed during this period by

323 On these responsa, see Emanuel, *Shivrei Luḥot*, 219 (n. 2).

324 See Fraenkel, *Ha-Tefillah veha-Piyyut be-Maḥzor Nuernberg*, 6, 77.

325 R. Ḥayyim's *piyyutim* are collected in ms. Bodl. 1150, fols. 161r–169v: אודה יוצר חסד נוצר (a *yozer* for the Sabbath of the ten commandments); חלק ה' עמו בצבאיו הוא אות (an *'ofan* for this same portion of *Yitro*); אני אלוף רגז אלוף ככבש אלוף וכדעת נשבה (an *'ahavah* for *parashat Yitro*); אני ביום עברה איד נכון לצלעי (a *ge'ulah* with a refrain, for *Yitro*); ארנן לבקר מופתים וחסדי א-ל (a *yozer* for *Shabbat shirah*, the portion of *Beshalaḥ*); חסין י-ה הווה והיה וכל נהיה יעידהו (an *'ofan* for *Shabbat shirah*); חצי יגונים עזר מונים (an *'ahavah* for *Shabbat shirah*); חסד צור לבי אומר (a *zulat* for *Shabbat shirah*); גאוני תהום שחו וחיו יבשה / גאולים שבחו שירה חדשה (a *ge'ulah* for *Shabbat shirah*). Note that the custom of R. Ḥayyim Palti'el cited in this manuscript on fol. 13v belongs to the *minhag* collection by R. Ḥayyim Palti'el b. Jacob; cf. Goldschmidt, *Meḥqerei Tefillah u-Piyyut*, n. 322.

326 See E. Fleischer, *Shirat ha-Qodesh ha-'Ivrit Bimei ha-Benayim*, 447, 450–59; idem, *Ha-Yozerot*, 673–83; and Fraenkel, *Ha-Tefillah veha-Piyyut be-Maḥzor Nuernberg*, 76–78.

327 Cf. Zunz, *LG*, 493. R. Moses b. Eleazar *ha-Kohen*, a relative of R. Meir's leading student in Germany, R. Asher b. Yeḥi'el (Rosh), and author of a work on *minhagim* titled *Sefer Ḥasidim Qatan* or *Sefer ha-Maskil*, composed several *seliḥot* and *qinot* to commemorate a series of persecutions. See M. M. Hoenig, "'Al Mahadurato ha-Ḥadashah shel Sefer ha-Maskil" (above, n. 284), 197 (n. 2).

328 On R. Avigdor, see above, Introduction, n. 90; and below, chapter 6, nn. 104–20.

329 See *Maḥzor Sukkot*, ed. Fraenkel, 327, אנצח על השמינית בקרב / עם מצא חן שרידי חרב.

330 א-ל דרכיו נועם מתנדבים בעם (with a *ḥaruz 'aḥid*). See Zunz, *LG*, 314; ms. Verona 34, fol. 40v; and cf. above, n. 138.

331 אקרא בכל יום ואהמה לאבי ובלילות על משכבי (Davidson, *Ozar ha-Shirah veha-Piyyut*, 4:111, 1962*: א). On the uncommon nature of this *piyyut* venue, see above, n. 78.

332 א-ל מי נקרא; see Zunz, *LG*, 313 (and Davidson, ibid., 1:175, 3789:א), and א-ל מי ימלל גבורתיך (Davidson, 3785:א).

"specialists" such as *ḥazzanim* and *naqdanim*, who were not also significant Tosafists or halakhic authorities.[333] A number of these specialists may have been associated in some way with the Tosafist academies, but their proficiency and productivity in talmudic studies remains unclear. Nonetheless, this review of the *piyyut* compositions by Tosafists and other significant halakhic scholars in northern France and Germany suggests that the writing of *piyyut* in Tosafist circles clearly remained a current and active area of scholarly endeavor throughout the twelfth and thirteenth centuries.

Not surprisingly, there are some differences between northern France and Germany in this regard. Most significant, of course, is the fact that the German Tosafists were more prolific on the whole than their northern French counterparts. As we have also seen, however, the rabbinic scholars in both areas adhered in large measure to the same basic models or compositional patterns. More than any other factor, the availability of opportunities or the needs of the discipline and the *genres* of *piyyut* shaped the interests of the Tosafists, as was the case in the pre-Crusade period. In brief, Tosafist *payyetanim* assiduously pursued available opportunities. At this juncture in the history of *piyyut* composition, the issue for these *payyetanim* was not principally one of "how much"; the question of "where" was much more significant.

We have also noticed that a number of the largest producers of *piyyut* in Germany fundamentally followed the *seliḥot/qinot* model that also included *zulatot* for *sefirat ha-ʿomer* and the like; the increasing number and extent of persecutions in medieval Ashkenaz, beginning in the late twelfth century, meant, unfortunately, that these opportunities were steadily if not increasingly available.[334] Throughout this chapter, we have also noted the significant extent of Spanish (or Sefardic) influence that appears to have been present in both Germany and northern France. This influence begins already in the mid-eleventh century and remains quite pronounced through the end of the thirteenth century. Indeed, *piyyutim* by R. Yosef ibn

333 For *piyyut* specialists in this period, such as R. Samuel Devlin *Ḥazzan* (of Erfurt, who died a martyr's death), see Zunz, *LG*, 465 (and above, nn. 152, 174); Fraenkel, *Ha-Tefillah veha-Piyyut be-Maḥzor Nuernberg*, 56, 60–61 (n. 334), 77 (n. 432). Cf. *ʿArugat ha-Bosem*, ed. Urbach, 4:60, and E. Hollender, *Piyyut Commentary in Medieval Ashkenaz*, 52–53; above, n. 285; and Introduction, n. 83.

334 With respect to personal "happy occasions" and festivals, *piyyutim* for the *Shabbat ḥatan* appear to have been more common in Germany than in northern France during the twelfth and thirteenth centuries (as Schmelzer has noted; see, e.g., his "Piyyutim le-Nisuʾin," 173–85, and idem, *Meḥqarim*, 190–208). On the other hand, *reshuyyot* connected with the Aramaic translations of the Torah and *Haftarah* readings on *Pesaḥ* and *Shavuʿot* are found mainly in northern France, as are *piyyutim* for occasions such as *Shabbat Ḥanukkah*. Clearly, these differences in *piyyut* composition may be rooted in different ritual and liturgical customs within these different geographic areas (as Schmelzer suggests as well).

Avitur, R. Solomon ibn Gabirol, R. Yehudah *ha-Levi*, and even R. Abraham Ezra were also part of medieval Ashkenazic prayer rites. The Tosafists apparently appreciated the meter and stylistic innovations that were present in Spanish *piyyut*, in general, and in the compositions of these Spanish authors in particular. They were quite comfortable importing and even occasionally expanding these techniques, as we have seen with regard to aspects of biblical interpretation as well, although increased Ashkenazic veneration of structural devices and more formal rules was surely the result of their own internal aesthetic values as well.[335]

As we have also seen, the German Pietists (*Ḥasidei Ashkenaz*) were far from the only Ashkenazic scholars in their day to be involved in substantive *piyyut* composition.[336] To be sure, a number of Tosafists from both Germany and northern France, including several leading figures, did not compose any *piyyutim*. In this case, however, a personal issue related to this discipline or field (i.e., whether the potential author had the ability or the proclivity to write liturgical poetry) rather than an ideological one (about whether *piyyut* still had a significant role within the rabbinic culture of Ashkenaz) was in all likelihood the key determinant, just as it was for those pre-Crusade figures who remained removed from the writing of *piyyut* even during its initial heyday in Ashkenaz.

The ebb and flow of medieval Ashkenazic *piyyut*, whether in the eleventh century or in the twelfth and thirteenth centuries, should be understood primarily as a function of liturgical opportunity and personal interest rather than as a curricular or ideological statement of change. As with the study of mysticism and magic that we shall discuss next, *piyyut* composition is another instance in which the Ashkenazic and Tosafist rabbinic culture of the twelfth and thirteenth centuries retained many of the wide disciplinary values of the pre-Crusade period. Leading rabbinic figures displayed, throughout, a broad range of interests and abilities in the realm of Torah study, creativity, and the search for religious truths, even as the impact of the Tosafists was felt most keenly in the realm of talmudic study, which remained the single largest focus of their intellectual efforts.

335 See, e.g., Elisabeth Hollender, "Late Ashkenazic Qinot in the Nuremberg Maḥzor," in *Giving a Diamond: Essays in Honor of Joseph Yahalom*, ed. W. Van Bekkum and N. Katsumata (Leiden, 2011), 265–78.

336 Cf. above, n. 155.

6

Magic and Mysticism in Tosafist Literature and Thought

As I have demonstrated at length in a book that appeared more than a decade ago, a significant group of northern French and German Tosafists and other rabbinic scholars were involved in the study of Jewish magic and mysticism.[1] Interest in these areas was typically combined with a tendency toward asceticism or *perishut*, as had been the case during the pre-Crusade period, especially within the academy of Mainz.[2] At the same time, however, the heavily talmudocentric orientation of several leading northern French Tosafists during the twelfth century and beyond, most notably Rabbenu Tam and R. Samson of Sens, as well as the near complete absence of any discussion of magic and mysticism in the standard *Tosafot* texts to the Babylonian Talmud, foster the incorrect impression that none of the Tosafists were involved in these disciplines.[3] It is not possible to review here all the data

[1] See my *"Peering through the Lattices": Mystical, Magical, and Pietistic Dimensions in the Tosafist Period* (Detroit, Mich., 2000). An updated and expanded Hebrew version was published by Merkaz Shazar under the title *Sod, Maggeyah u-Perishut be-Mishnatam shel Baʿalei ha-Tosafot* (Jerusalem, 2011).

[2] On asceticism and mysticism in pre-Crusade Mainz, see, e.g., Avraham Grossman, *Ḥakhmei Ashkenaz ha-Rishonim* (Jerusalem, 1981), 101, 211, 235, 247, 301, 310, 329, 334–36; my *"Peering through the Lattices,"* 131–57, and my "Hekkeruto shel Rashi be-Sifrut ha-Hekhalot uve-Torat ha-Sod," *Sefer Bar Ilan* 30–31 (2006), 491–500. Cf. Jeffrey Woolf, "The Prohibition of Gentile Bread during the Ten Days of Repentance: On the Genesis and Significance of a Custom," [Hebrew] in *Studies on the History of the Jews of Ashkenaz [Presented to Eric Zimmer]*, ed. G. Bacon et al. (Ramat Gan, 2008), 83–99; and E. Y. Brodt, *Bein Keseh le-ʿAsor* (Jerusalem, 2008), 21–22, 66–68.

[3] On the talmudic nature of the comments to the Torah put forward by Rabbenu Tam, see above, chapter 2, n. 6 (and chapter 3, nn. 190, 206), and see chapter 3, n. 217, for R. Samson of Sens, whose talmudic commentaries are exceptionally extensive. On the nearly complete absence of esoteric themes and teachings in the standard *Tosafot* to the Talmud and the reasons for that absence, see my *"Peering through the Lattices,"* 11–12.

presented in my earlier study, much of it from manuscript, or to pursue all the possible directions suggested there for further research. Nonetheless, it is worthwhile to describe briefly and to highlight, adding a number of new sources and details, those Tosafists and rabbinic scholars in both northern France and Germany who were most involved in these disciplines as well as those who were not, to assess the trends of these developments, and to point to some suggestive correlations between interest in these areas and the others that have been discussed in the present work.

Twelfth-Century Tosafists Who Avoided Mysticism: A Reaction to Pre-Crusade Ashkenazic Rabbinic Culture

Despite the tendency of quite of a number of pre-Crusade Ashkenazic rabbinic scholars to involve themselves in aspects of *torat ha-sod* in both Germany and northern France,[4] three prominent and outstanding twelfth-century Tosafists who were well aware of mystical texts and teachings nonetheless chose to distance themselves from this discipline: Rashbam, Raban, and Rabbenu Tam. As Sarah Kamin has demonstrated, Rashbam's interpretation of the Creation story was intended to bypass any possibility of cosmogonic or theosophic speculation.[5] In his commentary to *Qohelet* (2:3, 2:13), Rashbam asserts that only exoteric wisdom (which is absolutely necessary for mankind to master) should be pursued. On the other hand, "the deep and additional wisdom" (חכמה עמוקה ויתירה), which Rashbam (7:24) identifies as the wisdom contained in *Ma'aseh Merkavah* and *Sefer Yezirah*, is not needed by mankind and should not be pursued.[6]

In addition to diminishing the roles or importance of the supernatural and demonic worlds in his commentary to Job, which had been included by Rashi,[7] Rashbam specifically rejects Rashi's exegetical approach to Job

[4] See the indexes to A. Grossman, *Ḥakhmei Ashkenaz ha-Rishonim*, 449, and idem, *Ḥakhmei Ẓarefat ha-Rishonim* (Jerusalem, 1995), 617, s.v. *torat ha-sod*.

[5] See S. Kamin, "Rashbam's Conception of the Creation in the Light of the Intellectual Currents of His Time," *Scripta Hierosolymitana* 31 (1986), 91–132. Cf. Eleazar Touitou, *Exegesis in Perpetual Motion* [Hebrew] (Ramat Gan, 2003), 54, n. 11, 69, and Moshe Greenberg, "Darkah shel Sarah Kamin ba-Meḥqar," in *Ha-Miqra bi-Re'i Mefarshav [Sefer Zikkaron le-Sarah Kamin]*, ed. S. Japhet (Jerusalem, 1995), 25.

[6] See *Perush R. Shmu'el b. Meir le-Qohelet*, ed. S. Japhet and R. Salters (Jerusalem, 1985), 52–53 (and n. 187); and Gila Rozen, "Perush Rashi le-Qohelet" (M.A. thesis, Bar Ilan University, 1996), 57, 111, 162.

[7] See S. Japhet, *Perush Rabbenu Shmu'el b. Meir (Rashbam) le-Sefer Iyyov* (Jerusalem, 2000), 134–46. On Rashbam's tendency to explain away talmudic superstitions and folk magic, see, e.g., Louis Rabinowitz, *The Social History of the Jews in Northern France in the 12th–14th Centuries* (New York, 1972), 197, 206–7, and E. E. Urbach, *Meḥqarim be-Madda'ei ha-Yahadut* (Jerusalem, 1986), 17–18.

28, which involves mystical doctrines found in *Sefer Yeẓirah*.[8] Rashbam was clearly aware of the mystical powers inherent in Divine names and the existence and contents of various mystical texts. He defines the term *sitrei Torah* in his talmudic commentary to *'Arvei Pesaḥim* as מעשה מרכבה ומעשה בראשית ופירושו של שם כדכתיב זה שמי לעלם.[9] In doing so, Rashbam connects speculation on the Divine chariot with the mystical knowledge of the Divine name, which *Ḥasidei Ashkenaz* did as well, albeit with greater emphasis.[10] Thus Rashbam's attempt to distance himself and his readers from mystical speculation and symbolism was not at all due to ignorance or unawareness. Rather, it was a conscious strategy on his part.

Rashbam's German contemporary, R. Eliezer b. Nathan (Raban) of Mainz, also avoided recourse to *sod*. The introduction to his commentary on the prayers and to *piyyutim* is strikingly similar in both style and content to that of R. Eleazar of Worms's introduction to his prayer commentary, which was composed two generations later. Indeed, these two introductions have been arrayed side by side in contemporary scholarship,[11] a comparison that points out a glaring difference. While R. Eleazar of Worms expresses a keen interest in elucidating *sodot ha-tefillah* and *sod ha-berakhah*, Raban makes no mention of these dimensions at all, asserting only that he intends to provide basic, exoteric interpretations of the prayers and blessings.[12]

[8] See Japhet, *Perush Rabbenu Shmu'el b. Meir (Rashbam) le-Sefer Iyyov*, 153–59. On Rashi's greater openness to the use of mystical teachings (at least in exegetical contexts), see my "Rashi's Awareness of Jewish Mystical Literature and Tradition," in *Raschi und sein Erbe*, ed. D. Krochmalnik et al. (Heidelberg, 2007), 23–34.

[9] See Rashbam's commentary to *Pesaḥim* 119a, s.v. *sitrei ha-Torah*.

[10] See, e.g., *Sefer Roqeaḥ [Hilkhot Ḥasidut], Shoresh Qedushat ha-Yiḥud u-Shemo u-Merkavah ve-Sodotav* (Jerusalem, 1967), 23: וכל השמות יוצאין משם הנכבד ב"ה וב"ש ספר המרכבה וספר מעשה בראשית וספר יצירה וס' שמות וס' הכבוד אין לכתוב בס' הזה. Cf. Elliot Wolfson, *Through a Speculum That Shines* (Princeton, 1994), 235, and Haviva Pedaya, "Pegam ve-Tikkun shel ha-E-lohut be-Qabbalat R. Yiẓḥaq Sagi Nahor," *Jerusalem Studies in Jewish Thought* 6 [3–4] (1987), 157 (n. 2). Rashi to *Pesaḥim* (loc. cit.) merely mentions *ma'aseh merkavah* and *ma'aseh bereshit* as exemplars of *sitrei Torah*. A formulation similar to Rashbam's is found in the commentary to *Avot* in *Maḥzor Vitry*, ed. S. Hurwitz (Nuremberg, 1923), 554–55, and see also Moshe Idel, "Tefisat ha-Torah be-Sifrut ha-Hekhalot ve-Gilgulehah ba-Qabbalah," *Jerusalem Studies in Jewish Thought* 1 (1981), 36 (n. 38). Rashbam may have had a hand in this *Avot* commentary, along with other students of Rashi such as R. Jacob b. Samson. See I. Ta-Shma, "'Al Perush Avot shebe-Maḥzor Vitry," *Qiryat Sefer* 42 (1977), 507–8, and cf. A. Grossman, *Ḥakhmei Ẓarefat ha-Rishonim*, 413–16, and below, chapter 7, n. 38.

[11] See A. Grossman, *Ḥakhmei Ashkenaz ha-Rishonim*, 348; and *Siddur Rabbenu Shelomoh mi-Germaiza ve-Siddur Ḥasidei Ashkenaz*, ed. M. Hershler (Jerusalem, 1972), editor's introduction, 29. See also *Sefer Raban/Even ha-'Ezer* (repr. Jerusalem, 1975), sec. 119 (fols. 86b–87a).

[12] On the absence of *sod* material in Raban's prayer and *piyyut* commentaries, see *'Arugat ha-Bosem*, ed. E. E. Urbach, vol. 4 (Jerusalem, 1963), 24–39, 73–74. Urbach concludes unequivocally that "[Raban] did not include in them matters of *torat ha-sod*." See also Stefan Reif, *Judaism and Hebrew Prayer* (Cambridge, 1993), 171–75; S. Emanuel, *Shivrei Luḥot*, 54–55 (Jerusalem, 2007); *Siddur Rabbenu Shelomoh mi-Germaiza*, ed. M. Hershler, 139–40, and esp. n.28; and Matania

In another methodological statement, Raban indicates that his omission of esoteric material was by design, even as he, like Rashbam, was well aware of this type of material: "I do not need [or, I am not worthy, in a manuscript variant] to interpret and explain (איני צריך/כדאי לפרשם) *'ofannim* [liturgical poems on the portion of the pre-*Shema* liturgy that refers to angelic and other heavenly beings, which often contained esoteric themes], because *ma'aseh Bereshit* and *ma'aseh Merkavah* may not be explicated [to others] even in private. Rather, I will explain the *peshat*, so that one can have a basic understanding of what he is saying" (אך הפשט אפרש כדי לכוין ולהשמיע מה שמוציא בפה).[13]

Moreover, Raban reports an interpretation by his brother Hezekiah which was intended, according to Elliot Wolfson, to vigorously deflect a mystical approach. Hezekiah did not bow in the presence of a Torah scroll because of any inherent Godliness in the Torah scroll itself but rather because the *Shekhinah* dwells within the Holy Ark. This explanation stands in clear opposition to the mystical tradition embraced and expanded upon by the German Pietists, which identifies the Torah with the Divine glory, the *Kavod.* According to this tradition, the Torah scroll is identified as the Divine footstool, and one bows in the presence of a Torah because it is in fact a manifestation of the Divine. In their formulation, Hezekiah and Raban wished to offset this view.[14]

Ben-Ghedaliah, "Ha-Reqa ha-Histori li-Ketivat Sefer Even ha-'Ezer" (M.A. thesis, Touro College, 2002), 21–24. The so-called pseudo-Raban prayer commentary does contain mystical material. See Chaim Levine, "Perush 'al ha-Maḥzor ha-Meyuḥas le-Raban," *Tarbiz* 29 (1959–60), 162–75, and cf. A. Y. Hershler, "Perush Siddur ha-Tefillah veha-Maḥzor Meyuḥas le-R. Eliezer b. Nathan mi-Magenẓa (ha-Ra'avan), Ketav Yad Frankfurt," *Genuzot* 3 (1991), 1–28; *'Arugat ha-Bosem*, ed. Urbach, 4:38 (n. 81); and Binyamin Hamburger, *Shorshei Minhag Ashkenaz*, vol. 2 (Bnei Brak, 2000), 241.

13 Urbach, *'Arugat ha-Bosem*, 4:29, cites this passage from ms. Hamburg 153 (fols. 32v–33r, with the reading איני צריך). However, the manuscript there (at the very beginning of fol. 33r) appears to me to read איני כדיי; see also the facsimile edition of this manuscript published by A. N. Z. Roth et al. (Jerusalem, 1980). In ms. Warsaw 258, fol. 182r, the passage also begins, אופנים איני כדאי לפרשם.

14 See Elliot Wolfson, "The Mystical Significance of Torah Study in German Pietism," *JQR* 84 (1993), 71–73; and idem, *Through a Speculum That Shines*, 248–50. Raban (*Sefer Raban*, sec. 127 [*massekhet Berakhot*, fol. 88b]) follows Rabbenu Ḥanan'el's view that certain human beings may perceive aspects of the Divine realm through the imaginative faculty of *re'iyat ha-lev*, but does not accept the position of Rabbenu Ḥanan'el that this is possible even with respect to the *Kavod* itself; see below, n. 103. Raban's dream experience in 1152, recorded in *Sefer Raban*, sec. 26 (fols. 26b–27a), perhaps earned for him the sobriquet of *ba'al Shem* in the late medieval *Ma'aseh Bukh*; see, e.g., A. J. Heschel, "'Al Ruaḥ ha-Qodesh Bimei ha-Benayim," in *Sefer ha-Yovel li-Khvod Alexander Marx*, ed. S. Lieberman (New York, 1950), 196, and Sarah Zfatman, *Bein Ashkenaz li-Sefarad: Le-Toledot ha-Sippur ha-Yehudi Bimei ha-Benayim* (Jerusalem, 1993), 82, n. 7, 105. Comparison of this episode, however, with other contemporary Ashkenazic dream experiences in halakhic contexts, such as those of R. Menaḥem b. Jacob of Worms (below,

Like his brother Rashbam, Rabbenu Tam tended to interpret talmudic passages in ways that eliminated the roles of superstition and *shedim*, even where these had been left intact by Rashi and other predecessors. Thus while Rashi interpreted the talmudic dictum that a misplaced *mezuzah* was harmful because it could not then serve to eliminate *shedim*, Rabbenu Tam saw the potential harm simply as the risk of injury if one bumped into the *mezuzah* owing to its poor placement.[15] As opposed to Rashi, Rabbenu Tam cites *Otiyyot de-R. Aqiva* only in halakhic contexts (e.g., as a source for the technically correct writing of *sifrei Torah*), with no concern for or interest in its mystical aspects and implications.[16]

As we have noted, Rabbenu Tam was unfailingly talmudocentric, which was undoubtedly a factor in his general avoidance of mystical topics and literature. Indeed, Rabbenu Tam was not even inclined, as Rashbam was, toward the study and interpretation of Scripture as a distinct discipline.[17] There are

---

n. 66), R. Ephraim b. Isaac of Regensburg (below, n. 77), and R. Isaiah b. Mali di Trani (below, n. 87), reveals that while Raban's experience was deeply spiritual, it also appears to have been largely psychosomatic and entails neither magical techniques nor distinctly mystical elements (which do characterize the other dreams and figures). Cf. Ḥida, *Shem ha-Gedolim* (Warsaw, 1876), *ma'arekhet ha-gedolim*, 26, sec. 199, and 62–64, sec. 224; and below, n. 69. See now my "Dreams as a Determinant of Jewish Law and Practice in Northern Europe during the High Middle Ages," in *Studies in Medieval Jewish Intellectual and Social History: A Festschrift for Robert Chazan*, ed. D. Engel, L. Schiffman, and E. Wolfson (Leiden, 2012), 111–43.

15 See, e.g., Rashi, *Menaḥot* 32b, s.v. *sakkanah*; *Tosafot Menaḥot* 32b, s.v. *sakkanah*; and R. Yeroḥam b. Meshullam, *Toledot Adam ve-Ḥavvah* (Venice, 1553), sec. 21, pt. 7 (fol. 179c). Cf. *Teshuvot R. Meir mi-Rothenburg* (Cremona, 1556), #108, and Daniel Sperber, *Minhagei Yisra'el*, vol. 1 (Jerusalem, 1989), 46–56.

16 See *Rashi 'al ha-Torah*, ed. Abraham Berliner (Frankfurt, 1905), 427 (*liqqutim* to Numbers 14:4); I. Ta-Shma, "Sifriyyatam shel Ḥakhmei Ashkenaz Bnei ha-Me'ah ha-Yod Alef/ha-Yod Bet," *Qiryat Sefer* 60 (1985), 307; idem, "Qavvim le-Ofiyyah shel Sifrut ha-Halakhah be-Ashkenaz ba-Me'ah ha-Yod Gimmel/ha-Yod Daled," *'Alei Sefer* 4 (1977), 26–27; Rabbenu Tam's *Hilkhot [Tiqqun] Sefer Torah* in *Ginzei Yerushalayim*, ed. S. A. Wertheimer, vol. 1 (Jerusalem, 1896), 97–99; *Sefer ha-Manhig*, ed. S. Raphael (Jerusalem, 1978), 2:587, 620; and cf. Aharon Mondschein, "The Massoretes Fabricated Explanations for Full and Defective Spellings: On Abraham Ibn Ezra's Struggles Against the (Ab)use of Biblical Spelling as an Exegetical Tool," [Hebrew] *Shenaton le-Ḥeqer ha-Miqra veha-Mizraḥ ha-Qadum* 19 (2009), 293 (n. 214). Note also the differences between Rabbenu Tam and R. Judah *he-Ḥasid* in defining the thirteen Divine attributes. See, e.g., *Tosafot Rosh ha-Shanah* 17b, s.v. *ve-shalosh*; *Sefer Ḥasidim* (Parma), ed. J. Wistinetski (Frankfurt, 1924), secs. 414–15; *Sefer ha-Manhig*, 1:277–78; *Tosafot ha-Shalem*, ed. Gellis, vol. 10 (Jerusalem, 1999), 124–25; S. E. Stern, "Perush Yod Gimmel Middot le-Rabbenu Tam," *Yeshurun* 3 (1997), 3–4; and cf. Ibn Ezra to Exodus 34:6; and my "Rabbinic Figures in Castilian Kabbalistic Pseudepigraphy," *Journal of Jewish Thought and Philosophy* 3 (1993), 93 (n. 57), 95(n. 67).

17 See, e.g., my "On the Role of Bible Study in Medieval Ashkenaz," in *The Frank Talmage Memorial Volume*, ed. B. Walfish (Haifa, 1993), 1:151–66. See also above, Introduction, nn. 51, 53–54, and in chapter 2, n. 6; and cf. Rami Reiner, "Rabbenu Tam u-Bnei Doro: Qesahrim, Hashpa'ot ve-Darkhei Limmudo ba-Talmud" (Ph.D. diss., Hebrew University, 2002), 283–317. Even Rabbenu Tam's extensive interest in *piyyut* (above, chapter 5) was at least partially motivated by his interest in *halakhah*. See, e.g., Urbach, *Ba'alei ha-Tosafot*, 1:107–10, and cf. A. Grossman, "Perush ha-Piyyutim le-R. Aharon b. Ḥayyim ha-Kohen," in *Be-Oraḥ Madda: Sefer Yovel*

only a handful of passages in Rabbenu Tam's substantial corpus that reflect mystical considerations, and their implications must be carefully considered. *Tosafot Ḥagigah* cites Rabbenu Tam as defining (the secret of) *maʿaseh Bereshit* as the Divine name of forty-two letters, which can be derived from the first two verses of the Torah and played a role in Creation. As we have noted, however, Rashbam was also aware of, and occasionally makes reference to, earlier Ashkenazic mystical traditions about Divine names. Moreover, this particular tradition, which had apparently not yet reached Ashkenaz by Rashi's day but was expanded upon later by R. Eleazar of Worms and ultimately by the Zohar, was also cited in the name of R. Hai Gaon.[18]

In his *Sefer ha-Qomah*, R. Moses b. Eleazar *ha-Darshan*, a grandson of R. Judah *he-Ḥasid*, attributes to Rabbenu Tam a mystical teaching (סוד שמי־ פורש בשם רבינו תם) that Metatron is to be identified with the *Shekhinah*.[19] Rabbenu Tam's actual formulation, however, was offered in a completely exoteric context. Rashi had interpreted the phrase in Exodus 23:21, "for My name is within him" (*ki shemi be-qirbo*), as an indication that the angel which the Almighty sent to guide the Jewish people following the sin of the golden calf was named Metatron, since the *gematria* of Metatron is equivalent to the

le-Aharon Mirsky, ed. Zvi Malachi (Lod, 1986), 453; Haym Soloveitchik, "Three Themes in the *Sefer Ḥasidim*," *AJS Review* 1 (1976), 345, 352 (n. 31); Z. Malachi, "Rashi and His Disciples in Relation to the Old Paytanim," in *Rashi, 1040–1990*, ed. Sed Rajna (Paris, 1993), 455–62.

[18] See *Tosafot Ḥagigah* 11b, s.v. *ʿein dorshin*; Elliot Wolfson, "Letter Symbolism and Merkavah Imagery in the Zohar," in *ʿAlei Shefer: Studies in the Literature of Jewish Thought*, ed. Moshe Hallamish (Ramat Gan, 1990), 217*–218*; and cf. ms. Bodl. 2344, fol. 3r. Cf. Rashi's commentary to *Sukkah* 45a, s.v. *ʾani va-ho*; *Qiddushin* 71a, s.v. *Shem ben shteim ʿesreh*; *Sefer ha-Bahir*, ed. Daniel Abrams (Los Angeles, 1994), sec. 76, 79; and my "Rashi's Awareness of Jewish Mystical Literature and Traditions," in *Raschi und sein Erbe* (above, n. 8).

[19] See E. Wolfson, *Through a Speculum That Shines*, 260, and the manuscript sources for this passage, cited in n. 309. As Wolfson notes, this passage also refers to the mystical treatise by an associate of the German Pietists, R. Neḥemyah b. Solomon (*ha-Navi*, of Erfurt), which explains and accounts for the various names of Metatron. Cf. Yehuda Liebes, "The Angels of the Shofar and Yeshua Sar ha-Panim," [Hebrew] *Jerusalem Studies in Jewish Thought* 6:1–2 (1987), 171–95; E. E. Urbach, "Sefer ʿArugat ha-Bosem le-R. Avraham b. ʿAzriʾel," *Tarbiz* 10 (1939), 50–51; *ʿArugat ha-Bosem*, ed. Urbach, 4:119; and Wolfson, *Through a Speculum That Shines*, 231–32, n. 177. In a lengthy series of exceptionally illuminating articles, Moshe Idel has recently uncovered R. Neḥemyah's voluminous mystical corpus, as well as the pivotal role that he played in the development and conceptualization of Ashkenazic mysticism, in ways that were related to but ultimately distinct from the German Pietists. See now Idel, "An Unknown Liturgical Poem for Yom Kippur by Neḥemia ben Shlomo the Prophet," [Hebrew] in *From Sages to Savants: Studies Presented to Avraham Grossman* (Jerusalem, 2010), 237–61 (and 237, n. 2, for a listing of many of his other studies to date on R. Neḥemyah). As far as I can tell, however, there was no interaction between R. Neḥemyah and Tosafist *battei midrash*, nor does R. Neḥemyah's name (or another name associated with him, R. Troestlin *ha-Navi*) appear in any Ashkenazic talmudic or halakhic writings. Cf. above, Introduction, n. 83; *Tosafot ha-Shalem*, ed. Gellis, 7:36, sec. 7 (from *Paʿaneaḥ Raza*); and my "*Peering through the Lattices*," 244, n. 67.

Divine name, *Sha-dai.*[20] The comment attributed to Rabbenu Tam, preserved in the Tosafist Torah compilation *Moshav Zeqenim*, suggests instead that the Almighty is referred to as Metatron according to a passage in the *Pesiqta* (to Ex. 13:21), in which the Almighty asserts that "He is the *manitor* [watchman] for his children."[21] There is no suggestion of any mystical methodology at work here; that connection is made by R. Moses *ha-Darshan* alone. Indeed, several *Tosafot* comments record Rabbenu Tam's exposition of the purely angelic nature and role of Metatron, as these nonesoteric aspects appear in the *Pesiqta* and in various talmudic sources.[22] Rabbenu Tam was interested in clarifying the role of Metatron and other heavenly figures on the basis of rabbinic texts. One of the positions he formulated in this endeavor may have been helpful to *baʿalei sod*, but it cannot be maintained on this basis that Rabbenu Tam was himself an active *baʿal sod.*

According to a text of the *Ḥug ha-Keruv ha-Meyuḥad*, a mystical circle that flourished in northern France and England and was associated with the German Pietists, Abraham ibn Ezra created a *golem* in the presence of Rabbenu Tam. The figure of Ibn Ezra was often co-opted by medieval Jewish mystics, including the German Pietists, just as Ibn Ezra himself was the subject of legends and tales involving *torat ha-sod* practices. As a leading medieval talmudist and rabbinic figure, Rabbenu Tam would seem to have been placed in the same kind of position in this instance, although he was certainly the more passive figure in this situation in any case.[23]

20 For Rashi's (earlier?) source, see *Midrash Tehillim*, ed. Buber, 17:3, n. 12, and *Torah Shelemah*, sec. 313. Cf. Wolfson, *Through a Speculum That Shines*, 260, n. 306. On Rashi's (limited) use of *gematria* in his Torah commentary, cf. above, chapter 2, n. 37.

21 See *Moshav Zeqenim ʿal ha-Torah*, ed. S. D. Sassoon (London, 1959), 198: ופר''ת שהקב''ה בעצמו נקרא מטטרון כדאמרינן בפסיקתא וה' הולך לפניהם יומם אמר הקב''ה אני הייתי מניטור לבני פי' שומר. Cf. Daniel Abrams, "The Boundaries of Divine Ontology: The Inclusion and Exclusion of Metatron in the Godhead," *Harvard Theological Review* 87 (1994), 299–300.

22 See, e.g., *Tosafot Yevamot* 16b, s.v. *pasuq zeh*; the parallel *Tosafot Ḥullin* 60a, s.v. *pasuq zeh*; and the variant in *Tosafot ha-Shalem ʿal Massekhet Yevamot*, ed. Abraham Shoshana (Jerusalem, 1994), 100. Cf. Reuven Margaliot, *Malʾakhei ʿElyon* (Jerusalem, 1964), 79–80; *Tosafot ha-Shalem*, ed. Gellis, 8:343–44, sec. 11; and 8:346–47, secs. 9, 11.

23 See Moshe Idel, *Golem* (Albany, N.Y., 1990), 81–82, 86–87, 92–93, nn. 4, 11, and see also the revised Hebrew edition (Jerusalem, 1996), 276–77. On the *Ḥug ha-Keruv ha-Meyuḥad*, see Y. Dan, "Ḥug ha-Keruv ha-Meyuḥad bi-Tenuʿat Ḥasidei Ashkenaz," *Tarbiz* 35 (1966), 349–72; and D. Abrams, "A History of the Unique Cherub," *JQR* 90 (2000), 397–403. Ibn Ezra praised Rabbenu Tam as a *malʾakh ha-E-lohim* (see A. J. Heschel, "ʿAl Ruaḥ ha-Qodesh Bimei ha-Benayim," 182, n. 34), and there was certainly literary contact between them; see Urbach, *Baʿalei ha-Tosafot*, 1:109–10, and above, Introduction, n. 3. On Ibn Ezra in the thought of *ḥasidut Ashkenaz*, see, e.g., Dan, *Torat ha-Sod shel Ḥasidut Ashkenaz* (Jerusalem, 1968), 29–31, 113–16, 138–43, and Wolfson. *Through a Speculum That Shines*, 177, 193, 215, 222, 247–47. Cf. A. Lifshitz, "R. Avraham ibn Ezra be-Perushei Baʿalei ha-Tosafot ʿal ha-Torah," *Hadarom* 28 (1968), 202–21; and above, chapter 4, n. 122. For legends about Ibn Ezra, see, e.g., Naftali ben Menaḥem, *Avraham Ibn Ezra—Siḥot va-Aggadot ʿAm* (Jerusalem, 1943), and idem, *ʿInyanei Ibn Ezra* (Jerusalem, 1978), 337–73.

Rabbenu Tam is paired in similar fashion with his older contemporary, R. Elijah b. Judah of Paris. R. Elijah of Paris, not to be confused with the northern French Pietist and *payyetan* from the first half of the eleventh century, R. Elijah b. Menaḥem *ha-Zaqen* of Le Mans,[24] was perceived to have affinities with esoteric lore owing to his deep piety and to his mystical traditions concerning the end of days, which were recorded by R. Jacob of Provins.[25] Several variant texts record a request that was made by R. Jacob to a R. Samuel (or R. Saul) *ha-Navi*, who was expounding certain Torah passages and ideas in the home of R. Menaḥem Vardimas (d. 1224), in the presence of other rabbinic figures and students, to inquire of *Mosheh Rabbenu* about whether Rabbenu Tam or R. Elijah was correct in his halakhic exposition concerning the need to tie the *kesher shel tefillin* (on the *tefillin shel yad*) anew each day.[26] This passage, which speaks to the spiritual virtuosity of R. Elijah in particular and to the mystical milieu in which some of his students and successors flourished, does not, however, demonstrate any mystical proclivities or tendencies on the part of Rabbenu Tam.[27]

There is one additional manuscript passage in which Rabbenu Tam is again paired with R. Elijah of Paris. In response to a request from a learned

[24] On R. Elijah b. Menaḥem, see A. Grossman, *Ḥakhmei Ẓarefat ha-Rishonim*, 86–87, 98, 104–5, and see also above, chapter 1, nn. 225, 231, regarding R. Elijah of Paris's view on the scope of logical applications to be pursued within talmudic interpretation.

[25] For R. Elijah of Paris's noteworthy piety, see Urbach, *Baʿalei ha-Tosafot*, 1:76, 79, 122, and *Sefer ha-Manhig*, ed. Raphel, 1:49, 1:337, 2:649. For his traditions concerning the end of days, see *Teshuvot u-Pesaqim*, ed. E. Kupfer (Jerusalem, 1973), 309–12.

[26] According to this passage, R. Samuel first sought to adjure the souls of R. Elijah and R. Tam, but was told by Metatron that R. Elijah could not descend, since he was offering sacrifices before the Almighty (and it was deemed inappropriate for the *Shekhinah* to descend together with R. Elijah). See Urbach, *Baʿalei ha-Tosafot*, 1:88; Norman Golb, *Toledot ha-Yehudim be-ʿIr Rouen* (Tel Aviv, 1976), 98–110; and Rami Reiner, "Rabbenu Tam u-Bnei Doro: Qesharim, Hashpaʿot ve-Darkhei Limmudo ba-Talmud," 72–76. After reviewing the contacts between Rabbenu Tam and R. Elijah with respect to various legal matters and halakhic rulings, Reiner (83–84) notes at least one instance in which these two rabbinic scholars actually met face to face, and further suggests that there were familial ties between them as well.

[27] Relatively little is known about (or has been preserved from) either R. Jacob b. Meir of Provins (who appears to have been a teacher of R. Isaac *Or Zaruʿa*; see Uzi Fuchs, "ʿIyyunim be-Sefer Or Zaruʿa le-R. Yiẓḥaq b. Mosheh me-Vienna" [M.A. thesis, Hebrew University, 1993], 19, n. 45, citing *Sefer Or Zaruʿa, hilkhot Pesaḥim*, sec. 235, and *pisqei Bava Meẓiʿa*, sec. 3) or R. Menaḥem Vardimas of Rouen/Dreux. Complicating this issue is that Vardimas is the equivalent of Menaḥem, and could have been linked to other rabbinic scholars of that name; see *Shabbat* 118b, and S. Emanuel, *Shivrei Luḥot*, 214. Indeed, this name has also been applied to R. Menaḥem b. Pereẓ of Joigny, a student of Rabbenu Tam (who appears to have lived a generation or so before R. Jacob of Provins), as well as a R. Menaḥem (*he-*)*Ḥasid*, who also had contact with German Tosafists in the thirteenth century. See, e.g., N. Golb, *The Jews in Medieval Normandy* (Cambridge, 1998), 387–99, 408–12; Gavriel Zinner, *Oẓar Pisqei ha-Rishonim ʿal Hilkot Pesaḥ* (New York, 1985), 19–20, 22, 39; *Perushim u-Pesaqim le-Rabbenu Avigdor [Katz]*, ed. Machon Harerei Qedem (Jerusalem, 1996), 41, 178, 193, 368, 370, 423, 473, and cf. I. Ta-Shma, *Knesset Meḥqarim* (Jerusalem, 2004), 1:131; my *"Peering through the Lattices,"* 98, 206–7; and below, nn. 52–53.

father, *ha-Rav R. Todros*, who had been unable to attend the burial of his murdered twenty-year-old son, Elijah of Chartres, and who refused to eat or drink until they acquiesced to his request as the leading scholars of the generation (*gedolei ha-dor*), Rabbenu Tam and R. Elijah allowed the use of a Divine name in order to resurrect the visage of the deceased son (שיתירו לו גדולי הדור רבינו תם מרמרו ורבינו אליהו מפריז להעלות לפניו בנו בשם המפורש . . . כך עשו והתירו לו.) This text further suggests that it was R. Todros who then washed and immersed himself, and donned white garments. In the presence of the community in the synagogue, R. Todros placed, or perhaps recited, the Divine name between the Torah scrolls, and thereby adjured the soul of his son. The son's face appeared from between the Torah scrolls, and he conversed with his father in the presence of the congregation and even emerged from the ark for a time, until his father returned his presence to the ark.[28]

According to this passage, Rabbenu Tam appears not only to be aware of magical adjurations, as Rashbam and Raban were, but also to support the use of these adjurations for appropriate purposes. At the same time, Rabbenu Tam was a relatively "silent partner" in this episode as well. As the text clearly notes, both Rabbenu Tam and R. Elijah responded to his request from afar, while remaining in their respective places of residence. Rabbenu Tam was not the initiator of any magical processes, nor was he necessarily involved in them. He was, however, undoubtedly aware of the venerable Ashkenazic traditions concerning the power and use of *Shemot*, although he would apparently countenance their usage only in especially weighty and poignant situations such as the one described. Indeed, a passage found in Rabbenu Tam's *Sefer ha-Yashar* is understood by some to mean that the remains of Rabbenu Tam's martyred brother-in-law, R. Samson of Falaise (grandfather of R. Samson of Sens and Riẓba), were found or handed over some six months after his death, through the efforts of a *ba'al ha-ḥalom*, who divined its location through a magical dream procedure. Here again, however, Rabbenu Tam was uninvolved with the procedure itself.[29]

Similarly, in the two instances in which Rabbenu Tam does mention aspects of *sod* or magic himself, he presents them in the name of the *Ḥakhmei*

[28] See ms. Vienna 152 (Hebr. 47; Italy, fifteenth century), fols. 1v–2r (following a section titled המפורש לשם פירוש), and cf. Urbach, *Ba'alei ha-Tosafot*, 1:123; and G. Scholem, *Reshit ha-Qabbalah bi-Provence*, 38–39, n.2; and idem, *Origins of the Kabbalah* (Princeton, 1987), 100–102. After this episode, the manuscript continues with a תפילת אליהו, which ends with the blessing of שומע תפלה. This account is also found in ms. JTS 8114 (Ashkenaz, fourteenth/fifteenth century), fols. 68r–v. Although the locale of the deceased in ms. Vienna is given as קרנות, the passage in ms. JTS makes it clear that he was from Chartres.

[29] See *Sefer ha-Yashar le-Rabbenu Tam* (*ḥeleq ha-teshuvot*), ed. Shraga Rosenthal (Berlin, 1898), 191, and cf. *Sefer Or Zaru'a, hilkhot 'agunah*, pt. 1, sec. 692 (fol. 97c); A. Aptowitzer, *Mavo la-Rabiah* (Jerusalem, 1938), 420; Urbach, *Ba'alei ha-Tosafot*, 1:19; and A. J. Heschel, "'Al Ruaḥ ha-Qodesh Bimei ha-Benayim," 182, n. 37 (end).

or *Ge'onei Lothaire* of the late eleventh century, as transmitted to him by his father, R. Meir b. Samuel. Rabbenu Tam endorses the custom that one should not eat after sunset on the day of the Sabbath because of the danger from *shedim* or *maziqin* that could befall those who did, as per the *Ḥakhmei Lothaire*, but his justification for this custom unfolds through the citation of completely exoteric rabbinic texts.[30] In the context of formulating the halakhic permissibility of reciting *piyyutim* within portions of the prayer service in which no other interruptions are permitted, Rabbenu Tam reports (from his father) the Lothaire tradition that describes how R. Eleazar *ha-Qallir* appeared when he composed *piyyutim* and made reference to the angels who surrounded the *kisse ha-merkavah*: a fire ignited and burned around R. Eleazar (ליהטה אש סביביו). It was in this context as well, the composition of *piyyutim* that had heavenly secrets and approbation, that Rabbenu Tam characterized R. Simeon b. Isaac *ha-Gadol* of Mainz (c. 1000) as "accustomed to performing miracles" (*melummad be-nisim*).[31] Rabbenu Tam makes no attempt to explain or to analyze these traditions. He accepts them simply as earlier rabbinic perceptions that should be upheld as a matter of proper custom and respect.

In light of all this, it is not surprising to discover that a series of mystical adjurations and requests that are attributed in several manuscripts to Rabbenu Tam, and that owe quite a bit to *Hekhalot* literature, belong in fact to a lesser-known northern French Tosafist of the thirteenth century, R. Isaac b. Isaac of Chinon. R. Isaac's demonstrated interest in mysticism and magic, and his possible connection to *ḥasidut Ashkenaz* through the Tosafist *beit midrash* at Evreux, as we shall see, are fully consistent with his authorship of these formulations.[32] Their attribution to Rabbenu Tam, on the other hand,

[30] See I. Ta-Shma, *Minhag Ashkenaz ha-Qadmon* (Jerusalem, 1992), 102, 203–13. Cf. *Teshuvot Ba'alei ha-Tosafot*, ed. I. A. Agus (New York, 1954), 56; *Shibbolei ha-Leqet*, sec. 127, ed. S. Buber (Vilna, 1887), fol. 50a (and ms. Bodl. 659, fol. 35); *Moshav Zeqenim 'al ha-Torah*, 144–45 (Ex. 16:5); (the parallel passage in) *Perushim u-Pesaqim le-Rabbenu Avigdor [Katz]*, 93–97 (*pesaq* 125, to *parashat va-Yaqhel*); and below n. 54, regarding the competing position strongly held (and argued) by Rabbenu Tam's student R. Menaḥem of Joigny.

[31] See *Maḥzor Vitry*, ed. Simon Hurwitz (Nuremberg, 1923), 364; *Shibbolei ha-Leqet ha-Shalem*, ed. Buber, sec. 28 (= ed. S. K. Mirsky [New York, 1966], 216); *Va-Yiqra Rabbah*, 16:4; *Sefer Or Zaru'a, Hilkhot Qeri'at Shema*, sec. 19; Ezra Fleischer, "Inyanim Qiliriyim," *Tarbiz* 50 (1981), 282–302; Ruth Langer, "Kalir Was a Tanna," *Hebrew Union College Annual* 67 (1996), 95–106; and Rami Reiner, "Rabbenu Tam: Rabbotav (ha-Ẓarefatim) ve-Talmidav Bnei Ashkenaz" (M.A. thesis, Hebrew University, 1997), 15–21, 45. Cf. Avraham Grossman, "Ẓemiḥat Parshanut ha-Piyyut," in *Sefer Yovel li-Shelomoh Simonsohn*, ed. A. Oppenheim et al. (Tel Aviv, 1993), 69; Moshe Idel, *Kabbalah: New Perspectives* (New Haven, Conn., 1988), 320, n. 119; *Ketav Tamim le-R. Mosheh Taku* in *Oẓar Neḥmad* 4(1863), 85 (in which Qallir is described as a *mal'akh E-lohim*); and the use of the phrase *melummad be-nissim* (about R. Shim'on Bar Yoḥai and R. Naḥum of Gimzo) in *Me'ilah* 17b and *Sanhedrin* 109a.

[32] See below, n. 131.

is a clear example of *teliyyah be-'ilan gadol* (attribution to a leading northern French Tosafist and rabbinic figure whose authorship cannot actually be demonstrated), as a means of enhancing their legitimacy and significance.

Renewed Interest in Mysticism among Students of Rabbenu Tam

As was the case with respect to the issue of treating *parshanut ha-miqra* as a distinct discipline,[33] several of Rabbenu Tam's students did not follow or endorse the relatively passive approach taken by their teacher with regard to mystical and magical studies but favored instead the more engaged approach that was found in rabbinic circles in Ashkenaz during the pre-Crusade period. R. Elḥanan b. Yaqar of London, who also spent time in northern France with fellow members of the mystical Circle of the Special Cherub (*Ḥug ha-Keruv ha-Meyuḥad*),[34] writes that he studied *Sefer Yeẓirah* with an unnamed scholar who had himself studied it with R. Isaac (Ri) *ha-Zaqen*. R. Isaac b. Samuel (Ri) of Dampierre (d. 1189) was Rabbenu Tam's nephew, and his most important student.[35] Indeed, R. Elḥanan b. Yaqar cites a formulation of Ri, on the fates and rewards in the world to come which await the sinners and the righteous, in his mystical commentary to *Sefer Yeẓirah*.[36]

Moreover, Ri was associated by the *Ḥug ha-Keruv ha-Meyuḥad* with the study of *Sefer Yeẓirah* for mystical and magical purposes in another instance as well. According to a variant of the *Ḥug*'s Pseudo-Sa'adyah commentary to *Sefer Yeẓirah*, Ri [ר"ז = ר"י הזקן] and his disciples wished to create a *golem* in the course of their study of *Sefer Yeẓirah*, but the students became endangered in the process. Ri directed them to reverse the letters of the alphabet that they had recited previously, and the students were spared.[37]

Ri is included among a list of Ashkenazic scholars who purportedly received and transmitted mystical prognostications: "Ri ascended to the heavens (*'alah la-marom*) and received things from the ministering angels (*mal'akhei ha-sharet*)."[38] He is the only figure on that list who was not

[33] See above, chapter 2.

[34] On R. Elḥanan, see above, Introduction, n. 83.

[35] On Ri's extreme pietism with respect to prayer practices and regular fasting, and the differing attitudes of Rabbenu Tam, see my *"Peering through the Lattices,"* 42–44, 193–94, and cf. Urbach, *Ba'alei ha-Tosafot*, 1:230–32.

[36] Ms. JTS Mic. 8118 (ENA 838), fol. 65v. See also my *"Peering through the Lattices,"* 191–92, n. 4.

[37] See Moshe Idel, *Golem*, 81–82, 91–92, n. 4.

[38] See Alexander Marx, "Ma'amar 'al Shenat Geulah," *Ha-Ẓofeh le-Ḥokhmat Yisra'el* 5 (1921), 194–202. Cf. Urbach, *Ba'alei ha-Tosafot*, 1:238, n. 45*, and my "Ḥishuvei ha-Qeẓ shel Ḥakhmei Ashkenaz me-Rashi u-Bnei Doro ve-'ad li-Tequafat Ba'alei ha-Tosafot," in *Rashi: Demuto ve-Yeẓirato*, ed. A. Grossman and S. Japhet (Jerusalem, 2008), vol. 2, 381–401.

otherwise closely associated with the German Pietists, although it is possible that he was visited in northern France by R. Judah *he-Ḥasid*, and that he met R. Samuel *he-Ḥasid* as well.[39] R. Abraham b. Nathan *ha-Yarḥi* (of Lunel), author of the *Sefer ha-Manhig*, traveled to Dampierre to study with Ri. It was within Ri's circle that R. Abraham observed certain pietistic and mystical practices in prayer that he attributes to scholars and Pietists in northern France.[40]

A talmudic passage that alludes to the tactics of *poterei ḥalomot* (dream interpreters) was understood by Ri as referring to those who arrived at their interpretations on the basis of the *mazal* under which a person was born rather than through the application of any type of *ḥokhmah*.[41] Where the Talmud prohibits the use of trees worshipped by idolaters even for medicinal purposes, Ri suggests that the potential effectiveness of these trees, as opposed to others of the same species or type, was unlocked through the idolaters' invocation of *shedim*.[42] Indeed, Ri permitted the magical summoning of *shedim* by nonidolaters in order to ascertain the whereabouts of lost objects through divination.[43] In light of Ri's familiarity with mystical teachings and magical techniques, it is likely that his support of the magical summoning of *shedim* to retrieve lost objects reflects more than a simple acceptance of popular beliefs or superstitions.[44]

Another important student of Rabbenu Tam, R. Eliezer b. Samuel of Metz (1115–98), has a lengthy discussion in his *Sefer Yere'im* about the adjuration of both *shedim* and angels (*hashba'at shedim u-mal'akhim*). He concludes that these techniques, which are akin to methodologies found in *Sefer Yeẓirah*, are not to be prohibited as forms of sorcery (*ma'aseh keshafim*). If, however, a person "creates an actual object or changes a person's mind

[39] See Urbach, *Ba'alei ha-Tosafot*, 1:237.

[40] See, e.g., *Sefer ha-Manhig*, ed. Y. Raphael (Jerusalem, 1978), 1:363, 2:475, 478, 519, 526. Cf. I. Ta-Shma, "Ḥasidut Ashkenaz bi-Sefarad: Rabbenu Yonah Gerondi, ha-Ish u-Po'alo," in *Galut Aḥar Golah*, ed. Aharon Mirsky et al. (Jerusalem, 1988), 171–73 (= idem, *Knesset Meḥqarim*, 2:117–19]), and Urbach, *Ba'alei ha-Tosafot*, 1:237–38.

[41] See *Tosafot Berakhot* 55b, s.v. *poterei ḥalomot*; *Tosafot R. Yehudah Sir Leon*, ad loc.; and cf. *She'elot u-Teshuvot min ha-Shamayim le-R. Ya'akov mi-Marvege*, ed. R. Margoliot (Jerusalem, 1957), #22, pp. 61–62; A. J. Heschel, "'Al Ruaḥ ha-Qodesh Bimei ha-Benayim," 179, n. 17; and *Shitah Mequbbeẓet le-Bava Meẓi'a* 85b, in which Ri is cited by *Tosafot Shanẓ*, אמר ר׳ [= רבי] שבחלום הראהו.

[42] See *Tosafot Pesaḥim* 25a, s.v. *ḥuẓ*, and *Tosafot Rash mi-Shanẓ*, ad loc.

[43] See *Semag*, *'aseh* 74 (fol. 154a); *Sefer Mordekhai ha-Shalem 'al Massekhet Bava Qamma*, ed. A. Halpern (Jerusalem, 1992), 213 (sec. 172, to *Bava Qamma* 116a); Urbach, *Ba'alei ha-Tosafot*, 1:238–39; and cf. *Sefer Or Zaru'a, pisqei Bava Qamma*, sec. 457.

[44] For additional examples of medieval Ashkenazic halakhic texts and manuscript passages that deal with the permissibility and practices of using magical techniques as well as *segullot* to apprehend thieves, see my "*Peering through the Lattices*," 195 (nn. 13–14).

through his own magical manipulations" (i.e., not via *hashba'at mal'akhim* or *hashba'at shedim*), that person is guilty of sorcery.[45]

R. Eliezer of Metz is cited by his student R. Eleazar of Worms as ruling that it is appropriate to stand during the recitation of the first portion of *Qeri'at Shema*. This ruling, which has pietistic overtones, is based on a passage in *Hekhalot* literature. All subsequent proponents of this view in Europe during the thirteenth century were associated in some way with *ḥasidut Ashkenaz*.[46]

R. Eliezer cautioned against a person saying, even in jest, that God had told him something directly. This warning is perhaps indicative of R. Eliezer's familiarity with quasi-prophetic experiences—of the kind experienced by Ri's student, R. Ezra *ha-Navi* of Moncontour and others—that will be discussed more fully below.[47] On the other hand, R. Eliezer permitted the binding of a dying individual by oath to return after his death, to report or to answer whatever he is asked (משביע את ההולך לשוב לאחר מיתה להגיד לו אשר ישאל). In R. Eliezer's view, this does not entail a violation of the prohibition against communicating with the dead (*doresh 'el ha-metim*), since this request was made of the individual while he was still alive. Although R. Eliezer cites two talmudic texts in support of this arrangement, he again displays a clear interest in occult practices.[48] Indeed, R. Eliezer's formulation adumbrates a lengthier passage in *Sefer Ḥasidim* about a commitment made between two people that the first of them to die would communicate with the other, either through a dream or in the even more vivid form of a vision.[49]

45 *Sefer Yere'im*, ed. A. A. Schiff (Vilna, 1892), sec. 239. On R. Eliezer's *Tosafot*, see S. Emanuel, *Shivrei Luḥot*, 293–97; *Tosafot ha-Rosh 'al Massekhet Nedarim*, ed. B. Deblitzky (Bnei Brak, 2001), 1, 6–9, 16, 28, 40–41, 44, 47, 52–54, 58, 65, 80, 82, 84, 88; and above, chapter 1. For R. Jacob of Corbeil's formulation concerning the recitation of the *Shema* prayer and its effect on *shedim*, see my "*Peering through the Lattices*," 197–200.

46 See Eric Zimmer, "Tenuḥot u-Tenu'ot ha-Guf bi-She'at Qeri'at Shema," *Assufot* 8 (1995), 346–48.

47 See *Sefer Yere'im*, sec. 241 (fol. 110a); *Haggahot Maimuniyyot, Hilkhot 'Avodah Zarah*, 5:8 [1]; Urbach, *Me-'Olamam shelo Hakhamim*, 22, n. 188; and below, nn. 122–24.

48 See *Sefer Yere'im*, secs. 334–35; *Haggahot Maimuniyyot, Hilkhot 'Avodah Zarah* 13:13 [8]; and *Beit Yosef, Yoreh De'ah*, sec. 179, s.v. *'ov*. This passage from *Sefer Yere'im* is also included by Zedekiah b. Abraham *ha-Rofe* in his *Shibbolei ha-Leqet* (*ha-ḥeleq ha-sheni*), ed. Simcha Hasida (Jerusalem, 1988), 43, sec. 11. Cf. my "Mysticism and Asceticism in Italian Rabbinic Literature of the Thirteenth Century," *Kabbalah*, 6 (2001), 135–49. Maimonides, *Hilkhot 'Avodah Zarah*, loc. cit., writes that any act intended to allow a dead person to inform a living one is punishable by lashes. Cf. *Shulḥan 'Arukh, Yoreh De'ah* 179:14, and the comment of *Shakh*, ad loc., sec. 16 (which notes the correlation between R. Eliezer of Metz's view and positions of the Zohar and *ḥakhmei ha-qabbalah*).

49 See *Sefer Ḥasidim* (Parma), ed. Wistinetski, sec. 324: אם שני אדם טובים בחייהם נשבעו או נתנו אמונתם יחד אם ימות אחד מהם שיודיע לחבירו היאך באותו עולם וכו'; and cf. Monford Harris, *Studies in Jewish Dream Interpretation* (Montvale, N.J., 1994), 20; Tamar Alexander-Frizer, *The Pious Sinner* (Tubingen, 1991), 87–94; and M. Idel, "On She'elat Ḥalom in Ḥasidei Ashkenaz: Sources and Influences," *Materia Giudaica* 10:1 (2005), 99–109.

R. Isaac b. Mordekhai (Ribam) of Bohemia and Regensburg, another devoted student of Rabbenu Tam, whose teachings are frequently recorded in the standard *Tosafot*,[50] was queried by R. Judah *he-Ḥasid* with regard to *torat ha-mal'akhim.* Whereas one biblical passage implies that many angels watch over a righteous person, another suggests that only one angel is involved. Ribam suggests that the single angel responsible for this is the so-called *Sar ha-Panim*, who instructs other angels under his control to traverse the world to insure that nothing will harm righteous people (שלא יזיק שום דבר לצדיקים).[51] A Tosafist student of Rabbenu Tam from northern France, R. Menaḥem b. Pereẓ of Joigny, transmitted a *siman* for the arrival of Elijah the prophet that is found in a Parma manuscript section laden with references to German Pietists and their predecessors, and to mystical techniques and *segullot.*[52] R. Menaḥem is cited in a *Tosafot* passage as suggesting that

[50] See ms. Paris 772 (R. Eleazar of Worms's prayer commentary), fol. 23v (= *Perushei Siddur ha-Tefillah la-Roqeaḥ*, ed. M. Hershler [Jerusalem, 1992], 1:87.) Cf. *'Arugat ha-Bosem le-R. Avraham b. 'Azri'el*, ed. E. E. Urbach, vol. 4 (Jerusalem, 1963), 99, n. 75; Urbach, *Ba'alei ha-Tosafot*, 1:199, n. 38; I. Ta-Shma, *Knesset Meḥqarim*, 1:246; my *"Peering through the Lattices,"* 201–2 (n. 29), and 213 (n. 51); my "R. Judah *he-Ḥasid* and the Rabbinic Scholars of Regensburg: Interactions, Influences and Implications," *JQR* 96 (2006), 26–30; and Michael Swartz, *Scholastic Magic* (Princeton, 1996), 135–47.

[51] See Urbach, *Ba'alei ha-Tosafot*, 1:196–98, and see Emanuel, *Shivrei Luḥot*, 83–86, for additional citations of Ribam's *Tosafot*. See also Rami Reiner, "Rabbenu Tam: Rabbotav (ha-Ẓarefatim) ve-Talmidav Benei Ashkenaz," 79–82, and above, Introduction, n. 19. For Ribam's pietistic ruling concerning the appropriateness of fasting on Rosh ha-Shanah, see my "R. Judah *he-Ḥasid* and the Rabbinic Scholars of Regensburg," 32–34, and *R. Eleazar mi-Vermaiza—Derashah le-Pesaḥ*, ed. S. Emanuel (Jerusalem, 2006), editor's introduction, 35–37. Care must be taken in distinguishing between R. Isaac b. Mordekhai and Rabbenu Tam's brother, R. Isaac b. Meir, who is also referred to in *Tosafot* texts as Ribam. See, e.g., *Tosafot Ketubot* 3b, s.v. *ve-lidrosh*; *Tosafot Sanhedrin* 74, s.v. *ve-ha*; *Tosafot Yoma* 82b, s.v. *mah*; *Tosafot Yeshanim le-Yoma* 82a, s.v. *ḥuz*; and cf. *Ḥiddushei ha-Ritva 'al Masskehet Ketubot*, ed. M. Goldstein (Jerusalem, 1982), 14–15; and Urbach, *Ba'alei ha-Tosafot*, 1:58, n. 116.

[52] See ms. Parma 541 (Ashkenaz, thirteenth century), fol. 266v (sec. 276): אור זרוע לצדיק ולישרי לב שמחה סופי תיבות ר׳ עקיבה. וכן אביר יעקב בגימטריה ר׳ עקיבה. והוא היה בן גר י-ה-ו-ה. וסימן אליהו הנביא קבלתי מר׳ מנחם מיואני. The *gematria* and *sofei tevot* derivations of the name and spelling of Aqiva that precede R. Menaḥem's *siman* in ms. Parma 541 also appear in ms. Parma 563 (Ashkenaz, thirteenth century), fol. 40v (without attribution); in R. Eleazar of Worms's *Rimzei Haftarot* (to Isaiah 61), published in *Perush ha-Roqeaḥ 'al ha-Torah*, ed. Y. Kanievsky, vol. 3 (Bnei Brak, 1981), 330; and in R. Isaac b. *Moses's 'alfa-beta* introduction to his *Sefer Or Zaru'a* (see below, n. 99). Cf. M. Idel, "Tefisat ha-Torah be-Sifrut ha-Hekhalot ve-Gilgulehah ba-Qabbalah," *Meḥqerei Yerushalayim be-Maḥshevet Yisra'el* 1 (1981), 36–37 (n. 39); idem, "Some Forlorn Writings of a Forgotten Ashkenazi Prophet, R. Neḥemiah ben Shlomo ha-Navi," *JQR* 95 (2005), 93–96; idem, "R. Neḥemiah b. Shlomo the Prophet of Erfurt's Commentary on the *Piyut E-l Na le-'Olam Tu'araz*," *Moreshet Yisra'el* 2 (2005), 221 (n. 122) ; and Ephraim Shoham-Steiner, "'For a prayer in that place would be most welcome': Jews, Holy Shrines, and Miracles—A New Approach," *Viator* 37 (2006), 369–95 (for his use of these two Parma manuscripts).

salt is put on bread to keep away the שטן,[53] and he argues strongly, against Rabbenu Tam, that the problem of eating on the Sabbath during twilight (*bein ha-shemashot*), because this disturbs the souls in both *gan ʿeden* and *gehinnom* (*gozel ʾet ha-metim*), applies to Friday evening at the beginning of the Sabbath rather than to Saturday afternoon.[54]

[53] See *Tosafot Berakhot* 40a, s.v. *have melaḥ*, and I. Ta-Shma, *Minhag Ashkenaz ha-Qadmon*, 257–59. Cf *Paʿaneaḥ Raza*, ed. Machon Torat ha-Rishonim (Jerusalem, 1998), *parashat Qedoshim* (Lev. 19:16), 377: שכן דרך ניחוש ההורגין את הנפש אוכלין עליו פת במלח שלא ינקמו נקמתו ממנו; *Sefer Ḥasidim* (Parma), secs. 1465–67; *Sefer Roqeaḥ*, 240 (sec. 353); Joshua Trachtenberg, *Jewish Magic and Superstition* (New York, 1939), 160; and Aaron Katchen, "The Covenantal Salt of Friendship," in *The Frank Talmage Memorial Volume*, ed. Barry Walfish, 1:167. For R. Menaḥem's *Tosafot* interpretations, see Urbach, *Baʿalei ha-Tosafot*, 1:146–49. On R. Menaḥem's masoretic treatise (Urbach, 149, n. 39), see Y. S. Penkower, "Baʿal ha-Tosafot R. Menaḥem mi-Joigny ve-Ḥibbur ha-Mesorah 'Okhlah ve-Okhlah' Mahadurat Ketav Yad Halle," *ʿIyyunei Miqra u-Parshanut* 3 (1993), 287–315 (and above, chapter 2, n. 10). Those Ashkenazic talmudists and Tosafists who were involved in masoretic studies typically had links to *ḥasidut Ashkenaz* or to esoteric studies and manifestations of *ḥasidut* in northern France. See my *"Peering through the Lattices,"* 117, n. 52. Ms. Bodl. 1150 (a collection of ritual law that includes several halakhists from the circle of R. Judah *he-Ḥasid*, on fols. 17v–20r), contains rulings by both R. Menaḥem and R. Yom Tov of Joigny (fol. 19v). Cf. I. Ta-Shma, *Knesset Meḥqarim*, 1:251–52, and ms. JNUL $8^0$476, fol. 107r. On R. Yom Tov's association with *perishut*, see my *"Peering through the Lattices,"* 46–47. N. Golb, *The Jews in Medieval Normandy*, identifies R. Menaḥem (Vardimas) b. Pereẓ as a teacher of the Tosafist R. Samuel of Falaise (which is somewhat problematic from the chronological standpoint; see above, n. 27, and cf. Urbach, *Baʿalei ha-Tosafot*, 1:462–63; as Urbach notes, R. Samuel refers to his teacher, R. Menaḥem of Dreux, as R. Menaḥem *Ḥasid*). See also the *ʿaqedah* composed by Menaḥem (Vardimas) b. Pereẓ, תמימיך אוהביך אברהם הוא אברם, published in *Leqet Piyyutim u-Seliḥot me-ʾet Payyetanei Ashkenaz ve-Ẓarefat*, ed. D. Goldschmidt and Y. Fraenkel (Jerusalem, 1993), 2:433–34.

[54] See *Moshav Zeqenim ʿal ha-Torah*, ed. Solomon Sassoon (London, 1959, 144 [on Ex. 16:5] (= *Perushim u-Pesaqim le-R. Avigdor [Ẓarefati]*, ed. E. F. Hershkowitz [Jerusalem, 1996], 95–96 [*pesaq* 125]): ורבינו זקינינו מיואני ורבינו משולם מנרבונא מוקים לה בבין השמשות של ערב שבת. והטעם נכון לפי שבאים מתים קרובים תוך שנתן י״ב חודש מדין שלהם וטובלין בנהר היוצא מגן עדן ונכנסין שם. ולכן כששותה מים אז [ז״א בבין השמשות בערב שבת] גוזל את קרוביו . . . וכן מנהג ביוני ובאשכנז ובארץ האי . . . כמו שנהגו קדמונים לעשות סעודת צהרים בשבת בין מנחה למעריב ואין פורשין לאכול ולשתות בהם. אך כל תלמידי רבני צרפת נהגו איסור לא לאכול ולא לשתות בין מנחה למעריב בשבת משום מעשה שהיה שאחד מת ששתה לאחר [ששתה]. The position taken by R. Menaḥem of Joigny was also held by R. Meshullam of Melun (and by R. Judah *he-Ḥasid*). Cf. *Sefer Or Zaruʿa*, vol. 2, *hilkhot moẓaʾei Shabbat*, sec. 89; S. E. Stern, "Shetiyyat Mayim be-Shabbat Bein ha-Shemashot," *Yeshurun* 2 (1996), 3–4; I. Ta-Shma, *Minhag Ashkenaz ha-Qadmon*, 203–5; and *Sefer Gematriʾot le-R. Yehudah he-Ḥasid*, ed. D. Abrams (Los Angeles, 1998), 49 (fol. 13r): וכל ערבי שבתות וימים טובים בין מנחה לתפלת מעריב מוציאין רוחות מבית גנזיהם ומרעין אותם בשדה הבושם ושותין מאותו הנחל. לכך כל השותה מים בין מחנה למעריב כאילו גוזל המתים. As Ta-Shma notes, R. Jacob of Marvege undertook a *sheʾelat ḥalom* to ascertain whether one who ate on the Sabbath between the afternoon and evening prayers had "sinned," as R. Jacob [Tam] had ruled (*Sheʾelot u-Teshuvot min ha-Shamayim*, ed. Margoliot, #39). The answer he received was clearly in the negative. Cf. *Shibbolei ha-Leqet*, *ʿinyan Shabbat*, sec. 127, who cites this dream of the "*ẓaddiq*," R. Jacob of Marvege, to counter the claim of Rabbenu Tam. In his *Gilgulei Minhag be-ʿOlam ha-Halakhah* (Jerusalem, 1995), 183–89, Y. Gartner notes the insistence of the kabbalists that the third meal take place following the *minḥah* prayer on the Sabbath afternoon.

Parallel Developments among German Tosafists and the Circle of חכמי שפירא: The Impact of *Ḥasidei Ashkenaz*

German Tosafists such as R. Judah b. Qalonymus (Rivaq, d. c. 1199),[55] who lived in Speyer during the period in which R. Samuel *he-Ḥasid* (b. 1115) and his son, R. Judah *he-Ḥasid*, also lived there (Judah b. Samuel left Speyer for Regensburg only in 1195), participated in disciplines or forms of exoteric Torah study that were recommended or favored by the German Pietists, such as the study and interpretation of the Tannaitic components of *Seder Qodashim* as well as the interpretation of *midreshei halakhah*.[56] They also refer to pieces of *torat ha-sod* which they received from R. Judah *he-Ḥasid*. Rivaq's *Sefer Yiḥusei Tanna'im va-Amora'im* contains a lengthy passage that cites *Hekhalot* literature, and interprets the activities of R. Yishma'el *Kohen Gadol* based on the *torat ha-Kavod* of the German Pietists. Rivaq's passage also deals with the role of Akatri'el as a representation of the Divine or as an angel, another issue dealt with extensively by the Pietists.[57]

R. Ephraim b. Jacob (b. Qalonymus) of Bonn (c. 1132–97), a contemporary of Rivaq and R. Judah *he-Ḥasid*, succeeded his teacher R. Joel *ha-Levi* as *'av beit din* in Bonn, having also served as a judge on the important rabbinic court in Mainz.[58] As we have seen in the preceding chapter, R. Ephraim composed a large number of *piyyutim*, in addition to commenting on them. His liturgical compositions also contain a number of rulings and decisions concerning proper prayer practices and the laws of the festivals, and additional rulings in other areas of Jewish law.[59]

R. Ephraim of Bonn was in contact with R. Judah *he-Ḥasid* and with Rivaq, and he may even have received material from Judah's father, R. Samuel *he-Ḥasid*.[60] In addition to counting words and letters in prayers, and

[55] On Rivaq's talmudic writings and *Tosafot*, see Urbach, *Ba'alei ha-Tosafot*, 1:366–74, 378; I. Ta-Shma, *Ha-Sifrut ha-Parshanit la-Talmud*, vol. 2 (Jerusalem, 2000), 116–18; S. Emanuel, *Shivrei Luḥot*, 13, 287–88, 307–8; and above, chapter 1 (nn. 6, 19, 25, 94), for his judicial activities.

[56] See Yaacov Sussmann, "Masoret Limmud u-Masoret Nosaḥ shel Talmud ha-Yerushalmi," in *Studies in Talmudic Literature in Honor of the Eightieth Birthday of Shaul Lieberman* (Jerusalem, 1983), 14 (n. 11), 34–35; idem, "Perush ha-Rabad le-Massekhet Sheqalim: Ḥiddah Bibliografit—Be'ayah Historit," in *Me'ah She'arim: Studies in Medieval Jewish Spirituality in Memory of Isadore Twersky*, ed. E. Fleischer et al. (Jerusalem, 2001), 166–67; S. Emanuel, *Shivrei Luḥot*, 317 (n. 46); and my "The Scope of Talmudic Commentary in Europe during the High Middle Ages," in *Printing the Talmud*, ed. S. L. Mintz and G. M. Goldstein (New York, 2005), 43–52. Cf. Emanuel, *Shivrei Luḥot*, 56–59, 157 (n. 15), 317 (n. 46), and below, n. 77.

[57] See Urbach, *Ba'alei ha-Tosafot*, 1:375–77. Cf. *Sefer Or Zaru'a* (below, n. 102), and below, chapter 7.

[58] See above, chapter 1, nn. 11, 42.

[59] See *'Arugat ha-Bosem*, ed. Urbach, 4:39–51, and above, Introduction, nn. 88–90.

[60] See *'Arugat ha-Bosem*, 4:40, 110 (n. 30).

interpreting the prayers based on these sequences as R. Judah *he-Ḥasid* and other *Ḥasidei Ashkenaz* did,[61] R. Ephraim offers a description of the *kisse ha-kavod* in a liturgical commentary that is quite similar to later esoteric formulations of R. Eleazar of Worms and versions of *Sod ha-Egoz.*[62] The response of the Almighty during the *kedushah*, as expressed in *Hekhalot* literature, is alluded to by R. Ephraim in an *ʾofan*: ינשק צור דמות היצור בכס עצור והוא נכבד.[63]

R. Menaḥem b. Jacob (d. 1203) was the senior member of the Worms rabbinical court in the late twelfth century; his activities as a judge and halakhist, as well as his stature as a prolific *payyetan*, have been discussed above. R. Menaḥem's direct teachers are not clearly known to us, although he appears to have had contact with R. Ephraim of Regensburg.[64] The circumcision manuals of R. Jacob *ha-Gozer* and his son R. Gershom, which were compiled or edited in the first half of the thirteenth century by a third, unnamed *mohel* who had studied with both Jacob and Gershom,[65] record a heavenly explanation put forward by their relative, R. Menaḥem of Worms (טעם זה כתב מפי דודו ר' מנחם שאמר לו בעל החולם/כתבתי טעם מפי ר' מנחם זצ"ל שאמר לו בעל החלום), as to why the blessing recited over a circumcision should not be recited in the more active form, *lamul* ("to circumcise"), but rather should

[61] See *Siddur Rabbenu Shelomoh mi-Germaiza ve-Siddur Ḥasidei Ashkenaz*, ed. M. Hershler (Jerusalem, 1972), 60, 98, 109 (n. 38), 114, 154; and S. Emanuel, "Ha-Polmos ʿal Nosaḥ ha-Tefillah shel Ḥasidei Ashkenaz," *Meḥqerei Talmud* 3 (2005), 2:592 (n. 2).

[62] See *Siddur Rabbenu Shelomoh*, 70–71; Elliot Wolfson, "Demut Yaʿakov Ḥaquqah be-Kisse ha-Kavod: ʿIyyun Nosaf be-Torat ha-Sod shel Ḥasidut Ashkenaz," in *Massuʾot*, ed. M. Oron and A. Goldreich (Jerusalem, 1994, 140 (n. 44) (= idem, *Along the Path* [Albany, N.Y., 1995], 121 [n. 65]); and Daniel Abrams, *Sexual Symbolism and Merkavah Speculation in Medieval Germany* (Tubingen, 1997), 47–52. See also *Sefer Or Zaruʿa*, pt. 2, sec. 276 (*hilkhot Rosh ha-Shanah*), where R. Ephraim of Bonn is identified as the (written) source of the dream story surrounding the transmission of *U-netnaeh Toqef* by R. Amnon ("מצאתי מכתב ידו של ה"ר אפרים מבונא ב"ר יעקב שר' אמנון ממגנצא יסד ונתנה תוקף על מקרה רע שאירע לו). Whatever the historicity of this account (see my *"Peering through the Lattices,"* 106–7, n. 26, and 132–33, n. 3), R. Ephraim was considered by R. Isaac *Or Zaruʿa* (who studied with both R. Judah *he-Ḥasid* and R. Eleazar of Worms) as a credible figure in the transmission process. R. Eliʿezer b. Joel *ha-Levi* of Cologne and Bonn (Rabiah, d. c. 1225) seems to have been more a Pietist than a mystic, even though a quasi-mystical experience is attributed to him (see below, n. 100). A more intensely mystical dream, however, is reported involving Rabiah's martyred brother, Uri. See ms. Bodl. 1155. fol. 171v; A. Aptowitzer, *Mavo la-Rabiah*, 67; and *Leqet Piyyutei Seliḥot*, ed. D Goldschmidt and A. Fraenkel (Jerusalem, 1993), 445–46. According to this report, Uri dictated a liturgical poem after his death to a R. Mordekhai b. Eliʿezer, via a dream in which he appeared to R. Mordekhai. Cf. my *"Peering through the Lattices,"* 47–51, 165, 214–17.

[63] See A. M. Habermann, *Piyyutei R. Ephraim b. Yaʿaqov mi-Bonn* (Jerusalem, 1969), 16–18 (esp. lines 12 and 13); and see above, chapter 5, n. 109.

[64] See Aptowitzer, *Mavo la-Rabiah*, 382–83; above, Introduction, n. 90; chapter 1, nn. 12, 57, 145; and chapter 5, nn. 203–21.

[65] See *Zikhron Berit la-Rishonim*, ed. Jacob Glassberg (Berlin, 1892; repr. Jerusalem, 1971), introduction (by Joel Mueller), xii–xix); I. Ta-Shma, *Knesset Meḥqarim*, 1:320–22; Elisheva Baumgarten, *Mothers and Daughters* (Princeton, 2004), 46.

always be made as *ʿal mizvat milah* ("on the precept of circumcision"): The word *ʿal* is equal to 100 in *gematria*, which was the age of Abraham when he was commanded to circumcise Isaac, and the word *ha-milah* equals 90, which was Sarah's age at the time; thus this blessing reflects their great merit.[66]

The transmission provided by the heavenly *baʿal ha-ḥalom* to R. Menaḥem is also found, and indeed may have originated, in *Sefer Assufot*, a halakhic compendium composed by an anonymous student of Rabiah (d. c. 1225) and R. Eleazar of Worms (d. c. 1230; author of *Sefer Roqeaḥ* and R. Judah *he-Ḥasid*'s leading Pietist student).[67] *Sefer Assufot*, which treats R. Menaḥem b. Jacob as a significant decisor of Jewish law along with other

[66] See *Zikhron Berit la-Rishonim*, ed. Glassberg, 80, 130–31. For the identification of R. Menaḥem in this passage as R. Menaḥem b. Jacob of Worms, see Mueller, introduction to *Zikhron Berit la-Rishonim*, ed. Jacob Glassberg, xv, and A. Aptowitzer, *Mavo la-Rabiah*, 76–77, 382. Aptowitzer's evidence for the relationship between R. Menaḥem of Worms and R. Jacob and R. Gershom is based on *Sefer Assufot*, ms. Montefiore 134, fol. 22r (col. 2): כך כתוב בתופס שלי. שמעתי מאבא מורי שהעיד על דודי ר' מנחם מגרמייזא [מעשה] ועכבו בבית הכנסת מאוד, ולא רצה להמתין מן פלדונש שלו ואכל מן התבשיל הירקות ואחר כך אכל פלדונש ולא שהה בנתיים אבל נטל ידיו ועשה קינוח בטיבול פת ביין. Two other passages in *Zikhron Berit la-Rishonim* (62, 74) further establish R. Menaḥem as the uncle of R. Gershom *ha-Gozer* (אלו דרשות העתיק הגוזר בדרשה של דוד ה"ר מנחם ז"ל; פעם אחת מל רבנו גרשם המוהל ביום הכיפורים והורה לו דודו רבנו מנחם ז"ל לעשות כן ושהה הכוס של ברכה עד הלילה וטעם בלילה ואם הילד). See also ibid., 77, 84 (וכן הורה רבנו מנחם), and cf. E. E. Urbach, *Baʿalei ha-Tosafot*, 1:369–70; Aptowitzer also maintains, based on another passage in *Zikhron Berit la-Rishonim* (61), that R. Jacob *ha-Gozer* was the nephew of Ephraim of Bonn, son of Ephraim's brother, Gershom. On the issue of the proper *milah* blessing, cf. *Haggahot Maimuniyyot* to *Mishneh Torah, hilkhot milah*, 3:1 [2], citing Rashi, R. Eliʿezer of Metz, and R. Simḥah of Speyer. The suggestion by R. Menaḥem (and other of his colleagues) is that the blessing *ʿal ha-milah* is always made, even if the father is (actively) performing the circumcision himself.

[67] See *Sefer Assufot*, ms. Montefiore 134 (sec. 389), fol. 84v (col. 4): ואין אומ' למול אלא על המילה כגון על ביעור חמץ על נטילת ידים על נטילת לולב על מקרא מגילה. כתבתי הטעם מפי רבי' מנחם זצ"ל שאמ' לו בעל החלום מפני מה מברכים על המילה כנגד השנים שהיו אברהם ושרה כשניתן לאברהם מצות המילה. ע"ל זה מאה רמז לאברהם שהיה בן ק' שנה דכת' ואברהם בן מאת שנה וגו' וכת' וימל אברהם את יצחק וגו'. ה"מ"י"ל"ה עולה צ' רמז לשרה שהיתה בת צ' שנים שנא' ואם שרה הבת תשעים שנה וגו'. מכאן שמברכים ע'ל ה'מי'ל'ה זכר לאברהם ושרה שהיו ראשונים שקיימו מצות מילה. Moritz Gudemann, *Ha-Torah veha-Ḥayyim* (Warsaw, 1897), 62 (n. 4), assumed that the *baʿal ha-ḥalom* in this passage is a reference to R. Jacob of Marvege, the Provençal author of *She'elot u-Teshuvot min ha-Shamayim* (and a precise contemporary of R. Menahem of Worms); see also *She'elot u-Teshuvot min ha-Shamayim*, ed. R. Margoliot (Jerusalem, 1957), editor's introduction, 22. It is more reasonable to suggest, however, that this term is a rabbinic or talmudic one, which connotes the angel who oversees the content of dreams (and that R. Menaḥem's dream had no particular connection with R. Jacob or his work). See, e.g., *Sanhedrin* 30a (ובא בעל החלום ואמר לו כך וכך הן במקום פלוני הן); Rashi's comment, s.v. *baʿal ha-halom* (שר המראה חלומות בלילה); and above, n. 29. Although the majority of rabbinic figures cited by *Sefer Assufot* are German Tosafists from the Rhineland, this work will occasionally cite French students of Rabbenu Tam and Ri, such as R. Ḥayyim *Kohen* and R. Barukh b. Isaac, author of *Sefer ha-Terumah* (see, e.g., fols. 41r, 91r), not to mention R. Eliʿezer of Metz (who was also a teacher of Rabiah and R. Eleazar of Worms). On the decidedly German provenance of this work, however, see also the collection of *shetarot* and judicial procedures found on fols. 135–42 (secs. 468–500), and cf. S. E. Stern, *Sefer Me'orot ha-Rishonim* (Jerusalem, 2002), 92–98, 222–30; and above, chapter 1.

contemporary German authorities,[68] contains a number of halakhic rulings by R. Menaḥem,[69] as well as other passages that contain mystical and magical materials. These include the recitation of various Divine names and angelic adjurations, and even the eating of certain foods and verses (which were written on eggs or cakes) in order to neutralize Potaḥ, the angel of forgetfulness, and to achieve a state of *petiḥat ha-lev*, which allows for a more comprehensive and permanent understanding of Torah teachings.[70]

[68] For additional passages in *Sefer Assufot* dealing with circumcision which mention R. Jacob and R. Gershom *ha-Gozer* by name, see, e.g., ms. Montefiore 134 (sec. 388), fol. 78v, col. 3, and fol. 80r; and especially fol. 81r, col. 1: סליק סדר המילה כאשר סדרו ר׳ גרשם ב״ר יעקב הגוזר לפי סברתו ולפי דעתו. גם זה מצרכי המילה . . . ומפי ר׳ יעקב כתב פעם אחת בא לידו למול והוא ינוקא דאתייליד ליה נגיעא בבישרא וכו׳ . . . [דף 18, עמ׳ ב] אחרי כן הוקרה ר׳ לר׳ גרשם כשמל את בנו כם בתתקע״ה [5121] לפרט שלא יכול לעשות פריעה עד שחתך אותו העור פעם שנית וכו׳. ר׳ גרשם הגוזר הנהיג לרחוץ הילד ביום השלישי למילתו כשחל להיות בשבת וכו׳ . . . כך קבל גרשם הגוזר וכך נראה לו. See also fols. 86r–88v, and below, n. 70. For references to contemporary Ashkenazic halakhists in matters of circumcision, see, e.g., fol. 82r, col. 2: בספר אבי״ה מצאתי ששמע בשם ר׳ יהוד׳ חסיד כוכבים שעומדים שלשה זה תחת זה וכו׳ [ליציאת השבת ולתענית]; and fol. 83r, col. 1: מנהג הוא בוורמיישא שאין או׳ למנצח ביום המילה לפי שנא בו יענך ה׳ ביום צרה וכו׳ אבל במגנצא או׳ למנצח משום שאית ביה צערא לינוקא וכו׳ [דף 38א, עמ׳ ב]. On the rabbinic figures in the final passage, cf. S. Emanuel, *Shivrei Luḥot*, 60, 68; and *Piyyutei R. Yeḥi'el b. Avraham mi-Roma*, ed. A. Fraenkel (Jerusalem, 2007), editor's introduction, 1–2. See also ms. Montefiore 134, fol. 45r (col. 2), citing R. Judah *he-Ḥasid* (on the *remazim* for the ten plagues in the Passover haggadah); 45v (col. 4), citing R. David of Muenzburg in a matter of fulfilling one's obligation through a *kos shel berakhah*; and fol. 61v (col. 3), for an interpolation from R. Meir of Rothenburg (cited by R. Menaḥem b. Meir) regarding the drinking of water in the afternoon on the Sabbath (to achieve *petiḥat ha-lev*; cf. below, n. 70). On this last practice, cf. ms. Montefiore 130, fols. 54v–55r, cited and discussed by I. Ta-Shma, *Minhag Ashkenaz ha-Qadmon*, 213–14; and cf. S. E. Stern, *Sefer Me'orot ha-Rishonim* (Jerusalem, 2002), 58–59; and below, n. 139.

[69] See *Sefer Assufot*, ms. Montefiore 134, fol. 26r (col. 1): אבל מורינו מנחם ב״ר יעקב היה מורה לתלמידיו שצריך לבדוק כשנשבר הנוצה בכנפים אע״פ שאינו יוצא בחוץ; fol. 36r (regarding a procedure for *hekhsher kelim*, cited in S. Emanuel, *R. Eleazar mi-Vermaiza—Derashah le-Pesaḥ*, 72–73 [n. 36]); fol. 55r (col. 2, on patching a hole in a *shofar*); fol. 66r (col. 2, on the order of the blessings in the *Sukkah* on the first two nights of the festival); fol. 83r (col. 1, permitting a mourner to go to the synagogue after the third day of his mourning in order to attend the circumcision of his son, rather than requiring the congregation to come to his home); fol. 114r (col. 1, in agreement with the view held later by both Rabiah and R. Eleazar of Worms, whose names are not mentioned, concerning the placement of certain types of Divine names on the exterior covering of the *mezuzah*). Cf. fol.17 (col. 1, וכן הנהיג הרב בוורמייזא, a characterization that perhaps refers to R. Menaḥem, on inflating certain blemishes in a slaughtered animal's lung to determine the animal's status as a *terefah*). See also *Sefer ha-Qushyot*, ed. Y. Y. Stal (Jerusalem, 2007), 167–68 (sec. 215), for a *siman le-nerot Ḥanukkah* by R. Menaḥem of Worms (based on a talmudic passage), and *Germania Judaica*, vol. 1, ed. I. Elbogen et al. (Tubingen, 1963), 452.

[70] See these elements as contained in the educational initiation ceremony found in ms. Mont. 134 (fols. 67r–v), published in S. E. Stern, *Me'orot ha-Rishonim*, 18–21 (including also the concerns of R. Judah *he-Ḥasid*); I. Marcus, *Rituals of Childhood* (New Haven, Conn., 1996), 29–31; my *"Peering through the Lattices,"* 140–41, 155–57, 227 (n. 16), 236–38 (nn. 46–47); and above, n. 68 (end). See also ms. Montefiore 134, fol. 56r (regarding *neḥush* practices on Rosh ha-Shanah); fol. 56v (col. 4, for R. Samuel *he-Ḥasid*'s *gematria* derivation, which establishes that R. Aqiva composed the *Avinu Malkenu* prayer, published in S. E. Stern, *Me'orot ha-Rishonim*, 111, and see below, n. 112); and see also fol. 59r (col. 1, regarding certain *perushim* who stood

Moreover, as we shall soon see, R. Menaḥem of Worms was also not the only Ashkenazic scholar at this time to have had the kind of dream or visionary experience that he did.[71]

R. Barukh b. Samuel of Mainz (d. 1221), a leading German halakhist and judge, authored the voluminous but no longer extant *Sefer ha-Ḥokhmah*, as well as numerous *piyyutim.* R. Barukh studied with Rivaq of Speyer, R. Eliezer of Metz, and R. Moses b. Solomon *ha-Kohen* of Mainz, a teacher of R. Eleazar of Worms—Moses *ha-Kohen* was replaced by Barukh as a member of the Mainz rabbinic court—and perhaps with R. Ephraim b. Isaac of Regensburg as well.[72] R. Barukh queried R. Judah *he-Ḥasid* about how to deal with the obligation of reciting *Qeri'at Shema* in the morning by the prescribed halalkhic time, on those festivals and occasions when the length of the prayer service made reaching the deadline impossible, assuming that one prayed at a slow, deliberate pace, as R. Barukh seems to have done. R. Judah, whose penchant for the slow recitation of the prayers in order to enhance *kavvanah* is well documented, responded that he relied on the *Shema* that was recited at the very beginning of the morning service for this purpose.[73] Urbach suggests that the influence of R. Judah's teachings can be detected in Barukh's ample array of *piyyutim* as well, although he does not provide any specific examples. There are, however, a number of citations and paraphrases from *Hekhalot* literature that are found in R. Barukh's *piyyutim.*[74]

---

for the entire night on Yom Kippur and through the day as well); and fols. 61r–v (cols. 2–3) regarding fasting for two days for Yom Kippur (and cf. "*Peering through the Lattices,*" 44–51). See also ms. Montefiore 134, fol. 86r (col. 1): סליק הלכות גרים. הרוצה ללמוד אומנות המילה ילמד מזה הספר כאשר כתב אותו ר' גרשם הגוזר לפי סברתו ולפי דעתו ולפי חכמתו וכאשר קבל מרבותיו ובאובנת[א] בדליבה . . . [עמ' ב] ברפואות שעושין למילות . . . כך קבל ר' גרשם הגוזר מרבו ר' יעקב הגוזר ומשאר חכמים היודעים בעיניין. Beginning on fol. 88v, a list of *refu'ot*, herbal potions, and amulets are listed which are characterized as *baduq u-menuseh*. Fol. 89r (col. 2) contains an amulet from R. Judah *he-Ḥasid* for a woman who was having difficulty delivering a child: מקשה לילד בלידת הילד או השליא מקבלת ר' יהודה החסיד כתב בקלף אלה שמות [הנזכרים בתוך הטקסט] ומניחין הקלף על בטנה ותלד מיד בע[זרת] השם. ללידת השליא נותנין לה לשתות מעט שמן זית. Fols. 150v–154r contain a lengthy series of penitential regimens (*sidrei teshuvah*) by R. Eleazar of Worms, including the most demanding form of *teshuvat ha-mishqal.*

[71] Cf. above, n. 14, and below, nn. 76, 99.

[72] See E. E. Urbach, *Ba'alei ha-Tosafot*, 1:25–29. S. Emanuel, *Shivrei Luḥot*, 104–41, adds much detail, especially with regard to *Sefer ha-Ḥokhmah* and its contents. See also above, chapter 1, nn. 6, 144; and chapter 5, nn. 187–99.

[73] See *'Arugat ha-Bosem*, ed. Urbach, 4:94–96. Cf. Haym Soloveitchik, "Three Themes in the *Sefer Ḥasidim*," 333 (n. 70), and I. Ta-Shma, "Barukh ben Samuel of Mainz," *Encyclopedia Judaica*, 4:280–81.

[74] See A. M. Habermann, "Piyyutei R. Barukh b. Shmu'el mi-Magenẓa," *Yedi'ot ha-Makhon le-Ḥeqer ha-Shirah ha-'Ivrit* 6 (1946), 56, 60–61, 79–82; my "Esotericism and Magic in Ashkenaz during the Tosafist Period," in *Studies on the History of the Jews in Ashkenaz Presented to Eric Zimmer*, ed. G. Bacon et al. (Ramat Gan, 2008) [Hebrew], 203–15; and above, chapter 5, n. 200. Urbach, *Ba'alei ha-Tosafot*, 2:638–39, notes the view of Y. N. Epstein that the standard *Tosafot* to tractate *Sotah* were edited by R. Barukh. For a reference by these *Tosafot* to a magical *leḥishah* (albeit in the name of Rabbenu Ḥanan'el), see below, n. 113.

Interestingly, both R. Judah *he-Ḥasid* and R. Barukh of Mainz reported on a quasi-mystical experience of R. Ephraim of Regensburg.[75] R. Ephraim decided to permit the consumption of a fish called *barbuta* (or *balbuta*), a species that his teacher, Rabbenu Tam, as well as Rashbam, had ruled was kosher in northern France, despite the fact that its scales either disappeared when the fish was removed from water or were found only in the area of the gills. R. Judah and R. Barukh report, with only slight variation, that an elderly man with flowing hair and a lengthy beard appeared to R. Ephraim that night in a dream. He held out a plate of insects or crustaceans (*sheraẓim*), and bid R. Ephraim to eat them. When R. Ephraim protested, the old man suggested that these *sherazim* "are as permitted as those that you ate today." When R. Ephraim awoke, he knew that Elijah had appeared to him, and from then on, he refrained from eating that species of fish (*piresh mehem*). In the other version of this account, R. Ephraim immediately smashed the vessels in which the fish had been prepared and eaten, and declared that anyone who did not eat this species would be blessed.[76]

R. Barukh of Mainz's son, R. Samuel Bamberg, who studied with R. Eliezer of Metz and R. Simḥah of Speyer,[77] strongly supported the prayer

[75] R. Ephraim, a German student of Rabbenu Tam, was a contemporary of Ribam of Bohemia, and served with him on the rabbinic court in Regensburg. See Urbach, *Baʿalei ha-Tosafot*, 1:199–206; S. Emanuel, *Shivrei Luḥot*, 289–91 (on Ephraim's lost halakhic work, *ʾArbaʿah Panim*); R. Reiner, "Rabbenu Tam," 89–92; above, chapter 1, nn. 27–28; and chapter 5, nn. 162–72.

[76] According to *Sefer Tashbeẓ*, sec. 252 (= R. Meir b. Barukh of Rothenburg, *Teshuvot, Pesaqim u-Minhagim*, ed. I. Z. Kahana, vol. 2 [Jerusalem, 1959], 196, sec. 60), the account of R. Ephraim's dream was related by R. Barukh of Mainz. According to *Sefer Or Zaruʿa* (*pisqei ʿavodah zarah*, sec. 200), however, it was R. Judah *he-Ḥasid* who initially recounted the dream of R. Ephraim of Regensburg: ואני המחבר שמעתי מפי הקדוש רבינו יהודה החסיד שאמר בלשון הזה שכל מי שיאכל בלבוטא לא יזכה לאכול לויתן. The passage in *Sefer Or Zaruʿa* then continues with an account of Ephraim's dream. R. Eleazar of Worms records the same statement in the name of R. Judah *he-Ḥasid*, בשם רבי׳ יהודה חסיד נאמ׳ כל האוכל בלבוטא לא מן הלויתן הוא אוכל (albeit without any reference to R. Ephraim's dream), as well as the *siman* that a split or crack in the tail is the sign of a kosher fish. See S. Emanuel, *R. Eleazar mi-Vermaiza—Derashah la-Pesaḥ*, 26–27. In n. 97, Emanuel notes a passage in ms. Bodl. 875 (fol. 6v), in which Rabbenu Pereẓ of Corbeil records R. Judah as prohibiting the eating of the *barbuta* (mentioned also by Rabbenu Pereẓ in his glosses to *Semaq*), and that R. Yeḥiʾel of Paris was also careful not to eat this fish; cf. below, n. 129. See also *Semaq mi-Ẓurikh*, ed. Y. Y. Har-Shoshanim, vol. 2 (Jerusalem, 1977), 293 (n. 135); Urbach, *Baʿalei ha-Tosafot*, 1:204; A. J. Heschel, "ʿAl Ruaḥ ha-Qodesh Bimei ha-Benayim," 199; Tamar Alexander, "Rabbi Judah the Pious as a Legendary Figure," in *Mysticism, Magic and Kabbalah in Ashkenazi Ḥasidism*, ed. K. Grozinger (Berlin, 1995), 135–36; and my "R. Judah *he-Ḥasid* and the Rabbinic Scholars of Regensburg," 29–30. R. Ephraim of Regensburg and R. Judah *he-Ḥasid* also proposed similar regimens of *tiqqunei teshuvah* for a penitent murderer. See ms. B.M. 477/3, fol. 165r (= M. Hershler, "Teshuvot ve-Tiqqun Geonim ve-Qadmonim mi-tokh Ktav Yad," *Sinai* 66 [1970], 177); ms. Parma (de Rossi) 180, fol. 362v; ms. Parma 1237, fol. 36v; and my "R. Judah *he-Ḥasid*," 27–28. R. Ephraim's son Moses expressed his own pietistic view on the matter of fasting on Rosh ha-Shanah. See my "R. Judah *he-Ḥasid*," 32–33, and above, n. 51.

[77] R. Simḥah of Speyer studied with R. Eliʿezer of Metz, R. Abraham b. Samuel *he-Ḥasid*, Rivaq of Speyer, and R. Moses *ha-Kohen* of Mainz (see Urbach, *Baʿalei ha-Tosafot*, 1:411–20, and

interpretations, wordings, and numerical analysis of *Ḥasidei Ashkenaz* and earlier Qalonymides.[78] He exchanged a series of letters on halakhic matters with R. Simḥah—who regarded R. Samuel as the worthy successor to his father—and he also sent queries to Rabiah.[79] Although it is unknown whether R. Samuel composed any halakhic monographs or *Tosafot*, a number of his responsa have survived, mostly in the collections of his student R. Meir of Rothenburg. Many of his *pesaqim* are found in a collection edited by one of his students, in which R. Samuel is referred to as *mori ha-ro'eh*.[80]

R. Samuel of Bamberg appears to have composed a full-fledged prayer commentary, of which remnants are extant.[81] The comments by R. Samuel

---

S. Emanuel, *Shivrei Luḥot*, 154–66, with special focus on R. Simḥah's lost halakhic work, *Seder 'Olam*), and had a similar career path to both R. Barukh of Mainz and R. Eleazar of Worms. As Urbach notes (1:412–13), R. Simḥah responded to a halakhic query from R. Judah *he-Ḥasid*; cf. ms. Bodl. 659, fol. 82v. One of R. Simḥah's closest students, R. Avigdor Katz, compared (and followed) the position of his teacher, who did not fast on Rosh ha-Shanah, to that of R. Judah *he-Ḥasid*, who did fast in his day (*be-doro*; see Urbach, *Ba'alei ha-Tosafot*, 1:419). Moreover, Urbach notes the similarity of an interpretation by R. Simḥah to a passage found in *Midrash Tadshe* concerning the degree of *'ahavat ha-bore* experienced by the soul (cited in the quasi-mystical *'alfa beta* introduction to *Sefer Or Zaru'a*, sec. 44; see below, n. 98) to that of R. Eleazar of Worms in his pietistic introduction to his *Sefer Roqeaḥ* (*shoresh 'ahavat ha-Shem*); cf. my *"Peering through the Lattices,"* 224 (n. 8). R. Simḥah authored a commentary to the *Sifra* that typifies the scholarly endeavors of the circle of Tosafists in Speyer, who subscribed to the curricular concerns and initiatives of the German Pietists; see above, n. 56. See also the parallels in approach between R. Eleazar of Worms and R. Simḥah of Speyer with regard to the *tiqqunei teshuvah* recommended for a returning apostate in my "Returning to the Jewish Community in Medieval Ashkenaz: History and Halakhah," in *Turim: Studies in Jewish History and Literature Presented to Dr. Bernard Lander*, ed. M. Shmidman (New York, 2007), 81–89.

[78] See, e.g., ms. Cambr. Add. 394, fols. 18v (cf. *Siddur R. Shelomoh mi-Germaiza*, ed. Hershler, 119), and 20v; Cambr. Add. 561, fol. 50r (margin); Bodl. 1103, fols. 40r–v, 54v, 75r–v; Bodl. 1205, fol. 48v; Bodl. 2274, fol. 24v; B.M. 534, fols. 13r–15v; B.M. 754, fols. 130r–136v; Paris 646, fol. 6 (and cf. C. Sirat, "Un rituel Juif de France: Le manuscrit hébreu 633 de la bibliothèque nationale de Paris," *REJ* 119 [1961], 11). See also *Perushei Siddur ha-Tefillah la-Roqeaḥ*, ed. Hershler, 1:359, and 2:403, 442, 471–73, 543; *Siddur R. Shelomoh mi-Germaiza*, 136 (based on a *piyyut* by R. Simeon *ha-Gadol*); 184 (אבל ה"ר שמואל מצא מכתיבת ידו של רבינו יודא החסיד; Hershler suggests that this is R. Samuel of Evreux [see also *Siddur R. Shelomoh mi-Germaiza*, 88], although R. Samuel Bamberg is clearly the more likely reference), 221–23, 296. A number of these texts also contain pieces of the liturgical polemic associated with *Ḥasidei Ashkenaz*. See *'Arugat ha-Bosem*, ed. Urbach, 4:92–97; I. Ta-Shma, "Quntresei 'Sodot ha-Tefillah' le-R. Yehudah he-Ḥasid," *Tarbiz* 65 (1996), 65–77; and S. Emanuel, "Ha-Polmos 'al Nosaḥ ha-Tefillah shel Ḥasidei Ashkenaz," in *Meḥqerei Talmud* 3, ed. Y. Sussmann and D. Rosenthal (Jerusalem, 2005), 591–625.

[79] See Urbach, *Ba'alei ha-Tosafot*, 1:429–32, and cf. Emanuel, *Shivrei Luḥot*, 106–7 (n. 17), 164. See also the halakhic ruling issued by R. Samuel Bamberg and R. Moses Taku in *Siddur Rabbenu Shelomoh mi-Germaiza*, 296.

[80] See "Pisqei Halakhot le-Rabbenu Yosef ve-Hora'ot le-Rabbo Rabbenu Shmu'el ha-Ro'eh," in *Shitat ha-Qadmonim*, ed. M. Y. Blau (New York, 1992), 319–95, based on ms. Cambr. Or. 786 (Ashkenaz, 1282), fols. 176d–186b. Cf. Emanuel, *Shivrei Luḥot*, 127, 262, 266–69, and Ta-Shma, *Knesset Meḥqarim*, 1:239.

[81] See Ta-Shma (above, n. 78), 70–77; idem, "'Al Kammah 'Inyanei Maḥzor Vitry," *'Alei Sefer* 11 (1984), 81–89, and *'Alei Sefer* 12 (1985), 131–32; Emanuel (above, n. 78), 609–21; idem, *'Alei Sefer* 12 (1985), 129–30; and *'Arugat ha-Bosem*, ed. Urbach, 4:70–72.

of Bamberg demonstrate his familiarity not only with the liturgical interpretations of the German Pietists but also with their insistence that particular *nusha'ot* be preserved precisely. Moreover, R. Samuel put forward a scriptural derivation of a significant aspect of German Pietism, which was cited elsewhere in the name of R. Judah *he-Ḥasid.* Part of the German Pietists' search for the larger Divine will entailed an emphasis on the thoughts and feelings that lay behind an act, as well as the notion that the intellectual ability to discern, rather than the fixed age of legal adulthood alone, determined responsibility for one's deeds. This principle was derived, in two passages in *Sefer Ḥasidim*, from the case of ʿEr and Onan, following the approach of one version of *Midrash Tanhuma* indicating that they were eight or nine years old, and from instances involving other biblical figures. This derivation is also cited in R. Judah *he-Ḥasid*'s Torah commentary that was compiled by his son R. Moses Zal(t)man, and in the name of R. Judah in several of the so-called Tosafist Torah commentaries.[82]

One formulation preserved by R. Judah's son reads, "My father queried, why were ʿEr and Onan punished, since they had not yet reached the age of punishment? He responded that these are the laws of Heaven (*dinei shamayim*), that a person is punished according to [the level of] his intelligence. If a minor is as perspicacious as a twenty-year-old, then he is punished. Proof may be derived from Samuel [the prophet], whom Eli wished to punish for issuing a halakhic ruling in his presence, even though he [Samuel] was only two years old." This passage is cited in a Tosafist Torah compilation, in shorter form but with precise linguistic parallels, in the name of R. Samuel Bamberg.[83]

Other students of R. Simḥah of Speyer, who had origins in or close connections with Italy, as part of the network of Ashkenazic rabbinic centers during the twelfth and thirteenth centuries,[84] shared this interest in esoteric studies. R. Isaiah di Trani (Rid), who cites rabbinic figures from both Germany and northern France, ruled in a responsum that a particular adhesion

82 See H. Soloveitchik, "Three Themes in the *Sefer Ḥasidim*," 324–25 (and esp. n. 33); *Perushei ha-Torah le-R. Yehudah he-Ḥasid*, ed. Y. S. Lange (Jerusalem, 1975), 52–53; *Tosafot ha-Shalem*, ed. J. Gellis, vol. 4 (Jerusalem, 1985), 63–64; and ms. Moscow 348, fol. 25v (קטן שדעתו כגדול מענישין אותו בדין שמים וראיה מעלי שרצה לענוש את שמואל). Cf. *Nimmuqei Ḥumash le-Rabbenu Yeshayah [di Trani]*, ed. C. B. Chavel (Jerusalem, 1972), 28; and above, chapter 3, nn. 114–15.

83 See ms. B.M. Or. 9931 (Gaster 730; Ashkenaz, fourteenth century), fol. 16r. As noted above (chapter 2, n. 193), this Tosafist Torah collection was preserved by a student of R. Yedidyah b. Israel of Nuremberg; see also Urbach, *Baʿalei ha-Tosafot*, 2:569 (n. 25). It includes interpretations from Tosafists such as R. Jacob and R. Yosef of Orleans and R. Yom Tov of Joigny, and it also cites R. Judah *he-Ḥasid* frequently, as well as others who were connected to his circle and teachings, such as R. Yaqar of Cologne (fols. 26v–27r), and R. Isaac Fuller (fol. 121r). Another interpretation by R. Samuel Bamberg is cited on fol. 76r.

84 See, e.g., S. Emanuel, *Shivrei Luḥot*, 65–81; and my "Mysticism and Asceticism in Italian Rabbinic Literature of the Thirteenth Century," (above, n. 48).

of the lungs renders an animal a *terefah*, unfit for ritual slaughter, on halakhic grounds. But in addition, Rid writes, Elijah the prophet appeared to him in a dream and confirmed his ruling.[85] Although R. Isaiah stresses that dreams are not authoritative in and of themselves (as per *Gittin* 52a, דברי חולומות לא מעלין ולא מורידין), and that his ruling is well based within talmudic law, R. Isaiah writes that when Elijah appeared to him in his dream, he asked for Elijah's guidance: אליהו זכור לטוב נדמה לי בחלום ושאלתי את פיו, connoting that this was not merely a "passive" dream experience. Moreover, R. Isaiah provided a scriptural indicator (*siman*) for the lenient and strict positions in his case, a technique that was commonly employed by R. Jacob of Marvege in his collection of responsa that were purportedly received from heaven, *She'elot u-Teshuvot min ha-Shamayim*.[86]

R. Isaiah is cited by the *'Arba'ah Turim* as allowing forms of divination (כדי לידע את העתידות) that are done using holy Divine names (שמותיו הקדושים), since "this is the greatness and might of the Almighty." The conjuring of demons (*shedim*) for this purpose is prohibited, however, since the manipulation of *shedim* was deemed, in Isaiah's view, to be a form of sorcery.[87]

Rid records a mystical interpretation, found also in the so-called French or Rhenish version of *Sefer Ḥasidim*,[88] and in other texts of the German

[85] See *Teshuvot R. Yeshayah di Trani*, ed. A. Y. Wertheimer (Jerusalem, 1975), 511–12 (#112). Cf. I. Ta-Shma, "Ha-Rav Yeshayah di Trani ha-Zaqen u-Qesharav 'im Bizantiyyon ve-Ereẓ Yisra'el," *Shalem* 4 (1984), 409–16; and idem, "Sefer Shibbolei ha-Leqet u-Kefelav," *Italia* 11 (1996), 46–48 (= idem, *Knesset Meḥqarim*, vol. 3 [Jerusalem, 2005], 9–19, 71–72). On Rid's place within the Tosafist enterprise, cf. Urbach, *Ba'alei ha-Tosafot*, 1:413; Isadore Twersky, "The Contribution of Italian Sages to Rabbinic Literature," *Italia Judaica* (Rome, 1983), 399–400; my "Progress and Tradition in Medieval Ashkenaz," *Jewish History* 14 (2000), 287–92, 302–7; Ta-Shma, "R. Yeshayah di Trani ve-Sifro 'Tosafot Rid,'" *Meḥqerei Talmud* 3 (2005), 916–43 (= idem, *Knesset Meḥqarim*, 3:24–54); and above, chapter 3.

[86] See Ta-Shma, "Ha-Rav Yeshayah di Trani ha-Zaqen," 415 (n. 25) (= *Knesset Meḥqarim*, 16 [n. 28]). Cf. idem, "She'elot u-Teshuvot min ha-Shamayim, ha-Qoveẓ ve-Tosfotav," *Tarbiz* 57 (1988), 57–63, and *She'elot u-Teshuvot min ha-Shamayim le-Ya'aqov mi-Marvege*, ed. R. Margoliot, 77–79 (#62–64, 68).

[87] See R. Jacob b. Asher, *'Arba'ah Turim*, *Yoreh De'ah*, sec. 179, and *Beit Yosef*, ad loc., s.v. *katav ha-Ramah*. Jacob cites his father, R. Asher b. Yeḥi'el, as having allowed a form of divination that utilized *shedim* to locate a lost object. The manipulation of *shedim* to retrieve lost objects (and in other magical contexts) was also permitted by two of Rabbenu Tam's students, Ri of Dampierre and R. Eli'ezer of Metz; see above, nn. 41–43. Cf. *Tosafot Rid* to *Qiddushin* 71a.

[88] See *Sefer Ḥasidim* (Bologna), ed. R. Margoliot (Jerusalem, 1957), sec. 18. (On this version of *Sefer Ḥasidim*, see Ivan Marcus, "The Recensions and Structure of *Sefer Ḥasidim*," *Proceedings of the American Academy for Jewish Research* 45 [1978], 131–53. See also *Maḥzor Vitry*, ed. S. Hurwitz [Nuremberg, 1923], 97 [sec. 126]. For magical adjurations and aspects of *Hekhalot* mysticism in *Maḥzor Vitry*, see my "*Peering through the Lattices*," 153–57, 162.) *Sefer ha-Manhig*, ed. Y. Raphael (Jerusalem, 1978), 1:31–32, cites this interpretation in the name of Rashbam. For Rashbam's awareness of esoteric teachings and traditions related to Divine names, see above, nn. 9–10. This particular attribution has been cogently questioned, however, by David Rosin, in the introduction to his edition of Rashbam's *Perush 'al ha-Torah* (Breslau, 1882), xvii (n. 4), in light of Rashbam's decidedly rationalistic and nonmystical bent (as noted above).

Pietists and their students,[89] concerning the response of *Amen* to a blessing. In the words of the Talmud (*Berakhot* 53b), "One who answers *Amen* to a blessing is greater than the one who recites the blessing." The interpretation advanced by Isaiah di Trani maintains that this is so because the letters in the word *Amen* are the *gematria* equivalent of the total of the letters of the Tetragrammaton according to both its written and vocalized forms. Thus one who answers *Amen* has, in effect, invoked the name of God twice, while the one making the blessing has done so only once.[90]

R. Isaac b. Moses *Or Zaruʿa* and R. Avigdor Katz of Vienna

R. Isaac b. Moses *Or Zaruʿa*, one of the leading Tosafist halakhists in the first half of the thirteenth century, ultimately served as rabbi of Vienna. As noted in the first chapter, R. Isaac represents the "reunification" of the German and the French Tosafist schools in the thirteenth century, following more than a generation of relative detachment and separation.[91] R. Isaac studied in Germany with leading Tosafists including Rabiah, R. Simḥah of Speyer, and R. Jonathan b. Isaac of Wurzburg, and in northern France with R. Judah Sirleon, R. Samson of Coucy, and R. Jacob b. Meir of Provins, among others. He also studied with R. Judah *he-Ḥasid* and R. Abraham b. Moses in Regensburg, and apparently with R. Eleazar of Worms as well.[92]

[89] These include *Sefer ha-Roqeaḥ*, *Sefer ʿArugat ha-Bosem*, and *Sefer Or Zaruʿa*, and are conveniently collected in *Tosafot R. Yehudah Sirleon le-Massekhet Berakhot*, ed. N. Zaks (Jerusalem, 1969), 2:599 (nn. 316–17). Ri's student, the Tosafist R. Judah Sirleon (d. 1224), presents and then rejects this interpretation as *lo nehira*; see also the rationalistic explanation by R. Menaḥem *ha-Meiri* (cited by Zaks in n. 316). As further noted by Zaks, the Ashkenazic view espoused by Rid and the German Pietists makes its way into the Zohar (and should thus be added to the list of examples compiled by I. Ta-Shma, *Ha-Nigleh shebe-Nistar* [Tel Aviv, 1995], 21–26), and into the mystically inclined Torah commentary of R. Baḥya b. Asher (to Ex. 14:31). Rashba (*Responsa*, 5:53) refers to the esoteric interpretation of this talmudic passage (*ʿinyan neʿelam le-Baʿalei ḥokhmah*). In his aggadic commentary to *Berakhot*, Rashba links the esoteric interpretation of the passage to the *sefirot*. See also the formulation of Rabbenu Yonah, cited in *Beit Yosef le-Oraḥ Ḥayyim*, sec. 124, and the commentary of Maharsha to *Sotah* 40b, s.v. *minayin she-ʾein ʾomrim*.

[90] See *Pisqei R. Yeshayah di Trani le-Massekhet Berakhot*, ed. A. Y. Wertheimer (Jerusalem, 1964), 164–65. See also R. Isaiah's *Sefer ha-Makhriʿa*, ed. S. A. Wertheimer (Jerusalem, 1998), 543–48 (sec. 87). There is little, if any, esoteric material in Rid's Torah commentary (above, chapter 3), other than a small amount of *gematria* interpretations and *remazim*, although note Rid's anti-anthropomorphic comment to Deut. 21:23 (ed. Chavel, 67); his *Tosafot ha-Rid* to *Ḥagigah* 16a; and below, chapter 7.

[91] See above, chapter 1, n. 128 (and the works cited there), esp. Rami Reiner, "From Rabbenu Tam to R. Isaac of Vienna: The Hegemony of the French Talmudic School in the Twelfth Century," in *The Jews of Europe in the Middle Ages*, ed. C. Cluse (Turnhout, 2004), 273–82.

[92] See Urbach, *Baʿalei ha-Tosafot*, 1:436–37; Uzi Fuchs, "ʿIyyunim be-Sefer Or Zaruʿa le-R. Yiẓḥaq b. Moshe me-Vienna" (M.A. thesis, Hebrew University of Jerusalem, 1993), 11–19, 29–32; idem, "Shalosh Teshuvot Ḥadashot shel R. Yiẓḥaq b. Mosheh baʿal Or Zaruʿa," *Tarbiz* 70 (2001),

R. Isaac embraced a number of aspects of Ashkenazic pietism,[93] including the *harḥaqot* for a *niddah* prescribed in Ashkenazic sources according to the so-called *Baraita de-Masskeht Niddah*, which was associated with the *Hekhalot* corpus.[94] R. Isaac was attuned not only to the existence of *shedim* and *maziqin* but also to the magical nature of their powers. He cites R. Eleazar of Worms on the custom that the *shaliaḥ ẓibbur* sustains the chanting of *barekhu* at the conclusion of the Sabbath, since the souls who reside in *gehinnom* return there after this point. As long as the chanting continues, they do not return.[95]

In his discussion of a talmudic passage implying that *shedim* do not observe Jewish law—and interpreted in this way by Rashi—R. Isaac *Or Zaruʿa* cites R. Judah *he-Ḥasid*, who maintained that *shedim* "believe in the Torah and [also] do whatever the *ḥakhamim* decreed." Thus they would not willingly violate even a rabbinic prohibition such as *teḥum Shabbat.* In a situation where it appears that they traveled on the Sabbath, they were merely communicating through long tubes.[96] When R. Judah was asked, in light of the notion that *shedim* observe even the rabbinic requirements of the Oral Law, how *shedim* could engage in illicit sexual relations with certain women, he responded that *shedim* have an arrangement whereby their observance of the Torah is contingent on their being treated properly by human beings. If someone harms or bothers them, however, they can harm that person in turn. The discussions in *Sefer Or Zaruʿa* concerning *shedim* correspond closely to material found in *Sefer Ḥasidim* and in an esoteric text from *Ḥasidei Ashkenaz, Sefer ha-Kavod.*[97]

109–31; S. Emanuel, *Shivrei Luḥot*, 155–58, 176–77, 250–52; I. Ta-Shma, *Knesset Meḥqarim*, 1:157–66, 232–33; idem, *Ha-Sifrut ha-Parshanit la-Talmud*, 2:109 (n. 27), 117; and Rami Reiner, "'Mi-Gan Eden' ve-ʿad 'Ẓeror ha-Ḥayyim': Birkot ha-Metim ba-Maẓevot me-Ashkenaz Bimei ha-Benayim," *Zion* 76 (2011), 19–23.

[93] See U. Fuchs, "'Iyyunim be-Sefer Or Zaruʿa," 33–40. Fuchs focuses on aspects of prayer, physical acts of expiation (*kapparah*) to atone for sin, the proper distribution (and destination) of charity (and other ethical imperatives), as well as exegetical techniques.

[94] See my *"Peering through the Lattices,"* 128–30. R. Isaac also presents the pietistic discussion by Tosafists in Central and Eastern Europe about fasting on Rosh ha-Shanah, and he expresses his own view as well. A version of this is also presented in R. Eleazar of Worms's *Maʿaseh Roqeaḥ*. See my *"Peering,"* 111–15, and above, nn. 48, 74.

[95] See *Sefer Or Zaruʿa, hilkhot moza'ei Shabbat*, pt. 2, sec. 89 (fol. 24a). Eleazar of Worms had noted that this was also done by R. Eliʿezer b. Meshullam *Ḥazzan* (of Speyer). R. Eliʿezer *Ḥazzan* was a direct link in the esoteric chain of tradition of the German Pietists. See I. Ta-Shma, *Minhag Ashkenaz ha-Qadmon*, 307; and my *"Peering through the Lattices,"* 143, 154 (n. 56).

[96] See *Sefer Or Zaruʿa, hilkhot ʿeruvin*, pt. 2, sec. 147. Cf. Y. L. Zlotnick, *Maʿaseh Yerushalmi* (Jerusalem, 1947), 29–30. On the association of R. Isaac *Or Zaruʿa*'s teacher, R. Jonathan of Wurburg, with *torat ha-sod* material, see Gershom Scholem, *Reshit ha-Qabbalah* (Tel Aviv, 1948), 197–98, and Urbach, *Baʿalei ha-Tosafot*, 1:222, 438.

[97] See Yosef Dan, *Torat ha-Sod shel Ḥasidut Ashkenaz* (Tel Aviv, 1968), 186–88. The notion that *shedim* observe *mizvot* is part of the larger view of the German Pietists (which conflicts with the

R. Isaac begins his *Sefer Or Zaru'a* with an analytical treatise on the Hebrew alphabet (*le-falpel be-'otiyyot shel 'alfa beta*). In addition to citing several mystical and esoteric texts such as *Otiyyot de-R. Aqiva*, *'Alfa Beta de-R. Aqiva*, and *Sefer Yezirah*,[98] this treatise refers to letter combinations, *gematriyyot*, and *sofei tevot* utilized by other Ashkenazic *sod* literature;[99] to pietistic

---

views of both philosophers and kabbalists) that demonic powers emerge from the positive aspect or side of the Divine realm. Cf. *Sefer Ḥasidim* (Parma), ed. Wistinetski, secs. 733, 1763, 379; Barbara Newman, "Possessed by the Spirit: Devout Women, Demoniacs, and the Apostolic Life in the Thirteenth Century," *Speculum* 74 (1998), 749–57; and Dorit Alloro-Cohen, "Ha-Maggeyah veha-Kishuf be-Sefer ha-Zohar" (Ph.D. diss., Hebrew University of Jerusalem, 1989). See also *Sefer Or Zaru'a*, pt. 2, sec. 50 (end); I. Ta-Shma, *Minhag Ashkenaz ha-Qadmon*, 299–308; M. B. Lerner, "Ma'aseh ha-Tanna veha-Met: Gilgulav ha-Sifrutiyyim veha-Hilkhatiyyim," *Assufot* 2 (1988), 29–68; and *Sippurei Gilgulim ve-Ruḥot*, ed. M. Y. Blau (New York, 1995), 40–41.

[98] R. Isaac *Or Zaru'a* cites the *'Alfa Beta de-R. Aqiva* twice in the first section of his treatise (and again in secs. 21, 28, 33), and suggests that he is modeling his discussion after that work. The introductory mnemonic alphabets that R. Isaac presents reflect the talmudic discussion in *Shabbat* 104a, which itself has clear affinities with *Sefer Yezirah*. See I. Ta-Shma, *Knessest Meḥqarim*, 1:36–37; Ivan Marcus, *Rituals of Childhood*, 138–39 (n. 41); and cf. Y. Dan, *Torat ha-Sod shel Ḥasidut Ashkenaz*, 69–70. The passage in sec. 28 mentions both the *'Alfa Beta de-R. Aqiva* and *Sefer Yezirah* concerning a letter derivation of שם המפורש שבו נברא העולם.

[99] R. Isaac begins his treatise by expressing the joy he felt at being able to identify the correct spelling of the Hebrew name Aqiva (עקיבה rather than עקיבא) on the basis of a *sofei tevot* analysis of the verse אור זרוע לצדיק ולישרי לב שמחה. According to the eighteenth-century *Seder ha-Dorot* (by R. Yechiel Halperin), R. Isaac was unsure of how to spell this name in a bill of divorce, and the solution came to him in a dream. His gratitude for this heavenly edification caused him to name his book *Sefer Or Zaru'a*; see *She'elot u-Teshuvot min ha-Shamayim*, ed. R. Margoliot, editor's introduction, 8. Although this later source cannot be seen as evidence that this actually occurred (i.e., that R. Isaac's discovery of this spelling resulted from a mystical experience), the fact that several other mystical dreams are found and recorded in *Sefer Or Zaru'a*—including Ephraim of Regensburg's dream concerning the *barbuta* fish, citing R. Judah *he-Ḥasid* (above, n. 76); the dream procedure used to locate the remains of R. Simeon *ha-Qadosh* of Falaise (above, n. 31); and Ephraim of Bonn's account of R. Amnon's transmission of the *U-natenneh toqef* prayer (above, n. 62)—heighten the possibility of R. Isaac's own mystical dream experiences. See also R. Margoliot, 8–9, and below, n. 160. The *sofei tevot* derivation for the spelling of "Aqiva" presented by R. Isaac is similar to the *gematria* formulation that R. Isaac (among others) attributes to R. Samuel *he-Ḥasid* (see *Sefer Or Zaru'a*, pt. 2, sec. 281, and below, n. 110): ור' שמואל החסיד היה אומר אבי"נו מלכי"נו חטא"נו לפני"ך עולה בגי' רב"י עקיב"ה (הו"א) יס"דו וחד חסר הקריאה. Note Urbach's observation (*Ba'alei ha-Tosafot*, 1:439) that R. Isaac's *'Alfa Beta* treatise demonstrates that he was indeed a disciple of both R. Judah *he-Ḥasid* and R. Eleazar of Worms, who began his own halakhic work, *Sefer Roqeaḥ*, with a pietistic introduction. Cf. Ivan Marcus, *Piety and Society* (Leiden, 1981), 131–32. In the first section of his introduction, and in secs. 11–13 and 21, R. Isaac makes use of the *gematria* technique of *millui*, which is associated especially with the German Pietists. See Marcus, "Exegesis for the Few and for the Many: Judah he-Ḥasid's Biblical Studies," *Meḥqerei Yerushalayim be-Maḥshevet Yisra'el* 8 (1989), 1*–24*, and Joseph Dan, "The Ashkenazic Concept of Language," in *Hebrew in Ashkenaz*, ed. L. Glinert (New York, 1993), 17. For the possible esoteric connotations of the notion in sec. 12, that circumcision constitutes a seal of the Divine name, see Elliot Wolfson, "Circumcision and the Divine Name: A Study in the Transmission of Esoteric Doctrine," *JQR* 78 (1987), 85–112 (esp. 110–11).

prayer practices based on *Hekhalot* texts;[100] and to additional mystical teachings including *torat ha-mal'akhim.*[101] R. Isaac *Or Zaru'a* interprets the talmudic account of R. Yishma'el and Akatri'el in terms of the *torat ha-Kavod* of the German Pietists, perhaps influenced also by a passage in *Sefer Yiḥusei Tanna'im va-Amora'im.*[102]

R. Avigdor b. Elijah *ha-Kohen* (d. c. 1275), the successor to R. Isaac *Or Zaru'a* in Vienna, apparently studied in northern France as a youth. His

[100] See sec. 2, for the raising of the eyes during the *kedushah*, a practice based on *Hekhalot* texts that became fairly widespread in Ashkenaz. Cf. *Sefer Rabiah*, ed. Aptowitzer, 1:70 (citing *Sefer Hekhalot*), and n. 19; Eric Zimmer, *'Olam ke-Minhago Noheg* (Jerusalem, 1996) 77–78; and below, n. 120. Although Rabiah does not display affinities with mysticism and magic to the same extent as other Ashkenazic figures included in this discussion, this is one of several practices that Rabiah (one of R. Isaac *Or Zaru'a*'s leading talmudic teachers) adopts on the basis of *Hekhalot* and related literature. See also *Sefer Rabiah* 1:26, regarding the movement of the head during the recitation of *Shema* as an indication of proper intention, a practice with roots in *Sefer Yeẓirah*; and cf. Zimmer, "Tenuḥot u-Tenu'ot ha-Guf bi-She'at Qeri'at Shema," 360–61; and above, n. 46. See also *Sefer Rabiah*, 2:196–97 (citing *sefarim ḥizoniyyim*), and *Sefer Or Zaru'a*, pt. 2, sec. 281 (citing *Sefer shel Qedushot = Hekhalot Rabbati*), on prostrating oneself during the Yom Kippur liturgy, when the sequence of the recitation of the *Shem ha-Meforash* by the *Kohen Gadol* is described.

[101] According to R. Isaac's formulation in sec. 3, the letter *'alef* (which is פלא spelled backward) teaches one to pay attention to the wonders of the Torah, לידע סוד הדבר ולעמוד על עיקרו. Torah study is referred to several times in this treatise as a means of acquiring special or secret knowledge. See, e.g., the theme repeated in sec. 6 (Torah study leads to the revelation of *ta'amei Torah*), and cf. sec. 24. Note the reference to *mal'akh Sar ha-Torah* (a highly significant angelic figure in *Hekhalot* literature) in sec. 29 (and cf. secs. 35, 41), and see also the last section (50), which discusses the proper manipulation of angels so that *mal'akhei havalah* will not be granted control over a person. An annotated version of this treatise was published by Yosef Movshowitz in *Sefer ha-Zikkaron le-R. Shiloh Raphael*, ed. Movshowitz (Jerusalem, 1998), 95–144. For two passages in R. Isaac's text that are also found in the pietistic introduction to *Sefer Roqeaḥ*, see Movshowitz's notes on 134–45.

[102] See *Sefer Or Zaru'a, hilkhot qeri'at shema*, secs. 7–8; I. Ta-Shma, *Ha-Sifrut ha-Parshanit la-Talmud*, 1:133–35, 2:191–92; above, n. 57; and below, chapter 7. R. Isaac rejects the view of Rabbenu Ḥanan'el that R. Yishma'el saw Akatri'el only in his mind (through an imaginative faculty), as well as the view that Akatri'el is only an angel (who could therefore be perceived). He accepts the notion (in accordance with *ḥasidut Ashkenaz*) that Akatri'el is the *Kavod*, which is Divine but nonetheless revealed. Cf. Gershom Scholem, *Major Trends in Jewish Mysticism* (New York, 1941), 110–16; Reuven Margoliot, *Torat ha-Mal'akhim* (Jerusalem, 1988), 12; Elliot Wolfson, *Through a Speculum That Shines*, 127, 147, 262 (nn. 314–15); Arthur Green, *Keter* (Princeton, 1997), 62–65; Daniel Abrams, "Sefer Shaqod le-R. Shmu'el b. Qalonymus ve-Torat ha-Kavod shel Talmud R. Eleazar Worms," *Assufot* 14 (2002), 231–32; and idem, "From Divine Shape to Angelic Being: The Career of Akatriel in Jewish Literature," *Journal of Religion* 76 (1994), 50–55. Yehudah Liebes, *Studies in Jewish Myth and Jewish Mysticism* (Albany, N.Y., 1993), 50–51, suggests that the approach of R. Isaac *Or Zaru'a* (whom he characterizes as "one of the leading Ashkenazic halakhists in the twelfth and thirteenth centuries who knew nothing about Kabbalah"), in the way that he highlights the connections between women and the (new) moon, was one step removed from the (fully mystical) approach found in *Sefer Ḥasidim*, which was itself quite close to the view of the kabbalists. In light of the material assembled here, R. Isaac's affinity for these teachings is hardly surprising. See also *Darkhei Mosheh* to *'Arba'ah Turim, Oraḥ Ḥayyim*, sec. 426 (end).

most important teacher, however, was R. Simḥah of Speyer. R. Avigdor subsequently taught in Ferrara and Verona, and was in close contact with R. Zedekiah b. Abraham *ha-Rofe* of Rome, author of *Shibbolei ha-Leqet.*[103] Like R. Isaac *Or Zaruʿa*, R. Avigdor was also a teacher (or senior colleague) of R. Meir of Rothenburg. Although R. Avigdor is barely mentioned in *Tosafot* texts,[104] his talmudic and halakhic interpretations circulated widely. R. Avigdor also composed a commentary to the *megillot* that has survived, as well as a lengthy, multifaceted commentary to the Torah, which includes discussions of legal practices and customs that have been published for the most part.[105] These commentaries often reflect the exegetical methods of

103 See I. Ta-Shma, *Knesset Meḥqarim*, 3:21, 23, 46, 70; my "Mysticism and Asceticism in Italian Rabbinic Literature" (above, n. 48); and S. Emanuel, *Shivrei Luḥot*, 175–76 (n. 103).

104 See, e.g., Urbach, *Baʿalei ha-Tosafot*, 2:607, 628, and above, Introduction, nn. 9, 90.

105 See H. J. Zimmels, "Le-Toledot R. Avidgor b. Eliyyahu ha-Kohen Katz me-Vienna," *Ha-Ẓofeh me-Ereẓ Hagar* 15 (1931), 110–26; idem, "Ketav Yad Hamburg Cod. Hebr. 45 ve-Yiḥuso le-R. Avigdor Katz," in *Maʾamarim le-Zikkaron R. Ẓevi Pereẓ Chajes*, ed. A. Aptowitzer and Z. Schwarz (Vienna, 1933), 248–61; I. A. Agus, "Avigdor b. Elijah *ha-Kohen*," *Encyclopedia Judaica*, 2:963; *Shibbolei ha-Leqet ha-Shalem*, ed. S. K. Mirsky (New York, 1966), editor's introduction, 13–25; *Shibbolei ha-Leqet*, vol. 2, ed. Hasida, editor's introduction, 23–26, 32–35; I. Ta-Shma, "Sefer Shibbolei ha-Leqet u-Kefelav," 46–47; S. Emanuel, *Shivrei Luḥot*, 175–81. In addition to noting that R. Avigdor apparently studied for a time in Halle, Germany, as well (176, n. 104), which is quite distant from Speyer, Ms. Hamburg 45, which contains the (mostly) halakhic Torah commentary of R. Avigdor, refers on several occasions to the customs of *Ẓarefat/Ẓarefatim* (see, e.g., *Perushim u-Pesaqim le-Rabbenu Avigdor*, ed. Machon Harerei Qedem [Jerusalem, 1996], 8, 354, 453, 459, 467, 490), and to a series of northern French rabbinic authorities; see the index to *Perushim u-Pesaqim*, 536–37. There is, however, an element of doubt as to whether R. Avigdor of Vienna is the author of the *peshatim* that appear alongside the *perushim u-pesaqim* in this manuscript. Complicating this question is the existence of another R. Avigdor in northern France in the early thirteenth century who was also the author of a Torah commentary (found in ms. Bodl. 2273) that was of a much deeper mystical nature. On these issues, see my *"Peering through the Lattices"* 94 (n. 2), and 97–98 (n. 9); Emanuel, *Shivrei Luḥot*, 172–75; M. Idel, "On R. Neḥemiah ben Shlomo the Prophet's Commentaries on the Name of Forty-Two," [Hebrew] *Kabbalah* 14 (2006), 211, 215, 217, 219–22, 225; and the next note. Urbach has no sustained discussion of R. Avigdor Katz; see *Baʿalei ha-Tosafot*, 1:433, 435–36 (R. Avigdor as a student of R. Eleazar b. Samuel of Verona), 565 (n. 4); and the above note. A number of sections from ms. Hamburg 45 (from among the labeled *pesaqim*) have been published separately. See, e.g., S. E. Stern, "Pisqei Rabbenu Avigdor Kohen Zedeq be-ʿInyanei Shemitah ve-Yovel," *Moriah* 19:10–12 (1944), 10–14; idem, *Sefer Qiddush ve-Havdalah le-Rabbotenu ha-Rishonim* (Bnei Brak, 1991), 51–57; Y. Lifshitz, "Hilkhot Qinyan ve-Halippin le-Baʿalei ha-Tosafot," in *Sefer Zikkaron li-Khevodo ule-Zikhro shel R. Yaʿaqov Bezalel Zolty*, ed. Y. Buksboim (Jerusalem, 1987), 181–85; idem, "Hilkhot Hagʿalah mi-Ketav Yad le-Rabbenu Avigdor Kohen Ẓedeq," in *Sefer Zikkaron li-Khevod R. Shmuʾel Barukh Verner*, ed. Y. Buksboim (Jerusalem, 1996), 131–35. See also *Teshuvot u-Pesaqim*, ed. E. Kupfer, 108, 320–21. For additional responsa and *pesaqim* of R. Avigdor, see, e.g., ms. Parma 918, fol. 26r; Paris 1408, fols. 56v–57r; Parma 425, fols. 31v–32r; Parma 1237, fols. 47v, 143v; Parma 929, fols. 96, 150, 223; and cf. E. Lichtenstein, "Beʾur Yerushalmi le-R. Avigdor Kohen Ẓedeq," *Bi-Netivot Yam* 3 (Petach Tikva, 1972), 171–73.

the German Pietists, and there are specific parallels in interpretation and doctrine.[106]

Like R. Judah *he-Ḥasid* and R. Samuel Bamberg, R. Avigdor interpreted that ʿEr and Onan were fully culpable for their actions, even at the ages of eight or nine.[107] R. Avigdor cites approvingly the view held by R. Judah *he-Ḥasid*, found in both *Sefer Ḥasidim* and in Judah's Torah commentary, that one who writes a Torah scroll must gather together a quorum and write the Divine names in their presence.[108] R. Avigdor also cites a passage from *Midrash Avkir*, a midrashic collection associated with the German Pietists in particular.[109] He recognized the Pietist practice of regarding the night of *Hoshana Rabbah* as the *leil ha-ḥittum*, the final sealing of one's judgment for those who did not repent fully on Yom Kippur. On that night, the fullness of a person's shadow as seen in the moonlight was an indicator of what a person's judgment would be.[110]

R. Avigdor authored a commentary to *Avinu Malkenu* that includes the *gematria* by R. Samuel *he-Ḥasid* which serves to demonstrate R. Aqiva's role in the formulation or dissemination of this prayer. This commentary was copied after R. Eleazar of Worms's esoteric treatise, *Ḥokhmat ha-Nefesh.* The

[106] Although R. Avidgor refers to R. Judah *he-Ḥasid* and R. Eleazar of Worms by name in only a handful of instances (see *Perushim u-Pesaqim le-R. Avigdor*, editor's introduction, 15–16), numerous parallels show that he was clearly aware of and attuned to their biblical comments and other writings. See *Perushim u-Pesaqim*, 12–15, 21, 28, 32 (esp. n. 8), 37, 52, 70, 82, 84, 90, 107, 111 (including the pietist conception of the *Kavod*), 131, 166, 176, 208, 220, 230, 263, 265, 321, 324, 339, 344. A similar pattern can be seen in *Perush R. Avigdor Katz li-Megillat Esther*, ed. Z. Leitner (Jerusalem, 1994), and *Perush R. Avigdor Katz le-Shir ha-Shirim*, ed. S. A. Wertheimer (Jerusalem, 1971), which was based on the edition of Y. Bamberger (Frankfurt, 1899). See also Y. Gellis, "Qetaʿim mi-Baʿalei ha-Tosafot ʿal Megillat Esther," *Moriah* 21:5–6 (1997), 3–4. The *peshatim* in ms. Hamburg 45 also contain interpretations from (and parallels to) R. Judah *he-Ḥasid*, as well as those of leading northern French Tosafists and biblical exegetes. See above, chapter 4, nn. 134, 149, 181, 193.

[107] See *Perushim u-Pesaqim*, 13. For R. Judah and R. Samuel, see above, nn. 82–83.

[108] See *Perushim u-Pesaqim*, 109 (nn. 20–21), and cf. *Perushei ha-Torah le-R. Yehudah he-Ḥasid*, ed. Lange, 132–33.

[109] See *Perushim u-Pesaqim*, 123–24. On the association of *Midrash Avkir* with the German Pietists, see Adolph Neubauer, "Le Midrasch Tanhuma," *REJ* 14 (1887), 109–10; M. Idel, "Ha-Maḥshavah ha-Ra'ah shel ha-E-l," *Tarbiz* 49 (1980), 358–59; Urbach, *Baʿalei ha-Tosafot*, 1:395; idem, *ʿArugat ha-Bosem*, 4:173–74; Amos Geulah, "Midrash Avkir: Mevo'ot u-Muva'ot" (M.A. thesis, Hebrew University of Jerusalem, 1998), 112–22, 183–84; and idem, "Midreshei Aggadah Avudim ha-Yeduʿim me-Ashkenaz Bilvad: Avkir, Esfah, u-Devarim Zuta" (Ph.D. diss., Hebrew University of Jerusalem, 2007), 24–27, 111–13.

[110] See *Perushim u-Pesaqim*, 240; I. Ta-Shma, *Ha-Nigleh shebe-Nistar*, 22–23; idem, *Sefer Gematri'ot le-R. Yehudah he-Ḥasid*, 16 (introduction), 58 (fol. 17v); and M. Idel, "Gazing at the Head in Ashkenazi Hasidism," *Journal of Jewish Thought and Philosophy* 6 (1997), 276–79. Avidgor's discussions (*Perushim u-Pesaqim*, 315, 462, from the parallel ms. Mantua 36) about giving charity on behalf of the sick and the departed, and the expression of *ḥazaq* for each person who is called to participate in the public reading of the Torah (*Perushim u-Pesaqim*), are also consonant with views of the German Pietists. See my "*Peering through the Lattices*," 53–54, 92 (n. 78).

commentary refers to esoteric dimensions of *Avinu Malkenu*, in addition to describing exoteric concepts of repentance and redemption. It also identifies parts of this prayer that are associated with *Hekhalot* literature.[111]

R. Avigdor Katz is cited by *Shibbolei ha-Leqet* as espousing the notion of directing prayer through angels who could serve as intermediaries (תהיו מליצי יושר לפניו).[112] R. Simḥah of Speyer permitted R. Avigdor to perform a *leḥishah* over R. Simḥah's eyes on the Sabbath, when R. Simḥah experienced severe discomfort. R. Avigdor learned the *leḥishah* technique from a woman, and he performed it twice a day.[113]

Moreover, ten manuscripts that contain Italian or Ashkenazic prayer rites and date from the fourteenth and fifteenth centuries attribute a magical *tefillat/shemirat ha-derekh* to R. Avigdor. After a person has departed his city and he is at a distance of an arrow's flight, he should turn back to face the city and recite two verses (Gen. 32:2–3) that describe the appearance

111 See ms. Cambr. Add. 858, 1 (Ashkenaz, fifteenth century), fols. 45r–45v (פירוש אבינו מלכנו דקדוקי הרא"ך [=ה"ר אביגדור כ"ץ]). This passage is preceded, at the beginning of fol. 34r, by העתקתי מספר חכמת נפש סוד ה"ר אלעזר (and see also fol. 10v, הועתק מספרי מורי' הרב ר' אגיבדור כ"ץ צרפתי, and S. Emanuel, *Shivrei Luḥot*, 177–78, n. 111). Cf. *Synopse zur Hekhalot-Literatur*, ed. P. Schafer et al. (Tubingen, 1981), sec. 334. The *gematria* of R. Samuel *he-Ḥasid* is cited by *Sefer Rabiah*, ed. Aptowitzer, 2:232 (and n. 6): ושמעתי בשם ר' שמואל [החסיד אבינו מלכנו] חטאנו לפניך עולה בגימטריה רבי עקיבא הוא יסדו. Cf. Urbach, *Ba'alei ha-Tosafot*, 1:195 (n. 79); and see also ms. Hamburg 152, fol. 106v; *Sefer Assufot* (ms. Montefiore 134, transcribed in *Zekhor le-Avraham*, ed. A. Berger [Jerusalem, 1993], 27, and see also above, n. 70); and *Sefer Or Zaru'a*, 2:281. In this *gematria* the word חטאנו is counted as it is pronounced, without the (silent) *'alef*. Cf. D. Sperber, *Minhagei Yisra'el*, 4:49. Also, in most of the texts that record this *gematria*, "Aqiva" is spelled with a *heh* at the end, rather than with an *'alef*—as in Palestinian texts from the talmudic period and as this name was often spelled in texts of the German Pietsts. R. Avigdor Katz also favored prayer *nusha'ot* and variant readings that were followed by *Ḥasidei Ashkenaz*. See, e.g., Binyamin Hamberger, *Shorashei Minhag Ashkenaz*, vol. 1 (Bnei Brak, 1995), 61–62; Eric Zimmer, *'Olam ke-Minhago Noheg*, 123–27; and Naftali Wieder, "Yismah Moshe," in *Meḥqarim ba-Aggadah, Targumim u-Tefillot Yisra'el le-Zekher Yiẓḥaq Heinemann*, ed. E. Fleischer (Jerusalem, 1981), 96–98.

112 See *Shibbolei ha-Leqet*, ed. Buber, sec. 282. R. Avigdor bases his reading primarily on a talmudic interpretation of Rashi; see my "Hekkeruto shel Rashi be-Sifrut ha-Hekhalot uve-Torat ha-Sod," *Bar Ilan* 30–31 (2006), 491–500. For evidence of other Ashkenazic rabbinic figures who approved of this practice, see my *"Peering through the Lattices,"* 134 (n. 4), 147 (n. 38); and cf. 239 (n. 51).

113 See ms. Bodl. 666, *Mordekhai 'al Massekhet Shabbat*, at the end of *Pereq ha-Zoreq*; *Teshuvot Maharam* (Prague), #55; *Haggahot Maimuniyyot le-hilkhot Shabbat*, 21:28[4]; Urbach, *Ba'alei ha-Tosafot*, 1:414 (n. 20); I. Ta-Shma, *Knesset Meḥqarim*, 1:247–48; S. Emanuel, *Shivrei Luḥot*, 155–557; idem, "Ivvaron ke-'Eylah le-Gerushin," *Massekhet* 6 (2007), 31–42; Y. Yuval, *Ḥakhamim be-Doram*, 260–61; J. Trachtenberg, *Jewish Magic and Superstition*, 199–200; and cf. Ephraim Shoham-Steiner, *Involuntary Marginals* [Hebrew] (Jerusalem, 2008), 225–27. In response to a question from R. Zedekiah b. Abraham *ha-Rofe*, R. Avigdor prohibited *leḥishot* that invoked *shedim*, whether for personal needs or to divine the future. See *Shibbolei ha-Leqet*, part 2, ed. S. A. Hasida, 41–43 (sec. 2). I. Z. Kahana, "She'elot u-Teshuvot ha-Or Zaru'a u-Maharam b. Barukh," *Sinai* 25 (1939), 86 (sec. 127); *Tosafot Sotah* 11b, s.v. *she-haytah* (above, n. 74); and above, nn. 43, 87.

of the angels who came to accompany Jacob as he resumed his journey from Laban (*ve-Ya'akov halakh le-darko va-yifge'u bo mal'akhei E-lohim*). The petitioner then recites the formula: "Just as Jacob was not harmed by Laban or by his brother Esau who despised him, so too I and the members of my group should not be harmed in any way by any of my enemies or pursuers or agents of damage" (כן לא אהיה נזוק אני פב״פ וכל חבורתי מכל שונאי ומכל רודפי ומכל מזיקי ומציקי בשום היזק שבעולם).

In three of the manuscripts, Avigdor's formula ends here, and the standard prayer of the wayfarer (*tefillat ha-derekh*) is then recited.[114] In two others, the petitioner continues by reciting the verse that describes how the fear of God descended on the surrounding area, allowing the sons of Jacob to travel without anyone pursuing them (Gen. 35:5).[115] The five remaining manuscripts conclude with a list of the Divine names that can be derived from this verse through esoteric permutations, although we cannot be absolutely certain that this last portion was also composed by R. Avigdor.[116] An Italian manuscript contains a brief commentary on Ezekiel's vision of the chariot according to both *peshat* and *sod* that is ascribed to R. Avigdor of Rome.[117]

Finally, R. Avigdor authored a treatise of ethics and beliefs titled *Sha'arei Musar*, which contains a number of similarities to material in *Sefer Ḥasidim*. In this treatise, R. Avigdor stresses the development of fear of Heaven and resistance to sin by remembering that all of one's actions are performed under the watchful eye of the Creator. One needs to break the desire to sin (*le-shabber 'et libbo*) and to always consider the proximity of death (*yom ha-mitah*). He also describes the powerful efficacy of *kavvanah* in prayer even after one has sinned, the need to be extremely humble and self-effacing in dealing with others, and the paramount importance of penitence, which is to be accompanied by shame (*bushah*) and weeping.[118]

[114] See ms. Parma 112, fol. 46v; ms. Parma 997, fol. 297; ms. Vatican 243, fol. 12r.

[115] See ms. Sassoon 408, fols. 192–94; ms. Parma 671, fol. 93.

[116] See ms. Parma 292, fol. 164; ms. Parma 309, fols. 184v–186r; ms. Parma Perreau 22, fol. 112; ms. B.M. Or. 10169 (Gaster 438), fol. 23r; and ms. JTS Mic. 2095, fol. 16v. More than half of the ten manuscripts that record R. Avigdor's prayer do so in close proximity to magical *shemirot ha-derekh* or other prayers of protection attributed to Naḥmanides, R. Judah *he-Ḥasid*, R. Eleazar of Worms, and other Ashkenazic rabbinic figures such as R. Meir of Rothenburg. See my *"Peering through the Lattices,"* 226–27 (n. 16). See also ms. Livorno (Talmud Torah) 138, fols. 28r, 29r–v, 36r, 38r. Ms. Cambr.Or. 71 (Ashkenaz, 1398), fol. 166r, contains a similar kind of formula for protection that apparently involved a brother of the Tosafist (and student of Ri of Dampierre) R. Solomon *ha-Qadosh* b. Judah of Dreux: זאת מצאתי בירושלמי. שלח ה״ר יעקב מגרמוזייה אח הקדוש מדרוייש. חנוך ואליהו גיבורי א-ל מלך וחזק לא טעמו טעם מיתה הלכו ביום ובלילה ולא הוזקו. יה״ר מלפניך א-להי השמים כשם שלא הוזקו כך אני לא אזוק. For another reference to R. Jacob b. Judah of Dreux, see Urbach, *Ba'alei ha-Tosafot*, 2:519 (n. 47). On R. Solomon of Dreux, see above, chapter 3.

[117] See ms. Cambr. Add. 3111 (fifteenth century), fols. 63v–65r.

[118] See *Sha'arei Musar le-R. Avigdor Kohen Zedeq* in *Shitat ha-Qadmonim*, ed. M. Y. Blau (New York, 1989), 1–7 (based on ms. Rome Casanatense 159 [Italy, 1454], fols. 21r–25r). This treatise is also

A close parallel to *Sefer Ḥasidim* can be seen in a passage that recommends specific strategies and opportunities for engaging another's child or an adult in Torah study, even on a small scale, thereby preventing them from sitting idly by (כדי שלא ילכו בטלים).[119] R. Avigdor also cites the passage in *Hekhalot Rabbati* that he refers to as *Ma'aseh Merkavah*, which describes the lifting of the eyes and the body by those reciting the *kedushah*, as reflecting the response of the Almighty to these actions.[120] R. Avigdor's brother, Eliezer b. Elijah *ha-Kohen*, authored a rhymed treatise of rebuke (*tokhehah*).[121] In this work, Eliezer touches on many of the same specific issues that R. Avigdor discusses in *Sha'arei Musar* using similar terms and phrases.

Northern France during the Thirteenth Century, and R. Meir of Rothenburg and His Circle

Interest in mysticism and magic was present among northern French Tosafists of the thirteenth century as well. R. Ezra *ha-Navi* of Moncontour, who was a student of Ri of Dampierre, as noted above, lived long enough to be a teacher of R. Meir of Rothenburg (d. 1293), and is characterized as a *navi* even by *Tosafot* texts,[122] owing at least in part to the mystical *ḥishuv ha-qeẓ* episodes that he experienced. During these episodes, R. Ezra ascended to the heavens (*'alah la-shamayim*, a state also attributed to his teacher, Ri)[123]

---

found in ms. Paris 839 (Ashkenaz, fourteenth century), fol. 72 (which contains only the beginning); Sassoon 405 (Italy, 1415), fols. 82–85; and Vatican 251 (Italy, fourteenth century), fols. 28r–32v. A text of *Sha'arei Musar* was also published separately in Jerusalem in 1993. On R. Avigdor's pietism, cf. *Shibbolei ha-Leqet*, part 2, ed. S. Hasida, 226–27 (sec. 48).

119 See *Sefer Ḥasidim* (Parma), secs. 762–64.

120 See also the parallel citation in *Perush R. Avidgor Katz le-Shir ha-Shirim*, ed. Wertheimer, 27, and cf. above, n. 100. Rabiah is the earliest Ashkenazic rabbinic authority to cite this from *Sefer Hekhalot*, while R. Avigdor is the first to note *Ma'aseh Merkavah* as the source of this passage. Cf. my *"Peering through the Lattices,"* 109–10 (n. 34). For another reference to *Hekhalot* literature (along with the teachings of R. Eleazar of Worms) in R. Avigdor's commentary to *Shir ha-Shirim*, see *Perush R. Avigdor Katz*, ed. Wertheimer, 11, and cf. I. Ta-Shma, "Od li-Be'ayat ha-Meqorot ha-Ashkenaziyyim shel Sefer ha-Zohar," *Kabbalah* 3 (1998), 259–60.

121 See ms. Vatican Urb. 22, fols. 65r–66r (beginning זה יסד מה"ר אליעזר אחיו של ה"ר אביגדור כהן צדק. הבה נתחכמה לתור לנשמה מנוחה שלמה בשכבה ובקומה לעתיד לבוא), and cf. S. Emanuel, *Shivrei Luḥot*, 179, for *pesaqim* attributed to R. Eli'ezer. R. Eli'ezer's ethical treatise is also found in ms. Parma 147, fol. 145; ms. Bodl. 913, fols. 15r–16v; ms. Bodl. 914, fols. 182r–183v; ms. Bodl. 2287, fols. 19r–28r; and ms. Bodl. 2848, fols. 3r–14r.

122 See *Tosafot Gittin* 88a, s.v. *dilma*; *Tosafot Shavu'ot* 25a, s.v. *Rav de-'amar*; *Tosafot Rabbenu Pereẓ le-Bava Qamma* 23b, s.v. *temol*, citing *ha-Rav ha-Navi mi-Moncontour* (= *Da'at Zeqenim le-Rabbotenu Ba'alei ha-Tosafot* [Ex.] fol. 3a, and *Tosafot ha-Shalem*, ed. J. Gellis, 8:233, sec. 1). See also A. J. Heschel, "'Al Ruaḥ ha-Qodesh Bimei ha-Benayim," 184; Joseph Shatzmiller's addenda to *Gallia Judaica*, in *Qiryat Sefer* 45 (1970), 609–10; and Shraga Abramson, "Navi, Ro'eh ve-Ḥozeh," in *Sefer ha-Yovel li-Mugash li-Khvod Rav Mordekhai Kirschblum*, ed. D. Telsner (Jerusalem, 1983), 121–23.

123 See above, n. 38.

using *Hekhalot* magical techniques, and inquired about the time of the *qeẓ* from the biblical prophets Ḥaggai, Zekharyah, and Malʾakhi. In the course of these heavenly experiences, R. Ezra also received certain verses or songs that he was then able to transmit.[124]

R. Moses b. Jacob of Coucy (d. c. 1250) composed and apparently implemented a series of physically demonstrative penitential prayer supplications (*teḥinot*). These supplications reflect the *tiqqunei teshuvah* of *Ḥasidei Ashkenaz*, and contain parallels to penitential prayers authored by R. Eleazar of Worms and R. Yehudah *he-Ḥasid.* One of these penitential supplications was appended without attribution by R. Yonah of Gerona, who was clearly impacted by *ḥasidut Ashkenaz*, to his *Yesod ha-Teshuvah.*[125] Indeed, numerous pietistic affinities with the German Pietists, in prayer and other contexts, were displayed by R. Yonah's northern French teachers, R. Moses b. Shneʾur and R. Samuel b. Shneʾur of Evreux.[126] What remains unresolved, however, is the extent to which the *ḥasidut* that developed in northern France emerged on its own, based on developments in the pre-Crusade period and during the first part of the twelfth century, and was then further influenced or energized through personal or literary contacts with *Ḥasidei Ashkenaz*, or whether Ashkenazic pietism initially sprang from the same source but developed into fundamentally separate branches within northern France and Germany.[127] My sense is that the former path of development is the more likely one.

R. Yeḥiʾel b. Joseph of Paris (d. c. 1260–65), a northern French Tosafist contemporary of R. Moses of Coucy and the brothers of Evreux, provided a mystical commentary to the *Hekhalot*-based *E-l Adon* hymn. This commentary discusses the way the seventy-two letter Divine name, and the different perspectives of the Godhead (*Maʿaseh Merkavah*) experienced by Isaiah and Ezekiel are reflected in the structure and content of this hymn. This commentary by R. Yeḥiʾel is consistent with those offered by the early Spanish kabbalist R. Judah b. Yaqar, who studied in northern France with Riẓba and perhaps with other Tosafists as well, and by R. Eleazar of Worms, and it

124 See Urbach, *Baʿalei ha-Tosafot*, 1:336–37, 2:528; I. Ta-Shma, *Knesset Meḥqarim*, 1:150–51; G. Scholem, *Origins of the Kabbalah*, 239–40; M. Idel, *Kabbalah: New Perspectives*, 91–92; and my "Ḥishuvei ha-Qeẓ" (above, n. 38). R. Troestlin *ha-Navi* is linked to some of these experiences as well; cf. my *"Peering through the Lattices,"* 211, 244–25, and above, n. 19.

125 See my *"Peering through the Lattices,"* 70–81. Cf. Y. T. Langermann, "From Private Devotion to Communal Prayer: New Light on Abraham Maimonides's Synagogue Reforms," in *Ginzei Qedem*, ed. R. Brody, vol. 1 (Jerusalem, 2005), 46*–48*.

126 See the literature cited in S. Emanuel, *Shivrei Luḥot*, 193 (n. 38).

127 This question is sharpened by the level of separation between Tosafist circles in northern France and Germany in the late twelfth and early thirteenth centuries, as discussed above in chapter 1.

apparently reached R. Aaron *ha-Levi* of Barcelona through the exposition of R. Yeḥi'el.[128]

R. Yeḥi'el is reported, in a collection of *pesaqim* most likely compiled by his leading student, Rabbenu Pereẓ of Corbeil, to have had contact with a departed soul who described how angels would throw him into the air and let him fall without catching him, as punishment for his practice of talking during the cantor's recitation of the *berakhah 'aḥat me-'en sheva* on the eve of the Sabbath. An almost identical passage is found in *Sefer Ḥasidim.*[129] The notion of forty-nine distinct approaches to every halakhic issue, associated by both Ritva and R. Solomon Luria (Maharshal, d. 1572) with esoteric

128 See ms. Paris l'Alliance 133, cited in Colette Sirat, "Un nouveau manuscrit du *Maḥzor Vitry*," *REJ* 125 (1966), 262; I. Ta-Shma, "Li-Meqorotav ha-Sifrutiyyim shel Sefer ha-Zohar," *Tarbiz* 60 (1991), 663–64; and idem, *Ha-Nigleh shebe-Nistar* (Tel Aviv, 2001), 30, 67. Although the inclusion of *E-l Adon* in the *siddurim* of R. Judah b. Yaqar and R. Eleazar of Worms means, as noted by Ta-Shma, that it was known by Tosafists (such as Riẓba) well before the days of R. Yeḥi'el of Paris, R. Yeḥi'el's interest in this particular hymn and his comments are nonetheless significant and suggestive. On the *Hekhalot* aspects of *E-l Adon* that can be discerned from the prayer commentaries of *Ḥasidei Ashkenaz* and R. Judah b. Yaqar as well, see Meir Bar-Ilan, *Sitrei Tefillah ve-Hekhalot* (Jerusalem, 1987), 115–20.

129 See H. S. Sha'anan, "Pisqei Rabbenu Pereẓ ve-Aḥerim be-'Inyanei Oraḥ Ḥayyim," *Moriah* 17:9–10 (1991), 14, sec. 26 (from ms. Paris BN 407, fol. 237r). See also *Sefer Ḥasidim* (Parma), sec. 1073, cited in *'Arba'ah Turim, Oraḥ Ḥayyim*, sec. 268. R. Yeḥi'el is best known for his involvement in the Trial of the Talmud in Paris, in 1240. See also ms. Vatican 324, fol. 278r; and above, chapter 4, n. 101. In addition, a large number of R. Yeḥi'el's *piseqei halakhah* have been published, while others are still in manuscript, including a group of his *pesaqim* that was collected and supplemented by the brothers of Evreux. There is also evidence for *Tosafot* of R. Yeḥi'el to several tractates. See Urbach, *Ba'alei ha-Tosafot*, 1:458–60; Emanuel, *Shivrei Luḥot*, 187–98; idem, "R. Yeḥi'el mi-Paris: Toledotav ve-Ziqato le-Ereẓ Yisra'el," *Shalem* 8 (2008), 86–89; I. Ta-Shma, *Ha-Sifrut ha-Parshanit la-Talmud*, 2:110–12; and above, chapter 1, nn. 112–16. In the present study, we have noted R. Yeḥi'el's interest in *peshat* aspects of *miqra*, alongside his halakhic and midrashic exegesis, and his awareness of comments by Abraham ibn Ezra. See, e.g., ms. Paris BN 353, fol. 77r; Shraga Abramson, "Iggeret ha-Qodesh ha-Meyuḥeset la-Ramban," *Sinai* 90 (1982), 244–49; and above, chapter 4, n. 122. Moreover, R. Yeḥi'el was involved with *piyyut* commentary; see, e.g., the above note; *'Arugat ha-Bosem*, ed. Urbach, 4:39 (n. 82); and above, chapter 5, nn. 283–84. (The *tiqqunei teshuvah*, however, seemingly attributed to R. Yeḥi'el in S. E. Stern, *Me'orot ha-Rishonim*, 55–56, on the basis of ms. Cambr. 377, do not belong to R. Yeḥi'el; his halakhic formulation in this manuscript begins only in the passage that follows the *tiqqunei teshuvah.*) As such, far from being solely a talmudist or halakhist, R. Yeḥi'el was involved with virtually all of the areas and fields discussed in the this book; see below, Conclusion. To be sure, as we have seen with regard to a Torah interpretation (above, chapter 4, n. 151), there are instances in which formulations by R. Judah *he-Ḥasid* and R. Yeḥi'el may have become intertwined, perhaps due to a copyist's error in understanding the abbreviation ר"ח as a reference to R. Yeḥi'el rather than to R. Yehudah *he-Ḥasid*. This is perhaps the case for the very similar discussion that both R. Yehudah and R. Yeḥi'el were reported to have had with a departed soul, although there is no literary or textual remnant that suggests such a mixup. Nonetheless, virtually all of the remaining mystical phenomena associated here with R. Yeḥi'el are correctly attributed to him. Moreover, R. Yehudah and R. Yeḥi'el on occasion held the same position with regard to a (quasi-)mystical issue, and each of their positions can be confirmed independently; see, e.g., above, n. 76.

traditions (although Ritva cites the talmudic interpretation itself from otherwise unidentified *Tosafot*), is cited by the *Tosafot* of R. Pereẓ of Corbeil from the *Tosafot R. Yeḥi'el mi-Paris* (on the basis of a passage in *Midrash Tehillim*).[130] R. Isaac b. Isaac of Chinon, a productive northern French Tosafist during the mid-thirteenth century who authored *Tosafot* texts as well as *piyyutim* (and studied at Evreux), composed a series of magical supplications and adjurations that he copied into liturgical texts.[131] R. Isaac b. Joseph of Corbeil (d. 1280), the son-in-law of R. Yeḥi'el of Paris and another student of the academy at Evreux, displayed a number of affinities with the German Pietists in terms of both pietistic behaviors and the magical use of Divine names.[132]

R. Elijah Menaḥem b. Moses of London (1220–84), a contemporary English Tosafist of R. Meir of Rothenburg, studied in northern France as R. Meir did,[133] and was a descendant of the leading talmudic scholar and mystic at Mainz c. 1000, R. Simeon *ha-Gadol*.[134] R. Elijah inserted formulae involving Divine names into *mezuzot* (literally, "he carved Names on the doorpost") that protected the home from fire. R. Elijah is also credited with transmitting two magical adjurations that included both Divine and angelic names. One of them was designed to induce a dream that would answer particular questions, a *she'elat ḥalom*. This procedure involved the release of a Divine name that could be found by pronouncing formulae

[130] See *Tosafot Rabbenu Pereẓ ha-Shalem ʿal Massekhet ʿEruvin*, ed. H. Dickman (Jerusalem, 1991), 48 (*ʿEruvin* 13b). For a full discussion of the origins and intentions of this repercussive Tosafist passage, see above, Introduction. For the presence of this and additional material of significance from R. Yeḥi'el of Paris (which reached *Ḥiddushei ha-Ritva* through the *Tosafot* or *beit midrash* of Rabbenu Pereẓ), see my "Between Ashkenaz and Sefarad: Tosafist Teachings in the Talmudic Commentaries of Ritva," in *Between Rashi and Maimonides: Themes in Medieval Jewish Thought, Literature and Exegesis*, ed. E. Kanarfogel and M. Sokolow (New York, 2010), 237–73. On the mystical dimensions of *Midrash Tehillim* and its use in medieval Ashkenaz, see my *"Peering through the Lattices,"* 198–99.

[131] See *"Peering through the Lattices,"* 174–77; my "Esotericism and Magic in Ashkenazic Prayer during the Tosafist Period" (above, n. 74), 208–10; Colette Sirat, "Un rituel Juif de France," *REJ* 125 (1966), 7–40; and above, at n. 32.

[132] See *"Peering through the Lattices,"* 81–92, and my "German Pietism in Northern France: The Case of R. Isaac of Corbeil," in *Ḥazon Naḥum: Studies in Jewish Law, Thought, and History Presented to Dr. Norman Lamm*, ed. Y. Elman and J. Gurock (New York, 1997), 207–27.

[133] The precise identity of R. Elijah's teacher(s) is unclear; see Cecil Roth, "Toledot Rabbenu Eliyyahu mi-Londrish," in *Perushei Rabbenu Eliyyahu mi-Londrish u-Pesaqav*, ed. M. Y. Zaks (Jerusalem, 1956), 20–22, 29, and Urbach, *Baʿalei ha-Tosafot*, 2:499–505. However, there does appear to have been a strong connection between Elijah's father, R. Moses of London, and R. Moses of Evreux. See my *"Peering through the Lattices,"* 233 (n. 39), and cf. Ta-Shma, *Knesset Meḥqarim*, 1:372–79.

[134] See A. Grossman, *Ḥakhmei Ashkenaz ha-Rishonim*, 87–88. A contemporary mystic, R. Elḥanan b. Yaqar of London (see above, Introduction, n. 83), wrote in his *Sod ha-Sodot* that he too was a descendant of R. Simeon.

over certain grasses or herbs (*Shem ha-katuv ba-yereq*) and was described as *seder ha-she'elah.*[135] R. Elijah also reports a prophetic dream that he had (והנה אקיץ משנתי והנה חלום נבואה ולא אחת משמים) in which he offered (in response to a question, נשאלתי בחלומי . . . ואען בחלומי) an interpretation of a problematic passage in the grace after meals.[136]

R. Meir of Rothenburg was a student of R. Isaac *Or Zaru'a* in Wurzburg, and of other Tosafist rabbinic figures linked to magic and *sod* in northern France, including R. Ezra *ha-Navi* of Moncontour, R. Yeḥi'el of Paris, and R. Samuel of Evreux, and he was in contact with R. Avigdor Katz of Vienna. R. Meir also exhibited affinities with the German Pietists, and with R. Judah *he-Ḥasid* in particular, on a wide range of issues. These included conservatism in halakhic decision-making, spiritual conceptions of *qiddush ha-Shem*, biblical interpretations characterized as *ta'amei massoret*, liturgical practices and *nosaḥ ha-tefillah* for which R. Meir adduced passages in *Hekhalot* literature in support of readings favored by R. Judah, procedures for repentance and *tiqqunei teshuvah*, and even protection of women from spousal abuse and attitudes toward settling in *Ereẓ Yisra'el.*[137]

135 See A. Marmorstein, "Some Hitherto Unknown Jewish Scholars of Angevin England," *JQR* 19 (1928–29), 32: להציל בית ר' [אליהו] מנחם חזן מלונדון חקק על משקוף הבית בסכין את השמות וניצל כל הבית (and cf. V. Aptowitzer, "Les Noms de Dieu et des Anges dans la Mezouza," *REJ* 60 [1910], 39–52, and *REJ* 65 (1913), 54–60), and ms. Sassoon 290, fol. 381r (sec. 1003): זה מה שיסד ה"ר אליהו מלונדריש כשתרצה לעשות שאלתך וכו'.

136 See Urbach, *Ba'alei ha-Tosafot*, 2:505–6. Urbach makes no note of the prophetic experience reflected in this passage, citing it with respect to another issue entirely. Interestingly, R. Elijah also appears to have been a medical doctor who wrote glosses to the grammatical work *Sefer ha-Shoham*, and whose rabbinic writings include a commentary to the Mishnah. See C. Roth (above, n. 133), 23–40.

137 See, e.g., ms. Cambr. Add. 1022.1, fol. 100v (ולכן נוהגין חסידי אשכנז להתפלל קריאת שמע מתוך הכתב ובפרט שליח ציבור. מה"ר מאיר מרוטברוק כתב שאסור לקראתו שלא מן הכתב וכ"ש שאר פרשיות של תורה. ולכן בכל מקום שלוחי ציבור האשכנזים קוריו ק"ש בלחש, discussed in my "Levels of Literacy in Ashkenaz and Sefarad as Reflected in the Recitation of Biblical Verses Found in the Liturgy," in *From Scholars to Savants: Studies Presented to Avraham Grossman* [Hebrew], ed. J. Hacker et al. [Jerusalem, 2009], 189–90); *Sefer Tashbeẓ* (ed. Lemberg), sec. 553 (Maharam cautioned his students not to say [לך] אכול בשמחה לחמך following a *hatavat ḥalom* because he had a tradition [*qabbalah*] from R. Judah he-*Ḥasid* in this regard, since the first letters of each of these words spell out א'ב'ל, a mourner); the addenda to *Sefer Tashbeẓ*, ed. Machon Yerushalayim (Jerusalem, 2011), sec. 2 ([מהר"ם] אומר פסוקים של אליהו במוצאי שבת. ואומר ג' פעמים אליהו קודם שקורא הפסוקים כי אמר ששמע משם ר' רבינו יהודה חסיד שטובים להצלחה. וגם שמע משמו שטוב לומר בכל יום כל הפסוקים של עשרים וארבעה [ספרי התנ"ך] שיש בהן זכירה כמו זכרון או זכר, והוא טוב לשכחה); Urbach, *Ba'alei ha-Tosafot*, 2:522, 536, 547, 564; *Sefer Mordekhai 'al Massekhet Megillah*, sec. 781, ed. M. A. Rabinowitz (Jerusalem, 1997), 16; *Ta'amei Masoret ha-Miqra le-R. Yehudah he-Ḥasid*, ed. Y. S. Lange (Jerusalem, 1981), 11; Lange, "Perushei Ba'alei ha-Tosafot 'al ha-Torah—Ketav Yad Paris 48," *'Alei Sefer* 5 (1978), 73; I. Marcus, *Rituals of Childhood*, 114–16; *Teshuvot u-Pesaqim le-R. Meir mi-Rothenburg*, ed. I. Z. Kahana, vol. 1 (Jerusalem, 1957), 14–15; my "Preservation, Creativity, and Courage: The Life and Works of R. Meir of Rothenburg," *Jewish Book Annual* 50 (1992–93), 249–59; I. Ta-Shma, "'Al Odot Yaḥasam shel Qadmonei Ashkenaz le-'Erekh ha-'Aliyyah le-Ereẓ Yisra'el," *Shalem* 6

As reflected in a number of manuscript passages, R. Meir was involved in aspects of magic and practical esoteric applications, through the recitation of *Shemot* and mystical formulae, the writing of amulets involving letter combinations, and the use of Divine names. In some instances, his formulae are recorded in manuscripts in close proximity to those of R. Yehudah *he-Ḥasid*, R. Eleazar of Worms, and other Ashkenazic students, including R. Meir's own student, R. Dan, who fled Germany for Toledo, Spain, as Rosh and his family did, in the early years of the fourteenth century.[138] The purpose of several of these formulae was to achieve the state of *petiḥat ha-lev*, in which a person was able to remember and understand the Torah they had studied or would study, without forgetting it.[139] The concept of *petiḥat ha-lev* is well attested in medieval Ashkenazic texts, and harkens back to formulations of R. Sa'adyah Gaon and R. Eleazar *ha-Qallir*, as well as *Hekhalot* rituals and texts.[140]

Other magical formulae recorded in the name of R. Meir of Rothenburg sought to secure protection from physical harm and danger, whether caused by rulers or *maziqin*, or due to incarceration.[141] Maharam decided

(1992), 315–17, but cf. my "The *'Aliyyah* of 'Three Hundred Rabbis' in 1211: Tosafist Attitudes toward Settling in the Land of Israel," *JQR* 76 (1986), 205–9; A. Grossman, "Ziqato shel Maharam mi-Rothenburg 'el Ereẓ Yisra'el," *Cathedra* 84 (1997), 63–84; idem, "Yaḥasam shel Ḥakhmei Yemei ha-Benayim 'el Hakka'at Nashim," in *Proceedings of the Tenth World Congress of Jewish Studies*, Div. B, vol. 1 (Jerusalem, 1990), 121–23 (= "Medieval Rabbinic Views on Wife Beating," *Jewish History* 5 [1991], 57–61); idem, "Haggahot R. Shemayah be-Nosaḥ Perush Rashi," *Tarbiz* 60 (1991), 91–92; Naftali Wieder, "Be-'ityah shel Gematria Anti-Noẓerit ve-Anti Islamit," *Sinai* 76 (1975), 5–10; idem, "Tiqqunim be-Nosaḥ ha-Tefillah be-Hashpa'at Leshonot Lo'aziyyot," *Sinai* 81 (1977), 27–29; *Sefer Berakhot le-Maharam*, ed. S. Spitzer (Jerusalem, 1988), 133; *Teshuvot Maharam defus Prague*, #517 (וכן אמר מהר"ם מאחר שגמר אדם למסור את נפשו על קידוש השם, מכאן ואילך כל מיתה שעושים לו אינו מרגיש כלל. וראיה מן המסורה הכוני ב' . . . ומביא ראיה מספר היכלות שר' חנניה בן תרדיון היה במקום קיסר וכו'); *'Arugat ha-Bosem le-R. Avraham b. 'Azri'el*, ed. Urbach, 4:59–60; and cf. Ruth Langer, *To Worship God Properly* (Detroit, Mich., 1998), 215–24.

[138] On R. Dan, see I. Ta-Shma in *Knesset Meḥqarim*, 2:157–66; *Perush Rabbenu Baḥya 'al ha-Torah*, ed. C. D. Chavel (Jerusalem, 1977), 2:19, and the editor's introduction, 1:10; S. Z. Havlin, "Teshuvot Ḥadashot leha-Rashba," in *Sefer Zikkaron le-R. Y. B. Zolty*, ed. Y. Buksboim (Jerusalem, 1987), 220–21 (n. 5); and my "Tosafist Teachings in the Talmudic Commentaries of Ritva," 247–48, 257–59.

[139] See ms. Vatican 243, fol. 4v (and cf. Ta-Shma, *Knesset Meḥqarim*, 162–63, and above, n. 68), and ms. Livorno Talmud Torah 138, fol. 36r; and above, n. 137. A *qabbalah* (for salvation) from R. Dan is found in ms. Vatican 243, fol. 6v, and see also fol. 10 (for a *segullah*). Cf. ms. JNUL 8*476, fol. 50v, and ms. Moscow-Guenzberg 182, fol. 156r, in the name of [מהר"ם נ"ע נשמתו עדן]. See also ms. Sassoon 290, fol. 254 (sec. 565, שמירה מופלאה בשם ה"ר דן), and ms. Bodl. 916, fol. 40. R. Dan transmitted a *sod* formulation concerning resurrection and the miracles of the messianic era, although to be sure some of these passages by R. Dan might have been composed in Spain (under the influence of Spanish Kabbalah), rather than in Germany.

[140] See my *"Peering through the Lattices,"* 140–42, 155–56; and above, n. 70.

[141] See Gershom Scholem in *Qiryat Sefer* 4 (1927–29), 317, based on ms. Camb. Add. 664, fol. 72r. See also ms. Moscow-Guenzberg 717, fol. 185, and ms. Bodl. 1936, fols. 72r–72v, for

a matter of monetary law, which he had not studied or discussed with his teachers, based on what he learned from the angelic *ba'al ha-ḥalom* in a dream he had while being held captive in the tower of Ensisheim.[142] Moreover, R. Meir issued a *she'elat ḥalom* and a *goral* for predicting or knowing the future.[143]

Although some manuscripts that contain magical material attributed to Mahram are relatively late or are of non-Ashkenazic provenance, R. Meir's involvement with *torat ha-sod* can be further confirmed from the writings of a number of his students and followers, in addition to R. Dan.[144] R. Solomon Simḥah b. Eli'ezer of Troyes, author of a lengthy work titled *Sefer ha-Maskil*, studied rabbinic literature with Maharam and with Rabbenu Pereẓ of Corbeil. R. Solomon Simḥah displays a great familiarity with the *torat ha-Kavod* of *ḥasidut Ashkenaz*, and with a form of the doctrine of the ether that he refers to as *'avir mufla barukh Hu u-varukh Shemo*, which was akin to the *'avir* recognized by the German Pietists.[145] R. Solomon was also interested in the use of Divine names to achieve certain effects, including *petiḥat ha-lev*, which he describes in physiological terms, and in the manipulation

adjurations and amulets from R. Meir of Rothenburg that could be employed to ease childbirth, thwart enemies, make a person beloved by all, and secure the assistance of the Almighty. Cf. *Sefer Tashbeẓ* (Lemberg, 1858), secs. 60, 257–58; *Teshuvot Maharam*, ed. Cremona, 108; and *'Arba'ah Turim, Yoreh De'ah*, sec. 286 (= R. Asher b. Yeḥi'el, *Halakhot Qetanot, hilkhot mezuzah*, sec. 10.)

142 See *Teshuvot Maimuniyyot le-sefer qinyan* (*hilkhot sekhirut*, ch. 5), #31; *Sefer Mordekhai 'al Massekhet Bava Qamma*, sec. 1; and *Sefer ha-Parnas le-R. Mosheh Parnas Rothenburg* (Vilna, 1891), sec. 415. Cf. *She'elot u-Teshuvot min ha-Shamayim*, ed. Margoliot, editor's introduction, 9, and *Teshuvot Maharam*, ed. M. A. Bloch (Berlin, 1891), 201 (#108, end).

143 See ms. Parma 1221 (Spain, fifteenth century), fols. 189r–190v; the manuscript is described in *Ohel Ḥayyim*, ed. M. Hallamish and E. Hurvitz, vol. 1, 193–94 (fols. 21r, 44r, 92r–v), and includes formulations from both R. Meir and R. Judah *he-Ḥasid*. See also ms. Paris 776 (Sefarad, fifteenth century), fols. 174v–175r; ms. Parma 563, fols. 95r–96r. Cf. Jonathan Elukin, "The Ordeal of Scripture," *Exemplaria* 5.1 (1993), 142–60; and the references to *goralot* in *Sefer Ḥasidim* (Parma), secs. 169, 255, 371.

144 On R. Meir's spirituality, cf. *Teshuvot Maharam*, ed. Bloch, 57 (#476, by R. Meir's student, R. Ḥayyim b. Makhir); Michael Fishbane, *The Kiss of God* (Seattle, Wash., 1994), 51–55; and idem, "The Imagination of Death in Jewish Spirituality," in *Death, Ecstasy, and Other Wordly Journeys*, ed. J. Collin and M. Fishbane (Albany, N.Y., 1995), 191. The passage that appears in *Teshuvot Maharam*, ed. Bloch, 325–26 (#5), which decries the magical use of adjurations that are composed of Divine or angelic names, is actually a passage that was interpolated from *Sefer Malmad ha-Talmidim* (Lyck, 1866, fol. 68a) by the Provençal rationalist R. Jacob Anatoli (who later settled in Italy). See Marc Saperstein, *Decoding the Rabbis* (Cambridge, Mass., 1980), 192; idem, "Christians and Christianity in the Sermons of Jacob Anatoli," in *The Frank Talmage Memorial Volume*, ed. B. Walfish (Haifa, 1993), 2:236, 238 (nn. 10, 24); and cf. J. Trachtenberg, *Jewish Magic and Superstition*, 243, 311 (n. 23), who was unaware that this was an interpolation from Jacob's work (which does not at all represent or reflect Meir of Rothenburg's own view).

145 For R. Solomon Simḥah of Troyes's views concerning anthropomorphism, see below, chapter 7.

of both demonic and angelic forces. He mentions as the greatest authorities in these areas (*ha-me'orot ha-gedolim*) R. Yehudah *he-Ḥasid* and Rabbenu Meir *ha-Gadol* (meaning his own teacher, R. Meir of Rothenburg). Indeed, R. Solomon's consistent application of the addendum *barukh Hu u-varukh Shemo* of the *'avir ha-mufla*, which he considered to be an aspect of the Divine Being, also reflects a convention associated with *Ḥasidei Ashkenaz*. In addition, R. Solomon provides a physiological description of the state of *petiḥat ha-lev* and suggests the ways this phenomenon facilitates the understanding and retention of Torah knowledge and other wisdom.[146]

According to R. Solomon, the Almighty gave man the ability to control *shedim* through the aegis of two fallen angels (Shemḥazai and Azza'el),[147] and also by invoking Divine names that were known to some. Indeed, the correct recitation of a sequence of *Shemot* has the capacity to bring the Messiah. At the same time, however, use of these powers might cause men to lose sight of their origin from the Divine, and to experience a diminution of *yir'at shamayim*. Morever, the power of Divine names over demons is effective even when activated *be-tum'ah*, by sorcerers or by those who err in their ways, because all is derived from the Almighty and from the power of His six names.[148] Therefore, Divine names should not be utilized in practice, although learning or teaching their powers is permitted.[149]

Two decades ago, Mark Verman identified a *Ḥug ha-'Iyyun* text, found in a fourteenth-century manuscript, in which R. Meir of Germany (*me-Allemagne*) and Rabbenu Pereẓ of France (*mi-Ẓarefat*) offered definitions and explanations of an unusual celestial figure and name, *Ara'ayeta*, an appellation for the Primal Ether (*'avir ha-qadmon*). R. Meir identified this Divine representation as *'or qadmon*: "It is from the pure and holy Name, and it corresponds to One, His unity, First, His unity, His transformation, One." R. Pereẓ called its name "Tenth level . . . there is in this name the secret of the

[146] See I. Ta-Shma, *Knesset Meḥqarim*, 1:150–54; Gad Freudenthal, "Ha-Avir Barukh Hu u-Barukh Shemo be-Sefer ha-Maskil le-R. Shelomoh Simḥah mi-Troyes," *Da'at* 32–33 (1994), 187–234, and *Da'at* 34 (1995), 87–129; idem, "Stoic Physics in the Writings of R. Sa'adia Gaon al-Fayyumi and Its Aftermath in Medieval Jewish Mysticism," *Arabic Sciences and Philosophy* 6 (1996), 133–36; Joseph Davis, "R. Yom Tov Lipmann Heller, Joseph b. Isaac *ha-Levi* and Rationalism in Ashkenazic Culture, 1550–1650" (Ph.D. diss., Harvard University, 1990), 67; and cf. G. Scholem, *Origins of the Kabbalah*, 251.

[147] For earlier versions of this motif, and for its presence in the Zohar as well, see R. Margoliot, *Mal'akhei 'Elyon*, 274–75, 292; M. Idel, "Ha-Maḥshavah ha-Ra'ah shel ha-E-l," 359 (n. 8); Rashi to Numbers 13:33; and B. J. Bamberger, *Fallen Angels* (Philadelphia, 1952), 129–33, 177–81.

[148] See *Tosafot ha-Shalem*, ed. Gellis, 2:289–90 (to Gen. 25:6).

[149] See ms. Moscow-Guenzberg 508, fol. 47v (transcribed by Freudenthal in *Da'at* 34 [1995], 118). See also fol. 46v, transcribed by Ta-Shma in *Knesset Meḥqarim*, 1:156; fols. 32r–33v; and cf. M. Idel, "Shelomoh Molkho ke-Magiqqon," *Sefunot* 18 (1985), 199–200. Solomon Simḥah, who offered an almost immediate date for the beginning of the redemption, refers to the prophetic activities of R. Ezra *ha-Navi* of Moncontour; see above, n. 124.

Cherubs." Verman cites this text, and a related one, as proof for the impact of *Ḥasidei Ashkenaz* on the *Ḥug ha-ʿIyyun.* At the same time, Verman notes two mystical techniques attributed to an "unidentified" R. Meir, one recorded in ms. Vatican 243 and the other in ms. Paris 776, in close proximity to a prophylactic technique attributed to R. Yehudah *he-Ḥasid.*[150]

In light of the evidence presented here, there can be little doubt that the R. Meir of Germany this text refers to is R. Meir of Rothenburg, just as R. Pereẓ of France is probably the Tosafist R. Pereẓ b. Elijah of Corbeil.[151] R. Pereẓ studied with R. Samuel of Evreux, Maharam, and R. Isaac of Corbeil, who all affected ascetic practices and disciplinary techniques similar to those of *Ḥasidei Ashkenaz*,[152] and whose connections to magic and mysticism have been described above.[153]

Additional manuscript evidence suggests that several other students of Maharam may have been involved with *sod* or magic. These include R. Yeḥiʾel b. Uri, the father of R. Asher (Rosh), who adopted the practice of reciting *barukh Hu u-varukh Shemo* each time a Divine name was mentioned, a practice that originated with the German Pietists and was also followed by R. Solomon Simḥah of Troyes.[154] Magical *segullot* as well as *sodot* are also attributed to Rosh himself, although the presence of this material only in relatively late manuscripts, and the specific contents in certain instances, weaken some of these attributions.

According to one manuscript text, Rosh transmitted a formula that would protect an individual and his money from thieves or demonic forces.[155] The authenticity of this passage is perhaps heightened by the fact

150 See M. Verman, *The Books of Contemplation* (Albany, N.Y., 1992), 201 (n. 32).

151 These identifications would further support Verman's dating of the text of the *ʿIyyun* circle as originating between 1230 and 1270, contra Scholem, who argued for the first quarter of the thirteenth century (in Provence). Cf. my "Rabbinic Figures in Castilian Kabbalistic Pseudepigraphy" (above, n. 16), 83 (n. 24), and Elliot Wolfson, *Along the Path*, 179 (n. 351). An easily identified (contemporary) name mentioned in the texts of the *Ḥug ha-ʿIyyun* is that of R. Eleazar of Worms. For the influence of *Ḥasidei Ashkenaz* on the *Ḥug ha-ʿIyyun*, see the literature cited in my "Rabbinic Figures," 80 (n. 13) and 104 (n. 96).

152 See my *"Peering through the Lattices,"* 59–63, 115–24, and above, n. 132.

153 One of the three references in *Tosafot* texts to R. Ezra of Moncontour as *ha-Navi* is found in *Tosafot Rabbenu Pereẓ* to *Bava Qamma* 23b. See above, n. 122, and cf. Urbach, *Baʿalei ha-Tosafot*, 1:336 (nn. 14*, 16).

154 See N. Wieder, "Barukh Hu u-Barukh Shemo—Meqoro, Zemanno ve-Nosaḥo," in *ʿIyyunim be-Sifrut Ḥazal, ba-Miqra uve-Toledot Yisraʾel muqdash li-Prof. Ezra Zion Melammed*, ed. Y. D. Gilat et al. (Ramat Gan, 1982), 287–90. Cf. Y. S. Zachter, "Kavvanat Shema," *Yeshurun* 2 (1996), 29 (n. 9); and *Teshuvot ha-Rosh*, 4:20.

155 See ms. Warsaw 9 (Ashkenaz, sixteenth century), fols. 152r–153r. Rosh also ruled that one who drinks *yayn nesekh*, even unwittingly, must fast for five days. This penance was also prescribed by R. Judah *he-Ḥasid* on the basis of the number of times the word "wine," or products of the vine, are referred to in Deuteronomy 32:32 (which begins with the phrase, כי מגפן סדום גפנם). See ms. Bodl. 784, fol. 99v, and cf. my "Rabbinic Attitudes toward Nonobservance in the

that R. Asher is cited by his son, R. Jacob *Ba'al ha-Turim*, who also studied with R. Meir of Rothenburg, as having allowed divination that utilized *shedim* as a means for finding and recovering lost or stolen property, just as Ri of Dampierre and R. Isaiah of Trani had, in the late twelfth and early thirteenth centuries,[156] and as R. Isaac b. Elijah, a contemporary of Maharam of Rothenburg, had as well.[157] Also likely to be authentic is a *sod* that R. Jacob b. Asher received from his father, in a passage that describes R. Asher as *mequbbal ve-hakham*,[158] as well as a *shemirat ha-derekh* attributed to Rosh.[159]

The response of R. Ḥayyim Eli'ezer b. Isaac *Or Zaru'a*, a student of Maharam, records the mystical experience of R. Isaac b. Elijah, who dreamed that Maharam appeared to him (even though R. Isaac had never actually met or seen R. Meir during his lifetime). In this dream, R. Meir of Rothenburg communicated to R. Isaac the need to retain a particular talmudic *girsa*.[160] Given these mystical views and experiences of R. Isaac b. Elijah, Jacob Katz's contention that R. Isaac's criticism of those students who engaged in *'iyyun ve-lo gemara*, as recorded in the responsa of R. Ḥayyim *Or Zaru'a*, refers to those who generated excessive *pilpul* without concern for the halakhic ramifications appears to be more plausible than Urbach's suggestion that *'iyyun* connotes the study of philosophy and/or *sod*.[161] R. Yaqar of Cologne, a contemporary of Maharam and a leading judge, halakhist, and *payyetan*, like R. Meir himself, is mentioned in two parallel manuscript passages (from *Seder Sodot/Raza Rabba*, a mystical work associated with *Ḥasidei Ashkenaz*) regarding esoteric derivations and uses of *Shemot*.[162]

The Tosafist period comes to a close with R. Meir of Rothenburg, his contemporaries, and his students. We have seen that there was sustained

---

Medieval Period," in *Jewish Tradition and the Nontraditional Jew*, ed. J. J. Schacter (Northvale, N.J., 1992), 25–26 (nn. 64–66). For other dimensions of R. Asher's piety, see A. H. Freimann, *Ha-Rosh ve-Ze'eza'av* (Jerusalem, 1986), 82–84, and H. J. Zimmels, *Ashkenazim and Sephardim* (London, 1976), 22, 32–33.

156 See *'Arba'ah Turim* to *Yoreh De'ah*, sec. 179 (end); *Beit Yosef*, ad loc.; and above, nn. 44, 87. On R. Jacob *ba'al ha-Turim*'s connection to *Ḥasidei Ashkenaz* and their *sod* interpretation, see my *"Peering through the Lattices,"* 247.

157 See *Teshuvot Ba'alei ha-Tosafot*, ed. Agus, 223–24, and and cf. Urbach, *Ba'alei ha-Tosafot*, 2:543–44. In his responsum, R. Isaac also approves of the adjuration of demons to know the future (לידע עתידות).

158 See ms. JTS Mic. 1852 (Sefarad, fifteenth century), fols. 1r–v.

159 See ms. Moscow-Guenzberg 1302 (Mizrah, 1431), fol. 14r: שמירת הדרך לרא"ש כשתראה לסטים או [איש] שאתה ירא ממנו, תאמר ששה פעמים על סדר אצבעות . . . ותזקוף ידך ותתחיל מן הזרת וכו'.

160 See *She'elot u-Teshuvot Maharaḥ Or Zaru'a*, #164.

161 See *She'elot u-Teshuvot Maharaḥ Or Zaru'a*, #163; J. Katz, *Halakhah ve-Qabbalah* (Jerusalem, 1986); and Urbach, *Ba'alei ha-Tosafot*, 2:586 (n. 2).

162 See ms. JTS Mic. 1885 (Italy, fifteenth century), fols. 71–73; ms. Paris BN 843 (fifteenth century), fols. 69–70; and G. Scholem, *Reshit ha-Qabbalah*, 197–98. On R. Yaqar as rabbinic judge and *payyetan*, see above, chapter 1 (n. 114), and chapter 5, nn. 309–21.

interest among Tosafists in the study of *torat ha-sod* and in magical theories and practices. While the talmudic methodologies of Tosafists such as Rabbenu Tam, Raban, and Rash *mi-Shanz* dominated the entire period, their downplaying of magic and mysticism among other pre-Crusade disciplines was often not accepted by their students and colleagues in either northern France or Germany. Indeed, *sod* interests among the Tosafists appear to have expanded as the thirteenth century unfolds, in part due to the influence of the German Pietists, whose own extensive interests and involvement in *torat ha-sod* were, of course, even more formally developed. Although *Ḥasidei Ashkenaz*, and related mystical circles such as the *Ḥug ha-Keruv ha-Meyuḥad* and the circle led by R. Neḥemyah b. Solomon of Erfurt, put forward a unique and sophisticated theosophical system in which Tosafists were generally not involved, the common level of mystical and magical interests among leading talmudists in medieval Ashkenaz was significantly higher than contemporary scholarship originally thought, and comports fully with the broader disciplinary interests that we have seen among the Tosafists throughout this study. Indeed, the next chapter will argue that even in the realm of Jewish thought and belief, it is possible to detect focused involvement and the formulation of a range of positions by various Tosafists.

7

Tosafist Approaches to Matters of Belief and the Implications for Popular Culture

Although there has been some renewed discussion about the extent to which medieval Ashkenazic rabbinic scholars were familiar with scientific knowledge and rationalistic modes of thought, the Tosafists surely did not study philosophy as a formal discipline, away from the pages of the Talmud or the verses of the Bible.[1] Moreover, even though mystical studies and practices, especially as found in and encouraged by the *Hekhalot* corpus, were discussed and pursued by a number of Tosafists in northern France, Germany, Italy, and England—as described in the previous chapter—there is no evidence in medieval Ashkenaz, except among the German Pietists and members of related circles, such as the Circle of the Special Cherub or that of R. Neḥemyah b. Solomon (the Prophet) of Erfurt, for an overarching body of theosophic or theurgic teachings and theories akin to the nascent

[1] See, e.g., David Berger, "Polemic, Exegesis, Philosophy and Science: On the Tenacity of Ashkenazic Modes of Thought," *Simon Dubnow Institute Yearbook* 8 (2009), 27–39; idem, "Judaism and General Culture in Medieval and Early Modern Times," in *Judaism's Encounter with Other Cultures*, ed. J. J. Schacter (Northvale, N.J., 1997), 93–98, 117–22; Gad Freudenthal, "The Place of Science in Medieval Hebrew Communities," in *Rashi 1090–1990: Hommage à Ephraim Urbach*, ed. G. Sed-Rajna (Paris, 1993), 599–613; Avraham Grossman, "Rashi's Rejection of Philosophy—Divine and Human Wisdoms Juxtaposed," *Simon Dubnow Institute Yearbook* 8 (2009), 95–118; idem, *Emunot ve-De'ot be-'Olamo shel Rashi* (Alon Shvut, 2008), 14–15, 91–93, 112–16, 124–30, 178–80, 245–49; and cf. my *"Peering through the Lattices": Mystical, Magical, and Pietistic Dimensions in the Tosafist Period* (Detroit, Mich., 2000), 19 (n. 1), 160–61, 166, 208 (n. 40), 219–20. As much of this literature also indicates, certain members of *Ḥasidei Ashkenaz* were more enlightened in terms of these disciplines. See also Elliot Wolfson, *Through a Speculum That Shines* (Princeton, 1994), 193–205; Israel Ta-Shma, *Knesset Meḥqarim*, vol. 1 (Jerusalem, 2004), 181–207; and the next note.

kabbalistic systems that developed in Provence and Spain during the late twelfth and early thirteenth centuries, and beyond.[2]

Nonetheless, the notion that the Tosafists did not consider issues of belief or the nature of the Divine in thoughtful and consistent ways is a misconception, especially in light of the presentation in prior chapters of palpable Tosafist interests in a variety of non-talmudic or extra-talmudic areas of inquiry and endeavor. A case in point to be discussed here is the attitude of medieval Ashkenazic rabbinic scholarship toward anthropomorphism. The general consensus of modern scholarship has been that the Tosafists were essentially corporealists (*magshimim*).[3]

A significant methodological issue that impacts any discussion of anthropomorphism has to do with the way the Tosafists understood or interpreted aggadic portions of the Talmud. The approach to aggadic interpretation in medieval Ashkenaz appears to have been relatively uniform. E. E. Urbach has shown that the Tosafists often brought proofs to their talmudic interpretations from post-biblical and post-talmudic works, which were essentially aggadic.[4] At the same time, the Tosafists took talmudic *ʾaggadah* seriously, even investing it with halakhic valence,[5] and, as legalists, they tended to interpret this material literally or according to its plain sense,

[2] See, e.g., Moshe Idel, "Bein Ashkenaz le-Qastilyah ba-Meʾah ha-Shelosh ʿEsreh—Hashbaʿot: Reshimot ve-Shaʿarei Derashot be-Ḥugo shel R. Neḥemyah b. Shlomo ha-Navi ve-Hashpaʿoteihen," *Tarbiz* 77 (2008), 475–554; Mark Verman, *The Books of Contemplation* (Albany, N.Y., 1992), 101, 200–204; and cf. Joseph Dan, *Torat ha-Sod shel Ḥasidut Ashkenaz* (Jerusalem, 1968), 116–43, 205–10, 245–62.

[3] See, e.g., Yonah Fraenkel, *Darkhei ha-Aggadah veha-Midrash* (Jerusalem, 1991), 511–15; *ʿArugat ha-Bosem*, ed. Urbach, vol. 4 (Jerusalem, 1963), 74–81; Marc Saperstein, *Decoding the Rabbis* (Cambridge, Mass., 1980), 7–13; Israel Ta-Shma, *Ha-Sifrut ha-Parshanit la-Talmud*, vol. 2 (Jerusalem, 2000), 191–94; and Yair Lorberbaum, *Ẓelem E-lohim* (Tel Aviv, 2004), 27–31. See also Shamma Friedman, "Ẓelem, Demut ve-Tavnit," *Sidra* 22 (2007), 89–152. Moritz Gudemann (writing in the late nineteenth century) is a notable exception; see below, nn. 71, 120.

[4] E. E. Urbach, *Baʿalei ha-Tosafot* (Jerusalem, 1980), 2:713–18. Cf. Yair Lorberbaum, *Ẓelem E-lohim*, 111.

[5] Thus, for example, both Avraham Grossman, "Shorashav shel Qiddush ha-Shem be-Ashkenaz ha-Qedumah," in *Qedushat ha-Ḥayyim ve-Ḥeruf ha-Nefesh*, ed. Isaiah Gafni and Aviezer Ravitzky (Jerusalem, 1992), 99–130, and Israel Ta-Shma, "Hitabdut ve-Rezaḥ ha-Zulat ʿal Qiddush ha-Shem: Li-Sheʾelat Meqomah shel ha-Aggadah be-Massoret ha-Pesiqah ha-Ashkenazit," in *Yehudim Mul ha-Ẓelav*, ed. Y. T. Assis et al. (Jerusalem, 2000), 150–56, have argued with respect to preemptive acts of martyrdom (including suicide and the killing of others) that Ashkenazic rabbinic leaders decided these difficult matters of Jewish law on the basis of aggadic passages within the talmudic corpus. Without undermining in any way the validity of this approach, I have demonstrated that Ashkenazic martyrdom was (subsequently) justified by leading rabbinic decisors on the basis of precise halakhic grounds and categories as well. See my "Halakhah and *Meẓiʾut* (Realia) in Medieval Ashkenaz: Surveying the Parameters and Defining the Limits," *Jewish Law Annual* 14 (2003), 201–16.

following the approach of Rashi in his talmudic commentary.[6] Nonetheless, the fact that the Tosafists (and Rashi) do not seem to have been particularly troubled in their talmudic commentaries by anthropomorphic statements in the*'aggadah* should not be taken as a proof that they endorsed this position.[7] Indeed, as Urbach also maintains, the Tosafist approach to *'aggadah* and to midrash was akin to their approach to *halakhah* in another respect as well. The Tosafists (taking their cue in all likelihood once again from Rashi) did not often pursue the spiritual dimensions or religious depths of aggadic texts when they interpreted these texts as part of their talmudic comments (as we saw in the previous chapter, with regard to possible mystical dimensions within the Talmud).[8] Only the German Pietists addressed talmudic

[6] Note, e.g., the comment of R. Samson of Sens (*Kitab 'al Rasa'il*, ed. Yehiel Brill [Paris, 1871], 136): ואיך יעלה על לב [איש] לומר שלא נקח דברי ה[א]גדה כפשטה, cited and briefly discussed by Bernard Septimus, *Hispano-Jewish Culture in Transition* (Cambridge, Mass., 1982), 57–58. Cf., however, *Shitah Mequbbeẓet* to *Bava Meẓi'a* 85b. The Talmud recounts an incident in which Elijah showed a rabbinic scholar the members of the heavenly academy in their heavenly abode, with the proviso that this scholar not look at the throne on which R. Hiyya sat. The scholar could not restrain himself, and his eyes were injured. Although the standard *Tosafot* (B.M. 86a, s.v. *itsei*) appears to understand this passage in literal terms, *Shitah Mequbbeẓet* records a passage from *Tosafot Shanẓ* in which "our teacher" (*rabbenu*, either R. Samson himself or his main teacher, Ri of Dampierre) maintained that Elijah revealed this sight to the rabbinic scholar only in a dream.

[7] Cf. Marc Saperstein and Israel Ta-Shma, above, n. 3. In one instance, Ta-Shma contrasts Rashi's silence on the aggadic sections that present anthropomorphic challenges early in the first chapter of *Berakhot* (fols. 6–7) with the vigorous anti-anthropomorphic interpretation of his North African predecessor, Rabbenu Ḥanan'el. It should be noted, however, that R. Eliezer b. Nathan (Raban), an early German Tosafist from the mid-twelfth century, reproduces a significant part of R. Ḥanan'el's commentary in his own talmudic commentary (*Sefer Raban, massekhet Berakhot* [repr. Jerusalem, 1975], sec. 126). Rabbenu Ḥanan'el's passage is also cited at the end of the twelfth century by R. Judah b. Qalonymus of Speyer, in his *Sefer Yiḥusei Tanna'im va-Amoraim* (see Urbach, *Ba'alei ha-Tosafot*, 1:376–77), and in the thirteenth century (in even greater detail) by R. Isaac b. Moses of Vienna, in his *Sefer Or Zaru'a*; see below, n. 84. Ta-Shma also notes Rashi's relatively uncritical acceptance of R. Yishma'el's heavenly journey and conversation with the angel Suri'el (*Berkahot* 51a), which Rashi, citing the *Beraita de-Ma'aseh Merkavah*, suggests was achieved by adjuring a Divine name. As I have described elsewhere, however, Rashi interprets several other heavenly journeys mentioned by the Talmud in the same manner. These interpretations reflect Rashi's familiarity with *Hekhalot* literature and other mystical practices and procedures, and are not the result of a simple, literal, or unsophisticated approach to the talmudic passage. See my *"Peering through the Lattices,"* 144–53, and my "Hekkeruto shel Rashi be-Sifrut ha-Hekhalot uve-Torat ha-Sod," *Sefer Bar Ilan* 30–31 (2006), 491–500. At the same time, *Tosafot Ḥagigah* 14b, s.v. *nikhnesu le-pardes*, interprets another of these heavenly journeys (which in Rashi's view occurred again by means of an adjured Divine name) as happening only in the minds of the sages involved, an interpretation consonant with the (anti-anthropomorphic) approach of R. Ḥanan'el referred to above. For this passage and other relevant *Tosafot* variants, see my *"Peering through the Lattices,"* 189 (n. 2).

[8] As I have noted in *"Peering through the Lattices,"* 4–5, 217–18, even those Tosafists who were interested in mysticism and other forms of spirituality hardly expressed themselves within the genre of *Tosafot*. These ideas found their expression (with minor exceptions) only in other

and halakhic questions, not to mention aggadic considerations, in ways that Urbach characterized as more spiritual or theological than halakhic.[9]

Tosafot passages do gather aggadic statements and compare them to each other, and attempt to resolve contradictions among them.[10] However, as Urbach correctly maintains, these comparisons and conclusions should be viewed, in the absence of any other indication, as typical specimens of Tosafist interpretation of the talmudic corpus rather than as specific evidence for Tosafist religious thought or beliefs. In order to argue that something is in fact an actual or personal theological position or belief of the Tosafists, one must be able to demonstrate that such a belief is not simply the result of the Tosafist resolutions of talmudic contradictions or the textual problems at hand but rather a systematically held position that is not dependent on or linked to particular talmudic *sugyot*.[11] The fact that Urbach devotes

---

kinds of compositions and Tosafist literature. Although this development is somewhat striking, it is not surprising, given the decidedly halakhic nature of the talmudic corpus. Indeed, Naḥmanides, who was a leading kabbalist and whose Torah commentary is replete with kabbalistic material, barely refers to kabbalistic issues in his talmudic commentaries. Cf. Judah Galinsky, "'Ve-Lihyot Lefanekha 'Eved Ne'eman kol ha-Yamim': Pereq be-Haguto ha-Datit shel R. Mosheh mi-Coucy," *Da'at* 42 (1999), 13–14.

[9] See Urbach, *Ba'alei ha-Tosafot*, 1:391–93, 412–13. Within Ashkenaz only the German Pietists were consistently committed to a level of allegorical interpretation as well. See Joseph Davis, "Philosophy, Dogma, and Exegesis in Medieval Ashkenazic Judaism: The Evidence of *Sefer Hadrat Qodesh*," *AJS Review* 18 (1993), 216–18. At the trial of the Talmud held at Paris in 1240, R. Yeḥi'el b. Joseph of Paris asserted that *'aggadah* does not have the same binding force as talmudic law (and need not be taken as literally), although the polemical pressure of the trial was undoubtedly a factor in his formulation. See Davis, 217, n. 80, and D. Berger, "Judaism and General Culture," 97–98. Israel Ta-Shma's interesting theory, that Nicholas Donin, prior to his apostasy, was part of a group that wished to rebel against the "'talmudism' of the Tosafists, in part by reading the written Torah allegorically," has not been sufficiently demonstrated. See Ta-Shma, "R. Yeḥiel de Paris: L'homme et l'oeuvre, religion et societe," *Annuaire des Ecole pratique des hautes etudes* 99 (1990–91), 215–19. The Jewish allegorists referred to by R. Yosef b. Isaac *Bekhor Shor* in his biblical commentary (Lev. 17:11 and Deut. 6:9, and cf. Nu. 12:8), and by R. Solomon Simḥah of Troyes (in his *Sefer ha-Maskil*), as noted by Ta-Shma, were in all likelihood from a Spanish or Sefardic milieu, with which *Bekhor Shor* (and Solomon Simḥah) were familiar. See below, nn. 19, 42, 45; my "Rabbinic Attitudes toward Non-Observance in the Medieval Period," in *Jewish Tradition and Nontraditional Jews*, ed. J. J. Schacter (Montvale, N.J., 1992), 3–35 (and esp. 10, n. 17); D. Berger, "Judaism and General Culture," 119 (n. 107); Judah Galinsky, "Mishpat ha-Talmud bi-Shenat 1240 be-Paris, ve-Sefer ha-Miẓvot shel R. Mosheh mi-Coucy," *Shenaton ha-Mishpat ha-'Ivri* 22 (2001–3), 45–48, 65–69; and cf. Martin Lockshin, *Rashbam's Commentary on Exodus* (Atlanta, 1997), 129 (n. 10).

[10] For example, Urbach, *Ba'alei ha-Tosafot*, 2:714 (n. 79), notes *Tosafot Bava Mezi'a* 58b, s.v. *ḥuz*, which presents a fairly systematic treatment of the order of the punishments that are meted out in *gehinnom*. For a similar treatment concerning the locale of *gan 'eden*, see *Tosafot Bava Batra* 84b, s.v. *be-zafra*; *Tosafot Bekhorot* 55b, s.v. *mitra*; and *Tosafot Qiddushin* 71b, s.v. *'ad*.

[11] Tosafists do occasionally yield fairly systematic glimpses into their actual beliefs. See, e.g., my "Medieval Rabbinic Conceptions of the Messianic Age: The View of the Tosafists," in *Me'ah She'arim: Studies in Medieval Jewish Spiritual Life in Memory of Isadore Twersky*, ed. Ezra Fleischer et al. (Jerusalem, 2001), 147–70. My methodological contention there is that by detecting

fewer than a handful of pages in his work to this issue further supports the sense that aggadic interpretation was not, in any event, a major scholarly activity or concern of the *Baʿalei ha-Tosafot.*[12]

Nonetheless, and despite the tendency in medieval Ashkenaz to understand talmudic *ʾaggadah* according to its literal or plain sense, uniformity of position among Tosafists with respect to anthropomorphism should not be presumed. Indeed, contrary to the impression given by the defenders of Maimonides, a number of Tosafists and rabbinic figures in both northern France and Germany plainly assert that the Divine form cannot be accurately characterized or properly defined by anthropomorphic terms or physical dimensions. To be sure, these rabbinic scholars had to contend with the various biblical and talmudic passages which suggest that God appeared in different modalities and forms to prophets and certain rabbinic figures. Although most people reading this book might not be inclined to attribute actual physical or human dimensions to God, the Bible and the Talmud certainly seem to suggest that God has the ability to appear to human beings in various guises or forms that they can apprehend. Like all other medieval rabbinic scholars who chose to confront this issue, those Tosafists who did so needed to balance their own intuitive sense of the unique nature of the Divine existence with the way that God's thoughts and actions are depicted in traditional Jewish texts.

R. Joseph b. Isaac *Bekhor Shor* of Orleans

In an effort to reconcile these disparate conceptions, R. Joseph b. Isaac *Bekhor Shor*, the late twelfth-century northern French *peshat* exegete and Tosafist (who studied with Rabbenu Tam, and is known in the literature of the *Tosafot* as R. Yosef of Orleans),[13] offers the following as the first of two interpretations to Genesis 1:26, "Let us make man in our image" (נעשה אדם בצלמנו כדמותנו): "Let us create man in such a way that through intimidation, he will rule and dominate all on earth, just as the Almighty and other heavenly beings dominate in their realms." *Bekhor Shor* then continues: "This

repetitive phrases and conceptions in different Tosafist genres and contexts that cannot be attributed purely to the resolution or interpretation of talmudic texts, it is possible to discover an authentic "personal position" within Tosafist thought. Tosafist materials on the messianic age contain characteristics and constructs that are diametrically opposed to those of Rambam (which is not surprising in and of itself). Highly significant, however, is the fact that these materials were presented by the Tosafists in an equally consistent and nuanced way.

[12] A comparison to the first edition of Urbach, *Baʿalei ha-Tosafot* (Jerusalem, 1956), 551–53, shows that little was added to or changed on this topic for the revised edition. See also Yonah Frenkel, *Darkhei ha-Aggadah veha-Midrash* (Givʿatayim, 1991), 2:512–23.

[13] See Urbach, *Baʿalei ha-Tosafot*, 1:132–40, and above, chapter 2.

[verse] does not mean that these [God and man] actually have a comparable physical image, for no physical conception or image can be attributed to the One above."

Bekhor Shor cites several biblical verses (in the Torah, and in Isaiah 40) that suggest that God cannot be described in physical terms or compared with physical beings. The biblical phrases that refer to the eyes or hands of God and so on are merely a convention devised to convey Divine actions to man (*le-sabber ʾet ha-ʾozen*), who comprehends intelligent existence and functions only in human terms. The vision reported by Ezekiel in which God appears to the prophet in human form is only so in the prophet's mind's eye. "For God and the heavenly entourage can make themselves appear in any form that they would like man to see." The same holds true for the various rabbinic figures as reported by the Talmud and other prophets to whom the Almighty or other heavenly figures appeared. Thus the comparison of forms in Genesis 1:26 is made only with respect to the ability to intimidate other beings, even though, in this case as well, the comparison is imprecise.[14]

One is tempted to suggest that R. Yosef *Bekhor Shor* of Orleans had access to Maimonides' *Mishneh Torah.* In *Hilkhot Yesodei ha-Torah* 1:8, Maimonides writes that Scripture explicitly indicates that God has no body or bodily form. Two of the three verses that Rambam cites to prove his contention are Deuteronomy 4:15 and Isaiah 40:25, the key prooftexts adduced by *Bekhor Shor.* In *Yesodei ha-Torah* 1:9, Maimonides goes on to explain, just as *Bekhor Shor* does, that the Torah's phrases that describe the various limbs and parts of God are meant only as illustrations, expressed in human terms that are the only ones which man can appreciate and understand (הכל לפי דעתן של בני אדם שאינם מכירין אלא הגופות), and are not meant to be taken literally. On the other hand, since Yosef of Orleans probably died before Maimonides' death in 1204, and the earliest citation of *Mishneh Torah* by French Tosafists does not occur before the turn of the twelfth century,[15] it is unlikely, and impossible to demonstrate, that Yosef derived his formulation from this work.[16]

[14] See *Perushei R. Yosef Bekhor ʿal ha-Torah*, ed. Yehoshafat Nevo (Jerusalem, 1994), 6: כי אין לתת דמיון ודמות ותמונה למעלה . . . אינו אלא לשבר את האוזן . . . שהקב"ה ופמליא של מעלה מדמין עצמן . . . בכל עניין שירצו להראות לאדם, and see also *Bekhor Shor*'s commentary to Numbers 23:22 (א-ל מוציאו ממצרים כתועפות ראם לו, ed. Nevo, 286): ואע"פ שראם כאין נגד הבורא, בן אדם אינו יכול לדמות משלו אלא במה שעיני בני אדם רואות כמו ה' . . . כאריה ישאג, ואריה אינו כלום [נגד הבורא]. Note the conceptual and literary similarities found in Torah comments by Rashi, cited below, n. 102.

[15] See Ephraim Kanarfogel and Moshe Sokolow, "Rashi ve-Rambam Nifgashim ba-Genizah he-Qahirit: Hafnayah ʾel Sefer 'Mishneh Torah' be-Kikhtav Eḥad mi-Baʿalei ha-Tosafot," *Tarbiz* 67 (1998), 411–16.

[16] The Tosafist exegetical comment to Genesis 1:26 (*Tosafot ha-Shalem*, ed. Jacob Gellis, vol. 1 [Jerusalem, 1982], 65–66), which Israel Ta-Shma had maintained (in his *Ha-Sifrut ha-Parshanit la-Talmud*, vol. 2 [Jerusalem, 2000], 106, n. 22) demonstrates *Bekhor Shor*'s use of *Mishneh Torah*,

To be sure, Yosef *Bekhor Shor* (as we have seen above in chapter 2) is known as one of the more "rationalistic" Tosafists and *peshat* exegetes.[17] He attempted, in a number of verses, to eliminate anthropomorphic references.[18] Yosef had access to works of Spanish biblical exegesis and thought, including those of Ibn Ḥayyuj, Abraham bar Ḥiyya, and Baḥya ibn Paquda, if not to the commentaries of Abraham ibn Ezra.[19] Nonetheless, *Bekhor Shor* does not express himself here in philosophical terms,[20] and cannot be characterized as anything more than a rationalistic rabbinic scholar who had to confront the vexing but obvious dilemma outlined above: How can God, who is essentially noncorporeal, appear to man in seemingly human form? *Bekhor Shor*'s solution appears similar to that of Rambam in *Mishneh Torah*, as noted, and in Maimonides' *Guide to the Perplexed* as well.[21] Good Tosafist that he was, however, *Bekhor Shor* was also concerned with identifying and explaining relevant talmudic sources, and he marshals them to support his claim that God appears to man in physical form only by way of some type of mental imagery (*medammeh/idmei*). The notion of a paranormal or psychologistic revelation, directed by God, through which a vision appears in the mind of the prophet without anything actually happening in the external world, is held also by R. Hai Gaon, R. Ḥanan'el b. Ḥushi'el of Kairwan,

is in fact an addendum or an interpolation made by *Sefer ha-Gan* (in ms. Nuremberg 5) to *Bekhor Shor*'s core comment on this verse; for this comment, see below, n. 78. *Sefer ha-Gan*, written by Aaron b. Yosef *ha-Kohen*, was completed circa 1240, when *Mishneh Torah* was already more widely available in northern France. For the heavy influence of *Bekhor Shor*'s commentary on *Sefer ha-Gan*, see *Sefer ha-Gan*, ed. Y. M. Orlian (Jerusalem, 2009), editor's introduction, 42–48. Orlian's edition (which does not contain this reference to Maimonides) is based on ms. Vienna Heb. 28 (Cat. Schwartz, 19/5); see the editor's introduction, 13, 107. This manuscript of *Sefer ha-Gan* cites *Mishneh Torah* (only) in a comment to Leviticus 21:4 (as does the parallel manuscript of *Sefer ha-Gan*, ms. Nuremberg 5). See *Sefer ha-Gan*, ed. Orlian, 283, and cf. *Tosafot ha-Shalem*, ed. Gellis, vol. 8 (Jerusalem, 1990), 119.

[17] See also my *"Peering through the Lattices,"* 160–61 (n. 69); 166–67 (n. 86), and my "Anthropomorphism and Rationalist Modes of Thought in Medieval Ashkenaz: The Case of R. Yosef Bekhor Shor," *Simon Dubnow Institute* 8 (2009), 119–38.

[18] See, e.g., S. A. Poznanski, *Mavo ʿal Hakhmei Ẓefon Ẓarefat Mefarshei ha-Miqra* (repr. Jerusalem, 1965), 66; and E. E. Urbach, *Baʿalei ha-Tosafot*, 1:134.

[19] See e.g., *Perushei R. Yosef Bekhor Shor ʿal ha-Torah*, ed. Y. Nevo, editor's introduction, 3; Moshe Idel, "Perush Mizmor Yod Tet bi-Tehillim le-Rav Yosef Bekhor Shor," *ʿAlei Sefer* 9 (1981), 63–69; Avraham Grossman, "Ha-Qesharim bein Yahadut Sefarad le-Yahadut Ashkenaz Bimei ha-Benayim," in *Moreshet Sefarad*, ed. Haim Beinart (Jerusalem, 1992), 176–77; idem, *Ḥakhmei Ẓarefat ha-Rishonim* (Jerusalem, 1995), 472–73; and cf. Abraham Lifshitz, "R. Avraham ibn Ezra be-Ferushei Baʿalei ha-Tosafot ʿal ha-Torah," *Hadarom* 28 (1968), 219–21, and above, chapter 2, nn. 51, 87. As Idel notes, however, *Bekhor Shor* also retained an interest in astrology that was hardly typical of Spanish rationalists.

[20] Cf. Galinsky (above, n. 8), 20–22.

[21] See *Moreh Nevukhim* 1:46, 2:44–45.

and R. Nathan b. Yeḥi'el of Rome (author of the *'Arukh*).[22] Clearly, the Tosafist R. Yosef (*Bekhor Shor*) of Orleans was an Ashkenazic rabbinic scholar who did not wish to attribute forms of corporeality or anthropomorphism to God.[23]

R. Moses Taku and R. Solomon Simḥah of Troyes

R. Moses b. Ḥisdai Taku, a German Tosafist writing (circa 1220) in his rather idiosyncratic treatise of Jewish thought titled *Ketav Tamim*,[24] describes the Almighty in terms that are, at first blush, strikingly similar to those of Yosef *Bekhor Shor.* Moreover, Taku's underlying concerns are the same as those of *Bekhor Shor.* Nonetheless, Taku reaches a conclusion that is decidedly different.[25]

Although R. Moses Taku begins, as *Bekhor Shor* did, with an assertion that God cannot be accurately characterized by or compared to any particular physical form (*lo yedammeh lo shum demut*), Taku goes on to suggest,

[22] See, e.g., Elliot Wolfson, *Through a Speculum That Shines*, 144–48; Y. Lorberbaum, *Ẓelem Elohim*, 29–30; and cf. below, nn. 52, 55. Wolfson characterizes what the prophets saw, according to this theory, as a mental image (*dimyon*). A text of R. Judah *he-Ḥasid* defines this conception of a prophetic vision as an *'aḥizat 'enayim* (illusion). See Joseph Dan, "Ashkenazi Hasidism and the Maimonidean Controversy," *Maimonidean Studies* 3 (1995), 38–39; idem, *'Iyyunim be-Sifrut Ḥasidei Ashkenaz* (Ramat Gan, 1975), 165; and cf. below, n. 53.

[23] The first northern French Tosafist and biblical exegete to deny Divine anthropomorphism was actually Rashbam; see below, nn. 76–77, and cf. M. Lockshin, "Ha-Im Yosef Bekhor Shor Hayah Pashtan?" in *Iggud* 1, ed. A. Melammed et al. (Jerusalem, 2008), 169–72. Since Ramban was aware of the Torah commentary of *Bekhor Shor* (see Hillel Novetzky, "The Influence of Rabbi Joseph Bekhor Shor and Radak on Ramban's Commentary on the Torah" [M.A. thesis, Yeshiva University, 1992], 6–33), *Bekhor Shor* is perhaps to be counted as part of the "minority position" among northern French rabbis to which Ramban alludes in his letter of 1232; see below, n. 101.

[24] On R. Moses as Tosafist and halakhist, see Urbach, *Ba'alei ha-Tosafot*, 1:420–23; Ta-Shma, *Sifrut ha-Parshanit la-Talmud Bimei ha-Benayim*, vol. 2 (Jerusalem, 2000), 116; idem, *Knesset Meḥqarim*, 1:232,236, 241, 244–45; S. Emanuel, *Shivrei Luḥot: Sefarim Avudim shel Ba'alei ha-Tosafot* (Jerusalem, 2007), 138 (n. 157), 222 (n. 18), 312, 315 (n. 34). See also J. N. Epstein, "R. Mosheh Taku b. Ḥisdai ve-Sifro Ketav Tamim," in his *Meḥqarim be-Sifrut ha-Talmud uvi-Leshonot Shemiyyot*, vol. 1 (Jerusalem, 1983), 294–302; my "The Development and Diffusion of Unanimous Agreement in Medieval Ashkenaz," in *Studies in Medieval Jewish History and Literature*, vol. 3, ed. I. Twersky and J. Harris (Cambridge, Mass., 2000), 29–31; above, Introduction, n. 22, and chapter 5, n. 186.(A condensed version of the key responsum by R. Moses on the issue of communal government discussed in my "The Development and Diffusion" appears in ms. JTS Rab. 1489 [Paris, 1390], in a marginal gloss to *Sefer Miẓvot Qatan* copied across the tops of fols. 228v–229r). See also ms. Bodl. 678, fols. 47r–v.

[25] *Ketav Tamim* (facsimile edition of ms. Paris H711, with an introduction by Joseph Dan [Jerusalem, 1984]), *53–55* (fols. 27a–28a): ולא ידמה לו שום דמות . . . וכשרצונו להראות עצמו למלאכים מראה עצמו בקומה זקופה . . . ופעמים מראה להם אור משונה בלא דמות . . . וכשרוצה הקב''ה לדבר עם נביא יוצא קול במקום שזורחת שכינתו.

against the view of *Bekhor Shor* and Maimonides,[26] that when God decides to show himself in a particular form to angels or to prophets, he actually adopts that form. He does not create a separate form, often referred to as the *kavod ha-nir'eh*, to represent Him, which is the view held by R. Saʿadyah Gaon and, with modification, by the leaders of the German Pietists, as we shall see. Moreover, while God sometimes adopts a well-defined form, in other instances He does not, appearing instead as "an unusual light without form,"[27] or even through a voice, without any visual imagery.[28] In addition, R. Moses asserts that God has the power of movement (נידה וניעה), an assessment that once again puts him at odds with both Maimonides and Saʿadyah, who believe that this possibility would compromise God's infinitude.[29]

In the course of this passage, then, R. Moses Taku rejects almost all other contemporary Jewish approaches toward eliminating or minimizing anthropomorphism, a contrarian approach taken throughout his *Ketav Tamim* for which R. Moses is well known by modern scholarship.[30] It must be pointed out and emphasized, however, that R. Moses himself does not believe that God is consistently or grossly anthropomorphic.[31] Rather, just

[26] Cf. M. M. Kasher, *Torah Shelemah*, vol. 16 (New York, 1955), 315–19. Because of the similarities in terminology between *Bekhor Shor* and Taku, Kasher posits that they share the same overall view (that God, despite the fact that He has no physical form per se, can choose different guises to adopt, including physical ones), against the view of Maimonides that God cannot have any corporeal characteristics whatsoever.

[27] Saʿadyah, in the second section (*ma'amar ha-yiḥud*) of his *Emunot ve-Deʿot* (Leipzig, 1859), 62, writes that the *kavod* sometimes appears as "a [great] light, and not in a human form." Shabbetai Donnolo, the tenth-century Byzantine scholar whose *Sefer Ḥakhmoni* was available (and cited) in medieval Ashkenaz, interprets the *demut ha-E-lohim* of Genesis 1:26 as "light that has no measure or [dimension] of greatness." According to Donnolo, however, the boundless light is to be identified with the invisible "upper glory," and is not the Divine manifestation that was revealed to created beings, prophetic or angelic. See E. Wolfson, *Through a Speculum That Shines*, 127–34.

[28] Texts from the Circle of the Special Cherub (*Ḥug ha-Keruv ha-Meyuḥad*) identify the revealed (or emanated) Divine glory as having "neither form nor image, only voice, spirit and speech." See Joseph Dan, "The Emergence of Mystical Prayer," in *Studies in Jewish Mysticism*, ed. Dan and Frank Talmage (Cambridge, Mass., 1982), 93–99. See also *Sefer ha-Maskil*, below, n. 42. Again, however, the reference here is to the Divine glory and not to a direct appearance of the Almighty Himself.

[29] For Rambam, see, e.g., *Perush ha-Mishnayyot le-Sanhedrin*, ch. 10, *yesod shelishi*; *MT Yesodei ha-Torah* 1:11; and *Moreh Nevukhim*, 1:54. For Saʿadyah, see his *Emunot ve-Deʿot*, ed. Yosef Kafih (Jerusalem, 1970), 108.

[30] See, e.g., Joseph Dan's introduction to the facsimile edition of *Ketav Tamim* (above, n. 25), 11–27, and the studies cited in the next note.

[31] Because of R. Moses's negative attitude toward *Shiʿur Qomah* (see the next note), Urbach, *Baʿalei ha-Tosafot*, 1:423–24, argues that Taku did not advocate a pronounced or extreme version of Divine anthropomorphism, as does D. J. Silver, *Maimonidean Criticism and the Maimonidean Controversy, 1180–1240* (Leiden, 1965), 138–40. Similarly, David Berger, "Judaism and General Culture in Medieval and Early Modern Times," 93, suggests that Taku "affirmed a moderate

as God has the ability or possibility of appearing in various forms, He has the ability to move in certain ways.

This observation explains the somewhat surprising fact that R. Moses, unlike several other Ashkenazic thinkers, including Eleazar of Worms and members of the *Ḥug ha-Keruv ha-Meyuḥad*, denies completely the authority of the highly anthropomorphic *Shiʿur Qomah*, even on a nonliteral or symbolic plane.[32] Some have understood this as a function of Taku's extreme respect for the canonized biblical and talmudic corpus, and his concomitant discounting of any conflicting rabbinic traditions or interpretations to be found outside of that corpus.[33]

Although this may be so (and we will see another example of this attitude below, in Taku's interpretation of Genesis 1:26), the more compelling ideological reason for Taku's view, to my mind, is based on the notion that God does not have a singular, permanent form that can be precisely traced or consistently described, as the work *Shiʿur Qomah* attempts to do. What God does have, according to Taku, is the possibility of adopting different forms as the situation warrants. As Israel Ta-Shma puts it, Taku's approach "does not reject the anti-anthropomorphic conception (*ha-tefisah ha-mufshetet*) of the Godhead, but rather sees it as one possibility, alongside His appearance in anthropomorphic form (*ha-hitgalut ha-magshimah*), which is also not exclusive but only one possibility. The Godhead can choose for itself the type of appearance that is most appropriate at a particular time and does not require the approval of the philosophers in order to adopt for itself the option of anthropomorphism, [which can be done by the Almighty] as warranted or desired."[34]

---

kind of anthropomorphism" (that was nonetheless corporeal by Maimonidean standards). Joseph Dan, "Ashkenazi Hasidism and the Maimonidean Controversy," 43, writes that Taku "most probably . . . did not believe in an anthropomorphic God." According to Joseph Davis, "Philosophy, Dogma, and Exegesis in Medieval Ashkenazic Judaism," 213, "to suppose that the Ashkenazic rabbis, even R. Moses Taku, the author of *Ketav Tamim* and the most vocal opponent of philosophy, held a corporealist view of God's nature is to credit him and them with a doctrinal or dogmatic approach to theology that they did not in fact take." On the other hand, Haim Hillel Ben-Sasson, in his review of Urbach's *Baʿalei ha-Tosafot* in *Beḥinot be-Biqqoret ha-Sifrut* 9 (1956), 51–52, characterizes Taku as an outright *magshim*, as do J. N. Epstein (above, n. 24, 298–99); B. Septimus, *Hispano-Jewish Culture in Transition* (Cambridge, Mass., 1982), 79; Gad Freudenthal in *Daʿat* 32–33 (1994), 193; and M. Saperstein, *Decoding the Rabbis*, 7–9.

[32] R. Moses expresses his opinion on *Shiʿur Qomah* in *Ketav Tamim*, 5 (fol. 3a). For the views of *Ḥasidei Ashkenaz* and the associated *Ḥug ha-Keruv ha-Meyuḥad* and their contemporaries, see, e.g., Alexander Altmann, "Moses Narboni's 'Epistle on *Shiʿur Qoma*,'" 225–39; Moshe Idel, "'Olam ha-Mal'akhim bi-Demut Adam," *Meḥqerei Yerushalayim be-Maḥshevet Yisra'el* 3 [1–2] (1984), 1–2, 8–11, 15–19; and Elliot Wolfson, *Through a Speculum That Shines*, 214–34.

[33] See E. E. Urbach, J. Dan, and J. Davis, above, n. 31.

[34] See Ta-Shma, *Ha-Sifrut ha-Parshanit la-Talmud*, vol. 2, 194, n. 8, and cf. J. Davis, "Philosophy, Dogma, and Exegesis in Medieval Ashkenazic Judaism," 213, and M. M. Kasher, *Torah Shelemah*, vol. 16, 319, 321. Ta-Shma implies, however, that this approach to anthropomorphism is virtually ubiquitous within Ashkenaz, an assessment that the present study argues should be qualified.

For this reason, in my view, R. Moses is equally unhappy with the more "permanent" solutions proposed by Saʿadyah (that God appears through the created *kavod*), R. Judah *he-Ḥasid* (that God appears through the emanated *kavod*), and Maimonides (that God appears to the prophet in a vision that is in the prophet's mind).[35] For R. Moses, God actually appears to the prophet in a particular form at a specific point and time, even though He has no fixed, permanent form that can be sketched or described. Indeed, R. Moses distinguishes elsewhere in *Ketav Tamim* between a *ẓelem*, which God has, and a fixed *demut*, which He does not have. *Ẓelem* for R. Moses denotes the fact that the Almighty exists in a way that can be recognized, as opposed to *demut*, which by itself conveys the notion of a fixed image, a characteristic that is not applicable to God.[36]

This distinction, which allows for the physical appearance of God at a particular moment in human history even though He has no fixed form, is found in Taku's interpretation of Genesis 1:26, where Taku presents additional examples of God's ability to appear in different forms.[37] R. Moses Taku, and a northern French predecessor, R. Jacob b. Samson,[38] whose view R. Moses cites approvingly in this passage, could certainly have been a target of the Maimunists' critique during the so-called Maimonidean controversy. Nonetheless, it should be noted that while R. Moses Taku was not completely atypical in his

[35] *Ketav Tamim*, 17–18 (fols. 9a–b). Cf. below, n. 53.

[36] Note that the distinction between these terms (carrying similar meanings) is also made by Maimonides in *Moreh Nevukhim* 1:1, in support of his diametrically opposed position with respect to anthropomorphism. Cf. Zev Harvey, "Qeẓad le-Hatḥil Lilmod ʾet Moreh ha-Nevukhim 1:1," *Daʿat* 21 (1988), 5–23; Yair Lorberbaum, "ʿAl Daʿatam shel Hakhamim z"l lo Altah ha-Hagshamah me-ʿOlam (Moreh ha-Nevukhim 1:46): Anthropomorphiyyut be-Sifrut Ḥazal—Seqirat Meḥqar Biqortit," *Maddaʿei ha-Yahadut* 40 (2000), 41–45; and idem, *Ẓelem E-lohım*, 33–34, 58–61, 70–73.

[37] *Ketav Tamim*, 7–11 (fols. 4a–6a, and cf. Kasher, *Torah Shelemah*, vol. 16, 310–11): ויראהו על הים כבחור . . . נלחם ובסיני כזקן מלא רחמים . . . וכן כשבא לברות עולם נראה דמות ובקומה שהרי בדיבור בראו . . . ואם תאמר בהקב"ה שכתוב בו והלא את השמים ואת הארץ אני מלא כיצד היה מתראה בצימצום קומת אדם. On the changeable forms assumed by the angels that Taku describes toward the end of this passage, see below, n. 56.

[38] On R. Jacob b. Solomon (1070–1140) and his commentary to *Avot*, see Grossman, *Ḥakhmei Ẓarefat ha-Rishonim*, 412–16. From this passage in *Ketav Tamim*, we learn that Jacob was a student of Rashi and a teacher of Rabbenu Tam in northern France. Grossman also sees this passage as proof of Jacob's authorship of the *Avot* commentary found in *Maḥzor Vitry*, because there is a parallel passage in that portion of *Maḥzor Vitry* (ed. S. Hurwitz, 514, cited by Grossman, 414, n. 215): כי בצלם א-להים עצמו עשאו המקום. ואית דלא גרסי הא כיון דאין לצור דמיון ולא תמונה [כי] מי שאומר כזה חיישינן שמא מין הוא. The *Maḥzor Vitry* passage continues: ואף כי בצלם אית דמתרגם ארי בצלמא ה' עבד ולא בצלמא דה'. ובעברי היקף [הזקף] גדול בצדיק (בצידו) של בצלם לפיס[ו]ק הטעם להבין פתרונו. On the variants of this passage (and their implications), see Kasher, *Torah Shelemah*, vol. 16, 310 (n. 3); and *ʿArugat ha-Bosem*, ed. Urbach, 4:79–80. On the authorship of the *Avot* commentary in *Maḥzor Vitry*, cf. I. Ta-Shma, "ʿAl Perush Avot shebe-Maḥzor Vitry," *Qiryat Sefer* 42 (1967), 507–8, and Urbach, 4:80, n. 50.

view, he does not represent a monolithic position within medieval Ashkenaz, as we shall continue to see in this discussion.[39] Moreover, Moses is not arguing for absolute Divine corporealism, nor does he believe that God can be fairly and accurately characterized in crude anthropomorphic terms. Indeed, if we are looking purely from the standpoint of methodology, the distance between Taku and *Bekhor Shor* is not all that great.[40]

R. Solomon Simḥah b. Eliezer of Troyes (c.1235–1300) was a descendant of Rashi, and a direct student of both R. Meir of Rothenburg and R. Pereẓ of Corbeil. He was also a self-described literary student of R. Judah *he-Ḥasid* and a prolific *payyetan*, although he was not a halakhic authority (or *rosh yeshivah*) of the rank of his teachers.[41] Displaying a keen interest in

[39] See J. Davis, "Philosophy, Dogma, and Exegesis in Medieval Ashkenazic Judaism," 212–13, n. 65 (citing M. Saperstein, who describes Taku as "anachronistic and isolated"), and J. Dan (with whom Davis fundamentally agrees), who argues that Taku was unexceptional (as does Ta-Shma, above, n. 34). Septimus (above, n. 31) writes that "it would perhaps be rash to assert that R. Moses was fully representative of mainstream Franco-German tradition." D. Berger (above, n. 31), 93, characterizes Taku as "not entirely a marginal figure" (although on p. 118 he calls *Ketav Tamim* an unusual work). Dan (in the introduction to the facsimile edition of *Ketav Tamim*, 8–11, and in "Ashkenazi Hasidism and the Maimonidean Controversy," 40–47) stresses that Taku's *Ketav Tamim* predates the Maimonidean controversy and reflects none of its actual struggles (even as Taku does argue strongly against the "heretical" views of Sa'adyah, Maimonides, Ibn Ezra, and the German Pietists), and that *Ketav Tamim* does not seem to have caused a stir within Ashkenaz. Urbach maintains (*'Arugat ha-Bosem*, 4:80), specifically with regard to anthropomorphism, that Taku saw himself as fighting against a "new heresy" within Ashkenaz that wished to label those who supported the "incumbent" position of anthropomorphism as heretics. Urbach bases his formulation on a passage in *Ketav Tamim* (facsimile ed., 61, = fol. 31a): כי זו הדת החדש וחכמתם מקרוב באו ויאמרו מה שראו הנביאים הם צורות הברואים. As we have seen, Taku himself insists that wherever the biblical corpus, as explicated by the rabbis of the talmudic period, indicates that God appeared, it was God Himself who appeared, rather than a figure that He created and dispatched, הבורא ולא הברואים.

[40] See above, n. 26. The extent to which Provençal anti-Maimunists (such as those in the circle of R. Solomon Montpellier) embraced a crude or simplistic form of anthropomorphism is also a matter of conjecture. See, e.g., Scholem, *Origins of the Kabbalah* (Princeton, 1987), 204–16, 404–8; Isadore Twersky, *Rabad of Posquieres* (Philadelphia, 1980), 282–86 (and the addendum on p. 358); B. Septimus, *Hispano-Jewish Culture in Transition*, 80–81 (and esp. n. 45); Berger, "Judaism and General Culture in Medieval and Early Modern Times, 94–95; D. J. Silver, *Maimonidean Criticism and the Maimonidean Controversy*, 156–63; and Moshe Halbertal, *Bein Torah le-Ḥokhmah* (Jerusalem, 2000), 114. Scholem, ibid., and Urbach (above, n. 31) attempt to correlate the events and positions in Ashkenaz during the Maimonidean controversy with the oft-cited gloss of Rabad on anthropomorphism (*Hilkhot Teshuvah*, 3:7). Cf. Z. Harvey, above, n. 36.

[41] See Israel Ta-Shma, "'Sefer ha-Maskil'—Ḥibbur Yehudi Ẓarefati Bilti-Yadu'a mi-Sof ha-Me'ah ha-Yod Gimmel," *Meḥqerei Yerushalayim be-Ereẓ Yisra'el* 2:3 (1983), 417–19; my "*Peering through the Lattices*," 239–40; and Susan Einbinder, *Beautiful Death: Jewish Poetry and Martyrdom in Medieval France* (Princeton, 2002), 126–48. R. Solomon Simḥah was interested in the powers and use of Divine names and mentions his teacher, R. Meir of Rothenburg, and R. Judah *he-Ḥasid* as the greatest authorities in this area. He displays clear familiarity with the *torat ha-kavod* of the German Pietists (as well as that of R. Sa'adyah Gaon), and with a form of the doctrine of the ether (referred to by Solomon as אויר מופלא ברוך הוא וברוך שמו) that was akin to

maintaining an anti-allegorical approach to Scripture, R. Solomon analyzes and addresses the dilemma of Divine anthropomorphism in his voluminous *Sefer ha-Maskil*, which remains largely unpublished. Solomon utilizes terms and texts found in both *Bekhor Shor* and Taku, but ultimately stakes out a unique and different position from either of these predecessors. In two places in his work, Solomon criticizes the view held by rabbinic scholars and philosophers that when the Torah asserts that God spoke, it is merely a *mashal*, since speech only emanates from a being that has a body. According to this view, God's words weren't heard at Sinai, but rather they were apprehended and understood by the intellects of Moses and the Jewish people. Solomon rejects this possibility, arguing that it is not the physical mouth that gives a human being the power of speech but rather the *ruaḥ*, the essential being or existence of the person. Similarly, God's existence gives Him the ability to speak (although the speech of God is obviously produced in a different manner than human speech is). Thus, even though God is incorporeal, He did actually speak to the Jewish people.[42]

---

versions of "*torat ha-ʾAvir*" found in the writings of these and other medieval Jewish thinkers, and in Stoic thought as well. See Gad Freudenthal, "Ha-Avir Barukh Hu u-Varukh Shemo be-Sefer ha-Maskil," *Daʿat* 32–33 (1994), 208–29, and idem, "Stoic Physics in the Writings of R. Saʿadyah Gaon al-Fayyumi and Its Aftermath in Medieval Jewish Mysticism," *Arabic Science and Philosophy* 6 (1996), 133–36. Although Solomon did not have access to Rambam's writings (see the next note), Freudenthal shows that he was aware of non-Ashkenazic sources such as Ibn Gabirol's *Keter Malkhut* and various Provençal philosophical writings (in addition to Saʿadyah's *Sefer Emunot ve-Deʿot* and Donnolo's *Sefer Ḥakhmoni*). Einbinder (*Beautiful Death*, 132) notes Solomon's awareness of Sefardic *piyyut*. Cf. above, chapter 5, nn. 291, 296, 305.

42 See the introductory section to *Sefer ha-Maskil*, ms. Moscow 508, fol. 1v (transcribed in Gad Freudenthal, "Ha-Avir Barukh Hu u-Varukh Shemo be-Sefer ha-Maskil," [part two] *Daʿat* 34 [1995], 87–88): . . . וראיתי דברי בני אדם אשר נקראו בשם גדולים חכמים ופילוסופים אשר יצאתה מהם שגגה באמרם ויאמר ה׳ וידבר ה׳ אין זה אלא משל שאין מאמר ודיבור יוצא אלא מפי מי שיש לו פה ובקב״ה אין לנו לומר שום גשמות וחיתוך איברים ודימו הדבר למשל ואמרו כי לא היה בזה רק דעה של משה ודעה של ישראל. ומי הוא אשר לא ימצא בזה עקירת הנפש מן האמונה השלימה . . . ועוד כי כבר ידענו שאין הפה מדבר ואין העין רואה. אבל הרוח כל זמן שהוא נתון בלב [האדם] רואה דרך עינים ומדבר דרך הפה. וכל זה גורם לו הרוח כי לאחר שמת האדם מי מעכבו מלדבר הלא יש לו פה. וכן בהמות וחיות ועופות יש להם פה מי מעכבן מלדבר אלא הרוח הוא שמגבר. Cf. Rashi's commentary to *Niddah* 31a, s.v. *marʾeh ha-ʿayin* (noted by Freudenthal, "Ha-Avir Barukh Hu u-Varukh Shemo be-Sefer ha-Maskil," *Daʿat* 32–33 [1994], 221, n. 120): שאע״פ שנבראת העין מן האב והאם אינו רואה [בלא שהקב״ה נותן לו רוח ונשמה וכו׳]. תדע שהרי המת יש לו עינים ויש לו שפתים ויש לו אזנים ואינו רואה ולא שומע ולא מדבר. On this section in *Sefer ha-Maskil*, see also Ta-Shma, "Sefer ha-Maskil," 420. Ta-Shma argues, correctly in my view, that those scholars who hold the position rejected by Solomon were Jewish thinkers (rather than non-Jewish philosophers). Indeed, Freudenthal, *Daʿat* 32–33,192–93, suggests that Solomon is critcizing the view of Rambam himself, although he also maintains that Solomon does not seem to have had *Mishneh Torah* in front of him. Rather, Solomon became aware of Rambam's views on anthropomorphism (as they appear in *Mishneh Torah*) from another Ashkenazic source that had this work (such as Abraham b. Azriʾel's *ʿArugat ha-Bosem*). Solomon certainly did not have a copy of *Moreh Nevukhim*. Cf. Freudenthal, ibid., 205, and see below, n. 106. A more detailed version of the passage just cited (which further supports the notion that R. Solomon Simḥah is arguing against learned Jewish allegorists) is found in *Sefer ha-Maskil* on fols. 48a–b. See Freudenthal, *Daʿat* 32–33, 195, and *Daʿat* 34, 121–22.

In another passage, Solomon chides those who go astray by presuming that God actually revealed Himself in the various physical forms and imageries that the Torah intimates and that the prophets describe. Rather, Solomon insists, God has no image or form (אין לה' יתברך גוף וצורה). Solomon cites the verses in Isaiah 40 to this effect, and he also notes that the biblical descriptions of various Divine limbs are simply to facilitate their understanding (לשבר את האוזן מה שהיא יכולה לשמוע). Moving forward, Solomon characterizes the physical forms that the prophets saw in their prophetic visions in a different way. What they saw was a temporary image (*demut she-hu lefi sha'ah*), which they understood through a lesser, not fully clear degree of prophecy (*'ispaqlaryah she-'einah me-'irah*). But again, Solomon insists, this vision was only temporary (*le-ẓorekh ha-sha'ah*), "for God does not have a standing, permanent form or shape."[43]

Gad Freudenthal notes that one of the verses cited by *Sefer ha-Maskil* is found in Rambam's treatment of anthropomorphism in *Hilkhot Yesodei ha-Torah* 1:8 (and both are found in Shabbetai Donnolo's treatment of Genesis 1:26, in his *Sefer Ḥakhmoni*).[44] More significant, however, both verses are also found in *Bekhor Shor*'s commentary to Genesis 1:26, as is the phrase "*le-sabber 'et ha-'ozen*."[45] The question here is whether Solomon's use of the concept of *demut le-fi ẓorekh ha-sha'ah* (even though, at the same time, *'ein lo demut 'omedet*) signifies that God actually adopted the temporary physical form (in line with the view of Moses Taku) or whether Solomon, in accordance with the view of *Bekhor Shor*, means that God has no real image or form (*demut 'omedet*) and that the temporary prophetic image he refers to is not a corporeal manifestation of God.

[43] Ms. Moscow 508, fol. 9r (Freudenthal, *Da'at*, 89): העיקר הוא להעשיר את עניי הדת אשר לבם פונה והולך אנה ואנה . . . וכבר ידענו כי אין להש"י דמות וצורה כמו שנ' אל מי תדמיוני ואשוה ואל מי תדמיון א-ל ומה מדות תעלנו לו כי אע"פ שנא' עיני ה' פני ה' ידי ה' . . . והארץ הדום רגליו, לשבר את האוזן מה שהיא יכולה לשמוע נכתב כי ודאי אין להקב"ה דמות וצורה עומד. ומה שנגלה ליחזקאל ולישעיה לא נגלה להם בדמות אמתית עומדת אלא בדמות לפי שעה ובאספקלריא שאינה מאירה היו רואים ולא היו יכולים לכוין להשיג אמיתת עצמותו והמראה ההיא לא היתה אלא לפי צורך השעה כי ודאי אין להקב"ה עצמותו והמראה ההיא לא היתה אלא לפי צורך השעה כי ודאי אין להקב"ה דמות וצורה עומדת. Phrases in this passage are reminiscent of formulations by Rabbenu Ḥanan'el in his talmudic commentary. See E. Wolfson, *Through a Speculum That Shines*, 147–48, and above, n. 22. See also the introductory section of *Sefer ha-Maskil*, cited by Ta-Shma, "Sefer ha-Maskil," (above, n. 41), 420–21: עוד נפלאו כי עמדו הנביאים ואמר אחד מהם ראיתי את ה' יושב על כסאו וכל צבא השמים עומדים עליו מימינו ומשמאלו אם כן נראה כמייחס להם גבול שיש לו ימין ושמאל וכן נאמר ביחזקאל . . . וכל העם יוד־עים כי אין לו חקר וקצבה ברוך הוא; and ms. Moscow 508, fol. 12a (Freudenthal, *Da'at* 34, 90): לא תוכל לראות את פני אינו רוצה לומר פנים ממש כי הכל יודעים שאין להקב"ה דמות פנים אלא כך אמר לו וכו'.

[44] See Freudenthal in *Da'at* 32–33 (1994), 195(n. 19), and above, n. 27.

[45] Freudenthal, *Da'at* 32–33, 193–94 (n. 15a), also notes that the phrase used by R. Solomon Simḥah has parallels in *Mishneh Torah*, Sa'adyah's *Emunot ve-De'ot*, and works of R. Eleazar of Worms (including his *Sefer Roqeaḥ*). In this instance, however, there are also parallels to the passage by R. Yosef *Bekhor Shor* (see above, n. 14), and in Moses Taku's *Ketav Tamim* (above, n. 39). See also below, n. 102.

Freudenthal holds that, as opposed to Taku, Solomon was not a *magshim* even though Solomon, like Taku, was strongly against allegorical interpretation.[46] Indeed, Freudenthal demonstrates that *Sefer ha-Maskil* also developed a unique approach in angelology which informs his view. According to Solomon, there are three classes of angels who do the will of the Almighty. The "permanent" or "existing" ones (*mal'akhim kayamim*) are those such as Mikha'el, Refa'el, and Gavri'el. The second and third classes are called the "temporary angels" (*mal'akhim le-sha'ah*) and the "separate air" (*ruaḥ nifrad*), respectively. The temporary angels are appointed for a particular mission or activity. When their mission is completed, they are consumed by fire. This type of angel is also described as "a separate air from the secret source, from the mysterious Divine air, blessed be He" (*ruaḥ ha-mufla barukh Hu*). Similarly, the members of the third class (the *ruaḥ nifrad*) were also mobilized specially in order to do His bidding but, following their missions, they are returned to their place. As opposed to the "permanent angels," the latter two classes of angels are derived from the essence of the Almighty (*ruaḥ ha-'iqqar*). While the "permanent" angels have set responsibilities, the latter two groups do not, serving in limited capacities and particular one-time situations.[47]

Most important for our purposes, however, is Solomon's view that the Divine essence (*ha-E-l ha-'iqqar*, which in Solomon's cosmological scheme is to be identified with the cosmic Air that fills the entire world, *ha-E-l ha-'avir/ha-'avir ha-mufla*)[48] can be manifested through various physical forms. The different "separate airs," each of which has a unique and finite mission, do not compromise Divine corporeality on the one hand, but are responsible, on the other hand, for the many forms through which the Almighty reveals Himself to the prophets and to others.[49] It is these groups of angels who are responsible for the "temporary manifestations" (*demut she-hu lefi sha'ah*) of God that appeared to the prophets as needed (*le-ẓorekh ha-sha'ah*), but who then receded. As Solomon concludes, all of these various representations of God are angelic, and they are therefore not permanent.

Although Solomon's solution to the problem of anthropomorphism in situations where God appeared to prophets and others seems to be closer empirically to the approach of Yosef *Bekhor Shor* than to the position of Moses Taku, there is one additional factor that must be considered. The identification made by Solomon between God and the cosmic Air is itself

[46] See Freudenthal, *Da'at* 32–33 (1994), 193.

[47] See ms. Moscow 508, fol. 9v (Freudenthal, *Da'at* 34 [1995], 89–90).

[48] Freudenthal, *Da'at* 32–33 (1994), 189–92. See also Ta-Shma, "Sefer ha-Maskil," 429: האויר המופלא ברוך הוא וברוך שמו הוא הקב"ה והוא הממלא את הכל ונמצא בכל.

[49] See Freudenthal, *Da'at* 32–33 (1994), 196.

at least partly anthropomorphic. Saʿadyah's comparisons between God and the *ʾavir* that fills the entire world, found especially in his commentary to *Sefer Yezirah*, were figurative and were meant only as metaphor. Solomon invested this comparison with real, physical properties—the substance of God is to be found in the air and in the light above the firmament—moving him closer overall to the position of Taku, and perhaps even beyond.[50]

The German Pietists and Related Mystical Circles in Ashkenaz

There were, however, a number of other leading scholars in northern France and Germany during the twelfth and thirteenth centuries whose views are more closely in line with the position of *Bekhor Shor*. *Ḥasidei Ashkenaz*, whose leadership also practiced a method of biblical interpretation that was not far from the *peshat* approach of *Bekhor Shor*, as we have seen in earlier chapters, were quite interested in eliminating anthropomorphism by distinguishing between the hidden essence of God and the Divine glory (*kavod*) that was created or emanated (and therefore distinct) from God. Beginning with R. Judah *he-Ḥasid*, and employing the ideas of Saʿadyah Gaon[51] and other early medieval rabbinic figures such as R. Nathan b. Yeḥiʾel, R. Ḥananʾel b. Ḥushiʾel, R. Shabbetai Donnolo, and also R. Abraham ibn Ezra (and, to a lesser extent, Abraham bar Ḥiyya), the Pietists were thus able to explicitly and repeatedly reject anthropomorphism, and to assert that God has no material or representable form.[52]

In a treatise attributed to R. Judah *he-Ḥasid*, three approaches are presented regarding which manifestation of God the prophets saw: (1) they saw the created Glory (following R. Saʿadyah Gaon); (2) they saw a vision in their own minds, directed by God, but which never actually occurred (*ʾaḥizat ʿenayim*; this position is held by R. Hai and by Rambam); (3) they saw an emanated Divine power, the Divine glory (*kavod*). The upper aspect of this emanation cannot be seen, but the lower aspect is the subject of prophetic vision. This is the position that R. Judah *he-Ḥasid* preferred, although

[50] See Ta-Shma, "Sefer ha-Maskil," 427–31; D. Berger, "Judaism and General Culture in Medieval and Early Modern Times," 95; and cf. above, n. 41.

[51] On the availability of a Hebrew paraphrase of Saʿadyah's *Emunot ve-Deʿot* in medieval Ashkenaz, see, e.g., Ronald Kiener, "The Hebrew Paraphrase of Saʿadiah Gaon's *Kitab ʿal Amanat waʾl-Iʿtiqadat*," *AJS Review* 11 (1986), 1–25, and cf. my "*Peering through the Lattices*," 219, n. 68.

[52] See, e.g., Gershom Scholem, *Major Trends in Jewish Mysticism* (New York, 1941), 110–16; J. Dan, *Torat ha-Sod shel Ḥasidut Ashkenaz*, 104–16, 129–30; E. Wolfson, *Through a Speculum That Shines*, 134, n. 30, 193–94, 214–15; and Daniel Abrams, "Ha-Shekhinah ha-Mitpalelet Lifnei ha-Qadosh Barukh Hu—Maqor Ḥadash li-Tefisah Teʾosofit ʾeẓel Ḥasidei Ashkenaz," *Tarbiz* 63 (1994), 510–11.

he was not unalterably opposed to the others. Judah's preferred position follows the approach of Abraham ibn Ezra.[53]

The phrase אין שייך בו [לבורא] לא צלם ולא דמות and its variants are found repeatedly in the treatise titled *Sha'arei ha-Sod veha-Yiḥud veha-Emunah*, composed by Judah's leading pupil, R. Eleazar of Worms. Eleazar also decries those who insisted on radical anthropomorphism by attributing various limbs to the Almighty (אין לבורא לא גוף וגושם / אין לו מידת הגושמ[נים] / אין לדמותו לבריותיו), categorizing them as grave sinners (חוטאים בנפשם). Biblical phrases that describe God's actions in anthropomorphic terms were formulated only so that human beings would be able to grasp their meaning (ומה שנאמר מילות בקרייה עינינים גושמנים לא נכתבו כי אם להבין לבני אדם).[54] R. Eleazar mentions those earlier rabbinic authorities (including Sa'adyah Gaon, Rabbenu Ḥanan'el, R. Nissim Gaon, and R. Nathan b. Yeḥi'el) who agreed that God has no physical image or form. Like R. Judah *he-Ḥasid*, R. Eleazar is fundamentally comfortable with their views, even as he, like R. Judah, advocates the model of the emanated (or revealed) *kavod*, which appeared to the prophets in various forms (including human ones) as needed (כפי צורך [ה]שעה).[55]

In this same treatise, R. Eleazar also offers a related interpretation of Genesis 1:26–27 which blunts the possible anthropomorphic reference suggested by these verses. According to Eleazar, these verses do not imply that the Creator has the form or image of His creations. Rather, the meaning of making man "in our image" is that "we [= the angels, who are implied in the plural form of the verse] wish to be revealed to the prophets in the most desirable countenance, which is the human face." Thus man was created in the cherished humanlike countenance or image of the angels, which is the image that God shows to the prophets.[56]

[53] See J. Dan, *'Iyyunim be-Sifrut Ḥasidei Ashkenaz*, 165–73, and idem, "Ashkenazi Hasidism and the Maimonidean Controversy," 38–39. As Dan notes in the latter study (42–43), R. Moses Taku was aware of this treatise, referring to it as *Sefer ha-Kavod*. See also above, n. 35.

[54] See Joseph Dan, "Sefer 'Sha'arei ha-Sod ha-Yiḥud veha-Emunah' le-R. Eleazar mi-Worms," *Temirin* 1 (1972), 141–56; Gad Freudenthal (above, n. 45); and *'Arugat ha-Bosem*, ed. Urbach, 4:74.

[55] Dan, "Sefer 'Sha'arei ha-Sod ha-Yiḥud veha-Emunah' le-R. Eleazar mi-Worms," esp. 146–47, 151. Cf. D. Abrams, "'Sod Kol ha-Sodot': Tefisat ha-Kavod ve-Kavvanat ha-Tefillah be-Kitvei R. Eleazar mi-Worms," *Da'at* 34 (1995), 61–72, and idem, "From Divine Shape to Angelic Being: The Career of Akatriel in Jewish Literature," *The Journal of Religion* 76 (1996), 50–55. It is important to note that *Bekhor Shor*, Moses Taku, and the author of *Sefer ha-Maskil*, like the German Pietists, were all very much aware of the various approaches to anthropomorphism held by Spanish (Sefardic) rationalists. See above, nn. 33, 41, 49, 55, and see J. Dan, "Ashkenazi Hasidism and the Maimonidean Controversy," 34–38. The awareness of these materials is perhaps one of the elements that distinguishes these rabbinic figures (including Moses Taku) from those Ashkenazic Jews who may have been simple *magshimim*.

[56] Dan, "Sefer 'Sha'arei ha-Sod ha-Yiḥud,'" 146: ... ומה שכתב ויאמר א-להים נעשה אדם בצלמנו כדמותינו ויברא את האדם בצלמו בצלם א-להים ברא אותו ... כי בצלם א-להים עשה את האדם. לא שיש לבורא ית' דמות וצלם

Ramban, in his letter of 1232 to the *rabbanei Ẓarefat* during the so-called Maimonidean controversy, cites extensively from this treatise by R. Eleazar of Worms in an effort to show that the view of a leading Ashkenazic scholar, and a sometime-Tosafist as well, is compatible or consonant with that of Maimonides.[57] He also notes that this work of R. Eleazar was readily available to the rabbis of northern France.[58]

In his commentary to *Sefer Yeẓirah*, Eleazar states unequivocally that God has no bodily image and cannot be seen. Nonetheless, God "appears to the prophets by means of the presence of His glory through many images (נראה לנביאים על ידי שכינת כבודו בדמיונות הרבה), according to His desire and will." The prophets, according to Eleazar, did not simply see a figurative image of God in their minds. Rather, the Divine glory assumed a concrete shape or form in the mind of the one seeing the vision.[59]

It must be noted, however, as this last example intimates, that the German Pietists also had to deal with earlier esoteric materials that tended to support anthropomorphic descriptions. Within their more exoteric writings (such as the treatise of R. Eleazar of Worms cited by Naḥmanides, which

---

בריותיו אלא פיר' בצלמינו שאנו חפיצים להראות לנביאים בפרצוף אדם החמוד הוא מפני אדם צלם המיוחד לנו דמות דמיון הנראה לנו מכובד ויקר זה בצלמו המכובד בעיניו בצלם מלאכים נראים בו שהוא יקר. E. Wolfson, *Through a Speculum That Shines*, 210–11, also records another instance of this interpretation in Eleazar's writings. He notes (n. 89) that Eleazar follows the interpretation of Ibn Ezra to Genesis 1:26 ("the expression 'in God's image' refers to an angel"). This is the interpretation of Rashbam as well; see below, n. 76. (Wolfson mentions the view of the German Pietists [and others] implied in their interpretation of Genesis 1:26—and against the philosophical view of Maimonides—that the angels, like man, are composed of both matter and form. Cf. Moses Taku (above, n. 37); *Tosafot Bava Meẓi'a* 85b, s.v. *nir'in ke-'okhlin*; *Perushei R. Yosef Bekhor Shor 'al ha-Torah* to Genesis 18:1 (ed. Nevo, 30); *Tosafot ha-Shalem*, ed. Gellis, vol. 2 (Jerusalem, 1983), 110. Not surprisingly, Rashbam and *Bekhor Shor* (and *Sefer ha-Gan*; see below, at n. 80) are closer to the Maimonidean view, but without the philosophical dimension. Cf. below, n. 77.]

[57] *Kitvei ha-Ramban*, ed. C. D. Chavel (Jerusalem, 1968), 1:346–47: כי אין קץ ותכלית לכל אשר יש בו ואין לו גבול ולא איברים לבורא העולמים . . . וכתבו שאין דמות וגשם לבורא וקללו המאמין בזה . . . לא יהיה כוונתם בדבר הנראה לעין מלאכים או לעין נביאים לקרותו א-ל כי אם ביוצר הכל אשר אין לו דמות ואין לו קץ. On Ramban's contention that the teachings of Eleazar of Worms with respect to anthropomorphism are fully consonant with those of Maimonides, cf. Dan, "Ashkenazi Hasidism and the Maimonidean Controversy," 31. On R. Eleazar's activities as a Tosafist and halakhist, see, e.g., Urbach, *Ba'alei ha-Tosafot*, 1:392–408, and Simcha Emanuel, "Ḥibburav ha-Hilkhatiyyim shel R. Eleazar mi-Vermaiza," *Te'udah* 16–17 (2001), 203–54.

[58] *Kitvei ha-Ramban*, 1:348 (ידעתי כי הספר ההוא מצוי אצלכם). On the diffusion of this work, see Urbach, "Ḥelqam shel Ḥakhmei Ashkenaz ve-Ẓarefat ba-Polmos 'al ha-Rambam ve-'al Sefarav," *Zion* 12 (1947), 151; idem, *Ba'alei ha-Tosafot*, 1:408–9; and my *"Peering through the Lattices,"* 19–20. On the understanding and use of *Shi'ur Qomah* by *Ḥasidei Ashkenaz* as referring to the *kavod ha-nir'eh* (in a manner similar to that of R. Sa'adyah Gaon), see above, n. 32.

[59] See *Perush Sefer Yeẓirah le-R. Eleazar mi-Worms*, cited and analyzed in Wolfson, *Through a Speculum That Shines*, 207–8. *Dimyon(ot)* in this context denotes that the invisible is made visible. Cf. Moshe Idel, "Le-Gilgulehah shel Tekhniqah Qedumah shel Ḥazon Nevu'i Bimei ha-Benayim," *Sinai* 86 (1980), 1–3.

was part of the so-called *sifrut ha-Yiḥud*),[60] the Pietists were able to firmly maintain their commitment to eliminating anthropomorphism. In their esoteric writings, however, the Pietists developed strongly mythical formulations in accordance with the symbolism of the earlier esoteric material. Thus, anthropomorphic speculations can be found in the esoteric writings of Eleazar of Worms and others, especially with respect to the prophetic and visionary experiences that were cultivated and achieved in connection with pronouncing and understanding certain Divine names. Anthropomorphic beliefs can also perhaps be found within the intentions of prayer (*kavvanot ha-tefillah*) of a related mystical circle, the *Ḥug ha-Keruv ha-Meyuḥad.* All of these various mystical practices and experiences were, however, highly private and deeply secret, and were taught and shared only in limited ways.[61]

In the same vein, a leading member of the *Ḥug ha-Keruv ha-Meyuḥad*, R. Elḥanan b. Yaqar, included in his mystical treatise on creation and cosmology, *Sod ha-Sodot*, one formulation concerning the way God appeared to the prophets that is markedly different from his other treatments of this subject, even those within the same work. Although Elḥanan does not mention R. Moses Taku or his *Ketav Tamim* by name, the more radical formulation of R. Elḥanan contains several close similarities and parallels to anthropomorphic passages in *Ketav Tamim.*[62]

[60] See J. Dan, "'Sifrut ha-Yiḥud' shel Ḥasidei Ashkenaz," *Qiryat Sefer* 41 (1966), 533–44; idem, *Torat ha-Sod shel Ḥasidut Ashkenaz*, 164–68.

[61] See Elliot Wolfson, *Through a Speculum That Shines*, 192–95, 234–69; Moshe Idel, "Gazing at the Head in Ashkenazi Hasidism," *Journal of Jewish Thought and Philosophy* 6 (1997), 280–94; Arthur Green, *Keter* (Princeton, 1997), 106–20; Joseph Dan, "Ashkenazi Hasidism and the Maimonidean Controversy," 31–32; idem, *Torat ha-Sod shel Ḥasidut Ashkenaz*, 156–64; idem, "*Pesaq ha-Yirah veha-Emunah* and the Intention of Prayer in Ashkenazi Esotericism," *Frankfurter Judaistische Beitrage* 19 (1991–92), 185–215; although cf. D. Abrams, "The Evolution of the Intention of Prayer to the 'Special Cherub,'" *Frankfurter Judaistische Beitrage* 22 (1995), 1–14. Ramban also appears to be anti-anthropomorphic in his letter to the *rabbanei Ẓarefat* (and in several passages in his biblical commentary; see, e.g., Bernard Septimus, "'Open Rebuke and Concealed Love': Naḥmanides and the Andalusian Tradition," in *R. Moses Naḥmanides (Ramban): Explorations in His Religious and Literary Virtuosity*, ed. Isadore Twersky [Cambridge, Mass., 1983], 24–29, and esp. n. 45). In certain kabbalistic contexts, however, his stance becomes more complex as well, and he becomes more supportive of an anthropomorphic orientation. See Yair Lorberbaum, "Qabbalat ha-Ramban ʿal Beriʾat ha-Adam be-Ẓelem E-lohim," *Kabbalah* 5 (2000), 287–326.

[62] See J. Dan, "Seridei Polmos ʿal Torat ha-E-lohut be-Sefer 'Sod ha-Sodot' le-R. Elḥanan b. Yaqar mi-London," *Tarbiz* 61 (1992), 249–71. The passage under discussion was published by Dan, 265–67 (from ms. JTS 8118, fols. 53a–b): על דברת בני אדם האומרים כי שכינה בכל מקום פתרון דבריהם בכל מקום טהור שרצונו לזרוח שם שכינתו. כי השמש בשמים זורח בכל מקום נקלה ונכבד ועל בתי האלילים ועל מקומות מטונפים בכל. הבורא יתברך שמו אינו כן כי זריחתו בכל מקום אשר יבחר כי אינו נראה במקדש העליון בזריחתו בכל עת כי אם בעת הצורך . . . ומראיו מתהפכים ברצונו לענינים רבים כאשר קבלו מפי רבותינו ע"ה. See Dan's analysis, esp. 267, 270–71, and cf. above, nn. 25, 37. On R. Elḥanan b. Yaqar, see also my "*Peering through the Lattices*," 191–92.

In commenting on a *piyyut* that refers to the Divine *kavod*, R. Eleazar of Worms's Pietist student, R. Abraham b. Azri'el of Bohemia (a leading commentator on *piyyutim* who composed his *'Arugat ha-Bosem* c. 1234 and was also a student of the German Tosafist R. Simḥah of Speyer),[63] reviews and briefly describes the theories that were known to him with respect to the forms through which God revealed himself to man.[64] Abraham b. Azri'el begins by stating that God never revealed His essence, about which one cannot make comparisons or offer formulations. The talmudic passages in the first chapter of tractate *Berakhot* which refer to God putting on *tefillin* and the like speak about the manifest form of God, the *Shekhinah* (= the *kavod*). Indeed, one Gaon (= R. Hai) understands the talmudic passages in *Berakhot* to mean that God showed the *kavod* to His prophets and adherents (and indeed to Moses), and they perceived it through an understanding of the heart (*'ovanta de-libba*). That is, they received a mental image of a seated person (or any other vision that was meant to represent God) but did not see it with their eyes (*lo re'iyyah be-'ayin*). R. Abraham relates (with approval) the approach of this Gaon to the manner in which God appeared to Moses following the sin of the golden calf, and also mentions the similar approach of his teacher R. Eleazar of Worms, and of R. Neḥemyah b. Solomon.[65]

Abraham next presents the view of Maimonides on this issue, as it is found in *Hilkhot Yesodei ha-Torah*, 1:8–9. God cannot possibly have any anthropomorphic form. The anthropomorphic phrases found in the Torah are written in this way only so that human beings can have a proper understanding of God's functions and powers. A proof for this approach is that one prophet saw a vision of God dressed in pristine clothing, another prophet saw God in soiled clothes, Moses saw God at the crossing of the Red Sea as a fighting warrior, and God appeared at Sinai as a prayer leader wrapped in a *tallit.* All of these diverse visions show that God has no physical image or form, only the nonphysical manifestations that are seen in prophetic visions.

R. Abraham turns next to Sa'adyah Gaon. Sa'adyah stresses that the Divine form that appears to the prophets, the form that speaks to them

[63] On R. Simḥah and his students, see, e.g., A. Aptowitzer, *Mavo la-Rabiah* (Jerusalem, 1938), 412–14; Urbach, *Ba'alei ha-Tosafot*, 1:411–20; I. Ta-Shma, *Creativity and Tradition* (Cambridge, Mass., 2006), 70–79; S. Emanuel, *Shivrei Luḥot*, 154–58; above, Introduction, n. 79; and in chapter 1, nn. 19–22.

[64] See *'Arugat ha-Bosem*, ed. E. E. Urbach, vol. 1 (Jerusalem, 1939), 197–201.

[65] See Urbach, "Sefer 'Arugat ha-Bosem le-R. Avraham b. Azri'el," *Tarbiz* 10 (1939), 50–51, and M. Idel, "R. Neḥemiah ben Shlomo the Prophet of Erfurt's Commentary on the Piyyut *E-l Na le-'Olam Tu'araz*," [Hebrew] in *Moreshet Yisra'el*, ed. O. Bartana, vol. 2 (2005), 5–41; idem, "From Italy to Ashkenaz and Back: On the Circulation of Jewish Mystical Traditions," *Kabbalah* 14 (2006), 77–80.

and that sits on the throne and so on, is a created, distinct form (*ha-ẓurah beru'ah hi ve-ḥadashah*). This created, luminous form is the Divine *kavod*, also known as the *Shekhinah*. At times, the light of the *Shekhinah* shines without embracing any image or form, and the Divine voice is heard from the luminous form. Abraham then distinguishes among the ways Moses and other prophets heard this voice. He then cites R. Ḥanan'el b. Ḥushi'el who held (like R. Hai) that prophetic visions were mental images (*'avna de-libba*) and not actual ones, since God has no real, physical form. Rabbenu Nissim Gaon and Shabbetai (Donnolo) *ha-Rofe* also held this view. Moving to a related issue, R. Abraham describes a tradition of his teacher R. Judah *he-Ḥasid* on the way that Moses more clearly perceived the *kavod* (*be-'ispaqlarya ha-me'irah*) than did all other prophets (*be-'ispaqlarya she-'einah me'irah*), and he also cites a passage from Rabbenu Ḥanan'el on this issue.

Finally, R. Abraham cites a passage from Moses of Taku's *Ketav Tamim* on the same subject. As Urbach notes,[66] this passage is not found in the version of *Ketav Tamim* that is extant, a development that is not particularly troubling since we know that there are (large) sections of the original work that have not survived.[67] More suggestive, however, is the fact that R. Abraham, who cites *Ketav Tamim* with some frequency in his work and without any fanfare, omits R. Moses's anthropomorphic approach to the appearance of God in prophetic visions.[68] R. Abraham chose not to present this approach in his survey which, in accordance with the somewhat eclectic style of his Pietist teachers in this matter, is otherwise quite thorough and complete. Indeed, Abraham had no difficulty including the rationalistic position of Maimonides.[69]

As noted in the previous chapter, R. Isaac b. Moses, author of the Tosafist compendium *Sefer Or Zaru'a*, was a student of Rabiah, R. Simḥah of Speyer, R. Judah Sirleon of Paris, and R. Samson of Coucy, among other Tosafists in northern France and Germany. He also studied with R. Judah *he-Ḥasid* and with others associated with the German Pietists, including R. Eleazar of Worms and R. Abraham b. Azri'el of Bohemia.[70] In the course of his halakhic commentary to tractate *Berakhot*, R. Isaac cites at length the explanation and approach of Rabbenu Ḥanan'el, which was mentioned

66 *'Arugat ha-Bosem*, ed. Urbach, 1:201, n. 8.

67 See, also, e.g., J. Dan's introduction to the facsimile edition of *Ketav Tamim* (above, n. 25), 7; and I. Ta-Shma, *Knesset Meḥqarim*, 1:134, 148 (n. 23), 229 (n. 16).

68 See Urbach, "Sefer 'Arugat ha-Bosem," 47–49; Dan, "Ashkenazi Hasidism and the Maimonidean Controversy," 46–47.

69 Cf. Urbach, "Sefer 'Arugat ha-Bosem," 49–50.

70 See Urbach, *Ba'alei ha-Tosafot*, 1:436–39; *'Arugat ha-Bosem*, ed. Urbach, 4:112, 119–20, 126–27; and cf. my *"Peering through the Lattices,"* 111–13.

briefly by R. Abraham in his *'Arugat ha-Bosem*, to two talmudic passages that seemingly attribute physical forms to God. In light of the fact that God does not project an actual physical image (according to the verses in Isaiah and so on), R. Ḥanan'el interprets the claim that the Almighty wears phylacteries in accordance with the concept that God provides a mental or psychological image of Himself (as represented by the lower *kavod*) to the prophets (בראיית הלב ולא בראיית העין). Similarly, when the Talmud maintains that God prays, the reference is to a mental image of God (ראיית הלב), represented by the *kavod.* R. Isaac also ratifies the view of R. Ḥanan'el that the figure of Akatri'el, who appeared to R. Yishma'el the High Priest in the Holy of Holies, was a manifestation of the *kavod* (seen by R. Yishma'el in his mind's eye), and was not merely an angelic figure.[71]

Tosafist Torah Commentaries

R. Isaac b. Judah *ha-Levi*, the northern French compiler of the Tosafist biblical commentary *Pa'aneaḥ Raza*, which appeared in the late thirteenth century, was strongly influenced by the Torah commentary of R. Yosef *Bekhor Shor*, and he also included much exegetical (and pietistic) material from the German Pietists.[72] According to one of the comments to Genesis 1:26 found in *Pa'aneaḥ Raza*, God's intention to create man in "our image" refers to the image of the angels (who have a human form). God appears to the

[71] *Sefer Or Zaru'a*, vol. 1, *hilkhot qeri'at shema*, secs. 7–8. Cf. I. Ta-Shma, *Ha-Sifrut ha-Parshanit la-Talmud*, vol. 2, 191–92. Moritz Gudemann, *Ha-Torah veha-Ḥayyim*, vol. 1 (Warsaw, 1897), 56, n. 4, notes this material from *Sefer Or Zaru'a* as part of the evidence for his larger contention that no leading Ashkenazic rabbinic figures supported any form of anthropomorphism. A less elaborate version of the interpretation of Rabbenu Ḥanan'el, as recorded by R. Isaac b. Moses *Or Zaru'a* in sec. 7, is found already in the commentary of the mid-twelfth-century German Tosafist R. Eliezer b. Nathan (*Sefer Raban* [repr. Jerusalem, 1975], *massekhet Berakhot*, sec. 126). The material in sec. 8 on R. Yishma'el and the identity of Akatri'el is found in the *Seder Tanna'im va-Amora'im* by R. Isaac b. Moses's German predecessor, R. Judah b. Qalonymus (Rivaq) of Speyer (d.c. 1200); see Urbach, *Ba'alei ha-Tosafot*, 1:376–77. Like R. Isaac *Or Zaru'a*, Rivaq offers talmudic proofs for R. Ḥanan'el's claim that Akatri'el represents the *kavod* (and is not an angel), although Isaac's proofs are somewhat different. Cf. my *"Peering through the Lattices,"* 163–64, n. 75, and E. Wolfson, *Through a Speculum That Shines*, 261–62. On R. Isaac *Or Zaru'a*'s tendencies toward pietism and mysticism, see my *"Peering through the Lattices,"* 128–30, 221–25 (and in the above note); Uziel Fuchs, "'Iyyunim be-Sefer Or Zaru'a le-R. Yishaq b. Mosheh me-Vienna" (M.A. thesis, Hebrew University, 1993), 18–19, 29, 33–40; and above, chapter 6.

[72] See my *"Peering through the Lattices,"* 248–49 (n. 79), and Joy Rochwarger, "Sefer Pa'aneaḥ Raza and Biblical Exegesis in Medieval Ashkenaz" (M.A. thesis, Touro College, 2000), chapter 4. Cf. Sara Japhet, "The Nature and Distribution of Medieval Compilatory Commentaries in Light of Rabbi Joseph Kara's Commentary on the Book of Job," in *The Midrashic Imagination*, ed. Michael Fishbane (Albany, N.Y., 1993), 98–122; idem, "Perush ha-Ḥizquni la-Torah—Li-Demuto shel ha-Ḥibbur ule-Mattarato," in *Sefer ha-Yovel le-Rav Mordekhai Breuer*, ed. Moshe Bar-Asher (Jerusalem, 1992), 91–111; and above, chapter 2, n. 143.

prophets via this angelic human form so that the prophets will not become disoriented or terrified.

Paʿaneaḥ Raza emphasizes that all intelligent people must understand that the Creator Himself has no structure or form (as the verses in Isaiah 40 indicate). He sees but is not seen, just as the human soul, which is infused with His spirit but has no form, allows a person to see but is itself not seen, even as it fills the entire human body. Similarly, there is no finitude to the greatness of God. He is unlimited and has no limbs, but He fills everything. All references to the hands and ears and heart and mouth (of God) are merely representations (*mashal*, as many verses indicate) of His ability to hear, think, and speak in order that the human ear hear what it is capable to understand. The prophets saw only the splendor of the lower part of the *kavod.* Moses saw this through a clear speculum (as Rabbenu Ḥanan'el explains in tractate *Yevamot*), but no one ever saw the upper *kavod.* Furthermore, Rabbenu Ḥanan'el and Rabbenu Nissim, among others, wrote that the Creator has no form, and they castigated anyone who claims that He does. One who believes that the Creator has no form is fortunate, and one who does not believe thusly will be afflicted and is close to being a heretic. In the work of Rambam, it is stated that whoever posits a form for the Creator is among those who will be severely punished. The comparable forms (of God and man) alluded to in Genesis 1:26 only establish the comparison with respect to the ability to intimidate others, so that their fear will extend to created beings.[73]

This passage in *Paʿaneaḥ Raza*, like the passage in Abraham b. Azri'el's *ʿArugat ha-Bosem*, includes virtually every one of the approaches that we have encountered in medieval Ashkenaz to address the problem of anthropomorphism. It begins with the interpretation of R. Eleazar of Worms, that the human image adopted by those angels who are sent by God to appear to the prophets constitutes the "common image" between the Divine and the human realms. The passage refers to the Saʿadyanic theory of the *kavod*, and mentions by name the early medieval talmudists who subscribed to a form of this view. Maimonides' position is cited directly, and the verses and principles gathered to explain the references to anthropomorphic characteristics in the Torah follow both the specifics in *Mishneh Torah* and in the commentary of R. Yosef *Bekhor Shor.* The exegetical approach that locates the common ground between God and human beings in their ability to intimidate and control other creatures also comes from the commentary

[73] This passage is included in *Tosafot ha-Shalem*, ed. Gellis, 1:61–62, sec. 13, from ms. Warsaw 260 and ms. Bodl. 2344. Cf. Elliot Wolfson, *Through a Speculum That Shines*, 211. A transcription of this passage is also found in Rochwarger, "Sefer Paʿaneaḥ Raza and Biblical Exegesis in Medieval Ashkenaz," 79 (from ms. Bodl. 2344, fol. 8r).

of *Bekhor Shor.*[74] Interestingly, *Pa'aneah Raza* (again like *'Arugat ha-Bosem*) found no need or opportunity to include the approach of R. Moses Taku. In a comment to Exodus 20:4 ("you shall not recognize the gods of others in my presence"), *Pa'aneah Raza* rejects completely the possibility that God possesses an actual physical form.[75]

To be sure, *Pa'aneah Raza* was composed well after the Maimonidean controversy of the 1230s, and was perhaps influenced in its interpretation of Genesis 1:26 by that complex of events as well. Nonetheless, there are other, earlier Ashkenazic interpretations of Genesis 1:26 (aside from that of R. Eleazar of Worms) which express their rejection of anthropomorphism in this verse by invoking a comparison to the images of the angels, using even simpler terms. The earliest example is the commentary of Rashbam: "in our image [means] in the image of the angels." Similarly, Rashbam interprets that the Divine image in which man was created (in Genesis 1:27) refers to the image of the angels.[76] Rashbam makes his comment from the standpoint of rationalistic *peshat* exegesis, without any recourse to any formal philosophical (or mystical) concepts or terms.[77]

[74] Cf. Rochwarger, "Sefer Pa'aneaḥ Raza and Biblical Exegesis in Medieval Ashkenaz," 80.

[75] This passage is cited in *Tosafot ha-Shalem*, ed. Gellis, vol. 8 (Jerusalem, 1990), 84 (and see also *Moshav Zeqenim*, ad loc.): לא תחשבו שום דמות להב"ה. והא דכתיב בצלם א-להים [בראשית ט:ו] ר"ל בצלם חשוב שהיה לו ולכן יש אתנחתא תחת צלם.

[76] בצלמנו, בצלם המלאכים. Cf. M. Lockshin, *Rabbi Samuel ben Meir's Commentary on Genesis* (Lewiston, N.Y., 1989), 53–54. A similar comment (to 1:26) is recorded anonymously, in a manuscript variant (ms. Paris 260) of the Tosafist Torah commentary, *Moshav Zeqenim* (published by Y. S. Lange in *Ha-Ma'ayan* 12 [1972], 81, and also in *Tosafot ha-Shalem*, ed. Gellis, 1:65, sec. 25): כדמותינו. ר"ל דמות מלאכים דאין לומר דמות הבורא יתברך דהא כתיב ואל מי תדמיוני ואשוה יאמר קדוש.

[77] On Rashbam's rationalism (including his awareness of aspects of Spanish biblical exegesis), and his rejection of mystical teachings, see my *"Peering through the Lattices,"* 159–61; and cf. J. Davis, "Philosophy, Dogma, and Exegesis in Medieval Ashkenazic Judaism," 213, n. 67; and above, n. 23. Sara Japhet has noted (see her *Perush Rashbam le-Sefer Iyyov* [Jerusalem, 2000], 127–35, that Rashbam also attempts to eliminate or re-interpret anthropomorphic depictions of God in his Job commentary, although she maintains that Rashbam is not fully consistent in this effort. In his review of Japhet's book (*AJS Review* 27 [2003], 128–32), Mordechai Cohen attributes the inconsistency to the fact that Rashbam did not have the rigorously philosophical outlook that Rambam did. Cf. Lockshin, *Rabbi Samuel ben Meir's Commentary*, 338–39, n. 3, and above, n. 1. A good example of the similarities (and differences) between the exegetical/philosophical approaches of Rashbam and Rambam can be seen in their interpretations of Genesis 18, the story of the three angels who came to visit Abraham. Coming mostly from the exegetical (*peshat*) perspective but reflecting a degree of rationalism as well, Rashbam puts forward (in his commentary to Genesis 18:1, against the view of Rashi) the fairly radical interpretation that the appearance of the three angels in physical form, as the Torah describes, constitutes the appearance of God mentioned by the Torah at the beginning of this episode. In *Moreh Nevukhim* 2:42, Maimonides, like Rashbam, maintains that God appeared to Abraham in the guise of the angels. A philosophical issue, however, rather than an exegetical one was at the core of Rambam's interpretation. In Maimonides' rigorous philosophical model, angels, like God, do not have a corporeal form. Thus they appeared to Abraham, as representatives of

The views of Rashbam and Rambam, as well as *Bekhor Shor*, are brought together in an interpretation of the northern French Tosafist Torah commentary *Sefer ha-Gan*, compiled by Aaron b. Yose[f] *ha-Kohen*, circa 1240, to Genesis 1:26.[78] *Sefer ha-Gan* begins by presenting, without attribution, the essence of *Bekhor Shor*'s interpretation of this verse. It is inappropriate to refer to the form of the Creator, as various biblical verses indicate. The references to Divine eyes or speech is a *mashal* to convey the notion that God can communicate, just as Scripture compares the voice of God to the sound of deep, rushing water. The claim that man is made in God's image refers only to the ability to intimidate, that the fear of man—like the fear of God—will be placed over other creatures.[79] *Sefer ha-Gan* describes the punishment for one who believes that God has a physical image according to Rambam (בספר הר"ר משה אבן מיימון), in what appears to be a paraphrase of *Hilkhot Teshuvah*, 3:6–7.

Sefer ha-Gan then links Rashbam's interpretation of Genesis 1:26 (that the form attributed to man is the unique form of the angels) to Rambam's description of the category of angels in *Yesodei ha-Torah* 2:7 called איש (anthropos), who appear in prophetic visions.[80] The sense of the verse is that God created man in the image of the Divine (*be-ẓelem E-lohim*), meaning in the image of the angels (*be-ẓelem mal'akhim*), since in many (biblical) contexts, angels are referred to as *'elohim.* These passages from Maimonides are also cited in several subsequent Tosafist Torah commentaries from the mid- and late thirteenth century.[81]

God, in a prophetic dream. See also *Mishneh Torah, Hilkhot Yesodei ha-Torah*, 2:7, and M. Lockshin, *Rabbi Samuel ben Meir's Commentary*, 338–39, n. 3.

78 Ms. Nuremberg 5, cited in *Tosafot ha-Shalem*, ed. Gellis, vol. 1, 65–66 (sec. 26): אין נכון לומר בדמות הבורא כי אין לו לאדם לתת לו דמות ותמונה דכתיב כי לא ראיתם כל תמונה וכתיב ואל מי תדמיוני ואשוה ואל מי תדמיון א-ל. ומה שמצינו גבי הבורא עינים ולשון אין זה כי אם דרך משל להשמיע לאזנים כמו שכתוב קולו כקול מים רבים. והא דאמר בצלמינו כדמותינו אין זה כי אם על האיום כלומר שתהיה אימתו מוטלת על הבריות. ובספר ה"ר משה אבן מיימון מצאתי כל הערוך דמות לבורא הוא מאותם שגיהנום כלה ואינם כלים. וביסודו של רבי שמואל ראיתי צלמו בצלם המיוחד לו, כדמותינו כדמות המלאכים. ועוד ראיתי בספר ה"ר מיימון כי עשה מיני משמשין של הקב"ה לכדמותינו של מטה הקרובים אלינו הנזכרים בפסוק גבי הגר גבי יהושע וגבי מנוח ובהרבה מקומות מלאכים אלהים. Because it is found only in ms. Nuremberg 5 (and not at all in ms. Vienna Heb. 28 = Cat. Schwartz, 19/5), this passage does not appear in *Sefer ha-Gan*, ed. Orlian, 119 (which made systematic use only of the Vienna manuscript). Cf. above, n. 16.

79 See above, n. 6.

80 The examples that are given in *Sefer ha-Gan*, from the angels that appeared to Hagar, Joshua, and Manoah, are not specifically mentioned in this passage in *Mishneh Torah* but are mentioned in *Moreh Nevukhim* 2:42. This suggests that the author of *Sefer ha-Gan* had access to *Moreh Nevukhim* as well. See below, n. 90.

81 *Tosafot ha-Shalem*, ed. Gellis, 1:65, sec. 21, records two other Tosafist Torah commentaries, ms. Bodl. 271 and ms. Paris 48, which cite the first reference to Rambam found in *Sefer ha-Gan* (on the punishment for believing God is corporeal), together with Rashbam's comment. Both these collections were put together after *Sefer ha-Gan*, and one of them cites material directly

R. Isaiah di Trani

As noted above in chapter 3, R. Isaiah b. Mali (= Emanuel) di Trani (Rid, c.1175–1240) was an Italian halakhist who studied in his youth with the German Tosafist R. Simḥah of Speyer. Israel Ta-Shma has reviewed R. Isaiah's large corpus and has sketched the contours of his scholarship.[82] Rid was especially familiar with the talmudic writings of Rashi, Rashbam, and Rabbenu Tam (and those of one of Rabbenu Tam's leading students, R. Isaac b. Mordekhai of Regensburg). He also cites leading earlier authorities from the Sefardic world, such as *Halakhot Gedolot*, Rabbenu Ḥanan'el, and Rif, as well as several important rabbinic figures from his homeland in southern Italy. In terms of overall methodology, however, Rid behaves for the most part like an Ashkenazic scholar, as indicated not only by his extensive *Tosafot* but also in his *pesaqim* and other halakhic compositions as well.[83]

One of Rid's first compositions—written, according to Ta-Shma, before any of his *Tosafot* and talmudic novellae, and in all probability shortly after he returned to Italy from his studies in Germany, sometime in the early years of the thirteenth century—was his commentary to the Pentateuch

---

from *Sefer ha-Gan*. See Gellis's introduction, 22–23, 34. The second Rambam passage found in *Sefer ha-Gan*, on the angels who appear in human form in prophetic visions, is cited in *Perushei ha-Torah le-R. Ḥayyim Palti'el*, ed. Y. S. Lange (Jerusalem, 1981), 4. Lange notes in his introduction (10–11) that this commentary contains a significant amount of material from both Yosef *Bekhor Shor* and *Pa'aneaḥ Raza*. Ḥayyim Palti'el was a student of R. Meir of Rothenburg, who ultimately settled in eastern Germany. His collection of *minhagim* followed those of R. Judah *he-Ḥasid*, including a number that reflect earlier practices in northern France rather than those of Rhineland Germany. R. Ḥayyim Palti'el himself appears to have spent some time in northern France, and is also referred to as R. Ḥayyim of Falaise. Indeed, somewhat ironically, he may have been the son-in-law of R. Samuel of Falaise (see below, n. 107). See Lange in *'Alei Sefer* 8 (1980), 142–45; Eric Zimmer, *'Olam ke-Minhago Noheg* (Jerusalem, 1996), 271, 277, 283, 286, 296–97; and my *"Peering through the Lattices,"* 113. Rambam's statement of the principle of Divine incorporeality (based on *Mishneh Torah*) is quoted by Jacob b. Judah *Ḥazzan* of London in his *Ez Ḥayyim*, ed. Israel Brodie (Jerusalem, 1962), vol. 1, 5–6 (אינו גוף וגויה). Cf. J. Davis, "Philosophy, Dogma, and Exegesis in Medieval Ashkenazic Judaism," 217–18. On the increased use of *Mishneh Torah* in Ashkenaz in the mid- and late thirteenth century, see, e.g., my "Preservation, Creativity, and Courage: The Life and Works of R. Meir of Rothenburg," *Jewish Book Annual* 50 (1992–93), 250–52.

82 See Ta-Shma, "Ha-Rav Yeshayah di Trani ha-Zaqen u-Qesharav 'im Byzantiyyon ve-Ereẓ Yisra'el," *Shalem* 4 (1984), 409–16; idem, "Ha-Sefer Shibbolei ha-Leqet u-Kfelav," *Italia* 11 (1994), 39–51; idem, "R. Yeshayah di Trani u-Mif'alo ha-Sifruti," *Meḥqerei Talmud* 3 (2005), 916–43. The synopsis presented here follows primarily Ta-Shma's treatment of R. Isaiah in his *Ha-Sifrut ha-Parshanit la-Talmud*, vol. 2, 174–87. See also my *"Peering through the Lattices,"* 223, and my "Progress and Tradition in Medieval Ashkenaz," *Jewish History* 14 (2001), 287–92.

83 Indeed, as noted by Ta-Shma, *Ha-Sifrut ha-Parshanit la-Talmud*, 2:185, Ritva and other Spanish scholars refer to him as R. Yeshayah *ha-Ashkenazi*. Cf. above, chapter 3, n. 107.

titled *Nimmuqei Ḥumash.*[84] Not surprisingly, this work betrays a heavy dose of Ashkenazic influence. Virtually all of the rabbinic figures whom Rid cites in this work, which comports with the genre of Tosafist Torah commentary and includes halakhic and talmudic material, as well as *gematria* and the like, are from either northern France or Germany,[85] with one notable exception. In three places, R. Isaiah reproduces passages from Maimonides' *Moreh Nevukhim.*[86] Indeed, Ta-Shma notes the rather curious phenomenon that Rid hardly quotes Maimonides' *Mishneh Torah* in his vast halakhic corpus—and this is true for Rid's successors in Italy for quite a while—but does quote *Moreh Nevukhim* at length on these three occasions. Typically, Ashkenazic halakhists and rabbinic figures in the thirteenth century quoted freely from *Mishneh Torah* but tended to ignore *Moreh Nevukhim.* Rid's unusual pattern of citation shows that Rambam's philosophy was not what kept Rid away from Rambam's halakhic writings. Rather, Ta-Shma suggests that the rejection or displacement of Maimonidean *halakhah* in Italy was due to the dominance of the Franco-German halakhic tradition in Italy during this time. Nonetheless, Rid's use of *Moreh Nevukhim* is suggestive.[87]

Assessing the availability of *Moreh Nevukhim* in its Hebrew translation in thirteenth-century Ashkenaz is difficult at best. It seems from the various letters mentioned earlier in connection with the Maimonidean controversy that parts, if not all, of *Moreh Nevukhim* were shown to groups of *rabbanei Ẓarefat* (some of whom voiced specific criticisms), and that it was therefore available in some form to Ashkenazic rabbinic scholars who wished to use it.[88] Nonetheless, Tosafists in northern France and Germany, including those who were supportive of *Mishneh Torah*, do not cite the *Moreh.*[89] Included in

84 See Ta-Shma, "Sefer 'Nimmuqei Ḥumash' le-R. Yeshayah di Trani," *Qiryat Sefer* 64 (1992–93), 751–75. Ta-Shma maintains that a more complete version of this work is preserved in ms. Moscow 303. Cf. above, chapter 3, nn. 109, 121.

85 See Ta-Shma, "Sefer 'Nimmuqei Ḥumash' le-R. Yeshayah di Trani," 752, and idem, "The Acceptance of Maimonides' *Mishneh Torah* in Italy," *Italia* 13–15 (2001), 82. These figures include R. Yosef Qara, R. Yosef *Bekhor Shor*, R. Judah *he-Ḥasid* and R. Eleazar of Worms, Rabbenu Tam, Ri, R. Eliezer of Metz (in his *Sefer Yere'im*), R. Samson of Coucy, Rid's correspondent, R. Isaac *Or Zaru'a* (and R. Isaac's teacher R. Jonathan b. Isaac of Wurzburg), as well as eastern European scholars such as R. Moses Fuller. R. Sa'adyah and Maimonides (see at the next note), and one or two Italian scholars, are also mentioned.

86 Ms. Moscow 303, fols. 59v, 64r, and 80r.

87 See Ta-Shma, "The Acceptance of Maimonides' *Mishneh Torah* in Italy," 79–90. Cf. Jacob Dienstag, "Yaḥasam shel Ba'alei ha-Tosafot leha-Rambam," in *Sefer ha-Yovel le-S. K. Mirsky*, ed. Simon Bernstein and Gershon Churgin (New York, 1955), 365.

88 Cf. below, nn. 113, 114, 117.

89 See Joseph Davis, "Philosophy, Dogma, and Exegesis in Medieval Ashkenazic Judaism," 210 (n. 58), and J. Dienstag, "Yaḥasam shel Ba'alei ha-Tosafot leha-Rambam," 350–79.

this pattern are figures such as R. Moses of Coucy and R. Isaac *Or Zaru'a*,[90] and even the more philosophically inclined R. Eleazar of Worms[91] and R. Abraham b. Azri'el of Bohemia (author of *'Arugat ha-Bosem*),[92] as well as the eclectic *Sefer ha-Maskil*.[93] Although it is possible that R. Isaiah di Trani received a copy of the *Moreh* through Italian channels,[94] it would appear that he is, given the point in his career when he wrote *Nimmuqei Ḥumash*, the first Tosafist and rabbinic scholar trained in Ashkenaz to cite the *Moreh* with authority and consistency.

Rid's use of *Moreh Nevukhim* must therefore be closely studied. Ta-Shma maintains that Rid, as reflected in his commentary to Genesis 1:26, encountered some radical Ashkenazic *magshimim* who believed that God

[90] On the frequent citation of *Mishneh Torah* by Tosafists in the mid-thirteenth century, see Ta-Shma, "The Acceptance of Maimonides' *Mishneh Torah*" (above, n. 87), and cf. above, nn. 16, 81, 120. (On R. Moses of Coucy's possible awareness of the existence of *Moreh Nevukhim*, see J. Woolf, "Maimonides Revised: The Case of the *Sefer Miswot Gadol*," *Harvard Theological Review* 90 [1997], 186.) The so-called *perushei Ba'alei ha-Tosafot 'al ha-Torah* (with the exception of the passage in *Sefer ha-Gan*, above, n. 78, which betrays an awareness of *Moreh Nevukhim*), also follow this pattern for the most part. Indeed, these commentaries do not even cite *Mishneh Torah* with much frequnecy. See, e.g., Gellis, *Tosafot ha-Shalem*, vol. 1, 61–62, 65–66 (the pieces from *Mishneh Torah* cited in connection with Genesis 1:26; see above, nn. 73, 78, 81); 121 (a possible parallel to *Moreh Nevukhim* on the angelic powers of the primordial snake); 183 (a possible parallel to *Moreh Nevukhim* from a passage in *Bekhor Shor*; cf. above, n. 21); vol. 6 (Jerusalem, 1986), 42 (*Mishneh Torah* on the laws of inheritance); vol. 9 (Jerusalem, 1993), 101 (a citation from *MT Hilkhot 'Avodah Zarah*); 172 (the making of the *hoshen*, based on *MT Hilkhot Kelei ha-Mikdash*).

[91] R. Eleazar of Worms's pietistic introductory section to his halakhic work *Sefer Roqeaḥ* (*Hilkhot Ḥasidut*) was patterned, to some extent, after Rambam's *Sefer ha-Madda'*; cf. Urbach, *Ba'alei ha-Tosafot*, 1:393. Maimonides' *Hilkhot Teshuvah* is also cited extensively in the so-called *Sefer Ḥasidim* I (ed. Bologna, secs. 1–152); see, e.g., Ivan Marcus, "The Recensions and Structure of 'Sefer Ḥasidim,'" *PAAJR* 45 (1978), 131–53. Cf. J. Dan, *Torat ha-Sod shel Ḥasidut Ashkenaz*, 31. And yet the German Pietists do not cite *Moreh Nevukhim* as far as I can tell.

[92] *'Arugat ha-Bosem* cites liberally from *Mishneh Torah*, including the theological portions of *Sefer ha-Madda'*; see Ta-Shma (above, n. 87), and Urbach, *'Arugat ha-Bosem* 4:166, 177. Somewhat surprisingly, R. Moses Taku does not refer to *Moreh Nevukhim* in his attack on Maimonides' philosophy but works only with material found in *Mishneh Torah*. Cf. Dan, "Ashkenazi Hasidism and the Maimonidean Controversy," 31–34, 40–41; D. J. Silver, *Maimonidean Criticism and the Maimonidean Controversy, 1180–1240*, 138; and cf. above, nn. 37, 41. Reference is made to a passage in *Moreh Nevukhim* in a gloss found in the Paris manuscript of *Ketav Tamim* (see the facsimile edition, 43–44 [= fol. 22a–b]). Although the identity of the author of this gloss is unclear, it does not appear to have been R. Moses himself.

[93] See Freudenthal in *Da'at* 32–33 (1994) [above, n. 31], 193.

[94] To be sure, however, there are no Italian halakhists prior to R. Isaiah who can be positively identified as the conduits. Note that the kabbalist Abraham Abulafia apparently taught or explained pieces of *Moreh Nevukhim* in Rome to Rid's grandson (and namesake), R. Isaiah the younger (Ri'az), and to the Italian halakhist R. Zedekiah b. Abraham *ha-Rofe* (author of *Shibbolei ha-Leqet*, d.c. 1260), who had a strong literary connection with Rid (although he did not actually study with him). See Ta-Shma, "Ha-Rav Yeshayah di Trani," 411; Moshe Idel, *R. Menaḥem Reqanati ha-Mekubbal* (Tel Aviv, 1998), 36; and my "*Peering through the Lattices*," 228, n. 21.

had a corporeal form in the literal or simplest sense. Given the inability until now to identify and pinpoint such groups, this would be a discovery of great significance. Rid does not espouse this position himself, and he seeks to defuse it using a lengthy citation from *Moreh Nevukhim*, while not rebuking its adherents too sharply or too directly. Indeed, it would appear that Rid also wished to explain how these *magshimim* (mistakenly) came to embrace their position. Owing to the importance of this passage, which Ta-Shma considers to be the first instance of a leading rabbinic scholar looking from the "outside" into a group of this type of committed *magshimim*, Ta-Shma reproduces the opening lines of the passage which, in his view, are a record or reflection of this encounter.[95]

In fact, however, this entire passage is a faithful, virtually verbatim reproduction of the translation of *Moreh Nevukhim* 1:1, although Rid does not note this source in his commentary nor does he indicate that this is a citation. Thus, there is no exchange of any kind taking place here between Rid and Ashkenazic *magshimim.* Rather, Rid is presenting only the words of Maimonides, explaining why some Jews, who were presumably not from Ashkenaz, incorrectly felt that they must attribute a physical form to God, in order to have certain biblical verses make sense. To be sure Rid, in citing this passage, may have sought to undercut the view that existed in Ashkenaz as well among those who believed in pronounced anthropomorphism, but their voices are not being heard here. The main point of *Moreh Nevukhim* 1:1 is to distinguish philosophically between *ẓelem*, which denotes the essential existence of a being (in this instance, the Divine Being and Intellect) without signifying corporeality, and *demut*, a comparative term that does imply a measure of similarity between God and man in Genesis 1:26. Maimonides' (and Rid's) conclusion is that the similarity is to be found in the intellects of God and man, and not in the physical realm.[96] Nonetheless,

[95] Ta-Shma, "Sefer Nimmuqei Ḥumash," 752: צלם ודמות כבר חשבו בני אדם כי צלם בלשון העברי יורה על תמונת הדבר ותוארו והביא זה להגשמה גמורה לאומ׳ נעשה אדם בצלמנו כדמותנו וחשבו שהשם על צורת האדם ר״ל תמונתו ותוארו והתחייבה להם ההגשמה הגמורה והאמינו בה וראו שאם הם יפרדו מזאת האמונה יכזיבו הכתוב וגם ישימו את השם נעדר אם לא יהיה לו גוף בעל פנים ויד כמותם בתמונה ובתואר אלא שהוא גדול ויותר בהיר לפי סברתם וחומר שלו גם כן אינו בשר ודם. וזהו תכלית מה שיחשבוהו רוממות בחוקי השם. Cf. Ta-Shma, *Ha-Sifrut ha-Parshanit la-Talmud*, vol. 2, 194. After citing Ta-Shma in his "Sefer Nimmuqei Ḥumash," Yair Lorberbaum, "Al Da'atam shel Ḥakhamim z"l lo Altah ha-Hagshamah me-'Olam," 6 (nn. 17–18), and 42 (n. 170), notes that the passage in *Nimmuqei Ḥumash* is taken word for word from *Moreh Nevukhim* 1:1, but maintains nonetheless that it helps to demonstrate that "many rabbis" in Ashkenaz took anthropomorphism literally. These assessments are repeated in idem, *Ẓelem E-lohim*, 31 (n. 18, end), and 86 (n. 5).

[96] The passage in ms. Moscow 303 reads, נאמר [בצלמנו כדמותינו] באדם מפני זה הענין, ר״ל מפני השכל הא-להי המודבק בו שהוא בצלם א-להים ובדמות[ו] לא שהוא ית׳ גוף שיהיה [א״כ] בעל תמונה. This kind of distinction between *zelem* and *demut* was followed to a very different conclusion by R. Moses Taku and R. Jacob b. Samson. See above, nn. 37–38.

despite the fact that Rid has not helped us to pinpoint an identifiable group of Ashkenazic *magshimim*, we have in Rid another important Ashkenazic thinker who is supportive of the Maimonidean position on anthropomorphism, citing it for the first time not from *Mishneh Torah* but from *Moreh Nevukhim*.

Rid copies extensively from *Moreh Nevukhim* in two additional instances. In his commentary to the *ʿaqedah* in *parashat Va-Yera* (Genesis 22:1, "And the Almighty tested Abraham"), Rid reproduces Rambam's unique interpretation of the test that the binding of Isaac presented to Abraham, and he lists where this chapter is found in *Moreh Nevukhim*.[97] In his commentary to *parashat Ki Tissa*, Rid again refers his reader to a specific, albeit brief, chapter in *Moreh Nevukhim* and reproduces it faithfully, in which Maimonides explains the biblical phrase that the tablets containing the Ten Commandments were the product of the Almighty (*maʿaseh E-lohim*). This issue has an anthropomorphic tinge as well, and Rid again seems to be endorsing the Maimonidean view by citing the appropriate chapter from *Moreh Nevukhim* in full.[98]

Rid expresses an anti-anthropomorphic view in his commentary to Ezekiel as well, although in this case it is closer to the *kavod ha-neʾezal* found in *Shaʿarei ha-Sod ha-Yiḥud veha-Emunah* and in other exoteric writings of R. Eleazar of Worms—while also harkening back to the *kavod ha-nivra* of R. Saʿadyah Gaon—than it is to the view of Maimonides. Commenting on Ezekiel's description of the *Merkavah*, at the point where a form or image that appears to be human is seen above the image of the throne (Ezekiel 1:26, *ve-ʿal demut ha-kisse demut ke-marʾeh ʾadam ʿalav mi-lemaʿalah*), R. Isaiah asserts that this refers to the *Shekhinah* (= the *kavod*). It is inappropriate, however to ascribe any form or image to the Creator Himself. Rather, this form that is seen is a temporary one by which the Creator appears to His prophets. Indeed, we find the Creator appearing in a number of different forms to His prophets, and each of these forms is created for a particular instance. He appeared to Moses as the burning fire within the bush. And at Mount Sinai as well, the appearance of the Divine glory was as a consuming fire. Nonetheless, a person should not say that any of these are His actual form, nor should he spend a lot of time pondering these issues since one cannot fully grasp the properties of God and the glory of the *Shekhinah*. In conclusion, a person should fully believe that the Creator has no form and no image. What appeared to the prophets is a form that was developed

[97] Ms. Moscow 303, fol. 64r: רבי' משה בן מיימון ז"ל דבר על זה הפסוק וייסד עליו פרק כ"ד בחלק שלישי לספר מורה נבוכים. ענין הנסיון גם כן מסופק מאוד וכו'. The rest of Rid's commentary to *Va-Yera* consists of the full citation of this chapter, ending on fol. 65v.

[98] Ms. Moscow 303, fols. 80–v, citing *Moreh Nevukhim*, 1:66.

specifically for that moment, so that the prophet could say that God sent him and the voice of the Divine came directly to the prophet.[99]

Assessing the Nature and Extent of the Maimonidean Controversy in Ashkenaz

R. Samuel b. Mordekhai of Marseilles, a little-known Provençal scholar writing in defense of Maimonides and against his detractors in light of the Maimonidean controversy of the 1230s, records in an epistle that "the majority of the rabbinic scholars in northern France [accept] anthropomorphism, with the exception of Rashi whose writings consistently deflect seeming anthropomorphic interpretations by employing the prinicple, *dibrah Torah ki-leshon bnei ʾadam.*"[100] Naḥmanides, in his better-known letter of 1232 to the *rabbanei Ẓarefat*, notes that Ashkenazic scholars leveled the charge that Maimonides was mistaken in insisting (in his *Sefer ha-Maddaʿ*) that God has no form or shape. These rabbinic scholars apparently believed that God did

[99] See Rid to Ezekiel 1:26 (ed. Ha-Keter, Jerusalem, 2000): וחלילה חלילה שנתאר דמות או תמונה לבורא אלא זו הצורה ברואה היא לפי שעה שהבורא מדבר לנביאיו. וכמה צורות משונות מצינו שנדמה לנביאיו והכל הם נבראים לפי שעה . . . כמה יסמוך ויאמין כל אדם כי אין דמות לבורא לא דמות ולא תמונה ואין לו חקר מרוב דקותו והעלמו ומה שנדמה לנביאיו הוא דמיון נוצר לפי שעה (partially cited in E. Z. Melammed, "Le-Perush Nakh shel R. Yeshayah mi-Trani," in *Meḥqarim ba-Miqra uba-Mizraḥ ha-Qadmon Muggashim li-Shmuʾel Leonstam bi-Melot lo Shivʿim Shanah*, ed. Y. Avishur and J. Blau [Jerusalem, 1978], 292). Rid is referring here to a form of the כבוד הנברא. Rid's last sentence is also quite similar to a formulation of Saʿadyah Gaon in *Emunot ve-Deʿot*, ed. Kafih, 103. For a similar notion of a lower Divine form that is created (or emanated) for a short period of time in order to be shown to a prophet in a particular situation, see, e.g., R. Eleazar of Worms's *Sefer Shaʿarei ha-Sod ha-Yiḥud veha-Emunah*, ed. Dan (above, n. 54), 147, 151, and see also above, n. 55. Cf. the analysis of the German Pietists' *Shir ha-Kavod* in Arthur Green, *Keter*, 111 (to line 11): "God's appearance changes as is appropriate to human need in each particular situation." Rid cites a pietistic biblical interpretation of R. Eleazar in his *Nimmuqei Ḥumash*, ms. Moscow 508, fol. 81v, and interpretations of R. Judah *he-Ḥasid* (fols. 63r, 68v, 85r, 98r). Moreover, Naḥmanides noted the availability of Eleazar's *Shaʿarei ha-Sod* within Ashkenaz; see above, n. 58. Note also *Tosafot Rid* to *Ḥagigah* 16a, where Rid refers to man's inability to ponder and to ascertain a full understanding and description of the *Shekhinah*. In the final section of that discussion (s.v. *di-khtiv ke-marʾeh ha-qeshet*), Rid concludes: כך מראה השכינה אינם יכולים לכוין בבירור מה הוא, and cf. *Nimmuqei Torah le-Rabbenu Yeshayah*, ed. C. D. Chavel (Jerusalem, 1972), 67 (to Deut. 21:23): כי קללת א-להים. פירש המורה [=רש"י] זלזולו של מלך שהאדם בדמות דיוקנו וכו'. ובפרשת בראשית [א:כז] פירש ויברך את האדם בצלמו בדפוס העשוי לו. ולמה לא פירש בצלמו ממש. ויש לומר ודאי כי אין אדם עשוי בדמות הבורא, ויפה פירש בדפוס העשוי לו. וזה שפירש שאדם עשוי במדות דיוקנו מפני שכשהמקום נראה לאנשים כדמות אדם נראה, אבל דמות הק' לא נודע. ולפי הפשט, כי קללת אלהים תלוי כל העובר מקלל את הדיינים כמו אלהים לא תקלל. Cf. above, chapter 3, n. 167.

[100] Ms. Neofiti 11, fol. 210v: כי רוב חכמי צרפת מגשימים, זולתי הרב רש"י כי הוא לבדו נשאר וספריו מעידין עליו וכל מקום הנראה לגשמות הוא מפרש כי על דרך שאמרו דברה תורה כלשון בני אדם. See Gershom Scholem, *Origins of the Kabbalah*, 406–7. On R. Samuel b. Mordekhai and his epistle, cf. Scholem, 224–26, and Moshe Idel, "Qeta ʿIyyunim le-R. Asher b. Meshullam mi-Lunel," *Qiryat Sefer* 50 (1975), 148–53. I thank my student Pinchas Roth of Hebrew University for sharing his transcription of this manuscript with me.

have some kind of physical form.[101] Rashi is singled out by a Provençal rationalist, Asher b. Gershom (perhaps of Beziers), as holding, in consonance with the view of Maimonides but against the general tenor within the rabbinic circles of northern France, that the physical or anthropomorphic descriptions of God reported by the prophets were products of their prophetic imagination rather than actual images.[102]

Although no one questions the reliability per se of the Provençal and Spanish rabbinic writers who made these assertions, it is problematic to learn about the positions that northern French anti-Maimunists or anti-rationalists allegedly espoused primarily from the pens of those whose mission it was to defend Maimonides.[103] The fact is that accusations during this phase of the Maimonidean controversy were never made to or about a particular Tosafist or Ashkenazic rabbinic scholar. Naḥmanides does not mention the names of any northern French rabbinic figures in his letter

[101] See the text of Naḥmanides' letter published in *Kitvei ha-Ramban*, ed. Chavel, 345–46 (= *Qovez Teshuvot ha-Rambam* [Leipzig, 1859], sec. 3, fols. 9d–10b). Just prior to his discussion of anthropomorphism, Naḥmanides notes the approbation for *Mishneh Torah* implicit in the writings of the leading Tosafist, R. Isaac b. Abraham (Riẓba) of Dampierre (d. 1210). Cf. Bernard Septimus, *Hispano-Jewish Culture in Transition*, 79: "Not only rationalist polemicists but even an anti-rationalist like Naḥmanides indicates that anthropomorphism played an important role in the condemnation of Maimonides' works [in Ashkenaz]." Shortly thereafter, Naḥmanides cites extensively from the treatise of R. Eleazar of Worms to show that Eleazar did not subscribe to the anthropomorphic view; see above, nn. 57–58.

[102] See ms. Cambridge Add. 507.1, fols. 75r–v, transcribed in Joseph Shatzmiller, "Les Tossafistes et la Première Controverse Maïmonidienne," in *Rashi et la culture juive en France du Nord au moyen âge*, ed. G. Dahan and G. Nahon (Paris, 1997), 75. Later in his letter (fols. 78r–v; Shatzmiller, 79–80), Asher claims that the rabbis of northern France decreed that the Bible and the Talmud must be studied only according to the commentaries of Rashi, ostensibly because Rashi tends to interpret according to the literal sense and in accordance with rabbinic teachings. (This claim is also found in the letter to the rabbis of northern France sent by Samuel b. Abraham Saporta; see B. Septimus, *Hispano-Jewish Culture in Transition*, 78.) And yet, Asher notes, there are instances in which Rashi interprets a biblical verse according to its context, differently than Onkelos does and without any support from talmudic literature. Moreover, Rashi maintains in "many instances" that Scripture is phrased in a manner that "appeases the ear" (לשכך את האוזן) so that it can be understood, "which comports with the words of our teacher (Maimonides)." Shatzmiller (n. 229) suggests that an example of this last point can be found in Rashi's commentary to Exodus 15:8, "And with a blast of Thy nostrils the waters [of the Red Sea] were piled up." Rashi's comment is that "Scripture speaks as if this [the blast that goes forth from the nostrils of the nose] were possible of the Divine Presence in the way of a king of flesh and blood only in order to let the ears of people hear in accordance with what usually happens, in order that they will be able to understand the matter. When a person is angry, his breath emerges from his nostrils." See also Shatzmiller, n. 167 (and Rashi to Ex. 19:18).

[103] That the position of the northern French anti-rationalists on anthropomorphism is not found explicitly in any of their writings but is recorded only in documents written by the Maimunists is noted in a number of studies. See, e.g., Septimus, *Hispano-Jewish Culture in Transition*, 79; and Shatzmiller, "Iggarto shel R. Asher b. Gershom le-Rabbanei Ẓarefat mi-Zeman ha-Maḥloqet 'al Kitvei ha-Rambam," in *Meḥqarim be-Toledot 'Am Yisra'el ve-Ereẓ Yisra'el le Zekher Zvi Avneri*, ed. A. Gilboa et al. (Haifa, 1970), 134–35.

to them—in which he asks that their ban on the study of *Sefer ha-Madda*ʿ and *Moreh Nevukhim* be lifted or modified—although at one point he does refer to the *herem* as having been agreed upon by "all the land of northern France, its Rabbis and Torah leaders."[104] The letter sent by Asher b. Gershom was titled אגרת שלוחה מאת ר׳ אשר ב״ר גרשום על אודות מורה נבוכים לרבני צרפת.[105]

[104] *Kitvei ha-Ramban*, ed. Chavel, 1:338. To be sure, Ramban, throughout his talmudic *ḥiddushim*, refers to the interpretations of *rabboteinu ha-Ẓarefatim/hakhmei ha-Ẓarefatim* (not to mention [*baʿal ha-*] *Tosafot*), titles that often denote specific and recognized Tosafist authors and compositions. These designations, however, do not represent Tosafists beyond the era of Ri (d. 1189) and R. Samson of Sens (d. 1214). See, e.g, *Ḥiddushei ha-Ramban le-Massekhet Ketubot*, ed. Ezra Schwat (Jerusalem, 1993), editor's introduction, 31–38. As Schwat notes, Ramban also had access, through his cousin Rabbenu Yonah, to *Tosafot* and talmudic interpretations from the study halls of the brothers of Evreux and R. Yeḥi'el of Paris. These rabbinic figures, however, are never mentioned in connection with the *herem* and do not seem to have had any involvement in the Maimonidean controversy. Cf. I. Ta-Shma, *Ha-Sifrut ha-Parshanit la-Talmud*, 2:36, 49–50. On Naḥmanides' goals and strategy in writing his letter, see David Berger, "How Did Naḥmanides Propose to Resolve the Maimonidean Controversy?" in *Me'ah She'arim: Studies in Medieval Jewish Spiritual Life in Memory of Isadore Twersky*, ed. Ezra Fleischer et al. (Jerusalem, 2001), 135–46.

[105] For the title of Asher's letter, see Shatzmiller, "Les Tossafistes," 63. In the body of the letter, Asher refers to רבותי רבני צרפת וחכמיה, and he mentions passages and ideas in both *Mishneh Torah* and *Moreh Nevukhim*, cf. Shatzmiller, 62, 72, 74–78. He also makes reference to the anti-Maimonidean stance taken by the rabbinic scholars in Orleans (וחכמי אורליינש אשר כתבו כי יש לאל ידם למסרנו), without mentioning a single scholar by name, and he refers to an unidentified French anti-Maimonidean rabbinic figure by the derogatory epithet הרב ר׳ משה ליצון. Moreover, Asher alleges that no fewer than thirty-six *rabbanei Zarefat* set out to defame (the Maimunist) R. David Kimḥi (Radak). Needless to say, we cannot name even one of these rabbis. See Shatzmiller, "Iggarto shel R. Asher b. Gershom" (above, n. 103), 135–37, and idem, "Le Tossafistes et la Premiere Controverse Maimonidienne," 60–61. (Shatzmiller's suggestion in his French article that the derisively characterized הרב ר׳ משה ליצון referred to by Asher may perhaps be a relative of the Tosafist R. Joseph of Clisson [קליצון] is interesting but improbable; in any event, there is no known Tosafist from Clisson by this name.) Corbeil and Orleans were important locales during the Tosafist period, and each produced a number of important Tosafists. The fact that no known scholars from these places can be identified as overtly anti-Maimunist heightens the dilemma. In short, there were obviously some northern French talmudic scholars who held this position, but none have been identified as leading Tosafists. And yet a number of contemporary scholars refer consistently to the anti-Maimonidean stance of "the Tosafists." Indeed, Shatzmiller titled his French article "The Tosafists and the First Maimonidean Controversy" (and see esp. pp. 55–57), and Septimus writes (63–64) that "Solomon [of Montpellier]'s circle turned for support to the Tosafist schools of northern France . . . [and] discoveries by Joseph Shatzmiller have shown that at least some of the Tosafists responded with sharp condemnation of Provençal rationalism." See also Jeffrey Woolf, "Maimonides Revised: The Case of the *Sefer Miswot Gadol*," 178, 189. (Shatzmiller, "Les Tossafistes," 79, cites Asher as referring to a group of *rabbanei Ẓarefat* who were able to see Samuel ibn Tibbon's Hebrew translation of *Moreh Nevukhim* only after they arrived in Marseilles. Cf. Simon Schwarzfuchs, *Yehudei Ẓarefat Bimei ha-Benayim* [Tel Aviv, 2001], 186.) Similarly, the letter sent by Samuel Saporta is titled כתב אשר שלח הרב ר׳ שמואל ב״ר אברהם [ספורטא] לרבני צרפת וקנאתו על מה שהשיגו על הרב רבינו משה ז״ל. This letter contains a strong critique of the anthropomorphic view that was supposedly held by these unidentified rabbis (and a list of rabbinic predecessors who held the anti-anthropomorphic view), and refers to passages in *Moreh Nevukhim* that were apparently available to them. See *Yeshurun*, ed. Joseph Kobak, vol. 8 (Bamberg, 1875), 132–39, 152–53.

Similarly, when the anti-Maimunist R. Solomon b. Abraham of Montpellier wished to bring his case against Maimonides and his philosophical writings to the rabbis of northern France for their opinion—in Solomon's words, חשבנו בלבו להראות צרותינו לרבני צרפת וגדוליה . . . גם הגיע אליהם ספר מורה וחרה אפם מאוד—he did so without designating a particular rabbinic figure as the addressee. R. Solomon dispatched R. Yonah of Gerona, who had studied in northern France at the Tosafist academy at Evreux, to carry out this mission. In this instance as well, however, there is no record of any specific rabbinic figures with whom Rabbenu Yonah interacted.[106]

The only known Tosafist to have penned a letter during this phase of the Maimonidean controversy seems to have been R. Samuel b. Solomon of Falaise.[107] R. Samuel's brief document focuses mainly on the importance of the literal interpretation of *'aggadah*, and the negative influences of Maimonides' works; literal versus nonliteral interpretation of *'aggadah* was certainly a

[106] See Azriel Shohat, "Berurim be-Farashat ha-Polmos ha-Rishon," *Zion* 36 (1971), 30–31, and D. J. Silver, *Maimonidean Criticism and the Maimonidean Controversy, 1180–1240*, 159, n. 1. On Rabbenu Yonah's student days at Evreux, see my *"Peering through the Lattices,"* 27, 63–64, 70–72. It should be noted that the study hall at Evreux was linked in a number of respects to the German Pietists, whose anti-anthropomorphic views have been noted. Whether Rabbenu Yonah would have found this academy particularly receptive to his mission is therefore highly questionable. Cf. Septimus, *Hispano-Jewish Culture in Transition*, 64: "It would seem that R. Jonah, a former student at the French academies, personally brought the case before his old teachers"; and above, n. 104. The absence of leading Ashkenazic rabbinic (Tosafist) names associated with the purported northern French *herem* against *Sefer ha-Madda'* and *Moreh Nevukhim* is noted by D. Berger, "Judaism and Culture," 109, n. 107 (in the name of Haym Soloveitchik), and by Simon Schwarzfuchs, *Yehudei Ẓarefat Bimei ha-Benayim*, 196 (and I also heard this from Israel Ta-Shma). See also J. Dan, "Ashkenazi Hasidism and the Maimonidean Controversy," (above, n. 22), 31.

[107] The letter was published by Joseph Shatzmiller, "Li-Temunat ha-Maḥloqet ha-Rishonah 'al Kitvei ha-Rambam," *Zion* 35 (1969), 139, from ms. B.M. Add. 27131, and cf. Shatzmiller, 127–30. The preamble begins with the phrase, וזאת אגרת אחת מאגרות רבני צרפת אשר נתקבצו כולם והסכימו לנדות כל מי שקורא בספר מורה הנבוכים וספר המדע אשר חבר הרב הגדול רבינו משה בן מיימון זצ"ל. The letter is signed by שמואל בן הנדיב ר' שלמה שיחיה, who is presumed to be the Tosafist of this name, and by (his brother?) יצחק בן הנדיב ר' שלמה שיחיה. Falaise is proximate to Evreux, and perhaps Samuel was in touch with Rabbenu Yonah, although, as indicated, there is no evidence for any such contact. Note that during the so-called resurrection controversy that took place in the early years of the thirteenth century, (the anti-Maimunist) R. Meir *ha-Levi* Abulafia (Ramah) sent Maimonidean material to R. Samson of Sens (and his Tosafist brother Riẓba), among other rabbinic figures, and received a relatively mild response composed by R. Samson. Although the letter of Ramah ultimately reached R. Eleazar of Worms, three of the other five northern French figures to whom Ramah addressed his letter, Samson of Corbeil, David of Chateau Thierry, and Abraham of Toques, are otherwise unknown to us. See B. Septimus, *Hispano-Jewish Culture in Transition*, 48–50, and Norman Golb, *The Jews in Medieval Normandy* (Cambridge, 1998), 402, n. 75. Of the remaining two, Solomon (*ha-Qadosh*) b. Judah of Dreux was a Tosafist who had studied with Ri (see Urbach, *Ba'alei ha-Tosafot*, 1:337–40; Golb, 400–403; and my *"Peering through the Lattices,"* 97–98), and Eliezer b. Aaron of Bourgogne apparently authored a treatise on *'issur ve-heter* titled *Sha'arei ha-Panim*, which is cited (once) by two late medieval halakhic compendia. Cf. Simcha Emanuel, *Shivrei Luḥot*, 240–41.

core issue of the Maimonidean controversy.[108] Nonetheless, R. Samuel's letter does not refer at all to the issue of anthropomorphism.[109]

Moreover, R. Samuel's leading Tosafist contemporaries and colleagues in northern France, R. Yeḥi'el of Paris and R. Moses of Coucy, can hardly be characterized as anti-Maimonidean in the way that R. Samuel was.[110]

108 This is evident throughout the studies of the Maimonidean controversy (with special emphasis on the events of the 1230s) that have appeared over the last four decades. See, e.g., D. J. Silver, *Maimonidean Criticism and the Maimonidean Controversy*, chs. 8–9; Shatzmiller, "Li-Temunat ha-Maḥloqet ha-Rishonah ʿal Kitvei ha-Rambam," (in the above note), 126–44; idem, "Iggarto shel R. Asher b. Gershom le-Rabbanei Ẓarefat mi-Zeman ha-Maḥloqet ʿal Kitvei ha-Rambam," in *Meḥqarim be-Toledot ʿAm Yisraʾel ve-Ereẓ Yisraʾel le Zekher Ẓvi Avneri*, ed. A. Gilboa et al. (Haifa, 1970), 129–40; idem, "Les Tossafistes et la Première Controverse Maïmonidienne," 54–82; Azriel Shohat, "Berurim be-Farashat ha-Polmos ha-Rishon ʿal Sifrei ha-Rambam," 26–60; B. Septimus, *Hispano-Jewish Culture in Transition*, chs. 4–5; David Berger, "Judaism and General Culture in Medieval and Early Modern Times," 85–100. See also Moshe Halbertal, *Bein Torah le-Ḥokhmah*, above, n. 40.

109 Samuel's father, R. Solomon b. Samuel *ha-Ẓarefati*, traveled to Germany, where he was a student of both R. Samuel and R. Judah *he-Ḥasid*. He authored a Torah commentary in the style of the German Pietists, replete with *gematria* and *sod* interpretations, and he also composed interpretations of difficult passages within Abraham ibn Ezra's biblical commentaries, especially those dealing with Divine names. Among the *sodot* that R. Solomon explains is the notion mentioned cryptically by Ibn Ezra that Moses did not write all the verses of the Torah himself, but that several phrases or expressions were added by others (a concept also found in the biblical commentaries of R. Judah *he-Ḥasid* and other members of his circle). He also preserved various *sodot ha-tefillah*. See my *"Peering through the Lattices,"* 94–96, 100–102, and see above, chapter 4, n. 121. R. Samuel b. Solomon studied with the Tosafist R. Solomon *ha-Qadosh* of Dreux, one of the recipients of the letter from Ramah to northern France (above, n. 107, and see also above, chapter 3, nn. 212–15). R. Samuel cites two *gematria* interpretations from his father but displays no overt tendencies toward *ḥasidut* or *perishut*, except that he was much more hesitant than his colleague R. Yeḥi'el of Paris in declaring accepted stringencies invalid, even those that were found not to be well based. See my *"Peering through the Lattices,"* 96–100, and cf. N. Golb, *The Jews in Medieval Normandy*, 396–407, 463–74, and Gavriel Zinner, *Oẓar Pisqei ha-Rishonim ʿal Hilkhot Pesaḥ* (New York, 1985), 14–21, 31. On the tendency toward *ḥumra* in the writings of Rabbenu Yonah, see, e.g., Israel Ta-Shma, *Ha-Sifrut ha-Parshanit la-Talmud*, vol. 2, 28–29; idem, "Ḥasidut Ashkenaz bi-Sefarad: Rabbenu Yonah Gerondi—ha-Ish u-Foʿalo," in *Galut Aḥar Golah*, ed. A. Mirsky et al. (Jerusalem, 1988), 180–91; and my *"Peering through the Lattices,"* 66–67.

110 On R. Yeḥi'el of Paris, cf. above, n. 9, and E. E. Urbach, "Ḥelqam shel Ḥakhmei Ashkenaz ve-Ẓarefat ba-Polmos ʿal ha-Rambam ve-ʿal Sefarav," 158–59. R. Yeḥi'el had a particular interest in the biblical teachings of Ibn Ezra. See my *"Peering through the Lattices,"* 96, n. 8; 235, n. 43; and cf. D. Berger, "Judaism and General Culture," 119, n. 107; I. Ta-Shma, "Mashehu ʿal Biqqoret ha-Miqra be-Ashkenaz Bimei ha-Benayim," in *Ha-Miqra bi-Reʾi Mefarshav*, ed. Sara Japhet (Jerusalem, 1994), 456, n. 21; and Abraham Lifshitz, "R. Avraham ibn Ezra be-Perushei Baʿalei ha-Tosafot ʿal ha-Torah," *Hadarom* 28 (1968), 202–21. On the brothers of Evreux, see above, nn. 104, 106. On R. Moses of Coucy, see Urbach, *Baʿalei ha-Tosafot*, 1:471–73, and the next note. R. Yeḥi'el of Paris, R. Moses of Coucy, and R. Samuel b. Solomon of Falaise are mentioned and linked together in a passage from Qershavyah (Crespia) *ha-Naqdan* b. Isaac *ha-Sofer* concerning the writing of bills of divorce in Paris; see, e.g., *Teshuvot u-Fesaqim*, ed. Efraim Kupfer (Jerusalem, 1973), 325–26. A fourth rabbinic scholar, R. Judah b. David of Melun (or Metz), is also mentioned by Qershavyah as having been involved in this process. As E. E. Urbach notes (*Baʿalei ha-Tosafot*,

R. Moses makes extensive use of *Mishneh Torah* in his *Sefer Mizvot Gadol.* Indeed, *Sefer Mizvot Gadol* appears to be dependent on *Mishneh Torah* in many ways. To be sure, R. Moses plays down and even ignores many of the philosophical aspects of *Mishneh Torah.*[111] This pattern is not surprising, however, given that the Tosafists, and Ashkenazic rabbinic scholars on the whole, received neither legacy nor training in the formal discipline of philosophy, and displayed no real interest in its study.[112] Although Maimonides' philosophical teachings and *Moreh Nevukhim* were certainly not part of the curriculum of the Tosafists,[113] our inability to identify any known Tosafists who were involved in the Maimonidean controversy should cause us to resist the temptation and the tendency to lump all Tosafists and Ashkenazic rabbinic figures together when it comes to the issues that surrounded this controversy, such as anthropomorphism.

Indeed, all of the previous discussion in this chapter suggests that the impression engendered by the various letters on behalf of Maimonides dur-

---

1:461), however, Judah is referred to only once in the literature of the *Tosafot* (although these four scholars were also invited to participate in the Disputation of Paris in 1240; see Galinsky, "Mishpat ha-Talmud be-Paris," (above, n. 9). There is no way, therefore, of knowing Judah's view (or the view of other lesser-known scholars like him) on anthropomorphism. Urbach, "Ḥelqam shel Ḥakhmei Ashkenaz ve-Ẓarefat," 149–59, also attempts to document the stance of German Tosafists during the Maimonidean controversy of the 1230s. The matter requires further elucidation, however, in light of the numerous documents and studies that have appeared in the half-century since this article was published.

[111] See J. Woolf, "Maimonides Revised: The Case of the *Sefer Miswot Gadol,*" 175–203; J. Galinsky, "Ve-lihyot Lefanekha 'Eved Ne'eman," (above, n. 8), 16–22; and cf. Urbach, *Ba'alei ha-Tosafot*, 1:468–69; and Zev Harvey, "She'elat I-Gashmiyyut ha-E-l Ezel Rambam, Rabad, Crescas u-Spinoza," in *Meḥqarim be-Hagut Yehudit*, ed. S. O. Heller Wilensky and M. Idel (Jerusalem, 1989), 69–74. Urbach points out that there is not the slightest reference to the Maimonidean controversy in *Sefer Mizvot Gadol* (in addition to noting Moses's effusive praise of Rambam's scholarship in the introduction to *Sefer Mizvot Gadol*, although the pitfalls of allegorical interpretation may have been behind Moses's vigorous sermons and exhortations to ensure the performance of various precepts). Cf. J. Dan, "Ashkenazi Hasidism and the Maimonidean Controversy," 33–34, 46–47, and Urbach, "Ḥelqam shel Ḥakhmei Ashkenaz ve-Ẓarefat ba-Polmos 'al ha-Rambam," 154. Galinsky (16, n. 19) notes the veneration for *Mishneh Torah* demonstrated by associates of R. Moses of Coucy in Paris (circa 1240), who seem to have been unmoved and unaffected by the developments of the Maimonidean controversy. In the absence of a clear and direct statement by R. Moses about anthropomorphism, Galinsky (20, n. 41) is unsure as to where R. Moses stands on this issue. It should be noted, however, that in *Sefer Mizvot Gadol*, in both the (second) introduction to the positive commandments and the third positive commandment (citing extensively from an introductory passage in Shabbetai Donnolo's *Sefer Ḥakhmoni*, which interprets the phrase in Genesis 1:26, *na'aseh 'adam be-zalmenu*; see Shraga Abramson, "'Inyanut be-Sefer Miẓvot Gadol," *Sinai* 80 [1977], 210–14, and cf. above, n. 27), R. Moses characterizes in detail the pronounced physicality of the human being, as compared to the presumed noncorporeal existence of the Almighty.

[112] See above, n. 1. J. Woolf (in the preceding note) suggests that R. Moses of Coucy handled the philosophical material in *Mishneh Torah* in the way he did in order to render the halakhic material in *Mishneh Torah* more suitable and acceptable to his audience.

[113] Cf. above, nn. 89–90.

ing the controversy of the 1230s—that many or most of the *rabbanei Ẓarefat* believed in Divine anthropomorphism—is a rather exaggerated one, certainly with respect to the leading scholars or the rabbinic elite of the day.[114] Against this impression, we have encountered a wide range of positions within the rabbinic literature of medieval Ashkenaz during the twelfth and thirteenth centuries, from the relatively anthropomorphic views of R. Moses Taku and R. Solomon b. Simḥah of Troyes, to the essentially Maimonidean view held by R. Yosef *Bekhor Shor* of Orleans and *Sefer ha-Gan* (and other *perushei Baʿalei ha-Tosafot ʿal ha-Torah*). Other Tosafists, especially those with connections to the German Pietists, were somewhere in the middle, espousing different versions of the doctrine of the derivative Divine glory (*kavod*) that appeared to the prophets and others in real or imagined form. We have found these positions expressed in a number of different Tosafist genres and contexts as well, an important factor when trying to determine the personal beliefs and positions of the Tosafists.

If the criteria set forth by Naḥmanides in his letter of 1232 are used as a measuring stick, only those Ashkenazic scholars who held positions more anthropomorphic than the nonesoteric (*sifrut ha-Yiḥud*) views of R. Eleazar of Worms and R. Judah *he-Ḥasid* would be considered as corporealists (*magshimim*), although, to be sure, fully committed Maimunists (or Jewish Aristotelians) might have had a lower threshold for measuring anthropomorphism than Ramban did.[115] Indeed, we have been unable to positively identify any Ashkenazic rabbinic scholars who espoused radical or crude forms of anthropomorphism. The positions of R. Moses Taku and *Sefer ha-Maskil* did not include overt or fixed Divine corporeality, and in any case, these positions do not seem to have had much of an impact on subsequent Ashkenazic rabbinic literature.

It has been suggested that the question sent by R. Abraham Klausner of Vienna to R. Menaḥem Agler of Prague in the late fourteenth century concerning which characterization of God's nature is more correct, the corporeal or the noncorporeal, meant that this basic question had never

114 A letter written from Narbonne to Spain in the 1230s severely ridicules the "great men of Israel among the *Ẓarefatim* and their scholars, their heads and men of understanding," for their magical uses of Divine names, angels, and demons through conjuration, referring to them as "madmen full of delusions" and the like. See, e.g., B. Septimus, *Hispano-Jewish Culture in Transition*, 86–87; M. Halbertal, *Bein Torah le-Ḥokhmah*, 115. As I have demonstrated throughout my *"Peering through the Lattices,"* these practices, found among many (but certainly not all) of the Tosafists in Ashkenaz, were undertaken with the same kind of care and precision that typified the talmudic scholarship of Ashkenaz; see also above, chapter 6.

115 In addition, the unique version of the *Kavod* theory held by the *Ḥug ha-Keruv ha-Meyuḥad* might have been considered closer to anthropomorphism than the other versions of this theory we have seen. See Scholem, *Origins of the Kabbalah* (above, n.40), and cf. above, n. 62.

been fully resolved in Ashkenaz, and that the anthropomorphic view had at least remained current.[116] As R. Abraham indicates, however, he raised his question on the basis of having read the writings of R. Saʿadyah Gaon and R. Abraham ibn Ezra, as well as the pietistic *Shir ha-Yiḥud*, which all held the nonanthropomorphic view, followed by R. Moses Taku's *Ketav Tamim*, which challenges this view. R. Abraham was impressed by the array of biblical and talmudic texts that Taku cites and, as a result, posed his question. It would seem that Abraham became aware of the anthropomorphic view mostly from his reading of this unusual and erudite book, which was not often cited in the thirteenth century. Troubled by the impressive argumentation of this work against such luminaries as Saʿadyah Gaon and Maimonides, Abraham sends his query to his colleague R. Menaḥem Agler, who was partial to philosophy. R. Menaḥem rejects *Ketav Tamim*'s view on anthropomorphism out of hand in favor of the view of Maimonides, referring to Taku's work derisively as כתב טמא. As this exchange demonstrates as well, the view of *Ketav Tamim* on anthropomorphism was not widely accepted within medieval Ashkenaz, even as the existence of *Ketav Tamim* and the position on anthropomorphism that it represents were known to some rabbinic scholars.[117]

Formulations of R. Eleazar of Worms and other German Pietists regarding their *torat ha-Kavod* appear to assume that there were individuals in Ashkenaz who did support the more radical position.[118] Somewhat paradoxically, the more esoteric writings of the German Pietists and associated mystical circles (such as the *Ḥug ha-Keruv ha-Meyuḥad*) themselves convey a greater inclination toward anthropomorphism, at least on the symbolic level. This position, however, held only by a small, inner group of Pietist followers, was hidden from non-Ashkenazic Jewry and probably from the bulk of Ashkenazic Jewry as well.[119] R. Isaiah di Trani, and any of the Tosafists who held a middle position, may have been writing to bring people away from the edge, but there is no evidence for direct interaction with any individuals who actually held the more radical anthropomorphic position.

[116] See D. Berger, "Judaism and General Culture in Medieval and Early Modern Times," 95–96. The correspondence between R. Abraham and R. Menaḥem Agler was published by Efraim Kupfer, "Li-Demutah ha-Tarbutit shel Yahadut Ashkenaz ve-Ḥakhamehah ba-Me'ot ha-Yod Daled—ha-Tet-Vav," *Tarbiz* 42 (1972–73), 114–15. See also Y. Y. Yuval, *Ḥakhamim be-Doram* (Jerusalem, 1989), 301.

[117] Cf. above, nn. 39, 62, 68, 75. On the limited reception of *Ketav Tamim* during the early modern period in eastern Europe, see, e.g., *She'elot u-Teshuvot ha-Ramo*, ed. Asher Siev (New York, 1971), #126, sec. 3; and cf. Jacob Elbaum, *Petiḥut ve-Histagrut* (Jerusalem, 1990), 166, n. 46.

[118] See *'Arugat ha-Bosem*, ed. Urbach, 4:74–81.

[119] See above, n. 61.

From the larger perspective of medieval Jewish intellectual history, the range of views in Ashkenaz with regard to anthropomorphism helps to diminish the "backward" image—as compared, for example, to Maimonides, Naḥmanides, and other Spanish talmudists—that has sometimes been assigned to the talmudic scholars of this region. Without benefit of a sustained philosophical tradition, the Tosafists, not to mention the German Pietists who were much more aware of philosophical teachings, were able nonetheless to respond to important theological questions that stood before them, against the backdrop of the complete corpus of talmudic and rabbinic literature. The positions they developed are interesting and even innovative, and they speak to a more varied and sophisticated rabbinic culture in medieval Ashkenaz than has been imagined until now.

Perhaps there were members of the second-level intelligentsia in Ashkenaz—who qualified as rabbinic scholars of some ability or note but were not represented by, and did not contribute to, the writings of the Tosafists—who believed in radical anthropomorphism, if not in the position advocated by R. Moses Taku; there were many such rabbinic scholars and students present in northern France and Germany during the Tosafist period.[120] These figures may have been less aware of Spanish and Sefardic sources related to anthropomorphism, as compared to those leading Ashkenazic authors who presented nonanthropomorphic views. To be sure, there may also have been a degree of simple or crude anthropomorphism present within the less-educated and less-learned strata of Ashkenazic society. Alas, the paucity of sources that record popular religious belief in medieval Ashkenaz does not allow us at this time to assess the situation in this part of Ashkenazic society in more concrete terms.[121]

[120] See Moritz Gudemann, above, n. 71; and cf. Moshe Idel, "Kabbalah and Elites in Thirteenth-Century Spain," *Medieval Historical Review* 9 (1994), 5–19. On the relatively small size of the Tosafist academies (especially in northern France), and the distinction between Tosafist academies and other (lesser) *battei midrash* and Torah scholars within medieval Ashkenaz, see my *Jewish Education and Society in the High Middle Ages* (Detroit, Mich., 1992), 16–18, 49–51, 66–68; and my "Bein Yeshivot Ba'alei ha-Tosafot le-Battei Midrashot Aḥerim be-Ashkenaz Bimei ha-Benayim," in *Yeshivot u-Battei Midrashot*, ed. I. Etkes (Jerusalem, 2006), 85–108. Cf., e.g., *Tosafot ha-Shalem*, ed. Gellis, 1:262, sec. 1. Unknown and unnamed Ashkenazic rabbinic figures expressed and implemented their views with regard to a complex, highly charged (and tragic) application of the precept of *kiddush ha-Shem.* Interestingly, the lives and achievements of those who wrote the letters to *rabbanei Ẓarefat* on behalf of the Maimonidean corpus, with the obvious exception of Ramban, are also barely known to us.

[121] Cf. my "Levels of Literacy in Ashkenaz and Sefarad as Reflected by the Recitation of Biblical Verses Found in the Liturgy," [Hebrew] in *From Sages to Savants—Studies Presented to Avraham Grosssman*, ed. Y. Hacker et al. (Jerusalem, 2009), 187–211. On the composition, role, and impact of the secondary elite in medieval Ashkenaz, see also above, chapter 4.

Finally, with regard to anthropomorphism and the rabbinic elite, there appears to have been something of a regional distinction between northern France and Germany; the former area boasted a number of Tosafists who pursued an almost Maimonidean view, while their German counterparts preferred to espouse a form of the Divine *kavod*, although this distinction becomes somewhat blurred by the second half of the thirteenth century as the so-called Tosafist Torah compilations included both positions together. This array is rather different from what I have found regarding Tosafist attitudes toward the messianic era, where northern French and German Tosafists alike, and *Ḥasidei Ashkenaz* as well, consistently supported an approach, *sugya* in and *sugya* out, that viewed this era as a relatively miraculous one, parting ways at every opportunity, and in every detail, from the position developed by Maimonides, which depicted a completely natural era in human history.[122]

As we have noticed, however, in other realms of Tosafist endeavor, including their major interest in talmudic interpretation and halakhic rulings and legislation, there are issues or topics for which all Tosafists appear to express a similar view as their personalist position, just as there are any number of instances in which their preferred approaches varied.[123] What is significant about the issues of anthropomorphism and the nature of the messianic era is that Tosafists were certainly sophisticated enough to use their methods and outlook to address matters of belief as well, in enlightened ways. To be sure, the Tosafists did not follow the Maimonidean interpretational strategy with respect to *ʾaggadah*, which typically understood many passages as hypberbolic if not as metaphoric or allegorical. Nonetheless, just as the talmudic *peshat* approach favored by the Tosafists was applied with the rigor and consistency that are evident in halakhic contexts, it should not be surprising to discover that, on occasion, it is possible to adduce Tosafist views in matters of faith as well.

Indeed, as I have also shown, it is possible with respect to the messianic era to locate the views of R. Meir *ha-Levi* Abulafia (Ramah), R. David Kimḥi (Radak), and Naḥmanides, all systematic thinkers in their own right, between the more polar positions held by Maimonides and the Tosafists. Moving forward, it may well be possible to identify additional positions of faith

122 See my "Medieval Rabbinic Conceptions of the Messianic Ages: The View of the Tosafists," in *Me'ah She'arim: Studies in Medieval Jewish Spiritual Life in Memory of Isadore Twersky*, ed. Ezra Fleischer et al. (Jerusalem, 2001), 147–70.

123 See above, chapter 1, nn. 161–69. As I indicated there (in n. 166), my study of messianic calculations by Tosafists has also revealed that the two disparate approaches to these calculations favored in medieval Ashkenaz were adopted by rabbinic scholars from both Germany and northern France.

and belief among the Tosafists, whether they all appear to be of one mind or whether they are of different minds, as in the case of anthropomorphism. Although the views of the Tosafists may not break down along geographic lines in a particular matter, we have seen that this possibility must always be considered in both halakhic and non-halakhic contexts.[124]

124 See e.g., *Ḥiddushei R. Beẓal'el b. Joel Ranschburg: Pitḥei Niddah* (Jerusalem, 1957), to *Niddah* 16, for his discussion of free will versus Divine omniscience. The Tosafist view is, of course, essentially Talmud-based, and is not couched at all in philosophic terms, as it was for Rambam or even for Saʿadyah. Nonetheless, there appear to be certain commonly held axioms or postulates, and some differences of view that can be consistently identified. Thus, R. Beẓal'el Ranschburg is able, at least broadly, to effectively compare and contrast the Tosafist view with that of Maimonides.

Conclusion

Ashkenazic Rabbinic Culture in Its Plenitude

More than a quarter-century ago, Ivan Marcus published a suggestive article in which he maintained that the intellectual history of medieval Spanish or Sefardic Jewry has received a disproportionate share of scholarly attention as compared to the learned endeavors within Ashkenazic society.[1] Sefardic authors created works in philosophy and poetry, both religious and secular, which appealed much more to modern tastes—beginning already with the period of the *Wissenschaft des Judenthums*—than did the heavy talmudism of the Ashkenazic rabbinic elite. Indeed, the only areas of medieval Ashkenazic intellectual endeavor that received significant attention from *Wissenschaft* scholars such as Abraham Geiger and Leopold Zunz were liturgical poetry and other synagogue texts, and northern French biblical interpretation, which was highlighted by an enlightened devotion to *peshuto shel miqra* or *peshat.*

Marcus's sensitivity to this imbalance may have been heightened, at least in part, by his own concurrent studies on the social thought and penitential programs of the German Pietists.[2] The nuanced theories of religious and social hierarchics and reforms espoused by *Ḥasidei Ashkenaz*, as well as their approaches to all kinds of popular beliefs and practices, not to mention their mystical teachings and writings and varied forms of biblical exegesis, clearly showed that there was much more to Ashkenazic intellectual life and rabbinic culture than the study of Talmud and *halakhah* alone. The older

[1] See I. Marcus, "Beyond the Sefardic Mystique," *Orim* 1 (1985), 35–53.

[2] See, e.g., I. Marcus, "The Recensions and Structure of *Sefer Ḥasidim*," *Proceedings of the American Academy for Jewish Research* 45 (1978), 131–53; idem, "The Politics and Ethics of Pietism in Judaism: The *Ḥasidim* of Medieval Germany," *Journal of Religious Ethics* 8 (1980), 227–59; idem, *Piety and Society: The Jewish Pietists of Medieval Germany* (Leiden, 1981); idem, "*Ḥasidei Ashkenaz* Private Penitentials: An Introduction and Descriptive Catalogue of Their Manuscripts and Early Editions," in *Studies in Jewish Mysticism*, ed. J. Dan and F. Talmage (Cambridge, Mass., 1982), 57–84; and see also idem, "Hierarchies, Religious Boundaries and Jewish Spirituality in Medieval Germany," *Jewish History* 1 (1986), 7–25.

stereotype, however, had been in vogue essentially from the medieval period onward. *Ashkenazim* referred to *Sefaradim* (derisively) as poets, even as *Sefaradim* complimented *Ashkenazim* for their talmudic prowess and little else, certainly not for the literary style in which the *Ashkenazim* expressed themselves, nor for the approaches they employed in interpreting the Bible.[3]

As we noted at the outset of this study, a good deal of the most substantive twentieth-century scholarship on Tosafist creativity tended to ignore or downplay these extra-talmudic disciplines and developments as well, opting perhaps unwittingly for a form of the medieval Spanish model, in which talmudists were often uninvolved with other disciplines (with some notable exceptions), while leading philosophers, mystics, and poets were often not especially adept at talmudic studies and interpretation.[4] This perception may also help to explain why there has been relatively little sustained scholarly treatment of Spanish talmudic studies from the twelfth and thirteenth centuries, at least prior to the recently published volumes by Israel Ta-Shma, *Ha-Sifrut ha-Parshanit la-Talmud.*[5] Indeed, Ta-Shma elsewhere pointedly criticized Yitzhak Baer for neglecting to integrate in any way the voluminous talmudic commentaries of Naḥmanides or Rashba into his classic study on the history of the Jews in Christian Spain.[6]

[3] See e.g., the exchange between Rabbenu Tam and R. Abraham ibn Ezra (as noted by E. E. Urbach, *Ba'alei ha-Tosafot* [Jerusalem, 1980], 1:109–10). Cf. Bernard Septimus, *Hispano-Jewish Culture in Transition: The Career and Controversies of Ramah* (Cambridge, Mass., 1982), 79–89; Moshe Halbertal, *People of the Book* (Cambridge, Mass., 1997), 109–19; idem, *Bein Torah le-Ḥokhmah* (Jerusalem, 2000), 114–15; David Malkiel, *Reconstructing Ashkenaz* (Stanford, Calif., 2009), 2–5; the assessment of Profiat Duran, as cited and discussed in my *Jewish Education and Society in the High Middle Ages* (Detroit, Mich., 2007), 85; Uriel Simon, "Transplanting the Wisdom of Spain to Christian Lands: The Failed Efforts of R. Abraham Ibn Ezra," *Yearbook of the Simon Dubnow Institute* 8 (2009), 181–89; Aharon Mondschein, "The Massoretes Fabricated Explanations for Full and Defective Spellings: On Abraham Ibn Ezra's Struggles Against the (Ab)use of Biblical Spelling as an Exegetical Tool," [Hebrew] *Shenaton le-Ḥeqer ha-Miqra veha-Mizraḥ ha-Qadum* 19 (2009), 289–301; and above, Introduction, n. 55.

[4] On the sharp tension between talmudists and *pashtanim* in medieval Spain, see, e.g., Moses ibn Ezra, *Sefer ha-'Iyyunim veha-Diyyunim*, ed. A. Halkin (Jerusalem, 1975), 257; Yonah ibn Janah, *Sefer ha-Riqmah*, ed. M. Wilensky (Berlin, 1929), 10–19; and Judah b. Barzilai al-Barzeloni, *Perush Sefer Yeẓirah*, ed. S. Z. H. Halberstam (Berlin, 1888), 5.

[5] Volume 1 (Jerusalem, 2001), and volume 2 (Jerusalem, 2003). Cf. Chaim Tchernowitz, *Toledot ha-Posqim*, vol. 2 (New York, 1947), 106–34. Studies of individual Spanish talmudists include, e.g., Septimus's work on Ramah (above, n. 3); *Ḥiddushei ha-Ramban le-Massekhet Ketubot*, ed. Ezra Chwat (Jerusalem, 1993), editor's introduction, 1–45 (and see also M. Halbertal, *'Al Derekh ha-Emet* [Jerusalem, 2006], *passim*); Leon Feldman, "Studies in the Life and Times of R. Nissim b. Reuben Gerondi of Barcelona (Ph.D. diss., Columbia University, 1968); and cf. my "Between Ashkenaz and Sefarad: Tosafist Teaching in the Talmudic Commentaries of Ritva," in *Between Rashi and Maimonides: Themes in Medieval Jewish Thought, Literature and Exegesis*, ed. E. Kanarfogel and M. Sokolow (New York, 2010), 237–73.

[6] See Ta-Shma, *Knesset Meḥqarim*, vol. 2 (Jerusalem, 2004), 279–96. Cf. *R. Moses Naḥmanides: Explorations in His Religious and Literary Virtuosity* (Cambridge, Mass., 1983), ed. I. Twersky,

These prior assessments notwithstanding, this study has demonstrated that Ashkenazic rabbinic scholarship was interested in an array of disciplines well beyond those of talmudic studies and halakhic decision-making, which in and of themselves differed between northern France and Germany in a number of ways. The difficulty in fully locating the various extra-talmudic interests stems in part from the fact that they were often cultivated according to methods and goals that were not fully enunciated. Moreover, these non-talmudic writings remained mostly in manuscript. It was the talmudic studies of the Tosafists that were of the greatest interest to subsequent rabbinic and lay scholarship. Their Torah commentaries were never as popular as Rashi's commentary; their *piyyutim* were never as well known as those of classical *payyetanim* such as Qallir, or even as those of leading pre-Crusade *payyetanim* such as R. Simeon *ha-Gadol* or R. Meir *Shaẓ* of Worms; and their forays into magic and mysticism paled against the protean efforts of R. Eleazar of Worms and his associates, not to mention subsequent kabbalists.

Nonetheless, as we have seen, significant efforts and contributions in all these disciplines were in fact realized and achieved during the Tosafist period, and they constitute an important dimension of the intellectual history and rabbinic culture of medieval Ashkenaz, and of the search within Ashkenazic rabbinic scholarship for multiple and variegated Torah truths and interpretations. Moreover, the literary remains of these efforts can also help to explain a number of cultural developments whose parameters and reasons have been unclear to this point. We now have a much better idea of where and how *peshat* interpretation moved at the end of the twelfth century and beyond. The significant patterns of authorship that emerge for a large cohort of Tosafists in both northern France and Germany suggest that *piyyut* composition in medieval Ashkenaz was not the sole purview of particular families, such as the descendants of Rashi or *Ḥasidei Ashkenaz*, although to be sure, the original intent of *payyetanim* is not always clear, and there are many additional *piyyutim* in manuscript whose authors have not yet been identified.[7] In addition, Spanish forms and materials clearly exerted influence in this discipline. Indeed, this influence appears to have grown with the passage of time, albeit in different ways than was the case for biblical interpretation. The notion that Ashkenazic rabbinic scholars were all vivid corporealists had hardly been scrutinized by modern scholarship

editor's introduction, 8 (n. 20), where Dubnow's statement that Naḥmanides' "report on the disputation of Barcelona has historic and religious value and will certainly live longer than his big books in the field of halakhah" is deservedly critiqued.

[7] See, e.g., *Leqet Piyyutei Seliḥot*, ed, D. Goldschmidt and A. Fraenkel (Jerusalem, 1996), 662–768.

in the past. We now know that at least among the first-level rabbinic elite this was simply not the case.

Several recent studies have suggested that *piyyut* commentary (and perhaps even prayer commentary more generally) was taught and developed within the talmudic *battei midrash* or *yeshivot* in medieval Ashkenaz, and there is both textual and conceptual evidence to support this contention, given that *piyyut* commentary required a thorough knowledge and understanding of the full spectrum of both biblical and rabbinic texts.[8] In his constructive critique of E. E. Urbach's oeuvre, Ya'acov Sussmann argued for the importance of noting with greater precision the distinctions, as well as the similarities, between the Tosafists of northern France and their German counterparts. As Sussmann further suggests, this reevaluation must also include a fuller assessment of the extra-talmudic disciplines such as *torat ha-sod*, as well as liturgical interpretations and compositions, in which various Tosafists were involved.[9]

This study has also shown that Ashkenazic rabbinic scholarship was aware and appreciative of some of the larger interpretational strategies employed by Christian scholars and intellectuals during the twelfth century and beyond. Ashkenazic rabbinic culture was not as isolated or as insulated as has been thought, although the areas in which other influences may have permeated must be carefully drawn. The Tosafists were undoubtedly aware of significant intellectual developments within Christian society, even as they could not read about the details and specifics found in the vast majority of Christian religious and scholarly works that were composed in Latin. The area of legal dialectic, as we have seen, is an especially fertile realm in this regard.

Indeed, the breadth of Ashkenazic rabbinic scholarship itself, in the pre-Crusade period and especially beyond, may owe something to the expansion of Christian learning in northern France and Germany, although it would be incorrect to attribute the breadth of the rabbinic scholarship solely or even mainly to this influence. Rather, the relatively broad rabbinic values that were active during the pre-Crusade period in Ashkenaz continued to play a significant role during the twelfth and thirteenth

[8] See Avraham Grossman, *Ḥakhmei Ẓarefat ha-Rishonim* (Jerusalem, 1995), 507–9, 522–28, 531–38; I. Ta-Shma, *Ha-Tefillah ha-Ashkenazit ha-Qedumah* (Jerusalem, 2003), 33–42 (and below, n. 10); Mordechai Breuer, *Be-Ohalei Ya'aqov* (Jerusalem, 2004), 164–65, 516; Elisabeth Hollender, "Commentary on a 'Lost' Piyyut: Considering the Transmission of Teaching and Texts in Rashi's Bet Midrash," in *Raschi und sein Erbe*, ed. D. Krochmalnik et al. (Heidelberg, 2007), 47–63; and idem, *Piyyut Commentaries in Medieval Ashkenaz* (Berlin, 2008), 6–9.

[9] See Sussmann, "The Scholarly Oeuvre of Professor Ephraim Elimelekh Urbach," [Hebrew] in *Ephraim Elimelekh Urbach: A Bio-Bibliography* [Supplementary Jewish Studies, Forum of the World Union for Jewish Studies, vol. 1] (Jerusalem, 1993), 39–40, 47–54, 61.

centuries. Although there is reason to believe that more than a few pieces of pre-Crusade scholarship may have been lost, the commitment of leading scholars during that period, especially in Mainz, to disciplines aside from talmudic studies appears to have remained in vogue. Indeed, Israel Ta-Shma has written that:

> Beginning with the eleventh century, [Ashkenazic rabbinic] literature was produced that dealt with *piyyut* interpretation and the interpretation of prayer, as well as the major *midreshei halakhah* and *midreshei ʾaggadah*. In the thirteenth century, an extensive corpus of biblical exegesis (especially on the Pentateuch) was added. Various literary indicators suggest that there were also *shiʿurim* taught in these subjects, within the main study hall [of the Tosafist academies] or at least in the private living quarters of the teacher, and certain Torah figures specialized in, and often referred to, these particular exegetical contexts. However, despite this widespread presence of supplementary disciplines—as clearly reflected by the vast amount of material that can be found in manuscript—and despite the fact that the number of students and teachers who participated in these disciplines was not trivial, these disciplines did not occupy a place in the fixed curriculum or main schedule of studies of the *yeshivah*. Those teachers who specialized in these subjects did not share in the leadership and representation of the *yeshivah*. From all the documents that we have in our hands dealing with the nature of the Tosafist academies, one person alone [who was dedicated to talmudic studies in particular] served as the *rosh yeshivah*.

Ta-Shma concludes that it was "the deep-seated Jewish recognition of the exclusive status of the Babylonian Talmud" that prevented the Tosafist academies from developing as full-fledged multidisciplinary institutions, as the medieval universities did.[10]

Although the results of the present study suggest that the involvement of certain leading Tosafists with disciplines beyond talmudic and halakhic interpretation was even more widespread and wide-ranging than Ta-Shma imagined, the resistance of Rabbenu Tam and others to some of these other disciplines, especially mysticism and non-talmudic biblical interpretation, may well have stemmed from his overarching, singular commitment to the hegemony of the Babylonian Talmud. Indeed, Rabbenu Tam's father, R. Meir b. Samuel, had been a student at Worms, where some of the non-talmudic disciplines had receded by the eleventh century and where nascent talmudic

[10] See Ta-Shma, "Maqbilim she-Einam Nifgashim: Yeshivot Baʿalei ha-Tosafot veha-Sevivah ha-Aqademaʾit be-Ẓarefat ba-Meʾah ha-Shteim ʿEsreh veha-Shelosh ʿEsreh," in *Yeshivot u-Battei Midrashot*, ed. I. Etkes (Jerusalem, 2006), 83–84.

dialectic, on the other hand, was being developed. A significant part of the "revolutionary" aspect of Rabbenu Tam's intellectual leadership during the mid-twelfth century was to approach all Jewish learning through the prism of the talmudic corpus. Although a number of important Tosafists such as R. Samson b. Abraham of Sens (d. 1214) and his brother Riẓba remain as paragons of this focused talmudism, Tosafists such as R. Yom Tov of Joigny, R. Yeḥiʾel of Paris, R. Ephraim of Regensburg, and R. Meir of Rothenburg, among many others in both northern France and Germany, emerge from our study as first-rate talmudists who nonetheless evinced significant interest in and made impressive contributions to a range of other disciplines within the larger pantheon of Torah study.

Ashkenazic rabbinic culture in the High Middle Ages began with the Talmud, but it was about much more than talmudic scholarship alone. These other interests had the potential to impact rabbinic scholarship at every level, and to impact medieval Ashkenazic society as a whole. As we have noted, the Tosafist exegetes on the Torah in the late twelfth and early to mid-thirteenth centuries whose comments we have highlighted served as a kind of bridge between the classical twelfth-century *pashtanim* in northern France (beginning with the commentary of Rashi) and the compilatory *perushei Baʿalei ha-Tosafot ʿal ha-Torah* that began to appear in the mid-thirteenth century and extended into the early fourteenth century and beyond.[11]

A full-scale study dedicated solely to these compilatory works, which can be found in more than two hundred manuscripts all told, remains a desideratum.[12] On a certain level, relatively little progress has been made in evaluating this corpus since the brief but perceptive treatment by Samuel Poznanski nearly a century ago, in the context of his larger study of biblical exegesis in northern France.[13] Although Poznanski correctly saw these compilatory works as much greater repositories of *derash* than *peshat* which did not appear in any way to be a continuation of the work of the twelfth-century northern French *pashtanim*, Sara Japhet has shown that *peshat* was

[11] We have noted that the classical twelfth-century northern French *pashtanim* were also engaged to a significant degree in commenting on biblical books beyond the Torah, a pursuit that was not shared, for the most part, by the Tosafist commentators from the late twelfth century and beyond whose work we have highlighted. See above, chapter 2, nn. 28, 42, 199; and chapter 3, nn. 97, 110, 120

[12] I have written a lengthy article on the midrashic methods of these collections titled "Midrashic Texts and Methods in Tosafist Torah Commentaries," in *Re-Visioning Midrash: Transformations and Cultural Innovations*, ed. Michael Fishbane and Joanna Weinberg (Oxford, 2012). Nonetheless, there remains much to be done with this corpus.

[13] S. Poznanski, *Mavo ʿal Ḥakhmei Ẓarefat Mefarshei ha-Miqra* (Jerusalem, 1965), originally published in conjunction with his edition of *Perush R. Eliʿezer mi-Belgenẓi le-Sefer Yeḥezqel* (Warsaw, 1913).

nonetheless a recognizable component of a number of these collections, with particular emphasis on the *Ḥizzequni* commentary that was completed in northern France around 1275.[14]

While we have seen that those Tosafists and leading Ashkenazic rabbinic figures who served as significant, independent Torah commentators effectively filled this gap and also produced a significant stratum or component of the broader *Perushei Ba'alei ha-Tosafot 'al ha-Torah*, it is fairly clear that the corpus of the Tosafist Torah commentaries as a whole was meant to serve or to accommodate members of the second-level intelligentsia, and perhaps those below them as well. Indeed, a similar phenomenon and pattern can be detected in the appearance of a series of abridged Ashkenazic halakhic treatises, some of which were organized according to the weekly portions of the Torah, from the mid-thirteenth century onward. This popularization of Ashkenazic rabbinic culture, which coincided with the decline of the physical and personal fortunes of Ashkenazic Jewry in the mid-thirteenth century, also requires further study.[15]

As I have suggested throughout this study, the regnant perception of Ashkenazic rabbinic scholarship and culture must be thoroughly revised in a number of ways. Most significantly, the absence of formal, rigorous philosophical training in medieval Ashkenaz should not be construed as evidence for an absence of intellectualism. Indeed, the charge leveled in the 1230s during the so-called Maimonidean controversy, that "the rabbis of northern France" fully espoused and endorsed a belief in anthropomorphism, cannot be documented for any known Tosafists or their students. In this instance as well, the ability to locate and isolate the views of the second-level intelligentsia, whose presence has also been raised with regard to the so-called Tosafist Torah compilations, may yet prove to be crucial.[16]

[14] See Japhet, "The Commentary of Ḥizkuni to the Pentateuch," [Hebrew] in *Sefer ha-Yovel le-R. Mordekhai Breuer*, ed. Moshe Bar-Asher et al. (Jerusalem, 1992), 1:91–111.

[15] See my "Bein Yeshivot Ba'alei ha-Tosafot le-Battei Midrashot Aḥerim be-Ashkenaz Bimei ha-Benayim," in *Yeshivot u-Battei Midrashot*, ed. Etkes, 85–108; and above, chapter 4, nn. 193–96. On the nature of compilatory works in this period in medieval Europe, see A. J. Minnis, "Late-Medieval Discussion of *Compilatio* and the Role of the Compilator," *Beitrage zur Geshichte de deutschen Sprache und Literatur* 101:3 (Tubingen, 1979), 385–421; and Neil Hathaway, "Compilatio: From Plagiarism to Compiling," *Viator* 20 (1990), 19–44. Cf. Judah Galinsky, "On Popular Halakhic Literature and the Jewish Reading Audience in Fourteenth-Century Spain," *Jewish Quarterly Review* 98 (2008), 305–27; C. F. Biggs, "Literacy, Reading and Writing in the Medieval West," *Journal of Medieval History* 26 (2000), 397–420; and my "Prayer, Literacy and Literary Memory in the Jewish Communities of Medieval Europe," in *Jewish Studies at the Crossroads of Anthropology and History*, ed. R. S. Boustan et al. (Philadelphia, 2011), 250–70, 397–404.

[16] Cf. M. Idel, *Messianic Mystics* (New Haven, Conn., 1998), 265–69; idem, "R. Neḥemiah ben Shlomo the Prophet of Erfurt's Commentary on the *Piyyut El Na le-'Olam Tu'araz*," [Hebrew] *Moreshet Yisra'el* 2 (2005), 40–41; and above, in the Introduction, n. 84.

In addition, this study has identified a number of possible Spanish (and Provençal) influences upon the Tosafists, although, again, distinctions among disciplines are crucial. In talmudic studies, for example, there seems to have been relatively little movement from southern Europe northward. Contemporary scholarship disagrees a bit about some of the details, but it is clear that R. Isaac Alfasi's work is not cited in any significant way in Ashkenaz until the late twelfth or early thirteenth centuries, and Maimonides' *Mishneh Torah* lags even behind that.[17] Ashkenazic Jewry believed that their underlying traditions and innovative methods in the realm of talmudic and halakhic studies were most effective, and it would appear that rabbinic scholarship in the south agreed to a large extent.

Indeed, a number of rabbinic scholars from Provence made their way north during the late twelfth century to study with R. Isaac of Dampierre and other Tosafists, even though there were several outstanding talmudists active precisely at that time in Provence, including R. Zeraḥyah *ha-Levi* and Rabad of Posquieres. These wandering Provençal rabbinic scholars then brought the Tosafist material southward to the leading circles of talmudic study in Catalonia and Aragon, where it became tremendously influential throughout the thirteenth century, as reflected by the talmudic writings of Ramban, Rashba, and others.[18]

In biblical studies, on the other hand, the Spanish center exerts a measure of influence already in the pre-Crusade period,[19] and this influence continues throughout the twelfth and thirteenth centuries.[20] As opposed to the realm of talmudic studies, Tosafists and other Ashkenazic rabbinic

[17] See, e.g. Urbach, *Baʿalei ha-Tosafot* (Jerusalem, 1980), 1:56–57, 251, 326, 617–18, 663–64; Avraham Grossman, "Me-Andalusia le-Eiropah: Yaḥasam shel Ḥakhmei Ashkenaz ve-Ẓarefat ba-Meʾot ha-Yod Bet/ha-Yod Gimmel ʾel Sifrei ha-Halakhah shel ha-Rif veh-Rambam," *Peʿamim* 80 (1999), 14–24; I. Ta-Shma, *Knesset Meḥqarim*, vol. 1 (Jerusalem, 2004), 43–61; idem, *Ha-Sifrut ha-Parshanit la-Talmud*, vol. 1 (Jerusalem, 1999), 60–61, 74–75, and vol. 2 (Jerusalem, 107, 109, 112); Simcha Emanuel, *Shivrei Luḥot* (Jerusalem, 2006), 67, 77, 116; E. Kanarfogel and M. Sokolow, "Rashi and Maimonides Meet in a Geniza Fragment," [Hebrew] *Tarbiz* 67 (1998), 411–16; and cf. Jeffrey Woolf, "Admiration and Apathy: Maimonides' 'Mishneh Torah' in High and Late Medieval Ashkenaz," in *Be'erot Yitzhak: Studies in Memory of Isadore Twersky*, ed. J. Harris (Cambridge, Mass., 2005), 427–53; and Haym Soloveitchik, "The Halakhic Isolation of the Ashkenazic Community," *Yearbook of the Simon Dubnow Institute* 8 (2009), 41–47.

[18] See I. Ta-Shma, *Rabbenu Zeraḥyah ha-Levi Baʿal ha-Maʾor u-Bnei Ḥugo* (Jerusalem, 1992), 84–86, 166; Shalem Yahalom, "R. Nathan b. R. Meir Moro shel ha-Ramban," *Peʿamim* 91 (2002), 5–7, 15–18, 20–22; idem, "R. Yehudah b. Yaqar—Toledotav u-Meqomo be-Mishnat ha-Ramban," *Sidra* 17 (2002), 79–86, 93–100, 105–7; and my "Between Ashkenaz and Sefarad: Tosafist Teachings in the Talmudic Commentaries of Ritva," above, n. 5.

[19] See, e.g., A. Grossman, *Ḥakhmei Ẓarefat ha-Rishonim* (Jerusalem, 1995), 457–77; and cf. Eleazar Touitou, *Ha-Peshatot ha-Mitḥadshim be-khol Yom* (Ramat Gan, 2003), 11–47; and Mordechai Cohen, "Meqor Sefaradi Efshari li-Tefisat Peshuto shel Miqra ʾeẓel Rashi," in *Rashi: The Man and His Work* [Hebrew], ed. A. Grossman and S. Japhet (Jerusalem, 2008), 2: 353–79.

[20] See above, chapter 2, nn. 51, 56, 100; chapter 3, nn. 14, 19, 88; and chapter 4, nn. 48, 93, 96.

figures were apparently more than willing to receive "outside information" and methodological assistance in this and other disciplines. This is certainly the case for *piyyut* composition as well, where in a number of respects German *payyetanim* take the lead from their French counterparts in adopting Spanish conventions and styles.[21]

With regard to magic and mysticism, research over the last several decades has pointed to the large amount of *Hekhalot*-based and other magical and mystical teachings and practices that moved from the north to the south, often by way of Provence, a pattern that appears to be contrary to the largely separate or parallel tracks of development that had been assumed by Scholem and others.[22] There is also evidence, however, for Ashkenazic figures (such as R. Abraham of Cologne, author of the kabbalistic work *Keter Shem Tov*) who made their way to northern Spain and then to Castile as the Zoharic corpus was being formulated in the late thirteenth century, in order to participate in the more formalized development of theosophic kabbalah.[23]

There is no evidence to suggest that the strongly anti-anthropomorphic position taken by Rashbam and *Bekhor Shor* was influenced overtly by Sefardic rationalism, although a more subtle form of influence was surely possible. Beginning, however, with *Sefer ha-Gan* and continuing through the thirteenth century, a number of *Perushei Baʿalei ha-Tosafot ʿal ha-Torah* introduce the view of Maimonides, from *Mishneh Torah* and in some instances from *Moreh Nevukhim* as well, to support their position, just as Saʿadyah Gaon's *torat ha-Kavod* clearly impacted the views of *Ḥasidei Ashkenaz* and R. Solomon Simḥah of Troyes. Once again, in non-talmudic

[21] See above, chapter 5, nn. 25, 27, 32, 42, 66, 135, 141, 162, 183, 201, 257, 318; and at n. 334.

[22] See, e.g., I. Ta-Shma, *Ha-Nigleh shebe-Nistar* (Tel Aviv, 2001); M. Idel, *Ben: Sonship and Jewish Mysticism* (New York, 2007), 194–97, 218–43, 276–87; idem, "Ha-Tefillah be-Qabbalat Provence," *Tarbiz* 62 (1993), 265–86; idem, "From Italy to Ashkenaz and Back: On the Circulation of Jewish Mystical Traditions," *Kabbalah* 14 (2006), 86–94; and idem, "Bein Ashkenaz le-Qastilyah ba-Me'ah ha-Shelosh ʿEsreh: Hashbaʿot, Reshimot ve-Shaʿarei Derashot be-Ḥugo shel R. Neḥemyah b. Shelomoh ha-Navi ve-Hashpa'oteihen," *Tarbiz* 77 (2008), 475–554; Elliot Wolfson, "Demut Yaʿaqov Ḥaquqah be-Kisse ha-Kavod: ʿIyyun Nosaf be-Torat ha-Sod shel Ḥasidei Ashkenaz," in *Massu'ot: Meḥqarim be-Sifrut ha-Qabbalah ube-Hagut ha-Yehudit le-Zikhro shel Ephraim Gottlieb*, ed. M. Oron and A. Goldreich (Jerusalem, 1994), 131–95; *The Commentaries to Ezekiel's Chariot of R. Eleazar of Worms and R. Jacob ben Jacob ha-Kohen* [Hebrew], ed. A. Farber-Ginat and D. Abrams (Los Angeles, 2004), editors' introduction, 9–31; and Daniel Abrams, "From Germany to Spain: Numerology as a Mystical Technique," *Journal of Jewish Studies* 47 (1996), 85–101.

[23] See Idel, *Kabbalah: New Perspectives* (New Haven, Conn., 1988), 211–12. Cf. idem, "The Kabbalah's 'Window of Opportunities,' 1270–1290," in *Me'ah She'arim: Studies in Medieval Jewish Spiritual Life in Memory of Isadore Twersky*, ed. E. Fleischer (Jerusalem, 2001), 201–6; Jacob Elbaum, *Openness and Insularity* [Hebrew] (Jerusalem, 1990), 16–17, 40–41, 183–200; and Joseph Davis, *Yom Tov Lipmann Heller* (Oxford, 2004), 39–43.

realms there was room at the Ashkenazic intellectual banquet even for Maimonides. Whatever the impact of the Maimonidean controversy in Ashkenaz, it did not disqualify Maimonides per se and certainly not in the areas of Jewish thought and beliefs, even as the Tosafists often moved in other directions.[24]

[24] In a forthcoming study, I account in detail for the noticeable avoidance in Ashkenaz rabbinic works of Maimonides' halakhic materials until the mid- to late thirteenth century along the lines suggested here, which accounts at the same time for their use of a number of his teachings in Jewish thought. Especially suggestive is the appearance of Maimonides in the *Perushei Ba'alei ha-Tosafot 'al ha-Torah*; see, e.g., Jacob Dienstag, "Yaḥasam shel Ba'alei ha-Tosafot leha-Rambam," in *Sefer Yovel likhvod Shmu'el Kalman Mirsky*, ed. S. Bernstein and G. Churgin (New York, 1958), 350–79. Note also that R. Qershavyah *ha-Naqdan* (see above, Introduction, n. 83, and in chapter 1, n. 116) produced a full copy of *Mishneh Torah* in Paris in 1242–43, along with his own rhymed introduction that included אזהרות מיימוניות. See ms. Cambridge Add. 1564; and Norman Golb, *The Jews in Medieval Normandy* (Oxford, 1997), 441–44.

Index of Manuscript References

Berlin (National Library)

9 430

37 76

Bodleian (Oxford)

Cat. Neubauer—

268 260, 268, 332

270 187, 218, 238, 257, 278, 346

271 104, 272, 277, 285, 329, 333, 337, 351, 356, 513

274 283, 333

283 275

352 54

659 454, 460

666 475

667 45

672 60, 434

696 83

784 485

847 81

875 66, 465

884 59

913 477

914 477

916 482

970 17

1025 389, 403, 418, 424, 430, 437

1038 400

1083 279

1098 404, 415

1099 22, 380, 396–97, 405, 407, 415, 419, 421–22, 424, 435, 437–39

1103 466

1104 22, 24, 400

1105 415

1106 439

1128 439–40

1147 22, 393, 419, 422

1148 440

1149 380, 396, 402–3, 407–13, 421–22, 424, 427, 429, 439

1150 431, 441, 459

1151 394

1154 430

1155 459

1205 466

1206 28

1207 28

1208 398

1211 435

1250 435

1442 15

1449 15

1606 399

1936 482

2273 473

2274 466

2287 477

2343 168, 211, 276m 336–40, 353

2344 164–65, 168, 170, 180, 212, 228, 244, 256, 268, 276–77, 337–363, 450, 511

2373 406

2502 434

Bodleian (Oxford) (*continued*)
2679 111
2797 399
2848 477
Qu. Opp. Add. 635 328

Bologna (National Archive)
165 409, 423

Breslau (*Beit ha-Midrash la-Rabbanim*)
102 241–42, 244–45, 247–48, 250–55, 257–58, 261, 264, 266, 282, 304, 367

British Museum (London)
Cat. Margoliouth—
190 (Add. 22092) 272, 294, 299–300, 323, 353
243 (Or. 2853) 274, 279–80, 306, 343, 360
477 (Add. 27075) 465
534 (Harley 5529) 466
537 (Add. 19972) 40, 64
640 (Add. 26883) 415
754 (Harley 5510) 466
1056 (Add. 11369) 408

Add. 27131 522
Or. 2735 397, 408
Or. 9931 (Gaster 730) 114, 157, 163, 174, 179–84, 190, 193, 201, 209, 218, 226, 229, 232, 234, 236–38, 268, 273–74, 286, 333, 345, 363, 467
Or. 10619 476

Budapest
Kaufman A 31
National Library [2^{0}] 1 40, 62, 79

Cambridge (University Library)
Add. 377 248, 251, 257, 262, 479
Add. 394 434, 466
Add. 404 273
Add. 490 45
Add. 507.1 520
Add. 561 127, 431, 466
Add. 664 482
Add. 667.1 59, 435
Add. 669.2 170, 211, 218, 226, 231, 246, 273, 278, 285
Add. 858.1 475
Add. 1022.1 481
Add. 1564 540
Add. 3111 476
Add. 3127 63
Dd. 13.7 420
Or. 71 60, 476
Or. 786 466
Or. 791 361

Cluny (Museum)
12290 396, 405, 413, 423, 440

Cremona (National Archive)
32 429
56 427

Florence, Laurenziana
Acq. e. Doni. 121 119
Plut. 88.9 15
Plut. II.20 17, 190, 268, 276, 278, 293, 329–32, 352

Frankfurt (National and University Library)
Hebr. Oct. 100 312, 327

Giessen (University Library)
Cod. 892 387

Hamburg (National and University Library)
13 22
39 427
40 295, 298, 308, 316
45 65, 157, 190–91, 223–24, 237, 244, 253, 274, 279, 285–86, 289, 339, 343–44, 356, 360, 363–64, 473–74
86 439
130 410
137 395
144 329, 435

152 28, 399, 475
156 448
189 438

Jerusalem (National Library)
Heb. $4^0$1125 409, 423
Heb. $8^0$476 459, 482
Karlin 688 346
private collection C (IMHM film #41225) 424, 429
Schocken 19522 400, 423

Leiden (University Library)
Scaliger 4 403
Warner 27 113, 157–58, 184, 237, 242, 244, 268, 277, 289, 351–52, 355

Leipzig (University Library)
1099 22
B.H. 1 114

Livorno (Talmud Torah)
138 476, 482

Los Angeles/UCLA (University Library)
779 (bx. 3.3) 65–66

Lund (University Library)
L. O. 2 127, 162, 398

Mantua (Community Library)
36 274, 280, 360, 474

Melun (Municipal Library)
14 435

Modena (Municipal Archive)
20 427
30 425
2416 405
769 397

Montefiore (London)
101 403
130 41
134 56, 368, 462–63, 475
140 66
220 279
479 329

Moscow (Guenzberg Collection)
74 54
82 15, 28, 205, 211, 218, 226, 231, 238, 272, 289, 345, 355
109 394
121 234, 237, 284, 286, 364, 369, 371–72
182 482
186 49
187 76
201 415
268 271, 275, 279, 353–55
303 158, 240, 244–48, 250–62, 264–67, 273–74, 279, 282, 284, 303, 310, 313, 363, 367, 515, 517–18
333 33
348 467
362 16, 113, 174, 237, 268, 287, 289, 358
365 272
508 484, 501–3, 519
611 380, 394–97, 416–19, 423, 427
717 482
774 10
898 278, 353, 363
983 361
1041 399
1302 48

Munich (National Library)
5 237
50 113, 163, 180, 188–202, 274, 285–86, 344–45, 353
52 127, 156, 227, 244, 256, 274, 299, 3–8, 344, 352
62 225, 291
422 22, 338

New York—JTS
Lutzki 778 123
Lutzki 787 291

New York—JTS (*continued*)
Lutzki 791 169, 179, 279, 290, 295–96, 300, 302, 305, 307–8, 313–19, 321–27, 353
Lutzki 794 179, 251, 294, 303, 311, 313, 316, 318–21, 323
Mic. 1852 486
Mic. 1885 486
Mic. 2095 476
Mic. 4460 127
Mic. 8114 453
Mic. 8118 456, 507
Mic. 8972 379, 422, 437
Mic. 9303 380, 389
Rab. 673 44, 47, 54, 56, 60, 62 67
Rab. 678 50
Rab. 1489 420, 496
Rab. 1923 83

Nuremberg (Municipal Library)
5 269, 356, 495, 513

Paris (Biblioteque Nationale, heb.)
48 285, 513
167 15–16, 113, 158, 163, 268, 277, 287, 289, 358
168 277
260 208, 212–13, 215, 225, 232, 241, 284, 286, 347, 362–63, 365–66, 368–73, 512
312 329
343 110
353 334–35, 479
391 437
405 436
407 479
633 466
634 433
644 392
646 413, 466
647 396
648 392, 424
660 240–44, 246, 252, 265, 274
752 162
772 458
776 483, 485
839 477
843 486
1292 118
1408 473
1467 (=Warsaw 260) 49
1480 62

Paris (l'Alliance)
H 133 A 435, 479
H 482 A 22, 415
H711A 496

Parma
Cat. de Rossi—
86 48, 52, 64, 79
99 476
112 476
147 477
159 391
180 465
254 434
292 476
309 476
352 394, 405–6, 412–13
365 403, 409
403 162
425 473
541 14, 113–14, 184, 195, 278, 333, 337, 340–42, 344, 398, 458
563 458, 483
585 403, 421, 430
586 97, 403, 415, 426
588 395, 399, 404, 427, 430
605 394, 396, 413, 424
654 398, 407–9, 411, 433–34
655 28, 440
671 476
740 434
855 395, 409, 433
885 433
908 403, 415
918 473
924 394
929 473
963 434
1051 185–86, 193, 273–74, 278
1104 416, 429, 438

1117 427
1131 420
1138 395, 415
1198 393–94
1221 483
1237 410, 465, 473
1259 435
1264 429
1265 394
1274 397, 415
1318 395
1334 66
1654 435
Palatina 3505 15
Palatina 3515 434
Perreau 22 476

Pesaro (National Archive)
31 435

Prague (Jewish Museum)
45 415
120 438
246 407, 413, 423, 429
250 409, 423, 429

Prague (National Library)
VI EA 2 398, 403
XVII F 7 22

Rome, Casanatense
159 476

Sassoon
290 481–82
405 477
408 476

Strasbourg (National Library)
44 218, 272

St. Petersburg (National Library)
EVR I 22 180–81, 185–85, 274, 344
EVR I 134 433
EVR I 192 15
EVR IV 1 413–14, 433

St. Petersburg (Institute of Oriental Studies)
D 101 395

Toronto (University, Freidberg Collection)
3—013 434

Vatican
Ebr.
45 157, 212, 216, 218, 221–22, 229, 236, 247, 289, 311, 341, 346, 355
48 30, 353
123 207, 363
138 184
183 361
214 410
243 476, 482, 485
251 477
285 435
301 15
312 403, 426, 429, 438
315 438
316 409, 423
319 403–4, 426, 429
320 398
323 412, 432
324 22, 162, 329, 479
326 400
402 15
506 208, 223
553 427

Neofiti
8 268
11 519

Rossiana
356 415

Urb.
21 166–67, 294, 300, 305–6, 312, 315, 318, 323, 326
27 432
122 477

Vercelli (Bishop's seminary)
C235 40, 58, 62, 64, 67

Verona (Municipal Library)
34 380, 388–90, 394, 396, 401, 406, 413, 417, 422–24, 427, 441

Vienna (National Library)
19 (Heb. 28) 269, 356, 495, 513
72 (Heb. 2) 40, 64
73 (Heb. 208) 40, 65
152 (Heb. 47) 453

Warsaw (Jewish Studies Institute)
9 485
204 212, 241
240 420
260 269, 511

Warsaw (University Library)
258 67, 361, 448

Zurich (Central Library)
Heid. 51 22, 127

Subject Index

Note: For ease of reading, books, chapter and verse of the Hebrew Bible are italicized. Books are shown in the order they appear in the Hebrew Bible. Scriptural interpretations and commentaries by rabbinic scholars are included in the index as the last subheading under the scholar's name.

Aaron b. Yose[f] *ha-Kohen*. See *Sefer ha–Gan* (Aaron b. Yose *ha–Kohen*)
Aaron of Regensburg, 45, 48–49
Abelard, Peter, 94–95, 105–6, 109–10
Abraham b. Azri'el of Bohemia, 24–25, 215, 377, 508–11
Abraham b. Moses of Regensburg, 44–45, 50
Abraham b. Nathan *ha-Yarḥi* of Lunel, 456
Abraham b. Samuel *he-Ḥasid*, 416
Abraham Klausner of Vienna, 525–26
Abun, 27
academies. *See* Tosafist academies
Amen response, 469
Amoraic dialectic, 90
angels: classes of, 503; eating by, 267–68; of mercy, 226; Mikha'el, 364; temporary, permanent, and separate air, 503. *See also* biblical stories
Anselm of Canterbury, 92
Anselm of Laon, 92
anthropomorphism: Isaac b. Moses *Or Zaru'a* of Vienna on, 509–10; Isaiah b. Mali [Emanuel] di Trani (Rid) on, 514–20; Joseph b. Isaac *Bekhor Shor* of Orleans on, 493–96; Judah *ha-Ḥasid* on, 504–6; Maimonides on, 508–9; Tosafists and, 496, 525–28
anti-anthropomorphic position, 539
'Arygat ha-Bosem (Abraham b. Azri'el), 511
Asher b. Gershom, 520–21
Asher b. Yeḥi'el (Rosh), 29n100, 72n137–72n138, 287, 468n87, 485–86
Avigdor b. Elijah Katz *ha-Kohen* of Vienna: consultations between Germany and northern France, 64n111; magic and mysticism, 469–77; *Perushim u-Pesaqim*, 360–61; *piyyut* composition, 441; on Song of Songs, 30n104
'Avi ha-'Ezri (Ibn Ezra), 326
Avinu Malkenu, 474–75
'avon, defined, 229
Avot, Bekhor Shor's efforts to defend behavior of, 152–53
'Azri'el b. Yehi'el *he-Ḥasid*, 53

Ba'alei ha-Tosafot (Urbach), 2, 24–25, 87–88
Babylonian Talmud, 1, 283, 535

Barukh b. Isaac: cited in *Sefer ha-Gan,* 267; interactions with other rabbinic courts, 50, 63–64n110; rabbinic/halakhic interpretations by, 267–68; Regensburg rabbinic court and, 44–45; *Sefer ha-Terumah,* 3; in *siddur mishpatim,* 330; on song of *Ha'azinu,* 270–71; scriptural interpretation and commentary: *Genesis: 2:9,* 269; *3:22,* 269–70; *18:8,* 267–68; *Exodus: 21:28-29,* 268; *Numbers: 12:14,* 268; *Deuteronomy: 32:1-6,* 270–71

Barukh b. Samuel of Mainz: interactions with Worms court, 50; and Judah b. Qalonymus (Rivaq) b. Meir of Speyer, 20, 39; and litigant's right to appeal court's decision, 78–79; Mainz rabbinic court and, 39; ordinance regarding use of secular courts *('arka'ot),* 72n138; *piyyut* composition, 376–77, 420–23; rabbinic courts of northern France and, 59; as rabbinic scholar and decisor, 74; on recitation of *Qeri'at Shema,* 464–65; *Sefer ha-Ḥokhmah,* 74, 361–62

Bava Meẓi'a, 21

beit din (primary court), 57–58

beit din 'ara'i (secondary or temporary court), 46

beit din ha-gadol (supreme court), 62

Beit Hillel, conflicts with *Beit Shammai,* 26–27

Bekhor Shor. See Joseph (Yosef) b. Isaac *Bekhor Shor* of Orleans

Ben-Sasson, Haim Hillel, 13

Berekhyah b. Natronai *ha-Naqdan* of Normandy, 23n83, 86

Berekhyah *ha-Naqdan,* 326

Bereshit Rabbah: on angels eating, 267–68; brothers of Evreux and, 352–54; citation in standard *Tosafot* to Talmud, 118n25; on Noah and the flood, 166–67; on Noah's *tanim* status, 340; *peshat* comment to Genesis 3:1, 212

Bernard, abbot of Clairvaux, 94–95

Bernard of Chartres, 107

Bible scholars, interaction between Jewish and Christian, 105

biblical exegesis: in 13th century, 535; Joseph (Yosef) b. Isaac *Bekhor Shor* of Orleans, 126–79; pre-Crusade period, 538; in Spain, 495; Tosafist in northern France at end of 12th century: between *peshat* and *derash: overview,* 111–26; Yom Tov b. Isaac of Joigny (Teitav), 179–203

biblical interpretation: developments in realms of *derash* and talmudic Torah interpretation, 267–88; in early 13th century, 205–88; Isaiah b. Mali [Emanuel] di Trani (Rid), 238–67; Judah *he-Ḥasid* and, 32; northern French, 531; by student of Yeḥi'el b. Joseph of Paris, 340; by Yosef Qara, 86

biblical redaction theories, 32, 33n112

biblical stories: Aaron and sin of the golden calf, 366; Abraham, age of, 341–42; Abraham and Sodom, 248; Bil'am and the angel, 198–99; counting of the tribes, 176–77, 231; covenant between Jacob and Laban, 357; covenant of stone, 357; Creation, 165–66, 446; 'Er and Onan, 242–43, 467, 474; the flood, 166; Isaac, binding of, 144; Isaac and Esau, 168; Jacob and Esau, 153–54, 249; Joseph, the selling of, 150–51, 169, 188, 349–51; Joseph, the shaving of, 187; Joseph and Potiphar's wife, 353; Moses, as baby, 221–22; Moses is given the Torah, 28–29; Noah: *age of,* 275–77; *and the flood,* 166–67; *tamin status,* 340; Rivka, gift of jewelry to, 337–38; sin of the golden calf, 152–53, 227–28, 233–34, 327, 366; sin of the

spies, 231, 233–34, 312–13; Tamar, 216–17, 333. *See also* plagues
blowing of the *shofar,* 195
Bonfant. *See* Samuel b. Abraham *ha-Levi* of Worms (Bonfant)
Bonn rabbinic court, 46
Burchard of Worms, 108

cathedral schools: development of, in Germany and northern France, 102–3; goal of educational process, 92; in Paris, 33; proximity to Tosafist study halls, 105–6; shift from monastic schools to, 38, 91
censuses, 279
Chartres cathedral school, 91, 102–3
Christian dialectical method: influence of Jewish scholarship on, 109; Jewish awareness of and comfort with, 102–3, 108; Tosafists's contacts with, 103–9; uses and criticisms, 92–94
Christians: interactions with Jews, 85; *peshat* principles learned through talking with Jews, 105–6; rabbinic scholarship and interpretational strategies of, 534
Christian scholarship: influence of, 106–8; monasteries as center of, 91; parallels with Jewish methods, 87–90, 106–8; and talmudic method of the Tosafists, 84–110
Circle of the Special Cherub *(Ḥug ha-Keruv ha-Meyuḥad),* 455
circumcision: in the desert, 263–64; Menaḥem of Worms on, 461–62; of Moses's son Eliezer, 273; precept of, 165–66; on the Sabbath, 283
Cologne academy, 103
Cologne rabbinic court, 45–48, 50
Concordia discordantium canonum. See *Decretum* (Gratian)
corporealists, 525
corporeality. *See* anthropomorphism
cosmic Air, 503–4
courts. *See* rabbinic courts

Da'at Zeqenim, 173, 346
David b. Qalonymus of Muenzberg, 50, 430
David b. She'alti'el, 52
David Kimḥi (Radak), 121, 208, 521n105, 528
deception, biblical examples for, 151–52
Decretum (Gratian), 109
derash approach: in early 13th-century Tosafist developments, 267–88; Eleazar b. Judah of Worms, 362; Joseph *Bekhor Shor* of Orleans, 126–61; in late 12th century, northern France, 111–26; in middle 13th-century Tosafist Torah commentaries, 359–61; Rid and, 265
Derashot u-Pisqei Halakhot (Ḥayyim b. Isaac *Or Zaru'a*), 361
dialectical method: in Christian and Jewish circles, 90, 92–94, 98–99, 102–3; as dominant approach in Tosafist *battei midrash,* 97; fundamental aim of, 34; practice among rabbinic scholars, 103–4; talmudic scholars and, 106; Tosafists and, 110
Divine essence, 503
Divine form, 493
Divine love, 30
Divine names, 450, 453, 468, 484
Divine presence, 192
Divine truth, 92
Divine voice, 509
Divine wisdom, 28
divorce *(gittin),* 57, 65–69
dreams and interpretations, 154–55, 456

Eleazar b. Judah of Worms: and constructs of leprosy, 366–67; *derash* commentary, 362; on Divine corporeality, 498, 505, 511; exoteric and midrashic interpretation, 206–7; on impurity of *kohen gadol vs. kohen hedyot,* 368; influence of Christian scholars on, 108; in *Moshav Zeqenim,* 363; mysticism,

Eleazar b. Judah of Worms (*continued*) 470; mysticism, avoidance of, 447; in *parashat Va-Yiqra,* 364–65; *peshat* approach, 281, 369; *piyyut* composition, 416–20; and rabbinic courts, 40–41, 50; Ramban's citation, 506; *remez* interpretation, 363; *Sha'arei ha-Sod veha-Yihud veh-Emunah,* 505; in standard *Tosafot,* 4n9; scriptural interpretation and commentary: *Genesis: 1:26-27,* 505; *12:13,* 363; *Exodus: 4:3,* 372; *4:24,* 372; *40:35,* 363–64; *Leviticus: 1:9,* 365; *4:24,* 365; *8:2-3,* 365; *9:1,* 366; *14:4,* 367; *14:34-53,* 367; *19:19,* 367; *19:27,* 367–68; *24:11,* 368–69; *Numbers: 5:2-3,* 369; *8:12,* 369; *10:2,* 370; *10:35,* 370; *11:1,* 370; *13:19,* 370; *17:23,* 371; *18:31,* 371; *20:6,* 371; *20:8,* 372; *20:10,* 372; *21:8,* 372; *24:4,* 371–72; *78:9,* 369; *Deuteronomy: 19:19,* 364; *32:6,* 364

Eleazar b. Simeon, 426

Eleazar b. Yeḥi'el, 49

Eleazar *ha-Qallir,* 454

Elḥanan b. *ha-Ri:* exegetical model, 271–75; interdisciplinary scholarship, 23n83; *piyyut* composition, 376, 407; scriptural interpretation and commentary: *Genesis: 4:10,* 271–72; *18:2,* 272; *41:50,* 272–73; *Exodus: 4:24,* 273; *12:6,* 273; *19:17,* 274; *Deuteronomy: 2:9,* 274–75

Elḥanan b. Yaqar of London, 86, 455, 507

Eliezer b. Aaron of Burgundy, 410–11

Eliezer b. Elijah *ha-Kohen,* 477

Eliezer b. Joel (Yo'el) *ha-Levi* (Rabiah): disciplinary concentration, 19; and German *payyetanim,* 375; *piyyut* composition, 403–5; and rabbinic courts, 39, 41–42, 45–47, 49–50, 59–60, 69, 78–79; *Sefer Avi'asaf,* 3n7; and standard *Tosafot,* 4n9, 7

Eliezer b. Nathan (Raban) of Mainz: on absence of *beit din ha-gadol* or *beit ḥa-va'ad,* 80n158–80n159; avoidance of mysticism, 447–48; consultations with rabbinical courts, 54n79; disciplinary concentration, 19; ordinance regarding use of secular courts (*'arka'ot*), 72; *piyyut* composition and commentary, 25–26, 376, 396–97

Eliezer b. Samson of Cologne, 45, 72, 397–98

Eliezer b. Samuel of Metz: mysticism, 456–57; *piyyut* composition, 411–12; rabbinic courts of northern France and, 62–64; *Sefer Yere'im,* 3

Eliezer b. Solomon *mi-Tukh,* 3, 5, 267–68, 409

Eliezer of Beaugency, 155

Elijah b. Judah *ha-Kohen* of Paris, 54, 99–101, 452–53

Elijah b. Menaḥem *ha-Zaqen* of Le Mans, 452

Elijah Menaḥem b. Moses of London, 480–81

Eliyyahu Mizraḥi, 243

Elyaqim b. Asher *ha-Levi,* 43

Ephraim b. Isaac of Regensburg: Barukh b. Samuel and, 39; extra-talmudic studies, 536; mysticism, 465; *piyyut* composition, 376–77, 412–14; rabbinic courts of northern France and, 59; as rabbinic scholar, decisor, and teacher, 74–75; Regensburg rabbinic court, 43–44

Ephraim b. Jacob (b. Qalonymus) of Bonn: Bonn rabbinic court and, 46; interdisciplinary scholarship, 24–25; mysticism, 460–61; *piyyut* composition and commentary, 377, 399–403

Ephraim b. Joel, 49

Ephraim b. Samson, 73; interdisciplinary scholarship, 23n83

Evreux, brothers of, 76, 107, 328, 330, 352–55, 478. *See also* Moses b. Shne'ur of Evreux

Evreux academy, 348–59

Ezra *ha-Navi* of Moncontour, 477–78

gematria, 170, 202, 215, 248–49
German Pietists: affinity for *piyyut,* 377, 414–16, 443; approach to talmudic and halakhic questions, 491–92; *beit din* policy, late 13th century, 70; "conservatism," 83n168; on Divine corporeality, 497, 504, 506, 526–27; esoteric tradition, 206; *Ḥug ha-Keruv ha-Meyuḥad Ḥullin* associated with, 451; influence of Christian scholars on, 107–8; institutions, identification of, 75; magic and mysticism, 99, 448, 504–10, 531; Moses b. Shne'ur of Evreux and, 478; penitential doctrine of, 366; Qalonymide family, 20; search for the larger Divine, 467
Gershom b. Isaac, 46, 404, 461
gittin (divorce) cases, 57, 65–69
Gratian, 109–10
Grossman, Avraham, 9–10, 83n168, 89–90, 102–3, 152

Ha'azinu, 13
Hadar Zeqenim compilation, 277–78, 353, 355–56
Hai Gaon, 450, 495, 508
Hakhel, 182
Ḥakhmei Lothaire, 453–54
halakhic and talmudic studies: rabbinic courts of Germany, 38–53
halakhic questions: German Pietists's approach to, 491–92; notion of 49 approaches to, 479–80
halakhic works: by Barukh b. Isaac, 267–68; Christian influence on responsa of Rid, 106–7; debates of *Beit Hillel* and *Beit Shammai,* 26–27; German and Austrian, 3, 5–7; innovations by *Bekhor Shor,* 162; by northern French Tosafists, 69n128; Tosafists's sensitivity to use of talmudic texts in, 135; treatises, abridged series, 537; Yom Tov b. Isaac of Joigny (Teitav), 202
Halakhot Gedolot, 514
Ḥanan'el b. Ḥushi'el of Kairwan, 495, 509–11, 514
Ḥanokh, 104
Ḥasidei Ashkenaz (mystical circle), 202, 460–69, 504, 531, 539
hata'ah, defined, 229
Ḥayyim b. Yeḥi'el *Ḥefeẓ Zahav,* 48, 53, 73
Ḥayyim Eli'ezer b. Isaac *Or Zaru'a,* 361, 486
Ḥayyim *Kohen,* 68
Ḥayyim Palti'el b. Barukh, 440–41
Ḥayyim Palti'el b. Jacob, 440
Ḥayyim Palti'el of Falaise, 342–43
Ḥayyim Yosef David Azulai (Ḥida), 242, 294
ḥayyot (nondomesticated animals), 185
Ḥazak, 227
Ḥazal, 13
he-Ḥaver Joseph b. *he-Ḥaver* Solomon, 61
Henri Rozenne of Champagne, 104
ḥerem ha-qehillot (communal rule prohibiting judges from choosing not to serve), 79n156, 80
Hezekiah b. Jacob of Madgeburg, 48–49, 64
Hezekiah b. Manoaḥ, 121, 124, 167, 208, 359
Hillel b. Azri'el, 49, 175
Ḥizzequni (Hezekiah b. Manoaḥ), 121, 167, 208, 359
Ḥug ha-Keruv ha-Meyuḥad (Circle of the Special Cherub), 451, 455, 507
Ḥumash circle, 223

Ibn Ezra, Abraham: *'Avi ha-'Ezri,* 326; on blessings given by Moses to the tribes, 178–79; influence on *Bekhor Shor*'s Torah commentary, 141; *piyyut* composition, 443; and *torat ha-sod* practices, 451; on verses added to Torah after revelation at Sinai, 32; scriptural interpretation and commentary: *Genesis: 3:1,* 208; *32:2,* 145; *43:17,* 285; *45:28,* 188;

Ibn Ezra, Abraham (*continued*) *46:23,* 251–52; *Exodus: 1:20,* 170; *2:6,* 252; *20:13,* 301; *20:22,* 286; *33:18–20,* 192; *Leviticus: 19:27,* 367; *20:19,* 308; *Deuteronomy: 5:17,* 301; *16:12,* 323–24; *26:5,* 236; *33:13,* 237
Ibn Gabirol, 440
'Imrei No'am, 242–43, 344–45
intellectual ability to discern, 467
Isaac *(Or Zaru'a). See* Isaac b. Moses *Or Zaru'a* of Vienna
Isaac Alfasi, 538
Isaac b. Abraham (Riẓba) of Dampierre, 97–98; 1 Genesis 6:9, 275; 1 Genesis 9:28, 275–77; cited in ms. Parma (De Rossi) 541, 340; and focused talmudism, 536; *piyyut* composition, 376; rabbinic courts of northern France and, 59, 61; in *siddur mishpatim,* 330
Isaac b. Asher (Riba) *ha-Levi* of Speyer, 18–19, 41, 43, 80n160
Isaac b. Eliezer *ha-Levi,* 97
Isaac b. Elijah, 486
Isaac b. Ezekiel *mi-Morat* of Russia, 205
Isaac b. Ḥayyim, 336–39
Isaac b. Isaac of Chinon, 432–33, 454–55, 480
Isaac b. Jacob (Ri) *ha-Lavan* of Prague and Regensburg, 44, 284–85, 411
Isaac b. Joseph of Corbeil, 480
Isaac b. Judah *ha-Levi,* 163–64, 206, 510–13
Isaac b. Mordekhai (Ribam) of Bohemia, 43, 54n79, 74–75, 411, 458
Isaac b. Moses *Or Zaru'a* of Vienna: on Divine corporeality, 509–10; Isaiah di Trani and, 239; mysticism, 469–72; and rabbinic courts, 44, 48, 52, 55–56n83, 56n86, 59n96, 62–64, 69; in standard *Tosafot,* 4n9
Isaac b. Samuel (Ri) *ha-Zaqen* of Dampierre: Christian influence on, 107; dominance of, 2; mysticism, 455–56; *piyyut* composition, 17–18, 376, 405–7; and rabbinic courts, 57–61; in *siddur mishpatim,* 330; students of, 2–3, 18; use of *shedim,* 486; scriptural interpretation and commentary: *Deuteronomy 2:9,* 274
Isaac b. Shne'ur, 348–59
Isaac *ha-Lavan,* 44
Isaac *ha-Navi* of *Ẓarefat,* 361–62
Isaac of Bohemia. *See* Isaac b. Jacob (Ri) *ha-Lavan* of Prague and Regensburg
Isaac of Corbeil, 6, 361
Isaac of Evreux (Ri), 352–55
Isaac of Russia, 224, 233
Isaiah b. Mali [Emanuel] di Trani (Rid): Barukh b. Isaac compared to, 270; biography of, 239; commentary categories and statistics, 244–45; commentary to *parashat Yitro,* 256; on Divine corporeality, 514–19; exegetical characteristics, 240–41; *halakhah*-based comments on Passover sacrifice, 254; halakhic responsa of, 106–7; linguistic interpretation by, 265; methodology of, 243; in *Moshav Zeqenim,* 242–43, 250n140, 362; mysticism, 467–68; *Nimmuqei Ḥumash,* 514–15; on sacrificial order, 260–61; Speyer rabbinic court and, 42; in Tosafist Torah compilations, 242–43; use of Christian educational methods, 106–7; use of *gematria,* 249; use of *peshat,* 250, *250,* 281; use of *shedim,* 486; scriptural interpretation and commentary: *Genesis: 1:26,* 516–17; *2:16-17,* 240–41, 246; *3:22,* 240; *4:15,* 245; *9:3,* 246; *12:7,* 247; *12:8,* 250; *13:11,* 246–47; *13:14,* 247; *14:4,* 251; *18:4,* 241; *18:29,* 248; *22:1,* 518; *23:16,* 248; *25:19,* 248; *25:22,* 249; *26:25,* 250; *28:5,* 249; *32:11,* 249; *32:32,* 241–42; *33:19,* 250; *35:19,* 250; *38:7,* 242; *41:7,* 251; *46:23,* 251–52; *Exodus: 3:6,* 260; *7:22,* 253;

7:24, 253; *9:14*, 254; *10:14*, 255; *12:25*, 263–64; *12:26*, 254; *15:25*, 255; *16:5*, 255–56; *16:22*, 255–56; *18:2*, 256; *18:18*, 258; *19:13*, 259; *19:17*, 273–74; *20:21*, 259; *33:18*, 260; *40:35*, 363–64; *summary of comments to*, 260; *Leviticus: 13:55*, 261; *19:16*, 261; *summary of comments to*, 260–61; *Numbers: 8:2*, 262–63; *9:1*, 263–64; *11:4*, 264; *11:23*, 264; *17:25*, 265; *21:30*, 265; *24:2*, 265; *26:8*, 252; *26:9*, 252; *35:32*, 265–66; *summary of comments to*, 262; *Deuteronomy: 18:2*, 266; *33:9*, 266–67; *summary of comments to*, 266; *Judges: 13:8*, 253; *Jeremiah: 46:20*, 261–62; *Ezekiel: 1:26*, 518; *Psalms: 78:46-47*, 255; *Chronicles: 1:2:8*, 252

Ivo of Chartres, 92, 110

Jacob *Ba'al ha-Turim*, 486

Jacob b. Isaac *ha-Levi* (Ya'avetz), 403

Jacob b. Joseph of Verdun, 48, 65, 66n122

Jacob b. Meir of Ramerupt. *See* Rabbenu Tam (Jacob b. Meir of Ramerupt)

Jacob b. Mordekhai, 46, 53

Jacob b. Samson, 390–91, 499

Jacob b. Solomon of Courson, 48–49

Jacob *ha-Gozer*, 461

Jacob of Marvege, 468

Jacob of Orleans (Rabbenu Jacob Tam), 1, 55, 162–79, 242, 254, 259

Jerusalem Talmud, 283

Jewish learning in the Muslim and Christian worlds, 84–87

Joel b. Isaac *ha-Levi* of Bonn: Cologne rabbinic court, 46; interactions with other rabbinic courts, 50; *piyyut* composition, 403–4; rabbinic courts of northern France and, 59; as rabbinic scholar and decisor, 74

Jonathan b. Isaac of Wurzburg, 44, 284

Joseph (Yosef) b. Isaac *Bekhor Shor* of Orleans: *Avot* behavior defended by, 152–53; Barukh b. Isaac compared to, 270; commentary by, 158, 162–63; on Divine corporeality, 493–96, 511–12, 525; exegetical method, 159–61; on hail damage, 173; halakhic innovations, 162; interest in *miqra* as distinct discipline, 179; Isaiah di Trani and, 240; methods favored by, 359–61; in *Moshav Zeqenim*, 362; *peshat* approach, 143, 203; *piyyut* composition, 409–10; and rabbinic courts, 55, 68; Rashi's Torah commentary and, 130–37, 155–57, 165–79; rational *severa* approach, 154–55; on the selling of Joseph, 150–51; on *yibbum* between Tamar and Judah, 159–61; scriptural interpretation and commentary: *Genesis: 1:26*, 252, 493–94, 502, 513; *3:1*, 208; *3:11*, 148; *3:14*, 148; *10:9*, 130; *11:2*, 133; *11:7*, 133–34; *12:15*, 246–47; *15:6*, 134; *17:7*, 214; *18:2*, 142; *18:13*, 214; *22:1*, 144–45; *23:1*, 149; *25:29*, 150–51; *25:31*, 151; *25:33-34*, 151, 159; *28:5*, 155; *32:2*, 145; *35:18*, 131; *37:2*, 148; *37:9–10*, 153; *37:25*, 350; *37:28*, 139, 350; *38:13*, 159, 161; *38:26*, 159; *41:7*, 139; *41:16*, 130–31; *41:51*, 218; *41:56*, 130; *42:2*, 130; *45:4*, 150–51; *45:28*, 188; *46:15*, 252; *Exodus: 1:20*, 170; *2:14*, 138; *3:14*, 138; *7:22*, 253; *9:6*, 134–35; *9:14*, 254; *10:4*, 299–300; *12:43*, 135; *12:45*, 135, 138–39; *12:48*, 135–36; *15:11*, 173; *15:20*, 149; *16:15*, 136–37; *18:2*, 257; *19:13*, 259; *19:17*, 273–74; *21:10*, 139; *24:14*, 143; *25:10*, 227; *33:18–20*, 192; *Leviticus: 14:13*, 143; *19:27*, 368; *25:1*, 193; *Numbers: 8:2*, 263; *10:2*, 370; *13:3*, 312; *13:19*, 370; *22:6*, 197–98; *23:13*, 133; *27:17*, 178; *30:15*, 132–33; *31:19*, 139; *Deuteronomy: 12:19*, 136; *21:23*, 139; *31:28*, 142–43; *32:6*, 131; *33:24*, 132; *34:2*, 132; *34:5*, 132; *Judges: 3:16*, 142

Joseph b. Moses, 54
Joseph b. Nathan *Ḥazzan* of Wurzberg, 398–99
Joseph Kimḥi, 16, 338
Joseph of Chartres, 294
Joseph of Paris, 341
Joseph *Tov 'Elem,* 63
Judah b. Abraham, 54
Judah b. David of Melun, 65
Judah b. Eliezer, 166, 168, 290, 292–93
Judah b. Moses *ha-Kohen* of Friedberg and Wurzburg, 52, 429–30
Judah b. Qalonymus (Rivaq) b. Meir of Speyer, 20, 39, 41–43, 460
Judah b. Qalonymus (Rivaq) b. Moses of Mainz, 39, 418–19
Judah (Yehudah) b. Samuel *ha-Levi,* 415, 440, 443
Judah b. Samuel *he-Ḥasid:* citations in Tosafist Torah compilations, 237–38; exegetical strategies, 207–8; Isaiah di Trani and, 240; masoretic interpretation, 227; methodological assumptions regarding works by, 211–12; *midrash* interpretations, 208, 228; *peshat* approach, 208–10, 216, 281; *peshat* method, "syncopated," 216, 221–22; realia-based interpretations, 230; Regensburg rabbinic court and, 44–45; *remez* interpretation, 208; scholarly interests, 20; on Tamar's punishment, 217; Torah commentary, 32, 205, 210–11, 238; Tosafist *pashtanim,* second wave, 237; use of *gematria,* 215; use of *remez* techniques, 221; scriptural interpretation and commentary: *Genesis: 3:1,* 208–9; *4:15,* 245–46; *6:3,* 228; *35:22,* 216; *38:7,* 242; *38:24,* 216; *46:26-27,* 219; *47:7,* 220; *47:8,* 219–20; *47:10,* 220; *48:22,* 220–21; *Exodus: 1:7,* 221; *2:6,* 221–22; *15:26,* 223; *16:1,* 229; *16:32-34,* 223–24; *16:35,* 223–24; *18:3-4,* 222; *19:21,* 224; *19:23,* 224–25; *23:20,* 226; *24:1,* 225–26; *24:7,* 226; *27:20,* 227; *28:37,* 228; *32:32,* 228; *32:34,* 233–34; *34:7,* 229; *39:31,* 228; *Leviticus: 10:3,* 229; *21:14,* 229–30; *Numbers: 1:10,* 231; *1:14,* 231; *1:22-23,* 231; *2:14,* 231; *4:18,* 231; *12:6,* 232–33; *13:8,* 231; *13:11,* 231; *14:20,* 233; *19:2,* 227; *22:2,* 234–35; *25:14,* 231; *Deuteronomy: 7:12,* 223; *14:13-14,* 235; *21:18-21,* 236; *26:5,* 236; *33:13,* 237; *Joshua: 24:9,* 234–35; *Judges: 11:24,* 234–35; *13:8,* 253; *Chronicles: 1:4:17,* 221; *2:26:16-21,* 234
Judah *ha-Ḥasid:* cited in *Te'amim shel Ḥumash,* 334; on Divine corporeality, 499, 504–5; in *Moshav Zeqenim,* 362; mysticism, 470; *piyyut* composition, 415; on recitation of *Qeri'at Shema,* 464–65; scriptural interpretation and commentary: *Genesis: 37:28,* 350; *40:15,* 350–51; *45:4,* 351; *Genesis 40:15,* 350–51; *Leviticus: 25:17,* 283; *27:3,* 311; *Numbers: 26:59,* 319; *Deuteronomy: 23:2,* 345
Judah *ha-Kohen,* 96
Judah Sirleon of Paris, 3, 60, 61n105, 66n122, 69
Judah the Prince, 249

kabbalists, first-level, 23
Ketav Tamin (Moses b. Ḥisdai Taku), 496–500, 509
kiddush, German and French approaches, 82–83n167
Kol Bo (Shemaryah b. Simḥah of Speyer), 361

Lafranc of Bec, 92
laws of purity, 306
legal dialectic, 534
leprosy constructs, 366–67
Levites, 178–79, 266–67, 296, 311–12, 314, 327
liqqutim, 6

liturgical rites, differences between northern France and Germany, 81n165
Lombard, Peter, 109–10

Madgeburg rabbinic court, 48–49
magic and mysticism: in 13th-century northern France, 477–87; asceticism (*perishut*) and, 445; Avigdor b. Elijah Katz *ha-Kohen* of Vienna, 469–77; avoidance of, 446–47; avoidance of, by Rashbam, Raban, and Rabbenu Tam, 446–55; Bernard, abbot of Clairvaux and, 95; German Pietists and, 504–10; *Ḥasidei Ashkenaz* (mystical circle), 202, 460–69, 504, 531, 539; *Hekhalot*-based, 539; Isaac b. Moses *Or Zaru'a* of Vienna and, 469–77; Meir of Rothenburg and, 477–87; mystical circles, 506, 526; parallel developments among German Tosaifists, 460–69; in *piyyut*, 383; rite of *shedim*, 142, 456; secondary elite and, 21–23; students of Rabbenu Tam and, 455–59; in Tosafist literature and thought, 553; in Tosafist literature and thought, overview, 445–46
Maimonidean controversy: anthropomorphism and, 537; early phases of, 29; nature and extent in Ashkenaz, 519–29; Ramban's view, 506. *See also* Maimonides
Maimonides: avoidance of halakhic materials in Ashkenaz rabbinic works, 540n24; on Divine corporeality, 494, 497, 499, 508–9, 511; *Mishneh Torah*, 494, 511, 515, 538; *Moreh Nevukhim*, 515–18; in *Perushei Ba'alei ha-Tosafot 'al ha-Torah*, 539; Tosafists in messianic era and, 528
Maimunists, 525
Mainz academy, 10, 96–97
Mainz rabbinic court, 39–41, 50, 52–53
marriage: between Jewish women and Amonite or Moabite men, 293–94; prohibition on marital relations during famine, 218
masoretic interpretations, 195–97, 202, 206, 227, 235, 237
masoretic studies, 459n53
Mattatyahu, and Paris rabbinic court, 54
Meir b. Isaac *Shaliaḥ Ẓibbur (Shaẓ)*, 385–89
Meir b. Samuel, 90, 395, 535
Meir *ha-Levi* Abulafia (Ramah), 29, 528
Meir of Germany. *See* Meir (Maharam) of Rothenburg
Meir (Maharam) of Rothenburg: extra-talmudic studies, 536; magic and mysticism, 477–87; *piyyut* composition and commentary, 377, 436–38; rabbinic courts of northern France and, 50–51, 63
Meir of Speyer, 42
Mekhilta, 222
Melun rabbinic court, 54n79
Menaḥem Agler of Prague, 525–26
Menaḥem b. Abraham of Oberlingen, 53
Menaḥem b. David, 47, 49
Menaḥem b. Jacob of Worms: interactions with Speyer rabbinic court, 50; mysticism, 461–64; *piyyut* composition, 420, 423–26, 440; as rabbinic scholar and decisor, 74; references in *Ba'alei ha-Tosafot*, 25; Worms rabbinic court, 40–41
Menaḥem b. Makhir of Regensburg, 389–90, 396
Menaḥem b. Natronai (Qovil), 49
Menaḥem b. Pereẓ of Joigny, 458–59
Menaḥem of London, 67n123
Meshullam b. David, 50, 52
Meshullam b. Nathan, 54
Meshullam of Melun, 54n79, 99–101
messianic era, 82n166, 310, 493n11, 528–29
Metatron, 226, 450–51
midrashic approach and interpretations: academy at Evreux and,

midrashic approach and interpretations (*continued*)
358–59; Eleazar b. Judah of Worms and, 206–7; in Germany, 361–73; Judah b. Samuel *he-Ḥasid* and, 228; by Moses b. Shne'ur of Evreux, 352; Moses b. Shne'ur of Evreux and, 355–56; by secondary rabbinic elite, 360; Urbach on Tosafists and, 490–93
Midrash Rabbah, 353
Midrash Shoḥer Tov, 27
Midrash Tadshe, 185
Mikha'el (angel of mercy), 226
Minḥat Yehudah (Judah b. Eliezer), 166, 168, 290, 292–93
Mishneh Torah (Maimonides), 494, 511, 515, 538
monasteries, 38, 91
Mordekhai b. Joseph, 41
Mordekhai of Poland, 205
Moreh Nevukhim (Maimonides), 515–18
Moses: blessing to the tribe of Levi, 178–79, 266–67; divorce of Ẓipporah, 256–57; lifespan, 201–2
Moses Azri'el b. Eleazar *ha-Darshan,* 49, 450–51
Moses b. Ḥisdai Taku, 496–500, 509, 524–25
Moses b. Jacob of Coucy, 478
Moses b. Joel, 43, 54n79, 74–75
Moses b. Mordekhai of Mainz, 39, 50
Moses b. Naḥman (Naḥmanides): on Divine corporeality, 519–20, 525; intersection of *peshat* and *sod,* 160; responses to Rashi's commentary, 243; views in messianic era, 528; scriptural interpretation and commentary: *Genesis: 32:2,* 145
Moses b. Samuel, 46
Moses b. Shne'ur of Evreux: Genesis 31:52, 357; Numbers 11:21-23, 358; on educational conventions, 76; midrashic interpretations by, 352, 355–56; piestistic affinities with German Pietists, 478; and *Sefer ha-Gan,* 356–58; in *siddur mishpatim,* 330
Moses b. Solomon *ha-Kohen* of Mainz, 19, 39, 41–42, 64n110
Moses b. Yeḥi'el, 54
Moses b. Yom Tov of London, 67n123
Moses *ha-Kohen* ibn Chiqatilia, 338
Moses of Coucy: on Divine corporeality, 523; exegetical interpretations, 292, 305–11; French Tosafist contemporaries, 328; parable of incense test, 315–16; on *parashat Ḥuqqat,* 316; and Rabbenu Tam's commentary, 310; and Rashi's Torah commentary, 291–93, 295–98, 300, 302–4; *Sefer Miẓvot Gadol (Semag),* 3, 292–94; on term *'eved kena'ani,* 302; scriptural interpretation and commentary: *Genesis: 3:14,* 282; *7:6,* 296–97; *9:6-7,* 327; *9:21,* 297–98; *14:24,* 292; *18:9,* 292–93; *29:34,* 295–96; *38:26,* 332–33; *Exodus: 1:1,* 302; *1:7,* 300; *2:12,* 303; *2:26,* 303–4; *2:29,* 327; *3:5,* 304; *4:6-8,* 304–5; *4:11,* 298; *5:15,* 318; *6:2,* 312; *10:4,* 299–300; *20:13,* 301; *Leviticus: 1:3,* 309; *1:10-12,* 305; *1:11,* 306; *2:2,* 306; *2:9,* 309; *3:46,* 307; *4:34,* 307; *6:3,* 307; *6:8,* 310–11; *6:29,* 307; *8:28,* 308; *Numbers: 1:2,* 321; *1:3,* 311–12; *2:3,* 318; *2:20,* 318; *3:3-16,* 312–13; *5:11,* 319; *6:1-2,* 314; *6:6,* 314; *6:10,* 315; *6:11,* 314–15; *6:16,* 314–15; *6:32,* 315; *6:59,* 319; *6:64,* 320; *19:3,* 316–17; *20:1,* 316; *20:11,* 316; *20:14,* 316; *20:17,* 317; *20:21,* 316; *30:2,* 320–21; *Deuteronomy: 1:4,* 322; *1:7,* 325; *1:44,* 322; *2:9,* 318; *2:18,* 325–26; *2:28-30,* 293; *2:29,* 316; *2:30,* 310–11; *2:39,* 326; *2:42,* 326; *3:4-5,* 293–94; *3:6,* 326; *3:11,* 323; *3:37,* 327; *5:17,* 301; *5:18,* 323; *6:12,* 323–24; *8:18-19,* 309; *20:5-7,* 324; *28:30,* 324; *Kings: 7:51,*

305; *Isaiah: 16:14*, 323; *Psalms: 6:2*, 326
Moses Zal(t)man, 205
Moshav Zeqenim (Tosafist Torah compilation): *Bekhor Shor*'s commentary in, 156–57, 227, 256n159; on circumcision of Moses's son, Eliezer, 273; Eleazar of Worms's commentary in, 362–65, 368–69, 372–73; Judah *he-Ḥasid*'s commentary in, 212, 231, 236; on naming of Isaac, 282–83; Paris manuscript version, 215; Rashi's commentary in, 264–65n177, 274; Rid's commentary in, 242–43, 257n161, 260n167; Yehi'el of Paris's commentary in, 343
Moshe b. Mordekhai, 67n124

Naḥmanides. *See* Moses b. Naḥman (Naḥmanides)
Nathan b. Isaac of Mainz, 426–27
Nathan b. Simeon, 42, 49–50
Nathan b. Yeḥi'el of Rome, 496
Neḥemyah b. Solomon, 23n83, 487, 489–90
Netan'el of Chinon, 340, 434–35
Nimmuqei Ḥumash, 203, 242–44, 514–15
Nissim Gaon, 358, 509, 511
Noachides, 216–17

'omeq peshuto shel miqra approach, 202
Onkelos, 355–56
Oral Law, 35
Orleans rabbinic court, 55
Ovadyah b. Samuel, 140

Pa'aneaḥ Raza (Issac b. Judah *ha-Levi*), 163–65, 168, 179, 206, 510–13
parables: incense test, 315–16; midget standing on the shoulders of a giant, 106–7; test of the incense (Moses of Coucy), 315–16
parashat Ḥuqqat, 316
parashat Mishpatim, 301–2, 329–32
parashat Va-Yiqra, 364–65
Paris rabbinic court, 54, 99
Passover sacrifice, 254, 263–64
payyetanim, 436, 533
Pereẓ b. Elijah of Corbeil: on halakhic debates of *Beit Hillel* and *Beit Shammai*, 26–27; interactions with other rabbinic courts, 50–51; mysticism, 480, 484–85; in *siddur mishpatim* (Exodus 21:1-24:18), 329–30
Pereẓ of France. *See* Pereẓ b. Elijah of Corbeil
Perushei Ba'alei ha-Tosafot 'al ha-Torah, 539
perushei Magenza, 97
Perush ha-Roqeaḥ 'al ha-Torah, 298, 361
Perushim u-Pesaqim (Avigdor b. Elijah Katz *ha-Kohen* of Vienna), 360–61
peshat approach: in 12th century, 9n28; in commentary by Eleazar of Worms, 369; figures associated with, 238; forms pursued by Rhineland rabbinic scholars, 281; Jacob of Orleans, 170, 176–78; Joseph *Bekhor Schor* of Orleans, 126–61; Judah b. Samuel *he-Ḥasid*, 208; in late 12th century, northern France, 111–26; masoretic patterns used in support, 229n73; Moses b. Naḥman (Naḥmanides) and, 160; movement for study of, 202–3; principles learned by Christians through talking with Jews, 105–6; Rashbam, 184; Tosafists and, 161–62, 528; Yom Tov b. Isaac of Joigny (Teitav), 179–203
Peshatim la-Torah (Isaac b. Ḥayyim), 336–38
peshuto shel miqra approach, 185, 287
Peter of Blois, 107
Petiḥat ha-lev, 482
piyyut composition: in 12th century, 393–405; in late 13th century, 436–43; in 13th-century Germany, 414–31; in 13th-century northern France, 431–36; innovations

piyyut composition (*continued*)
by Meir *Shaz* of Worms, 388–89; Isaac b. Samuel (Ri) of Dampierre, 17–18, 405–7; lack of, from Rashbam, 14; in medieval Ashkenaz, 533; northern French and German, compared, 442–43; overview of genres and strategies among Tosafists, 375–81; pre-Crusade antecedents, 381–93; in pre-Crusade period, 9–10, 405; Rabbenu Tam, 16, 393–94; *seliḥot*-only model, 384, 433; Spanish, 386–87, 539; students of Rabbenu Tam, 405–14; Urbach on, 375–78
piyyutim: Aramaic *(reshuyyot),* 387–88; *bikkur* and *ʿaqedah* forms, 388; commentators, 23–24; *ḥaruz mavriaḥ* or *ḥaruz ʾaḥid* technique, 383; interpretation by secondary elite, 21–22; issue of novelty, 392; *maʿarivim,* as genre, 385; *meʾorah,* 393–94; for personal, celebratory occasions, 378–79; teaching and commentary development, 534; venues for, 379–80
plagues: of boils, 171; of the firstborn, 172, 254, 300; of frogs, 172; hail, 172–73, 254; of hail, 299–300; of leprosy, 307; of locusts, 254–55, 299
pogroms at York (March 1190), 179
Provençal rabbinic scholars, 538
punishments: for blaspheming, 280; capital, 216, 331; corporal and noncorporal, rabbinic courts and, 236; to prevent commission of future sins, 242; by stoning, 357

Qalonymide family of German Pietists, 20
Qalonymus b. Gershom, 41, 50
Qalonymus b. Judah *(ha-baḥur)* of Worms, 391–92
Qalonymus of Rome, 12
qehillot Shu"m, 52
Qershavyah (Cresbia) b. Isaac *ha-Naqdan,* 22n83, 65
qinot (elegies), 378n13, 379, 382–83, 390–91, 396–97, 400, 403–4, 416–17, 419, 426–27, 430, 438–43

Rabad of Posquieres, 538
Raban. *See* Eliezer b. Nathan (Raban) of Mainz
Rabbenu Gershom b. Judah, 96–97, 382
Rabbenu Jacob Tam. *See* Jacob of Orleans (Rabbenu Jacob Tam)
Rabbenu Tam (Jacob b. Meir of Ramerupt): Christian scholars' influence on, 107; commentaries on Torah and other biblical verses, 15; conflicts with Elijah and Meshullam, 99–101; dialectical method of, 16; disciplinary concentration, 14; on discovering the truth of Torah, 30; dominance of, 2; intellectual biography of, 10; intellectual leadership, revolutionary aspect, 536; Isaiah di Trani and, 239–40; mysticism, avoidance of, 449–55; and northern French *payyetanim,* 375; *piyyut* composition, 393–97; and rabbinic courts, 55–57, 59, 68, 72; resistance to extra-talmudic studies, 535; *Sefer Hakhraʿot,* 15n52; *Sefer ha-Yashar,* 15n54; students of, 2–3, 5n9, 16–17, 43–44, 405–14, 455–59; talmudic interpretation, 14–15n51, 99–101; scriptural interpretation and commentary: *Leviticus: 26:8,* 310–11; *Deuteronomy: 32:30,* 310–11
rabbinic courts: cases before, 78–79; interactions between northern French and German, 64–65, 69–70; litigant's right to appeal, 57, 61–62, 78–79, 80n158; rulings *(pesaqim),* 47, 57–59, 71; *zabla* practices, 62–63, 70, 78–79. *See also names of individual courts;* rabbinic courts,

Germany; rabbinic courts, northern France
rabbinic courts, Germany: *beit din* policy, 70; communal policy, 78–80; interaction among, 46, 49–51; locales, 38; principle for providing court services by larger to smaller communities, 71; as seat of religious leadership and power within communities, 74–75; secondary or temporary *(beit din 'ara'i)*, 50; talmudic and halakhic studies, 38–53
rabbinic courts, northern France: Jewish divorce law and bills of divorce *(gittim)*, 65–69; judicial structure, 58; locations and members, 54–59; Meir (Maharam) of Rothenburg and, 50–51; monetary law, 69; nature and power of local courts, 60–61; talmudic approach of, 54–70; transitory status of, 71; *zabla* practices, 62–63, 70, 78–79
rabbinic culture: multiple truths and interpretations, 26–35; popularization of, 537; during Tosafist period, 2–26; values during pre-Crusade period, 534–35
rabbinic institutions, identification of, 75
rabbinic leadership and power, 77
rabbinic scholars: burden of serving as rabbinic decisor, 73; distinction between first-level and secondary elite, 21–23, 534; from Provence, 538; and rabbinic court *vs.* academy as seat of religious leadership, 74; religious authority of, 37; in Tosafist period, 97–98
rabbinic scholarship: Christian scholars' strategies and, 534; distinctions between northern France and Germany, 80–84; extra-talmudic interests and writings, 533; influence on Christian dialectal methods, 109; parallels with Christian scholarship, 87–90
Rabiah. *See* Eliezer b. Joel *ha-Levi* (Rabiah)
Radak. *See* David Kimḥi (Radak)
rainbows, 292
Ramah. *See* Meir *ha-Levi* Abulafia (Ramah)
Rambam, 494, 502, 511–13
Ramban, 160, 304, 334n119, 506, 525
Rashba (Samson b. Abraham of Sens or Solomon b. Abraham of Troyes), 330
Rashbam: avoidance of mysticism, 446–47; *Bava Batra* commentary, 10n35; on Book of Judges 13:8, 252–53; on Divine corporeality, 512; on hail damage, 173; influence on *Bekhor Shor*'s Torah commentary, 138–41, 144–48; intellectual biography of, 10; interpretational strategies, 31–32; interpretation rejected by *Bekhor Shor*, 130–31; ordinance regarding use of secular courts *('arka'ot)*, 72; participation on *beit din* ruling, 57–58; *peshat* interpretations, 184; rabbinic courts of northern France and, 68; rabbinic courts of Paris and Troyes, 54; Rashi compared to, 31; scriptural interpretation, 11–14; on story of selling of Joseph, 150–51; Vulgate translation and, 86; scriptural interpretation and commentary: *Genesis: 1:27*, 512; *12:3*, 337; *22:1*, 144–45; *23:1*, 149; *23:20*, 337; *25:29*, 150–51; *25:31*, 151; *25:33-34*, 151, 159; *32:2*, 145; *37:28*, 139, 349; *37:36*, 349; *41:7*, 139; *45:4*, 349–51; *45:28*, 188; *47:6*, 189; *Exodus: 1:20*, 170; *2:6*, 252; *2:14*, 138; *2:45*, 138–39; *3:14*, 138; *9:14*, 254; *14:2*, 151–52; *14:5*, 151–52; *15:20*, 149–50; *16:15*, 137; *18:2*, 256; *19:13*, 259; *21:10*, 139; *Leviticus: 26:19*, 176; *Numbers:*

Rashbam (*continued*)
12:1, 186; *16:1-2*, 314; *17:20*, 177; *31:19*, 139; *Deuteronomy: 3:11*, 323; *21:23*, 139; *32:8*, 201; *32:14*, 182–83; *Judges: 13:8*, 252

Rashbat. *See* Samuel b. Natronai (Rashbat)

Rashi: approach in talmudic commentary as model for Tosafists, 490–91; commentary to Psalms, 11n37; and dialectic, 90; on Divine corporeality, 519; influence on *Bekhor Shor*, 137, 141–42; intellectual biography of, 10; methods favored by northern French *pashtanim* in mid-13th century, 359–61; rabbinic court in Troyes, 77n153; Rashbam compared to, 31; Rid, 263–64; Rid's responses to commentary by, 243–44; on sacrificial order, 260–61; scriptural interpretation, 12; *seliḥot* and *qinot* compositions, 382–83; on term *'eved kena'ani*, 302; Tosafists' analysis of Torah commentary by, 161; on tractate to *Ḥullin*, 29; use of *gematria*, 215; scriptural interpretation and commentary: *Genesis: 1:1*, 165; *2:16-17*, 246; *3:1*, 208, 212; *3:14*, 281–82, 336; *4:10*, 271–72; *4:15*, 212; *5:29*, 212; *7:23*, 346; *9:3*, 246; *9:18*, 213; *10:9*, 130; *11:2*, 133; *11:7*, 133–34; *12:3*, 337; *13:7*, 341; *13:11*, 246–47; *13:14*, 247; *15:6*, 134; *17:19*, 283; *18:2*, 272; *18:4*, 241; *18:8*, 214; *18:29*, 248; *24:47*, 337–38; *25:22*, 249; *25:26*, 282–83; *28:5*, 155, 249; *28:12*, 145; *28:17*, 277; *29:34*, 295–96; *32:2*, 145; *35:18*, 131; *38:24*, 216; *38:26*, 332–33; *41:14*, 187; *41:16*, 130–31; *41:50*, 218, 272–73; *41:56*, 130; *42:2*, 130; *46:23*, 251–52; *47:6*, 189, 296–97; *49:21*, 297–98; *Exodus: 1:20*, 170; *2:6*, 252; *2:12*, 222; *2:16*, 222; *4:24*, 273, 355; *9:6*, 134–35; *9:14*, 254; *10:14*, 254–55; *12:6*, 273; *12:15*, 355; *12:40*, 341; *12:43*, 135; *12:45*, 135; *12:48*, 135–36; *14:7*, 339; *15:8*, 355–56; *15:15*, 318; *15:26*, 339–40; *16:15*, 136–37; *16:22*, 255–56; *18:2*, 256; *18:18*, 258; *19:13*, 259; *19:17*, 273; *20:21*, 259; *21:1*, 302; *21:6*, 330; *22:12*, 303; *23:21*, 450–51; *30:14-16*, 279; *Leviticus: 8:24*, 330; *11:11*, 306; *12:2*, 306; *12:8*, 345; *13:46*, 306–7; *16:3*, 307; *18:28*, 308; *21:3*, 309; *22:9*, 309; *25:9*, 195; *Numbers: 8:2*, 262–63; *9:1*, 263–64; *10:35*, 195; *11:1*, 196; *11:23*, 264; *12:6*, 232; *13:19*, 370; *16:1-2*, 314; *16:6*, 314; *20:10*, 284; *20:11*, 316; *21:1*, 197; *21:34*, 346; *22:24*, 357; *23:13*, 133; *25:11*, 319; *26:64*, 320; *30:15*, 132–33; *35:32*, 265–66; *Deuteronomy: 1:4*, 322; *1:44*, 322; *2:9*, 274, 318; *2:28-30*, 293; *12:19*, 136; *15:18*, 323; *16:12*, 323–24; *18:2*, 266; *26:5*, 236; *27:15*, 181; *32:6*, 131; *32:8*, 201; *33:16*, 183; *33:24*, 132; *34:2*, 132; *34:5*, 132; *Jeremiah: 46:20*, 261–62

Rash *mi-Shanz*. *See* Samson b. Abraham of Sens (Rash *mi Shandz*)

realia-based interpretations, 171, 232

Regensburg rabbinic court, 43–45, 50, 54n79

remez interpretation, 31, 207–8, 221, 227, 271, 286, 297–98, 363

reshuyyot (Aramaic *piyyutim*), 379, 387–88

responsa *(she'elot u-teshuvot)*, 71

Ri. *See* Isaac b. Jacob (Ri) *ha-Lavan* of Prague and Regensburg; Isaac b. Samuel (Ri) *ha-Zaqen* of Dampierre; Isaac of Evreux (Ri)

Riba. *See* Isaac b. Asher (Riba) *ha-Levi* of Speyer

Riba *ha-Levi ha-Zaqen*, 103

Ribam. *See* Isaac b. Mordekhai (Ribam) of Bohemia

Rid. *See* Isaiah b. Mali [Emanuel] di Trani (Rid)

Ritva. *See* Yom Tov b. Abraham al-Ishvilli (Ritva)
Rivaq b. Meir of Speyer. *See* Judah b. Qalonymus (Rivaq) b. Meir of Speyer
Rivaq b. Moses of of Mainz, 42, 59
Rivaq of Mainz. *See* Judah b. Qalonymus of Mainz (Rivaq b. Moses)
Riẓba. *See* Isaac b. Abraham (Riẓba) of Dampierre
Robert of Melun, 92
Rosh. *See* Asher b. Yeḥi'el (Rosh)
rosh yeshivah (academy head), 75–77
Rupert, abbot of Deutz, 92–93, 95

Sa'adyah Gaon, 224, 497, 499, 504, 508–9
sacrifice, animals suitable for, 175, 185
sacrifice, Passover, 254, 263–64
sacrificial order, 260–61
Samson b. Abraham of Sens (Rash *mi-Shanz*): on absence of *beit din ha-gadol* or *beit ḥa-va'ad,* 80n159; Christian influence on, 107; commentaries by, 18, 28–29; on educational conventions, 76; focused talmudism, 536; on local courts chosen via *zabla,* 79; rabbinic courts of northern France and, 57–58, 60, 61–62; rulings by, 58–59
Samson b. Ẓadoq, 70
Samson of Coucy, 64n111
Samson of Falaise, 453
Samuel b. Abraham *ha-Levi* of Worms (Bonfant), 67n124, 428–30
Samuel b. Elḥanan, 60
Samuel b. Meir, 224
Samuel b. Menaḥem *(ha-Levi),* 49
Samuel b. Menaḥem of Wurzburg, 436
Samuel b. Mordekhai of Marseilles, 519
Samuel b. Natronai (Rashbat), 45, 59, 376
Samuel b. Qalonymus *he-Ḥasid,* 202
Samuel b. Shne'ur of Evreux, 76, 330, 478
Samuel b. Solomon of Falaise, 64–65, 114–15, 384n31, 522
Samuel *he-Ḥasid* of Speyer, 20, 235, 334, 415
Samuel of Bamberg, 465–67
secondary rabbinic elite: distinction between first-level and, 534; on Divine corporeality, 527–28; midrashic interpretations and expansions, 360; *piyyut* interpretation, 21–22; popularization of rabbinic culture and, 537; and shift in Tosafist interpretation, 287–88
secular courts *('arka'ot),* 71
Seder Eliyyahu Rabbah, 267–68
Seder 'Olam, 342
Seder Qodashim, 162
Seder Sodot/Raza Rabba, 486
Sefardic influence on German and northern French *payyetanim,* 442–43
Sefardic Jewry, scholarly attention given to, 531–32
Sefer Assofot (anonymous student), 462–63
Sefer Avi'asaf (Rabiah), 3n7
Sefer Avi ha-'Ezri (Rabiah), 3, 4n9, 179, 286–87
Sefer ha-Gan (Aaron b. Yose[f] *ha-Kohen*): Barukh b. Isaac's commentary in, 267–68; as earliest Tosafist Torah compilation, 287; influence of *Bekhor Shor,* 289; Moses of Evreux and, 356–58; and transition to diffuse Tosafist Torah compilatory commentaries, 328; view of Maimonides in, 539; scriptural interpretation and commentary: *Genesis: 1:26,* 513; *9:28,* 276–77; *31:52,* 277–78; *37:36,* 351; *39:1,* 351
Sefer ha-Ḥokhmah (Barukh b. Samuel of Mainz), 74, 361–62
Sefer Hakhra'ot (Rabbenu Tam), 15n52
Sefer ha-Manhig (Abraham b. Nathan *ha-Yarḥi* of Lunel), 456

Sefer ha-Maskil (Solomon Simḥah b. Eli'ezer of Troyes), 483, 501, 503, 525
Sefer ha-Qomah (Moses b. Eleazar *ha-Darshan*), 450–51
Sefer Ḥasidim: on Divine miracles, 214; on Divine will, 467; *ḥerem ha-qehillot,* 79–80; influence of Christian scholars on, 108; mysticism in, 468–69, 470; objections to unrestrained dialectic, 108–9; Rashi omitted in, 210; and Regensburg rabbinic Court, 44–45; on *zabla* selections for rabbinic courts, 70
Sefer ha-Terumah (Barukh b. Isaac), 3
Sefer ha-Yashar (Rabbenu Tam), 15n54, 453
Sefer Mizvot Gadol (Semag) (Moses of Coucy), 3, 292–94, 524
Sefer Mizvot Qatan (Semaq) (Isaac of Corbeil), 6, 361
Sefer Mordekhai, 6n14
Sefer Or Zaru'a (Isaac b. Moses *Or Zaru'a* of Vienna), 3, 59, 79n157, 470–72
Sefer Rabiah. See *Sefer Avi ha-'Ezri* (Rabiah)
Sefer Roqeaḥ (Eleazar of Worms), 4n9
Sefer Yere'im (Eliezer of Metz), 3
Sefer Yezirah, 455, 506
Sefer Yiḥusei Tanna'im va-Amora'im (Rivaq), 460
seliḥot (penitential prayers), 379, 382–84, 433
Semag. See *Sefer Mizvot Gadol (Semag)* (Moses of Coucy)
Sha'arei ha-Sod veha-Yihud veh-Emunah (Eleazar of Worms), 505
Sha'arei Musar (Avigdor b. Elijah Katz *ha-Kohen* of Vienna), 476–77
Shabbetai (Donnolo) *ha-Rofe,* 509
Shavu'ot festival, 28, 230
She'alti'el b. Menaḥem of Cologne, 40, 47, 430
shedim: behavior of, 470; control of, 484; danger from, 454; rite of, 142, 456–57; use of, 449, 486
Shemaryah b. Mordekhai of Speyer, 19, 42, 56
Shemaryah b. Simḥah of Speyer, 361
shemitah, 181
Shibbolei ha-Leqet (Zedekiah b. Abraham *ha-Rofe*), 242, 473
shirshur (stylistic convention), 382
Shi'ur Qomah, 498
Sic et Non (Abelard), 109–10
siddur mishpatim, 329–30
Simeon b. Isaac *ha-Gadol* of Mainz, 27, 96, 382–83, 454
Simḥah b. Gershom, 49
Simḥah b. Samuel of Speyer: Isaiah di Trani and, 239; Judah *he-Ḥasid* and, 203; mysticism, 467–68, 475–76; *piyyut* composition, 377, 427–30; rabbinic courts and, 42, 46, 49–50, 59, 61n107, 69; scholarly interests, 19–20; in standard *Tosafot,* 4n9; Torah commentary, 281–82; scriptural interpretation and commentary: *Genesis: 17:19,* 283; *Leviticus: 12:3,* 283; *21:2,* 283; *23:28,* 283; *25:17,* 283; *Numbers: 20:10,* 284; *Deuteronomy: 22:10,* 284; *Isaiah: 1:15,* 283–84
Simmanei Or Zaru'a (Ḥayyim), 6n12
slaves, ear-piercing procedure for, 190, 331
snakes, 208–9, 212, 281–82
Sod ha-Sodot (Elḥanan b. Yaqar), 507
sod interpretation, 160, 208, 485, 487
Solomon b. Abraham of Montpellier, 522
Solomon b. Abraham of Troyes, 277–78
Solomon b. Isaac, 55
Solomon b. Judah *(ha-Qadosh)* of Dreux, 271–80; scriptural interpretation and commentary: *Genesis: 6:9,* 275; *9:28,* 275–77; *28:17,* 277; *Exodus: 21:12,* 278; *21:28,* 278–79; *Leviticus: 23:14,* 280; *24:12-15,* 280; *27:30,* 280; *Numbers: 15:32-34,* 280
Solomon b. Samson of Worms, 90

Solomon b. Samuel *ha-Ẓarefat*, 334–35, 431–32
Solomon *ha-Qadosh* b. Judah of Dreux, 330, 431
Solomon ibn Gabriol, 443
Solomon of Chateau-Landon, 342
Solomon Simḥah b. Eliezer of Troyes, 23n83, 483–84, 500–504, 525
song of *Ha'azinu*, 270–71
Song of Songs, 30n104, 355–56
Spain: biblical exegesis and thought, 495; Golden Age of, 22–23; *piyyut* composition, 382–84, 386–87, 442–43
Speyer cathedral school, 102–3
Speyer rabbinic court, 41–43, 49–50, 52–53
Stephen of Tournai, 94
study of midrash: by Yeḥi'el b. Joseph of Paris, 347–48

Ta'amei Mesoret ha-Miqra (Judah *he-Ḥasid*), 206
talmudic approach to interpretation and commentary: overview, 37–38; aim of, in pre-Crusade period, 95–96; Christian scholarship and, 84–110; dialectical method, 106; German Pietists and, 491–92; Isaac b. Asher (Riba) *ha-Levi* of Speyer, 18–19; Joseph (Yosef) b. Isaac *Bekhor Shor* of Orleans, 158; northern French and German, compared, 71–83; Rabbenu Tam and, 14–15n51, 99–101; rabbinic courts in Germany, 38–53; rabbinic courts of northern France and, 54–70; Rashi's approach as model for Tosafists, 490–91; by Ri, in case involving liability of nonprofessional coin evaluation, 59; Ta-Shma on goal of in High Middle Ages, 31; Tosafists and, 267–88, 533; Urbach on methods of Tosafists, 9; Yom Tov b. Isaac of Joigny (Teitav), 202
Talmud Yerushalmi, 283
Tanna R. Yehoshua b. Qorhah, 191
Targum Yonatan b. Uzi'el, 325
Ta-Shma, Israel: on Ashkenazic rabbinic literature, 535; on Christian scholars, 34n116; on distinctions in rabbinic scholarship between northern France and Germany, 83–84; on goal of talmudic interpretation in High Middle Ages, 31; parallels between methods of Jewish and Christian scholarship, 88–89; scholarly treatment of Spanish talmudic subjects, 532; studies on life and works of Isiah di Trani (Rid), 238–67
Te'amim shel Ḥumash (Solomon b. Samuel *ha-Ẓarefati*), 334
teḥinnot (penitential prayers), venues for, 382
Ten Commandments, 226
Tetragrammaton, 285, 335
theosophic kabbalah, Ashkenazim in development of, 539
three crowns, 227
Todros *ha-Rav*, 453
Torah studies: possibility of multiple truths in, 26–30; Tosafist exegetes in late 12th and 13th centuies, 536; ways of ascertaining and presenting truths of, 31
torat ha-sod, 22n83
Tosafist academies: and Babylonian Talmud, 535; at Cologne, 103; at Evreux, 348–59; heads of, in northern France, 75–77; at Mainz, 10, 97; significance of, 96; Worms, 90
Tosafist dialectic, 6–7
Tosafist *payyetanim*, German and northern French, 443
Tosafists: approach to aggadic interpretation, 490–91; approach to *halakhah*, 491; attitudes toward messianic era, 528; developments in *derash* and talmudic interpretations, 267–88; on Divine corporeality, 527–28; extra-talmudic interests,

Tosafists (*continued*)
533; French, 61, 280–81, 375–78; French and German, compared, 5–7, 37–38, 82–84, 534; German, 19, 281, 380–81, 460–69; influences on, 103–9, 538; involvement in other disciplines, 21, 110; language familiarity, 85–87; main pursuits of, 20–21; *piyyut* composition, 378; prominent figures of 12th and 13th centuries, 1; rabbinic literature, 61; sensitivity to use of talmudic texts in halakhic contexts, 135; students' identification by teachers, 38; talmudic method of, 9. *See also names of individual Tosafists*
Tosafist Torah commentaries, approaches to matters of belief and implications for popular culture, 510–13; *derash* approach in middle13th-century, 359–61; exoteric, by Judah *he-Ḥasid*'s, 207–38; mid-13th century, 359–61; purpose of, 537; Rabbenu Tam and, 15. *See also names of individual scholars; titles of specific commentaries;* Tosafist Torah compilations
Tosafist Torah compilations, 163, 287–88, 340. *See also titles of specific compilations*
Tosafot, 2–4n8, 7–8n24, 37. *See also titles of specific Tosafot*
Tosafot Bava Meẓi'a (Eliezer b. Solomon *mi-Tukh*), 267–68
Tosafot Evreux, 354
Tosafot Ḥagigah, 450
Tosafot Ḥakhmei Evereux, 3
Tosafot ha-Rid, 243
Tosafot Rabbenu Pereẓ, 3, 27n95
Tosafot Rid, 239–40
Tosafot R. Yehudah Sirleon, 3
Tosafot Shanẓ, 3
Tosafot Yeshanim, 4
Tree of Knowledge, 240, 269
Tree of Life, 240, 269
tribe of Levi, 178–79, 266–67, 296, 311–12, 314, 327
Troyes rabbinic court, 57
Tuvyah of Vienne, 68n125, 433–34

Urbach, E. E.: on Abraham b. Azri'el of Bohemia, 24; *Ba'alei ha-Tosafot,* 2, 8, 24–25, 87–88; on *piyyut* composition by German and northern French Tosafists, 375–78; on talmudic method of Tosafists, 9; on Tosafist approach to *'aggadah* and to midrash, 490–93; and *Tosafot* to Babylonian Talmud, 3–4

William of Champeaux, 92
William of Conches, 107
Wissenschaft scholars, 531
Worms academy, 90, 96
Worms rabbinic court, 40–41, 50, 52–53
Wurzburg rabbinic court, 49

Ya'aqov b. Yaqar, 12
Yaqar b. Samuel *ha-Levi* of Cologne: Cologne rabbinic court, 48; interaction with other rabbinic courts, 52; mysticism, 486; *piyyut* composition, 429, 438–40; rabbinic courts of northern France and, 64–65; Rabiah and, 40
Yeḥezqel b. Meir of Rothenburg, 45
Yeḥi'el (Blois martyr), 408
Yeḥi'el b. Joseph of Paris: overview, 328–29; biblical interpretations compiled by student of, 340; in consultations from Germany to northern France, 64; on Divine corporeality, 523; extra-talmudic studies, 536; mysticism, 478–79; *piyyut* commentary, 435; rabbinic courts of northern France and, 54, 65, 69; *shitot* composition, 8n24; study of midrash, 347–48; scriptural interpretation and commentary: *Genesis:*

7:23, 346–47; *11:11,* 344–45; *17:1,* 341–42; *38:26,* 333; *Exodus: 10:14,* 343; *14:7,* 339; *15:26,* 339–40; *18:3-4,* 343–44; *21:6,* 330; *27:4,* 344; *Leviticus: 8:24,* 330; *12:6-8,* 345; *24:15-16,* 335; *Numbers: 20:27,* 346; *Joel: 2:2,* 343
Yehudah *ha-Levi. See* Judah (Yehuda) b. Samuel *ha-Levi*
Yehudah *he-Ḥasid,* 202, 215, 232
Yequti'el (Blois martyr), 408
yeshiva studies, in 13th century, 535
yibbum, 159–61, 333
Yo'el *ha-Levi. See* Eliezer b. Joel *ha-Levi* (Rabiah)
Yom Tov b. Abraham al-Ishvilli (Ritva), 26
Yom Tov b. Isaac of Joigny (Teitav): biblical exegesis of, 179–203; exegetical techniques, 202; extra-talmudic studies, 536; masoretic and *gematria* interpretations, 202; in *Pa'aneaḥ Raza,* 164; *peshat* approach, 179, 181, 184, 202–3; on piercing slave's ear, 331; *piyyut* composition, 407–8; on *Sefer Bamidbar,* 195; talmudic and halakhic interpretations, 202; scriptural interpretation and commentary: *Genesis: 41:14,* 187; *45:28,* 188; *47:6,* 189; *Exodus: 30:12,* 190; *33:18–20,* 190–92; *Leviticus: 23:13,* 193; *23:34,* 193; *25:1,* 193; *25:3,* 195; *25:9,* 195; *25:15,* 195; *26:14,* 195; *Numbers: 7:12,* 195; *8:26,* 195; *10:35,* 195; *11:1,* 196; *14:27,* 196–97; *14:34,* 201; *17:2,* 196–97; *18:21,* 197; *18:23,* 197; *20:11,* 197; *21:1,* 197; *22:6,* 197–98; *22:34,* 198; *31:18,* 199; *31:30,* 199; *31:38,* 199; *31:44,* 199; *31:51,* 199; *Deuteronomy: 21:15,* 200; *22:14,* 200; *22:19,* 200; *27:15,* 181; *28:2,* 200; *28:15,* 200; *32:8,* 201; *33:1,* 201; *34:7,* 201
Yom Tov b. Judah of Falaise, 54
Yonah of Gerona, 478, 522
Yosef *Bekhor Shor. See* Joseph (Yosef) b. Isaac *Bekhor Shor* of Orleans
Yosef b. Ḥayyim, 53
Yosef b. Samuel *Tov 'Elem* (Bonfils), 384–85
Yosef ibn Avitur, 442–43
Yosef Qara, 22n83, 83n167, 86, 140, 264
yoẓerot, venues for, 380

ẓabla practices, in rabbinic courts of northern France, 62–63, 70, 78–79
ẓabla principle, 62
Zal(t)man, 217, 223–24, 228, 233–34
Zedekiah b. Abraham *ha-Rofe,* 107, 242, 473
Zeraḥyah *ha-Levi,* 538
ẓulatot, venues for, 380, 382

www.ingramcontent.com/pod-product-compliance
Lightning Source LLC
LaVergne TN
LVHW010356080826
844660LV00016B/983/J

* 9 7 8 0 8 1 4 3 3 0 2 4 1 *